COMMERCIAL ARBITRATION: CASES AND PROBLEMS

COMMERCIAL ARBITRATION: CASES AND PROBLEMS

Third Edition

Christopher R. Drahozal
John M. Rounds Professor of Law
University of Kansas School of Law

ISBN: 978–0–7698–5987–3 (hardbound)
ISBN: 978–0–7698–5988–0 (loose-leaf)
ISBN: 978–0–3271–7919–1 (eBook)

Library of Congress Cataloging-in-Publication Data

Drahozal, Christopher R.
  Commercial arbitration : cases and problems / Christopher R. Drahozal, John M. Rounds Professor of Law,
University of Kansas School of Law. -- Third Edition.
     pages cm
  Includes index.
  ISBN 978-0-7698-5987-3 (hardbound)
  1. Arbitration and award--United States--Cases. 2. Arbitration and award--United States. I. Title.
   F9085.D73 2013 347.73'9--dc23
2012050156

NOTE TO USERS
To ensure that you are using the latest materials available in this area, please be sure to periodically check the LexisNexis Law School web site for downloadable updates and supplements at www.lexisnexis.com/lawschool.

Editorial Offices
121 Chanlon Rd., New Providence, NJ 07974 (908) 464-6800
201 Mission St., San Francisco, CA 94105-1831 (415) 908-3200
www.lexisnexis.com

MATTHEW◆BENDER

(2013–Pub.3126)

Dedication

For Kaye

Preface

This book provides an overview of the law and practice of commercial arbitration. By agreeing to arbitrate, parties "opt out" of the public court system in favor of having a private judge (or judges) resolve their dispute. Courts can continue to play a role — by enforcing arbitration agreements and awards, as well as by providing assistance to the arbitrators during the course of the proceeding. But in most cases, arbitration provides an alternative to judicial dispute resolution that operates without any court involvement.

Commercial arbitration has grown rapidly as a form of alternative dispute resolution. (I use the term "commercial arbitration" broadly, to include arbitration between businesses and consumers or employees as well as arbitration among businesses — and to exclude labor arbitration.) The use of arbitration to resolve international commercial disputes is commonplace and will continue to grow with the increasing "globalization" of national economies. In the last several decades, however, a series of decisions by the United States Supreme Court — expanding the arbitrability of federal statutory claims and restricting the power of states to regulate commercial arbitration — have led to the increasing use of arbitration to resolve consumer and employment disputes. The policy issues raised by this "consumerization" of arbitration recur in various contexts throughout the book.

The book addresses four main topics: enforcing agreements to arbitrate (Chapters 1-5); the arbitration proceeding (Chapter 6); enforcing arbitration awards (Chapter 7); and drafting arbitration clauses (Chapter 8). Each chapter contains a number of problems that require careful analysis of the relevant statutes, cases, and rules. The problems provide a focal point for class discussion, as well as setting the legal and policy issues in a practical context. Some of the problems (or at least some of the sub-parts of the problems) are quite easy. That is intentional. I have tried to design the problems so that they begin with the easy cases and progress to the more difficult ones, rather than presenting only the difficult (albeit often more interesting) cases.

The materials in the book consist largely of court cases, with some secondary materials. I have included the leading United States Supreme Court cases dealing with commercial arbitration, as well as other cases that contain either useful discussions of the issues or particularly interesting facts. Omissions from the text of cases and articles are indicated by ellipses. I have deleted citations and footnotes without so indicating, and have used short citation forms when the case appears elsewhere in the text. The governing treaties and statutes are reprinted in the accompanying Documentary Supplement, as are a number of sets of arbitration rules and related materials.

The book also includes a handful of arbitration awards. Unlike judicial opinions, arbitration awards generally are not published. Indeed, one of the important attributes of commercial arbitration is its greater degree of confidentiality, which precludes routine publication of awards. I have tried to choose court cases and secondary readings that describe arbitration proceedings and typical practices in arbitration, in an attempt to deal with the limited availability of arbitration awards. I also include or refer to empirical studies on commercial arbitration (particularly ones examining the terms of arbitration clauses) to add further insight into actual arbitration practice.

I am grateful to a number of people for assistance and support. My thanks to Roger

Preface

Alford, Ken Dunham, Michael Helfand, Rusty Park, Bo Rutledge, Amy Schmitz, Steve Ware, and Mark Weidemaier for helpful comments on and discussions about the book. Thanks also to my commercial arbitration classes for their questions and comments both in and out of class. I appreciate the research assistance of John Richer and Jeff Stowell on the first edition, Matt Koenigsdorf on the second edition, and Richard Shie on the third edition, as well as financial support from the University of Kansas School of Law and the University of Kansas General Research Fund.

I hope you find this material as interesting and challenging as I do.

Christopher R. Drahozal
August 2012
Lawrence, Kansas

Acknowledgments

I am grateful to the following for granting permission to reprint excerpts contained in this book:

BRUCE L. BENSON, THE ENTERPRISE OF LAW: JUSTICE WITHOUT THE STATE 221-222 (1990). Copyright © 1990 by the Pacific Research Institute for Public Policy. Reprinted with permission.

George A. Bermann, *The "Gateway" Problem in International Commercial Arbitration*, 37 YALE J. INT'L L. 1, 13-28 (2012). Copyright © 2012 by the Yale Journal of International Law. Reprinted with permission.

Stephen R. Bond, *How to Draft an Arbitration Clause (Revisited)*, ICC INTERNATIONAL COURT OF ARBITRATION BULLETIN (vol. 1/no. 2), Dec. 1990, at 14, 16–21. Copyright © 1990 by the International Chamber of Commerce. Reprinted with permission.

Christopher R. Drahozal, *In Defense of* Southland: *Reexamining the Legislative History of the Federal Arbitration Act*, 78 NOTRE DAME L. REV. 101, 105–07 (2002). Copyright © 2002 by the Notre Dame Law Review. Reprinted with permission.

Paul D. Friedland, *Combining Civil Law and Common Law Elements in the Presentation of Evidence in International Commercial Arbitration*, MEALEY'S INT'L ARB. REP., Sept. 1997. Copyright © 1997 by Paul D. Friedland. Reprinted with permission.

Stephen L. Hayford, *Law in Disarray: Judicial Standards for Vacatur of Commercial Arbitration Awards*, 30 GA. L. REV. 731, 751–56 (1996). Copyright © 1996 by the Georgia Law Review Association, Inc. Reprinted with permission.

William M. Landes & Richard A. Posner, *Adjudication as a Private Good*, 8 J. LEGAL STUD. 235, 235–40 (1979). Copyright © 1979 by The University of Chicago. Reprinted with permission.

William W. Park, *Private Adjudicators and the Public Interest: The Expanding Scope of International Arbitration*, 12 BROOK. J. INT'L L. 629, 635–40 (1986). Copyright © 1986 by William W. Park. Reprinted with permission.

Rand Institute of Civil Justice, Business-to-Business Arbitration in the United States: Perceptions of Corporate Counsel 2 22 (2011). Copyright © 2011 by the Rand Corporation. Reprinted with permission.

Alan Scott Rau, *The New York Convention in American Courts*, 7 AM. REV. INT'L ARB. 213, 251–56 (1996). Copyright © 1996 by the Parker School of Foreign & Comparative Law. Reprinted with permission.

Peter B. Rutledge & Christopher R. Drahozal, *Contract and Choice*, 2013 BYU L. REV. ___ (forthcoming). Copyright © 2013 by Peter B. Rutledge and Christopher R. Drahozal. Reprinted with permission.

David S. Schwartz, *Enforcing Small Print to Protect Big Business: Employee and Consumer Rights Claims in an Age of Compelled Arbitration*, 1997 WIS. L. REV. 33, 60–61. Copyright © 1997 by the Board of Regents of the University of Wisconsin System. Reprinted with permission.

Acknowledgments

Jean R. Sternlight, Gateway *Widens Doorway to Imposing Unfair Binding Arbitration on Consumers*, FLA. BAR J., Nov. 1997, at 8, 8–12. Copyright © 1997 by the Florida Bar *Journal.* Reprinted with permission.

Jean R. Sternlight, *Panacea or Corporate Tool?: Debunking the Supreme Court's Preference for Binding Arbitration*, 74 WASH. U. L.Q. 637, 686–93 (1996). Copyright © 1996 by Washington University. Reprinted with permission.

John M. Townsend, *Drafting Arbitration Clauses: Avoiding the 7 Deadly Sins*, DISP. RESOL. J. Feb./Apr. 2003. Copyright © 2003 by the American Arbitration Association. Reprinted with permission.

GORDON TULLOCK, TRIALS ON TRIAL: THE PURE THEORY OF LEGAL PROCEDURE 127–129 (1980). Copyright © 1980 by the Columbia University Press. Reprinted with permission.

Katherine Van Wezel Stone, *Rustic Justice: Community and Coercion Under the Federal Arbitration Act*, 77 N. CAR. L. REV. 931, 969–91 (1999). Copyright © 1999 by Katherine Van Wezel Stone. Reprinted with permission.

Stephen J. Ware, *The Case for Enforcing Adhesive Arbitration Agreements — with Particular Consideration of Class Actions and Arbitration Fees*, 5 J. AM. ARB. 251, 254–64 (2006). Copyright © 2006 by the Journal of American Arbitration. Reprinted with permission.

W. Mark C. Weidemaier, *Toward a Theory of Precedent in Arbitration*, 51 WM. & MARY L. REV. 1895 (2010). Copyright © 2010 by the William & Mary Law Review. Reprinted with permission.

Summary Table of Contents

Table of Contents

Table of Contents

Table of Contents

Table of Contents

Table of Contents

Table of Contents

Table of Contents

Table of Contents

Table of Contents

Table of Contents

Table of Contents

Chapter 1

INTRODUCTION TO COMMERCIAL ARBITRATION

§ 1.01 OVERVIEW

Commercial arbitration is a form of private dispute resolution. Instead of going to court, parties agree among themselves to hire a private judge — or arbitrator — to adjudicate their dispute. By agreeing to arbitrate, the parties ordinarily give up their right to have a public judge (or jury) decide the case.

Arbitration is a matter of contract between the parties. The parties must agree or they will not be bound to arbitrate. The parties' agreement likewise defines the scope of the disputes subject to arbitration. The parties control how the arbitrators are selected, what procedures will be followed, and what remedial powers the arbitrators will have. Indeed, some courts (although not the United States Supreme Court) permit the parties to contract to expand the scope of judicial review of arbitration awards beyond that provided by law. The limits on the parties' "freedom of contract" in arbitration is one of the recurring issues addressed in this book.

This chapter provides an introduction to commercial arbitration as a form of contractual dispute resolution. First, it addresses private versus public dispute resolution. Is dispute resolution a governmental function? Can dispute resolution be "privatized"? What is the appropriate role of government in resolving disputes? Second, it considers what exactly is arbitration. Private dispute resolution can take a number of forms, not all of which strictly are "arbitration." Third, it looks at why parties arbitrate. Given the variety of disputes that parties agree to arbitrate, it is not surprising that their reasons for agreeing to arbitrate vary as well. Fourth, it presents a brief history of commercial arbitration and traces how the use of arbitration to resolve disputes has changed over time. Although arbitration began as a device for resolving disputes between merchants, today it is commonly used to resolve consumer and employment disputes as well.

§ 1.02 A THEORY OF PRIVATE DISPUTE RESOLUTION

William M. Landes & Richard A. Posner, ADJUDICATION AS A PRIVATE GOOD,
8 J. Legal Stud. 235, 235–240 (1979)*

Adjudication is normally regarded as a governmental function and judges as public officials. Even economists who assign a highly limited role to government consider the provision of judicial services an indisputably apt function of government; this was, for example, Adam Smith's view. Few economists (and few lawyers) realize that the provision of judicial services precedes the formation of the state; that many formally public courts long had important characteristics of private institutions (for example, until 1825 English judges were paid out of litigant's fees as well as general tax revenues); and that even today much adjudication is private (commercial arbitration being an important example). Further, most cases, both civil and criminal, in the public courts are settled out of court rather than litigated to judgment, and most of the inputs into the litigation of such cases are private.

. . .

1. *Introduction.* A court system (public or private) produces two types of service. One is dispute resolution — determining whether a rule has been violated. The other is rule formulation — creating rules of law as a by-product of the dispute-settlement process. When a court resolves a dispute, its resolution, especially if embodied in a written opinion, provides information regarding the likely outcome of similar disputes in the future. This is the system of precedent, which is so important in the Anglo-American legal system.

. . .

The two judicial services are in principle severable and in practice often are severed. Jury verdicts resolve disputes but do not create precedents. Legislatures create rules of law but do not resolve disputes. In the Anglo-American legal system rule formation is a function shared by legislatures and (especially appellate) courts; elsewhere judicial law making tends to be less important.

2. *Dispute Resolution.* Imagine a purely private market in judicial services. People would offer their services as judges, and disputants would select the judge whom they mutually found most acceptable. The most popular judges would charge the highest fees, and competition among judges would yield the optimum amount and quality of judicial services at minimum social cost. This competitive process would produce judges who were not only competent but also impartial — and would thus fulfill the ideals of procedural justice — because a judge who was not regarded as impartial could not get disputes submitted to him for resolution: one party would always refuse.

A voluntary system of dispute resolution does not presuppose that the dispute has arisen from a consensual relationship (landlord-tenant, employer-employee, seller-buyer, etc.) in which the method of dispute resolution is agreed on before the

---

dispute arose. All that is necessary is that when a dispute does arise the parties to it choose a judge to resolve it. Even if they are complete strangers, as in the typical accident case, the parties can still choose a judge to determine liability.

Although dispute resolution could thus be provided (for criminal as well as civil cases) in a market that would operate free from any obvious elements of monopoly, externality, or other sources of "market failure," it may not be efficient to banish public intervention entirely. Public intervention may be required (1) to ensure compliance with the (private) judge's decision and (2) to compel submission of the dispute to adjudication in the first place. The first of these public functions is straightforward, and no more compromises the private nature of the adjudication system described above than the law of trespass compromises the private property rights system. The second function, compelling submission of the dispute to judge, is more complex. If A accuses B of breach of contract, the next step in a system of private adjudication is for the parties to select a judge. But suppose B, knowing that any impartial judge would convict him, drags his feet in agreeing to select a judge who will hear the case, rejecting name after name submitted by A for his consideration. Although a sanction for this kind of foot-dragging (a sanction analogous to the remedies that the National Labor Relations Board provides for refusals to bargain collectively in good faith) is conceivable, there may be serious difficulty in determining when the bargaining over the choice of the judge is in bad faith — it is not bad faith, for example, to reject a series of unreasonable suggestions by the other side.

Two ways of overcoming the submission problem come immediately to mind. The first is for the parties to agree on the judge (or on the method of selecting him) before the dispute arises, as is done in contracts with arbitration clauses. This solution is available, however, only where the dispute arises from a preexisting voluntary relationship between the parties; the typical tort or crime does not. The second solution is to randomize the choice of the judge; then the parties do not have to negotiate over his selection. But randomization undermines the competitive process which generates an optimal level of judicial services. With random selection even an incompetent judge can anticipate an income as a result of the process by which judges are chosen to hear cases. And there is still the problem of compelling the party who fears the outcome of impartial adjudication to submit to the random-selection process.

Another type of private solution to the problem of enforcement and the selection of a private judge is available when both parties to the dispute are members of the same (private) group or association. The group can expel any member who unreasonably refuses to submit to an impartial adjudication (perhaps by a judge selected by the group) or to abide by the judge's decision. To the extent that membership in the group confers a value over and above alternative opportunities, members will have incentives to bargain in good faith over the selection of the judge and to abide by his decision. In these circumstances dispute resolution can operate effectively without public intervention.

. . .

3. *Rule Production.* Private production of rules or precedents involves two problems. First, because of the difficulty of establishing property rights in a

precedent, private judges may have little incentive to produce precedents. They will strive for a fair result between the parties in order to preserve a reputation for impartiality, but why should they make any effort to explain the result in a way that would provide guidance for future parties? To do so would be to confer an external, an uncompensated, benefit not only on future parties but also on competing judges. If anything, judges might deliberately avoid explaining their results because the demand for their services would be reduced by rules that, by clarifying the meaning of the law, reduced the incidence of disputes. Yet, despite all this, private judges just might produce precedents. We said earlier that competitive private judges would strive for a reputation for competence and impartiality. One method of obtaining such a reputation is to give reasons for a decision that convince the disputants and the public that the judge is competent and impartial. Competition could lead private judges to issue formal or informal "opinions" declaring their interpretation of the law, and these opinions — though intended simply as advertising — would function as precedents, as under a public judicial system. But this scenario is no more than plausible. If there were cheaper methods of advertising one's impartiality as an adjudicator than by writing opinions, those methods would be chosen and precedents would not be produced. . . .

The second problem with a free market in precedent production is that of inconsistent precedents which could destroy the value of a precedent system in guiding behavior. If there are many judges, there is likely to be a bewildering profusion of precedents and no obvious method of harmonizing them. An individual contemplating some activity will have difficulty discovering its legal consequences because they will depend on who decides any dispute arising out of the activity. Stated otherwise, there would appear to be tremendous economies of standardization in the precedent market, akin to those that have given us standard dimensions for electrical sockets and railroad gauges. While many industries have achieved standardization without monopoly, it is unclear how the requisite standardization or commonality could be achieved in the precedent market without a single source for precedent production — without, that is to say, a monopoly: by what competitive process would the precedents of competing judges converge to a social optimum? Suppose the socially optimal rule for internalizing the costs of sonic boom is to make the airplane owner strictly liable for sonic-boom damage. Nevertheless, any judge who adopted such a rule would be certain to have no sonic-boom business, for no airplane owner would submit to the jurisdiction of such a judge. The problem — and it appears to be a general one in a system of private precedent production — is that the private benefit of the sonic-boom rule to one of the "customers" whose voluntary agreement to purchase judicial services from the judge is essential if the judge is to sell his services diverges radically from the social benefit of the rule.

A related problem is that a system of voluntary adjudication is strongly biased against the creation of precise rules of any sort. Any rule that clearly indicates how a judge is likely to decide a case will assure that no disputes subject to the rule are submitted to that judge since one party will know that it will lose. Judges will tend to promulgate vague standards which give each party to a dispute a fighting chance.

This problem disappears if the parties agree in advance to the submission of disputes to a particular judge applying a known set of rules. It can also be overcome, in the association setting, simply by the association's monopolizing the production of the relevant rules or precedents. It is overcome in the traditional family by the monopoly of authority enjoyed by the head of the family.

Of course, without a rigorous empirical study of the costs of public dispute resolution and precedent production relative to those of private provision of these services, we cannot conclude that private provision, with all its problems, is less efficient than public. What is clear is that, outside of the association setting (an important qualification), a private market is more likely to emerge in dispute resolution than in rule creation. . . .

This article by Landes and Posner is a classic examination of the competing roles of the private sector and the public sector in resolving disputes. It touches on a variety of issues that have important implications for policy discussions about commercial arbitration.

Incentives of arbitrators. One such issue is how the incentives of arbitrators compare to the incentives of public court judges. Landes and Posner present an optimistic view of arbitrators' incentives, arguing that competition among arbitrators will tend to result in awards that are in both parties' best interests. The following excerpt from Professor Gordon Tullock identifies a circumstance in which competition among arbitrators for business might not be so beneficial — when one of the parties to the arbitration proceeding is a "repeat player."

Gordon Tullock, TRIALS ON TRIAL: THE PURE THEORY OF LEGAL PROCEDURE 127–129 (1980)*

When we turn to the arbitrator, the incentive system is quite different [from that of a public court judge]. The professional arbitrator is unlike a judge in that his decision in a given case increases or decreases the likelihood of his being employed in the future. Since he wants to be employed in the future — he is making money from his arbitration practice — he will attempt to choose that decision which is most likely to lead to his being selected for arbitration in the future. Where the two parties to any future contract have roughly equal levels of information, . . . this leads him to choose an economical and accurate procedure if that is possible for him. If, however, one of the parties to future contracts is apt to hold superior information, it may lead to a very strong element of bias on the part of the arbitrator.

The point is, I suppose, fairly obvious; but a little discussion may not be out of place. If the arbitrator, for example, deals exclusively in small-scale consumer complaints, he may feel that most consumers will not know anything at all about the arbitrator and therefore will be willing to accept the arbitrator suggested by the retailer. Under the circumstances, a bias toward the retailer might be the arbitrator's profit-maximizing course of action. It might not, however, because the retailer might be interested in his general reputation and want an arbitrator who was either impartial or, for that matter, actually procustomer.

I have noticed that when I have a complaint in my dealings with retail

---

establishments, their usual reaction is not one of making a fair judicial decision between themselves and me but of giving me every benefit of the doubt. Presumably one reason for this is that careful consideration of the issue would be an expensive process, and the complaints desk would have to be greatly enlarged if they attempted it. Even more important is their feeling that damaging their relations with the customer is a good deal more expensive for them than the cost of replacing some piece of merchandise which the customer claims is defective. They do not accept the customer's position in every single case, but they very decidedly tend to favor him. They might select arbitrators with the same set of biases. On the other hand, the fact that the complaints desk is lenient, and therefore that only cases the complaints desk thought were fake were transferred to the arbitrator, might mean they wanted an arbitrator who normally decided for them. In any event, the arbitrator would not aim at true accuracy but at whatever outcomes were favored by the retailer. The customer might or might not benefit from that.

NOTES

1. In a study of awards in employment arbitrations administered by the American Arbitration Association, Professor Lisa Bingham has identified "significantly different outcomes based on whether an employer is a repeat player." Lisa B. Bingham, *Employment Arbitration: The Repeat Player Effect*, 1 EMPL. RTS. & EMPLOYMENT POL'Y J. 189, 220 (1997). She found that employees won in only 16 percent of the arbitrations against repeat player employers (defined as those arbitrating in more than one case in the sample) as compared with 63 percent of the arbitrations against all employers. Similarly, employees recovered only 11 percent of what they demanded in arbitrations against repeat players, while they recovered 48 percent of what they demanded from non-repeat players. *Id.* at 213. She identified a variety of possible causes for this differing likelihood of success, only one of which was the incentives of the arbitrators. Other possibilities included: differing quality of representation in the hearing; "systematic differences in the merits of these cases" (her study did not control for the merits); and the possibility that "employers may get better at screening cases with repeat experience in the process, and learn to settle the cases they otherwise would lose." *Id.* She presented no comparable data for public courts, so there is no way to tell whether her results are due to the nature of the arbitration process. In a follow-up study, however, Professor Bingham found that the "patterns largely correspond with differences in the nature of the basis for arbitration. Repeat player employers get to arbitration based on an implied contract stemming from a personnel or employee handbook," cases that employees more frequently lose. Lisa B. Bingham, *Unequal Bargaining Power: An Alternative Account for the Repeat Player Effect in Employment Arbitration*, INDUS. REL. RES. ASS'N 50TH ANN. PROC. 33, 39 (1999). In other words, "[a]n employee arbitrating pursuant to a personnel manual may have a substantively weaker legal claim which contributes to the relatively weak employee outcomes." *Id.* at 40.

2. Lewis Maltby has compared some of Professor Bingham's results to data from employment cases in federal court. He reported that (based on Professor Bingham's data) employees won 63 percent of their cases in arbitration, but only 15 percent in federal court. Lewis Maltby, *Employment Arbitration: Is It Really*

Second Class Justice?, Disp. Resol. Mag., Fall 1999, at 23. But in arbitration, successful employees recovered on average only 25 percent of the amount they demanded, while in court the successful employee recovered 70 percent of his or her demand. *Id.* Maltby finds this latter comparison misleading, however, because the vast majority of cases in federal court never make it to trial, being resolved on summary judgment almost uniformly in favor of the employer. Adjusting for that fact, he concluded: "The entire class of employees who take their dispute to court receive 10.4 percent of their total demand. Employees who take their disputes to arbitration receive 18 percent of their total demand. Employees who take their dispute to arbitration receive almost twice as much of their demands as the employees who take their dispute to court." *Id.* at 24. Given that the fees parties pay in arbitration are based on the amount demanded, these numbers may reflect no more than the fact that parties in arbitration have a strong incentive to be more realistic about their initial demands than parties in court.

3. A more recent study by Theodore Eisenberg and Elizabeth Hill, also examining AAA employment arbitration awards, found outcomes in arbitration to be roughly comparable with outcomes of similar cases in court. Theodore Eisenberg & Elizabeth Hill, *Arbitration and Litigation of Employment Claims: An Empirical Comparison*, Disp. Resol. J., Nov. 2003/Jan. 2004, at 44, 50. The median award to higher-pay employees in non-civil-rights cases in arbitration was $94,984 and the mean award was $211,720. By comparison, the median award in state court employment trials was $68,737 and the mean award was $462,307. In both cases, the difference in the amounts was not statistically significant, meaning that although the amounts were different, the difference could well be due to chance. When awards to lower-pay employees in arbitration were examined, the differences were statistically significant — the median award to lower-pay employees was only $13,450 and the mean was only $30,732. According to Eisenberg and Hill, their results "are consistent with the hypothesis that litigated non-discrimination employment cases are commenced mostly by higher-pay employees" and that arbitrators make similar awards in such cases as judges and juries. *Id.* at 53. Further, they conclude that "[l]ower-pay employees seem to be unable to attract the legal representation necessary for meaningful access to court," while many lower-pay employees in fact brought claims in arbitration. *Id.* They emphasize, however, that difficulties in controlling for types of cases and types of claimants "suggest caution in interpreting the findings." *Id.* For a criticism of the methodology of the Eisenberg and Hill study, see David S. Schwartz, *Mandatory Arbitration and Fairness*, 84 Notre Dame L. Rev. 1247, 1297-1309 (2009).

4. In March 2009, the Searle Civil Justice Institute issued the first in-depth study of consumer arbitrations administered by the American Arbitration Association, published as Christopher R. Drahozal & Samantha Zyontz, *An Empirical Study of AAA Consumer Arbitrations*, 25 Ohio St. J. on Disp. Resol. 843 (2010); and Christopher R. Drahozal & Samantha Zyontz, *Private Regulation of Consumer Arbitration*, 79 Tenn. L. Rev. 289 (2012). The study found that consumer claimants won some relief in 53.3% of the cases studied, and that prevailing consumer claimants were awarded 52.1% of the amount they sought. Business claimants won some relief in 83.6% of the cases studied, and prevailing business claimants were awarded 93.0% of the amount they sought. 25 Ohio St. J. on Disp. Resol. at 898-99.

The study cautions, however, that the fact that business claimants did better in arbitration does not itself show that the process is biased in favor of businesses. Instead, "the differing outcomes are likely due to the types of cases brought by business claimants and consumer claimants rather than any form of systematic bias." *Id.* at 901.

The Searle study also tested for a repeat-player effect in AAA consumer arbitrations. Using a traditional definition of repeat player (based on the number of cases arbitrated by the business), the study found no statistically significant repeat-player effect — i.e., repeat businesses fared essentially the same as non-repeat businesses. *Id.* at 909. Using an alternative definition of repeat player (based on AAA administration of its Consumer Due Process Protocol), the study found a weakly statistically significant repeat-player effect, with consumer claimants winning some relief in 43.4% of awarded claims against repeat businesses and 56.1% of awarded claims against non-repeat businesses. *Id.* at 911. But, again, these differing win-rates, the study concluded, do not necessarily provide evidence of bias in favor of repeat players. Instead, the study found evidence that the repeat-player effect "may result from case selection by repeat businesses, who settle meritorious claims and arbitrate only weaker ones, while non-repeat businesses are more likely to arbitrate all claims, even meritorious ones." *Id.* at 913. For a recent study examining outcomes in AAA employment arbitrations, see Alexander J.S. Colvin, *An Empirical Study of Employment Arbitration: Case Outcomes and Processes*, 8 J. EMP. LEGAL STUD. 1 (2011).

5. More generally, Professor Marc Gallanter has identified a number of advantages that repeat players in the legal system have over what he calls "one-shotters." Marc Gallanter, *Why the "Haves" Come Out Ahead: Speculations on the Limits of Legal Change*, 9 LAW & SOC'Y REV. 95 (1974); see also Carrie Mendel-Meadow, *Do the "Haves" Come Out Ahead in Alternative Judicial Systems? Repeat Players in ADR*, 15 OHIO ST. J. ON DISP. RESOL. 19 (1999). The advantages Gallanter identifies include not only greater expertise and resources, but also the ability to "play for rules in litigation itself," seeking to establish precedents that would aid in future litigation. Gallanter, *supra*, at 100. How would this advantage apply in arbitration?

6. Professor Tullock contends that, while an arbitrator may have an incentive to favor repeat players in his or her decisions, it is not clear that the repeat player will want decisions biased in its favor. Tullock notes that businesses, for example, may be sufficiently concerned about maintaining a reputation for good quality products that they would prefer fair adjudication or even adjudication biased in favor of the other party (for example: "the customer is always right"). Do you agree?

7. Another critique of arbitration also is linked to the self-interest of arbitrators: the perception that arbitrators have an incentive to make compromise awards. Professor Alan Scott Rau explains:

> The dynamic of arbitrator self-interest has long been familiar in collective bargaining cases and is thought, for example, to provide one explanation for the apparently common practice of compromise awards. Repeat business for the arbitrator is likely only if he is able to retain the future goodwill of both union and management; the desire to do so may give him an incentive

(in the hallowed phrase) to "split the baby" in a single arbitration, or it may be "reflected in a *course* of decisions by the same arbitrator which over time, taken together, appears to show a rough balance between awards favorable to labor and those favorable to management."

Alan Scott Rau, *Integrity in Private Judging*, 38 S. TEX. L. REV. 485, 523 (1997); Rand Institute for Civil Justice, Business-to-Business Arbitration in the United States: Perceptions of Corporate Counsel 11-12 (2011) (reporting results of survey of 121 corporate counsel as "suggest[ing] that there is widespread belief that arbitration leads to compromised awards"). In labor arbitration, both the corporation and the union may be repeat players. What about in arbitrations between employers and individual employees? While the employer may well be a repeat player, it is likely that any individual employee will not be. Are there any repeat players on the employee's side? What about plaintiffs' lawyers?

In an empirical study of international arbitration awards, Stephanie Keer and Richard Naimark found that, on average, claimants recovered 46.66% of the amount sought, a percentage that would seem consistent with a practice of compromise awards. But "a careful examination of the frequency distribution of cases revealed a bimodal distribution" — in other words, in most cases claimants were awarded either all or none of what they sought. Stephanie E. Keer & Richard W. Naimark, *Arbitrators Do Not "Split the Baby" — Empirical Evidence from International Business Arbitration*, 18 J. INT'L ARB. 573, 574 (2001). Keer and Naimark therefore conclude that "the results from this study show emphatically that arbitrators do not engage in the practice of 'splitting the baby.' " *Id.* at 578. A much earlier study by Soia Mentschikoff reached similar conclusions. Soia Mentschikoff, *Commercial Arbitration*, 61 COLUM. L. REV. 846, 861 (1961). If so, why does a belief that arbitrators make compromise awards persist?

Precedent in arbitration. A second issue is the extent to which commercial arbitration can replicate the role courts play (in common law systems) of making law. Landes and Posner question whether a system of precedent would arise in commercial arbitration. Professor Mark Weidemaier disagrees in the following excerpt.

W. Mark C. Weidemaier, TOWARD A THEORY OF PRECEDENT IN ARBITRATION,
51 WM. & MARY L. REV. 1895, 1899, 1903–14(2010)[*]

INTRODUCTION

Do arbitrators create precedent? The claim that they do not recurs throughout the arbitration literature. Yet this claim conflicts with a small but growing body of evidence that, in some arbitration systems, arbitrators frequently cite to other arbitrators, claim to rely on past awards, and promote adjudicatory consistency as

---

an important system goal. Thus, although not every system of arbitration generates precedent, some clearly do.

. . .

I. ARBITRATION AS CAPABLE OF GENERATING PRECEDENT

A. A Traditional View (with Caveats): Arbitration as Particularized, Ad Hoc Decision Making

A number of arguments support the claim that arbitration does not generate precedent. For one thing, participants in private dispute resolution systems may lack sufficient lawmaking incentives. Judges and litigants generally do not obtain, and in any event would have difficulty enforcing, property rights in precedent. The production of law thus confers an uncompensated benefit on third parties, and "[w]hy would litigants who engage the services of a rent-a-judge want to pay extra for a reasoned opinion enunciating a rule that benefits only future litigants?"

The claim that arbitration does not generate precedent also is based on certain structural characteristics that are commonly — though perhaps too readily — associated with arbitration. For example, it is often said that arbitrators need not follow the law and may instead resolve disputes in whatever fashion they deem just. Arbitrators need not issue reasoned awards explaining the basis of their decisions. Many arbitration proceedings and awards are kept private, denying the public and future disputants information about past decisions. Arbitration also lacks formal legal mechanisms for ensuring that arbitrators reach consistent decisions, such as a doctrine of stare decisis or an appellate mechanism. And finally, parties to arbitration agreements may exercise control over the system's capacity to generate precedent. Their contracts may limit the precedential value of past awards or require each party to keep arbitration results confidential.

For those who attribute these characteristics to the institution of arbitration generally, the resulting picture naturally is one of particularized, ad hoc decision making. In this picture, arbitrators do justice (at best) within the unique confines of individual cases; they do not apply, much less create, legal rules. Unlike courts, which "are bound by precedent" and, even when not bound, "should give serious consideration" to other judicial opinions, arbitrators are presumed unwilling or unable to situate the disputes over which they preside within a wider body of similar disputes. As a result, past awards do not inform, much less control, future arbitrators. It follows, too, that arbitrators cannot change existing law; they cannot announce new legal rules to guide future behavior.

Though accurate to a degree, the foregoing picture of arbitration is quite stylized. It proffers a vision of "folklore arbitration" that primarily reflects assumptions about domestic arbitration practices within the United States. Even within that sphere, it corresponds imperfectly to a market reality in which arbitrators and arbitral institutions offer a diverse range of arbitration products. For example, parties often do pay arbitrators to produce reasoned awards, and these awards are often made available to the public. Future parties may seek to use these awards as "persuasive evidence" of the appropriate outcome to their dispute.

They may even require arbitrators to follow prior arbitration awards, potentially yielding, over time, a "sophisticated, comprehensive," and entirely private system of laws. Given the resulting diversity of arbitration practices, some arbitration scholars have recognized that arbitration systems have the capacity to generate precedent. Evidence from a number of arbitration systems, both international and within the United States, supports this view.

The following Section describes the evidence relevant to three such systems: international investment arbitration conducted by the International Centre for Settlement of Investment Disputes (ICSID), international commercial arbitration, and labor arbitration within the United States. In many respects, these three systems of arbitration have little in common. Thus, I do not offer them as examples of "arbitration" writ large, or to suggest an equivalence among them. To the contrary, their differences help to illustrate an important fact: that each system of arbitration represents a unique institutional context, the particulars of which undoubtedly will influence how (and whether) arbitral precedent evolves. . . .

B. The Creation of Arbitral Precedent: Three Case Studies

1. ICSID as an Evolved System of International Investment Law

The use of arbitration to resolve disputes between states and foreign investors has a lengthy history. Most early investment arbitrations were conducted pursuant to bilateral treaties that created tribunals empowered to adjudicate existing disputes involving foreign nationals. But absent such a treaty between the investor's home state and the host or borrower state, disappointed investors often had little recourse.

ICSID's major innovation was to create a formal mechanism for resolving investment disputes, one in which foreign investors assert claims directly against states. Although there is probably no such thing as a "typical" investment dispute, consider claims asserted by a foreign oil company arising out of a sovereign state's cancelation of the company's contract to extract oil from the sovereign's territory. The ICSID Convention itself does not create an obligation to arbitrate such disputes. States must consent to arbitration, either in particular contracts or by consenting generally to arbitration in a statute or treaty. In our example dispute, ICSID jurisdiction might be founded on an arbitration clause in a bilateral investment treaty between the investor's home state and the host country. Such arbitrations are "typically governed by international law, whether that law takes the form of treaty terms or customary international law as incorporated by the treaty."

At least from the perspective of capital-exporting states, ICSID was a pragmatic, procedural solution to a long-standing concern: the failure to reach multilateral agreement on substantive standards of investor protection. But ICSID was not consciously designed to create a body of investment law precedent. There is no doctrine of stare decisis in investment or any other kind of arbitration. Yet despite the formally nonbinding nature of past awards, ICSID tribunals frequently cite to and engage with awards issued by investment or other international tribunals. In an analysis of ICSID awards issued between 1990 and 2006, Jeffery Commission found that tribunals cited to awards rendered by other ICSID panels nearly 80 percent of the time. Commission also found that, over that time period, ICSID panels grew increasingly likely to cite prior awards and that the number of such citations per award increased. Through this engagement with past awards, ICSID tribunals have gradually fashioned what has been called an investment treaty "case law or jurisprudence."

2. International Commercial Arbitration's Weaker System of Precedent

Unlike international investment arbitration, which involves disputes between states and foreign investors, international commercial arbitration generally refers to "nonspecialized arbitration between private parties involved in international commercial transactions." As an example, consider a dispute between a U.S. importer and its purchasing agent in Hong Kong arising out of the importer's refusal to pay sales commissions. Although parties may contract for the application of transnational commercial law, the limited empirical evidence suggests that national law governs most commercial arbitrations.

As with investment arbitration, international commercial arbitration awards sometimes cite to and engage with other awards. Yet the existing evidence, although quite limited, suggests that international commercial arbitration features a much less robust system of arbitral precedent than investment arbitration. For example, in a survey of awards interpreting the United Nations Convention on Contracts for the International Sale of Goods, Professor Gabrielle Kaufmann-Kohler found that only 6 of 100 awards cited to other awards. A separate survey of International Chamber of Commerce awards found that about 15 percent cited past awards, mostly on questions of jurisdiction and procedure.

3. An Example from the United States: Labor Arbitration

Labor arbitrators, of course, adjudicate disputes between an employer and the union representing its employees. The arbitrator's authority derives from the arbitration clause contained in the collective bargaining agreement (CBA) between the union and the employer. Most CBAs require "cause" or "just cause" for any disciplinary action, and most labor arbitrations feature an employee challenging the employer's action under that standard. These are contract disputes, but of a somewhat unique sort. In most contracts, but for the arbitration clause, claims for breach of contract would be litigated in court. In that sense, arbitration serves as a substitute for litigation. By contrast, the traditional understanding of labor arbitration is that the CBA represents a bargain in which the union limits its right to strike in exchange for the employer's agreement to replace its traditional discretion over discipline and discharge decisions with arbitration under a "just cause" standard. Because the CBA grants unionized employees protection from discipline and discharge not enjoyed by most nonunionized employees, this bargain — "no strikes in exchange for arbitration of grievances" — means that most grievance arbitrations "involve[] claims that would not have been asserted in litigation had the parties not agreed to arbitrate."

Although labor arbitration otherwise has little in common with international investment arbitration, each system appears to have produced a fairly robust system of arbitral precedent. Labor arbitration scholars and industry professionals widely believe that labor arbitrators treat past awards as legitimate sources of authority and as building blocks in a "common law of the workplace." Surveys of labor arbitrators, reports of cases in which arbitrators have relied on prior awards, and a modest body of empirical evidence all support this belief.

4. Precedent's Role Across Different Systems of Arbitration

ICSID, international commercial, and labor arbitration are not the only arbitration systems in which some form of precedent has evolved. Some maritime arbitrators, for example, take prior awards into consideration, and it appears that the same is true in class arbitration. At one level, it should be no surprise that such a diverse array of arbitration systems have generated some form of precedent. Assume, for example, that members of a trade association want to have disputes resolved according to a set of trade rules rather than state-supplied law. Because arbitrators can be chosen for their diligence, acumen, or industry expertise, association members might prefer arbitration to litigation. Assume further that members want their arbitration system to produce rulings that bind future arbitrators, perhaps because they believe this will lend certainty to future transactions and facilitate dispute settlement. To accomplish these goals, the arbitration contract might require arbitrators to set forth the reasoning underlying their awards and even to follow precedent established in prior arbitrations. Structured in this manner, an arbitration system might produce "a sophisticated, comprehensive [and private] legal system."

But most users of arbitration do not consciously seek to create a system of private legal rules. Certainly that is true of ICSID, international commercial, and labor arbitration. Nevertheless, past awards receive precedential weight in each system. Indeed, at first glance, this appears to be one of the few things the three systems have in common. . . .

. . .

That each of these very different systems of arbitration has generated some form of precedent illustrates the wide range of contexts in which arbitral precedent may evolve. . . .

NOTE

The legal frameworks governing two of the three types of arbitration discussed by Professor Weidemaier — ICSID arbitration and labor arbitration — are largely beyond the scope of this book. Investment arbitrations conducted by ICSID are subject to the ICSID Convention (the Convention on the Settlement of Investment Disputes Between States and Nationals of Other States (opened for signature Mar. 18, 1965, 17 U.S.T. 1270, 575 U.N.T.S. 159)) rather than the New York Convention (the Convention on the Recognition and Enforcement of Foreign Arbitral Awards). The New York Convention, which applies to most international commercial arbitrations (including investment arbitrations not subject to the ICSID Convention), is discussed beginning in Chapter 5. For a brief overview of the ICSID Convention, see GARY B. BORN, INTERNATIONAL COMMERCIAL ARBITRATION 105-107 (2009).

The legal framework governing labor arbitration in the United States likewise is separate from the legal framework governing commercial arbitration. "[T]he [Supreme] Court has studiously avoided applying the FAA to collective bargaining agreements," and has instead "constructed an entire realm of jurisprudence under Section 301" of the Labor-Management Relations Act. Dennis R. Nolan, *Employment Arbitration After* Circuit City, 41 BRANDEIS L.J. 853, 883 n.138 (2003); *see* Textile Workers Union v. Lincoln Mills, 353 U.S. 448, 451-52 (1957). That said, "the federal courts have often looked to the [FAA] for guidance in labor arbitration cases," United Paperworkers Int'l Union v. Misco, Inc., 484 U.S. 29, 40 n.9 (1987), while the Supreme Court on a number of occasions has cited to labor arbitration cases in construing the FAA, *see, e.g.*, Stolt-Nielsen S.A. v. AnimalFeeds Int'l Corp., 130 S. Ct. 1758, 1767-68 (2010); Howsam v. Dean Witter Reynolds, Inc., 537 U.S. 79, 84 (2002). *See generally* Stephen L. Hayford, *Unification of the Law of Labor Arbitration and Commercial Arbitration: An Idea Whose Time Has Come*, 52 BAYLOR L. REV. 781 (2000).

Despite the differences in legal framework, the fact remains that both ICSID arbitration and labor arbitration (as well as international commercial arbitration) are private forms of dispute resolution in which a system of precedent apparently has developed.

Role of government. Landes and Posner argue that the use of government power may be necessary, at least in some circumstances, for commercial arbitration to be a viable alternative to public courts. Not all agree that such government intervention is beneficial.

Bruce L. Benson, THE ENTERPRISE OF LAW: JUSTICE WITHOUT THE STATE 221–222 (1990)*

Many observers contend that these [arbitration] laws make arbitration viable. Landes and Posner, for example, argued that the arbitration clauses in contracts are "effective, in major part anyway, only because the public courts enforce such contracts; if they did not, there would often be no effective sanction against the party who simply breaches the contract to arbitrate." In other words, private arbitration is a viable option to public courts, because it is backed by those public courts. This claim is demonstrably false. The historic development of the Law Merchant demonstrates that a significant boycott sanction can be produced by the commercial community. In fact, the international Law Merchant continues to survive and flourish without the backing of a coercive government authority. Beyond that, however, it was during the years prior to 1920 that arbitration began to catch on, particularly among trade associations, so the process was well established before government coercion was available. The merchant community backed the rulings with sanctions similar to those that evolved under the medieval law merchant.

---

* Copyright © 1990 by the Pacific Research Institute for Public Policy. Reprinted with permission.

Anyone who refused to accept an arbiter's decision found access to his trade association's arbitration tribunal withdrawn or saw his name released to the association's membership: "these penalties were far more fearsome than the cost of the award with which he disagreed. Voluntary and private adjudications were voluntarily and privately adhered to if not out of honor, out of self interest." This does not mean, however, that the New York statute and all those that followed have not had an impact on arbitration. In fact, the effect is precisely the opposite of that suggested by Landes and Posner: *Arbitration became a less attractive alternative to the public courts than it would have otherwise been in the absence of these laws.*

How can this be? The problem is that what statute law protected, government also controlled. An enormous number of court cases were filed after the New York statute was passed, for instance, as businessmen tried to determine what characteristics of arbitration would be considered "legal" by the courts. Cases involved such issues as the appropriate way to select arbitrators, whether lawyers had to be present (lawyers became active in arbitration because of these statutes), whether stenographic notes of the proceedings should be taken, and so on. . . . Businessmen, forced to pay attention to the prospect of judicial review, had to make their arbitration processes compatible with statute and precedent law, including public court procedure.

Some of the most attractive aspects of the arbitration alternative were substantially weakened as a direct result of the statutory legalization of the process. In particular, arbitration has taken a much more complex "legalistic" character, arbitration is less a summary proceeding, concern for government imposed laws is relatively more significant, and arbitration is costlier. The government has not eliminated arbitration as a competitor, but the arbitration statutes have limited its competitiveness.

PROBLEM 1.1

One of the clients of your firm is a high government official in a country that recently has privatized many formerly state-owned enterprises: public utilities, railroads, manufacturing operations, and so on. The client has hired several consultants in the United States to evaluate whether other governmental services might be privatized, such as schools and prisons. Your firm has been retained as a consultant to evaluate the extent to which the country's court system might be privatized as well. Your assignment is to consider whether and to what extent a system of commercial arbitration could take the place of the country's court system. If complete privatization is not feasible, in your view, consider what the government might do to promote and foster commercial arbitration as an alternative to the public courts.

————

Is dispute resolution a traditional governmental function? Whether it is a traditional governmental function is important for several reasons, not the least of which is whether constitutional due process protections apply. One ground on which otherwise private activity can be treated as "state action" — and thus subject to constitutional constraints — is when the "private entity has exercised powers that are 'traditionally the exclusive prerogative of the State.' " Blum v. Yaretsky, 457 U.S. 991, 1005 (1982).

SMITH v. AMERICAN ARBITRATION ASSOCIATION, INC.
United States Court of Appeals for the Seventh Circuit
233 F.3d 502 (2000)

POSNER, *Circuit Judge.*

The plaintiff appeals from the dismissal under Fed. R. Civ. P. 12(b)(6) of her far-ranging challenge to standard arbitration procedure. She had made a contract to sell defendant Argenbright her controlling interest in the PIMMS Corporation for some $65 million. The contract provided that disputes under it would be resolved by arbitration in Chicago "in accordance with the rules and regulations of the American Arbitration Association" . . . . Shortly after the sale, Argenbright gave notice to Smith that it believed that she had exaggerated PIMMS's revenue potential, that the exaggeration constituted a breach of warranty, that Argenbright had sustained damages of $14 million, and that it wanted to arbitrate the claim. It filed the claim with the American Arbitration Association's Chicago office, which responded by sending the parties a list of 15 arbitrators taken from the Association's roster for "Large and Complex Commercial Cases." The list contained 14 men and one woman. Pursuant to the Association's rules, the parties were asked to strike the names of any of the persons on the list whom they did not want to have on the arbitration panel and to rank the remaining ones. One of the names struck by Argenbright was that of the woman on the list (whom Smith had listed as her first choice), and as a result a panel of three male arbitrators was selected — whereupon Smith brought this suit in federal district court . . . complaining primarily that the lack of gender diversity of the list, coupled with Argenbright's action in excluding the only woman on it, was a breach of contract. . . .

. . .

Smith expresses concern that because she is a woman and her opponent is a corporation presumably controlled by men (though there is no allegation to that effect), an all-male panel will be unsympathetic to her. No effort to substantiate the suggestion that male judges or arbitrators are prejudiced against wealthy women who have purely commercial disputes with corporations has been made; nor has Smith pointed to any issue in this litigation to which a man might be insensitive. The relief sought, which seems premised on the belief that a female litigant is entitled to be judged by a panel that includes at least one woman, borders on the fantastic.

But we do not suppose that there is anything in the law that would forbid private parties to stipulate to a mode of private dispute resolution that specified a particular gender composition of the tribunal, assuming the arbitrators are not employees of the American Arbitration Association or of some other dispute-resolution agency conducting the arbitration, which might bring Title VII into play. So if Smith has a contractual right to be judged by an arbitration panel that contains at least one woman, she can enforce it, though just how and when are questions . . . .

. . .

So viewed, however, Smith's claim against Argenbright is premature. The time to challenge an arbitration, on whatever grounds, including bias, is when the arbitration is completed and an award rendered. To allow a party to bring an independent suit to enjoin the arbitration is inconsistent with fundamental procedural principles that apply with even greater force to arbitration than to conventional litigation. If during jury voir dire a *Batson* objection to the exercise of a peremptory challenge is rejected by the trial judge, the disappointed litigant cannot bring a suit to enjoin the litigation. But that is what Smith tried to do here. It is true that in rare instances a litigant can interrupt the litigation by filing an interlocutory appeal or seeking mandamus. But a party who wants to have such an option should not (and of course need not) consent to arbitration, which generally and here does not have an appellate component. The choice of arbitration is a choice to trade off certain procedural safeguards, such as appellate review, against hoped-for savings in time and expense (other than the expense of the tribunal), a measure of procedural simplicity and informality, and a differently constituted tribunal. That choice would be disrupted by allowing a party to arbitration to obtain an interlocutory appeal to a federal district court, as Smith has tried to do.

The parties are of diverse citizenship, so Argenbright if it obtains an award in the arbitration will be able to seek confirmation (that is, enforcement) of the award in federal district court under the Federal Arbitration Act. 9 U.S.C. § 9. Smith points out that while she will be able to object to confirmation, the grounds for objection permitted by the act . . . are extremely limited, and though one of them is "evident partiality" by the arbitrators, 9 U.S.C § 10(a)(2), this will be impossible as a practical matter to prove; therefore she should be permitted to sue now. That's a non sequitur. The right to object to the composition of the tribunal on broader grounds than evident partiality was one of the procedural rights that Smith gave up when she agreed to the arbitration clause in the stock purchase agreement. By agreeing to arbitrate in a setting in which Argenbright if it prevailed could seek confirmation under the Federal Arbitration Act, Smith bound herself to accept the limited judicial review which that act allows.

We mentioned the principle of *Batson v. Kentucky*, 476 U.S. 79 (1986), that peremptory challenges cannot be based on racial or other invidious grounds, now including gender. J.E.B. v. Alabama, 511 U.S. 127 (1994). Smith argues that this principle, which is based on the equal protection clause (more precisely, where federal rather than state action is concerned, on the due process clause of the Fifth Amendment, interpreted as containing an equal-protection component), should be extended to arbitration, since the courts through the Federal Arbitration Act and cognate state statutes lend their assistance to arbitration. We disagree. Arbitration is a private self-help remedy. The American Arbitration Association is a private organization selling a private service to private parties who are under no legal obligation to agree to arbitrate their disputes or, if they decide to use arbitration to resolve disputes, to use the services of the Association, which is not the only provider of such services. When arbitrators issue awards, they do so pursuant to the disputants' contract — in fact the award is a supplemental contract obligating the losing party to pay the winner. The fact that the courts enforce these contracts, just as they enforce other contracts, does not convert the contracts into state or federal action and so bring the equal protection clause into play. This is not Shelley v.

Kraemer, 334 U.S. 1 (1948), or Marsh v. Alabama, 326 U.S. 501 (1946), cases in which the enforcement of private contracts had the effect of establishing private governments exercising governmental power under delegation from the state.

. . .

Affirmed.

NOTES

1. All of the federal courts that have addressed the issue have held that commercial arbitration is not "state action" to which constitutional protections apply. *See, e.g.,* Perpetual Securities, Inc. v. Tang, 290 F.3d 132, 137–39 (2d Cir. 2002); Desiderio v. National Ass'n of Securities Dealers, 191 F.3d 198 (2d Cir. 1999), *cert. denied,* 531 U.S. 1069 (2001); Koveleskie v. SBC Capital Markets, Inc., 167 F.3d 361, 368 (7th Cir.), *cert. denied,* 528 U.S. 811 (1999); Duffield v. Robertson Stephens & Co., 144 F.3d 1182 (9th Cir.), *cert. denied,* 525 U.S. 982 (1998); Davis v. Prudential Sec., Inc., 59 F.3d 1186, 1190–91 (11th Cir. 1995); *see also* Sarah Rudolph Cole, *Arbitration and State Action,* 2005 BYU L. REV. 1, 4 (citing cases). The same holds for state courts, as well. *Id.* at 4 n.11; *see, e.g.,* MedVal USA Health Programs, Inc. v. MemberWorks, Inc., 872 A.2d 423, 434–36 (Conn.), *cert. denied,* 546 U.S. 960 (2005).

2. Several commentators, however, argue to the contrary. Professor Richard Reuben, for example, contends that "[a]n ADR process, like arbitration, often involves not only the mere resolution of disputes but . . . the *state-enforced* resolution of disputes. It is this element of state enforcement that distinguishes matters of constitutional moment from those of purely private concern. The binding resolution of disputes is, of course, a traditionally exclusive public function." Richard C. Reuben, *Public Justice: Toward a State Action Theory of Alternative Dispute Resolution,* 85 CALIF. L. REV. 577, 621 (1997); *see also* Jean R. Sternlight, *Rethinking the Constitutionality of the Supreme Court's Preference for Binding Arbitration: A Fresh Assessment of Jury Trial, Separation of Powers, and Due Process Concerns,* 72 TUL. L. REV. 1, 40–47 (1997). *Compare* Cole, *supra,* at 28–48 (arguing for finding of state action in agency-initiated arbitration, such as securities arbitration, but not in contractual arbitration).

PROBLEM 1.2

One evening, Elsie Patrick receives a phone call from Hilton Cubitt, a principal in the brokerage firm of Cubitt Investments, Inc. Cubitt convinces Elsie to use her retirement nest egg of $50,000 to set up a brokerage account for Cubitt to administer. On Cubitt's advice, Elsie invests all $50,000 in ostrich egg futures, which Cubitt assures her will be a highly profitable investment. Indeed, Cubitt tells her, she is fortunate to be among the first purchasers of these investments because "the early bird gets the worm."

When her investment proves not to be as profitable as she had hoped, Elsie comes to see you. Elsie asks you to look into her investment account, and says that she fears "she has egg on her face" from relying on Cubitt. You discover that, not only were ostrich egg futures a grossly inappropriate investment for Elsie's retirement savings, in fact there were no ostrich egg futures. Instead, Cubitt used the money to "feather his own nest," so to speak: to buy expensive cars, to take vacations at ritzy resorts, and to maintain a very expensive lifestyle.

As required by the account agreement, Elsie submits her claim against Cubitt to arbitration. The arbitration panel finds in her favor, awarding her $50,000 in compensatory damages and $15,000,000 in punitive damages against Cubitt. When you go to court to confirm the arbitration award, Cubitt opposes confirmation on the ground that the punitive damages award is excessive under a line of recent United States Supreme Court decisions, including BMW v. Gore, 517 U.S. 559 (1996). How would you respond to Cubitt's argument?

§ 1.03   WHAT IS ARBITRATION?

Neither the Federal Arbitration Act nor state arbitration statutes define "arbitration." In Rush Prudential HMO, Inc. v. Moran, 536 U.S. 355 (2002), the Supreme Court stated that "[i]n the classic sense, arbitration occurs when 'parties in dispute choose a judge to render a final and binding decision on the merits of the controversy and on the basis of proofs presented by the parties.' " *Id.* at 382 (*quoting* 1 IAN R. MACNEIL ET AL., FEDERAL ARBITRATION LAW § 2.1.1 (1995)). A similar definition comes from the Restatement, which defines an "arbitral tribunal" as "a body consisting of one or more persons designated directly or indirectly by the parties to an arbitration agreement and empowered by them to adjudicate a dispute that has arisen between or among them." Restatement (Third) of the U.S. Law of International Commercial Arbitration § 1-1(b). The Restatement makes clear that "arbitration differs from collaborative forms of ADR, such as mediation, which do not produce a binding resolution of disputes and which require the parties' continuing willingness to participate in the proceedings." *Id.* § 1-1, rptrs. note to cmt. c.

The following cases discuss forms of dispute resolution that fall between mediation and arbitration so defined. Consider whether these forms of dispute resolution, or ones like them, are "arbitration" within the meaning of the Federal Arbitration Act and the Uniform Arbitration Act.

AMF INC. v. BRUNSWICK CORP.
United States District Court for the Eastern District of New York
621 F. Supp. 456 (1985)

WEINSTEIN, CHIEF JUDGE.

In this case of first impression, AMF Incorporated seeks to compel Brunswick Corporation to comply with their agreement to obtain a non-binding advisory opinion in a dispute over the propriety of advertising claims. For reasons indicated below, the agreement to utilize an alternative dispute resolution mechanism must be enforced.

. . .

AMF and Brunswick compete nationally in the manufacture of electronic and automatic machinery used for bowling centers. In earlier litigation before this court, AMF alleged that Brunswick had advertised certain automatic scoring devices in a false and deceptive manner. Brunswick responded with counterclaims regarding advertisements for AMF's pinspotter, bowling pins and automatic scorer. In 1983 the parties ended the litigation with a settlement agreement filed with the court. Any future dispute involving an advertised claim of "data based comparative superiority" of any bowling product would be submitted to an advisory third party, the National Advertising Division ("NAD") of the Council of Better Business Bureaus, to determine whether there was experimental support for the claim.

. . .

NAD was created in 1971 by the American Advertising Federation, American Association of Advertising Agencies, Association of National Advertisers, and the Council of Better Business Bureaus "to help sustain high standards of truth and accuracy in national advertising." . . . If NAD finds that the advertising claims are unsupported, and the advertiser refuses to modify or discontinue the advertising, the organization will complain to the appropriate governmental authority. Voluntary compliance with NAD's decisions has been universal. Reportedly no advertiser who has participated in the complete process of a NAD investigation and NARB appeal has declined to abide by the decision.

In March and April 1985, Brunswick advertised its product, Armor Plate 3000, in a trade periodical called *Bowler's Journal.* Armor Plate is a synthetic laminated material used to make bowling lanes. It competes with the wood lanes produced by AMF. "The wood lane. A relic of the past," claims the advertisement, under a sketch of a horse and buggy. It goes on to detail the advantages of Armor Plate; and, as indicated in the footnote to the advertisement, strongly suggests that research supports the claim of durability as compared to wood lanes.

. . .

AMF, disputing the content of the advertisement, sought from Brunswick the underlying research data referred to in the footnote. Brunswick replied that having undertaken the expense of research it would not make the results available to AMF. Thereupon AMF informed Brunswick that it was invoking Paragraph 9 of the settlement agreement and requested that Brunswick provide substantiation to an independent third party. Brunswick responded that its advertisement did not fall within the terms of the agreement. AMF now brings this action to compel Brunswick to submit its data to the NAD for nonbinding arbitration.

. . .

AMF characterizes the settlement agreement as one subject to the Federal Arbitration Act. The Act provides for enforcement of agreements to "settle" disputes arising after the agreement was entered into. . . . The issue posed is whether "a controversy" would be "settled" by the process set forth in the agreement.

Brunswick argues that the parties did not contemplate the kind of arbitration envisaged by the Act because the opinion of the third party is not binding on AMF and Brunswick and the agreement cannot settle the controversy. Arbitration,

Brunswick argues, must present an alternative to litigation; that is, it must provide "a final settlement of the controversy between the parties."

Arbitration is a term that eludes easy definition. One commentator has pointed out that "difficulty with terminology seems to have persisted throughout the entire development of arbitration." . . . Case law has done little to sharpen the definition.

The Federal Arbitration Act, adopted in 1925, made agreements to arbitrate enforceable without defining what they were. Contemporary cases provide a broad description of arbitration: "[a] form of procedure whereby differences may be settled." At no time have the courts insisted on a rigid or formalistic approach to a definition of arbitration.

Case law following the passage of the Act reflects unequivocal support of agreements to have third parties decide disputes — the essence of arbitration. No magic words such as "arbitrate" or "binding arbitration" or "final dispute resolution" are needed to obtain the benefits of the Act.

. . .

An adversary proceeding, submission of evidence, witnesses and cross-examination are not essential elements of arbitration. The Second Circuit has set a standard of "fundamental fairness" in arbitration; rules of evidence and procedure do not apply with the same strictness as they do in federal courts.

Arbitration is a creature of contract, a device of the parties rather than the judicial process. If the parties have agreed to submit a dispute for a decision by a third party, they have agreed to arbitration. The arbitrator's decision need not be binding in the same sense that a judicial decision needs to be to satisfy the constitutional requirement of a justiciable case or controversy.

. . .

Under the circumstances of this case, the agreement should be characterized as one to arbitrate. Obviously there is a controversy between the parties — is there data supporting Brunswick's claim of superiority. Submission of this dispute will at least "settle" that issue, even though the parties may want to continue related disputes in another forum.

It is highly likely that if Brunswick's claims are found by NAD to be supported that will be the end of AMF's challenge to the advertisement. Should the claims not be found to be supported, it is probable that Brunswick will change its advertising copy. Viewed in the light of reasonable commercial expectations the dispute will be settled by this arbitration. That it may not end all controversy between the parties for all times is no reason not to enforce the agreement.

The mechanism agreed to by the parties does provide an effective alternative to litigation, even though it would not employ an adversary process. That the arbitrator will examine documents in camera and ex parte does not prevent recognition of the procedure as arbitration since the parties have agreed to this special practice in this unique type of dispute. Courts are fully familiar with the practice since prosecutorial and business secrets often require protection by ex parte and in camera proceedings during the course of a litigation.

In a confidential-submission scheme, such as the one agreed to here, adversarial hearings cannot take place. But this fact does not militate against application of the Act. Rather it supports arbitration since the special arbitrator may be more capable of deciding the issue than is a court which relies so heavily on the adversary process. Moreover, the particular arbitrator chosen by these parties is more capable than the courts of finding the faint line that separates data supported claims from puffery in the sometimes mendacious atmosphere of advertising copy.

. . .

AMF's petition to compel the submission of data pursuant to Paragraph 9 of the settlement agreement of June 30, 1983 is enforceable under the Federal Arbitration Act. . . .

NOTES

1. In Harrison v. Nissan Motor Corp., 111 F.3d 343 (3d Cir. 1997), the United States Court of Appeals for the Third Circuit distinguished *AMF* and held that nonbinding arbitration required under the Pennsylvania Automobile Lemon Law was not arbitration within the meaning of the FAA. The court of appeals found that "the essence of arbitration . . . is that, when the parties agree to submit their disputes to it, they have agreed to arbitrate these disputes through to completion, i.e. to an award made by a third-party arbitrator." *Id.* at 350. Because "a claimant cannot be barred from pursuing litigation under the Lemon Law if the mechanism delays for more than forty days," the court concluded that the "claimant would not . . . pursue the procedure to completion in all cases." *Id.* at 350–51. Therefore, the court held, "the informal dispute resolution mechanism provided for by Nissan pursuant to the Lemon Law does not constitute arbitration." *Id.* at 351.

For the views of other courts, compare Brennan v. King, 139 F.3d 258, 266 n.7 (1st Cir. 1998) (because employment contract "imposes strict constraints on the scope of the arbitrator's authority and severely limits the effect of the arbitral decision, there is little ground for a 'reasonable . . . expectation' that the procedure will resolve the dispute") (citing *Harrison*); Dluhos v. Strasberg, 321 F.3d 365, 372–73 (3d Cir. 2003) (holding non-binding domain name dispute resolution not subject to the FAA); and Salt Lake Tribune Publishing Co. v. Mgmt. Planning, Inc., 390 F.3d 684, 690 (10th Cir. 2004) (appraisal that would "not definitively settle the dispute" is not "arbitration" within the meaning of the FAA) with Wolsey, Ltd. v. Foodmaker, Inc., 144 F.3d 1205, 1209 (9th Cir. 1998) (agreement providing for non-binding arbitration enforceable under the FAA because it provides for submission of claims to a third party but does not "explicitly permit" one party to go to court before the arbitration is completed) (distinguishing *Harrison*); Dow Corning Corp. v. Safety Nat'l Casualty Corp., 335 F.3d 742, 747–48 (8th Cir. 2003), *cert. denied*, 540 U.S. 1219 (2004) (finding authority to review non-binding arbitration award under the FAA); and Liberty Mut. Group, Inc. v. Wright, 2012 U.S. Dist. LEXIS 29414, at *19-*20 (D. Md. Mar. 5, 2012) (distinguishing *Salt Lake Tribune* and holding that appraisal process constituted arbitration when "[s]ubmission of the dispute to the appraisers will ultimately settle that issue, as the appraisers — perhaps through involvement of the umpire — will reach a binding decision through that process").

2.   Several courts have held that clauses requiring mediation are enforceable under the applicable arbitration statute. *See* CB Richard Ellis, Inc. v. American Envt'l Waste Mgmt., 1998 U.S. Dist. LEXIS 20064 (E.D.N.Y. Dec. 4, 1998) (FAA) ("Because the mediation clause in the case at bar manifests the parties' intent to provide an alternative method to 'settle' controversies arising under the parties' 1997 agreement, this mediation clause fits within the Act's definition of arbitration"); Fisher v. GE Medical Sys., 276 F. Supp. 2d 891, 893 (M.D. Tenn. 2003) (FAA); Cecala v. Moore, 982 F. Supp. 609, 613 (E.D. Ill. 1997) (Illinois Arbitration Act). *But see* Advanced Bodycare Solutions, L.L.C. v. Thione Int'l, Inc., 524 F.3d 1235, 1240 (11th Cir. 2008) ("because the mediation process does not purport to adjudicate or resolve a case in any way, it is not 'arbitration' within the meaning of the FAA"); Lynn v. General Electric Co., 2005 U.S. Dist. LEXIS 5108 (D. Kan. Jan. 20, 2005) (rejecting "proposition that the word 'arbitration' as used in the FAA includes the process of mediation"). So is mediation really "arbitration" after all?

CHENG-CANINDIN v. RENAISSANCE HOTEL ASSOCIATES
California Court of Appeal
57 Cal. Rptr. 2d 867 (1996)

HAERLE, ASSOCIATE JUSTICE.

I. INTRODUCTION

Respondent Georgina Cheng-Canindin brought a wrongful termination suit against the owners and management of her former employer, the Parc Fifty Five Hotel (the Hotel). Appellants Renaissance Hotel Associates and Lawrence Chan are two of the defendants in the wrongful termination action who petitioned the trial court to compel respondent to participate in "mandatory contractual arbitration" of her claims. Appellants contend the trial court erred by denying their petition and refusing to compel respondent to submit her dispute to the Hotel's "Review Committee" for a final and binding resolution of her claims. We hold that respondent did not agree to arbitrate her claims against the Hotel and therefore affirm the trial court's order denying the petition to compel arbitration.

II. STATEMENT OF FACTS

A. Respondent's Employment by the Hotel

Respondent was hired by the Hotel on January 30, 1985, and was employed in its Human Resources Department. In February 1987, she signed a document entitled "Receipt of Employee Handbook." That document states, in part: "I have this day received a copy of the Renaissance Employee Handbook. I agree to fully and completely read the Employee Handbook and to abide by the rules and regulations contained therein. I agree to resolve all disputes concerning my employment with the Hotel by the procedures outlined in this Handbook."

B. The Hotel's "Internal Problem Solving Procedure"

. . .

The [Renaissance Employee] Handbook outlines the Hotel's four "step" internal problem solving procedure. Step No. 1 instructs the employee to bring all problems to his or her immediate department head unless the complaint concerns that person. Step No. 2 is to advise the employee's division head of the problem. If the problem is not solved, Step No. 3 is to contact the personnel manager. If the employee is "still not satisfied with the outcome" he or she is instructed to go to Step No. 4, which is described as follows:

> You may bring your problem or concern to the Renaissance Review Committee. We hope that most disagreements or problems you have concerning your employment with the Renaissance can be satisfactorily resolved by the three steps listed above. However, we realize that some disputes are better handled by an impartial group of individuals with no 'stake' in the outcome. Therefore, the Renaissance Review Committee has been developed to be the final decision-maker in all disputes arising out of your employment with the Hotel. The Renaissance Review Committee is made up of employees and members of management, all from outside of your department. After all facts are presented to the Committee, it will discuss the dispute and reach a binding decision based on a majority vote by the members of the Committee. The decision of the Committee will be final for all parties involved.

. . .

C. The Present Action

On March 10, 1994, respondent, who was five months pregnant, was terminated from her employment. Respondent filed a wrongful termination complaint alleging, among other things, sex and race discrimination, violations of public policy and defamation. Instead of answering the complaint, respondents filed a "petition to compel plaintiff's compliance with contractual alternative dispute resolution, including arbitration pursuant to California Code of Civil Procedure § 1281.2" (the petition).

In their petition, appellants alleged that respondent was terminated for breaching company policy concerning confidentiality of personnel information.

The petition further alleged that respondent refused to resolve her dispute concerning the basis for her termination by participating in the mandatory internal problem solving procedures which she had previously agreed to follow. The petition requested that the trial court stay court proceedings pending completion of "arbitration in the form of the Parc Fifty Five Review Committee procedures."

At the hearing on their petition, appellants argued that respondent, by agreeing to comply with the terms of the Handbook, did not simply agree to participate in the Review Committee procedure before filing suit, but that she effectively waived her right to a judicial forum with respect to any claim relating to her employment. Appellants also challenged any notion that the Review Committee procedure was "inherently biased." According to appellants, federal law preempts state law regarding the enforceability of this agreement and federal law requires proof of actual bias. After the hearing, the trial court issued a minute order denying appellants' petition to compel arbitration. . . .

III. DISCUSSION

Appellants contend the trial court erroneously concluded that the agreement at issue in this case is not governed by the Federal Arbitration Act (the FAA), that the FAA mandates that an arbitration agreement be enforced absent proof of actual bias, and that there is no evidence of actual bias in this case. We find it unnecessary to address these contentions because we conclude that the parties to this appeal did not enter into an arbitration agreement at all.

Under both federal and state law, the threshold question presented by a petition to compel arbitration is whether there is an agreement to arbitrate. . . .

. . .

In the present case, neither the alleged agreement nor any of the literature describing the Hotel's Review Committee procedure employs the term arbitration. "[T]he failure of the agreement to identify the grievance procedure as 'arbitration' is not fatal to its use as a binding mechanism for resolving disputes between the parties. More important is the nature and intended effect of the proceeding." Here, the nature and intended effect of the Review Committee procedure compel the conclusions that the parties did not in fact enter into an arbitration agreement nor did they even intend to do so.

A. The Nature of the Review Committee Procedure Does Not Evince an Agreement to Arbitrate

Appellants contend the Review Committee procedure constitutes arbitration. Our review of the relevant authorities defining arbitration leads us to a decidedly contrary conclusion. Indeed, the nature of the Review Committee procedure is inconsistent with the concept of arbitration.

1. "Arbitration" Defined

California statutory law pertaining to the validity and enforceability of arbitration agreements does not define "arbitration." The only California case we have found which purports to do so . . . offers little guidance as to the requisite attributes of a true arbitration agreement.

The most useful definition of arbitration we have found is contained in Black's Law Dictionary which defines arbitration as: "A process of dispute resolution in which a neutral third party (arbitrator) renders a decision after a hearing at which both parties have an opportunity to be heard. Where arbitration is voluntary, the disputing parties select the arbitrator who has the power to render a binding decision." (Black's Law Dictionary (6th ed., 1990) p. 105.) We glean from this definition several attributes of a true arbitration agreement: (1) a third party decision maker; (2) a mechanism for ensuring neutrality with respect to the rendering of the decision; (3) a decision maker who is chosen by the parties; (4) an opportunity for both parties to be heard, and (5) a binding decision. Although we have not found a California case which adopts Black's definition, we have found that the procedures which are characterized by California courts as "arbitrations" possess the attributes set forth in Black's definition.

. . .

All of this authority confirms our strong view that a third party decision maker and some decree of impartiality must exist for a dispute resolution mechanism to constitute arbitration. This conclusion is reinforced by authority from several other states which define the arbitration process as requiring an impartial third party decision maker with authority to render a final and binding decision. . . .

For the foregoing reasons, we conclude that, although arbitration can take many procedural forms, a dispute resolution procedure is not an arbitration unless there is a third party decision maker, a final and binding decision, and a mechanism to assure a minimum level of impartiality with respect to the rendering of that decision.

2. The Review Committee Procedure is Not an Arbitration Procedure

Arbitration is the submission of a dispute to a third party. Under the Review Committee procedure at issue in this case, the Hotel is the sole decision maker. Everyone involved in the decision making process is employed by, selected by, and under the control of the Hotel. Employees of the Hotel sit on the Committee; the General Manager of the Hotel breaks tie votes; the Committee is chaired by an employee from the Personnel Department. The employee does not select any Committee member and must accept the roles that the Hotel has assigned to the General Manager and the Personnel Department.

For a procedure to constitute arbitration there must be some mechanism for ensuring a minimum level of impartiality. . . . [T]his mechanism can take many different forms. Party-affiliated representatives or otherwise partial decision makers can play a role in an arbitration when the procedure also contains some impartial means of resolving those disagreements which cannot be resolved by the partial decision makers. In the present case, the effective decision makers are not simply party-affiliated; they are one of the parties to the dispute. The other party, the employee, has no representative among the decision makers to counter-balance the Hotel's inherent, substantial and obvious power. Nor is there any provision in the Review Committee procedure which even purports to afford, much less assure, impartiality.

Indeed, contrary to the Hotel's contentions on appeal, the entire Review Committee procedure is inherently slanted in management's direction. The General Manager decides, according to some unknown standards, the jurisdiction of the Committee, breaks tie votes and makes the final decision about whether a witness should be required to testify. The Personnel Department chooses the Committee members, makes relevancy decisions and also has control over who may testify. It is even suggested that Committee members need not to be objective; their job is to "ensure that major decisions affecting the employment of individual employees is [sic] made in accordance with Hotel policy." Hotel policies may never be challenged by employees or altered by the Committee.

Arbitration should give both parties an opportunity to be heard. Contrary to appellants' contention on appeal, the Review Committee procedure does not guarantee the employee such an opportunity. Indeed we are dismayed by appellants' bold contention that their procedures "provide all of the procedures that Plaintiff would have in a trial court, without the consequent delay or expense." A terminated employee is expressly precluded from challenging Hotel policy, procedure or rules. She is strongly discouraged from retaining counsel and is advised to seek assistance from the Personnel Department if she needs help presenting her case. And, in stark contrast to the trial procedures with which we are familiar, under Hotel procedure the jurisdiction of the Committee, the relevancy of evidence and the presentation of witnesses are all matters within the unfettered discretion of one of the parties to the dispute, the Hotel.

. . .

B. The Parties Did Not Intend that the Review Committee Procedure Constitute Binding Arbitration

Several factors support our additional conclusion that the parties did not intend to enter into a binding arbitration agreement. First, the Hotel's literature describing the Review Committee procedure suggests that the Hotel viewed the procedure as an "internal problem solving" mechanism and not as a substitute for litigation. Of course, the Hotel was not required to use the term "arbitration," but we cannot infer an intent to arbitrate when the procedure described by the Hotel is inconsistent with the definition of arbitration. . . .

By the same token, evidence that an employee has accepted its employer's "request" to agree to participate in an *internal* grievance procedure is not evidence the employee intended to enter into a binding arbitration agreement. Notwithstanding the statements in Hotel literature that Committee decisions will be final and binding, we simply cannot accept the proposition that the average employee who agrees to comply with the terms of the Handbook views the Review Committee procedure as a binding arbitration or intends to waive his or her right to a judicial forum.

We also find support in the record for respondent's contention that the Review Committee procedure was not mandatory but voluntary and therefore was not intended to be tantamount to an arbitration agreement. This contention is supported by the permissive language used in the Handbook to describe the procedure; e.g., "[y]ou *may* bring your problem or concern to the Renaissance Review Committee." In addition, respondent submitted evidence that she and other employees, including members of management, believed that participation in the Review Committee procedure was optional. Indeed, appellants' own evidence indicates the Hotel viewed the procedure as voluntary. Appellants have included in this record a copy of their petition to confirm an arbitration award made by the Review Committee against a former employee named Henry Tran, and a trial court order confirming that award. In the Tran petition, appellants characterized the final step of their "internal problem solving procedure" as the "voluntary submission of a dispute" to their Review Committee.

In summary, we conclude that there is no arbitration agreement between the parties in this case. The Review Committee procedure is not an arbitration procedure because there is no third party decision maker, the procedure totally lacks impartiality, and it is controlled exclusively by one of the parties to the dispute. Further, evidence that the procedure was conceived as a way for the Hotel to resolve internal problems and that participation in the Review Committee procedure was intended to be voluntary is additional support for the conclusion that the parties did not intend to enter into a mandatory arbitration agreement. Since there is no arbitration agreement between the parties in this case, appellants' petition to compel arbitration was properly denied.

IV. DISPOSITION

The August 3, 1995, order denying appellants' motion to compel arbitration is affirmed.

NOTE

This case illustrates one way that courts review "arbitration" agreements for fairness. If a court finds that an agreement is so one-sided that it cannot properly be called arbitration, it will refuse to enforce the agreement and permit the parties to proceed in court instead. As you read the rest of the material on enforcing arbitration agreements, keep an eye out for other ways courts police the fairness of arbitration agreements.

KABIA v. KOCH
Civil Court of the City of New York
713 N.Y.S.2d 250 (2000)

Norman C. Ryp, J.

A. ISSUE

Whether . . . a videotaped episode of "The People's Court," presided by "Judge" Edward I. Koch, is an arbitration under CPLR Art. 75? If so, is the "Judge" subject to arbitral immunity, privilege(s), absolute or qualified? Socratic issues of first impression for the 21st century!

B. FACTS & PROCEDURAL HISTORY

Defendant, Edward I. Koch, moves under CPLR 3212, for summary judgment dismissing the complaint. Claimant, (a/k/a plaintiff), Idris Kabia, alleges he was libeled and slandered, as a "kidnapper" of his then infant son in his native country (Sierra Leone) Africa on national television. On January 19, 1999, claimant sued his son, Ahmed Kabia, for $2,000.00 (originally $200.00) for alleged failure to return property (i.e., photos of them together) in the Small Claims Part . . . , with an initial hearing scheduled for February 24, 1999. Between January 19 and February 9, 1999, both were contacted by Ralph Edwards Productions ("Producer") and afforded the opportunity to resolve their dispute on "The People's Court" then presided over by former New York City Mayor, Chief Magistrate and now "Arbitrator" Edward I. Koch (a/k/a "Arbitrator") rather than in this Court. They were each sent an Agreement to Arbitrate ("A/A"). Producer also requested that claimant, who did, write a statement, dated February 2, 1999, justifying his version of the facts and requested relief.

Thereafter, on February 9, 1999, both claimant and defendant signed the A/A with Ralph Edwards productions d/b/a "The People's Court" (hereinafter "The People's Court") at The People's Court studios just prior to the scheduled videotaping. Under the A/A, any award by the Arbitrator (defendant herein) is paid to the winning party only by The People's Court not the losing party. If no award is made, both parties are each paid $250.00 (as herein) from a fund provided by the Producer. The A/A includes three paragraphs (paras. 7[a], 7[b] and 8) releasing the Producer and Arbitrator (para. 8) including for "statements during . . . the arbitration which plaintiff and/or defendant . . . feel rightly or wrongly to be derogatory, defamatory or in some other way injurious to themselves . . ." . . . Attached to the A/A were "The People's Court Rules" including 'The Judgment' (para. 3) which exclaimed that the Arbitrator's Decision shall be "FINAL AND BINDING."

Thereafter, on February 9, 1999, after the parties signed the above documents, the "arbitration" proceeding occurred. At the end of the "arbitration proceeding," the Arbitrator-defendant found in favor of defendant-son therein and awarded claimant-plaintiff no money. Immediately following the "arbitration" proceeding and before claimant left the Producer's studio, claimant signed a "Litigant Acknowledgment" of his entitlement to $250.00 from the Producer. Subsequently, on February 22, 1999, Producer's check (# 46846 dated 2/22/99) in the sum of $250.00 payable to claimant was received, endorsed and deposited by claimant-plaintiff on February 27, 1999. During March, 1999, an edited videotape version of subject videotape was broadcast on national network television.

On April 2, 1999, claimant filed subject action . . . against defendant Edward Koch, alleging a claim to "defame, liable, slander." At the motional hearing, the only contested triable factual issue was whether defendant "Arbitrator" Edward I. Koch, uttered the words "kidnapped" or "kidnapper" or a word(s) of similar import, claimed by plaintiff. . . . The Court requested and received, along with claimant, unedited and edited videotaped versions, with transcript(s) of the subject televised program. After televiewing, while the Court did not see nor hear the controverted words, the Court assumes such utterance for the purpose of this CPLR 3212 summary judgment motion herein, since evidence is construed most favorable to defendant, motional opponent.

C. APPLICABLE LAW

This Court's mission is to do substantial justice between the parties according to the rules of substantive law (CCA § 1804) in fairness to plaintiff, whose birth language was not English. . . .

. . .

1. "People's Court" — Arbitration Proceeding under CPLR Art. 75?

. . .

BLACK'S LAW DICTIONARY 105 (6th ed. 1991) defines arbitration as "A process of dispute resolution in which a neutral third party (arbitrator) renders a decision after a hearing at which both parties have the opportunity to be heard." Arbitration is a form of alternative dispute resolution almost wholly independent of the court system. It requires a written agreement to submit a present or future controversy to arbitration and that the parties "expressly" and "unequivocally" enter into such agreement. Arbitration is a legally legitimate means to resolve disputes because it neither unlawfully deprives a party of access to the courts nor divests them of the constitutional right to trial by jury as these rights are waivable and the agreement to arbitrate waives them.

. . .

. . . Judge Philip S. Straniere in Doo Wop Shoppe Ltd. v. Ralph Edwards Productions D/B/A The People's Court, 691 N.Y.S.2d 253 (Civ. Ct. Richmond Co. — 1998), using the above Black's definition of "arbitration," found that "the 'People's Court' is not a form of arbitration recognized in New York State and the rights and protection afforded persons who engage in arbitration are not available to the participants in that program." The Court therein found that A/A had "all the trappings of an arbitration contract except" payment of an award by the losing litigant but let the "arbitrator's" award stand. This Court respectfully disagrees with such finding so that the People's Court proceeding of February 9, 1999 herein was an "arbitration proceeding" in accordance with CPLR Art. 75 and New York State public policy, which encourages arbitration.

Judge Straniere, in *Doo Wop*, reasoned that People's Court "Arbitration" is not a form of arbitration recognized in New York State because the ultimate award or "judgment" by the arbitrator was paid by a third party (the People's Court), and not the losing party . . . . Nowhere in CPLR Art. 75 . . . or case law does it state that an arbitration agreed to by both parties, in writing, fails to be an arbitration under CPLR Art. 75 because the award/judgment is paid by a third party. Second, Judge Straniere suggested that parties submitting to arbitration by the People's Court are not afforded the rights and protections of parties to an Article 75 arbitration. No language in the A/A distinguishes the People's Court from any other Art. 75 proceeding in New York State. Rather People's Court arbitration is an Art. 75 arbitration and subject to its rules and procedures. . . . Although "Final and Binding" is seemingly exclusionary language, and noting arbitrator's awards are not generally reviewable, such language and policy do not unilaterally "sacrifice any right [the parties] have to redress of the courts," but simply limits parties' redress under CPLR § 7511. Such limits are the essence of arbitration and allow for its economical and expeditious resolution of disputes.

2. Defamation: Slander

As noted above, for CPLR 3212 motional purposes, it is assumed, without conceding, though it is not visible or audible on the videotape or transcript as required by CPLR 3016(a) that the below words were uttered by the Arbitrator.

It is uncontroverted that one who has "kidnapped" or is a "kidnapper," in 1990 in Sierra Leone, Africa, even his own son, under Penal Law ("P.L.") Art. 135 may or may not be guilty of a felony or serious crime in New York. . . . If a "serious crime," such a statement published on national television may be slanderous, per se, and unnecessary to allege special damages.

3. "Judicial Proceeding"? — Arbitral Immunity Privileges — Absolute or Qualified?

Although not judges, arbitrators exercise judicial functions and are protected from civil liability for acts done in the exercise of judicial functions whether general or special damages are sought. Under this doctrine of arbitral immunity, arbitrators in contractually agreed upon arbitration proceedings are absolutely immune from liability for all acts within the scope of the arbitral process. Such acts include questions from "Judge-Arbitrator" Edward I. Koch to ascertain factual background to determine issues and their resolution.

In addition, an arbitration association cannot be held liable for the actions of arbitrators who enjoy judicial immunity from civil liability for acts complained of since the doctrine of arbitral immunity protects not only arbitrators but their organizations from civil liability for all acts performed within their arbitral capacity.

D. CONCLUSION

For the foregoing reasons, claimant's complaint is dismissed, with prejudice.

NOTE

Kabia v. Koch illustrates another reason why it may matter whether a particular form of dispute resolution is "arbitration": arbitrators (and arbitration institutions) may be absolutely immune from civil liability for various forms of alleged wrongdoing. For example, section 14(a) of the Revised Uniform Arbitration Act provides that "[a]n arbitrator or an arbitration organization acting in that capacity is immune from civil liability to the same extent as a judge of a court of this State acting in a judicial capacity." Why should an arbitrator have the same degree of immunity as a judge?

PROBLEM 1.3

In which of the following cases have the parties provided for "arbitration" within the meaning of the Federal Arbitration Act, 9 U.S.C. § 2?

(a) Violet Smith and Bob Carruthers have a dispute over who owns a vintage used bicycle. They agree to have Jack Woodley, an "impartial mediator," resolve their dispute and to abide by his decision.

(b) Same as (a) except that Smith and Carruthers agree to have Woodley help them settle their dispute. Woodley's role is to be a facilitator; he is not to decide how the dispute should come out.

(c) Same as (a) except that Smith and Carruthers agree to appear before Judge Judy on her syndicated television show and to abide by her resolution of their dispute.

(d) Same as (a) except that Carruthers files suit in small claims court seeking to recover the bicycle. The court requires all parties in pending cases to present their evidence before a neutral third party selected by the court, who issues a nonbinding ruling on the merits. The court selects Woodley to be the third party.

(e) Same as (a) except that Smith and Carruthers agree between themselves to have Woodley issue an advisory ruling on the merits of their dispute. If either party is dissatisfied with Woodley's decision, he or she is free to go to small claims court.

(f) Same as (a) except that before any dispute arises Smith and Carruthers agree to have disputes between themselves decided by three people chosen by Carruthers.

§ 1.04 WHY ARBITRATE?

Why do parties agree to arbitrate their disputes? The answer varies, depending on the context. Let's start with a contract between two sophisticated commercial parties, both located in the United States. Why would those parties agree to have their disputes resolved in arbitration rather than in court? The following survey results suggest that there are a variety of reasons why commercial parties might agree (and might not agree) to arbitration.

Rand Institute for Civil Justice, BUSINESS-TO-BUSINESS ARBITRATION IN THE UNITED STATES: PERCEPTIONS OF CORPORATE COUNSEL 2-22 (2011)*

The purpose of this study was to assess corporate counsel's opinions on the relative advantages of arbitration and litigation . . . .

. . .

Our approach was to field a survey of corporate counsel and then conduct follow-up interviews with a subset of survey respondents to further explore the

---

* Copyright © 2011 by the Rand Corporation. Reprinted with permission.

issues revealed by our findings. The survey consisted of 28 questions to explore respondents' perspectives on the benefits of arbitration compared with litigation, the factors that encourage or discourage them to use arbitration clauses in B2B contracts, and their experiences with arbitration. . . .

. . .

We received 121 responses to our survey. We were unable to calculate a precise response rate, however, because we do not know the total number of people who received the invitation. Nevertheless, the number of returned survey responses would represent an upper-bound response rate of no more than 13 percent if we consider only direct recipients. Our response rate was likely affected by corporate counsel's desire to avoid revealing sensitive information about their companies' work.

. . .

Our study was exploratory research of limited scope and scale. Consequently, the survey is a sample of convenience that limits the extent to which results can be construed broadly. Our sample is the product of non-random selection of individuals with email accounts included in select company, friend network, and professional association lists who felt inclined to participate. Also, our sample is not representative of corporate attorneys, because over 50 percent of respondents had over 15 years of experience in litigation. For these reasons, our results are only suggestive of the factors that may explain why arbitration clauses are not common in B2B contracts.

PERCEPTIONS OF ARBITRATION COMPARED WITH LITIGATION

Most Believe Arbitration Is at Least Somewhat Better Than Litigation

A slight majority of respondents indicated that they believe contractual arbitration for domestic B2B disputes is better than litigation, and most of those respondents believe it is only somewhat better . . . .

These findings comport with prior research suggesting that there is general belief in the efficiency and utility of arbitration as opposed to litigation. However, despite the ostensible benefits of arbitration, about 44 percent of respondents had no, neutral, or negative attitudes regarding arbitration. The neutral and no-opinion responses may be reflective of respondents not having enough experience to form a judgment, or of being able to identify both systems' benefits and disadvantages in different circumstances but not to identify which system is better or worse overall. The large percentage of respondents who believe arbitration is worse than litigation may also be a result of potential bias in favor of litigation stemming from the respondents' large amount of litigation experience.

Our subsequent interviews revealed that many believe that arbitration is becoming increasingly akin to litigation, requiring substantial time in protracted pre-hearing efforts for discovery and money to pay for outside counsel and arbitrator(s). Both the interviewees who favor arbitration and those who do not expressed similar concerns. This perception of arbitration's trend toward litigation-style procedures, and respondents' experiences with it, may account for the significant proportion of negative perspectives revealed by the study.

. . .

Most Believe Arbitration Saves Time Compared with Litigation

Almost 60 percent of respondents agreed that arbitration saves time relative to litigation for B2B disputes . . . . These findings are consistent with previous research suggesting that many believe arbitration is a speedier process than litigation. Interestingly, in contrast to the responses to the general question on whether arbitration or litigation is better, nearly all respondents had an opinion about arbitration's time-saving potential.

. . .

Most Believe Arbitration Saves Money Compared with Litigation

As for whether arbitration saves money compared with litigation in B2B contexts, a bare majority of respondents agreed that it does, one-third of them disagreed, and 17 percent had neutral opinions . . . .

Every respondent had an opinion on this question, suggesting the importance of cost to corporate attorneys. The fact that so many respondents disagreed about cost savings was somewhat surprising given prior opinion research.

. . .

FACTORS ENCOURAGING THE USE OF ARBITRATION

A majority of respondents indicated that four factors encourage them to add an arbitration clause to a B2B contract:

- avoiding potentially excessive or emotionally driven jury awards

- controlling the arbitrator's qualifications

- confidentiality of proceedings and decisions

- contract complexity.

The Most Important Factor Encouraging the Use of Arbitration Is Avoiding Excessive or Emotionally Driven Jury Awards

For 75 percent of respondents, the risk of excessive or emotionally driven jury awards encourages including arbitration clauses in B2B contracts . . . . Only 7 percent of respondents disagreed, and only 15 percent had neutral opinions.

. . .

Our findings suggest support for the idea that corporate counsel prefer arbitration in cases that risk disproportionate jury awards. Concerns about unpredictable jury awards are already reflected in the fact that many companies now require people to waive their rights to a jury trial as a condition of employment. Previous research also suggests that litigation is preferred for resolving a dispute in cases where legal precedent would dictate a favorable outcome. However, arbitration is preferred in cases where the jury is likely to decide because of unfavorable or unclear legal precedent.

. . .

Control over Arbitrator Qualifications Strongly Encourages Arbitration

Nearly 70 percent of respondents indicated that the ability to control the arbitrator's qualifications encouraged the use of contractual arbitration . . . . While this result was not surprising, the 18 percent of respondents believing that this kind of control actually discourages the use of arbitration raised some interesting questions.

. . .

Confidentiality Is Another Key Factor Encouraging Arbitration

Two-thirds of the survey respondents indicated that confidentiality encourages using contractual arbitration . . . .

Again, this result is generally as we expected; it comports with previous research in which over 40 percent of respondents were found to believe that companies elect arbitration because of the confidential proceedings.

Our interviewees considered confidentiality the second most important benefit of arbitration. They cited two key benefits of confidential proceedings:

*   lack of publicity over a dispute and its outcome

*   reduced risk of divulging trade secrets or other commercially sensitive information.

. . .

B2B Contract Complexity Also Encourages Arbitration

A majority of respondents indicated that the complexity of B2B contracts encourages using arbitration . . . . This finding is consistent with responses to related questions on our survey. For instance, respondents may believe arbitrators will understand complex contracts better than juries will, because arbitrators are selected based on their subject-matter experience. The choice to include arbitration clauses in complex contracts may also tie into concerns about confidentiality and technical trade secrets. In general, our findings show that many factors can influence whether a corporate attorney chooses arbitration over litigation.

. . .

FACTOR DISCOURAGING THE USE OF ARBITRATION

Preserving the Right to Appeal Discourages Using Arbitration

Preserving the right to appeal was the only factor cited by a majority of respondents as discouraging arbitration . . . .

This view, which is not surprising, is akin to the findings of a study in which almost 55 percent of surveyed respondents cited the difficulty of appeal as a deterrent to using arbitration. In our survey, this factor was cited by a smaller majority (63 percent) than the factors discussed above as encouraging arbitration, except for complex contracts. This may indicate that corporate counsel are less concerned about being able to appeal an arbitration decision than about possible excessive jury awards (which can be appealed) and the qualifications of the people hearing the case.

. . .

INFLUENCE OF BUSINESS RELATIONSHIPS ON ARBITRATION DECISIONS

Good Business Relationships Mainly Encourage or Have No Effect on Arbitration Decisions

We also analyzed the effect that having a good previous or existing relationship with the other company had on the decision to include an arbitration clause. As might be expected, a near majority of respondents believed a good relationship with another company encouraged adding an arbitration clause to the contract, whereas another sizable proportion believed this factor had no effect . . . .

The logic is that if companies have good relationships with one another, they might be more inclined to use a dispute resolution process other than litigation, because they will be more likely to resolve disputes informally or can better predict the nature and magnitude of potential disputes. We asked the same question about whether an expected future relationship with the company would encourage choosing arbitration and got a very similar breakdown of responses.

. . .

Poor Business Relationships Have a Mixed Effect on Arbitration Decisions

Respondents were even more divided on whether a poor relationship with a company discouraged including an arbitration clause: 36 percent felt it did, and 36 percent reported that it had no effect. Another 23 percent felt a poor previous or existing relationship might encourage using arbitration . . . .

This result may mean that our respondents believe arbitration can better handle difficult disputes in certain situations. For example, arbitration's confidentiality may be appealing for resolving disputes when a poor relationship is involved. . . .

NOTES

1.   The majority of the survey respondents (who were corporate counsel) stated their belief that arbitration saves time and saves money. (Interestingly, though, a substantial percentage disagreed with both propositions.) Why might arbitration be faster and cheaper than litigation? Why not? One reason that arbitration might be faster is that typically (although not always) it has less discovery than litigation, which would reduce the time it takes to resolve a dispute as well as the cost. Indeed, one would expect cost and speed to be closely related, if for no other reason than that delay is costly.

2.   Another reason why arbitration might result in faster dispute resolution than litigation is that it enables the parties to avoid a queue. In court, a lawsuit is added to the judge's docket behind previously filed cases. In arbitration, if the parties wish, they can choose an arbitrator who has no backlog, or at least less of a backlog than there would be in court. Of course, it may be that the best known arbitrators are as busy or busier than judges, so the parties may face tradeoffs in choosing the arbitration panel.

3.   The survey did not ask whether cost and time savings encouraged the use of arbitration; presumably it took that proposition for granted. The factors that the survey respondents identified as most encouraging the use of arbitration between businesses were (1) avoiding excessive jury verdicts; (2) having more control over the choice of the decision maker; (3) the heightened confidentiality in arbitration; and (4) greater complexity of the contract. Why would each of these factors encourage the use of arbitration?

4.   By comparison, the only factor that a majority of respondents identified as discouraging the use of arbitration was the lack of a right to appeal in arbitration. But of course the lack of an appeals process is another reason why arbitration might be faster and cheaper than litigation. And at least some respondents indicated that each of the factors listed above (avoiding juries, choosing the decision maker, increased confidentiality, and contract complexity) discouraged rather than encouraged the use of arbitration. In short, the reasons parties agree to arbitrate will depend very much on the circumstances, with no form of dispute resolution being best for all parties at all times.

C & L ENTERPRISES, INC. v. CITIZEN BAND POTAWATOMI INDIAN TRIBE
United States Supreme Court
532 U.S. 411 (2001)

JUSTICE GINSBURG delivered the opinion of the Court.

. . . This case concerns the impact of an arbitration agreement on a tribe's plea of . . . immunity [from suit in a state court]. The document on which the case centers is a standard form construction contract signed by the parties to govern the installation of a foam roof on a building, the First Oklahoma Bank, in Shawnee, Oklahoma. The building and land are owned by an Indian Tribe, the Citizen Potawatomi Nation (Tribe). The building is commercial, and the land is off-reservation, nontrust property. The form contract, which was proposed by the Tribe and accepted by the contractor, C & L Enterprises, Inc. (C & L), contains an arbitration clause.

The question presented is whether the Tribe waived its immunity from suit in state court when it expressly agreed to arbitrate disputes with C & L relating to the contract, to the governance of Oklahoma law, and to the enforcement of arbitral awards "in any court having jurisdiction thereof." We hold that, by the clear import of the arbitration clause, the Tribe is amenable to a state-court suit to enforce an arbitral award in favor of contractor C & L.

I

Respondent Citizen Potawatomi Nation is a federally recognized Indian Tribe. In 1993, it entered into a contract with petitioner C & L for the installation of a roof on a Shawnee, Oklahoma, building owned by the Tribe. The building, which housed the First Oklahoma Bank, is not on the Tribe's reservation or on land held by the Federal Government in trust for the Tribe. The contract at issue is a standard form agreement copyrighted by the American Institute of Architects. The Tribe proposed the contract; details not set out in the form were inserted by the Tribe and its architect. Two provisions of the contract are key to this case. First, the contract contains an arbitration clause:

"All claims or disputes between the Contractor [C & L] and the Owner [the Tribe] arising out of or relating to the Contract, or the breach thereof, shall be decided by arbitration in accordance with the Construction [I]ndustry Arbitration Rules of the American Arbitration Association currently in effect unless the parties mutually agree otherwise.

. . . The award rendered by the arbitrator or arbitrators shall be final, and judgment may be entered upon it in accordance with applicable law in any court having jurisdiction thereof." The American Arbitration Association Rules to which the clause refers provide: "Parties to these rules shall be deemed to have consented that judgment upon the arbitration award may be entered in any federal or state court having jurisdiction thereof."

Second, the contract includes a choice-of-law clause that reads: "The contract shall be governed by the law of the place where the Project is located." Oklahoma has adopted a Uniform Arbitration Act, which instructs that "[t]he making of an agreement . . . providing for arbitration in this state confers jurisdiction on the court to enforce the agreement under this act and to enter judgment on an award thereunder." The Act defines "court" as "any court of competent jurisdiction of this state."

After execution of the contract but before C & L commenced performance, the Tribe decided to change the roofing material from foam (the material specified in the contract) to rubber guard. The Tribe solicited new bids and retained another company to install the roof. C & L, claiming that the Tribe had dishonored the contract, submitted an arbitration demand. The Tribe asserted sovereign immunity and declined to participate in the arbitration proceeding. It notified the arbitrator, however, that it had several substantive defenses to C & L's claim. On consideration of C & L's evidence, the arbitrator rendered an award in favor of C & L for $25,400 in damages (close to 30% of the contract price), plus attorney's fees and costs.

Several weeks later, C & L filed suit to enforce the arbitration award in the District Court of Oklahoma County, a state court of general, first instance, jurisdiction. The Tribe appeared specially for the limited purpose of moving to dismiss the action on the ground that the Tribe was immune from suit. The District Court denied the motion and entered a judgment confirming the award.

The Oklahoma Court of Civil Appeals affirmed, holding that the Tribe lacked immunity because the contract giving rise to the suit was "between an Indian tribe and a non-Indian" and was "executed outside of Indian Country." The Oklahoma Supreme Court denied review, and the Tribe petitioned for certiorari in this Court.

While the Tribe's petition was pending here, the Court decided [Kiowa Tribe of Okla. v. Manufacturing Technologies, Inc., 523 U.S. 751 (1998)], holding: "Tribes enjoy immunity from suits on contracts, whether those contracts involve governmental or commercial activities and whether they were made on or off a reservation." *Kiowa* reconfirmed: "[A]n Indian tribe is subject to suit only where Congress has authorized the suit or the tribe has waived its immunity." Thereafter, we granted the Tribe's petition in this case, vacated the judgment of the Court of Civil Appeals, and remanded for reconsideration in light of *Kiowa*.

On remand, the Court of Civil Appeals changed course. It held that, under *Kiowa*, the Tribe here was immune from suit on its contract with C & L, despite the contract's off-reservation subject matter. The court then addressed whether the Tribe had waived its immunity. . . . Concluding that the Tribe had not waived its suit immunity with the requisite clarity, the appeals court instructed the trial court to dismiss the case. The Oklahoma Supreme Court denied C & L's petition for review.

Conflicting with the Oklahoma Court of Civil Appeals' current decision, several state and federal courts have held that an arbitration clause, kin to the one now before us, expressly waives tribal immunity from a suit arising out of the contract. We granted certiorari to resolve this conflict, and now reverse.

II

. . .

. . . [T]o relinquish its immunity, a tribe's waiver must be "clear." We are satisfied that the Tribe in this case has waived, with the requisite clarity, immunity from the suit C & L brought to enforce its arbitration award.

The construction contract's provision for arbitration and related prescriptions lead us to this conclusion. The arbitration clause requires resolution of all contract-related disputes between C & L and the Tribe by binding arbitration; ensuing arbitral awards may be reduced to judgment "in accordance with applicable law in any court having jurisdiction thereof." For governance of arbitral proceedings, the arbitration clause specifies American Arbitration Association Rules for the construction industry, and under those Rules, "the arbitration award may be entered in any federal or state court having jurisdiction thereof."

The contract's choice-of-law clause makes it plain enough that a "court having jurisdiction" to enforce the award in question is the Oklahoma state court in which C & L filed suit. By selecting Oklahoma law ("the law of the place where the Project is located") to govern the contract, the parties have effectively consented to confirmation of the award "in accordance with" the Oklahoma Uniform Arbitration Act.

The Uniform Act in force in Oklahoma prescribes that, when "an agreement . . . provid[es] for arbitration in this state," *i.e.*, in Oklahoma, jurisdiction to enforce the agreement vests in "any court of competent jurisdiction of this state." On any sensible reading of the Act, the District Court of Oklahoma County, a local court of general jurisdiction, fits that statutory description.

In sum, the Tribe agreed, by express contract, to adhere to certain dispute resolution procedures. In fact, the Tribe itself tendered the contract calling for those procedures. The regime to which the Tribe subscribed includes entry of judgment upon an arbitration award in accordance with the Oklahoma Uniform Arbitration Act. That Act concerns arbitration in Oklahoma and correspondingly designates as enforcement forums "court[s] of competent jurisdiction of [Oklahoma]." C & L selected for its enforcement suit just such a forum. In a case involving an arbitration clause essentially indistinguishable from the one to which the Tribe and C & L agreed, the Seventh Circuit stated:

> There is nothing ambiguous about th[e] language [of the arbitration clause]. The tribe agrees to submit disputes arising under the contract to arbitration, to be bound by the arbitration award, and to have its submission and the award enforced in a court of law.
>
>   . . .
>
> The [tribal immunity] waiver . . . is implicit rather than explicit only if a waiver of sovereign immunity, to be deemed explicit, must use the words 'sovereign immunity.' No case has ever held that." Sokaogon Gaming Enterprise Corp. v. Tushie-Montgomery Associates, Inc., 86 F.3d 656, 659–60 (7th Cir. 1996).

That cogent observation holds as well for the case we confront.[3]

The Tribe strenuously urges, however, that an arbitration clause simply "is not a waiver of immunity from suit." The phrase in the clause providing for enforcement of arbitration awards "in any court having jurisdiction thereof," the Tribe maintains, "begs the question of what court has jurisdiction." As counsel for the Tribe clarified at oral argument, the Tribe's answer is "no court," on earth or even on the moon. No court — federal, state, or even tribal — has jurisdiction over C & L's suit, the Tribe insists, because it has not expressly waived its sovereign immunity in any judicial forum.

Instead of waiving suit immunity in any court, the Tribe argues, the arbitration

---

[3] Instructive here is the law governing waivers of immunity by foreign sovereigns. "Under the law of the United States . . . an agreement to arbitrate is a waiver of immunity from jurisdiction in . . . an action to enforce an arbitral award rendered pursuant to the agreement. . . ." Restatement (Third) of the Foreign Relations Law of the United States § 456(2)(b)(ii) (1987).

clause waives simply and only the parties' rights to a court trial of contractual disputes; under the clause, the Tribe recognizes, the parties must instead arbitrate. The clause no doubt memorializes the Tribe's commitment to adhere to the contract's dispute resolution regime. That regime has a real world objective; it is not designed for regulation of a game lacking practical consequences. And to the real world end, the contract specifically authorizes judicial enforcement of the resolution arrived at through arbitration.

. . .

For the reasons stated, we conclude that under the agreement the Tribe proposed and signed, the Tribe clearly consented to arbitration and to the enforcement of arbitral awards in Oklahoma state court; the Tribe thereby waived its sovereign immunity from C & L's suit. The judgment of the Oklahoma Court of Civil Appeals is therefore reversed, and the case is remanded for further proceedings not inconsistent with this opinion.

It is so ordered.

NOTES

1.   A significant use of arbitration, and one which is discussed at various points in this book, is to resolve disputes between parties from different sovereigns (including Indian tribes such as in the *C & L Enterprises* case). International commercial contracts, for example, often provide for arbitration as the dispute resolution mechanism. The most commonly given reason for using arbitration in international contracts is that neither party wants to litigate in the other parties' home court. Another important reason is the well-developed legal framework for enforcing international arbitration awards, which is discussed in detail in Chapter 7. For example, Christian Bühring-Uhle concludes, based on his survey of international arbitration practitioners, that "[c]learly the two most significant advantages and presumably the two most important reasons for choosing arbitration as a means of international commercial dispute resolution seem to be the *neutrality of the forum*, i.e., the possibility to avoid being subjected to the jurisdiction of the home court of one of the parties, and the superiority of its legal framework, with treaties like the New York Convention guaranteeing the *international enforcement* of awards." *See* Christian Bühring-Uhle, Arbitration and Mediation in International Business 136 (1996). Other advantages of international commercial arbitration cited by survey respondents included the confidentiality of the proceedings, the arbitrators' expertise, the lack of a right to appeal, and the limited availability of discovery. *Id.* at 136–37. By comparison, the majority of respondents believed that any cost advantages of arbitration over litigation in the international context were non-existent. *Id.* at 138. Why do you suppose the parties in *C & L Enterprises* included an arbitration clause in their contract?

2.   Some international contracts (again, like the contract in *C & L Enterprises*) are not merely between parties from different sovereigns, but are between a foreign party and the sovereign itself. As Bühring-Uhle explains, such parties may be particularly likely to agree to arbitration "because on the one hand governments are reluctant — and sometimes prevented by constitutional constraints — to submit to

the jurisdiction of another government and on the other hand private entities tend to abhor the prospect of confronting a sovereign in its own courts." *Id.* at 142.

3.   One barrier to litigation against a sovereign is sovereign immunity, the defense raised by the tribe in *C & L Enterprises.* In that case, the Supreme Court held that agreeing to arbitration constituted a waiver of sovereign immunity in an action to enforce the arbitration award. With respect to foreign sovereigns, the issue is addressed in the United States by the Foreign Sovereign Immunities Act, 28 U.S.C. § 1605:

> (a) A foreign state shall not be immune from the jurisdiction of courts of the United States or of the States in any case —
>
> . . .
>
> (6) in which the action is brought, either to enforce an agreement made by the foreign state with or for the benefit of a private party to submit to arbitration all or any differences which have arisen or which may arise between the parties with respect to a defined legal relationship, whether contractual or not, concerning a subject matter capable of settlement by arbitration under the laws of the United States, or to confirm an award made pursuant to such an agreement to arbitrate, if (A) the arbitration takes place or is intended to take place in the United States, (B) the agreement or award is or may be governed by a treaty or other international agreement in force for the United States calling for the recognition and enforcement of arbitral awards, (C) the underlying claim, save for the agreement to arbitrate, could have been brought in a United States court under this section or section 1607, or (D) paragraph (1) of this subsection is otherwise applicable. . . .

See also 9 U.S.C. § 15 (act of state doctrine inapplicable to enforcement of arbitration agreements and awards).

The previous excerpts addressed the use of arbitration to resolve disputes among relatively sophisticated commercial parties. The following excerpt considers arbitration between a business and a consumer.

David S. Schwartz, ENFORCING SMALL PRINT TO PROTECT BIG BUSINESS: EMPLOYEE AND CONSUMER RIGHTS CLAIMS IN AN AGE OF COMPELLED ARBITRATION,

1997 WIS. L. REV. 33, 60–61 *

There are several reasons why corporate defendants would prefer arbitration to litigation for their patterned, repetitive disputes with minor players — customers, employees and smaller business entities with whom they deal through standardized adhesion contracts:

Lower defense costs. Corporate defendants generally find it cheaper to arbitrate than litigate their disputes. Arbitration generally eliminates pretrial motion and discovery practice, and the informality of arbitration means less time preparing for hearing and presenting evidence.

Lower plaintiff's attorneys fees. For the same reasons, attorney's fees on the plaintiff's side are less in arbitration. Because a prevailing plaintiff may be entitled to recover her attorneys fees under a number of state and federal laws regulating business entities, lower plaintiff's attorneys fees mean less potential expense to the corporate defendant. Moreover, because plaintiffs' attorneys view arbitration as an unfavorable forum, they are less likely to take on arbitration cases; thus, plaintiffs are less likely to get legal assistance.

Lower damage awards. While the jury is probably still out on this issue, there is a general perception that arbitrators give smaller awards than juries. Arbitrators may be more jaded, and hence make lower awards, particularly in more egregious cases where punitive damages are available. Corporate defendants, with some empirical justification, may believe that they are likely to get more sympathy from arbitrators, if not downright bias in their favor. There is a historical tendency to draw arbitrators from the business community. In some sectors, like the securities industry, arbitrators are drawn from the industry itself. Even where they are not, individual arbitrators have an economic stake in being selected again, and their judgment may well be shaded by a desire to build a "track record" of decisions that corporate repeat-users will view approvingly. Even the independent arbitration companies have an economic interest in being looked on kindly by large institutional corporate defendants who can bring repeat business. An individual plaintiff is likely to have one arbitration in his or her entire life, and a plaintiffs' lawyer will have a handful of arbitrations in a year. A large company, however, will not only have numerous arbitrations, but can also refer arbitration business in a variety of legal fields where business disputes arise. Unsurprisingly, at least one study has detected that corporate defendants have a repeat-player advantage in arbitration.

The greater reluctance of plaintiffs' attorneys to accept compelled arbitration cases will also tend to result in lower awards, if one assumes that legally-represented parties tend to fare better.

Higher threshold costs to plaintiff. With arbitration filing and administrative fees as high as thousands of dollars per case, and hourly rates for arbitrators ranging from $200 to $700, arbitration can be extremely expensive, particularly in more complicated cases. Plaintiffs generally are expected to cover half of these costs.

Privacy. Arbitrations are private proceedings. Papers filed with arbitrators are not part of any public record; proceedings take place in private offices rather than in public courtrooms; and they tend to be less interesting to the media.

No discovery. The unavailability of discovery skews the system in favor of the corporate defendant. The plaintiff has the burden of production of evidence, much of which the defendant may well possess. In addition, the ethical prohibition against lawyers' "ex parte" contacts with opposing parties (i.e., informal, and without opposing counsel present) extends to many current, and possibly some former, employees of a corporate defendant. This sharply curtails a plaintiff's ability to develop evidence through informal investigation rather than discovery.

The combination of these factors make arbitration a highly attractive alternative to litigation for corporate defendants in many circumstances. Because corporations will typically interact with small players through contracts of adhesion, there is a substantial incentive to use form terms to lock in the advantages of arbitration in advance of any dispute.

NOTES

1.   Schwartz identifies a number of reasons why corporations might prefer arbitration over litigation for resolving disputes with consumers and employees, such as lower awards to plaintiffs, higher costs for bringing claims, limited availability of discovery, and the privacy of arbitration proceedings. Other reasons he might have cited are the limited grounds for appeal of an arbitration award and the general lack of class relief in arbitration. Schwartz' view is that these characteristics of arbitration unfairly disadvantage consumers and employees to the benefit of corporations. Do you agree?

In a more recent article, Schwartz emphasizes what he calls the "claim-suppressing" effect of arbitration clauses:

> The compelling logic of what is commonly called "mandatory arbitration" is that it is intended to suppress claims. . . .

>   . . .

> The motivation of employers and sellers to use arbitration as a claim-suppressing technique is borne out by their positions with regard to class actions. Nothing is more claim-suppressing than a ban on class actions, particularly in cases where the economics of disputing make pursuit of individual cases irrational. Two paradigm examples are all too common. In the consumer setting, low-dollar-value rip-offs that generate large revenues because practiced on a wide scale — unauthorized charges to credit card holders for unsolicited "credit insurance," for example — can go entirely unremedied without a class action. Small, quotidian violations of wage and hour laws by mass employers would likewise go unremedied if relegated to

individual suits. Professor Eisenberg has shown that barring class actions has become a primary factor in companies' choice to use pre-dispute arbitration.

David S. Schwartz, *Claim-Suppressing Arbitration: The New Rules*, 87 IND. L.J. 239, 240-42 (2012). The policy debate over consumer and employment arbitration is considered in more detail at the end of this Chapter.

2. Schwartz describes a different (but related) sort of repeat-player problem from the one discussed in Section 1.02: that the institutions that administer arbitrations may "have an economic interest in being looked on kindly by large institutional corporate defendants who can bring repeat business." How likely is it that arbitration institutions will administer arbitration programs so as to favor corporations? In an Alabama lawsuit challenging their arbitration agreement with First USA N.A. (a large credit card issuer), a class of cardholders argued that the National Arbitration Forum (NAF) was biased in favor of First USA because of the sizable fees First USA paid the NAF. As evidence of bias, the plaintiffs relied on data showing that of 19,705 NAF awards in arbitrations initiated by First USA, the arbitrators ruled in favor of the bank in 19,618 (99.6 percent) and in favor of the cardholder in 87 (0.4 percent). *See* Caroline E. Mayer, *Win Some, Lose Rarely?; Arbitration Forum's Rulings Called One Sided*, WASH. POST, March 1, 2000, at E01. Does that discrepancy show bias? In response, the NAF contended that (1) the proceedings brought by First USA were collection actions, in which creditors have a 98 percent success rate in court; and (2) more than 28,000 additional First USA claims "expired" for failure to timely notify the cardholder, and those claims should be treated as victories for cardholders. *Id.* Are you persuaded? The data also showed that only four cardholders had brought actions against First USA. Of those four claims, the arbitrators ruled in favor of the cardholder in two, one was settled, and one was still pending. *Id.* What is the significance of those results? Is it evidence that Professor Schwartz is right about the claim-suppressing nature of arbitration? What additional facts might you want to know?

3. A second study by the Searle Civil Justice Institute compared business claims against consumers resolved in AAA arbitrations with business claims against consumers resolved in court. *See* Christopher R. Drahozal & Samantha Zyontz, *Creditor Claims in Arbitration and in Court*, 7 HASTINGS BUS. L.J. 77 (2011). The study found a high win-rate for businesses in AAA consumer arbitrations, with business claimants being awarded some relief in 86.2% to 97.1% of cases going to an award and being awarded from 92.9 to 99.2% of the amount sought. *Id.* at 91. But the win-rate of business claimants was even higher in court (ranging from 98.4% to 100.0%), with business claimants being awarded an equal or higher percentage of the amount sought (ranging from 96.2% to 99.5%) in court as well. *Id.* The study concludes that

> nothing in our study provides any evidence of biased outcomes in arbitration. The outcomes we observe appear to be the result of the type of case being adjudicated rather than differences between arbitration and litigation. Moreover, the study does definitively demonstrate that win rates in arbitration alone do not show that arbitration is biased. The win rates for

creditors in claims they brought in court are as high as or higher than the win rates for claims brought by creditors in arbitration.

Id. at 83.

4.   In July 2009, the Minnesota Attorney General filed suit against the National Arbitration Forum, asserting claims for fraud and deceptive practices. Complaint, Minnesota v. National Arbitration Forum, Inc., No. 27-CV-09-18559 (Minn. Dist. Ct. July 14, 2009), *available at* http://www.ag.state.mn.us/PDF/PressReleases/ SignedFiledComplaintArbitrationCompany.pdf. The AG's complaint alleged that the NAF had failed to disclose that it was affiliated with a major debt collection firm that appeared in arbitrations it administered. Less than a week later, the NAF settled the litigation, in part by agreeing permanently to stop administering new consumer arbitration cases. Consent Judgment, ¶ 3, Minnesota v. National Arbitration Forum, Inc., No. 27-CV-09-18559 (Minn. Dist. Ct. July 17, 2009), *available at* http://pubcit.typepad.com/files/nafconsentdecree.pdf.

Shortly thereafter, the American Arbitration Association announced its own moratorium on the administration of most consumer debt collection cases (although not claims brought by consumers against businesses). American Arbitration Association, Notice on Consumer Debt Collection Arbitrations, *available at* http://www. adr.org/cs/idcplg?IdcService=GET_FILE&dDocName=ADRSTG_ 012244&RevisionSelectionMethod=LatestReleased 36427 (last visited August 9, 2012). The AAA's action was not in response to any actual or threatened litigation, but rather was based on its "experiences administering debt collection arbitrations" and "its consideration of a number of policy concerns that have been raised." Testimony of Richard W. Naimark on Behalf of the American Arbitration Association, *Hearing on Arbitration or Arbitrary: The Misuse of Mandatory Arbitration to Collect Consumer Debts*, Subcommittee on Domestic Policy, House Oversight Committee, 111th Cong., 1st Sess. (July 22, 2009). In October 2010, a task force convened by the AAA issued a Consumer Debt Collection Due Process Protocol, supplementing its Consumer Due Process Protocol with additional protections for consumer debtors. *See* National Task Force on the Arbitration of Consumer Debt Collection Disputes, Consumer Debt Collection Due Process Protocol — Statement of Principles (Oct. 2010). The AAA has not, however, ended its moratorium on administering most such cases.

5.   Do the views of corporate counsel about arbitration vary depending on the type of dispute? Researchers at Cornell University surveyed general counsel and chief litigators of Fortune 1000 companies in 2011 about their views on alternative dispute resolution.* One question asked the respondents to specify the principal reasons companies did not use arbitration, and broke down the responses by type of dispute (based on 368 responses, with respondents permitted to identify more than one reason):

---

* The study is a follow-up study to David B. Lipsky & Ronald L. Seeber, The Appropriate Resolution of Corporate Disputes: A Report on the Growing Use of ADR by U.S. Corporations 17, 26 (1998). The results of the 2011 study are not yet published, but were kindly provided by Professor Lipsky.

Principal Reasons Companies Did Not Use Arbitration, By Type of Dispute

	2011 Consumer	2011 Corp. & Comm'l	2011 Employment
Difficult to appeal	41%	52%	41%
Not confined to legal rules	33%	44%	36%
Unwillingness of opposing party	53%	45%	43%
Results in compromise outcomes	42%	47%	43%
Lack of confidence in neutrals	29%	34%	24%
Lack of qualified neutrals	16%	11%	8%
Too costly	28%	23%	18%

The survey respondents expressed more concern about the difficulty of appealing awards in commercial disputes than in consumer and employment disputes, and more concern about costs and the lack of qualified arbitrators in consumer disputes than in commercial disputes (but not employment disputes, interestingly). Why might that be? What other conclusions can you draw from the survey results?

PROBLEM 1.4

You recently started work as an Associate General Counsel in the legal department of Anerly Oil, Inc. (Anerly), with its principal place of business in Houston, Texas. Anerly is a multinational oil company that is involved in all aspects of the oil production process: exploration, refining, and distribution. Anerly asks you to review its usual approach to dispute resolution matters in negotiating contracts, which turns out to be to ignore the issue entirely and refuse to include any sort of dispute resolution clause in its contracts. (1) What means of dispute resolution has Anerly chosen by its contractual silence? (2) In which of the following contracts, if any, would you recommend that Anerly include an arbitration clause?

(a) A contract between Anerly and a computer equipment supplier, governing a sizable but one-time purchase of computer equipment by Anerly.

(b) A contract between Anerly and another oil company for the purchase of oil on the spot market. Anerly and the other oil company deal with each other on a regular basis.

(c) A contract between Anerly and an oil pipeline company located in Turkey concerning the transport of oil using the pipeline.

(d) A contract between Anerly and the government of Uzbekistan concerning the development of a newly discovered oilfield in Uzbekistan.

(e) A contract between Anerly Finance Corp., a subsidiary of Anerly that issues gas station credit cards, and an individual who wishes to use the credit card.

(f) A contract between Anerly and one of its franchisees, which runs an Anerly gas station.

§ 1.05   A BRIEF HISTORY OF COMMERCIAL ARBITRATION

Katherine Van Wezel Stone, RUSTIC JUSTICE: COMMUNITY AND COERCION UNDER THE FEDERAL ARBITRATION ACT,
77 N. Car. L. Rev. 931, 969–91 (1999)[*]

A. The Genesis of Arbitration

Private dispute resolution dates back hundreds of years in the Western world. Arbitration originated in Roman and Canon law and was revived in the Middle Ages in European civil law systems. In the common law, arbitration has been a feature of dispute resolution since the fourteenth century, if not before. Early forms of arbitration were dispute resolution procedures created and administered by trade groups — merchant or producer communities. These groups set norms of conduct and business standards for members of a trade or a business community, and they established procedures whereby respected members of the community resolved disputes between members. Disputes often blended allegations of contractual breaches with allegations of breaches of customary practices of the trade. In the arbitration, community elders were expected to resolve the dispute by drawing on the formal and informal norms of the community.

. . .

In England from the seventeenth century onward, many mercantile disputes were resolved by arbitration conducted by the merchant and craft guilds. The merchant guilds established arbitration tribunals because they felt that the courts were not sufficiently knowledgeable about commercial customs and were excessively slow and cumbersome. The arbitration tribunals were composed of experts in the trade, who applied the usages and practices of the trade as their source of law. Later, these informal tribunals were reorganized by the trade associations, together with the municipal authorities, and became the London Court of Arbitration, which is jointly managed by the London Chamber of Commerce and the City of London.

. . .

The use of private arbitration in the United States has a similar history. In the colonial period, arbitration was used within a common industry in a particular locality to settle internal disputes. For example, the New York Chamber of Commerce set up an arbitration system in 1768 in order to "settl[e] business disputes according to trade practice rather than legal principles," and it is considered the oldest surviving arbitration committee in the United States.

. . .

---

[*] Copyright © 1999 by Katherine Van Wezel Stone. Reprinted with permission.

B. Arbitration Under the Common Law in the Nineteenth Century

Despite the proliferation of arbitration in commercial communities in the United States in the late nineteenth and early twentieth century, arbitration remained outside of and in tension with the legal system. Common law courts would not grant specific performance on agreements to arbitrate because they said agreements to arbitrate were revocable by either party until the arbitral award was rendered. According to the "revocability doctrine," the arbitrator was an agent of the parties acting jointly, so that the agency agreement could be revoked by either party at any time before an arbitral award. Thus, if one party to an arbitration agreement refused to arbitrate, the other party was powerless to compel arbitration, or to obtain a stay of litigation if the other side brought suit in court. In most states, the party seeking arbitration could go to court for damages for breach of the promise to arbitrate, but the courts awarded only nominal amounts — at most the cost of preparing for the arbitration that never occurred. Thus, a party seeking to arbitrate had no effective remedy against a party who refused to abide by an arbitration agreement.

The American doctrine of revocability had its origins in English arbitration law and is thought to have originated in a 1609 decision by Lord Coke in *Vynior's Case*. This case involved the enforcement of a bond to ensure compliance with arbitration procedures that the parties had established. The King's Bench enforced the bond, but Lord Coke stated, in dicta, that the promise to arbitrate established a revocable agency relationship with the arbitrator. This dicta became the basis for the revocability doctrine.

The revocability doctrine was not particularly problematic for the early merchant craft guilds because they could, like the plaintiff in *Vynior's Case*, include a hefty bond that would be forfeited by any party resisting arbitration. In 1697, however, Parliament enacted the Statute of Fines and Penalties, which forbade the use of penalty bonds to remedy a breach of contract. Thereafter, a party with an arbitration clause could only sue for damages for its breach — damages that were at best a nominal amount to compensate for the expense of preparing for arbitration. At that point, parties who wanted to enforce arbitration agreements needed to obtain specific performance, and for that the revocability doctrine was a serious obstacle.

Gradually, with a series of enactments beginning at the end of the eighteenth century and continuing throughout the nineteenth century, the English Parliament abandoned the revocability doctrine. The earliest of these statutory measures enabled parties to make arbitration submissions a Rule of Court, for which noncompliance was punishable by contempt. The English arbitration act of 1854, also known as the Common Law Procedure Act, provided that parties were entitled to judicial review of arbitral decisions on issues of law, and in 1889, Parliament enacted a statute making all agreements to arbitrate future or present disputes irrevocable, "except by leave of a court or judge."

In America, by contrast, the revocability doctrine held firm throughout the nineteenth century. There were two quite different justifications offered for it. The first was that parties are not competent, by private contract, to "oust the court of jurisdiction." The "ouster" rationale for the doctrine actually originated in England, but quickly took firm hold in both federal and state courts in the United States. For example, the Supreme Court stated in 1874 in *Insurance Co. v. Morse*: "Agreements in advance to oust the courts of the jurisdiction conferred by law are illegal and void." It further stated that parties could neither create nor diminish the jurisdiction of the courts by contract. The ouster rationale became the primary explanation for U.S. courts' refusal to grant specific performance to agreements to arbitrate.

There was another rationale articulated for the courts' stance on arbitration in the nineteenth century. In *Tobey v. County of Bristol*, Justice Story explained that while a court of equity had no objections to arbitration tribunals, it would not compel parties to participate in an arbitration because it could not ensure that the process would be fair and equitable. He stated:

> [W]hen [courts of equity] are asked to proceed farther and to compel the parties to appoint arbitrators whose award shall be final, they necessarily pause to consider, whether such tribunals possess adequate means of giving redress, and whether they have a right to compel a reluctant party to submit to such a tribunal, and to close against him the doors of the common courts of justice, provided by the government to protect rights and to redress wrongs. One of the established principles of courts of equity is not to entertain a bill for the specific performance of any agreement where it is doubtful whether it may not thereby become the instrument of injustice, or to deprive parties of rights which they are otherwise fairly entitled to have protected.

Despite this alternate rationale, by the 1920s, the ouster-of-jurisdiction explanation for the revocability doctrine became the dominant, if not universal, understanding of arbitration law. Story's view — that the courts disapproved of executory promises to arbitrate because they wanted to ensure a fair hearing — was almost totally forgotten or ignored. Thus narrowed in its interpretation, the revocability doctrine became a straw man that courts and commentators set out to attack.

C. Arbitration and the Rise of Trade Associations

In the early twentieth century, the commercial bar in New York initiated a campaign to overturn the common law rule of revocability. Commercial lawyers saw arbitration as essential to enable the business community to resolve disputes quickly, and they wanted the courts to facilitate rather than thwart its use. . . .

. . .

The growth of commercial arbitration went hand in hand with the explosive growth of trade associations in the 1920s. By 1927, the American Arbitration Association compiled information on over 1000 trade associations that had systems of arbitration for their members. These internal arbitration systems were designed to resolve disputes over contract interpretation and industry standards. They were means to achieve uniformity, articulate ethics, and police malfeasance among trading partners. One advocate noted that arbitration was integral to the mission of trade associations because it facilitated uniform enforcement of industry standards and at the same time dispersed knowledge of trade standards and evolving trade customs to members of the trade. Arbitration was also praised for its ability to resolve disputes between trade association members in a manner that preserved the cohesiveness of the organization. Arbitration, it was said, could restore confidence, promote trust, and keep business running smoothly. It created goodwill between members in an association and between the industry and the rest of society. Trade-association arbitrations were touted as proceedings with fewer technicalities, "much more with an aim to homespun justice, than . . . actions in the courts." For these reasons, some contemporaries claimed that the availability of arbitration was the most valuable feature of trade-association membership.

Early twentieth century trade associations urged and even sometimes required their members to use form contracts with a standard arbitration clause for their business transactions. In these standard clauses, parties agreed to use an industry-specific arbitration system to adjudicate all disputes. The characteristic trade-association arbitration was an informal proceeding headed by a respected member of the trade group in which the "elder" would resolve disputes between group members on the basis of the norms, customary practices, and unstated understandings of the community.

D. The New York City Chamber of Commerce's Campaign to Overturn the Revocability Doctrine

As the trade association movement picked up momentum in the early years of the twentieth century, business leaders and their lawyers mounted pressure to eliminate the revocability doctrine and make agreements to arbitrate enforceable by specific performance. They were reinforced in their determination by a 1915 decision of Judge Charles Hough in *U.S. Asphalt Refining Co. v. Trinidad Lake Petroleum Co.*, in which the court criticized the revocability doctrine and stated that there was no reasoned basis for it other than stare decisis. The *U.S. Asphalt Refining* decision emboldened the New York Chamber of Commerce to initiate a concerted effort to reverse the revocability doctrine. . . .

     . . .

     . . . In the following years, the New York Chamber of Commerce joined with the New York Bar Association to propose a statute to the New York legislature to change the common law rule. The statute . . . was patterned on the English arbitration law of 1889, with one significant difference: the proposed New York law did not contain a provision for de novo judicial review of questions of law. This difference was not accidental, for the New York Chamber of Commerce vehemently opposed any judicial review of arbitral awards.

In 1920, [the] bill passed the New York legislature and became the New York Arbitration Act. The New York statute made arbitration agreements "valid, irrevocable, and enforceable save on such grounds as exist at Law or in Equity for the revocation of any contract." The New York statute served as a template for the Federal Arbitration Act, enacted five years later.

     . . .

The New York Court of Appeals upheld the 1920 Act against a constitutional challenge in *In re Herman Berkovitz*. . . . Judge Cardozo, writing for the court, held that the statute did not abrogate the right to a jury trial, did not subvert the "dignity and power" of the state court, nor did it impair the obligation of contract. Comparing arbitration to a release or covenant not to sue, Cardozo held that arbitration was consistent with the public policy of the state.

E. From the New York Statute to the Federal Arbitration Act

After the enactment of the New York arbitration statute, the Arbitration Society of America was formed to promote the use of arbitration in industry. By 1924, over 1000 leading businesses and over sixty-five trade groups had joined, and the Society had decided over 500 arbitration cases. This group, which later became the American Arbitration Association ("AAA"), advocated that parties include pre-dispute promises to arbitrate as standardized terms in their business dealings. This simple device, they claimed, would "compel the parties to arbitrate." The AAA also drafted a model arbitration act — the "Draft Act" — which, like the New York statute, made agreements to arbitrate irrevocable and specifically enforceable.

Within three years of the enactment of the New York statute, New Jersey and Massachusetts adopted similar measures. By 1933, twelve states, including New Jersey and Massachusetts, had enacted the Draft Act. Some states, however, resisted the New York approach on the ground that to enforce predispute arbitration agreements would permit stronger parties to coerce weaker ones. They were also critical of the New York approach for its failure to provide judicial review on matters of law. Illinois rejected the New York approach and enacted an arbitration law that permitted the enforcement of agreements to arbitrate that were made *after* the dispute arose. Further, Illinois adopted the English rule of providing judicial review of arbitral awards on matters of law. In 1924, after considerable internal debate between the two competing approaches, the Commissioners on Uniform State Laws rejected the New York approach and adopted the Illinois approach.

Also in the early 1920s, the American Bar Association ("ABA") debated which type of arbitration law to recommend to the states. In 1921, it delegated the task of drafting a model state arbitration act to its Committee on Commerce, Trade and Commercial Law. That Committee drafted a model bill that tracked the language of the New York statute. Despite the efforts of the Commissioners on Uniform State Laws to sway the ABA to the Illinois approach, the ABA opted in 1922 for the approach of its own Committee.

In 1922, the ABA Committee on Commerce, Trade and Commercial Law also drafted a federal statute, the Commercial Arbitration Act, based on the New York statute, to submit to Congress. . . . In 1923, Congress held hearings on the proposed act. The ABA Committee revised the bill in 1923 and 1924 to accommodate congressional criticisms. Then, in 1925, five years after the enactment of the New York statute, the United States Arbitration Act (later renamed the Federal Arbitration Act) passed both Houses of Congress unanimously.

The United States Arbitration Act contained all the essential features, and most of the wording, of the New York Arbitration Act. Like the New York statute, the federal statute made agreements to arbitrate present or future disputes "valid, irrevocable, and enforceable"; it provided that when there is a contract containing an arbitration clause, a court must stay litigation and grant specific performance of the promise to arbitrate; and it provided only four narrow grounds for judicial review.

NOTES

1.   Justice Story's opinion in *Tobey v. County of Bristol*, from which Professor Stone quotes, is a classic statement of the common law view of arbitration. As Professor Stone notes, Justice Story expresses skepticism whether arbitration will be fair, skepticism that some continue to share today. In addition, Justice Story plainly states the common law doctrine that arbitration clauses are revocable until an award is made:

> It is certainly the policy of the common law, not to compel men to submit their rights and interests to arbitration, or to enforce agreements for such a purpose. Nay, the common law goes farther, and even if a submission has been made to arbitrators, who are named, by deed or otherwise, with an express stipulation, that the submission shall be irrevocable, it still is revocable and countermandable, by either party, before the award is actually made, although not afterwards.

Tobey v. County of Bristol, 23 F. Cas. 1313, 1321 (C.C.D. Mass. 1845). Almost all current arbitration statutes overrule this revocability doctrine by making arbitration agreements "valid, irrevocable, and enforceable." *See, e.g.*, 9 U.S.C. § 2. Additionally, Justice Story expressed concern about the ability of courts to fill gaps in arbitration agreements:

> How can a court of equity compel the respective parties to name arbitrators; and *a fortiori*, how can it compel the parties mutually to select arbitrators, since each must, in such a case, agree to all the arbitrators? If one party refuses to name an arbitrator, how is the court to compel him to name one? . . . Take the present case, where the arbitrators are to be mutually selected, when and within what time are they to be appointed? How many shall they be, — two, three, four, five, seven, ten, or even twenty? The resolve is silent as to the number. Can the court fix the number, if the parties do not agree upon it? That would be doing what has never yet been done. If either party should refuse to name any arbitrator, or to agree upon any named by the other side, has the court authority, of itself, to appoint arbitrators, or to substitute a master for them? That would be . . . to bind the parties contrary to their agreement. . . . So that we abundantly see, that the very impracticability of compelling the parties to name arbitrators, or upon their default, for the court to appoint them, constitutes, and must forever constitute, a complete bar to any attempt on the part of a court of equity to compel the specific performance of any agreement to refer to arbitration.

23 F. Cas. at 1322. Most current arbitration statutes address this concern by setting out default rules to govern issues such as how arbitrators are to be selected in the event the parties' arbitration agreement is silent. Arbitration statutes also provide

for the courts to serve as the "appointing authority," acting for a party who fails or refuses to appoint an arbitrator under the agreement.

2.   Professor Bruce Benson takes a somewhat different view from that of Professor Stone as to the origins of the FAA. He argues that at least some lawyers supported legislation like the FAA because they saw such legislation as an opportunity to expand their role in arbitration, which previously had been a hostile forum for lawyers. Rather than viewing arbitration as a "competitive threat" to be "squelch[ed]," these lawyers, he contends, sought instead to "establish a lucrative role for themselves in arbitration." Bruce L. Benson, *An Exploration of the Impact of Modern Arbitration Statutes on the Development of Arbitration in the United States*, 11 J. L. & ECON. ORG. 479, 491–92 (1995). What sorts of provisions would you expect to find in arbitration statutes under Professor Benson's theory? Is there any other explanation possible for such provisions?

3.   Modern trade associations continue to use arbitration to resolve disputes among their members. For a description of the procedure before the New York Diamond Dealers Club (DDC), see Lisa Bernstein, *Opting Out of the Legal System: Extralegal Contractual Relations in the Diamond Industry*, 21 J. LEGAL STUD. 115, 124–29 (1992); *see also* Lisa Bernstein, *The Questionable Empirical Basis of Article 2's Incorporation Strategy: A Preliminary Study*, 66 U. CHI. L. REV. 710 (1999); Lisa Bernstein, *Merchant Law in a Merchant Court: Rethinking the Code's Search for Immanent Business Norms*, 144 U. PA. L. REV. 1765 (1996) (National Feed and Grain Association).

———————

Today, arbitration has outgrown its merchant roots. In part due to a series of United States Supreme Court cases that you will read in the next several chapters, businesses regularly include arbitration clauses in their standard form contracts for use in transactions with consumers, employees, and franchisees. As Tom Stipanowich puts it, arbitration has become "consumerized." See Thomas J. Stipanowich, *The Growing Debate over 'Consumerized' Arbitration: Adding Cole to the Fire*, DISP. RESOL. MAG., Summer 1997, at 20.

The previous sections in this chapter have given you a taste of the controversy over the use of arbitration clauses in consumer contracts. The following two excerpts address a central issue in the debate: do arbitration clauses make consumers better off by enabling businesses to lower prices (or increase wages), or are corporations using arbitration simply to line their own pockets at the expense of consumers?

Jean R. Sternlight, PANACEA OR CORPORATE TOOL?: DEBUNKING THE SUPREME COURT'S PREFERENCE FOR BINDING ARBITRATION,
74 WASH. U. L.Q. 637, 686–93 (1996)*

Some defenders of mandatory binding arbitration, while recognizing that businesses would perhaps like to use form contracts and binding arbitration to benefit themselves at the expense of the consumer, argue that competitive market forces will prevent companies from achieving those goals. These free marketeers argue that if the terms of consumer contracts were in fact unduly and inefficiently biased toward the supplier, then other suppliers, in order to benefit themselves, would step in and offer a contractual provision that treated the consumer more generously. The free marketeers further contend that the market will ensure that any benefits secured by the suppliers through imposition of an arbitration provision will be passed on to the consumers. Thus, if mandatory arbitration provisions are common in form contracts, it is because the greater speed and lower cost of arbitration benefits all parties and is therefore efficient and preferable.

. . .

This story of "free market to the rescue" is significantly flawed in that it rests on a set of assumptions that cannot be shown to exist. Most importantly, the competitive defense of form contracts depends on an assumption that consumers read, understand, and evaluate the cost of the binding arbitration clause being imposed by the seller. Instead, it seems generally true that while consumers may be well informed about certain key contractual terms, such as price or color or engine size, they generally know very little about the subordinate contract terms, commonly known as "boilerplate." If the consumer is not aware of the existence or significance of the clause, the supplier is free to impose a term that benefits the supplier but significantly harms the consumer. In fact, economists generally recognize that where one party lacks information as to the cost of a non-price term in a contract, there will be two inefficiencies: a quantity effect and a quality effect. The quantity effect will cause the consumer to purchase too much of the item because she will not recognize its full cost. The quality effect will cause the parties to enter into the wrong contract — one containing a binding arbitration clause — even in circumstances where a fully knowledgeable consumer would have refused to accept such an agreement.

Further, one cannot fairly argue that the consumer made the deliberate choice to forego reading the contract and thus may rightly be penalized. Given the high cost of obtaining and understanding information in a complex economy, the consumer's behavior may reflect rational economic behavior. Specifically, the marginal cost of obtaining information about a particular contractual clause may exceed the expected marginal benefit from such information. To obtain such information the consumer would not only have to read the fine print, but would also likely have to obtain legal advice to assist her in understanding its significance. Given her limited knowledge and her hope that she will not need to sue the seller, and also recognizing

---

the difficulty of finding or negotiating an alternative clause in any event, the rational consumer will not attempt to comprehend most form contractual terms.

The free market advocates have responded to this lack of information with several arguments, none of which is convincing. According to the "knowledgeable minority" defense, even though many consumers do not read form contracts, enough consumers do read such contracts and evaluate the advantages and disadvantages of their respective terms to ensure that suppliers will not be able to inflict unfair terms. If a supplier did try to impose a detrimental arbitration clause without lowering its price sufficiently to make the clause acceptable to a knowledgeable consumer, the portion of consumers who read such clauses would notice the detrimental provision and either insist on its being changed or switch to another supplier.

There are several flaws to this Pollyannaish defense. First, it seems likely that the "knowledgeable minority" is an extremely small minority. Arbitration clauses are often buried in seemingly insignificant places, camouflaged as insignificant junk mail, written in very small print, and written in technical terms not likely to be meaningful to most. If the knowledgeable minority is sufficiently small, the supplier may well make enough money from taking advantage of the majority to more than justify losing the minority's business. Further, if the seller is in a position to be able to discriminate as to contractual terms between consumers, the seller could satisfy the well-informed consumers while still imposing a binding arbitration clause on the other more ignorant consumers. In addition, because different consumers have different tastes for risk and other features, a knowledgeable minority cannot necessarily look out for the interests of the majority.

The free marketeers may also seek to counter the fact that consumers lack knowledge with the argument that sellers will use advertising to educate the consumers. Some economists argue that where one seller seeks to gain a competitive advantage by lowering quality in order to lower price, the underpriced seller will expose the tactic through advertising. The problem with this argument is that, realistically, no seller is likely to call attention to possible problems with its own product by telling consumers that "if it explodes you can sue us in court, not just through an arbitration." In other words, by publicizing the risks relevant to the arbitration clause the seller might well cause sales as a whole to plummet. Moreover, sellers may be reluctant to expend a significant portion of their advertising budget on subordinate terms when they could likely achieve greater inroads by focusing on terms more likely to influence consumer choice. Furthermore, the free marketeers ignore the fact that in many industries barriers to entry have apparently discouraged new suppliers from joining the industry, and that all the suppliers in the industry may well employ essentially the same arbitration clause.

In addition to the flaws of lack of information, transaction costs, and barriers to entry outlined above, the free market advocates must also confront a growing literature demonstrating that individuals may be quite far from the rational profit maximizers economists like to hypothesize. Professor Robert Ellickson, in particular, has recently done some pathbreaking work showing that policymakers must consider culture and human frailties, as well as self-interest, in developing legal rules and policies. If consumers do not act rationally, one cannot assume that their actions will ensure efficient operation of the market.

In sum, because the market for most consumer goods differs substantially from the perfectly competitive, perfect information, zero transaction cost market envisioned by some economists, there is little or no reason to believe that market forces will prevent sellers from using arbitration clauses to take unfair advantage of consumers and other little guys. Rather, given the high cost of information and consumers' behavior with respect to risk, it appears that failing to regulate the market with respect to arbitration clauses is likely to lead to an inefficient result that benefits those who impose form arbitration agreements.

Stephen J. Ware, THE CASE FOR ENFORCING ADHESIVE ARBITRATION AGREEMENTS — WITH PARTICULAR CONSIDERATION OF CLASS ACTIONS AND ARBITRATION FEES,
5 J. AM. ARB. 251, 254–64 (2006)*

A. Reducing Costs and Passing on the Savings

Few doubt that enforcement of adhesive arbitration agreements benefits the businesses that use such agreements. This consensus is unsurprising; if businesses using these agreements did not benefit from them, why would they continue to use them? The consensus view is that businesses using adhesive arbitration agreements do so because those businesses generally find that those agreements lower their dispute-resolution costs.

In the case of consumer arbitration agreements, this benefit to businesses is also a benefit to consumers. That is because whatever lowers costs to businesses tends over time to lower prices to consumers. While the entire cost-savings is passed on to consumers only under conditions of perfect competition, some of the cost-savings is passed on to consumers under non-competitive conditions, even monopoly. The extent to which cost-savings are passed on to consumers is determined by the elasticity of supply and demand in the relevant markets. Therefore, the size of the price reduction caused by enforcement of consumer arbitration agreements will vary, as will the time it takes to occur. But it is inconsistent with basic economics to question the existence of the price reduction.

The analogous point can be made about the effect on wages of the enforcement of employment arbitration agreements. While one can question the size or timing of the wage increase caused by this enforcement, it is inconsistent with basic economics to question the existence of it. This point applies similarly with respect to adhesive arbitration agreements in other contexts as well. It is merely an example of the general insight that contract terms favorable to sellers go hand-in-hand with lower prices. "Recognition of this has been standard in the law-and-economics literature for at least a quarter of a century."

B. The Source(s) of the Cost Reduction

While there is consensus that the enforcement of adhesive arbitration agreements lowers the dispute-resolution costs of the businesses that use them, there is uncertainty about the source(s) of this cost-reduction. One possible source is that comparable cases brought by adhering parties, such as consumers and employees, generally lead to lower awards in arbitration than in litigation. This is the story of arbitration as "self-help deregulation" for business. If a business wants to reduce the legal liability imposed by, for example, consumer protection regulation, the business does not need to work for change through the political system; it can use self help to reduce its liability by requiring its customers to agree to arbitration. If this "self-help deregulation" story is true, then enforcement of arbitration agreements has costs to consumers and employees (lower awards and, therefore, lower settlements), as well as benefits (lower prices or higher wages).

By contrast, a different possible source of arbitration's cost-savings to business defendants is that arbitration reduces the business defendant's process costs — the time and legal fees spent on pleadings, discovery, motions, trial or hearing, and appeal. It is possible that the amount of awards is identical in arbitration and litigation but the business defendant's cost of getting to the award is lower in arbitration. If this is true — if all arbitration's benefits to the business defendant come from lower process costs — then arbitration benefits both parties to the contract. The process-cost savings benefit consumers and employees, who receive better prices or wages, and benefit the business defendant to the extent the business did not pass on the cost-savings arbitration produced.

. . . So the happy story about adhesive arbitration agreements is that they are all about reducing process costs. They do not affect the outcomes of cases in any significant or systematic way; they merely get to the outcomes more efficiently . . .

Of course, the happy story that adhesive arbitration agreements just reduce process costs and the "self-help deregulation" story that such agreements just lower awards are not the only two possibilities. It is possible that adhesive arbitration results in *both* lower process costs for the business defendant and generally lower awards for adhering parties like consumers and employees. And it is possible — the following section suggests likely — that, in addition to lowering process costs, adhesive arbitration tends to result in lower awards for some types of cases but higher awards in other types of cases.

C. Empirical Studies and Their Inherent Limits

The previous paragraphs show that the sources of arbitration's benefit to the business defendant matter in assessing the costs and benefits to adhering parties of enforcing arbitration agreements. It would be useful if empirical studies could reveal the extent to which each possible source is, in fact, contributing to arbitration's benefit to the business defendant. Unfortunately, this is not possible. . . .

. . . In sum, "[e]mpirical studies are vulnerable to the possibility that the studied cases going to arbitration are systematically different from the studied cases going to litigation." Therefore, in comparing arbitration and litigation, we must be cautious about how much weight we give empirical studies.

That said, the empirical evidence supports the aforementioned hypotheses that (1) reduced process costs are a significant source of the cost-savings businesses derive from arbitration, and (2) that arbitration tends to result in lower awards for some types of cases but higher awards in other types of cases. The empirical studies, which have been in the area of employment arbitration, indicate that employees win a higher percentage of their claims in arbitration than in litigation but employees who win in litigation win more money than employees who win in arbitration. The anecdotes I have heard from practicing lawyers suggest similar results in consumer arbitration: claims that would result in big-dollar jury awards tend to see lower awards in arbitration, but smaller-yet-meritorious claims, some of which might not be cost-effective to pursue at all in litigation, tend to see higher awards in arbitration.

If this empirical/anecdotal picture is accurate, then adhesive arbitration agreements give consumers and employees (1) better prices or wages and (2) extra leverage in small-yet-meritorious cases, but (3) reduced leverage in cases that could lead to a big-dollar jury award. For the vast majority of consumers and employees, the benefits of (1) and (2) outweigh the costs of (3) because it is the rare consumer or employee who actually has a claim that could lead to a big-dollar jury award. If such a dispute has already arisen, however, the price that particular consumer or employee will charge for giving up (3) increases dramatically. In other words, it is entirely rational for a consumer, or employee, or other adhering party to prefer, at the time of contracting, that an arbitration clause be in the contract even if, at the time of a particular dispute, the adhering party prefers that an arbitration clause not be in the contract.

D. The Importance of Enforcing Pre-Dispute Agreements to Arbitrate

In discussing arbitration agreements, it is crucial to distinguish between pre-dispute agreements formed at the time of contracting and post-dispute agreements formed after a particular dispute has arisen. Critics of adhesive arbitration agreements conclude that arbitration must be bad for consumers and employees if businesses have to impose it through pre-dispute adhesion contracts in which the arbitration clause is unlikely to be noticed by the consumer or employee, let alone the focus of attention. If arbitration really was good for them, consumers and employees would choose it post-dispute, when they have had time to consider (perhaps in consultation with a lawyer) the pros and cons of arbitration versus litigation. According to this view, only post-dispute arbitration agreements should be enforced.

Limiting enforcement to post-dispute agreements, however, would fail to produce all the social gains produced by enforcing pre-dispute arbitration agreements. That is because the social gains resulting from arbitration's lower process costs will not be realized nearly as often if an enforceable arbitration agreement can only be made after a dispute arises. Neither party is likely to agree, post-dispute, to arbitrate claims for which arbitration is expected to be less favorable to that party than litigation would be. Thus post-dispute arbitration agreements are unlikely to occur even if both parties believe that the process costs (for both sides) are lower in arbitration than litigation.

By contrast, pre-dispute agreements are formed at a time when both parties are uncertain about whether there will be a dispute and, if so, what sort of dispute it will be. That is the time when both sides have an incentive to choose the forum that reduces process costs. This explains why enforcement of predispute arbitration agreements benefits consumers and employees as a whole even though it would be against some particular consumers' and employees' interests to agree to arbitration once a dispute has arisen. In sum, the general enforcement of adhesive arbitration agreements benefits society as a whole by reducing process costs and, in particular, benefits most consumers, employees, and other adhering parties.

NOTES

1. The controversy over arbitration of consumer disputes manifests itself throughout the law of commercial arbitration. Courts (and legislatures) continue to struggle with whether and how much to regulate arbitration clauses in contracts between businesses and consumers, employees, and others. You will have many opportunities throughout this book to revisit the question of whether more or less regulation is needed.

2. As discussed in Chapter 3, in recent years Congress has enacted a number of statutes limiting the enforceability of pre-dispute arbitration agreements in particular types of contracts and types of claims. It also has considered but not enacted bills that would restrict the use of arbitration clauses in nursing home contracts and consumer lending agreements, among others. In addition, the proposed Arbitration Fairness Act provides more broadly that "no predispute arbitration agreement shall be valid or enforceable if it requires arbitration of an employment dispute, consumer dispute, or civil rights dispute." H.R. 1873, 112th Cong., § 3 (2011) (adding 9 U.S.C. § 402(a)). Congress has held several hearings on the Arbitration Fairness Act, but has not passed it.

The Dodd-Frank Wall Street Reform and Consumer Protection Act, Pub. L. No. 111-203 (2010), gives both the SEC and the newly created Consumer Financial Protection Bureau authority to prohibit or impose conditions on the use of pre-dispute arbitration agreements in contracts they regulate, *id.* §§ 921 & 1028. The CFPB currently is preparing a study of arbitration clauses in consumer financial services contracts, which Dodd-Frank required it to do prior to regulating. Is Congress or an administrative agency the better institution to consider whether to regulate arbitration?

Several states also have enacted statutes in response to concerns about the fairness of consumer and employment arbitration. See, for example, the 2002 California arbitration laws reprinted in the Documentary Supplement. The California statutes regulate the arbitration process, rather than making pre-dispute arbitration clauses unenforceable (perhaps due, as we will see in Chapter 4, to concerns about preemption by the Federal Arbitration Act). Preemption concerns aside, which form of regulation is preferable?

3.   There also have been a variety of private efforts to promote the fairness of consumerized arbitration. See, for example, the Due Process Protocol for Mediation and Arbitration of Statutory Disputes Arising Out of the Employment Relationship and the Consumer Due Process Protocol, both reprinted in the Documentary Supplement. How effective do you think these private efforts will be?

4.   Professor Sternlight uses the phrase "mandatory arbitration" as a shorthand for pre-dispute arbitration clauses in standard form contracts. Pre-dispute arbitration agreements are ones entered into before a dispute arises between the parties. Post-dispute arbitration agreements, also called submission agreements, are ones entered into after a dispute has arisen. The authors of a leading treatise have criticized the use of phrases such as "mandatory arbitration" or "compulsory arbitration" in this context:

> Where . . . the very issue is the genuineness of consent or the harshness of the alternatives to consent, using such terms as *compulsory* or *mandatory* in such circumstances is, at best, highly confusing. At worst, it constitutes question-begging: The very question at stake where such questions arise is whether whatever consent to arbitrate as has been manifested should or should not be given full contractual effect. To call the arbitration compulsory or mandatory is to answer by label, not by attention to the facts and by analysis. It is far better to call these terms "pre-dispute arbitration agreements."

See 2 Ian R. Macneil et al., Federal Arbitration Law § 17.1.2.2, at 17:8 to 17:9 (Supp. 1999).

PROBLEM 1.5

You are a staff person for Senator Grace Dunbar, a newly elected member of the United States Senate. She tells you that one of her colleagues has asked her to co-sponsor two bills. The first bill is entitled the "Employment Arbitration Choice Act," and would amend the FAA to add a new section 17 as follows:

Section 17. Resolution of Controversy

(a)   Notwithstanding an employment contract that provides for the use of arbitration to resolve a controversy arising out of or relating to the employment relationship, arbitration may be used to settle such a dispute only if —

(1)   The employer or employee submits a written request after the dispute arises to the other party to use arbitration; and

(2)   The other party consents in writing not later than 60 days after the receipt of the request to use arbitration.

(b)   An employer subject to this Act may not require an employee to arbitrate a dispute as a condition of employment.

The second bill would repeal the FAA altogether, at least as applied to wholly domestic disputes. She asks you whether she should agree to be a cosponsor of either of the bills. What do you advise her?

Chapter 2

ENFORCING DOMESTIC AGREEMENTS TO ARBITRATE

§ 2.01 OVERVIEW

Most arbitration agreements are complied with voluntarily. A party may prefer arbitration to court litigation, either because it is cheaper, more accurate, or for some other reason. A party may decide that trying to avoid arbitration is not worth the effort because it likely will be ordered to arbitrate anyway. Or a party may not want to develop a reputation for trying to avoid its agreements.

In some cases, however, one of the parties to a pre-dispute arbitration agreement will decide that it does not want to proceed to arbitration once a dispute has arisen. At common law, courts generally would not stand in the way of parties that sought to avoid arbitration. With the enactment of the Federal Arbitration Act (FAA) (formerly known as the United States Arbitration Act) and various state arbitration statutes (many of which are based on the Uniform Arbitration Act (UAA)), however, arbitration agreements — whether entered into before or after a dispute arises — are now "valid, irrevocable, and enforceable." 9 U.S.C. § 2; UAA § 1; *see also* Revised Uniform Arbitration Act (RUAA) § 6. According to the United States Supreme Court, the Federal Arbitration Act espouses an "emphatic federal policy in favor of arbitral dispute resolution," *see* Mitsubishi Motors Corp. v. Soler Chrysler-Plymouth, Inc., 473 U.S. 614, 631 (1985), a policy that is cited frequently by courts interpreting and applying the Act.

As a procedural matter, disputes over whether parties must arbitrate can end up in court in various ways. First, the party that prefers to go to court might simply ignore the arbitration clause and file a lawsuit in court. If it does so, the other party can seek a stay of the litigation under section 3 of the Federal Arbitration Act and an order compelling arbitration under section 4 of the FAA. *See also* UAA § 2; RUAA § 7. Second, the party that wants arbitration to go forward can file a freestanding action to compel arbitration under section 4 of the FAA. Third, the party that prefers to go to court may request a court to enjoin the arbitration proceeding. Although the FAA does not expressly authorize injunctions against arbitration, a number of courts have recognized such an action. *See* 2 IAN R. MACNEIL ET AL., FEDERAL ARBITRATION LAW § 23.5 (1994 & Supp. 1999); *see also* UAA § 2(b) ("court may stay an arbitration proceeding commenced or threatened on a showing that there is no agreement to arbitrate"). *But see* Rodarte v. FINRA, 2011 U.S. Dist. LEXIS 59636, at *12-*13 (D.S.C June 1, 2011) ("An interpretation of the FAA according to the plain language of its relevant provisions convinces the court that the FAA does not authorize a cause of action to stay or enjoin arbitration.").

The FAA and the UAA do not require courts to enforce all agreements to arbitrate. The arbitration agreement must be in writing: only "written provisions" to settle disputes by arbitration are enforceable. *See* 9 U.S.C. § 2; *see also* UAA § 1. The party seeking arbitration must not be "in default in proceeding with such arbitration." *See* 9 U.S.C. § 3. In addition, the enforceability of the arbitration agreement can be challenged "upon such grounds as exist at law or in equity for the revocation of any contract." 9 U.S.C. § 2; *see also* UAA § 1; RUAA § 6(a). In other words, in ruling on the enforceability of an agreement to arbitrate, courts generally "apply ordinary state-law principles that govern the formation of contracts." First Options of Chicago, Inc. v. Kaplan, 514 U.S. 938, 944 (1995).

This chapter first addresses the preliminary question of who — the court or the arbitrator — decides whether a dispute is subject to arbitration. Second, it examines the circumstances under which a party waives its right to arbitrate. Third, it considers the scope of the arbitration agreement: how have the parties defined by their agreement which disputes are arbitrable. Fourth, it looks at general state contract law principles as applied to arbitration agreements. Fifth, it examines when non-signatories to the arbitration agreement nonetheless are bound to arbitrate. Finally, it takes an initial look at some of the procedural issues that arise in enforcing domestic arbitration agreements.

§ 2.02   WHO DECIDES ARBITRABILITY

PRIMA PAINT CORP. v. FLOOD & CONKLIN MFG. CO.
United States Supreme Court
388 U.S. 395 (1967)

Mr. Justice Fortas delivered the opinion of the Court.

This case presents the question whether the federal court or an arbitrator is to resolve a claim of "fraud in the inducement," under a contract governed by the United States Arbitration Act of 1925, where there is no evidence that the contracting parties intended to withhold that issue from arbitration.

The question arises from the following set of facts. On October 7, 1964, respondent, Flood & Conklin Manufacturing Company, a New Jersey corporation, entered into what was styled a "Consulting Agreement," with petitioner, Prima Paint Corporation, a Maryland corporation. This agreement followed by less than three weeks the execution of a contract pursuant to which Prima Paint purchased F & C's paint business. The consulting agreement provided that for a six-year period F & C was to furnish advice and consultation "in connection with the formulae, manufacturing operations, sales and servicing of Prima Trade Sales accounts." These services were to be performed personally by F & C's chairman, Jerome K. Jelin, "except in the event of his death or disability." F & C bound itself for the duration of the contractual period to make no "Trade Sales" of paint or paint products in its existing sales territory or to current customers. To the consulting agreement were appended lists of F & C customers, whose patronage was to be taken over by Prima Paint. In return for these lists, the covenant not to compete, and the services of Mr. Jelin, Prima Paint agreed to pay F & C certain percentages of its receipts from the listed customers and from all others, such payments not to exceed $225,000 over the life of the agreement. The agreement took into account the possibility that Prima Paint might encounter financial difficulties, including bankruptcy, but no corresponding reference was made to possible financial problems which might be encountered by F & C. The agreement stated that it "embodies the entire understanding of the parties on the subject matter." Finally, the parties agreed to a broad arbitration clause. . . .

The first payment by Prima Paint to F & C under the consulting agreement was due on September 1, 1965. None was made on that date. Seventeen days later, Prima Paint did pay the appropriate amount, but into escrow. It notified attorneys for F & C that in various enumerated respects their client had broken both the consulting agreement and the earlier purchase agreement. Prima Paint's principal contention, so far as presently relevant, was that F & C had fraudulently represented that it was solvent and able to perform its contractual obligations, where as it was in fact insolvent and intended to file a petition under Chapter XI of the Bankruptcy Act . . . shortly after execution of the consulting agreement. Prima Paint noted that such a petition was filed by F & C on October 14, 1964, one week after the contract had been signed. F & C's response, on October 25, was to serve a "notice of intention to arbitrate." On November 12, three days before expiration of its time to answer this "notice," Prima Paint filed suit in the United States District Court for the Southern District of New York, seeking rescission of the consulting agreement on the basis of the alleged fraudulent inducement. The complaint asserted that the federal court had diversity jurisdiction.

Contemporaneously with the filing of its complaint, Prima Paint petitioned the District Court for an order enjoining F & C from proceeding with the arbitration. F & C cross-moved to stay the court action pending arbitration. F & C contended that the issue presented — whether there was fraud in the inducement of the consulting agreement — was a question for the arbitrators and not for the District Court. . . .

The District Court granted F & C's motion to stay the action pending arbitration, holding that a charge of fraud in the inducement of a contract containing an arbitration clause as broad as this one was a question for the arbitrators and not for the court. The Court of Appeals for the Second Circuit dismissed Prima Paint's appeal. It held that the contract in question evidenced a transaction involving interstate commerce; that under the controlling [circuit precedent] a claim of fraud in the inducement of the contract generally — as opposed to the arbitration clause itself — is for the arbitrators and not for the courts; and that this rule — one of "national substantive law" — governs even in the face of a contrary state rule. We agree, albeit for somewhat different reasons, and we affirm the decision below.

The key statutory provisions are §§ 2, 3, and 4 of the United States Arbitration Act of 1925. . . .

In *Bernhardt v. Polygraphic Co.*, this Court held that the stay provisions of § 3, invoked here by respondent F & C, apply only to the two kinds of contracts specified in §§ 1 and 2 of the Act, namely those in admiralty or evidencing transactions in "commerce." Our first question, then, is whether the consulting agreement between

F & C and Prima Paint is such a contract. We agree with the Court of Appeals that it is. Prima Paint acquired a New Jersey paint business serving at least 175 wholesale clients in a number of States, and secured F & C's assistance in arranging the transfer of manufacturing and selling operations from New Jersey to Maryland. The consulting agreement was inextricably tied to this interstate transfer and to the continuing operations of an interstate manufacturing and wholesaling business. There could not be a clearer case of a contract evidencing a transaction in interstate commerce.

Having determined that the contract in question is within the coverage of the Arbitration Act, we turn to the central issue in this case: whether a claim of fraud in the inducement of the entire contract is to be resolved by the federal court, or whether the matter is to be referred to the arbitrators. . . .

With respect to cases brought in federal court involving maritime contracts or those evidencing transactions in "commerce," we think that Congress has provided an explicit answer. That answer is to be found in § 4 of the Act, which provides a remedy to a party seeking to compel compliance with an arbitration agreement. Under § 4, with respect to a matter within the jurisdiction of the federal courts save for the existence of an arbitration clause, the federal court is instructed to order arbitration to proceed once it is satisfied that "the making of the agreement for arbitration or the failure to comply [with the arbitration agreement] is not in issue." Accordingly, if the claim is fraud in the inducement of the arbitration clause itself — an issue which goes to the "making" of the agreement to arbitrate — the federal court may proceed to adjudicate it.[12] But the statutory language does not permit the federal court to consider claims of fraud in the inducement of the contract generally. Section 4 does not expressly relate to situations like the present in which a stay is sought of a federal action in order that arbitration may proceed. But it is inconceivable that Congress intended the rule to differ depending upon which party to the arbitration agreement first invokes the assistance of a federal court. We hold, therefore, that in passing upon a § 3 application for a stay while the parties arbitrate, a federal court may consider only issues relating to the making and performance of the agreement to arbitrate. In so concluding, we not only honor the plain meaning of the statute but also the unmistakably clear congressional purpose that the arbitration procedure, when selected by the parties to a contract, be speedy and not subject to delay and obstruction in the courts.

There remains the question whether such a rule is constitutionally permissible. The point is made that, whatever the nature of the contract involved here, this case is in federal court solely by reason of diversity of citizenship, and that since the decision in Erie R. Co. v. Tompkins, 304 U.S. 64 (1938), federal courts are bound in diversity cases to follow state rules of decision in matters which are "substantive" rather than "procedural," or where the matter is "outcome determinative." The

---

[12] This position is consistent both with the decision in Moseley v. Electronic Facilities, 374 U.S. 167, 171, 172 (1963), and with the statutory scheme. As the "saving clause" in § 2 indicates, the purpose of Congress in 1925 was to make arbitration agreements as enforceable as other contracts, but not more so. To immunize an arbitration agreement from judicial challenge on the ground of fraud in the inducement would be to elevate it over other forms of contract — a situation inconsistent with the "saving clause."

question in this case, however, is not whether Congress may fashion federal substantive rules to govern questions arising in simple diversity cases. Rather, the question is whether Congress may prescribe how federal courts are to conduct themselves with respect to subject matter over which Congress plainly has power to legislate. The answer to that can only be in the affirmative. And it is clear beyond dispute that the federal arbitration statute is based upon and confined to the incontestable federal foundations of "control over interstate commerce and over admiralty."[13]

In the present case no claim has been advanced by Prima Paint that F & C fraudulently induced it to enter into the agreement to arbitrate "[a]ny controversy or claim arising out of or relating to this Agreement, or the breach thereof." This contractual language is easily broad enough to encompass Prima Paint's claim that both execution and acceleration of the consulting agreement itself were procured by fraud. Indeed, no claim is made that Prima Paint ever intended that "legal" issues relating to the contract be excluded from arbitration, or that it was not entirely free so to contract. Federal courts are bound to apply rules enacted by Congress with respect to matters — here, a contract involving commerce — over which it has legislative power. The question which Prima Paint requested the District Court to adjudicate preliminarily to allowing arbitration to proceed is one not intended by Congress to delay the granting of a § 3 stay. Accordingly, the decision below dismissing Prima Paint's appeal is affirmed.

NOTES

1.   Under the separability doctrine as adopted by the Supreme Court in *Prima Paint*, an arbitration clause is separable from the main contract entered into by the parties. In other words, the agreement to arbitrate is treated as a separate contract from the underlying contract, so that the arbitration agreement is untainted by any fraudulent inducement as to the underlying contract. What is the basis for the Court's adoption of the separability doctrine? Do you agree with its interpretation of the FAA?

2.   The doctrine of separability, as applied by the Court in *Prima Paint*, allocates decision making authority between courts and arbitrators. Because the arbitration clause is separable from the underlying contract, the Court holds that allegations of fraudulent inducement of that underlying contract are to be decided by the arbitrator, not by the court. The Court does not rule on the merits of the allegations; instead, it holds that those allegations are to be considered by the arbitrator, along with any other arguments on the merits the parties might raise. Why did the parties in *Prima Paint* care enough about this issue to litigate it all the way to the Supreme Court?

---

[13] It is true that the Arbitration Act was passed 13 years before this Court's decision in *Erie R. Co.* v. *Tompkins, supra*, brought to an end the regime of Swift v. Tyson, 16 Pet. 1 (1842), and that at the time of enactment Congress had reason to believe that it still had power to create federal rules to govern questions of "general law" arising in simple diversity cases — at least, absent any state statute to the contrary. If Congress relied at all on this "oft-challenged" power, it was only supplementary to the admiralty and commerce powers, which formed the principal bases of the legislation. . . .

3.   Although allegations of fraudulent inducement directed at the contract as a whole are to be decided by the arbitrator, the Court in *Prima Paint* indicates that allegations of fraudulent inducement directed at the making of the agreement to arbitrate itself need not be submitted to arbitration. Instead, such a defense can be decided by a court. In Moseley v. Electronic & Missile Facilities, Inc., 374 U.S. 167 (1963), cited in *Prima Paint*, the petitioner alleged "not only the subcontracts, but also the arbitration clauses contained therein as having been procured through fraud." *Id.* at 170–71. "[T]he insertion in the subcontracts of an arbitration clause requiring arbitration of disputes in New York" was alleged to be part of "a fraudulent scheme to obtain a great amount of work and material from petitioner and the other subcontractors without making payment therefor and to 'browbeat' petitioner and his fellow subcontractors into accepting much less than the value of their claims." *Id.* at 171. On those facts, the Supreme Court concluded that it was appropriate for the court to decide the fraud issue in advance of arbitration.

What if the party seeking to avoid arbitration alleged that it did not realize it was even signing a contract because of the other party's trickery? This defense, sometimes called fraud in the execution, differs from fraudulent inducement, in which the party admits that it formed a contract but did so only because the other party lied about material facts. The defense of fraud in the execution, like the defense of fraudulent inducement in *Prima Paint*, is directed at the contract as a whole, not at the arbitration clause itself. But it differs from fraudulent inducement in that the party raising the defense denies there was ever a contract. Some courts have held that the defense of fraud in the execution can be decided by the court. *See, e.g.*, Rosenthal v. Great Western Financial Sec. Corp., 926 P.2d 1061 (Cal. 1996). Do you agree?

4.   *Prima Paint* involved allegations of fraudulent inducement. What about other contract defenses such as illegality, lack of consideration, or lack of assent? How should the separability doctrine apply to those defenses?

5.   Not all states have adopted the separability doctrine as a matter of state arbitration law. In Shaffer v. Jeffery, 915 P.2d 910 (Okla. 1996), for example, the Oklahoma Supreme Court held that a defense of fraudulent inducement of the contract as a whole was for the court, not the arbitrator, to decide. The court reasoned as follows:

> The question before us is whether we should give the Oklahoma Arbitration Act the same construction as given to the Federal Arbitration Act by the Supreme Court in *Prima Paint*. Courts in most states where it has come up have followed *Prima Paint*. Courts in Louisiana, Minnesota, and Tennessee have declined to do so.
>
> . . .
>
> [Some state] courts embraced the separability doctrine because of *Prima Paint* and because an unsupported allegation of fraud could cause delay by allowing its resolution by the [court]. In other words, unsupported allegations of fraud would frustrate the parties' intent to a speedy remedy by arbitration. One problem with this approach is that even where the separability doctrine is enforced there are still certain claims that may be

made, including those that are unsupported, resulting in judicial adjudication and delay of arbitration. For example, allegations concerning the formation of the arbitration agreement itself must be judicially adjudicated prior to arbitration, even when it is ultimately determined that those allegations were insufficient.

. . .

[We hold that a] court must determine the existence of an arbitration agreement in the first instance. At this early stage the court is best suited to determine issues such as fraud. . . . "[C]ourts have far more expertise in resolving legal issues which go to the validity of a contract than do arbitrators." We have recently recognized that a strong public policy favors arbitration in Oklahoma. Resolution of claims such as fraud by those who are best suited to perform the task will enhance the arbitration process.

Id. at 916–17. For a critical view of separability under the FAA, see Stephen J. Ware, *Employment Arbitration and Voluntary Consent*, 25 HOFSTRA L. REV. 83, 128–38 (1996).

PROBLEM 2.1

John Openshaw has developed a new type of self-repairing bicycle tire, for which he wants to obtain a patent. He enters into a contract with an attorney, James Fordham, to have Fordham handle all legal aspects of obtaining the patent and licensing the product. The written fee contract contains a clause providing that all disputes arising out of or relating to the contract are subject to arbitration. Fordham botches the patent application, and a competitor obtains all legal rights to the self-repairing bicycle tire. Openshaw files suit against Fordham for damages alleging a variety of claims, including legal malpractice and breach of contract. Fordham files a motion for stay of the proceedings pending arbitration. Which of the following defenses that Openshaw might raise could a court consider in ruling on a motion for stay, and which are for the arbitrator?

(a) Openshaw alleges that the only reason he signed the contract was because he relied on statements Fordham made about his vast experience in doing patent work, which all proved to be lies.

(b) Openshaw alleges that the only reason he agreed to include an arbitration clause in the contract was that Fordham told him such a clause was required by law, which proved to be a lie.

(c) Openshaw alleges that he never signed a written contract with Fordham, and that the written contract that Fordham produced is a forgery.

(d) Openshaw alleges that as a matter of state law, his legal malpractice claim is not subject to arbitration.

(e) Openshaw alleges that Fordham was disbarred several years before the parties signed the fee contract, and that Fordham was practicing law without a license at the time he signed the contract to do legal work for Openshaw.

(f) Assume that Openshaw filed suit in state court in Oklahoma and that the transaction is governed solely by the Oklahoma Arbitration Act. Which of your answers to the above questions would change, if any?

FIRST OPTIONS OF CHICAGO, INC. v. KAPLAN
United States Supreme Court
514 U.S. 938 (1995)

JUSTICE BREYER delivered the opinion of the Court.

In this case we consider . . . how a district court should review an arbitrator's decision that the parties agreed to arbitrate a dispute. . . .

I

The case concerns several related disputes between, on one side, First Options of Chicago, Inc., a firm that clears stock trades on the Philadelphia Stock Exchange, and, on the other side, three parties: Manuel Kaplan; his wife, Carol Kaplan; and his wholly owned investment company, MK Investments, Inc. (MKI), whose trading account First Options cleared. The disputes center around a "workout" agreement, embodied in four separate documents, which governs the "working out" of debts to First Options that MKI and the Kaplans incurred as a result of the October 1987 stock market crash. In 1989, after entering into the agreement, MKI lost an additional $1.5 million. First Options then took control of, and liquidated, certain MKI assets; demanded immediate payment of the entire MKI debt; and insisted that the Kaplans personally pay any deficiency. When its demands went unsatisfied, First Options sought arbitration by a panel of the Philadelphia Stock Exchange.

MKI, having signed the only workout document (out of four) that contained an arbitration clause, accepted arbitration. The Kaplans, however, who had not personally signed that document, denied that their disagreement with First Options was arbitrable and filed written objections to that effect with the arbitration panel. The arbitrators decided that they had the power to rule on the merits of the parties' dispute, and did so in favor of First Options. The Kaplans then asked the Federal District Court to vacate the arbitration award, see 9 U.S.C. § 10, and First Options requested its confirmation, see § 9. The court confirmed the award. Nonetheless, on appeal the Court of Appeals for the Third Circuit agreed with the Kaplans that their dispute was not arbitrable; and it reversed the District Court's confirmation of the award against them.

We granted certiorari to consider . . . the standard[] that the Court of Appeals used to review the determination that the Kaplans' dispute with First Options was arbitrable. . . . [T]he Court of Appeals said that courts "should *independently* decide whether an arbitration panel has jurisdiction over the merits of any particular dispute." First Options asked us to decide whether this is so (*i.e.*, whether courts, in "reviewing the arbitrators' decision on arbitrability," should "apply a *de novo* standard of review or the more deferential standard applied to arbitrators' decisions on the merits") when the objecting party "submitted the issue to the arbitrators for decision." . . .

II

Th[is] . . . question — the standard of review applied to an arbitrator's decision about arbitrability — is a narrow one. To understand just how narrow, consider three types of disagreement present in this case. First, the Kaplans and First Options disagree about whether the Kaplans are personally liable for MKI's debt to First Options. That disagreement makes up the *merits* of the dispute. Second, they disagree about whether they agreed to arbitrate the merits. That disagreement is about the *arbitrability* of the dispute. Third, they disagree about *who should have the primary power to decide the second matter.* Does that power belong primarily to the arbitrators (because the court reviews their arbitrability decision deferentially) or to the court (because the court makes up its mind about arbitrability independently)? We consider here only this third question.

Although the question is a narrow one, it has a certain practical importance. That is because a party who has not agreed to arbitrate will normally have a right to a court's decision about the merits of its dispute (say, as here, its obligation under a contract). But, where the party has agreed to arbitrate, he or she, in effect, has relinquished much of that right's practical value. The party still can ask a court to review the arbitrator's decision, but the court will set that decision aside only in very unusual circumstances. *See, e.g.*, 9 U.S.C. § 10 (award procured by corruption, fraud, or undue means; arbitrator exceeded his powers); *Wilko v. Swan* (parties bound by arbitrator's decision not in "manifest disregard" of the law), overruled on other grounds, *Rodriguez de Quijas v. Shearson/American Express, Inc.* Hence, who — court or arbitrator — has the primary authority to decide whether a party has agreed to arbitrate can make a critical difference to a party resisting arbitration.

We believe the answer to the "who" question (*i.e.*, the standard-of-review question) is fairly simple. Just as the arbitrability of the merits of a dispute depends upon whether the parties agreed to arbitrate that dispute, so the question "who has the primary power to decide arbitrability" turns upon what the parties agreed about *that* matter. Did the parties agree to submit the arbitrability question itself to arbitration? If so, then the court's standard for reviewing the arbitrator's decision about *that* matter should not differ from the standard courts apply when they review any other matter that parties have agreed to arbitrate. That is to say, the court should give considerable leeway to the arbitrator, setting aside his or her decision only in certain narrow circumstances. *See, e.g.*, 9 U.S.C. § 10. If, on the other hand, the parties did not agree to submit the arbitrability question itself to arbitration, then the court should decide that question just as it would decide any other question that the parties did not submit to arbitration, namely independently. These two answers flow inexorably from the fact that arbitration is simply a matter of contract between the parties; it is a way to resolve those disputes — but only those disputes — that the parties have agreed to submit to arbitration.

We agree with First Options, therefore, that a court must defer to an arbitrator's arbitrability decision when the parties submitted that matter to arbitration. Nevertheless, that conclusion does not help First Options win this case. That is because a fair and complete answer to the standard-of-review question requires a word about how a court should decide whether the parties have agreed to submit the arbitrability issue to arbitration. And, that word makes clear that the Kaplans did not agree to arbitrate arbitrability here.

When deciding whether the parties agreed to arbitrate a certain matter (including arbitrability), courts generally (though with a qualification we discuss below) should apply ordinary state-law principles that govern the formation of contracts. The relevant state law here, for example, would require the court to see whether the parties objectively revealed an intent to submit the arbitrability issue to arbitration.

This Court, however, has (as we just said) added an important qualification, applicable when courts decide whether a party has agreed that arbitrators should decide arbitrability: Courts should not assume that the parties agreed to arbitrate arbitrability unless there is "clea[r] and unmistakabl[e]" evidence that they did so. In this manner the law treats silence or ambiguity about the question "*who* (primarily) should decide arbitrability" differently from the way it treats silence or ambiguity about the question "*whether* a particular merits-related dispute is arbitrable because it is within the scope of a valid arbitration agreement" — for in respect to this latter question the law reverses the presumption. *See Mitsubishi Motors* (" 'Any doubts concerning the scope of arbitral issues should be resolved in favor of arbitration' " (*quoting Moses H. Cone Memorial Hospital v. Mercury Constr. Corp.*)).

But this difference in treatment is understandable. The latter question arises when the parties have a contract that provides for arbitration of some issues. In such circumstances, the parties likely gave at least some thought to the scope of arbitration. And, given the law's permissive policies in respect to arbitration, one can understand why the law would insist upon clarity before concluding that the parties did not want to arbitrate a related matter. On the other hand, the former question — the "who (primarily) should decide arbitrability" question — is rather arcane. A party often might not focus upon that question or upon the significance of having arbitrators decide the scope of their own powers. And, given the principle that a party can be forced to arbitrate only those issues it specifically has agreed to submit to arbitration, one can understand why courts might hesitate to interpret silence or ambiguity on the "who should decide arbitrability" point as giving the arbitrators that power, for doing so might too often force unwilling parties to arbitrate a matter they reasonably would have thought a judge, not an arbitrator, would decide.

On the record before us, First Options cannot show that the Kaplans clearly agreed to have the arbitrators decide (*i.e.*, to arbitrate) the question of arbitrability. First Options relies on the Kaplans' filing with the arbitrators a written memorandum objecting to the arbitrators' jurisdiction. But merely arguing the arbitrability issue to an arbitrator does not indicate a clear willingness to arbitrate that issue, *i.e.*, a willingness to be effectively bound by the arbitrator's decision on that point. To the contrary, insofar as the Kaplans were forcefully objecting to the arbitrators deciding their dispute with First Options, one naturally would think that they did *not* want the arbitrators to have binding authority over them. This conclusion draws added support from (1) an obvious explanation for the Kaplans' presence before the arbitrators (i.e., that MKI, Mr. Kaplan's wholly owned firm, was arbitrating workout agreement matters); and (2) Third Circuit law that suggested that the Kaplans might argue arbitrability to the arbitrators without losing their right to independent court review.

First Options makes several counterarguments: (1) that the Kaplans had other ways to get an independent court decision on the question of arbitrability without arguing the issue to the arbitrators (*e.g.*, by trying to enjoin the arbitration, or by refusing to participate in the arbitration and then defending against a court petition First Options would have brought to compel arbitration, see 9 U.S.C. § 4); (2) that permitting parties to argue arbitrability to an arbitrator without being bound by the result would cause delay and waste in the resolution of disputes; and (3) that the Arbitration Act therefore requires a presumption that the Kaplans agreed to be bound by the arbitrators' decision, not the contrary. The first of these points, however, while true, simply does not say anything about whether the Kaplans intended to be bound by the arbitrators' decision. The second point, too, is inconclusive, for factual circumstances vary too greatly to permit a confident conclusion about whether allowing the arbitrator to make an initial (but independently reviewable) arbitrability determination would, in general, slow down the dispute resolution process. And, the third point is legally erroneous, for there is no strong arbitration-related policy favoring First Options in respect to its particular argument here. After all, the basic objective in this area is not to resolve disputes in the quickest manner possible, no matter what the parties' wishes, but to ensure that commercial arbitration agreements, like other contracts, "are enforced according to their terms," and according to the intentions of the parties. That policy favors the Kaplans, not First Options.

We conclude that, because the Kaplans did not clearly agree to submit the question of arbitrability to arbitration, the Court of Appeals was correct in finding that the arbitrability of the Kaplan/First Options dispute was subject to independent review by the courts.

. . .

The judgment of the Court of Appeals is affirmed.

It is so ordered.

NOTES

1.   Unlike *Prima Paint*, which involved a challenge to the enforceability of an arbitration agreement before the arbitration proceeding took place, *First Options* arose out of a challenge to an arbitration award after it was made. The question in *First Options*, as posed by the Supreme Court, is whether the arbitrators' finding that the Kaplans had agreed to arbitrate was entitled to deference. The Court held that it was not entitled to deference but instead was subject to de novo review by a court. In other words, a court, rather than the arbitrator, was entitled to make the ultimate decision.

Accordingly, despite the differing procedural posture, the fundamental issue in both *First Options* and *Prima Paint* essentially is the same: who ultimately decides whether a dispute is subject to arbitration, a court or the arbitrator. In *Prima*

Paint, the Supreme Court held that a defense of fraud in the inducement of the contract is to be decided by the arbitrator. In *First Options*, the Court held that whether a party has assented to arbitrate can be decided by a court. What does *First Options* suggest about who should decide the other contract law defenses we discussed earlier?

2.   The Court in *First Options* states that the arbitrators' decision on arbitrability would have been entitled to deference had the Kaplans "clearly agreed to have the arbitrators decide (*i.e.*, to arbitrate) the question of arbitrability." What sort of evidence is required to make that showing? The Court holds that merely arguing the issue to the arbitrators does not constitute clear and unmistakable evidence that a party agrees to have the arbitrators decide arbitrability. What if the arbitration clause in *First Options* had provided that "all issues and disputes as to the arbitrability of claims must also be resolved by the arbitrator." Would that have changed the Court's decision?

3.   In Howsam v. Dean Witter Reynolds, Inc., 537 U.S. 79 (2002), the Supreme Court resolved a circuit court split over whether courts or arbitrators are to apply the six-year limit for filing claims under the securities industry's arbitration rules, holding that the matter is one for the arbitrator. The Court's reasoning was as follows:

> This Court has determined that "arbitration is a matter of contract and a party cannot be required to submit to arbitration any dispute which he has not agreed so to submit." Steelworkers v. Warrior & Gulf Nav. Co., 363 U.S. 574, 582 (1960); *see also First Options*. Although the Court has also long recognized and enforced a "liberal federal policy favoring arbitration agreements," *Moses H. Cone Memorial Hospital v. Mercury Constr. Corp.*, it has made clear that there is an exception to this policy: The question whether the parties have submitted a particular dispute to arbitration, *i.e.*, the "*question of arbitrability*," is "an issue for judicial determination unless the parties clearly and unmistakably provide otherwise." AT&T Technologies, Inc. v. Communications Workers, 475 U.S. 643, 649 (1986) (emphasis added); *First Options*. We must decide here whether application of the NASD time limit provision falls into the scope of this last-mentioned interpretive rule.

> Linguistically speaking, one might call any potentially dispositive gateway question a "question of arbitrability," for its answer will determine whether the underlying controversy will proceed to arbitration on the merits. The Court's case law, however, makes clear that, for purposes of applying the interpretive rule, the phrase "question of arbitrability" has a far more limited scope. The Court has found the phrase applicable in the kind of narrow circumstance where contracting parties would likely have expected a court to have decided the gateway matter, where they are not likely to have thought that they had agreed that an arbitrator would do so, and, consequently, where reference of the gateway dispute to the court avoids the risk of forcing parties to arbitrate a matter that they may well not have agreed to arbitrate.

[A] gateway dispute about whether the parties are bound by a given arbitration clause raises a "question of arbitrability" for a court to decide. *See [First Options]* (holding that a court should decide whether the arbitration contract bound parties who did not sign the agreement); John Wiley & Sons, Inc. v. Livingston, 376 U.S. 543, 546–547 (1964) (holding that a court should decide whether an arbitration agreement survived a corporate merger and bound the resulting corporation). Similarly, a disagreement about whether an arbitration clause in a concededly binding contract applies to a particular type of controversy is for the court. *See, e.g., AT&T Technologies* (holding that a court should decide whether a labor-management layoff controversy falls within the arbitration clause of a collective-bargaining agreement); Atkinson v. Sinclair Refining Co., 370 U.S. 238, 241–243 (1962) (holding that a court should decide whether a clause providing for arbitration of various "grievances" covers claims for damages for breach of a no-strike agreement).

At the same time the Court has found the phrase "question of arbitrability" *not* applicable in other kinds of general circumstance where parties would likely expect that an arbitrator would decide the gateway matter. Thus " 'procedural' questions which grow out of the dispute and bear on its final disposition" are presumptively *not* for the judge, but for an arbitrator, to decide. *John Wiley* (holding that an arbitrator should decide whether the first two steps of a grievance procedure were completed, where these steps are prerequisites to arbitration). So, too, the presumption is that the arbitrator should decide "allegations of waiver, delay, or a like defense to arbitrability." *Moses H. Cone Memorial Hospital.* Indeed, the Revised Uniform Arbitration Act of 2000 (RUAA), seeking to "incorporate the holdings of the vast majority of state courts and the law that has developed under the [Federal Arbitration Act]," states that an "arbitrator shall decide whether a condition precedent to arbitrability has been fulfilled." RUAA § 6(c) and comment 2. And the comments add that "in the absence of an agreement to the contrary, issues of substantive arbitrability . . . are for a court to decide and issues of procedural arbitrability, *i.e.*, whether prerequisites such as *time limits*, notice, laches, estoppel, and other conditions precedent to an obligation to arbitrate have been met, are for the arbitrators to decide." *Id.*, § 6, comment 2 (emphasis added).

Following this precedent, we find that the applicability of the NASD time limit rule is a matter presumptively for the arbitrator, not for the judge. The time limit rule closely resembles the gateway questions that this Court has found not to be "questions of arbitrability."

Id. at 83–86.

4.   Courts often have "distinguished between substantive arbitrability, that is, whether the dispute falls within the scope of a valid arbitration agreement, and procedural arbitrability, that is, whether the procedural requirements for submitting the dispute to arbitration are met." 2 Ian R. Macneil et al., Federal Arbitration Law § 15.1.4.2 (1994). Questions of substantive arbitrability ordinarily are for the court; questions of procedural arbitrability ordinarily are for the

arbitrator. *Id.* §§ 15.1.4.2 & 21.1.2.1. This distinction is reflected in the Revised Uniform Arbitration Act, quoted in *Howsam*, which provides that "[t]he court shall decide whether an agreement to arbitrate exists or a controversy is subject to an agreement to arbitrate" and "[a]n arbitrator shall decide whether a condition precedent to arbitrability has been fulfilled and whether a contract containing a valid agreement to arbitrate is enforceable." RUAA § 6(b) & (c). How does this usage of the word "arbitrability" compare to how the Supreme Court uses it in *First Options* and *Howsam*?

BUCKEYE CHECK CASHING, INC. v. CARDEGNA
United States Supreme Court
546 U.S. 440 (2006)

JUSTICE SCALIA delivered the opinion of the Court.

We decide whether a court or an arbitrator should consider the claim that a contract containing an arbitration provision is void for illegality.

I

Respondents John Cardegna and Donna Reuter entered into various deferred-payment transactions with petitioner Buckeye Check Cashing (Buckeye), in which they received cash in exchange for a personal check in the amount of the cash plus a finance charge. For each separate transaction they signed a "Deferred Deposit and Disclosure Agreement" (Agreement), which included [an arbitration provision].
. . .

Respondents brought this putative class action in Florida state court, alleging that Buckeye charged usurious interest rates and that the Agreement violated various Florida lending and consumer-protection laws, rendering it criminal on its face. Buckeye moved to compel arbitration. The trial court denied the motion, holding that a court rather than an arbitrator should resolve a claim that a contract is illegal and void *ab initio*. The District Court of Appeal of Florida for the Fourth District reversed, holding that because respondents did not challenge the arbitration provision itself, but instead claimed that the entire contract was void, the agreement to arbitrate was enforceable, and the question of the contract's legality should go to the arbitrator.

Respondents appealed, and the Florida Supreme Court reversed, reasoning that to enforce an agreement to arbitrate in a contract challenged as unlawful " 'could breathe life into a contract that not only violates state law, but also is criminal in nature. . . . ' " We granted certiorari.

II

A

To overcome judicial resistance to arbitration, Congress enacted the Federal Arbitration Act (FAA). Section 2 embodies the national policy favoring arbitration and places arbitration agreements on equal footing with all other contracts. . . . Challenges to the validity of arbitration agreements "upon such grounds as exist at law or in equity for the revocation of any contract" can be divided into two types. One type challenges specifically the validity of the agreement to arbitrate. *See, e.g., Southland Corp. v. Keating* (challenging the agreement to arbitrate as void under California law insofar as it purported to cover claims brought under the state Franchise Investment Law). The other challenges the contract as a whole, either on a ground that directly affects the entire agreement (e.g., the agreement was fraudulently induced), or on the ground that the illegality of one of the contract's provisions renders the whole contract invalid.[1] Respondents' claim is of this second type. The crux of the complaint is that the contract as a whole (including its arbitration provision) is rendered invalid by the usurious finance charge.

In *Prima Paint Corp. v. Flood & Conklin Mfg. Co.*, we addressed the question of who — court or arbitrator — decides these two types of challenges. The issue in the case was "whether a claim of fraud in the inducement of the entire contract is to be resolved by the federal court, or whether the matter is to be referred to the arbitrators." Guided by § 4 of the FAA, we held that "if the claim is fraud in the inducement of the arbitration clause itself — an issue which goes to the making of the agreement to arbitrate — the federal court may proceed to adjudicate it. But the statutory language does not permit the federal court to consider claims of fraud in the inducement of the contract generally." We rejected the view that the question of "severability" was one of state law, so that if state law held the arbitration provision not to be severable a challenge to the contract as a whole would be decided by the court.

Subsequently, in *Southland Corp.*, we held that the FAA "created a body of federal substantive law," which was "applicable in state and federal court." We rejected the view that state law could bar enforcement of § 2, even in the context of state-law claims brought in state court.

B

Prima Paint and *Southland* answer the question presented here by establishing three propositions. First, as a matter of substantive federal arbitration law, an

---

[1] The issue of the contract's validity is different from the issue of whether any agreement between the alleged obligor and obligee was ever concluded. Our opinion today addresses only the former, and does not speak to the issue decided in the cases cited by respondents (and by the Florida Supreme Court), which hold that it is for courts to decide whether the alleged obligor ever signed the contract, Chastain v. Robinson-Humphrey Co., 957 F.2d 851 (CA11 1992), whether the signor lacked authority to commit the alleged principal, Sandvik AB v. Advent Int'l Corp., 220 F.3d 99 (CA3 2000); Sphere Drake Ins. Ltd. v. All American Ins. Co., 256 F.3d 587 (CA7 2001), and whether the signor lacked the mental capacity to assent, Spahr v. Secco, 330 F.3d 1266 (CA10 2003).

arbitration provision is severable from the remainder of the contract. Second, unless the challenge is to the arbitration clause itself, the issue of the contract's validity is considered by the arbitrator in the first instance. Third, this arbitration law applies in state as well as federal courts. The parties have not requested, and we do not undertake, reconsideration of those holdings. Applying them to this case, we conclude that because respondents challenge the Agreement, but not specifically its arbitration provisions, those provisions are enforceable apart from the remainder of the contract. The challenge should therefore be considered by an arbitrator, not a court.

In declining to apply *Prima Paint*'s rule of severability, the Florida Supreme Court relied on the distinction between void and voidable contracts. "Florida public policy and contract law," it concluded, permit "no severable, or salvageable, parts of a contract found illegal and void under Florida law." *Prima Paint* makes this conclusion irrelevant. That case rejected application of state severability rules to the arbitration agreement without discussing whether the challenge at issue would have rendered the contract void or voidable. Indeed, the opinion expressly disclaimed any need to decide what state-law remedy was available (though Justice Black's dissent asserted that state law rendered the contract void). Likewise in *Southland*, which arose in state court, we did not ask whether the several challenges made there — fraud, misrepresentation, breach of contract, breach of fiduciary duty, and violation of the California Franchise Investment Law — would render the contract void or voidable. We simply rejected the proposition that the enforceability of the arbitration agreement turned on the state legislature's judgment concerning the forum for enforcement of the state-law cause of action. So also here, we cannot accept the Florida Supreme Court's conclusion that enforceability of the arbitration agreement should turn on "Florida public policy and contract law."

C

Respondents assert that *Prima Paint*'s rule of severability does not apply in state court. They argue that *Prima Paint* interpreted only §§ 3 and 4 — two of the FAA's procedural provisions, which appear to apply by their terms only in federal court — but not § 2, the only provision that we have applied in state court. This does not accurately describe *Prima Paint*. Although § 4, in particular, had much to do with *Prima Paint*'s understanding of the rule of severability, this rule ultimately arises out of § 2, the FAA's substantive command that arbitration agreements be treated like all other contracts. The rule of severability establishes how this equal-footing guarantee for "a written [arbitration] provision" is to be implemented. Respondents' reading of *Prima Paint* as establishing nothing more than a federal-court rule of procedure also runs contrary to *Southland*'s understanding of that case. One of the bases for *Southland*'s application of § 2 in state court was precisely *Prima Paint*'s "reliance for [its] holding on Congress' broad power to fashion substantive rules under the Commerce Clause." *Southland* itself refused to "believe Congress intended to limit the Arbitration Act to disputes subject only to federal-court jurisdiction."

Respondents point to the language of § 2, which renders "valid, irrevocable, and enforceable" "a written provision in" or "an agreement in writing to submit to arbitration an existing controversy arising out of" a "contract." Since, respondents argue, the only arbitration agreements to which § 2 applies are those involving a "contract, and since an agreement void *ab initio* under state law is not a "contract," there is no "written provision" in or "controversy arising out of" a "contract," to which § 2 can apply. This argument echoes Justice Black's dissent in *Prima Paint*: "Sections 2 and 3 of the Act assume the existence of a valid contract. They merely provide for enforcement where such a valid contract exists." We do not read "contract" so narrowly. The word appears four times in § 2. Its last appearance is in the final clause, which allows a challenge to an arbitration provision "upon such grounds as exist at law or in equity for the revocation of any *contract.*" (Emphasis added.) There can be no doubt that "contract" as used this last time must include contracts that later prove to be void. Otherwise, the grounds for revocation would be limited to those that rendered a contract voidable — which would mean (implausibly) that an arbitration agreement could be challenged as voidable but not as void. Because the sentence's final use of "contract" so obviously includes putative contracts, we will not read the same word earlier in the same sentence to have a more narrow meaning. We note that neither *Prima Paint* nor *Southland* lends support to respondents' reading; as we have discussed, neither case turned on whether the challenge at issue would render the contract voidable or void.

. . .

It is true, as respondents assert, that the *Prima Paint* rule permits a court to enforce an arbitration agreement in a contract that the arbitrator later finds to be void. But it is equally true that respondents' approach permits a court to deny effect to an arbitration provision in a contract that the court later finds to be perfectly enforceable. *Prima Paint* resolved this conundrum — and resolved it in favor of the separate enforceability of arbitration provisions. We reaffirm today that, regardless of whether the challenge is brought in federal or state court, a challenge to the validity of the contract as a whole, and not specifically to the arbitration clause, must go to the arbitrator.

The judgment of the Florida Supreme Court is reversed, and the case is remanded for further proceedings not inconsistent with this opinion.

It is so ordered.

NOTES

1. In *Buckeye*, the Supreme Court resolved a split among the lower courts as to how *Prima Paint* applies to a claim that the underlying contract is void for illegality. The Court held that, like the fraudulent inducement claim involved in *Prima Paint*, the illegality claim also must be resolved by the arbitrator. As the Court explained, "a challenge to the validity of the contract as a whole, and not specifically to the arbitration clause, must go to the arbitrator." Are there any exceptions to this principle?

2. What does the Court's decision suggest about how *Prima Paint* applies to other challenges to the underlying contract as a whole, such as lack of capacity or duress? In footnote one, the Court distinguishes the illegality issue in *Buckeye* from

the "issue of whether any agreement between the alleged obligor and obligee was ever concluded." It continues:

> Our opinion today addresses only the former, and does not speak to the issue decided in the cases cited by respondents (and by the Florida Supreme Court), which hold that it is for courts to decide whether the alleged obligor ever signed the contract, Chastain v. Robinson-Humphrey Co., 957 F.2d 851 (CA11 1992), whether the signor lacked authority to commit the alleged principal, Sandvik AB v. Advent Int'l Corp., 220 F.3d 99 (CA3 2000); Sphere Drake Ins. Ltd. v. All American Ins. Co., 256 F.3d 587 (CA7 2001), and whether the signor lacked the mental capacity to assent, Spahr v. Secco, 330 F.3d 1266 (CA10 2003).

Is the Court indicating that lack of mental capacity goes to "whether any agreement between the alleged obligor and obligee was ever concluded" and thus could be decided by a court? Should duress be treated the same way?

The Texas Supreme Court, in In re Morgan Stanley & Co., 293 S.W.3d 182 (Tex. 2009), held that the defense of lack of capacity was a matter that could be decided by a court. The Texas court recognized that footnote 1 in *Buckeye* expressly reserved the question. *Id.* at 186. But it found lack of capacity indistinguishable from the other "formation defenses identified in *Buckeye*," which the "overwhelming weight of authority" had held were matters that the court could decide. *Id.* at 189. In dissent, Justice Hecht agreed with the majority that issues of contract formation were issues the court could decide. *Id.* at 193 (Hecht, J., dissenting). But, he argued:

> The issue whether a party who executed a contract lacked the mental capacity to do so is different. The rule in Texas and most other jurisdictions is that the contract exists and can be ratified or avoided. . . . The issue is not "the making of the agreement"; an agreement with a person lacking capacity exists — it happened. Rather, the issue is whether the agreement is valid and enforceable.

Id. Who gets the better of the argument, the majority or the dissent?

3.   Why didn't the *Buckeye* Court cite *First Options*? Doesn't *First Options* also deal with the question of whether "any agreement . . . was ever concluded" — between the Kaplans and First Options? *See* Howsam v. Dean Witter Reynolds, Inc., 537 U.S. 79, 84 (2002) (describing *First Options* as "holding that a court should decide whether the arbitration contract bound parties who did not sign the agreement"). In Granite Rock Co. v. International Brotherhood of Teamsters, 130 S. Ct. 2847 (2010), the United States Supreme Court stated that "[i]t is well settled in both commercial and labor cases that . . . where the dispute at issue concerns contract formation, the dispute is generally for courts to decide," citing both *First Options* and *Buckeye*. Id. at 2855-56.

4.   The Court in *Buckeye* finds the statutory basis for the *Prima Paint* rule to be section 2 of the FAA rather than sections 3 and 4 — which are the provisions on which *Prima Paint* apparently had relied. The reason it matters is that *Buckeye* was from a state court (the Florida Supreme Court) while *Prima Paint* came from a federal court, and the U.S. Supreme Court in *Buckeye* seems to concede that only

section 2 of the FAA (and not sections 3 and 4) apply in state court. Even that latter proposition (that section 2 of the FAA applies in state court) remains controversial, and we will discuss it more in Chapter 4. For now, though, it is worth noting *Buckeye*'s holding that the *Prima Paint* separability doctrine applies in state court as well as in federal court.

5. The Supreme Court rejected an attempt to limit *Buckeye* in Preston v. Ferrer, 552 U.S. 346 (2008). In that case, Ferrer (TV's "Judge Alex") argued that his contract with Preston (which included an arbitration clause) was void because Preston was acting as an unlicensed talent agent contrary to California law. Preston denied that he was a talent agent, asserting instead that he was a personal manager who did not need a license. According to the Supreme Court, "[t]he dispositive issue . . . is simply who decides whether Preston acted as personal manager or as talent agent." *Id.* at 352. The Court concluded that "*Buckeye*, largely, if not entirely, resolves the dispute before us." *Id.* at 354. It rejected Ferrer's attempts to distinguish *Buckeye* as follows:

> Ferrer contends that the TAA is . . . compatible with the FAA because § 1700.44(a) merely postpones arbitration until after the Labor Commissioner has exercised her primary jurisdiction. The party that loses before the Labor Commissioner may file for *de novo* review in Superior Court. At that point, Ferrer asserts, either party could move to compel arbitration . . . and thereby obtain an arbitrator's determination prior to judicial review.

> . . .

> . . . Arbitration, if it ever occurred following the Labor Commissioner's decision, would likely be long delayed, in contravention of Congress' intent "to move the parties to an arbitrable dispute out of court and into arbitration as quickly and easily as possible." . . .

> A prime objective of an agreement to arbitrate is to achieve "streamlined proceedings and expeditious results." That objective would be frustrated even if Preston could compel arbitration in lieu of *de novo* Superior Court review. Requiring initial reference of the parties' dispute to the Labor Commissioner would, at the least, hinder speedy resolution of the controversy.

> Ferrer asks us to overlook the apparent conflict between the arbitration clause and § 1700.44(a) because proceedings before the Labor Commissioner are administrative rather than judicial. . . .

> . . .

> [W]e disapprove the distinction between judicial and administrative proceedings drawn by Ferrer and adopted by the appeals court. When parties agree to arbitrate all questions arising under a contract, the FAA supersedes state laws lodging primary jurisdiction in another forum, whether judicial or administrative.

Id. at 356-59.

PROBLEM 2.2

Recall the facts of Problem 2.1 involving John Openshaw's dispute with James Fordham. Fordham seeks a stay of Openshaw's legal malpractice action based on an arbitration clause in the written fee agreement.

(a)   Openshaw alleges that he never signed a written contract with Fordham, and that the written contract that Fordham produced is a forgery (see Problem 2.1(c)). Under *First Options*, can a court consider Openshaw's forgery defense, or is that a matter for the arbitrator?

(b)   Same as (a) except that Openshaw alleges that Fordham was practicing law without a license at the time he signed the contract to do legal work for Openshaw (see Problem 2.1(e)). Can a court consider Openshaw's illegality defense, or is that a matter for the arbitrator?

In *First Options*, the Supreme Court suggested that parties could contract for a different allocation of authority between courts and arbitrators, as long as "there is 'clea[r] and unmistakabl[e] evidence' that they did so." What sort of evidence is necessary? Are there any limits on the parties' contractual authority? The Supreme Court considered those questions in the next case.

RENT-A-CENTER, WEST, INC. v. JACKSON
United States Supreme Court
130 S. Ct. 2772 (2010)

Justice Scalia delivered the opinion of the Court.

We consider whether, under the Federal Arbitration Act . . . , a district court may decide a claim that an arbitration agreement is unconscionable, where the agreement explicitly assigns that decision to the arbitrator.

I

On February 1, 2007, the respondent here, Antonio Jackson, filed an employment-discrimination suit . . . against his former employer in the United States District Court for the District of Nevada. The defendant and petitioner here, Rent-A-Center, West, Inc., filed a motion under the FAA to dismiss or stay the proceedings and to compel arbitration. Rent-A-Center argued that the Mutual Agreement to Arbitrate Claims (Agreement), which Jackson signed on February 24, 2003 as a condition of his employment there, precluded Jackson from pursuing his claims in court. The Agreement provided for arbitration of all "past, present or future" disputes arising out of Jackson's employment with Rent-A-Center, including "claims for discrimination" and "claims for violation of any federal . . . law." It also provided that "[t]he Arbitrator, and not any federal, state, or local court or agency, shall have exclusive authority to resolve any dispute relating to the interpretation, applicability, enforceability or formation of this Agreement including, but not limited to any claim that all or any part of this Agreement is void or voidable."

Jackson opposed the motion on the ground that "the arbitration agreement in question is clearly unenforceable in that it is unconscionable" under Nevada law. Rent-A-Center responded that Jackson's unconscionability claim was not properly before the court because Jackson had expressly agreed that the arbitrator would have exclusive authority to resolve any dispute about the enforceability of the Agreement. It also disputed the merits of Jackson's unconscionability claims.

The District Court granted Rent-A-Center's motion to dismiss the proceedings and to compel arbitration. The court found that the Agreement " " 'clearly and unmistakenly *[sic]*' " " gives the arbitrator exclusive authority to decide whether the Agreement is enforceable, and, because Jackson challenged the validity of the Agreement as a whole, the issue was for the arbitrator. . . .

Without oral argument, a divided panel of the Court of Appeals for the Ninth Circuit . . . reversed on the question of who (the court or arbitrator) had the authority to decide whether the Agreement is enforceable. It noted that "Jackson does not dispute that the language of the Agreement clearly assigns the arbitrability determination to the arbitrator," but held that where "a party challenges an arbitration agreement as unconscionable, and thus asserts that he could not meaningfully assent to the agreement, the threshold question of unconscionability is for the court." . . . Judge Hall dissented on the ground that "the question of the arbitration agreement's validity should have gone to the arbitrator, as the parties 'clearly and unmistakably provide[d]' in their agreement."

We granted certiorari.

II

A

The Agreement here contains multiple "written provision[s]" to "settle by arbitration a controversy." § 2. Two are relevant to our discussion. First, the section titled "Claims Covered By The Agreement" provides for arbitration of all "past, present or future" disputes arising out of Jackson's employment with Rent-A-Center. Second, the section titled "Arbitration Procedures" provides that "[t]he Arbitrator . . . shall have exclusive authority to resolve any dispute relating to the . . . enforceability . . . of this Agreement including, but not limited to any claim that all or any part of this Agreement is void or voidable." The current "controversy" between the parties is whether the Agreement is unconscionable. It is the second provision, which delegates resolution of that controversy to the arbitrator, that Rent-A-Center seeks to enforce. Adopting the terminology used by the parties, we will refer to it as the delegation provision.

The delegation provision is an agreement to arbitrate threshold issues concerning the arbitration agreement. We have recognized that parties can agree to arbitrate "gateway" questions of "arbitrability," such as whether the parties have agreed to arbitrate or whether their agreement covers a particular controversy. . . . An agreement to arbitrate a gateway issue is simply an additional, antecedent agreement the party seeking arbitration asks the federal court to enforce, and the FAA operates on this additional arbitration agreement just as it does on any other. The additional agreement is valid under § 2 "save upon such grounds as exist at law or in equity for the revocation of any contract," and federal courts can enforce the agreement by staying federal litigation under § 3 and compelling arbitration under § 4. The question before us, then, is whether the delegation provision is valid under § 2.

B

There are two types of validity challenges under § 2: "One type challenges specifically the validity of the agreement to arbitrate," and "[t]he other challenges the contract as a whole, either on a ground that directly affects the entire agreement (e.g., the agreement was fraudulently induced), or on the ground that the illegality of one of the contract's provisions renders the whole contract invalid." In a line of cases neither party has asked us to overrule, we held that only the first type of challenge is relevant to a court's determination whether the arbitration agreement at issue is enforceable.[2] See *Prima Paint Corp.* v. *Flood & Conklin Mfg. Co.; Buckeye; Preston* v. *Ferrer.* That is because § 2 states that a "written provision" "to settle by arbitration a controversy" is "valid, irrevocable, and enforceable" without mention of the validity of the contract in which it is contained. Thus, a party's challenge to another provision of the contract, or to the contract as a whole, does not prevent a court from enforcing a specific agreement to arbitrate. "[A]s a matter of substantive federal arbitration law, an arbitration provision is severable from the remainder of the contract." *Buckeye.*

Here, the "written provision . . . to settle by arbitration a controversy" that Rent-A-Center asks us to enforce is the delegation provision — the provision that gave the arbitrator "exclusive authority to resolve any dispute relating to the . . . enforceability . . . of this Agreement." The "remainder of the contract" is the rest of the agreement to arbitrate claims arising out of Jackson's employment with Rent-A-Center. To be sure this case differs from *Prima Paint, Buckeye,* and *Preston,* in that the arbitration provisions sought to be enforced in those cases were contained in contracts unrelated to arbitration — contracts for consulting services, see *Prima Paint,* check-cashing services, see *Buckeye,* and "personal management" or "talent agent" services, see *Preston.* In this case, the underlying contract is itself an arbitration agreement. But that makes no difference. Application of the severability rule does not depend on the substance of the remainder of the contract. Section 2 operates on the specific "written provision" to "settle by arbitration a controversy" that the party seeks to enforce. Accordingly, unless Jackson challenged the delegation provision specifically, we must treat it as valid under § 2, and must enforce it under §§ 3 and 4, leaving any challenge to the validity of the Agreement as a whole for the arbitrator.

---

[2] The issue of the agreement's "validity" is different from the issue whether any agreement between the parties "was ever concluded," and, as in *Buckeye Check Cashing, Inc.* v. *Cardegna,* we address only the former.

C

The District Court correctly concluded that Jackson challenged only the validity of the contract as a whole. Nowhere in his opposition to Rent-A-Center's motion to compel arbitration did he even mention the delegation provision. . . .

. . . As required to make out a claim of unconscionability under Nevada law, he contended that the Agreement was both procedurally and substantively unconscionable. It was procedurally unconscionable, he argued, because it "was imposed as a condition of employment and was non-negotiable." But we need not consider that claim because none of Jackson's substantive unconscionability challenges was specific to the delegation provision. First, he argued that the Agreement's coverage was one sided in that it required arbitration of claims an employee was likely to bring — contract, tort, discrimination, and statutory claims — but did not require arbitration of claims Rent-A-Center was likely to bring — intellectual property, unfair competition, and trade secrets claims. This one-sided-coverage argument clearly did not go to the validity of the delegation provision.

Jackson's other two substantive unconscionability arguments assailed arbitration procedures called for by the contract — the fee-splitting arrangement and the limitations on discovery — procedures that were to be used during arbitration under both the agreement to arbitrate employment-related disputes and the delegation provision. It may be that had Jackson challenged the delegation provision by arguing that these common procedures as applied to the delegation provision rendered that provision unconscionable, the challenge should have been considered by the court. To make such a claim based on the discovery procedures, Jackson would have had to argue that the limitation upon the number of depositions causes the arbitration of his claim that the Agreement is unenforceable to be unconscionable. That would be, of course, a much more difficult argument to sustain than the argument that the same limitation renders arbitration of his factbound employment-discrimination claim unconscionable. Likewise, the unfairness of the fee-splitting arrangement may be more difficult to establish for the arbitration of enforceability than for arbitration of more complex and fact-related aspects of the alleged employment discrimination. Jackson, however, did not make any arguments specific to the delegation provision; he argued that the fee-sharing and discovery procedures rendered the entire Agreement invalid.

*   †   *

We reverse the judgment of the Court of Appeals for the Ninth Circuit.

It is so ordered.

JUSTICE STEVENS, with whom JUSTICE GINSBURG, JUSTICE BREYER, and JUSTICE SOTO-MAYOR join, dissenting.

Neither petitioner nor respondent has urged us to adopt the rule the Court does today: Even when a litigant has specifically challenged the validity of an agreement to arbitrate he must submit that challenge to the arbitrator unless he has lodged an objection to the particular line in the agreement that purports to assign such challenges to the arbitrator — the so-called "delegation clause."

. . .

Prima Paint and its progeny allow a court to pluck from a potentially invalid contract a potentially valid arbitration agreement. Today the Court adds a new layer of severability — something akin to Russian nesting dolls — into the mix: Courts may now pluck from a potentially invalid arbitration agreement even narrower provisions that refer particular arbitrability disputes to an arbitrator. I do not think an agreement to arbitrate can ever manifest a clear and unmistakable intent to arbitrate its own validity. But even assuming otherwise, I certainly would not hold that the *Prima Paint* rule extends this far.

In my view, a general revocation challenge to a standalone arbitration agreement is, invariably, a challenge to the " 'making' " of the arbitration agreement itself, and therefore, under *Prima Paint*, must be decided by the court. A claim of procedural unconscionability aims to undermine the formation of the arbitration agreement, much like a claim of unconscionability aims to undermine the clear-and-unmistakable-intent requirement necessary for a valid delegation of a "discrete" challenge to the validity of the arbitration agreement itself. Moreover, because we are dealing in this case with a challenge to an independently executed arbitration agreement — rather than a clause contained in a contract related to another subject matter — any challenge to the contract itself is also, necessarily, a challenge to the arbitration agreement. They are one and the same.

. . . [T]he Court now declares that *Prima Paint*'s pleading rule requires more: A party must lodge a challenge with even greater specificity than what would have satisfied the *Prima Paint* Court. A claim that an entire arbitration agreement is invalid will not go to the court unless the party challenges the particular sentences that delegate such claims to the arbitrator, on some contract ground that is particular and unique to those sentences.

. . .

NOTES

1.   Although the Supreme Court in *Rent-A-Center* (as it did in *Buckeye Check Cashing*) refers to an arbitration clause as "severable" from the contract in which it is included, the more accepted terminology is "separability" rather than "severability." Indeed, as ordinarily used, "severability" refers to whether an invalid clause in a contract has the effect of invalidating the entire contract; if the invalid clause is "severable," it does not. "Separability" refers to the converse question of whether an (allegedly) invalid contract also invalidates the arbitration clause contained therein. Keeping the terminology separate avoids confusing these two, distinct ideas. Indeed, in omitted footnote four to the majority opinion in *Rent-A-Center*, the Court seems to get the two mixed up, discussing the effect (or lack thereof) of a severability provision in the contract on the separability doctrine under the FAA.

2.   Be clear how the use of the separability doctrine in *Rent-A-Center* differs from how we have seen it used before. Previous cases (such as *Prima Paint* itself) involved a challenge to the main contract — such as for the sale of a business — between the parties, which included an arbitration clause. In *Rent-A-Center*, the

"main" contract analyzed by the Court is a freestanding arbitration agreement, while the arbitration clause in that contract is a clause providing that the arbitrator has authority to rule on issues such as unconscionability challenges to the main arbitration agreement.

3. How are employees likely to respond to the *Rent-A-Center* decision? One would expect them to start challenging the delegation clause itself as unconscionable. What sorts of challenges to the delegation clause are they likely to bring? Can they challenge the agreement to arbitrate the arbitrator's authority itself as unconscionable? One possible response for businesses is to put language in their arbitration agreements making challenges to the delegation clause subject to arbitration. Would *Rent-A-Center* in turn make those provisions separable from the delegation clause? Will employees in turn challenge those provisions as unconscionable? This sort of dynamic is what the dissent refers to as the "Russian nesting doll" effect of the majority's opinion. Is there any limit to this sort of back-and-forth? Or will it continue on indefinitely? Courts since *Rent-A-Center* have rejected arguments that delegation clauses are unconscionable, with varying degrees of sympathy toward the position. Howard v. Rent-A-Center, Inc., 2010 U.S. Dist. LEXIS 76342, at *15 (E.D. Tenn. July 28, 2010) (holding that "allowing arbitrators [to] determine their own jurisdiction is neither contrary to public policy nor unconscionable"); Spears v. Mid-America Waffles, Inc., 2012 U.S. Dist. LEXIS 90902, at * 6 (D. Kan. July 2, 2012) ("[T]he court determines that the delegation provision (requiring individual claims) is not unconscionable. Plaintiffs agreed to submit questions of interpretation and enforceability to the arbitrator, and that agreement is enforceable."); Chin v. Advanced Fresh Concepts Franchise Corp., 194 Cal. App. 4th 704, 710-11 (Cal. App. 2011) (asserting that "[t]here is substantial authority that a delegation clause in an adhesion contract is unconscionable," but refusing to invalidate clause because franchisee "makes no colorable claim that any other provision of the arbitration provision is unconscionable").

4. What about language like that in AAA Commercial Arbitration Rule R-7(a), which provides that "[t]he arbitrator shall have the power to rule on his or her own jurisdiction, including any objections with respect to the existence, scope or validity of the arbitration agreement"? Is that language sufficient to give the arbitrator final say over challenges to the enforceability of the arbitration agreement under *Rent-A-Center*? Most courts have held that the language is sufficient. *See, e.g.,* Awuah v. Coverall N. Am., Inc., 554 F.3d 7, 11 (1st Cir. 2009) (describing AAA Rule R-7(a) as containing language "about as 'clear and unmistakable' as language can get, meeting the standard we have followed"). The language in *Rent-A-Center* itself was much stronger, however, providing that the arbitrators had "exclusive authority to resolve any dispute relating to the . . . enforceability . . . of this Agreement."

The Restatement (Third) of the U.S. Law of International Commercial Arbitration distinguishes the language in the institutional rules from the language in *Rent-A-Center*, concluding:

> Although those rules give the arbitrators the authority to determine their own jurisdiction, they do not expressly provide that the arbitrators have the final and unreviewable authority to determine either the claims or issues encompassed by the arbitration agreement or the effect or validity of the

restriction on the arbitral tribunal's authority. Under such provisions, if a case proceeds to arbitration and a party raises a jurisdictional objection, the tribunal has the authority to entertain and resolve the jurisdictional question, and does not have to suspend proceedings so that a court may first resolve the issue. But the provisions do not prescribe any particular standard of review or measure of deference to the tribunal on questions of the matters submitted to arbitration when the question comes subsequently before a court. Accordingly, they do not show that the parties "clearly agreed to have the arbitrators decide (*i.e.*, to arbitrate) the question of arbitrability." First Options, 514 U.S. at 946. Instead, the language must not only grant the arbitral tribunal the authority to resolve such questions, but must also indicate that the tribunal's determination is final and entitled to deference by the courts.

Restatement (Third) of the U.S. Law of International Commercial Arbitration, § 4-14, rptrs. note to cmt. e. Is the Restatement consistent with the Supreme Court's decision in *Rent-A-Center*?

PROBLEM 2.3

Consider one last time James Fordham's request for a stay of John Openshaw's legal malpractice action, based on an arbitration clause in their written fee agreement (from Problems 2.1 and 2.2):

(a) Openshaw alleges that the only reason he agreed to include an arbitration clause in the contract was that Fordham told him such a clause was required by law, which proved to be a lie (see Problem 2.1(b)). The arbitration clause provides that "the arbitrator, and not a court, shall have exclusive authority to resolve any dispute relating to the enforceability or formation of this Agreement including, but not limited to, any claim that all or any part of this Agreement is void or voidable." Can a court consider Openshaw's fraudulent inducement defense, or is that a matter for the arbitrator?

(b) Same as (a) except that the arbitration clause does not mention the authority of the arbitrator; instead it incorporates by reference the AAA Commercial Arbitration Rules (see especially Rule R-7). Can a court consider Openshaw's fraudulent inducement defense, or is that a matter for the arbitrator?

(c) Same as (a) except that Openshaw alleges that he never signed a written contract with Fordham, and that the written contract that Fordham produced is a forgery (see Problem 2.2(a)). Can a court consider Openshaw's forgery defense, or is that a matter for the arbitrator?

(d) Same as (c) except that after Openshaw raises the forgery defense, Openshaw and Fordham both agree in writing to have an arbitrator decide that defense. Can a court consider Openshaw's forgery defense, or is that a matter for the arbitrator?

§ 2.03   DEFAULT IN PROCEEDING WITH ARBITRATION

Section 3 of the FAA provides for the court to stay litigation pending arbitration "providing the applicant for the stay is not in default in proceeding with such arbitration." When is a party in "default" in proceeding with arbitration such that a court should refuse to grant a stay?

PERRY HOMES v. CULL
Supreme Court of Texas
258 S.W.3d 580 (2008)

JUSTICE BRISTER delivered the opinion of the Court . . . .

Since 1846, Texas law has provided that parties to a dispute may choose to arbitrate rather than litigate. But that choice cannot be abused; a party cannot substantially invoke the litigation process and then switch to arbitration on the eve of trial. There is a strong presumption against waiver of arbitration, but it is not irrebuttable and was plainly rebutted here. The Plaintiffs vigorously opposed (indeed spurned) arbitration in their pleadings and in open court; then they requested hundreds of items of merits-based information and conducted months of discovery under the rules of court; finally only four days before the trial setting they changed their minds and decided they would prefer to arbitrate after all. Having gotten what they wanted from the litigation process, they could not switch to arbitration at the last minute like this.

The Plaintiffs argue — and we agree — that sending them back to the trial court not only deprives them of a substantial award but also wastes the time and money spent in arbitration. But they knew of this risk when they requested arbitration at the last minute because all of the Defendants objected. Accordingly, we vacate the arbitration award and remand the case to the trial court for a prompt trial.

I. Background

In 1996, Robert and Jane Cull bought a house from Perry Homes for $233,730. They also bought a warranty from Home Owners Multiple Equity, Inc. and Warranty Underwriters Insurance Company. The warranty agreement included a broad arbitration clause providing that all disputes the Culls might have against Perry Homes or the warranty companies were subject to the Federal Arbitration Act, and would be submitted to the American Arbitration Association (AAA) or another arbitrator agreed upon by the parties.

Over the next several years, the home suffered serious structural and drainage problems. According to the Culls, the Defendants spent more effort shifting blame than repairing the home. When the Culls sued in October 2000, the warranty companies (but not Perry Homes) immediately requested arbitration; the Culls vigorously opposed it, and no one ever pressed for a ruling. At the same time, the Culls' attorneys began seeking extensive discovery from all of the Defendants.

After most of the discovery was completed and the case was set for trial, the Culls changed their minds about litigating. Instead they asked the trial court to compel arbitration under precisely the same clause and conditions to which they had originally objected. The trial judge expressed reservations . . . . Nevertheless, the trial court ordered arbitration because the Defendants had not shown any prejudice from litigation conduct . . . . The order was signed December 6, 2001, four days before the case was set for trial. The Defendants filed petitions for mandamus in the court of appeals and this Court, both of which were denied without opinion within a few days.

After a year in arbitration, on December 24, 2002, the arbitrator awarded the Culls $800,000, including restitution of the purchase price of their home ($242,759), mental anguish ($200,000), exemplary damages ($200,000), and attorney's fees ($110,000). The Defendants moved to vacate the award, again arguing (among other things) that the case should never have been sent to arbitration after so much activity in court. The trial court overruled the objection, confirmed the award, and added post-judgment interest duplicating that already in the award; the court of appeals affirmed after deleting the duplicative interest. We granted the Defendants' petition to consider whether the arbitration award should be set aside because the Culls waived their right to arbitration.

II. When Should Orders Compelling Arbitration Be Reviewed?

. . . [T]he Culls argue that an order compelling arbitration can only be reviewed *before* arbitration occurs. The Culls address none of the cases in which this Court and the United States Supreme Court have reviewed such orders *after* arbitration. Nor do they address the general rule that parties waive nothing by foregoing interlocutory review and awaiting a final judgment to appeal.

But most important, the Culls do not address section 16 of the Federal Arbitration Act, which expressly prohibits pre-arbitration appeals . . . . This ban on interlocutory appeals of orders compelling arbitration was added by Congress in 1988 to prevent arbitration from bogging down in preliminary appeals. We have held that routine mandamus review of such orders in state court would frustrate this federal law.

The Culls assert that post-arbitration review is unavailable because an arbitration award can be vacated only for statutory grounds like corruption, fraud, or evident partiality. But reviewing the trial court's initial referral to arbitration is not the same as reviewing the arbitrator's final award; as the United States Supreme Court has held, courts conduct ordinary review of the former and deferential review only of the latter.

We agree that post-arbitration review of referral may create (as the Culls allege) a "huge waste of the parties' resources." But if review is available before arbitration, parties may also waste resources appealing every referral when a quick arbitration might settle the matter. Frequent pre-arbitration review would inevitably frustrate Congress's intent "to move the parties to an arbitrable dispute out of court and into arbitration as quickly and easily as possible." We recognize the potential for waste, but that is a risk a party must take if it moves for arbitration after substantially invoking the litigation process.

III. Do Courts or Arbitrators Decide Waiver?

The Culls also assert that waiver of arbitration by litigation conduct is an issue to be decided by arbitrators rather than courts. To the contrary, this Court and the federal courts have held it is a question of law for the court. Rather than referring such claims to arbitrators, we have decided them ourselves at least eight times, as does every federal circuit court.

The Culls argue this was all changed in 2002 by *Howsam v. Dean Witter Reynolds*, in which the United States Supreme Court said the "presumption is that the arbitrator should decide 'allegation[s] of waiver, delay, or a like defense to arbitrability.' " For several reasons, we disagree that this single sentence changed the federal arbitration landscape.

First, "waiver" and "delay" are broad terms used in many different contexts. *Howsam* involved the National Association of Securities Dealers' six-year limitations period for arbitration claims, not waiver by litigation conduct; indeed, it does not appear the United States Supreme Court has ever addressed the latter kind of waiver. Although the federal courts do not defer to arbitrators when waiver is a question of litigation conduct, they consistently do so when waiver concerns limitations periods or waiver of particular claims or defenses. As *Howsam* involved the latter rather than the former, its reference to waiver must be read in that context.

Second, the *Howsam* court specifically stated that "parties to an arbitration contract would normally expect a forum-based decisionmaker to decide forum-specific procedural gateway matters." . . . By contrast, when waiver turns on conduct in court, the court is obviously in a better position to decide whether it amounts to waiver. "Contracting parties would expect the court to decide whether one party's conduct before the court waived the right to arbitrate."

Third, as the *Howsam* Court itself stated, parties generally intend arbitrators to decide matters that "grow out of the dispute and bear on its final disposition," while they intend courts to decide gateway matters regarding "whether the parties have submitted a particular dispute to arbitration." Waiver of a substantive claim or delay beyond a limitations deadline could affect final disposition, but waiver by litigation conduct affects only the gateway matter of where the case is tried.

Finally, arbitrators generally must decide defenses that apply to the whole contract, while courts decide defenses relating solely to the arbitration clause. Thus, for example, arbitrators must decide if an entire contract was fraudulently induced, while courts must decide if an arbitration clause was. As waiver by litigation conduct goes solely to the arbitration clause rather than the whole contract, consistency suggests it is an issue for the courts.

Every federal circuit court that has addressed this issue since *Howsam* has continued to hold that substantial invocation of the litigation process is a question for the court rather than the arbitrator — including the First, Third, Fifth, and Eighth[34] Circuits. Legal commentators appear to agree. So do we.

---

[34] The Eighth Circuit did refer to *Howsam* in one case as requiring waiver to be referred to

IV. When Is the Litigation Process Substantially Invoked?

We have said on many occasions that a party waives an arbitration clause by substantially invoking the judicial process to the other party's detriment or prejudice. Due to the strong presumption against waiver of arbitration, this hurdle is a high one. To date, we have never found such a waiver, holding in a series of cases that parties did not waive arbitration by:

- filing suit;

- moving to dismiss a claim for lack of standing;

- moving to set aside a default judgment and requesting a new trial;

- opposing a trial setting and seeking to move the litigation to federal court;

- moving to strike an intervention and opposing discovery;

- sending 18 interrogatories and 19 requests for production;

- requesting an initial round of discovery, noticing (but not taking) a single deposition, and agreeing to a trial resetting; or

- seeking initial discovery, taking four depositions, and moving for dismissal based on standing.

These cases well illustrate the kind of conduct that falls short. But because none amounted to a waiver, they are less instructive about what conduct suffices. We have stated that "allowing a party to conduct full discovery, file motions going to the merits, and seek arbitration only on the eve of trial" would be sufficient. But what if (as in this case) only two out of these three are met? And how much is "full discovery"?

We begin by looking to the standards imposed by the federal courts. They decide questions of waiver by applying a totality-of-the-circumstances test on a case-by-case basis. In doing so, they consider a wide variety of factors including:

- whether the movant was plaintiff (who chose to file in court) or defendant (who merely responded);

- how long the movant delayed before seeking arbitration;

- whether the movant knew of the arbitration clause all along;

- how much pretrial activity related to the merits rather than arbitrability or jurisdiction;

- how much time and expense has been incurred in litigation;

- whether the movant sought or opposed arbitration earlier in the case;

- whether the movant filed affirmative claims or dispositive motions;

- what discovery would be unavailable in arbitration;

---

arbitrators, but that case involved an allegation of waiver by previous arbitration, not litigation. *See Nat'l Am. Ins. Co. v. Transamerica Occidental Life Ins. Co.*, 328 F.3d 462, 463-66 (8th Cir. 2003).

- whether activity in court would be duplicated in arbitration; and

- when the case was to be tried.

Of course, all these factors are rarely presented in a single case. Federal courts have found waiver based on a few, or even a single one.

We agree waiver must be decided on a case-by-case basis, and that courts should look to the totality of the circumstances. Like the federal courts, this Court has considered factors such as:

- when the movant knew of the arbitration clause;

- how much discovery has been conducted;

- who initiated it;

- whether it related to the merits rather than arbitrability or standing;

- how much of it would be useful in arbitration; and

- whether the movant sought judgment on the merits.

Thus, we disagree with the court of appeals that waiver is ruled out in this case solely because the Culls "did not ask the court to make any judicial decisions on the merits of their case." While this is surely a factor, it is not the only one. Waiver involves substantial invocation of the judicial *process*, not just judgment on the merits.

. . .

We recognize, as we have noted before, "the difficulty of uniformly applying a test based on nothing more than the totality of the circumstances." But there appears to be no better test for "substantial invocation." . . . How much litigation conduct will be "substantial" depends very much on the context; three or four depositions may be all the discovery needed in one case, but purely preliminary in another.

. . .

The answer to most questions regarding arbitration "flow inexorably from the fact that arbitration is simply a matter of contract between the parties." Like any other contract right, arbitration can be waived if the parties agree instead to resolve a dispute in court. Such waiver can be implied from a party's conduct, although that conduct must be unequivocal. And in close cases, the "strong presumption against waiver" should govern.

V. Is a Showing of Prejudice Required?

Although convinced that the Culls had substantially invoked the litigation process, the trial court compelled arbitration because the Defendants did not prove an arbitrator would not have allowed the same discovery. "Even substantially invoking the judicial process does not waive a party's arbitration rights unless the opposing party proves that it suffered prejudice as a result." On at least eight occasions, we have said prejudice is a necessary requirement of waiver by litigation conduct.

The Defendants ask us to reconsider this requirement. They point out that Texas law does not require a showing of prejudice for waiver, but only an intentional relinquishment of a known right. Waiver "is essentially unilateral in its character" and "no act of the party in whose favor it is made is necessary to complete it." Thus, they argue we cannot impose a waiver rule for arbitration contracts that does not apply to all others.

We decline the Defendants' invitation based on both federal and state law. The Defendants say the federal courts are split on the issue, but the split is not very wide. Of the twelve regional circuit courts, ten require a showing of prejudice, and the other two treat it as a factor to consider. We have noted before the importance of keeping federal and state arbitration law consistent.

Under Texas law, waiver may not include a prejudice requirement, but estoppel does. In cases of waiver by litigation conduct, the precise question is not so much when waiver occurs as when a party can no longer take it back. . . . Texas estoppel law does not allow a party to withdraw a representation once the other party takes "action or forbearance of a definite and substantial character." Using precisely the same terms, the Restatement does not allow a party to withdraw an option contract when the offeree has taken substantial action based upon it. In these contexts, prejudice is an element of the normal contract rules.

VI. Was Arbitration Waived Here?

A. Did the Culls Waive Arbitration?

It remains only to apply these rules to this case.

Unquestionably, the Culls substantially invoked the litigation process, as their conduct here far exceeds anything we have reviewed before. Before arbitration was ordered, the Culls did not deny taking ten depositions, and the court's file (of which the trial judge took judicial notice) included:

- their initial objection to arbitration covering 79 pages;

- the Defendants' responses to requests for disclosure;

- the Culls' five motions to compel, attached to which were 76 requests for production of documents regarding complaints, inspections, repairs, and settlements relating to eight other homes in the same subdivision;

- Perry Homes' two motions for protective orders regarding six designees noticed for deposition by the Culls on nine issues (including purchase and preparation of the lot, design and construction of the foundation, sale of this home and others in the subdivision, and attempts to deal with the Culls' and other foundation complaints), with an attachment requesting categories of documents (including all photos, videos, correspondence, insurance policies, plans, soil tests, permits, subcontractors, contracts for sale, and repairs relating to the house or the suit, all complaints about any house in the subdivision, and Perry Homes' articles of incorporation, by-laws, minutes, and financials); and

- the Culls' notices of depositions for three of the Defendants' experts with 24 categories of documents requested from each (including all documents relating to this case, all their articles, publications, or speeches given in their fields of expertise, all courses or seminars they had attended, all persons they had studied under, and all reference books or treatises in their libraries).

There is simply no question on this record that the Culls conducted extensive discovery about every aspect of the merits.

But under the totality-of-the-circumstances test, discovery is not the only measure of waiver. Here, when the warranty defendants initially moved to compel arbitration, the Culls filed a 79-page response opposing it, asserting that the AAA "is incompetent, is biased, and fails to provide fair and appropriate arbitration panels." They complained of the AAA's fees, and asserted that as a result the "purported arbitration clause is unconscionable and unenforceable, and this Court's enforcement of such would be nothing short of ridiculous and absurd." This, plus their prayer asking the trial court to deny the motion to compel arbitration "in its entirety," belies the court of appeals' conclusion that "the Culls merely opposed the use of the AAA" rather than arbitration itself. In some federal courts, the Culls' objection alone could suffice to waive arbitration.

The Culls also moved for arbitration very late in the trial process. It is true that Perry Homes moved to continue the trial setting when the Culls sought arbitration, requesting about ten weeks to finish deposing experts. Because the trial court ordered arbitration, no one knows whether the case would have gone to trial . . . . But in view of the written discovery and depositions already completed, the record is nevertheless clear that most of the discovery in the case had already been completed before the Culls requested arbitration. The rule that one cannot wait until "the eve of trial" to request arbitration is not limited to the evening before trial; it is a rule of proportion that is implicated here.

Then 14 months after filing suit and shortly before the December 2001 trial setting, the Culls changed their minds and requested arbitration. They justified their change of heart on the basis that they wanted to avoid the delays of an appeal. But their change unquestionably delayed adjudication of the merits; instead of a trial beginning in a few days or weeks, the plenary arbitration hearing did not begin until late September of 2002 — almost ten months after the Culls abandoned their trial setting. Moreover, to the extent arbitration reduces delay, it does so by severely limiting *both* pretrial discovery *and* post-trial review. Having enjoyed the benefits of extensive discovery for 14 months, the Culls could not decide only then that they were in a hurry.

It is also unquestionably true that this conduct prejudiced the Defendants. "Prejudice" has many meanings, but in the context of waiver under the FAA it relates to inherent unfairness — that is, a party's attempt to have it both ways by switching between litigation and arbitration to its own advantage:

[F]or purposes of a waiver of an arbitration agreement[,] prejudice refers to the inherent unfairness in terms of delay, expense, or damage to a party's legal position that occurs when the party's opponent forces it to litigate an issue and later seeks to arbitrate that same issue.

Thus, "a party should not be allowed purposefully and unjustifiably to manipulate the exercise of its arbitral rights simply to gain an unfair tactical advantage over the opposing party."

Here, the record before the trial court showed that the Culls objected to arbitration initially, and then insisted on it after the Defendants acquiesced in litigation. They got extensive discovery under one set of rules and then sought to arbitrate the case under another. They delayed disposition by switching to arbitration when trial was imminent and arbitration was not. They got the court to order discovery for them and then limited their opponents' rights to appellate review. Such manipulation of litigation for one party's advantage and another's detriment is precisely the kind of inherent unfairness that constitutes prejudice under federal and state law.

. . .

Accordingly, we reverse the court of appeals' judgment, vacate the arbitration award, and remand this case to the trial court for a prompt trial.

NOTES

1.   Who decides whether there has been a waiver, the court or the arbitrator? Section 3 of the FAA provides for a stay pending arbitration, "providing the applicant for the stay is not in default in proceeding with such arbitration," suggesting that the decision is one for the court. Section 4 of the FAA contains no similar language, however. In *Howsam v. Dean Witter Reynolds, Inc.* (see note 3 after *First Options*), the Supreme Court stated that "the presumption is that the arbitrator should decide 'allegations of waiver, delay, or a like defense to arbitrability.' " According to the court in *Perry Homes*, the dicta in *Howsam* (which did not involve a claim of waiver) should be limited to waiver of claims rather than waiver of the right to arbitrate by conduct in litigation. Is that a sensible distinction?

2.   What is the appropriate standard to apply in evaluating a claim of waiver? As the court notes, courts often examine a variety of factors, making a determination of waiver dependent on the facts of the individual case. How does that affect the ability of attorneys to advise their clients on whether a party has waived the right to arbitrate?

3.   The court in *Perry Homes* held that prejudice was required to find waiver. As the court noted, not all federal courts require a finding of prejudice. For an example, see the Seventh Circuit's decision in Cabinetree of Wisconsin, Inc. v. Kraftmaid Cabinetry, Inc., 50 F.3d 388 (7th Cir. 1995), which reasoned as follows:

 [W]e . . . hold that an election to proceed before a nonarbitral tribunal for the resolution of a contractual dispute is a presumptive waiver of the right to arbitrate. Although not compelled by our previous cases, this presumption is consistent with them; for we have deemed an election to proceed in court a waiver of a contractual right to arbitrate, without insisting on evidence of prejudice beyond what is inherent in an effort to change forums in the middle (and it needn't be the exact middle) of a litigation. . . .

. . .

We have said that invoking judicial process is *presumptive waiver.* For it is easy to imagine situations — they have arisen in previous cases — in which such invocation does not signify an intention to proceed in a court to the exclusion of arbitration. There might be doubts about arbitrability, and fear that should the doubts be resolved adversely the statute of limitations might have run. Some issues might be arbitrable, and others not. The shape of the case might so alter as a result of unexpected developments during discovery or otherwise that it might become obvious that the party should be relieved from its waiver and arbitration allowed to proceed. We need not try to be exhaustive. It is enough to hold that while normally the decision to proceed in a judicial forum is a waiver of arbitration, a variety of circumstances may make the case abnormal, and then the district court should find no waiver or should permit a previous waiver to be rescinded. In such a case prejudice to the other party, the party resisting arbitration, should weigh heavily in the decision whether to send the case to arbitration, as should the diligence or lack thereof of the party seeking arbitration — did that party do all it could reasonably have been expected to do to make the earliest feasible determination of whether to proceed judicially or by arbitration?

Id. at 390–91; *see* Madison Foods, Inc. v. Fleming Cos., 325 B.R. 687, 692 (Bankr. D. Del. 2005) (describing Seventh Circuit approach as the "minority view").

In February 2011, the Supreme Court granted certiorari in *Stok & Assocs., P.A. v. Citibank* (No. 10-514), to resolve the conflict. The question presented in the case, as stated by the petitioner, was: "Under the Federal Arbitration Act, should a party be required to demonstrate prejudice after the opposing party waived its contractual right to arbitrate by participating in litigation, in order for such waiver to be binding and irrevocable?" The case settled, however, and the Court dismissed it, leaving resolution of the conflict to another day.

4. What about the timing of court review of claims of waiver? In *Perry Homes*, the Supreme Court did not review the trial court's finding of no waiver until after the arbitration proceeding had been completed. Why did the appellate courts wait until after the arbitration was over instead of reviewing the order compelling arbitration before the arbitration had begun?

5. Rule R-48(a) of the Commercial Arbitration Rules of the American Arbitration Association provides that "[n]o judicial proceeding by a party relating to the subject matter of the arbitration shall be deemed a waiver of the party's right to arbitrate." Does that mean that *Perry Homes* should have been decided differently if the parties there had agreed to arbitrate under the AAA Rules? Courts generally have refused to give "no waiver" provisions that effect. As the Second Circuit explained in S&R Co. of Kingston v. Latona Trucking, Inc., 159 F.3d 80, 85–86 (2d

Cir. 1998), *cert. dismissed*, 528 U.S. 1058 (1999):

> . . . [W]e agree with those courts and authorities that have interpreted this "no waiver" clause as intended to permit parties to seek provisional remedies or other judicial proceedings that would not function to displace arbitration on the underlying dispute. Thus, the fact that an arbitration agreement incorporates such a clause would not prevent a court from finding that a party has waived arbitration by actively participating in protracted litigation of an arbitrable dispute. . . .

> We agree with the Massachusetts Supreme Court's observation that to allow the "no waiver" clause to preclude a finding of waiver would

>> permit the parties to waste scarce judicial time and effort and hamper judges' authority to control the course of proceedings before them and to correct any abuse of those proceedings and then demand arbitration. Further, delay in demanding arbitration until after judicial proceedings are almost complete permits the losing party to test[] the water before taking the swim.

> [Home Gas Corp. v. Walter's of Hadley, Inc., 403 Mass. 772, 532 N.E.2d 681, 685 (1989).] Accordingly, we hold that the presence of the "no waiver" clause does not alter the ordinary analysis undertaken to determine if a party has waived its right to arbitration.

PROBLEM 2.4

Cushing Cushions, Inc. enters into a written contract with Browner Box Company to purchase custom-sized boxes to use for shipping its cushions to buyers. The contract contains a pre-dispute arbitration clause. Browner fails to deliver the boxes when required by the contract. Browner files suit in federal court against Cushing seeking a declaration that its failure to deliver the boxes was excused on grounds of commercial impracticability. After participating in the lawsuit for some amount of time, Cushing seeks a stay of the suit pending arbitration, relying on section 3 of the FAA, and an order compelling arbitration under section 4 of the FAA. Browner responds by arguing that Cushing has waived its right to arbitrate by participating in the court litigation. Is the waiver issue for the court or the arbitrator to decide?

PROBLEM 2.5

Stoner Accessories, Inc. enters into a contract to purchase a variety of imported scarves and neckties from Roylott Apparel, Ltd. The sales contract contains an arbitration clause. When the neckwear arrives, Stoner is dissatisfied with its quality, while Roylott insists that the neckwear fully meets the contract specifications. Which of the following actions by Roylott would constitute a waiver of its right to arbitrate under the contract?

(a) Instead of initiating arbitration, Roylott engages in lengthy negotiations with Stoner trying to resolve the dispute.

(b) Instead of initiating arbitration, Roylott agrees to several sessions with a mediator in an attempt to resolve its dispute with Stoner.

(c) After Stoner files suit against Roylott, both parties engage in limited discovery in the court action before Roylott seeks to compel arbitration. The extent of the discovery does not exceed what likely would have taken place in arbitration.

(d) Same as (c), except that both parties engage in extensive discovery in the court action, well beyond what would have taken place in arbitration.

(e) After Stoner files suit against Roylott and discovery is complete, Roylott files a motion for summary judgment. Not until the court denies the motion does Roylott seek to compel arbitration.

(f) Same as (e), except that the parties provided for arbitration under the AAA Commercial Arbitration Rules (see especially Rule R-48(a)).

§ 2.04   THE SCOPE OF THE ARBITRATION AGREEMENT

Because arbitration is a matter of contract, the parties are free to define what disputes will be arbitrated. Only claims that the parties agree to arbitrate can be resolved by an arbitrator; other claims remain subject to court resolution.

Sometimes parties agree to arbitrate only particular substantive claims (e.g., claims for breach of contract) or only claims arising out of particular provisions of their contract. More commonly, parties use general language to describe the disputes subject to arbitration. The sample pre-dispute arbitration clause suggested by the American Arbitration Association, for example, provides:

> Any controversy or claim arising out of or relating to this contract, or the breach thereof, shall be settled by arbitration administered by the American Arbitration Association under its Commercial Arbitration Rules, and judgment on the award rendered by the arbitrator(s) may be entered in any court having jurisdiction thereof.

When a dispute arises, what claims are subject to arbitration under this clause? What if the language of the parties' arbitration agreement is different from that suggested by the AAA? How does the "emphatic federal policy in favor of arbitration" figure in?

SIMULA, INC. v. AUTOLIV, INC.
United States Court of Appeals for the Ninth Circuit
175 F.3d 716 (1999)

TASHIMA, CIRCUIT JUDGE:

This appeal presents the question of how broadly an arbitration clause containing the phrase "arising in connection with this Agreement" should be construed. The district court held that it encompassed all disputes having their origin or genesis in the contract and granted appellees' motion to compel arbitration. We have jurisdiction under 28 U.S.C. § 1291 and we affirm.

I.

In 1992, Simula, Inc., and Simula Automotive Safety Devices, Inc. (together "Simula"), invented the Inflatable Tubular Structure ("ITS"), an automotive side impact head protection air bag system. In 1993, Simula approached BMW, a German automaker, about purchasing the ITS. BMW instructed Simula to work through Autoliv, AB, and its subsidiaries, Autoliv, Inc., Autoliv Development GMBH, Autoliv ASP, Inc., and Autoliv North America (collectively "Autoliv"), a previously-approved "first-tier" vendor/supplier of automotive components, to present Simula's technology for incorporation into BMW's cars.

As directed by BMW, Simula approached Autoliv about the ITS technology. In May 1993, Autoliv and Simula signed nondisclosure agreements. Thereafter, Simula disclosed to Autoliv confidential, proprietary, and trade secret information regarding the ITS, as well as testing data illustrating the enhanced safety advantages it offered.

In January 1994, Autoliv and Simula signed a letter of intent outlining the proposed relationship between them. Under the proposal, Simula would manufacture the ITS and give a conditional license of confidential, proprietary, and trade secret technology to Autoliv. In return, Autoliv would integrate the ITS into the BMW automobile. Autoliv was to pay Simula for each ITS unit delivered by Simula to Autoliv and pay royalties on the sales of the ITS integrated systems. In July 1994, Autoliv received a contract and a sum of money from BMW to fund a portion of the ITS integration cost.

In August 1994, with Simula's permission, Autoliv presented the Simula ITS system to Mercedes Benz. Because BMW and Mercedes Benz were head-to-head competitors and viewed one another as leaders in European automotive safety, Mercedes Benz suggested to Autoliv that it begin development of a product that differed from the ITS. Autoliv agreed. As Simula alleges, Autoliv subsequently began to replicate features of the ITS into a competing "inflatable curtain," accelerated its efforts to develop the inflatable curtain as a competitive "first-to-the-market" product, and undertook a scheme to disparage the ITS to automotive manufacturers and to represent favorably the qualities of Autoliv's own side protective technology.

. . .

In January 1995, Simula and Autoliv entered into three related agreements including: (1) a Joint Development and Cooperation Agreement; (2) a Licensing Agreement; and (3) a Frame Supply Agreement (collectively, the "1995 Agreement"). At the time that Simula signed the agreements, Simula did not know of and Autoliv did not disclose its inflatable curtain concept. Under the Joint Development and Cooperation Agreement and the Frame Supply Agreement, the first customer project between Simula and Autoliv was BMW. Under the Licensing Agreement, Autoliv maintains it acquired the exclusive rights to all marketing and sales of any ITS system for all automobile manufacturers and that Simula may not market the ITS itself.

In February 1998, Simula brought suit against Autoliv alleging causes of action for: (1) violation of the Sherman Act, 15 U.S.C. §§ 1 and 2; (2) violation of the

Trademark Act of 1946 ("Lanham Act"), 15 U.S.C. § 1125; (3) misappropriation of trade secrets and breach of the non-disclosure agreements; (4) defamation; and (5) breach of the Arizona Trade Secrets Act, Ariz. Rev. Stat. § 44-401. Simula sought preliminary and permanent injunctive relief, treble damages for antitrust violations, punitive damages, compensatory damages, attorney's fees, and costs.

Autoliv moved to compel arbitration pursuant to the Federal Arbitration Act ("FAA"), 9 U.S.C. §§ 3–4, and either to dismiss the complaint or stay the action pending the resolution of arbitration proceedings. The district court granted Autoliv's motion to compel arbitration and its motion to dismiss. It held that all of Simula's claims against Autoliv were subject to the arbitration clause contained in the 1995 Agreement because all of Simula's claims relate to, derive from, and arise in connection with that contract. Simula appeals.

II.

Determinations of arbitrability, like the interpretation of any contractual provision, are subject to de novo review. Therefore, we review de novo the district court's interpretation of the contract language in the parties' 1995 Agreement.

Federal substantive law governs the question of arbitrability. *See Moses H. Cone Mem'l Hosp. v. Mercury Constr. Corp.* The FAA reflects Congress' intent to provide for the enforcement of arbitration agreements within the full reach of the Commerce Clause. The FAA embodies a clear federal policy in favor of arbitration. "[A]ny doubts concerning the scope of arbitrable issues should be resolved in favor of arbitration." *Moses H. Cone.*

The standard for demonstrating arbitrability is not high. The Supreme Court has held that the FAA leaves no place for the exercise of discretion by a district court, but instead mandates that district courts direct the parties to proceed to arbitration on issues as to which an arbitration agreement has been signed. . . .

We must first determine the breadth of the disputed arbitration clauses. The three arbitration clauses in the 1995 Agreement identically state in relevant part:

> *All disputes arising in connection with this Agreement* shall be finally settled under the Rules of Conciliation and Arbitration of the International Chamber of Commerce by three arbitrators appointed in accordance with the said rules.

(Emphasis added). Although we have not yet construed this precise language, we have expansively interpreted similar language and other courts have construed identical language liberally.

In Republic of Nicaragua [v. Standard Fruit Co., 937 F.2d 469, 479 (9th Cir. 1991),] we held that an arbitration clause containing the phrase "any and all disputes arising under the arrangements contemplated hereunder" must be interpreted liberally.[3] . . .

---

[3] Simula cites both Mediterranean Enter.[, Inc. v. Ssangyong Corp., 708 F.2d 1458, 1464 (9th Cir. 1988),] and Tracer Research Corp. v. National Envt'l Servs. Co., 42 F.3d 1292 (9th Cir.1994), to support its contention that the disputed arbitration clause should be narrowly construed. Neither of these cases,

. . .

Every court that has construed the phrase "arising in connection with" in an arbitration clause has interpreted that language broadly. We likewise conclude that the language "arising in connection with" reaches every dispute between the parties having a significant relationship to the contract and all disputes having their origin or genesis in the contract.

III.

To require arbitration, Simula's factual allegations need only "touch matters" covered by the contract containing the arbitration clause and all doubts are to be resolved in favor of arbitrability. Accordingly, we must examine the factual allegations raised to determine which of Simula's causes of action are arbitrable.

A. Antitrust Claims

Simula brought two claims under the Sherman Act, 15 U.S.C. §§ 1 and 2, alleging that: (1) the January 1995 licensing agreement unreasonably restrains trade in the development, marketing and selling of automobile side-impact neck and head protection systems; and (2) Autoliv possesses significant monopoly power in the side-impact protection system markets. [Simula] [c]ontend[s] that its antitrust claims do not fall within the scope of the arbitration clause . . . .

. . . In short, Simula accuses Autoliv of using the 1995 Agreement as an anti-competitive tool to restrain trade, to the detriment of itself and U.S. automobile drivers in general.

. . .

. . . [R]esolution here of Simula's antitrust claims will necessitate interpreting the 1995 Agreement to determine its meaning and whether the contracts between Autoliv and Simula actually do suppress competition as alleged. The same reasoning applies to the allegations of improper marketing and disparaging remarks, as these disputes also implicate Autoliv's performance under the 1995 Agreement as the exclusive dealer of Simula's ITS system. All of the agreements between Autoliv and Simula would have to be closely examined in order to determine whether Autoliv performed its contractual obligations in a manner consistent with the various agreements. This job is for the arbitrator, however, not for the courts.

. . .

B. Lanham Act Claims

Simula alleges that under the Lanham Act, 15 U.S.C. § 1125, Autoliv intentionally made false and misleading representations while promoting Simula's ITS system.

---

however, controls the language in the present clause: *Mediterranean Enter.* interpreted a clause providing for any disputes "arising hereunder," and *Tracer Research* involved an arbitration clause providing for arbitration of claims "arising out of" the agreement. Such language is considerably more narrow in scope than the language at issue here.

Simula contends that its Lanham Act claims are not arbitrable because they are separate tort claims relating to conduct occurring prior to the date on which the parties entered into the arbitration clause. Therefore, Simula argues, the claims are governed by the parties' previous agreements, the 1993 nondisclosure agreement and January 1994 letter of intent.

The 1995 Agreement, however, effectively subsumed the prior contracts. . . . Thus any obligation of Autoliv under the 1993 nondisclosure agreement and January 1994 letter of intent was incorporated into the 1995 Agreement under the merger clause, and is subject to the arbitration clause.

Further, the alleged misrepresentations relate directly to Autoliv's capacity as the exclusive dealer of Simula's ITS system under the 1995 Agreement; all the disparagement claims pertain to statements made regarding the ITS in the course of Autoliv's promotional efforts. Therefore, resolving Simula's factual allegations against Autoliv requires interpreting Autoliv's performance and conduct under the 1995 Agreement.

. . .

C. Defamation

Simula alleges that Autoliv made false, malicious, and defamatory statements about Simula, its engineering staff and its products in public fora. These statements, Simula contends, prejudice it in the conduct of its business, deter others from dealing with it, and have defamed its reputation.

Like its Lanham Act claims, Simula's defamation claims hinge upon the allegedly false statements made by Autoliv about the ITS system. Simula's defamation claims are similarly referable to arbitration because the purported defamatory conduct arose out of Autoliv's performance as exclusive distributor of the ITS system, a performance which is controlled by the arbitration clause in the 1995 Agreement. Simula's assertion that Autoliv improperly marketed the ITS, and that this improper marketing included Autoliv's purposeful defamation of Simula's product, is integrally related to Autoliv's duties to use its "best endeavors" to sell the ITS under the 1995 Agreement.

We have held that defamation claims are arbitrable if the claim arises out of the agreement. Therefore, we hold that Simula's defamation claims are arbitrable.

D. Misappropriation of Trade Secrets/Breach of Nondisclosure Agreements/Breach of Arizona Trade Secrets Act

. . .

Simula relies upon the violation of the May 1993 nondisclosure agreements as the basis for its misappropriation of trade secrets claim. As with its Lanham Act claims, however, those nondisclosure agreements were a key part of the 1995 Agreement, which expressly prohibited the misuse of proprietary information, including technical information and trade secrets. If Autoliv had fully complied with the contract, as interpreted by Simula, there would be no tort claims. Thus Simula's claims will necessitate a review of the contracts between Autoliv and Simula to determine whether Autoliv improperly breached the nondisclosure agreements and misappropriated trade secrets.

Further, it is unlikely that without the disclosure agreements, Simula would have ever dealt with Autoliv. Indeed, the entire business relationship between Simula and Autoliv was dependent, in part, on the rights and obligations under the nondisclosure agreements and reaffirmed by the 1995 Agreement. Autoliv gained access to Simula's confidential and proprietary information because of the parties' contractual relationship. Although the nondisclosure agreements themselves do not have arbitration clauses, they are a significant part of the business relationship between Simula and Autoliv which was subsumed by the 1995 Agreement, and thus subject to arbitration.

. . .

Accordingly, we hold that Simula's claims of trade secret misappropriation are dependent on the 1995 Agreement and subject to arbitration.

. . .

VII. Conclusion

As the Supreme Court has made abundantly clear, the emphatic federal policy in favor of arbitral dispute resolution applies with special force in the field of international commerce. The broadly-worded arbitration clause mandates the submission of these claims to arbitration. Accordingly, we affirm the district court's order compelling arbitration and dismissing Simula's complaint.

AFFIRMED.

NOTES

1.   As previously noted, most courts treat the scope of the arbitration agreement as an issue of substantive arbitrability, which can be decided by a court. 2 IAN R. MACNEIL ET AL., FEDERAL ARBITRATION LAW § 15.1.4.2 (1994 & Supp. 1999); see also RUAA § 6(b) ("The court shall decide whether . . . a controversy is subject to an agreement to arbitrate.").

2.   Although *Simula* involved an international dispute, the court of appeals interpreted the arbitration clause using standards applicable to domestic arbitration agreements as well.

3.   The *Simula* court quoted from Moses H. Cone Memorial Hospital v. Mercury Constr. Corp., 460 U.S. 1, 24 (1983), to the effect that "any doubts concerning the scope of arbitrable issues should be resolved in favor of arbitration." Despite that presumption, the precise language of an arbitration clause remains important. The *Simula* court distinguished between the language at issue in the case — "arising in connection with" — which it construed broadly, and other language — "arising hereunder" and "arising out of" — which it found "considerably more narrow in scope." Do you agree?

4.   More generally, courts often distinguish between "broad" arbitration clauses and "narrow" arbitration clauses. The characterization of an arbitration clause as "broad" or "narrow" can be decisive, as the following commentary explains:

> [T]he form of an arbitration agreement may assume an unfortunate talismanic function, going somewhat beyond simply looking at the language to ascertain party intention. Learned Hand's statement that if the arbitration clause is "general in form, it makes no difference what may come up under it," all disputes are subject to arbitration, illustrates this point. On the other hand, if the arbitration clause is narrow in form or possibly if it contains an explicit exclusion, its judicial characterization as narrow may lead to the exclusion of arbitration that might possibly have been within the realm of the probable intention of the parties.

2 Ian R. Macneil et al., Federal Arbitration Law § 20.2.1 (1994).

5.   The Ninth Circuit's decision in Tracer Research Corp. v. National Environmental Services Co., 42 F.3d 1292 (9th Cir. 1994), *cert. dismissed*, 515 U.S. 1187 (1995), cited in *Simula*, provides an example of a court interpreting an arbitration clause as a narrow one. In *Tracer*, the arbitration clause provided for arbitration of "any controversy or claim arising out of this Agreement." The court of appeals, following its earlier decision in Mediterranean Enterprises, Inc. v. Ssangyong Corp., 708 F.2d 1458 (9th Cir. 1983), found that this language "covered only those disputes 'relating to the interpretation and performance of the contract itself.' " 42 F.3d at 1295 (quoting *Mediterranean Enterprises*). As a result, it held that a tort claim of misappropriation of trade secrets was not within the scope of the arbitration clause, even though "the tort claim would not have arisen 'but for' the parties' licensing agreement." *Id.* Instead, "defendants' continuing use of [plaintiff's] trade secrets would constitute an independent wrong from any breach of the licensing and nondisclosure agreements" and "does not require interpretation of the contract." *Id.* Other circuits have interpreted similar language more broadly than the Ninth Circuit in *Tracer Research*, finding tort claims arbitral under clauses providing for arbitration of "any dispute . . . which may arise hereunder," Gregory v. Electro-Mechanical Corp., 83 F.3d 382, 385–86 (11th Cir. 1996), and any dispute "arising out of the agreement," Sweet Dreams Unlimited, Inc. v. Dial-A-Mattress Int'l, Ltd., 1 F.3d 639, 642 (7th Cir. 1993); Dialysis Access Center, LLC v. RMS Lifeline, Inc., 638 F.3d 367, 380-81 (1st Cir. 2011) ("any dispute that may arise under" the contract). *See* Simitar Entertainment, Inc. v. Silva Entertainment, Inc., 44 F. Supp. 2d 986, 995–96 (D. Minn. 1999) (recognizing conflict); Efund Capital Partners v. Pless, 59 Cal. Rptr. 3d 340, 353 (Cal. App. 2007) (describing *Tracer Research* and *Mediterranean Enterprises* as reflecting a "distinctly minority rule").

6.   In a highly publicized case, Halliburton Co. sought to compel arbitration of claims brought by Jamie Leigh Jones, who alleged that she was raped by Halliburton employees while she was working in Iraq. The Fifth Circuit eventually held that Jones's sexual assault claims were not "related to" employment and so did not fall within the scope of the arbitration clause between Jones and Halliburton. Jones v. Halliburton Co., 583 F.3d 228, 241 (5th Cir. 2009). Jones's case led Congress to adopt the so-called "Franken Amendment," restricting the use of arbitration clauses by defense contractors, discussed in § 3.02.

PROBLEM 2.6

Percy Phelps is employed by Holdhurst, Inc. in its business records department. He has a two-year employment contract with Holdhurst, which provides that he can only be fired for cause and contains an arbitration clause. After Phelps has been on the job for only a short time, Holdhurst fires him. Holdhurst tells Phelps that the reason he was fired was because he misplaced several key business documents containing extremely valuable trade secrets. Phelps disputes the allegation, and believes that he was fired because of the woman he was dating. He files suit in federal court asserting (1) a claim for breach of contract and (2) tort claims for libel and slander based on oral and written statements Holdhurst allegedly made to prospective employers about the events that led to Phelps' firing. Holdhurst responds by seeking a stay of the proceedings pending arbitration.

Under each of the following arbitration clauses, determine which, if any, of Phelps' claims are subject to arbitration:

(a) Any claim for breach of this contract shall be settled by arbitration.

(b) Any controversy or claim arising out of or relating to this contract, or the breach thereof, including tort claims, shall be settled by arbitration.

(c) Any controversy or claim arising out of or relating to this contract, or the breach thereof, shall be settled by arbitration.

(d) Any controversy or claim arising out of or relating to this contract shall be settled by arbitration.

(e) Any controversy or claim arising in connection with this contract shall be settled by arbitration.

(f) Any controversy or claim arising out of this contract shall be settled by arbitration.

(g) Same as (f), except that the arbitration clause incorporates by reference the AAA Commercial Arbitration Rules. Can a court still decide the scope issue?

§ 2.05 GENERAL CONTRACT LAW DEFENSES

Section 2 of the FAA makes written agreements to arbitrate enforceable "save upon such grounds as exist at law or in equity for the revocation of any contract." The Supreme Court has construed this language as making arbitration agreements subject to "general contract law principles." Allied-Bruce Terminix Cos. v. Dobson, 513 U.S. 265, 281 (1995). This section examines a number of general contract law defenses — lack of assent, lack of consideration, unconscionability, fraud, and material breach — on which courts have relied in finding arbitration agreements unenforceable. In addition to the merits of the defenses, make sure to consider whether the court should even have ruled on the defense under *Prima Paint* and *First Options*, or whether the defense is one for the arbitrator.

[A]   Assent and Formalities

SPECHT v. NETSCAPE COMMUNICATIONS CORP.
United States Court of Appeals for the Second Circuit
306 F.3d 17 (2002)

SOTOMAYOR, CIRCUIT JUDGE:

This is an appeal from a judgment . . . denying a motion by defendants-appellants Netscape Communications Corporation and its corporate parent, America Online, Inc. (collectively, "defendants" or "Netscape"), to compel arbitration and to stay court proceedings. In order to resolve the central question of arbitrability presented here, we must address issues of contract formation in cyberspace. Principally, we are asked to determine whether plaintiffs-appellees ("plaintiffs"), by acting upon defendants' invitation to download free software made available on defendants' webpage, agreed to be bound by the software's license terms (which included the arbitration clause at issue), even though plaintiffs could not have learned of the existence of those terms unless, prior to executing the download, they had scrolled down the webpage to a screen located below the download button. We agree with the district court that a reasonably prudent Internet user in circumstances such as these would not have known or learned of the existence of the license terms before responding to defendants' invitation to download the free software, and that defendants therefore did not provide reasonable notice of the license terms. In consequence, plaintiffs' bare act of downloading the software did not unambiguously manifest assent to the arbitration provision contained in the license terms.

. . .

DISCUSSION

. . .

III. Whether the User Plaintiffs Had Reasonable Notice of and Manifested Assent to the SmartDownload License Agreement

Whether governed by the common law or by Article 2 of the Uniform Commercial Code ("UCC"), a transaction, in order to be a contract, requires a manifestation of agreement between the parties. Although an onlooker observing the disputed transactions in this case would have seen each of the user plaintiffs click on the SmartDownload "Download" button, a consumer's clicking on a download button does not communicate assent to contractual terms if the offer did not make clear to the consumer that clicking on the download button would signify assent to those terms. California's common law is clear that "an offeree, regardless of apparent manifestation of his consent, is not bound by inconspicuous contractual provisions of which he is unaware, contained in a document whose contractual nature is not obvious."

Arbitration agreements are no exception to the requirement of manifestation of assent. "This principle of knowing consent applies with particular force to provisions for arbitration." Clarity and conspicuousness of arbitration terms are important in securing informed assent. "If a party wishes to bind in writing another to an agreement to arbitrate future disputes, such purpose should be accomplished in a way that each party to the arrangement will fully and clearly comprehend that the agreement to arbitrate exists and binds the parties thereto." Thus, California contract law measures assent by an objective standard that takes into account both what the offeree said, wrote, or did and the transactional context in which the offeree verbalized or acted.

A. The Reasonably Prudent Offeree of Downloadable Software

Defendants argue that plaintiffs must be held to a standard of reasonable prudence and that, because notice of the existence of SmartDownload license terms was on the next scrollable screen, plaintiffs were on "inquiry notice" of those terms. We disagree with the proposition that a reasonably prudent offeree in plaintiffs' position would necessarily have known or learned of the existence of the SmartDownload license agreement prior to acting, so that plaintiffs may be held to have assented to that agreement with constructive notice of its terms. It is true that "[a] party cannot avoid the terms of a contract on the ground that he or she failed to read it before signing." But courts are quick to add: "An exception to this general rule exists when the writing does not appear to be a contract and the terms are not called to the attention of the recipient. In such a case, no contract is formed with respect to the undisclosed term."

. . .

[R]eceipt of a physical document containing contract terms or notice thereof is frequently deemed, in the world of paper transactions, a sufficient circumstance to place the offeree on inquiry notice of those terms. "Every person who has actual notice of circumstances sufficient to put a prudent man upon inquiry as to a particular fact, has constructive notice of the fact itself in all cases in which, by prosecuting such inquiry, he might have learned such fact." Cal. Civ. Code § 19. These principles apply equally to the emergent world of online product delivery, pop-up screens, hyperlinked pages, clickwrap licensing, scrollable documents, and urgent admonitions to "Download Now!" What plaintiffs saw when they were being invited by defendants to download this fast, free plug-in called SmartDownload was a screen containing praise for the product and, at the very bottom of the screen, a "Download" button. Defendants argue that under the principles set forth in the cases cited above, a "fair and prudent person using ordinary care" would have been on inquiry notice of SmartDownload's license terms.

We are not persuaded that a reasonably prudent offeree in these circumstances would have known of the existence of license terms. Plaintiffs were responding to an offer that did not carry an immediately visible notice of the existence of license terms or require unambiguous manifestation of assent to those terms. Thus, plaintiffs' "apparent manifestation of . . . consent" was to terms "contained in a document whose contractual nature [was] not obvious." Moreover, the fact that, given the position of the scroll bar on their computer screens, plaintiffs may have been aware that an unexplored portion of the Netscape webpage remained below the download button does not mean that they reasonably should have concluded that this portion contained a notice of license terms. In their deposition testimony, plaintiffs variously stated that they used the scroll bar "only if there is something that I feel I need to see that is on — that is off the page," or that the elevated position of the scroll bar suggested the presence of "mere[ ] formalities, standard lower banner links" or "that the page is bigger than what I can see." Plaintiffs testified, and defendants did not refute, that plaintiffs were in fact unaware that defendants intended to attach license terms to the use of SmartDownload.

We conclude that in circumstances such as these, where consumers are urged to download free software at the immediate click of a button, a reference to the existence of license terms on a submerged screen is not sufficient to place consumers on inquiry or constructive notice of those terms. The SmartDownload webpage screen was "printed in such a manner that it tended to conceal the fact that it was an express acceptance of [Netscape's] rules and regulations." Internet users may have, as defendants put it, "as much time as they need[ ]" to scroll through multiple screens on a webpage, but there is no reason to assume that viewers will scroll down to subsequent screens simply because screens are there. When products are "free" and users are invited to download them in the absence of reasonably conspicuous notice that they are about to bind themselves to contract terms, the transactional circumstances cannot be fully analogized to those in the paper world of arm's-length bargaining. In the next two sections, we discuss case law and other legal authorities that have addressed the circumstances of computer sales, software licensing, and online transacting. Those authorities tend strongly to support our conclusion that plaintiffs did not manifest assent to SmartDownload's license terms.

B. Shrinkwrap Licensing and Related Practices

Defendants cite certain well-known cases involving shrinkwrap licensing and related commercial practices in support of their contention that plaintiffs became bound by the SmartDownload license terms by virtue of inquiry notice. For example, in *Hill v. Gateway 2000, Inc.*, the Seventh Circuit held that where a purchaser had ordered a computer over the telephone, received the order in a shipped box containing the computer along with printed contract terms, and did not return the computer within the thirty days required by the terms, the purchaser was bound by the contract. In *ProCD, Inc. v. Zeidenberg*, the same court held that where an individual purchased software in a box containing license terms which were displayed on the computer screen every time the user executed the software program, the user had sufficient opportunity to review the terms and to return the software, and so was contractually bound after retaining the product. [86 F.3d 1447 (7th Cir. 1996)]; *cf.* Brower v. Gateway 2000, Inc., 676 N.Y.S.2d 569, 572 (1st Dep't 1998) (buyer assented to arbitration clause shipped inside box with computer and software by retaining items beyond date specified by license terms); M.A. Mortenson Co. v. Timberline Software Corp., 970 P.2d 803, 809 (Wash. Ct. App. 1999) (buyer manifested assent to software license terms by installing and using software), *aff'd*, 998 P.2d 305 (Wash. 2000).

These cases do not help defendants. To the extent that they hold that the purchaser of a computer or tangible software is contractually bound after failing to object to printed license terms provided with the product, *Hill* and *Brower* do not differ markedly from the cases involving traditional paper contracting. . . . Insofar as the purchaser in *ProCD* was confronted with conspicuous, mandatory license terms every time he ran the software on his computer, that case actually undermines defendants' contention that downloading in the absence of conspicuous terms is an act that binds plaintiffs to those terms. In *Mortenson*, the full text of license terms was printed on each sealed diskette envelope inside the software box, printed again on the inside cover of the user manual, and notice of the terms appeared on the computer screen every time the purchaser executed the program. In sum, the foregoing cases are clearly distinguishable from the facts of the present action.

C. Online Transactions

Cases in which courts have found contracts arising from Internet use do not assist defendants, because in those circumstances there was much clearer notice than in the present case that a user's act would manifest assent to contract terms. *See, e.g.*, Caspi v. Microsoft Network, L.L.C., 732 A.2d 528, 530, 532-33 (N.J. Super. Ct. App. Div. 1999) (upholding forum selection clause where subscribers to online software were required to review license terms in scrollable window and to click "I Agree" or "I Don't Agree"); Barnett v. Network Solutions, Inc., 38 S.W.3d 200, 203-04 (Tex. App. 2001) (upholding forum selection clause in online contract for registering Internet domain names that required users to scroll through terms before accepting or rejecting them).

After reviewing the California common law and other relevant legal authority, we conclude that under the circumstances here, plaintiffs' downloading of SmartDownload did not constitute acceptance of defendants' license terms. Reasonably conspicuous notice of the existence of contract terms and unambiguous manifestation of assent to those terms by consumers are essential if electronic bargaining is to have integrity and credibility. We hold that a reasonably prudent offeree in plaintiffs' position would not have known or learned, prior to acting on the invitation to download, of the reference to SmartDownload's license terms hidden below the "Download" button on the next screen. We affirm the district court's conclusion that the user plaintiffs . . . are not bound by the arbitration clause contained in those terms.

. . .

CONCLUSION

For the foregoing reasons, we affirm the district court's denial of defendants' motion to compel arbitration and to stay court proceedings.

NOTES

1. Section 2 of the FAA makes enforceable a "written provision" to settle future disputes by arbitration and an "agreement in writing" to submit existing disputes to arbitration. Why are oral agreements to arbitrate not enforceable under the FAA?

2. What sort of writing is needed to satisfy section 2? This question is increasingly important because of the growth of electronic commerce, as illustrated in *Specht*. Arguably, electronic communications do not constitute writings unless printed out on paper, which defeats one of the major benefits of communicating electronically. The Revised Uniform Arbitration Act deals with the issue by using the word "record" instead of "writing," RUAA § 6(a), and defining "record" to mean "information that is inscribed on a tangible medium or that is stored in an electronic or other medium and is retrievable in perceivable form." *Id.* § 1(6). Effective October 1, 2000, the Electronic Signatures in Global and National Commerce Act, Pub. L. No. 106-229, provides:

> Notwithstanding any statute, regulation, or other rule of law . . . , with respect to any transaction in or affecting interstate or foreign commerce —
>
> (1) a signature, contract, or other record relating to such transaction may not be denied legal effect, validity, or enforceability solely because it is in electronic form; and
>
> (2) a contract relating to such transaction may not be denied legal effect, validity, or enforceability solely because an electronic signature or electronic record was used in its formation.

15 U.S.C. § 7001(a). Do electronic communications now satisfy the FAA? *See* Campbell v. General Dynamics Gov't Systems Corp., 407 F.3d 546, 556 (1st Cir. 2005) ("This statute definitively resolves the issue . . . as to whether an e-mail agreement to arbitrate is unenforceable under the FAA because it does not satisfy the FAA's 'written provision' requirement, 9 U.S.C. § 2. By its plain terms, the E-Sign Act prohibits any interpretation of the FAA's 'written provision' requirement that would preclude giving legal effect to an agreement solely on the basis that it was in electronic form.").

3. The writing requirement of the FAA is distinct from any statute of frauds that might otherwise apply to the transaction. Article 2 of the UCC, for example, provides that "a contract for the sale of goods for the price of $500 or more is not enforceable by way of action or defense unless there is some writing sufficient to indicate that a contract for sale has been made between the parties and signed by the party against whom enforcement is sought or by his authorized agent or broker." UCC § 2-201(1). In addition, remember that the requirement of assent is separate from either of the two writing requirements. Merely because there is a writing that satisfies both the statute of frauds and section 2's requirement of a writing does not necessarily mean that the parties have agreed to arbitrate.

4. As already noted, courts use general contract law principles in determining whether an agreement to arbitrate has been formed. In *Specht*, the court of appeals held that the consumers did not accept Netscape's offered license terms (which

included an arbitration clause) by downloading the SmartDownload software. According to the court, "a reasonably prudent offeree in plaintiffs' position would not have known or learned, prior to acting on the invitation to download, of the reference to SmartDownload's license terms hidden below the 'Download' button on the next screen." By comparison, courts have consistently held that a contract is formed when a buyer clicks "I accept" in response to contract terms made available by a seller on its web page (so-called "clickwrap" licenses). *E.g.*, Caspi v. Microsoft Network, LLC, 732 A.2d 528, 532-33 (N.J. Super. Ct. 1999) (forum selection clause), cited in *Specht*. What might Netscape have done to increase the likelihood that its license terms would be enforceable?

PROBLEM 2.7

Violet Hunter orders various trees and shrubs from the Westaway's Nursery web page. After she selects the items she wishes to purchase, a screen listing the items appears on her computer. At the end of the list it states: "By clicking 'I Accept' you agree to the terms stated in Westaway's Standard Terms & Conditions. In order to complete your purchase, you must agree to those terms. If you do not wish to complete your purchase, click on 'I Decline.' " Two "buttons" are presented. One states "I Accept"; when clicked it continues to the next page where the buyer provides credit card information to pay for the purchase. The other states "I Decline"; when clicked it returns to the Westaway's home page without completing the transaction. The phrase "Westaway's Standard Terms & Conditions" is a link to a page that lists a number of contract terms, including an arbitration clause. By clicking on the link, a buyer can review the contract terms before agreeing to them. Hunter clicks the "I Accept" button without reviewing Westaway's Standard Terms and Conditions. Westaway's charges her credit card and ships the trees and shrubs. Hunter plants the trees and shrubs according to Westaway's instructions, but soon they are all dead. Hunter wants to assert a claim against Westaway's for breach of warranty. Has she made an enforceable agreement to arbitrate that claim under section 2 of the FAA?

PROBLEM 2.8

Prosper's Greengrocer, Inc. (Prosper) decides to expand its grocery business. It begins negotiations on a contract to purchase several thousand dollars of fresh fruits and vegetables weekly from Holder's Harvest Company (Holder), a large food distributor. Prosper and Holder exchange successive drafts of a contract. Thinking that a deal is imminent, Holder sends a signed draft to Prosper for its signature. Prosper does not sign the contract, but has a lengthy discussion with Holder on the phone about the terms of the contract. Holder comes away from the phone conversation believing that Prosper has agreed to the contract. Two days later, however, Prosper faxes a letter to Holder saying that it has decided not to agree to the contract.

All of the drafts of the contract, including the one signed by Holder, contained an arbitration clause. Accordingly, Holder initiates an arbitration proceeding against Prosper alleging breach of contract. Prosper responds by filing suit in federal court seeking to enjoin the arbitration proceeding, at all times denying that it agreed to the contract. Can the court rule on Prosper's contention that it did not agree to the contract, or is that a matter for the arbitrator? What defenses to arbitration, in addition to lack of assent, might Prosper raise? If the court determines that Prosper did agree to the contract during the phone conversation, how should the court rule on Prosper's request for injunctive relief?

BADIE v. BANK OF AMERICA
California Court of Appeal
79 Cal. Rptr. 2d 273 (1998)

PHELAN, PRESIDING JUSTICE.

Plaintiffs, four individuals and two consumer-oriented organizations, Consumer Action and California Trial Lawyers Association, challenge the validity of an alternative dispute resolution (ADR) clause which Bank of America (the Bank) sought to add to existing account agreements between itself and its deposit account and credit card account customers by sending those customers an insert with their monthly account statements (hereafter, "bill stuffer"), notifying them of the new term. None of the individual plaintiffs had a deposit account with the Bank, but all had the Bank's credit cards.

Plaintiffs filed their complaint shortly after the Bank began sending the "bill stuffers" to its customers. . . .

After a 17-day nonjury trial, the trial court entered judgment in favor of the Bank, ruling that the change of terms provision in the original account agreements permitted the addition of the ADR clause. . . .

Plaintiffs timely appealed. . . .

BACKGROUND

Starting in June 1992 and for a period of several months thereafter, the Bank mailed half-page "bill stuffers" to its personal credit card and deposit account customers, informing them that, from that time forward, any dispute between a customer and the Bank regarding customer accounts would be resolved either "by arbitration or by reference" if either the Bank or customer so requested. . . . The Bank's intention in sending the "bill stuffer" was to add a new provision to the existing account agreements. In attempting to add the ADR clause to the existing agreements, the Bank relied upon the change of terms provision included in the original account agreements, which gave the Bank the unilateral right to modify the agreements after customers entered into them. It is undisputed that the account agreements were contracts of adhesion.

The contract documents comprising the original credit account agreements consisted of either an application or, if the account was opened in response to a direct mail solicitation to accept a "pre-approved" credit card, an "Acceptance Certificate," plus a document referred to as an account agreement and disclosure statement, which was sent to the customer after the account was opened. A change of terms provision was included in each of these documents. . . .

The account agreement and disclosure statement provided a . . . description of the account features, including fees, the method of calculating balances and finance charges, how payments were applied, the circumstances under which the Bank would close an account, and so forth. . . . All versions of the agreement presented at trial included a provision labeled "Change of Terms," which was set forth in a section headed "Other Important Information." In most versions, which were dated between April 1988 and June 1992, the change of terms provision stated, "We may change any term, condition, service or feature of your Account at any time. We will provide you with notice of the change to the extent required by law." In two versions of the agreement, . . . the change of terms provision [included the following language:] . . . "We may also add new terms, conditions, services or features to your Account." . . . The language expressly allowing the Bank to add new terms was deleted from the versions of the agreement and disclosure statement that were in effect at the time the ADR "bill stuffers" were mailed to credit account customers. . . .

None of the agreements admitted into evidence contained any provision regarding the method or forum for resolving disputes. . . .

DISCUSSION

[1] California's Public Policy Favoring ADR Is Not Operative Unless the Parties Have First Entered Into An Enforceable Agreement to Arbitrate.

. . .

In its statement of decision, the trial court asserted that California public policy favors arbitration . . . and implied that the need for consent with respect to such ADR procedures has been eroded. . . .

. . .

When the trial court glossed over the threshold issue of consent and concluded that the validity of the Bank's modification of its account agreements depends on the manner in which ADR in general, and arbitration in particular, are viewed under California law, it put the cart before the horse. Whether there is an agreement to submit disputes to arbitration or reference does not turn on the existence of a public policy favoring ADR, as the trial court apparently believed. That policy, whose existence we readily acknowledge, does not even come into play unless it is first determined that the Bank's customers agreed to use some form of ADR to resolve disputes regarding their deposit and credit card accounts, and that determination, in turn, requires analysis of the account agreements in light of ordinary state law principles that govern the formation and interpretation of contracts.

[2] Whether the ADR Clause Became Part of the Account Agreements Depends Upon the Meaning and Scope of the Change of Terms Provision in the Original Account Agreements.

Although the trial court characterized plaintiffs' action as a "facial challenge to the ADR Clause," the action is more appropriately described as a challenge to the

Bank's interpretation of the change of terms provision in the original account agreements. Whether the Bank's customers can be said to have agreed to allow the Bank to add the ADR clause to those agreements simply by sending them notice of the change depends, as a threshold matter, on the meaning and scope of the change of terms provision itself. . . . The Bank appears to contend that . . . the new ADR provision is a valid part of the contract as long as the prescribed procedure for making the modification was followed. In this case, the only procedural requirement set forth in the change of terms provision was that the Bank would notify the customer of the change. Thus, the Bank argues, because it sent notice in the form of the "bill stuffer," it met the sole procedural requirement of the change of terms provision, and the modification was therefore valid because it was made "in accordance with the terms of the contract." We cannot agree.

. . .

. . . Plaintiffs contend that the change of terms provision did not authorize the addition of new terms, but only modification of what they refer to as the "price terms" of the credit account agreement, by which they mean the matters required to be disclosed under the Truth in Lending Act. When the trial court rejected this argument, it focused on construing the meaning of the word "change," rather than on construing the meaning of the word "terms." [T]he trial court ruled that the word "change" was equivalent to the word "amend," and included the concepts "add," "delete," "revise," "replace," or "modify." Not only does using the somewhat legalistic word "amend" to define the garden-variety word "change" appear to run counter to the spirit of [California law], but the conclusion that "change" was intended to mean "add" is questionable in light of the fact that the phrase stating that the Bank could "add" new terms had been deleted from the revised version of the change of terms provision in the account agreements in effect when the ADR "bill stuffer" was mailed. In any event, whether the change of terms provision permitted the Bank to add the ADR clause simply by sending a "bill stuffer" depends principally on what the parties intended by the word "terms," not on whether the word "change" also means "add," or on whether the Bank used the word "add" in the change of terms provision. Yet the trial court made no serious attempt to ascertain the meaning attributed by the parties to the word "terms" as of the time the account agreements were entered into. Instead, it simply stated that "the word 'terms' is not, as plaintiffs argue, limited purely to price terms for already existing services," and that the Bank had the ability "to modify any of the relevant terms of the contract." But without a threshold determination of what the parties intended when they agreed that the Bank could change the "terms" of the account agreement, the validity of the ADR clause cannot be properly assessed. In order to make that determination, we must apply the standard statutory rules of contract interpretation in order to ascertain the mutual intention of the parties as it existed at the time the original account agreements were entered into.

[3] Application of the Standard Rules of Contract Interpretation Demonstrates That the Customers' Consent to Allow the Bank to Change the Terms of the Credit Account Agreement Did Not Constitute Consent to Addition of an ADR Clause by a Unilateral Notice.

. . .

As noted, the Bank contends the change of terms provision authorizes any modification whatsoever, as long as the procedure set forth in the account agreements is followed, while plaintiffs contend there are substantive limitations on the kinds of changes authorized by the provision. . . .

. . .

Based solely on the language of the credit account agreement, we cannot conclude that either party's interpretation of the change of terms provision is clearly untenable. Although the Bank's interpretation is supported by the fact that the change of terms provision is broadly worded and contains no express limitation on its application, plaintiffs' narrower interpretation is supported by the fact that all the terms, conditions, services and features discussed in the original agreements pertain to matters that are integral to the Bank/creditor relationship, whereas the method and forum for dispute resolution — a matter which is collateral to that relationship — is not discussed at all.

Having determined that the credit account agreement is reasonably susceptible to the interpretations offered by both sides, we proceed to determine the construction of the ambiguous language by applying the appropriate canons of construction. . . .

. . . [T]he change of terms provision is employed in the context of consumer credit agreements between the Bank and its customers. All the provisions of the original credit account agreements concerned matters that were integral to that relationship. In this context, there is nothing about the original terms that would have alerted a customer to the possibility that the Bank might one day in the future invoke the change of terms provision to add a clause that would allow it to *impose* ADR on the customer. . . . All this is not to say that the Bank could not have included an ADR clause in the original account agreement simply because such a provision is not integral to the financial relationship between the Bank and its credit account customers in the same way interest rates or finance charges are. But the validity of an ADR provision included in an account agreement in the first instance is a different issue, which we are not required to address here. Our focus is on whether the words of the original account agreements mean that the Bank's customers, by agreeing to a unilateral change of terms provision, intended to give the Bank the power in the future to terminate its customers' existing right to have disputes resolved in the civil justice system, including their constitutionally based right to a jury trial. In our view, the object, nature and subject matter of these agreements strongly support the conclusion that the customers did not so intend, and that they, as promisors with respect to the change of terms provision, had no inkling that the Bank understood the provision differently. In short, the original agreements do not suggest that ADR was one of "those things concerning which . . . the parties intended to contract."

. . .

A narrow interpretation of the change of terms provision, which limits its operation to matters that are integral to the Bank/creditor relationship, does not render the provision inoperative or cause it to be mere surplusage. The Bank may still invoke it to modify fees, grace periods, annual percentage rates and so forth, subject to the Bank's duty of good faith and fair dealing. . . .

Thus, after analyzing the credit account agreements in light of the standard canons of contract interpretation, we conclude that when the account agreements were entered into, the parties did not intend that the change of terms provision should allow the Bank to add completely new terms such as an ADR clause simply by sending out a notice. Further, to the extent that application of these canons of construction has not removed all uncertainty concerning the meaning of the provision, we resort to the rule that ambiguous contract language must be interpreted most strongly against the party who prepared it, a rule that applies with particular force to the interpretation of contracts of adhesion, like the account agreements here. Application of this rule strengthens our conviction that the parties did not intend that the change of terms provision should permit the Bank to add new contract terms that differ *in kind* from the terms and conditions included in the original agreements.

To reach the contrary conclusion, i.e., that the original account agreements *did* authorize addition of the ADR clause, we would have to assume that by agreeing to the change of terms provision, the Bank's customers intended to permit a modification that would amount to waiver of their constitutionally-based right to a jury trial (Cal. Const., art. I, § 16). In order to be enforceable, a contractual waiver of the right to a jury trial "must be clearly apparent in the contract and its language must be unambiguous and unequivocal, leaving no room for doubt as to the intention of the parties." . . .

. . .

We recognize that not every dispute concerning a deposit account or credit card account invariably implicates the right to a *jury* trial because in some instances only injunctive relief might be sought, or only the resolution of purely legal issues might be required. However, the Bank's interpretation of the change of terms provision would dispense with the requirement for a clear and unmistakable indication that the customer intended to waive the right to a jury trial. Because we find no unambiguous and unequivocal waiver of that right here, and because the right to select a *judicial* forum, whether a bench trial or a jury trial, as distinguished from arbitration or some other method of dispute resolution, is a substantial right not lightly to be deemed waived, the Bank's interpretation of the change of terms provision must be rejected.

DISPOSITION

The judgment entered in favor of the Bank on the plaintiffs' third cause of action with respect to the validity and enforceability of the ADR clause is reversed. That clause is not a part of the Bank's contract with the four individual plaintiffs here and may not be enforced against them. The judgment is affirmed in all other respects.

Costs are awarded to the individual appellants.

NOTES

1.   Not all courts agree with the *Badie* court's analysis. *E.g.*, Hutherson v. Sears Roebuck & Co., 793 N.E.2d 886, 900 (Ill. App. 2003) ("Although we agree with *Badie* that the parties did not intend for SNB to make additions or deletions to the credit card agreement that would essentially convert the credit card agreement to something else entirely, we do not read the 'change of terms' provision so narrowly as to preclude an amendment containing an arbitration provision."); *see* Union Planters Bank v. Rogers, 912 So. 2d 116 (Miss. 2005) (noting "split in authority" on the issue). For a critical view of so-called "unilateral revision" of contracts, see David Horton, *The Shadow Terms: Contract Procedure and Unilateral Amendments*, 57 UCLA L. REV. 605 (2010).

2.   Delaware, in which many banks that issue credit cards are located, rejects the *Badie* approach by statute:

> Unless the agreement governing a revolving credit plan otherwise provides, a bank may at any time and from time to time amend such agreement in any respect, whether or not the amendment or the subject of the amendment was originally contemplated or addressed by the parties or is integral to the relationship between the parties. Without limiting the foregoing, such amendment may change terms by the addition of new terms or by the deletion or modification of existing terms, whether relating to plan benefits or features, the rate or rates of periodic interest, the manner of calculating periodic interest or outstanding unpaid indebtedness, variable schedules or formulas, interest charges, fees, collateral requirements, methods for obtaining or repaying extensions of credit, attorney's fees, plan termination, the manner for amending the terms of the agreement, *arbitration or other alternative dispute resolution mechanisms*, or other matters of any kind whatsoever. . . .

Del. Code Ann. tit. 5, § 952(a) (emphasis added). What effect, if any, might this statute have in cases like *Badie*?

3.   Although the FAA makes only written arbitration agreements enforceable, it does not require that arbitration agreements be signed. *See* Caley v. Gulfstream Aerospace Corp., 428 F.3d 1359, 1369 (11th Cir. 2005) ("the overwhelming weight of authority supports the view that no signature is required to meet the FAA's 'written' requirement"). If the FAA required a signature, an arbitration clause added by a change-in-terms notice such as that involved in *Badie* could well be unenforceable because the consumer never signs the arbitration agreement (although presumably he or she does sign the original credit card agreement). Should the FAA be amended to apply only to arbitration agreements signed by both parties?

PROBLEM 2.9

The City & Suburban Bank issues a credit card to John Clay. The original account agreement signed by Clay provides: "We may change any term, condition, service or feature of your Account at any time. We will provide you notice of the change to the extent required by law."

(a) The bank sends notice to Clay that the terms of the account agreement are changed to provide for all disputes to be resolved by arbitration. Is Clay bound to arbitrate?

(b) Same as (a) except that the original account agreement also contains a forum selection clause, which provides that any dispute must be litigated in federal court or state court in California. The bank sends notice to Clay that the terms of the account agreement are changed to provide for all disputes to be resolved by arbitration. Is Clay bound to arbitrate?

(c) Same as (a) except that the agreement includes the following language: "We may also add new terms, conditions, services or features to your Account." The bank sends notice to Clay that a term is being added to the account agreement providing for all disputes to be resolved by arbitration. Is Clay bound to arbitrate?

HILL v. GATEWAY 2000, INC.
United States Court of Appeals for the Seventh Circuit
105 F.3d 1147 (1997)

EASTERBROOK, CIRCUIT JUDGE.

A customer picks up the phone, orders a computer, and gives a credit card number. Presently a box arrives, containing the computer and a list of terms, said to govern unless the customer returns the computer within 30 days. Are these terms effective as the parties' contract, or is the contract term-free because the order-taker did not read any terms over the phone and elicit the customer's assent?

One of the terms in the box containing a Gateway 2000 system was an arbitration clause. Rich and Enza Hill, the customers, kept the computer more than 30 days before complaining about its components and performance. They filed suit in federal court arguing, among other things, that the product's shortcomings make Gateway a racketeer (mail and wire fraud are said to be the predicate offenses), leading to treble damages under RICO for the Hills and a class of all other purchasers. Gateway asked the district court to enforce the arbitration clause; the judge refused, writing that "[t]he present record is insufficient to support a finding of a valid arbitration agreement between the parties or that the plaintiffs were given adequate notice of the arbitration clause." Gateway took an immediate appeal, as is its right. 9 U.S.C. § 16(a)(1)(A).

The Hills say that the arbitration clause did not stand out: they concede noticing the statement of terms but deny reading it closely enough to discover the agreement to arbitrate, and they ask us to conclude that they therefore may go to court. Yet an agreement to arbitrate must be enforced "save upon such grounds as exist at law or in equity for the revocation of any contract." 9 U.S.C. § 2. . . . A contract need not be read to be effective; people who accept take the risk that the unread terms may in retrospect prove unwelcome. Terms inside Gateway's box stand or fall together. If they constitute the parties' contract because the Hills had an opportunity to return the computer after reading them, then all must be enforced.

ProCD, Inc. v. Zeidenberg, 86 F.3d 1447 (7th Cir.1996), holds that terms inside a box of software bind consumers who use the software after an opportunity to read the terms and to reject them by returning the product. Likewise, Carnival Cruise Lines, Inc. v. Shute, 499 U.S. 585 (1991), enforces a forum-selection clause that was included among three pages of terms attached to a cruise ship ticket. *ProCD* and *Carnival Cruise Lines* exemplify the many commercial transactions in which people pay for products with terms to follow; *ProCD* discusses others. The district court concluded in *ProCD* that the contract is formed when the consumer pays for the software; as a result, the court held, only terms known to the consumer at that moment are part of the contract, and provisos inside the box do not count. Although this is one way a contract could be formed, it is not the only way: "A vendor, as master of the offer, may invite acceptance by conduct, and may propose limitations on the kind of conduct that constitutes acceptance. A buyer may accept by performing the acts the vendor proposes to treat as acceptance." Gateway shipped computers with the same sort of accept-or-return offer ProCD made to users of its software. . . .

Plaintiffs ask us to limit *ProCD* to software, but where's the sense in that? *ProCD* is about the law of contract, not the law of software. Payment preceding the revelation of full terms is common for air transportation, insurance, and many other endeavors. Practical considerations support allowing vendors to enclose the full legal terms with their products. Cashiers cannot be expected to read legal documents to customers before ringing up sales. If the staff at the other end of the phone for direct-sales operations such as Gateway's had to read the four-page statement of terms before taking the buyer's credit card number, the droning voice would anesthetize rather than enlighten many potential buyers. Others would hang up in a rage over the waste of their time. And oral recitation would not avoid customers' assertions (whether true or feigned) that the clerk did not read term X to them, or that they did not remember or understand it. Writing provides benefits for both sides of commercial transactions. Customers as a group are better off when vendors skip costly and ineffectual steps such as telephonic recitation, and use instead a simple approve-or-return device. Competent adults are bound by such documents, read or unread. For what little it is worth, we add that the box from Gateway was crammed with software. The computer came with an operating system, without which it was useful only as a boat anchor. Gateway also included many application programs. So the Hills' effort to limit *ProCD* to software would not avail them factually, even if it were sound legally — which it is not.

For their second sally, the Hills contend that *ProCD* should be limited to executory contracts (to licenses in particular), and therefore does not apply because both parties' performance of this contract was complete when the box arrived at their home. This is legally and factually wrong: legally because the question at hand concerns the *formation* of the contract rather than its *performance*, and factually because both contracts were incompletely performed. *ProCD* did not depend on the fact that the seller characterized the transaction as a license rather than as a contract; we treated it as a contract for the sale of goods and reserved the question whether for other purposes a "license" characterization might be preferable. All debates about characterization to one side, the transaction in *ProCD* was no more executory than the one here: Zeidenberg paid for the software and walked out of the store with a box under his arm, so if arrival of the box with the product ends the time for revelation of contractual terms, then the time ended in *ProCD* before Zeidenberg opened the box. But of course ProCD had not completed performance with delivery of the box, and neither had Gateway. One element of the transaction was the warranty, which obliges sellers to fix defects in their products. The Hills have invoked Gateway's warranty and are not satisfied with its response, so they are not well positioned to say that Gateway's obligations were fulfilled when the motor carrier unloaded the box. What is more, both ProCD and Gateway promised to help customers to use their products. Long-term service and information obligations are common in the computer business, on both hardware and software sides. Gateway offers "lifetime service" and has a round-the-clock telephone hotline to fulfil this promise. Some vendors spend more money helping customers use their products than on developing and manufacturing them. The document in Gateway's box includes promises of future performance that some consumers value highly; these promises bind Gateway just as the arbitration clause binds the Hills.

Next the Hills insist that *ProCD* is irrelevant because Zeidenberg was a "merchant" and they are not. Section 2-207(2) of the UCC, the infamous battle-of-the-forms section, states that "additional terms [following acceptance of an offer] are to be construed as proposals for addition to a contract. Between merchants such terms become part of the contract unless . . . ." Plaintiffs tell us that *ProCD* came out as it did only because Zeidenberg was a "merchant" and the terms inside ProCD's box were not excluded by the "unless" clause. This argument pays scant attention to the opinion in *ProCD*, which concluded that, when there is only one form, "sec. 2-207 is irrelevant." The question in *ProCD* was not whether terms were added to a contract after its formation, but how and when the contract was formed — in particular, whether a vendor may propose that a contract of sale be formed, not in the store (or over the phone) with the payment of money or a general "send me the product," but after the customer has had a chance to inspect both the item and the terms. *ProCD* answers "yes," for merchants and consumers alike. Yet again, for what little it is worth we observe that the Hills misunderstand the setting of *ProCD*. A "merchant" under the UCC "means a person who deals in goods of the kind or otherwise by his occupation holds himself out as having knowledge or skill peculiar to the practices or goods involved in the transaction," § 2-104(1). Zeidenberg bought the product at a retail store, an uncommon place for merchants to acquire inventory. His corporation put ProCD's database on the Internet for anyone to browse, which led to the litigation but did not make Zeidenberg a software merchant.

At oral argument the Hills propounded still another distinction: the box containing ProCD's software displayed a notice that additional terms were within, while the box containing Gateway's computer did not. The difference is functional, not legal. Consumers browsing the aisles of a store can look at the box, and if they are unwilling to deal with the prospect of additional terms can leave the box alone, avoiding the transactions costs of returning the package after reviewing its contents. Gateway's box, by contrast, is just a shipping carton; it is not on display anywhere. Its function is to protect the product during transit, and the information on its sides is for the use of handlers ("Fragile!" "This Side Up!") rather than would-be purchasers.

Perhaps the Hills would have had a better argument if they were first alerted to the bundling of hardware and legal-ware after opening the box and wanted to return the computer in order to avoid disagreeable terms, but were dissuaded by the expense of shipping. What the remedy would be in such a case — could it exceed the shipping charges? — is an interesting question, but one that need not detain us because the Hills knew before they ordered the computer that the carton would include *some* important terms, and they did not seek to discover these in advance. Gateway's ads state that their products come with limited warranties and lifetime support. How limited was the warranty — 30 days, with service contingent on shipping the computer back, or five years, with free onsite service? What sort of support was offered? Shoppers have three principal ways to discover these things. First, they can ask the vendor to send a copy before deciding whether to buy. The Magnuson-Moss Warranty Act requires firms to distribute their warranty terms on request, 15 U.S.C. § 2302(b)(1)(A); the Hills do not contend that Gateway would have refused to enclose the remaining terms too. Concealment would be bad for business, scaring some customers away and leading to excess returns from others. Second, shoppers can consult public sources (computer magazines, the Web sites of vendors) that may contain this information. Third, they may inspect the documents after the product's delivery. Like Zeidenberg, the Hills took the third option. By keeping the computer beyond 30 days, the Hills accepted Gateway's offer, including the arbitration clause.

The Hills' remaining arguments, including a contention that the arbitration clause is unenforceable as part of a scheme to defraud, do not require more than a citation to *Prima Paint Corp. v. Flood & Conklin Mfg. Co.* Whatever may be said pro and con about the cost and efficacy of arbitration (which the Hills disparage) is for Congress and the contracting parties to consider. Claims based on RICO are no less arbitrable than those founded on the contract or the law of torts. *Shearson/American Express, Inc. v. McMahon.* The decision of the district court is vacated, and this case is remanded with instructions to compel the Hills to submit their dispute to arbitration.

NOTES

1. The arbitration clause contained in Gateway 2000's terms and conditions provided as follows:

> Any dispute or controversy arising out of or relating to this Agreement or its interpretation shall be settled exclusively and finally by arbitration. The arbitration shall be conducted in accordance with the Rules of Conciliation and Arbitration of the International Chamber of Commerce. The arbitration shall be conducted in Chicago, Illinois, U.S.A. before a sole arbitrator. Any award rendered in any such arbitration proceeding shall be final and binding on each of the parties, and judgment may be entered thereon in a court of competent jurisdiction.

See Brower v. Gateway 2000, Inc., 676 N.Y.S.2d 569, 570 (1998).

2.   Professor Jean Sternlight has strongly criticized the decision in *Gateway 2000*:

> *Hill v. Gateway* is but the most extreme example of a series of court decisions that allow large companies to impose potentially unfair binding arbitration agreements on unwitting consumers. . . .

> The outcome in *Gateway*, however, is questionable on federal statutory, common law, and constitutional grounds. First, the Magnuson-Moss Act, passed in 1974 "to improve the adequacy of information available to consumers, [and] prevent deception," provides that consumers cannot, prior to their assertion of a claim, be deprived of their right to sue merchants in court. While the Act allows merchants to establish informal dispute settlement procedures, the Act and the accompanying regulations and legislative history imply that these procedures must be nonbinding. In comments issued together with the regulations the FTC explicitly rebutted claims of some industry representatives that warrantors ought, in advance of a dispute, be allowed to require consumers to resort to binding arbitration. . . .

> . . .

> *Gateway* is also questionable as a matter of contract law. . . . [P]ursuant to the more traditional contract analysis offered by the buyers, the contract was formed when, by accepting payment, faxing a confirmation, and shipping the computer, Gateway accepted the purchase offer made by the Hills over the phone. Buyers argue that because their offer did not contain an arbitration clause, the supplemental terms contained in the box were simply a proposal for additional or modifying terms which the buyers did not accept. Uniform Commercial Code § 2-207 governs such situations. Where, as in *Gateway*, the contract was not between two merchants, § 2-207 provides that if a party accepts a contract but also states different or additional terms than were offered, those terms are regarded as mere "proposals for addition" and not modifications to the contract. Here, because the contract was entered between consumers and merchant prior to the shipment of the computer, it would seem that the Hills should not be bound by the proposal for an arbitration clause.

> . . .

> Finally, *Gateway* is unwise as a matter of policy. Judge Easterbrook based his conclusion that "[p]ractical considerations support allowing vendors to enclose the full legal terms with their products," on a "straw man," asserting that requiring cashiers to read such terms over the phone would simply "anesthetize" or anger potential customers. This analysis is flawed because it fails to consider alternative ways to regulate dealer conduct and because it ignores the potential significance of allowing companies to require consumers to trade their litigation rights for arbitration. Companies can use such clauses not only to take away a consumer-friendly jury but also to force consumers to bring claims in a distant and thus expensive forum, to impose high extra arbitration costs, to deny

consumers needed discovery, to deprive consumers of recovery for punitive damages, and to prevent consumers from using the economical class action procedures that would be available in court. The *Gateway* provision itself was unfair in some of these ways. It required that the dispute would be heard under International Chamber of Commerce rules which demand the filing party to pay at least $2,000 for the services of the ICC and its arbitrator. What kind of sense would it make for a consumer with a dispute over a $4,000 computer to pay half that amount in arbitration fees alone? The clause also required all claims to be brought in Chicago, which would certainly be quite expensive for those customers who, unlike the Hills, did not live in Chicago. Finally, the ICC rules make no provision for discovery, which could well prove crucial to a consumer's claim of fraud or defect.

Jean R. Sternlight, Gateway *Widens Doorway to Imposing Unfair Binding Arbitration on Consumers*, FLA. BAR J., Nov. 1997, at 8, 8–12.*

3.   Other courts dealing with cases involving Gateway 2000 generally have approved of the Seventh Circuit's conclusion on contract formation. *See, e.g.*, Brower v. Gateway 2000, Inc., 676 N.Y.S.2d 569 (N.Y. App. Div. 1998); Westendorf v. Gateway 2000, Inc., 2000 Del. Ch. LEXIS 54, *aff'd*, 763 A.2d 92 (Del. 2000); Levy v. Gateway 2000, Inc., 1997 WL 823611 (N.Y. Sup. Ct. 1997). *But see* Klocek v. Gateway, Inc., 104 F. Supp. 2d 1332 (D. Kan. 2000) (refusing to enforce arbitration clause), *dismissed for lack of subject matter jurisdiction*, 2000 U.S. Dist. LEXIS 21854 (D. Kan. Sept. 6, 2000). But a New York court has held that the requirement of arbitration under the rules of the International Chamber of Commerce was unconscionable because of high arbitration fees. *See Brower*, 676 N.Y.S. 2d at 574.

PROBLEM 2.10

Westaway's Nursery (from Problem 2.7) also sells plants by phone. Customers can call a toll free number and place an order using a credit card. Westaway's then ships the plants to the customer using whatever delivery service the customer wants. Your firm represents Westaway's. The president of Westaway's tells you that he would like the company's phone transactions to be subject to the same terms and conditions (including an arbitration clause) that its Internet transactions are. How might Westaway's try to accomplish that end? What are the risks and benefits of the various options available to Westaway's?

[B] Lack of Consideration

GIBSON v. NEIGHBORHOOD HEALTH CLINICS, INC.
United States Court of Appeals for the Seventh Circuit
121 F.3d 1126 (1997)

FLAUM, CIRCUIT JUDGE.

Mona Gibson appeals the district court's dismissal of her claims under Title VII and the Americans with Disabilities Act ("ADA") against her former employer, Neighborhood Health Clinics ("NHC"). The district court dismissed Gibson's claims on the ground that she had contractually agreed to submit any claims against NHC to arbitration. We reverse and remand.

I.

Gibson, who had previously been employed by NHC under circumstances not relevant to the instant case, was rehired by NHC on December 22, 1994. On December 30, 1994, at which time Gibson, although rehired, had not yet returned to work, NHC held a meeting at which all employees were presented with a new Associates Policy Manual (the "Manual"), and required to sign a new Associates Understanding (the "Understanding"). Gibson was not required to attend the meeting and in fact she did not. The Understanding included the following language:

> I agree to the grievance and arbitration provisions set forth in the Associates Policy Manual. I understand that I am waiving my right to a trial, including a jury trial, in state or federal court of the class of disputes specifically set forth in the grievance and arbitration provisions on pages 8–10 of the Manual.

The Manual states that when an employee alleges a violation of her rights under the ADA or Title VII (or other provisions not relevant here):

> THEN IT IS CLEARLY INTENDED AND AGREED THAT THE SOLE AND EXCLUSIVE MEANS FOR THE RESOLUTION OF ALL DISPUTES, ISSUES, CONTROVERSIES, CLAIMS, CAUSES OF ACTION OR GRIEVANCES BY AN EMPLOYEE AGAINST NEIGHBORHOOD HEALTH CLINICS SHALL BE THROUGH THE PROCESS OF ARBITRATION AND PURSUANT TO . . . THE INDIANA UNIFORM ARBITRATION ACT.

. . .

The arbitration provisions were not part of the terms of employment during Gibson's previous tenure with NHC.

When Gibson was hired in December 1994, she was informed that she should report to work on January 9, 1995. On that date, she met with NHC's personnel director, Chris Baxter, who handed Gibson a stack of papers to sign, including insurance and tax forms. Among the papers was the Understanding. Gibson testified at her deposition that when she asked Baxter about the Understanding, Baxter told her that it was a form that everybody signed so that complaints about time off could be settled through a grievance procedure.

The Manual referenced in the Understanding was not given to Gibson at that time; Baxter was only able to locate a copy of the Manual later that day, at which time she provided it to Gibson. Although she signed the Understanding, Gibson never signed the Manual.

NHC fired Gibson on April 6, 1995. On May 15, 1995, Gibson filed a discrimination claim with the Equal Employment Opportunity Commission, alleging sex and disability discrimination. NHC was informed of this charge shortly thereafter. Gibson then filed her complaint in the district court. NHC moved to dismiss Gibson's complaint on the ground that she had waived her right to a judicial determination of her claims against NHC by agreeing to submit such disputes to arbitration. The district court agreed, concluding that the Manual in connection with the Understanding created an enforceable arbitration agreement, and granted the motion to dismiss. In addition, because Gibson failed to abide by the deadline for submitting her claim to arbitration, the dismissal effectively foreclosed her ability to obtain redress. The district court therefore entered final judgment, from which Gibson now appeals. We have jurisdiction pursuant to 28 U.S.C. § 1291.

. . .

III.

The parties agree that an employee and employer may contractually agree to submit federal claims, including Title VII and ADA claims, to arbitration. An agreement to arbitrate is treated like any other contract. If there is no contract there is to be no forced arbitration. In determining whether a valid arbitration agreement arose between the parties, a federal court should look to the state law that ordinarily governs the formation of contracts. 9 U.S.C. § 2; *First Options of Chicago, Inc. v. Kaplan.* . . .

. . .

It is a basic tenet of contract law that in order for a promise to be enforceable against the promisor, the promisee must have given some consideration for the promise. Consideration is defined as a bargained for exchange whereby the promisor (here Gibson) receives some benefit or the promisee (here NHC) suffers a detriment. Thus, in order for Gibson's agreement to be enforceable, there must be detriment to NHC or benefit to Gibson that was bargained for in exchange for Gibson's promise to arbitrate all disputes.

Often, consideration for one party's promise to arbitrate is the other party's promise to do the same. In the present case, however, NHC cannot point to its own promise to arbitrate in order to make enforceable Gibson's promise to do likewise. The Understanding contains no promise on NHC's part to submit claims to arbitration. It is worded entirely in terms of Gibson's obligation to submit her claims to arbitration (using phrases such as "I agree" "I understand" "I am waiving"); it contains no promise on NHC's part. In order for a contract to be enforceable, both parties must be bound by its terms. Although Indiana courts will not find that there was a lack of obligation on the part of one party when "a reasonable and logical interpretation will render the contract valid and enforceable," there is no gloss we can apply to the language of the Understanding that would suggest that NHC was also required to forgo a judicial forum in favor of arbitration. To find that NHC was required to arbitrate any claim brought by Gibson would not give recognition to an obligation that was clearly present yet imperfectly expressed, Licocci v. Cardinal Assocs., Inc., 445 N.E.2d 556, 559 (Ind. 1983) (citing Wood v. Lucy, Lady Duff-Gordon, 222 N.Y. 88, 118 N.E. 214, 214 (N.Y. 1917)), but rather would lend arcane meaning to the clear language chosen by NHC; to find an obligation here would be to weave a contract out of loose threads. Therefore, we conclude that the Understanding itself did not contain consideration for Gibson's promise in the form of a promise by NHC to submit disputes to arbitration.

In contrast to the one-sided obligation contained in the wording of the Understanding, the Manual contains language that arguably could be read to bind NHC. We conclude, however, that any promise NHC made in the Manual cannot serve as consideration for Gibson's promise to arbitrate. The absence of a meaningful link between Gibson's promise, contained in the Understanding, and NHC's obligation, set forth in the Manual, precludes reading these provisions as complementary components of a bargained for exchange. To be sure, contract terms may be incorporated by reference to a separate document, including an employee handbook, and consideration for the promise in one instrument may be contained in another. Nevertheless, whatever the physical form by which a contract is memorialized (if any), proper consideration must consist of benefit or detriment given in exchange for the promise in question. The principal purposes of this consideration requirement are the "cautionary function of bringing home to the promisor the fact that his promise is legally enforceable and an evidentiary function . . . of making it more likely that an enforceable promise was intended." Neither of these functions is served when a promisor does not know of the promise that purportedly serves as consideration. Here, Gibson was unaware of the terms of the Manual (even if the Understanding's reference to the Manual alerted her to its existence) at the time she signed the Understanding. The promise that she made in the Understanding, therefore, was not given in exchange for any promise that NHC made in the Manual. In addition, although the Manual contains language that could be read to bind Gibson as well as NHC, Gibson did not (even in the objective or constructive sense) assent to the terms of the Manual, either when she signed the Understanding (at which point the Manual was not made available), or when she received the Manual. Consequently, there is no promise on the part of NHC that can serve as consideration for Gibson's promise to arbitrate.

Nor was Gibson's promise to submit claims to arbitration supported by consideration in the form of NHC's promise to hire her or to continue to employ her, or by its reasonable reliance on her promise. An initial offer of employment may constitute consideration for an employee's promise, such as a covenant not to compete. However, NHC's offer of employment to Gibson was not made in exchange for her promise to arbitrate, for she had already been hired at the time she made the promise. Once again, the element of bargained for exchange is lacking. An employer's specific promise to continue to employ an at-will employee may provide valid consideration for an employee's promise to forgo certain rights. In the present case, however, NHC never made a promise to continue Gibson's employment in exchange for her promise to submit claims to arbitration. That is, it never communicated to her that if she signed the Understanding she could continue to work there, and that if she did not her status would be uncertain. It is true that NHC continued to employ her. Yet when an employer has made no specific promise, the mere fact of continued employment does not constitute consideration for the employee's promise. Finally, while in the employment context it has been held that one party's partial performance in reliance upon the other party's promise may be sufficient consideration to make the promise enforceable, there is no indication in the present case that NHC was induced to rely on Gibson's promise. It had made its decision to hire her prior to her agreeing to the terms of the Understanding, and there is no evidence that its decision to continue to employ her following her signing of the Understanding (on the day she returned to work) was based upon her agreeing to the terms contained therein. We therefore conclude that Gibson's promise to submit her claims against NHC to arbitration did not give rise to an enforceable contract.

REVERSED and REMANDED.

PROBLEM 2.11

Mawson & Williams (M&W), is an investment banking firm seeking to hire a new employee, Hall Pycroft. In which of the following cases is Pycroft's promise to arbitrate supported by consideration?

(a) Before Pycroft begins work, he signs a two-year employment contract. One of the terms in the employment contract is a pre-dispute arbitration clause. The arbitration clause provides that both M&W and Pycroft agree to submit to arbitration all disputes arising out of or relating to the employment contract.

(b) Same as (a), except that the arbitration clause provides that Pycroft must arbitrate all disputes but that M&W has the option to proceed in court.

(c) During Pycroft's job interview, M&W tells Pycroft that it will not hire him unless he agrees to a pre-dispute arbitration agreement. Pycroft does not respond in the interview, but before starting work he signs a form promising to arbitrate all of his claims against M&W. M&W does not promise to arbitrate any disputes it might have against Pycroft, but it does hire him as an employee.

(d) After Pycroft starts work, M&W and Pycroft enter into a written agreement providing that all disputes shall be subject to arbitration.

(e) After Pycroft starts work, M&W requires him to sign a form promising that he will arbitrate all disputes against M&W. M&W does not promise to arbitrate any disputes it might have against Pycroft, but makes clear that any employee who does not sign the form will not be eligible for any future raises or promotions. Shortly after signing the form, Pycroft is promoted and receives a large raise.

(f) Same as (e), except that Pycroft has not yet received any promotion or raise.

(g) Same as (e), except that M&W does not make future raises or promotions conditional on signing the form. Instead, M&W tells Pycroft that he will be fired if he does not sign the form. Pycroft signs. (Assume for purposes of your answer that under the governing law Pycroft is an at-will employee.)

(h) Same as (g) except that M&W does not threaten to fire any employee who does not sign. Instead, M&W simply hands the form to Pycroft, who signs it.

[C] Unconscionability and Contracts of Adhesion

SAMANIEGO v. EMPIRE TODAY, LLC
Court of Appeal of California
140 Cal. Rptr. 3d 492 (2012)

Siggins, J. — Empire Today, LLC (Empire), a national carpet and flooring business, appeals from the superior court's refusal to compel contractual arbitration of claims by carpet installers that Empire violated multiple provisions of the Labor Code. The court found the arbitration provision was unconscionable under California law. We affirm. We hold the provision is unconscionable and unenforceable under *Armendariz v. Foundation Health Psychcare Services, Inc.* (2000) 24 Cal.4th 83 (*Armendariz*); . . . and that the recent decision of the Supreme Court of the United States in *AT&T Mobility LLC v. Concepcion* (2011) 563 ___ U.S. ___ (*Concepcion*) does not change our analysis. We also hold the trial court did not abuse its discretion when it declined to sever the unconscionable contract provisions in order to otherwise enforce the arbitration clause or when it rejected Empire's late-filed reply declarations.

BACKGROUND

Plaintiffs Salome Samaniego and Juventino Garcia work or worked as carpet installers for Flooring Install, Inc., an alleged subsidiary or affiliate of Empire. When they were initially hired, and again later during their employment, plaintiffs were given form contracts and told to sign them if they wanted to work for Empire. The second contract (the Agreement), which is at issue here, was captioned "Flooring Install, Inc. Subcontractor Installer Agreement." Both contracts were presented only in English, although Garcia cannot read English and Samaniego has difficulty reading more than simple written English. The contracts were offered on a nonnegotiable, take it or leave it basis, with little or no time for review.

The Agreement is 11 single-spaced pages of small-font print riddled with complex legal terminology. The arbitration provision is set forth in the 36th of 37 sections. It provides: "Any dispute or claim arising from any provision of this Agreement or relating in any way to the business relationship between Flooring Install and the Subcontractor shall be submitted to arbitration before a single arbitrator pursuant to the Commercial Arbitration Rules of the American Arbitration Association. . . . [¶] **Both Flooring Install and the Subcontractor are hereby agreeing to choose arbitration, rather than litigation or some other means of dispute resolution, to address their grievances or alleged grievances with the expectation that this resolution process may be more cost-effective**

and expedient for the parties than litigation. By entering into this Agreement and the arbitration provisions of this section, both parties are giving up their constitutional right to have any dispute decided in a court of law before a jury and, instead, are accepting the use of arbitration, other than as set forth immediately below. [¶] DUE TO THE POSSIBLE IMMEDIATE AND IRREPARABLE NATURE OF THE HARM, THE PARTIES AGREE THAT THIS SECTION SHALL NOT APPLY TO ANY CLAIMS BROUGHT BY ANY PARTY FOR DECLARATORY OR PRELIMINARY INJUNCTIVE RELIEF INVOLVING [specified sections] **OF THIS AGREEMENT."**

The Agreement also includes a shortened six-month statute of limitations for subcontractors to sue under the Agreement and a unilateral fee-shifting provision that requires them to pay any attorneys' fees Empire might incur "to enforce any of its rights hereunder or to collect any amounts due." Although the Agreement directs that arbitration will be governed by the commercial rules of the American Arbitration Association, those rules were not attached to it or otherwise provided to plaintiffs.

Samaniego and Garcia filed this putative class action challenging Empire's allegedly unlawful misclassification of its carpet installers as independent contractors. The complaint alleges numerous Labor Code violations, including that Empire failed to pay minimum wage and overtime compensation; refused to indemnify employees for job-related expenses; wrongfully deducted from employee pay; coerced employees to make purchases from the company; failed to provide required meal periods; and failed to pay all wages due upon installers' termination.

Empire moved to stay the action and compel arbitration pursuant to the Agreement. The court found the Agreement was "highly unconscionable from a procedural standpoint" and demonstrated "strong indicia of substantive unconscionability," and therefore denied Empire's motion to compel. It also denied Empire's request for reconsideration in light of the United States Supreme Court's decision in *Concepcion*, which was issued several weeks after the denial of Empire's motion. Empire timely appealed.

DISCUSSION

I. The Trial Court Correctly Refused to Compel Arbitration

The primary questions presented for our consideration are (1) whether the agreement to arbitrate is unconscionable and, therefore, unenforceable under California law; [and] (2) whether the court properly declined to enforce the entire arbitration clause rather than sever unconscionable provisions . . . .

    . . .

B. Unconscionability

California law on unconscionability is well established. " ' " [U]nconscionability has generally been recognized to include an absence of meaningful choice on the part of one of the parties together with contract terms which are unreasonably favorable to the other party." Phrased another way, unconscionability has both a "procedural" and a "substantive" element.' ' "The procedural element requires oppression or surprise. Oppression occurs where a contract involves lack of negotiation and meaningful choice, surprise where the allegedly unconscionable provision is hidden within a prolix printed form. The substantive element concerns whether a contractual provision reallocates risks in an objectively unreasonable or unexpected manner." Under this approach, both the procedural and substantive elements must be met before a contract or term will be deemed unconscionable. Both, however, need not be present to the same degree. A sliding scale is applied so that "the more substantively oppressive the contract term, the less evidence of procedural unconscionability is required to come to the conclusion that the term is unenforceable, and vice versa." ' "

1. Procedural Unconscionability

. . .

. . . Here, based on properly admitted, uncontroverted evidence, the superior court found as follows. "After being hired but before starting work, both Plaintiffs were required to take computer tests and complete certain paperwork, including a subcontractor agreement. They were told that they were 'required' to sign these documents, including the agreement, if they wanted to work for Empire. Both Plaintiffs are not able to read English (at all, or sufficiently well) and both Plaintiffs asked for a Spanish translation of the documents (including the agreement) in Spanish [*sic*] but were told none were available. Plaintiffs both signed all of the paperwork as instructed, but were not provided a copy." Plaintiffs were later presented with new agreements, also in English only, "and told that they were required to sign it if they wanted to keep working. Mr. Samaniego was directed to sign it immediately, and was told that he could not take it home for review. Mr. Garcia was permitted 24 hours to review and return his agreement, signed, which he did." In short, "[p]laintiffs perform manual labor, do not speak English as a first language, have limited or no literacy in English, and were told they could not continue employment if they did not sign the agreements."

Moreover, Empire failed to provide plaintiffs with a copy of the relevant arbitration rules. This is significant. . . . "Numerous cases have held that the failure to provide a copy of the arbitration rules to which the employee would be bound supported a finding of procedural unconscionability."

The Agreement was comprised of [sic] 11 pages of densely worded, single-spaced text printed in small typeface. The arbitration clause is the penultimate of 37 sections which . . . were neither flagged by individual headings nor required to be initialed by the subcontractor. Taken together, these factors amply support the trial court's finding that the Agreement was procedurally unconscionable.

. . .

2. Substantive Unconscionability

The Agreement also demonstrates "strong indicia of substantive unconscionability," as the trial court found. " 'Substantive unconscionability focuses on the one-sidedness or overly harsh effect of the contract term or clause.' " Empire asserts that none of the contractual terms amount[s] to substantive unconscionability. But it supports its argument only with authority for the general proposition that a contractual provision that unilaterally shortens a limitations period to six months, taken alone, does not necessarily render an adhesion contract substantively unconscionable. The import of such a clause is quite different in the context of the statutory wage and hour claims asserted here. The Labor Code provides the bases for the class claims, and it affords employees three or four years to assert them. Where, as in this case, arbitration provisions undermine statutory protections, courts have readily found unconscionability. As noted in *Armendariz*, "an arbitration agreement cannot be made to serve as a vehicle for the waiver of statutory rights created by the FEHA."

In any event, the limitations period is just one of several one-sided provisions. The Agreement also requires plaintiffs to pay any attorneys' fees incurred by Empire, but imposes no reciprocal obligation on Empire. Again, such a clause contributes to a finding of unconscionability. Empire argues this clause is of no moment because, after all, one-way fee-shifting provisions that benefit only employers violate both the Labor Code and commercial arbitration rules, "which means that Empire cannot recover its attorney's fees from plaintiffs even if it prevails in arbitration." In other words, according to Empire, it is not unconscionable because it is illegal and, hence, unenforceable. To state the premise is to refute Empire's logic. The argument is unpersuasive.

In addition, the Agreement exempts from the arbitration requirement claims typically brought by employers — namely, those seeking declaratory and preliminary injunctive relief to protect Empire's proprietary information and noncompetition/nonsolicitation provisions — while restricting to arbitration any and all claims plaintiffs might bring. Empire notes in this regard that "not all lack of mutuality in an adhesive arbitration agreement is invalid." True enough. But at issue here is whether the multiple one-sided provisions in the Agreement, considered together, support the trial court's finding that it exhibits strong indicia of substantive unconscionability. They do, and we therefore have no difficulty affirming the denial of Empire's motion to compel arbitration.

. . .

III. Severability

Empire argues that, even if the "carve-out" from arbitration for injunctive and declaratory relief, shortened limitations period and fee-shifting provisions are unconscionable, the court abused its discretion when it declined to sever them and otherwise enforce arbitration. We disagree.

. . . "An arbitration agreement can be considered permeated by unconscionability if it 'contains more than one unlawful provision . . . . Such multiple defects indicate a systematic effort to impose arbitration . . . not simply as an alternative to litigation, but as an inferior forum that works to the [stronger party's] advantage.' 'The overarching inquiry is whether " 'the interests of justice . . . would be furthered' " by severance.' " On this record, the trial court could, and presumably did, make that inquiry and conclude, reasonably, that severance would not serve the interests of justice.

IV. *Concepcion*

Finally, Empire contends the United States Supreme Court's recent decision in *Concepcion*, 131 S. Ct. 1740, extends the Federal Arbitration Act so broadly as to preempt each "unconscionability-based rationale" that supported the trial court's refusal to compel arbitration here. Empire reads *Concepcion* too broadly.

In *Discover Bank v. Superior Court* (2005) 36 Cal.4th 148 (*Discover Bank*), the California Supreme Court held that arbitration agreements in adhesive consumer contracts that forbid classwide arbitration are, as a general matter, unconscionable. . . .

Concepcion addresses whether the FAA preempts the *Discover Bank* rule. The United States Supreme Court held that it does, because "[r]equiring the availability of classwide arbitration interferes with fundamental attributes of arbitration and thus creates a scheme inconsistent with the FAA." But at the same time as the court repudiated the categorical rule in *Discover Bank*, it explicitly reaffirmed that the FAA "permits agreements to arbitrate to be invalidated by 'generally applicable contract defenses, such as fraud, duress, or unconscionability,' [although] not by defenses that apply only to arbitration or that derive their meaning from the fact that an agreement to arbitrate is at issue." In short, arbitration agreements remain subject, post-*Concepcion*, to the unconscionability analysis employed by the trial court in this case.

DISPOSITION

The order denying Empire's motion for a stay and to compel arbitration is affirmed.

NOTES

1.   In recent years, the majority of all unconscionability cases involve challenges to arbitration clauses. Susan Randall, *Judicial Attitudes Toward Arbitration and the Resurgence of Unconscionability*, 52 BUFFALO L. REV. 185, 194 (2004) (68.5% of unconscionability cases from 2002-2003 involved arbitration clauses). And unconscionability challenges to arbitration clauses — at least prior to the Supreme Court's decision in *AT&T Mobility LLC v. Concepcion* (see note 6) — were much more likely to succeed than unconscionability challenges to other contract clauses. Does that say more about the terms of arbitration clauses or about courts' views of arbitration, do you think?

2.   The California court in *Samaniego* analyzed the unconscionability issue by looking at both procedural unconscionability (an unfair bargaining process) and substantive unconscionability (unfair contract terms). Most courts require both

procedural and substantive unconscionability, albeit sometimes using a sliding scale such that a lot of one makes up for less of another. Which is more important here, procedural unconscionability or substantive unconscionability?

3. Some arbitration clauses (although not the clause in *Samaniego*) permit consumers or employees to opt out of the arbitration clause within some period of time after entering the contract. In Circuit City Stores, Inc. v. Ahmed, 283 F.3d 1198 (9th Cir. 2002), for example, the arbitration clause provided that as long as an employee returned an "opt-out" form to Circuit City within 30 days of receipt, he or she was excluded from the arbitration program and retained the right to go to court to resolve any dispute. Ahmed did not return the opt-out form, and when he later sought to bring a court action against Circuit City, he challenged the arbitration agreement as unconscionable. The court of appeals rejected the argument on the ground that "this case lacks the necessary element of procedural unconscionability." *Id.* at 1199. The court explained:

> Ahmed was not presented with a contract of adhesion because he was given the opportunity to opt-out of the Circuit City arbitration program by mailing in a simple one-page form. Moreover, and apart from its nonadhesive nature, the arbitration agreement here also lacked any other indicia of procedural unconscionability. The terms of the arbitration agreement were clearly spelled out in written materials and a videotape presentation; Ahmed was encouraged to contact Circuit City representatives or to consult an attorney prior to deciding whether to participate in the program; and he was given 30 days to decide whether to participate in the program.

> Ahmed argues that he was not given a meaningful opportunity to opt out of the arbitration program because he did not have the degree of sophistication necessary to recognize the meaning of the opt-out provision or to know how to avoid it, and because 30 days was too short a period in which to make a decision because "an employee is thinking positively about the employment relationship in the first 30 days." Ahmed cites no cases in support of these arguments. Moreover, the general rule is that "one who signs a contract is bound by its provisions and cannot complain of unfamiliarity with the language of the instrument." Ahmed was given ample opportunity to investigate any provisions he did not understand before deciding whether to opt out of Circuit City's arbitration program.

Id. at 1199-1200. How often do you suppose consumers or employees in fact opt out of arbitration clauses in their contracts? How, if at all, is that fact relevant to the issue of procedural unconscionability?

4. As for substantive unconscionability, the court of appeal found several provisions in the arbitration clause to be unconscionable: the clause shortened the time period in which the employee could file a claim, carved out actions for injunctive and declaratory relief from the obligation to arbitrate (i.e., it permitted parties to go to court to bring such actions), and contained a one-sided fee-shifting provision to the benefit of the employer. What is unfair about those provisions? Would the court have invalidated the arbitration clause if it had contained only some but not all of those provisions? What other types of provisions in arbitration clauses should be held to be unconscionable? What about the limited discovery available in

arbitration or the lack of a jury trial? Are those enough to make an arbitration clause unconscionable?

5. For a skeptical view of applying the doctrine of unconscionability to arbitration clauses (based at least in part on FAA preemption, which is the topic of Chapter 4), see Judge Frank Easterbrook's opinion in Carbajal v. H. & R. Block Tax Servs., Inc., 372 F.3d 903 (7th Cir. 2004):

> Section 2 of the Federal Arbitration Act says that an agreement to arbitrate "shall be valid, irrevocable, and enforceable, save upon such grounds as exist at law or in equity for the revocation of any contract." Thus arbitration specified in a form contract must be treated just like any other clause of the form. Unless Delaware (whose law applies) would refuse to enforce limited warranties, clauses curtailing the time available to file suit, and the like, then this arbitration clause must be enforced. Carbajal does not offer any reason to think that Delaware generally refuses to enforce details on the back of an auto-rental contract or equivalent form; thus this agreement to arbitrate is valid. The cry of "unconscionable!" just repackages the tired assertion that arbitration should be disparaged as second-class adjudication. It is precisely to still such cries that the Federal Arbitration Act equates arbitration with other contractual terms. *See Allied-Bruce Terminix Cos. v. Dobson.* People are free to opt for bargain-basement adjudication — or, for that matter, bargain-basement tax preparation services; air carriers that pack passengers like sardines but charge less; and black-and-white television. In competition, prices adjust and both sides gain. "Nothing but the best" may be the motto of a particular consumer but is not something the legal system foists on all consumers.

Id. at 906.

6. In *AT&T Mobility, LLC v. Concepcion,* discussed in *Samaniego* and examined at length in Chapter 4, the United States Supreme Court held that the FAA precludes states from invalidating arbitration clauses that contain class arbitration waivers as unconscionable. The extent to which unconscionability remains available as a ground for challenging the enforceability of an arbitration clause after *Concepcion* remains an open question, one that you should revisit after reading *Concepcion.*

PROBLEM 2.12

Mawson & Williams (see Problem 2.11) adopts a new dispute resolution program to cover all of its current and future employees. The program provides for all disputes between M & W and any employee to be arbitrated subject to the following provisions:

(1) All arbitrators must have at least 25 years of experience in the financial services industry;

(2) M & W retains the ability to go to court to seek provisional relief to enforce covenants not to compete entered into by employees; and

(3) Damages awarded in arbitration are limited to past wages owed to the employee.

If an employee challenges the arbitration agreement as unconscionable, is he or she likely to succeed? What might M & W do to enhance the likelihood that a court will uphold the program?

[D]   Fraud and Breach of Fiduciary Duty

ENGALLA v. PERMANENTE MEDICAL GROUP, INC.
Supreme Court of California
938 P.2d 903 (1997)

Mosk, Justice.

In this case we consider the circumstances under which a court may deny a petition to compel arbitration because of the petitioner's fraud in inducing the arbitration agreement. . . . Plaintiffs are family members and representatives of the estate of Wilfredo Engalla (hereafter sometimes the Engallas). Engalla was enrolled, through his place of employment, in a health plan operated by the Permanente Medical Group, Inc., Kaiser Foundation Hospitals, and the Kaiser Foundation Health Plan (hereafter Kaiser).

Prior to his death, Engalla was engaged in a medical malpractice dispute with Kaiser, which, according to the terms of Kaiser's "Group Medical and Hospital Services Agreement," was submitted to arbitration. After attempting unsuccessfully to conclude the arbitration prior to Engalla's death, the Engallas filed a malpractice action against Kaiser in superior court, and Kaiser filed a petition to compel arbitration pursuant to Code of Civil Procedure section 1281.2. In opposing the petition, plaintiffs claimed that Kaiser's self-administered arbitration system was corrupt or biased in a number of respects, that Kaiser fraudulently misrepresented the expeditiousness of its arbitration system, and that Kaiser engaged in a course of dilatory conduct in order to postpone Engalla's arbitration hearing until after his death, all of which should be grounds for refusing to enforce the arbitration agreement. The trial court found in the Engallas' favor, denying Kaiser's petition to compel arbitration on grounds of fraud, but the Court of Appeal reversed.

We conclude that there is indeed evidence to support the trial court's initial findings that Kaiser engaged in fraudulent conduct justifying a denial of its petition to compel arbitration, but we further conclude that questions of fact remain to be resolved by the trial court before it can be determined whether Kaiser's conduct was actually fraudulent. . . . We accordingly reverse the judgment of the Court of Appeal and direct it to remand the case to the trial court for such factual determinations. As will appear, although we affirm the basic policy in favor of enforcement of arbitration agreements, the governing statutes place limits on the extent to which a party that has committed misfeasance in the performance of such an agreement may compel its enforcement.

. . .

II. PROCEDURAL ISSUES

. . . The trial court was apparently of the view that it did not have to definitively decide the fraud issue in order to dispose of the petition, because that issue would be ultimately decided by a jury in the context of the Engallas' damages action. Because the trial court, understandably confused by case law, apparently abdicated its role as trier of fact in deciding the petition to compel arbitration, the case must be remanded to that court to resolve any factually disputed issues, unless there is no evidentiary support for the Engallas' claims. We turn then to the question whether there was such support.

III. FRAUD IN THE INDUCEMENT OF THE ARBITRATION AGREEMENT

The Engallas claim fraud in the inducement of the arbitration agreement and therefore that "[g]rounds exist for the revocation of the agreement" within the meaning of section 1281.2, subdivision (b). . . . Fraud is one of the grounds on which a contract can be rescinded. In order to defeat a petition to compel arbitration, the parties opposing a petition to compel must show that the asserted fraud claim goes specifically "to the 'making' of the agreement to arbitrate," rather than to the making of the contract in general. In the present case, the Engallas do allege, and seek to show, fraud in the making of the arbitration agreement.

The Engallas claim that Engalla was fraudulently induced to enter the arbitration agreement — in essence a claim of promissory fraud. . . . The elements of fraud that will give rise to a tort action for deceit are: " '(a) misrepresentation (false representation, concealment, or nondisclosure); (b) knowledge of falsity (or 'scienter'); (c) intent to defraud, i.e. to induce reliance; (d) justifiable reliance; and (e) resulting damage.' " . . .

Here the Engallas claim (1) that Kaiser misrepresented its arbitration agreement in that it entered into the agreement knowing that, at the very least, there was a likelihood its agents would breach the part of the agreement providing for the timely appointment of arbitrators and the expeditious progress towards an arbitration hearing; (2) that Kaiser employed the above misrepresentation in order to induce reliance on the part of Engalla and his employer; (3) that Engalla relied on these misrepresentations to his detriment. The trial court found evidence supporting those claims. We examine each of these claims in turn.

First, evidence of misrepresentation is plain. . . . [S]ection 8.B. of the arbitration agreement provides that party arbitrators "shall" be chosen within 30 days and neutral arbitrators within 60 days, and that the arbitration hearing "shall" be held "within a reasonable time thereafter." . . .

Here there are facts to support the Engallas' allegation that Kaiser entered into the arbitration agreement with knowledge that it would not comply with its own contractual timelines, or with at least a reckless indifference as to whether its agents would use reasonable diligence and good faith to comply with them. . . . [A] survey of Kaiser arbitrations between 1984 and 1986 submitted into evidence showed that a neutral arbitrator was appointed within 60 days in only 1 percent of the cases, with only 3 percent appointed within 180 days, and that on average the neutral arbitrator was appointed 674 days — almost 2 years — after the demand for arbitration. Regardless of when Kaiser became aware of these precise statistics, which were part of a 1989 study, the depositions of two of Kaiser's in-house attorneys demonstrate that Kaiser was aware soon after it began its arbitration program that its contractual deadlines were not being met, and that severe delay was endemic to the program. Kaiser nonetheless persisted in its contractual promises of expeditiousness.

Kaiser now argues that most of these delays were caused by the claimants themselves and their attorneys, who procrastinated in the selection of a neutral arbitrator. But Kaiser's counterexplanation is without any statistical support, and is based solely on anecdotal evidence related by Kaiser officials. Moreover, the explanation appears implausible in view of the sheer pervasiveness of the delays. . . . It is, after all, the defense which often benefits from delay, thereby preserving the status quo to its advantage until the time when memories fade and claims are abandoned. Indeed, the present case illustrates why Kaiser's counsel may sometimes find it advantageous to delay the selection of a neutral arbitrator. There is also evidence that Kaiser kept extensive records on the arbitrators it had used, and may have delayed the selection process in order to ensure that it would obtain the arbitrators it thought would best serve its interests. Thus, it is a reasonable inference from the documentary record before us that Kaiser's contractual representations of expeditiousness were made with knowledge of their likely falsity, and in fact concealed an unofficial policy or practice of delay.

The systemwide nature of Kaiser's delay comes into clearer focus when it is contrasted with other arbitration systems. As the Engallas point out, many large institutional users of arbitration, including most health maintenance organizations (HMO's), avoid the potential problems of delay in the selection of arbitrators by contracting with neutral third party organizations, such as the American Arbitration Association (AAA). These organizations will then assume responsibility for administering the claim from the time the arbitration demand is filed, and will ensure the arbitrator or arbitrators are chosen in a timely manner. Though Kaiser is not obliged by law to adopt any particular form of arbitration, the record shows that it did not attempt to create within its own organization any office that would neutrally administer the arbitration program, but instead entrusted such administration to outside counsel retained to act as advocates on its behalf. In other words, there is evidence that Kaiser established a self-administered arbitration system in which delay for its own benefit and convenience was an inherent part, despite express and implied contractual representations to the contrary.

A fraudulent state of mind includes not only knowledge of falsity of the misrepresentation but also an "intent to . . . induce reliance" on it. It can be reasonably inferred in the present case that these misrepresentations of expeditiousness, which are found not only in the contract but in newsletters periodically sent to subscribers touting the virtues of the Kaiser arbitration program, were made by Kaiser to encourage these subscribers to believe that its program would function efficiently. . . .

Kaiser also claims that the Engallas failed to demonstrate actual reliance on its misrepresentations . . .

. . .

. . . [W]e conclude that Kaiser's representations of expeditiousness in the arbitration agreement were not "so obviously unimportant" as to render them immaterial as a matter of law. We have recognized that expeditiousness is commonly regarded as one of the primary advantages of arbitration. . . . The explicit and implicit representations contained in Kaiser's arbitration agreement serve to confirm to the reasonable potential subscriber that Kaiser has an efficient system of arbitration, in which what is lost in terms of jury trial rights would be gained in part by a swifter resolution of the dispute. If it is indeed the case that these representations were false, and concealed an arbitration process in which substantial delay was the rule and timeliness the rare exception, then we cannot say these misrepresentations were so trivial that they would not have influenced a reasonable employer's decision as to which among the many competing employee health plans it would choose for its employees.

. . .

We turn then to the question of injury. A defrauded party has the right to rescind a contract, even without a showing of pecuniary damages, on establishing that fraudulent contractual promises inducing reliance have been breached. . . . Of course, the Engallas cannot defeat a petition to compel arbitration on the mere showing that Kaiser has engaged generally in fraudulent misrepresentation about the speed of the arbitration process.

Rather, they must show that in their particular case, there was substantial delay in the selection of arbitrators contrary to their reasonable, fraudulently induced, contractual expectations. Here, there is ample evidence to support the Engallas' contention that Kaiser breached its arbitration agreement by repeatedly delaying the timely appointment of an available party arbitrator and a neutral arbitrator.

. . .

In sum, we conclude there is evidence to support the Engallas' claims that Kaiser fraudulently induced Engalla to enter the arbitration agreement in that it misrepresented the speed of its arbitration program, a misrepresentation on which Engalla's employer relied by selecting Kaiser's health plan for its employees, and that the Engallas suffered delay in the resolution of its malpractice dispute as a result of that reliance, despite Engalla's own reasonable diligence. The trial court, on remand, must resolve conflicting factual evidence in order to properly adjudicate Kaiser's petition to compel arbitration.

. . .

NOTES

1.   While the *Engalla* case was pending, and to a large degree in response to the *Engalla* litigation, the California legislature enacted section 1373.20(a) of the California Health & Safety Code:

> If a plan uses arbitration to settle disputes with enrollees or subscribers, and does not use a professional dispute resolution organization independent

of the plan that has a procedure for a rapid selection, or default appointment, of neutral arbitrators, the following requirements shall be met by the plan with respect to the arbitration of the disputes and shall not be subject to waiver:

> (1) If the party seeking arbitration and the plan against which arbitration is sought, in cases or disputes requiring a single neutral arbitrator, are unable to select a neutral arbitrator within 30 days after service of a written demand requesting the designation, it shall be conclusively presumed that the agreed method of selection has failed and the method provided in Section 1281.6 of the Code of Civil Procedure [providing for court appointment of arbitrators] may be utilized.

> (2) In cases or disputes in which the parties have agreed to use a tripartite arbitration panel consisting of two party arbitrators and one neutral arbitrator, and the party arbitrators are unable to agree on the designation of a neutral arbitrator within 30 days after service of a written demand requesting the designation, it shall be conclusively presumed that the agreed method of selection has failed and the method provided in Section 1281.6 of the Code of Civil Procedure may be utilized. . . .

Will the availability of court appointment of arbitrators eliminate the delays in *Engalla*? Does it make sense to distinguish between independent and nonindependent administrators, as the California statute does?

2. Did Kaiser have a duty to disclose to the Engallas anything about possible differences between arbitration and litigation? Or simply to refrain from affirmative misrepresentations?

HODGES v. REASONOVER
Louisiana Supreme Court
2012 La. LEXIS 1962 (July 2, 2012)

KNOLL, J.

We are called on to decide whether a binding arbitration clause in an attorney-client retainer agreement is enforceable where the client has filed suit for legal malpractice. This case presents two important countervailing public policies: Louisiana and federal law explicitly favor the enforcement of arbitration clauses in written contracts; by the same token, Louisiana law also imposes a fiduciary duty of the highest order requiring attorneys to act with the utmost fidelity and forthrightness in their dealings with clients, and any contractual clause which may limit the client's rights against the attorney is subject to close scrutiny.

After our careful study, we hold there is no *per se* rule against arbitration clauses in attorney-client retainer agreements, provided the clause is fair and reasonable to the client. However, the attorneys' fiduciary obligation to the client encompasses ethical duties of loyalty and candor, which in turn require attorneys to fully disclose the scope and the terms of the arbitration clause. An attorney must clearly explain the precise types of disputes the arbitration clause is meant to cover and must set forth, in plain language, those legal rights the parties will give up by agreeing to arbitration. In this case, the defendants did not make the necessary disclosures, thus, the arbitration clause is unenforceable. Accordingly, the judgment of the lower courts is affirmed.

FACTS AND PROCEDURAL HISTORY

For completeness, we will briefly describe the underlying representation by defendants. Jacqueline Hodges is the founder, sole shareholder, and Chief Executive Officer of Med-Data Management, Inc. ("Med-Data") and its successor entity, HRC Solutions, Inc. This dispute ultimately arises out of a 2005 asset sale between Med-Data and a company known as MedAssets, Inc. Med-Data developed software used by hospitals to manage their billing and medical insurance claims. Med-Data sold the rights to the software to MedAssets, Inc., in exchange for an upfront cash payment and a portion of any future sales of the former Med-Data software, provided a certain minimum threshold was met. On September 25, 2007, MedAssets informed Hodges it had not met the threshold of sales necessary to trigger additional payments.

Plaintiffs retained Kirk Reasonover, of the law firm of Reasonover & Olinde, to sue MedAssets in federal court in Atlanta, Georgia. Reasonover and the Hodges had an ongoing business relationship since 1998. The parties agreed to a "blended" fee schedule, meaning the firm charged a reduced hourly rate in exchange for taking a contingency interest in the case. The retainer agreement contained the following arbitration clause:

> Any dispute, disagreement or controversy of any kind concerning this agreement, the services provided hereunder, or any other dispute of any nature or kind that may arise among us, shall be submitted to arbitration, in New Orleans, Louisiana. Such arbitration shall be submitted to the American Arbitration Association.

The retainer agreement was dated August 27, 2007, and signed by both Jacqueline and Stephen Hodges. On December 3, 2007, the Hodges filed a complaint against MedAssets in the Northern District of Georgia federal court, alleging breach of contract and breach of the duty of good faith and fair dealing. MedAssets filed a motion to dismiss, citing the binding alternative dispute resolution clause in the asset purchase agreement. The court found the clause only applied to disputes over the amount of the payout, and not to allegations of breach of the duty of good faith and fair dealing, and denied the motion.

In August 2009, Stephen Hodges approached Kirk Reasonover and asked whether Reasonover & Olinde would be open to renegotiating the original retainer agreement. Defendants agreed, and the parties entered into a "revised fee agreement" based purely on a contingency fee. The revised fee agreement contained an arbitration clause identical to the one in the original agreement and stated "[b]ecause this agreement involves the acquisition of an additional interest in your case, and your interests in this transaction are adverse to ours, you should review this agreement with independent counsel." The Hodges chose not to retain independent counsel and signed the revised fee agreement on August 31, 2009.

Plaintiffs' claims against MedAssets ultimately failed to survive a motion for summary judgment. This suit for legal malpractice followed. Defendants filed declinatory exceptions alleging improper venue and lack of subject matter jurisdiction based on the binding arbitration clause.

The District Court denied defendants' exceptions . . . . The court found the mandatory arbitration clause was a prospective limitation of liability [contrary to Louisiana Rule of Professional Conduct 18(h)(1)] and, because the Hodges were not represented by independent counsel, the arbitration clause was invalid. The court of appeal denied defendants' request for supervisory writs, Judge Bonin dissenting. We granted writs to address the enforceability of mandatory arbitration clauses in attorney-client agreements.

Applicable Legal Principles

The positive law of Louisiana favors arbitration as a preferred method of alternative dispute resolution. . . . Similarly, the Federal Arbitration Act ("FAA") reflects a "liberal federal policy favoring arbitration agreements, notwithstanding any state substantive or procedural policies to the contrary." To the extent that federal and state law differ, the FAA preempts state law as to any written arbitration agreement in a contract involving interstate commerce.

At the same time, agreements between law firms and clients are held to higher scrutiny than normal commercial contracts because of the fiduciary duties involved. "The relation of attorney and client is more than a contract. It superinduces a trust status of the highest order and devolves upon the attorney the imperative duty of dealing with the client on the basis of the strictest fidelity and honor." "In no other agency relationship is a greater duty of trust imposed than in that involving an attorney's duty to his client." An attorney is also bound by the ethical requirements set forth in the Louisiana Rules of Professional Conduct, which have the force of substantive law. An attorney-client contract which directly violates a disciplinary rule is unenforceable. . . .

Analysis

Louisiana Rule of Professional Conduct 1.8(h)(1) prohibits a lawyer from "prospectively limiting the lawyer's liability to a client for malpractice unless the client is independently represented in making the agreement." The question of whether an arbitration clause is a prospective limitation of liability is *res nova* in Louisiana, but has arisen in other jurisdictions. The American Bar Association Ethics Committee issued a formal opinion stating that an arbitration clause does not violate Model Rule of Professional Conduct 1.8(h)(1), which is identical to the Louisiana rule, unless some aspect of the arbitration clause limits the lawyer's substantive liability:

> [M]andatory arbitration provisions are proper unless the retainer agreement insulates the lawyer from liability or limits the liability to which

she otherwise would be exposed under common or statutory law. For example, if the law of the jurisdiction precludes an award of punitive damages in arbitration but permits punitive damages in malpractice lawsuits, the provision would violate Rule 1.8(h) unless that client is independently represented in making the agreement.

ABA Formal Ethics Opinion 02-425.

We agree. Unless otherwise limited by the parties' contract or the rules of the specific arbitral tribunal, arbitrators have the power to render whatever relief is justified by the record, to the full extent provided for by law and equity. "By agreeing to arbitrate a statutory claim, a party does not forgo the substantive rights afforded by the statute; it only submits to their resolution in an arbitral, rather than a judicial, forum. It trades the procedures and opportunity for review of the courtroom for the simplicity, informality, and expedition of arbitration." *Mitsubishi Motors.* Provided the arbitrator retains full authority to render an award fully compensating a client for his injuries, most state ethics committees have held an arbitration clause is not a true limitation of an attorney's liability . . . .

Reasonover & Olinde argue this clause does not insulate defendants from liability because it does not purport to hold the firm harmless, change the standard of care, exclude any category of damages, or create any unreasonable procedural requirements which will effectively prevent plaintiffs from seeking recovery. The agreement specifically calls for the application of Louisiana substantive law to the arbitral proceedings, meaning the Hodges are entitled to the same rights and remedies as if the case were being heard in state court.

Plaintiffs admit the arbitration clause places no explicit limitations on defendants' substantive liability but claim there are unreasonable procedural barriers which may deter clients from bringing claims in arbitration. Specifically, plaintiffs claim the initial filing fees for the American Arbitration Association ("AAA") are $18,800, compared with the roughly $500 fee for filing a petition in Orleans Parish Civil District Court. Plaintiffs contend the substantial upfront costs of AAA arbitration may discourage would-be litigants from filing arbitration claims against their attorneys, thus protecting the attorneys from malpractice liability. The Hodges admit they can afford the AAA initial filing fee, but there are many potential litigants who cannot pay such a significant sum.

Nonetheless, we do not believe the initial filing fee constitutes a "prospective limitation of liability" under the meaning of Rule 1.8(h)(1). We note the AAA allows parties whose income is below 200% of the federal poverty guidelines to seek a waiver of the initial filing fees, and the arbitrator, in his discretion, may apportion the arbitration expenses at the close of the proceedings.

It is an unfortunate reality that litigation can be a costly endeavor, whether in state court, federal court, or arbitration. Initial filing fees are only a small part of the costs associated with high-stakes commercial litigation. Indeed, comparatively low cost is often touted as one of the primary benefits of arbitration over litigation. Arbitration generally provides for streamlined discovery, little to no motion practice, and flexible procedure, all of which may potentially save significant amounts of time and money and thus recoup the initial filing costs. Given these factors, we cannot say the overall costs of arbitration will be so clearly burdensome to the client as to constitute an effective limit of liability.

. . .

. . . An arbitration clause does not inherently limit or alter either party's substantive rights; it simply provides for an alternative venue for the resolution of disputes. The AAA is a well-known alternative dispute resolution organization, and there is no evidence that arbitration conducted in accordance with AAA rules, before AAA-approved arbitrators, would be presumptively unfair or biased. In summary, a binding arbitration clause between an attorney and client does not violate Rule of Professional Conduct 1.8(h) provided the clause does not limit the attorney's substantive liability, provides for a neutral decision maker, and is otherwise fair and reasonable to the client.

Our analysis, however, does not end here. The Hodges also urge this Court to find the arbitration clause unenforceable because Reasonover & Olinde did not adequately disclose the full scope of the arbitration clause and the potential consequences of agreeing to binding arbitration.

An attorney's fiduciary duties include the duties of candor and loyalty in all dealings with a client. The duty of candor requires a lawyer to "explain a matter to the extent reasonably necessary to permit the client to make informed decisions regarding the representation." ABA Model Rule of Professional Conduct 1.4(b). The duty of loyalty forbids a lawyer from taking any action in his own self-interest which would have an adverse effect on the client.

Inherent in these duties is the principle that an attorney cannot take any action adversely affecting the client's interest unless the client has been fully apprised, to the extent reasonably practicable, of the risks and possible consequences thereof — that is, the client must give informed consent. Louisiana Rule of Professional Conduct 1.0(e) defines "informed consent" as consent given after a "lawyer has communicated adequate information and explanation about the material risks of and reasonably available alternatives to the proposed course of conduct." In the context of attorney-client arbitration clauses, this means the lawyer has an obligation to fully explain to the client the possible consequences of entering into an arbitration clause, including the legal rights the client gives up by agreeing to binding arbitration. Without clear and explicit disclosure of the consequences of a binding arbitration clause, the client's consent is not truly "informed."

Louisiana law has long required attorneys to fully disclose all risks to the client before entering into a contract with the potential to negatively affect the client's rights. This is certainly the case with binding arbitration clauses, which affect the client's rights to a jury and appeal. Attorneys, by virtue of their legal education and training, have an advantage over clients, who may not understand the arbitration process and the full effects of an arbitration clause. At a minimum, the attorney must disclose the following legal effects of binding arbitration, assuming they are applicable:

- Waiver of the right to a jury trial;

- Waiver of the right to an appeal;

- Waiver of the right to broad discovery under the Louisiana Code of Civil Procedure and/or Federal Rules of Civil Procedure;

- Arbitration may involve substantial upfront costs compared to litigation;

- Explicit disclosure of the nature of claims covered by the arbitration clause, such as fee disputes or malpractice claims;

- The arbitration clause does not impinge upon the client's right to make a disciplinary complaint to the appropriate authorities;

- The client has the opportunity to speak with independent counsel before signing the contract.

Given these principles, we find Reasonover & Olinde failed to make the necessary full disclosures to the Hodges. The arbitration clause did not specifically enumerate the types of disputes it was meant to cover, including malpractice claims. Defendants never mentioned malpractice while negotiating the contract, and Stephen Hodges testified that, to his understanding, the arbitration clause was only intended to cover fee disputes: "I was not even contemplating malpractice. It was not even considered. We didn't even know to ask the question . . . . We assumed that it was an arbitration of fees. And I would say again that we had a ten year relationship with Kirk Reasonover and paid him. And I will tell you that we had no fee disputes in ten years, so it seemed largely inconsequential." Although the fee agreement does advise the Hodges of their right to speak with independent counsel, it does not warn of the waiver of the right to a jury trial, the right to appeal, and the right to broad discovery.

Defendants argue these disclosures were unnecessary because the Hodges are sophisticated businesspeople who understood the effects of arbitration, as the applicability of an arbitration clause was a major issue in the Hodges' lawsuit against MedAssets. We decline to find the extent of an attorney's fiduciary duty depends on the sophistication of the client. To do so would create two classes of clients and implicitly hold that well-educated, business-savvy clients are somehow less deserving of an attorney's full candor and loyalty. This rule would be directly contrary to the high ethical standards set forth in the Rules of Professional Conduct and repugnant to Louisiana public policy. Thus, the Hodges' alleged sophistication and familiarity with arbitration are irrelevant; they are entitled to the same warnings and disclosures as any client.

Conclusion

In summary, we find arbitration clauses in attorney-client agreements may be enforceable, provided the contract does not limit the attorney's substantive liability, is fair and reasonable to the client, and does not impose any undue procedural barrier to a client seeking relief. However, an attorney must make full and complete disclosure of the potential effects of an arbitration clause, including the waiver of a jury trial, the waiver of the right to appeal, the waiver of broad discovery rights, and the possible high upfront costs of arbitration. The contract must explicitly list the types of disputes covered by the arbitration clause, e.g., legal malpractice, and make clear that the client retains the right to lodge a disciplinary complaint. Because those requirements were not met in this case, the arbitration clause is not enforceable.

The judgment of the lower courts is affirmed, and the matter is remanded to the district court for further proceedings.

AFFIRMED AND REMANDED.

NOTE

How do the disclosure obligations of attorneys under *Hodges* compare to the disclosure obligations of Kaiser under *Engalla*? Does the distinction make sense? Who is more likely to understand the differences between arbitration and litigation, Engalla or the Hodges? Should that affect the extent of required disclosures?

PROBLEM 2.13

Mawson & Williams (see Problem 2.12) undertakes an extensive informational campaign among its employees, seeking to convince them to agree to arbitration by informing them of its benefits. Prominent in the informational literature is the statement that "you are more likely to recover in arbitration than you are in court." The campaign is very successful, with virtually all M&W employees signing pre-dispute arbitration agreements by the time the campaign ends. Shortly thereafter, an internal management memo is leaked to the employees. The memo reports management's estimates that juries find in favor of employees 60 percent of the time in court cases against M&W, while arbitrators find in favor of employees only 10 percent of the time.

A group of employees, relying on *Engalla*, seeks to have the arbitration agreements they signed invalidated because of fraud. They make two arguments. First, they rely on the internal memo to argue that M&W misrepresented to them that "you are more likely to recover in arbitration than you are in court." Second, they argue that M&W misled the employees by not telling them that by agreeing to arbitration, they effectively give up the right to be party to a class action. How is a court likely to rule on the employees' arguments? How would your analysis differ if Mawson & Williams was a law firm entering into fee agreements with its clients?

[E]   Material Breach

HOOTERS OF AMERICA, INC. v. PHILLIPS
United States Court of Appeals for the Fourth Circuit
173 F.3d 933 (1999)

WILKINSON, CHIEF JUDGE:

Annette R. Phillips alleges that she was sexually harassed while working at a Hooters restaurant. After quitting her job, Phillips threatened to sue Hooters in court. Alleging that Phillips agreed to arbitrate employment-related disputes, Hooters preemptively filed suit to compel arbitration under the Federal Arbitration Act, 9 U.S.C. § 4. Because Hooters set up a dispute resolution process utterly lacking in the rudiments of even-handedness, we hold that Hooters breached its agreement to arbitrate. Thus, we affirm the district court's refusal to compel arbitration.

I.

Appellee Annette R. Phillips worked as a bartender at a Hooters restaurant in Myrtle Beach, South Carolina. She was employed since 1989 by appellant Hooters of Myrtle Beach (HOMB), a franchisee of appellant Hooters of America (collectively Hooters).

Phillips alleges that in June 1996, Gerald Brooks, a Hooters official and the brother of HOMB's principal owner, sexually harassed her by grabbing and slapping her buttocks. After appealing to her manager for help and being told to "let it go," she quit her job. Phillips then contacted Hooters through an attorney claiming that the attack and the restaurant's failure to address it violated her Title VII rights. Hooters responded that she was required to submit her claims to arbitration according to a binding agreement to arbitrate between the parties.

This agreement arose in 1994 during the implementation of Hooters' alternative dispute resolution program. As part of that program, the company conditioned eligibility for raises, transfers, and promotions upon an employee signing an "Agreement to arbitrate employment-related disputes." The agreement provides that Hooters and the employee each agree to arbitrate all disputes arising out of employment, including "any claim of discrimination, sexual harassment, retaliation, or wrongful discharge, whether arising under federal or state law." The agreement further states that the employee and the company agree to resolve any claims pursuant to the company's rules and procedures for alternative resolution of employment-related disputes, as promulgated by the company from time to time ("the rules"). Company will make available or provide a copy of the rules upon written request of the employee.

The employees of HOMB were initially given a copy of this agreement at an all-staff meeting held on November 20, 1994. HOMB's general manager, Gene Fulcher, told the employees to review the agreement for five days and that they would then be asked to accept or reject the agreement. No employee, however, was given a copy of Hooters' arbitration rules and procedures. Phillips signed the agreement on November 25, 1994. When her personnel file was updated in April 1995, Phillips again signed the agreement.

After Phillips quit her job in June 1996, Hooters sent to her attorney a copy of the Hooters rules then in effect. Phillips refused to arbitrate the dispute.

Hooters filed suit in November 1996 to compel arbitration under 9 U.S.C. § 4. Phillips defended on the grounds that the agreement to arbitrate was unenforceable. . . .

In March 1998, the district court denied Hooters' motions to compel arbitration and stay proceedings on the counterclaims. The court found that there was no meeting of the minds on all of the material terms of the agreement and even if there were, Hooters' promise to arbitrate was illusory. In addition, the court found that the arbitration agreement was unconscionable and void for reasons of public policy. Hooters filed this interlocutory appeal, 9 U.S.C. § 16.

II.

The benefits of arbitration are widely recognized. Parties agree to arbitrate to secure "streamlined proceedings and expeditious results [that] will best serve their needs." The arbitration of disputes enables parties to avoid the costs associated with pursuing a judicial resolution of their grievances. By one estimate, litigating a typical employment dispute costs at least $50,000 and takes two and one-half years to resolve. Further, the adversarial nature of litigation diminishes the possibility that the parties will be able to salvage their relationship. For these reasons parties agree to arbitrate and trade "the procedures and opportunity for review of the courtroom for the simplicity, informality, and expedition of arbitration."

. . .

III.

. . . The question remains whether a binding arbitration agreement between Phillips and Hooters exists and compels Phillips to submit her Title VII claims to arbitration. . . .

Hooters argues that Phillips gave her assent to a bilateral agreement to arbitrate. That contract provided for the resolution by arbitration of all employment-related disputes, including claims arising under Title VII. Hooters claims the agreement to arbitrate is valid because Phillips twice signed it voluntarily. Thus, it argues the courts are bound to enforce it and compel arbitration.

We disagree. The judicial inquiry, while highly circumscribed, is not focused solely on an examination for contractual formation defects such as lack of mutual assent and want of consideration. Courts also can investigate the existence of "such grounds as exist at law or in equity for the revocation of any contract." However, the grounds for revocation must relate specifically to the arbitration clause and not just to the contract as a whole. *Prima Paint Corp. v. Flood & Conklin Mfg. Co.* In this case, the challenge goes to the validity of the arbitration agreement itself. Hooters materially breached the arbitration agreement by promulgating rules so egregiously unfair as to constitute a complete default of its contractual obligation to draft arbitration rules and to do so in good faith.

Hooters and Phillips agreed to settle any disputes between them not in a judicial forum, but in another neutral forum — arbitration. Their agreement provided that Hooters was responsible for setting up such a forum by promulgating arbitration rules and procedures. To this end, Hooters instituted a set of rules in July 1996.

The Hooters rules when taken as a whole, however, are so one-sided that their only possible purpose is to undermine the neutrality of the proceeding. The rules require the employee to provide the company notice of her claim at the outset, including "the nature of the Claim" and "the specific act(s) or omissions(s) which are the basis of the Claim." Hooters, on the other hand, is not required to file any responsive pleadings or to notice its defenses. Additionally, at the time of filing this notice, the employee must provide the company with a list of all fact witnesses with a brief summary of the facts known to each. The company, however, is not required to reciprocate.

The Hooters rules also provide a mechanism for selecting a panel of three arbitrators that is crafted to ensure a biased decisionmaker. The employee and Hooters each select an arbitrator, and the two arbitrators in turn select a third. Good enough, except that the employee's arbitrator and the third arbitrator must be selected from a list of arbitrators created exclusively by Hooters. This gives Hooters control over the entire panel and places no limits whatsoever on whom Hooters can put on the list. Under the rules, Hooters is free to devise lists of partial arbitrators who have existing relationships, financial or familial, with Hooters and its management. In fact, the rules do not even prohibit Hooters from placing its managers themselves on the list. Further, nothing in the rules restricts Hooters from punishing arbitrators who rule against the company by removing them from the list. Given the unrestricted control that one party (Hooters) has over the panel, the selection of an impartial decision maker would be a surprising result.

Nor is fairness to be found once the proceedings are begun. Although Hooters may expand the scope of arbitration to any matter, "whether related or not to the Employee's Claim," the employee cannot raise "any matter not included in the Notice of Claim." Similarly, Hooters is permitted to move for summary dismissal of employee claims before a hearing is held whereas the employee is not permitted to seek summary judgment. Hooters, but not the employee, may record the arbitration hearing "by audio or videotaping or by verbatim transcription." The rules also grant Hooters the right to bring suit in court to vacate or modify an arbitral award when it can show, by a preponderance of the evidence, that the panel exceeded its authority. No such right is granted to the employee.

In addition, the rules provide that upon 30 days notice Hooters, but not the employee, may cancel the agreement to arbitrate. Moreover, Hooters reserves the right to modify the rules, "in whole or in part," whenever it wishes and "without notice" to the employee. Nothing in the rules even prohibits Hooters from changing the rules in the middle of an arbitration proceeding.

If by odd chance the unfairness of these rules were not apparent on their face, leading arbitration experts have decried their one-sidedness. George Friedman, senior vice president of the American Arbitration Association (AAA), testified that the system established by the Hooters rules so deviated from minimum due process standards that the Association would refuse to arbitrate under those rules. George Nicolau, former president of both the National Academy of Arbitrators and the International Society of Professionals in Dispute Resolution, attested that the Hooters rules "are inconsistent with the concept of fair and impartial arbitration." He also testified that he was "certain that reputable designating agencies, such as the AAA and Jams/Endispute, would refuse to administer a program so unfair and one-sided as this one." Additionally, Dennis Nolan, professor of labor law at the

University of South Carolina, declared that the Hooters rules "do not satisfy the minimum requirements of a fair arbitration system." He found that the "most serious flaw" was that the "mechanism [for selecting arbitrators] violates the most fundamental aspect of justice, namely an impartial decision maker." Finally, Lewis Maltby, member of the Board of Directors of the AAA, testified that "This is without a doubt the most unfair arbitration program I have ever encountered."

. . .

We hold that the promulgation of so many biased rules — especially the scheme whereby one party to the proceeding so controls the arbitral panel — breaches the contract entered into by the parties. The parties agreed to submit their claims to arbitration — a system whereby disputes are fairly resolved by an impartial third party. Hooters by contract took on the obligation of establishing such a system. By creating a sham system unworthy even of the name of arbitration, Hooters completely failed in performing its contractual duty.

Moreover, Hooters had a duty to perform its obligations in good faith. *See* Restatement (Second) of Contracts § 205 (1981) ("Every contract imposes upon each party a duty of good faith and fair dealing in its performance and its enforcement."). Good faith "emphasizes faithfulness to an agreed common purpose and consistency with the justified expectations of the other party." Restatement (Second) of Contracts § 205 cmt. a. Bad faith includes the "evasion of the spirit of the bargain" and an "abuse of a power to specify terms." *Id.* § 205 cmt. d. By agreeing to settle disputes in arbitration, Phillips agreed to the prompt and economical resolution of her claims. She could legitimately expect that arbitration would not entail procedures so wholly one-sided as to present a stacked deck. Thus we conclude that the Hooters rules also violate the contractual obligation of good faith.

Given Hooters' breaches of the arbitration agreement and Phillips' desire not to be bound by it, we hold that rescission is the proper remedy. Generally, "rescission will not be granted for a minor or casual breach of a contract, but only for those breaches which defeat the object of the contracting parties." As we have explained, Hooters' breach is by no means insubstantial; its performance under the contract was so egregious that the result was hardly recognizable as arbitration at all. We therefore permit Phillips to cancel the agreement and thus Hooters' suit to compel arbitration must fail.

IV.

We respect fully the Supreme Court's pronouncement that "questions of arbitrability must be addressed with a healthy regard for the federal policy favoring arbitration." Our decision should not be misread: We are not holding that the agreement before us is unenforceable because the arbitral proceedings are too abbreviated. An arbitral forum need not replicate the judicial forum. . . .

Nor should our decision be misunderstood as permitting a full-scale assault on the fairness of proceedings before the matter is submitted to arbitration. Generally, objections to the nature of arbitral proceedings are for the arbitrator to decide in the first instance. Only after arbitration may a party then raise such challenges if they meet the narrow grounds set out in 9 U.S.C. § 10 for vacating an arbitral award. In the case before us, we only reach the content of the arbitration rules because their promulgation was the duty of one party under the contract. The material breach of this duty warranting rescission is an issue of substantive arbitrability and thus is reviewable before arbitration. This case, however, is the exception that proves the rule: fairness objections should generally be made to the arbitrator, subject only to limited post-arbitration judicial review as set forth in section 10 of the FAA.

By promulgating this system of warped rules, Hooters so skewed the process in its favor that Phillips has been denied arbitration in any meaningful sense of the word. To uphold the promulgation of this aberrational scheme under the heading of arbitration would undermine, not advance, the federal policy favoring alternative dispute resolution. This we refuse to do.

The judgment of the district court is affirmed, and the case is remanded for further proceedings consistent with this opinion.

NOTES

1. What evidence was there in *Hooters* about how the arbitration system operated in practice? Should the court have required such evidence before refusing to enforce the arbitration agreement?

2. What if the arbitration rules that the court found objectionable had been included in an employment contract signed by Phillips at the time she was hired? Would the court's reasoning have been the same? Would the court have ordered Phillips to arbitrate?

3. For another application of the doctrine of material breach to arbitration agreements, see Brown v. Dillard's, Inc., 430 F.3d 1004 (2005) (holding that Dillard's could not enforce arbitration agreement against employee when it had previously breached agreement by refusing to arbitrate dispute brought by employee).

PROBLEM 2.14

The City and Suburban Bank (see Problem 2.9) revises its standard credit card account agreement to provide as follows: "We may change any term, condition, service or feature of your Account at any time. We may also add new terms, conditions, services or features to your Account. We will provide you notice of the change to the extent required by law." Under which of the following circumstances do the bank's credit card customers have any argument under *Hooters* that the arbitration agreement is unenforceable?

(a) The Bank's standard account agreement also provides that all disputes are to be resolved by arbitration under arbitration rules promulgated by the bank. When the bank subsequently promulgates its arbitration rules, those rules require all arbitrators currently to be employed by a bank that issues credit cards.

(b) The Bank sends its customers notice that the terms of the account agreement are changed to provide for all disputes to be resolved by arbitration and to require all arbitrators currently to be employed by a bank that issues credit cards.

(c) The Bank's standard account agreement also provides that all disputes are to be resolved by arbitration and requires all arbitrators currently to work for a bank that issues credit cards.

PROBLEM 2.15

After Percy Phelps clears up his previous difficulties (see Problem 2.6), he begins work at Harrison, Inc. On his first day of work, Phelps is given a copy of the Harrison Employee Handbook, which he is told contains important company policies. The first page of the Handbook states: "The terms and policies contained in this Handbook are subject to change by Harrison, Inc. at any time. The change will take effect two weeks after you receive notice of it." Phelps knew nothing about the Handbook before he started work. But while signing a number of other forms in the Human Resources Department, he signs (without reading what he is signing) a form agreeing to comply with the policies in the Handbook.

After Phelps has worked at Harrison for less than a month, and before he receives any sort of promotion or raise, Harrison gives all of its employees notice of the terms of a new Alternative Dispute Resolution Program to be added to the Employee Handbook. The notice touts the ADR program as a "fair, fast, and low cost" way of resolving disputes between the company and employees. Under the terms of the ADR program, "all disputes or claims arising under the contract" are to be resolved by arbitration. Although the description of the program is quite vague about the precise procedures to be followed in arbitration, it does make clear that (1) when employees file a claim they must pay half of the administrative and arbitrators' fees that result; and (2) Harrison, but not the employee, can go to court to seek injunctive relief on any legally permissible ground.

Phelps soon gets fired when he allegedly misplaces several more highly confidential documents. He still has not gotten a promotion or raise. Phelps files suit against Harrison, alleging breach of contract and slander and libel. Harrison files an answer in the lawsuit and engages in some perfunctory discovery practice, and only then files a motion to stay the proceedings pending arbitration. How should the court rule on Harrison's motion? Be sure and consider the full array of arguments that Phelps might make in seeking to avoid arbitration.

§ 2.06 BINDING NON-SIGNATORIES TO AGREEMENTS TO ARBITRATE

This section addresses the circumstances under which a person or entity is bound by an agreement to arbitrate even though not a signatory to the agreement. We have already seen one example. In *First Options of Chicago, Inc. v. Kaplan*, the arbitrator concluded that the Kaplans were bound to arbitrate under an agreement signed only by their wholly owned investment company. The issue is one of assent. As always, a party cannot be required to arbitrate if it did not agree to do so. The following case examines a variety of theories under which such assent can be found even though the party was not a signatory to the arbitration agreement at issue.

THOMSON-CSF, S.A. v. AMERICAN ARBITRATION ASSOCIATION
United States Court of Appeals for the Second Circuit
64 F.3d 773 (1995)

ALTIMARI, CIRCUIT JUDGE:

Plaintiff-appellant Thomson-CSF, S.A. ("Thomson") appeals from a judgment entered in the United States District Court for the Southern District of New York . . . , denying its request for declaratory and injunctive relief and granting defendant-appellee Evans & Sutherland Computer Corporation's ("E & S") cross-motion to compel arbitration. Thomson asserts that the district court improvidently compelled it to arbitrate against E & S based upon an arbitration agreement between E & S and Thomson's subsidiary, to which Thomson was not a signatory. Because, under ordinary principles of contract and agency law, Thomson cannot be said to have voluntarily submitted to arbitrate its disputes with E & S, we reverse the judgment of the district court and remand for proceedings consistent with this opinion.

BACKGROUND

Rediffusion Simulation Limited ("Rediffusion") was a British company engaged in the business of building flight simulators for the training of pilots. In 1986, Rediffusion entered into a "Working Agreement" with E & S, located in Salt Lake City, Utah. Under the Working Agreement, Rediffusion agreed to purchase computer-generated image equipment (the computer "brain" of the flight simulator) exclusively from E & S and to use its best efforts to market those systems containing E & S equipment; in return, E & S agreed to supply its imaging equipment only to Rediffusion.

Subsequent to entering into the Working Agreement, Rediffusion was sold to Hughes Aircraft Company. Hughes amended and extended the Working Agreement between Rediffusion and E & S. On December 31, 1993, Hughes sold Rediffusion to Thomson, which renamed it Thomson Training and Simulation Limited. Prior to purchasing Rediffusion, Thomson maintained a division engaged in the business of building flight simulation equipment (the Training and Simulation Systems Division) into which it began integrating Rediffusion.

At the time Thomson began publicly contemplating the acquisition of Rediffusion, E & S informed Thomson that, if it purchased Rediffusion, E & S intended to bind Thomson and its flight simulation division to the Working Agreement. Specifically, E & S told Thomson that upon purchasing Rediffusion both Rediffusion and Thomson's Training and Simulation Systems Division would be required to purchase all needed computer-generated image equipment from E & S. In response, Thomson wrote to E & S seeking to have it waive those provisions of the Working Agreement that E & S believed to be binding upon Thomson. Thomson did not, however, concede that it would be bound by Rediffusion's Working Agreement. In fact, when it became clear that Thomson and E & S could reach no agreement prior to Thomson's acquisition of Rediffusion, Thomson explicitly informed E & S that it was not adopting the Working Agreement and did not consider itself bound by Rediffusion's Agreement which it had neither negotiated nor signed.

. . .

Injunctive Relief

While under Thomson's ownership, Rediffusion's share of the flight simulator market drastically decreased. On August 8, 1994, E & S filed a demand for arbitration under the Working Agreement against both Rediffusion and its parent-company Thomson, asserting a breach of their obligations arising out of the Working Agreement. Despite Thomson's insistence that it was not bound by the Working Agreement (and the arbitration clause contained therein), E & S filed a demand for arbitration against both Rediffusion and Thomson on August 8, 1994. While Rediffusion did not contest the applicability of the arbitration clause to it, Thomson refused to answer E & S's demand for arbitration. On August 29, 1994, Thomson commenced this action in the Southern District of New York, seeking 1) a declaration that it was not bound by the arbitration clause of the Working Agreement and 2) an injunction prohibiting further proceedings against it under the Working Agreement. E & S cross-moved to compel Thomson to arbitrate.

The district court granted E & S's cross-motion to compel arbitration. In doing so, the district court stated that while E & S's claims did not fall under any of the traditional categories for binding a nonsignatory to an arbitration clause, Thomson was bound nonetheless. Adopting a hybrid approach to binding a nonsignatory to an arbitration agreement, the district court accepted E & S's assertion that "the Court may bind Thomson based on its conduct in voluntarily becoming . . . an affiliate, on the degree of control Thomson exercises over [Rediffusion], and on the interrelatedness of the issues."

Thomson now appeals the judgment of the district court.

DISCUSSION

Arbitration is contractual by nature — "a party cannot be required to submit to arbitration any dispute which he has not agreed so to submit." Thus, while there is a strong and "liberal federal policy favoring arbitration agreements," *Mitsubishi Motors Corp. v. Soler Chrysler-Plymouth, Inc.*, such agreements must not be so broadly construed as to encompass claims and parties that were not intended by the original contract. "It does not follow, however, that under the [Federal Arbitration] Act an obligation to arbitrate attaches only to one who has personally signed the written arbitration provision." This Court has made clear that a nonsignatory party may be bound to an arbitration agreement if so dictated by the "ordinary principles of contract and agency."

I. *Traditional Bases For Binding Nonsignatories*

This Court has recognized a number of theories under which nonsignatories may be bound to the arbitration agreements of others. Those theories arise out of common law principles of contract and agency law. Accordingly, we have recognized five theories for binding nonsignatories to arbitration agreements: (1) incorporation by reference; (2) assumption; (3) agency; (4) veil-piercing/alter ego; and (5) estoppel. The district court properly rejected each of these traditional theories as sufficient justification for binding Thomson to the arbitration agreement of its subsidiary.

A. *Incorporation by Reference*

A nonsignatory may compel arbitration against a party to an arbitration agreement when that party has entered into a separate contractual relationship with the nonsignatory which incorporates the existing arbitration clause. *See* Import Export Steel Corp. v. Mississippi Valley Barge Line Co., 351 F.2d 503, 505–506 (2d Cir. 1965) (separate agreement with nonsignatory expressly "assum-[ing] all the obligations and privileges of [signatory party] under the . . . subchar-ter" constitutes grounds for enforcement of arbitration clause by nonsignatory). As the district court noted, E & S has not attempted to show that the Working Agreement was incorporated into any document which Thomson adopted. Thus, Thomson cannot be bound under an incorporation theory.

B. *Assumption*

In the absence of a signature, a party may be bound by an arbitration clause if its subsequent conduct indicates that it is assuming the obligation to arbitrate. *See* Gvozdenovic v. United Air Lines, Inc., 933 F.2d 1100, 1105 (2d Cir.) (flight attendants manifested a clear intention to arbitrate by sending a representative to act on their behalf in arbitration process), *cert. denied*, 502 U.S. 910 (1991). While Thomson was aware that the Working Agreement purported to bind it as an "affiliate" of Rediffusion, at no time did Thomson manifest an intention to be bound by that Agreement. In fact, Thomson explicitly disavowed any obligations arising out of the Working Agreement and filed this action seeking a declaration of non-liability under the Agreement. Accordingly, it cannot be said that Thomson assumed the obligation to arbitrate.

C. *Agency*

Traditional principles of agency law may bind a nonsignatory to an arbitration agreement. Because the Working Agreement was entered into well before Thomson purchased Rediffusion, Thomson could not possibly be bound under an agency theory.

D. *Veil Piercing/Alter Ego*

In some instances, the corporate relationship between a parent and its subsidiary are sufficiently close as to justify piercing the corporate veil and holding one corporation legally accountable for the actions of the other. As a general matter, however, a corporate relationship alone is not sufficient to bind a nonsignatory to an arbitration agreement. Nonetheless, the courts will pierce the corporate veil "in two broad situations: to prevent fraud or other wrong, or where a parent dominates and controls a subsidiary." . . . While E & S concedes that it can make no showing of fraud, it argues that Thomson sufficiently dominated Rediffusion as to justify veil piercing.

Veil piercing determinations are fact specific and "differ[ ] with the circumstances of each case." This Court has determined that a parent corporation and its subsidiary lose their distinct corporate identities when their conduct demonstrates a virtual abandonment of separateness. "[T]he factors that determine the question of control and domination are less subjective than 'good faith'; they relate to how the corporation was actually operated."

E & S has not demonstrated that Thomson exerted the degree of control over Rediffusion necessary to justify piercing the corporate veil. While the district court found that "Thomson has common ownership with [Rediffusion]; that Thomson actually controls [Rediffusion]; . . . [and] that Thomson incorporated [Rediffusion] into its own organizational and decision-making structure," the district court did not find an abandonment of the corporate structure. E & S has not shown an absence of corporate formalities, nor has it shown an intermingling of corporate finances and directorship. Rather, as the district court found, Rediffusion continued to function as a distinct entity closely incorporated into the existing corporate structure of its parent company, Thomson. Accordingly, in light of the totality of the circumstances, Thomson cannot be bound by Rediffusion's arbitration agreement under a veil piercing/alter ego theory.

E. *Estoppel*

This Court has also bound nonsignatories to arbitration agreements under an estoppel theory. In Deloitte Noraudit A/S v. Deloitte Haskins & Sells, U.S., 9 F.3d 1060, 1064 (2d Cir. 1993), a foreign accounting firm received a settlement agreement concerning the use of the trade name "Deloitte" in association with accounting practices. Under the agreement — containing an arbitration clause — local affiliates of the international accounting association Deloitte Haskins & Sells International were entitled to use the trade name "Deloitte" in exchange for compliance with the dictates of the agreement. A Norwegian accounting firm received the agreement, made no objection to the terms of the agreement, and proceeded to utilize the trade name. This Court held that by knowingly exploiting the agreement, the accounting firm was estopped from avoiding arbitration despite having never signed the agreement. . . .

. . . E & S asserts a theory of benefit under the Working Agreement which in essence amounts to an anti-trust violation — according to E & S, Thomson purchased Rediffusion (its only serious competitor in the flight simulation industry) so that it could keep Rediffusion from competing; by incorporating Rediffusion into its own structure, Thomson was able to eliminate all simulators utilizing E & S imaging equipment from the market; because E & S was contractually bound to supply only Rediffusion with imaging equipment, it was effectively shut out of the market; thus, E & S contends that Thomson benefitted from the Working Agreement by eliminating E & S as a competitor.

This indirect benefit which E & S asserts — and the district court implicitly adopts — is not the sort of benefit which this Court envisioned as the basis for estopping a nonsignatory from avoiding arbitration. Had Thomson *directly* benefitted from the Working Agreement by seeking to purchase equipment from E & S or enforcing the exclusivity provisions of the Agreement, it would be estopped from avoiding arbitration. The benefit which E & S asserts, however, derives directly from Thomson's purchase of Rediffusion, and not from the Working Agreement itself; Thomson received no benefit at all from the Working Agreement (as opposed to the acquisition). Thus, Thomson is not bound by its subsidiary's arbitration agreement under *Deloitte.*

Several courts of appeal have recognized an alternative estoppel theory requiring arbitration between a signatory and nonsignatory. In these cases, a signatory was bound to arbitrate with a nonsignatory at the nonsignatory's insistence because of "the close relationship between the entities involved, as well as the relationship of the alleged wrongs to the nonsignatory's obligations and duties in the contract . . . and [the fact that] the claims were 'intimately founded in and intertwined with the underlying contract obligations.' " . . . Thomson can not be bound to arbitrate under this line of cases.

As these cases indicate, the circuits have been willing to estop a *signatory* from avoiding arbitration with a nonsignatory when the issues the nonsignatory is seeking to resolve in arbitration are intertwined with the agreement that the estopped party has signed. As the district court pointed out, however, "[t]he situation here is inverse: E & S, as signatory, seeks to compel Thomson, a non-signatory." While E & S suggests that this is a non-distinction, the nature of arbitration makes it important. Arbitration is strictly a matter of contract; if the parties have not agreed to arbitrate, the courts have no authority to mandate that they do so. In the line of cases discussed above, the courts held that the parties were estopped from avoiding arbitration because they had entered into written arbitration agreements, albeit with the affiliates of those parties asserting the arbitration and not the parties themselves. Thomson, however, cannot be estopped from denying the existence of an arbitration clause to which it is a signatory because no such clause exists. At no point did Thomson indicate a willingness to arbitrate with E & S. Therefore, the district court properly determined these estoppel cases to be inapposite and insufficient justification for binding Thomson to an agreement that it never signed.

Moreover, these estoppel cases all involve claims which are integrally related to the contract containing the arbitration clause. The same cannot be said of the case at hand. As discussed above, E & S's claims against Thomson amount to the assertion that Thomson purchased Rediffusion in order to eliminate it as a competitor. While a cause of action may lie against Thomson for such alleged predatory business practices, the violation can hardly be characterized as arising out of or being integrally related to the Working Agreement between E & S and Rediffusion. Thus, the analogy to this line of estoppel cases again must fail.

II. *The District Court's Hybrid Approach*

Despite properly determining that E & S's claims did not fall within any of the traditional theories for binding a nonsignatory, the district court stated, "[n]evertheless, E & S asserts that the Court may bind Thomson based on its conduct in 'voluntarily bec[oming] . . . an affiliate,' on the degree of control Thomson exercises over [Rediffusion], and on the interrelatedness of the issues. This Court agrees." In so doing, the district court improperly extended the law of this Circuit and diluted the protections afforded nonsignatories by the "ordinary principles of contract and agency." A nonsignatory may not be bound to arbitrate except as dictated by some accepted theory under agency or contract law.

. . .

The district court below improperly extended the limited theories upon which this Court is willing to enforce an arbitration agreement against a nonsignatory. The district court's hybrid approach dilutes the safeguards afforded to a nonsignatory by the "ordinary principles of contract and agency" and fails to adequately protect parent companies, the subsidiaries of which have entered into arbitration agreements. Anything short of requiring a *full* showing of some accepted theory under agency or contract law imperils a vast number of parent corporations. . . .

CONCLUSION

Accordingly, the judgment of the district court is reversed and remanded for proceedings consistent with the foregoing.

NOTES

1. As this case suggests, a variety of contract and agency theories may be used to bind a party to an arbitration agreement even though it is not a signatory. In applying those theories, however, it is important to identify whether the non-signatory is trying to avoid arbitration or trying to force a signatory to arbitrate. In *Thomson*, a signatory to the arbitration agreement (E&S) was trying to force a non-signatory (Thomson) to arbitrate their dispute. In such a case, the non-signatory is claiming it did not agree to arbitrate at all. The court of appeals distinguishes cases in which a non-signatory is trying to force a signatory to arbitrate. In those cases, the signatory is claiming it did not agree to arbitrate with the non-signatory. *See, e.g.*, Grigson v. Creative Artists Agency, L.L.C., 210 F.3d 524, 525 (5th Cir.) (requiring signatory to arbitrate under "intertwined claims" theory), *cert. denied*, 531 U.S. 1013 (2000). Which sort of case is more problematic in your view?

2. In Arthur Andersen LLP v. Carlisle, 556 U.S. 624 (2009), the Supreme Court recognized that nonsignatories could enforce arbitration agreements (to the extent permitted by general state contract law). The Court explained as follows:

> "[S]tate law," therefore, is applicable to determine which contracts are binding under § 2 and enforceable under § 3 "*if* that law arose to govern issues concerning the validity, revocability, and enforceability of contracts generally." *Perry v. Thomas*. Because "traditional principles" of state law allow a contract to be enforced by or against nonparties to the contract through "assumption, piercing the corporate veil, alter ego, incorporation by reference, third-party beneficiary theories, waiver and estoppel," 21 R.

Lord, Williston on Contracts § 57:19, p. 183 (4th ed. 2001), the Sixth
Circuit's holding that nonparties to a contract are categorically barred from
§ 3 relief was error.

Id. at 630-31.

PROBLEM 2.16

Pompey Computers, Inc. enters into a contract with Armstrong Distributing Co.
under which Armstrong agrees to buy 150 computers from Pompey. The contract
further permits Armstrong to order up to an additional 150 computers at the same
price, and provides for all disputes to be resolved by arbitration.

(a) A third company, Staunton Supply, now buys 150 computers from Pompey.
The Pompey-Staunton contract does not contain an arbitration clause, but provides
that it is subject to all the terms of the Pompey-Armstrong contract. When
Pompey delivers the computers to Staunton, Staunton claims they are defective.
Can Pompey compel Staunton to arbitrate the dispute?

(b) Armstrong repudiates its contract with Pompey and then files for
bankruptcy. Pompey discovers that when Armstrong signed the contract it was
acting on behalf of Staunton. Can Pompey compel Staunton to arbitrate the
dispute?

(c) Same as (b), except that Armstrong did not sign the contract with Pompey on
behalf of Staunton. Instead, Pompey discovers that Staunton owns 100 percent of
the shares of Armstrong and has failed to maintain any separate corporate or
financial structure for the two companies. Can Pompey compel Staunton to
arbitrate the dispute?

(d) Same as (b), except that Armstrong did not sign the contract with Pompey on
behalf of Staunton. Instead, before filing for bankruptcy, Armstrong sells the
computers to Staunton. When the computers prove to be defective, Staunton sues
Pompey alleging that Pompey breached the warranty contained in the sales
contract between Pompey and Armstrong. Can Pompey compel Staunton to
arbitrate the dispute?

(e) With Armstrong's permission, Staunton orders an additional 150 computers
directly from Pompey under the Pompey-Armstrong contract. When the
computers arrive, Staunton claims they are defective. Can Pompey compel
Staunton to arbitrate the dispute?

(f) Armstrong repudiates its contract with Pompey. Rather than proceed against
Armstrong, Pompey sues Staunton alleging that Staunton induced Armstrong to
repudiate the contract. Can Staunton compel Pompey to arbitrate the dispute?

§ 2.07 PROCEDURAL ISSUES IN ENFORCING DOMESTIC
ARBITRATION AGREEMENTS — PART 1

In actions to enforce domestic arbitration agreements, the FAA provides "for an
expeditious and summary hearing, with only restricted inquiry into factual issues."
Moses H. Cone Memorial Hosp. v. Mercury Constr. Corp., 460 U.S. 1, 22 (1983).

Section 6 of the FAA contains a general statement of the applicable procedure: "Any application to the court hereunder shall be made and heard in the manner provided by law for the making and hearing of motions, except as herein otherwise expressly provided." 9 U.S.C. § 6. Procedure under the Uniform Arbitration Act and the Revised Uniform Arbitration Act is similar. *See* UAA § 16; RUAA § 5(a). Thus, in general, courts will resolve disputes about the enforceability of arbitration agreements on a paper record — "based upon the petition and answer, affidavits, documentary evidence, and legal memoranda submitted by the parties to the court." 2 IAN R. MACNEIL ET AL., FEDERAL ARBITRATION LAW § 24.3.1 (1994).

A potentially significant exception is in section 4 of the FAA, which provides for a right to jury trial for certain issues raised in opposition to a petition to compel arbitration:

> If the making of the arbitration agreement or the failure, neglect, or refusal to perform the same be in issue, the court shall proceed summarily to the trial thereof. . . . Where such an issue is raised, the party alleged to be in default may, except in cases of admiralty, on or before the return day of the notice of application, demand a jury trial of such issue, and upon such demand the court shall make an order referring the issue or issues to a jury in the manner provided by the Federal Rules of Civil Procedure, or may specially call a jury for that purpose.

9 U.S.C. § 4. Section 3 of the FAA contains no similar language. 9 U.S.C. § 3. Likewise, the UAA and RUAA do not provide for a right to jury trial, instead requiring only that the court "proceed summarily" to determine any issues raised. UAA § 2(a), (b); RUAA § 7.

Under section 4, "[a] party resisting arbitration cannot obtain a jury trial merely by demanding one; rather he bears the burden of showing that he is entitled to a jury trial." Doctor's Assocs., Inc. v. Jabush, 89 F.3d 109, 114 (2d Cir. 1996) (internal quotations omitted). The party "must make at least some showing that under prevailing law, he would be relieved of his contractual obligation to arbitrate if his allegations proved to be true," and he must "produce at least some evidence to substantiate his factual allegations." Dillard v. Merrill Lynch, Pierce, Fenner & Smith, Inc., 961 F.2d 1148, 1154 (5th Cir. 1992), *cert. denied*, 506 U.S. 1079 (1993). Some courts have described the standard as a "summary judgment type standard," *see* Kreimer v. Delta Faucet Co., 2000 U.S. Dist. LEXIS 9610 (S.D. Ind. June 2, 2000) (request for evidentiary hearing), and refused to order a jury trial when there was "no material dispute of fact" as to the making of the arbitration agreement, Great Western Mortgage Corp. v. Peacock, 110 F.3d 222, 231 n.36 (3d Cir.), *cert. denied*, 522 U.S. 915 (1997); *see also Jabush*, 89 F.3d at 114 (must be "genuine issue entitling a party to a jury trial"). For a case in which the court held that a trial was required under section 4, see Magnolia Capital Advisors Inc. v. Bear Stearns & Co., 2008 U.S. App. LEXIS 7455, at *13 (11th Cir. Apr. 3, 2008) (unpublished) (reversing district court and "find[ing] that Magnolia produced evidence sufficient to substantiate its unequivocal denial of having made any such [arbitration] agreement").

The timing of an appeal also can be important to a party seeking (or resisting) arbitration. Section 16 of the FAA governs the appealability of trial court orders dealing with arbitration. *See* 9 U.S.C. § 16; *see also* UAA § 19; RUAA § 28. In many circumstances, the application of section 16 is straightforward. The following case addresses one circumstance that had proven not to be so clear.

GREEN TREE FINANCIAL CORP.-ALABAMA v. RANDOLPH
United States Supreme Court
531 U.S. 79 (2000)

CHIEF JUSTICE REHNQUIST delivered the opinion of the Court.

In this case we first address whether an order compelling arbitration and dismissing a party's underlying claims is a "final decision with respect to an arbitration" within the meaning of § 16 of the Federal Arbitration Act, 9 U.S.C. § 16, and thus is immediately appealable pursuant to that Act. Because we decide that question in the affirmative, we also address the question whether an arbitration agreement that does not mention arbitration costs and fees is unenforceable because it fails to affirmatively protect a party from potentially steep arbitration costs. We conclude that an arbitration agreement's silence with respect to such matters does not render the agreement unenforceable.

I

Respondent Larketta Randolph purchased a mobile home from Better Cents Home Builders, Inc., in Opelika, Alabama. She financed this purchase through petitioners Green Tree Financial Corporation and its wholly owned subsidiary, Green Tree Financial Corp.-Alabama. Petitioners' Manufactured Home Retail Installment Contract and Security Agreement required that Randolph buy Vendor's Single Interest insurance, which protects the vendor or lienholder against the costs of repossession in the event of default. The agreement also provided that all disputes arising from, or relating to, the contract, whether arising under case law or statutory law, would be resolved by binding arbitration.

Randolph later sued petitioners, alleging that they violated the Truth in Lending Act (TILA), 15 U.S.C. § 1601 *et seq.*, by failing to disclose as a finance charge the Vendor's Single Interest insurance requirement. She later amended her complaint to add a claim that petitioners violated the Equal Credit Opportunity Act, 15 U.S.C. §§ 1691–1691f, by requiring her to arbitrate her statutory causes of action. She brought this action on behalf of a similarly situated class. In lieu of an answer, petitioners filed a motion to compel arbitration, to stay the action, or, in the alternative, to dismiss. The District Court granted petitioners' motion to compel arbitration, denied the motion to stay, and dismissed Randolph's claims with prejudice. The District Court also denied her request to certify a class. She requested reconsideration, asserting that she lacked the resources to arbitrate and as a result, would have to forgo her claims against petitioners. The District Court denied reconsideration. Randolph appealed.

The Court of Appeals for the Eleventh Circuit first held that it had jurisdiction to review the District Court's order because that order was a final decision. The Court of Appeals looked to § 16 of the Federal Arbitration Act (FAA), 9 U.S.C. § 16, which governs appeal from a District Court's arbitration order, and specifically

§ 16(a)(3), which allows appeal from "a final decision with respect to an arbitration that is subject to this title." The Court determined that a final, appealable order within the meaning of the FAA is one that disposes of all the issues framed by the litigation, leaving nothing to be done but execute the order. The Court of Appeals found the District Court's order within that definition.

The court then determined that the arbitration agreement failed to provide the minimum guarantees that respondent could vindicate her statutory rights under the TILA. Critical to this determination was the court's observation that the arbitration agreement was silent with respect to payment of filing fees, arbitrators' costs, and other arbitration expenses. On that basis, the court held that the agreement to arbitrate posed a risk that respondent's ability to vindicate her statutory rights would be undone by "steep" arbitration costs, and therefore was unenforceable. We granted certiorari, and we now affirm the Court of Appeals with respect to the first conclusion, and reverse it with respect to the second.

II

Section 16 of the Federal Arbitration Act, enacted in 1988, governs appellate review of arbitration orders. [The Court here quoted 9 U.S.C. § 16.] The District Court's order directed that arbitration proceed and dismissed respondent's claims for relief. The question before us, then, is whether that order can be appealed as "a final decision with respect to an arbitration" within the meaning of § 16(a)(3). Petitioners urge us to hold that it cannot. They rely, in part, on the FAA's policy favoring arbitration agreements and its goal of "mov[ing] the parties to an arbitrable dispute out of court and into arbitration as quickly and easily as possible." *Moses H. Cone Memorial Hospital v. Mercury Constr. Corp.* In accordance with that purpose, petitioners point out, § 16 generally permits immediate appeal of orders hostile to arbitration, whether the orders are final or interlocutory, but bars appeal of interlocutory orders favorable to arbitration.

Section 16(a)(3), however, preserves immediate appeal of any "final decision with respect to an arbitration," regardless of whether the decision is favorable or hostile to arbitration. And as petitioners and respondent agree, the term "final decision" has a well-developed and longstanding meaning. It is a decision that "ends the litigation on the merits and leaves nothing more for the court to do but execute the judgment." Because the FAA does not define "a final decision with respect to an arbitration" or otherwise suggest that the ordinary meaning of "final decision" should not apply, we accord the term its well-established meaning.

The District Court's order directed that the dispute be resolved by arbitration and dismissed respondent's claims with prejudice, leaving the court nothing to do but execute the judgment. That order plainly disposed of the entire case on the merits and left no part of it pending before the court. The FAA does permit parties to arbitration agreements to bring a separate proceeding in a district court to enter judgment on an arbitration award once it is made (or to vacate or modify it), but the existence of that remedy does not vitiate the finality of the District Court's resolution of the claims in the instant proceeding. 9 U.S.C. §§ 9, 10, 11. The District Court's order was therefore "a final decision with respect to an arbitration" within the meaning of § 16(a)(3), and an appeal may be taken.[2]

Petitioners contend that the phrase "final decision" does not include an order compelling arbitration and dismissing the other claims in the action, when that order occurs in an "embedded" proceeding, such as this one. "Embedded" proceedings are simply those actions involving both a request for arbitration and other claims for relief. "Independent" proceedings, by contrast, are actions in which a request to order arbitration is the sole issue before the court. Those Courts of Appeals attaching significance to this distinction hold that an order compelling arbitration in an "independent" proceeding is final within the meaning of § 16(a)(3), but that such an order in an "embedded" proceeding is not, even if the district court dismisses the remaining claims. Petitioners contend that the distinction between independent and embedded proceedings and its consequences for finality were so firmly established at the time of § 16's enactment that we should assume Congress meant to incorporate them into § 16(a)(3).

We disagree. It does not appear that, at the time of § 16(a)(3)'s enactment, the rules of finality were firmly established in cases like this one, where the District Court both ordered arbitration and dismissed the remaining claims. We also note that at that time, Courts of Appeals did not have a uniform approach to finality with respect to orders directing arbitration in "embedded" proceedings. The term "final decision," by contrast, enjoys a consistent and longstanding interpretation. Certainly the plain language of the statutory text does not suggest that Congress intended to incorporate the rather complex independent/embedded distinction, and its consequences for finality, into § 16(a)(3). We therefore conclude that where, as here, the District Court has ordered the parties to proceed to arbitration, and dismissed all the claims before it, that decision is "final" within the meaning of § 16(a)(3), and therefore appealable.

III

[The portion of the Court's opinion addressing the issue of arbitration costs is reprinted in § 3.03[C]. — Ed.]

NOTES

1. The policy behind section 16 was described by its drafters as follows:

    Under present doctrine, appeal from orders with respect to arbitration depends not only on the final judgment rule, but also on antique distinctions arising from the days when law and equity were administered by separate courts. The appealability of orders that direct arbitration, stay arbitration, or stay judicial proceedings depends on accidents of procedure that do not respond to any rational needs of either appeals timing or arbitration. The rules as to appealability, moreover, often are obscure.

---

[2] Had the District Court entered a stay instead of a dismissal in this case, that order would not be appealable. 9 U.S.C. § 16(b)(1). The question whether the District Court should have taken that course is not before us, and we do not address it.

This section permits arbitration to proceed without appeal if the district court orders that arbitration precede litigation, and by permitting immediate appeal if the district court orders that litigation precede arbitration. Denial of appeal when arbitration is given precedence should not often be costly: district courts usually will be correct, and the arbitration process is apt to produce considerable savings in the process of preparing for trial if the dispute is ultimately found nonarbitrable. If the dispute is found to be arbitrable, of course, great saving will be made.

Section-by-Section Analysis on the Judicial Improvements and Access to Justice Act, CONG. REC. S16298, S16309 (Oct. 14, 1988).

2. In footnote 2 in *Green Tree*, the Supreme Court reserved the question whether district courts can dismiss rather than stay cases in which the parties have agreed to arbitrate. Since *Green Tree*, the circuits have split on that question, as the Third Circuit explained in Lloyd v. Hovensa, LLC, 369 F.3d 263 (3d Cir. 2004):

Courts of Appeals have reached different resolutions of the issue of whether a District Court has discretion to deny a motion for a stay pending arbitration and dismiss a complaint where it finds all claims before it to be arbitrable. We have not heretofore had occasion to resolve the issue. Today, we side with those courts that take the Congressional text at face value.

. . .

In accordance with the Supreme Court's instruction in *Green Tree*, we apply the "the plain language of the statutory text" in interpreting the FAA. Here, the plain language of § 3 affords a district court no discretion to dismiss a case where one of the parties applies for a stay pending arbitration. The directive that the Court "shall" enter a stay simply cannot be read to say that the Court shall enter a stay in all cases except those in which all claims are arbitrable and the Court finds dismissal to be the preferable approach. On the contrary, the statute clearly states, without exception, that whenever suit is brought on an arbitrable claim, the Court "shall" upon application stay the litigation until arbitration has been concluded. In this case, Wyatt requested a stay of the proceeding as part of his motion to compel arbitration. Accordingly, we hold that the District Court was obligated under 9 U.S.C. § 3 to grant the stay once it decided to order arbitration.

We are free to disregard an unambiguous directive of Congress only in the rare instances where failing to do so produces a nonsensical result that could not have been intended. This is not one of those rare exceptions. Congress adopted the FAA to establish, promote and facilitate a national policy strongly favoring arbitration as a process for resolving disputes. Holding that Congress intended to deprive the District Court of discretion to deny a stay produces results that effectively promote and facilitate arbitration.

. . . [T]he District Court has a significant role to play under the FAA even in those instances in which the District Court orders the arbitration of all claims. Even in those instances, the parties are entitled to seek the

Court's assistance during the course of arbitration. For example, the FAA allows arbitrating parties to return to court for resolution of disputes regarding the appointment of an arbitrator or the filling of an arbitrator vacancy, 9 U.S.C. § 5. Similarly, parties may ask the court to compel the attendance of witnesses, or to punish the witnesses for contempt, 9 U.S.C. § 7. Then, after an arbitration award is rendered, a party is entitled to seek relief in the District Court in the form of a judgment on the award or an order vacating or modifying the award. *See* 9 U.S.C. §§ 9, 10, 11. If the plaintiff's case has been dismissed rather than stayed, the parties will have to file a new action each time the Court's assistance is required, with the attendant risk of having their case assigned to a new judge. On the other hand, if the court enters a stay of the action and retains jurisdiction, then proceedings under §§ 5, 7, 9, 10, or 11 may be expedited, as the parties may simply return . . . to the same district judge presiding over the plaintiff's case.

There is an even more important reason, however, to hold that Congress meant exactly what it said. Whenever a party is subjected to litigation on any issue and is found to be entitled to arbitrate that issue, § 3 of the FAA, as we have noted, mandates that a stay be entered by the District Court. The effect of that stay is twofold: it relieves the party entitled to arbitrate of the burden of continuing to litigate the issue while the arbitration process is on-going, and it entitles that party to proceed immediately to arbitration without the delay that would be occasioned by an appeal of the District Court's order to arbitrate. Under § 16 of the FAA, whenever a stay is entered under § 3, the party resisting arbitration is expressly denied the right to an immediate appeal. The legislative scheme of the FAA thus reflects a policy decision that, if a district court determines that arbitration of a claim is called for, the judicial system's interference with the arbitral process should end unless and until there is a final award.

. . .

In short, a literal reading of § 3 of the FAA not only leads to sensible results, it also is the only reading consistent with the statutory scheme and the strong national policy favoring arbitration.

Id. at 268-71.

3.   If the district court refuses to order arbitration and the party seeking arbitration takes an immediate appeal, does the district court have to stay its proceedings while the appeal is pending? The circuits are divided on the issue. *See* Weingarten Realty Investors v. Miller, 661 F.3d 904, 907-08 (5th Cir. 2011) (adopting minority view):

Whether an appeal from a denial of a motion to compel arbitration divests the district court of jurisdiction to proceed to the merits is the subject of a circuit split. The Second and Ninth Circuits have held that a stay is not automatic. . . . In the absence of an automatic stay, the district court nonetheless retains the power to determine, on a case-by-case basis, whether proceedings should be stayed until the appeal regarding arbitrability has been resolved.

The Seventh Circuit, later joined by the Third, Fourth, Tenth, and Eleventh, has held that a notice of appeal automatically stays proceedings in the district court. . . . These courts analogize arbitrability appeals to appeals regarding double jeopardy, sovereign immunity, and qualified immunity, reasoning that because a district court cannot proceed past these issues when there are interlocutory appeals, it similarly cannot proceed when arbitrability is appealed.

4.   Does a party's failure to take an interlocutory appeal as permitted under section 16 preclude that party from arguing after trial that the case should have been arbitrated? The circuits again appear to be in some disagreement, as described by the First Circuit in Colon v. R.K. Grace & Co., 358 F.3d 1 (1st Cir. 2003):

> Denials of arbitration under the Federal Arbitration Act are, unlike most interlocutory rulings, immediately appealable. Nothing in the statute requires an immediate appeal but three circuits [the Second, Fifth, and Eighth Circuits] have held that the failure to promptly appeal such a denial may by estoppel foreclose the demanding party's right to arbitration, although this is not automatic and depends on a showing of prejudice to the other side. The reason is that it is wasteful to have a full trial and then determine by a post-trial appeal that the whole matter should have been arbitrated and so start again. [The Fourth Circuit appears to have rejected this view.]
>
>   . . .
>
> We are sympathetic to the approach of the Second, Fifth and Eighth Circuits, and it is wise for us to make this clear by dictum so as to give warning to the bar. Yet this case is a perfect example of why one would not employ a mechanical forfeiture rule. Because in this case the district judge did not definitively deny the arbitration request until after trial began — indeed, until all the evidence was taken — any holding by us that the defendants had to appeal the denial immediately so as to avoid an unnecessary trial would be ridiculous: the trial had already occurred.

Id. at 4. Subsequently, the First Circuit adopted the rule it foreshadowed in *Colon,* holding that "failure to promptly appeal a denial of arbitration will, if prejudicial to the opposing party, operate to forfeit the demanding party's right to arbitration." Franceschi v. Hospital General San Carlos, Inc., 420 F.3d 1, 4 (1st Cir. 2005).

5.   The Supreme Court held in Arthur Andersen LLP v. Carlisle, 556 U.S. 624, 627 (2009), that nonsignatories may rely on section 16 to bring an immediate appeal from the denial of their request for a stay of the underlying lawsuit. The Court explained:

> Ordinarily, courts of appeals have jurisdiction only over "final decisions" of district courts. 28 U.S.C. § 1291. The FAA, however, makes an exception to that finality requirement, providing that "an appeal may be taken from . . .

an order . . . refusing a stay of any action under section 3 of this title." 9 U.S.C. § 16(a)(1)(A). By that provision's clear and unambiguous terms, any litigant who asks for a stay under § 3 is entitled to an immediate appeal from denial of that motion — regardless of whether the litigant is in fact eligible for a stay. Because each petitioner in this case explicitly asked for a stay pursuant to § 3, the Sixth Circuit had jurisdiction to review the District Court's denial.

Id. at 627. Did Congress intend for nonsignatories to be able to bring an immediate appeal, do you suppose? Or is that outcome simply the result of poor drafting (i.e., excessive use of passive voice — "an appeal may be taken")?

PROBLEM 2.17

Howells Enterprises and Tregellis, Inc. enter into a consulting contract that contains an arbitration clause. Howells becomes dissatisfied with Tregellis' performance and threatens litigation.

(a) Howells files suit in federal court. Tregellis moves for a stay pending arbitration under section 3 of the FAA. The district court denies the motion. Is the order immediately appealable?

(b) Tregellis files a petition in federal court under section 4 of the FAA seeking an order compelling Howell to arbitrate. The district court denies Tregellis' petition. Is the order immediately appealable?

(c) Howell files suit in federal court seeking an injunction against an arbitration proceeding initiated by Tregellis. The district court grants the injunction. Is the order immediately appealable?

(d) Same as (a) except that the district court grants Tregellis' motion and stays the proceedings pending arbitration. Is the order immediately appealable?

(e) Same as (b) except that the district court grants Tregellis' petition to compel arbitration. Is the order immediately appealable?

(f) Same as (c) except that the district court denies Howells' motion to enjoin the arbitration. Is the order immediately appealable?

(g) Same as (a) except that Tregellis files a motion to stay the proceedings and a petition to compel arbitration. The district court grants the petition to compel arbitration, but instead of staying the proceedings the court dismisses Howells' complaint with prejudice. Is the order immediately appealable?

(h) Same as (g) except that instead of dismissing the complaint the district court grants the motion to stay. Is the order immediately appealable?

Chapter 3

FEDERAL LAW RESTRICTIONS ON THE ENFORCEABILITY OF ARBITRATION AGREEMENTS

§ 3.01 OVERVIEW

This chapter addresses whether it is appropriate to use arbitration to resolve every sort of claim that might arise between the parties, or whether federal law should make some arbitration agreements unenforceable. In the past, this discussion typically focused on whether federal statutory claims could be resolved in arbitration (the so-called "non-arbitrability doctrine"). If a federal statutory claim was non-arbitrable, courts would not enforce pre-dispute agreements to arbitrate those claims (although they would enforce post-dispute agreements). Recent federal legislation has more commonly focused on making arbitration agreements unenforceable in certain types of contracts (e.g., motor vehicle franchise contracts, consumer mortgage contracts). This chapter considers both — federal laws that make arbitration agreements unenforceable as to certain types of claims or in certain types of contracts.

In each such case, two conflicting federal statutes are involved: the Federal Arbitration Act on the one hand, and some other federal statute on the other. The Federal Arbitration Act broadly makes agreements to arbitrate enforceable. The argument in these cases essentially is that the competing federal statute overrides the general provisions of the FAA (either expressly or impliedly) and makes arbitration agreements unenforceable, again, either as to certain claims or in certain contracts. Similar issues can arise under state laws, but conflicts between the FAA and state statutes that make arbitration agreements unenforceable present different issues and are taken up in Chapter 4.

This chapter first examines federal statutes that expressly make arbitration agreements unenforceable, most often in a particular type of contract. It then considers whether federal statutes that do not expressly address arbitration might nonetheless impliedly make arbitration agreements unenforceable. (Most of these cases focus on the arbitrability of federal statutory claims.) The United States Supreme Court, in *Wilko v. Swan*, initially took a strong stand against arbitrability; subsequent cases eroded that stand, ultimately leading to *Wilko* being overruled. After tracing that history, the chapter examines selected areas in which arbitrability remains uncertain. Finally, it addresses conflicts between particular arbitration procedures and statutory rights and remedies, a more recent variation on this same theme. Even if in general parties can agree to arbitrate statutory claims, under what circumstances might particular arbitration procedures unlawfully interfere with the claimant's ability to vindicate his or her statutory rights?

Before we look at the relevant statutes and case law, however, first think about the broader policy question: when is arbitration an appropriate method of resolving disputes? We discussed some of the policy considerations in § 1.05, focusing on possible costs and benefits of arbitration clauses in consumer and employment contracts. The following excerpt continues that discussion by looking at some of the competing considerations involved in deciding whether for public policy reasons a statutory claim should be arbitrable. Its focus is on international arbitration. How much of the analysis applies to domestic arbitration as well?

William W. Park, PRIVATE ADJUDICATORS AND THE PUBLIC INTEREST: THE EXPANDING SCOPE OF INTERNATIONAL ARBITRATION,
12 BROOK. J. INT'L L. 629, 635–40 (1986)*

All laws implicate public interests, in the sense that they further societal goals, such as ensuring respect for contracts or the orderly inheritance of public property. Yet some laws appear to bear upon public interests to a greater degree than others.

Private parties may negotiate away some rights by an arbitration clause or a choice of law clause — even before any dispute arises — and courts will enforce this bargain. The right to demand payment for goods sold and delivered might, for example, be bargained away. As to other rights, however, courts might hesitate to permit a waiver, before the dispute arises, of rights that implicate what might be referred to as "non-negotiable" public interests. Indeed, the vindication of some claims involves widespread effects, external to the parties, which are so significant that adjudication becomes a matter of public concern.

. . .

The goal of these "non-negotiable" legal rules is not merely justice between the parties. They also create benefits for all society — such as a fair stock market or an orderly way to deal with bankruptcies. For this reason, courts consider that these rules implicate what might be called "public rights."

The first refrain that appears in arguments against arbitrability of public disputes is that public dispute resolution will fertilize judicial precedent. The development of the legal system, it may be argued, requires implementation and interpretation of statutes by courts that create precedents open for all to see. However, this argument seems to put the cart before the horse. Public interpretation of statutes does create precedent that may guide businessmen. However, courts elaborate the law to deal with disputes; they do not entertain litigation in order to permit lawyers to elaborate the law.

The second and more central theme that runs through the non-arbitrability cases is a concern that society at large will be injured by arbitration of public law claims. Courts express this fear in a variety of ways. They may say that the legal and factual issues are too complicated for arbitrators; that arbitration proceedings are too

---

informal, providing inadequate discovery; that arbitrators, like foxes guarding the chicken coop, have a pro-business bias and will under-enforce laws designed to protect the public; that arbitrators are less connected to the democratic process than judges; that lack of appeal to arbitral awards makes arbitration a "black hole" to which rights are sent and never heard from again.

No empirical evidence suggests that arbitrators are necessarily less trustworthy or competent than judges. There may, however, be merit in holding "public law issues" non-arbitrable under a slightly different alternative analysis, which starts with a recognition that arbitrators are paid only to do justice between or among the parties before them. "Public rights" belong not to the litigants, but to society at large. Society never signed the arbitration agreement, and is not a party to the arbitration. If the arbitration, which is a consensual process, affects only the consenting adults who signed the agreement, they alone are hurt by the arbitrators' folly. But if the dispute affects the property of one who never signed the arbitration agreement, the arbitration takes on a different case. Indeed, the right to proper enforcement of antitrust laws may be analogous to a third person's property right. Furthermore, the societal interest in the vindication of claims relating to matters such as free economic competition and the securities markets belongs not to the businessmen in the controversy, but to a community which never agreed to arbitrate.

. . .

[O]ne might articulate three competing objectives: (1) freedom of contract to provide for private dispute resolution, which calls for an efficient arbitral process; (2) protection of society against under-enforcement of law by private adjudicators; and (3) meeting the needs of international trade and investment for a system of neutral non-national binding dispute resolution.

Underlying the first objective is the assumption that the enforcement of a freely accepted bargain to arbitrate — entered into by parties with equal negotiating power — will provide the business community with the benefits of confidential, economical and speedy dispute resolution. A different result might be reached in the case of "contracts of adhesion" imposed on weaker parties with little bargaining power. . . .

The second goal, protecting the public against under-enforcement of mandatory public norms, relates to a concern of many judges that arbitrators will be less likely than courts to apply our competition law correctly, or at least less likely to find liability and to assess treble damages. Incorrect application of the law may hurt those segments of society that have a stake in the outcome of the arbitration.

The final objective — meeting the needs of international commercial and investment transactions — presumes that business people will be more likely to enter into trans-border contracts, resulting in more efficient allocation of global resources, if they feel confident that potential disputes will be settled in a forum more neutral than the other party's national courts. While transborder business will continue even if assertion of public law claims can defeat the arbitration agreement, it would seem reasonable to expect that many wealth-creating transactions might fail if business people lack confidence that they can avoid the "home town justice" of the other party's national courts.

NOTES

1. Professor Thomas Carbonneau has proposed the following amendment to the FAA, which would make many federal statutory claims nonarbitrable:

> Cases involving the enforcement of fundamental statutory rights cannot be the subject of an arbitration agreement or an arbitral proceeding. Fundamental statutory rights include those arising from antitrust statutes, the securities legislation, RICO, labor statutes, and other regulatory legislative frameworks deemed essential by Congress. Arbitral agreements or awards that pertain to international commercial arbitration or maritime arbitration are exempted from this prohibition.

Thomas E. Carbonneau, *Arbitration and the U.S. Supreme Court: A Plea for Statutory Reform*, 5 Ohio St. J. on Disp. Resol. 231, 273 (1990). Why those claims and not others? Why the exemption for international commercial arbitration and maritime arbitration?

2. Courts typically will enforce post-dispute agreements to arbitrate federal statutory claims, even if the claim is non-arbitrable. *See* Shearson/American Express, Inc. v. McMahon, 482 U.S. 220, 223 (1987) ("courts uniformly . . . concluded that *Wilko* [did] not apply to the submission to arbitration of existing disputes"). And parties surely can settle federal statutory claims, can they not? Should arbitration agreements be treated differently than settlements? Conversely, courts regularly disallow pre-dispute waivers of various statutory rights. Perhaps that is the closer analogy.

Professor Keith Hylton takes the latter view but draws the opposite conclusion:

> Commentators and courts sometime take pains to distinguish waivers from arbitration agreements, usually noting that the arbitration agreement does not involve a waiver of legal claims, but rather only an agreement to carry on the dispute within the arbitral forum. My analysis shows that this distinction means little from an economic perspective. If the arbitral forum is heavily biased in favor of the defendant, then an arbitration agreement may be effectively equivalent to a waiver. Given this, if potential plaintiffs and defendants can make any arbitration agreements they desire, then they should be able to enter into waiver agreements.

Keith N. Hylton, *Agreements to Waive or to Arbitrate Legal Claims: An Economic Analysis*, 8 Sup. Ct. Econ. Rev. 209, 230 (2000). Do you agree with Professor Hylton? Does the fact that some arbitration agreements might serve as waivers of the statutory rights at issue mean that all arbitration of statutory claims should be precluded? Or is there some intermediate position?

3. Professor Park points out that some statutes set forth "mandatory" rules, which cannot ordinarily be varied by the parties' agreement, while others merely set out "default" rules, which control only in the absence of the parties' agreement. He also distinguishes between statutes that protect the interests of third parties and

those that protect one of the parties to the contract from the other. Are these distinctions helpful in deciding which statutory claims should be arbitrable? *See, e.g.*, Stephen J. Ware, *Default Rules from Mandatory Rules: Privatizing Law Through Arbitration*, 83 MINN. L. REV. 703, 732–33 (1999) (arguing that mandatory common law rules (as well as mandatory statutory rules) should not be arbitrable, while default statutory rules should be subject to arbitration).

4. Does it matter whether enforcement actions by the government remain available for claims that are subject to arbitration? In EEOC v. Waffle House, Inc., 534 U.S. 279 (2002), the United States Supreme Court by a 6-3 vote held that an employee's agreement to arbitrate does not preclude the EEOC from seeking to recover in court relief such as damages, back pay, or reinstatement on behalf of the employee. Thus, even if an employee agrees to arbitration, the EEOC remains able to recover on behalf of the employee the exact same remedies the employee was bound to seek in arbitration. The Court's opinion noted, however, that in 2000 the EEOC filed only 291 lawsuits and intervened in another 111 cases. *Id.* at 290 n.7. Does that affect your view? What about actions brought by a private plaintiff acting as a "private attorney general"? Should those be subject to arbitration?

5. Recall the discussion in § 1.02 about whether a system of precedent can arise in arbitration. What effect does the arbitration of federal statutory claims (or any claims, for that matter) have on the development of the law? Professor Charles Knapp has (colorfully) expressed concern about the future development of the common law of contract in a world with widespread use of arbitration:

> If all contract disputes which the parties could not settle between themselves had to be submitted to arbitration for resolution, rather than to a court of law, the common law of contract would cease to be a living organism. It would become merely an historical relic, a legal King Tut in its elaborately detailed Restatement (Second) sarcophagus, a ruler to be exhumed and displayed — even admired, perhaps — but not obeyed. This might not be altogether a bad thing, but it would mean that our legal system in this respect at least had become vastly different from the one we had (or imagined ourselves to have) for the past century or so.

Charles L. Knapp, *Taking Contracts Private: The Quiet Revolution in Contract Law*, 71 FORDHAM L. REV. 761, 785-86 (2002). Do you agree with those concerns? What is Professor Park's view? Are the potential risks greater for common law claims or for federal statutory claims? How widespread would the use of arbitration need to be to turn an area of law into a "legal King Tut"?

PROBLEM 3.1

Senator Grace Dunbar (see Problem 1.5) once again asks for your advice on arbitration matters. This time, she tells you about a group of constituents asking her to introduce legislation that would make some types of claims nonarbitrable. She wants to know what claims, if any, should be included in the bill. She also asks you whether, instead of precluding arbitration of certain types of claims, it would be better to make arbitration agreements entered into by certain classes of parties (employees and consumers, for example) unenforceable. How do you advise the Senator?

§ 3.02 EXPRESS STATUTORY RESTRICTIONS ON THE ENFORCEABILITY OF ARBITRATION AGREEMENTS

Congress can, of course, expressly make arbitration agreements enforceable or unenforceable, as to certain claims or in certain types of contracts. *See, e.g.*, 35 U.S.C. § 294(a) (provision in contract involving "a patent or any right under a patent" that requires "arbitration of any dispute relating to patent validity or infringement arising under the contract" "shall be valid, irrevocable, and enforceable"). In recent years, a growing number of federal statutes have restricted the enforceability of arbitration agreements — most often, although not exclusively, by making pre-dispute arbitration agreements unenforceable in certain types of contracts.

The first such statute was enacted in 2002, when President Bush signed into law a bill making pre-dispute arbitration clauses unenforceable in motor vehicle franchise agreements — contracts governing the business relationship between car dealers and car manufacturers. *See* Motor Vehicle Franchise Contract Arbitration Fairness Act, 15 U.S.C. § 1226. The legislation does not address the use of arbitration clauses in contracts between car dealers and their customers (or car dealers and their employees, for that matter). Are car dealers the sort of party one would most expect to need protection from pre-dispute arbitration agreements? Why do you suppose this legislation passed while other bills prohibiting pre-dispute arbitration clauses in consumer and employment contracts did not?

In 2006, Congress restricted the enforceability of arbitration agreements in consumer credit contracts with military personnel and their dependents. *See* Military Lending Act, 10 U.S.C. § 987(e)(3). More recently, the 2008 Farm Bill (passed by Congress over President Bush's veto) required any "livestock or poultry contract" with a pre-dispute arbitration clause to include "a provision that allows a producer or grower, prior to entering the contract to decline to be bound by the arbitration provision," and to provide conspicuous notice of the provision. 7 U.S.C. § 197c(a), (b). Thereafter, in response to *Jones v. Halliburton* (noted in § 2.04), Congress provided that "[n]one of the funds appropriated or otherwise made available by this Act may be expended for any Federal contract for an amount in excess of $1,000,000 that is awarded more than 60 days after the effective date of [the 2010 Defense Department Appropriations Act], unless the contractor agrees not to" require or enforce any pre-dispute clause to "resolve through arbitration any claim under title VII of the Civil Rights Act of 1964 or any tort related to or arising out of sexual assault or harassment, including assault and battery, intentional infliction of emotional distress, false imprisonment, or negligent hiring, supervision, or retention." Department of Defense Appropriations Act, 2010, Pub. L. No. 111-118, § 8116(a) (2009) (also known as the "Franken amendment"). The provision has been reenacted in subsequent defense appropriations acts and implemented by DoD regulations, which are reprinted in the Documentary Supplement.

Most recently, the Dodd-Frank Wall Street Reform and Consumer Protection Act, Pub. L. No. 111-203 (2010), contains a variety of provisions dealing with arbitration. It precludes residential mortgage agreements from including pre-dispute arbitration clauses, *id.* § 1414; makes several causes of action created by the Act nonarbitrable, *id.* §§ 748, 922, & 1057; and gives both the SEC and the newly created Consumer Financial Protection Bureau authority to prohibit or impose conditions on the use of pre-dispute arbitration agreements in contracts they regulate, *id.* §§ 921 & 1028.

The cases that follow highlight issues that have arisen in the application of some of these statutes.

VOLKSWAGEN OF AMERICA, INC. v. SUD'S OF PEORIA, INC.
United States Court of Appeals for the Seventh Circuit
474 F.3d 966 (2007)

RIPPLE, *Circuit Judge.*

Volkswagen of America, Inc. ("Volkswagen") brought this diversity action against one of its car dealerships, Sud's of Peoria, Inc. ("Sud's"), for breach of contract. Invoking the Federal Arbitration Act, Sud's moved to stay the entire action pending arbitration. The district court denied the motion in part; Sud's now has appealed. For the reasons set forth in the following opinion, we affirm the judgment of the district court.

I

BACKGROUND

A. Facts

In the summer of 2003, Sud's, through its three principal owners, contracted with Volkswagen to open an authorized Volkswagen vehicle dealership. At the time negotiations began, Sud's was conducting its operations in a vehicle showroom in Peoria, Illinois. In the 2003 agreement, in exchange for the right to sell Volkswagen automobiles, Sud's agreed to redesign its existing facility according to Volkswagen's uniform design specifications. Additionally, the parties' arrangement contemplated that Sud's soon would move its operations to a new site in nearby Pekin, Illinois.

The parties signed three additional agreements. First, a "Facility Construction Agreement" ("Construction Agreement") outlined a timetable and general design specifications for the construction of the new facility. According to the terms of the Construction Agreement, Sud's had twenty-one months from the date on which it acquired the new property to complete construction of the facility and have it ready for use. The agreement set intermediate deadlines for Sud's to complete a land survey, to prepare design plans and to furnish a warranty deed for the new property. The Construction Agreement also contained the following arbitration clause:

In the event of any dispute concerning any matter arising under this Agreement, the parties consent to mandatory binding arbitration to be held in Oakland County, Michigan, under the auspices of a nationally recognized arbitration service reasonably mutually acceptable to the parties.

The parties also entered into a financing arrangement to fund construction of the new facility. Under the terms of a "Memorandum of Understanding — Capital Loan Agreement" (the "Loan Agreement"), Volkswagen agreed to extend to Sud's a $500,000 loan at an interest rate of 4.25%. In paragraph two of the Loan Agreement, Sud's, in turn, promised to service the loan with monthly interest payments and to repay the principal in five annual installments of $100,000 due at the end of each year. In paragraph four of the Loan Agreement, Sud's also agreed to execute and comply fully with the terms of the Construction Agreement. Failure to do so, the provision stated, required immediate repayment of the loan balance and accumulated interest.

Lastly, the parties agreed to a "Performance Incentive Program" (the "Incentive Program"), which allowed Sud's to earn five, annual "incentive" payments of $100,000 from Volkswagen, in addition to a $60,000 bonus incentive at the end of the five-year period. The incentive payments were timed to coincide with Sud's loan obligations so that Sud's could use its yearly $100,000 earned incentive to make its annual, $100,000 loan payment. To earn the incentives, Sud's was required to comply with the minimum requirements of the Volkswagen Dealer Operating Standards, a component of the parties' franchise agreement that governed the general design and operations of authorized Volkswagen dealerships. Additionally, the earning of incentives depended on Sud's execution of, and full compliance with, the Construction Agreement. If Sud's violated the Construction Agreement in year one, it would not earn the incentive payment for that year and also would be disqualified from earning future payments. As construction of the new facility began, Volkswagen paid Sud's a $20,000 advance to be earned later under the Incentive Program.

B. District Court Proceedings

On September 7, 2004, Volkswagen filed this diversity action for breach of contract against Sud's and its three principal owners, each of whom had executed guarantees on Sud's performance. . . . At the heart of the complaint were allegations that Sud's had failed to meet the time line set forth in the parties' Construction Agreement; Sud's allegedly did not begin construction on time, failed to acquire property for the new facility and did not tender the construction plans required by that agreement. According to Count I of the complaint, this breach of the Construction Agreement placed Sud's in default of its loan obligations; Count I also asserted, in the alternative, that Sud's had defaulted on its loan obligations by failing to remit its first annual payment on time. Volkswagen sought full repayment of the $500,000 loan principal.

Count II of the complaint alleged breach of the Incentive Program and sought recovery of the $20,000 advance. According to Count II, Sud's had violated the Incentive Program in two ways. First, Sud's allegedly had disqualified itself from earning incentives by violating the terms of the Construction Agreement. Second, Sud's allegedly had not complied with the franchise agreement's Dealer Operations

Standards, a precondition to receiving incentives, because it failed "to order, install, or display at its current dealership premises a Volkswagen facade dealer nameplate that complies with [Volkswagen's] current corporate identity standards."

Relying upon the Construction Agreement's arbitration provision, Sud's notified Volkswagen of its intent to submit the matter to arbitration. It then moved, under the FAA, to stay the action in the district court pending an arbitrator's resolution of the dispute. The district court granted the motion in part and denied it in part. Addressing Count I of Volkswagen's complaint — breach of the Loan Agreement — the court stayed the issues related to Sud's compliance with the Construction Agreement because of that contract's arbitration clause. However, the court refused to stay the question of whether Sud's had made its loan payments on time. In the court's view, the Loan Agreement did not provide for arbitration and did not incorporate the Construction Agreement's arbitration clause for matters unrelated to construction.

With respect to Count II — breach of the Incentive Program — the court also stayed one issue but not the other. The court held that failure to install a dealer nameplate was non-arbitrable because the Motor Vehicle Franchise Contract Arbitration Fairness Act of 2002 ("Fairness Act"), 15 U.S.C. § 1226, requires the parties to arbitrate disputes only if both parties assent to arbitration *after* a controversy arises under a dealer franchise agreement. The district court held that the nameplate issue arose under a franchise agreement within the meaning of the statute. Because only Sud's, not Volkswagen, had agreed to proceed to arbitration after the dispute had arisen, the issue could not be sent to arbitration. With respect to the alternate theory, however, the court held that Volkswagen's theory that Sud's had breached the Incentive Program because it failed to comply with the Construction Agreement was arbitrable because of the Construction Agreement's arbitration clause.

In short, all issues related to Sud's performance of the Construction Agreement were stayed pending arbitration, but the balance of the case was set to move forward in the district court.

II

DISCUSSION

. . .

In its brief before this court, Sud's submits that the district court, having determined that certain issues are arbitrable, was "require[d]" to stay proceedings in their entirety pending arbitration. . . .

For arbitrable issues, a § 3 stay is mandatory. For remaining non-arbitrable issues, however, the FAA does not give courts express guidance on how to proceed. To fill this gap in the statute, Sud's proposes a rule that would require the district court to stay the *entire case* whenever it finds at least one arbitrable issue. . . .

The courts, however, generally have not interpreted § 3 in this fashion. "[T]he cases, perhaps concerned lest the tail wag the dog, treat the question whether to stay the entire case as discretionary in cases involving both arbitrable and nonarbitrable issues."

The Supreme Court has indicated its support for this interpretation of § 3 on at least two occasions. In *Dean Witter Reynolds, Inc. v. Byrd*, 470 U.S. 213, 221 (1985), the Court was untroubled by the prospect of "piecemeal" litigation resulting from the stay of some issues but not others. "The preeminent concern of Congress in passing the Act was to enforce private agreements into which parties had entered, and that concern requires that we rigorously enforce agreements to arbitrate, even if the result is 'piecemeal' litigation, at least absent a countervailing policy manifested in another federal statute." Similarly, in *Moses H. Cone Memorial Hospital*, the Court noted that, at the district court's discretion, litigation may proceed against parties who were not subject to the arbitration agreement, even though claims against the arbitrating parties have been stayed. "That decision," the Court held, "is one left to the district court (or to the state trial court under applicable state procedural rules) as a matter of its discretion to control its docket."

. . .

. . . In light of Sud's independent obligation to make payments on the Loan Agreement, we cannot say that the district court abused its discretion in failing to stay litigation concerning this issue.

The district court also was faced with another issue which, in its view, was not subject to arbitration . . . Under the Incentive Agreement, receiving the incentives is conditioned upon compliance with the "Dealer Operating Standards," a component of the Volkswagen Dealer Agreement. These standards required Sud's to display a Volkswagen facade dealer nameplate that meets Volkswagen's corporate identity requirements. Volkswagen's complaint asserts that, by failing to comply with this requirement, Sud's disqualified itself from earning incentives. . . .

The district court held that arbitration of this claim was not authorized under the Motor Vehicle Franchise Contract Arbitration Fairness Act of 2002, 15 U.S.C. § 1226. . . .

The Fairness Act requires that, before car manufacturers and their dealerships settle a dispute through arbitration, "all parties" must consent in writing "*after* such controversy arises." *Id.* § 1226(a)(2) (emphasis added). The district court determined that, because only Sud's desired arbitration of this issue, the parties had not executed the bilateral, *post-dispute, written* agreement necessary for the name plate issue to be submitted to arbitration.

Sud's nevertheless urges that, despite the term "after" in the statute, we should infer the requisite consent in Volkswagen's act of drafting the original franchise agreement. Invoking the legislative history of the Fairness Act, Sud's submits that the Act is intended to "*protect* motor vehicle *dealers*" against automobile manufacturers" and to ensure dealers "the remedy of arbitration that a dealer desires." When it is the dealership who wishes to arbitrate a dispute, Sud's contends, we should interpret the statute more leniently.

The legislative history cited by Sud's — a Senate Committee Report to the Fairness Act — provides an enlightening history of automotive franchise arrangements. As the report describes, for over half a century, Congress has understood "the imbalances in bargaining power" inherent in the relationship between car dealers and manufacturers. S. Rep. No. 107-266, at 7 (2002). According to the Senate Report, unlike other types of franchisees that have a wide selection of franchisers with whom to contract, automotive dealerships "may only obtain the right to merchandise and sell their product from an extremely limited group of manufacturers." Leveraging this disparity in bargaining power, motor vehicle manufacturers historically have forced dealers into boilerplate franchise contracts "on a 'take it or leave it' basis." Prominent in these "contracts of adhesion" are mandatory arbitration clauses that remained enforceable under the FAA, despite attempts by state legislatures to prohibit unfair dealer-manufacturer arbitration.

Even if we accept Sud's submission that the drafters of the Fairness Act likely intended to equalize the bargaining equation in favor of the dealer, we cannot ignore that this same Senate Committee Report insists repeatedly, consistent with the statutory text, that *"both parties"* must consent to arbitration, and only *"after"* a controversy arises. Indeed, if the legislative history confirms anything, it is that Congress intended such boilerplate arbitration clauses to be displaced in favor of "forums otherwise available" under federal or local law. In view of this history, we refuse to depart from the Fairness Act's plain wording. As the statute provides, *both* parties must consent voluntarily to arbitrate a dispute under a manufacturer-dealer agreement and that consent must be expressed only *after* that dispute has arisen. The district court determined correctly that the record revealed that only Sud's has consented to arbitration at this stage. Accordingly, we must affirm the court's refusal to stay the dealer nameplate issue pending arbitration.

Conclusion

In short, while the district court had the discretion to stay judicial proceedings until the arbitration was completed, we cannot say that the district court abused its discretion when it decided not to do so. . . .

For these reasons, we affirm the judgment of the district court.

AFFIRMED.

NOTES

1.   As the court acknowledged, the Motor Vehicle Franchise Contract Arbitration Fairness Act was enacted to protect car dealers from having to arbitrate claims with manufacturers under pre-dispute arbitration agreements. But here, it was the car dealer who sought to have the case resolved in arbitration, not the manufacturer. If arbitration is unfair to car dealers, why did the dealer here want to arbitrate?

2.   The issue in the Supreme Court's decision in *Byrd*, cited by the court of appeals in *Volkswagen*, was whether a court could proceed to adjudicate all issues in a case if arbitrable claims were intertwined with nonarbitrable claims. The Supreme Court held that the court lacks the discretion to try all the claims (both nonarbitrable and arbitrable) in one lawsuit, reasoning as follows:

The preeminent concern of Congress in passing the Act was to enforce private agreements into which parties had entered, and that concern requires that we rigorously enforce agreements to arbitrate, even if the result is "piecemeal" litigation, at least absent a countervailing policy manifested in another federal statute. By compelling arbitration of state-law claims, a district court successfully protects the contractual rights of the parties and their rights under the Arbitration Act.

Dean Witter Reynolds, Inc. v. Byrd, 470 U.S. 213, 221 (1985). For a more recent case presenting the same issue, see KPMG LLP v. Cocchi, 132 S. Ct. 23, 25-26 (2011) (per curiam).

In *Volkswagen*, by contrast, the district court had held that some of the claims were subject to arbitration; the issue was whether the other claims could proceed in court on a parallel track to the arbitration, or whether those claims should be stayed pending the outcome in arbitration. The court of appeals held that the district court did not abuse its discretion in permitting the parallel proceedings.

COX v. COMMUNITY LOANS OF AMERICA, INC.
United States District Court for the Middle District of Georgia
2012 U.S. Dist. LEXIS 31448 (Mar. 8, 2012)

CLAY D. LAND, UNITED STATES DISTRICT JUDGE.

This putative class action involves vehicle title pawns. Plaintiffs Jason M. Cox, Estevan Castillo and Leo Thomas Tookes Jr. (collectively, "Plaintiffs") are members of the United States Military who entered vehicle title pawn transactions with one of the Defendants and were later unable to redeem their car titles. Plaintiffs' vehicles have either been repossessed or are subject to repossession. Plaintiffs allege that their vehicle title pawn transactions are void from the inception because they are prohibited by the federal Military Lending Act ("MLA"), 10 U.S.C. § 987. Defendants Community Loans of America, Inc., Alabama Title Loans, Inc. and Georgia Auto Pawn, Inc. (collectively, "Defendants") filed a Motion to Dismiss relying on an arbitration clause in the relevant contracts. Defendants maintain that the arbitration clauses are enforceable and the transactions do not violate the MLA. As the Court announced during the hearing on the motion, Defendants' motion is denied. This Order sets forth the reasons for the ruling.

. . .

In the present context, the Court must determine whether Plaintiffs have sufficiently alleged that their title pawn transactions violated the MLA, and thus the arbitration clauses in their agreements are unenforceable. Defendants argue that the transactions in question involve Plaintiffs actually selling their vehicles to Defendants while retaining the right to repurchase them by paying back the sale price plus a fee that is a percentage of the sale price. Defendants maintain that such title pawn transactions are not consumer credit transactions within the meaning of the MLA, and therefore, are not prohibited by the MLA. Plaintiffs contend that the transactions are loans that are secured by the titles to their vehicles, and as such, are prohibited consumer credit transactions under the MLA. At this stage of the proceedings, the Court examines Plaintiffs' factual allegations in the Complaint along with any exhibits to the Complaint. Construing all reasonable inferences in Plaintiffs' favor, the Court must determine whether Plaintiffs have sufficiently alleged that the transactions are credit transactions prohibited by the MLA.

FACTUAL ALLEGATIONS

The Plaintiffs allege the following in their Complaint. Plaintiffs are members of the United States military. Defendants are businesses that make vehicle title loans. A vehicle title loan is a transaction in which the customer pledges or signs over his car title to a vehicle title loan company, and in return the customer receives cash. The customer gets his car title back if he pays the loan amount plus a percentage within a certain number of days. Each Plaintiff obtained a vehicle title loan from one of the Defendants.

. . .

DISCUSSION

The central issue in this case is whether Plaintiffs have adequately alleged violations of the Military Lending Act ("MLA"), 10 U.S.C. § 987. It is undisputed that if the MLA applies, then the arbitration provisions in the relevant contracts are unenforceable, 10 U.S.C. § 987(e)(3), and the Motion to Dismiss based on the arbitration provision must be denied.

I. Military Lending Act Background

In 2006, the U.S. Department of Defense issued a report to Congress entitled "Report On Predatory Lending Practices Directed at Members of the Armed Forces and Their Dependents" ("DoD Report"). The report focused on "predatory lending" to military personnel, including car title loans. The report concluded that predatory lending to military personnel, including car title loans, "undermines military readiness, harms the morale of troops and their families, and adds to the cost of fielding an all volunteer fighting force." The report recommends prohibiting lenders from using "car title pawns as security for obligations." The report also notes a steady and significant increase in the rate of revoked or denied security clearances for military personnel due to financial problems; "At a time when we are at war, this is an unacceptable loss of valuable talent and resources."

In response to the DoD Report, Congress enacted the MLA. The MLA provides that a "creditor who extends consumer credit" to a "covered member of the armed services" "may not impose an annual percentage rate of interest greater than 36 percent" with respect to the credit extended. 10 U.S.C. § 987(a), (b). The MLA also makes it unlawful for a "creditor to extend consumer credit to a covered member . . . with respect to which" the creditor uses "the title of a vehicle as security for the obligation." 10 U.S.C. § 987(e)(5).

The MLA requires certain mandatory disclosures in connection with the "extension of consumer credit." 10 U.S.C. § 987(c). The MLA expressly preempts inconsistent state or federal laws. 10 U.S.C. § 987(d). As noted above, Defendants concede that if the MLA applies to the transactions at issue in this case, then the arbitration clauses in the relevant agreements are unenforceable. *See* 10 U.S.C. § 987(e)(3). If a "creditor" knowingly violates the MLA, that is a misdemeanor. 10 U.S.C. § 987(f)(1). Also, "[a]ny credit agreement, promissory note, or other contract prohibited under [the MLA] is void from the inception of such contract." 10 U.S.C. § 987(f)(3).

The MLA does not define "creditor" or "consumer credit." Rather, the statute directed the Secretary of Defense to prescribe regulations establishing those definitions after consultation with the Department of Treasury, Office of the Comptroller of the Currency, Office of Thrift Supervision, Board of Governors of the Federal Reserve System, Federal Trade Commission, Federal Deposit Insurance Corporation, and the National Credit Union Administration. 10 U.S.C. § 987(h)(2)(D), (3). In the final rule adding new regulations to implement the provisions of the MLA, the Department of Defense stated that "vehicle title loans should be included within the definition of consumer credit, and that covering such transactions is consistent with the law's purpose." Limitations on Terms of Consumer Credit Extended to Service Members and Dependents, 72 Fed. Reg. 50,580, 50,586 (Aug. 31, 2007).

. . .

II. Did Plaintiffs Allege "Vehicle Title Loans"?

The question for the Court is whether, taking the factual allegations in Plaintiffs' Complaint to be true and resolving all reasonable inferences in Plaintiffs' favor, Plaintiffs have alleged that the transactions they entered with Defendants are "vehicle title loans" within the meaning of the MLA. Based on the allegations in the Complaint and the attachments to the Complaint, the Court concludes that they have.

Defendants contend that the transactions at issue here are not "vehicle title loans" within the meaning of the MLA because the transactions here are creatures of state law that do not involve "credit" within the meaning of the MLA. . . . [U]nder the MLA, "credit" is "the right granted by a creditor to a debtor to defer payment of debt or to incur debt and defer its payment." 32 C.F.R. § 232.3(d). Defendants' main argument is that Plaintiffs did not take on "debt" because there is no promissory note or other form of promise to pay; rather, the transaction was actually a sale of a vehicle with the opportunity to buy it back and the right to continue to use the vehicle until the time for re-purchasing it expired.

Construing Defendants' own documents in Plaintiffs' favor, however, Plaintiffs have plausibly alleged consumer credit transactions within the meaning of the MLA. First, the agreements state the "cost of [Plaintiffs'] credit," "[t]he dollar amount the credit will cost [Plaintiffs]," and the "amount of credit provided to [Plaintiffs]." Second, the agreements state that Plaintiffs were "giving a security interest in the certificate of title" to their vehicles. Third, the agreements state that Defendants may register a lien on the certificate of title. Fourth, [two of the

Plaintiffs] each received a notice reiterating that his "automobile title has been pledged as security for the pawn," stating that pawning "is a more expensive way of borrowing money," asking that he acknowledge the amount "borrowed," and asking him to acknowledge that "continued ownership of [his] automobile" would be "at risk" if the amount due was not paid.

In other words, construing the factual allegations in the Complaint and the attached agreements in Plaintiffs' favor, each Plaintiff deposited his vehicle title with a Defendant as security for the payment of a debt. Defendants' own documents state that Plaintiffs "borrowed" money. Moreover, a specific sum of money is due by agreement, and if it is not paid, then the Plaintiff loses the title to his car and the car itself. For all of these reasons, the Court concludes that Plaintiffs sufficiently alleged that the transactions they entered with Defendants are "vehicle title loans" within the meaning of the MLA.

Defendants focus on Georgia and Alabama law and repeatedly argue that the transactions in this case "are not loans." Under the law of both states, a "pawn transaction" is defined as either a "loan on the security of pledged goods" or a "purchase of pledged goods on the condition that the pledged goods may be redeemed or repurchased by the pledgor or seller for a fixed price within a fixed period of time." O.C.G.A. § 44-12-130(3); *accord* Ala. Code § 5-19A-2(3). . . .

The express preemption clause in the MLA "preempts any State or Federal law, rule, or regulation, including any State usury law, to the extent that such law, rule, or regulation is inconsistent with this section[.]" 10 U.S.C. § 987(d)(1). Therefore, to the extent that Georgia or Alabama law conflicts with the MLA, the state law is preempted. Accordingly, it does not matter that Alabama and Georgia would categorize the transactions as "pawns" rather than "loans." What matters is that Plaintiffs sufficiently alleged that the transactions they entered with Defendants involve "credit" and are "vehicle title loans" within the meaning of the federal law. Thus, even though the transactions may not be considered "credit" transactions under state law, they may be considered "consumer credit" transactions within the meaning of the MLA.

Defendants argue that even if the Court finds that Plaintiffs have sufficiently alleged claims under the MLA, the law is so vague and ambiguous that Defendants did not have notice that "pawn transactions" like the ones alleged in Plaintiffs' Complaint were covered under the MLA. Construing the factual allegations in the Complaint and the attachments to the Complaint in Plaintiffs' favor, however, Defendants did have notice that the transactions would be covered under the MLA. As discussed above, Defendants' own documents reference the "credit" provided to the Plaintiffs and state that Plaintiffs were "giving a security interest in the certificate of title" to their vehicles. Also, Defendants appear to acknowledge that the "pawn transactions" are a type of "closed-end credit transaction" within the meaning of the TILA, which has the same definition of "closed-end credit transaction" as the MLA.

. . .

Given that Plaintiffs sufficiently alleged claims under the MLA, the arbitration provisions in their agreements are unenforceable. 10 U.S.C. § 987(e)(3). Accordingly, Defendants' Motion to Dismiss based on the arbitration provisions must be denied.

. . .

NOTE

The Military Act was designed to protect military personnel from predatory lending activity. Why include a prohibition on arbitration clauses as well?

The DoD Report (at p. 51) discussed in *Cox* explained:

> Service members should maintain full legal recourse against unscrupulous lenders. Loan contracts to Service members should not include mandatory arbitration clauses or onerous notice provisions, and should not require the Service member to waive his or her right of recourse, such as the right to participate in a plaintiff class. Waiver is not a matter of "choice" in take-it-or-leave-it contracts of adhesion.

If that is true for members of the military, isn't it also true for all consumers? Or is there a reason to treat military personnel and their families differently?

HOLMES v. AIR LIQUIDE USA LLC

United States District Court for the Southern District of Texas
2012 U.S. Dist. LEXIS 10678 (Jan. 30, 2012)

KEITH P. ELLISON, UNITED STATES DISTRICT JUDGE.

MEMORANDUM AND ORDER

. . .

I. BACKGROUND

Plaintiff Jamie V. Holmes ("Holmes" or "Plaintiff") was employed by Defendant Air Liquide America ("Air Liquide") as Manager of Strategic Projects. Holmes' employment was terminated in February 2011. In July 2011, Holmes filed this lawsuit against Defendants for discrimination in violation of the Americans with Disabilities Act ("ADA"), the Texas Commission on Human Rights Act ("TCHRA"), and Title VII of the Civil Rights Act of 1964 ("Title VII"). Holmes' Complaint alleges that Air Liquide discriminated against her for her association with a person with a disability — in this case, Holmes' daughter — in violation of the ADA and the TCHRA. She alleges that Air Liquide also discriminated against her on the basis of her gender in violation of Title VII and the TCHRA. Finally, Holmes alleges that Air Liquide retaliated against her for exercising her rights in violation of the TCHRA and the Family & Medical Leave Act ("FMLA").

. . .

III. ANALYSIS

. . .

Plaintiff argues that . . . [even if a predispute arbitration agreement exists between the parties, it was rendered invalid and unenforceable by the 2010 Dodd-Frank Wall Street Reform and Consumer Protection Act ("Dodd-Frank").]

1. Plain meaning of the statute

Plaintiff argues that two sections of Dodd-Frank invalidate any predispute arbitration agreement that she might have had with Defendants. Plaintiff cites 7 U.S.C. § 26(n)(2) [§ 748 of Dodd-Frank] (adding new whistleblower protections under the Commodity Exchange Act) and 18 U.S.C. § 1514A(e) [§ 922 of Dodd-Frank] (enhancing scope of the Sarbanes-Oxley whistleblower provisions). Plaintiff contends that, if an arbitration agreement requires arbitration of disputes arising under those sections, then the entire agreement is invalid, and no dispute (including disputes *not* arising under the relevant sections and entirely unrelated to Dodd-Frank) is subject to it.

Plaintiff supports her reading of 7 U.S.C. § 26(n)(2) and 18 U.S.C. § 1514A(e) by comparing those Sections of Dodd-Frank to a third Section, 12 U.S.C. § 5567(d)(2) [§ 1057 of Dodd-Frank], which states that "no predispute arbitration agreement shall be valid or enforceable **to the extent that** it requires arbitration of a dispute arising under this section.") (emphasis added). Plaintiff argues that Congress is aware of the difference between "if" and "to the extent that," and that "[w]here Congress includes particular language in one section of a statute but omits it in another section of the same Act, it is generally presumed that Congress acts intentionally and purposely in the disparate inclusion or exclusion." Thus, Plaintiff concludes that, as 7 U.S.C. § 26(n)(2) and 18 U.S.C. § 1514A(e) use broader language than 12 U.S.C. § 5567(d)(2), their meaning likewise must be broader.

Plaintiff contends that the arbitration agreement at issue in this case, which requires arbitration of any federal statutory claim, necessarily (if unintentionally) requires arbitration of claims arising under 7 U.S.C. § 26 and 18 U.S.C. § 1514A. By requiring arbitration of disputes under those sections, Plaintiff argues that the arbitration agreement violates those sections, and is therefore invalid and unenforceable. Defendants dispute this reading of the statute, and argue that such a reading would invalidate every pre-Dodd-Frank arbitration agreement that does not specifically account for Dodd-Frank. Defendants contend that Plaintiff's reading of the statute is "nonsensical, and such an interpretation cannot be accepted because it is unreasonable and would lead to an absurd result."

The Court emphasizes that this is not a case in which the dispute arises under Dodd-Frank — it is clear that any agreement requiring the arbitration of such a dispute would be invalid. What is far less clear is whether agreements requiring the arbitration of all federal statutory claims are rendered invalid by the passage of Dodd-Frank simply because, without having anticipated the statute, the agreements implicitly require arbitration of claims arising under it. The Court is not aware of any courts to have considered such an argument. However, as the Court ultimately concludes that Plaintiff's argument must fail because the portions of

Dodd-Frank upon which she relies do not apply retroactively, it does not issue an opinion on whether Plaintiff's reading of Dodd-Frank is correct.

2. Retroactive Application of Dodd-Frank

a. Legal Standard

Generally, statutes are presumed to operate prospectively, not retrospectively. In *Landgraf v. USI Film Prods.*, 511 U.S. 244 (1994), the Supreme Court provided the framework by which courts are to determine the retroactivity of federal statutes. Noting the "particular concerns" raised by retroactive statutes, the Supreme Court instructs that courts must consider "whether the new provision attaches new legal consequences to events completed before its enactment." If it does, a presumption against statutory retroactivity exists. The presumption against retroactivity can be rebutted by "specific legislative authorization;" that is, where a statute unambiguously applies to preenactment conduct, "there is no conflict between that principle and a *presumption* against retroactivity," and the statute is to be applied as it indicates.

The presumption of retroactivity can be rebutted in other situations, as well. For example, "[w]hen the intervening statute authorizes or affects the propriety of prospective relief," the new provision is not retroactive, and the statute may be applied. Statutes conferring or ousting jurisdiction or changing procedural rules similarly may, in some cases, be applied retroactively. However, where a new statute would have a "genuinely 'retroactive' effect," that is, where its application would "impair rights a party possessed when he acted, increase a party's liability for past conduct, or impose new duties with respect to transactions already completed," it may not be applied retroactively. Thus, the Court must determine whether Congress manifested clear intent for Dodd-Frank to apply retroactively; if it did not, the Court must consider whether the provisions at issue would have a genuinely retroactive effect if applied to past conduct.

b. Case Law

↓ ↓ ↓

Only two courts have evaluated the retroactive application of portions of Dodd-Frank restricting mandatory predispute arbitration. *See Henderson v. Masco Framing Corp.*, 2011 U.S. Dist. LEXIS 80494 (D. Nev. July 22, 2011); *Pezza v. Investors Capital Corp.*, 767 F. Supp. 2d 225 (D. Mass. 2011). These courts reached opposite conclusions: *Henderson* held that 18 U.S.C. § 1514A(e) could not apply retroactively under the principles set forth in *Langraf*. The court determined that the arbitration agreement at issue was a contract, and that predictability was therefore of paramount importance. It concluded that retroactive application of the provisions at issue would "impair rights [the parties] possessed when [they] acted." *Pezza*, in contrast, concluded that retroactive application of a provision regarding arbitration would affect only the conferral of jurisdiction; under *Landgraf*, the court concluded, the effect of the provision was therefore not genuinely retroactive.

c. Analysis

The Court begins its analysis by agreeing with both the *Pezza* and *Henderson* courts that the portions of Dodd-Frank addressing predispute arbitration do not evidence any intent to apply retroactively. Thus, the Court proceeds to considering whether the presumption against retroactivity is rebutted in this case. Ultimately, the Court cannot agree with the holding in *Pezza* that the portions of Dodd-Frank at issue affect only procedural rights. Instead, as the court held in *Henderson*, this Court finds that the rights of contracting parties are substantive, and that a statute affecting those rights undoubtedly impairs rights that existed at the time the parties acted. As the court in *Henderson* explained, retroactive application in this case "would not merely affect the jurisdictional location in which [the parties'] claims could be brought; it would fundamentally interfere with the parties' contractual rights and would impair the 'predictability and stability' of their earlier agreement." Indeed, *Landgraf* explicitly mentioned "contractual or property rights" as "[t]he largest category of cases in which . . . the presumption against retroactivity has been applied," as these are areas "in which predictability and stability are of prime importance." Because Dodd-Frank would have a "genuinely 'retroactive' effect," the Court concludes that neither 7 U.S.C. § 26(n)(2) nor 18 U.S.C. § 1514A(e) affects the enforceability of the arbitration agreement between Plaintiff and Defendants.

. . .

IV. CONCLUSION

Because a valid arbitration agreement exists and is enforceable, Defendants' motion to compel arbitration must be **GRANTED**. The case is therefore **DISMISSED WITH PREJUDICE.**

IT IS SO ORDERED.

NOTES

1.   The provisions of Dodd-Frank at issue in *Holmes* are different from the other federal statutes restricting the enforcement of arbitration agreements we have looked at. The Dodd-Frank provisions make the enforceability of the arbitration agreement turn on the type of federal statutory claim at issue. By comparison, the other statutes we have looked at (as well as another provision of Dodd-Frank, dealing with consumer mortgage agreements) make arbitration agreements unenforceable in certain types of contracts. Which approach is better?

2.   What do you think of Holmes's interpretation of the Dodd-Frank nonarbitrability provisions? The district court avoids the issue by holding that the provisions were not retroactive and so not applicable to Holmes's arbitration agreement. How should a court address the argument on its merits? Do you think Congress intended to invalidate all arbitration clauses that do not expressly exclude Dodd-Frank claims from their scope, even if no such claim could plausibly be brought in the case?

3. *Holmes* does identify an important distinction between the Dodd-Frank nonarbitrability provisions: whether they invalidate the entire arbitration agreement or whether they make the agreement unenforceable only as to the particular federal statutory claim. Under the former type of statute, the entire case will proceed in court (because the arbitration agreement is unenforceable in its entirety), while under the later type of statute, only the federal statutory claim will be adjudicated in court while the rest of the case will proceed in arbitration. Keep this distinction in mind while working through the materials in the rest of this Chapter.

PROBLEM 3.2

Captain J.H. Watson recently was honorably discharged from the U.S. Army and now has joined his parents in the family automobile business (their car dealership is known as Watson Motor Cars ("WMC")). During his first day at work, his mother tells him about a dispute that WMC is having with Hansom Motors, the manufacturer of the automobiles that WMC sells. The amount of the claim is too small to hire a lawyer, she says, and wonders whether it would be easier for the family to file a claim in arbitration than to sue (the franchise agreement has an arbitration clause, she tells him).

Watson has his own troubles to worry about as well. Hanging over him from his time in the military are some payday loans he took out to provide extra cash when his Army paycheck ran a little short. Watson believes that the interest rate on the loans exceeds the maximum permitted by law and wants to file suit against the payday lender. But his mother's mention of arbitration prompts him to look at his payday loan agreement, and he notices an arbitration clause there, too.

You are a friend of Watson's family, and he asks you both about his and about WMC's options. What do you tell him?

§ 3.03 IMPLIED STATUTORY RESTRICTIONS ON THE ENFORCEABILITY OF ARBITRATION AGREEMENTS

The express statutory limitations on the enforceability of arbitration agreements discussed in the previous section are a relatively recent development. Most federal statutes do not mention arbitration, yet many provide statutory causes of action. Can those claims be arbitrated? Or are they non-arbitrable?

[A]   The Rise and Decline of the Nonarbitrability Doctrine

WILKO v. SWAN
United States Supreme Court
346 U.S. 427 (1953)

Mr. JUSTICE REED delivered the opinion of the Court.

This action by petitioner, a customer, against respondents, partners in a securities brokerage firm, was brought in the United States District Court for the Southern District of New York, to recover damages under § 12(2) of the Securities Act of 1933. The complaint alleged that on or about January 17, 1951, through the instrumentalities of interstate commerce, petitioner was induced by Hayden, Stone and Company to purchase 1,600 shares of the common stock of Air Associates, Incorporated, by false representations that pursuant to a merger contract with the Borg Warner Corporation, Air Associates' stock would be valued at $6.00 per share over the then current market price, and that financial interests were buying up the stock for the speculative profit. It was alleged that he was not told that Haven B. Page (also named as a defendant but not involved in this review), a director of, and counsel for, Air Associates was then selling his own Air Associates' stock, including some or all that petitioner purchased. Two weeks after the purchase, petitioner disposed of the stock at a loss. Claiming that the loss was due to the firm's misrepresentations and omission of information concerning Mr. Page, he sought damages.

Without answering the complaint, the respondent moved to stay the trial of the action pursuant to § 3 of the United States Arbitration Act until an arbitration in accordance with the terms of identical margin agreements was had. An affidavit accompanied the motion stating that the parties' relationship was controlled by the terms of the agreements and that while the firm was willing to arbitrate petitioner had failed to seek or proceed with any arbitration of the controversy.

Finding that the margin agreements provide that arbitration should be the method of settling all future controversies, the District Court held that the agreement to arbitrate deprived petitioner of the advantageous court remedy afforded by the Securities Act, and denied the stay. A divided Court of Appeals concluded that the Act did not prohibit the agreement to refer future controversies to arbitration, and reversed.

The question is whether an agreement to arbitrate a future controversy is a "condition, stipulation, or provision binding any person acquiring any security to waive compliance with any provision" of the Securities Act which § 14 declares "void." We granted certiorari to review this important and novel federal question affecting both the Securities Act and the United States Arbitration Act.

As the margin agreement in the light of the complaint evidenced a transaction in interstate commerce, no issue arises as to the applicability of the provisions of the United States Arbitration Act to this suit, based upon the Securities Act.

In response to a Presidential message urging that there be added to the ancient rule of *caveat emptor* the further doctrine of "let the seller also beware," Congress passed the Securities Act of 1933. Designed to protect investors, the Act requires issuers, underwriters, and dealers to make full and fair disclosure of the character of securities sold in interstate and foreign commerce and to prevent fraud in their sale. To effectuate this policy, § 12(2) created a special right to recover for misrepresentation which differs substantially from the common-law action in that the seller is made to assume the burden of proving lack of scienter. The Act's special right is enforceable in any court of competent jurisdiction — federal or state — and removal from a state court is prohibited. If suit be brought in a federal court, the purchaser has a wide choice of venue, the privilege of nation-wide service of process and the jurisdictional $3,000 requirement of diversity cases is inapplicable.

The United States Arbitration Act establishes by statute the desirability of arbitration as an alternative to the complications of litigation. The reports of both Houses on that Act stress the need for avoiding the delay and expense of litigation, and practice under its terms raises hope for its usefulness both in controversies based on statutes or on standards otherwise created. This hospitable attitude of legislatures and courts toward arbitration, however, does not solve our question as to the validity of petitioner's stipulation by the margin agreements . . . to submit to arbitration controversies that might arise from the transactions.

. . .

Respondent is in agreement with the Court of Appeals that the margin agreement arbitration paragraph does not relieve the seller from either liability or burden of proof imposed by the Securities Act. We agree that in so far as the award in arbitration may be affected by legal requirements, statutes or common law, rather than by considerations of fairness, the provisions of the Securities Act control. This is true even though this proposed agreement has no requirement that the arbitrators follow the law. . . .

The words of § 14 void any "stipulation" waiving compliance with any "provision" of the Securities Act. This arrangement to arbitrate is a "stipulation," and we think the right to select the judicial forum is the kind of "provision" that cannot be waived under § 14 of the Securities Act. . . . While a buyer and seller of securities, under some circumstances, may deal at arm's length on equal terms, it is clear that the Securities Act was drafted with an eye to the disadvantages under which buyers labor. Issuers of and dealers in securities have better opportunities to investigate and appraise the prospective earnings and business plans affecting securities than buyers. It is therefore reasonable for Congress to put buyers of securities covered by that Act on a different basis from other purchasers.

When the security buyer, prior to any violation of the Securities Act, waives his right to sue in courts, he gives up more than would a participant in other business transactions. The security buyer has a wider choice of courts and venue. He thus surrenders one of the advantages the Act gives him and surrenders it at a time when he is less able to judge the weight of the handicap the Securities Act places upon his adversary.

Even though the provisions of the Securities Act, advantageous to the buyer, apply, their effectiveness in application is lessened in arbitration as compared to judicial proceedings. Determination of the quality of a commodity or the amount of money due under a contract is not the type of issue here involved. This case requires subjective findings on the purpose and knowledge of an alleged violator of the Act. They must be not only determined but applied by the arbitrators without judicial instruction on the law. As their award may be made without explanation of their reasons and without a complete record of their proceedings, the arbitrators' conception of the legal meaning of such statutory requirements as "burden of proof," "reasonable care" or "material fact," cannot be examined. Power to vacate an award is limited. While it may be true, as the Court of Appeals thought, that a failure of the arbitrators to decide in accordance with the provisions of the Securities Act would "constitute grounds for vacating the award pursuant to section 10 of the Federal Arbitration Act," that failure would need to be made clearly to appear. In unrestricted submission, such as the present margin agreements envisage, the interpretations of the law by the arbitrators in contrast to manifest disregard are not subject, in the federal courts, to judicial review for error in interpretation. The United States Arbitration Act contains no provision for judicial determination of legal issues such as is found in the English law. As the protective provisions of the Securities Act require the exercise of judicial direction to fairly assure their effectiveness, it seems to us that Congress must have intended § 14 to apply to waiver of judicial trial and review.

. . .

Two policies, not easily reconcilable, are involved in this case. Congress has afforded participants in transactions subject to its legislative power an opportunity generally to secure prompt, economical and adequate solution of controversies through arbitration if the parties are willing to accept less certainty of legally correct adjustment. On the other hand, it has enacted the Securities Act to protect the rights of investors and has forbidden a waiver of any of those rights. Recognizing the advantages that prior agreements for arbitration may provide for the solution of commercial controversies, we decide that the intention of Congress concerning the sale of securities is better carried out by holding invalid such an agreement for arbitration of issues arising under the Act.

Reversed.

NOTES

1. Relying on *Wilko*, courts of appeals held that a wide array of federal statutory claims could not be arbitrated: antitrust, *see, e.g.*, American Safety Equip. Corp. v. J.P. Maguire & Co., 391 F.2d 821 (2d Cir. 1968); Securities Exchange Act of 1934, McMahon v. Shearson/American Exp., Inc., 788 F.2d 94, 96 (2d Cir. 1986), *rev'd*, 482 U.S. 220 (1987); Commodities Exchange Act, Marchese v. Shearson Hayden Stone, Inc., 734 F.2d 414, 419–21 (9th Cir. 1984); racketeering (RICO), Page v. Moseley, Hallgarten, Estabrook & Weeden, Inc., 806 F.2d 291, 298–300 (1st Cir. 1986); patent, Beckman Instruments, Inc. v. Technical Dev. Corp., 433 F.2d 55, 63 (7th Cir. 1970), *cert. denied*, 401 U.S. 976 (1971); copyright, Kamakazi Music Corp. v. Robbins Music Corp., 522 F. Supp. 125, 137 (S.D.N.Y. 1981), *aff'd*, 684 F.2d 228 (2d Cir. 1982); non-core bankruptcy proceedings, Zimmerman v. Continental Airlines, 712 F.2d 55, 59 (3d Cir. 1983), *overruled*, Hays & Co. v. Merrill Lynch, Pierce,

Fenner & Smith, Inc., 885 F.2d 1149, 1155 (3d Cir. 1989); Title VII, Utley & Goldman Sachs & Co., 883 F.2d 184, 187 (1st Cir. 1989), *cert. denied*, 493 U.S. 1045 (1990); age discrimination, Nicholson v. CPC Int'l Inc., 877 F.2d 221, 231 (3d Cir. 1989); ERISA, Barrowclough v. Kidder, Peabody & Co., 752 F.2d 923, 941 (3d Cir. 1985), *overruled*, Pritzker v. Merrill Lynch, Pierce, Fenner & Smith, Inc., 7 F.3d 1110 (3d Cir. 1993).

2. The majority opinion in *Wilko* reflects a strong distrust of arbitration as a means of resolving statutory claims: arbitrators may not understand the law, and courts are not in a position to review the arbitrators' decisions to ensure that they comply with the law. Compare the Court's analysis in *Wilko* with the following argument from Professor Stephen Ware:

> [A]rbitrators often do not [apply the law]. Soia Mentschikoff's seminal survey of arbitrators found that eighty percent of the studied commercial arbitrators "thought they ought to reach their decisions within the context of the principles of substantive rules of law, but almost ninety percent believed that they were free to ignore these rules whenever they thought that more just decisions would be reached by doing so."
>
> A more recent survey of construction arbitrators found that twenty-eight percent of surveyed arbitrators reported that they do not always follow the law in formulating their awards. . . . And even those arbitrators who try to apply the law will sometimes fail; they will make honest mistakes of law. In both of these cases — conscious disregard of the law and honest mistakes about the law — the arbitrator has not applied the law. In neither of these cases, however, is a court likely to vacate the arbitrator's award. In sum, an arbitration award that does not apply the law will probably be confirmed by courts.

Stephen J. Ware, *Default Rules from Mandatory Rules: Privatizing Law Through Arbitration*, 83 MINN. L. REV. 703, 719–22 (1999). Do you share these concerns? How do you think judges would respond to the survey questions asked of arbitrators? How, if at all, might the incentives facing arbitrators affect whether they apply the law in their decisions?

3. One clause from the *Wilko* opinion, which has little to do with the Court's actual holding, continues to be cited frequently by courts: that "the interpretations of the law by the arbitrators in contrast to *manifest disregard* are not subject, in the federal courts, to judicial review for error in interpretation" (emphasis added). Courts have picked up on this phrase to review arbitral awards for "manifest disregard of the law," even though no such ground for judicial review is provided in the FAA. *See infra* § 7.03[A].

4. Beginning in the 1970s, the United States Supreme Court started backing away from *Wilko v. Swan* and permitted some statutory claims to be arbitrated. The first such case was Scherk v. Alberto-Culver Co., 417 U.S. 506 (1974), in which the Court held that a claim under the Securities Exchange Act of 1934 arising out of an international transaction was arbitrable. The Court reasoned:

> Accepting the premise . . . that the operative portions of the language of the 1933 Act relied upon in *Wilko* are contained in the Securities

Exchange Act of 1934, the respondent's reliance on *Wilko* in this case ignores the significant and, we find, crucial differences between the agreement involved in *Wilko* and the one signed by the parties here. Alberto-Culver's contract to purchase the business entities belonging to Scherk was a truly international agreement. Alberto-Culver is an American corporation with its principal place of business and the vast bulk of its activity in this country, while Scherk is a citizen of Germany whose companies were organized under the laws of Germany and Liechtenstein. The negotiations leading to the signing of the contract in Austria and to the closing in Switzerland took place in the United States, England, and Germany, and involved consultations with legal and trademark experts from each of those countries and from Liechtenstein. Finally, and most significantly, the subject matter of the contract concerned the sale of business enterprises organized under the laws of and primarily situated in European countries, whose activities were largely, if not entirely, directed to European markets.

Such a contract involves considerations and policies significantly differ- ent from those found controlling in *Wilko*. In *Wilko*, quite apart from the arbitration provision, there was no question but that the laws of the United States generally, and the federal securities laws in particular, would govern disputes arising out of the stock-purchase agreement. The parties, the negotiations, and the subject matter of the contract were all situated in this country, and no credible claim could have been entertained that any international conflict-of-laws problems would arise. In this case, by con- trast, in the absence of the arbitration provision considerable uncertainty existed at the time of the agreement, and still exists, concerning the law applicable to the resolution of disputes arising out of the contract.

Such uncertainty will almost inevitably exist with respect to any contract touching two or more countries, each with its own substantive laws and conflict-of-laws rules. A contractual provision specifying in advance the forum in which disputes shall be litigated and the law to be applied is, therefore, an almost indispensable precondition to achievement of the orderliness and predictability essential to any international business trans- action. Furthermore, such a provision obviates the danger that a dispute under the agreement might be submitted to a forum hostile to the interests of one of the parties or unfamiliar with the problem area involved.

A parochial refusal by the courts of one country to enforce an interna- tional arbitration agreement would not only frustrate these purposes, but would invite unseemly and mutually destructive jockeying by the parties to secure tactical litigation advantages. In the present case, for example, it is not inconceivable that if Scherk had anticipated that Alberto-Culver would be able in this country to enjoin resort to arbitration he might have sought an order in France or some other country enjoining Alberto-Culver from proceeding with its litigation in the United States. Whatever recognition the courts of this country might ultimately have granted to the order of the foreign court, the dicey atmosphere of such a legal no-man's-land would surely damage the fabric of international commerce and trade, and imperil the willingness and ability of businessmen to enter into international commercial agreements.

The exception to the clear provisions of the Arbitration Act carved out by *Wilko* is simply inapposite to a case such as the one before us. . . .

Id. at 515–17.

Thus, the Court in *Scherk* distinguished *Wilko* based not on the statute involved, but on the nature of the transaction. Because the transaction involved in *Scherk* was an international one, rather than a domestic one, submitting the statutory claim to arbitration was permissible. In the following case, the Court revisited that distinction.

MITSUBISHI MOTORS CORP. v. SOLER CHRYSLER-PLYMOUTH, INC.
United States Supreme Court
473 U.S. 614 (1985)

JUSTICE BLACKMUN delivered the opinion of the Court.

The principal question presented by these cases is the arbitrability, pursuant to the Federal Arbitration Act and the Convention on the Recognition and Enforcement of Foreign Arbitral Awards (Convention), of claims arising under the Sherman Act, 15 U.S.C. § 1 *et seq.*, and encompassed within a valid arbitration clause in an agreement embodying an international commercial transaction.

I

Petitioner-cross-respondent Mitsubishi Motors Corporation (Mitsubishi) is a Japanese corporation which manufactures automobiles and has its principal place of business in Tokyo, Japan. Mitsubishi is the product of a joint venture between, on the one hand, Chrysler International, S.A. (CISA), a Swiss corporation registered in Geneva and wholly owned by Chrysler Corporation, and, on the other, Mitsubishi Heavy Industries, Inc., a Japanese corporation. The aim of the joint venture was the distribution through Chrysler dealers outside the continental United States of vehicles manufactured by Mitsubishi and bearing Chrysler and Mitsubishi trademarks. Respondent-cross-petitioner Soler Chrysler-Plymouth, Inc. (Soler), is a Puerto Rico corporation with its principal place of business in Pueblo Viejo, Guaynabo, Puerto Rico.

On October 31, 1979, Soler entered into a Distributor Agreement with CISA which provided for the sale by Soler of Mitsubishi-manufactured vehicles within a designated area, including metropolitan San Juan. On the same date, CISA, Soler, and Mitsubishi entered into a Sales Procedure Agreement (Sales Agreement) which, referring to the Distributor Agreement, provided for the direct sale of Mitsubishi products to Soler and governed the terms and conditions of such sales. Paragraph VI of the Sales Agreement, labeled "Arbitration of Certain Matters," provides: "All disputes, controversies or differences which may arise between [Mitsubishi] and [Soler] out of or in relation to Articles I-B through V of this

Agreement or for the breach thereof, shall be finally settled by arbitration in Japan in accordance with the rules and regulations of the Japan Commercial Arbitration Association."

Initially, Soler did a brisk business in Mitsubishi-manufactured vehicles. As a result of its strong performance, its minimum sales volume, specified by Mitsubishi and CISA, and agreed to by Soler, for the 1981 model year was substantially increased. In early 1981, however, the new-car market slackened. Soler ran into serious difficulties in meeting the expected sales volume, and by the spring of 1981 it felt itself compelled to request that Mitsubishi delay or cancel shipment of several orders. About the same time, Soler attempted to arrange for the transshipment of a quantity of its vehicles for sale in the continental United States and Latin America. Mitsubishi and CISA, however, refused permission for any such diversion, citing a variety of reasons, and no vehicles were transshipped. Attempts to work out these difficulties failed. Mitsubishi eventually withheld shipment of 966 vehicles, apparently representing orders placed for May, June, and July 1981 production, responsibility for which Soler disclaimed in February 1982.

The following month, Mitsubishi brought an action against Soler in the United States District Court for the District of Puerto Rico under the Federal Arbitration Act and the Convention. Mitsubishi sought an order, pursuant to 9 U.S.C. §§ 4 and 201, to compel arbitration in accord with ¶ VI of the Sales Agreement. Shortly after filing the complaint, Mitsubishi filed a request for arbitration before the Japan Commercial Arbitration Association.

Soler denied the allegations and counterclaimed against both Mitsubishi and CISA. . . . In the counterclaim premised on the Sherman Act, Soler alleged that Mitsubishi and CISA had conspired to divide markets in restraint of trade. To effectuate the plan, according to Soler, Mitsubishi had refused to permit Soler to resell to buyers in North, Central, or South America vehicles it had obligated itself to purchase from Mitsubishi. . . .

After a hearing, the District Court ordered Mitsubishi and Soler to arbitrate each of the issues raised in the complaint and in all the counterclaims save two and a portion of a third. With regard to the federal antitrust issues, it recognized that the Courts of Appeals, following *American Safety Equipment Corp. v. J.P. Maguire & Co.*, 391 F.2d 821 (CA2 1968), uniformly had held that the rights conferred by the antitrust laws were "of a character inappropriate for enforcement by arbitration." The District Court held, however, that the international character of the Mitsubishi-Soler undertaking required enforcement of the agreement to arbitrate even as to the antitrust claims[, relying] on *Scherk v. Alberto-Culver Co.* . . .

The United States Court of Appeals for the First Circuit affirmed in part and reversed in part. . . .

. . . [A]fter endorsing the doctrine of *American Safety*, precluding arbitration of antitrust claims, the Court of Appeals concluded that neither this Court's decision in *Scherk* nor the Convention required abandonment of that doctrine in the face of an international transaction. Accordingly, it reversed the judgment of the District Court insofar as it had ordered submission of "Soler's antitrust claims" to arbitration. Affirming the remainder of the judgment, the court directed the

District Court to consider in the first instance how the parallel judicial and arbitral proceedings should go forward. We granted certiorari primarily to consider whether an American court should enforce an agreement to resolve antitrust claims by arbitration when that agreement arises from an international transaction.

II

At the outset, we address the contention raised in Soler's cross-petition that the arbitration clause at issue may not be read to encompass the statutory counter-claims stated in its answer to the complaint. . . . [I]t argues that as a matter of law a court may not construe an arbitration agreement to encompass claims arising out of statutes designed to protect a class to which the party resisting arbitration belongs "unless [that party] has expressly agreed" to arbitrate those claims, by which Soler presumably means that the arbitration clause must specifically mention the statute giving rise to the claims that a party to the clause seeks to arbitrate. . . .

We do not agree, for we find no warrant in the Arbitration Act for implying in every contract within its ken a presumption against arbitration of statutory claims.
. . .

. . . By agreeing to arbitrate a statutory claim, a party does not forgo the substantive rights afforded by the statute; it only submits to their resolution in an arbitral, rather than a judicial, forum. It trades the procedures and opportunity for review of the courtroom for the simplicity, informality, and expedition of arbitration. We must assume that if Congress intended the substantive protection afforded by a given statute to include protection against waiver of the right to a judicial forum, that intention will be deducible from text or legislative history. Having made the bargain to arbitrate, the party should be held to it unless Congress itself has evinced an intention to preclude a waiver of judicial remedies for the statutory rights at issue. Nothing, in the meantime, prevents a party from excluding statutory claims from the scope of an agreement to arbitrate.

In sum, the Court of Appeals correctly conducted a two-step inquiry, first determining whether the parties' agreement to arbitrate reached the statutory issues, and then, upon finding it did, considering whether legal constraints external to the parties' agreement foreclosed the arbitration of those claims. We endorse its rejection of Soler's proposed rule of arbitration-clause construction.

III

We now turn to consider whether Soler's antitrust claims are nonarbitrable even though it has agreed to arbitrate them. In holding that they are not, the Court of Appeals followed the decision of the Second Circuit in *American Safety Equipment Corp. v. J.P. Maguire & Co.* Notwithstanding the absence of any explicit support for such an exception in either the Sherman Act or the Federal Arbitration Act, the Second Circuit there reasoned that "the pervasive public interest in enforcement of the antitrust laws, and the nature of the claims that arise in such cases, combine to make . . . antitrust claims . . . inappropriate for arbitration." We find it unnecessary to assess the legitimacy of the *American Safety* doctrine as applied to agreements to arbitrate arising from domestic transactions. As in *Scherk v.*

Alberto-Culver Co., we conclude that concerns of international comity, respect for the capacities of foreign and transnational tribunals, and sensitivity to the need of the international commercial system for predictability in the resolution of disputes require that we enforce the parties' agreement, even assuming that a contrary result would be forthcoming in a domestic context.

. . .

At the outset, we confess to some skepticism of certain aspects of the *American Safety* doctrine. . . . [T]he doctrine comprises four ingredients. First, private parties play a pivotal role in aiding governmental enforcement of the antitrust laws by means of the private action for treble damages. Second, "the strong possibility that contracts which generate antitrust disputes may be contracts of adhesion militates against automatic forum determination by contract." Third, antitrust issues, prone to complication, require sophisticated legal and economic analysis, and thus are "ill-adapted to strengths of the arbitral process, i.e., expedition, minimal requirements of written rationale, simplicity, resort to basic concepts of common sense and simple equity." Finally, just as "issues of war and peace are too important to be vested in the generals, . . . decisions as to antitrust regulation of business are too important to be lodged in arbitrators chosen from the business community — particularly those from a foreign community that has had no experience with or exposure to our law and values."

Initially, we find the second concern unjustified. The mere appearance of an antitrust dispute does not alone warrant invalidation of the selected forum on the undemonstrated assumption that the arbitration clause is tainted. A party resisting arbitration of course may attack directly the validity of the agreement to arbitrate. *See Prima Paint Corp. v. Flood & Conklin Mfg. Co.* Moreover, the party may attempt to make a showing that would warrant setting aside the forum-selection clause — that the agreement was "[a]ffected by fraud, undue influence, or overweening bargaining power"; that "enforcement would be unreasonable and unjust"; or that proceedings "in the contractual forum will be so gravely difficult and inconvenient that [the resisting party] will for all practical purposes be deprived of his day in court." But absent such a showing — and none was attempted here — there is no basis for assuming the forum inadequate or its selection unfair.

Next, potential complexity should not suffice to ward off arbitration. We might well have some doubt that even the courts following *American Safety* subscribe fully to the view that antitrust matters are inherently insusceptible to resolution by arbitration, as these same courts have agreed that an undertaking to arbitrate antitrust claims entered into after the dispute arises is acceptable. And the vertical restraints which most frequently give birth to antitrust claims covered by an arbitration agreement will not often occasion the monstrous proceedings that have given antitrust litigation an image of intractability. In any event, adaptability and access to expertise are hallmarks of arbitration. The anticipated subject matter of the dispute may be taken into account when the arbitrators are appointed, and arbitral rules typically provide for the participation of experts either employed by the parties or appointed by the tribunal. Moreover, it is often a judgment that streamlined proceedings and expeditious results will best serve their needs that causes parties to agree to arbitrate their disputes; it is typically a desire to keep the effort and expense required to resolve a dispute within manageable bounds that prompts them mutually to forgo access to judicial remedies. In sum, the factor of potential complexity alone does not persuade us that an arbitral tribunal could not properly handle an antitrust matter.

For similar reasons, we also reject the proposition that an arbitration panel will pose too great a danger of innate hostility to the constraints on business conduct that antitrust law imposes. International arbitrators frequently are drawn from the legal as well as the business community; where the dispute has an important legal component, the parties and the arbitral body with whose assistance they have agreed to settle their dispute can be expected to select arbitrators accordingly.[18] We decline to indulge the presumption that the parties and arbitral body conducting a proceeding will be unable or unwilling to retain competent, conscientious, and impartial arbitrators.

We are left, then, with the core of the *American Safety* doctrine — the fundamental importance to American democratic capitalism of the regime of the antitrust laws. Without doubt, the private cause of action plays a central role in enforcing this regime. . . . The treble-damages provision wielded by the private litigant is a chief tool in the antitrust enforcement scheme, posing a crucial deterrent to potential violators.

The importance of the private damages remedy, however, does not compel the conclusion that it may not be sought outside an American court. Notwithstanding its important incidental policing function, the treble-damages cause of action conferred on private parties by § 4 of the Clayton Act, and pursued by Soler here by way of its third counterclaim, seeks primarily to enable an injured competitor to gain compensation for that injury. . . .

. . . And, of course, the antitrust cause of action remains at all times under the control of the individual litigant: no citizen is under an obligation to bring an antitrust suit, and the private antitrust plaintiff needs no executive or judicial approval before settling one. It follows that, at least where the international cast of a transaction would otherwise add an element of uncertainty to dispute resolution, the prospective litigant may provide in advance for a mutually agreeable procedure whereby he would seek his antitrust recovery as well as settle other controversies.

There is no reason to assume at the outset of the dispute that international arbitration will not provide an adequate mechanism. To be sure, the international arbitral tribunal owes no prior allegiance to the legal norms of particular states; hence, it has no direct obligation to vindicate their statutory dictates. The tribunal, however, is bound to effectuate the intentions of the parties. Where the parties have

---

[18] We are advised by Mitsubishi and amicus International Chamber of Commerce, without contradiction by Soler, that the arbitration panel selected to hear the parties' claims here is composed of three Japanese lawyers, one a former law school dean, another a former judge, and the third a practicing attorney with American legal training who has written on Japanese antitrust law. The Court of Appeals was concerned that international arbitrators would lack "experience with or exposure to our law and values." The obstacles confronted by the arbitration panel in this case, however, should be no greater than those confronted by any judicial or arbitral tribunal required to determine foreign law. Moreover, while our attachment to the antitrust laws may be stronger than most, many other countries, including Japan, have similar bodies of competition law.

agreed that the arbitral body is to decide a defined set of claims which includes, as in these cases, those arising from the application of American antitrust law, the tribunal therefore should be bound to decide that dispute in accord with the national law giving rise to the claim.[19] And so long as the prospective litigant effectively may vindicate its statutory cause of action in the arbitral forum, the statute will continue to serve both its remedial and deterrent function.

Having permitted the arbitration to go forward, the national courts of the United States will have the opportunity at the award-enforcement stage to ensure that the legitimate interest in the enforcement of the antitrust laws has been addressed. The Convention reserves to each signatory country the right to refuse enforcement of an award where the "recognition or enforcement of the award would be contrary to the public policy of that country." Art. V(2)(b). While the efficacy of the arbitral process requires that substantive review at the award-enforcement stage remain minimal, it would not require intrusive inquiry to ascertain that the tribunal took cognizance of the antitrust claims and actually decided them.

As international trade has expanded in recent decades, so too has the use of international arbitration to resolve disputes arising in the course of that trade. The controversies that international arbitral institutions are called upon to resolve have increased in diversity as well as in complexity. Yet the potential of these tribunals for efficient disposition of legal disagreements arising from commercial relations has not yet been tested. If they are to take a central place in the international legal order, national courts will need to "shake off the old judicial hostility to arbitration," Kulukundis Shipping Co. v. Amtorg Trading Corp., 126 F.2d 978, 985 (CA2 1942), and also their customary and understandable unwillingness to cede jurisdiction of a claim arising under domestic law to a foreign or transnational tribunal. To this extent, at least, it will be necessary for national courts to subordinate domestic notions of arbitrability to the international policy favoring commercial arbitration.

Accordingly, we "require this representative of the American business commu-

---

[19] In addition to the clause providing for arbitration before the Japan Commercial Arbitration Association, the Sales Agreement includes a choice-of-law clause which reads: "This Agreement is made in, and will be governed by and construed in all respects according to the laws of the Swiss Confederation as if entirely performed therein." The United States raises the possibility that the arbitral panel will read this provision not simply to govern interpretation of the contract terms, but wholly to displace American law even where it otherwise would apply. The International Chamber of Commerce opines that it is "[c]onceivabl[e], although we believe it unlikely, [that] the arbitrators could consider Soler's affirmative claim of anti-competitive conduct by CISA and Mitsubishi to fall within the purview of the choice-of-law provision, with the result that it would be decided under Swiss law rather than the U.S. Sherman Act." At oral argument, however, counsel for Mitsubishi concede that American law applied to the antitrust claims and represented that the claims had been submitted to the arbitration panel in Japan on that basis. The record confirms that before the decision of the Court of Appeals the arbitral panel had taken these claims under submission.

We therefore have no occasion to speculate on this matter at this stage in the proceedings, when Mitsubishi seeks to enforce the agreement to arbitrate, not enforce an award. Nor need we consider now the effect of an arbitral tribunal's failure to take cognizance of the statutory cause of action on the claimant's capacity to reinitiate suit in federal court. We merely note that in the event the choice-of-forum and choice-of-law clauses operated in tandem as a prospective waiver of a party's right to pursue statutory remedies for antitrust violations, we would have little hesitation in condemning the agreement as against public policy.

nity to honor its bargain," by holding this agreement to arbitrate "[enforceable] . . . in accord with the explicit provisions of the Arbitration Act."

The judgment of the Court of Appeals is affirmed in part and reversed in part, and the cases are remanded for further proceedings consistent with this opinion.

It is so ordered.

NOTES

1.   Compare the Supreme Court's view of arbitration, as expressed in *Scherk* and *Mitsubishi*, with the view expressed in *Wilko*. Can the more favorable view expressed in *Scherk* and *Mitsubishi* be explained solely because of the factual differences between those cases and *Wilko*? Or is there a more fundamental shift?

2.   Both *Scherk* and *Mitsubishi* involved international arbitration instead of strictly domestic arbitration. Should that distinction matter? Is there any basis in the text of the statutes for the distinction?

3.   One issue in *Mitsubishi* was whether the parties had agreed to arbitrate federal antitrust claims at all. The Court rejected the plaintiff's argument that parties must specifically identify federal statutory claims in their arbitration agreement before the agreement will be construed to cover those claims. But if the scope of the parties' agreement, properly construed, did not include federal antitrust claims, certainly it is correct that there is no obligation to arbitrate those claims. As always, arbitration is a matter of contract, and if the parties did not agree to arbitrate a certain claim or claims, they cannot be forced to do so under the FAA.

PROBLEM 3.3

The year is 1986. Last year, the Supreme Court issued its decision in *Mitsubishi*. You are preparing for oral argument before the Court on the question whether a purely domestic claim under the 1934 Securities Exchange Act is arbitrable. The 1934 Act is like the 1933 Securities Act at issue in *Wilko* in that it voids any provision that waives compliance with a provision of the Act. But in *Scherk*, the Supreme Court held that claims under the 1934 Act were arbitrable in international contracts. How would you argue that claims under the 1934 Act arising out of domestic contracts are arbitrable? Are not arbitrable? After you prepare your answer to this problem, read the following materials and see how the argument came out.

The next case in the progression presented exactly the issue raised in Problem 3.3 — can a claim under 1934 Securities Exchange Act (like that in *Scherk*) be arbitrated when the arbitration clause was contained in a domestic contract (like that in *Wilko*)? Or would the distinction between domestic and international transactions persist?

In Shearson/American Express, Inc. v. McMahon, 482 U.S. 220 (1987), the Court held that the 1934 Securities Exchange Act claim could be arbitrated, even in a domestic contract:

When Congress enacted the Exchange Act in 1934, it did not specifically address the question of the arbitrability of § 10(b) claims. The McMahons contend, however, that congressional intent to require a judicial forum for the resolution of § 10(b) claims can be deduced from § 29(a) of the Exchange Act, 15 U.S.C. § 78cc(a), which declares void "[a]ny condition, stipulation, or provision binding any person to waive compliance with any provision of [the Act]."

First, we reject the McMahons' argument that § 29(a) forbids waiver of § 27 of the Exchange Act, 15 U.S.C. § 78aa, [which provides for exclusive federal court jurisdiction over violations of the Act]. . . .

. . .

We do not read *Wilko v. Swan* as compelling a different result. . . . The conclusion in *Wilko* was expressly based on the Court's belief that a judicial forum was needed to protect the substantive rights created by the Securities Act. . . . *Wilko* must be understood, therefore, as holding that the plaintiff's waiver of the "right to select the judicial forum" was unenforceable only because arbitration was judged inadequate to enforce the statutory rights created by § 12(2).

Indeed, any different reading of *Wilko* would be inconsistent with this Court's decision in *Scherk v. Alberto-Culver Co.* . . . *Scherk* supports our understanding that *Wilko* must be read as barring waiver of a judicial forum only where arbitration is inadequate to protect the substantive rights at issue. At the same time, it confirms that where arbitration does provide an adequate means of enforcing the provisions of the Exchange Act, § 29(a) does not void a predispute waiver of § 27 — *Scherk* upheld enforcement of just such a waiver.

. . .

The other reason advanced by the McMahons for finding a waiver of their § 10(b) rights is that arbitration does "weaken their ability to recover under the [Exchange] Act." That is the heart of the Court's decision in *Wilko*, and respondents urge that we should follow its reasoning. *Wilko* listed several grounds why, in the Court's view, the "effectiveness [of the Act's provisions] in application is lessened in arbitration." . . .

. . . [T]he reasons given in *Wilko* reflect a general suspicion of the desirability of arbitration and the competence of arbitral tribunals — most apply with no greater force to the arbitration of securities disputes than to the arbitration of legal disputes generally. It is difficult to reconcile *Wilko*'s mistrust of the arbitral process with this Court's subsequent decisions involving the Arbitration Act.

Indeed, most of the reasons given in *Wilko* have been rejected subsequently by the Court as a basis for holding claims to be nonarbitrable. In *Mitsubishi*, for example, we recognized that arbitral tribunals are readily capable of handling the factual and legal complexities of antitrust claims, notwithstanding the absence of judicial instruction and supervision. Likewise, we have concluded that the streamlined procedures of arbitration do not entail any consequential restriction on substantive rights. Finally, we have indicated that there is no reason to assume at the outset that arbitrators will not follow the law; although judicial scrutiny of arbitration awards necessarily is limited, such review is sufficient to ensure that arbitrators comply with the requirements of the statute.

The suitability of arbitration as a means of enforcing Exchange Act rights is evident from our decision in *Scherk*. Although the holding in that case was limited to international agreements, the competence of arbitral tribunals to resolve § 10(b) claims is the same in both settings. . . . And courts uniformly have concluded that *Wilko* does not apply to the submission to arbitration of existing disputes, even though the inherent suitability of arbitration as a means of resolving § 10(b) claims remains unchanged.

Id. at 227-32. The Court also upheld the arbitrability of a claim under the Racketeer Influenced and Corrupt Organizations Act (RICO), 18 U.S.C. § 1961 et seq., relying heavily on its decision in *Mitsubishi*. Indeed, the Court found "even more reason to suppose that arbitration will adequately serve the purposes of RICO than that it will adequately protect private enforcement of the antitrust laws":

Antitrust violations generally have a widespread impact on national markets as a whole, and the antitrust treble-damages provision gives private parties an incentive to bring civil suits that serve to advance the national interest in a competitive economy. RICO's drafters likewise sought to provide vigorous incentives for plaintiffs to pursue RICO claims that would advance society's fight against organized crime. But in fact RICO actions are seldom asserted "against the archetypal, intimidating mobster." The special incentives necessary to encourage civil enforcement actions against organized crime do not support nonarbitrability of run-of-the-mill civil RICO claims brought against legitimate enterprises. The private attorney general role for the typical RICO plaintiff is simply less plausible than it is for the typical antitrust plaintiff, and does not support a finding that there is an irreconcilable conflict between arbitration and enforcement of the RICO statute.

Id. at 241-42. As to both claims, then, the Court extended precedent based on international contracts (*Scherk* and *Mitsubishi*) into the domestic realm.

The Supreme Court's decision in *McMahon* cast serious doubt on the continuing validity of *Wilko* itself. The Court soon resolved that uncertainty by overruling *Wilko* in Rodriguez de Quijas v. Shearson/American Express, Inc., 490 U.S. 477 (1989). The Court explained:

We do not think [the *Wilko* Court's] reasons justify an interpretation of § 14 that prohibits agreements to arbitrate future disputes relating to the purchase of securities. The Court's characterization of the arbitration process in *Wilko* is pervaded by what Judge Jerome Frank called "the old judicial hostility to arbitration." Kulukundis Shipping Co. v. Amtorg Trading Corp., 126 F.2d 978, 985 (CA2 1942). That view has been steadily eroded over the years, beginning in the lower courts. The erosion intensified in our most recent decisions upholding agreements to arbitrate federal claims raised under the Securities Exchange Act of 1934, under the Racketeer Influenced and Corrupt Organizations (RICO) statutes, and under the antitrust laws. The shift in the Court's views on arbitration away from those adopted in *Wilko* is shown by the flat statement in *Mitsubishi*: "By agreeing to arbitrate a statutory claim, a party does not forgo the substantive rights afforded by the statute; it only submits to their resolution in an arbitral, rather than a judicial, forum." To the extent that *Wilko* rested on suspicion of arbitration as a method of weakening the protections afforded in the substantive law to would-be complainants, it has fallen far out of step with our current strong endorsement of the federal statutes favoring this method of resolving disputes.

Once the outmoded presumption of disfavoring arbitration proceedings is set to one side, it becomes clear that the right to select the judicial forum and the wider choice of courts are not such essential features of the Securities Act that § 14 is properly construed to bar any waiver of these provisions. Nor are they so critical that they cannot be waived under the rationale that the Securities Act was intended to place buyers of securities on an equal footing with sellers. . . .

. . .

Indeed, in *McMahon* the Court declined to read § 29(a) of the Securities Exchange Act of 1934, the language of which is in every respect the same as that in § 14 of the 1933 Act, to prohibit enforcement of predispute agreements to arbitrate. . . .

. . . We now conclude that *Wilko* was incorrectly decided and is inconsistent with the prevailing uniform construction of other federal statutes governing arbitration agreements in the setting of business transactions. Although we are normally and properly reluctant to overturn our decisions construing statutes, we have done so to achieve a uniform interpretation of similar statutory language, and to correct a seriously erroneous interpretation of statutory language that would undermine congressional policy as expressed in other legislation. Both purposes would be served here by overruling the *Wilko* decision.

Id. at 480–82, 484.

PROBLEM 3.4

Congress enacts the Internet Fraud Act (IFA), which creates a private right of action for victims of fraud perpetrated using the Internet. The IFA provides for suit to be brought in any court of competent jurisdiction, and it precludes removal of suits filed in state court. If suit is brought in federal court, the Act provides for nationwide service of process and a wide choice of venue. Further, under the IFA, the seller has the burden of proving that it lacks scienter (a change from the common law, which requires buyers to prove scienter as an element of common law fraud).

Slaney Securities, Inc. (Slaney) offers financial planning software available for downloading online. Elsie Patrick (see Problem 1.2) downloads and installs Slaney's software (after paying the required $69.95 by credit card). When Patrick runs the software, all it does is show a flashing screen that says: "You need to avoid making foolish purchases over the Internet." Patrick files suit in federal court against Slaney alleging a violation of the IFA. Slaney moves to stay the proceedings pending arbitration and to compel arbitration, relying on a provision of its license agreement with Patrick providing that all disputes shall be subject to arbitration.

(a) In addition to the above provisions, the IFA provides that disputes arising under the Act shall not be subject to arbitration. How should the court rule on Slaney's motions?

(b) Same facts as (a) except that instead of prohibiting arbitration of IFA claims, the Act makes "void" any "condition, stipulation, or provision binding any person to waive compliance with any provision of this Act." How should the court rule on Slaney's motions?

(c) Same facts as (a) except that instead of prohibiting arbitration of IFA claims, the Act provides that federal courts shall have exclusive jurisdiction of all claims arising under the IFA. How should the court rule on Slaney's motions?

PROBLEM 3.5

Patricia Cairns sells used greeting cards under a franchise from the Send-A-Wreck Used Greeting Card Company. Her franchise agreement with Send-A-Wreck requires her to use correcting fluid (the liquid that covers up the handwriting inside the greeting cards) she purchases from Send-A-Wreck itself. Cairns would rather use a lower-cost alternative she can buy at a local office supply store. When Send-A-Wreck refuses her request to use the alternative correcting fluid, Cairns files suit in federal court alleging that the franchise agreement violates the federal antitrust laws because it constitutes an unlawful tying arrangement. Send-A-Wreck responds by seeking to compel arbitration, based on a provision in the franchise agreement which provides that the parties agree to arbitrate "any dispute due to a breach of this contract." What arguments should Cairns make in opposing arbitration? How is the court likely to rule?

From *McMahon* and *Rodriguez de Quijas*, it was clear that many, if not most, federal statutory claims were arbitrable. The final major Supreme Court case addressing the arbitrability of federal statutory claims dealt with a very different type of claim from the previous ones: a claim for employment discrimination in violation of the Age Discrimination in Employment Act. The outcome, however, was the same.

GILMER v. INTERSTATE/JOHNSON LANE CORP.

United States Supreme Court

500 U.S. 20 (1991)

JUSTICE WHITE delivered the opinion of the Court.

The question presented in this case is whether a claim under the Age Discrimination in Employment Act of 1967 (ADEA), can be subjected to compulsory arbitration pursuant to an arbitration agreement in a securities registration application. The Court of Appeals held that it could, and we affirm.

I

Respondent Interstate/Johnson Lane Corporation (Interstate) hired petitioner Robert Gilmer as a Manager of Financial Services in May 1981. As required by his employment, Gilmer registered as a securities representative with several stock exchanges, including the New York Stock Exchange (NYSE). His registration application, entitled "Uniform Application for Securities Industry Registration or Transfer," provided, among other things, that Gilmer "agree[d] to arbitrate any dispute, claim or controversy" arising between him and Interstate "that is required to be arbitrated under the rules, constitutions or by-laws of the organizations with which I register." Of relevance to this case, NYSE Rule 347 provides for arbitration of "[a]ny controversy between a registered representative and any member or member organization arising out of the employment or termination of employment of such registered representative."

Interstate terminated Gilmer's employment in 1987, at which time Gilmer was 62 years of age. After first filing an age discrimination charge with the Equal Employment Opportunity Commission (EEOC), Gilmer subsequently brought suit in the United States District Court for the Western District of North Carolina, alleging that Interstate had discharged him because of his age, in violation of the ADEA. In response to Gilmer's complaint, Interstate filed in the District Court a motion to compel arbitration of the ADEA claim. In its motion, Interstate relied upon the arbitration agreement in Gilmer's registration application, as well as the Federal Arbitration Act (FAA). The District Court denied Interstate's motion, based on this Court's decision in Alexander v. Gardner-Denver Co., 415 U.S. 36 (1974), and because it concluded that "Congress intended to protect ADEA claimants from the waiver of a judicial forum." The United States Court of Appeals for the Fourth Circuit reversed, finding "nothing in the text, legislative history, or underlying purposes of the ADEA indicating a congressional intent to preclude enforcement of arbitration agreements." We granted certiorari to resolve a conflict among the Courts of Appeals regarding the arbitrability of ADEA claims.

II

. . .

It is by now clear that statutory claims may be the subject of an arbitration agreement, enforceable pursuant to the FAA. Indeed, in recent years we have held enforceable arbitration agreements relating to claims arising under the Sherman Act; § 10(b) of the Securities Exchange Act of 1934; the civil provisions of the Racketeer Influenced and Corrupt Organizations Act (RICO); and § 12(2) of the Securities Act of 1933. In these cases we recognized that "[b]y agreeing to arbitrate a statutory claim, a party does not forgo the substantive rights afforded by the statute; it only submits to their resolution in an arbitral, rather than a judicial, forum."

Although all statutory claims may not be appropriate for arbitration, "[h]aving made the bargain to arbitrate, the party should be held to it unless Congress itself has evinced an intention to preclude a waiver of judicial remedies for the statutory rights at issue." In this regard, we note that the burden is on Gilmer to show that Congress intended to preclude a waiver of a judicial forum for ADEA claims. If such an intention exists, it will be discoverable in the text of the ADEA, its legislative history, or an "inherent conflict" between arbitration and the ADEA's underlying purposes. Throughout such an inquiry, it should be kept in mind that "questions of arbitrability must be addressed with a healthy regard for the federal policy favoring arbitration."

III

Gilmer concedes that nothing in the text of the ADEA or its legislative history explicitly precludes arbitration. He argues, however, that compulsory arbitration of ADEA claims pursuant to arbitration agreements would be inconsistent with the statutory framework and purposes of the ADEA. Like the Court of Appeals, we disagree.

A

Congress enacted the ADEA in 1967 "to promote employment of older persons based on their ability rather than age; to prohibit arbitrary age discrimination in employment; [and] to help employers and workers find ways of meeting problems arising from the impact of age on employment." To achieve those goals, the ADEA, among other things, makes it unlawful for an employer "to fail or refuse to hire or to discharge any individual or otherwise discriminate against any individual with respect to his compensation, terms, conditions, or privileges of employment, because of such individual's age." This proscription is enforced both by private suits and by the EEOC. In order for an aggrieved individual to bring suit under the ADEA, he or she must first file a charge with the EEOC and then wait at least 60 days. An individual's right to sue is extinguished, however, if the EEOC institutes an action against the employer. Before the EEOC can bring such an action, though, it must "attempt to eliminate the discriminatory practice or practices alleged, and to effect voluntary compliance with the requirements of this chapter through informal methods of conciliation, conference, and persuasion."

As Gilmer contends, the ADEA is designed not only to address individual grievances, but also to further important social policies. We do not perceive any inherent inconsistency between those policies, however, and enforcing agreements to arbitrate age discrimination claims. It is true that arbitration focuses on specific disputes between the parties involved. The same can be said, however, of judicial resolution of claims. Both of these dispute resolution mechanisms nevertheless also can further broader social purposes. The Sherman Act, the Securities Exchange Act of 1934, RICO, and the Securities Act of 1933 all are designed to advance important public policies, but, as noted above, claims under those statutes are appropriate for arbitration. "[S]o long as the prospective litigant effectively may vindicate [his or her] statutory cause of action in the arbitral forum, the statute will continue to serve both its remedial and deterrent function."

We also are unpersuaded by the argument that arbitration will undermine the role of the EEOC in enforcing the ADEA. An individual ADEA claimant subject to an arbitration agreement will still be free to file a charge with the EEOC, even though the claimant is not able to institute a private judicial action. Indeed, Gilmer filed a charge with the EEOC in this case. In any event, the EEOC's role in combating age discrimination is not dependent on the filing of a charge; the agency may receive information concerning alleged violations of the ADEA "from any source," and it has independent authority to investigate age discrimination. Moreover, nothing in the ADEA indicates that Congress intended that the EEOC be involved in all employment disputes. Such disputes can be settled, for example, without any EEOC involvement. Finally, the mere involvement of an administrative agency in the enforcement of a statute is not sufficient to preclude arbitration. For example, the Securities Exchange Commission is heavily involved in the enforcement of the Securities Exchange Act of 1934 and the Securities Act of 1933, but we have held that claims under both of those statutes may be subject to compulsory arbitration.

Gilmer also argues that compulsory arbitration is improper because it deprives claimants of the judicial forum provided for by the ADEA. Congress, however, did not explicitly preclude arbitration or other nonjudicial resolution of claims, even in its recent amendments to the ADEA. . . . Moreover, Gilmer's argument ignores the ADEA's flexible approach to resolution of claims. The EEOC, for example, is directed to pursue "informal methods of conciliation, conference, and persuasion," which suggests that out-of-court dispute resolution, such as arbitration, is consistent with the statutory scheme established by Congress. In addition, arbitration is consistent with Congress' grant of concurrent jurisdiction over ADEA claims to state and federal courts, because arbitration agreements, "like the provision for concurrent jurisdiction, serve to advance the objective of allowing [claimants] a broader right to select the forum for resolving disputes, whether it be judicial or otherwise."

B

In arguing that arbitration is inconsistent with the ADEA, Gilmer also raises a host of challenges to the adequacy of arbitration procedures. Initially, we note that in our recent arbitration cases we have already rejected most of these arguments as insufficient to preclude arbitration of statutory claims. Such generalized attacks on arbitration "res[t] on suspicion of arbitration as a method of weakening the protections afforded in the substantive law to would-be complainants," and as such, they are "far out of step with our current strong endorsement of the federal statutes favoring this method of resolving disputes." Consequently, we address these arguments only briefly.

Gilmer first speculates that arbitration panels will be biased. However, "[w]e decline to indulge the presumption that the parties and arbitral body conducting a proceeding will be unable or unwilling to retain competent, conscientious and impartial arbitrators." In any event, we note that the NYSE arbitration rules, which are applicable to the dispute in this case, provide protections against biased panels. The rules require, for example, that the parties be informed of the employment histories of the arbitrators, and that they be allowed to make further inquiries into the arbitrators' backgrounds. In addition, each party is allowed one peremptory challenge and unlimited challenges for cause. Moreover, the arbitrators are required to disclose "any circumstances which might preclude [them] from rendering an objective and impartial determination." The FAA also protects against bias, by providing that courts may overturn arbitration decisions "[w]here there was evident partiality or corruption in the arbitrators." There has been no showing in this case that those provisions are inadequate to guard against potential bias.

Gilmer also complains that the discovery allowed in arbitration is more limited than in the federal courts, which he contends will make it difficult to prove discrimination. It is unlikely, however, that age discrimination claims require more extensive discovery than other claims that we have found to be arbitrable, such as RICO and antitrust claims. Moreover, there has been no showing in this case that the NYSE discovery provisions, which allow for document production, information requests, depositions, and subpoenas will prove insufficient to allow ADEA claimants such as Gilmer a fair opportunity to present their claims. Although those procedures might not be as extensive as in the federal courts, by agreeing to arbitrate, a party "trades the procedures and opportunity for review of the courtroom for the simplicity, informality, and expedition of arbitration." Indeed, an important counterweight to the reduced discovery in NYSE arbitration is that arbitrators are not bound by the rules of evidence.

A further alleged deficiency of arbitration is that arbitrators often will not issue written opinions, resulting, Gilmer contends, in a lack of public knowledge of employers' discriminatory policies, an inability to obtain effective appellate review, and a stifling of the development of the law. The NYSE rules, however, do require that all arbitration awards be in writing, and that the awards contain the names of the parties, a summary of the issues in controversy, and a description of the award issued. In addition, the award decisions are made available to the public. Furthermore, judicial decisions addressing ADEA claims will continue to be issued because it is unlikely that all or even most ADEA claimants will be subject to arbitration agreements. Finally, Gilmer's concerns apply equally to settlements of ADEA claims, which, as noted above, are clearly allowed.

It is also argued that arbitration procedures cannot adequately further the purposes of the ADEA because they do not provide for broad equitable relief and class actions. As the court below noted, however, arbitrators do have the power to fashion equitable relief. Indeed, the NYSE rules applicable here do not restrict the types of relief an arbitrator may award, but merely refer to "damages and/or other relief." The NYSE rules also provide for collective proceedings. But "even if the arbitration could not go forward as a class action or class relief could not be granted by the arbitrator, the fact that the [ADEA] provides for the possibility of bringing a collective action does not mean that individual attempts at conciliation were intended to be barred." Finally, it should be remembered that arbitration agreements will not preclude the EEOC from bringing actions seeking class-wide and equitable relief.

C

An additional reason advanced by Gilmer for refusing to enforce arbitration agreements relating to ADEA claims is his contention that there often will be unequal bargaining power between employers and employees. Mere inequality in bargaining power, however, is not a sufficient reason to hold that arbitration agreements are never enforceable in the employment context. Relationships between securities dealers and investors, for example, may involve unequal bargaining power, but we nevertheless held in *Rodriguez de Quijas* and *McMahon* that agreements to arbitrate in that context are enforceable. . . . "Of course, courts should remain attuned to well-supported claims that the agreement to arbitrate resulted from the sort of fraud or overwhelming economic power that would provide grounds 'for the revocation of any contract.' " There is no indication in this case, however, that Gilmer, an experienced businessman, was coerced or defrauded into agreeing to the arbitration clause in his registration application. As with the claimed procedural inadequacies discussed above, this claim of unequal bargaining power is best left for resolution in specific cases.

IV

In addition to the arguments discussed above, Gilmer vigorously asserts that our decision in Alexander v. Gardner-Denver Co., 415 U.S. 36 (1974), and its progeny . . . preclude arbitration of employment discrimination claims. Gilmer's reliance on these cases, however, is misplaced.

In *Gardner-Denver*, the issue was whether a discharged employee whose grievance had been arbitrated pursuant to an arbitration clause in a collective-bargaining agreement was precluded from subsequently bringing a Title VII action based upon the conduct that was the subject of the grievance. . . .

. . .

There are several important distinctions between the *Gardner-Denver* line of cases and the case before us. First, those cases did not involve the issue of the enforceability of an agreement to arbitrate statutory claims. Rather, they involved the quite different issue whether arbitration of contract-based claims precluded subsequent judicial resolution of statutory claims. Since the employees there had not agreed to arbitrate their statutory claims, and the labor arbitrators were not authorized to resolve such claims, the arbitration in those cases understandably was held not to preclude subsequent statutory actions. Second, because the arbitration in those cases occurred in the context of a collective-bargaining agreement, the claimants there were represented by their unions in the arbitration proceedings. An important concern therefore was the tension between collective representation and individual statutory rights, a concern not applicable to the present case. Finally, those cases were not decided under the FAA, which, as discussed above, reflects a "liberal federal policy favoring arbitration agreements." Therefore, those cases provide no basis for refusing to enforce Gilmer's agreement to arbitrate his ADEA claim.

V

We conclude that Gilmer has not met his burden of showing that Congress, in enacting the ADEA, intended to preclude arbitration of claims under that Act. Accordingly, the judgment of the Court of Appeals is

Affirmed.

NOTES

1. Although the Supreme Court has never addressed the question, the Circuits unanimously have applied *Gilmer* to claims under Title VII of the Civil Rights Act of 1964 and held that they can be arbitrated. *See* EEOC v. Luce, Forward, Hamilton & Scripps, 345 F.3d 742, 748-49, 754 (9th Cir. 2003) (en banc) (citing cases and rejecting prior Ninth Circuit precedent to the contrary).

2. The Ninth Circuit took a different approach to the arbitrability of Title VII claims in Prudential Insurance Co. v. Lai, 42 F.3d 1299 (9th Cir. 1994), *cert. denied*, 516 U.S. 812 (1995). In that case, the court of appeals held that "a Title VII plaintiff may only be forced to forego her statutory remedies and arbitrate her claim if she has knowingly agreed to submit such disputes to arbitration." *Id.* at 1305. Because the "employment contract . . . that plaintiffs executed did not describe any disputes the parties agreed to arbitrate," *id.*, the plaintiffs did not knowingly agree to arbitrate their Title VII claims. *See also* Walker v. Ryan's Family Steak Houses, Inc., 400 F.3d 370, 381 (6th Cir.), *cert. denied*, 126 S. Ct. 730 (U.S. 2005). Other circuits have rejected the *Lai* court's view. *See* Caley v. Gulfstream Aerospace Corp., 428 F.3d 1359, 1371 (11th Cir. 2005) ("general contract principles govern the enforceability of arbitration agreements" and "no heightened 'knowing and voluntary' standard applies"); Morales v. Sun Constructors, Inc., 541 F.3d 218, 224 (3d Cir. 2008).

3. In Wright v. Universal Maritime Service Corp., 525 U.S. 70 (1998), the United States Supreme Court held that a general arbitration clause in a collective bargaining agreement (CBA) did not require an employee to arbitrate his claim under the Americans with Disabilities Act. The Court concluded that an agreement to arbitrate a statutory claim in a CBA must be "clear and unmistakable," *id.* at 80, a standard that the arbitration clause at issue did not meet. The Court in *Wright* took "no position . . . on the effect of [section 118 of the 1991 Civil Rights Act] . . . in areas outside collective bargaining." *Id.* at 82 n.2. Subsequently, the Tenth Circuit refused to extend *Wright's* requirement of a "clear and unmistakable" agreement to individual employment contracts. Williams v. Imhoff, 203 F.3d 758 (10th Cir. 2000). Such contracts, according to the Tenth Circuit, are governed by the Federal Arbitration Act, so that " 'any doubts concerning the scope of arbitrable issues should be resolved in favor of arbitration.' " *Id.* at 764 (quoting *Mitsubishi Motors*);

see also American Heritage Life Ins. Co. v. Orr, 294 F.3d 702, 711 (5th Cir. 2002), *cert. denied*, 537 U.S. 1106 (2003) (likewise distinguishing *Wright* as limited to collective bargaining agreements).

4. Subsequently, the Supreme Court held in 14 Penn Plaza LLC v. Pyett, 556 U.S. 247, 274 (2009), "that a collective-bargaining agreement that clearly and unmistakably requires union members to arbitrate ADEA claims is enforceable as a matter of federal law." The Court quoted *Gilmer* in distinguishing *Gardner-Denver* as " 'involv[ing] the quite different issue whether arbitration of contract-based claims precluded subsequent judicial resolution of statutory claims. Since the employees there had not agreed to arbitrate their statutory claims, and the labor arbitrators were not authorized to resolve such claims, the arbitration in those cases understandably was held not to preclude subsequent statutory actions." *Id.* at 265. According to the *Pyett* Court, "*Gardner-Denver* and its progeny thus do not control the outcome where, as is the case here, the collective-bargaining agreement's arbitration provision expressly covers both statutory and contractual discrimination claims." *Id.* The Court also rejected an argument that sometimes had been made against the arbitration of Title VII claims outside of the collective bargaining context:

> Respondents' contention that § 118 of the Civil Rights Act of 1991 precludes the enforcement of this arbitration agreement also is misplaced. Section 118 expresses Congress' support for alternative dispute resolution: "Where appropriate and to the extent authorized by law, the use of alternative means of dispute resolution, including . . . arbitration, is encouraged to resolve disputes arising under" the ADEA. Respondents argue that the legislative history actually signals Congress' intent to preclude arbitration waivers in the collective-bargaining context. In particular, respondents point to a House Report that, in spite of the statute's plain language, interprets § 118 to support their position. See H. R. Rep. No. 102-40, pt. 1, p 97 (1991) ("[A]ny agreement to submit disputed issues to arbitration . . . in the context of a collective bargaining agreement . . . does not preclude the affected person from seeking relief under the enforcement provisions of Title VII. This view is consistent with the Supreme Court's interpretation of Title VII in *Alexander* v. *Gardner-Denver Co.*, 415 U.S. 36, 94 S. Ct. 1011, 39 L. Ed. 2d 147 (1974)"). But the legislative history mischaracterizes the holding of *Gardner-Denver*, which does not prohibit collective bargaining for arbitration of ADEA claims. Moreover, reading the legislative history in the manner suggested by respondents would create a direct conflict with the statutory text, which encourages the use of arbitration for dispute resolution without imposing any constraints on collective bargaining. In such a contest, the text must prevail.

Id. at 259 n.6.

Since *Gilmer*, the Supreme Court has consistently upheld the enforceability of arbitration agreements in the face of allegedly conflicting federal statutes. In 1995, the Court avoided the question whether the Carriage of Goods by Sea Act (COGSA) conflicted with the FAA by construing a provision of COGSA not to preclude resolution of disputes by arbitration in a foreign forum. *See* Vimar Seguros y Reaseguros v. M/V Sky Reefer, 515 U.S. 528 (1995). The Court made the following comments on petitioner's argument that Japanese arbitrators might not apply the substantive provisions of COGSA to the parties' dispute:

> Whatever the merits of petitioner's comparative reading of COGSA and its Japanese counterpart, its claim is premature. At this interlocutory stage it is not established what law the arbitrators will apply to petitioner's claims or that petitioner will receive diminished protection as a result. The arbitrators may conclude that COGSA applies of its own force or that Japanese law does not apply so that, under another clause of the bill of lading, COGSA applies. Respondents seek only to enforce the arbitration agreement. The District Court has retained jurisdiction over this case and "will have the opportunity at the award enforcement stage to ensure that the legitimate interest in the enforcement of the . . . laws has been addressed." *Mitsubishi Motors.*

Id. at 540.

Most recently, in 2012, the Supreme Court concluded that claims under the Credit Repair Organizations Act (CROA), 15 U.S.C. § 1679 et seq., could be arbitrated pursuant to a pre-dispute agreement. CompuCredit Corp. v. Greenwood, 132 S. Ct. 665 (2012). The CROA does not expressly address whether claims under the Act can be arbitrated. Nor do the remedial provisions of the Act contain any language that precludes arbitration of CROA claims; the only possible such arguments had already been rejected in prior Supreme Court cases. Instead, the focus of the case was on the disclosure provisions of the Act, which required credit repair organizations to inform consumers that "[y]ou have a right to sue a credit repair organization that violates the Credit Repair Organizations Act." The Ninth Circuit held that this language showed Congress' intent that parties not be required to arbitrate CROA claims, since a "right to sue" necessarily means a right to proceed in court, rather than arbitration.

The Supreme Court reversed. It stated that "the flaw in [the Ninth Circuit's] argument is its premise: that the disclosure provision provides consumers with a right to bring an action in a court of law." *Id.* at 669-70. Rather, it only requires companies to make certain disclosures; the substantive and procedural rights created by the statute must be found elsewhere — in provisions that do not preclude arbitration. Instead, the language in the disclosure provision "is meant to describe the law to consumers in a manner that is concise and comprehensible to the lay-man — which necessarily means that it will be imprecise." *Id.* at 670. In the Court's words: the "right to sue" language is "a colloquial method of communicating to consumers that they have the legal right, enforceable in court to recover damages from credit repair organizations that violate the CROA." *Id.* at 672. Given how common arbitration clauses were at the time the CROA was enacted, the Court concluded, if Congress had intended to prohibit them it would have done so more clearly than in the disclosure language cited.

PROBLEM 3.6

Percy Phelps (see Problem 2.15) files suit challenging his firing by his most recent employer, which he alleges was unlawful under both the Age Discrimination in Employment Act (ADEA) and the Americans with Disabilities Act (ADA). Note that 42 U.S.C. § 12212, a provision of the ADA, provides as follows:

> Where appropriate and to the extent authorized by law, the use of alternative means of dispute resolution, including settlement negotiations, conciliation, facilitation, mediation, factfinding, minitrials, and arbitration, is encouraged to resolve disputes arising under this chapter.

Phelps and his employer signed an agreement to arbitrate all disputes arising out of the employment relationship. Must Phelps arbitrate his ADEA claim? Must he arbitrate his ADA claim?

[B] Current Issues in the Arbitrability of Federal Statutory Claims

After *Gilmer*, it appeared that virtually all federal statutory claims were arbitrable. Indeed, a leading American arbitration scholar described the "category of 'inarbitrable disputes' " in the United States as a "null set." Alan Scott Rau, *The Culture of American Arbitration and the Lessons of ADR*, 40 TEX. INT'L L.J. 449, 452 (2005). It certainly is true that the vast majority of claims that a plaintiff might seek to bring in a U.S. court can be resolved in arbitration if the parties so agree. But there remain several areas where the arbitrability of federal statutory claims has not been finally resolved, which this section addresses.

IN RE AMERICAN HOMESTAR OF LANCASTER, INC.
Supreme Court of Texas
50 S.W.3d 480 (2001)

JUSTICE JAMES A. BAKER delivered the opinion of the Court.

The issue in this mandamus proceeding is whether the Magnuson-Moss Warranty Act prohibits enforcing predispute binding arbitration agreements in warranty disputes involving a consumer-product purchase. The court of appeals held that the Magnuson-Moss Act prohibits such agreements. We disagree. Accordingly, we conditionally grant a writ of mandamus and direct the court of appeals to vacate its order.

I. BACKGROUND

In May 1997, James and Clara Van Blarcum bought a manufactured home from Nationwide Housing System. American Homestar manufactured the home, and Associates Housing Financing Services financed it. At closing, Nationwide Housing provided the Van Blarcums with a written warranty. The parties also signed a "Retail Installment Contract-Security Agreement" and a separate "Arbitration Provision". . . .

After their manufactured home was installed, the Van Blarcums complained about various alleged defects with the home. Despite receiving assurances that these defects would be remedied, nine months later, the defects remained. Accordingly, in July 1998, the Van Blarcums sued American Homestar, Nationwide Housing, and Associates Financing, alleging Magnuson-Moss Warranty Act, Texas Deceptive Trade Practices Act, and Texas Manufactured Housing Standards Act violations. The Van Blarcums also alleged breach of express and implied warranties.

American Homestar and Nationwide Housing moved to compel binding arbitration. The trial court granted the motion, stayed the litigation, and ordered the parties to proceed to arbitration. The Van Blarcums filed a petition for a writ of mandamus with the court of appeals, arguing that the Magnuson-Moss Act prohibits binding arbitration of consumer warranty disputes. The court of appeals, sitting en banc, conditionally granted a writ, holding that the trial court abused its discretion by compelling arbitration. . . . . The court reasoned that, because the arbitration provision in the contract violates the Magnuson-Moss Act, the agreement was invalid and unenforceable in its entirety for all the Van Blarcums' claims.

. . .

American Homestar and Nationwide Housing petitioned this Court for mandamus relief, requesting that we vacate the court of appeals' order. Because we hold that the Magnuson-Moss Act does not override the Federal Arbitration Act's mandate to enforce binding arbitration agreements, we conditionally grant mandamus relief.

II. APPLICABLE LAW

. . .

The United States Supreme Court has recognized an "emphatic federal policy in favor of arbitral dispute resolution." *Mitsubishi Motors Corp. v. Soler Chrysler-Plymouth, Inc.* To further this purpose, the FAA compels judicial enforcement of a wide range of written arbitration agreements.

Only a contrary congressional command can override the FAA's mandate to enforce arbitration agreements. *Shearson/American Express, Inc. v. McMahon.* Thus, to overcome the presumption favoring arbitration agreements, the party opposing arbitration must show that Congress intended to preclude a party's waiving a statute's judicial remedies. *McMahon.* A party may show this intent through the statute's text or legislative history or through an inherent conflict between arbitration and the statute's underlying purposes. . . .

. . .

III. ANALYSIS

American Homestar and Nationwide Housing argue that the Van Blarcums did not meet their burden of proof under *McMahon* to show that the Magnuson-Moss Act prohibits predispute binding arbitration under the FAA. The Van Blarcums disagree and argue that, despite the Supreme Court's palpable resistance to override the FAA, the Magnuson-Moss Act is substantially different from the [other statutes the Court has considered] in that its text, legislative history, and purposes all support a conclusion that, in passing the Magnuson-Moss Act, Congress intended to override the FAA and prohibit binding arbitration.

First, the Van Blarcums point out that the FTC has determined that decisions of an informal dispute settlement mechanism shall not be binding on any person, 16 C.F.R. § 703.5(j), and argue that this regulation evidences the FTC's position that the Magnuson-Moss Act precludes enforcing a binding arbitration agreement. Second, they cite section 15 U.S.C. § 2310(d)(1)(A), providing a statutory right to "bring suit for damages and other legal and equitable relief . . . in any court of competent jurisdiction," to argue that an informal dispute settlement mechanism can only serve as a prerequisite and not a bar to filing suit. Third, they cite to legislative history indicating "an adverse decision in any informal dispute settlement proceeding would not be a bar to a civil action on the warranty involved in the proceeding." *See* Wilson v. Waverlee Homes, Inc., 954 F. Supp. 1530, 1538 (M.D. Ala. 1997) (quoting H.R. REP. No. 93-1107, at 41 (1974)), *aff'd*, 127 F.3d 40 (11th Cir. 1997).

Indeed, several federal district courts have followed similar reasoning to hold that the Magnuson-Moss Act prohibits enforcing binding arbitration agreements. *See* Wilson, 954 F. Supp. at 1539; Boyd v. Homes of Legend, Inc., 981 F. Supp. 1423, 1440 (M.D. Ala. 1997), *remanded on jurisdictional grounds*, 188 F.3d 1294 (11th Cir. 1999); Rhode v. E&T Invs, Inc., 6 F. Supp. 2d 1322, 1332 (M.D. Ala. 1998). But this reasoning has been refuted. *See, e.g.*, Southern Energy Homes, Inc. v. Lee, 732 So. 2d 994, 1012 (Ala. 1999) (See, J., dissenting) (concluding that, under the Supreme Court's analytical framework, the Magnuson-Moss Act does not prohibit enforcing binding arbitration agreements) (opinion adopted in Southern Energy Homes, Inc. v. Ard, 772 So. 2d 1131, 1135 (Ala. 2000) ("We now opine that Justice See's dissent in *Lee* is correct and the majority opinion is incorrect. Therefore, we overrule the majority opinion in *Lee* and adopt Justice See's dissent.")). And we agree that Supreme Court precedent follows a different rationale and warrants a different conclusion.

A. THE TEXT

In determining legislative intent, we look first to the plain and common meaning of the statute's words. The Magnuson-Moss Act does not expressly prohibit binding arbitration. In fact, the Magnuson-Moss Act does not mention arbitration.

The Van Blarcums rely on 15 U.S.C. § 2310(a)(3) to support their position. This section provides that if a warrantor elects to have an informal dispute settlement mechanism, it must "incorporate[] in [its] written warranty a requirement that the consumer resort to [the informal mechanism] before pursuing any legal remedy under this section respecting such warranty." 15 U.S.C. § 2310(a)(3)(C). Then, "the consumer may not commence a civil action . . . unless he initially resorts to such procedure." 15 U.S.C. § 2310(a)(3). Moreover, "in any civil action arising out of a warranty obligation and relating to a matter considered in such a procedure, any decision in such procedure shall be admissible in evidence." 15 U.S.C. § 2310(a)(3). These provisions, according to the Van Blarcums, evidence congressional intent that any alternative dispute-resolution procedure act only as a prerequisite to suit — not a bar from bringing claims in a judicial forum.

However, expressly providing for one type of out-of-court settlement mechanism does not necessarily preclude enforcing an agreement to participate in another. In *Gilmer*, the Supreme Court noted that the ADEA imposes a similar prerequisite. Specifically, a claimant must file a charge with the EEOC before pursuing a claim in court, and the EEOC must engage in "informal methods of conciliation, conference, and persuasion." 29 U.S.C. § 626(b). The Supreme Court nevertheless concluded that the ADEA's expressly providing for "out-of-court dispute resolution" is not inconsistent with allowing arbitration under the FAA. Similarly, enforcing the parties' binding arbitration agreement is not inconsistent with the Magnuson-Moss Act's providing an out-of-court informal dispute settlement mechanism.

Contrary to the Van Blarcums's position, section 2310(a)(3) merely gives a warrantor the *option* to include an informal dispute settlement mechanism in its written warranty. It does not speak to other means of settling disputes between parties, such as binding arbitration. In enacting section 2310(a)(3), Congress sought to provide warrantors an incentive to establish informal procedures to fairly and expeditiously resolve consumer warranty disputes. 15 U.S.C. § 2310(a)(1). The Magnuson-Moss Act does not mention or prohibit other dispute-resolution procedures. And, neither the Magnuson-Moss Act nor the FTC regulations mention arbitration or the FAA. Accordingly, we conclude that nothing in the Magnuson-Moss Act's text suggests congressional intent to override the FAA.

B. LEGISLATIVE HISTORY

We next look to the Magnuson-Moss Act's legislative history for evidence of clear congressional intent to preclude enforcing binding arbitration under the FAA. The Van Blarcums rely on legislative history stating that "an adverse decision in any informal dispute settlement proceeding would not be a bar to a civil action on the warranty involved in the proceeding." They contend this statement indicates congressional intent that compulsory agreements to arbitrate warranty disputes are unenforceable.

However, this legislative history is not dispositive. . . .

. . . The Magnuson-Moss Act's history cited by the Van Blarcums is even less clear about an intent to prohibit binding arbitration than the Exchange Act's history considered in *McMahon*[, in which a conference committee report indicated an intent to leave *Wilko v. Swan* unaffected]. In fact, unlike the Exchange Act's history, the Magnuson-Moss Act's history does not expressly refer to arbitration proceedings; it only discusses informal dispute settlement proceedings as the Magnuson-Moss Act contemplates. If the Supreme Court concluded that the Exchange Act's history did not show an intent to prohibit arbitration, we must reach the same conclusion given the language in the Magnuson-Moss Act's history. . . .

Additionally, legislative history from an earlier version of the Magnuson-Moss Act further supports our conclusion that the legislative history cited by the Van Blarcums is not dispositive. Interpreting that earlier version, the Senate Report states that "it is Congress' intent that warrantors of consumer products cooperate with government and private agencies to establish informal dispute settlement mechanisms that take care of consumer grievances *without the aid of litigation or formal arbitration.*" S. REP. No. 91-876, at 22–23 (1970) (emphasis added). This passage arguably demonstrates that Congress contemplated a consumer's resort to courts *or* binding arbitration if the informal dispute settlement mechanism did not resolve the dispute. Or, at minimum, it shows the legislative history is ambiguous. Accordingly, we conclude that the Magnuson-Moss Act's legislative history does not show a clear intent to preclude enforcing predispute binding arbitration agreements under the FAA.

C. INHERENT CONFLICT

We next consider whether an inherent conflict exists between the Magnuson-Moss Act and binding arbitration under the FAA. The Van Blarcums do not identify an inherent conflict. Instead, they only cite to the Magnuson-Moss Act's three stated purposes: "to improve the adequacy of information available to consumers, prevent deception, and improve competition in the marketing of consumer products." 15 U.S.C. § 2302(a). However, we are not convinced that enforcing binding arbitration agreements would circumvent any of these purposes. A warrantor could honestly market a consumer product with full disclosure to the consumer about the product and still present a predispute binding arbitration agreement to the consumer. These are not inherently inconsistent positions for the warrantor. To so conclude would be tantamount to adopting the now-rejected *Wilko* mentality that binding arbitration is inherently unfair to consumers. And it would ignore that "Congress, when enacting [the FAA], had the needs of consumers . . . in mind." *Allied-Bruce Terminix Cos. v. Dobson.*

The Magnuson-Moss Act's legislative history does indicate a concern about unequal bargaining power. . . . But the Supreme Court has recognized that perceived uneven bargaining power is not a justifiable reason to hold that arbitration agreements are never enforceable. . . . [B]ecause the FAA's purpose was to place arbitration clauses on the same footing as other contractual agreements, courts can resolve unequal bargaining power claims on a case-by-case basis. However, the Van Blarcums do not allege that their arbitration agreement resulted from fraud or uneven economic power. And the arbitration provision does not restrict the arbitrator's ability to grant relief.

Accordingly, we conclude that there is no inherent conflict between the FAA and the Magnuson-Moss Act's purposes. Finding nothing in the Magnuson-Moss Act's text, legislative history, or purposes that preclude[s] enforcement of predispute binding arbitration agreements under the FAA, we hold that the arbitration clause in this case is valid and enforceable.

D. FEDERAL TRADE COMMISSION'S INTERPRETATION

The Van Blarcums point out that the FTC has determined that decisions rendered through an informal dispute settlement mechanism shall not be binding on any person. *See* 16 C.F.R. § 703.5(j). They argue that the FTC's regulation demonstrates its position that the Magnuson-Moss Act precludes enforcing a binding arbitration agreement.

The FTC has promulgated regulations about informal dispute settlement mechanisms. But no FTC regulation expressly prohibits binding arbitration. Rather, when the FTC first published its rules and interpretations in 1975, the agency recognized that industry representatives hoped the FTC would allow warrantors and consumers to agree to binding arbitration. The FTC refused. It noted that it was Congress' intent that informal dispute settlement mechanisms not be legally binding, and, even if binding arbitration were contemplated under the statute, the FTC was not prepared at that time to develop guidelines for such a system. The FTC further noted that warrantors are not precluded from offering a binding arbitration option after a warranty dispute has arisen. In 1999, after reviewing its rules and interpretations, the FTC concluded that predispute binding arbitration agreements are still not permissible under the Magnuson-Moss Act.

. . . Here, Congress has not spoken to the precise question — whether the Magnuson-Moss Act precludes enforcing binding arbitration under the FAA. And, while we may defer to an agency's interpretation of the statute it administers, *see generally* Chevron U.S.A., Inc. [v. Natural Resources Defense Council, Inc., 467 U.S. 837 (1984)], we owe no such deference when the agency's interpretation is unreasonable.

In this case, we are not persuaded that the FTC's position results from a permissible or reasonable construction of the Magnuson-Moss Act. In fact, the Supreme Court, in an analogous context [in *McMahon*], has rejected arguments similar to those upon which the FTC relies to conclude the statute prohibits binding arbitration. . . .

Moreover, the FTC's position about binding arbitration has been less than consistent. For example, in its commentary to Rule 703.5(j), the FTC recognized that some witnesses in the 1975 hearing suggested the warrantor and consumer might agree to binding arbitration. The FTC encouraged this by emphatically stating "*nothing in the rule precludes the parties from agreeing to use some avenue of redress* other than the mechanism if they feel it is more appropriate." (Emphasis added). And, even though the FTC is empowered to restrain warrantors from failing to comply with a Magnuson-Moss Act requirement, neither the parties nor the FTC as amicus have identified an FTC enforcement action to restrain these allegedly-standard predispute binding arbitration agreements. For these reasons, we need not defer to the FTC's current position about binding arbitration.

IV. CONCLUSION

The Supreme Court has mandated that the FAA's policy favoring enforcing arbitration agreements trumps other federal statutes absent a clear congressional command. . . . Because we find no clear congressional intent in the Magnuson-Moss Act to override the FAA policy favoring arbitration, we hold that the trial court did not abuse its discretion in compelling arbitration. Thus, the court of appeals erred in granting mandamus relief and invalidating the parties' arbitration agreement. . . .

NOTES

1. The Magnuson-Moss Warranty Act creates a cause of action for any "consumer who is damaged by the failure of a supplier, warrantor, or service contractor to comply with any obligation under this [Act], or under a written warranty, implied warranty, or service contract." 15 U.S.C. § 2310(d)(1). A "consumer" means a "buyer (other than for purposes of resale) of any consumer product or any person to whom such product is transferred during the duration of an implied or written warranty (or service contract) applicable to the product." *Id.* § 2301(3). A "consumer product" is "any tangible personal property which is distributed in commerce and which is normally used for personal, family, or household purposes." *Id.* § 2301(1). The consumer's cause of action under the Act is expressly made subject to section 2310(a)(3), which permits a warrantor to "establish an informal dispute settlement procedure which meets the requirements of the Commission's rules." *Id.* § 2310(a)(3). If a warrantor establishes such an informal dispute resolution procedure, if the procedure complies with the FTC's rules, and if the warrantor "incorporates in a written warranty a requirement that the consumer resort to such procedure before pursuing any legal remedy under this section respecting such warranty," then "the consumer may not commence a civil action . . . under subsection (d) of this section unless he initially resorts to such procedure." *Id.* As the court explains in *American Homestar*, the FTC's regulations promulgated under the authority of the Magnuson-Moss Act state that "[d]ecisions of the [informal dispute resolution] Mechanism shall not be legally binding on any person," 16 C.F.R. § 703.5(j), although the warrantor shall "act in good faith in determining to whether, and to what extent, it will abide by a Mechanism decision." *Id.* § 703.2(g).

2. Are the Van Blarcums arguing that Magnuson-Moss claims are not arbitrable, or that Magnuson-Moss invalidates the entire arbitration agreement? Which is their stronger argument?

3. Most courts now agree with the Texas Supreme Court that Magnuson-Moss claims can be arbitrated and that the Act does not invalidate pre-dispute arbitration clauses in consumer warranties. *See, e.g.*, Davis v. Southern Energy Homes, Inc., 305 F.3d 1268 (11th Cir.), *cert. denied*, 538 U.S. 945 (2003); Walton v. Rose Mobile Homes LLC, 298 F.3d 470 (5th Cir. 2002); Patriot Mfg., Inc. v. Jackson, 2005 Ala. LEXIS 207 (Ala. Nov. 18, 2005); Borowiec v. Gateway 2000, Inc., 808 N.E.2d 957 (Ill.), *cert. denied*, 543 U.S. 869 (2004). *But see* Parkerson v. Smith, 817 So. 2d 529, 534 (Miss. 2002) ("the Magnuson-Moss Warranty Act has superceded the FAA in regard to breach of consumer warranties, and binding arbitration cannot be compelled in this case without contravening the purposes of the Act"); Koons Ford of Baltimore, Inc. v. Lobach, 919 A.2d 722, 736 (Md. Ct. App. 2007) ("Congress made clear, in § 2310(a)(3)(c), that consumers must retain the ability to adjudicate their claims in court, even if they must first resort to informal dispute settlement procedures").

4. One additional issue on which a federal agency has expressed its views on arbitrability is whether securities issuers can include arbitration clauses in their corporate governance documents, effectively requiring arbitration of securities fraud suits against the issuers. Given *McMahon* and *Rodriguez de Quijas*, there

would seem to be a good argument that such an arbitration clause would be enforceable. But for a number of years the Securities and Exchange Commission (SEC) has refused to accelerate securities filings that included an arbitration clause, effectively killing the offering unless the arbitration clause was removed. *See* Carl W. Schneider, *Change, the SEC and Me: Reflections from the Loyal Opposition*, Bus. L. Today, May/June 1999, at 32; Thomas L. Riesenberg, *Arbitration and Corporate Governance: A Reply to Carl Schneider*, Insights, Aug. 1990, at 2. In February 2012, for example, the Carlyle Group withdrew an arbitration clause from its initial public offering documents in the face of SEC (and other) opposition. *See, e.g.*, Kevin Roose, *Carlyle Drops Arbitration Clause from I.P.O. Plans*, N.Y. Times DealBook, Feb. 3, 2012. Is the SEC's practice consistent with Supreme Court precedent? Does it reflect sound policy? For further discussion, see Barbara Black, *Arbitration of Investors' Claims Against Issuers: An Idea Whose Time Has Come?*, 75 Law & Contemp. Probs. 107 (2012).

PROBLEM 3.7

Recall the facts of *Hill v. Gateway 2000, Inc.* from § 2.05[A]. The Hills ordered a Gateway 2000 computer by phone. Included with the computer shipped by Gateway was a list of terms and conditions, one of which was an arbitration clause. Assume that another was a written warranty within the meaning of the Magnuson-Moss Warranty Act. The form containing the terms and conditions provided that continued use of the computer after 30 days would constitute acceptance of the terms and conditions contained in the form. The Hills did not return the computer within thirty days. When Gateway failed to resolve problems with the computer to their satisfaction, the Hills filed suit in federal court, raising claims for breach of a written warranty, breach of the implied warranty of merchantability, fraud, and racketeering, as well as a claim under the Magnuson-Moss Warranty Act. Aside from the issue of assent, which we have discussed before, do the Hills have any other argument they might make that their claims are not subject to arbitration? Are they likely to prevail on that argument?

CLARY v. HELEN OF TROY, L.P.

United States District Court for the Western District of Texas
2011 U.S. Dist. LEXIS 151479 (Dec. 20, 2011)

Kathleen Cardone, United States District Judge.

ORDER

On this day, the Court considered "Defendant's Motion to Stay Proceedings and to Compel Arbitration." For the reasons set forth below, the Motion is **DENIED**.

I. BACKGROUND

Plaintiff Edith Clary was an employee of Defendant Helen of Troy Nevada Corporation. On April 15, 2011, Plaintiff received a federal jury summons informing her she would be on call for jury duty from June 1, 2011 to July 1, 2011. The next day, Plaintiff told Defendant's representative about the summons. According to Plaintiff, Defendant's representative and Plaintiff examined the possibility of claiming an exemption from jury duty, but ultimately agreed that none of the exemptions applied. In response to the possibility of Plaintiff missing work, Defendant allegedly started looking for outside help and gave some of Plaintiff's work to Plaintiff's assistant.

On May 26, 2011, Defendant fired Plaintiff despite her claims that she was a "good employee." Defendant allegedly told her that the reason for the firing was a violation of company policy, but Plaintiff alleges she was actually fired because she was summoned for federal jury service. Plaintiff therefore alleges the firing violated 28 U.S.C. § 1875, The Jury System Improvements Act of 1978 ("Jury Act").

II. DISCUSSION

Defendant argues that there is a mutual, binding agreement between Plaintiff and Defendant to resolve all disputes relating to Plaintiff's employment in arbitration. Both parties appear to agree that the dispute in this case relates to Plaintiff's employment. Therefore, Defendant maintains that the Federal Arbitration Act ("FAA"), requires the Court to compel arbitration and stay the proceedings based on the arbitration clause in the employment agreement.

Plaintiff responds that arbitration is inappropriate because her claims arise under the Jury Act. According to Plaintiff, the Jury Act is a unique federal statute that is incompatible with arbitration because Congress enacted the Jury Act to give federal courts, not arbitrators, the power to protect the integrity of the judicial system. Thus, the issue presented to the Court is whether a claim under the Jury Act is arbitrable. This appears to be a question of first impression among courts in the Fifth Circuit.

A. FAA

. . .

"Like any statutory directive, the Arbitration Act's mandate may be overridden by a contrary congressional command." In other words, the FAA mandates arbitration unless the party opposing arbitration can show that Congress intended to preclude arbitration for the given statutory claim. *Gilmer.* "If such an intention exists, it will be discoverable in the text of the [statute], its legislative history, or an 'inherent conflict' between arbitration and the [statute's] underlying purposes." *Id.*

Here, Plaintiff does not contend that the text of the Jury Act or the legislative history shows such an intention. Rather, Plaintiff argues there is an inherent conflict between the Jury Act's purpose and requiring resolution of this claim through arbitration. According to Plaintiff, Congress enacted the Jury Act to give federal courts the power to protect the integrity of their juries, and thus the integrity of the judicial process as a whole. Plaintiff argues that arbitration of Jury Act violations inherently conflicts with Congress's intent. Thus, the Court examines the purposes of the Jury Act to decide if those purposes conflict with resolving this claim through arbitration.

B. The Jury Act

The Jury Act states:

(a) No employer shall discharge, threaten to discharge, intimidate, or coerce any permanent employee by reason of such employee's jury service, or the attendance or scheduled attendance in connection with such service, in any court of the United States.

(b) Any employer who violates the provisions of this section —

(1) shall be liable for damages for any loss of wages or other benefits suffered by an employee by reason of such violation;

(2) may be enjoined from further violations of this section and ordered to provide other appropriate relief, including but not limited to the reinstatement of any employee discharged by reason of his jury service; and

(3) shall be subject to a civil penalty of not more than $5,000 for each violation as to each employee, and may be ordered to perform community service.

28 U.S.C. § 1875(a)-(c).

The Jury Act serves two critical purposes. First, the Jury Act protects an employee from any employer who is "hostile to the idea of jury duty, or who believes that the interests of his business outweigh the obligation for jury service imposed by law." H.R. Rep. No. 95-1652, at 1 (1978). The Jury Act "impose[s] on the employer a duty to ensure that an employee is aware that the employee could report for jury duty without fear of reprisal."

There is no conflict between arbitration and protecting individual jurors in their employment. The Supreme Court has explained that "so long as the prospective litigant effectively may vindicate its statutory cause of action in the arbitral forum, the statute will continue to serve both its remedial and deterrent function." *Mitsubishi Motors.* Based on the jurisprudence of the Supreme Court and the Fifth Circuit, there is no reason to suspect a juror's substantive rights under the Jury Act will not be adequately protected by arbitration.

However, the Jury Act has a second purpose — to give federal courts the power to protect the judicial process.

To say that the federal courts could not operate without juries is not an exaggeration. The Founding Fathers considered the jury to be "the very palladium of free government" and a critical barrier to tyranny. The Federalist No. 83 (A. Hamilton). To ensure the jury remains a barrier to tyranny, the Founders included three jury rights in the Constitution. . . . Thus, under the Constitution, "the jury . . . has an awesome responsibility in American justice. It determines the fate of men — their property, their freedom, and sometimes their lives."

Given that federal courts cannot constitutionally function without juries, federal courts must be able to protect the integrity of the jury system from interfering employers. The court in *In re Adams*[, 421 F. Supp. 1027 (E.D. Mich. 1976),] explained the problem:

> A jury cannot be expected to listen in the relaxed, attentive manner required to absorb the evidence presented and to discriminate among that evidence, nor to take the time to deliberate and argue in a rational way to reach a unanimous verdict if the members of the jury are worried about the security of their employment positions as a result of threats made by their employers involving jury service.

421 F. Supp. at 1031.

Before the enactment of the Jury Act, some courts had attempted to protect their juries via the court's criminal contempt power. But Congress recognized the contempt power was insufficient. Federal courts can only use the criminal contempt power when the conduct occurred within "its presence or so near thereto as to obstruct the administration of justice." 18 U.S.C. § 401. Congress was so focused on giving the federal courts additional power to protect their juries that Congress initially proposed criminal penalties in the Jury Act. Although Congress eventually opted only for civil penalties and a civil statutory remedy, courts have used the Jury Act to sua sponte enjoin an employer or order an employer to show cause without the employee filing an independent civil suit. In sum, the Jury Act protects the jury process that is fundamental to our system of justice.

There is an inherent conflict between arbitration and the Jury Act. Binding arbitration agreements take the power to protect the integrity of the jury system out of the hands of the courts and places it into the hands of private parties. This directly contradicts Congress's intentions and a critical purpose of the Jury Act — to give power to the federal courts to protect the integrity of the jury system beyond a court's inherent contempt power. Thus, despite the federal policy in favor of arbitration generally, arbitration is not appropriate under the Jury Act.

Defendant attempts to rebut this argument by analogizing the Jury Act to other federal employment statutes that are arbitrable. Defendant is correct that claims under the Age Discrimination in Employment Act, Fair Labor Standards Act, and Title VII are all arbitrable. Moreover, claims under the Sherman Act; section 10(b) of the Securities Exchange Act of 1934; the civil provisions of the Racketeer Influenced and Corrupt Organizations Act ("RICO"); section 12(2) of the Securities Act of 1933; and the Uniformed Services Employment and Reemployment Rights Act, 38 U.S.C. § 4301 *et seq.*, have all been found to be subject to binding arbitration agreements despite each statute's strong public policy purposes. But critically, none of those statutes impacted the federal court's ability to protect the integrity of its own juries, and thus in turn, the power to protect the judicial process itself.

In this way, the Jury Act is more similar to the federal Bankruptcy Code. The Fifth Circuit in *In re National Gypsum Co.* held that arbitration can conflict with the purposes of the Bankruptcy Code. 118 F.3d 1056, 1069 (5th Cir. 1999). The Fifth Circuit reasoned that an exception to mandatory arbitration was necessary to preserve the Bankruptcy Code's purpose of creating a centralized and efficient bankruptcy court system. Moreover, the Fifth Circuit explained that the "undisputed power of a bankruptcy court to enforce its own orders" also suggests mandatory arbitration is inappropriate.

Arbitration of the Jury Act poses the same two concerns. First, like in the bankruptcy context, arbitration of the Jury Act conflicts with Congress's intent to provide federal courts with additional power to ensure the courts operate smoothly. Given the constitutional necessity of juries, federal courts can only operate smoothly if the federal courts can protect the integrity of their juries.

Second, like in the bankruptcy context, arbitration could interfere with a court's ability to enforce its own orders. As discussed above, federal courts have the inherent power to protect the integrity of juries via the criminal contempt power. Congress enacted the Jury Act to supplement that power. If the FAA requires federal courts to send an alleged violation of the Jury Act to arbitration, federal courts could lose the Jury Act's power to protect the integrity of juries.

. . .

If Defendant is correct that the FAA requires arbitration of [Jury Act] violations when there is a binding arbitration agreement, the power of the courts [to protect the judicial process] . . . would be diminished. An employer's decision to invoke an arbitration clause in response to an order to show cause could frustrate the court's ability to enforce its own orders and protect the integrity of the jury system. Thus, like in the bankruptcy context, arbitration and the Jury Act inherently conflict because arbitration could impact the court's ability to effectively control its own cases and enforce its own orders.

Defendant correctly notes that the only two courts that appear to have addressed this issue both held that claims under the Jury Act are arbitrable. Def.'s Reply (citing *Shaffer v. ACS Gov't Servs., Inc.*, 321 F. Supp. 2d 682 (D. Md. 2004); *McNulty v. Prudential-Bache Sec., Inc.*, 871 F. Supp. 567 (E.D.N.Y. 1994)). However, *Shaffer* did not analyze the issue — instead, the court simply concluded that it "agrees with" the *McNulty* decision. The court in *McNulty* did analyze the issue. The court concluded that "[t]here is no evidence in the statute's text or legislative history that Congress intended to remove claims under the [Jury] Act from arbitration; nor is there an inherent conflict between arbitration and the purposes of the Act." When analyzing the inherent conflict factor, the court focused on the Jury Act's provision that provides for appointment of counsel. The court reasoned persuasively that this provision cannot foreclose arbitration because Title VII also has a provision appointing counsel, and Title VII claims are arbitrable.

Although the Court finds the *McNulty* opinion well-reasoned, the *McNulty* court did not address a critical purpose of the Jury Act — Congress's intent to give federal courts the power to protect the judicial process. As explained above, placing the power of the Jury Act in the hands of arbitrators inherently conflicts with Congress's intention to give that power to the federal courts. Accordingly, the Court holds that Plaintiff has shown that Congress intended to preclude arbitration from the Jury Act because arbitration inherently conflicts with a purpose of the Jury Act.

III. CONCLUSION

For the foregoing reasons, Defendant's Motion is **DENIED**.

SO ORDERED.

PROBLEM 3.8

J.H. Watson (from Problem 3.2) gets called to jury duty by the local federal court, but his parents (who run Watson Motor Cars (WMC)) refuse to let him take time off work to serve. Law-abiding citizen that he is, Watson shows up for jury duty any way, gets selected, and ends up serving as jury foreman for a complex (and long) federal criminal case. When he calls to tell his parents he is not going to be able to be at work for several weeks, they tell him not to bother coming back to the dealership because he no longer has a job there.

The marshal at the courthouse tells Watson about a federal law that protects jurors from losing their jobs because of their jury service. When Watson tells his parents about the federal law, they each say "so sue me," which he does. He files suit in federal court asserting a claim for violation of the Jury System Improvements Act of 1978, 28 U.S.C. § 1875. His parents respond to the lawsuit by moving to stay the suit and to compel arbitration of Watson's claim. (It turns out that the employment contract Watson had signed with WMC included a broad arbitration clause.) Is Watson's claim arbitrable?

IN RE UNITED STATES LINES, INC.
United States Court of Appeals for the Second Circuit
197 F.3d 631 (1999)

WALKER, CIRCUIT JUDGE:

The United States Lines, Inc. and United States Lines (S.A.) Inc. Reorganization Trust (the "Trust") sued in the Bankruptcy Court for the Southern District of New York . . . seeking a declaratory judgment to establish the Trust's rights under various insurance contracts. The bankruptcy court held that the action was within its core jurisdiction and denied the defendants' motion to compel arbitration of the proceedings. The District Court for the Southern District of New York . . . reversed and held that the insurance contract disputes were not core proceedings. After ordering arbitration to go forward, the district court certified its order for interlocutory appeal pursuant to 28 U.S.C. § 1292(b). We now reverse and remand.

BACKGROUND

. . . On November 24, 1986, United States Lines, Inc. and United States Lines (S.A.) Inc., as debtors, filed a voluntary petition for bankruptcy relief under Chapter 11 of the Bankruptcy Code, 11 U.S.C. §§ 101 *et seq.* The Trust is their successor-in-interest pursuant to a plan of reorganization that was confirmed by the bankruptcy court on May 16, 1989.

Among the creditors are some 12,000 employees who have filed more than 18,000 claims, most of which are for asbestos-related injuries sustained while sailing on different ships in debtors' fleet over four decades. Many additional claims are expected to mature in the future. The Trust asserts that these claims are covered by several Protection & Indemnity insurance policies (the "P & I policies") issued by four domestic and four foreign mutual insurance clubs ("the Clubs"). Generally, a single club insured the debtors' entire fleet for a particular year, but there were exceptions when certain ships were insured independently of fleet coverage by another club or under a different policy. All of the P & I policies were issued before the debtors petitioned for bankruptcy relief.

The proceeds of the P & I policies are the only funds potentially available to cover the above employees' personal injury claims. At the heart of each of the P & I policies is a pay-first provision by which the insurers' liability is not triggered until the insured pays the claim of the personal injury victim. The deductibles for each accident or occurrence vary among the different policies, ranging from $250 to $100,000.

. . . [O]n January 5, 1993, the Trust began this action as an adversarial proceeding in bankruptcy, pursuant to 28 U.S.C. § 2201, seeking a declaratory judgment of the parties' respective rights under the various P & I policies. Nine of the ten counts in the complaint seek a declaration from the court of the Clubs' contractual obligations under the P & I policies in light of the stipulation of conditional settlement. The tenth claim seeks punitive damages for creating an "insurance maze."

The bankruptcy court held, *inter alia*, that the Trust's declaratory judgment action was "core," and thus could be tried to binding judgment in the bankruptcy court, and that the bankruptcy court had discretion to deny the motion to compel arbitration filed by the four foreign Clubs. The district court, exercising appellate jurisdiction, reversed both determinations. . . . On March 4, 1998, the district court entered an order certifying its November 26, 1997 order for interlocutory appeal pursuant to 28 U.S.C. § 1292(b), and we accepted the appeal.

DISCUSSION

. . .

II. Whether the Declaratory Judgment Action Is "Core"

The Bankruptcy Code divides claims in bankruptcy proceedings into two principal categories: "core" and "non-core." *See* 28 U.S.C. § 157. "Bankruptcy judges have the authority to 'hear and determine all . . . core proceedings arising under title 11 . . . and may enter appropriate orders and judgments, subject to review under section 158 of [title 28.]' " With respect to non-core claims, unless the parties otherwise agree, the bankruptcy court can only recommend findings of fact and conclusions of law to the district court. In this case the bankruptcy court held that the Trust's declaratory judgment action was a core proceeding pursuant to 28 U.S.C. § 157(b)(2), and the district court held that it was non-core. We review the latter ruling *de novo.* Unlike the district court, we conclude that the bankruptcy court has core jurisdiction over the proceedings.

The origin of the core/non-core distinction is found in Northern Pipeline Construction Co. v. Marathon Pipe Line Co., 458 U.S. 50 (1982), in which the Supreme Court struck down provisions of the 1978 Bankruptcy Act that vested authority in Article I bankruptcy courts to hear cases that, absent the parties' consent, constitutionally could only be heard by Article III courts — so-called "non-core" proceedings. . . .

The principal holding of *Marathon* is that Congress has minimal authority to control the manner in which "a right created by *state* law, a right independent of and antecedent to the reorganization petition that conferred jurisdiction upon the Bankruptcy Court" may be adjudicated.

Therefore, under *Marathon*, whether a contract proceeding is core depends on (1) whether the contract is antecedent to the reorganization petition; and (2) the degree to which the proceeding is independent of the reorganization. The latter inquiry hinges on "the nature of the proceeding." Proceedings can be core by virtue of their nature if either (1) the type of proceeding is unique to or uniquely affected by the bankruptcy proceedings, or (2) the proceedings directly affect a core bankruptcy function. Core bankruptcy functions of particular import to the instant proceedings include "[f]ixing the order of priority of creditor claims against a debtor," "plac[ing] the property of the bankrupt, wherever found, under the control of the court, for equal distribution among the creditors," and "administer[ing] all property in the bankrupt's possession."

. . .

Notwithstanding that the Trust's claims are upon pre-petition contracts, we conclude that the impact these contracts have on other core bankruptcy functions nevertheless render the proceedings core. Indemnity insurance contracts, particularly where the debtor is faced with substantial liability claims within the coverage of the policy, "may well be . . . 'the most important asset of [i.e., the debtor's] estate.' " As such, resolving disputes relating to major insurance contracts are bound to have a significant impact on the administration of the estate. . . .

The insurance proceeds are almost entirely earmarked for paying the personal injury claimants and represent the only potential source of cash available to that group of creditors. However, under the pay-first provisions of the P & I policies, those proceeds will not be made available until the Trust has paid the claims. Debtors' insolvency makes that threshold requirement difficult to meet; as is typical, their lack of assets leaves them unable to pay all of the claims first and seek indemnification later. . . . The insolvent insured is therefore often forced to satisfy the pay-first requirement by means of complex, creative payment schemes. In addition to the difficulties involved in paying the claims, the Trust faces a significant risk that the payment scheme ultimately employed will be deemed not to satisfy the pay-first requirement.

If the Trust were initially to pay the claimants with assets earmarked for other creditors only to be informed afterwards that the payments did not trigger the Clubs' indemnification obligation, the result would be an inequitable distribution among the creditors. Therefore, in order to effectuate an equitable distribution of the bankruptcy estate, a comprehensive declaratory judgment is required to determine (1) whether a chosen payment plan will trigger the indemnification obligation and (2) the amounts payable under the insurance contracts. Thus, the declaratory proceedings brought by the Trust in this case directly affect the bankruptcy court's core administrative function of asset allocation among creditors, and for that reason they are core.

. . .

III. Annulment of the Arbitration Clauses

The parties have entered into valid agreements to arbitrate their contract disputes, some of which call for international arbitration. Arbitration is favored in our judicial system, and the Arbitration Act mandates enforcement of valid arbitration agreements. The arbitration preference is particularly strong for international arbitration agreements. The Clubs therefore argue that the bankruptcy court cannot enjoin arbitration of the proceedings. We disagree.

"Like any statutory directive, the Arbitration Act's mandate may be overridden by a contrary congressional command." *Shearson/Am. Express*. That is true even where arbitration is sought subject to an international arbitration agreement. In the bankruptcy setting, congressional intent to permit a bankruptcy court to enjoin arbitration is sufficiently clear to override even international arbitration agreements.

The Bankruptcy Court has broad, well-established powers premised upon 28 U.S.C. §§ 1334 and 157 to preserve the integrity of the reorganization process. Section 105 of the Bankruptcy Code states that where it has jurisdiction, the bankruptcy "court may issue any order, process, or judgment that is necessary or appropriate to carry out the provisions of this title." The language of § 362, the automatic stay provision, is equally encompassing: "Except as provided in subsection (b) of this section, a petition [for bankruptcy protection] . . . operates as a stay, applicable to all entities, of — the commencement or continuation . . . of a judicial, administrative or other action or proceeding against the debtor. . . ." 11 U.S.C. § 362(a)(1). "As the legislative history of the automatic stay provision reveals, the scope of section 362(a)(1) is broad, staying all proceedings, including arbitration. . . ." Finally, one of the core purposes of bankruptcy "effectuated by Sections 362 and 105 of the Code" is to "allow the bankruptcy court to centralize all disputes concerning property of the debtor's estate so that reorganization can proceed efficiently, unimpeded by uncoordinated proceedings in other arenas." However, by not granting the bankruptcy court exclusive jurisdiction over non-core matters, "it is clear that in 1984 Congress did not envision all bankruptcy related matters being adjudicated in a single bankruptcy court."

Thus, there will be occasions where a dispute involving both the Bankruptcy Code and the Arbitration Act "presents a conflict of near polar extremes: bankruptcy policy exerts an inexorable pull towards centralization while arbitration policy advocates a decentralized approach towards dispute resolution."

Such a conflict is lessened in non-core proceedings which are unlikely to present a conflict sufficient to override by implication the presumption in favor of arbitration. Core proceedings implicate more pressing bankruptcy concerns, but even a determination that a proceeding is core will not automatically give the bankruptcy court discretion to stay arbitration. "Certainly not all core bankruptcy proceedings are premised on provisions of the Code that 'inherently conflict' with the Federal Arbitration Act; nor would arbitration of such proceedings necessarily jeopardize the objectives of the Bankruptcy Code." However, there are circumstances in which a bankruptcy court may stay arbitration, and in this case the bankruptcy court was correct that it had discretion to do so.

In exercising its discretion over whether, in core proceedings, arbitration provisions ought to be denied effect, the bankruptcy court must still "carefully determine whether any underlying purpose of the Bankruptcy Code would be adversely affected by enforcing an arbitration clause." The Arbitration Act as interpreted by the Supreme Court dictates that an arbitration clause should be enforced "unless [doing so] would seriously jeopardize the objectives of the Code." That inquiry constitutes a mixed question of law and fact with legal conclusions being reviewed *de novo*, and factual determinations being reviewed for clear error. Where the bankruptcy court has properly considered the conflicting policies in accordance with law, we acknowledge its exercise of discretion and show due deference to its determination that arbitration will seriously jeopardize a particular core bankruptcy proceeding. We see no basis for disturbing the bankruptcy court's determination to that effect here.

In the instant case, the declaratory judgment proceedings are integral to the bankruptcy court's ability to preserve and equitably distribute the Trust's assets. Furthermore, as we have previously pointed out, the bankruptcy court is the preferable venue in which to handle mass tort actions involving claims against an insolvent debtor. The need for a centralized proceeding is further augmented by the complex factual scenario, involving multiple claims, policies and insurers. The bankruptcy court was not clearly erroneous in finding that "arbitration of the disputes raised in the Complaint would prejudice the Trust's efforts to preserve the Trust as a means to compensate claimants." It was within the bankruptcy court's discretion to refuse to refer the declaratory judgment proceedings, which it properly found to be core, to arbitration.

CONCLUSION

The opinion and order of the district court is reversed, and the case is remanded for further proceedings consistent with this opinion. Costs of the appeal are awarded to the Trust.

PROBLEM 3.9

King & Saunders (K&S) had a corporate stock trading account with Slaney Securities, Inc. (see Problem 3.4), a brokerage firm. One of the terms of the brokerage agreement was that the parties would arbitrate any and all disputes arising out of or relating to the agreement. After a series of business setbacks, K&S filed for Chapter 11 bankruptcy. The Bankruptcy Trustee, standing in the shoes of K&S, filed a claim against Slaney alleging that Slaney "churned" K&S's account, running up excessive fees and resulting in substantial trading losses. The Trustee asserted various causes of action against Slaney for fraud, and sought to have the bankruptcy court adjudicate its claims. Slaney responded that the claims should be submitted to arbitration per the parties' arbitration agreement. Are K&S's claims subject to arbitration?

[C]   Arbitrability and Statutory Rights and Remedies

As discussed above, in recent years the United States Supreme Court has consistently held that federal statutory claims are subject to arbitration. In each case, however, the Court emphasized (or at least assumed) that it was possible for "the prospective litigant effectively [to] vindicate [his or her] statutory cause of action in the arbitral forum." *See, e.g., Gilmer* (quoting *Mitsubishi*). When might that not be the case? What sorts of arbitration procedures might prevent a party from "effectively vindicat[ing]" his or her statutory rights? How should a court deal with problematic arbitration clauses — by severing the offending procedures, interpreting the arbitration clause to avoid any conflict, or invalidating the clause altogether? The following cases address these questions.

GREEN TREE FINANCIAL CORP.-ALABAMA v. RANDOLPH
United States Supreme Court
531 U.S. 79 (2000)

CHIEF JUSTICE REHNQUIST delivered the opinion of the Court.

[For the Court's statement of the facts, see § 2.07.]

We now turn to the question whether Randolph's agreement to arbitrate is unenforceable because it says nothing about the costs of arbitration, and thus fails to provide her protection from potentially substantial costs of pursuing her federal statutory claims in the arbitral forum. . . . In considering whether respondent's agreement to arbitrate is unenforceable, we are mindful of the FAA's purpose "to reverse the longstanding judicial hostility to arbitration agreements . . . and to place arbitration agreements upon the same footing as other contracts." *Gilmer v. Interstate/Johnson Lane Corp.*

In light of that purpose, we have recognized that federal statutory claims can be appropriately resolved through arbitration, and we have enforced agreements to arbitrate that involve such claims. We have likewise rejected generalized attacks on arbitration that rest on "suspicion of arbitration as a method of weakening the protections afforded in the substantive law to would-be complainants." *Rodriguez de Quijas.* These cases demonstrate that even claims arising under a statute designed to further important social policies may be arbitrated because " 'so long as the prospective litigant effectively may vindicate [his or her] statutory cause of action in the arbitral forum,' " the statute serves its functions. *See Gilmer* (quoting *Mitsubishi*).

In determining whether statutory claims may be arbitrated, we first ask whether the parties agreed to submit their claims to arbitration, and then ask whether Congress has evinced an intention to preclude a waiver of judicial remedies for the statutory rights at issue. In this case, it is undisputed that the parties agreed to arbitrate all claims relating to their contract, including claims involving statutory rights. Nor does Randolph contend that the TILA [Truth in Lending Act] evinces an intention to preclude a waiver of judicial remedies. She contends instead that the arbitration agreement's silence with respect to costs and fees creates a "risk" that she will be required to bear prohibitive arbitration costs if she pursues her claims in an arbitral forum, and thereby forces her to forgo any claims she may have against petitioners. Therefore, she argues, she is unable to vindicate her statutory rights in arbitration.

It may well be that the existence of large arbitration costs could preclude a litigant such as Randolph from effectively vindicating her federal statutory rights in the arbitral forum. But the record does not show that Randolph will bear such costs if she goes to arbitration. Indeed, it contains hardly any information on the matter. As the Court of Appeals recognized, "we lack . . . information about how claimants fare under Green Tree's arbitration clause." The record reveals only the arbitration agreement's silence on the subject, and that fact alone is plainly insufficient to render it unenforceable. The "risk" that Randolph will be saddled with prohibitive costs is too speculative to justify the invalidation of an arbitration agreement.

To invalidate the agreement on that basis would undermine the "liberal federal policy favoring arbitration agreements." It would also conflict with our prior holdings that the party resisting arbitration bears the burden of proving that the claims at issue are unsuitable for arbitration. We have held that the party seeking to avoid arbitration bears the burden of establishing that Congress intended to preclude arbitration of the statutory claims at issue. *See Gilmer; McMahon.* Similarly, we believe that where, as here, a party seeks to invalidate an arbitration agreement on the ground that arbitration would be prohibitively expensive, that party bears the burden of showing the likelihood of incurring such costs. Randolph did not meet that burden. How detailed the showing of prohibitive expense must be before the party seeking arbitration must come forward with contrary evidence is a matter we need not discuss; for in this case neither during discovery nor when the case was presented on the merits was there any timely showing at all on the point. The Court of Appeals therefore erred in deciding that the arbitration agreement's silence with respect to costs and fees rendered it unenforceable.

The judgment of the Court of Appeals is affirmed in part and reversed in part.

It is so ordered.

NOTES

1.　If a statutory scheme does not allow pre-dispute waivers of statutory rights, presumably the parties should not be allowed to achieve such a waiver indirectly through use of an arbitration clause. The more difficult question is identifying when an arbitration clause effects such an impermissible waiver. The Supreme Court in *Green Tree* recognized that "[i]t may well be that the existence of large arbitration costs could preclude a litigant . . . from effectively vindicating her federal statutory rights in the arbitral forum." But, the Court held, when "a party seeks to invalidate an arbitration agreement on the ground that arbitration would be prohibitively expensive, that party bears the burden of showing the likelihood of incurring such costs." What must a party show to carry that burden? The Supreme Court did not resolve that issue in *Green Tree* because Ms. Randolph presented essentially no evidence on the costs she was likely to incur.

2. The arbitration agreement in *Green Tree* did not specify any set of institutional rules to govern the arbitration. Would it have made a difference had it done so? The leading case prior to *Green Tree* dealing with the costs of arbitration was Cole v. Burns International Security Services, 105 F.3d 1465 (D.C. Cir. 1997). The arbitration agreement in *Cole*, between an employee and an employer, provided that the arbitration would be governed by the Employment Arbitration Rules of the American Arbitration Association.

The employee argued that high arbitration fees precluded him from arbitrating his civil rights claims against the employer. The D.C. Circuit's analysis was as follows:

> There is no doubt that parties appearing in federal court may be required to assume the cost of filing fees and other administrative expenses, so any reasonable costs of this sort that accompany arbitration are not problematic. However, if an employee like Cole is required to pay arbitrators' fees ranging from $500 to $1,000 per day or more, in addition to administrative and attorney's fees, is it likely that he will be able to pursue his statutory claims? We think not. There is no indication in AAA's rules that an arbitrator's fees may be reduced or waived in cases of financial hardship. These fees would be prohibitively expensive for an employee like Cole, especially after being fired from his job, and it is unacceptable to require Cole to pay arbitrators' fees, because such fees are unlike anything that he would have to pay to pursue his statutory claims in court.

> Arbitration will occur in this case only because it has been mandated by the employer as a condition of employment. Absent this requirement, the employee would be free to pursue his claims in court without having to pay for the services of a judge. In such a circumstance — where arbitration has been imposed by the employer and occurs only at the option of the employer — arbitrators' fees should be borne solely by the employer.

> Some commentators have suggested that it would be a perversion of the arbitration process to have the arbitrator paid by only one party to the dispute. We fail to appreciate the basis for this concern. If an arbitrator is likely to "lean" in favor of an employer — something we have no reason to suspect — it would be because the employer is a source of future arbitration business, and not because the employer alone pays the arbitrator. It is doubtful that arbitrators care about who pays them, so long as they are paid for their services.

> Furthermore, there are several protections against the possibility of arbitrators systematically favoring employers because employers are the source of future business. For one thing, it is unlikely that such corruption would escape the scrutiny of plaintiffs' lawyers or appointing agencies like AAA. Corrupt arbitrators will not survive long in the business. In addition,

wise employers and their representatives should see no benefit in currying the favor of corrupt arbitrators, because this will simply invite increased judicial review of arbitral judgments. Finally, if the arbitrators who are assigned to hear and decide statutory claims adhere to the professional and ethical standards set by arbitrators in the context of collective bargaining, there is little reason for concern. . . .

In sum, we hold that Cole could not be required to agree to arbitrate his public law claims as a condition of employment if the arbitration agreement required him to pay all or part of the arbitrator's fees and expenses. In light of this holding, we find that the arbitration agreement in this case is valid and enforceable. We do so because we interpret the agreement as requiring Burns Security to pay all of the arbitrator's fees necessary for a full and fair resolution of Cole's statutory claims.

. . . [T]he disputed agreement does not explicitly address this issue; it merely incorporates the provisions of the AAA Rules. However, the AAA Rules are also silent on this point, so there is no clear allocation of responsibility for payment of arbitrator's fees. It is well understood that, where a contract is unclear on a point, an interpretation that makes the contract lawful is preferred to one that renders it unlawful. It is also accepted that ambiguous provisions are construed against the drafter of the contract, in this case, Burns. Therefore, in order to uphold the validity of the parties' contract, we interpret the arbitration agreement between Cole and Burns as requiring Burns to pay all arbitrators' fees in connection with the resolution of Cole's claims.

Id. at 1484–86. How should *Cole* be decided after *Green Tree*? *See* Brown v. Wheat First Secs., Inc., 257 F.3d 821 (D.C. Cir.) (assuming without deciding that *Green Tree* "leaves *Cole* fully intact," but refusing to extend *Cole* to nonstatutory claims), *cert. denied*, 534 U.S. 1067 (2001).

3. What if the institutional arbitration rules permit claimants to seek a waiver of the administrative or arbitrator's fees? Does a claimant have to seek such a waiver before requesting a court to set aside an arbitration agreement on grounds of excessive cost? Or what if the institutional rules permit the arbitrator to allocate the costs of arbitration in the award? Is the possibility that a claimant might recover the costs of arbitration from the respondent if the claimant prevails sufficient for a court to order arbitration to proceed?

4. Since *Green Tree*, a number of cases have addressed what sort of showing claimants must make to prevail on a claim that arbitration would be prohibitively expensive. For example, in Morrison v. Circuit City Stores, Inc., 317 F.3d 646 (6th Cir. 2003) (en banc), the en banc Sixth Circuit held that "potential litigants must be given an opportunity, prior to arbitration on the merits, to demonstrate that the potential costs of arbitration are great enough to deter them and similarly situated individuals from seeking to vindicate their federal statutory rights in the arbitral forum." *Id.* at 663. The court of appeals elaborated on its approach as follows:

[I]f the reviewing court finds that the cost-splitting provision would deter a substantial number of similarly situated potential litigants, it should refuse to enforce the cost-splitting provision in order to serve the underlying functions of the federal statute. In conducting this analysis, the reviewing court should define the class of such similarly situated potential litigants by job description and socioeconomic background. It should take the actual plaintiff's income and resources as representative of this larger class's ability to shoulder the costs of arbitration. But . . . *Green Tree* "does not necessarily mandate a searching inquiry into an employee's bills and expenses." "Nothing in *Green Tree* requires courts to undertake detailed analyses of the household budgets of low-level employees to conclude that arbitration costs in the thousands of dollars deter the vindication of employees' claims in arbitral fora."

Moreover, in addressing the effect of arbitration costs on a class, the reviewing court should look to average or typical arbitration costs, because that is the kind of information that potential litigants will take into account in deciding whether to bring their claims in the arbitral forum. In considering the decision-making process of the typical member of a class, it is proper to take into account the typical or average costs of arbitration.

In analyzing this issue, reviewing courts should consider the costs of litigation as the alternative to arbitration, . . . but they must weigh the potential costs of litigation in a realistic manner. . . . Reviewing courts must consider whether the litigant will incur th[e] additional expense [of the arbitrator's fees and costs] and whether that expense, taken together with the other costs and expenses of the differing fora, would deter potential litigants from bringing their statutory claims in the arbitral forum. The issue is not "the fact that [the] fees would be paid to the arbitrator," but rather whether the "overall cost of arbitration," from the perspective of the potential litigant, is greater than "the cost of litigation in court."

Finally, under this analysis, the reviewing court should discount the possibilities that the plaintiff will not be required to pay costs or arbitral fees because of ultimate success on the merits, either because of cost-shifting provisions in the arbitration agreement or because the arbitrator decides that such costs or fees are contrary to federal law. . . . In many cases, if not most, employees considering the consequences of bringing their claims in the arbitral forum will be inclined to err on the side of caution, especially when the worst-case scenario would mean not only losing on their substantive claims but also the imposition of the costs of the arbitration.

Id. at 663-65. As applied, the court of appeals concluded: "This analysis will yield different results in different cases. It will find, in many cases, that high-level managerial employees and others with substantial means can afford the costs of arbitration, thus making cost-splitting provisions in such cases enforceable. In the case of other employees, however, this standard will render cost-splitting provisions unenforceable in many, if not most, cases." *Id.* at 665.

GRAHAM OIL CO. v. ARCO PRODUCTS CO.
United States Court of Appeals for the Ninth Circuit
43 F.3d 1244 (9th Cir. 1995)

REINHARDT, CIRCUIT JUDGE:

I. INTRODUCTION

Graham Oil Co. ("Graham Oil") appeals the judgment of the district court, which dismissed, with prejudice, all of its claims against ARCO Products Co. ("ARCO"). The claims were dismissed because Graham Oil refused to submit to arbitration as required by an arbitration clause in its distributorship agreement with ARCO.

Graham Oil contends that the arbitration clause is invalid because it requires the surrender of certain rights provided under the Petroleum Marketing Practices Act ("PMPA"), 15 U.S.C. §§ 2801–2806. Accordingly, it argues that the district court — not an arbitrator — must decide the merits of its claims under the PMPA. We agree.

II. FACTS

For nearly forty years, Graham Oil was a branded distributor of ARCO gasoline in Coos Bay, Oregon. On October 2, 1990, Graham Oil and ARCO entered into a Branded Distributor Gasoline Agreement ("Agreement"), which was effective from January 1, 1991, to December 31, 1993. Among other things, the parties agreed that Graham Oil would purchase a minimum amount of gasoline each month during the two-year period of the Agreement.

On November 10, 1991, ARCO notified Graham Oil that it intended to terminate the Agreement as of October 31, 1991, because Graham Oil had not been purchasing the required minimum amount of gasoline as specified in the Agreement. On November 27, 1991, Graham Oil filed a motion for a preliminary injunction against ARCO in federal district court. Graham Oil argued that ARCO had violated the PMPA by deliberately raising its prices so that Graham Oil would be unable to meet the minimum gasoline requirements. Accordingly, Graham Oil argued that ARCO should not be allowed to terminate the Agreement.

On December 3, 1991, the district court issued a preliminary injunction that prohibited ARCO from terminating the Agreement for 90 days. Instead of reaching the merits of Graham Oil's claims under the PMPA, however, the court found that arbitration was Graham Oil's exclusive remedy. The court required the parties to complete the arbitration within 90 days.

Graham Oil appealed the district court's order and refused to submit to arbitration. Upon the expiration of the 90 days, ARCO moved for summary judgment. Graham Oil filed a cross-motion to keep the court's preliminary injunction in force pending the resolution of its appeal. The court denied Graham Oil's cross-motion and granted summary judgment in favor of ARCO. On appeal, Graham Oil argues that the arbitration clause in the Agreement is invalid and that the court must determine the merits of its claims under the PMPA.

III. ANALYSIS

This case involves the validity of an arbitration clause that, in addition to specifying arbitration as the means by which disputes are to be resolved, purports to waive certain statutory rights conferred upon petroleum franchisees by the PMPA. We conclude that the clause is invalid. As a result, we strike it and remand for further proceedings.

A. *Validity of the Clause.*

1. Purpose of the PMPA. In determining the validity of the arbitration clause, we first review the purpose of the PMPA. Congress enacted the PMPA with the primary goal of "protecting franchisees." Such protection was needed in order to correct the great "disparity of bargaining power" between petroleum franchisors and franchisees. According to the legislative history of the PMPA, petroleum franchise agreements generally are nothing more than "contracts of adhesion" that perpetuate the "continuing vulnerability of the franchisee to the demands and actions of the franchisor."

In order to correct some of the effects of this disparity in bargaining power, Congress enacted certain protections for franchisees like Graham Oil. Essentially, the Act affords franchisees statutory remedies for the arbitrary or discriminatory termination (or non-renewal) of franchises by their franchisors. Among other things, these protections include exemplary damages, reasonable attorney's fees, and a one-year statute of limitations. These rights and benefits are, of course, not only designed to compensate for injury, but also to deter unfair conduct.

2. Arbitration Clause. Turning to the arbitration clause, we note as an initial matter that arbitration is a form of dispute resolution that finds favor in the courts. In a number of instances, the Supreme Court has upheld agreements to submit statutory claims to arbitration, including claims involving unfair business practices. Among the claims in that category are those arising under the Sherman Act, the Securities Exchange Act of 1934, and the Securities Act of 1933. Some of the arbitration provisions — like the provisions here — have been contained in form agreements executed before the dispute arose.

3. Analysis. Nothing in the PMPA suggests that Congress intended to change the general presumption in favor of upholding agreements to submit statutory claims to arbitration. A simple agreement for arbitration of disputes is valid, whether or not contained in a franchise agreement. Such a provision constitutes nothing more than an agreement to substitute one legitimate dispute resolution *forum* for another and involves no surrender of statutory protections or benefits.

However, the fact that franchisees may agree to an arbitral forum for the resolution of statutory disputes in no way suggests that they may be forced by those with dominant economic power to surrender the statutorily-mandated rights and benefits that Congress intended them to possess. This is certainly true in cases arising under the PMPA, which was enacted to shield franchisees from the gross "disparity of bargaining power" that exists between them and franchisors. If franchisees could be compelled to surrender their statutorily-mandated protections as a condition of obtaining franchise agreements, then franchisors could use their superior bargaining power to deprive franchisees of the PMPA's protections. In effect, the franchisors could simply continue their earlier practice of presenting prospective franchisees with contracts of adhesion that deny them the rights and benefits afforded by Congress. In that way, the PMPA would quickly be nullified.

Here, the arbitration clause purports to forfeit certain important statutorily-mandated rights or benefits afforded to Graham Oil and other franchisees by the PMPA. First, the arbitration clause expressly forfeits Graham Oil's statutorily-mandated right to recover exemplary damages from ARCO if Graham Oil prevails on certain claims. The clause provides that neither party can be awarded exemplary damages. *Compare* 15 U.S.C. § 2805(d)(1)(B) ("If the franchisee prevails in [certain] action[s] . . . such franchisee shall be entitled . . . to *exemplary damages*, where appropriate. . . ." (emphasis added)) *with* Agreement § 22(b) ("The arbitrator(s) *may not assess* punitive or *exemplary damages*. . . ." (emphasis added)).

Second, the arbitration clause expressly forfeits Graham Oil's statutorily-mandated right to recover reasonable attorney's fees from ARCO if Graham Oil prevails on certain claims. The clause provides that each party will bear its own attorney's fees. *Compare* 15 U.S.C. § 2805(d)(1)(C) ("If the franchisee prevails in [certain] action[s] . . . such franchisee shall be entitled . . . to *reasonable attorney* and expert witness *fees* to be paid by the franchisor. . . ." (emphasis added)) *with* Agreement § 22(a) ("*Each party shall pay its own costs and expenses, including attorneys' fees related to such arbitration*. . . ." (emphasis added)).

Third, the arbitration clause expressly forfeits Graham Oil's statutorily-mandated right to a one-year statute of limitations on its claims against ARCO. The clause reduces the time in which a claim can be brought from one year to 90 days, or in some cases six months. *Compare* 15 U.S.C. § 2805(a) ("[N]o such action may be maintained unless commenced *within 1 year* after . . . the date the franchisor fails to comply with [certain] requirements . . . of this title." (emphasis added)) *with* Appendix, EXHIBIT E § A ("The party waives the right to seek any relief or pursue any claim not included in an arbitration demand filed . . . *within 90 days* following the date the party knew or should have known of the facts giving rise to the claim [and in no event more than six months after the occurrence of the facts giving rise to the claim]" (emphasis added)).

Each of the three statutory rights is important to the effectuation of the PMPA's policies. The purpose of exemplary damages is to deter franchisors from engaging in improper terminations of franchise agreements. The purpose of attorney's fees is to deter franchisors from improperly contesting meritorious claims. Finally, the purpose of a one-year statute of limitations is to afford franchisees a reasonable period of time in which to seek relief for improper terminations and other abuses by petroleum franchisors. In attempting to strip franchisees of these statutory rights and benefits by means of an arbitration clause included in the franchise agreement, ARCO violated the purpose as well as the specific terms of the PMPA.

Because the arbitration clause employed by ARCO compels Graham Oil to surrender important statutorily-mandated rights afforded franchisees by the PMPA, we hold that the clause contravenes the Act.

B. Severability of the Clause.

Having determined that ARCO's arbitration clause violates federal law, we turn to the question of its severability. "Arbitration clauses [must] be treated as severable from the documents in which they appear unless there is clear intent to the contrary." Here, there is no evidence of any contrary intent. More important from a practical standpoint, neither party suggests that if the arbitration clause is unlawful, the entire contract must be invalidated. Accordingly, we conclude that, as in the usual case, the arbitration clause here is severable.

The more difficult question is whether the *entire* arbitration clause should be severed, or simply the provisions pertaining to exemplary damages, attorney's fees, and the statute of limitations. Relying on principles that are analogous to those we use in determining whether a particular clause is severable from an entire contract, we conclude that in this case the *entire* clause must be eliminated.

It is a well-known principle in contract law that a clause cannot be severed from a contract when it is an integrated part of the contract. . . .

Here, the offending parts of the arbitration clause do not merely involve a single, isolated provision; the arbitration clause in this case is a highly integrated unit containing three different illegal provisions. Unlike the other clauses, the arbitration clause here includes a survival provision that expressly preserves the entire clause in the event the contract is declared invalid. Moreover, it establishes a unified procedure for handling all disputes, and its various unlawful provisions are all a part of that overall procedure. Thus, we conclude that the clause must be treated as a whole and that its various provisions are not severable.

Our decision to strike the entire clause rests in part upon the fact that the offensive provisions clearly represent an attempt by ARCO to achieve through arbitration what Congress has expressly forbidden. Congress enacted the PMPA precisely to prevent the type of agreement that ARCO included in the arbitration clause of its franchise contract. ARCO attempted to use an arbitration clause to achieve its unlawful ends. Such a blatant misuse of the arbitration procedure serves to taint the entire clause. As a leading treatise notes, severance is inappropriate when the entire clause represents an "integrated scheme to contravene public policy." *See* E. ALLAN FARNSWORTH, FARNSWORTH ON CONTRACTS § 5.8, at 70 (1990). For the above reasons, we conclude that the entire arbitration clause, and not merely the offensive provisions, must be stricken from the contract. We remand to the district court, which is the proper forum for the resolution of this underlying dispute.

IV. CONCLUSION

The district court improperly dismissed Graham Oil's claims. The arbitration provision contained in the franchise agreement is invalid, and the court — not an arbitrator — must decide the merits of the claims. Accordingly, the judgment is reversed, and the case is remanded for further proceedings not inconsistent with this opinion.

REVERSED and REMANDED.

FERNANDEZ, CIRCUIT JUDGE, dissenting:

I agree with the majority that arbitration of PMPA disputes is appropriate. Where we part company is at the point where the majority decides to strike down the arbitration provision in its entirety because that provision purports to remove some remedies that would otherwise be available under the PMPA. . . .

I will assume, without deciding, that the arbitration provision's removal of attorneys fees and punitive damages and its changing of the date to bring a claim are all provisions which, as a matter of law, cannot be agreed to by these contracting parties. I will also assume that those questions should not be submitted to the arbitrator in the first instance, although I find that question to be a knotty one indeed. Even given those assumptions, I disagree with the conclusion that the arbitration provision should be stricken in its entirety.

. . .

Here the contract itself does not provide the specific severance clause that we find in many commercial contracts. Nevertheless, as I see it, the arbitration provision can and does stand up quite well without the offending provisions and would have been acceptable to both parties in that form. I have not the slightest doubt that to the extent arbitration is desirable it would have been just as desirable without those provisions. They are not a sine qua non of arbitral attractiveness and are not intertwined with the arbitration provision. If arbitration is a beauty, it is no less a one because it has lost a slipper. That indicates that arbitration should be required in this case.

Nor do I believe that this blinks at reality. Had the arbitration provision been offered without the offending provisions, Graham would surely have accepted it in that more favorable form. It would have been less favorable to ARCO, but that company would undoubtedly have still offered the provision, even without that which it could not have.

In *fine*, the parties agreed upon arbitration. Some of the terms they agreed to may not be possible. However, on the whole, arbitration *is* possible, and the real point of this litigation — should ARCO pay damages for breaching the agreement by mispricing its products — can and should be submitted to the arbitrators, as agreed. Thus, I do not agree that we should elide the arbitration provision and bring the whole of this contractual dispute into the federal courts based upon an idea that a picaresque oil company wronged its franchisee when it asked for arbitration of disputes between them. Arbitration is a favored procedure, and we should favor it here.

Therefore, I respectfully dissent.

NOTES

1.   Is the decision in *Graham Oil* consistent with the Supreme Court's decision in *Green Tree*?

2.   Compare the *Graham Oil* court's approach to a conflict between statutory rights and arbitration procedures with the D.C. Circuit's approach in *Cole*.

In *Graham Oil*, the court of appeals found that certain provisions of the arbitration agreement conflicted with the rights and remedies provided by the Petroleum Marketing Practices Act. Because in the court's view those provisions were not severable from the rest of the arbitration clause, the entire arbitration agreement was invalid. In *Cole*, to uphold the validity of the parties' arbitration agreement, the court construed the arbitration agreement to require the employer to pay all the arbitration costs. Could the court in *Graham Oil* have construed the arbitration agreement to avoid any of the conflicts with the statute? Should it have done so?

One possibility is the punitive damages provision of the arbitration agreement in *Graham Oil*, which provided that "[t]he arbitrator(s) may not assess punitive or exemplary damages." Does that language constitute a waiver of the right to recover punitive damages, or does it merely define the scope of the arbitrator's authority, permitting a court later to award punitive damages if appropriate? *Compare* Stephen J. Ware, *Punitive Damages in Arbitration: Contracting Out of the Government's Role in Punishment and Federal Preemption of State Law*, 63 FORDHAM L. REV. 529, 540–42 (1994) (arguing that language denying arbitrator authority to award punitive damages waives altogether claim for punitive damages) *with* Thomas J. Stipanowich, *Punitive Damages and the Consumerization of Arbitration*, 92 NW. U. L. REV. 1, 35 (1997) (arguing that punitive damages remain available in court after arbitration proceeding is completed).

In PacifiCare Health Systems, Inc. v. Book, 538 U.S. 401 (2003), the Supreme Court held that resolving such an ambiguity was a matter for the arbitrator, not the court. The district court in *PacifiCare* had refused to compel arbitration of a claim under the Racketeer Influenced and Corrupt Organizations Act (RICO) because of a provision in the arbitration agreement that precluded the award of "punitive damages." The district court concluded that the provision would prevent the arbitrator from awarding treble damages as provided for under RICO, and so might deny the claimant "meaningful relief for allegations of statutory violations in an arbitration forum." The Supreme Court reversed, explaining that the language in the arbitration agreement was ambiguous and that "we should not, on the basis of 'mere speculation' that an arbitrator might interpret these ambiguous agreements in a manner that casts their enforceability into doubt, take upon ourselves the authority to decide the antecedent question of how the ambiguity is to be resolved." *Id.* at 406–07. The Court explained that "the preliminary question whether the remedial limitations at issue here prohibit an award of RICO treble damages is not a question of arbitrability" that a court could decide." *Id.* at 407 n.2. "[S]ince we do not know how the arbitrator will construe the remedial limitations," the Court concluded, "the proper course is to compel arbitration." *Id.* at 407.

3.   The severability of unenforceable provisions in an arbitration clause was the subject of an opinion by now-Chief Justice John Roberts while serving on the D.C. Circuit. In Booker v. Robert Half Int'l, Inc., 413 F.3d 77 (D.C. Cir. 2005), the court of appeals held that the district court had properly severed a provision precluding the award of punitive damages, which the parties agreed was unenforceable. In so doing, the court surveyed the law on severability and distinguished *Graham Oil*:

Booker next argues that enforcing the remainder of the arbitration clause contravenes the federal policy interest in ensuring the effective vindication of statutory rights. He contends that responding to illegal provisions in arbitration agreements by judicially pruning them out leaves employers with every incentive to "overreach" when drafting such agreements. If judges merely sever illegal provisions and compel arbitration, employers would be no worse off for trying to include illegal provisions than if they had followed the law in drafting their agreements in the first place. On the other hand, because not every claimant will challenge the illegal provisions, some employees will go to the arbitral table without all their statutory rights.

We have never addressed this issue, but Booker's argument — bolstered by support from the EEOC — has helped persuade some circuits to strike arbitration clauses in their entirety, rather than simply sever offending provisions. Other circuits, however, have invoked the federal policy in favor of enforcing agreements to arbitrate to reject policy arguments like Booker's and uphold severance of illegal provisions. The differing results may well reflect not so much a split among the circuits as variety among different arbitration agreements. Decisions striking an arbitration clause entirely often involved agreements without a severability clause, or agreements that did not contain merely one readily severable illegal provision, but were instead pervasively infected with illegality. Decisions severing an illegal provision and compelling arbitration, on the other hand, typically considered agreements with a severability clause and discrete unenforceable provisions.

. . .

We agree with the district court that severing the punitive damages bar and enforcing the arbitration clause was proper here. Not only does the agreement contain a severability clause, but Booker identifies only one discrete illegal provision in the agreement. . . . This one unenforceable provision does not infect the arbitration clause as a whole. The district court did not unravel "a highly integrated" complex of interlocking illegal provisions, but rather removed a punitive damages bar that appears to have been grafted onto an intact and functioning framework, for the AAA commercial rules — incorporated by reference in the clause — already contain provisions on remedies that do not prohibit punitive damages. Indeed, by severing a remedial component of the arbitration clause, the district court removed a provision generally understood as not being essential to a contract's consideration, and thus more readily severable.

The *Graham Oil* decision, on which Booker relies, struck the entire arbitration agreement after noting that "the offensive provisions clearly represent an attempt . . . to achieve through arbitration what Congress has expressly forbidden." There is no evidence of that here. At the time the parties signed the agreement . . . the law of this circuit was unclear as to whether bars on punitive damages in arbitration clauses were enforceable in this context. Moreover, the AAA did not promulgate the employment arbitration rules favored by Booker — and assented to by RHI in pre-litigation negotiations — until after the parties signed the employment agreement.

By invoking the severability clause to remove a discrete remedial provision, the district court honored the intent of the parties reflected in the employment agreement, which included not only the punitive damages bar but the explicit severability clause as well. In doing so, the court was also faithful to the federal policy which "requires that we rigorously enforce agreements to arbitrate."

Id. at 84-86.

4. This "vindication of statutory rights" doctrine often overlaps with unconscionability as a basis for challenging the enforceability of arbitration agreements. How do the theories differ? In one sense, the vindication of statutory rights doctrine is narrower because it requires the challenge to the arbitration agreement to be based on an inconsistency with a particular (usually federal) statute. Unconscionability has no such limitation. But since the Supreme Court's decision in *Concepcion* (discussed in Chapter 4) — holding that the FAA preempts at least some unconscionability challenges to arbitration agreements — the vindication of statutory rights doctrine has gained increased prominence. Because the doctrine is based on a conflict between the arbitration agreement (and the FAA) and another federal statute, preemption doctrine does not apply. As a result, some courts have held that *Concepcion* does not apply. See the further discussion in § 4.04.

PROBLEM 3.10

In addition to providing for binding arbitration, the Send-A-Wreck franchise agreement (see Problem 3.5) also provides that (1) the arbitration shall be conducted under the Commercial Arbitration Rules of the American Arbitration Association; (2) the arbitrator shall have no authority to award punitive damages; (3) each party shall bear its own attorney's fees; and (4) any claim not filed within one year shall be barred as untimely. Patricia Cairns now files suit alleging an unlawful tying arrangement in violation of the federal antitrust laws and claiming actual damages of $150,000. She seeks recovery of treble damages (three times actual damages) and of her attorney's fees, both of which are statutorily authorized for successful antitrust plaintiffs. Her suit is filed more than a year after the claim arose, but within the time permitted by the statute of limitations under the federal antitrust laws. In opposing Send-A-Wreck's petition to compel arbitration, Cairns' attorney also submits (1) an affidavit from Cairns asserting that she cannot afford to arbitrate the dispute because her annual income is only $20,000; and (2) biographies of prospective arbitrators showing that they charge a minimum of $1,000 per day to serve as arbitrator. Should a court order Cairns to arbitrate her antitrust claim?

PROBLEM 3.11

The State of New York enacts its own version of the Internet Fraud Act (see Problem 3.4), creating a state cause of action for Internet-related fraud and prohibiting arbitration of claims under the Act. Is the analysis of the arbitrability issue for this statute any different than the analysis in Problem 3.4?

Chapter 4

THE FEDERAL ARBITRATION ACT AND STATE LAW

§ 4.01   OVERVIEW

The previous chapter examined how courts have reconciled possible conflicts between the Federal Arbitration Act and other federal statutes that arguably affect the enforceability of arbitration agreements. This chapter looks at conflicts between the FAA and state laws. It begins by examining *Southland Corp. v. Keating*, in which the United States Supreme Court held that the FAA applies in state court and preempts conflicting state laws. Next, it considers the scope of the FAA — both the nexus with interstate commerce required for the statute to apply and the meaning of a statutory exception for at least some employment contracts. Then, the chapter looks at the extent to which the FAA preempts the use of generally applicable contract law defenses, focusing on the Supreme Court's decision in *AT&T Mobility LLC v. Concepcion*. It next discusses a possible exception from FAA preemption for insurance contracts, various further applications of FAA preemption doctrine, and the effect of choice-of-law clauses on FAA preemption. Finally, it examines procedural issues that arise in enforcing arbitration agreements in state and federal court.

§ 4.02   PREEMPTION AND THE FAA

In *Prima Paint*, discussed in § 2.02, the Supreme Court stated that "[f]ederal courts are bound to apply rules enacted by Congress with respect to matters — here, a contract involving commerce — over which it has legislative power." Accordingly, when the FAA applies it governs in federal court, even in the face of contrary state law. Although the FAA was enacted in 1925, not until 1984 did the Supreme Court consider whether the FAA applied in state courts as well as federal courts. The Supreme Court's decision in *Southland*, which follows, was controversial at the time and remains controversial today.

SOUTHLAND CORP. v. KEATING
United States Supreme Court
465 U.S. 1 (1984)

Chief Justice Burger delivered the opinion of the Court.

This case presents the [question] . . . whether the California Franchise Investment Law, which invalidates certain arbitration agreements covered by the Federal

Arbitration Act, violates the Supremacy Clause. . . .

I

Appellant The Southland Corporation is the owner and franchisor of 7-Eleven convenience stores. Southland's standard franchise agreement provides each franchisee with a license to use certain registered trademarks, a lease or sublease of a convenience store owned or leased by Southland, inventory financing, and assistance in advertising and merchandising. The franchisees operate the stores, supply bookkeeping data, and pay Southland a fixed percentage of gross profits. The franchise agreement also contains . . . [a] provision requiring arbitration. . . .

Appellees are 7-Eleven franchisees. Between September 1975 and January 1977, several appellees filed individual actions against Southland in California Superior Court alleging, among other things, fraud, oral misrepresentation, breach of contract, breach of fiduciary duty, and violation of the disclosure requirements of the California Franchise Investment Law. Southland's answer, in all but one of the individual actions, included the affirmative defense of failure to arbitrate.

In May 1977, appellee Keating filed a class action against Southland on behalf of a class that assertedly includes approximately 800 California franchisees. Keating's principal claims were substantially the same as those asserted by the other franchisees. After the various actions were consolidated, Southland petitioned to compel arbitration of the claims in all cases, and appellees moved for class certification.

The Superior Court granted Southland's motion to compel arbitration of all claims except those claims based on the Franchise Investment Law. The court did not pass on appellees' request for class certification. Southland appealed from the order insofar as it excluded from arbitration the claims based on the California statute. . . .

The California Court of Appeal reversed the trial court's refusal to compel arbitration of appellees' claims under the Franchise Investment Law. That court interpreted the arbitration clause to require arbitration of all claims asserted under the Franchise Investment Law, and construed the Franchise Investment Law not to invalidate such agreements to arbitrate. Alternatively, the court concluded that if the Franchise Investment Law rendered arbitration agreements involving commerce unenforceable, it would conflict with § 2 of the Federal Arbitration Act, and therefore be invalid under the Supremacy Clause. . . .

The California Supreme Court, by a vote of 4-2, reversed the ruling that claims asserted under the Franchise Investment Law are arbitrable. The California Supreme Court interpreted the Franchise Investment Law to require judicial consideration of claims brought under that statute and concluded that the California statute did not contravene the federal Act. . . .

. . . We reverse.

. . .

III

. . . The California Franchise Investment Law provides: "Any condition, stipulation or provision purporting to bind any person acquiring any franchise to waive compliance with any provision of this law or any rule or order hereunder is void." Cal. Corp. Code § 31512. The California Supreme Court interpreted this statute to require judicial consideration of claims brought under the State statute and accordingly refused to enforce the parties' contract to arbitrate such claims. So interpreted the California Franchise Investment Law directly conflicts with § 2 of the Federal Arbitration Act and violates the Supremacy Clause.

In enacting § 2 of the federal Act, Congress declared a national policy favoring arbitration and withdrew the power of the states to require a judicial forum for the resolution of claims which the contracting parties agreed to resolve by arbitration. . . . Congress has thus mandated the enforcement of arbitration agreements.

We discern only two limitations on the enforceability of arbitration provisions governed by the Federal Arbitration Act: they must be part of a written maritime contract or a contract "evidencing a transaction involving commerce" and such clauses may be revoked upon "grounds as exist at law or in equity for the revocation of any contract." We see nothing in the Act indicating that the broad principle of enforceability is subject to any additional limitations under State law.

The Federal Arbitration Act rests on the authority of Congress to enact substantive rules under the Commerce Clause. . . .

. . . The statements of the Court in *Prima Paint* [*Corp. v. Flood & Conklin Mfg. Co.*] that the Arbitration Act was an exercise of the Commerce Clause power clearly implied that the substantive rules of the Act were to apply in state as well as federal courts. As Justice Black observed in his dissent, when Congress exercises its authority to enact substantive federal law under the Commerce Clause, it normally creates rules that are enforceable in state as well as federal courts.

In *Moses H. Cone Memorial Hospital v. Mercury Construction Corp.*, we reaffirmed our view that the Arbitration Act "creates a body of federal substantive law" and expressly stated what was implicit in *Prima Paint*, i.e., the substantive law the Act created was applicable in state and federal court. . . .

Although the legislative history is not without ambiguities, there are strong indications that Congress had in mind something more than making arbitration agreements enforceable only in the federal courts. The House Report plainly suggests the more comprehensive objectives:

> "The purpose of this bill is to make valid and enforcible [sic] agreements for arbitration contained *in contracts involving interstate commerce* or within the jurisdiction or [sic] admiralty, or which may be the subject of litigation in the Federal courts." (emphasis added).

This broader purpose can also be inferred from the reality that Congress would be less likely to address a problem whose impact was confined to federal courts than a problem of large significance in the field of commerce. The Arbitration Act sought to "overcome the rule of equity, that equity will not specifically enforce an[y] arbitration agreement." . . .

. . . Congress also showed its awareness of the widespread unwillingness of state courts to enforce arbitration agreements, and that such courts were bound by [inadequate] state laws. . . . The problems Congress faced were therefore twofold: the old common law hostility toward arbitration, and the failure of state arbitration statutes to mandate enforcement of arbitration agreements. To confine the scope of the Act to arbitrations sought to be enforced in federal courts would frustrate what we believe Congress intended to be a broad enactment appropriate in scope to meet the large problems Congress was addressing.

JUSTICE O'CONNOR argues that Congress viewed the Arbitration Act "as a procedural statute, applicable only in federal courts." If it is correct that Congress sought only to create a procedural remedy in the federal courts, there can be no explanation for the express limitation in the Arbitration Act to contracts "involving commerce." 9 U.S.C. § 2. For example, when Congress has authorized this Court to prescribe the rules of procedure in the federal Courts of Appeals, District Courts, and bankruptcy courts, it has not limited the power of the Court to prescribe rules applicable only to causes of action involving commerce. We would expect that if Congress, in enacting the Arbitration Act, was creating what it thought to be a procedural rule applicable only in federal courts, it would not so limit the Act to transactions involving commerce. On the other hand, Congress would need to call on the Commerce Clause if it intended the Act to apply in state courts. Yet at the same time, its reach would be limited to transactions involving interstate commerce. We therefore view the "involving commerce" requirement in § 2, not as an inexplicable limitation on the power of the federal courts, but as a necessary qualification on a statute intended to apply in state and federal courts.

Under the interpretation of the Arbitration Act urged by JUSTICE O'CONNOR, claims brought under the California Franchise Investment Law are not arbitrable when they are raised in state court. Yet it is clear beyond question that if this suit had been brought as a diversity action in a federal district court, the arbitration clause would have been enforceable. The interpretation given to the Arbitration Act by the California Supreme Court would therefore encourage and reward forum shopping. We are unwilling to attribute to Congress the intent, in drawing on the comprehensive powers of the Commerce Clause, to create a right to enforce an arbitration contract and yet make the right dependent for its enforcement on the particular forum in which it is asserted. And since the overwhelming proportion of all civil litigation in this country is in the state courts, we cannot believe Congress intended to limit the Arbitration Act to disputes subject only to *federal*-court jurisdiction.[9] Such an interpretation would frustrate Congressional intent to place "[a]n arbitration agreement . . . upon the same footing as other contracts, where it belongs."

---

[9] While the Federal Arbitration Act creates federal substantive law requiring the parties to honor arbitration agreements, it does not create any independent federal-question jurisdiction under 28 U.S.C. § 1331 or otherwise. This seems implicit in the provisions in § 3 for a stay by a "court in which such suit is pending" and in § 4 that enforcement may be ordered by "any United States district court which, save for such agreement, would have jurisdiction under Title 28, in a civil action or in admiralty of the subject matter of a suit arising out of the controversy between the parties."

In creating a substantive rule applicable in state as well as federal courts,[10] Congress intended to foreclose state legislative attempts to undercut the enforceability of arbitration agreements.[11] We hold that § 31512 of the California Franchise Investment Law violates the Supremacy Clause.

IV

The judgment of the California Supreme Court denying enforcement of the arbitration agreement is reversed . . .

JUSTICE STEVENS, concurring in part and dissenting in part.

The Court holds that an arbitration clause that is enforceable in an action in a federal court is equally enforceable if the action is brought in a state court. I agree with that conclusion. Although JUSTICE O'CONNOR's review of the legislative history of the Federal Arbitration Act demonstrates that the 1925 Congress that enacted the statute viewed the statute as essentially procedural in nature, I am persuaded that the intervening developments in the law compel the conclusion that the Court has reached. I am nevertheless troubled by one aspect of the case that seems to trouble none of my colleagues.

For me it is not "clear beyond question that if this suit had been brought as a diversity action in a Federal District Court, the arbitration clause would have been enforceable." The general rule prescribed by § 2 of the Federal Arbitration Act is that arbitration clauses in contracts involving interstate transactions are enforceable as a matter of federal law. That general rule, however, is subject to an exception based on "such grounds as exist at law or in equity for the revocation of any contract." I believe that exception leaves room for the implementation of certain substantive state policies that would be undermined by enforcing certain categories of arbitration clauses.

. . .

---

[10] The contention is made that the Court's interpretation of § 2 of the Act renders §§ 3 and 4 "largely superfluous." This misreads our holding and the Act. In holding that the Arbitration Act preempts a state law that withdraws the power to enforce arbitration agreements, we do not hold that §§ 3 and 4 of the Arbitration Act apply to proceedings in state courts. Section 4, for example, provides that the Federal Rules of Civil Procedure apply in proceedings to compel arbitration. The Federal Rules do not apply in such state court proceedings.

[11] . . . . JUSTICE STEVENS dissents in part on the ground that § 2 of the Arbitration Act permits a party to nullify an agreement to arbitrate on "such grounds as exist at law or in equity for the revocation of any contract." We agree, of course, that a party may assert general contract defenses such as fraud to avoid enforcement of an arbitration agreement. We conclude, however, that the defense to arbitration found in the California Franchise Investment Law is not a ground that exists at law or in equity "for the revocation of any contract" but merely a ground that exists for the revocation of arbitration provisions in contracts subject to the California Franchise Investment Law. Moreover, under this dissenting view, "a state policy of providing special protection for franchisees . . . can be recognized without impairing the basic purposes of the federal statute." If we accepted this analysis, states could wholly eviscerate Congressional intent to place arbitration agreements "upon the same footing as other contracts," simply by passing statutes such as the Franchise Investment Law. We have rejected this analysis because it is in conflict with the Arbitration Act and would permit states to override the declared policy requiring enforcement of arbitration agreements.

A state policy excluding wage claims from arbitration, *cf.* Merrill Lynch, Pierce, Fenner & Smith v. Ware, 414 U.S. 117 (1973), or a state policy of providing special protection for franchisees, such as that expressed in California's Franchise Investment Law, can be recognized without impairing the basic purposes of the federal statute. Like the majority of the California Supreme Court, I am not persuaded that Congress intended the pre-emptive effect of this statute to be "so unyielding as to require enforcement of an agreement to arbitrate a dispute over the application of a regulatory statute which a state legislature, in conformity with analogous federal policy, has decided should be left to judicial enforcement."

Thus, although I agree with most of the Court's reasoning and specifically with its jurisdictional holdings, I respectfully dissent from its conclusion concerning the enforceability of the arbitration agreement. On that issue, I would affirm the judgment of the California Supreme Court.

JUSTICE O'CONNOR, with whom JUSTICE REHNQUIST joins, dissenting.

Section 2 of the Federal Arbitration Act (FAA) provides that a written arbitration agreement "shall be valid, irrevocable, and enforceable, save upon such grounds as exist at law or in equity for the revocation of any contract." Section 2 does not, on its face, identify which judicial forums are bound by its requirements or what procedures govern its enforcement. The FAA deals with these matters in §§ 3 and 4.

. . .

Today, the Court takes the facial silence of § 2 as a license to declare that state as well as federal courts must apply § 2. In addition, though this is not spelled out in the opinion, the Court holds that in enforcing this newly discovered federal right state courts must follow procedures specified in § 3. The Court's decision is impelled by an understandable desire to encourage the use of arbitration, but it utterly fails to recognize the clear congressional intent underlying the FAA. Congress intended to require federal, not state, courts to respect arbitration agreements.

I

. . . Today's case is the first in which this Court has had occasion to determine whether the FAA applies to state court proceedings. One statement on the subject did appear in *Moses H. Cone Memorial Hospital,* . . . but that case involved a federal, not a state, court proceeding; its dictum concerning the law applicable in state courts was wholly unnecessary to its holding.

II

The majority opinion decides three issues. First, it holds that § 2 creates federal substantive rights that must be enforced by the state courts. Second, though the issue is not raised in this case, the Court states that § 2 substantive rights may not be the basis for invoking federal court jurisdiction under 28 U.S.C. § 1331. Third, the Court reads § 2 to require state courts to enforce § 2 rights using procedures that mimic those specified for federal courts by FAA §§ 3 and 4. The first of these conclusions is unquestionably wrong as a matter of statutory construction; the second appears to be an attempt to limit the damage done by the first; the third is unnecessary and unwise.

A

One rarely finds a legislative history as unambiguous as the FAA's. That history establishes conclusively that the 1925 Congress viewed the FAA as a procedural statute, applicable only in federal courts, derived, Congress believed, largely from the federal power to control the jurisdiction of the federal courts.

In 1925 Congress emphatically believed arbitration to be a matter of "procedure." . . .

Since *Bernhardt*, a right to arbitration has been characterized as "substantive," and that holding is not challenged here. But Congress in 1925 did not characterize the FAA as this Court did in 1956. Congress *believed* that the FAA established nothing more than a rule of procedure, a rule therefore applicable only in the federal courts.

If characterizing the FAA as procedural was not enough, the draftsmen of the Act, the House Report, and the early commentators all flatly stated that the Act was intended to affect only federal court proceedings. . . .

Yet another indication that Congress did not intend the FAA to govern state-court proceedings is found in the powers Congress relied on in passing the Act. The FAA might have been grounded on Congress' powers to regulate interstate and maritime affairs, since the Act extends only to contracts in those areas. There are, indeed, references in the legislative history to the corresponding federal powers. More numerous, however, are the references to Congress's pre-*Erie* power to prescribe "general law" applicable in all federal courts. At the congressional hearings, for example: "Congress rests solely upon its power to prescribe the jurisdiction and duties of the Federal courts." . . . Plainly, a power derived from Congress' Article III control over federal court jurisdiction would not by any flight of fancy permit Congress to control proceedings in state courts.

. . .

B

The structure of the FAA itself runs directly contrary to the reading the Court today gives to § 2. Sections 3 and 4 are the implementing provisions of the Act, and they expressly apply only to federal courts. Section 4 refers to the "United States district court[s]," and provides that it can be invoked only in a court that has jurisdiction under Title 28 of the United States Code. As originally enacted, § 3 referred, in the same terms as § 4, to "courts [or court] of the United States." There has since been a minor amendment in § 4's phrasing, but no substantive change in either section's limitation to federal courts.

None of this Court's prior decisions has authoritatively construed the Act otherwise. It bears repeating that both *Prima Paint* and *Moses H. Cone* involved federal court litigation. The applicability of the FAA to state court proceedings was simply not before the Court in either case. . . .

The *Prima Paint* majority gave full but precise effect to the original congressional intent — it recognized that notwithstanding the intervention of *Erie* the FAA's restrictive focus on maritime and interstate contracts permits its application in federal diversity courts. Today's decision, in contrast, glosses over both the careful crafting of *Prima Paint* and the historical reasons that made *Prima Paint* necessary, and gives the FAA a reach far broader than Congress intended.[19]

III

Section 2, like the rest of the FAA, should have no application whatsoever in state courts. Assuming, to the contrary, that § 2 *does* create a federal right that the state courts must enforce, state courts should nonetheless be allowed, at least in the first instance, to fashion their own procedures for enforcing the right. Unfortunately, the Court seems to direct that the arbitration clause at issue here must be *specifically* enforced; apparently no other means of enforcement is permissible.[20]

. . .

V

Today's decision adds yet another chapter to the FAA's already colorful history. In 1842 this Court's ruling in *Swift v. Tyson* set up a major obstacle to the enforcement of state arbitration laws in federal diversity courts. In 1925 Congress sought to rectify the problem by enacting the FAA; the intent was to create uniform law binding only in the federal courts. In *Erie* (1938), and then in *Bernhardt* (1956), this Court significantly curtailed federal power. In 1967 our decision in *Prima Paint* upheld the application of the FAA in a *federal-court* proceeding as a valid exercise of Congress's Commerce Clause and Admiralty powers. Today the Court discovers a federal right in FAA § 2 that the state courts must enforce. Apparently confident that state courts are not competent to devise their own procedures for protecting the newly discovered federal right, the Court summarily prescribes a specific procedure, found nowhere in § 2 or its common law origins, that the state courts are to follow.

Today's decision is unfaithful to congressional intent, unnecessary, and, in light of

---

[19] The Court suggests that it is unlikely that Congress would have created a federal substantive right that the state courts were not required to enforce. But it is equally rare to find a federal substantive right that cannot be enforced in federal court under the jurisdictional grant of 28 U.S.C. § 1331. Yet the Court states that the FAA must be so construed. The simple answer to this puzzle is that in 1925 Congress did not believe it was creating a substantive right at all.

[20] If my understanding of the Court's opinion is correct, the Court has made § 3 of the FAA binding on the state courts. But as we have noted, § 3 by its own terms governs only federal court proceedings. Moreover, if § 2, standing alone, creates a federal right to specific enforcement of arbitration agreements §§ 3 and 4 are, of course, largely superfluous. And if § 2 implicitly incorporates §§ 3 and 4 procedures for making arbitration agreements enforceable before arbitration begins, why not also § 9 procedures concerning venue, personal jurisdiction, and notice for enforcing an arbitrator's award after arbitration ends? One set of procedures is of little use without the other.

the FAA's antecedents and the intervening contraction of federal power, inexplicable. Although arbitration is a worthy alternative to litigation, today's exercise in judicial revisionism goes too far. I respectfully dissent.

NOTES

1. The language in the California Franchise Investment Law, which the California Supreme Court construed as precluding arbitration, is very similar to the language in the Securities Act of 1933, construed by the U.S. Supreme Court in *Wilko*. Given that the Supreme Court ultimately overruled *Wilko*, why didn't it review the California court's interpretation of the statute here?

2. For a detailed examination of the legislative history of the FAA, see IAN R. MACNEIL, AMERICAN ARBITRATION LAW 102–121 (1992). Professor Macneil concludes:

> In sum, the hearings confirm what is already clear from the prior background and the bills themselves: the proposed USAA was intended to apply only in federal courts. It was never intended to create substantive federal regulatory law superseding state law under the Supremacy Clause of the federal constitution.

Id. at 117.

For a contrary view, consider the following:

> . . . Chief Justice Burger's analysis in *Southland* of the FAA's legislative history leaves much to be desired. But that is because it is incomplete, not because the conclusion it reaches is wrong. In my view, the Chief Justice reached the correct conclusion about the FAA's legislative history: that "although the legislative history is not without ambiguities, there are strong indications that Congress had in mind something more than making arbitration agreements enforceable only in the federal courts." . . .

> (1) Materials submitted to Congress by the principal drafter of the FAA, Julius Henry Cohen, provide strong evidence that the FAA was intended to apply in state court. In the materials, Cohen argued that Congress had the power to make arbitration agreements enforceable in state court. The context of the argument makes clear that it does not reflect merely a "wish in [Cohen's] heart of hearts" or "lawyerly caution," as Macneil argues. Indeed, Cohen identified the "primary purpose" of the FAA as making arbitration agreements enforceable in federal court, implying that a secondary purpose of the Act was to make arbitration agreements enforceable in state court.

> (2) Cohen discussed Congress's power to make arbitration agreements enforceable in state court not only in the materials he submitted to Congress, but also in two law review articles he co-authored after the enactment of the FAA. In addition, at least one other contemporaneous commentary, which Macneil does not mention, flatly concludes that "the act is broad enough to apply to actions commenced in state courts as well as to those instituted in federal courts, and it was so intended by those who drafted it." Such statements belie the commonly asserted notion that no

one at the time the FAA was enacted believed it applied in state court, either because arbitration matters were procedural or because it would have been too great an infringement on state sovereignty.

(3) The vast majority of statements in the legislative history, relied on by Justice O'Connor and Professor Macneil to argue that the FAA applies only in federal court, state simply that the FAA applies in federal court, not that it applies only in federal court. Given that the "primary purpose" of the FAA was to make arbitration agreements enforceable in federal court, such statements are not surprising. But they do not exclude the possibility that the Act applies in state court as well. Likewise, supporters' arguments that the Act was constitutional based on Congress's power to establish rules of procedure in federal court do not demonstrate that the Act applies only in federal court. Because of doubts about the constitutionality of the FAA, its supporters relied on both Congress's power to regulate the federal courts and its power to regulate interstate commerce. The applicability of the Act in state court, by comparison, obviously could be grounded (and was in fact grounded) solely on the commerce power. . . .

(4) The usual discussions of the historical setting of the FAA incorrectly focus on the fact that the Act predates the decision in *Erie Railroad v. Tompkins.* . . . Instead, the more important historical reason for such transformation of the FAA as has occurred is the post-New Deal expansion in the scope of Congress's commerce power. Today, the FAA applies to a vastly wider array of cases than it did in 1925, both in federal court and in state court. Thus, the lack of opposition to the Act at the time of enactment is much less surprising than it otherwise might seem. Likewise, a plausible reason for the lack of reported state court cases considering the FAA for several decades after its enactment is the narrow reach of the Act during much of that time. Indeed, the first reported state court case to consider the FAA was decided in 1944, only two years after the Supreme Court's expansive interpretation of the scope of the commerce power in *Wickard v. Filburn.*

To be clear: I do not claim that the legislative history of the FAA unambiguously demonstrates that Congress intended the Act to apply in state court. As Chief Justice Burger wrote in *Southland*, the legislative history is "not without ambiguities." Instead, my argument is more limited. First, I conclude that the legislative history does not unambiguously demonstrate the opposite — *i.e.*, it does not demonstrate that, as Professor Macneil has contended, the FAA applies only in federal court. Second, in my view, construing the Act as applicable in state court is more consistent with the legislative history — that is, it leaves fewer ambiguities unexplained — than the Macneil interpretation.

Christopher R. Drahozal, *In Defense of* Southland: *Reexamining the Legislative History of the Federal Arbitration Act*, 78 NOTRE DAME L. REV. 101, 105-07 (2002).*

3. In Bernhardt v. Polygraphic Co. of America, 350 U.S. 198 (1956), referred to

in the dissenting opinion, an employee filed suit in Vermont state court against his employer, a New York corporation, alleging breach of an employment contract. The employee entered into the contract while a New York resident but then moved to Vermont, where his duties under the contract were to be performed. The employer removed the action to Vermont federal court on grounds of diversity of citizenship. The lower court held that the arbitration agreement was revocable, applying Vermont law under Erie R.R. v. Tompkins, 304 U.S. 64 (1938).

The Supreme Court first held that the Federal Arbitration Act did not apply:

> No maritime transaction is involved here. Nor does this contract evidence "a transaction involving commerce" within the meaning of § 2 of the Act. There is no showing that petitioner while performing his duties under the employment contract was working "in" commerce, was producing goods for commerce, or was engaging in activity that affected commerce, within the meaning of our decisions.

Id. at 200–01.

It then proceeded to address the *Erie* question, holding that the Vermont district court was required to apply Vermont law on the enforceability of arbitration agreements:

> If the federal court allows arbitration where the state court would disallow it, the outcome of litigation might depend on the courthouse where suit is brought. For the remedy by arbitration, whatever its merits or shortcomings, substantially affects the cause of action created by the State. The nature of the tribunal where suits are tried is an important part of the parcel of rights behind a cause of action. The change from a court of law to an arbitration panel may make a radical difference in ultimate result. Arbitration carries no right to trial by jury that is guaranteed both by the Seventh Amendment and by Ch. 1, Art. 12th, of the Vermont Constitution. Arbitrators do not have the benefit of judicial instruction on the law; they need not give their reasons for their results; the record of their proceedings is not as complete as it is in a court trial; and judicial review of an award is more limited than judicial review of a trial. . . . There would in our judgment be a resultant discrimination if the parties suing on a Vermont cause of action in the federal court were remitted to arbitration, while those suing in the Vermont court could not be.

Id. at 203–04. Is the view of arbitration expressed in *Bernhardt* consistent with that in the Supreme Court's more recent arbitrability cases?

4.   The Supreme Court revisited the preemption issue from *Southland* in Perry v. Thomas, 482 U.S. 483 (1987). In *Perry*, the Court held that the FAA preempted a California statute providing that wage collection actions could be brought "without regard to the existence of any private agreement to arbitrate." It declined to follow its earlier decision in Merrill Lynch, Pierce, Fenner & Smith v. Ware, 414 U.S. 117 (1973) (cited above in Justice Stevens' concurring and dissenting opinion in

Southland), which, the Court concluded, did not deal with preemption by the FAA. Justice Stevens, who joined Justice O'Connor in dissent, wrote separately as follows:

> Despite the striking similarity between this case and *Merrill Lynch, Pierce, Fenner & Smith, Inc. v. Ware*, the Court correctly concludes that the precise question now presented was not decided in *Ware*. Even though the Arbitration Act had been on the books for almost 50 years in 1973, apparently neither the Court nor the litigants even considered the possibility that the Act had pre-empted state-created rights. It is only in the last few years that the Court has effectively rewritten the statute to give it a pre-emptive scope that Congress certainly did not intend.

Id. at 492.

PROBLEM 4.1

As a law clerk for one of the Justices, you are responsible for preparing a bench memo on the *Southland* case. How would you recommend that he or she vote on the case, and why?

PROBLEM 4.2

Assume that *Southland* had come out the other way, with a majority agreeing with Justice O'Connor that the FAA did not apply in state court. Your client is a California franchisee with a claim under the California Franchise Investment Law against Southland, the franchisor. The franchise agreement contains an arbitration clause, but for tactical reasons you would prefer not to arbitrate. How do you proceed? If instead you represented Southland, how would you proceed?

ALLIED-BRUCE TERMINIX COS. v. DOBSON
United States Supreme Court
513 U.S. 265 (1995)

JUSTICE BREYER delivered the opinion of the Court.

This case concerns the reach of § 2 of the Federal Arbitration Act. That section makes enforceable a written arbitration provision in "a contract *evidencing* a transaction *involving* commerce." 9 U.S.C. § 2 (emphasis added). Should we read this phrase broadly, extending the Act's reach to the limits of Congress' Commerce Clause power? Or, do the two underscored words — "involving" and "evidencing" — significantly restrict the Act's application? We conclude that the broader reading of the Act is the correct one; and we reverse a State Supreme Court judgment to the contrary.

I

In August 1987 Steven Gwin, a respondent, who owned a house in Birmingham, Alabama, bought a lifetime "Termite Protection Plan" (Plan) from the local office of Allied-Bruce Terminix Companies, a franchise of Terminix International Company.

In the Plan, Allied-Bruce promised "to protect" Gwin's house "against the attack of subterranean termites," to reinspect periodically, to provide any "further treatment found necessary," and to repair, up to $100,000, damage caused by new termite infestations. Terminix International "guarantee[d] the fulfillment of the terms" of the Plan. The Plan's contract document provided in writing that "*any controversy or claim . . .* arising out of or relating to the interpretation, performance or breach of any provision of this agreement *shall be settled exclusively by arbitration.*" (emphasis added). In the Spring of 1991 Mr. and Mrs. Gwin, wishing to sell their house to Mr. and Mrs. Dobson, had Allied-Bruce reinspect the house. They obtained a clean bill of health. But, no sooner had they sold the house and transferred the Termite Protection Plan to Mr. and Mrs. Dobson than the Dobsons found the house swarming with termites. Allied-Bruce attempted to treat and repair the house, but the Dobsons found Allied-Bruce's efforts inadequate. They therefore sued the Gwins, and (along with the Gwins, who cross-claimed) also sued Allied-Bruce and Terminix in Alabama state court. Allied-Bruce and Terminix, pointing to the Plan's arbitration clause and § 2 of the Federal Arbitration Act, immediately asked the court for a stay, to allow arbitration to proceed. The court denied the stay. Allied-Bruce and Terminix appealed.

The Supreme Court of Alabama upheld the denial of the stay on the basis of a state statute making written, predispute arbitration agreements invalid and "unenforceable." To reach this conclusion, the court had to find that the Federal Arbitration Act, which pre-empts conflicting state law, did not apply to the termite contract. It made just that finding. The court considered the federal Act inapplicable because the connection between the termite contract and interstate commerce was too slight. In the court's view, the Act applies to a contract only if " 'at the time [the parties entered into the contract] and accepted the arbitration clause, they *contemplated* substantial interstate activity.' " Despite some interstate activities (*e.g.*, Allied-Bruce, like Terminix, is a multistate firm and shipped treatment and repair material from out of state), the court found that the parties "contemplated" a transaction that was primarily local and not "substantially" interstate.

Several state courts and federal district courts, like the Supreme Court of Alabama, have interpreted the Act's language as requiring the parties to a contract to have "contemplated" an interstate commerce connection. Several federal appellate courts, however, have interpreted the same language differently, as reaching to the limits of Congress' Commerce Clause power. We granted certiorari to resolve this conflict, and, as we said, we conclude that the broader reading of the statute is the right one.

II

Before we can reach the main issues in this case, we must set forth three items of legal background.

First, the basic purpose of the Federal Arbitration Act is to overcome courts' refusals to enforce agreements to arbitrate. . . .

Second, some initially assumed that the Federal Arbitration Act represented an exercise of Congress' Article III power to "ordain and establish" federal courts, U.S.

Const., Art. III, § 1. In 1967, however, this Court held that the Act "is based upon and confined to the incontestable federal foundations of 'control over interstate commerce and over admiralty.' " *Prima Paint Corp. v. Flood & Conklin Mfg. Co.*

Third, the holding in *Prima Paint* led to a further question. Did Congress intend the Act also to apply in state courts? Did the Federal Arbitration Act pre-empt conflicting state antiarbitration law, or could state courts apply their antiarbitration rules in cases before them, thereby reaching results different from those reached in otherwise similar federal diversity cases? In *Southland Corp. v. Keating*, this Court decided that Congress would not have wanted state and federal courts to reach different outcomes about the validity of arbitration in similar cases. The Court concluded that the Federal Arbitration Act pre-empts state law; and it held that state courts cannot apply state statutes that invalidate arbitration agreements.

We have set forth this background because respondents, supported by 20 state attorneys general, now ask us to overrule *Southland* and thereby to permit Alabama to apply its antiarbitration statute in this case irrespective of the proper interpretation of § 2. The *Southland* Court, however, recognized that the pre-emption issue was a difficult one, and it considered the basic arguments that respondents and *amici* now raise (even though those issues were not thoroughly briefed at the time). Nothing significant has changed in the 10 years subsequent to *Southland*; no later cases have eroded *Southland*'s authority; and, no unforeseen practical problems have arisen. Moreover, in the interim, private parties have likely written contracts relying upon *Southland* as authority. Further, Congress, both before and after *Southland*, has enacted legislation extending, not retracting, the scope of arbitration. *See, e.g.*, 9 U.S.C. § 15 (eliminating the Act of State doctrine as a bar to arbitration); 9 U.S.C. §§ 201–208 (international arbitration). For these reasons, we find it inappropriate to reconsider what is by now well-established law.

We therefore proceed to the basic interpretive questions aware that we are interpreting an Act that seeks broadly to overcome judicial hostility to arbitration agreements and that applies in both federal and state courts. We must decide in this case whether that Act used language about interstate commerce that nonetheless limits the Act's application, thereby carving out an important statutory niche in which a State remains free to apply its antiarbitration law or policy. We conclude that it does not.

III

. . .

The initial interpretive question focuses upon the words "involving commerce" [in § 2 of the FAA]. These words are broader than the often-found words of art "in commerce." They therefore cover more than " 'only persons or activities *within the flow* of interstate commerce.' " But, how far beyond the flow of commerce does the word "involving" reach? Is "involving" the functional equivalent of the word "affecting?" That phrase — "affecting commerce" — normally signals a congressional intent to exercise its Commerce Clause powers to the full. We cannot look to other statutes for guidance for the parties tell us that this is the only federal statute that uses the word "involving" to describe an interstate commerce relation.

After examining the statute's language, background, and structure, we conclude that the word "involving" is broad and is indeed the functional equivalent of "affecting." For one thing, such an interpretation, linguistically speaking, is permissible. The dictionary finds instances in which "involve" and "affect" sometimes can mean about the same thing. For another, the Act's legislative history, to the extent that it is informative, indicates an expansive congressional intent.

Further, this Court has previously described the Act's reach expansively as coinciding with that of the Commerce Clause.

Finally, a broad interpretation of this language is consistent with the Act's basic purpose, to put arbitration provisions on "the same footing" as a contract's other terms. Conversely, a narrower interpretation is not consistent with the Act's purpose, for (unless unreasonably narrowed to the flow of commerce) such an interpretation would create a new, unfamiliar, test lying somewhere in a no-man's land between "in commerce" and "affecting commerce," thereby unnecessarily complicating the law and breeding litigation from a statute that seeks to avoid it.

We recognize arguments to the contrary: The pre-New Deal Congress that passed the Act in 1925 might well have thought the Commerce Clause did not stretch as far as has turned out to be so. But, it is not unusual for this Court in similar circumstances to ask whether the scope of a statute should expand along with the expansion of the Commerce Clause power itself, and to answer the question affirmatively — as, for the reasons set forth above, we do here.

. . .

IV

Section 2 applies where there is "a contract *evidencing a transaction* involving commerce." 9 U.S.C. § 2 (emphasis added). The second interpretive question focuses on the underscored words. Does "evidencing a transaction" mean only that the transaction (that the contract "evidences") must turn out, *in fact*, to have involved interstate commerce? Or, does it mean more?

Many years ago, Second Circuit Chief Judge Lumbard said that the phrase meant considerably more. He wrote:

> "The significant question . . . is not whether, in carrying out the terms of the contract, the parties did cross state lines, but whether, at the time they entered into it and accepted the arbitration clause, they contemplated substantial interstate activity. Cogent evidence regarding their state of mind at the time would be the terms of the contract, and if it, on its face, evidences interstate traffic . . . , the contract should come within § 2. In addition, evidence as to how the parties expected the contract to be performed and how it was performed is relevant to whether substantial interstate activity was contemplated." Metro Industrial Painting Corp. v. Terminal Constr. Co., 287 F.2d 382, 387 (Lumbard, C.J., concurring).

The Supreme Court of Alabama, and several other courts, have followed this view, known as the "contemplation of the parties" test.

We find the interpretive choice difficult, but for several reasons we conclude that the first interpretation ("commerce in fact") is more faithful to the statute than the second ("contemplation of the parties"). First, the "contemplation of the parties" interpretation, when viewed in terms of the statute's basic purpose, seems anomalous. That interpretation invites litigation about what was, or was not, "contemplated." Why would Congress intend a test that risks the very kind of costs and delay through litigation (about the circumstances of contract formation) that Congress wrote the Act to help the parties avoid?

Moreover, that interpretation too often would turn the validity of an arbitration clause on what, from the perspective of the statute's basic purpose, seems happenstance, namely whether the parties happened to think to insert a reference to interstate commerce in the document or happened to mention it in an initial conversation. After all, parties to a sales contract with an arbitration clause might naturally think about the goods sold, or about arbitration, but why should they naturally think about an interstate commerce connection?

Further, that interpretation fits awkwardly with the rest of § 2. That section, for example, permits parties to agree to submit to arbitration "an existing controversy arising out of" a contract made earlier. Why would Congress want to risk non-enforceability of this *later* arbitration agreement (even if fully connected with interstate commerce) simply because the parties did not properly "contemplate" (or write about) the interstate aspects of the earlier contract? The first interpretation, requiring only that the "transaction" *in fact* involve interstate commerce, avoids this anomaly, as it avoids the other anomalous effects growing out of the "contemplation of the parties" test.

Second, the statute's language permits the "commerce in fact" interpretation. That interpretation, we concede, leaves little work for the word "evidencing" (in the phrase "a contract evidencing a transaction") to perform, for every contract evidences some transaction. But, perhaps Congress did not want that word to perform much work. . . . Early drafts made enforceable a written arbitration provision "in *any contract* or maritime transaction or transaction involving commerce." S. 4214, 67th Cong., 4th Sess., § 2 (1922) (emphasis added). Members of Congress, looking at that phrase, might have thought the words "any contract" standing alone went beyond Congress's constitutional authority. And, if so, they might have simply connected those words with the later words "transaction involving commerce," thereby creating the phrase that became law. Nothing in the Act's history suggests any other, more limiting, task for the language.

Third, the basic practical argument underlying the "contemplation of the parties" test was, in Judge Lumbard's words, the need to "be cautious in construing the act lest we excessively encroach on the powers which Congressional policy, if not the Constitution, would reserve to the states." The practical force of this argument has diminished in light of this Court's later holdings that the Act does displace state law to the contrary. *See Southland Corp. v. Keating; Perry v. Thomas.*

Finally, we note that an *amicus curiae* argues for an "objective" ("reasonable person" oriented) version of the "contemplation of the parties" test on the ground that such an interpretation would better protect consumers asked to sign form contracts by businesses. We agree that Congress, when enacting this law, had the needs of consumers, as well as others, in mind. Indeed, arbitration's advantages often would seem helpful to individuals, say, complaining about a product, who need a less expensive alternative to litigation. And, according to the American Arbitration Association (also an *amicus* here), more than one-third of its claims involve amounts below $10,000, while another third involve claims of $10,000 to $50,000 (with an average processing time of less than six months).

We are uncertain, however, just how the "objective" version of the "contemplation" test would help consumers. Sometimes, of course, it would permit, say, a consumer with potentially large damage claims, to disavow a contract's arbitration provision and proceed in court. But, if so, it would equally permit, say, local business entities to disavow a contract's arbitration provisions, thereby leaving the typical consumer who has only a small damage claim (who seeks, say, the value of only a defective refrigerator or television set) without any remedy but a court remedy, the costs and delays of which could eat up the value of an eventual small recovery.

In any event, § 2 gives States a method for protecting consumers against unfair pressure to agree to a contract with an unwanted arbitration provision. States may regulate contracts, including arbitration clauses, under general contract law principles and they may invalidate an arbitration clause "upon such grounds as exist at law or in equity for the revocation of *any* contract." 9 U.S.C. § 2 (emphasis added). What States may not do is decide that a contract is fair enough to enforce all its basic terms (price, service, credit), but not fair enough to enforce its arbitration clause. The Act makes any such state policy unlawful, for that kind of policy would place arbitration clauses on an unequal "footing," directly contrary to the Act's language and Congress's intent.

For these reasons, we accept the "commerce in fact" interpretation, reading the Act's language as insisting that the "transaction" in fact "involve[]" interstate commerce, even if the parties did not contemplate an interstate commerce connection.

V

The parties do not contest that the transaction in this case, in fact, involved interstate commerce. In addition to the multistate nature of Terminix and Allied-Bruce, the termite-treating and house-repairing material used by Allied-Bruce in its (allegedly inadequate) efforts to carry out the terms of the Plan, came from outside Alabama.

Consequently, the judgment of the Supreme Court of Alabama is reversed and the case is remanded for further proceedings consistent with this opinion.

It is so ordered.

JUSTICE O'CONNOR, concurring.

    . . .

I continue to believe that Congress never intended the Federal Arbitration Act to apply in state courts, and that this Court has strayed far afield in giving the Act so broad a compass. . . . I have no doubt that Congress could enact, in the first instance, a federal arbitration statute that displaces most state arbitration laws. But I also have no doubt that, in 1925, Congress enacted no such statute.

Were we writing on a clean slate, I would adhere to that view and affirm the Alabama court's decision. But, as the Court points out, more than 10 years have passed since *Southland*, several subsequent cases have built upon its reasoning, and parties have undoubtedly made contracts in reliance on the Court's interpretation of the Act in the interim. After reflection, I am persuaded by considerations of *stare decisis*, which we have said "have special force in the area of statutory interpretation," to acquiesce in today's judgment. Though wrong, *Southland* has not proved unworkable, and, as always, "Congress remains free to alter what we have done."

Today's decision caps this Court's effort to expand the Federal Arbitration Act. Although each decision has built logically upon the decisions preceding it, the initial building block in *Southland* laid a faulty foundation. I acquiesce in today's judgment because there is no "special justification" to overrule *Southland*. It remains now for Congress to correct this interpretation if it wishes to preserve state autonomy in state courts.

JUSTICE SCALIA, dissenting.

I have previously joined two judgments of this Court which rested upon the holding of *Southland Corp. v. Keating. See Volt Information Sciences, Inc. v. Board of Trustees of Leland Stanford Junior Univ.; Perry v. Thomas.* In neither of those cases, however, did any party ask that *Southland* be overruled, and it was therefore not necessary to consider the question. In the present case, by contrast, one of respondents' central arguments is that *Southland* was wrongly decided, and their request for its overruling has been supported by an amicus brief signed by the attorneys general of 20 States. For the reasons set forth in JUSTICE THOMAS' opinion, which I join, I agree with the respondents (and belatedly with JUSTICE O'CONNOR) that *Southland* clearly misconstrued the Federal Arbitration Act.

I do not believe that proper application of *stare decisis* prevents correction of the mistake. Adhering to *Southland* entails a permanent, unauthorized eviction of state-court power to adjudicate a potentially large class of disputes. Abandoning it does not impair reliance interests to a degree that justifies this evil. Primary behavior is not affected: no rule of conduct is retroactively changed, but only (perhaps) the forum in which violation is to be determined and remedied. I doubt that many contracts with arbitration clauses would have been forgone, or entered into only for significantly higher remuneration, absent the *Southland* guarantee. Where, moreover, reliance on *Southland* did make a significant difference, rescission of the contract for mistake of law would often be available.

I shall not in the future dissent from judgments that rest on *Southland*. I will, however, stand ready to join four other Justices in overruling it, since *Southland* will not become more correct over time, the course of future lawmaking seems unlikely to be affected by its existence, and the accumulated private reliance will not likely increase beyond the level it has already achieved (few contracts not terminable at will have more than a 5-year term).

For these reasons, I respectfully dissent from the judgment of the Court.

Justice Thomas, with whom Justice Scalia joins, dissenting.

I disagree with the majority at the threshold of this case, and so I do not reach the question that it decides. In my view, the Federal Arbitration Act (FAA) does not apply in state courts. I respectfully dissent.

. . .

II

Rather than attempting to defend *Southland* on its merits, petitioners rely chiefly on the doctrine of stare decisis in urging us to adhere to our mistaken interpretation of the FAA. In my view, that doctrine is insufficient to save *Southland.*

. . . I see no reason to think that the costs of overruling *Southland* are unacceptably high. Certainly no reliance interests are involved in cases like the present one, where the applicability of the FAA was not within the contemplation of the parties at the time of contracting. In many other cases, moreover, the parties will simply comply with their arbitration agreement, either on the theory that they should live up to their promises or on the theory that arbitration is the cheapest and best way of resolving their dispute. In a fair number of the remaining cases, the party seeking to enforce an arbitration agreement will be able to get into federal court, where the FAA will apply. And even if access to federal court is impossible (because § 2 creates no independent basis for federal-question jurisdiction), many cases will arise in States whose own law largely parallels the FAA. Only Alabama, Mississippi, and Nebraska still hold all executory arbitration agreements to be unenforceable, though some other States refuse to enforce particular classes of such agreements.

. . . Justice O'connor nonetheless acquiesces in the majority's judgment "because there is no 'special justification' to overrule *Southland.*" Even under this approach, the necessity of "preserv[ing] state autonomy in state courts" seems sufficient to me.

. . .

NOTES

1.   In addition to reaffirming *Southland,* the Court in *Allied-Bruce* interpreted the language defining the scope of section 2 of the FAA, a subject addressed in the next section. What test did the Court adopt? Why? On the facts of the case, the Court and the parties agreed that the test was satisfied. What are the facts that made the FAA applicable?

2.   One year after *Allied-Bruce,* the Supreme Court held that the following Montana statute was preempted by the FAA: "Notice that a contract is subject to arbitration . . . shall be typed in underlined capital letters on the first page of the contract; and unless such notice is displayed thereon, the contract may not be

subject to arbitration." Doctor's Associates, Inc. v. Casarotto, 517 U.S. 681 (1996). The Court's analysis was brief. After quoting section 2 of the FAA, the Court explained:

> Repeating our observation in *Perry*, the text of § 2 declares that state law may be applied "if that law arose to govern issues concerning the validity, revocability, and enforceability of contracts generally." Thus, generally applicable contract defenses, such as fraud, duress, or unconscionability, may be applied to invalidate arbitration agreements without contravening § 2.

> Courts may not, however, invalidate arbitration agreements under state laws applicable only to arbitration provisions. By enacting § 2, we have several times said, Congress precluded States from singling out arbitration provisions for suspect status, requiring instead that such provisions be placed "upon the same footing as other contracts." Montana's § 27-5-114(4) directly conflicts with § 2 of the FAA because the State's law conditions the enforceability of arbitration agreements on compliance with a special notice requirement not applicable to contracts generally. The FAA thus displaces the Montana statute with respect to arbitration agreements covered by the Act.

Id. at 686–87.

3. One interesting aspect of the *Casarotto* case is a concurring opinion written by a Montana Supreme Court justice in an earlier iteration of the case. *See* Casarotto v. Lombardi, 886 P.2d 931 (Mont. 1994) (Trieweiler, J., specially concurring). The following excerpts give an indication of the hostility that *Southland* has inspired in some state court judges:

> To those federal judges who consider forced arbitration as the panacea for their "heavy case loads" and who consider the reluctance of state courts to buy into the arbitration program as a sign of intellectual inadequacy, I would like to explain a few things.

> In Montana, we are reasonably civilized and have a sophisticated system of justice which has evolved over time and which we continue to develop for the primary purpose of assuring fairness to those people who are subject to its authority.

> . . .

> While our system of justice and our rules are imperfect, they have as their ultimate purpose one overriding principle. They are intended, and continue to evolve, for the purpose of providing fairness to people, regardless of their wealth or political influence.

> What I would like the people in the federal judiciary, especially at the appellate level, to understand is that due to their misinterpretation of congressional intent when it enacted the Federal Arbitration Act, and due to their naive assumption that arbitration provisions and choice of law provisions are knowingly bargained for, all of these procedural safeguards and substantive laws are easily avoided by any party with enough leverage

to stick a choice of law and an arbitration provision in its pre-printed contract and require the party with inferior bargaining power to sign it.

. . .

These insidious erosions of state authority and the judicial process threaten to undermine the rule of law as we know it.

Nothing in our jurisprudence appears more intellectually detached from reality and arrogant than the lament of federal judges who see this system of imposed arbitration as "therapy for their crowded dockets." These decisions have perverted the purpose of the FAA from one to accomplish judicial neutrality, to one of open hostility to any legislative effort to assure that unsophisticated parties to contracts of adhesion at least understand the rights they are giving up.

It seems to me that judges who have let their concern for their own crowded docket overcome their concern for the rights they are entrusted with should step aside and let someone else assume their burdens. The last I checked, there were plenty of capable people willing to do so.

PROBLEM 4.3

You have just begun work as a staff attorney for a consumer advocacy group when the Supreme Court grants certiorari in *Allied-Bruce*. You are asked to prepare an *amicus curiae* brief on behalf of the group seeking to have the Supreme Court overrule *Southland*. What arguments do you make in your brief?

PROBLEM 4.4

The Attorney General of Alabama asks your advice on how Alabama can protect its consumers against what she perceives as unfair arbitration clauses, given the *Southland* and *Allied-Bruce* decisions. What do you suggest?

§ 4.03 SCOPE OF THE FAA

Allied-Bruce clarified the interstate commerce nexus required for the FAA to apply, holding that the Act extends to the full reach of Congress's Commerce Power. Shortly thereafter, the Supreme Court decided United States v. Lopez, 514 U.S. 549 (1995), and for the first time since the 1930s struck down a federal statute as exceeding the scope of the Commerce Power. Thereafter, courts struggled with cases on the margin in trying to decide whether the particular transaction was governed by the FAA or by state arbitration law.

CITIZENS BANK v. ALAFABCO, INC.
United States Supreme Court
539 U.S. 52 (2003)

PER CURIAM.

The question presented is whether the parties' debt-restructuring agreement is "a contract evidencing a transaction involving commerce" within the meaning of the Federal Arbitration Act (FAA). As we concluded in *Allied-Bruce Terminix Cos. v. Dobson*, there is a sufficient nexus with interstate commerce to make enforceable, pursuant to the FAA, an arbitration provision included in that agreement.

I

Petitioner The Citizens Bank — an Alabama lending institution — seeks to compel arbitration of a financial dispute with respondents Alafabco, Inc. — an Alabama fabrication and construction company — and its officers. According to a complaint filed by respondents in Alabama state court, the dispute among the parties arose out of a series of commercial loan transactions made over a decade-long course of business dealings. In 1986, the complaint alleges, the parties entered into a quasi-contractual relationship in which the bank agreed to provide operating capital necessary for Alafabco to secure and complete construction contracts. That relationship began to sour in 1998, when the bank allegedly encouraged Alafabco to bid on a large construction contract in Courtland, Alabama, but refused to provide the capital necessary to complete the project. In order to compensate for the bank's alleged breach of the parties' implied agreement, Alafabco completed the Courtland project with funds that would otherwise have been dedicated to repaying existing obligations to the bank. Alafabco in turn became delinquent in repaying those existing obligations.

On two occasions, the parties attempted to resolve the outstanding debts. On May 3, 1999, Alafabco and the bank executed "renewal notes" in which all previous loans were restructured and redocumented. The debt-restructuring arrangement included an arbitration agreement covering "all disputes, claims, or controversies." That agreement provided that the FAA "shall apply to [its] construction, interpretation, and enforcement." Alafabco defaulted on its obligations under the renewal notes and sought bankruptcy protection in federal court in September 1999.

In return for the dismissal of Alafabco's bankruptcy petition, the bank agreed to renegotiate the outstanding loans in a second debt-restructuring agreement. On December 10, 1999, the parties executed new loan documents encompassing Alafabco's entire outstanding debt, approximately $430,000, which was secured by a mortgage on commercial real estate owned by the individual respondents, by Alafabco's accounts receivable, inventory, supplies, fixtures, machinery, and equipment, and by a mortgage on the house of one of the individual respondents. As part of the second debt-restructuring agreement, the parties executed an arbitration agreement functionally identical to that of May 3, 1999.

Within a year of the December 1999 debt restructuring, Alafabco brought suit in the Circuit Court of Lawrence County, Alabama, against the bank and its officers. Alafabco alleged, among other causes of action, breach of contract, fraud, breach of fiduciary duties, intentional infliction of emotional distress, and interference with a contractual or business relationship. Essentially, the suit alleged that Alafabco detrimentally "incur[red] massive debt" because the bank had unlawfully reneged on its agreement to provide capital sufficient to complete the Courtland project. Invoking the arbitration agreements, the bank moved to compel arbitration of the parties' dispute. The Circuit Court ordered respondents to submit to arbitration in accordance with the arbitration agreements.

The Supreme Court of Alabama reversed over Justice See's dissent. Applying a test it first adopted in Sisters of the Visitation v. Cochran Plastering Co., 775 So. 2d 759 (2000), the court held that the debt-restructuring agreements were the relevant transactions and proceeded to determine whether those transactions, by themselves, had a "substantial effect on interstate commerce." Because there was no showing "that any portion of the restructured debt was actually attributable to interstate transactions; that the funds comprising that debt originated out-of-state; or that the restructured debt was inseparable from any out-of-state projects," the court found an insufficient nexus with interstate commerce to establish FAA coverage of the parties' dispute.

Justice See in dissent explained why, in his view, the court had erred by using the test formulated in *Sisters of the Visitation*, in which the Supreme Court of Alabama read this Court's opinion in United States v. Lopez, 514 U.S. 549 (1995), to require that "a particular contract, in order to be enforceable under the Federal Arbitration Act must, by itself, have a substantial effect on interstate commerce." Rejecting that stringent test and assessing the evidence with a more generous view of the necessary effect on interstate commerce, Justice See would have found that the bank's loans to Alafabco satisfied the FAA's "involving commerce" requirement.

II

. . . Echoing Justice See's dissenting opinion, petitioner contends that the decision below gives inadequate breadth to the "involving commerce" language of the [FAA]. We agree.

We have interpreted the term "involving commerce" in the FAA as the functional equivalent of the more familiar term "affecting commerce" — words of art that ordinarily signal the broadest permissible exercise of Congress' Commerce Clause power. *Allied-Bruce Terminix Cos.* Because the statute provides for "the enforcement of arbitration agreements within the full reach of the Commerce Clause," it is perfectly clear that the FAA encompasses a wider range of transactions than those actually "in commerce" — that is, "within the flow of interstate commerce," *Allied-Bruce Terminix Cos.*

The Supreme Court of Alabama was therefore misguided in its search for evidence that a "portion of the restructured debt was actually attributable to interstate transactions" or that the loans "originated out-of-state" or that "the restructured debt was inseparable from any out-of-state projects." Such evidence might be required if the FAA were restricted to transactions actually "in commerce," but, as we have explained, that is not the limit of the FAA's reach.

Nor is application of the FAA defeated because the individual debt-restructuring transactions, taken alone, did not have a "substantial effect on interstate commerce." Congress' Commerce Clause power "may be exercised in individual cases without showing any specific effect upon interstate commerce" if in the aggregate the economic activity in question would represent "a general practice . . . subject to federal control." Only that general practice need bear on interstate commerce in a substantial way.

This case is well within our previous pronouncements on the extent of Congress' Commerce Clause power. Although the debt-restructuring agreements were executed in Alabama by Alabama residents, they nonetheless satisfy the FAA's "involving commerce" test for at least three reasons. First, Alafabco engaged in business throughout the southeastern United States using substantial loans from the bank that were renegotiated and redocumented in the debt-restructuring agreements. Indeed, the gravamen of Alafabco's state court suit was that it had incurred "massive debt" to the bank in order to keep its business afloat, and the bank submitted affidavits of bank officers establishing that its loans to Alafabco had been used in part to finance large construction projects in North Carolina, Tennessee, and Alabama.

Second, the restructured debt was secured by all of Alafabco's business assets, including its inventory of goods assembled from out-of-state parts and raw materials. If the Commerce Clause gives Congress the power to regulate local business establishments purchasing substantial quantities of goods that have moved in interstate commerce, it necessarily reaches substantial commercial loan transactions secured by such goods.

Third, were there any residual doubt about the magnitude of the impact on interstate commerce caused by the particular economic transactions in which the parties were engaged, that doubt would dissipate upon consideration of the "general practice" those transactions represent. No elaborate explanation is needed to make evident the broad impact of commercial lending on the national economy or Congress' power to regulate that activity pursuant to the Commerce Clause.

The decision below therefore adheres to an improperly cramped view of Congress' Commerce Clause power. That view, first announced by the Supreme Court of Alabama in *Sisters of the Visitation*, appears to rest on a misreading of our decision in *United States v. Lopez*. *Lopez* did not restrict the reach of the FAA or implicitly overrule *Allied-Bruce Terminix Cos.* — indeed, we did not discuss that case in *Lopez*. Nor did *Lopez* purport to announce a new rule governing Congress' Commerce Clause power over concededly economic activity such as the debt-restructuring agreements before us now. To be sure, "the power to regulate commerce, though broad indeed, has limits," but nothing in our decision in *Lopez* suggests that those limits are breached by applying the FAA to disputes arising out of the commercial loan transactions in this case.

Accordingly, the petition for writ of certiorari is granted, the judgment of the Supreme Court of Alabama is reversed, and the case is remanded for further proceedings not inconsistent with this opinion.

It is so ordered.

NOTES

1. The Supreme Court's decision in *Alafabco* was unusual in that the Court summarily reversed the Alabama Supreme Court — without requiring briefing on the merits or oral argument. The Court issues only a handful of summary reversals each term, usually in criminal cases.

2. After *Alafabco*, is any arbitration agreement governed solely by state law? For the views of the Supreme Court of Alabama on the question, see Service Corp. Int'l v. Fulmer, 883 So. 2d 621, 629 (Ala. 2003):

> Given this background, and in light of the continued vitality of Wickard [v. Filburn, 317 U.S. 111 (1942)] (which represents the outer limits of Congress's commerce power), it would be difficult indeed to give an example of an economic or commercial activity that one could, with any confidence, declare beyond the reach of Congress's power under the Commerce Clause, and, by extension, under the FAA. While there can be no per se rule that would preclude a trial court's role in evaluating whether a contract "evidences a transaction involving commerce," given the above, a trial court evaluating a contract connected to some economic or commercial activity would rarely, if ever, refuse to compel arbitration on the ground that the transactions lacked "involvement" in interstate commerce.

But see Baronoff v. Kean Dev. Co., 2006 N.Y. Misc. LEXIS 784 (Sup. Ct. Apr. 11, 2006) (contracts to renovate home and apartment "cannot be said to 'affect commerce' " even though materials used came from out-of-state); Bruner v. Timberlane Manor L.P., 155 P.3d 16, 30 (Okla. 2006) ("declin[ing] to join Alabama, Mississippi and Texas in treating the federal distribution of medicare insurance funds and state distribution of federal-state-matching medicaid funds as indicia of commerce that triggers the FAA").

3. The Supreme Court summarily reversed another state court's narrow interpretation of the FAA in Marmet Health Care Center v. Brown, 132 S. Ct. 1201 (2012). In *Marmet*, the West Virginia Supreme Court had held that "as a matter of public policy under West Virginia law, an arbitration clause in a nursing home admission agreement adopted prior to an occurrence of negligence that results in a personal injury or wrongful death, shall not be enforced to compel arbitration of a dispute concerning the negligence." Such a state law rule would ordinarily be preempted by the FAA — assuming it applies — under *Southland*. But the West Virginia court, after criticizing the Court's preemption jurisprudence as "created from whole cloth," construed the FAA as not extending to "personal injury or wrongful death suits that only collaterally derive from a written agreement that evidences a transaction affecting interstate commerce, particularly where the agreement involves a service that is a practical necessity for members of the public." The U.S. Supreme Court summarily reversed, concluding that "[t]he West Virginia court's interpretation of the FAA was both incorrect and inconsistent with clear instruction in the precedents of this Court." The FAA plainly applied to the

contracts at issue in *Marmet*, and there was no basis in the Act for the exclusion adopted by the West Virginia court.

4.   In National Federation of Independent Business v. Sebelius, 132 S. Ct. 2566 (2012), the majority of the Supreme Court concluded that the mandate that individuals buy health insurance contained in the Patient Protection and Affordable Care Act was beyond the scope of Congress's Commerce power (although the Court upheld the individual mandate under the taxing power instead). Given that the scope of the FAA is coextensive with Congress's Commerce power, to what extent does the Court's decision constrain the scope of the FAA? The five Justices concluding that the Affordable Care Act was beyond Congress's Commerce power based their decision on the view that "the individual mandate . . . does not regulate commercial activity. It instead compels individuals to *become* active in commerce by purchasing a product, on the ground that their failure to do so affects interstate commerce." *Id.* at 2587. By comparison, the FAA only applies when the parties have engaged in an activity — agreeing to arbitrate. So unless *NFIB v. Sebelius* foreshadows a broader retrenchment of the Commerce power, it is likely to have little or no effect on the scope of the FAA.

PROBLEM 4.5

Which of the following contracts "evidenc[e] a transaction involving commerce" within the meaning of the FAA?

(a) A contract between Gateway 2000 (a South Dakota company) and a consumer in Massachusetts who has ordered a Gateway 2000 computer over the phone.

(b) A contract between Gateway 2000 and a Massachusetts consumer who bought a Gateway 2000 computer at a local Gateway 2000 store. Assume that the computer was in stock and the consumer purchased the computer at the store and took it home with her, but that the computer was manufactured in South Dakota.

(c) A contract between the Massachusetts consumer and a Massachusetts contractor who agrees to finish the consumer's basement. The contractor does business only in Massachusetts, but the materials the contractor uses come from all over the United States.

(d) A contract between the Massachusetts consumer and a Massachusetts home cleaning service. The cleaning service does business only in Massachusetts and employs only Massachusetts residents. The cleaning supplies used, however, come from all over the United States.

(e) Same as (d) except that the contract at issue is the one between the Massachusetts home cleaning service and its employees.

————

Section 1 of the FAA provides that the Act does not apply to "contracts of employment of seamen, railroad employees, or any other class of workers engaged in foreign or interstate commerce." 9 U.S.C. § 1. How broadly that exception is interpreted is important. A broad reading of the language, as excluding all employment contracts from the scope of the FAA, would leave to state law the enforceability of arbitration agreements in employment contracts. In the following case, the Supreme Court resolved a split among the circuits over the question.

CIRCUIT CITY STORES, INC. v. ADAMS
United States Supreme Court
532 U.S. 105 (2001)

JUSTICE KENNEDY delivered the opinion of the Court.

Section 1 of the Federal Arbitration Act (FAA) excludes from the Act's coverage "contracts of employment of seamen, railroad employees, or any other class of workers engaged in foreign or interstate commerce." 9 U.S.C. § 1. All but one of the Courts of Appeals which have addressed the issue interpret this provision as exempting contracts of employment of transportation workers, but not other employment contracts, from the FAA's coverage. A different interpretation has been adopted by the Court of Appeals for the Ninth Circuit, which construes the exemption so that all contracts of employment are beyond the FAA's reach, whether or not the worker is engaged in transportation. It applied that rule to the instant case. We now decide that the better interpretation is to construe the statute, as most of the Courts of Appeals have done, to confine the exemption to transportation workers.

I

In October 1995, respondent Saint Clair Adams applied for a job at petitioner Circuit City Stores, Inc., a national retailer of consumer electronics. Adams signed an employment application which included [an arbitration clause]. . . . Adams was hired as a sales counselor in Circuit City's store in Santa Rosa, California.

Two years later, Adams filed an employment discrimination lawsuit against Circuit City in state court, asserting claims under California's Fair Employment and Housing Act and other claims based on general tort theories under California law. Circuit City filed suit in the United States District Court for the Northern District of California, seeking to enjoin the state-court action and to compel arbitration of respondent's claims pursuant to the FAA. The District Court entered the requested order. . . . An appeal followed.

While respondent's appeal was pending in the Court of Appeals for the Ninth Circuit, the court ruled on the key issue in an unrelated case. The court held the FAA does not apply to contracts of employment. See Craft v. Campbell Soup Co., 177 F.3d 1083 (1999). In the instant case, following the rule announced in *Craft*, the Court of Appeals held the arbitration agreement between Adams and Circuit City was contained in a "contract of employment," and so was not subject to the FAA. Circuit City petitioned this Court, noting that the Ninth Circuit's conclusion that all employment contracts are excluded from the FAA conflicts with every other Court of Appeals to have addressed the question. We granted certiorari to resolve the issue.

II

A

. . .

We had occasion in [*Allied-Bruce Terminix Cos. v. Dobson*] to consider the significance of Congress' use of the words "involving commerce" in § 2. The analysis began with a reaffirmation of earlier decisions concluding that the FAA was enacted pursuant to Congress' substantive power to regulate interstate commerce and admiralty, and that the Act was applicable in state courts and pre-emptive of state laws hostile to arbitration. Relying upon these background principles and upon the evident reach of the words "involving commerce," the Court interpreted § 2 as implementing Congress' intent "to exercise [its] commerce power to the full."

The instant case, of course, involves not the basic coverage authorization under § 2 of the Act, but the exemption from coverage under § 1. The exemption clause provides the Act shall not apply "to contracts of employment of seamen, railroad employees, or any other class of workers engaged in foreign or interstate commerce." 9 U.S.C. § 1. Most Courts of Appeals conclude the exclusion provision is limited to transportation workers, defined, for instance, as those workers "actually engaged in the movement of goods in interstate commerce." As we stated at the outset, the Court of Appeals for the Ninth Circuit takes a different view and interprets the § 1 exception to exclude all contracts of employment from the reach of the FAA. . . .

B

Respondent, at the outset, contends that we need not address the meaning of the § 1 exclusion provision to decide the case in his favor. In his view, an employment contract is not a "contract evidencing a transaction involving interstate commerce" at all, since the word "transaction" in § 2 extends only to commercial contracts. This line of reasoning proves too much, for it would make the § 1 exclusion provision superfluous. If all contracts of employment are beyond the scope of the Act under the § 2 coverage provision, the separate exemption for "contracts of employment of seamen, railroad employees, or any other class of workers engaged in . . . interstate commerce" would be pointless. The proffered interpretation of "evidencing a transaction involving commerce," furthermore, would be inconsistent with *Gilmer v. Interstate/Johnson Lane Corp.*, where we held that § 2 required the arbitration of an age discrimination claim based on an agreement in a securities registration application, a dispute that did not arise from a "commercial deal or merchant's sale." Nor could respondent's construction of § 2 be reconciled with the expansive reading of those words adopted in *Allied-Bruce*. If, then, there is an argument to be made that arbitration agreements in employment contracts are not covered by the Act, it must be premised on the language of the § 1 exclusion provision itself.

Respondent, endorsing the reasoning of the Court of Appeals for the Ninth Circuit that the provision excludes all employment contracts, relies on the asserted breadth of the words "contracts of employment of . . . any other class of workers engaged in . . . commerce." Referring to our construction of § 2's coverage provision in *Allied-Bruce* — concluding that the words "involving commerce" evidence the congressional intent to regulate to the full extent of its commerce power — respondent contends § 1's interpretation should have a like reach, thus exempting all employment contracts. The two provisions, it is argued, are coterminous; under this view the "involving commerce" provision brings within the FAA's scope all contracts within the Congress' commerce power, and the "engaged in . . . commerce" language in § 1 in turn exempts from the FAA all employment contracts falling within that authority.

This reading of § 1, however, runs into an immediate and, in our view, insurmountable textual obstacle. Unlike the "involving commerce" language in § 2, the words "any other class of workers engaged in . . . commerce" constitute a residual phrase, following, in the same sentence, explicit reference to "seamen" and "railroad employees." Construing the residual phrase to exclude all employment contracts fails to give independent effect to the statute's enumeration of the specific categories of workers which precedes it; there would be no need for Congress to use the phrases "seamen" and "railroad employees" if those same classes of workers were subsumed within the meaning of the "engaged in . . . commerce" residual clause. The wording of § 1 calls for the application of the maxim *ejusdem generis*, the statutory canon that "where general words follow specific words in a statutory enumeration, the general words are construed to embrace only objects similar in nature to those objects enumerated by the preceding specific words." Under this rule of construction the residual clause should be read to give effect to the terms "seamen" and "railroad employees," and should itself be controlled and defined by reference to the enumerated categories of workers which are recited just before it; the interpretation of the clause pressed by respondent fails to produce these results.

Canons of construction need not be conclusive and are often countered, of course, by some maxim pointing in a different direction. The application of the rule *ejusdem generis* in this case, however, is in full accord with other sound considerations bearing upon the proper interpretation of the clause. For even if the term "engaged in commerce" stood alone in § 1, we would not construe the provision to exclude all contracts of employment from the FAA. Congress uses different modifiers to the word "commerce" in the design and enactment of its statutes. The phrase "affecting commerce" indicates Congress' intent to regulate to the outer limits of its authority under the Commerce Clause. *See, e.g., Allied-Bruce.* The "involving commerce" phrase, the operative words for the reach of the basic coverage provision in § 2, was at issue in *Allied-Bruce.* That particular phrase had not been interpreted before by this Court. Considering the usual meaning of the word "involving," and the pro-arbitration purposes of the FAA, *Allied-Bruce* held the "word 'involving,' like 'affecting,' signals an intent to exercise Congress' commerce power to the full." Unlike those phrases, however, the general words "in commerce" and the specific phrase "engaged in commerce" are understood to have a more limited reach. In *Allied-Bruce* itself the Court said the words "in commerce" are "often found words of art" that we have not read as expressing congressional intent to regulate to the outer limits of authority under the Commerce Clause.

It is argued that we should assess the meaning of the phrase "engaged in commerce" in a different manner here, because the FAA was enacted when congressional authority to regulate under the commerce power was to a large extent confined by our decisions. When the FAA was enacted in 1925, respondent reasons, the phrase "engaged in commerce" was not a term of art indicating a limited assertion of congressional jurisdiction; to the contrary, it is said, the formulation came close to expressing the outer limits of Congress' power as then understood. Were this mode of interpretation to prevail, we would take into account the scope of the Commerce Clause, as then elaborated by the Court, at the date of the FAA's enactment in order to interpret what the statute means now.

A variable standard for interpreting common, jurisdictional phrases would contradict our earlier cases and bring instability to statutory interpretation. The Court has declined in past cases to afford significance, in construing the meaning of the statutory jurisdictional provisions "in commerce" and "engaged in commerce," to the circumstance that the statute predated shifts in the Court's Commerce Clause cases. . . .

The Court's reluctance to accept contentions that Congress used the words "in commerce" or "engaged in commerce" to regulate to the full extent of its commerce power rests on sound foundation, as it affords objective and consistent significance to the meaning of the words Congress uses when it defines the reach of a statute. To say that the statutory words "engaged in commerce" are subject to variable interpretations depending upon the date of adoption, even a date before the phrase became a term of art, ignores the reason why the formulation became a term of art in the first place: The plain meaning of the words "engaged in commerce" is narrower than the more open-ended formulations "affecting commerce" and "involving commerce." It would be unwieldy for Congress, for the Court, and for litigants to be required to deconstruct statutory Commerce Clause phrases depending upon the year of a particular statutory enactment.

In rejecting the contention that the meaning of the phrase "engaged in commerce" in § 1 of the FAA should be given a broader construction than justified by its evident language simply because it was enacted in 1925 rather than 1938, we do not mean to suggest that statutory jurisdictional formulations "necessarily have a uniform meaning whenever used by Congress." . . . We must, of course, construe the "engaged in commerce" language in the FAA with reference to the statutory context in which it is found and in a manner consistent with the FAA's purpose. These considerations, however, further compel that the § 1 exclusion provision be afforded a narrow construction. As discussed above, the location of the phrase "any other class of workers engaged in . . . commerce" in a residual provision, after specific categories of workers have been enumerated, undermines any attempt to give the provision a sweeping, open-ended construction. And the fact that the provision is contained in a statute that "seeks broadly to overcome judicial hostility to arbitration agreements," which the Court concluded in *Allied-Bruce* counseled in favor of an expansive reading of § 2, gives no reason to abandon the precise reading of a provision that exempts contracts from the FAA's coverage.

In sum, the text of the FAA forecloses the construction of § 1 followed by the Court of Appeals in the case under review, a construction which would exclude all employment contracts from the FAA. While the historical arguments respecting

Congress' understanding of its power in 1925 are not insubstantial, this fact alone does not give us basis to adopt, "by judicial decision rather than amendatory legislation," an expansive construction of the FAA's exclusion provision that goes beyond the meaning of the words Congress used. While it is of course possible to speculate that Congress might have chosen a different jurisdictional formulation had it known that the Court would soon embrace a less restrictive reading of the Commerce Clause, the text of § 1 precludes interpreting the exclusion provision to defeat the language of § 2 as to all employment contracts. Section 1 exempts from the FAA only contracts of employment of transportation workers.

C

As the conclusion we reach today is directed by the text of § 1, we need not assess the legislative history of the exclusion provision. We do note, however, that the legislative record on the § 1 exemption is quite sparse. Respondent points to no language in either committee report addressing the meaning of the provision, nor to any mention of the § 1 exclusion during debate on the FAA on the floor of the House or Senate. Instead, respondent places greatest reliance upon testimony before a Senate subcommittee hearing suggesting that the exception may have been added in response to the objections of the president of the International Seamen's Union of America. Legislative history is problematic even when the attempt is to draw inferences from the intent of duly appointed committees of the Congress. It becomes far more so when we consult sources still more steps removed from the full Congress and speculate upon the significance of the fact that a certain interest group sponsored or opposed particular legislation. We ought not attribute to Congress an official purpose based on the motives of a particular group that lobbied for or against a certain proposal — even assuming the precise intent of the group can be determined, a point doubtful both as a general rule and in the instant case. It is for the Congress, not the courts, to consult political forces and then decide how best to resolve conflicts in the course of writing the objective embodiments of law we know as statutes.

Nor can we accept respondent's argument that our holding attributes an irrational intent to Congress. "Under petitioner's reading of § 1," he contends, "those employment contracts *most* involving interstate commerce, and thus most assuredly within the Commerce Clause power in 1925 . . . are *excluded* from [the] Act's coverage; while those employment contracts having a *less* direct and less certain connection to interstate commerce . . . would come *within* the Act's affirmative coverage and would not be excluded."

We see no paradox in the congressional decision to exempt the workers over whom the commerce power was most apparent. To the contrary, it is a permissible inference that the employment contracts of the classes of workers in § 1 were excluded from the FAA precisely because of Congress' undoubted authority to govern the employment relationships at issue by the enactment of statutes specific to them. By the time the FAA was passed, Congress had already enacted federal legislation providing for the arbitration of disputes between seamen and their employers, *see* Shipping Commissioners Act of 1872. When the FAA was adopted, moreover, grievance procedures existed for railroad employees under federal law, *see* Transportation Act of 1920, and the passage of a more comprehensive statute providing for the mediation and arbitration of railroad labor disputes was imminent, *see* Railway Labor Act of 1926 (repealed). It is reasonable to assume that Congress excluded "seamen" and "railroad employees" from the FAA for the simple reason that it did not wish to unsettle established or developing statutory dispute resolution schemes covering specific workers.

As for the residual exclusion of "any other class of workers engaged in foreign or interstate commerce," Congress' demonstrated concern with transportation workers and their necessary role in the free flow of goods explains the linkage to the two specific, enumerated types of workers identified in the preceding portion of the sentence. It would be rational for Congress to ensure that workers in general would be covered by the provisions of the FAA, while reserving for itself more specific legislation for those engaged in transportation. Indeed, such legislation was soon to follow, with the amendment of the Railway Labor Act in 1936 to include air carriers and their employees.

III

Various *amici*, including the attorneys general of 22 States, object that the reading of the § 1 exclusion provision adopted today intrudes upon the policies of the separate States. They point out that, by requiring arbitration agreements in most employment contracts to be covered by the FAA, the statute in effect pre-empts those state employment laws which restrict or limit the ability of employees and employers to enter into arbitration agreements. It is argued that States should be permitted, pursuant to their traditional role in regulating employment relationships, to prohibit employees like respondent from contracting away their right to pursue state-law discrimination claims in court.

It is not our holding today which is the proper target of this criticism. The line of argument is relevant instead to the Court's decision in *Southland Corp. v. Keating*, holding that Congress intended the FAA to apply in state courts, and to pre-empt state antiarbitration laws to the contrary.

The question of *Southland*'s continuing vitality was given explicit consideration in *Allied-Bruce*, and the Court declined to overrule it. The decision, furthermore, is not directly implicated in this case, which concerns the application of the FAA in a federal, rather than in a state, court. The Court should not chip away at *Southland* by indirection, especially by the adoption of the variable statutory interpretation theory advanced by the respondent in the instant case. Not all of the Justices who join today's holding agreed with *Allied-Bruce, see* 513 U.S. at 284 (SCALIA, J., dissenting); *id.*, at 285 (THOMAS, J., dissenting), but it would be incongruous to adopt, as we did in *Allied-Bruce*, a conventional reading of the FAA's coverage in § 2 in order to implement pro-arbitration policies and an unconventional reading of the reach of § 1 in order to undo the same coverage. In *Allied-Bruce* the Court noted that Congress had not moved to overturn *Southland*, and we now note that it has not done so in response to *Allied-Bruce* itself.

Furthermore, for parties to employment contracts not involving the specific exempted categories set forth in § 1, it is true here, just as it was for the parties to the contract at issue in *Allied-Bruce*, that there are real benefits to the enforcement of arbitration provisions. We have been clear in rejecting the supposition that the advantages of the arbitration process somehow disappear when transferred to the employment context. Arbitration agreements allow parties to avoid the costs of litigation, a benefit that may be of particular importance in employment litigation, which often involves smaller sums of money than disputes concerning commercial contracts. These litigation costs to parties (and the accompanying burden to the Courts) would be compounded by the difficult choice-of-law questions that are often presented in disputes arising from the employment relationship, and the necessity of bifurcation of proceedings in those cases where state law precludes arbitration of certain types of employment claims but not others. The considerable complexity and uncertainty that the construction of § 1 urged by respondent would introduce into the enforceability of arbitration agreements in employment contracts would call into doubt the efficacy of alternative dispute resolution procedures adopted by many of the Nation's employers, in the process undermining the FAA's pro-arbitration purposes and "breeding litigation from a statute that seeks to avoid it." The Court has been quite specific in holding that arbitration agreements can be enforced under the FAA without contravening the policies of congressional enactments giving employees specific protection against discrimination prohibited by federal law; as we noted in *Gilmer*, " 'by agreeing to arbitrate a statutory claim, a party does not forgo the substantive rights afforded by the statute; it only submits to their resolution in an arbitral, rather than a judicial, forum.' " *Gilmer*, of course, involved a federal statute, while the argument here is that a state statute ought not be denied state judicial enforcement while awaiting the outcome of arbitration. That matter, though, was addressed in *Southland* and *Allied-Bruce*, and we do not revisit the question here.

.   .   .

For the foregoing reasons, the judgment of the Court of Appeals for the Ninth Circuit is reversed, and the case is remanded for further proceedings consistent with this opinion.

It is so ordered.

NOTE

The majority in *Circuit City*, by a 5-4 vote, construed the employment exception to the FAA narrowly, as applicable only to transportation workers. What were the key points in the Supreme Court's analysis? The Court reversed the Ninth Circuit, which had construed the exception to exclude all employment contracts from the FAA. Central to the Ninth Circuit's reasoning was its view that the exception would have excluded all employment contracts that were considered to be within the scope of the FAA at the time it was drafted. In other words, because the scope of the Commerce Power had expanded since the FAA was enacted, so, too, should the scope of the exception.

A third view has been asserted by Professor Richard Epstein:

Under current law, the right answer is that the FAA keeps to its 1925 contours, so that employment arbitrations are governed by state law, save to the extent that they involve interstate commerce as that phrase was understood in 1925. By venturing into the waters of partial translation, both sides to the present debate get the arguments confused. First, they wrongly expand the coverage "involving commerce" to keep the FAA in play; then they give the 1925 exemption its 1925 meaning. The second step is right, but the first is wrong. The upshot is that the Court wrongly applied the FAA to these arbitration contracts. Today state law should govern, even if it continues to show the hostility to the executory enforcement of arbitration contracts that the FAA was intended to combat. The right answer is to make Congress redraft the 1925 statute for the post-1937 era.

Richard A. Epstein, *Fidelity Without Translation*, 1 GREEN BAG 2D 21, 29 (1997). Who got it right — the Supreme Court, the Ninth Circuit, or Professor Epstein?

PROBLEM 4.6

An associate in an Iowa law firm enters into a written employment contract with her employer. The employment contract contains an arbitration clause. Part of the attorney's practice consists of representing national companies in litigation all over the country. The attorney asserts a breach of contract claim against the firm, and the firm seeks to have the dispute arbitrated. Iowa law provides:

A provision in a written contract to submit to arbitration a future controversy arising between the parties is valid, enforceable, and irrevocable unless grounds exist at law or in equity for the revocation of the contract. This subsection shall not apply to any of the following:

. . .

b. A contract between employers and employees.

IOWA CODE § 679A.1 (2004). Is the arbitration clause enforceable in state court in Iowa?

PROBLEM 4.7

Another female employee of a Hooters restaurant seeks to litigate her Title VII sexual harassment claim in federal court rather than going to arbitration. The Hooter's arbitration program is the same as the one described in the *Hooters* case. *See* § 2.05[E]. Identify *all* the arguments she might make in trying to avoid arbitration and evaluate the likelihood they will succeed. (In other words, make sure and consider arguments not only based on material in Chapter 4, but also Chapters 1, 2, and 3.)

§ 4.04   FAA PREEMPTION AND GENERALLY APPLICABLE CONTRACT DEFENSES

In *Doctor's Associates, Inc. v. Casarotto*, the Supreme Court stated (in dicta) that "generally applicable contract defenses, such as fraud, duress, or unconscionability, may be applied to invalidate arbitration agreements without contravening § 2." 517 U.S. 681, 686 (1996). The basis for the Court's statement was the "savings clause" of § 2, under which arbitration clauses are "valid, irrevocable, and enforceable, *save upon such grounds as exist at law or in equity for the revocation of any contract.*" 9 U.S.C. § 2 (emphasis added). Under this clause, if a party to an arbitration agreement fraudulently induces the other party to agree to arbitration, for example, a court need not enforce the arbitration agreement. (Recall from Chapter 2, though, that some contract defenses are for the arbitrator rather than the court to decide.)

Are there limits on the ability of courts to invalidate arbitration agreements using generally applicable contract defenses? What if, for example, a court held that arbitration clauses were per se unconscionable because they denied access to the courts? Unconscionabilty would seem to be a generally applicable contract defense — courts have held other types of contract provisions unconscionable, and the Court itself listed unconscionability as a generally applicable contract defense in *Casarotto*. But such a use of unconscionability doctrine would reflect precisely the sort of hostility toward arbitration on which the revocability doctrine and the state statutes discussed previously were based. Accordingly, the Court in *Perry v. Thomas* made clear (albeit again in dicta) that a court may not "rely on the uniqueness of an agreement to arbitrate as a basis for a state-law holding that enforcement would be unconscionable, for this would enable the court to effect what we hold today the state legislature cannot." 482 U.S. 483, 492 n. 9 (1987); *see also Casarotto*, 517 U.S.at 687 n. 3.

So how should a court determine whether a particular application of a generally applicable contract defense to invalidate an arbitration agreement is permitted or preempted? The Supreme Court addressed that issue in the next case.

AT&T MOBILITY LLC v. CONCEPCION
United States Supreme Court
131 S. Ct. 1740 (2011)

JUSTICE SCALIA delivered the opinion of the Court.

Section 2 of the Federal Arbitration Act (FAA) makes agreements to arbitrate "valid, irrevocable, and enforceable, save upon such grounds as exist at law or in equity for the revocation of any contract." We consider whether the FAA prohibits States from conditioning the enforceability of certain arbitration agreements on the availability of classwide arbitration procedures.

I

In February 2002, Vincent and Liza Concepcion entered into an agreement for the sale and servicing of cellular telephones with AT&T Mobility LCC (AT&T). The contract provided for arbitration of all disputes between the parties, but required that claims be brought in the parties' "individual capacity, and not as a plaintiff or class member in any purported class or representative proceeding." . . .

The . . . agreement provides that customers may initiate dispute proceedings by completing a one-page Notice of Dispute form available on AT&T's Web site. AT&T

may then offer to settle the claim; if it does not, or if the dispute is not resolved within 30 days, the customer may invoke arbitration by filing a separate Demand for Arbitration, also available on AT&T's Web site. In the event the parties proceed to arbitration, the agreement specifies that AT&T must pay all costs for nonfrivolous claims; that arbitration must take place in the county in which the customer is billed; that, for claims of $10,000 or less, the customer may choose whether the arbitration proceeds in person, by telephone, or based only on submissions; that either party may bring a claim in small claims court in lieu of arbitration; and that the arbitrator may award any form of individual relief, including injunctions and presumably punitive damages. The agreement, moreover, denies AT&T any ability to seek reimbursement of its attorney's fees, and, in the event that a customer receives an arbitration award greater than AT&T's last written settlement offer, requires AT&T to pay a $7,500 minimum recovery and twice the amount of the claimant's attorney's fees. [The guaranteed minimum recovery was increased in 2009 to $10,000.]

The Concepcions purchased AT&T service, which was advertised as including the provision of free phones; they were not charged for the phones, but they were charged $30.22 in sales tax based on the phones' retail value. In March 2006, the Concepcions filed a complaint against AT&T in the United States District Court for the Southern District of California. The complaint was later consolidated with a putative class action alleging, among other things, that AT&T had engaged in false advertising and fraud by charging sales tax on phones it advertised as free.

In March 2008, AT&T moved to compel arbitration under the terms of its contract with the Concepcions. The Concepcions opposed the motion, contending that the arbitration agreement was unconscionable and unlawfully exculpatory under California law because it disallowed classwide procedures. The District Court denied AT&T's motion. It described AT&T's arbitration agreement favorably, noting, for example, that the informal dispute-resolution process was "quick, easy to use" and likely to "promp[t] full or . . . even excess payment to the customer *without* the need to arbitrate or litigate"; that the $7,500 premium functioned as "a substantial inducement for the consumer to pursue the claim in arbitration" if a dispute was not resolved informally; and that consumers who were members of a class would likely be worse off. Nevertheless, relying on the California Supreme Court's decision in *Discover Bank* v. *Superior Court*, 113 P. 3d 1100 (2005), the court found that the arbitration provision was unconscionable because AT&T had not shown that bilateral arbitration adequately substituted for the deterrent effects of class actions.

The Ninth Circuit affirmed, also finding the provision unconscionable under California law as announced in *Discover Bank*. It also held that the *Discover Bank* rule was not preempted by the FAA because that rule was simply "a refinement of the unconscionability analysis applicable to contracts generally in California." . . .

We granted certiorari . . . .

    . . .

III

A

The Concepcions argue that the *Discover Bank* rule, given its origins in California's unconscionability doctrine and California's policy against exculpation, is a ground that "exist[s] at law or in equity for the revocation of any contract" under FAA § 2. Moreover, they argue that even if we construe the *Discover Bank* rule as a prohibition on collective-action waivers rather than simply an application of unconscionability, the rule would still be applicable to all dispute-resolution contracts, since California prohibits waivers of class litigation as well.

When state law prohibits outright the arbitration of a particular type of claim, the analysis is straightforward: The conflicting rule is displaced by the FAA. But the inquiry becomes more complex when a doctrine normally thought to be generally applicable, such as duress or, as relevant here, unconscionability, is alleged to have been applied in a fashion that disfavors arbitration. In *Perry* v. *Thomas*, 482 U.S. 483 (1987), for example, we noted that the FAA's preemptive effect might extend even to grounds traditionally thought to exist " 'at law or in equity for the revocation of any contract.' " We said that a court may not "rely on the uniqueness of an agreement to arbitrate as a basis for a state-law holding that enforcement would be unconscionable, for this would enable the court to effect what . . . the state legislature cannot."

An obvious illustration of this point would be a case finding unconscionable or unenforceable as against public policy consumer arbitration agreements that fail to provide for judicially monitored discovery. The rationalizations for such a holding are neither difficult to imagine nor different in kind from those articulated in *Discover Bank.* A court might reason that no consumer would knowingly waive his right to full discovery, as this would enable companies to hide their wrongdoing. Or the court might simply say that such agreements are exculpatory — restricting discovery would be of greater benefit to the company than the consumer, since the former is more likely to be sued than to sue. And, the reasoning would continue, because such a rule applies the general principle of unconscionability or public-policy disapproval of exculpatory agreements, it is applicable to "any" contract and thus preserved by § 2 of the FAA. In practice, of course, the rule would have a disproportionate impact on arbitration agreements; but it would presumably apply to contracts purporting to restrict discovery in litigation as well.

Other examples are easy to imagine. The same argument might apply to a rule classifying as unconscionable arbitration agreements that fail to abide by the Federal Rules of Evidence, or that disallow an ultimate disposition by a jury (perhaps termed "a panel of twelve lay arbitrators" to help avoid preemption). Such examples are not fanciful, since the judicial hostility towards arbitration that prompted the FAA had manifested itself in "a great variety" of "devices and formulas" declaring arbitration against public policy. And although these statistics are not definitive, it is worth noting that California's courts have been more likely to hold contracts to arbitrate unconscionable than other contracts.

The Concepcions suggest that all this is just a parade of horribles, and no genuine worry. "Rules aimed at destroying arbitration" or "demanding procedures incompatible with arbitration," they concede, "would be preempted by the FAA because they cannot sensibly be reconciled with Section 2." The "grounds" available under § 2's saving clause, they admit, "should not be construed to include a State's mere preference for procedures that are incompatible with arbitration and 'would wholly eviscerate arbitration agreements.' "

We largely agree. Although § 2's saving clause preserves generally applicable contract defenses, nothing in it suggests an intent to preserve state-law rules that stand as an obstacle to the accomplishment of the FAA's objectives. . . .

We differ with the Concepcions only in the application of this analysis to the matter before us. We do not agree that rules requiring judicially monitored discovery or adherence to the Federal Rules of Evidence are "a far cry from this case." The overarching purpose of the FAA, evident in the text of §§ 2, 3, and 4, is to ensure the enforcement of arbitration agreements according to their terms so as to facilitate streamlined proceedings. Requiring the availability of classwide arbitration interferes with fundamental attributes of arbitration and thus creates a scheme inconsistent with the FAA.

B

The "principal purpose" of the FAA is to "ensur[e] that private arbitration agreements are enforced according to their terms." *Volt.* . . . The point of affording parties discretion in designing arbitration processes is to allow for efficient, streamlined procedures tailored to the type of dispute. . . . Thus, in *Preston* v. *Ferrer,* holding preempted a state-law rule requiring exhaustion of administrative remedies before arbitration, we said: "A prime objective of an agreement to arbitrate is to achieve 'streamlined proceedings and expeditious results,' " which objective would be "frustrated" by requiring a dispute to be heard by an agency first. That rule, we said, would "at the least, hinder speedy resolution of the controversy."

California's *Discover Bank* rule similarly interferes with arbitration. Although the rule does not *require* classwide arbitration, it allows any party to a consumer contract to demand it *ex post.* The rule is limited to adhesion contracts, but the times in which consumer contracts were anything other than adhesive are long past.[6] The rule also requires that damages be predictably small, and that the consumer allege a scheme to cheat consumers. The former requirement, however, is toothless and malleable (the Ninth Circuit has held that damages of $4,000 are sufficiently small, and the latter has no limiting effect, as all that is required is an allegation. Consumers remain free to bring and resolve their disputes on a bilateral basis under *Discover Bank,* and some may well do so; but there is little incentive for lawyers to arbitrate on behalf of individuals when they may do so for a class and reap far higher fees in the process. And faced with inevitable class arbitration,

---

[6] Of course States remain free to take steps addressing the concerns that attend contracts of adhesion — for example, requiring class-action-waiver provisions in adhesive arbitration agreements to be highlighted. Such steps cannot, however, conflict with the FAA or frustrate its purpose to ensure that private arbitration agreements are enforced according to their terms.

companies would have less incentive to continue resolving potentially duplicative claims on an individual basis.

Although we have had little occasion to examine classwide arbitration, our decision in *Stolt-Nielsen* is instructive. In that case we held that an arbitration panel exceeded its power under § 10(a)(4) of the FAA by imposing class procedures based on policy judgments rather than the arbitration agreement itself or some background principle of contract law that would affect its interpretation. We then held that the agreement at issue, which was silent on the question of class procedures, could not be interpreted to allow them because the "changes brought about by the shift from bilateral arbitration to class-action arbitration" are "fundamental." This is obvious as a structural matter: Classwide arbitration includes absent parties, necessitating additional and different procedures and involving higher stakes. Confidentiality becomes more difficult. And while it is theoretically possible to select an arbitrator with some expertise relevant to the class-certification question, arbitrators are not generally knowledgeable in the often-dominant procedural aspects of certification, such as the protection of absent parties. The conclusion follows that class arbitration, to the extent it is manufactured by *Discover Bank* rather than consensual, is inconsistent with the FAA.

First, the switch from bilateral to class arbitration sacrifices the principal advantage of arbitration — its informality — and makes the process slower, more costly, and more likely to generate procedural morass than final judgment. . . .

Second, class arbitration *requires* procedural formality. The AAA's rules governing class arbitrations mimic the Federal Rules of Civil Procedure for class litigation. And while parties can alter those procedures by contract, an alternative is not obvious. . . .

We find it unlikely that in passing the FAA Congress meant to leave the disposition of these procedural requirements to an arbitrator. Indeed, class arbitration was not even envisioned by Congress when it passed the FAA in 1925; as the California Supreme Court admitted in *Discover Bank*, class arbitration is a "relatively recent development." And it is at the very least odd to think that an arbitrator would be entrusted with ensuring that third parties' due process rights are satisfied.

Third, class arbitration greatly increases risks to defendants. Informal procedures do of course have a cost: The absence of multilayered review makes it more likely that errors will go uncorrected. Defendants are willing to accept the costs of these errors in arbitration, since their impact is limited to the size of individual disputes, and presumably outweighed by savings from avoiding the courts. But when damages allegedly owed to tens of thousands of potential claimants are aggregated and decided at once, the risk of an error will often become unacceptable. Faced with even a small chance of a devastating loss, defendants will be pressured into settling questionable claims. Other courts have noted the risk of "in terrorem" settlements that class actions entail, and class arbitration would be no different.

Arbitration is poorly suited to the higher stakes of class litigation. In litigation, a defendant may appeal a certification decision on an interlocutory basis and, if unsuccessful, may appeal from a final judgment as well. Questions of law are reviewed *de novo* and questions of fact for clear error. In contrast, 9 U.S.C. § 10 allows a court to vacate an arbitral award *only* where the award "was procured by corruption, fraud, or undue means"; "there was evident partiality or corruption in the arbitrators"; "the arbitrators were guilty of misconduct in refusing to postpone the hearing . . . or in refusing to hear evidence pertinent and material to the controversy[,] or of any other misbehavior by which the rights of any party have been prejudiced"; or if the "arbitrators exceeded their powers, or so imperfectly executed them that a mutual, final, and definite award . . . was not made." The AAA rules do authorize judicial review of certification decisions, but this review is unlikely to have much effect given these limitations; review under § 10 focuses on misconduct rather than mistake. And parties may not contractually expand the grounds or nature of judicial review. *Hall Street Assocs.* We find it hard to believe that defendants would bet the company with no effective means of review, and even harder to believe that Congress would have intended to allow state courts to force such a decision.

. . .

The dissent claims that class proceedings are necessary to prosecute small-dollar claims that might otherwise slip through the legal system. But States cannot require a procedure that is inconsistent with the FAA, even if it is desirable for unrelated reasons. Moreover, the claim here was most unlikely to go unresolved. As noted earlier, the arbitration agreement provides that AT&T will pay claimants a minimum of $7,500 and twice their attorney's fees if they obtain an arbitration award greater than AT&T's last settlement offer. The District Court found this scheme sufficient to provide incentive for the individual prosecution of meritorious claims that are not immediately settled, and the Ninth Circuit admitted that aggrieved customers who filed claims would be "essentially guarantee[d]" to be made whole. Indeed, the District Court concluded that the Concepcions were *better off* under their arbitration agreement with AT&T than they would have been as participants in a class action, which "could take months, if not years, and which may merely yield an opportunity to submit a claim for recovery of a small percentage of a few dollars."

*   *   *

Because it "stands as an obstacle to the accomplishment and execution of the full purposes and objectives of Congress," California's *Discover Bank* rule is preempted by the FAA. The judgment of the Ninth Circuit is reversed, and the case is remanded for further proceedings consistent with this opinion.

It is so ordered.

JUSTICE THOMAS, concurring.

. . . Section 2 provides that "[a] written provision in . . . a contract . . . to settle by arbitration a controversy thereafter arising out of such contract . . . shall be valid, irrevocable, and enforceable, save upon such grounds as exist at law or in equity for the revocation of any contract." Significantly, the statute does not parallel the words "valid, irrevocable, and enforceable" by referencing the grounds as exist for the "invalidation, revocation, or nonenforcement" of any contract. Nor does the statute use a different word or phrase entirely that might arguably encompass validity, revocability, and enforceability. The use of only "revocation" and the conspicuous omission of "invalidation" and "nonenforcement" suggest that the exception does not include all defenses applicable to any contract but rather some subset of those defenses.

. . .

Examining the broader statutory scheme, § 4 can be read to clarify the scope of § 2's exception to the enforcement of arbitration agreements. When a party seeks to enforce an arbitration agreement in federal court, § 4 requires that "upon being satisfied that the making of the agreement for arbitration or the failure to comply therewith is not in issue," the court must order arbitration "in accordance with the terms of the agreement."

Reading §§ 2 and 4 harmoniously, the "grounds . . . for the revocation" preserved in § 2 would mean grounds related to the making of the agreement. This would require enforcement of an agreement to arbitrate unless a party successfully asserts a defense concerning the formation of the agreement to arbitrate, such as fraud, duress, or mutual mistake. Contract defenses unrelated to the making of the agreement — such as public policy — could not be the basis for declining to enforce an arbitration clause.

II

Under this reading, the question here would be whether California's *Discover Bank* rule relates to the making of an agreement. I think it does not.

. . .

The court's analysis and conclusion that the arbitration agreement was exculpatory reveals that the *Discover Bank* rule does not concern the making of the arbitration agreement. Exculpatory contracts are a paradigmatic example of contracts that will not be enforced because of public policy. . . . Refusal to enforce a contract for public-policy reasons does not concern whether the contract was properly made.

. . .

[Dissenting opinion of JUSTICE BREYER, joined by JUSTICES GINSBURG, SOTOMAYOR and KAGAN, omitted.]

NOTES

1. Will *Concepcion* "gut[] class actions," as the New York Times stated in an editorial after the decision? *Gutting Class Actions*, N.Y. TIMES (May, 12, 2011), *available at* http://www.nytimes.com/2011/05/13/opinion/13fri1.html. Are all consumer and employment contracts now likely to include arbitration clauses coupled with class arbitration waivers? If so, does that mean the decision is a "devastating blow to consumer [and employee] rights?" Are there other remedies available to consumers and employees? Are those remedies practical?

2. What about the statement in footnote 6 that "States remain free to take steps addressing the concerns that attend contracts of adhesion — for example, requiring class-action-waiver provisions in adhesive arbitration agreements to be high-lighted"? Is that statement consistent with the Court's decision in *Casarotto*, which held that a requirement that arbitration agreements be conspicuous was preempted by the FAA?

3. Does it matter whether the arbitration clause includes provisions like those in the AT&T Mobility clause, giving consumers incentives to bring claims on an individual basis? So far, at least, most lower courts applying *Concepcion* have not limited the holding to such clauses. *See, e.g.*, Bellows v. Midland Credit Mgmt., Inc., 2011 U.S. Dist. LEXIS 48237, at *11 (S.D. Cal. May 4, 2011); Day v. Persels & Assocs., LLC, 2011 U.S. Dist. LEXIS 49231, at *15-*16 (M.D. Fla. May 9, 2011); Zarandi v. Alliance Data Sys. Corp., 2011 U.S. Dist. LEXIS 54602, at *4-*5 (C.D. Cal. May 9, 2011). *But see* Feeney v. Dell, Inc., 28 Mass. L. Rep. 652, at *26-*30 (Mass. Super. Ct. 2011) (distinguishing *Concepcion* on ground that unlike the AT&T Mobility clause in *Concepcion*, "[t]he Dell Arbitration Clause provides no incentives and simply requires arbitration of all disputes, even those that could not possibly justify the expense in light of the amount in controversy").

4. After *Concepcion*, can courts still hold other provisions in arbitration agreements unconscionable — provisions such as punitive damages waivers, exceedingly short time limits for filing claims, and the like? Or would application of the unconscionability doctrine to those provisions in arbitration clauses be pre-empted as well? For one court's answer, take another look at *Samaniego v. Empire Today, LLC* in § 2.05[C].

5. What if the case involves a federal statutory claim? Can a court refuse to enforce an arbitration clause with a class arbitration waiver on the ground that the clause would prevent consumers from vindicating their federal statutory rights? *Compare* In re Am. Exp. Merchants' Litig., 667 F.3d 204, 218-19 (2d Cir. 2012) (finding arbitration clause unenforceable and distinguishing *Concepcion* because "the class action waiver in this case precludes plaintiffs from enforcing their statutory rights"), *cert. granted sub nom.*, Am. Express Co. v. Italian Colors Rest. 2012 LEXIS 8697 (U.S. Nov. 9, 2012) *with* Coneff v. AT&T Corp., 673 F.3d 1155, 1158-59 & nn. 2-3 (9th Cir. 2012) (applying *Concepcion* to reject argument that arbitration clause with class arbitration waiver prevented claimants from vindicating their federal statutory rights).

6. Other possible limits on *Concepcion* might come from other federal or state statutes. *See, e.g.*, D.R. Horton, Inc., 357 N.L.R.B. No. 184 (2012) (holding that an employer violates the NLRA "when it requires employees covered by the Act, as a condition of their employment, to sign an agreement that precludes them from filing joint, class, or collective claims addressing their wages, hours or other working conditions against the employer in any forum, arbitral or judicial"; such an agreement "unlawfully restricts employees' Section 7 right to engage in concerted action for mutual aid or protection, notwithstanding the Federal Arbitration Act (FAA), which generally makes employment-related arbitration agreements judi-cially enforceable"); Oliveira v. Citicorp N. Am., Inc., 2012 U.S. Dist. LEXIS 69573, at *7 (M.D. Fla. May 18, 2012) (citing district court cases following and refusing to

follow *D.H. Horton*). *Compare* Brown v. Ralphs Grocery Co., 128 Cal. Rptr. 3d 854, 863 (Cal. App. 2011) (holding that *Concepcion* "does not address a statute such as the PAGA [Private Attorney General Act], which is a mechanism by which the state itself can enforce state labor laws, because the employee suing under the PAGA 'does so as the proxy or agent of the state's labor law enforcement agencies' ") *with* Quevedo v. Macy's, Inc., 798 F. Supp. 2d 1122, 1142 (C.D. Cal. 2011) (holding "that [claimant's] PAGA claim is arbitrable, and that the arbitration agreement's provision barring him from bringing that claim on behalf of other employees is enforceable," relying on *Concepcion*); Iskanian v. CLS Transport. L.A., LLC, 142 Cal. Rptr. 3d 372, 384 (Cal. App. 2012) ("Respectfully, we disagree with the majority's holding in *Brown*"); *see also* Kilgore v. KeyBank, N.A., 673 F.3d 947, 959-63 (9th Cir. 2012) (holding based on *Concepcion* that "California's rule against arbitration of public injunctive claims is preempted by federal law"), *rehearing en banc granted*, 2012 U.S. App. LEXIS 19928 (9th Cir. Sept. 21, 2012).

7. Does *Concepcion* apply in state courts? Justice Thomas, who was the fifth vote in favor of finding preemption in *Concepcion*, has consistently dissented from decisions applying the FAA in state court. Had the lower court in *Concepcion* been a state court rather than a federal court the case might have come out differently. Can a state court refuse to apply *Concepcion* based on that possibility, even though the Court as a whole has consistently rejected Justice Thomas's position and held that the FAA does apply in state court?

8. What do you think of Justice Thomas's alternative reading of Section 2? As a textual matter, he certainly is right that the statute uses the word "revocation" in the savings clause without adding "invalid" or "unenforceable." Is unconscionability a ground for revoking a contract? Do you think Congress intended the savings clause to be narrower in reach than the rest of Section 2?

9. In response to *Concepcion*, Representative Hank Johnson and Senator Al Franken reintroduced into Congress the Arbitration Fairness Act, reprinted in the Documentary Supplement. Given the current composition of Congress, however, passage of the AFA is unlikely.

A more likely source of regulatory change is the Consumer Financial Protection Bureau (CFPB), created by the Dodd-Frank Wall Street Reform and Consumer Protection Act, Pub. L. No. 111-203 (2010). In Dodd-Frank, Congress directs the CFPB to study the use of pre-dispute arbitration clauses in consumer financial services contracts, *id.* § 1028(a), and then authorizes it to regulate such clauses if in the public interest and for the protection of consumers, *id.* § 1028(b). The Act specifies that the findings in the rulemaking "shall be consistent with the study conducted under subsection (a)." *Id.*

PROBLEM 4.8

In an arbitration agreement governed by the FAA, which of the following state common law rules would be preempted by federal law?

(a) Pre-dispute arbitration clauses are void as against the public policy of the state.

(b) Pre-dispute arbitration clauses are per se unconscionable unless they permit an individual to reject arbitration after a dispute arises.

(c) Before a consumer can be found to have assented to an arbitration clause, the clause must be conspicuous.

(d) A class arbitration waiver in an arbitration clause is unconscionable and stricken from the clause. As a result, the case is to proceed to class arbitration.

(e) An arbitration clause with a class arbitration waiver is unconscionable and the entire arbitration clause is invalidated. As a result, the case is to proceed as a putative class action in court.

(f) An arbitration clause with a punitive damages waiver is unconscionable and the entire arbitration clause is invalidated.

§ 4.05 EXCEPTIONS AND FURTHER APPLICATIONS

This part examines how FAA preemption applies in several additional contexts. First, it considers a possible exception to FAA preemption for insurance contracts. Second, it looks at how courts have dealt with state legislation that does not invalidate the arbitration agreement but merely regulates the arbitration process. Third, it examines state court procedures for enforcing arbitration agreements to see what sorts of preemption issues they may raise.

SOUTHERN PIONEER LIFE INSURANCE CO. v. THOMAS
Supreme Court of Arkansas
2011 Ark. 490 (2011)

KAREN R. BAKER, JUSTICE.

Appellant Southern Pioneer Life Insurance Co. ("Southern Pioneer") appeals the Greene County Circuit Court's denial of its motion to compel arbitration. . . . The circuit court denied Southern Pioneer's motion to compel arbitration after finding that the dispute was governed by Arkansas Code Annotated section 16–108–201(b), thereby preventing Southern Pioneer, as an insurer, from compelling appellees Danny and Irma Thomas to arbitrate a dispute under an insurance policy. . . . We affirm.

On February 19, 2007, appellees executed a credit application ("Application") and a retail installment contract ("RIC") for the purchase of a 2006 Chrysler PT Cruiser, which was financed by Chrysler Financial. The Application contained an arbitration agreement. . . . The RIC provided an option for appellees to purchase credit-life insurance coverage with Southern Pioneer by checking a box on the face of the form. The entire premium for the optional insurance coverage amounted to $1,450.54 and was financed with the purchase price of the vehicle into the life of the loan. The loan was set to expire on February 19, 2013, but appellees paid the loan off early on July 19, 2007.

On July 8, 2009, appellees, on their own behalf and on behalf of other putative class members, brought suit seeking the refund of unearned credit-life insurance premiums from the date they paid off their loan until the original maturity date of the loan, when the insurance was set to terminate. Southern Pioneer filed a motion to compel arbitration on September 23, 2010, attempting to force appellees to arbitrate their claims under the terms of the arbitration agreement that was a part of the Application. Southern Pioneer asserted that the suit involved a breach of the RIC and not the insurance contract. After a hearing the circuit court denied the motion to compel arbitration.

. . . On appeal, Southern Pioneer urges that [appellee's] claim "arise[s] out of or relate[s] to [the] Application, an installment sale contract or lease agreement, or any resulting transaction or relationship (including any such relationship with third parties who do not sign this Application and Contract of Arbitration)[.]" Further, Southern Pioneer points out that the language of the Application's arbitration agreement is broad and clearly evidences the intent of the parties to arbitrate disputes arising between the signatories and potential third parties. Southern Pioneer asserts that all of the claims for which appellees seek redress arise from the terms of the RIC, which developed from the Application. Appellees counter that all of their claims arise out of the insurance contract, which is not subject to arbitration under the AUAA and the McCarran-Ferguson Act, 15 U.S.C. §§ 1011 et seq. . . .

. . .

. . . Arkansas Code Annotated section 16–108–201(b) provided, at the time this cause of action arose, as follows:

> (1) A written provision to submit to arbitration any controversy there-after arising between the parties bound by the terms of the writing is valid, enforceable, and irrevocable, save upon such grounds as exist for the revocation of any contract.

> (2) This subsection shall have no application to personal injury or tort matters, employer-employee disputes, *nor to any insured or beneficiary under any insurance policy* or annuity contract. (emphasis supplied).

The FAA would ordinarily preempt conflicting state law, but the McCarran-Ferguson Act operates to bar application of the FAA and leave the regulation of the insurance industry to the states:

> No Act of Congress shall be construed to invalidate, impair or supersede any law enacted by any State for the purpose of regulating the business of insurance . . . unless such Act specifically relates to the business of insurance[.]

15 U.S.C. § 1012(b). The McCarran-Ferguson Act preserves state regulation of the insurance industry from any federal intrusion, subject only to certain express exceptions.[2] Under the McCarran-Ferguson Act, reverse preemption occurs if (1) the federal statute at issue does not specifically relate to the business of insurance; (2) the state law was enacted for the purpose of regulating the business of

---

[2] There is an important exception to the McCarran-Ferguson Act. Notably, the McCarran-Ferguson Act does not permit preemption where the federal law "specifically relates to the business of insurance." *See* 15 U.S.C. § 1012(b). No such exception applies here.

insurance; and (3) application of the federal statute will invalidate, impair, or supersede the state law. . . .

The FAA does not specifically relate to the business of insurance; therefore, the first factor is present.

As to the second factor . . . , the Supreme Court has provided a framework for resolving whether state law "regulates insurance." UNUM Life Ins. Co. of Am. v. Ward, 526 U.S. 358 (1999). First, the court must consider whether "from a 'common-sense view of the matter,' the contested prescription regulates insurance." Then, we must consider three factors:

> [F]irst, whether the practice has the effect of transferring or spreading a policyholder's risk; second, whether the practice is an integral part of the policy relationship between the insurer and the insured; and third, whether the practice is limited to entities within the insurance industry.

Id. While the three factors are relevant, they are merely guideposts, and all three need not be satisfied to save a state law from preemption.

Here, common sense dictates that section 16–108–201(b)(2) regulates the business of insurance by exempting arbitration agreements in insurance contracts from enforcement.

Next, we turn to the three factors of the framework. First, section 16–108–201(b)(2) affects policyholder risk by transferring or spreading the risk "by introducing the possibility of jury verdicts into the process for resolving disputed claims." Second, section 16–108–201(b)(2) regulates an integral part of the relationship between an insurer and insured by invalidating an otherwise mandatory insurance-contract term that would allow either party to compel arbitration of disputes arising thereunder. Third, section 16–108–201(b)(2) is *not* limited to entities within the insurance industry as it also exempts tort and employment claims from arbitration. However, all three factors do not need to be satisfied to resolve this question, and we hold that section 16–108–201(b)(2) regulates insurance within the meaning of the McCarran-Ferguson Act.

The third and final factor . . . is whether application of the federal statute will invalidate, impair, or supersede the state law. Application of the FAA to enforce the arbitration agreement between Southern Pioneer and appellees would clearly invalidate the operation of section 16–108–201(b)(2). Accordingly, we conclude that the McCarran-Ferguson Act does not allow the FAA to preempt section 16–108–201(b)(2), and section 16–108–201(b)(2) prohibits arbitration under these facts.

. . .

Affirmed.

COURTNEY HUDSON HENRY, JUSTICE, concurring.

I concur with the majority's opinion that the McCarranFerguson Act (MFA) reverse-preempts the Federal Arbitration Act (FAA) . . . However, the analysis does not end there. I write separately to emphasize that, after concluding that the

MFA reverse-preempts the FAA, we must apply Arkansas Code Annotated section 16–108–201(b) to the facts of this case.

. . .

I agree with the circuit court's ruling that section 16–108–201(b) governs this dispute. Based on the plain language of section 16–108–201, arbitration does not apply to "any insured or beneficiary under any insurance policy[.]" "Any insurance policy" includes appellees' credit-life insurance policy from Southern Pioneer for which they paid a single one-time premium of $1450.54, as reflected in the retail-installment-sales contract (RISC) containing the arbitration clause. I would hold that section 16–108–201 dictates that Southern Pioneer cannot compel arbitration of the insurance matter indirectly through the arbitration clause of the RISC.

This interpretation comports with the legislative intent of section 16–108–201. . . . Here, the General Assembly's intent was made quite clear by the emergency clause in Act 616 of 1981 that the Act "shall have no application to . . . any insured or beneficiary under any insurance policy[.]" . . . Thus, section 16–108–201 expresses the public policy of Arkansas that disputes relating to "any insurance polic[ies]" are not arbitrable. For these reasons, I would affirm the circuit court's ruling on this basis.

NOTES

1.   The vast majority of courts agree with the Arkansas Supreme Court that the McCarran-Ferguson Act preserves from FAA preemption (or, as the Arkansas court says, "reverse preempts") state laws that regulate the enforceability of arbitration clauses in insurance contracts. *See* American Bankers Ins. Co. of Florida v. Inman, 436 F.3d 490, 494 (5th Cir. 2006); Standard Sec. Life Ins. Co. v. West, 267 F.3d 821, 823 (8th Cir. 2001); Mutual Reinsurance Bureau v. Great Plains Mut. Ins. Co., 969 F.2d 931, 934-35 (10th Cir.), *cert. denied*, 506 U.S. 1001 (1992); McKnight v. Chicago Title Ins. Co., 358 F.3d 854, 859 (11th Cir. 2004); Allen v. Pacheco, 71 P.3d 375, 384 (Colo. 2003), *cert. denied*, 540 U.S. 1212 (2004); Love v. Money Tree, Inc., 614 S.E.2d 47, 50 (Ga. 2005); Friday v. Trinity Universal, 939 P.2d 869, 872-73 (Kan. 1997).

2.   One exception is the Vermont Supreme Court, which has held that the McCarran-Ferguson Act does not protect its state arbitration law from preemption. The Vermont Arbitration Act (VAA) provides that it "applies to all arbitration agreements to the extent not inconsistent with the laws of the United States," but that it "does not apply to . . . arbitration agreements contained in a contract of insurance." 12 Vt. Stat. Ann. § 5653. According to the court:

> The more difficult hurdle for plaintiffs is whether the VAA "regulates" the business of insurance. Implied in our [precedent] . . . is the holding that our common-law rule making arbitration agreements revocable up to the time of award is not a state law regulating the business of insurance. All the insurance contract exclusion from the VAA has done is to allow insurance arbitration agreements to continue to be governed by the common law.

Thus, the VAA regulates those arbitration agreements subject to its terms. Those that are excluded are not regulated by the VAA.

Little v. Allstate Ins. Co., 705 A.2d 538, 540-41 (1997). In other words, the Vermont Arbitration Act was not enacted for the purposes of regulating insurance; to the contrary, by its terms it excluded insurance contracts from its reach. Is the Arkansas Supreme Court's decision in *Thomas* consistent with *Little*? What if the Vermont court had construed the VAA exclusion as impliedly making arbitration agreements unenforceable in insurance contracts? Would that have changed its application of the McCarran-Ferguson Act?

KEYSTONE, INC. v. TRIAD SYSTEMS CORP.
Montana Supreme Court
971 P.2d 1240 (1998)

JUSTICE TERRY N. TRIEWEILER delivered the opinion of the Court.

¶ 1 Keystone, Inc., filed in the District Court of the Thirteenth Judicial District in Yellowstone County a complaint against Triad Systems Corp. for alleged breach of contract and other duties. In accordance with one of the contract provisions, Triad demanded that the parties arbitrate their dispute in California. Keystone filed a motion to compel arbitration in Montana, and Triad filed a cross-motion to compel arbitration in California. The District Court denied Keystone's motion and ordered the parties to submit to arbitration in California. Keystone appeals. We reverse the order of the District Court.

¶ 2 The sole issue on appeal is whether the contract provision which requires arbitration in California is void because it violates § 28-2-708, MCA, or § 27-5-323, MCA.

FACTUAL BACKGROUND

¶ 3 Triad Systems Corporation is a California corporation engaged in the sale of computer hardware, software, and support systems. Keystone, Inc., is a Montana corporation engaged in the distribution of automotive parts and supplies in Billings, Montana.

¶ 4 In November 1994, Keystone and Triad entered into a contract by which Keystone agreed to purchase a computer system from Triad for approximately $250,000. The system allegedly failed to work, and Triad was unable to correct the problems to Keystone's satisfaction. Keystone requested that Triad take back its computers and that it refund Keystone's payment. Triad refused.

¶ 5 In November 1996, Keystone filed a complaint against Triad in the District Court in which it alleged breach of warranty, breach of contract, negligence, and negligent misrepresentation. In response, Triad contended that pursuant to the parties' contract, they were required to arbitrate any dispute between them before the American Arbitration Association (AAA) in San Francisco, California. Keystone notified Triad that it was willing to arbitrate the matter before the AAA, but only in Montana.

¶ 6 In reliance on § 28-2-708, MCA, Keystone moved the District Court to compel arbitration in Montana. Triad filed a cross-motion to compel arbitration in California in accordance with the terms of the contract. The District Court reasoned that § 28-2-708, MCA, was preempted by the Federal Arbitration Act (FAA), and that as such, its only choice was to enforce the parties' agreement, which called for the parties to arbitrate in California. Accordingly, it granted Triad's motion to compel arbitration in California.

DISCUSSION

. . .

¶ 16 The basis of the parties' disagreement was the issue of whether § 28-2-708, MCA, applies to the arbitration provision in their contract and renders void the forum selection clause that requires the parties to arbitrate in California. Section 28-2-708, MCA, provides:

> Every stipulation or condition in a contract by which any party thereto is restricted from enforcing his rights under the contract by the usual proceedings in the ordinary tribunals or which limits the time within which he may thus enforce his rights is void. This section does not affect the validity of an agreement enforceable under Title 27, Chapter 5.

Keystone contends that, based on the statute, any forum selection clause that would require Montana residents to resolve disputes outside Montana when the usual procedure would be to resolve the dispute in Montana, is void, and that the statute applies to arbitration provisions, as well as other contracts. Triad, on the other hand, asserts that the statute does not apply to arbitration agreements. In addition to the preemption position taken by the District Court, Triad relies on what it contends is an express exclusion in the last sentence of the statute and on its assumption that arbitration is not a usual proceeding in the ordinary tribunals.

¶ 17 Section 28-2-708, MCA, has historically been applied for two distinct purposes: (1) to protect Montana residents from having to litigate outside of Montana; and (2) to invalidate pre-dispute arbitration agreements.

¶ 18 The first purpose reflects the fundamental public policy of this state to protect the "substantive rights of Montana residents to seek redress in the courts of [Montana]." Accordingly, § 28-2-708, MCA, has been applied to invalidate forum selection clauses that would have the effect of forcing Montana residents to litigate disputes outside of Montana. . . .

. . .

¶ 20 We conclude that § 27-5-323, MCA, provides the same protection in th[e] context [of arbitration clauses]. That statute, which pertains specifically to arbitration agreements, provides in relevant part as follows:

> No agreement concerning venue involving a resident of this state is valid unless the agreement requires that arbitration occur within the state of Montana. This requirement may only be waived upon the advice of counsel as evidenced by counsel's signature thereto.

¶ 21 There is no indication from the face of the contract at issue that the right to have disputes arbitrated in Montana was waived based on the advice of counsel.

¶ 22 Accordingly, we hold that the provision at issue which requires that a Montana resident arbitrate disputes related to a contract to be performed in Montana at a location outside Montana is void because it violates Montana law.

¶ 23 Our only remaining inquiry is whether Montana's controlling statutory law is preempted by the FAA which unquestionably applies. . . . The FAA generally preempts state law which restricts the application of arbitration agreements. However, when a state law does not conflict with the FAA so as to frustrate the objectives of Congress, it is not necessarily preempted. State law may be applied in spite of the FAA's preemptive effect "*if* that law arose to govern issues concerning the validity, revocability, and enforceability of contracts generally."

¶ 24 Keystone contends that § 28-2-708, MCA, governs the enforceability of contracts generally and, by logical extension, argues that applying the same restriction to arbitration agreements does not frustrate or conflict with the FAA. Therefore, it contends that the FAA should not preempt the statutes in question. Triad, like the District Court, relies on the general preemptive power of the FAA to avoid the effect of Montana's statutes. Upon review of the relevant statutes and case law, however, we conclude that the FAA does not preempt § 27-5-323, MCA.

¶ 25 In [*Doctor's Associates, Inc. v.*] *Casarotto*, the U.S. Supreme Court clarified the kind of state laws which are preempted by the FAA. . . . [W]e read *Casarotto* to stand for the proposition that a state law may not "place arbitration clauses on an unequal 'footing' " from general contract provisions.

¶ 26 As we stated above, § 28-2-708, MCA, invalidates choice of forum provisions in contracts generally. Section 27-5-323, MCA, does the same to arbitration agreements. Montana law, therefore, does not distinguish between forum selection clauses which are part of contracts generally and forum selection clauses found in agreements to arbitrate. Such a distinction, if one existed, would certainly manifest the kind of unequal treatment that *Casarotto* prohibits. The lack of such a distinction is evidence that the statute does not conflict with the FAA.

¶ 27 We are further persuaded that Montana's statutes are consistent with the FAA because neither statute nullifies either party's obligation to arbitrate their dispute. Rather, they preserve the obligation to arbitrate and constitute no more of an intrusion than on any other general contract entered into in this State. That ultimately distinguishes this case from those cases relied on by Triad in which application of the respective state laws invalidated altogether the parties' agreements to arbitrate.

¶ 28 The mere fact that in this case the statutes limit in part the enforceability of the agreement and nullify an agreement to resolve the parties' disputes in California does not create a conflict with the purpose of the FAA.

¶ 29 Accordingly, we hold that neither § 28-2-708, MCA, nor § 27-5-323, MCA, are preempted by the FAA. In addition, we hold that the combined effect of these statutes, as applied to the arbitration provision in this case, invalidates only that portion of the agreement which requires Keystone to arbitrate the dispute outside of Montana. We reverse the order of the District Court that requires the parties to arbitrate in California, and order that arbitration occur in Montana.

¶ 30 This case is remanded to the District Court for further proceedings consistent with this opinion.

NOTES

1.   Contrary to the Montana court's holding in *Keystone*, federal courts have consistently held preempted state laws that invalidate provisions requiring arbitration proceedings to be held in another state. *See* Bradley v. Harris Research, Inc., 275 F.3d 884, 890-92 (9th Cir. 2001); OPE Int'l LP v. Chet Morrison Contractors, Inc., 258 F.3d 443, 447-48 (5th Cir. 2001); KKW Enterprises, Inc. v. Gloria Jean's Gourmet Coffees Franchising Group, 184 F.3d 42, 50-52 (1st Cir. 1999); Doctor's Assocs., Inc. v. Hamilton, 150 F.3d 157, 163 (2d Cir. 1998); Management Recruiters Int'l v. Bloor, 129 F.3d 851, 856 (6th Cir. 1997) (dicta).

2.   The Montana Supreme Court in *Keystone* cited two reasons for holding that the FAA did not preempt the Montana statute in that case. The first reason was that "Montana law . . . does not distinguish between forum selection clauses which are parts of contracts generally and forum selection clauses found in agreements to arbitrate." In other words, the Montana law was not preempted because it did not "single out" arbitration clauses: the statute also invalidated clauses specifying an out-of-state forum for court litigation.

Under the court's reasoning, would a state law be preempted if it invalidated all clauses waiving the right to jury trial? Take a look again at the California statute at issue in *Southland*? Would that statute have been preempted under the reasoning in *Keystone*?

3.   In *Concepcion*, the U.S. Supreme Court at least implicitly rejected the "singling out" theory, holding California's *Discover Bank* rule preempted even though both class action waivers and class arbitration waivers were unconscionable under California law. Indeed, the Court mentioned the theory in explaining why the FAA would preempt a state court decision holding that an arbitration clause is unconscionable if it does not provide for "judicially monitored discovery": "In practice, of course, the rule would have a disproportionate impact on arbitration agreements; but it would presumably apply to contracts purporting to restrict discovery in litigation as well."

Previously, the Illinois Supreme Court expressly rejected the *Keystone* court's "singling out" theory, holding that the FAA preempts a provision of the Illinois Nursing Home Care Act that invalidates waivers of the right to a jury trial for claims under the Act. Carter v. SCC Odin Operating Co., 927 N.E.2d 1207 (Ill. 2010). The lower court had construed the Act as invalidating arbitration clauses in nursing home contracts, and held that the Act was not preempted because it did not "single out" arbitration. The Illinois Supreme Court concluded that it was immaterial that the statute did not mention, much less apply only to, arbitration:

> We believe that the antiwaiver provisions of the Nursing Home Care Act relied upon by the plaintiff are legally indistinguishable from the provisions

struck down by the Supreme Court in *Southland, Perry* and *Preston*. Here, just like the statutes in *Southland* and *Preston*, the Illinois statute required resolution of the dispute in a non-arbitral forum. Moreover, neither of the actual statutory provisions invalidated in *Southland* and *Preston* even mention arbitration. The appellate court erroneously believed that the Nursing Home Care Act had to specifically "target" or single out arbitration agreements for FAA preemption to apply. This is a misreading of *Perry* and *Casarotto*.

Id. at 1218. Indeed, the Illinois Supreme Court concluded that "*Southland* essentially held that state laws that may apply to more than arbitration clauses are nonetheless preempted," and that "[a]pplication of the 'singling out' theory in such cases would be nothing more than a 'backdoor attempt to have the Supreme Court overrule *Southland*, which it already has refused to do.' " *Id.* at 1219.

4.   The second reason the Montana court rejected the preemption challenge was that the state law did not "nullif[y] either party's obligation to arbitrate." Stated otherwise, after applying the statute, the parties still went to arbitration, they just did so in a different place than they had agreed. Does that rationale survive *Concepcion*?

Courts and commentators have suggested a variety of approaches to resolving preemption challenges to such sorts of statutes, which regulate the arbitration process rather than invalidate the parties' obligation to arbitrate (in whole or in part). At one extreme is the *Keystone* approach, under which such statutes would never be preempted. At the other extreme would be the view that the FAA preempts all state arbitration law, which some commentators have suggested but which the Supreme Court has rejected. *See* Volt Info. Sciences, Inc. v. Board of Trustees of the Leland Stanford Junior Univ., 489 U.S. 468, 477 (1989) (FAA does not "reflect a congressional intent to occupy the entire field of arbitration"). For a discussion of these and several intermediate approaches, see Christopher R. Drahozal, *Federal Arbitration Act Preemption*, 79 IND. L.J. 393, 416-20 (2004).

PROBLEM 4.9

Which of the following state statutes, if any, are preempted by the FAA? Assume for purposes of your analysis that the FAA applies to the transaction at issue.

(a) A statute providing that "Notice that a contract is subject to arbitration shall be typed in underlined capital letters on the first page of the contract; and unless such notice is displayed thereon, the contract may not be subject to arbitration."

(b) A statute providing that "A written agreement to submit an existing controversy to arbitration, or a provision in a written contract, other than a contract of insurance, to submit to arbitration any controversy, is valid, enforceable, and irrevocable."

(c) A statute providing that "An arbitration clause in a consumer contract shall be unenforceable unless it provides for arbitration to be held at a location convenient for the consumer."

(d) A statute providing that "Any arbitration proceeding between a business and a consumer shall be held in the consumer's home state."

(e) A statute providing that "All forum selection clauses, including arbitration clauses, are invalid and unenforceable."

———

Thus far, we have focused on section 2 of the FAA and its preemptive effect. What about other provisions of the FAA, such as sections 3 and 4? By their terms they apply only to federal courts, and the Supreme Court has insisted, in *Southland* for example, that they do not apply to state courts. But are there any circumstances under which state procedures for enforcing arbitration agreements would be preempted by the FAA?

ROSENTHAL v. GREAT WESTERN FINANCIAL SEC. CORP.
Supreme Court of California
926 P.2d 1061 (1996)

WERDEGAR, JUSTICE.

In this case involving the enforcement of a predispute arbitration clause in a client agreement executed in the purchase of securities, we address the procedures by which petitions to compel arbitration (Code Civ. Proc., § 1281.2) are to be determined in the superior courts. We conclude that while the client agreements here are subject to the United States Arbitration Act (9 U.S.C. §§ 1-16), the federal provision for a jury trial of questions regarding the existence of an arbitration agreement (9 U.S.C. § 4) does not operate in California state courts. . . . Rather, these questions are to be resolved by the trial court in the manner provided for the hearing and decision of motions (Code Civ. Proc., § 1290.2), either on the basis of affidavits or declarations or, in the exercise of the court's discretion where necessary to resolve material conflicts in the written evidence, upon live testimony.

. . .

FACTUAL AND PROCEDURAL BACKGROUND

Plaintiffs are 24 individuals, 23 of whom, through defendant Great Western Financial Securities Corporation (GWFSC), invested in stock and bond mutual funds. . . . Before making these investments, most plaintiffs were depositors with Great Western Bank (GWB), a separate corporation related to GWFSC. They allege representatives of both corporations led them to believe that the GWFSC representatives actually worked for GWB, that funds sold by GWFSC were, or were as secure as, insured deposits with GWB, and that the GWFSC funds were backed by GWB or by the United States Government. Plaintiffs allege the value of the GWFSC funds subsequently declined and they lost portions of their principal. . . .

GWFSC and four individual defendants employed by GWFSC (collectively GWFSC) petitioned the superior court for an order compelling arbitration of all claims made by most plaintiffs, on the ground these plaintiffs had executed client agreements containing a predispute arbitration clause. In opposition to the petition, plaintiffs asserted two grounds for not enforcing the arbitration agreement: "that there was fraud in the inception of the contract" and that "the contracts they signed were 'permeated with fraud.' "

. . .

GWFSC . . . argued that, although these agreements for the purchase of stock and bond funds were governed by the United States Arbitration Act (the USAA), the USAA's provision for jury trial on the existence of an arbitration agreement (9 U.S.C. § 4) does not apply in state court. . . .

. . . [T]he trial court agreed with GWFSC that the USAA's provision for jury trial did not apply in state court. Nonetheless, without holding an evidentiary hearing, the court denied the petition to arbitrate as to all but one of the plaintiffs "on grounds that each of the above-named plaintiffs presented sufficient evidentiary support for their allegations of fraud in the inception of the arbitration agreement."
. . .

GWFSC appealed the ruling denying its petition to compel as to 20 plaintiffs. The Court of Appeal held the superior court erred in determining plaintiffs were not entitled to a jury trial under section 4 of the USAA. Relying on prior Court of Appeal decisions, . . . the appellate court held the federal jury trial provision was applicable in a California court. The court did not address the merits of plaintiffs' fraud claims. Instead, it remanded for the trial court to determine whether plaintiffs have sufficiently alleged fraud in the making of the arbitration agreement, and if so to try, by jury if requested, the issue of whether the arbitration agreements were the result of fraud.

We granted GWFSC's petition for review.

I. Trial Court Procedure for Deciding a Petition to Compel Arbitration

A. Section 4 of the United States Arbitration Act

The parties correctly agree that because the transactions here involved interstate commerce, questions concerning arbitrability of the parties' dispute are governed by the USAA. . . .

. . .

In most important respects, the California statutory scheme on enforcement of private arbitration agreements is similar to the USAA; the similarity is not surprising, as the two share origins in the earlier statutes of New York and New Jersey. . . . In one important respect, however, section 1281.2 differs from section 4 of the USAA: the California statute does not provide for a jury trial of issues as to the making of the arbitration agreement or the resisting party's default thereunder. Instead, our statutory scheme requires petitions to compel arbitration to be determined "in the manner . . . provided by law for the making and hearing of motions." (Code Civ. Proc., § 1290.2.)

The question thus arises whether section 4 of the USAA, or sections 1281.2 and

1290.2, provide the procedure to be followed in a California court in a case where the USAA governs arbitrability of the controversy. . . . In light both of the specific language of the USAA and of general principles of federal preemption, we conclude the USAA does not require California courts to hold a jury trial on the existence of an arbitration agreement. . . .

Section 4 of the USAA does not explicitly govern the procedures to be used in state courts. As already noted, the statute contemplates a petition in "United States district court," and provides that certain steps are to be taken "in the manner provided by the Federal Rules of Civil Procedure." This language has led the United States Supreme Court to express its doubt that section 4 is applicable in state courts. . . .

Although the wording of section 4 of the USAA thus suggests it is limited to federal courts, that language is not completely dispositive, in that section 2 of the USAA, by contrast, has no such restricted range. Under the holding in *Southland Corp.*, section 2's rule of enforceability of arbitration clauses preempts contrary state law even in a state court proceeding. But the federal policy of ensuring enforcement of private arbitration agreements, centrally embodied in section 2, is not self-implementing; its effectuation requires that courts have available some procedure by which a party seeking arbitration may compel a resisting party to arbitrate. Section 4 of the USAA establishes one such procedure; state law may or may not provide for other equivalent or similar procedures. If no adequate state procedures are provided, state courts may, in order fairly to adjudicate a federal claim for enforcement of an arbitration agreement, be obliged to adopt a procedure similar in its essentials to that set out in the USAA. As the high court has previously explained (albeit with reference to section 3 of the USAA, rather than section 4), "[t]his is necessary to carry out Congress' intent to mandate enforcement of all covered arbitration agreements; Congress can hardly have meant that an agreement to arbitrate can be enforced against a party who attempts to litigate an arbitrable dispute in federal court, but not against one who sues on the same dispute in state court." That section 2 of the USAA does preempt contrary state law is established; it follows that a state procedural statute or rule that frustrated the effectuation of section 2's central policy would, where the federal law applied, be preempted by the USAA.

The question whether a jury trial is called for thus requires us to go beyond the language of section 4 of the USAA and apply broader principles of federal preemption. It is a "general and unassailable proposition . . . that States may establish the rules of procedure governing litigation in their own courts," even when the controversy is governed by substantive federal law. "By the same token, however, where state courts entertain a federally created cause of action, the 'federal right cannot be defeated by the forms of local practice.' " Thus, as we have previously recognized, a state procedural rule must give way "if it impedes the uniform application of the federal statute essential to effectuate its purpose, even though the procedure would apply to similar actions arising under state law." At a minimum the state procedure must be neutral as between state and federal law claims. More exactly, the state rule may be preempted if it would stand "as an obstacle to the accomplishment and execution of the full purposes and objectives of Congress." Uniform national application of a federal substantive law requires, in particular, that state courts not apply procedural rules that would "frequently and predictably produce different outcomes . . . based solely on whether the [federal] claim is asserted in state or federal court."

Like other federal procedural rules, therefore, "the procedural provisions of the [USAA] are not binding on state courts . . . provided applicable state procedures do not defeat the rights granted by Congress." We think it plain the California procedures for a summary determination of the petition to compel arbitration serve to further, rather than defeat, the enforceability policy of the USAA. Sections 1281.2 and 1290.2 are neutral as between state and federal law claims for enforcement of arbitration agreements. They display no hostility to arbitration as an alternative to litigation; to the contrary, the summary procedure provided, in which the existence and validity of the arbitration agreement is decided by the court in the manner of a motion, is designed to further the use of private arbitration as a means of resolving disputes more quickly and less expensively than through litigation. Finally, having a court, instead of a jury, decide whether an arbitration agreement exists will not "frequently and predictably produce different outcomes." Because the California procedure for deciding motions to compel serves to further, rather than defeat, full and uniform effectuation of the federal law's objectives, the California law, rather than section 4 of the USAA, is to be followed in California courts.

. . .

NOTES

1. The rest of the California Supreme Court's opinion in *Rosenthal* deals with whether the defense of fraud in the execution of the contract as a whole is for the court or the arbitrator. See the description in § 2.02.

2. Preemption issues also arise in connection with the conduct of the arbitration proceeding and enforcing arbitral awards. Those issues will be discussed in Chapters 6 and 7, respectively.

PROBLEM 4.10

Beryl Garcia owns a small pet store. She enters into a contract with Grimpen, Inc., a company that sells pet care supplies, to distribute Grimpen dog food in her store. A provision of her contract with Grimpen requires arbitration of any disputes arising out of or relating to the contract. When Grimpen terminates Beryl as a distributor, she files suit in state court against Grimpen alleging breach of contract. Grimpen files a motion seeking to have the state court stay its proceedings and to compel arbitration of their dispute. Assume that the distribution contract evidences a transaction involving interstate commerce.

(a) The state court grants the stay and the petition to compel arbitration. Beryl takes an immediate appeal of the order under a state law that makes the grant of an order compelling arbitration a final decision subject to immediate appeal. (*Compare* 9 U.S.C. § 16.) Does the state court of appeals have jurisdiction over the appeal?

(b) Assume instead that the state court denies the stay and petition to compel arbitration, and that, under state law, orders denying stays pending arbitration and petitions to compel arbitration are non-appealable interlocutory orders. (*Compare* 9 U.S.C. § 16.) Does the state court of appeals have jurisdiction over the appeal?

(c) Assume that Beryl has a contract with a local dog breeder, Stapleton's Hound Dogs, to supply Stapleton with its requirements of Grimpen dog food. When Beryl is terminated, Stapleton sues Beryl for breach of contract. Although Beryl's contract with Grimpen contains an arbitration clause, she has not agreed to arbitrate any disputes with Stapleton. Beryl seeks a stay of the arbitration proceeding with Grimpen, relying on a state statute that permits a court to stay arbitration pending resolution of related litigation between a party to the arbitration agreement and third parties not bound by it, when there is a possibility of conflicting rulings on a common issue of law or fact. Should the state court grant the stay of arbitration?

§ 4.06   CHOICE-OF-LAW ISSUES

Assume that a franchisor and a franchisee agree to arbitrate all claims relating to their contract, except for claims arising out of the state's franchise termination statute. Can the franchisor, relying on *Southland*, later force the franchisee to arbitrate its franchise termination act claim? Certainly not. The FAA does not require the parties to arbitrate any particular claims (or, with limited exceptions, to arbitrate those claims in any particular manner). Instead, it validates the parties' own arbitration agreement. *See* 9 U.S.C. § 4 (permitting the parties to an arbitration agreement to seek "an order directing that such arbitration proceed *in the manner provided for in such agreement*") (emphasis added). Thus, if the parties agree to exclude certain claims from arbitration, *Southland* does not require them to arbitrate those claims. Instead, what *Southland* holds is that if the parties agree to arbitrate certain claims, a state may not override that agreement and make those claims not subject to arbitration. The difficulty faced by the Court in the next two cases was to decide exactly what the parties provided in their agreements to arbitrate.

VOLT INFORMATION SCIENCES, INC. v. BOARD OF TRUSTEES OF THE LELAND STANFORD JUNIOR UNIVERSITY
United States Supreme Court
489 U.S. 468 (1989)

Chief Justice Rehnquist delivered the opinion of the Court.

Unlike its federal counterpart, the California Arbitration Act, Cal. Civ. Proc. Code Ann. § 1280 *et seq.* (1982), contains a provision allowing a court to stay arbitration pending resolution of related litigation. We hold that application of the California statute is not pre-empted by the Federal Arbitration Act (FAA or Act) in a case where the parties have agreed that their arbitration agreement will be governed by the law of California.

Appellant Volt Information Sciences, Inc. (Volt), and appellee Board of Trustees of Leland Stanford Junior University (Stanford) entered into a construction contract under which Volt was to install a system of electrical conduits on the Stanford campus. The contract contained an agreement to arbitrate all disputes between the parties "arising out of or relating to this contract or the breach thereof." The contract also contained a choice-of-law clause providing that "[t]he Contract shall be governed by the law of the place where the Project is located." During the course of the project, a dispute developed regarding compensation for extra work, and Volt made a formal demand for arbitration. Stanford responded by filing an action against Volt in California Superior Court, alleging fraud and breach of contract; in the same action, Stanford also sought indemnity from two other companies involved in the construction project, with whom it did not have arbitration agreements. Volt petitioned the Superior Court to compel arbitration of the dispute. Stanford in turn moved to stay arbitration pursuant to Cal. Civ. Proc. Code Ann. § 1281.2(c) (1982), which permits a court to stay arbitration pending resolution of related litigation between a party to the arbitration agreement and third parties not bound by it, where "there is a possibility of conflicting rulings on a common issue of law or fact." The Superior Court denied Volt's motion to compel arbitration and stayed the arbitration proceedings pending the outcome of the litigation on the authority of § 1281.2(c). . . .

The California Court of Appeal affirmed. The court acknowledged that the parties' contract involved interstate commerce, that the FAA governs contracts in interstate commerce, and that the FAA contains no provision permitting a court to stay arbitration pending resolution of related litigation involving third parties not bound by the arbitration agreement. However, the court held that by specifying that their contract would be governed by " 'the law of the place where the project is located,' " the parties had incorporated the California rules of arbitration, including § 1281.2(c), into their arbitration agreement. Finally, the court rejected Volt's contention that, even if the parties had agreed to arbitrate under the California rules, application of § 1281.2(c) here was nonetheless pre-empted by the FAA because the contract involved interstate commerce.

. . . The California Supreme Court denied Volt's petition for discretionary review. We postponed consideration of our jurisdiction to the hearing on the merits. We now hold that we have appellate jurisdiction and affirm.

Appellant devotes the bulk of its argument to convincing us that the Court of Appeal erred in interpreting the choice-of-law clause to mean that the parties had incorporated the California rules of arbitration into their arbitration agreement. Appellant acknowledges, as it must, that the interpretation of private contracts is ordinarily a question of state law, which this Court does not sit to review. But appellant nonetheless maintains that we should set aside the Court of Appeal's interpretation of this particular contractual provision for two principal reasons.

Appellant first suggests that the Court of Appeal's construction of the choice-of-law clause was in effect a finding that appellant had "waived" its "federally guaranteed right to compel arbitration of the parties' dispute," a waiver whose validity must be judged by reference to federal rather than state law. This argument fundamentally misconceives the nature of the rights created by the FAA. The Act was designed "to overrule the judiciary's longstanding refusal to enforce agreements to arbitrate," and place such agreements " 'upon the same footing as other contracts.' " Section 2 of the Act therefore declares that a written agreement to arbitrate in any contract involving interstate commerce or a maritime transaction "shall be valid, irrevocable, and enforceable, save upon such grounds as exist at law or in equity for the revocation of any contract," 9 U.S.C. § 2, and § 4 allows a party to such an arbitration agreement to "petition any United States district court . . . for an order directing that such arbitration proceed in the manner provided for in such agreement."

But § 4 of the FAA does not confer a right to compel arbitration of any dispute at any time; it confers only the right to obtain an order directing that "arbitration proceed *in the manner provided for in [the parties'] agreement*." 9 U.S.C. § 4 (emphasis added). Here the Court of Appeal found that, by incorporating the California rules of arbitration into their agreement, the parties had agreed that arbitration would not proceed in situations which fell within the scope of Calif. Code Civ. Proc. Ann. § 1281.2(c) (1982). This was not a finding that appellant had "waived" an FAA-guaranteed right to compel arbitration of this dispute, but a finding that it had no such right in the first place, because the parties' agreement did not require arbitration to proceed in this situation. Accordingly, appellant's contention that the contract interpretation issue presented here involves the "waiver" of a federal right is without merit.

Second, appellant argues that we should set aside the Court of Appeal's construction of the choice-of-law clause because it violates the settled federal rule that questions of arbitrability in contracts subject to the FAA must be resolved with a healthy regard for the federal policy favoring arbitration. . . . [Prior] cases of course establish that, in applying general state-law principles of contract interpretation to the interpretation of an arbitration agreement within the scope of the Act, due regard must be given to the federal policy favoring arbitration, and ambiguities as to the scope of the arbitration clause itself resolved in favor of arbitration.

But we do not think the Court of Appeal offended [this] principle by interpreting the choice-of-law provision to mean that the parties intended the California rules of arbitration, including the § 1281.2(c) stay provision, to apply to their arbitration agreement. There is no federal policy favoring arbitration under a certain set of procedural rules; the federal policy is simply to ensure the enforceability, according to their terms, of private agreements to arbitrate. Interpreting a choice-of-law clause to make applicable state rules governing the conduct of arbitration — rules which are manifestly designed to encourage resort to the arbitral process — simply does not offend the rule of liberal construction, nor does it offend any other policy embodied in the FAA.[5]

---

[5] [W]e think the California arbitration rules which the parties have incorporated into their contract generally foster the federal policy favoring arbitration. As indicated, the FAA itself contains no provision designed to deal with the special practical problems that arise in multiparty contractual disputes when some or all of the contracts at issue include agreements to arbitrate. California has taken the lead in fashioning a legislative response to this problem, by giving courts authority to consolidate or stay arbitration proceedings in these situations in order to minimize the potential for contradictory judgments.

The question remains whether, assuming the choice-of-law clause meant what the Court of Appeal found it to mean, application of Cal. Civ. Proc. Code Ann. § 1281.2(c) is nonetheless pre-empted by the FAA to the extent it is used to stay arbitration under this contract involving interstate commerce. It is undisputed that this contract falls within the coverage of the FAA, since it involves interstate commerce, and that the FAA contains no provision authorizing a stay of arbitration in this situation. Appellee contends, however, that §§ 3 and 4 of the FAA, which are the specific sections claimed to conflict with the California statute at issue here, are not applicable in this state-court proceeding and thus cannot pre-empt application of the California statute. While the argument is not without some merit,[6] we need not resolve it to decide this case, for we conclude that even if §§ 3 and 4 of the FAA are fully applicable in state-court proceedings, they do not prevent application of Cal. Civ. Proc. Code Ann. § 1281.2(c) to stay arbitration where, as here, the parties have agreed to arbitrate in accordance with California law.

The FAA contains no express pre-emptive provision, nor does it reflect a congressional intent to occupy the entire field of arbitration. But even when Congress has not completely displaced state regulation in an area, state law may nonetheless be pre-empted to the extent that it actually conflicts with federal law — that is, to the extent that it "stands as an obstacle to the accomplishment and execution of the full purposes and objectives of Congress." The question before us, therefore, is whether application of Cal. Civ. Proc. Code Ann. § 1281.2(c) to stay arbitration under this contract in interstate commerce, in accordance with the terms of the arbitration agreement itself, would undermine the goals and policies of the FAA. We conclude that it would not.

The FAA was designed "to overrule the judiciary's long-standing refusal to enforce agreements to arbitrate," and to place such agreements " 'upon the same footing as other contracts.' " While Congress was no doubt aware that the Act would encourage the expeditious resolution of disputes, its passage "was motivated, first and foremost, by a congressional desire to enforce agreements into which parties had entered." Accordingly, we have recognized that the FAA does not require parties to arbitrate when they have not agreed to do so, nor does it prevent parties who do agree to arbitrate from excluding certain claims from the scope of their arbitration agreement. It simply requires courts to enforce privately negotiated agreements to arbitrate, like other contracts, in accordance with their terms.

In recognition of Congress' principal purpose of ensuring that private arbitration agreements are enforced according to their terms, we have held that the FAA pre-empts state laws which "require a judicial forum for the resolution of claims which the contracting parties agreed to resolve by arbitration." But it does not follow that the FAA prevents the enforcement of agreements to arbitrate under different rules than those set forth in the Act itself. Indeed, such a result would be quite inimical to the FAA's primary purpose of ensuring that private agreements to arbitrate are enforced according to their terms. Arbitration under the Act is a

---

[6] While we have held that the FAA's "substantive" provisions — §§ 1 and 2 — are applicable in state as well as federal court, *see Southland Corp. v. Keating*, we have never held that §§ 3 and 4, which by their terms appear to apply only to proceedings in federal court, are nonetheless applicable in state court.

matter of consent, not coercion, and parties are generally free to structure their arbitration agreements as they see fit. Just as they may limit by contract the issues which they will arbitrate, *see Mitsubishi*, so too may they specify by contract the rules under which that arbitration will be conducted. Where, as here, the parties have agreed to abide by state rules of arbitration, enforcing those rules according to the terms of the agreement is fully consistent with the goals of the FAA, even if the result is that arbitration is stayed where the Act would otherwise permit it to go forward. By permitting the courts to "rigorously enforce" such agreements according to their terms, we give effect to the contractual rights and expectations of the parties, without doing violence to the policies behind by the FAA.

The judgment of the Court of Appeals is *Affirmed.*

NOTES

1. Follow the Supreme Court's analysis through step by step. First, the Court makes clear that it is not going to review the California court's interpretation of the parties' choice-of-law clause. That is a matter of state law, of which state courts are the highest authority. As a result, the Supreme Court takes as given that by agreeing to California law, the parties incorporated California arbitration law into their contract. Second, the Court recognizes that if the California court's contract interpretation violated federal law (including the FAA), the Court could step in. The Court refuses to do so here, however, for several reasons, including that "[i]nterpreting a choice-of-law clause to make applicable state rules governing the conduct of arbitration — rules which are manifestly designed to encourage resort to the arbitral process — simply does not offend the rule of liberal construction [of arbitration agreements], nor does it offend any other policy embodied in the FAA." Finally, the Court concludes that given the California court's interpretation of the choice-of-law clause, the California arbitration law was not preempted. As the Court explained: "Where, as here, the parties have agreed to abide by state rules of arbitration, enforcing those rules according to the terms of the agreement is fully consistent with the goals of the FAA, even if the result is that arbitration is stayed where the Act would otherwise permit it to go forward."

Professor Thomas A. Diamond finds this latter conclusion — "that the parties may agree to apply a state's arbitration rules, where in the absence of such an agreement the FAA would preempt state law" to be "unassailable." Thomas A. Diamond, *Choice of Law Clauses and Their Preemptive Effect Upon the Federal Arbitration Act: Reconciling the Supreme Court with Itself,* 39 ARIZ. L. REV. 35, 44 (1997). Instead, he takes issue with the second step of the Court's analysis — its "decision to refuse to review the California Court of Appeal's conclusion that the parties intended by their ambiguously worded choice of law clause to exclude the FAA." *Id.* He explains:

> By upholding an interpretation of the choice of law clause to exclude the FAA, the Court upheld a stay of arbitration pending litigation that left Volt with few options. It could wait, perhaps for years, for the litigation to be concluded and then proceed with arbitration; it could opt to waive its right to arbitrate and resolve the dispute through litigation; or it could decide that neither the option of delayed arbitration nor protracted litigation was

a viable alternative and choose to settle or drop its claim despite believing in the merits of its case. No matter what Volt decided, the effect would not be significantly dissimilar from a judicial decision to prevent arbitration by interpreting an ambiguously worded arbitration agreement not to encompass the dispute in issue — a result the Supreme Court acknowledged would have been impermissible.

Id. at 45. Do you agree?

2.   In Doctor's Associates, Inc. v. Casarotto, 517 U.S. 681 (1996), the Supreme Court distinguished the Montana requirement of conspicuous notice of an arbitration clause from the stay provision at issue in *Volt*:

> The Montana Supreme Court misread our *Volt* decision and therefore reached a conclusion in this case at odds with our rulings. *Volt* involved an arbitration agreement that incorporated state procedural rules, one of which, on the facts of that case, called for arbitration to be stayed pending the resolution of a related judicial proceeding. The state rule examined in *Volt* determined only the efficient order of proceedings; it did not affect the enforceability of the arbitration agreement itself. We held that applying the state rule would not "undermine the goals and policies of the FAA," because the very purpose of the Act was to "ensur[e] that private agreements to arbitrate are enforced according to their terms."
>
> Applying § 27-5-114(4) here, in contrast, would not enforce the arbitration clause in the contract between [Doctor's Associates] and Casarotto; instead, Montana's first-page notice requirement would invalidate the clause.

Id. at 687. Would the Court's distinction satisfy Professor Diamond?

MASTROBUONO v. SHEARSON LEHMAN HUTTON, INC.
United States Supreme Court
514 U.S. 52 (1995)

JUSTICE STEVENS delivered the opinion of the Court.

New York law allows courts, but not arbitrators, to award punitive damages. In a dispute arising out of a standard-form contract that expressly provides that it "shall be governed by the laws of the State of New York," a panel of arbitrators awarded punitive damages. The District Court and Court of Appeals disallowed that award. The question presented is whether the arbitrators' award is consistent with the central purpose of the Federal Arbitration Act to ensure "that private agreements to arbitrate are enforced according to their terms." *Volt Information Sciences, Inc. v. Board of Trustees of Leland Stanford Junior Univ.*

I

In 1985 petitioners, Antonio Mastrobuono, then an assistant professor of medieval literature, and his wife Diana Mastrobuono, an artist, opened a securities trading account with respondent Shearson Lehman Hutton, Inc. (Shearson), by executing Shearson's standard-form Client's Agreement. Respondent Nick Di-Minico, a vice president of Shearson, managed the Mastrobuonos' account until they closed it in 1987. In 1989, petitioners filed this action in the United States District Court for the Northern District of Illinois, alleging that respondents had mishandled their account and claiming damages on a variety of state and federal law theories.

Paragraph 13 of the parties' agreement contains an arbitration provision and a choice-of-law provision. Relying on the arbitration provision and on §§ 3 and 4 of the Federal Arbitration Act (FAA), respondents filed a motion to stay the court proceedings and to compel arbitration pursuant to the rules of the National Association of Securities Dealers. The District Court granted that motion, and a panel of three arbitrators was convened. After conducting hearings in Illinois, the panel ruled in favor of petitioners.

In the arbitration proceedings, respondents argued that the arbitrators had no authority to award punitive damages. Nevertheless, the panel's award included punitive damages of $400,000, in addition to compensatory damages of $159,327. Respondents paid the compensatory portion of the award but filed a motion in the District Court to vacate the award of punitive damages. The District Court granted the motion, and the Court of Appeals for the Seventh Circuit affirmed. Both courts relied on the choice-of-law provision in Paragraph 13 of the parties' agreement, which specifies that the contract shall be governed by New York law. Because the New York Court of Appeals has decided that in New York the power to award punitive damages is limited to judicial tribunals and may not be exercised by arbitrators, Garrity v. Lyle Stuart, Inc., 40 N.Y.2d 354, 353 N.E.2d 793 (1976), the District Court and the Seventh Circuit held that the panel of arbitrators had no power to award punitive damages in this case.

We granted certiorari because the Courts of Appeals have expressed differing views on whether a contractual choice-of-law provision may preclude an arbitral award of punitive damages that otherwise would be proper. We now reverse.

II

Earlier this Term, we upheld the enforceability of a predispute arbitration agreement governed by Alabama law, even though an Alabama statute provides that arbitration agreements are unenforceable. *Allied-Bruce Terminix Cos. v. Dobson.* Writing for the Court, JUSTICE BREYER observed that Congress passed the FAA "to overcome courts' refusals to enforce agreements to arbitrate." After determining that the FAA applied to the parties' arbitration agreement, we readily concluded that the federal statute pre-empted Alabama's statutory prohibition.

Petitioners seek a similar disposition of the case before us today. Here, the Seventh Circuit interpreted the contract to incorporate New York law, including the *Garrity* rule that arbitrators may not award punitive damages. Petitioners ask us to hold that the FAA pre-empts New York's prohibition against arbitral awards of punitive damages because this state law is a vestige of the "ancient" judicial hostility to arbitration. . . .

Respondents answer that the choice-of-law provision in their contract evidences the parties' express agreement that punitive damages should not be awarded in the arbitration of any dispute arising under their contract. Thus, they claim, this case is distinguishable from *Southland* and *Perry*, in which the parties presumably desired unlimited arbitration but state law stood in their way. Regardless of whether the FAA pre-empts the *Garrity* decision in contracts not expressly incorporating New York law, respondents argue that the parties may themselves agree to be bound by *Garrity*, just as they may agree to forgo arbitration altogether. In other words, if the contract says "no punitive damages," that is the end of the matter, for courts are bound to interpret contracts in accordance with the expressed intentions of the parties — even if the effect of those intentions is to limit arbitration.

We have previously held that the FAA's pro-arbitration policy does not operate without regard to the wishes of the contracting parties. . . . *Volt*.

Relying on our reasoning in *Volt*, respondents thus argue that the parties to a contract may lawfully agree to limit the issues to be arbitrated by waiving any claim for punitive damages. On the other hand, we think our decisions in *Allied-Bruce* [and] *Southland* make clear that if contracting parties agree to *include* claims for punitive damages within the issues to be arbitrated, the FAA ensures that their agreement will be enforced according to its terms even if a rule of state law would otherwise exclude such claims from arbitration. Thus, the case before us comes down to what the contract has to say about the arbitrability of petitioners' claim for punitive damages.

III

Shearson's standard-form "Client Agreement," which petitioners executed, contains 18 paragraphs. The two relevant provisions of the agreement are found in Paragraph 13. The first sentence of that paragraph provides, in part, that the entire agreement "shall be governed by the laws of the State of New York." The second sentence provides that "any controversy" arising out of the transactions between the parties "shall be settled by arbitration" in accordance with the rules of the National Association of Securities Dealers (NASD), or the Boards of Directors of the New York Stock Exchange and/or the American Stock Exchange. The agreement contains no express reference to claims for punitive damages. To ascertain whether Paragraph 13 expresses an intent to include or exclude such claims, we first address the impact of each of the two relevant provisions, considered separately. We then move on to the more important inquiry: the meaning of the two provisions taken together.

The choice-of-law provision, when viewed in isolation, may reasonably be read as merely a substitute for the conflict-of-laws analysis that otherwise would determine what law to apply to disputes arising out of the contractual relationship. Thus, if a similar contract, without a choice-of-law provision, had been signed in New York and was to be performed in New York, presumably "the laws of the State of New York" would apply, even though the contract did not expressly so state. In such event, there would be nothing in the contract that could possibly constitute evidence of an intent to exclude punitive damages claims. Accordingly, punitive damages would be allowed because, in the absence of contractual intent to the contrary, the FAA would pre-empt the *Garrity* rule.

Even if the reference to "the laws of the State of New York" is more than a substitute for ordinary conflict-of-laws analysis and, as respondents urge, includes the caveat, "detached from otherwise-applicable federal law," the provision might not preclude the award of punitive damages because New York allows its courts, though not its arbitrators, to enter such awards. In other words, the provision might include only New York's substantive rights and obligations, and not the State's allocation of power between alternative tribunals. Respondents' argument is persuasive only if "New York law" means "New York decisional law, including that State's allocation of power between courts and arbitrators, notwithstanding otherwise-applicable federal law." But, as we have demonstrated, the provision need not be read so broadly. It is not, in itself, an unequivocal exclusion of punitive damages claims.[4]

The arbitration provision (the second sentence of Paragraph 13) does not improve respondents' argument. On the contrary, when read separately this clause strongly implies that an arbitral award of punitive damages is appropriate. It explicitly authorizes arbitration in accordance with NASD rules; the panel of arbitrators in fact proceeded under that set of rules. The NASD's Code of Arbitration Procedure indicates that arbitrators may award "damages and other relief." NASD Code of Arbitration Procedure ¶ 3741(e) (1993). While not a clear authorization of punitive damages, this provision appears broad enough at least to contemplate such a remedy. Moreover, as the Seventh Circuit noted, a manual provided to NASD arbitrators contains this provision:

"B. Punitive Damages

"The issue of punitive damages may arise with great frequency in arbitrations. Parties to arbitration are informed that arbitrators can consider punitive damages as a remedy."

Thus, the text of the arbitration clause itself surely does not support — indeed, it contradicts — the conclusion that the parties agreed to foreclose claims for punitive damages.

Although neither the choice-of-law clause nor the arbitration clause, separately considered, expresses an intent to preclude an award of punitive damages, respondents argue that a fair reading of the entire Paragraph 13 leads to that conclusion. On this theory, even if "New York law" is ambiguous, and even if "arbitration in accordance with NASD rules" indicates that punitive damages are permissible, the juxtaposition of the two clauses suggests that the contract incorporates "New York law relating to arbitration." We disagree. At most, the choice-of-law clause introduces an ambiguity into an arbitration agreement that

---

[4] The dissent makes much of the similarity between this choice-of-law clause and the one in *Volt*, which we took to incorporate a California statute allowing a court to stay arbitration pending resolution of related litigation. In *Volt*, however, we did not interpret the contract *de novo*. Instead, we deferred to the California court's construction of its own state's law. In the present case, by contrast, we review a *federal* court's interpretation of this contract, and our interpretation accords with that of the only decision-maker arguably entitled to deference — the arbitrator.

would otherwise allow punitive damages awards. As we pointed out in *Volt*, when a court interprets such provisions in an agreement covered by the FAA, "due regard must be given to the federal policy favoring arbitration, and ambiguities as to the scope of the arbitration clause itself resolved in favor of arbitration."

Moreover, respondents cannot overcome the common-law rule of contract interpretation that a court should construe ambiguous language against the interest of the party that drafted it. Respondents drafted an ambiguous document, and they cannot now claim the benefit of the doubt. The reason for this rule is to protect the party who did not choose the language from an unintended or unfair result. That rationale is well-suited to the facts of this case. As a practical matter, it seems unlikely that petitioners were actually aware of New York's bifurcated approach to punitive damages, or that they had any idea that by signing a standard-form agreement to arbitrate disputes they might be giving up an important substantive right. In the face of such doubt, we are unwilling to impute this intent to petitioners.

Finally the respondents' reading of the two clauses violates another cardinal principle of contract construction: that a document should be read to give effect to all its provisions and to render them consistent with each other. We think the best way to harmonize the choice-of-law provision with the arbitration provision is to read "the laws of the State of New York" to encompass substantive principles that New York courts would apply, but not to include special rules limiting the authority of arbitrators. Thus, the choice-of-law provision covers the rights and duties of the parties, while the arbitration clause covers arbitration; neither sentence intrudes upon the other. In contrast, respondents' reading sets up the two clauses in conflict with one another: one foreclosing punitive damages, the other allowing them. This interpretation is untenable.

We hold that the Court of Appeals misinterpreted the parties' agreement.

The arbitral award should have been enforced as within the scope of the contract. The judgment of the Court of Appeals is, therefore, reversed.

It is so ordered.

[Dissenting opinion of JUSTICE THOMAS omitted.]

NOTES

1.	Rather than clearing up the confusion, *Mastrobuono* generated confusion of its own:

> In the wake of *Volt* and *Mastrobuono*, federal courts have developed a number of approaches to the choice-of-law question. Some courts have completely ignored state contract rules; others have too closely followed the Court's reasoning in *Mastrobuono*, applying Illinois and New York contract law to the contract at issue — regardless whether that contract had any ties to those states. Other courts have read *Mastrobuono* as mandating a categorical exclusion of state law — whether pro-or anti-arbitration — unless the contract language expressly departed from the FAA; still others have similarly relied on *Volt* to require application of the competing state

rule. The resulting confusion has produced a morass of inconsistent principles, expanding FAA preemption into areas traditionally reserved for the states, and departing from Congress's intent to place arbitration agreements on "equal footing" with all other contracts.

Note, *An Unnecessary Choice of Law:* Volt, Mastrobuono, *and Federal Arbitration Act Preemption*, 115 HARV. L. REV. 2250, 2260 (2002). The Justices themselves on occasion have been unsure of the proper interpretation of choice-of-law clauses. Both Justice Stevens (in Green Tree Fin'l Corp. v. Bazzle, 539 U.S. 444, 454 (2003) (Stevens, J., concurring in the judgment and dissenting in part)) and Justice Thomas (in Howsam v. Dean Witter Reynolds, Inc., 537 U.S. 79, 87 (2002) (Thomas, J., concurring in the judgment)) relied on general choice-of-law clauses to urge application of state arbitration rules, seemingly contrary to *Mastrobuono*.

2. The Supreme Court again addressed the interrelationship of choice-of-law clauses and arbitration clauses in Preston v. Ferrer, 552 U.S. 346 (2008) (for a description of the facts of *Preston*, see § 2.02):

> [Like *Volt*, Preston and Ferrer's contract also contains a choice-of-law clause, which states that the "agreement shall be governed by the laws of the state of California." A separate saving clause provides: "If there is any conflict between this agreement and any present or future law," the law prevails over the contract "to the extent necessary to bring [the contract] within the requirements of said law." Those contractual terms, according to Ferrer, call for the application of California procedural law, including § 1700.44(a)'s grant of exclusive jurisdiction to the Labor Commissioner.

> Ferrer's reliance on *Volt* is misplaced for two discrete reasons. First, arbitration was stayed in *Volt* to accommodate litigation involving third parties who were strangers to the arbitration agreement. Nothing in the arbitration agreement addressed the order of proceedings when pending litigation with third parties presented the prospect of inconsistent rulings. We thought it proper, in those circumstances, to recognize state law as the gap filler.

> Here, in contrast, the arbitration clause speaks to the matter in controversy; it states that "any dispute . . . relating to . . . the breach, validity, or legality" of the contract should be arbitrated in accordance with the American Arbitration Association (AAA) rules. Both parties are bound by the arbitration agreement; the question of Preston's status as a talent agent relates to the validity or legality of the contract; there is no risk that related litigation will yield conflicting rulings on common issues; and there is no other procedural void for the choice-of-law clause to fill.

> Second, we are guided by our more recent decision in *Mastrobuono v. Shearson Lehman Hutton, Inc.* Although the contract in *Volt* provided for "arbitration in accordance with the Construction Industry Arbitration Rules of the American Arbitration Association," Volt never argued that incorporation of those rules trumped the choice-of-law clause contained in the contract. Therefore, neither our decision in *Volt* nor the decision of the California appeals court in that case addressed the import of the contract's

incorporation by reference of privately promulgated arbitration rules.

In *Mastrobuono*, we reached that open question while interpreting a contract with both a New York choice-of-law clause and a clause providing for arbitration in accordance with the rules of the National Association of Securities Dealers (NASD). The "best way to harmonize" the two clauses, we held, was to read the choice-of-law clause "to encompass substantive principles that New York courts would apply, but not to include [New York's] special rules limiting the authority of arbitrators."

Preston and Ferrer's contract, as noted, provides for arbitration in accordance with the AAA rules. One of those rules states that "[t]he arbitrator shall have the power to determine the existence or validity of a contract of which an arbitration clause forms a part." AAA, Commercial Arbitration Rules R-7(b) (2007). The incorporation of the AAA rules, and in particular Rule 7(b), weighs against inferring from the choice-of-law clause an understanding shared by Ferrer and Preston that their disputes would be heard, in the first instance, by the Labor Commissioner. Following the guide *Mastrobuono* provides, the "best way to harmonize" the parties' adoption of the AAA rules and their selection of California law is to read the latter to encompass prescriptions governing the substantive rights and obligations of the parties, but not the State's "special rules limiting the authority of arbitrators."

Id. at 360-63. What is left of *Volt* after *Preston*?

PROBLEM 4.11

Recall the facts of Problem 4.10(c): Beryl Garcia seeks to stay an arbitration proceeding with Grimpen, Inc., pending resolution of a lawsuit that includes a related breach of contract claim brought by Stapleton's Hound Dogs. The arbitration agreement between Beryl and Grimpen is governed by the FAA; the arbitration law of the state where the action is filed (say, California) permits a court to stay an arbitration proceeding pending resolution of a related lawsuit.

In addition, assume that the contract between Beryl and Grimpen provides that the contract is governed by California law. How should the court rule on the request for a stay?

PROBLEM 4.12

Stoner Accessories (see Problem 2.5) decides to try a new supplier of neckwear. It enters into a contract with Farintosh Clothiers under which Stoner agrees to buy scarves and neckties from Farintosh. The contract provides that all disputes shall be decided by arbitration.

(a) Both Stoner and Farintosh are New York corporations, and the arbitration is to take place in New York. The arbitration clause is silent on the authority of the arbitrator to award punitive damages. New York arbitration law, however, precludes arbitrators from awarding punitive damages in arbitration proceedings. Assume that the transaction does not evidence a transaction involving interstate commerce. May the arbitrator award punitive damages?

(b) Same facts as sub-part (a) except that Farintosh is from New York, Stoner is from New Jersey, and their contract is for the interstate sale of neckwear. May the arbitrator award punitive damages?

(c) Same facts as sub-part (b) except that the parties' contract provides that "the arbitrator may not award punitive damages." May the arbitrator award punitive damages?

(d) Same facts as sub-part (b) except that the parties' contract provides that "New York law precluding the award of punitive damages in arbitration governs the arbitration proceeding." May the arbitrator award punitive damages?

(e) Same facts as sub-part (b) except that the parties' contract provides that "New York law on awarding punitive damages in arbitration governs the arbitration proceeding." May the arbitrator award punitive damages?

(f) Same facts as sub-part (b) except that the parties' contract provides that "New York law governs this contract." May the arbitrator award punitive damages?

(g) Same facts as sub-part (b) except that the parties' contract provides that "New York law governs this contract and its enforcement." May the arbitrator award punitive damages?

(h) Same facts as sub-part (b) except that the parties' contract provides that "New York law governs this contract" and that "any arbitration proceeding is governed exclusively by the Federal Arbitration Act."

PROBLEM 4.13

Recall the facts of *Southland* (see § 4.02): a franchisor seeks to compel arbitration of a claim under the California Franchise Investment Law. The California Supreme Court concludes that the claim is not arbitrable as a matter of state law, and the United States Supreme Court holds that the FAA preempts the California rule of nonarbitrability. Assume now that in addition to an arbitration clause, the franchise agreement contains a choice-of-law clause providing that California law governs the contract. Consistent with *Volt*, the California court construes the choice-of-law clause as incorporating California arbitration law as well as California substantive contract law, and holds that the dispute is not arbitrable because of the California Franchise Investment Law. Can the United States Supreme Court review the case? If so, how should it rule?

§ 4.07   PROCEDURAL ISSUES IN ENFORCING DOMESTIC ARBITRATION AGREEMENTS — PART 2

Some basic procedural issues in enforcing domestic arbitration agreements were discussed in Chapter 2. This part goes beyond those basics to examine the procedural issues arising from the choice of the proper court in which to enforce the arbitration agreement. As with any lawsuit, the court in which a party seeks to enforce an arbitration agreement must be one with personal jurisdiction, subject matter jurisdiction, and venue. The tactical significance of the choice of forum should be clear from the preceding materials in this chapter: some courts are more willing than others to enforce arbitration agreements.

VADEN v. DISCOVER BANK
Supreme Court of the United States
556 U.S. 49 (2009)

JUSTICE GINSBURG delivered the opinion of the Court.

Section 4 of the Federal Arbitration Act authorizes a United States district court to entertain a petition to compel arbitration if the court would have jurisdiction, "save for [the arbitration] agreement," over "a suit arising out of the controversy between the parties." We consider in this opinion two questions concerning a district court's subject-matter jurisdiction over a § 4 petition: Should a district court, if asked to compel arbitration pursuant to § 4, "look through" the petition and grant the requested relief if the court would have federal-question jurisdiction over the underlying controversy? And if the answer to that question is yes, may a district court exercise jurisdiction over a § 4 petition when the petitioner's complaint rests on state law but an actual or potential counterclaim rests on federal law?

The litigation giving rise to these questions began when Discover Bank's servicing affiliate filed a complaint in Maryland state court. Presenting a claim arising solely under state law, Discover sought to recover past-due charges from one of its credit cardholders, Betty Vaden. Vaden answered and counterclaimed, [asserting a class action] alleging that Discover's finance charges, interest, and late fees violated state law. Invoking an arbitration clause in its cardholder agreement with Vaden, Discover then filed a § 4 petition in the United States District Court for the District of Maryland to compel arbitration of Vaden's counterclaims. The District Court had subject-matter jurisdiction over its petition, Discover maintained, because Vaden's state-law counterclaims were completely preempted by federal banking law. The District Court agreed and ordered arbitration. Reasoning that a federal court has jurisdiction over a § 4 petition if the parties' underlying dispute presents a federal question, the Fourth Circuit eventually affirmed.

We agree with the Fourth Circuit in part. A federal court may "look through" a § 4 petition and order arbitration if, "save for [the arbitration] agreement," the court would have jurisdiction over "the [substantive] controversy between the parties." We hold, however, that the Court of Appeals misidentified the dimensions of "the controversy between the parties." Focusing on only a slice of the parties' entire controversy, the court seized on Vaden's counterclaims, held them completely preempted, and on that basis affirmed the District Court's order compelling arbitration. Lost from sight was the triggering plea — Discover's claim for the balance due on Vaden's account. Given that entirely state-based plea and the established rule that federal-court jurisdiction cannot be invoked on the basis of a defense or counterclaim, the whole "controversy between the parties" does not qualify for federal-court adjudication. Accordingly, we reverse the Court of Appeals' judgment.

. . .

A

The text of § 4 drives our conclusion that a federal court should determine its jurisdiction by "looking through" a § 4 petition to the parties' underlying substantive controversy. . . . The phrase "save for [the arbitration] agreement" [in § 4 of the FAA] indicates that the district court should assume the absence of the arbitration agreement and determine whether it "would have jurisdiction under title 28" without it. Jurisdiction over what? The text of § 4 refers us to "the controversy between the parties." That phrase, the Fourth Circuit said, and we agree, is most straightforwardly read to mean the "substantive conflict between the parties."

The majority of Courts of Appeals to address the question, we acknowledge, have rejected the "look through" approach entirely, as Vaden asks us to do here. The relevant "controversy between the parties," Vaden insists, is simply and only the parties' discrete dispute over the arbitrability of their claims. She relies, quite reasonably, on the fact that a § 4 petition to compel arbitration seeks no adjudication on the merits of the underlying controversy. Indeed, its very purpose is to have an arbitrator, rather than a court, resolve the merits. A § 4 petition, Vaden observes, is essentially a plea for specific performance of an agreement to arbitrate, and it thus presents principally contractual questions: Did the parties validly agree to arbitrate? What issues does their agreement encompass? Has one party dishonored the agreement?

Vaden's argument, though reasonable, is difficult to square with the statutory language. Section 4 directs courts to determine whether they would have jurisdiction "save for [the arbitration] agreement." How, then, can a dispute over the existence or applicability of an arbitration agreement be the controversy that counts?

The "save for" clause, courts espousing the view embraced by Vaden respond, means only that the "antiquated and arcane" ouster notion no longer holds sway. Adherents to this "ouster" explanation of § 4's language recall that courts traditionally viewed arbitration clauses as unworthy attempts to "oust" them of jurisdiction; accordingly, to guard against encroachment on their domain, they refused to order specific enforcement of agreements to arbitrate. The "save for" clause, as comprehended by proponents of the "ouster" explanation, was designed to ensure that courts would no longer consider themselves ousted of jurisdiction and would therefore specifically enforce arbitration agreements.

We are not persuaded that the "ouster" explanation of § 4's "save for" clause carries the day. To the extent that the ancient "ouster" doctrine continued to impede specific enforcement of arbitration agreements, § 2 of the FAA, the Act's "centerpiece provision," directly attended to the problem. Covered agreements to arbitrate, § 2 declares, are "valid, irrevocable, and enforceable, save upon such grounds as exist at law or in equity for the revocation of any contract." Having commanded that an arbitration agreement is enforceable just as any other contract, Congress had no cause to repeat the point.

In addition to its textual implausibility, the approach Vaden advocates has curious practical consequences. It would permit a federal court to entertain a § 4 petition only when a federal-question suit is already before the court, when the parties satisfy the requirements for diversity-of-citizenship jurisdiction, or when the dispute over arbitrability involves a maritime contract. Vaden's approach would not accommodate a § 4 petitioner who *could* file a federal-question suit in (or remove such a suit to) federal court, but who has not done so. In contrast, when the parties' underlying dispute arises under federal law, the "look through" approach permits a § 4 petitioner to ask a federal court to compel arbitration without first taking the formal step of initiating or removing a federal-question suit — that is, without seeking federal adjudication of the very questions it wants to arbitrate rather than litigate.

B

Having determined that a district court should "look through" a § 4 petition, we now consider whether the court "would have [federal-question] jurisdiction" over "a suit arising out of the controversy" between Discover and Vaden. . . .

. . .

. . . § 4 of the FAA instructs district courts asked to compel arbitration to inquire whether the court would have jurisdiction, "save for [the arbitration] agreement," over "a suit arising out of the controversy between the parties." We read that prescription in light of the well-pleaded complaint rule and the corollary rule that federal jurisdiction cannot be invoked on the basis of a defense or counterclaim. Parties may not circumvent those rules by asking a federal court to order arbitration of the portion of a controversy that implicates federal law when the court would not have federal-question jurisdiction over the controversy as a whole. It does not suffice to show that a federal question lurks somewhere inside the parties' controversy, or that a defense or counterclaim would arise under federal law. Because the controversy between Discover and Vaden, properly perceived, is not one qualifying for federal-court adjudication, § 4 of the FAA does not empower a federal court to order arbitration of that controversy, in whole or in part.

Discover, we note, is not left without recourse. Under the FAA, state courts as well as federal courts are obliged to honor and enforce agreements to arbitrate. Discover may therefore petition a Maryland court for aid in enforcing the arbitration clause of its contracts with Maryland cardholders.

True, Maryland's high court has held that §§ 3 and 4 of the FAA prescribe federal-court procedures and, therefore, do not bind the state courts. But Discover scarcely lacks an available state remedy. Section 2 of the FAA, which does bind the state courts, renders agreements to arbitrate "valid, irrevocable, and *enforceable*." This provision "carries with it duties [to credit and enforce arbitration agreements] indistinguishable from those imposed on federal courts by FAA §§ 3 and 4." Notably, Maryland, like many other States, provides a statutory remedy nearly identical to § 4. Even before it filed its debt-recovery action in a Maryland state court, Discover could have sought from that court an order compelling arbitration of any agreement-related dispute between itself and cardholder Vaden. At no time was federal-court intervention needed to place the controversy between the parties before an arbitrator.

* * *

For the reasons stated, the District Court lacked jurisdiction to entertain Discover's § 4 petition to compel arbitration. The judgment of the Court of Appeals affirming the District Court's order is therefore reversed, and the case is remanded for further proceedings consistent with this opinion.

It is so ordered.

NOTES

1. Prior to *Vaden*, the majority approach in the Circuits had been that a federal court does not have subject matter jurisdiction over a petition to compel arbitration solely on the basis of federal claims involved in the underlying dispute. *See* Westmoreland Capital Corp. v. Findlay, 100 F.3d 263 (2d Cir. 1996); Prudential Bache Secs., Inc. v. Fitch, 966 F.2d 981 (5th Cir. 1992); Smith Barney, Inc. v. Weinhold, 124 F.3d 199 (6th Cir. 1997) (unpublished). Under those cases, when would federal courts have had subject matter jurisdiction over a petition to compel arbitration? In what sorts of cases is the Supreme Court's decision in *Vaden* likely to matter?

2. What if the basis for federal court subject matter jurisdiction was diversity of citizenship rather than federal question jurisdiction? How, if at all, does *Vaden* affect that analysis?

> Prior to *Vaden*, all courts of appeals adopted the same approach in resolving § 4 diversity jurisdiction disputes. They determined . . . whether there is diversity of citizenship . . . by looking only to the parties in the federal action to compel arbitration, whether or not the claim(s) to be arbitrated were part of a parallel state court action that included other, non-diverse parties, unless a non-diverse party would be necessary and indispensable to the federal action under Rule 19 of the Federal Rules of Civil Procedure . . .
>
> . . .
>
> On appeal, Northport argues that *Vaden* did not mandate a new analysis for § 4 diversity jurisdiction disputes . . . . The representatives counter by arguing that, after *Vaden*, courts must "look through" to "the whole controversy as framed by the parties" in deciding § 4 diversity jurisdiction disputes. . . .
>
> The fundamental flaw in the representatives' contention that *Vaden* implicitly overruled prior circuit court diversity jurisdiction decisions . . . is that it ignores the underlying facts and the Supreme Court's decision in Moses H. Cone [Memorial Hosp. v. Mercury Constr. Corp., 460 U.S. 1 (1983)]. . . .
>
> *Moses H. Cone* is factually on all fours with these cases. [In that case, the Supreme Court stated that the independent basis of federal jurisdiction was diversity of citizenship. But it did not discuss that threshold issue, despite noting the presence of a non-diverse party who made the parallel

state court action non-removable.] Even if no party challenged diversity jurisdiction, that the Supreme Court did not even discuss the issue is telling because in other cases it has noted that federal courts are obligated to consider lack of subject matter jurisdiction sua sponte. Thus, the representatives' contention requires us to assume both that the Court overlooked a serious diversity jurisdiction issue in *Moses H. Cone* and then implicitly overruled *Cone*'s jurisdictional underpinnings in *Vaden*. This is contrary to well-established principles. The Supreme Court "does not normally overturn, or so dramatically limit, earlier authority *sub silentio.*"

In addition to a strong reluctance to assume that the Court implicitly overruled an earlier precedent, we find many clues in the majority opinion in *Vaden* that it did not intend to overrule *Moses H. Cone sub silentio.* The Court cited *Moses H. Cone* approvingly. It carefully limited its statement of the issues and holding to federal question jurisdiction. It cited the circuit court cases creating the federal question conflict but did not cite any of the circuit court § 4 diversity cases. This was not likely inadvertent because the circuit court opinions adopting the look through approach to federal question issues cited their earlier no-look-through diversity decisions approvingly.

. . .

For all these reasons, we decline to conclude that *Moses H. Cone* was implicitly overruled *sub silentio* in *Vaden*. . . . Therefore, we conclude that diversity of citizenship is determined in these cases by the citizenship of the parties named in the proceedings before the district court, plus any indispensable parties who must be joined pursuant to Rule 19.

Northport Health Servs. of Ark., LLC v. Rutherford, 605 F.3d 483, 486, 489-91 (8th Cir. 2010).

PROBLEM 4.14

In which of the following cases does the federal court have subject matter jurisdiction? In formulating your answers to this problem, examine 9 U.S.C. §§ 3 & 4, the selected sections of 28 U.S.C. reprinted in the Documentary Supplement, and the materials in this part.

(a) A New York franchisor files a petition to compel arbitration against a New York franchisee in New York federal court. The claims subject to arbitration are state law contract claims involving more than $75,000.

(b) Same facts as (a) except that the franchisee is in Connecticut.

(c) Same facts as (a) except that the franchisee is in Connecticut and the franchisor has a representative in Connecticut who is not a party to the arbitration agreement but who is sued by the franchisee in Connecticut state court.

(d) Same facts as (a) except that the claim that is subject to arbitration is a federal antitrust claim.

If the federal courts have subject matter jurisdiction of a particular case, which federal court is the proper one in which to file a petition to compel arbitration? The following case discusses a potentially important limitation on the power of federal courts to compel arbitration under § 4 of the FAA.

ANSARI v. QWEST COMMUNICATIONS CORP.
United States Court of Appeals for the Tenth Circuit
414 F.3d 1214 (2005)

McKAY, CIRCUIT JUDGE.

Plaintiffs Hamid Ansari and Broadband Utility Resources, L.P. (BUR) filed suit in Colorado district court against defendant Qwest Communications Corp. alleging several claims. Qwest petitioned to compel arbitration in Colorado based on the parties' agreement that disputes would be settled by arbitration. The district court denied the petition, concluding that it had no authority to compel arbitration in Colorado, because the parties had agreed that Washington, D.C. would be the arbitration forum. Also, the court concluded it had no authority to compel arbitration in Washington, D.C. Qwest appeals.

This appeal presents the following issue of first impression in this circuit: Whether § 4 of the Federal Arbitration Act (FAA) prohibited the Colorado district court from compelling arbitration in Colorado when the parties' contractual agreement designated Washington, D.C. as the arbitration forum. Like the district court, we conclude that § 4 did prohibit the district court from compelling arbitration in either Colorado or Washington, D.C. Accordingly, we affirm the district court's order denying arbitration.

. . .

DISCUSSION

Qwest argues that the district court erred in failing to consider the merits of its petition to compel arbitration and should not have required Qwest to initiate a new action in Washington, D.C. Qwest maintains that the plain language of the FAA, its purpose, and its legislative history direct a conclusion that the district court had the authority to compel arbitration in Colorado despite the language of the arbitration clause providing for arbitration to be held in Washington, D.C.

. . .

In considering the statutory language of § 4, courts have taken three different approaches when deciding whether a district court may compel arbitration when the arbitration agreement states that arbitration shall take place in another district. One court has held that a district court may compel arbitration in the district specified in the arbitration agreement, even though that district is outside its own district. Dupuy-Busching Gen. Agency, Inc. v. Ambassador Ins. Co., 524 F.2d 1275, 1276, 1278 (5th Cir. 1975) (recognizing Mississippi district court's order directing parties to proceed with arbitration in New Jersey was contrary to express terms of § 4, but finding district court acted correctly where plaintiff sought to avoid arbitration by bringing suit in Mississippi, rather than contract forum of New Jersey, and defendant sought arbitration under terms of agreement). Neither party to this appeal suggests that this is the correct approach. And we agree. No statutory language supports this approach.

Qwest favors a second approach, permitting the district court to compel arbitration in its own district and ignore the forum specified in the arbitration clause. The Ninth Circuit took this approach in Textile Unlimited, Inc. v. A. BMH & Co., 240 F.3d 781, 783 (9th Cir. 2001), holding that the FAA "does not require venue in the contractually-designated locale." In reaching this holding, the Ninth Circuit relied on *Cortez Byrd Chips, Inc. v. Bill Harbert Construction Co.*, which held that the venue provisions of §§ 9-11 of the FAA are permissive and allow a motion to confirm, vacate, or modify an arbitration award to be brought in any district court where venue is proper. The Ninth Circuit decided that the §§ 9-11 venue analysis of *Cortez Byrd Chips* should apply to the FAA as a whole. The Ninth Circuit therefore held that the § 4 venue provisions are discretionary, not mandatory. The court determined that on its face, "§ 4 only confines the *arbitration* to the district in which the petition to compel is filed. It does not require that the petition be filed where the contract specified that arbitration should occur."

This approach, however, fails to recognize that there is a difference between § 4 and §§ 9-11. And *Cortez Byrd Chips* specifically addresses §§ 9-11, not § 4. Although § 4 initially states a party "may petition any United States district court which, save for such agreement" has jurisdiction, it later, more narrowly, states "the hearing and proceedings, under such agreement, shall be within the district in which the petition for an order directing such arbitration is filed." Unlike §§ 9-11, which use the permissive language "may," § 4 uses the mandatory language "shall." Thus, the different sections have different venue provisions. Also, § 4 states that "the court shall make an order directing the parties to proceed to arbitration in accordance with the terms of the agreement." The Ninth Circuit ignores this statutory language. That court's approach fails to give effect to all of the § 4 statutory language directing that arbitration be in accordance with the terms of the agreement and that a district court can order arbitration only within its own district. Thus, we must reject this approach that Qwest favors.

Instead, we agree with plaintiffs and the district court that a third approach taken by a majority of courts is the correct approach. This majority view holds that where the parties agreed to arbitrate in a particular forum only a district court in that forum has authority to compel arbitration under § 4. *See, e.g.,* Inland Bulk Transfer Co. v. Cummins Engine Co., 332 F.3d 1007, 1018 (6th Cir. 2003); Mgmt. Recruiters Int'l, Inc. v. Bloor, 129 F.3d 851, 854 (6th Cir. 1997); Merrill Lynch, Pierce, Fenner & Smith, Inc. v. Lauer, 49 F.3d 323, 327 (7th Cir. 1995); *see also* Econo-Car Int'l, Inc. v. Antilles Car Rentals, Inc., 499 F.2d 1391, 1394, 11 V.I. 258 (3d Cir. 1974) (holding Virgin Islands district court could not compel arbitration in New York, forum agreed upon in arbitration clause, and noting restrictive reading of § 4 may preclude it from ordering arbitration in Virgin Islands). In other words, "a district court lacks authority to compel arbitration in other districts, or in its own district if another has been specified for arbitration." Any other result renders meaningless the § 4 mandate that arbitration and the order compelling arbitration issue from the same district.

. . . The legislative history of the FAA, albeit sketchy and incomplete, lends additional credence to this view. Describing the § 4 proviso that requires the hearings and the petition to issue from the same district, the Senate Committee on the Judiciary indicated that the statute was intended to require a party seeking to compel arbitration to apply to the proper court. S. Rep. No. 536, 68th Cong., 1st Sess. 3 (1924). Section 4 is aimed at streamlining the path toward arbitration and preventing scattered attacks in various judicial fora.

Qwest also argues that the district court's order contravenes the legislative intent to remove obstructions to arbitration where the parties have agreed to resolve their disputes by arbitration. The district court, however, did not obstruct Qwest's ability to obtain arbitration in the agreed-upon forum of Washington, D.C. Instead, the district court acted in accordance with the FAA's purpose to enforce private agreements, which requires rigorously enforcing agreements to arbitrate.

Next, Qwest argues that because plaintiffs chose to file suit in Colorado district court, they waived the forum selection clause in the arbitration section of the IRU Agreement. We do not address waiver in this appeal. It is presumed that the arbitrator will address any allegations concerning waiver. And nothing before us rebuts that presumption.

Finally, Qwest argues that the district court erred in ordering it to file a motion to compel arbitration in the District of Columbia district court, because a court in that district "may not" have personal jurisdiction over Qwest, and "apparently" would lack personal or subject matter jurisdiction over such a motion. Because Qwest failed to raise this argument at any time in the district court, we need not address it.

The order of the district court is AFFIRMED.

What if a defendant is unable to remove the action to federal court, perhaps because a non-diverse defendant was joined in state court? The following case discusses one course of action that defendants sometimes follow under such circumstances.

SPECIALTY BAKERIES, INC. v. ROBHAL, INC.
United States District Court for the Eastern District of Pennsylvania
961 F. Supp. 822 (1997)

BARTLE, DISTRICT JUDGE.

This matter may be succinctly summarized as a biting battle over bagels between a franchisor and franchisee. Not surprisingly, each side argues that the other's case is full of holes.

The court has subject matter jurisdiction based on diversity of citizenship under 28 U.S.C. § 1332. After a hearing on franchisor's motion for a preliminary injunction, the court makes the following findings of fact and conclusions of law, pursuant to Rule 52 of the Federal Rules of Civil Procedure.

I

The plaintiffs in this action are Specialty Bakeries, Inc. ("Specialty Bakeries") . . . and Manhattan Bagel Company, Inc. ("Manhattan Bagel Company") (herein-after collectively "franchisor"). Specialty Bakeries formerly traded as "Bagel Builders," a franchise system of retail bagel stores. On May 22, 1996, through a merger transaction, Specialty Bakeries became a wholly-owned subsidiary of Manhattan Bagel Company. . . . Defendants are HalRob, Inc. ("HalRob") and RobHal Management, Inc. ("RobHal") (hereinafter collectively "HalRob").

In September, 1995 HalRob and RobHal entered into a written franchise agreement with Specialty Bakeries entitled "Bagel Builders Franchise Agreement" as well as a first amendment thereto. As a result, HalRob obtained the right to operate a franchise for a Bagel Builders Restaurant in Broomall, Pennsylvania. The Broomall location, with which we are concerned here, opened as a Bagel Builders in April, 1996.

The franchise contract contains an arbitration provision which is at the heart of the controversy before the court. . . .

. . . [T]he parties also agreed to a non-compete clause which HalRob contends gave it an exclusive territory within a four mile radius of their Broomall restaurant. . . .

Prior to Manhattan Bagel Company's acquisition of Specialty Bakeries in May, 1996, the former had two franchisees operating under the name of "Manhattan Bagel" within four miles of HalRob's Bagel Builders Restaurant. Manhattan Bagel Company also had an agreement dated July, 1995, with a new franchisee. That franchisee opened a Manhattan Bagel store on June 18, 1996 within the same area.

The Bagel Builders trade name was discontinued after Manhattan Bagel Company acquired Specialty Bakeries. . . . Because of Manhattan Bagel Company's acquisition of Specialty Bakeries, four Manhattan Bagel stores now coexist in the Broomall vicinity. This state of affairs has led to the present controversy between HalRob and the franchisor.

Instead of immediately proceeding to arbitration as provided in the franchise agreement, HalRob filed suit on February 7, 1997 in the Superior Court of New Jersey, Camden County, Chancery Division. In the New Jersey complaint, HalRob alleges that as a result of Manhattan Bagel Company's ownership of Specialty Bakeries, three Manhattan Bagel businesses now illegally compete with HalRob's store within four miles of its situs. . . . It . . . seeks injunctive relief, compensatory damages, punitive damages, attorney's fees, and costs.

. . . [T]he New Jersey complaint also request[s] the court to "permanently enjoin Defendants Manhattan Bagel Company, Inc. and Specialty Bakeries, Inc. during the term of the [franchise] agreement and any extension or renewal of that agreement" [from having any dealings with the Manhattan Bagel outlets alleged to be in violation of the non-compete agreement]. . . .

. . . The New Jersey Superior Court has refused to stay the action pending arbitration. A hearing on HalRob's request for a preliminary injunction seeking the relief detailed above is scheduled before the state court in Camden, New Jersey on April 21, 1997.

In the meantime, on February 12, 1997, five days after the New Jersey action was instituted, the franchisor filed with this court a petition to compel arbitration, pursuant to the Federal Arbitration Act, 9 U.S.C. § 4. It claims that the issues in the New Jersey action are subject to, and can only be determined by, arbitration as set forth in the franchise agreement between the parties. The agreement specifically references the Federal Arbitration Act.

On March 26, 1997, this court entered an Order granting the petition to compel arbitration. . . .

On April 1, 1997, franchisor filed a motion for a temporary restraining order asking this court to enjoin HalRob from seeking the broad injunctive relief requested in the New Jersey action. . . . With the agreement of HalRob, the franchisor converted its motion for a temporary restraining order into a motion for a preliminary injunction. The court held an evidentiary hearing on April 9, 1997.

II

. . .

. . . [A] court may grant a preliminary injunction to preserve or restore the status quo so that the arbitration process may proceed unfettered, even when the parties' arbitration agreement does not contain a provision authorizing interim injunctive relief. . . . [T]he franchisor must establish: (1) reasonable probability of success on the merits; (2) irreparable harm if relief is not granted to prevent a change in the status quo; (3) possibility of harm to third parties from the grant or denial of the injunction; and (4) the public interest.

The franchisor has met all four prongs. It has demonstrated a reasonable probability of success on the merits, that is, that HalRob's resort to the New Jersey state court violates the arbitration provision of the parties' franchise agreement. Franchisor has also established that it will be irreparably harmed unless we enter a preliminary injunction. Interference with the functioning of the arbitration proceeding constitutes irreparable harm. Moreover, the harm to franchisor, including the individual plaintiffs, in not granting the preliminary injunction clearly outweighs the harm to HalRob in granting the requested relief. Third parties, those Manhattan Bagel Company franchisees who would be forced to close at least temporarily, would also be irreparably harmed. Finally, the public interest is served by preserving the integrity of the arbitration process under the Federal Arbitration Act.

The franchisor has established its right to a preliminary injunction to preserve the status quo and to prevent any interference with the arbitration to which the parties consented in their franchise agreement.

III

HalRob argues, however, that there is still a significant hole in the franchisor's case. HalRob contends that this court is barred because of the federal Anti-Injunction Act from issuing an injunction to interfere with or restrain a state court action. This Act states:

> A court of the United States may not grant an injunction to stay proceedings in a State court except as expressly authorized by Act of Congress, or where necessary in aid of its jurisdiction, or to protect or effectuate its judgments.

28 U.S.C. § 2283. The purpose of this statute is to recognize the "fundamental constitutional independence of the states and their courts" and "to prevent needless friction" between them and the federal courts. The Act may not be avoided by addressing the injunction to the parties, rather than to the state court. Thus, this court may not enjoin any portion of the New Jersey proceeding or the parties to it unless our order falls within one of the three exceptions of the Anti-Injunction Act.

The second exception, which allows this court to grant an injunction "where necessary in aid of its jurisdiction" is available and applicable in the present circumstances. Although this exception previously applied only to in rem proceedings, it has since been expanded to include situations "where the federal court has reached a judgment, but retains jurisdiction over the action to supervise the implementation of its order."

In our Order dated March 26, 1997, we "ORDERED that this court will retain jurisdiction until further order of court, pending completion of the arbitration proceeding." As such, we retained jurisdiction "to supervise implementation of [our] order." To allow HalRob to proceed to a preliminary injunction hearing in the state court seeking relief far beyond what the parties contemplated in that forum would eviscerate the arbitration process and make it a "hollow formality," with needless expense to all concerned. We do not have to wait until the state court acts. While the Supreme Court has not passed upon the applicability of the Anti-Injunction Act in the arbitration context, it has observed, "[c]ontracts to arbitrate are not to be avoided by allowing one party to ignore the contract and resort to the courts. Such a course could lead to prolonged litigation, one of the very risks the parties, by contracting for arbitration, sought to eliminate." *Southland Corp. v. Keating.*

We are sensitive to notions of federalism and comity. Yet, the integrity of arbitration under the Federal Arbitration Act constitutes an important federal policy. We do not believe that a contracting party or a state court may act in any way to undercut that policy, where as here a federal court order compelling arbitration has been issued. A preliminary injunction restraining the HalRob from proceeding in state court is necessary in aid of our jurisdiction so as to preserve the integrity of this arbitration process. Otherwise, HalRob can obtain full and complete injunctive relief and money damages in the state court, as it requests in its complaint there. Little or nothing would be left for the arbitrator.

Accordingly, we enjoin HalRob from proceeding in the New Jersey Superior Court to upset the status quo as it existed on February 7, 1997, pending the decision of the arbitrator. As we stated in our March 26, 1997 Order, the parties are to move promptly to resolve their dispute through arbitration.

NOTES

1. The United States Supreme Court has not addressed the use of antisuit injunctions in support of arbitration, as noted in *Specialty Bakeries*. The Court has indicated that a federal court should not abstain from ruling on a petition to compel arbitration because of a parallel state court proceeding, but has not considered whether the federal court should enjoin the state proceeding if it grants the petition to compel. *See* Moses H. Cone Memorial Hosp. v. Mercury Constr. Corp., 460 U.S. 1 (1983) (holding that under *Colorado River* abstention doctrine, no exceptional circumstances justified abstention; therefore federal district court abused its discretion in staying federal court action pending resolution of state court case seeking stay of arbitration); Quackenbush v. Allstate Ins. Co., 517 U.S. 706, 728 (1996) (remand of removed case to state court on grounds of *Burford* abstention inappropriate, in part because "motion to compel arbitration under the Federal Arbitration Act (FAA) implicates a substantial federal concern for the enforcement of arbitration agreements").

2. Not all federal courts are as willing to issue injunctions against state court litigation pending arbitration as the *RobHal* court. *See, e.g.*, THI of N.M. at Hobbs Ctr., LLC v. Patton, 2012 U.S. Dist. LEXIS 5252, at *74-*76 (D.N.M. Jan. 3, 2012):

> This Court is not persuaded that the FAA authorizes or requires such an injunction [against a state court suit pending compelled arbitration]. . . . Section 3 only provides that "the court in which such suit is pending" must stay proceedings if arbitration is required. Section 3 thus is not the express, unambiguous grant of authority by Congress for a federal court to stay state court proceedings. Nor is this Court persuaded that a stay of state court proceedings is necessary to aid its jurisdiction or to protect or effectuate its judgments. This case is before the Court under Section 4, which gives this Court authority to order *parties* to arbitrate where diversity or federal question jurisdiction is present. This Court has now resolved the issues of arbitration pending before it, and will order Defendant to arbitrate with Plaintiffs . . . . The Court fully expects the parties to comply with this Order, but should a party not so comply, dismissal of this case does not prevent a party from bringing a judgment enforcement action to compel compliance. This Court therefore has the tools at its disposal to protect and effectuate its judgment and to aid in its jurisdiction without resorting to an injunction against the state court. Moreover, the state court is bound to follow the FAA, just as is this Court, and there is no reason to believe the state court will force Defendant to proceed with the claims against Plaintiffs . . . in contravention of the FAA and this Order. The Court will therefore deny Plaintiffs' request for an order to stay the State Court Action.

3. Professor Jean Sternlight has criticized federal courts for being "overly willing to issue arbitral antisuit injunctions." Jean R. Sternlight, *Forum Shopping for Arbitration Decisions: Federal Courts' Use of Antisuit Injunctions Against State Courts*, 147 U. PA. L. REV. 91, 202 (1998). She highlights the "iron[y]" of federal

courts "us[ing] the force of federal supremacy to subordinate state interests in favor of a third forum, non-judicial private dispute resolution," and concludes that "when federal courts allow their great enthusiasm for arbitration to overwhelm their proper analysis of antisuit injunctions, they will inevitably issue decisions that are not only damaging to the relationship between federal and state courts, but also unjust." *Id.* at 203.

4.   For a detailed analysis of the procedural options for enforcing an arbitration agreement, from the perspective of a corporation seeking enforcement, see Mark R. Kravitz & Edward Wood Dunham, *Compelling Arbitration*, LITIGATION, Fall 1996, at 34.

PROBLEM 4.15

A Montana consumer purchases goods directly from an Illinois manufacturer (e.g., by using the manufacturer's web page). The sales contract provides that all disputes are to be settled by arbitration in Illinois. When a defect in the product injures the consumer, the consumer files suit in Montana state court, seeking $500,000 in damages. What procedural options should the manufacturer consider in seeking to compel arbitration? What options are available to the consumer? What other information do you need to know?

Chapter 5

ENFORCING INTERNATIONAL AGREEMENTS TO ARBITRATE

§ 5.01 OVERVIEW

Commercial arbitration is a particularly important means of resolving disputes in international transactions. As we have seen, none of the parties to an international contract ordinarily wants to have a dispute adjudicated in another party's home court. Arbitration provides a neutral forum on which all parties can agree. A significant proportion of many (albeit not all) types of international contracts provide for arbitration as a means of resolving disputes. GARY B. BORN, INTERNATIONAL COMMERCIAL ARBITRATION 71 (2009).

The enforceability of international arbitration agreements is governed by treaty and by national arbitration laws. The Convention on the Recognition and Enforcement of Foreign Arbitral Awards (the "New York Convention") broadly requires countries that are parties to the Convention to enforce arbitration agreements within its scope. Article II(1) of the New York Convention provides that "[e]ach Contracting State shall recognize an agreement in writing under which the parties undertake to submit to arbitration all or any differences which have arisen or which may arise between them in respect of a defined legal relationship, whether contractual or not, concerning a subject matter capable of settlement by arbitration." Further, Article II(3) requires that "[t]he court of a Contracting State, when seized of an action in a matter in respect of which the parties have made an agreement within the meaning of this article, shall, at the request of one of the parties, refer the parties to arbitration, unless it finds that the said agreement is null and void, inoperative or incapable of being performed." The United States has implemented its treaty obligation in Chapter 2 of Federal Arbitration Act. This chapter contains special provisions governing the enforcement of agreements to arbitrate that fall under the New York Convention. The United States also is a party to the Inter-American Convention on International Commercial Arbitration (the "Panama Convention"), which in most respects is similar to the New York Convention. The U.S. has implemented its obligations under the Panama Convention in Chapter 3 of the FAA.

Many of the issues raised in actions to enforce international arbitration agreements are analogous to those presented in the domestic arena. Indeed, the discussion in this chapter builds on what you now know about enforcing domestic arbitration agreements. This chapter focuses on the enforceability of international arbitration agreements under the Federal Arbitration Act, but also contains comparative materials that raise issues or suggest approaches from other countries. This chapter first addresses the prerequisites that must be met for the New York

Convention to apply. Second, it looks at possible defenses to the enforcement of agreements to arbitrate international disputes. Third, it examines procedural issues in enforcing international arbitration agreements, focusing on Chapter 2 of the FAA.

§ 5.02 SCOPE OF THE NEW YORK CONVENTION

Various requirements must be met for the New York Convention to apply. The following sections address those requirements, focusing principally (although not exclusively) on the implementation of the Convention in the United States. Note that even if the New York Convention does not apply, courts may enforce international arbitration agreements under national arbitration laws. As you review the materials in this chapter, try to identify differences between the enforceability of arbitration agreements under Chapter 1 of the FAA, dealing with domestic arbitration, and Chapters 2 and 3 of the FAA, dealing with international arbitration.

[A] "Agreement in Writing"

For the New York Convention to apply, there first must be an "agreement in writing" within the meaning of the Convention. Article II(2) of the Convention defines an "agreement in writing" as follows: "The term 'agreement in writing' shall include an arbitral clause in a contract or an arbitration agreement, signed by the parties or contained in an exchange of letters or telegrams." Difficulties arise in a variety of circumstances: "tacit or oral acceptance of a written purchase order or of a written sales confirmation; an orally concluded contract referring to written general conditions (e.g., oral reference to a form of salvage); or, certain brokers' notes, bills of lading and other instruments or contracts transferring rights or obligations to non-signing third parties (i.e., third parties who were not party to the original agreement." United Nations Commission on International Trade Law, Note by the Secretariat on Possible Future Work in the Area of International Commercial Arbitration A/CN.9/460, at ¶ 25 (Apr. 6, 1999). The following case provides an illustration.

KAHN LUCAS LANCASTER, INC. v. LARK INTERNATIONAL LTD.
United States Court of Appeals for the Second Circuit
186 F.3d 210 (1999)

PARKER, CIRCUIT JUDGE:

Defendant-Appellant Lark International, Ltd., ("Lark") appeals from a judgment of the United States District Court for the Southern District of New York . . . granting Plaintiff-Appellee Kahn Lucas Lancaster, Inc.'s ("Kahn Lucas") motion under 9 U.S.C. § 206 and the Convention on the Recognition and Enforcement of Foreign Arbitral Awards to compel arbitration. The judgment was entered in accordance with an Opinion and Order of the district court, dated August 6, 1997, which held that arbitration clauses in certain purchase orders sent by Kahn Lucas to Lark were enforceable under the Convention and bound Lark, despite the fact that Lark had not signed the purchase orders.

We reverse.

I. BACKGROUND

A. *Facts*

Lark is a Hong Kong corporation which acts as a purchasing agent for businesses seeking to buy and import clothing manufactured in Asia. Kahn Lucas is a New York corporation, with its principal place of business in New York, NY, engaged in the children's clothing business, primarily in reselling imported clothing to major retailers.

Kahn Lucas and Lark enjoyed a business relationship which began in 1988 and pursuant to which Lark would assist Kahn Lucas in arranging for overseas manufacturers to make garments ordered by Kahn Lucas. As part of this relationship, Lark processed Kahn Lucas's purchase orders and invoices. Pursuant to the terms of the purchase orders, as well as the parties' standing practice, the manufacturers would issue Kahn Lucas a seller's invoice for payment once the ordered garments were completed. Lark would then issue a separate invoice to Kahn Lucas for its commission, usually a set percentage of the amount charged by the manufacturer, on the order. Kahn Lucas paid both of these invoices through draw-downs on an existing letter of credit on which Lark was the named beneficiary. Lark would then remit payment to the manufacturer.

The dispute in this case arises from two purchase orders Kahn Lucas issued in early 1995 for children's fleece garments, manufactured in the Philippines, that it was to resell to Sears Roebuck, Inc. (the "Purchase Orders"). The Purchase Orders stated that the garments were "ordered from" Lark, listed "Lark International (Agent)" as seller, and were signed by Kahn Lucas. They were not signed by Lark. The Purchase Orders also clearly indicated that they contained a number of additional terms printed on the reverse side, and were made conditional upon the seller's acceptance of those terms. Included in these terms were clauses relating to arbitration. . . . Lark accepted the Purchase Orders without objection.

In July 1995, the manufacturers issued final invoices relating to the ordered garments, and Lark issued its commission invoice. But citing defective garments and failed deliveries, Kahn Lucas refused to release funds to Lark to pay either the seller's invoices or Lark's commission invoice.

B. *Proceedings Below*

Unable to achieve a satisfactory settlement with Lark and the manufacturers, Kahn Lucas sued Lark in the United States District Court for the Southern District of New York, invoking diversity jurisdiction and alleging breach of contract, breach of warranty, negligence, and breach of fiduciary duty. . . .

By motion brought pursuant to 9 U.S.C. § 206 and the Convention, Kahn Lucas converted its complaint into a motion to compel Lark to arbitrate the dispute in accordance with the Arbitration Clauses. Kahn Lucas also filed a demand for arbitration with the American Arbitration Association. Lark opposed the motion to compel arbitration . . . argu[ing] that the Arbitration Clauses were not enforceable under the Convention because Lark had not signed the Purchase Orders.

In an Opinion and Order dated August 6, 1997, the district court granted Kahn Lucas's motion to compel arbitration. The district court first noted that subject matter jurisdiction could only be properly based on section 203 of the implementing statutes of the Convention, 9 U.S.C. § 203, which provides an independent basis for subject matter jurisdiction; it could not be based on diversity (citing Matimak Trading Co. v. Khalily, 118 F.3d 76 (2d Cir. 1997) (holding that Hong Kong corporations are not citizens of a foreign state for purposes of diversity jurisdiction)). . . .

The court next focused on whether the Arbitration Clauses were enforceable under the Convention so as to vest the court with jurisdiction under section 203. . . . Although Lark had not signed the Purchase Orders, the district court held that the Purchase Orders represented an "arbitral clause in a contract," and therefore an "agreement in writing" to arbitrate sufficient to bring the dispute within the Convention. In holding that an arbitral clause in a contract need not be signed by the parties to be enforceable under the Convention, the district court relied on the only appellate case interpreting this section of the Convention, Sphere Drake Ins. PLC v. Marine Towing, Inc., 16 F.3d 666, 669 (5th Cir.1994). . . .

. . .

II. ANALYSIS

. . .

For the reasons that follow, we hold that the definition of "agreement in writing" in the Convention requires that such an agreement, whether it be an arbitration agreement or an arbitral clause in a contract, be signed by the parties or contained in a series of letters or telegrams. Therefore, the Arbitration Clauses are not enforceable under the Convention, and both the district court and this Court lack subject matter jurisdiction over the dispute. Because of this holding, . . . we accordingly reverse the judgment of the district court and dismiss Kahn Lucas's motion to compel arbitration for lack of subject matter jurisdiction.

A. *Applicable Principles of Construction*

Treaties are construed in much the same manner as statutes. The district court's construction of the Convention, like the construction of any statute, is a matter of law which we review *de novo*. Statutory construction is a "holistic endeavor" and must account for the statute's "full text, language as well as punctuation, structure and subject matter." Thus, the obvious starting point in construing a treaty is its text. And the plain meaning of a text "will typically heed the commands of its punctuation."

Among the rules of punctuation applied in construing statutes is this: When a modifier is set off from a series of antecedents by a comma, the modifier should be read to apply to each of those antecedents. As stated by the Eleventh Circuit, this rule is a "supplementary 'rule of punctuation' " to the "doctrine of the last antecedent," which states that a modifier generally applies only to the nearest, or last, antecedent.[1] Of course, "these doctrines are not absolute rules," and in applying them we are mindful of the Supreme Court's admonition that "a purported plain-meaning analysis based only on punctuation is necessarily incomplete and runs the risk of distorting a statute's true meaning."

In addition to utilizing rules of punctuation, we are aided in our plain-meaning analysis by the fact that the Convention exists in five official languages — French, Spanish, English, Chinese, and Russian — of equal authenticity. *See* New York Convention art. XVI, § 1. Because one purpose of the Convention is to unify the standards under which international agreements to arbitrate are observed, we should, if possible, adhere to an interpretation consistent with all of the official languages. That said, some of the official languages provide more insight into the drafters' intent than others: Of the five official languages, English, French, and Spanish were the working languages of the United Nations Conference on International Commercial Arbitration, which drafted the Convention. . . .

Finally, to the extent the drafters' intent is unclear from the text of the multiple versions of the Convention, we may turn to the Convention's legislative history for guidance.

B. *Construction of the New York Convention*

. . . Lark contends that the modifying clause "signed by the parties or contained in an exchange of letters or telegrams," modifies both: (1) "an arbitral clause in a contract" and (2) "an arbitration agreement" and, as a result, the dispute between the parties is not arbitrable due to the absence of Lark's signature on the Purchase Orders. Kahn Lucas contends, and the district court held, that "signed by the parties" modifies only the clause immediately preceding it, "an arbitration agreement," and not the previous clause. Thus, in Kahn Lucas's view, the unsigned Purchase Orders constitute an "agreement in writing" to arbitrate enforceable under the Convention.

As an initial matter, we must determine the meaning of the two elements in the series, namely "an arbitral clause in a contract" and "an arbitration agreement." We find the meaning of "an arbitral clause in a contract" to be self-evident. We also find that the phrase "an arbitration agreement," because it is used in conjunction with the phrase "an arbitral clause in a contract," refers to any agreement to arbitrate which is not a clause in a larger agreement, whether that agreement is part of a larger contractual relationship or is an entirely distinct agreement which relates to a non-contractual dispute. The parties agree that the Arbitration Clauses each

---

[1] These rules are illustrated by the following examples. Consider a sentence containing two antecedents — "A" and "B" — and one modifying phrase — "with C." The doctrine of the last antecedent suggests that if the sentence were structured "A or B with C," the phrase "with C" should be read to modify only "B." However, the "supplementary rule" . . . suggests that if the sentence were structured "A or B, with C", the phrase "with C" should be read to modify both "A" and "B."

constitute "an arbitral clause in a contract" and not "an arbitration agreement" under the Convention.

We turn, then, to the plain meaning of the English-language version of the Convention. Taking its lead from the Fifth Circuit's analysis in *Sphere Drake*, Kahn Lucas argues that the grammatical structure of section 2 compels the conclusion that its dispute with Lark falls within the Convention. We disagree. Section 2 takes the structure "A or B, with C." This structure is exactly that to which the "supplementary rule of punctuation" . . . applies. Grammatically, the comma immediately following "an arbitration agreement" serves to separate the series ("an arbitral clause in a contract or an arbitration agreement") from the modifying phrase ("signed by the parties or contained in an exchange of letters or telegrams"), and suggests that the modifying phrase is meant to apply to both elements in the series. Indeed, this comma can serve no other grammatical purpose. As a result, Kahn Lucas's reading of the statute would render the comma mere surplusage, a construction frowned upon.

Although the grammatical structure of the English-language version of the Convention suggests that the parties' dispute is not arbitrable, we are hesitant to use punctuation as the sole guide to the meaning of the text. But in this case, other available interpretive tools strongly support the conclusion the punctuation suggests.

First, the plain language of the other working-language versions of the Convention compels the conclusion that, in order to be enforceable under the Convention, both an arbitral clause in a contract and an arbitration agreement must be signed by the parties or contained in an exchange of letters or telegrams. In the French- and Spanish-language versions, the word for "signed" appears in the plural form, "*signes*" and "*firmados*" respectively. Because each of the two antecedents is couched in the singular, the modifier unambiguously applies to both of them. If, as Kahn Lucas argues, only an arbitration agreement need be signed by the parties, the French-language version would utilize the verb "*signe*" and the Spanish "*firmado.*"

The non-working official-language versions of the Convention do not offer similarly clear-cut support for this interpretation, but do not weigh strongly against it either. . . .

Finally, to the extent the plain meanings of the non-English language versions of the Convention do not resolve any ambiguity that exists in the English-language version, the legislative history of article II puts the matter to rest. The text of article II, as reported by the Conference's Working Group, and subject only to modification by the Drafting Committee for form, not substance, reverses the terms "arbitration agreement" and "arbitration clause in a contract." The Working Group text thus reads: "The expression 'agreement in writing' shall mean an arbitration agreement or an arbitration clause in a contract signed by the parties, or an exchange of letters or telegrams between those parties." Therefore, unless the modifier "signed" in the Convention applies to both antecedents, the Drafting Committee's editorial changes would amount to an unintended, and unauthorized, substantive amendment to article II, section 2.

Accordingly, although we are cognizant that the Convention "should be interpreted broadly to effectuate its recognition and enforcement purposes," the rules governing our construction do not allow us to follow the Fifth Circuit's interpretation of article II, section 2 as expressed in *Sphere Drake*. Upon review of the Convention's text, punctuation and subject matter, as well as an examination of the Convention's legislative history, we hold that the modifying phrase "signed by the parties or contained in an exchange of letters or telegrams" applies to both "an arbitral clause in a contract" and "an arbitration agreement."

C. *Application to the Facts*

. . .

As noted above, the Arbitration Clauses were contained in the Purchase Orders which were signed only by Kahn Lucas, and not by Lark. There is therefore no "arbitral clause in a contract . . . signed by the parties." Further, Kahn Lucas does not contend that the Purchase Orders, even together with Lark's Confirmation of Order forms, represent "an arbitral clause in a contract . . . contained in an exchange of letters or telegrams." As a result, there is no "agreement in writing" sufficient to bring this dispute within the scope of the Convention.

Because the dispute in question does not fall within the Convention, subject matter jurisdiction cannot properly be premised on 9 U.S.C. § 203. The district court and this Court thus lack subject matter jurisdiction over this dispute. The judgment of the district court is reversed, and Kahn Lucas's motion to compel arbitration is dismissed with prejudice.

III. CONCLUSION

For the foregoing reasons, the judgment of the district court is reversed, and Kahn Lucas's motion to compel arbitration is dismissed with prejudice for lack of subject matter jurisdiction.

NOTES

1. For a contrary interpretation of Article II(2), see the Fifth Circuit's opinion in Sphere Drake Insurance PLC v. Marine Towing, Inc., 16 F.3d 666 (5th Cir.), *cert. denied*, 513 U.S. 871 (1994):

> Marine Towing contends that, because it did not sign the insurance contract, the policy cannot provide the agreement in writing. Marine Towing would define an "agreement in writing" only as 1) a contract or other written agreement signed by the parties or 2) an exchange of correspondence between the parties demonstrating consent to arbitrate. We disagree with this interpretation of the Convention. We would outline the Convention definition of "agreement in writing" to include either
>
> (1) an arbitral clause in a contract or
>
> (2) an arbitration agreement,

(a) signed by the parties or

(b) contained in an exchange of letters or telegrams.

The insurance contract indisputably contains an arbitral clause. Because what is at issue here is an arbitral clause in a contract, the qualifications applicable to arbitration agreements do not apply. A signature is therefore not required. The district court properly did not require that the contract containing an arbitral provision be signed to constitute an agreement in writing under the Convention.

Id. at 669–70. *Compare* Standard Bent Glass Corp. v. Glassrobots Oy, 333 F.3d 440 (3d Cir. 2003) (following *Kahn Lucas* interpretation). For a critical analysis of *Sphere Drake*, published before the decision in *Kahn Lucas*, see Paul D. Friedland, *U.S. Courts' Misapplication of the "Agreement in Writing" Requirement for Enforcement of an Arbitration Agreement Under the New York Convention*, MEALEY'S INT'L ARB. REP., May 1998, at 21.

2.   Courts in a number of other countries have concluded that tacit acceptance does not satisfy Article II(2)'s requirement of an "agreement in writing." *See, e.g.*, Marc Rich & Co AG v. Italimpianti SpA (Corte di Cassazione 1991), *in* 17 Y.B. COMM. ARB. 554, 557 (1992) (Italy); James Allen Ltd. v. Marea Producten B.V. (Court of Appeal The Hague 1984), *in* 10 Y.B. COMM. ARB. 485, 486 (1985) (The Netherlands); Sté Confex v. Ets. Dahan (Cour de Cassation 1986), *in* 12 Y.B. COMM. ARB. 484, 485 (1987) (France). One exception is the Tribunal Fédéral of Switzerland, which has declined to apply the writing requirement strictly, reasoning that "with the development of modern means of communication, unsigned written documents have an increasing importance and diffusion, [and] . . . the need for a signature inevitably diminishes, especially in international commerce." Compagnie de Navigation et Transports SA v. MSC-Mediterranean Shipping Co. (Tribunal Fédéral 1995), *in* 21 Y.B. COMM. ARB. 690, 697 (1996) (Switzerland).

3.   In 2006, UNCITRAL issued a "recommendation" concerning the proper interpretation of Article II(2) — that it "be applied recognizing that the circumstances described therein are not exhaustive." UNCITRAL, Recommendation Regarding the Interpretation of Article II, Paragraph 2, and Article VII, Paragraph 1, of the Convention on the Recognition and Enforcement of Foreign Arbitral Awards, U.N. Doc. A/6/17 (July 7, 2006). Does the text of the Convention support such an interpretation? How much force should American (and other) courts give to the UNCITRAL recommendation? Does it undercut the holding in *Kahn Lucas*?

4.   The national arbitration laws of at least some countries (including the United States) have less demanding writing requirements than does the New York Convention as interpreted in *Kahn Lucas*. *See, e.g.*, German Arbitration Law 1998, § 1031(2), *in* 2 INT'L HANDBOOK ON COMMERCIAL ARBITRATION, *Germany*: Annex I-2 (Supp. June 2009); Arbitration Act 1996, sched. 1, art. 7(1) (New Zealand), *in* 3 INT'L HANDBOOK ON COMMERCIAL ARBITRATION, *New Zealand*: Annex I-11 (Supp. Mar. 2011) ("An arbitration agreement may be made orally or in writing"). *Compare* UNCITRAL Model Law on International Commercial Arbitration art. 7(2). Can a court enforce an arbitration agreement based on the national arbitration law even if the requirements of the New York Convention are not satisfied? Will enforcement of the

arbitration agreement under the national arbitration law interfere with the ability to enforce the arbitration award under the New York Convention? *See* N.Y. Convention arts. V(1); VII(1); *see also* Eric A. Schwartz, *The Effect of the Arbitration Agreement on the Enforcement of the Award: Issues for the Upcoming Decade*, ICC INT'L CT. ARB. BULL. 105, 107–09 (Special Supp. 1999).

5. For a discussion of whether electronic communications satisfy the requirement of an agreement in writing in the United States, see § 2.05[A].

PROBLEM 5.1

The Westhouse & Marbank Company (W&M), located in the United Kingdom, sends a purchase order to Bordeaux Wines, Inc., a French company, seeking to purchase fifty cases of wine. The purchase order provides for arbitration in the United States. Bordeaux ships and accepts payment for the wine; it does not, however, sign the purchase order or send any confirming paperwork to W&M. Does the New York Convention apply?

[B] Foreign or Non-Domestic

Next, the arbitration agreement must be either a foreign or a non-domestic one. Article I(1) of the Convention provides:

> This Convention shall apply to the recognition and enforcement of arbitral awards made in the territory of a State other than the State where the recognition and enforcement of such awards are sought, and arising out of differences between persons, whether physical or legal. It shall also apply to arbitral awards not considered as domestic awards in the State where their recognition and enforcement are sought.

By its terms, this Article speaks only of enforcing arbitration awards, not agreements to arbitrate. (To be clear, a foreign award is an award made outside of the country in which enforcement is sought, while a non-domestic award is an award made in the country in which enforcement is sought but with some international nexus.) But the Article is implemented in the United States through 9 U.S.C. § 202, which makes clear that it extends to agreements to arbitrate: "An agreement or award arising out of such a relationship [legal and commercial] which is entirely between citizens of the United States shall be deemed not to fall under the Convention unless that relationship involves property located abroad, envisages performance or enforcement abroad, or has some other reasonable relation with one or more foreign states." The negative implication of section 202 suggests that an agreement between an American party and a non-American party or between two non-American parties is within the scope of the Convention. Even if between two American parties, the agreement might be within the scope of the Convention if it has a clear relationship with international commerce. The sort of relationship that is necessary is the subject of the following case.

JONES v. SEA TOW SERVICES FREEPORT NY INC.

United State Court of Appeals for the Second Circuit

30 F.3d 360 (1994)

MINER, CIRCUIT JUDGE:

Plaintiffs-appellants Charles C. Jones and Clara E. Jones, his wife, appeal from an order entered in the United States District Court for the Eastern District of New York . . . denying their motion for summary judgment in their declaratory judgment action against defendant-appellee Sea Tow Services Freeport NY, Inc. ("Sea Tow") and staying the action pending arbitration in England. By their complaint, Mr. and Mrs. Jones sought a declaration of their rights and responsibilities under a Lloyd's Standard Form of Salvage Agreement, also known as Lloyd's Open Form ("LOF"). Sea Tow has counterclaimed for salvage fees claimed to be due and owing under the LOF.

In arriving at its conclusion, the district court determined that the Convention on the Recognition and Enforcement of Foreign Arbitral Awards ("Convention"), as implemented by the provisions of 9 U.S.C. §§ 201–208, applies to the LOF. According to the district court, the LOF provision for arbitration in England under English law provides a reasonable relation with a foreign state sufficient to allow arbitration to proceed under the Convention and the LOF. We think that the district court exceeded its jurisdiction in directing arbitration to proceed in England. We rest our conclusion on the fact that the parties to this action are U.S. citizens engaged in a purely domestic salvage dispute. In such circumstances, the relation with a foreign state that is required to invoke the Convention is lacking, despite the provisions in the LOF for arbitration in London under the English law of salvage.

BACKGROUND

The circumstances giving rise to this litigation comprise a cautionary tale for the owners of small vessels in distress. The lesson to be learned is that pleasure craft are just as much subject to the law of the sea, including the law of salvage, as their ocean-going commercial counterparts. The saving grace in this case is that the plaintiffs will be able to defend in the United States, rather than in a foreign forum, the salvage claim asserted against them.

Mr. and Mrs. Jones were the owners of the MISS JADE II, a thirty-three-foot pleasure craft whose home port was Freeport, New York. They apparently navigated the vessel too close to shore while on a voyage from Essex, Connecticut to Freeport on August 20, 1991. At some point during this navigation, the vessel was struck by a wave and rolled over, landing on Atlantic Beach, Long Island at about 8:30 p.m. on a cold and rainy night. Mr. and Mrs. Jones were assisted to shore by a passerby, who tied a line to the MISS JADE II to prevent her from drifting and then telephoned the Nassau County Police Department for assistance. Earlier, Mr. Jones had communicated with the Coast Guard by radio from his vessel regarding the situation. After determining that the Joneses were not seriously injured, the Coast Guard contacted Sea Tow, a professional salvage company.

The first to arrive at the scene was Officer Daly of the Nassau County Police Department. He attended to Mr. and Mrs. Jones, who had sustained minor injuries. He took Mrs. Jones into the police car to shelter her from the rain and cold. Thereafter, Captain Raia and Michael Marsh of Sea Tow arrived, and Marsh set the vessel's anchor to prevent drifting. Officer Daly then left the scene, whereupon Mr. and Mrs. Jones entered "Mobile I," a Sea Tow land vehicle. It was while they were inside the vehicle that the LOF was presented to the Joneses for their signatures. Mr. and Mrs. Jones contend that Mr. Jones was unable to read the LOF without his glasses and that Mrs. Jones thumbed through the document and was not able to comprehend it; that there was insufficient light in the vehicle to read; that Mrs. Jones returned the form unsigned to Captain Raia, who advised that it merely authorized Sea Tow to tow the vessel back to Freeport; that Captain Raia said that Boat/U.S., the insurer of the vessel, was familiar with the LOF and that there would be no problem if the form were signed; that they understood that they would be left stranded on the beach and would not be helped by Sea Tow if they refused to sign; and that they were unfamiliar with the term "salvage."

Captain Raia denies that he took advantage of Mr. and Mrs. Jones in any way. He asserts that Mrs. Jones read the form before signing her husband's name after he had fully explained the document and that he emphasized that the agreement was for salvage and not towage. He does not recall, however, whether he explained the LOF provision for arbitration. Although it was dark outside, he asserts that there was sufficient light in "Mobile I" for Mrs. Jones to read by. It seems undisputed that the conversation inside the vehicle lasted for 30-45 minutes. Captain Raia acknowledges that, after Mrs. Jones told him that she wished to consult with an attorney, he told her that he "would be unable to render assistance without a signed contract." As to the Boat/U.S. insurance, Captain Raia claims that he explained to Mrs. Jones that "her Boat/U.S. towing insurance would not cover salvage." After the LOF was signed, Captain Raia arranged for a vehicle to drive the Joneses home and later towed the MISS JADE II to Mako Marina, a full-service marina located about 400 yards from the vessel's usual mooring at Yachtman's Cove in Freeport. The vessel was towed a total distance of approximately six miles.

The LOF is a six-page document entitled "Lloyd's Standard Form of Salvage Agreement (Approved and Published by the Council of Lloyd's)." . . . Although the LOF was signed by Mrs. Jones in the Sea Tow land vehicle, the place of signing is filled in as "On board the MISS JADE II." In the first of 19 separate sections, some containing subdivisions within subdivisions, Sea Tow as "Contractor" agrees to use its "best endeavours . . . to salve the 'MISS JADE II' and/or her cargo[,] freight[,] bunkers[,] stores and other property." Section 1(c) provides that "[t]he Contractor's remuneration shall be fixed by Arbitration in London," and section 1(g) recites as follows: "This Agreement and Arbitration thereunder shall except as otherwise expressly provided be governed by the law of England, including the English law of salvage."

. . . Following the signature blocks on the last page of the LOF, there appears a legend printed by hand and subscribed by Captain Raia and by Mrs. Jones in the name of her husband: "I understand that this agreement is a salvage agreement, not a towerage [sic] agreement and that this agreement has been explained to me before I signed it."

It appears that Sea Tow sought to be paid in excess of $15,000 for its "salvage" services, based on a percentage of the value of MISS JADE II. . . .

Sea Tow instituted an arbitration proceeding against the Joneses in London on November 21, 1991, pursuant to the provisions of the LOF. The arbitration was stayed by stipulation of the parties, and Mr. and Mrs. Jones commenced the action giving rise to this appeal. . . .

. . . The [district] court stayed the action but retained jurisdiction to enforce any award later rendered. The substantive aspect of the summary judgment motion, including the issues of fraud, misrepresentation and mistake as well as Sea Tow's motion to amend the answer were referred to the arbitration proceeding in England. . . .

DISCUSSION

. . .

The Federal Arbitration Act declares valid and enforceable written provisions for arbitration in any maritime transaction and in any contract evidencing a transaction involving commerce. The Act defines "maritime transactions" as matters "embraced within admiralty jurisdiction" and "commerce" as including "commerce among the several States or with foreign nations." Ordinarily, agreements to arbitrate salvage disputes fall within these provisions. Where, however, an agreement to arbitrate involves the recognition and enforcement of arbitral awards made in the territory of a nation other than the nation where recognition and enforcement are sought, the Convention applies. Recognition and enforcement then must be pursued in accordance with the terms of the statutory provisions implementing the Convention. Chapter I, the original Federal Arbitration Act, applies to actions and proceedings to enforce the Convention to the extent that it is not in conflict with Chapter II, the Convention provisions. It is under these implementing provisions that Sea Tow invoked the jurisdiction of the district court to secure recognition of the arbitration provisions of the LOF. Despite Sea Tow's argument to the contrary, the district court lacked authority under Chapter I to direct that arbitration proceedings be held outside the Eastern District.

The LOF first appeared in the 1890s and since has become the most widely used form of salvage contract in the world. Even to those who should be among the cognoscenti, the Lloyd's Salvage Agreement is not a model of clarity. . . . Whether Mr. and Mrs. Jones were victims of fraud or misrepresentation we leave to another day. We hold here only that arbitration in London under the arbitration provisions of the LOF cannot be compelled in this case, and it is to that proposition that we now turn.

. . .

. . . The LOF provision for arbitration is part of an agreement involving a relationship that is entirely between citizens of the United States — Sea Tow and the Joneses. The relationship between these parties clearly did not involve property located abroad nor did it envisage performance abroad. Whether it envisages enforcement in England or has some other reasonable relation with England, as found by the district court, are the issues that require analysis in this case.

. . .

Neither the salvor-casualty relationship, nor the LOF agreement relationship has any *reasonable* relation with England in this case. The purported salvage operation took place just off the coast of the United States, and the LOF was presented to Mrs. Jones for signature in the United States. It is not sufficient that English law was to be applied in the resolution of the salvage dispute and that the arbitration proceeding was to be held before an English arbitrator in England. . . . It cannot be said that a significant portion of the making or performance of the LOF occurred or is to occur in England, and there is no basis for the application of English law.

The reasonable relation requirement necessary to make the arbitration provision in the LOF cognizable under the Convention cannot be fulfilled by the terms of the LOF itself. If it could, the LOF would become a self-generating basis for jurisdiction. In this case, there is no connection with England independent of the LOF. We therefore agree with those courts that have held the arbitration provisions of the LOF insufficient of themselves to confer jurisdiction under the Convention in accordance with section 202.

Although the district court determined that the LOF's designations of London as the arbitral forum, Lloyd's as the arbitrator and English law as governing the arbitration "indicate that the parties contemplated enforcement of this award in Great Britain," Sea Tow does not pursue this point on appeal. As a matter of fact, there is no "award" that can be enforced. Moreover, it seems clear that Sea Tow itself contemplated enforcement in New York. When it released the MISS JADE II, Sea Tow obtained a "Letter of Undertaking" from the Jones' insurance underwriter. Since this letter serves to protect Sea Tow's maritime lien and an enforcement of the lien can only take place where the property is located, Sea Tow obviously envisioned enforcement in New York.

The assets of Mr. and Mrs. Jones apparently are in New York. Certainly, there is no indication that they have any assets overseas. It therefore is difficult on the record before us to envision the enforcement of any arbitral award anywhere but in the United States. . . . Interestingly enough, the district court "retain[ed] jurisdiction to enforce any award eventually rendered." Again, there is no important foreign element involved. As between the parties in the case at bar, a United States forum is required for the enforcement of any arbitral award and even to compel arbitration. The district court's observation that the Committee of Lloyd's has a long history of experience in the arbitration of salvage disputes lends no support to the conclusion that the parties envisioned performance in England. There is no indication that competent salvage arbitrators are unavailable in the United States or that the necessary expertise is lacking here.

CONCLUSION

The judgment of the district court is reversed, and the case is remanded for further proceedings consistent with the foregoing.

NOTES

1. Examine the definition of "international" in the UNCITRAL Model Law art. 1(3). How would *Jones* have been decided under the Model Law?

2. Professor Alan Scott Rau offers the following commentary on *Jones*:

> In reading the Second Circuit's opinion in *Jones*, it is hard to escape the impression that for the court, the "real problem" in the case may have been that the owners "were amateurs presented with an adhesion contract in conditions of great stress, and [who were now] expected to present their case several thousand miles away." Warm sympathy for Charles and Clara Jones oozes not only from the court's statement of the facts (it was, by the way, a "cold and rainy night"), but from Judge Miner's unguarded comment that the litigation imparts a "cautionary tale for the owners of small vessels in distress" — with at least the "saving grace" that they can now defend against the salvage claim in the United States "rather than in a foreign forum." The holding that they could not be compelled to arbitrate in London may thus have served as an escape hatch for them, from an inflexible jurisprudence that regularly enforces arbitration clauses in adhesion contracts even at the cost of hardship to the "adhering" party. This is a plausible reading of *Jones*, and it calls for a few brief final comments.
>
> To begin with, to distort the regime of the Convention hardly seems the appropriate way of dealing with the thorny problem of the enforceability of forum-selection agreements. To the extent it announces a rule equally applicable to sophisticated commercial parties — who may knowingly have made the business decision to accept arbitration at Lloyd's — the holding in *Jones* sweeps far too broadly. More to the point, both the Convention and our general contract law are easily malleable enough to take principled account of the peculiar challenges posed by one-sided agreements: This can be done well within the structure of our present contract law by lawyers sufficiently competent to make an adequate record, and courts sufficiently willing to grapple with relevant factual distinctions.
>
> A sustained effort at a traditional contract analysis might in fact call for disparate results in the various cases that uniformly hold LOF agreements between American citizens to be outside the Convention. . . . With respect to the integrity of contractual "assent," . . . *Jones* might be a somewhat more appealing case for resisting arbitration than some of the other cases — where any challenge to the agreement process verges on the frivolous. For example, in one of the cases that have held the Convention inapplicable in this context, the LOF was signed by the yacht's captain one week after the salvage services had been completed! There is of course already a great deal of resonance in the term "yacht" itself, which is charged with all sorts of subterranean associations — but it is probably fair to say that the owner of a 53-foot vessel of that description is unlikely to be the paradigmatic babe

in the woods, of the kind to which our particular solicitude is often extended.

. . .

This leads us to the final point, and it is a fundamental one. The Second Circuit in *Jones* may have been casting about for some means of escape from [cases enforcing foreign forum selection clauses] — but it seems particularly indefensible to have done so without first taking account of some critical differences that may have justified enforcement of the contractual choice of forum. It is true that London is perhaps a "remote alien forum." It is not, however, self-evidently a more burdensome location for a Freeport yacht owner than for a Freeport salvor. And in any event what litigation like *Jones* seems to be "about" is in many respects less the world of "consumer protection," and much more about the incessant strategic jockeying for advantage between salvors and hull insurers, the true parties in interest. Nor can the process of assessing the LOF proceed in abstraction from the obvious institutional considerations: Itself a product of negotiation between salvor and underwriter interests, the LOF has become an industry standard — and a means of centralizing salvage determinations in such a way as to insure expertise and consistency. The Second Circuit may thus have mindlessly impaired the utility of a process that has been widely used and respected to the point that it may almost be said to have attained "a quasi-convention status."

Alan Scott Rau, *The New York Convention in American Courts*, 7 AM. REV. INT'L ARB. 213, 251–56 (1996).*

PROBLEM 5.2

Turner, Inc., an American company, enters into a written, signed contract with another American company, McCarthy Petroleum, Inc., under which Turner agrees to erect oil drilling equipment for McCarthy in Saudi Arabia. The contract provides for arbitration in England. Does the New York Convention apply? What if the oil drilling equipment were to be erected in Texas? Does the New York Convention apply?

[C] "Commercial"

In addition, in a number of countries the agreement must arise out of a "commercial" relationship. Article I(3) of New York Convention provides that a Contracting State may also "declare that it will apply the Convention only to differences arising out of legal relationships, whether contractual or not, which are considered as commercial under the national law of the State making such declaration." The United States made such a reservation; accordingly, section 202 makes clear that arbitration agreements must arise out of legal relationships which are "considered as commercial" under American law.

BAUTISTA v. STAR CRUISES
United States Court of Appeals for the Eleventh Circuit
396 F.3d 1289 (2005)

RESTANI, JUDGE:

The S/S Norway's steam boiler exploded on May 25, 2003, while the cruise ship was in the Port of Miami. Six of the crewmembers represented in this action were killed and four were injured. Each crewmember's employment agreement with Defendant NCL includes an arbitration clause, which the district court enforced pursuant to the United Nations Convention on the Recognition and Enforcement of Foreign Arbitral Awards (the "Convention"), and its implementing legislation, 9 U.S.C. §§ 202-208 (the "Convention Act"). Plaintiffs' appeal presents an issue of first impression in this Circuit: whether the crewmembers' employment agreements were shielded from arbitration by the seamen employment contract exemption contained in section 1 of the Federal Arbitration Act (the "FAA"). Because the FAA seamen exemption does not apply . . . , we affirm.

. . .

DISCUSSION

. . .

We have yet to determine whether the FAA exemption for seamen's employment contracts applies to arbitration agreements covered by the Convention Act. The district court determined that it does not. This conclusion is consistent with that of the Fifth Circuit — the only court of appeals to decide this issue — and several district courts. *See* Freudensprung v. Offshore Tech. Servs., Inc., 379 F.3d 327 (5th Cir. 2004); Francisco v. Stolt Achievement MT, 293 F.3d 270 (5th Cir. 2002), *cert. denied*, 537 U.S. 1030 (2002); Acosta v. Norwegian Cruise Line, Ltd., 303 F. Supp. 2d 1327 (S.D. Fla. 2003); Adolfo v. Carnival Corp., No. 02-23672, 2003 U.S. Dist. LEXIS 24143 (S.D. Fla. Mar. 17, 2003); Amon v. Norwegian Cruise Lines, Ltd., No. 02-21025, 2002 U.S. Dist. LEXIS 27064 (S.D. Fla. Sept. 26, 2002).

As we take up this issue of statutory interpretation, the first step is to determine whether the statutory language has a plain and unambiguous meaning by referring to "the language itself, the specific context in which that language is used, and the broader context of the statute as a whole." The inquiry ceases if the language is clear and "the statutory scheme is coherent and consistent." Such is the case here. The statutory framework of title 9 and the language and context of the Convention Act preclude the application of the FAA seamen's exemption, either directly as an integral part of the Convention Act or residually as a non-conflicting provision of the FAA.

A. The FAA Seamen Exemption Does Not Apply to the Convention Act Directly

1. Overview of the Convention and the Convention Act

. . . When the United States acceded to the Convention in 1970, it exercised its right to limit the Convention's application to commercial legal relationships as defined by the law of the United States . . . . Plaintiffs assert that the United States national law definition of "commercial" resides in section 1 of the FAA, which defines "commerce" and provides that "nothing herein contained shall apply to contracts of employment of seamen." 9 U.S.C. § 1. Although section 1 clearly exempts seamen's employment contracts from the FAA, see *Circuit City Stores, Inc. v. Adams*, the exemption's application outside the FAA is restricted by the second and third chapters of title 9.

2. The Statutory Framework of Title 9 of the United States Code

The three chapters of title 9 are closely interrelated, but, contrary to Plaintiffs' argument, they are not a seamless whole. As indicated, the FAA and the Convention Act comprise Chapter 1 and Chapter 2, respectively. Chapter 3 contains the legislation implementing the Inter-American Convention on International Commercial Arbitration (the "Inter-American Act"). Within the general field of arbitration, each act has a specific context and purpose. Congress, as it added the Convention Act and then the Inter-American Act to title 9, anticipated conflicts among these treaty-implementing statutes and the FAA. Congress addressed potential conflicts in two ways, each of which limits the degree to which title 9 may be considered a single statute.

The first is general in nature. The FAA applies residually to supplement the provisions of the Convention Act and the Inter-American Act. Rather than put the Convention Act and the Inter-American Act on equal footing with the FAA in the field of foreign arbitration, Congress gave the treaty-implementing statutes primacy in their fields, with FAA provisions applying only where they did not conflict. *See* 9 U.S.C. § 208 (the Convention Act residual provision); 9 U.S.C. § 307 (the Inter-American Act residual provision). This hierarchical structure accords with our understanding that, "as an exercise of the Congress' treaty power and as federal law, 'the Convention must be enforced according to its terms over all prior inconsistent rules of law.' "

The second technique for reconciling title 9's chapters is more specific. Certain provisions of the Convention Act and the Inter-American Act refer explicitly to specific sections of other chapters of title 9. Section 302 of the Inter-American Act, for example, directly incorporates several sections of the Convention Act: "sections 202, 203, 204, 205, and 207 of this title shall apply to this chapter [9 U.S.C. §§ 301-307] as if specifically set forth herein." 9 U.S.C. § 302. Most relevant for the instant case is the reference in section 202 of the Convention Act to section 2 of the FAA.

3. Section 202 of the Convention Act

In contrast to the Inter-American Act's direct incorporation of several Convention Act sections, section 202 does not incorporate section 2 of the FAA as an exhaustive description of the Convention Act's scope. Rather, section 202 uses section 2 as an illustration of the types of agreements covered by the Convention Act.

In articulating the Convention's commercial scope under the laws of the United States, section 202 of the Convention Act provides that an agreement falls under the Convention if it "arises out of a legal relationship, whether contractual or not, which is considered as commercial, including a transaction, contract, or agreement described in section 2 of this title [9 U.S.C. § 2]." Section 2 of the FAA makes valid and enforceable "[a] written provision in any maritime transaction or a contract evidencing a transaction involving commerce to settle by arbitration."

The Convention Act's reference to section 2 does not indicate an intent to limit the definition of "commercial" to those described in section 2 of the FAA as modified by section 1; the expansive term "including" would be superfluous if the FAA provided the full and complete definition. "Including" demonstrates that, at the very least, Congress meant for "commercial" legal relationships to consist of contracts evidencing a commercial transaction, as listed in section 2, as well as similar agreements.

We therefore understand the reference to section 2 of the FAA to be generally illustrative of the commercial legal relationships covered by section 202. The illustration rendered by section 2 includes employment agreements and makes no mention of the section 1 seamen exemption. Accordingly, the terms of the Convention Act do not provide that we read section 1 into section 202.

Plaintiffs cite committee testimony in the legislative history in the hope of demonstrating that Congress intended section 202 of the Convention Act to incorporate the FAA seamen exemption. Ambassador Richard Kearney, Chairman of the Secretary of State's Advisory Committee on Private International Law, testified before the Senate Foreign Relations Committee that

> the definition of commerce contained in section 1 of the original Arbitration Act is the national law definition for the purposes of the declaration. A specific reference, however, is made in section 202 to section 2 of title 9; which is the basic provision of the original Arbitration Act.

S. Comm. on Foreign Relations, Foreign Arbitral Awards, S. Rep. No. 91-702, at 6 (1970). Although it is plausible to infer from Ambassador Kearney's comments that he believed the section 1 exemptions should apply to the Convention Act, his views as a single State Department official are a relatively unreliable indicator of statutory intent. Plaintiffs nevertheless claim that, according to Udall v. Tallman, 380 U.S. 1, 16 (1965), his views are entitled to "great deference." *Udall*, however, accords such deference only to "the officers or agency charged with [the statute's] administration," and there is no indication that the State Department is so charged. Even if the above testimony were owed some deference, it could not alter the plain terms of the Convention Act. Rather than directly incorporate an FAA provision that Congress did not, we adhere to the framework Congress provided and evaluate the applicability of an unmentioned FAA section according to the Convention Act's residual application provision.

B. The FAA Seamen Exemption Does Not Apply Residually

As noted above, section 208 of the Convention Act provides that nonconflicting provisions of the Arbitration Act apply residually to Convention Act cases. . . . Under this residual provision, the issue is whether the FAA seamen exemption conflicts with the Convention Act or the Convention as ratified by the United States.

A conflict exists between the FAA seamen exemption, which is narrow and specific, and the language of the Convention and the Convention Act, which is broad and generic. Plaintiffs, under the impression that an FAA term may only be contradicted by name, argue that no conflict exists because section 202 of the Convention Act is silent as to seamen's employment contracts. According to this logic, a statutory provision pertaining to persons above the age of eighteen would not conflict with a provision that exempts thirty-year-olds. Because the Convention Act covers commercial legal relationships without exception, it conflicts with section 1, an FAA provision that exempts certain employment agreements that — but for the exemption — would be commercial legal relationships. The Fifth Circuit came to the same conclusion in *Francisco*:

> In short, the language of the Convention, the ratifying language, and the Convention Act implementing the Convention do not recognize an exception for seamen employment contracts. On the contrary, they recognize that the only limitation on the type of legal relationship falling under the Convention is that it must be considered "commercial," and we conclude that an employment contract is "commercial."

293 F.3d at 274. We see no reason to diverge from the sensible reasoning of our sister Circuit.

Indeed, to read industry-specific exceptions into the broad language of the Convention Act would be to hinder the Convention's purpose[, which "was to encourage the recognition and enforcement of commercial arbitration agreements in international contracts and to unify the standards by which agreements to arbitrate are observed and arbitral awards are enforced in the signatory countries."] Scherk v. Alberto-Culver Co., 417 U.S. 506, 520 n.15 (1974). In pursuing effective, unified arbitration standards, the Convention's framers understood that the benefits of the treaty would be undermined if domestic courts were to inject their "parochial" values into the regime. . . . *Id.* at 520 n.15. This concern is addressed by the broad language of section 202 of the Convention Act. Considering the language of the Convention Act in the context of the framework of title 9 and the purposes of the Convention, we find no justification for removing from the Convention Act's scope a subset of commercial employment agreements. The crewmembers' arbitration provisions constitute commercial legal relationships within the meaning of the Convention Act.

. . .

NOTES

1.   Roughly one-third of the signatories to the New York Convention have made the commercial reservation. The United States is one of those countries, as indicated above.

2.   A note to the UNCITRAL Model Law on International Commercial Arbitration explains that, as used in that statute, "[t]he term 'commercial' should be given a wide interpretation so as to cover matters arising from all relationships of a commercial nature, whether contractual or not." It then states:

> Relationships of a commercial nature include, but are not limited to, the following transactions: any trade transaction for the supply or exchange of goods or services; distribution agreement; commercial representation or agency; factoring; leasing; construction of works; consulting; engineering; licensing; investment; financing; banking; insurance; exploitation agreement or concession; joint venture and other forms of industrial or business co-operation; carriage of goods or passengers by air, sea, rail or road. Examples of disputes commonly treated as not "commercial" are family law disputes, state boundary disputes, and disputes presenting political issues.

3.   One type of relationship not included in the above list is the relationship between employer and employee. In many countries, the employment relationship is not viewed as "commercial." *See* 4 IAN R. MACNEIL ET AL., FEDERAL ARBITRATION LAW § 44.9.3.2 (1995). That is not true in the United States, however, as shown in *Bautista.*

4.   "[T]he commercial reservation generally has not caused problems as the courts tend to interpret the coverage of 'commercial' broadly." Albert Jan van den Berg, *New York Convention of 1958: Consolidated Commentary, in* 19 Y.B. COMM. ARB. 475, 495 (1994). One exception has been several decisions from courts in India, which concluded that consulting contracts were not "commercial" within the meaning of the New York Convention. The Supreme Court of India rejected those decisions in RM Investment & Trading Co. v. Boeing Co. (1994), *in* 22 Y.B. COMM. ARB. 710 (1995) (India), holding that a consulting contract was "commercial," at least when the consultant was providing services in connection with the sale of goods.

PROBLEM 5.3

Jonathan Small, an American, enters into a written, signed employment contract with Agra Enterprises, an Indian company. Small is to reside in India and provide services solely in India. The contract provides for arbitration in France. Agra files an action in India seeking to compel arbitration. Does the New York Convention apply? Would it matter if the contract were labeled a consulting contract? What would your answer be under chapter 2 of the FAA?

[D]   Reciprocity

Finally, it may be necessary that the arbitration agreement provide for arbitration in a country that is a party to the Convention. Article I(3) permits a country, when ratifying the Convention, "on the basis of reciprocity" to "declare that it will apply the Convention to the recognition and enforcement of awards made only in the territory of another Contracting State." This reciprocity reservation, which was made by the United States on ratifying the Convention, is considered in the next case.

E.A.S.T., INC. v. M/V ALAIA
United States Court of Appeals for the Fifth Circuit
876 F.2d 1168 (1989)

KING, CIRCUIT JUDGE:

Claimant-appellant Advance Co. appeals from the district court's order refusing to vacate the arrest of the M/V ALAIA and referring the parties to arbitration of their dispute in London pursuant to the terms of their charter party. We affirm the order of the district court.

I.

A. Facts

. . .

Briefly, plaintiff-appellee E.A.S.T. ("EAST") agreed in October of 1987 to charter the M/V ALAIA ("ALAIA"), owned by defendant-appellant Advance, Co. ("Advance"). . . . The charter party . . . stated that EAST's intention was to carry milk carton stock on pallets and soda ash in bulk from New Orleans and Port Arthur to Puerto Cabello, Venezuela. The charter party also contained an arbitration clause and specified that the place of arbitration would be London rather than New York and that the contract would be governed by English law.

EAST simultaneously entered into two voyage subcharters — one to carry milk carton stock and wood pulp on pallets from New Orleans to Puerto Cabello and one to carry bulk soda ash from Port Arthur to Puerto Cabello. . . .

The ALAIA was delivered under the time charter and went "on hire" at 001 hours on October 20, 1987. . . . On October 20 and 21, 1987, EAST's surveyor inspected the ALAIA and concluded that it was not suitable to carry the intended cargo. The surveyors for the subcharterers agreed.

EAST's surveyor found that rust, dirt, and debris made the vessel unfit to carry soda ash, that the vessel was not suitable for "grab discharge" — in violation of a specific warranty in the time charter, and that the hatch covers were so severely rusted that the vessel was unseaworthy. As a result of these findings, EAST rejected the ship and filed an *in rem* action, under the Federal Arbitration Act, 9 U.S.C. § 8, and Supplemental Admiralty Rule C, in the Federal District Court for the Eastern District of Louisiana to compel arbitration under the charter party and to obtain security for the arbitration award through the arrest of the vessel.

Two days after the arrest of the vessel, Advance filed a notice of appearance *in personam*, an answer and a counter-claim, and moved to vacate the arrest on the grounds first, that no valid time charter had come into existence and second, that no maritime lien could arise from the breach of the charter party as no cargo had yet been loaded on the vessel. Advance also argued that the district court could not order the parties to arbitration on the basis of *in rem* jurisdiction.

B. District Court Decision

After a post-seizure hearing, the district court first rejected the argument that no valid time charter existed. Then . . . the district court held that a maritime lien could arise from the breach of a *time* charter even when the breach occurs before the cargo has been loaded. Accordingly, the court found that the seizure was proper. Finally, the district court held that *in rem* jurisdiction provided a sufficient basis to refer the parties to arbitration under Section 8 of the Federal Arbitration Act. . . . The district court ordered each of the parties to post security for arbitration, ordered the parties to proceed to arbitration in London, and retained jurisdiction for purposes of enforcing any arbitration award. Advance filed a timely notice of appeal from the order of the district court.

. . .

II.

. . .

Before proceeding to the central issue of this case — whether there is a maritime lien arising from the alleged breach of a time charter — we must address [a] threshold question. Advance asserts on appeal that the pre-arbitration arrest of the ALAIA is inconsistent with the terms of the Convention on the Recognition and Enforcement of Foreign Arbitral Awards as implemented by 9 U.S.C. §§ 201-08. . . .

Advance relies on the Third Circuit's decision in McCreary Tire & Rubber Co. v. CEAT S.p.A., 501 F.2d 1032 (3d Cir.1974). In *McCreary*, the court held that resort to prejudgment attachment under state law was in violation of the parties' agreement to arbitrate their disputes and was therefore precluded by the Convention which "forbids the courts of a contracting state from entertaining a suit which violates an agreement to arbitrate." . . .

First, we note that EAST maintains that Advance may not avail itself of any defenses available under the Convention because Advance is a Liberian corporation and Liberia is not a signatory to the convention. EAST asserts that our decision in National Iranian Oil Co. v. Ashland Oil, Inc., 817 F.2d 326 (5th Cir.), *cert. denied*, 484 U.S. 983 (1987), supports this proposition. In that case, we held that the Convention did not confer on U.S. courts the power to compel arbitration in non-signatory nations.

EAST apparently concedes, however, that *Ashland Oil* does not hold the Convention inapplicable to arbitration agreements where one party is a citizen of a non-signatory nation. To the contrary, *Ashland Oil* recognizes that the Convention focuses on the situs of the arbitration, not upon the nationality of the parties. The court observed that if NIOC — a citizen of a non-signatory nation — had "chosen to negotiate a forum selection clause with a situs in any one of the . . . nations that are signatories to the Convention," that clause could have been enforced by U.S. courts.

The court further stated that "[w]hen the United States adhered to the Convention, it expressly chose the option available in Article I(3) to 'apply the Convention, on the basis of reciprocity, to the recognition and enforcement of *only* those awards made in the territory of another Contracting State.' " *Id.* at 335 (quoting Declaration of the United States upon Accession) (emphasis added). The principle of reciprocity is thus concerned with the forum in which the arbitration will occur and whether that forum state is a signatory to the Convention — not whether both parties to the dispute are nationals of signatory states.

EAST attempts to draw a distinction between enforcing an award rendered by a panel sitting in a signatory nation and allowing a national of a nonsignatory state to benefit from the Convention in the courts of the United States. Although we stated in *Ashland Oil* that "[c]oncerned with reciprocity, Congress must have meant only to allow signatories to partake of the Convention's benefits in U.S. courts," this does not mean that we will decline to apply the terms of the Convention to an arbitration clause that is governed by Convention and not "unenforceable *ab initio*" — as was the arbitration agreement in *Ashland Oil.*

In the instant case, the arbitration is to be conducted in London. Because Great Britain is a signatory to the Convention, we cannot conclude that Advance's Liberian nationality removes the arbitration provision in this charter party from the purview of the Convention.

. . .

. . . We conclude that prejudgment attachment under Section 8 — as an aid to arbitration — is manifestly not inconsistent with the aims of the Convention. We therefore reject Advance's argument that pre-arbitration arrest of the ALAIA was precluded by the Convention. . . .

. . .

III.

For the foregoing reasons, the order of the district court is AFFIRMED.

NOTES

1.   Roughly one-half of the signatories to the New York Convention, including the United States, have made the reciprocity reservation.

2.   Note that on December 15, 2005, the New York Convention entered into force in Liberia, effectively mooting E.A.S.T.'s argument (which was incorrect anyway). For the current list of signatories to the New York Convention, see the Documentary Supplement.

3.   Does the reciprocity reservation even apply to actions to enforce arbitration agreements? By its terms, it refers only to arbitration awards, not agreements to

arbitrate. American courts are split on the question. *Compare* National Iranian Oil Co. v. Ashland Oil, Inc., 817 F.2d 326 (5th Cir.) (court has no power to compel arbitration in Iran under the New York Convention because Iran is not a signatory), *cert. denied*, 484 U.S. 943 (1987) *with* Fuller Co. v. Compagnie des Bauxites de Guinee, 421 F. Supp. 938, 941 n.3 (W.D. Pa. 1976) (reciprocity limitation "clearly applies only to the recognition and enforcement of arbitral awards; it has no relevance to the problem pending before this court whether to order arbitration under the terms of the convention").

4.   If the reciprocity reservation does apply to agreements to arbitrate, the key fact, as the court in *E.A.S.T.* makes clear, is the seat of the arbitration — its legal home — rather than the nationality of the parties. *Cf.* Restatement (Third) of the U.S. Law of International Commercial Arbitration § 4-5 & cmt. a. Thus, if American and Iraqi parties agreed to arbitrate in Turkey, their agreement would be enforceable under the New York Convention even if reciprocity is required, because Turkey is a party to the Convention. If the same parties agreed to arbitrate in Iraq, the agreement would not be enforceable under the New York Convention — if reciprocity is required — because Iraq is not a party to the Convention. Does this differing treatment make sense?

PROBLEM 5.4

International Trading, Inc., located in the United States, enters into a written signed contract with Burma Manufacturing, Ltd., a company located in Myanmar, a southeast Asian country formerly known as Burma. The contract was for the purchase of clothing manufactured in Myanmar, and provided for arbitration in India. Does the New York Convention apply? What if International Trading entered a contract with Delhi Manufacturing, located in India, and the contract provided for arbitration in Myanmar? Does the New York Convention apply?

§ 5.03   DEFENSES TO ACTIONS TO ENFORCE INTERNATIONAL ARBITRATION AGREEMENTS

The enforceability of an international arbitration agreement raises many of the same issues as the enforceability of a domestic arbitration agreement, with the added complication of the varying national laws that may apply. Those issues include: Did the parties agree to arbitrate? Are there any other contract law defenses to arbitration? Is the subject matter of the dispute arbitrable? And who decides each of the preceding questions, the court or the arbitrator? We will consider the allocation of authority between courts and arbitrators first.

[A]   Who Decides Arbitrability

The following excerpt offers a comparative perspective on the doctrine of separability and the arbitrator's power to rule on his or her own jurisdiction.

George A. Bermann, THE "GATEWAY" PROBLEM IN INTERNATIONAL COMMERCIAL ARBITRATION,
37 Yale J. Int'l L. 1, 13-28 (2012)*

. . .

Generations of law students have been taught that the doctrines of Kompetenz-Kompetenz and separability — doctrines to which virtually all arbitration systems today purport to adhere — hold the keys to unlocking the mysteries associated with arbitral jurisdiction. I argue that, while these doctrines have a role to play, they fall far short of providing fully adequate answers. . . .

A. Kompetenz-Kompetenz

The doctrine of Kompetenz-Kompetenz, as generally understood, recognizes the authority of arbitral tribunals to determine their own jurisdiction. The breadth of this formulation has unfortunately generated much misunderstanding. All would appear to agree that Kompetenz-Kompetenz permits an arbitral tribunal to determine its own jurisdiction if it is challenged, and this of course is no minor achievement. But for this understanding, a tribunal arguably would be required to suspend proceedings whenever a party before it challenges its jurisdiction — whatever the basis of the challenge might be — and refer the jurisdictional issue to a court for determination. Allowing a party to unilaterally halt an arbitration merely by advancing a colorable reason in law why it should not go forward would dramatically impair the efficacy of arbitration.

Shall we, however, infer from the fact that an arbitral tribunal may determine its own jurisdiction when a party challenges it that a court may not address that question if a party raises it in court prior to the start of arbitration? Consider the [following] two scenarios . . . . In the first scenario, a party has initiated a claim in court, eliciting a motion to dismiss on the basis of an arbitration agreement between the parties. The immediate question for the court is *its own* jurisdiction, even if the answer will in turn depend on the court's assessment of the jurisdiction of an eventual arbitral tribunal. There is, a priori, no reason why the court should not be entitled to assess its own jurisdiction. In another era, in which courts were thought to be hostile to arbitration, that may have been a dangerous recipe. But that era is behind us.

Matters become more complicated in the second scenario. Here, a party has initiated arbitration and its opponent then goes to court — perhaps for a declaration that the dispute is not subject to arbitration, or for a stay of arbitration, or even for a ruling on a related claim of its own. That move has the effect, and often enough the purpose, of frustrating or at least delaying the arbitration. Arguably, the arbitral tribunal in this scenario is no less entitled to determine its own jurisdiction than the court in the first scenario. However, if we posit that the arbitral tribunal has not yet been fully constituted — and may not be for some time — permitting early judicial intervention on at least certain fundamental issues may be desirable. Moreover, it is not evident why as basic a question as jurisdiction to determine

---

jurisdiction should depend on who, as between the parties, was the first mover . . . . A more pertinent consideration is whether an arbitral tribunal is already fully in place and capable of exercising its Kompetenz-Kompetenz. Under neither of the scenarios I have posited is that the case.

I conclude that the doctrine of Kompetenz-Kompetenz need not preclude a court from entertaining a challenge to arbitral jurisdiction prior to constitution of the arbitral tribunal. I do not claim that a court may or should determine at this early stage *every* threshold issue that a party resisting arbitration might present to the arbitral tribunal itself — far from it. Some issues may particularly warrant threshold judicial determination and others not. Delineating between them in this regard is the very vocation of the distinction between gateway and non-gateway issues — a vocation to which the notion of separability, discussed in a later section, has traditionally been central.

1. Kompetenz-Kompetenz in French Law

The view of Kompetenz-Kompetenz I espouse here is far from universally shared. French law, notably, understands Kompetenz-Kompetenz very differently and has exerted considerable international influence on the matter, as it has on so many other matters in international commercial arbitration. . . .

Like U.S. law, French law accords arbitral tribunals the authority to decide the scope and validity of an arbitration agreement if either is called into question before the tribunal itself. But unlike U.S. law, French law treats the tribunal's authority to determine these issues as exclusive until after the arbitration is concluded and an award is rendered. According to French commentators, Kompetenz-Kompetenz thus has not only a *positive* dimension (authorizing arbitrators to determine their own competence at the outset), but also a *negative* one (barring courts from determining the competence of arbitrators at the outset). In its negative aspect, Kompetenz-Kompetenz requires courts to refrain from entertaining gateway challenges to an arbitration agreement, even if no arbitral tribunal has yet been formed. As Gaillard and Banifatemi put the matter, "the courts should refrain from engaging into [sic] the examination of the arbitrators' jurisdiction before the arbitrators themselves have had an opportunity to do so."

Negative Kompetenz-Kompetenz in French law is admittedly subject to an important exception. French law considers it intolerable to require a party to arbitrate a dispute when there is no plausible basis whatsoever for finding that it had bound itself to do so. Thus, if a French court determines that an arbitration clause *manifestly* does not exist or is *manifestly* null, it may so hold at the outset and, on that basis, decline to refer the parties to arbitration. . . .

The manifest nullity standard is meant to be — and is — very difficult to meet. As the term itself would suggest, a court must find, on the face of the proffered arbitration agreement itself, that it cannot serve as the basis for a valid arbitration. "The requirement that the clause be "manifestly null and void' means that this must be so clear that the court is not required to embark on any exercise of interpretation of the clause or its scope of application." French courts thus accept as sufficient what amounts to merely a prima facie showing on virtually all threshold issues. It would be an understatement to say that parties seeking relief in a French court from an apparent obligation to arbitrate face a seriously uphill battle.

The 2011 reform consolidates French case law with respect to the handling of threshold issues. The new Article 1465 forcefully reiterates the French version of Kompetenz-Kompetenz: "The arbitral tribunal has exclusive jurisdiction to rule on objections to its jurisdiction." Further, according to Article 1448, "when a dispute subject to an arbitration agreement is brought before a court, such court shall decline jurisdiction, except if an arbitral tribunal has not yet been seized of the dispute and if the arbitration agreement is manifestly void or manifestly not applicable." Thus, once the tribunal has been constituted, it exclusively resolves challenges to its own jurisdiction, whatever the basis of the objection. Before that time, a court is empowered only to determine whether an arbitration agreement is manifestly null or manifestly inapplicable.

In recognizing the "manifest nullity" exception, French law clearly acknowledges the legitimacy at stake in the enforcement of arbitration agreements. French law nevertheless strikes a very different balance between efficacy and legitimacy interests than U.S. law does. Its expansive understanding of Kompetenz-Kompetenz reduces to a bare minimum the inquiry that courts may make into the enforceability of arbitration agreements prior to enforcing them. This choice is a knowing one, crafted chiefly to thwart attempts by parties to delay or derail an arbitration. Efficacy concerns plainly prevail over legitimacy concerns at this stage of the proceedings. While sharing the vocabulary of Kompetenz-Kompetenz with American law, French law defines the concept differently and reaches strikingly different jurisdiction allocation outcomes.

Curiously, once an arbitration has ended in an award, French courts are permitted to make all the inquiries into arbitral jurisdiction that they were barred from making initially. If a party seeks to have the award annulled in a French court following an arbitration, it may raise each and every possible challenge to the existence and enforceability of the arbitration agreement. Moreover, it can expect the court to address those challenges without any deference to jurisdictional findings the arbitral tribunal may have previously made. Although French law postpones full judicial inquiry into arbitral jurisdiction until after an award has been issued, it obviously is not indifferent to the principle of consent or to the legitimacy concerns that underlie it.

However, postponing meaningful review of the arbitration agreement until after an award has been rendered imposes efficiency costs of its own. If a defect in the arbitration agreement is less than manifest (as it far more often than not will be), the arbitration will go forward, consuming time and resources — an expenditure that will have been wasted if a French court at the arbitral situs ultimately decides that the arbitration agreement did not exist or was not enforceable at the instance of the party invoking it, and thus annuls the award. French law appears to be indifferent to that efficacy cost. This arrangement is rational only if one assumes that annulment of an arbitral award in France, on the basis of one defect or another in the agreement to arbitrate, is truly a rarity.

2. Kompetenz-Kompetenz in German Law

German law more closely resembles American law in that it allows broad judicial intervention on certain issues at the threshold of arbitration, and expressly so provides in its Civil Procedure Code ("ZPO"). ZPO Section 1032(1) provides one avenue, entitling the defendant in a court action on a claim that it contends is subject exclusively to arbitration to seek a ruling that the court lacks jurisdiction to hear the matter on the merits. To prevail on the jurisdictional issue, plaintiff must demonstrate that the arbitration agreement is "null and void, inoperative or incapable of being performed." The court cannot content itself with a mere prima facie review of the arbitration agreement, i.e., with a determination that an agreement may at least plausibly be considered valid, operative and capable of being performed. Rather, the court makes a full and formal determination on the matter.

Second, section 1032(2) entitles a party against whom arbitration has been instituted to seek a ruling directly from an intermediate appellate court on "the admissibility or inadmissibility of arbitration," although it may do so only until such time as the arbitral tribunal has been constituted. Thereafter, the authority of the tribunal to make admissibility determinations becomes exclusive, though its determination is judicially challengeable on an interlocutory basis. Under section 1032(2), the court confines its inquiry to whether an effective and enforceable arbitration agreement exists, and whether the dispute falls within its ambit. While German law clearly posits "positive Kompetenz-Kompetenz," it equally clearly does not share French law's attachment to "negative Kompetenz-Kompetenz."

The system just described was introduced legislatively in 1998 as part of the modernization of German arbitration law. ZPO Section 1032(2) represents a conscious deviation from the UNCITRAL Model Law, which otherwise forms the basis of the German legislation. Prior to 1998, the ZPO made no specific reference to judicial intervention on matters of arbitral jurisdiction until after the tribunal had issued its final award. The reform's legislative purpose was clear, namely, to address the risk that parties might spend considerable time and resources in an arbitral forum, only to discover in an action for post-award relief that that forum lacked jurisdiction from the start. The German legislature plainly recognized that, while the arbitral process as such would run in a smoother and more streamlined fashion if the courts were essentially silenced on matters of arbitral jurisdiction during that process, that policy could prove highly inefficient in the long run, and so actually compromise arbitration's efficacy interest. So seriously is this "correction" taken that German law does not permit parties to agree in advance to assign final decision on the validity or enforceability of the arbitration agreement to the arbitrators.

On the other hand, the German legislature was sensitive to the cost of the new procedure in terms of delay in the event the arbitration commences only after the court upholds the arbitration agreement. It especially feared that jurisdictional challenges would be brought solely for purposes of delay, or otherwise frivolously. For this reason, the ZPO specifically provides that an arbitration, once initiated, must be allowed to proceed on its course, notwithstanding the respondent's having resorted to a court under section 1032(2). However serious the challenge, arbitral proceedings go forward concurrently with the judicial procedure. Indeed, even during the judicial proceedings, the party seeking arbitration is free to initiate it, thus simultaneously contesting judicial jurisdiction and triggering the arbitral process.

Germany has thus consciously produced a regime that enables courts to intervene on certain challenges, whether they take the form of a jurisdictional defense to a proceeding on a claim in court prior to any arbitration having been initiated or a stand-alone action brought in the period between initiation of arbitration and constitution of the tribunal. To this extent, the German mechanism reflects a commitment to party consent and to the legitimacy that such consent fosters. At the same time, under neither scenario are arbitral proceedings delayed, much less derailed, unless of course the court concludes that there exists no valid and enforceable agreement to arbitrate that is applicable to the dispute; in that circumstance, derailment is appropriate and will have been achieved on a reasonably timely basis. Kompetenz-Kompetenz under German law is evidently a highly calibrated instrument, and consciously so.

B. Separability

The traditional starting point for delineating gateway and non-gateway issues in American law is not Kompetenz-Kompetenz, but the doctrine of separability. That doctrine basically posits that an arbitration agreement constitutes an agreement separate and apart from the main contract. But, like Kompetenz-Kompetenz, separability has been asked to do too much work in assigning authority to determine arbitral jurisdiction between courts and arbitral tribunals. It has not proven equal to that task.

The difficulties associated with separability stem in part from the ambiguity surrounding it. Unlike elsewhere, separability in American law essentially serves two distinct purposes. One purpose — and indeed the one most widely ascribed to it in the international arbitral community — is to enable an arbitral tribunal to declare a contract invalid or unenforceable on the merits, without thereby necessarily destroying the basis of its authority to make that very ruling. As an agreement separate and apart from the main contract, an arbitration clause remains valid even though the contract of which it forms a part is not, thus permitting the former to survive the demise of the latter. Having survived, the arbitration clause remains a valid basis for the award. So understood, separability serves a highly salutary purpose. Party expectations concerning arbitration would clearly be disserved if arbitral tribunals were deemed, by virtue of deciding that a contract is invalid, to deprive themselves of the legal authority to make that very decision. Salutary though this purpose may be, it nonetheless has little if anything to do with delineating between gateway and non-gateway issues.

However, separability's second, and less universally acknowledged, function in U.S. law pertains directly to the demarcation between gateway and non-gateway issues. Under this species of separability, whether a court may initially determine a matter of arbitral jurisdiction depends on whether the jurisdictional challenge is based on a defect peculiar to the arbitration agreement, on the one hand, or applicable to the main contract as a whole, on the other. The Supreme Court, in the seminal *Prima Paint* case, traced that distinction to the language of the FAA, and its Section 4 in particular. But other considerations were surely also at play. The question whether a contract on which a claim in arbitration is predicated exists and is valid and enforceable clearly forms part of the merits of a case, and as such falls in principle within the arbitrators' province to resolve. The arbitration clause as such is situated differently. Not only does the arbitration clause not pertain to the merits of a contract dispute, but a challenge to that clause goes directly to the heart of the tribunal's authority to decide anything — including the validity and enforceability of the main contract. Separability thus permits courts to entertain challenges specifically applicable to the arbitration agreement, and not to the contract as a whole.

. . .

Although separability in U.S. law performs the twin functions I have described, only the first of them — namely, allowing an arbitration agreement and the authority it vests in an arbitral tribunal to survive the demise of the underlying contract — has won worldwide acceptance. Employing the notion to distinguish gateway from non-gateway issues is a distinctively, though not uniquely, American practice. . . .

1. Separability in French Law

French law is once again illuminating. At one time, the Cour de cassation, or Supreme Court, had posited a distinction between those threshold issues relating to the existence or validity of an arbitration agreement, on the one hand, and those relating to the scope of arbitral authority under that agreement, on the other. . . . Though advanced by the highest court, this approach did not, however, win favor with the Paris Court of Appeal, which considered it essential to arbitration's efficacy that, at its threshold, tribunals have exclusive authority to determine not only the scope of their authority to arbitrate, but also the existence and validity of the arbitration agreement upon which that authority rested.

That view eventually prevailed in the French courts. It also won favor with French legal scholars who, playing their customary role in conceptualizing the law, subsumed this emergent view under a more general principle of the "autonomy of the arbitration agreement." Article 1447 of the Civil Procedure Code now expressly affirms the principle of separability in this core sense. French and American law thus converge in advancing the autonomy of an arbitration agreement by insulating it from defects in the main contract.

Where French and American approaches part ways is over the additional role assigned to separability in American law, namely delineating between gateway and non-gateway issues. French courts deal with challenges to arbitral jurisdiction in the same way, regardless of whether they are directed at the main contract or at its arbitration clause in particular. Allowing courts to determine initially the existence or validity of the agreement to arbitrate is viewed in France as no less harmful to the autonomy of the arbitration agreement than allowing courts to determine initially the existence or validity of the main contract. France thus reaches the opposite conclusion from the United States on this point. It embraces the doctrine of separability in the way it is most widely understood internationally, but rejects it as a basis for allocating authority over issues of arbitral jurisdiction.

As a result, all objections to the obligation to arbitrate are reserved in France for the arbitral tribunal itself, subject only to the "manifest nullity" and "manifest inapplicability" exceptions — and even then, only if no tribunal has yet been constituted. Thus, French courts reject the assertion that a dispute falls outside the scope of an arbitration agreement, as long as it is at least arguable that the dispute falls within it. But the strong presumption in favor of arbitration comes into play whatever the reason advanced for resisting arbitration. It applies not only to the "whether" question (whether the parties agreed to arbitrate) and the "what" question (whether the parties agreed to arbitrate this type of dispute), but also the "who" question (whether a non-signatory is subject to the agreement to arbitrate), and indeed to any other objection to the obligation to arbitrate. In the French view, to require anything more than a *prima facie* showing on any threshold issue would impermissibly compromise the autonomy of the arbitration agreement.

French law thus offers a coherent model for reconciling efficacy and legitimacy interests in arbitration, albeit one that distinctly privileges efficacy over legitimacy values at the initial stage. The model proclaims an autonomy of the arbitration agreement built on the twin pillars of Kompetenz-Kompetenz and severability, as distinctively understood in French law.

2. Separability in German Law

As discussed earlier, German law carves out an important role for national courts in threshold determinations of arbitral jurisdiction. Under its Kompetenz-Kompetenz model, courts may examine the existence of a valid and enforceable agreement to arbitrate applicable to the case at hand, not only on the occasion of a jurisdictional objection to a court proceeding, but also in the immediate aftermath of a request for arbitration, though prior to constitution of a tribunal. The matters that a German court may examine on these occasions go by the global name of *Zulässigkeit*, or "issues of admissibility." Unfortunately, the term "admissibility" in German law suffers from much the same generality and over-inclusiveness as afflicts the term "arbitrability" when used loosely in U.S. case law and doctrine. Distinguishing specifically between gateway and non-gateway issues in German law is accordingly no simple matter.

German scholars appear to agree that an "admissibility" challenge must be directed at the existence of an effective and enforceable agreement to arbitrate that covers the dispute at hand. In principle, all issues related to the arbitration agreement's existence, validity, and scope are matters on which courts may rule under either Section 1032(1) or (2); all other threshold issues concerning the arbitration are reserved for the arbitrators. To that extent, German law embraces separability in its second as well as its first sense. But questions remain. How precisely is the universe of challenges to the arbitration agreement to be defined?

What specific kinds of challenges does it encompass? Most pertinent, for present purposes, must a challenge, in order to raise an admissibility issue, be directed uniquely at the arbitration agreement and not otherwise implicate the contract in which it is found? Neither the case law nor the doctrine offers very sharp answers.

One might say of German law that if an issue relates to the arbitration agreement, it is by definition a gateway issue. There are no further distinctions to be drawn.

Thus, unlike French law, German law does not confine the notion of separability to its core function, namely preventing an arbitral tribunal's invalidation of the main contract from thereby invalidating its authority to make that very determination. To be sure, it avoids using the same term for both functions (thus helping to avoid confusion). But just as U.S. law does through the notion of separability, German law organizes the allocation of authority over threshold issues around a distinction between the arbitration agreement and the main contract, albeit a distinction that is not drawn very finely and may entail some loss in predictability of results. Though the structure of German law is clear and crisp, the case law results are somewhat difficult to rationalize. We may put the matter this way. German law has constructed an institutionally and procedurally well-defined "gateway," but settled for a highly generalized notion of what distinguishes a "gateway" from a "non-gateway" issue.

Like domestic arbitration rules, the rules promulgated by international arbitration institutions commonly address the separability of the arbitration agreement and the arbitrators' authority to resolve challenges to their jurisdiction. *See, e.g.*, UNCITRAL Arbitration Rules, art. 23; AAA/ICDR Int'l Rules, art. 15; ICC Rules of Arbitration, art. 6. The next case provides one court's view of the significance of those rules.

APOLLO COMPUTER, INC. v. BERG
United States Court of Appeals for the First Circuit
886 F.2d 469 (1989)

Torruella, Circuit Judge.

The plaintiff appeals from a district court order refusing its request for a permanent stay of arbitration proceedings. The facts of the case are undisputed. On March 23, 1984, Apollo Computer, Inc. ("Apollo") and Dicoscan Distributed Computing Scandinavia AB ("Dico") entered into an agreement granting Dico, a Swedish company having its principal place of business in Stockholm, the right to distribute Apollo's computers in four Scandinavian countries. Helge Berg and Lars Arvid Skoog, the defendants in this action, signed the agreement on Dico's behalf in their respective capacities as its chairman and president. The agreement contained a clause stating that all disputes arising out of or in connection with the agreement would be settled in accordance with the Rules of Arbitration of the International Chamber of Commerce ("ICC"), and another clause that stated that the agreement was to be governed by Massachusetts law. The agreement also provided that it could not be assigned by Dico without the written consent of Apollo.

In September 1984, after disputes relating to the financing of Dico's purchases, Apollo notified Dico that it intended to terminate the agreement, effective immediately. Dico then filed for protection from its creditors under Swedish bankruptcy law and subsequently entered into liquidation, with its affairs being handled by its trustee in bankruptcy. The trustee assigned Dico's right to bring claims for damages against Apollo to the defendants. In May 1988, the defendants filed a complaint and a request for arbitration with the ICC.

On August 24, 1988, Apollo rejected arbitration, claiming that there was no agreement to arbitrate between it and the defendants, and that assignment of Dico's contractual right to arbitrate was precluded by the agreement's nonassignment clause. The ICC requested both parties to submit briefs on the issue. On December 15, 1988, the ICC's Court of Arbitration decided that pursuant to its rules, the arbitrator should resolve the issue of arbitrability, and directed the parties to commence arbitration proceedings to resolve that issue and, if necessary, the merits.

On January 11, 1989, Apollo filed the instant action in federal district court under diversity of citizenship jurisdiction. It sought a permanent stay of the arbitration . . . on the grounds that there is no arbitration agreement between the parties. The parties submitted a statement of material facts not in dispute. Apollo then moved for summary judgment. On May 11, 1989, the district court denied the request to stay arbitration and the motion for summary judgment. The court stated that "[a]s this order is determinative of the entire action, judgment for the defendants shall enter forthwith."

On May 16, 1989, Apollo filed a Notice of Appeal. . . .

. . .

Arbitrability

. . .

Apollo makes the following claims on appeal. First, it argues that the right to compel arbitration did not survive the termination of the agreement, so that even Dico would not have had the right to compel arbitration of the claims at issue. Second, it argues that even if Dico had the right to compel arbitration of the claims, it had not validly assigned that right to the defendants. Third, it argues that the agreement's nonassignment clause renders the purported assignment unenforceable against Apollo.

We do not reach any of these arguments because we find that the parties contracted to submit issues of arbitrability to the arbitrator. There is no question that this contract falls under the aegis of the Federal Arbitration Act. Both parties agree that under the Federal Arbitration Act, the *general* rule is that the arbitrability of a dispute is to be determined by the court. Parties may, however, agree to allow the arbitrator to decide both whether a particular dispute is arbitrable as well as the merits of the dispute.

In this case, the parties agreed that all disputes arising out of or in connection with their contract would be settled by binding arbitration "in accordance with the rules of arbitration of the International Chamber of Commerce." Article 8.3* of the ICC's Rules of Arbitration states:

---

* For the current version, see Articles 6.3-6.5 of the ICC Rules.

Should one of the parties raise one or more pleas concerning the existence or validity of the agreement to arbitrate, and should the [Court of Arbitration of the International Chamber of Commerce] be satisfied of the *prima facie* existence of such an agreement, the [Court of Arbitration of the International Chamber of Commerce] may, without prejudice to the admissibility or merits of the plea or pleas, decide that the arbitration shall proceed. In such a case, any decision as to the arbitrator's jurisdiction shall be taken by the arbitrator himself.

Article 8.4* of the ICC's Rules of Arbitration states:

Unless otherwise provided, the arbitrator shall not cease to have jurisdiction by reason of any claim that the contract is null and void or allegation that it is inexistent provided that he upholds the validity of the agreement to arbitrate. He shall continue to have jurisdiction, even though the contract itself may be inexistent or null and void, to determine the respective rights of the parties and to adjudicate upon their claims and pleas.

The contract therefore delegates to the arbitrator decisions about the arbitrability of disputes involving the existence and validity of a *prima facie* agreement to arbitrate.

Both the ICC's Court of Arbitration and the district court determined that a *prima facie* agreement to arbitrate existed. Therefore, they reasoned, Article 8.3 requires the arbitrator to determine the validity of the arbitration agreement in this specific instance — in other words, decide whether the arbitration agreement applies to disputes between Apollo and the assignees of Dico.

Apollo did not discuss this issue in its brief. At oral argument, it averred that Article 8.3 is inapplicable because no *prima facie* agreement to arbitrate exists between it and the defendants. We are unpersuaded by this argument. The relevant agreement here is the one between Apollo and Dico. The defendants claim that Dico's right to compel arbitration under that agreement has been assigned to them. We find that they have made the *prima facie* showing required by Article 8.3. Whether the right to compel arbitration survives the termination of the agreement, and if so, whether that right was validly assigned to the defendants and whether it can be enforced by them against Apollo are issues relating to the continued existence and validity of the agreement.

Ordinarily, Apollo would be entitled to have these issues resolved by a court. By contracting to have all disputes resolved according to the Rules of the ICC, however, Apollo agreed to be bound by Articles 8.3 and 8.4. These provisions clearly and unmistakably allow the arbitrator to determine her own jurisdiction when, as here, there exists a *prima facie* agreement to arbitrate whose continued existence and validity is being questioned. The arbitrator should decide whether a valid arbitration agreement exists between Apollo and the defendants under the terms of the contract between Apollo and Dico. Consequently, without expressing any opinion on the merits of the issues raised by Apollo, we affirm the district court's

---

*   For the current version, see Article 6.9 of the ICC Rules.

order denying a permanent stay of the arbitration proceedings.

Affirmed.

NOTES

1.   Is *Apollo* an illustration of the dictum in *First Options* that parties can agree to arbitrate arbitrability? Is it consistent with *Rent-A-Center*? Or is it instead a case that "[s]ome might suggest . . . represents an exercise in presuming one's own conclusion"? William W. Park, *Determining Arbitral Jurisdiction: Allocation of Tasks Between Courts and Arbitrators*, 8 AM. REV. INT'L ARB. 133, 141 n.23 (1997). Does it matter that the issue in *Apollo* is whether a non-signatory was bound to the arbitration agreement rather than, as in *Rent-A-Center*, whether the arbitration agreement was unconscionable?

2.   *Apollo* is an international arbitration case. Should the parties' ability to delegate issues to the arbitrator be broader in international settings than in domestic ones? How much does the language of the arbitration rules matter? Is there any material difference between the ICC Rules and the AAA/ICDR International Rules (or the AAA Commercial Arbitration Rules for that matter) in this regard?

3.   Recall from § 2.02 that the Restatement takes the position that institutional rules such as the ICC rules at issue in *Apollo* do not constitute a clear and unmistakable agreement to arbitrate arbitrability. Restatement (Third) of the U.S. Law of International Commercial Arbitration, § 4-14, rptrs. note to cmt. e.

4.   The Second Circuit followed *Apollo* in Contec Corp. v. Remote Solution Co., 398 F.3d 205 (2d Cir. 2005). The court of appeals "explicitly adopt[ed] *Apollo*" and held that "as a signatory to a contract containing an arbitration clause and incorporating by reference the AAA Rules, Remote Solution cannot now disown its agreed-to obligation to arbitrate all disputes, including the question of arbitrability." *Id.* at 211. Importantly, it seems, on its facts the case involved an attempt by a non-signatory to force a signatory to an arbitration agreement to arbitrate. The court of appeals in *Contec* distinguished Microchip Tech., Inc. v. U.S. Philips Corp., 367 F.3d 1350 (Fed. Cir. 2004), in which the Federal Circuit had refused to order a non-signatory to arbitrate the question of whether the parties had agreed to arbitrate, citing *First Options. Id.* at 1357-58. A subsequent district court in the Second Circuit likewise distinguished *Contec* in a case that involved "a signatory attempting to enforce an arbitration provision against a non-signatory." Masefield AG v. Colonial Oil Indus., Inc., 2005 U.S. Dist. LEXIS 7158, at *4 n.2 (S.D.N.Y. Apr. 26, 2005). *But see* Republic of Iran v. BNP Paribas USA, 2012 U.S. App. LEXIS 6264, *3-*5 (2d Cir. Mar. 28, 2012) (unpublished opinion) (holding that agreement to arbitrate under UNCITRAL Rules "does not provide clear and unmistakable evidence that the particular question of arbitrability at issue here — whether Iraq may invoke the arbitration clause as a third-party beneficiary of the contract — should be decided by arbitrators") (distinguishing *Contec* as based on "(1) the 'undisputed relationship between each corporate form of Contec and Remote Solution' and (2) the parties' continued conduct of themselves as subject to the agreement regardless of change in corporate form."). Why does it matter whether

the party seeking to avoid arbitration is a signatory or a non-signatory to the arbitration agreement?

PROBLEM 5.5

Millar Mining Company and Doran Drilling & Excavation Equipment, Inc. engage in extensive negotiations over a prospective contract for the purchase by Millar from Doran of several million dollars of highly sophisticated mining equipment. During the course of negotiations numerous drafts of a proposed contract are exchanged. Doran ultimately refuses to go forward with the deal. Millar responds by producing a contract allegedly signed by both parties. When Doran continues to refuse to perform, Millar threatens to initiate an arbitration proceeding (the alleged contract contains an arbitration clause) against Doran. Doran maintains that the purported contract is a forgery.

Doran retains your firm as counsel in the matter. During the course of your preliminary investigation, you determine that the country in which the arbitration would take place, as well as the most likely jurisdictions for any court actions concerning the contract, all have enacted the UNCITRAL Model Law on International Commercial Arbitration (see in particular Article 16). You further determine that the threatened arbitration between Millar and Doran falls within the scope of the Model Law.

Doran's general counsel, Clara St. Simon, who has had little experience with international commercial arbitration, asks you about the following:

(a) During discussions with Millar, Millar's general counsel (who also has had little experience with international commercial arbitration) told St. Simon that the arbitrators cannot address the forgery defense. "If they find the contract was a forgery, there won't be an agreement to arbitrate, and if there's no agreement to arbitrate, the arbitrators have no power," Millar's general counsel explained. Can the arbitrators rule on Doran's defense that the contract it purportedly signed was a forgery? How do you respond to the argument made by Millar's general counsel?

(b) In addition, St. Simon asks about Doran's alternatives if it goes ahead with the arbitration. She wants to know when, if at all, Doran can get court review of any ruling by the arbitrators on the forgery issue. "We'd like to get the forgery thing decided before we put in lots of time (and money) on the rest of the case, if we can, and then get a court to take a look at what the arbitrators did," she explains. What do you tell her? What would your answer be under U.S. law? French law?

[B] Assent

As with domestic arbitration, parties cannot be compelled to arbitrate an international dispute unless they have agreed to do so. Indeed, as already discussed, the New York Convention applies only if there is an "agreement in writing." Previously, we examined the necessity of a writing. This section looks at whether there is an "agreement."

FILANTO, S.P.A. v. CHILEWICH INTERNATIONAL CORP.
United States District Court for the Southern District of New York
789 F. Supp. 1229 (1992)

BRIEANT, CHIEF JUDGE.

. . .

This case is a striking example of how a lawsuit involving a relatively straight-forward international commercial transaction can raise an array of complex questions. . . .

Plaintiff Filanto is an Italian corporation engaged in the manufacture and sale of footwear. Defendant Chilewich is an export-import firm incorporated in the state of New York with its principal place of business in White Plains. On February 28, 1989, Chilewich's agent in the United Kingdom, Byerly Johnson, Ltd., signed a contract with Raznoexport, the Soviet Foreign Economic Association, which obligated Byerly Johnson to supply footwear to Raznoexport. Section 10 of this contract — the "Russian Contract" — is an arbitration clause. . . .

. . .

The first exchange of correspondence between the parties to this lawsuit is a letter dated July 27, 1989 from Mr. Melvin Chilewich of Chilewich International to Mr. Antonio Filograna, chief executive officer of Filanto. This letter refers to a recent visit by Chilewich and Byerly Johnson personnel to Filanto's factories in Italy, presumably to negotiate a purchase to fulfill the Russian Contract, and then states as follows:

> "Attached please find our contract to cover our purchase from you. Same is governed by the conditions which are enumerated in the standard contract in effect with the Soviet buyers [the Russian Contract], copy of which is also enclosed."

. . .

The next document in this case, and the focal point of the parties' dispute regarding whether an arbitration agreement exists, is a Memorandum Agreement dated March 13, 1990. This Memorandum Agreement, number 9003002, is a standard merchant's memo prepared by Chilewich for signature by both parties confirming that Filanto will deliver 100,000 pairs of boots to Chilewich at the Italian/Yugoslav border on September 15, 1990, with the balance of 150,000 pairs to be delivered on November 1, 1990. Chilewich's obligations were to open a Letter of Credit in Filanto's favor prior to the September 15 delivery, and another letter prior to the November delivery. This Memorandum includes the following provision:

> "It is understood between Buyer and Seller that USSR Contract No. 32-03/93085 [the Russian Contract] is hereby incorporated in this contract as far as practicable, and specifically that any arbitration shall be in accordance with that Contract."

Chilewich signed this Memorandum Agreement, and sent it to Filanto. Filanto at

that time did not sign or return the document. Nevertheless, on May 7, 1990, Chilewich opened a Letter of Credit in Filanto's favor in the sum of $2,595,600.00.
. . .

. . .

Then, on August 7, 1990, Filanto returned the Memorandum Agreement, sued on here, that Chilewich had signed and sent to it in March; though Filanto had signed the Memorandum Agreement, it . . . appended a covering letter, purporting to exclude all but three sections of the Russian Contract.

. . .

According to the Complaint, what ultimately happened was that Chilewich bought and paid for 60,000 pairs of boots in January 1991, but never purchased the 90,000 pairs of boots that comprise the balance of Chilewich's original order. It is Chilewich's failure to do so that forms the basis of this lawsuit, commenced by Filanto on May 14, 1991.

. . .

. . . [D]efendant Chilewich on July 24, 1991 moved to stay this action pending arbitration, while plaintiff Filanto on August 22, 1992 moved to enjoin arbitration.
. . .

. . .

. . . The central disputed issue . . . is whether the correspondence between the parties, viewed in light of their business relationship, constitutes an "agreement in writing."

Courts interpreting this "agreement in writing" requirement have generally started their analysis with the plain language of the [New York] Convention, . . . and have then applied that language in light of federal law, which consists of generally accepted principles of contract law, including the Uniform Commercial Code.

However, as plaintiff correctly notes, the "general principles of contract law" relevant to this action, do *not* include the Uniform Commercial Code; rather, the "federal law of contracts" to be applied in this case is found in the United Nations Convention on Contracts for the International Sale of Goods (the "Sale of Goods Convention"). This Convention, ratified by the Senate in 1986, is a self-executing agreement which entered into force between the United States and other signatories, including Italy, on January 1, 1988. . . . [A]bsent a choice-of-law provision, and with certain exclusions not here relevant, the Convention governs *all* contracts between parties with places of business in different nations, so long as both nations are signatories to the Convention. Sale of Goods Convention Article 1(1)(a). Since the contract alleged in this case most certainly was formed, if at all, after January 1, 1988, and since both the United States and Italy are signatories to the Convention, the Court will interpret the "agreement in writing" requirement of the Arbitration Convention in light of, and with reference to, the substantive international law of contracts embodied in the Sale of Goods Convention.

Not surprisingly, the parties offer varying interpretations of the numerous letters and documents exchanged between them. The Court will briefly summarize their respective contentions.

Defendant Chilewich contends that the Memorandum Agreement dated March 13 which it signed and sent to Filanto was an offer. It then argues that Filanto's retention of the letter, along with its subsequent acceptance of Chilewich's performance under the Agreement — the furnishing of the May 11 letter of credit — estops it from denying its acceptance of the contract. Although phrased as an estoppel argument, this contention is better viewed as an acceptance by conduct argument, e.g., that in light of the parties' course of dealing, Filanto had a duty timely to inform Chilewich that it objected to the incorporation by reference of all the terms of the Russian contract. Under this view, the return of the Memorandum Agreement, signed by Filanto, on August 7, 1990, along with the covering letter purporting to exclude parts of the Russian Contract, was ineffective as a matter of law as a rejection of the March 13 offer, because this occurred some five months after Filanto received the Memorandum Agreement and two months after Chilewich furnished the Letter of Credit. Instead, in Chilewich's view, this action was a proposal for modification of the March 13 Agreement. Chilewich rejected this proposal, by its letter of August 7 to Byerly Johnson, and the August 29 fax by Johnson to Italian Trading SRL, which communication Filanto acknowledges receiving. Accordingly, Filanto under this interpretation is bound by the written terms of the March 13 Memorandum Agreement; since that agreement incorporates by reference the Russian Contract containing the arbitration provision, Filanto is bound to arbitrate.

Plaintiff Filanto's interpretation of the evidence is rather different. While Filanto apparently agrees that the March 13 Memorandum Agreement was indeed an offer, it characterizes its August 7 return of the signed Memorandum Agreement with the covering letter as a counteroffer. While defendant contends that under Uniform Commercial Code § 2-207 this action would be viewed as an acceptance with a proposal for a material modification, the Uniform Commercial Code, as previously noted does not apply to this case, because the State Department undertook to fix something that was not broken by helping to create the Sale of Goods Convention which varies from the Uniform Commercial Code in many significant ways. Instead, under this analysis, Article 19(1) of the Sale of Goods Convention would apply. That section, as the Commentary to the Sale of Goods Convention notes, reverses the rule of Uniform Commercial Code § 2-207, and reverts to the common law rule that "A reply to an offer which purports to be an acceptance but contains additions, limitations or other modifications is a rejection of the offer and constitutes a counter-offer." Sale of Goods Convention Article 19(1). Although the Convention, like the Uniform Commercial Code, does state that non-material terms do become part of the contract unless objected to, Sale of Goods Convention Article 19(2), the Convention treats inclusion (or deletion) of an arbitration provision as "material," Sale of Goods Convention Article 19(3). The August 7 letter, therefore, was a counteroffer which, according to Filanto, Chilewich accepted by its letter dated September 27, 1990. Though that letter refers to and acknowledges the "contractual obligations" between the parties, it is doubtful whether it can be characterized as an acceptance.

More generally, both parties seem to have lost sight of the narrow scope of the inquiry required by the Arbitration Convention. All that this Court need do is to determine if a sufficient "agreement in writing" to arbitrate disputes exists between these parties. Although that inquiry is informed by the provisions of the Sale of Goods Convention, the Court lacks the authority on this motion to resolve all outstanding issues between the parties. Indeed, contracts and the arbitration clauses included therein are considered to be "severable," a rule that the Sale of Goods Convention itself adopts with respect to avoidance of contracts generally. Sale of Goods Convention Article 81(1). There is therefore authority for the proposition that issues relating to existence of the contract, as opposed to the existence of the arbitration clause, are issues for the arbitrators. . . .

. . .

The Court is satisfied on this record that there *was* indeed an agreement to arbitrate between these parties.

There is simply no satisfactory explanation as to why Filanto failed to object to the incorporation by reference of the Russian Contract in a timely fashion. As noted above, Chilewich had in the meantime commenced its performance under the Agreement, and the Letter of Credit it furnished Filanto on May 11 *itself* mentioned the Russian Contract. An offeree who, knowing that the offeror has commenced performance, fails to notify the offeror of its objection to the terms of the contract within a reasonable time will, under certain circumstances, be deemed to have assented to those terms. Restatement (Second) of Contracts § 69 (1981). The Sale of Goods Convention itself recognizes this rule: Article 18(1), provides that "A statement made by or other conduct of the offeree indicating assent to an offer is an acceptance." Although mere "silence or inactivity" does not constitute acceptance, Sale of Goods Convention Article 18(1), the Court may consider previous relations between the parties in assessing whether a party's conduct constituted acceptance, Sale of Goods Convention Article 8(3). In this case, in light of the extensive course of prior dealing between these parties, Filanto was certainly under a duty to alert Chilewich in timely fashion to its objections to the terms of the March 13 Memorandum Agreement — particularly since Chilewich had repeatedly referred it to the Russian Contract and Filanto had had a copy of that document for some time.

. . .

In light of these factors, and heeding the presumption in favor of arbitration, which is even stronger in the context of international commercial transactions, the Court holds that Filanto is bound by the terms of the March 13 Memorandum Agreement, and so must arbitrate its dispute in Moscow.

. . .

NOTES

1. In *Filanto*, the court applied the Convention on Contracts for the International Sale of Goods (CISG) in finding that there was an agreement to arbitrate. The United States and many major trading countries are parties to the CISG, which applies "to contracts of sale of goods between parties whose places of business are

in different States . . . when the States are Contracting States." CISG, art. 1(1)(a). The CISG does not apply to sales of goods to consumers, *id.* art 2(a), and expressly permits the parties to "exclude the application of this Convention," *id.* art. 6, in other words, to opt out of the CISG entirely. Because the CISG was applicable to the transaction, the *Filanto* court was able to avoid the difficult question of which law to apply in deciding whether there was sufficient assent. We will take a closer look at the question of the applicable law in the next section.

2.   Should the court in *Filanto* have decided whether there was a sufficient agreement or was that a matter for the arbitrators?

3.   What would be the result in *Filanto* if the court had applied *Kahn Lucas*?

4.   One fact pattern giving rise to assent issues, which may already be familiar to you, commonly is known as the "battle of the forms." One party submits a purchase order seeking to buy goods, and the other party responds with its own form, sometimes labeled a purchase order acknowledgment. Although the forms agree on the bargained-for terms, they differ in the fine print: for example, one of the forms, but not the other, contains an arbitration clause. The parties often then go ahead and perform. Is a contract formed on these facts? If so, have the parties agreed to arbitrate?

As the court in *Filanto* explains, the CISG takes a different approach to "battle of the forms" problems than does Article 2 of the Uniform Commercial Code (UCC). Article 19(1) of the CISG provides that "[a] reply to an offer which purports to be an acceptance but contains additions, limitations or other modifications is a rejection of the offer and constitutes a counter-offer." If the additional or different terms "do not materially alter the terms of the offer," however, the reply nonetheless "constitutes an acceptance," unless the offeror objects. CISG, art. 19(2). Terms relating to "the settlement of disputes," which would include an arbitration clause, always are considered to be material alterations, so no contract would be formed by the exchange of writings. *Id.* art. 19(3). If the parties go ahead and perform, that performance serves as an acceptance under article 18(1), such that a contract is formed on the terms of the last writing sent.

Under Article 2 of the UCC, by comparison, an additional term in the acceptance, even if material, does not prevent a contract from being formed, so long as the writings agree on the bargained for terms and acceptance is not "expressly made conditional on assent to the additional or different terms." UCC § 2-207(1). If the acceptance contains an additional term providing for arbitration, and both parties are merchants, the arbitration clause automatically becomes part of the contract unless the offer limits acceptance to its own terms, the arbitration clause "materially alters it," or the offeror objects. UCC § 2-207(2). Courts typically evaluate whether an arbitration clause is a material alteration on a case-by-case basis (indeed, a per se rule that an arbitration clause always is a material alteration likely would be preempted by the FAA). Aceros Prefabricados, S.A. v. TradeArbed, Inc., 282 F.3d 92, 100 (2d Cir. 2002) ("[A]rbitration agreements do not, as a matter of law, constitute material alterations to a contract; rather, the question of their inclusion in a contract under section 2-207(2)(b) is answered by examining, on a case-by-case basis, their materiality under a preponderance of the evidence standard as we would examine any other agreement.").

PROBLEM 5.6

Prendergast & Associates sends a Purchase Order to Armitage Armchairs for the purchase of 100 leather executive office chairs. Typed on the form purchase order are the item description, quantity, price, and delivery information. The rest of the form contains a number of standard terms, but is silent on dispute resolution. Armitage responds with its own form acknowledging Prendergast's order. The Purchase Order Acknowledgment correctly lists the item description, quantity, price, and delivery information from Prendergast's form. In addition, included in Armitage's form terms is a clause providing that all disputes are to be resolved by arbitration.

(a) Prendergast is from the United States; Armitage is from New Zealand. (Both those countries are parties to the Convention on Contracts for the International Sale of Goods.) After receiving the Purchase Order Acknowledgment, Prendergast changes its mind about the order, and sends Armitage a fax calling off the deal. Do Prendergast and Armitage have a contract? Can a court decide whether Prendergast and Armitage have a contract, or is that a matter for the arbitrator?

(b) Same as (a), except that Armitage also is from the United States. Do Prendergast and Armitage have a contract? Have they agreed to arbitrate their dispute?

(c) Same as (a), except that Prendergast does not change its mind about the order. Instead, Armitage ships the chairs and Prendergast pays for the chairs. Shortly after the chairs arrive, Prendergast discovers a defect in the chairs and demands its money back from Armitage. Do Prendergast and Armitage have a contract? Have they agreed to arbitrate their dispute?

(d) Same as (c), except that the arbitration clause in Armitage's Purchase Order Acknowledgment provides for the arbitration to be administered under the ICC Rules of Arbitration (see especially Article 6). Can a court decide whether Prendergast and Armitage have a contract, or is that a matter for the arbitrator?

[C] "Null and Void" Arbitration Agreement

Under Article II(3) of the New York Convention, a court need not direct the parties to arbitrate if "it finds that the said agreement is null and void, inoperative, or incapable of being performed." Presumably, this provision permits courts to consider contract law defenses to international agreements to arbitrate. But is there any limitation on which ones?

LINDO v. NCL (BAHAMAS), LTD.
United States Court of Appeals for the Eleventh Circuit
652 F.3d 1257 (2011)

HULL, Circuit Judge:

Plaintiff-Appellant Harold Leonel Pineda Lindo ("Lindo") appeals the district court's enforcement of the arbitration agreement in his employment contract with Defendant-Appellee NCL (Bahamas) Ltd. ("NCL"). Lindo sues NCL on a single count of Jones Act negligence, pursuant to 46 U.S.C. § 30104. He claims that NCL breached its duty to supply him with a safe place to work. The district court granted NCL's motion to compel arbitration and dismissed Lindo's complaint.

Given the New York Convention and governing Supreme Court and Circuit precedent, we must enforce the arbitration clause in Plaintiff Lindo's employment contract, at least at this initial arbitration-enforcement stage. After review and oral argument, we affirm the district court's order compelling arbitration of Lindo's Jones Act negligence claim.

I. FACTUAL BACKGROUND

Plaintiff Lindo is a citizen and resident of Nicaragua. Defendant NCL is a Bermuda corporation that operates cruise ships, with its principal place of business in Miami, Florida.

NCL employed Lindo to serve as a crewmember on the M/S Norwegian Dawn, which flies a Bahamian flag of convenience. The ship typically departs from ports in the United States and travels to international locales, such as Bermuda, Canada, and venues throughout the Caribbean.

Lindo alleges that in December 2008, while acting in the scope of his employment on NCL's private island in the Bahamas, he injured his back after he was ordered to transport heavy trash bags to the ship. He later underwent surgery to correct the injury.

. . .

Paragraph 12 of Lindo's [Employment] Contract specifies that all Jones Act claims will be resolved by binding arbitration pursuant to the United Nations Convention on Recognition and Enforcement of Foreign Arbitral Awards ("the New York Convention" or "the Convention") . . . . As to the place of arbitration, Lindo's Contract states that "[t]he place of the arbitration shall be the Seaman's country of citizenship, unless arbitration is unavailable under The Convention in that country, in which case, and only in that case, said arbitration shall take place in Nassau, Bahamas." As to the choice of law, Lindo's Contract provides, "The substantive law to be applied to the arbitration shall be the law of the flag state of the vessel." This entailed that any claim, including Lindo's Jones Act claim, would be arbitrated in Nicaragua (Lindo's country of citizenship) under Bahamian law (the law of the flag state of the vessel).

. . .

B. Procedural History

In 2009, Lindo filed suit in Florida state court. He asserted various claims [including a claim for Jones Act negligence, pursuant to 46 U.S.C. § 30104] . . . . NCL filed a motion to dismiss and compel arbitration.

Pursuant to 9 U.S.C. § 205, NCL also removed the action to the U.S. District Court for the Southern District of Florida and sought to compel arbitration. . . . Lindo opposed NCL's motion to dismiss and sought a remand to state court. Lindo argued that the arbitration provision in his Contract was void as against public policy because it operated as a prospective waiver of his Jones Act claim. . . .

The district court denied Lindo's motion to remand, granted NCL's motion to compel arbitration, and dismissed Lindo's . . . complaint. Lindo timely appealed.

II. THE NEW YORK CONVENTION

. . .

To implement the Convention, Chapter 2 of the FAA provides two causes of action in federal court for a party seeking to enforce arbitration agreements covered by the Convention: (1) an action to compel arbitration in accord with the terms of the agreement, 9 U.S.C. § 206, and (2) at a later stage, an action to confirm an arbitral award made pursuant to an arbitration agreement, 9 U.S.C. § 207.

The Convention contains defenses that correspond to the two separate stages of enforcement mentioned above. Article II contains the "null and void" defense, which — like 9 U.S.C. § 206 — is directed at courts considering an action or motion to "refer the parties to arbitration" . . . . Article II applies at the initial arbitration-enforcement stage.

Article V of the Convention, on the other hand, enumerates seven defenses that — like 9 U.S.C. § 207 — are directed at courts considering whether to recognize and enforce an arbitral award. Article V applies at the award-enforcement stage. One of Article V's seven defenses is the "public policy" defense . . . . After arbitration, a court may refuse to enforce an arbitral award if the award is contrary to the public policy of the country. . . .

Importantly, Article II contains no explicit or implicit public policy defense at the initial arbitration-enforcement stage. Meanwhile, Article V's public policy defense, by its terms, applies only at the award-enforcement stage.

Both parties agree that the Convention applies to Lindo's Contract. Applying the Convention, the district court recognized and enforced Lindo's agreement to arbitrate his dispute under Bahamian law in the country of his citizenship. On appeal, Lindo argues that his arbitration agreement, by selecting Bahamian law, effectively eliminates his U.S. statutory claim under the Jones Act and is unenforceable under the Convention. Lindo asserts that, despite his agreement binding him to do so, he cannot be required to arbitrate elsewhere under the Convention unless he can pursue a U.S. statutory claim under the Jones Act.

. . .

IV. ANALYSIS

. . . [W]e conclude that, at this initial arbitration-enforcement stage, the district court properly enforced Lindo's arbitration agreement in his Contract, which provided that his Jones Act claim would be arbitrated in a foreign forum (his own country of citizenship) under Bahamian law. We list the reasons why.

A. Strong Presumption of Arbitration Clause Enforcement

First, under the Convention and Supreme Court and Circuit precedent, there is a strong presumption in favor of freely-negotiated contractual choice-of-law and forum-selection provisions, and this presumption applies with special force in the field of international commerce. . . . Therefore, we necessarily start our analysis with a strong presumption in favor of the arbitration agreement in Lindo's Contract and, in fact, must view the choice clauses in Lindo's Contract as prima facie valid and enforceable.

B. U.S. Statutory Claims Are Arbitrable

. . . [B]oth the Supreme Court's and our Circuit's precedents have squarely held that contracts providing for arbitration of U.S. statutory claims are enforceable, absent a contrary intention clearly and specifically expressed by Congress. The fact that Lindo asserts a statutory Jones Act claim does not affect the strong presumption in favor of enforcement of the choice clauses in his Contract.

Because choice clauses encompassing U.S. statutory claims are enforceable, Lindo argues that his arbitration clause cannot be enforced . . . because it eliminates his Jones Act claim . . . .

C. Article II: "Null and Void" Defense at Arbitration-Enforcement Stage

Lindo's contentions are fundamentally flawed for several reasons. . . .

At the arbitration-enforcement stage, Article II(3) of the Convention recognizes only these affirmative defenses to that mandatory recognition: "The court of a Contracting State . . . shall, at the request of one of the parties, refer the parties to arbitration, unless it finds that the said agreement is *null and void, inoperative or incapable of being performed.*" New York Convention, art. II(3) (emphasis added).

In *Bautista [v. Star Cruises]*, this Court held that an arbitration agreement is "null and void" under Article II(3) of the Convention only where it is obtained through those limited situations, "such as fraud, mistake, duress, and waiver," constituting "standard breach-of-contract defenses" that "can be applied neutrally on an international scale." Lindo's Contract incorporates a union-negotiated CBA, and there is no claim — much less any showing — of fraud, mistake, duress, or waiver. To the extent Lindo relies on Article II, his claim fails.

Lindo argues that the arbitration provision is unconscionable, maintaining that he signed the Contract on a "take-it-or-leave-the-ship" basis. However, this was the same argument asserted by the plaintiff seamen in *Bautista*. This Court expressly rejected that argument, concluding that an unconscionability defense was not available under Article II of the Convention. See *id.* ("It is doubtful that there exists a precise, universal definition of the unequal bargaining power defense that may be applied effectively across the range of countries that are parties to the Convention, and absent any indication to the contrary, we decline to formulate one.").

. . .

E. Article V: Public Policy Defense at Arbitral Award-Enforcement Stage

Nevertheless, Lindo argues that his arbitration agreement is "contrary to the public policy" of the United States under Article V. . . .

. . . Article V applies only at the arbitral award-enforcement stage and not at the arbitration-enforcement stage at issue here. . . . When Art. II (3) was being discussed, the Israeli delegate pointed out that while a court could, under the draft Convention as it then stood, refuse enforcement of an award which was incompatible with public policy, " 'the court had to refer parties to arbitration whether or not such reference was lawful or incompatible with public policy.' " The German delegate observed that this difficulty arose from the omission in Art. II (3) " 'of any words which would relate the arbitral agreement to an arbitral award capable of enforcement under the convention.' " "When the German proposal was put to a vote, it failed to obtain a two-thirds majority (13 to 9) and the Article was thus adopted without any words linking agreements to the awards enforceable under the Convention. Nor was this omission corrected in the Report of the Drafting Committee. . . ."

For all the foregoing reasons, we hold that Lindo cannot raise an Article V public policy defense at this initial arbitration-enforcement stage.

F. Lindo's Public Policy Defense Lacks Merit at This Stage Anyway

Alternatively, even assuming, arguendo, that this timing infirmity were immaterial and Lindo could somehow raise an Article V public policy defense at the arbitration-enforcement stage, Lindo's challenge to his arbitration agreement still fails . . . because (1) Bahamian law itself recognizes negligence actions; and (2) even if, as Lindo claims, U.S. law under the Jones Act has a more relaxed causation standard for negligence claims than Bahamian law, these were precisely the same arguments lodged (and rejected) in [prior circuit precedent.]

. . .

V. CONCLUSION

For the foregoing reasons, we affirm the district court's order granting NCL's motion to dismiss and compel arbitration and denying Lindo's motion to remand.

AFFIRMED.

BARKETT, Circuit Judge, dissenting:

. . .

The threshold issue here is whether an arbitration agreement can be rendered "null and void, inoperative or incapable of being performed" on account of its inconsistency with the forum nation's public policy. If so, Lindo would be permitted to raise his prospective waiver argument at the initial agreement-enforcement stage.

As an initial matter, the meaning of the phrase "null and void" strongly suggests that public policy is a defense to arbitration. Indeed, Black's Law Dictionary provides that "[a] contract is *void* ab initio if it seriously offends law or public policy . . . ." (emphasis added). This common understanding — that a contractual provision contrary to public policy is void — must inform the meaning of the Convention's "null and void" clause.

This view is strengthened by Article V(2)(b) of the Convention, which provides that a court need not enforce an arbitral award if such enforcement would be contrary to public policy. Although one might initially wonder whether the Convention's express inclusion of a public policy exception at the award-enforcement stage implies a deliberate omission of such an exception at the agreement-enforcement stage, any such implication is dispelled by the proceedings of the New York Conference. In fact, the drafters of the Convention proceeded under the assumption that arbitration agreements would be addressed later in a separate Protocol, and thus they were chiefly concerned with the enforcement of arbitral awards, not agreements to arbitrate. It was "[n]ot until the final days of the Conference" that it was "realized that such a separation could seriously hamper the effectiveness of the new Convention." Article II was consequently "drafted in a race against time," and it was inserted "in the closing days of negotiations." As a result, and despite its importance, "[l]ittle thought, and less drafting attention, was given" to Article II, and the drafting history does "not reveal any discussion regarding th[e] words" of the "null and void" clause. It would therefore be a mistake to assume that the express inclusion of a public policy exception in Article V(2)(b) implies that such an exception is not encompassed by Article II(3), which was deliberately left broad.

. . . [I]t makes good sense to look to Article V(2)(b)'s public policy exception when interpreting Article II(3)'s "null and void" clause. . . . Interpreting the Convention this way makes sense because it congruously links the two stages of enforcement. For example, . . . [f]ailing to so interpret the Convention would require a court to compel arbitration in a dispute involving the sale of slaves, despite knowing full well that any resulting arbitral award would be unenforceable as a matter of public policy. While this example may be extreme, it illustrates the absurdity and inefficiency of requiring a court to refer a matter to arbitration where it is apparent from the face of the agreement that any subsequent award would be unenforceable as a matter of public policy.

. . .

Significantly, this interpretation of the "null and void" clause is also that of the political branches in the United States. When submitting the Convention to the

Senate for ratification in 1968, President Johnson attached a memorandum prepared by the Department of State, adopting [the] view that the "null and void" clause incorporated Article V(2)'s exceptions to the enforcement of arbitral awards.
. . .

. . .

Although the majority holds that Lindo may not raise his public policy defense at this initial stage, it gratuitously goes on to assert that the arbitration agreement does not violate public policy. Needless to say, this discussion is wholly unnecessary to the majority's resolution of this case and is plainly dicta. Nonetheless, I write to explain my contrary view that a faithful application of the Supreme Court's prospective waiver doctrine compels the conclusion that the arbitration agreement in this case contravenes public policy.

. . .

Enforcing the arbitration agreement in this case directly contravenes [the public policy reflected in the Jones Act]. The agreement unambiguously requires Lindo to submit his Jones Act claim to arbitration under Bahamian law. But there is no Jones Act in the Bahamas. Instead of a relaxed or featherweight causation standard, Bahamian law requires a seaman to prove a direct causal link between the employer's negligence and the injury, a much more stringent standard. The result is that the arbitral tribunal will neither "take cognizance of the statutory cause of action" nor "actually decide" a claim under the Jones Act, making the prospect of recovery substantially more difficult and unlikely. In short, the agreement results in the evisceration, not the vindication, of Lindo's statutory right under the Jones Act to establish causation by a mere featherweight.

NOTES

1.   In *Lindo*, the Eleventh Circuit (relying on a portion of its decision in *Bautista* omitted from the prior excerpt), interprets the "null and void" language in Article II(3) as applying only to "those limited situations, 'such as fraud, mistake, duress, and waiver,' constituting 'standard breach-of-contract defenses' that 'can be applied neutrally on an international scale.'" The court concludes that neither public policy nor unconscionability is such a defense. What is the basis for the court's conclusion? Do you agree?

2.   Is Article II(1) of the New York Convention (discussed in more detail in the next subsection) relevant to this discussion? Article II(1) requires contracting states to enforce arbitration agreements, but only as long as the dispute "concern[s] a subject matter capable of settlement by arbitration." Isn't that a form of public policy defense available at the agreement enforcement stage?

3.   How does the "prospective waiver doctrine," rejected in *Lindo*, compare to the "vindicating statutory rights doctrine" discussed in § 3.03[C]? If one is available should the other be?

4.   Does it make sense for a court to enforce an arbitration agreement when any award resulting from the arbitration might not be enforceable under Article V? Is the differing language between Article II and Article V of the Convention a

conscious choice or a drafting glitch? For a decision following *Lindo*, see Aggarao v. MOL Ship Mgmt. Co., Ltd., 675 F.3d 355, 373 (4th Cir. 2012) ("Aggarao is not entitled to interpose his public policy defense, on the basis of the prospective waiver . . . doctrine, until the second stage of the arbitration-related court proceedings — the award-enforcement stage.").

5.   In an omitted part of the opinion, the court of appeals discusses footnote 19 in *Mitsubishi*, which states:

> In addition to the clause providing for arbitration before the Japan Commercial Arbitration Association, the Sales Agreement includes a choice-of-law clause which reads: "This Agreement is made in, and will be governed by and construed in all respects according to the laws of the Swiss Confederation as if entirely performed therein." The United States raises the possibility that the arbitral panel will read this provision not simply to govern interpretation of the contract terms, but wholly to displace American law even where it otherwise would apply. The International Chamber of Commerce opines that it is "[c]onceivabl[e], although we believe it unlikely, [that] the arbitrators could consider Soler's affirmative claim of anti-competitive conduct by CISA and Mitsubishi to fall within the purview of the choice-of-law provision, with the result that it would be decided under Swiss law rather than the U.S. Sherman Act." At oral argument, however, counsel for Mitsubishi concede that American law applied to the antitrust claims and represented that the claims had been submitted to the arbitration panel in Japan on that basis. The record confirms that before the decision of the Court of Appeals the arbitral panel had taken these claims under submission.

> We therefore have no occasion to speculate on this matter at this stage in the proceedings, when Mitsubishi seeks to enforce the agreement to arbitrate, not enforce an award. Nor need we consider now the effect of an arbitral tribunal's failure to take cognizance of the statutory cause of action on the claimant's capacity to reinitiate suit in federal court. We merely note that in the event the choice-of-forum and choice-of-law clauses operated in tandem as a prospective waiver of a party's right to pursue statutory remedies for antitrust violations, we would have little hesitation in condemning the agreement as against public policy.

Doesn't the last sentence of footnote 19 speak directly to the issue in *Lindo*? The court of appeals in *Lindo* responded that "footnote 19 is undisputably dicta, and the Supreme Court has never once invalidated an arbitration agreement on that basis." 652 F.2d at 1278. Is that response persuasive?

6.   Are there any limits on the law that the parties can choose? What if the parties wished to avoid national laws altogether, and instead have their dispute resolved under some other standard? One often-discussed possibility is the law merchant, or *lex mercatoria* — "the embodiment of emerging customs and usages of international trade, supplemented in appropriate cases by resort to common-sense notions of justice and fairness." OKEZIE CHUKWUMERIJE, CHOICE OF LAW IN INTERNATIONAL COMMERCIAL ARBITRATION 107, 111 (1994). For one "tolerably complete account of the rules which are said to constitute the *lex mercatoria* in its present

form" (albeit "a rather modest haul for 25 years of international arbitration"), see Lord Justice Mustill, *The New Lex Mercatoria: The First Twenty-Five Years*, 4 ARB. INT'L 86, 110 (1988); *see also* KLAUS PETER BERGER, THE CREEPING CODIFICATION OF THE LEX MERCATORIA 278 annex I (1999). One "source" of the *lex mercatoria* is international arbitration awards. Does the new *lex mercatoria*, if there is such a thing, suggest that a system of precedent might, in fact, develop in arbitration?

The international arbitration literature contains extensive debates over whether there is a *lex mercatoria*, what its content is, and so on. *See, e.g.*, LEX MERCATORIA AND ARBITRATION (Thomas E. Carbonneau ed. rev. ed. 1998). A number of published arbitral awards have relied on the *lex mercatoria* as the basis for decision, although that number likely remains a small fraction of the total number of awards. *See* Christopher R. Drahozal, *Commercial Norms, Commercial Codes, and International Commercial Arbitration*, 33 VAND. J. INT'L L. 128 n.229 (2000) (collecting awards). In addition, national courts have on occasion upheld arbitral awards based on the *lex mercatoria*. *See, e.g.*, Norsolor S.A. v. Pabalk Ticaret Ltd. (Oberster Gerichtshof 1982), *in* 9 Y.B. COMM. ARB. 159 (1984) (Austria).

Despite all the discussions of the *lex mercatoria* in the international arbitration literature, few parties choose to have their contracts governed by "general principles of law" or the *lex mercatoria*. *See* Christopher R. Drahozal, *Contracting Out of National Law: An Empirical Look at the New Law Merchant*, 80 NOTRE DAME L. REV. 523 (2005). Indeed, one "extremely unscientific . . . survey" of international lawyers found that "[v]irtually every recipient replied that he had not had a client enter into a contract incorporating *lex mercatoria* as a choice of law in the past ten years. Most went on to add that they would strongly advise against such a provision, if a client were foolish enough to propose it." Barton S. Selden, Lex Mercatoria *in European and U.S. Trade Practice: Time to Take a Closer Look*, 2 ANN. SURV. INT'L & COMP. L. 111, 113–14 (1995). Why do you suppose that is?

PROBLEM 5.7

Egria Papier Gesellschaft is a German manufacturer of specialty paper products. It enters into a contract with an American company, Norton Distributors, Inc., for Norton to distribute its products in the United States. After two years, Egria terminates Norton as its distributor. Norton responds by filing suit in the United States alleging that the termination was a breach of contract and that it violated the American antitrust laws. Egria responds by moving to compel arbitration, based on a clause in the distribution agreement providing for arbitration in Germany. Should the court compel arbitration? How, if at all, would your answer change under the following circumstances?

(a) The contract provides that the law of the United States applies.

(b) The contract provides that law of Germany applies. (German law includes the competition laws of the European Union.)

(c) The contract provides that the law of Ormstein applies. (Ormstein is a fictitious country that has not enacted any sort of competition law, but that does have well-developed contract and tort law.)

(d) The contract provides that the contract shall be governed by the *lex mercatoria* to the exclusion of all national laws.

Assuming that a party raises an internationally recognized contract defense, what law should a court apply in adjudicating that defense? The next case addresses that issue.

RHONE MEDITERRANEE COMPAGNIA FRANCESE DI ASSICURAZIONI E RIASSICURAZIONI v. LAURO
United States Court of Appeals for the Third Circuit
712 F.2d 50 (1983)

GIBBONS, CIRCUIT JUDGE.

Rhone Mediterranee Compagnia Francese di Assicurazioni E Riassicurazioni (Rhone), a casualty insurer, appeals from an order of the District Court of the Virgin Islands staying Rhone's action pending arbitration. The action results from a fire loss which occurred when the vessel Angelina Lauro burned at the dock of the East Indian Co. Ltd. in Charlotte Amalie, St. Thomas. At the time of the fire the vessel was under time charter to Costa Armatori S.P.A. (Costa), an Italian Corporation. Rhone insured Costa and reimbursed it for property and fuel losses totaling over one million dollars. Rhone, as subrogee of Costa, sued the owner of the vessel, Achille Lauro (Lauro), and its master, Antonio Scotto di Carlo, alleging breach of the Lauro-Costa time charter, unseaworthiness, and negligence of the crew. The district court granted defendants' motion for a stay of the action pending arbitration, and Rhone appeals. . . . [W]e affirm.

. . .

As subrogee, Rhone stands in place of its insured, the time charterer Costa. In the time charter contract there is a clause:

23. *Arbitration*

Any dispute arising under the Charter to be referred to arbitration in London (or such other place as may be agreed according to box 24) one arbitrator to be nominated by the Owners and the other by the Charterers, and in case the Arbitrators shall not agree then to the decision of an Umpire to be appointed by them, the award of the Arbitrators or the Umpire to be final and binding upon both parties.

Box 24

Place of arbitration (only to be filled in if place other than London agreed (cl. 23)) NAPOLI

All the parties to the time charter agreement and the lawsuit are Italian. Italy and the United States are parties to the Convention on the Recognition and Enforcement of Foreign Arbitral Awards. . . .

. . . Rhone . . . [contends] that under the terms of the Convention the arbitration clause in issue is unenforceable. Rhone's argument proceeds from a somewhat ambiguous provision in Article II section 3 of the Convention. . . . Ambiguity occurs from the fact that no reference appears in section 3 to what law determines whether "said agreement . . . is null and void, inoperative or incapable of being performed."

Rhone contends that when the arbitration clause refers to a place of arbitration, here Naples, Italy, the law of that place is determinative. It then relies on the affidavit of an expert on Italian law which states that in Italy an arbitration clause calling for an even number of arbitrators is null and void, even if, as in this case, there is a provision for their designation of a tie breaker.

The ambiguity in Article II section 3 of the Convention with respect to governing law contrasts with Article V, dealing with enforcement of awards. . . . Article V unambiguously refers the forum in which enforcement of an award is sought to the law chosen by the parties, or the law of the place of the award.

Rhone and the defendants suggest different conclusions that should be drawn from the differences between Article II and Article V. Rhone suggests that the choice of law rule of Article V should be read into Article II. The defendants urge that in the absence of a specific reference Article II should be read so as to permit the forum, when asked to refer a dispute to arbitration, to apply its own law respecting validity of the arbitration clause.

There is some treaty history suggesting that a proposal to incorporate in Article II choice of law language similar to that in Article V was rejected because delegates to the United Nations organization which drafted it were concerned that a forum might then have an obligation to enforce arbitration clauses regardless of its "local" law. It thus appears that the ambiguity in Article II section 3 is deliberate. How it should be resolved has been a matter of concern to commentators, who suggest, variously, that the forum state should look to its own law and policy, to the rules of conflicts of laws, or to the law of the place of execution of the agreement.

None of the limited secondary literature sheds so clear a light as to suggest a certain answer. However, we conclude that the meaning of Article II section 3 which is most consistent with the overall purposes of the Convention is that an agreement to arbitrate is "null and void" only (1) when it is subject to an internationally recognized defense such as duress, mistake, fraud, or waiver, or (2) when it contravenes fundamental policies of the forum state. The "null and void" language must be read narrowly, for the signatory nations have jointly declared a general policy of enforceability of agreements to arbitrate. . . . In other words, signatory nations have effectively declared a joint policy that presumes the enforceability of agreements to arbitrate. Neither the parochial interests of the forum state, nor those of states having more significant relationships with the dispute, should be permitted to supersede that presumption. The policy of the Convention is best served by an approach which leads to upholding agreements to arbitrate. The rule of one state as to the required number of arbitrators does not implicate the fundamental concerns of either the international system or forum, and hence the agreement is not void.

Rhone urges that this rule may result in a Neopolitan arbitration award which, because of Italy's odd number of arbitrators rule, the Italian courts would not enforce. The defendants insist that even in Italy this procedural rule on arbitration is waivable and a resulting award will be enforced. Even if that is not the law of Italy, however, Rhone's objection does not compel the conclusion that we should read Article II section 3 as it suggests. The parties did agree to a non-judicial dispute resolution mechanism, and the basic purpose of the Convention is to discourage signatory states from disregarding such agreements. Rhone is not faced with an Italian public policy disfavoring arbitration, but only with an Italian procedural rule of arbitration which may have been overlooked by the drafters of the time charter agreement. Certainly the parties are free to structure the arbitration so as to comply with the Italian procedural rule by having the designated arbitrators select a third member before rather than after impasse. Even if that is not accomplished an award may still result, which can be enforced outside Italy.

Rhone urges that Article V section 1(d) prohibits such enforcement outside Italy, because it refers a non-Italian forum to the law of Italy. We disagree. Section 1 says only that "enforcement of an award may be refused" on the basis of the law of the country where it was made. Where, as here, the law of such a country generally favors enforcement of arbitration awards, and the defect is at best one of a procedural nature, Article V, section 1 certainly permits another forum to disregard the defect and enforce. That is especially the case when defendants come before the court and, relying on Article II, seek a stay of the action in favor of arbitration. They will hardly be in a position to rely on Italy's odd number of arbitrators rule if Rhone seeks to enforce an award in the District Court of the Virgin Islands.

The forum law implicitly referenced by Article II section 3 is the law of the United States, not the local law of the Virgin Islands or of a state. That law favors enforcement of arbitration clauses. . . . Since no federal law imposes an odd number of arbitrators rule — the only defect relied upon by Rhone — the district court did not err in staying the suit for breach of the time charter agreement pending arbitration. Moreover since the duty to provide a seaworthy vessel and to operate it non-negligently arises out of the charter relationship, it was proper to stay the entire case.

. . .

The order staying the action in the District Court of the Virgin Islands was in compliance with the Convention and with the law of the United States. It will be in all respects affirmed.

NOTE

In *Rhone*, the court points out that Article II(3) is silent on what law should be applied to determine if the arbitration agreement is null and void. It considers three possibilities: the law of the forum state, the law chosen under conflict of laws rules, and the law where the arbitration agreement was executed. Other possibilities include the law chosen in the parties' contract to apply to the arbitration proceeding, the law chosen to apply to the contract generally, the law of the arbitral seat, and the law where the arbitral award will be enforced. *See* Gary B. Born, International Commercial Arbitration 466-485 (2009). In the end the court in *Rhone* refused to apply the Italian law dealing with the number of arbitrators, even though Italy was the seat of the arbitration.

What law should courts apply? As a general matter, American courts have applied American law rather than foreign law to these sorts of issues. *See* 4 IAN R. MACNEIL ET AL., FEDERAL ARBITRATION LAW §§ 44.16.4 & 44.17.2.1 (1995). In *First Options*, the Supreme Court indicated that in cases under Chapter 1 of the FAA, courts should use "ordinary state-law principles that govern the formation of contracts." Is the same true in cases under Chapter 2? Or does the international character of the dispute require American courts to develop a federal common law of contracts when they rely on American law?

PROBLEM 5.8

Henry Baker Jewelers (Baker), of the United States, enters into a written contract with Morcar's Wholesale Gems (Morcar), from The Netherlands, to buy a variety of semiprecious gemstones. The contract provides that it will be governed by the laws of The Netherlands. When the gems are delivered, Baker determines that a number of them are fake, and files suit against Morcar in United States District Court for the Central District of California alleging breach of contract. Morcar files a motion to stay the proceedings and to compel arbitration, relying on an arbitration clause in the parties' contract, which provides for arbitration to take place in Great Britain. Baker opposes the motion, arguing that it was fraudulently induced to agree to arbitration by a variety of false representations Morcar made about the arbitration process.

Assume that the generally accepted elements of a defense of fraudulent inducement under American law are the following: the party claiming the defense must show (1) a misrepresentation of (2) material fact (3) made with an intent to deceive (scienter) on which (4) there was justifiable reliance and that (5) caused injury. Assume, however, that (1) Dutch law presumes scienter from the fact of a misrepresentation; (2) British law requires the party that made the misrepresentation to disprove reliance; and (3) California law holds that all misrepresentations about arbitration are per se material. What must Baker prove to establish its defense?

[D]   "Subject Matter Capable of Settlement by Arbitration"

Article II(1) of the New York Convention requires contracting states to enforce arbitration agreements, so long as the dispute "concern[s] a subject matter capable of settlement by arbitration." This language permits contracting states to define certain matters as not capable of settlement by arbitration — i.e., as nonarbitrable — without violating the Convention.

In Chapter 3, we examined federal statutes that (either expressly or impliedly) make arbitration agreements unenforceable in certain types of contracts or as to certain types of claims. Two key cases in the expansion of arbitrability under U.S. law, *Scherk v. Alberto-Culver Co.* and *Mitsubishi Motors Corp. v. Soler Chrysler-Plymouth, Inc.*, involved international arbitration. The outcomes of those cases reflected what at the time was a greater willingness to enforce international arbitration agreements than domestic ones. Subsequent cases, however, soon equalized the treatment of domestic and international arbitration (in favor of enforcing both types of arbitration agreements). The following case deals with one area in which a distinction between domestic and international arbitration may persist.

ESAB GROUP, INC. v. ZURICH INSURANCE PLC
United States Court of Appeals for the Fourth Circuit
685 F.3d 376 (2012)

FLOYD, Circuit Judge:

The Supreme Court has long recognized the importance of preserving the United States' ability to "speak with one voice" in regulating foreign commerce. Appellant . . . ESAB Group, Inc., urges us to allow the various views of the states to replace the federal government's singular voice regarding commercial arbitration of insurance disputes in foreign tribunals. Specifically, ESAB Group contends that South Carolina law "reverse preempts" federal law — namely, a treaty and its implementing legislation — pursuant to the McCarran-Ferguson Act, a federal statute directed at protecting state insurance regulations from implied preemption by federal domestic commerce legislation. We find such a reading of the pertinent law untenable. For this reason, we affirm as to the district court's exercise of subject-matter jurisdiction . . . .

. . .

I.

. . .

. . . South Carolina law establishes that, in general, written arbitration agreements are "valid, enforceable and irrevocable, save upon such grounds as exist at law or in equity for the revocation of any contract." S.C. Code Ann. § 15-48-10(a). But this rule does "not apply to . . . any insured or beneficiary under any insurance policy." *Id.* § 15-48-10(b)(4).

In analyzing the enforceability of domestic arbitration agreements in insurance policies, both the United States District Court for the District of South Carolina and the South Carolina Court of Appeals have held that, pursuant to the McCarran-Ferguson Act, South Carolina's law invalidating arbitration agreements in insurance policies reverse preempts chapter 1 of the FAA. ESAB Group's appeal presents the concomitant question with respect to the [New York] Convention and Convention Act [FAA chapter 2]: does the McCarran-Ferguson Act apply such that state law can reverse preempt federal law and invalidate a foreign arbitration agreement?

II.

. . .

ESAB Group is a South Carolina-based manufacturer of welding materials and equipment. . . .

Between 1989 and 1996, a Swedish insurer, Trygg-Hansa, issued seven global liability policies (the ZIP Policies or the Policies) to ESAB Group's Swedish parent, ESAB AB. . . . Special endorsements in the Policies specifically extended coverage to ESAB Group and its predecessors. . . . Five of the Policies, the 1989-1993 ZIP Policies, contain arbitration agreements, which mandate the resolution of disputes in Swedish arbitral tribunals in accordance with Swedish law. . . .

. . .

ESAB Group is currently facing numerous products liability suits arising from alleged personal injuries caused by exposure to welding consumables manufactured by ESAB Group or its predecessors. . . . ESAB Group requested that its insurers defend and indemnify it in these products liability actions. Several . . . refused coverage. As a result, ESAB Group brought suit against these insurers in South Carolina state court.

The defendant insurers removed the case to the United States District Court for the District of South Carolina pursuant to the Convention and the Convention Act's grant of removal jurisdiction. ESAB Group disputed the district court's subject-matter jurisdiction. . . . The district court . . . found that "the Convention, not the Convention Act, . . . directs courts to enforce international arbitration agreements," and because the McCarran-Ferguson Act's text limits its scope to federal statutes, McCarran-Ferguson could not disrupt the application of traditional preemption rules. . . . ESAB Group timely appealed the district court's exercise of subject-matter jurisdiction. . . .

III.

We . . . consider whether the federal courts have jurisdiction over the present action or whether, as ESAB Group claims, South Carolina law reverse preempts federal law and eliminates the basis for jurisdiction. Our review of questions of subject-matter jurisdiction is de novo.

ESAB Group asserts that the Convention is a non-self-executing treaty, i.e., one that requires implementing legislation to be given effect in domestic courts. According to ESAB Group, it follows from this that the Convention has legal effect only as incorporated into its implementing legislation — here, the Convention Act. And because the Convention Act is a federal statute that does not speak directly to insurance, ESAB contends, it is subject to reverse preemption under the McCarran-Ferguson Act.

A.

Two of our sister circuits, the Second and the Fifth, have examined whether a state law may preempt the Convention or Convention Act pursuant to the

McCarran-Ferguson Act and have reached divergent conclusions.

The Second Circuit visited the issue in *Stephens v. American International Insurance Co.*, 66 F.3d 41 (2d Cir. 1995). Citing only the Convention Act, the *Stephens* court stated, "[T]he Convention is not self-executing, and therefore, relies upon an Act of Congress for its implementation." The court then framed the question as whether the implementing legislation, the Convention Act, is subject to preemption by state law under the McCarran-Ferguson Act. Based on the text of the McCarran-Ferguson Act, the court concluded, without elaboration, that state laws precluding arbitration of disputes with a delinquent insurer reverse preempt the Convention Act.

. . .

The Fifth Circuit, sitting en banc, took up the issue of the interaction between the McCarran-Ferguson Act and the Convention in *Safety [National Cas. Corp. v. Certain Underwriters at Lloyd's, London*, 587 F.3d 714, 720 (5th Cir. 2009) (en banc), *cert. denied*, 131 S. Ct. 65 (2010)]. The majority in that case held that, even assuming the Convention was non-self-executing (and therefore did not have legal effect in domestic courts absent implementing legislation), reverse preemption did not apply. The majority first reasoned that the McCarran-Ferguson Act applied only to statutes, not treaties. It then concluded that, despite the presence of implementing legislation, the Convention, not the Convention Act, was being "construe[d]" to supersede state law. And because the McCarran-Ferguson Act did not apply to treaties, that Act could "not cause [state law] to reverse-preempt the Convention."

Judge Elrod, joined by two other judges, provided a strident dissent. She too assumed that the treaty was non-self-executing, finding that the parties failed to preserve this issue. But she observed that, as to non-self-executing treaties, "commentators overwhelmingly conclude that under current (and longstanding) law, it is only the implementing statute, not the non-self-executing treaty, that can be enforced by the courts so as to be capable of preemption." And because only the implementing legislation had preemptive effect, it was a statute — the Convention Act — that was being construed to supersede state law.

The dissent charged that the majority had misconstrued the appropriate inquiry by analyzing whether a treaty was an "Act of Congress" for purposes of McCarran-Ferguson; Judge Elrod agreed it was not. She further claimed that the majority had engaged in a "play on words" in finding that the Convention itself was being " 'construed' under the McCarran-Ferguson Act" to supersede state law. The Convention, as a non-self-executing treaty, was not judicially enforceable, so it lacked the power to preempt (or supersede) state law. Instead, the dissent argued, the Convention Act, which incorporated the Convention by reference, must be the source of the potentially preemptive federal law to which McCarran-Ferguson's reverse-preemption rule might apply. The proper question, according to the dissent, was whether the Convention Act was an "Act of Congress" within the meaning of McCarran-Ferguson, and the dissenters would have held that it was.

Judge Clement concurred in the judgment but rejected the majority's analysis. The dissent, she asserted, had "persuasively refute[d]" the majority's position that the provisions of a non-self-executing, implemented treaty "have full preemptive effect." Judge Clement argued that the court should instead have found that Article II of the Convention was self-executing based on its plain-language directive to domestic courts to enforce foreign arbitral agreements. Although she acknowledged that some factors indicated the Convention Act was intended as implementing legislation, she believed these were better explained by reading other portions of the Convention, particularly Article III, as non-self-executing. If Article II was self-executing, then the treaty itself preempted state law, and the McCarran-Ferguson Act, applicable only to statutes, could not disrupt the traditional rules of preemption.

B.

ZIP presents numerous arguments in support of its position that the McCarran-Ferguson Act does not authorize reverse preemption in this case. First, we quickly reject ZIP's contention that the South Carolina statute is not subject to McCarran-Ferguson because it is not a "law enacted . . . for the purpose of regulating the business of insurance." The Supreme Court has instructed that this category of laws is a "broad" one, encompassing "laws that possess the end, intention, or aim of adjusting, managing, or controlling the business of insurance." We agree with the district court and the South Carolina Court of Appeals that South Carolina's law, which governs the manner in which disputes regarding coverage are resolved, falls within this category.

The parties also spill significant ink disputing whether Article II of the Convention is a self-executing treaty provision. . . .

ZIP [Zurich Insurance PLC] asserts that Article II of the Convention is self-executing and, therefore, should be enforced and given preemptive effect independent of the Convention Act. There is much to recommend this position. Most notably, the starting point of treaty interpretation is the text, and the text of Article II instructs domestic courts to enforce foreign arbitral agreements. The Supreme Court has signaled that this sort of "directive to domestic courts" is indicative of a self-executing treaty provision. Judge Clement, in her *Safety National* concurrence, and the United States, in opposing the petition for certiorari in that case, see Brief for United States as Amicus Curiae at 9, *La. Safety Ass'n of Timbermen Self Insurers Fund v. Certain Underwriters at Lloyd's, London*, 131 S. Ct. 65 (2010) (No. 09-945), adopted the view that the instructive language in Article II rendered it self-executing.

But, as Judge Clement noted, there is an emerging presumption against finding treaties to be self-executing. And the legislative history of the Convention Act indicates that Congress viewed the Act as implementing legislation, at least as to some of the Convention's provisions. *Medellin* [*v. Texas*, 552 U.S. 491 (2008)], furthermore, cited the Convention Act as an example of implementing legislation. Although Judge Clement urged that the Convention Act served to implement other provisions of the Convention (particularly Article III), this is hardly clear because nothing in the Convention Act or legislative history differentiates between Article II and the remainder of the treaty.

. . .

But we need not wade into these murky waters to resolve the question before us. To the contrary, we hold that, even assuming Article II of the Convention is non-self-executing, the Convention Act, as implementing legislation of a treaty, does not fall within the scope of the McCarran-Ferguson Act. Instead, as detailed below, Supreme Court precedent dictates that McCarran-Ferguson is limited to legislation within the domestic realm, and prior precedent of this court and our sister circuits supports a narrow reading of the Act.

. . .

Where a statute touches upon foreign relations and the United States' treaty obligations, we must proceed with particular care in undertaking this interpretive task. As the Supreme Court observed in considering a prior potential conflict between the Convention Act and a federal statute, "[i]f the United States is to be able to gain the benefits of international accords and have a role as a trusted partner in multilateral endeavors, its courts should be most cautious before interpreting its domestic legislation in such manner as to violate international agreements." We seek, when possible, to "construe . . . statute[s] consistent with our obligations under international law."

ESAB Group urges that we must construe "Act of Congress," as that term is used in the McCarran-Ferguson Act, to apply to every federal statute, irrespective of the international implications. But the Supreme Court has recently explained that, in enacting the McCarran-Ferguson Act, Congress plainly did not intend the law to apply so broadly. In [*American Insurance Ass'n v. Garamendi*], 539 U.S. 396 (2003), the Supreme Court specified that McCarran-Ferguson was "directed to implied preemption by domestic commerce legislation."

Although in *Garamendi* the Court was examining the interaction between state law and an executive agreement, the Court's statements regarding congressional intent guide our understanding of Congress's intent to limit the Act's scope. Specifically, that case demonstrated that Congress did not intend for the McCarran-Ferguson Act to permit state law to vitiate international agreements entered by the United States.

. . .

The Convention Act, which provides, without exception, that the Convention "shall be enforced in United States courts," 9 U.S.C. § 201, similarly intends to replace all contrary state laws. The Supreme Court has opined that the Convention and Convention Act demand that courts "subordinate domestic notions of arbitrability to the international policy favoring commercial arbitration." *Mitsubishi Motors*. Thus, although the Court acknowledges that the Convention permits Congress to "specify categories of claims it wishes to reserve for decision by our own courts," it has "decline[d] to subvert the spirit of the United States' accession to the Convention by recognizing subject-matter exceptions where Congress has not expressly directed the courts to do so."

The McCarran-Ferguson Act contains no such express direction. Indeed, the Supreme Court has told us that the aim of McCarran-Ferguson is not arbitration or treaties, but "domestic commerce legislation." We therefore hold that the Convention Act, as legislation implementing a treaty, is not subject to reverse preemption, so insurance disputes are not exempt from the Convention Act pursuant to McCarran-Ferguson's reverse-preemption rule.

As we have observed, the federal government must be permitted to "speak with one voice when regulating commercial relations with foreign governments." With the Convention and Convention Act, the government has opted to use this voice to articulate a uniform policy in favor of enforcing agreements to arbitrate internationally, even when "a contrary result would be forthcoming in a domestic context." *Mitsubishi.* To allow "parochial refusal[s]" to enforce foreign arbitration agreements would frustrate the very purposes for which the Convention was drafted: achieving the predictable and orderly resolution of disputes "essential to any international business transaction" and ensuring parties are not haled into hostile or inappropriate forums. *Scherk v. Alberto-Culver Co.,*

Congress might opt to exclude insurance disputes from the Convention. But it has not done so with the McCarran-Ferguson Act. Nothing in McCarran-Ferguson suggests that, by enacting that statute, Congress intended to delegate to the states the authority to abrogate international agreements that this country has entered into and rendered judicially enforceable. We will not read it to do so.

. . .

For the foregoing reasons, we affirm.

NOTES

1.   Review the excerpt from Professor William Park in § 3.02, which discusses the arbitrability of statutory claims. Should courts be more willing or less willing to find certain types of claims nonarbitrable in international disputes than in domestic disputes? Why? To date, most international transactions involve relatively sophisticated parties. With the growing use of the Internet, however, it is likely that consumers will increasingly be involved in international commerce. Does that change your views?

2.   Why should the McCarran-Ferguson Act be construed differently for international transactions than domestic ones? Is there any support in the text of the Act for that distinction? What is the basis for the court of appeals' decision?

3.   Is the New York Convention self-executing? What does that mean? What difference would it make in *ESAB*? In other settings?

4.   In other countries, as in the U.S., "judicial and legislative decisions over the past several decades have progressively narrowed the scope of the non-arbitrability doctrine and the subjects which are considered to be non-arbitrable." GARY B. BORN, INTERNATIONAL COMMERCIAL ARBITRATION 788 (2009). For information on non-arbitrable disputes in a number of countries worldwide, see the national reports in INTERNATIONAL COUNCIL FOR COMMERCIAL ARBITRATION, INT'L HANDBOOK ON COMMERCIAL ARBITRATION (Jan Paulsson ed. 2011).

5. At one time, UNCITRAL had identified arbitrability as an area for possible future work in international commercial arbitration. It described the possible approaches as follows:

32. In some States the commercial subject matters that are reserved to the courts are determined by various statutes, for instance, those dealing with anti-trust or unfair competition, securities, intellectual property, labour or company law. Various States have included in their arbitration law a general provision going beyond the traditional formula of "what parties may compromise on or dispose of" to cover, for example, "any claim involving an economic interest." Uncertainty about, and differences among definitions of, which disputes are arbitrable may cause considerable difficulties in practice.

33. One way of approaching the problem may be to attempt to reach a world-wide consensus on a list of non-arbitrable issues. If that does not seem feasible, it may be considered whether it would be desirable to agree on a uniform provision setting out three or four issues that are generally considered non-arbitrable and then call upon States to list immediately thereafter any other issues deemed non-arbitrable by the State. Such an approach of channelled information, as used in article 5 of the UNCITRAL Model Law on International Commercial Arbitration, would provide certainty and easy access to information about those restrictions.

34. In searching for the best approach that would be workable worldwide and that would provide the desired degree of certainty and transparency, one would face a dilemma. The more general the formula, the greater would be the potential risk of divergent interpretations by courts of different States; the more detailed the list, the greater would be the risk of non-acceptance by States and, to the extent the list would be accepted, the greater would be the risk of solidifying matters and thus impeding further development toward limiting the realm of non-arbitrability. Nevertheless, a considered attempt seems desirable since the result of a world-wide discussion would in itself be revealing and useful.

United Nations Commission on International Trade Law, Note by the Secretariat on Possible Future Work in the Area of International Commercial Arbitration A/CN.9/460, at ¶¶ 32–34 (Apr. 6, 1999).

PROBLEM 5.9

You are a new member of the UNCITRAL working group considering whether to propose a uniform list of non-arbitrable disputes. Do you favor such a proposal? What sorts of disputes would you include on the list?

§ 5.04 PROCEDURAL ISSUES IN ENFORCING INTERNATIONAL ARBITRATION AGREEMENTS

As with domestic arbitration agreements, actions to enforce international arbitration agreements brought in United States courts must satisfy the same procedural requirements as other lawsuits: there must be personal jurisdiction, subject matter jurisdiction, and venue. Personal jurisdiction may be more problematic than with strictly domestic arbitration because of the international character of the transaction. For other procedural issues, chapter 2 of the Federal Arbitration Act contains specific provisions applicable only to arbitration agreements falling within the scope of the New York Convention.

First, unlike the domestic FAA, which requires an independent source of subject matter jurisdiction before an action can be brought in federal court, section 203 of the FAA provides for subject matter jurisdiction in federal court for any "action or proceeding falling under the Convention." 9 U.S.C. § 203. This provision can be particularly important in cases in which there is no jurisdiction on the basis of diversity of citizenship, such as when neither party is an American citizen. Section 205 of the FAA also permits removal to federal court of any state court action that "relates to an arbitration agreement or award falling under the Convention." *Id.* § 205.

Second, chapter 2 specifies two possible venues for any action brought under chapter 2: any court "in which save for the arbitration agreement an action or proceeding with respect to the controversy between the parties could be brought," and the court "for the district and division which embraces the place designated in the agreement as the place of arbitration if such place is within the United States." *Id.* § 204.

Third, American courts have broad power to order the parties to arbitrate in cases arising under the Convention. Section 206 of the Federal Arbitration Act provides that "[a] court having jurisdiction under this chapter may direct that arbitration be held in accordance with the agreement at any place therein provided for, whether that place is within or without the United States." *Id.* § 206. This broad power contrasts sharply with the much narrower power to order arbitration under the domestic FAA "within the district in which the petition for an order directing such arbitration is filed." *Id.* § 4. But what if the arbitration agreement is silent on the place of arbitration — in other words, no place of arbitration is "therein provided for"?

JAIN v. DE MÉRÉ
United States Court of Appeals for the Seventh Circuit
51 F.3d 686 (1995)

FLAUM, CIRCUIT JUDGE.

This case presents an issue of first impression: whether federal courts have power to compel arbitration between two foreign nationals where their arbitration agreement fails to specify a location for the arbitration. . . . We hold that federal courts have this power and therefore reverse the decision of the district court.

I.

Henri Courier de Méré, a citizen of France, owns a number of patents pertaining to electronic ballasts for fluorescent and gas discharge lamps that he invented. de Méré signed a contract with Ishwar D. Jain, a citizen of India, whereby Jain agreed to help market these inventions. The contract between de Méré and Jain provides that "Any disagreement arising out of this contract may only be presented to an arbitrary commission applying French laws." The contract is silent as to the location of the arbitration and the method of appointment of the arbitrator.

On August 25, 1993, de Méré entered into a license agreement with Motorola Lighting, Inc. of Illinois. This agreement, which Jain had helped promote and negotiate in Illinois, provided for certain royalty payments from Motorola to de Méré. According to the marketing contract, de Méré then paid Jain $25,000, ten percent of the first advanced royalty payment from Motorola. Jain believes that the marketing contract also entitles him to a percentage of other money Motorola has paid de Méré; de Méré disagrees and has refused to give Jain anything beyond the $25,000.

Pursuant to the contract, Jain served de Méré with a demand for arbitration on March 18, 1994. Jain sought arbitration in Illinois under the Commercial Arbitration Rules of the American Arbitration Association ("AAA"), and the AAA designated an arbitrator and scheduled a hearing for July 25–26, 1994. De Méré objected to the appointment of the AAA as the arbitrary commission and to its selection of an arbitrator. De Méré contended that the only appropriate jurisdiction under the contract lay in France.

Jain petitioned the District Court for the Northern District of Illinois to compel arbitration in Illinois. The district court held that it had jurisdiction under the Federal Arbitration Act (the "Act") and the Convention on the Recognition and Enforcement of Foreign Arbitral Awards (the "Convention"), but ruled that the Act did not permit it to compel arbitration in this case. The court determined that the contract's failure to specify . . . the location of the arbitration . . . left it powerless to enforce the arbitration agreement between de Méré and Jain. After the district court denied a motion for reconsideration, this appeal followed.

II.

Jain contends that the district court incorrectly determined that it could not compel arbitration in this case. Specifically, Jain asserts that 9 U.S.C. §§ 4 & 5, which empower a district court to compel arbitration in its own district and to appoint an arbitrator, give the district court all the authority it needs to refer the case to arbitration in the Northern District of Illinois. We review this question of statutory interpretation *de novo*.

The Federal Arbitration Act governs the enforcement, validity, and interpretation of arbitration clauses in commercial contracts in both state and federal courts. Chapter 2 of the Act, 9 U.S.C. §§ 201–208, which implements the Convention on the Recognition and Enforcement of Foreign Arbitral Awards, controls arbitration [of] disputes in the international context. In general, the Act creates a strong presumption in favor of arbitration, especially in international commercial agreements.

Mitsubishi Motors Corp. v. Soler Chrysler-Plymouth, Inc.; Scherk v. Alberto Culver Co.

The present arbitration dispute clearly lies within the domain of chapter 2. . . . De Méré and Jain are not United States citizens, and the relation between de Méré and Jain was commercial. Accordingly, Jain's suit meets chapter 2's jurisdictional requirements. Jurisdiction in this case also rests solely on chapter 2. Because they are both foreigners, Jain and de Méré are not diverse parties for the purposes of 28 U.S.C. § 1332, and Jain's royalty claim raises no federal question beyond arbitration. Chapter 2 thus demarcates the beginning and the end of our authority in this case.

Both Jain and de Méré concede that we cannot refer this matter to arbitration unless the district court has the authority to order arbitration to proceed in a particular place. Chapter 2 offers two potential statutory bases for compelling arbitration in this case. First, § 206 provides that any court with jurisdiction under chapter 2 "may direct that arbitration be held in accordance with the agreement at any place therein provided for, whether that place is within or without the United States. . . ." 9 U.S.C. § 206. Because the contract between Jain and de Méré does not identify an arbitration site, § 206 does not allow a court to grant Jain's motion to compel arbitration. *See* Bauhinia Corp. v. China Nat. Machinery & Equipment Import & Export Corp., 819 F.2d 247, 250 (9th Cir.1987).

Second, § 208 indicates that "Chapter 1 applies to actions and proceedings brought under [chapter 2] to the extent that [chapter 1] is not in conflict with this chapter or the Convention as ratified by the United States." . . . In contrast to § 206, § 4 not only permits but requires a court to compel arbitration in its own district when no other forum is specified. Indeed, a district court compelling arbitration under § 4 lacks the power to order arbitration to proceed outside its district. Thus, the court may only refer the case to arbitration in the Northern District of Illinois if § 4 applies.

Without question, chapter 2 incorporates § 4 to some degree. Where an arbitration agreement specifies an arbitration site, § 4 is admittedly incompatible with chapter 2. If the agreement calls for arbitration within the district in which the action is brought, both § 4 and § 206 permit the court to compel arbitration there; section 4 is at most redundant. If the agreement calls for arbitration outside of the district in which the action is brought, the limits of § 4 directly conflict with the district court's powers under § 206, and § 208 would render § 4 inapplicable.

Where, however, an arbitration agreement contains no provision for location, § 4 would supplement § 206 by giving a court the ability to compel arbitration in its own district. Under this circumstance, § 4 and § 206 conflict only if one assumes that Congress intended § 206 to be the exclusive method by which courts could order arbitration. But if § 206 were exclusive, courts would have less power to enforce arbitration agreements in international cases than in domestic ones whenever the agreement failed to stipulate an arbitration location. Chapter 2, by implementing the Convention on the Recognition and Enforcement of Foreign Arbitral Awards, was designed to increase the ability of district courts to compel arbitration in international commercial cases, and § 208 reflects that policy. Given that purpose, the absence of any explicit statement making § 206 exclusive, and the strong presumption in favor of arbitration in the sphere of private international law, we conclude § 4 is clearly applicable when an arbitration agreement fails to specify a place for arbitration.

The question then becomes *how* § 4 applies. Jain asserts that § 4 plainly states that when the district court determines that the parties have agreed to arbitrate a dispute, "the court shall make an order directing the parties to proceed to arbitration in accordance with the terms of the agreement[,]" and such arbitration "shall be within the district in which the petition for an order directing such arbitration is filed." Thus, Jain concludes, the district court should order arbitration in the Northern District of Illinois. De Méré replies that § 4 is inapplicable to this case on its own terms. He points out that the first sentence of § 4 allows a court to compel arbitration only where a court has jurisdiction over the subject matter of the case independent of any arbitration agreement. As noted earlier, Jain's place in federal court depends entirely on his arbitration contract with de Méré. Therefore, de Méré argues, the court cannot compel arbitration under § 4 and properly denied Jain's motion.

. . .

De Méré's position has some plausibility but is ultimately unconvincing. Section 208 requires the incorporation of chapter 1 provisions to the extent they do not conflict with chapter 2 or the Convention, and the jurisdictional restrictions of § 4 appear to conflict with jurisdictional grants of §§ 202 and 203 in international commercial arbitration disputes. Consequently, while the provision of § 4 allowing a court to order arbitration in its own district should apply to an action under chapter 2, its jurisdictional limits should not.

Other considerations also counsel the propriety of our conclusion. The jurisdictional requirement in § 4 ostensibly prevents the federalization of a vast number of arbitration disputes that were ordinarily the domain of state courts. This federalism concern has little force where Congress has otherwise determined that international commercial arbitration agreements are appropriate matters for federal courts. Moreover, compelling arbitration in cases like the present one better comports with the language of the Convention itself. . . . Given that the court is properly seized of this action [within the meaning of Article II(3) of the Convention], it should not then be left helpless to enforce the arbitration agreement. Finally, we note that under de Méré's argument, a federal court would have less power to compel arbitration under an international agreement than a state court. Jain could have filed suit in an Illinois state court based on the location of the royalty payments. De Méré, however, could then have removed the case to federal court under chapter 2's removal provision, 9 U.S.C. § 205. Once in federal court, under de Méré's reasoning, he could move to dismiss the case, as he has done here, whereas no such limit would necessarily apply in state court.

. . .

Last, it is important to note what is not at issue in this case. De Méré has not asserted that the district court lacked personal jurisdiction. Even if de Méré could have argued that he had never availed himself of anything in the Northern District of Illinois, *see* Asahi Metal Ind. v. Superior Ct. of California, Solano Cty., 480 U.S.

102 (1987), the time for making such an argument has passed. *See* Fed.R.Civ.P. 12(h)(1). Similarly, de Méré has not protested service of process. Nor has de Méré moved for dismissal on grounds of *forum non conveniens*, another reason for which district courts may dismiss a petition to compel arbitration. Finally, de Méré has not claimed that the agreement to arbitrate is an unenforceable nullity incapable of being performed. We pass judgment on the merits of none of these possible arguments.

In light of what is not at issue, the limited impact of our decision becomes clear. One foreign party can compel another foreign party to arbitrate in the United States only where the second party has expressly consented to a United States forum or has contacts with that forum sufficient to meet the requirements of personal jurisdiction. There will be no vast migration of foreign arbitration disputes to the United States, as de Méré prophecies, unless the defendant is already in some way connected to this country. Even in that event, the defendant may still invoke *forum non conveniens* arguments. To the extent future parties wish to avoid the uncertainty of leaving the forum question open, they can always specify the location of arbitration and the method of selecting an arbitrator in their initial agreement.

For the foregoing reasons, the decision of the district court is reversed and the case remanded.

NOTES

1.   Under section 206, a federal court in a case within the scope of the New York Convention can order arbitration "in accordance with the agreement at any place therein provided for, whether that place is within or without the United States." What if the parties' agreement provides for arbitration to be held in a country that is not a party to the New York Convention? The problem is reciprocity. As noted in § 5.02[D], American courts are split on whether the reciprocity limitation applies to enforcing agreements to arbitrate, with some requiring reciprocity, some not. If reciprocity is required, a court can only order arbitration to be held in a country that is a party to the New York Convention. If reciprocity is not required, the court can order arbitration to be held anywhere in the world.

2.   Neither party in *Jain* was American. But in cases with an American party, who usually benefits from the broad power of American courts to order arbitration under section 206, the American party or the non-American party?

3.   The result of the court's decision in *Jain v. de Méré* is that arbitration will take place in Illinois, the forum preferred by Jain but rejected by de Méré. Why should Jain's preferred forum be the one in which the court orders arbitration to be held? Doesn't section 4, as incorporated through section 208, permit a party to an arbitration agreement that is silent on location to choose an American arbitral forum unilaterally simply by filing an action to compel arbitration in the United States? Why not permit the court to order arbitration where it deems appropriate, regardless of whether the seat is in the same judicial district? Or leave the decision about the arbitral seat to the arbitrators, as does article 20(1) of the UNCITRAL Model Law?

4. What if the arbitration clause does not specify a place of arbitration, but does provide for arbitration under institutional rules that give the arbitrator the authority to determine the place of arbitration? In Tolaram Fibers, Inc. v. Deutsche Engineering der Voest-Alpine Industrieanlagenbau GmbH, 1991 U.S. Dist. LEXIS 3565 (M.D.N.C. Feb. 26, 1991), the district court held that such a clause "is not sufficiently specific so as to come within Section 206 of the Act" because it "does not select a definite forum." *Id.* at *11. Instead, under FAA section 4 the court compelled arbitration in the district in which the petition to compel had been brought. *Id.* at *12. Again, the party bringing the action was able to pick the place of arbitration unilaterally. Why shouldn't the arbitrator make that decision, as the parties agreed?

STORM LLC v. TELENOR MOBILE COMMUNICATIONS AS
United States District Court for the Southern District of New York
2006 U.S. Dist. LEXIS 90978 (Dec. 18, 2006)

GERARD E. LYNCH, District Judge:

Telenor Mobile Communications AS ("Telenor"), a Norwegian telecommunications company, and Storm LLC ("Storm"), a company organized under the laws of Ukraine, jointly own Kyivstar G.S.M. ("Kyivstar"), a Ukrainian telecommunications venture. Telenor and Storm are engaged in a dispute over, inter alia, the validity and effect of a 2004 shareholders' agreement (the "Shareholders Agreement" or "Agreement") related to the corporate governance and managment of Kyivstar. To resolve the dispute, Telenor invoked the arbitration provision of the Shareholders Agreement. . . . The issue now pending before the Court is Telenor's motion for relief in the form of a preliminary anti-suit injunction prohibiting Storm and its parent companies from further litigation in Ukraine in relation to the dispute.

. . .

BACKGROUND

The 2004 Agreement is the product of a series of negotiations and transactions among Telenor, Storm, and several other companies, some of which were formerly shareholders of Kyivstar. . . . [T]he negotiations arose from the desire of Alpha Telecommunications, a predecessor company of the "relief defendant" Altimo Holdings & Investment Limited ("Altimo"), to obtain a significant share of Kyivstar. Storm was the vehicle through which the acquisition was made. Because Storm obtained over 40% of the Kyivstar shares — which under Ukrainian law gave it substantial rights in corporate governance — Telenor negotiated an agreement obligating Storm not to exercise its rights in certain ways. Wary of the Ukrainian legal system, Telenor also negotiated an arbitration clause ("the Arbitration Agreement"), which provided that "[a]ny and all disputes and controversies arising under, relating to or in connection" with the Shareholders Agreement would be resolved by a tribunal of three arbitrators in New York in accordance with the Arbitration Agreement and the UNCITRAL rules.

Though the Agreement is nominally between Storm and Telenor, Storm is merely a holding company with no business other than holding the shares of Kyivstar for its ultimate corporate parent Altimo, which owns 50.1% of Storm through Hardlake, a Cyprus entity that is 100% owned by Altimo, and the remaining 49.9% through Alpren Limited, which is also 100% owned by Altimo.

. . .

After an initial honeymoon, Telenor and Storm developed differences, and Telenor now accuses Storm of violating the Shareholders Agreement in ways that effectively paralyze Kyivstar. Specifically, Telenor claims that Storm has violated the Shareholders Agreement by failing (1) to attend shareholder meetings, (2) to appoint candidates for election to the Kyivstar board, and (3) to attend board meetings and to participate in the management of Kyivstar. Telenor also claims that Storm's five percent ownership of a competitive company violates the Agreement. On February 7, 2006, Telenor sought redress for these alleged violations by invoking the arbitration clause.

. . . Storm responded to the arbitration demand by appointing an arbitrator and participating in proceedings before the arbitrators. Even as this process was developing, however, legal proceedings were instituted in Ukraine. In the Ukrainian proceedings, Alpren, the 49.9% owner of Storm, sought a declaration of the invalidity of the Shareholders Agreement. Telenor was not named as a defendant in the suit, and indeed neither Telenor nor the arbitrators were advised of its pendency. Storm did not retain counsel or file written opposition to the action. Instead, its current general director, Vadim Klymenko, appeared in person and registered oral opposition to Alpren's demands, a method of proceeding that Storm contends is permissible, and not unusual, in Ukraine.

Whether or not unusual under Ukrainian custom, the proceeding had a number of curious features. Although Klymenko, who acted for Storm in the matter, is not a lawyer, a resume submitted by him in connection with the arbitration notes that he is a Vice President of Altimo, the ultimate parent both of Storm and of Alpren, and that his responsibilities in that role include the management of "litigation[,] arbitration, representation and implementation of shareholders' interests." The initial Ukrainian proceeding appears to have lasted all of ten minutes, suggesting that Klymenko's oral opposition was somewhat perfunctory. It resulted in a judgment declaring the Shareholders Agreement invalid. Storm appealed the result, again without submitting any substantial defense of its position. An appellate court not only affirmed the lower court's decision against Storm, but broadened it by finding specifically that the Arbitration Agreement was invalid.

The arbitrators, however, did not accept the Ukrainian courts' conclusions as binding on them. In a well-reasoned decision, . . . the Tribunal denied Storm's motion to dismiss and held that it had jurisdiction to hear Telenor's claims.

After losing its motion to dismiss before the Tribunal, Storm obtained a "clarification" [from] the Ukrainian courts that broadened the scope of their initial rulings by specifically stating that the arbitration clause of the Shareholders Agreement was invalid . . . . Storm then quickly filed a petition in state court to enjoin the arbitration from continuing. Telenor removed the action to this Court, asserting subject matter jurisdiction under the New York Convention on the Recognition and Enforcement of Foreign Arbitral Awards. This Court denied preliminary relief, holding that the Court could not review an interlocutory order of an arbitral panel, and that to the extent Storm relied on the general equitable power of the Court, it was insufficiently likely to prevail on the merits, given the likely correctness of the arbitrators' ruling, the apparently collusive nature of the Ukrainian litigation, and the lack of conflict between the arbitrators' decision and the Ukrainian judgment, given that Storm had not been ordered by the Ukrainian court not to participate in the arbitration.

Following this decision, the Ukrainian parties returned to court. This time, Alpren sued not Storm but Klymenko himself as general director of Storm, and obtained in equally short order a ruling that not only barred Klymenko from participating in the arbitration, but that also purported to bar Storm and Telenor from proceeding with the arbitration — notwithstanding that Telenor had again not been notified of the action nor named as a party to it. Telenor has still not been served in Ukraine with any order of the Ukrainian court; it obtained a copy of the judgment only via New York counsel for Storm in connection with the arbitration proceedings and this litigation.

After this ruling, Telenor sought relief from this Court, counterpetitioning to compel arbitration, and simultaneously seeking an anti-suit injunction against Storm, Alpren and Altimo to prevent further litigation in the Ukraine. . . .

DISCUSSION

I. Legal Standards

The standard for issuing a preliminary injunction is well established. To obtain a preliminary injunction, the party seeking relief must demonstrate (1) that it will suffer irreparable harm absent injunctive relief, and (2) either (a) that it is likely to succeed on the merits, or (b) "that there are sufficiently serious questions going to the merits to make them a fair ground for litigation, and that the balance of hardships tips decidedly in favor of the moving party."

A federal court may enjoin a party from pursuing litigation in a foreign forum. "But principles of comity counsel that injunctions restraining foreign litigation be 'used sparingly' and 'granted only with care and great restraint.' " Two threshold requirements must be met before an anti-suit injunction is appropriate: (1) the parties must be the same in both matters; and (2) resolution of the case before the enjoining court must be dispositive of the action to be enjoined. If those requirements are satisfied, a court must then consider such factors as (1) the potential frustration of a policy in the enjoining forum; (2) the vexatiousness of the foreign litigation; (3) a threat to the issuing court's jurisdiction; (4) any prejudice caused by the foreign litigation to other equitable considerations; and (5) any delay, inconvenience, expense, inconsistency or unseemly race to judgment created by adjudication of the same issues in separate actions.

II. The Standards Applied

A. Threshold Requirements

1. The same parties

At the outset, there is some question in this case as to whether the threshold requirements are met. This is not a typical arbitration anti-suit scenario . . . , in which A seeks to compel arbitration against B in one jurisdiction while B seeks relief in the same dispute against A in a foreign court. In that situation, the parties will typically be the same in both proceedings, satisfying the first threshold requirement for an anti-suit injunction.

Here, in contrast, Telenor has demanded arbitration against Storm in New York, pursuant to the Shareholders Agreement. Unlike the typical anti-suit scenario, Storm did not refuse arbitration and seek converse relief against Telenor in the courts of Ukraine. Rather, Storm appointed an arbitrator, and appeared before the arbitration panel. Although the first issue presented to the arbitrators by Storm was a challenge to their jurisdiction, Storm has taken the position before this Court that it is ready and willing to proceed to the merits before the arbitrators — indeed, that it is eager for its "day in court" to vindicate its position on the merits — but for the fact that it has been placed in an untenable position by a lawsuit brought not by but *against* it in Ukraine. Telenor seeks to enjoin that litigation, which on its face is not a suit involving the same parties (Telenor and Storm) who are before the arbitrators here, but a suit between a third party, Alpren, and Storm. Thus, Storm argues, the first threshold requirement is not met, because the parties to the litigation in Ukraine are not the same as the parties here. Put another way, Storm argues that there is no basis for enjoining it from bringing litigation in Ukraine, because it has not brought any such litigation; rather, litigation has been brought against it there.

Telenor argues, however, that Storm's view of the litigation in Ukraine is at best formalistic, and at worst deceptive. According to Telenor, Alpren and Storm are mere alter egos of one another, and more importantly, they are both alter egos of their shared corporate parent, Altimo. And, Storm posits, even if the present record is insufficient to demonstrate that these various companies are alter egos of one another, the litigation between them is nevertheless collusive; it is, in effect, a friendly suit between Storm and its parent, in which the interests of the parties are aligned rather than adverse. In Telenor's view, Storm is in effect the plaintiff, having stimulated an action against itself in order to produce an order that serves its interests in the New York arbitration. And while Telenor is not formally a party to the Ukrainian lawsuit — indeed, it was deliberately left out of both actions in Ukraine, and given notice of neither until a judgment was obtained — its absence has not prevented the Ukrainian courts from entering an injunction that purports to bind Telenor. Thus, according to Telenor, the real parties in interest in the Ukrainian litigation are Storm (and its parents) on one side and Telenor on the other, the same parties as the New York arbitration.

. . .

. . . [T]he Court agrees that Telenor will likely succeed in establishing that Storm, Alpren and Altimo are alter egos of one another, at least to the extent necessary to warrant the relief Telenor seeks against them. Even if they are not, however, the parties in the two actions are sufficiently similar to satisfy the threshold requirement for a preliminary anti-suit injunction. The litigation in Ukraine, while nominally between Alpren and Storm, seeks to influence the arbitration proceedings and has resulted in orders that are directed at Telenor. Although Alpren is a participant in the Ukrainian litigation, Alpren is not merely a shareholder of Storm but is part of a family of affiliated corporations that collectively owns the entirety of Storm. The real parties in interest in the Ukrainian lawsuit are essentially the same entities that are involved in the arbitration here.

. . .

2. Dispositive litigation

The second threshold question is whether the present litigation will be dispositive of the issues being litigated in the foreign forum. As is frequently the case where arbitration is in issue, the litigation between Storm and Telenor in this Court does not in itself concern the merits of the issues that divide them, or that have been put in issue in Ukraine. Rather, this case concerns only the *arbitrability* of those issues. Nevertheless, courts have recognized that in this situation, the district court's judgment disposes of the foreign action by determining the arbitrability of the issues.

Here, the issue pending before this Court is the arbitrability of the very issues put before the Ukrainian court: Storm brought this action seeking to enjoin the arbitration, and Telenor counterpetitions to compel it. If the present action results in a judgment for Telenor and against Storm, then the issues before the Ukrainian courts will be, "by virtue of [that] judgment, . . . reserved to arbitration," and the threshold requirement for an anti-suit injunction will be met.

B. Factors Bearing on Injunctive Relief

The Court thus turns to the factors bearing on whether an injunction should issue . . . . If Storm had directly sued Telenor in the Ukrainian courts, balancing the factors involved here would be relatively easy, since several of the factors weigh heavily in favor of an injunction in this case.

With respect to the first factor, federal policy strongly favors the enforcement of arbitration agreements. This policy "applies with particular force in international disputes." To the extent that the litigation in Ukraine threatens to disrupt the arbitration process, it would have the effect of frustrating that policy. And there is no doubt that that litigation has been designed to, and has had the effect of, interfering in the arbitration process. The judgments issued in that litigation have been the basis for objections to the arbitrators' jurisdiction, appeals to this Court to enjoin the arbitration, and concerns on the part of Telenor that it or even the arbitrators themselves may be subject to penalties in Ukraine if the arbitration goes forward. This factor thus strongly favors an injunction.

. . .

Attempts to interfere with arbitration of international disputes are so powerfully disapproved that the Second Circuit has suggested, albeit not decided, that "an attempt to sidestep arbitration" might be "sufficient to support a foreign anti-suit injunction." Where this factor is present, little else is required to authorize an injunction. But here there is much else. The foreign litigation here has been conducted in the most vexatious way possible. Telenor has found its interests undermined by litigation to which it has not been made a party, and of which it has not even received notice until after orders have been entered. The Ukrainian orders have been used against Telenor in court and before the arbitrators here in New York, and have exposed it to potential criminal liability in Ukraine. As late as this very day, Telenor was receiving what appeared to be service of process in yet another lawsuit, only to be advised by Alpren's New York attorney during oral argument that there was no such lawsuit, and that the papers were a "mistake" of no legal significance. If a federal court may enjoin foreign litigation that straight-forwardly seeks to adjudicate the rights of a party to litigation, a fortiori it should be able to enjoin litigation being conducted by a kind of stealth attack. These facts also support a finding that the fourth factor favors an injunction: to the extent that the litigation in Ukraine purports to bind Telenor without notice or opportunity to be heard, it manifestly prejudices any equitable concern for fair play.

In addition, the foreign litigation threatens the jurisdiction of this Court. This case is here, at Storm's original instance, by virtue of the pending arbitration. Storm lost in its effort to derail that arbitration by a preliminary injunction. The Ukrainian litigation seeks to "sidestep" not merely the arbitration, but this Court's ruling. It further threatens the very existence of the arbitration, by threatening serious sanctions against Telenor if it proceeds with the arbitration. If Telenor were forced to yield to that pressure, this Court's jurisdiction would be at an end.

Moreover, continued litigation in Ukraine raises the distinct specter of delay, inconvenience, expense, inconsistency and an unseemly race to judgment. Arbitration is intended to be an expeditious and efficient means of resolving commercial disputes. Being forced to litigate in both American and Ukrainian courts not merely to enforce an arbitration agreement but to defend the existence of an arbitration already under way, has already created extensive delays in the arbitration proceeding and added considerable expense to the proceedings. The risk of inconsistent adjudications is acute, particularly because Alpren and Storm apparently insist on conducting their Ukrainian litigation without even notifying Telenor, such that Telenor's position has not even been heard. A proceeding in which Storm and Telenor vigorously contest the issues is highly likely to reach different conclusions than one in which the only participating parties share a common interest and the same analysis of the issues.

As for an "unseemly race to judgment," "unseemly" and "race" not begin to describe the situation here. After every setback in the arbitration or in this Court, parties associated with Storm have proceeded to the Ukrainian courts, seeking and obtaining broad rulings without any meaningful opposition. Telenor seeks to arbitrate the dispute in a neutral forum; Storm and its parents seek to coopt that process by resorting to a forum in which their home-court advantage is magnified by their willingness to play the game without letting the other team show up.

The factors relevant to an award of anti-suit relief thus strongly favor Telenor. And strongly favor Telenor they must, for as the courts have emphasized, even though "such an injunction in terms is leveled against the party bringing the suit, it nonetheless 'effectively restricts the jurisdiction of the court of a foreign sovereign.' " Considerations of comity thus always weigh against an anti-suit injunction.

Accordingly, to the extent that Storm can be held responsible for the Ukrainian litigation, the issue is clear-cut: Telenor is extremely likely to succeed in establishing that virtually all of the factors considered by courts in granting anti-suit injunctions favor its cause. Nevertheless, the entry of an anti-suit injunction against the *defendant* in foreign litigation is both unconventional, and, so far as the parties' or the Court's research can determine, unprecedented. The Court thus turns to consideration of that issue.

C. May an Anti-Suit Injunction Issue Against Storm?

. . . Telenor also claims that an injunction against Storm is appropriate because Storm is acting as the alter ego of its corporate parents Altimo and Alpren.

. . .

. . . [T]he Court is persuaded that Telenor is likely to succeed in establishing, at a minimum, that the litigation in Ukraine has been collusive, and not truly adversarial. The Ukrainian litigation was brought in Storm's as well as Alpren's interests, sought relief that Storm had every reason to desire, and was not meaningfully resisted by Storm or its general director. Storm has effectively conceded before this Court that it wants to preserve the Ukrainian judgment "against" it. Accordingly, it is a fair inference, and one that on this limited record the Court finds more likely true than not, that Storm colluded in the bringing of this litigation against itself. It can therefore be enjoined from continuing with such actions.

. . .

E. Irreparable Injury

The Court need not dwell on the issue of irreparable injury, for there is no question that the action to be enjoined places Telenor under threat of imminent and irreparable harm. To the extent the Ukrainian litigation interferes with the arbitration, Storm will be able to prolong its boycott of Kyivstar meetings, thereby making it impossible for that company — in which Telenor has a majority stake — to function. More importantly, however, the Ukrainian proceedings place Telenor under threat of criminal sanctions if it proceeds with the arbitration. Not only does Storm concede that this possibility exists, but it has exploited the possibility in its attempt to derail the arbitration.

. . .

CONCLUSION

For the foregoing reasons, the motion for a preliminary anti-suit injunction is granted. Storm, Altimo and Alpren are enjoined from bringing or attempting to cause the enforcement of any legal action in the Ukraine that would disrupt, delay or hinder in any way the arbitration proceedings between Telenor and Storm in New York.

SO ORDERED.

NOTES

1.   Recall the discussion in § 4.06 of federal court injunctions against state court litigation. How do the standards compare? Should federal courts be more willing to enjoin litigation in state courts or in foreign courts?

2.   The circuits currently are divided as to their willingness to enter anti-suit injunctions against foreign court litigation. The Eighth Circuit described the "conservative" and "liberal" approaches (while choosing the conservative approach) in Goss Int'l Corp. v. Man Roland Druckmaschinen Aktiengesellschaft, 491 F.3d 355, 359-61 (8th Cir. 2007):

> The propriety of issuing a foreign antisuit injunction is a matter of first impression for our circuit. Other circuits having decided the issue agree that "federal courts have the power to enjoin persons subject to their jurisdiction from prosecuting foreign suits." The circuits are split, however, on the level of deference afforded to international comity in determining whether a foreign antisuit injunction should issue.

> The First, Second, Third, Sixth, and District of Columbia Circuits have adopted the "conservative approach," under which a foreign antisuit injunction will issue only if the movant demonstrates (1) an action in a foreign jurisdiction would prevent United States jurisdiction or threaten a vital United States policy, and (2) the domestic interests outweigh concerns of international comity. Under the conservative approach, "[c]omity dictates that foreign antisuit injunctions be issued sparingly and only in the rarest of cases."

> In contrast, the Fifth and Ninth Circuits follow the "liberal approach," which places only modest emphasis on international comity and approves the issuance of an antisuit injunction when necessary to prevent duplicative and vexatious foreign litigation and to avoid inconsistent judgments.

> Under either the conservative or liberal approach, "[w]hen a preliminary injunction takes the form of a foreign antisuit injunction, [courts] are required to balance domestic judicial interests against concerns of international comity." We agree with the observations of the First Circuit that the conservative approach (1) "recognizes the rebuttable presumption against issuing international antisuit injunctions," (2) "is more respectful of principles of international comity," (3) "compels an inquiring court to balance competing policy considerations," and (4) acknowledges that " 'is-

suing an international antisuit injunction is a step that should 'be taken only with care and great restraint' and with the recognition that international comity is a fundamental principle deserving of substantial deference." Likewise, we agree with the Sixth Circuit's observation [that] the liberal approach "conveys the message, intended or not, that the issuing court has so little confidence in the foreign court's ability to adjudicate a given dispute fairly and efficiently that it is unwilling even to allow the possibility."

Although comity eludes a precise definition, its importance in our globalized economy cannot be overstated. Indeed, the "world economic interdependence has highlighted the importance of comity, as international commerce depends to a large extent on 'the ability of merchants to predict the likely consequences of their conduct in overseas markets.' " We also note the Congress and the President possess greater experience with, knowledge of, and expertise in international trade and economics than does the Judiciary. The two other branches, not the Judiciary, bear the constitutional duties related to foreign affairs. For these reasons, we join the majority of our sister circuits and adopt the conservative approach in determining whether a foreign antisuit injunction should issue.

Some commentators have identified a third, "middle-ground" approach:

[T]he First and Second Circuits have adopted a third, "middle-ground" standard which combines elements of both the conservative and liberal standards. Like the "conservative" standard, courts adhering to the "middle-ground" standard place great weight on comity considerations and have adopted a rebuttable presumption against the issuance of an injunction. On the other hand, these courts also consider the equitable factors underlying the "liberal standard" analysis, which might serve to rebut the presumption and favor the issuance of an injunction.

Arif Ali et al., *Anti-Suit Injunctions in Support of International Arbitration in the United States and the United Kingdom*, 2008 INT'L ARB. L. REV. 12, 15.

Which approach is superior? The cases on anti-suit injunctions reflect a variety of fact patterns, only some of which involve arbitration agreements. Should courts be more or less willing to issue anti-suit injunctions in support of an arbitration agreement than, say, a forum selection clause?

3. Other common law countries also have shown a willingess to grant anti-suit injunctions in support of arbitration, but civil law countries have not. GARY B. BORN, INTERNATIONAL COMMERCIAL ARBITRATION 1036-1043 (2009).

In Allianz SpA v. West Tankers Inc., Case C-185/07, [2009] E.C.R. I-663, the European Court of Justice (ECJ) held that Council Regulation 44/2001 on Jurisdiction and the Recognition and Enforcement of Judgments in Civil and Commercial Matters art. 1(2), 2001 O.J. L 12/1, at 3, precludes courts of one EU member state from issuing an anti-suit injunction in support of arbitration against litigation in another EU member state. The ECJ reasoned that "in no case is a court of one Member State in a better position to determine whether the court of another Member State has jurisdiction" and that such anti-suit injunctions "run[] counter to the trust which the Member States accord to one another's legal systems and judicial institutions and on which the system of jurisdiction under Regulation No 44/2001 is based." *Id.* ¶¶ 29 & 30. The ruling does not preclude courts in an EU member state from issuing an anti-suit injunction against litigation in the courts of a non-EU member state. Does *West Tankers* make EU member states such as the United Kingdom — whose courts otherwise have the authority to issue anti-suit injunctions in support of arbitration — more or less attractive as arbitral seats?

PROBLEM 5.10

Simpson Stables enters into a written contract with Ross Equine Sales to purchase a race horse for $100,000. The horse has not won any races yet, but Simpson has high hopes. After the horse is delivered, it turns up lame, ruining any racing prospects it might otherwise have had. Ross refuses to take the horse back. When Simpson threatens to begin an arbitration proceeding, Ross tells Simpson that it wants nothing to do with arbitration, even though their written contract contains an arbitration clause. Simpson thereafter files an action in United States District Court for the Southern District of New York seeking to compel Ross to arbitrate their dispute.

(a) Both Simpson and Ross are citizens of New York, and the contract provides for arbitration in New York, New York. How should the court rule on Simpson's motion?

(b) Simpson is a citizen of New York, Ross is a citizen of Kentucky, and the contract provides for arbitration in Kentucky. How should the court rule on Simpson's motion?

(c) Simpson is a citizen of New York, Ross is a citizen of Canada, and the contract provides for arbitration in Canada. How should the court rule on Simpson's motion?

(d) Simpson is a citizen of Great Britain, Ross is a citizen of Canada, and the contract provides for arbitration in Canada. How should the court rule on Simpson's motion?

(e) Simpson is a citizen of New York, Ross is a citizen of Canada, and the contract is silent on the place of arbitration. How should the court rule on Simpson's motion?

(f) Simpson is a citizen of New York, Ross is a citizen of Canada, and the contract is silent on the place of arbitration. The contract, however, provides that the arbitration is to be administered by the American Arbitration Association under the AAA/ICDR International Arbitration Rules (see especially Rule R-11). How should the court rule on Simpson's motion?

(g) Simpson is a citizen of New York, Ross is a citizen of Canada, and the contract provides for arbitration in New York. Before Simpson files its action in New York, Ross files suit against Simpson in Canada seeking damages for breach of contract from Simpson. Can the New York federal court enjoin Ross from pursuing its Canadian lawsuit?

PROBLEM 5.11

You are a new associate at a law firm that is trying to develop a practice in international commercial arbitration. One of the partners tells you that she is meeting tomorrow with a client to discuss an international arbitration matter. She has done some reading about the New York Convention to prepare for the meeting, but needs you to clear up one important point for her. She asks you: "What difference does it make in practice whether the New York Convention or the domestic FAA applies to a particular arbitration agreement?" What do you tell her?

Chapter 6

THE ARBITRATION PROCEEDING

§ 6.01 OVERVIEW

An arbitration proceeding follows many of the same steps as a civil case in court. The claimant must initiate the proceeding. The respondent is entitled to notice and an opportunity to respond. There is some opportunity for the parties to engage in discovery, and there may be pre-hearing procedures to streamline the case. The process culminates in some sort of hearing before the decision maker, who then decides the case.

At times, arbitration and civil litigation intersect. A continuing issue throughout this chapter is the extent to which courts can and should intervene in an arbitration proceeding before the award is made. Ordinarily, the purpose of court intervention is to provide assistance to the parties and the arbitrators. But too much "assistance" can undercut the authority of the arbitrators and interfere with the arbitration proceeding itself.

An important difference between an arbitration proceeding and a civil case is that arbitration is based on the agreement of the parties to proceed in that forum. Thus, the arbitration proceeding is governed by rules chosen by the parties, rather than rules of procedure adopted by courts and legislatures. Most commonly, the parties choose a set of rules promulgated by an institution that administers arbitrations, such as the American Arbitration Association or the International Chamber of Commerce. Some parties do not wish to involve an administering institution and instead agree to "ad hoc" arbitration. Such parties may agree on their own arbitration rules or may choose a set of rules developed by the United Nations Commission on International Trade Law (UNCITRAL). This chapter focuses on the AAA Commercial Arbitration Rules and the UNCITRAL Arbitration Rules, but occasionally highlights other rules that differ in interesting ways.

In essence, the arbitration rules are standard terms the parties incorporate by reference into their contracts. Because arbitration rules are merely standard contract terms, the parties can, and often do, change those rules in their contracts. Finding out how parties change the standard terms by contract can be difficult because contracts are not public documents. In some states, however, franchisors must file their franchise agreements with the state, so that the franchise agreements (and the arbitration clauses contained in those agreements) are available for public review. Relying on those public filings, this chapter presents some information on the actual terms of arbitration clauses in franchise agreements. (Information on some other sorts of contracts can be found in § 8.02.)

Even though arbitration is a matter of contract, arbitration laws nonetheless play several important roles in the course of arbitration proceedings. First, arbitration laws may contain default procedural rules that govern unless the parties' arbitration agreement specifies otherwise. Second, arbitration laws may include mandatory rules that the parties cannot change, either to protect one of the parties to the arbitration agreement or, less commonly, to protect someone who is not party to the agreement. The Revised Uniform Arbitration Act expressly recognizes the dichotomy between mandatory rules and default rules, stating that except as otherwise provided, "the parties to an agreement to arbitrate or to an arbitration proceeding may waive, or the parties may vary the effect of, the requirements of this [Act] to the extent permitted by law." RUAA § 4(a). Sections 4(b) and (c) of the RUAA then list the mandatory provisions of the statute.

Traditionally, arbitration is viewed as less formal than litigation. Some commentators have criticized what they view as the increasing "judicialization" of arbitration, arguing that arbitration is becoming too much like litigation. Professor Tom Carbonneau, for example, describes how "[l]awyering practices — extensive, party-conducted pre-trial discovery, depositions, direct and cross-examination — are redefining the character of arbitral procedure and justice," with "nefarious consequences" for the institution of arbitration. Thomas Carbonneau, *Arbitral Justice: The Demise of Due Process in American Law*, 70 Tul. L. Rev. 1945 (1996). As you proceed through this chapter, see what you think of that criticism.

Conversely, perhaps civil litigation should become more like arbitration (rather than the other way around). William Landes and Richard Posner state: "Because arbitration is a voluntary service provided in a competitive market, it may appear that any procedures widely used in arbitration must be efficient procedures for deciding the type of dispute in question." William M. Landes & Richard A. Posner, *Adjudication as a Private Good*, 8 J. Legal Stud. 235, 249 (1979). If so, it may be that the procedures in arbitration could "be used as a criterion for evaluating the efficiency of the public judicial system in areas such as contract and commercial law where most arbitrable disputes arise." *Id.* Again, as you proceed through this chapter, consider whether differences between arbitration and litigation suggest possible reforms to procedural rules in court.

§ 6.02 INITIATING THE PROCEEDING

To initiate an arbitration proceeding, a party files a demand for arbitration (the functional equivalent of a complaint in civil litigation) with the administering institution and serves a copy on the respondent. *See* AAA Commercial Arbitration Rules, Rules R-4(a), R-39; RUAA § 9(a) (requiring notice "by certified or registered mail, return receipt requested and obtained, or by service as authorized for the commencement of a civil action," unless otherwise agreed). Under the AAA Commercial Arbitration Rules, the demand "shall contain a statement setting forth the nature of the dispute, the names and addresses of all other parties, the amount involved, if any, the remedy sought, and the hearing locale requested." AAA Rule R-4(a). The respondent "may" file an answering statement to the demand, including any counterclaim. Rule 4(b). Unlike civil litigation, there is no requirement that the respondent in arbitration file an answering statement: "If no answering statement is filed within the stated time, respondent will be deemed to deny the claim." Rule R–4(c).

In international arbitrations, the initial filing is called a "request" or "notice" rather than a demand. *See* UNCITRAL Arbitration Rules, art. 3(1); ICC Rules of Arbitration, art. 4. The claimant also submits a statement of claim, if not included in the notice of arbitration, which is to include, among other things, "[a] statement of the facts supporting the claim" and "[t]he points at issue." UNCITRAL Arbitration Rules, art. 20(2). The respondent then submits a statement of defense, including any counterclaims. UNCITRAL Arbitration Rules, art. 21; ICC Rules of Arbitration, art. 5 ("Answer").

What if the respondent fails altogether to participate in the arbitration proceeding? Most arbitration rules provide for the proceeding to continue in the respondent's absence. AAA Commercial Arbitration Rules, Rule R-29; UNCITRAL Arbitration Rules, art. 30(2). Can such an arbitration process result in an enforceable award?

VAL-U CONSTRUCTION CO. v. ROSEBUD SIOUX TRIBE
United States Court of Appeals for the Eighth Circuit
146 F.3d 573 (1998)

WATERS, DISTRICT JUDGE.

The Rosebud Sioux Tribe (the "Tribe") appeals the district court's entry of summary judgment in favor of Val-U Construction Company of South Dakota ("Val-U") on the issue of whether an award Val-U obtained from an arbitration hearing, in which the Tribe chose not to participate, is valid. . . .

I. BACKGROUND

In July of 1989, the Tribe and Val-U entered into a contract for the construction of housing units on the Rosebud Sioux Indian Reservation. The contract contained an arbitration provision. Problems arose during the performance of the contract and the Tribe terminated the contract in September of 1990. . . . The following is an outline of the factual and procedural history relevant to the court's opinion in this case.

October 26, 1990	Val-U filed a demand for arbitration of the contract termination with the American Arbitration Association ("AAA").
December 11, 1990	The Tribe notified the AAA that it would not participate in arbitration based on principles of sovereign immunity.
March 5, 1991	The AAA advised the Tribe that a hearing in the matter would begin on May 6, 1991.
April 9, 1991	The Tribe filed suit in the United States District Court for the District of South Dakota against Val-U claiming, among other things, breach of contract.

May 3, 1991	Val-U filed an answer and pleaded as an affirmative defense the contract's arbitration clause. . . . (The district court did not compel arbitration of the Tribe's claims against Val-U, or stay the arbitration of Val-U's claims against the Tribe).
May 6, 1991	The AAA held an arbitration hearing and Val-U presented its case. The Tribe was not represented at the hearing.
May 23, 1991	The Tribe reasserted its position to the AAA that it did not believe it had to participate in arbitration based on principles of sovereign immunity.
May 29, 1991	The Tribe acknowledged receipt of the "proposed" arbitration award by the AAA and again stated its position that it was not bound by such an award under principles of sovereign immunity.
June 18, 1991	The AAA issued an award in favor of Val-U, finding the Tribe in breach of the contract and awarded Val-U $793,943.58, plus interest, fees, and costs. A copy of the award was forwarded to the Tribe on June 20, 1991.
March 30, 1994	The district court . . . dismissed the Tribe's claims with prejudice, and dismissed Val-U's breach of contract claim on the basis that it was barred by the Tribe's sovereign immunity to the extent it sought recovery beyond recoupment.
March 16, 1995	. . . On appeal, we held that the arbitration clause waived the Tribe's sovereign immunity as to all claims under the contract. Thus, we remanded to the district court to . . . determine the validity of the arbitration award Val-U obtained against the Tribe.
March 6, 1997	On remand, the district court . . . ordered the clerk to enter judgment in favor of Val-U in the amount of the arbitration award.

. . .

II. THE TRIBE'S APPEAL

. . .

A.

The Tribe's first argument on appeal concerns the court's previous opinion in this case on the issue of sovereign immunity. . . . [T]he Tribe contends that when this court held in *Rosebud* that the arbitration provision in the contract constituted a waiver of sovereign immunity, the decision was contrary to the prevailing federal law on what represents a waiver of sovereign immunity. Therefore, the Tribe asserts that our decision in *Rosebud* should only be applied prospectively.

. . .

[W]e hold that our opinion in *Rosebud* should be applied retroactively. As a result, the Tribe is not entitled to sovereign immunity from Val-U's breach of contract claims.

B.

The rest of the Tribe's arguments concern the validity of the arbitration award. First, the Tribe contends that the preferred disposition of a case is on the merits and not by default.[4] The Tribe asserts that the arbitration award should be vacated, and it should be given an opportunity to present its case because: (1) significant sums of money are involved; (2) significant facts exist that establish the Tribe has a meritorious defense against Val-U's claims; and (3) the Tribe did not participate in the arbitration proceedings based on its determination that the law at the time afforded it sovereign immunity from such a proceeding. We have already determined that the Tribe acted unreasonably in refusing to participate in the arbitration hearing based on its belief that it possessed immunity from suit, and thus, unless the Tribe can show that, under the Federal Arbitration Act (the "FAA"), it is entitled to have the award vacated, the award should be upheld.

. . .

The Tribe relies on the case of Food Handlers Local 425, Amalgamated Meat Cutters and Butcher Workmen of North America, AFL-CIO v. Pluss Poultry, Inc., 260 F.2d 835, 837 (8th Cir. 1958), where the court held that an arbitration clause must contain a provision that permits one party to initiate and prosecute to a conclusion an arbitration proceeding without the other party's participation. Otherwise, the court held, an award obtained under such circumstances is void and unenforceable.

. . .

We believe that *Food Handlers* is easily distinguished. In this case, the parties agreed that "[a]ll questions of dispute under this agreement shall be decided by arbitration in accordance with the Construction Industry Arbitration Rules of the American Arbitration Association." Rule 30 of the Construction Industry Arbitration Rules of the American Arbitration Association states that:

> [u]nless the law provides to the contrary, the arbitration may proceed in the absence of any party or representative who, after due notice, fails to be present or fails to obtain a postponement. An award shall not be made solely on the default of a party. The arbitrator shall require the party who is present to submit such evidence as the arbitrator may require for the making of an award.

Therefore, unlike the employer in *Food Handlers*, the Tribe agreed, via the arbitration clause, that an arbitration hearing may proceed in its absence as long as

---

[4] We note that this case was not decided by default. Val-U presented evidence to the arbitrator at the hearing, and the arbitrator issued an award based on the evidence submitted. This is in accordance with Rule 30 of the Construction Industry Arbitration Rules which forbids an award to be issued solely on the default of a party.

it was given notice of the hearing and an opportunity to obtain a postponement of the hearing. Val-U asserts that it presented evidence before the arbitrator and based on the evidence offered, the arbitrator entered a final award. In our view, the Tribe agreed to this possibility and is undeserving of an order vacating the award.

C.

The Tribe contends that because Val-U never sought to compel the Tribe to participate in the arbitration proceedings, the Tribe was not obligated to participate in the hearing. The Tribe asserts that Val-U clearly had this mechanism available to them, and because they did not use it, the Tribe had no duty to participate at the arbitration hearing.

. . .

We believe that § 4 of the FAA is clearly permissive. As such, Val-U was not required to petition the district court for an order compelling the Tribe to participate in the arbitration proceedings.

D.

The Tribe asserts that at the time that the arbitration hearing took place, this lawsuit was pending in federal district court. Thus, the Tribe contends that Val-U was required to move the district court to stay the federal lawsuit pending the outcome of the arbitration proceedings.

. . .

Section 3, like § 4, is permissive, not mandatory. Nowhere in the statute does it require either party to file a motion to stay. Thus, Val-U was not required to file a motion in district court to stay the lawsuit pending the outcome of the arbitration hearing.

. . .

The district court's entry of summary judgment in favor of Val-U is affirmed in full. . . .

NOTES

1.   The court stated in footnote 4 that the "case was not decided by default." Instead, awards that result from arbitration proceedings in which only one party participates commonly are called ex parte awards. As a practical matter, what is the difference? How often do you suppose an arbitrator finds in favor of the party that has not appeared?

2.   The *Rosebud Sioux* case emphasizes the importance of a contract provision or arbitration rule authorizing the arbitration to proceed in a party's absence. For a subsequent Eighth Circuit case in which such a provision evidently was lacking, see Hugs & Kisses, Inc. v. Aguirre, 220 F.3d 890 (8th Cir. 2000) (distinguishing *Rosebud Sioux* on the ground that there "the parties' arbitration agreement incorporated American Arbitration Association rules that allowed an arbitration

hearing to proceed in a party's absence if that party is given notice of the hearing and an opportunity to have it postponed. Here, the parties adopted no such rules, so the case before us cannot be distinguished from *Food Handlers*, on that ground").

3. In addition to contractual authorization, the party who does not participate must have received adequate notice of the proceeding for an ex parte award to be enforceable. The New York Convention and the Revised Uniform Arbitration Act expressly provide that lack of notice of the arbitration proceeding is a ground for non-enforcement or vacation of an award. *See* New York Convention, art. V(1)(b) ("[t]he party against whom the award is invoked was not given proper notice of the appointment of the arbitrator or the arbitration proceedings"); RUAA § 23(a)(6) ("the arbitration was conducted without proper notice of the initiation of an arbitration as required in Section 9 so as to prejudice substantially the rights of a party to the arbitration proceeding"). The FAA does not expressly make lack of notice a ground for vacatur, but lack of notice would likely satisfy section 10(a)(3) because "[t]he right to adequate notice is one part of a fundamentally fair hearing." Employers Insurance of Wausau v. Banco de Seguros del Estado, 199 F.3d 937, 942 (7th Cir. 1999) (citing Mullane v. Central Hanover Bank & Trust Co., 339 U.S. 306 (1950)), *cert. denied*, 530 U.S. 1215 (2000); *see* 3 IAN R. MACNEIL ET AL., FEDERAL ARBITRATION LAW § 32.9.1.2 (1994 & Supp. 1999).

4. In *Rosebud Sioux*, the court of appeals rejected the Tribe's argument that it did not have to participate in the arbitration proceeding unless compelled to do so by a court. On the Tribe's theory, when it did not appear in the arbitration, the arbitrators lacked authority to proceed without it in the absence of a court order. To the contrary, according to the court of appeals, sections 3 and 4 of the FAA are "permissive, not mandatory." A party may, but need not, obtain a court order requiring arbitration. Even without such a court order, the arbitration may proceed on an ex parte basis.

What if instead the Tribe had appeared in the arbitration and objected that it had not agreed to arbitrate? A handful of cases have concluded that "once [respondent] disputed the existence of an arbitration agreement, the [arbitrators] did not have jurisdiction to enter an arbitration award until [claimant] petitioned the courts to compel arbitration." MBNA America Bank, N.A. v. Christianson, 659 S.E.2d 209, 215 (S.C. Ct. App. 2008) *aff'd*, 2010 S.C. Unpub. LEXIS 3 (S.C. Feb. 1, 2010); *see also* MBNA America Bank, N.A. v. Credit, 132 P.3d 898, 900 (Kan. 2006) (same) (dicta); MBNA America Bank, N.A. v. Kay, 888 N.E.2d 288, 291-92 (Ind. App. 2008) (same). Commentators have been harshly critical of such decisions, finding them contrary to well established law. As Alan Scott Rau states:

> Is it possible even to imagine that an arbitration must grind to a halt whenever such an objection is made? Can it seriously be argued that — even where the court ultimately finds that the parties had indeed agreed to arbitrate — an award rendered prior to such a finding would still have to be vacated? Of course not . . . .

Alan Scott Rau, *Federal Common Law and Arbitral Power*, 8 NEV. L.J. 169, 200 (2007); *see also* William W. Park, *Determining an Arbitrator's Jurisdiction: Timing and Finality in American Law*, 8 NEV. L.J. 135, 152 n.68 (2007) ("The [court's] assertion has no foundation in logic, policy, or law.").

PROBLEM 6.1

The contract between Barker Business Supplies, Inc. (BBS). and Douglas Distribution Co. provides that all disputes arising out of or relating to the contract are to be resolved by arbitration under the Commercial Arbitration Rules of the American Arbitration Association. When a dispute occurs, BBS sends a demand for arbitration to Douglas by regular mail and files the demand with the AAA. At no point in the arbitration process does Douglas participate — neither BBS, the AAA, nor the arbitrator have ever heard anything from Douglas.

James Barker, the president of BBS and your client, comes to you shortly before the date scheduled for the hearing in the matter. He tells you that Douglas has not responded to the notice of the hearing. Barker says that he wants to know how BBS should proceed. "I've been involved in court cases where the other side hasn't shown up, and we've won by default or some such thing. But I've never seen that happen in arbitration before." He then asks you the following questions. How do you respond?

(a) Does it matter that BBS didn't use a process server to serve the original demand for arbitration? "I don't have any proof that Douglas ever got the thing in the first place," Barker says.

(b) Does Douglas' failure to file a response to the demand for arbitration preclude it from later challenging what BBS alleged in the demand?

(c) What if Douglas doesn't show up at the hearing? Does BBS win automatically? "I'm also worried that a court won't uphold an award if Douglas never shows," Barker tells you. "Douglas isn't going to comply with an award voluntarily, that's for sure."

§ 6.03 REPRESENTATION

Who can represent a party to an arbitration proceeding? If an action in court is necessary, such as to enforce (or challenge) an arbitration agreement or award, the representative will have to be a lawyer admitted to practice in the court. But what about in the arbitration proceeding itself? Institutional rules ordinarily permit parties to be represented by an attorney or "other authorized representative," so long as the represented party gives notice to the other side. AAA Commercial Arbitration Rules, Rule R-24; UNCITRAL Arbitration Rules, art. 5 ("by persons chosen by it").

The Federal Arbitration Act does not address who can represent a party to an arbitration proceeding. The Uniform Arbitration Act and the Revised Uniform Arbitration Act both provide that a party has the right to be "represented by an attorney," which cannot be waived before a dispute arises. UAA § 6; RUAA §§ 16, 4(b). The drafters of the RUAA "considered but rejected a proposal to add 'or any other person' after 'an attorney' " because of concerns "about incompetent and unscrupulous individuals, especially in securities arbitration, who hold themselves out as advocates." Comment 1 to RUAA § 16. Do such concerns justify a ban on non-lawyer representation in arbitration? What about in the following case?

NISHA, LLC v. TRIBUILT CONSTRUCTION GROUP, LLC
Supreme Court of Arkansas
2012 Ark. 130 (2012)

ROBERT L. BROWN, Associate Justice.

The issue in this case is whether a corporate officer, director, or employee, who is not a licensed attorney, engages in the unauthorized practice of law by representing the corporation in arbitration proceedings. We hold that such a person is so engaged, and we reverse the circuit court on this point. In addition, we reverse the circuit court's determination that an arbitrator, rather than the court, should determine issues regarding legal representation during arbitration proceedings.

This case began as a dispute over construction costs between TriBuilt Construction Group, LLC (TriBuilt), the appellee herein, and NISHA, LLC (NISHA) and Centennial Bank (formerly known as Community Bank) (Centennial), the appellants. TriBuilt was the general contractor hired by NISHA to build the Country Inn & Suites in Conway. Centennial entered into a Construction Loan and Security Agreement with NISHA, which assigned its interest in the construction contract with TriBuilt to Centennial as security for Centennial's entering into a construction mortgage for the project. After the project was completed, TriBuilt filed suit in the Sebastian County Circuit Court against NISHA and Centennial and asserted that when the project was completed, they refused to pay TriBuilt the $666,462.12 balance owed, defamed TriBuilt, and intentionally interfered with TriBuilt's ability to get bonding for the project.

NISHA moved to compel arbitration and contended that the contract with TriBuilt compelled the parties to arbitrate all disputes relating to the contract. . . . On January 12, 2010, the circuit court entered an order granting the motion to compel arbitration in part and denying it in part. The circuit court granted the motion to compel arbitration and stay proceedings with regard to TriBuilt's claims for breach of contract, quantum meruit, tortious interference with the contract, and conversion against Centennial and NISHA.

On January 26, 2011, the circuit court entered a second order permitting TriBuilt's counsel to withdraw from the case. TriBuilt's attorney subsequently withdrew from the arbitration proceedings as well. Rather than obtain new counsel to represent it in the arbitration proceedings, TriBuilt through its President, Alan Harrison, notified NISHA and Centennial that it intended to represent itself. Harrison, a nonlawyer, would present TriBuilt's case in the arbitration proceedings. On March 31, 2011, NISHA and Centennial filed a "Joint Petition for Permanent Injunction," seeking to prevent Harrison from representing TriBuilt in either the circuit court case or in the arbitration proceedings. In support of its petition, NISHA and Centennial contended that a corporate entity cannot represent itself in litigation and litigation-related matters through agents who are not licensed attorneys. They requested that the circuit court permanently enjoin TriBuilt from permitting, authorizing, or condoning Harrison, or any other officer, director, or employee, from engaging in the unauthorized practice of law by representing TriBuilt in the circuit court proceedings or in the court-ordered arbitration proceedings.

On April 13, 2011, International Fidelity Insurance Company (IFIC) filed a response to the joint petition for permanent injunction. IFIC claimed that TriBuilt was not prohibited by law from representing itself in an arbitration proceeding and that the representation in such a proceeding did not constitute the unauthorized practice of law. It maintained that under the American Arbitration Association (AAA) rules, which governed the arbitration proceeding at issue, any party could be represented by counsel, pro se, or "by any other representative of that party's choosing." IFIC claimed further that no Arkansas law prohibited a corporation from representing itself in arbitration proceedings.

On May 16, 2011, the circuit court entered an order granting NISHA and Centennial's joint petition so far as it pertained to proceedings before the circuit court but denying their petition for a permanent stay so far as it pertained to the arbitration proceedings for two reasons: (1) the circuit court did not agree that nonlawyer representation in an arbitration proceeding constituted the practice of law, and (2) the arbitration panel should decide that issue. NISHA and Centennial filed an interlocutory appeal to this court pursuant to Arkansas Rule of Appellate Procedure — Civil 2(a)(6). The circuit court issued a certificate under Arkansas Rule of Civil Procedure 54(b) and found that pro se representation by a corporate officer was an issue of first impression and that there was no just reason to delay entry of final judgment regarding whether Harrison could represent TriBuilt in the arbitration proceedings.

NISHA and Centennial raise two points in their brief on appeal: (1) this court should reverse the circuit court's finding that nonlawyer representation in arbitration proceedings does not constitute the unauthorized practice of law, and (2) that this court should reverse the circuit court's finding that the arbitrator should decide who can represent a party in arbitration proceedings. . . .

. . .

Although NISHA and Centennial present this as their second point for reversal, the question of whether the arbitrator or this court has the power to determine if a nonlawyer can represent a corporation during arbitration proceedings is jurisdictional and must be addressed first. The circuit court concluded that the arbitration body is entitled to determine what parties and representatives may participate in arbitration proceedings, as well as what rules apply in the process. That is in error. This court has the exclusive authority to regulate the practice of law. Likewise, the unauthorized practice of law falls within this court's constitutional authority to control and govern the practice of law. Because the issue is whether representation of a corporation by a nonlawyer during arbitration proceedings constitutes the unauthorized practice of law, the issue falls squarely within the ambit of this court's constitutional powers and may not be decided by an arbitration body. We reverse the circuit court on this point.

NISHA and Centennial's second argument is that a corporate entity cannot represent itself during arbitration proceedings because that constitutes the unauthorized practice of law. . . .

NISHA and Centennial claim that arbitration invokes the processes of the courts, is quasi-judicial in nature, and, thus, constitutes the practice of law. . . .

There is no doubt that under Arkansas's arbitration statutes, the circuit court remains involved to a degree in arbitration proceedings. Although arbitration proceedings can be initiated without court action, a court can compel parties to proceed to arbitration or stay already existing arbitration proceedings upon application of a party. The court may also send some claims to arbitration, while retaining other claims. Likewise, in some circumstances the court can appoint the arbitrator, if the parties have not agreed on a method for appointment or the agreed method fails or the arbitrator cannot continue.

In addition, a circuit court may, on request, direct the arbitrator to conduct a hearing promptly and render a timely decision. Plus, after a party to an arbitration proceeding receives notice of an award, that party may move the court for an order confirming the award, at which time the court shall issue a confirming order unless the award is modified, corrected, or is vacated. Except in certain limited situations, a valid and final award by an arbitrator has the same effect under the rules of res judicata as a judgment of a court. On appeal, this court will vacate an arbitration award only upon statutory grounds or a finding that the award violates a strong public policy. Based on this statutory scheme and this court's holding that arbitration awards have the same res judicata effect as a judgment of a court, NISHA and Centennial conclude that the courts of this state remain "actively involved" in arbitration and that it is an ancillary court process.

Although this court has never held that a nonlawyer's pro se representation of a corporation in arbitration proceedings constitutes the unauthorized practice of law, courts in other jurisdictions have so held. In *The Florida Bar re Advisory Opinion on Nonlawyer Representation in Securities Arbitration*, the Florida Supreme Court held that a nonlawyer who represented an investor during arbitration engaged in the unlicensed practice of law because the representation required, among other things: (1) conducting discovery and related depositions; (2) presenting evidence, raising objections, examining witnesses, voir dire of experts, and opening and closing arguments; and (3) preparing and filing the initial written statements of claims, answers, and counterclaims as well as written and oral motions and legal memoranda concerning the claims at issue. 696 So. 2d 1178, 1180 (Fla. 1997); *see also The Florida Bar v. Rapoport*, 845 So. 2d 874 (Fla. 2003) (holding that a lawyer who was not licensed in Florida engaged in the unauthorized practice of law by representing clients in securities proceedings in Florida).

The Ohio Supreme Court reached the same conclusion that a corporation, or its nonlawyer representative, could not represent individuals during securities arbitration proceedings. *See Disciplinary Counsel v. Alexicole, Inc.*, 822 N.E.2d 348 [(Ohio 2004)]. The Arizona Supreme Court similarly held that a disbarred attorney engaged in the unauthorized practice of law when he represented a motorist during arbitration proceedings against the motorist's insurance company. *In re Creasy*, 12 P.3d 214 (Ariz. 2000). In that case, the Arizona Supreme Court . . . determined that even a cursory review of the disbarred attorney's actions during the arbitration proceeding showed that he rendered the kind of core service that is and has been customarily given and performed from day to day in the ordinary practice of law.

This court has never formulated an all-encompassing definition for what constitutes the practice of law. In fact, we have specifically recognized the difficulty in creating a satisfactory definition. We have said, however:

> [W]hen one appears before a court of record for the purpose of transacting business with the court in connection with any pending litigation or when any person seeks to invoke the processes of the court in any matter pending before it, that person is engaging in the practice of law. . . . [A]ny one who assumes the role of assisting the court in its process or invokes the use of its mechanism is considered to be engaged in the practice of law. . . . We make it clear at this point that we are not holding that other activities aside from appearing in court do not constitute practicing law. It is uniformly held that many activities, such as writing and interpreting wills, contracts, trust agreements and the giving of legal advice in general, constitute practicing law.

Similarly, this court has stated that the practice of law is not confined to services by an attorney in a court of justice; it also includes any service of a legal nature rendered outside of courts and unrelated to matters pending in the courts. Finally, our statutory law provides in relevant part:

> It shall be unlawful for any corporation or voluntary association to practice or appear as an attorney at law for any person in any court in this state or before any judicial body, to make it a business to practice as an attorney at law for any person in any of the courts, to hold itself out to the public as being entitled to practice law, *to tender or furnish legal services or advice*, to furnish attorneys or counsel, to *render legal services of any kind in actions or proceedings of any nature or in any other way or manner*, or in any other manner to assume to be entitled to practice law or to assume or advertise the title of lawyer or attorney, attorney at law, or equivalent terms in any language in such a manner as to convey the impression that it is entitled to practice law or to furnish legal advice, service, or counsel or to advertise that either alone or together with or by or through any person, whether a duly and regularly admitted attorney at law or not, it has, owns, conducts, or maintains a law office or any office for the practice of law or for furnishing legal advice, services, or counsel.

Ark. Code Ann. § 16-22-211(a) (Supp. 2011) (emphasis added).

Although TriBuilt did not file a brief with this court in this appeal, IFIC did file a response with the circuit court and urged that representation during arbitration proceedings did not constitute the practice of law. In that response, IFIC relied primarily on cases where individuals were permitted to represent themselves in arbitration proceedings, cases refusing to vacate arbitration awards on the basis that a participant engaged in the unauthorized practice of law, AAA rules, the Federal Arbitration Act (FAA), and section 16-22-211(a) quoted above. *See Williamson v. John D. Quinn Construction Corp.*, 537 F. Supp. 613, 616 (S.D.N.Y. 1982) (rejecting a claim that a New Jersey law firm was precluded from recovering any fees for services performed in connection with an arbitration proceeding that took place in New York because it had engaged in the unauthorized practice of law); *Marino v. Tagaris*, 480 N.E.2d 286 (Mass. 1985) (noting that there is nothing inherently wrong with encouraging self-representation during arbitration proceedings); *Colmar, Ltd. v. Fremantlemedia N. Am., Inc.*, 801 N.E.2d 1017, 1022 (Ill. App. Ct. 2003) (holding that an out-of-state attorney's representation during arbitration proceedings did not constitute the unauthorized practice of law). All three of the cases cited by IFIC in circuit court are distinguishable on their facts from the case before us.

Though this court has never decided whether legal representation in an arbitration proceeding constitutes the practice of law in Arkansas, we have noted . . . that arbitration is designed to be a "less expensive and more expeditious means of settling litigation," and to relieve "docket congestion." We have also said that "[a]rbitration hearings are not analogous to trial proceedings." Those statements, though, do not decide the issue.

In reaching a decision on this matter, we are influenced by the fact that this court has been resolute in strictly enforcing the rule that a corporation through its nonlawyer officers cannot engage in the practice of law. We are further influenced by the fact that arbitration proceedings bear significant indicia of legal proceedings under the Uniform Arbitration Act, which has been adopted by this state. As already noted, if a hearing is held during arbitration, the parties have the right to be heard, present evidence material to the controversy, and cross-examine witnesses appearing at the hearing.

Bearing in mind the role of an advocate in arbitration proceedings, as just described, we are hard pressed to say that services of a legal nature are not being provided on behalf of the party in arbitration; in this case, TriBuilt. Accordingly, we reverse the decision of the circuit court on this point and hold that a nonlawyer's representation of a corporation in arbitration proceedings constitutes the unauthorized practice of law.

Reversed.

NOTE

Does the result here support Professor Benson's view (see § 1.02) that lawyers supported the enactment of arbitration laws in order to ensure themselves a "lucrative role" in the arbitration process? Is that the explanation for the right to counsel contained in the Uniform Arbitration Act and the Revised Uniform Arbitration Act as well? Is there any way to distinguish between regulation of the legal profession that protects consumers and regulation that merely keeps out unwanted competitors?

PROBLEM 6.2

To James Barker's (and your) surprise, Jack Douglas shows up at the hearing (see Problem 6.1) and manages to convince the arbitrator to give the company a short continuance to prepare for the arbitration. Representing Douglas at the hearing is Fred Porlock, whom you remember from law school — the first semester of law school, anyway. Porlock decided after the second week of school that studying wasn't for him and spent the rest of the semester making the rounds of the local bars and coffee shops. Needless to say, Porlock did not return for the spring semester, and certainly never graduated. When you ask Porlock what he's been up to, he tells you about the great practice he's built up representing parties in arbitration: "I don't need to worry about all those technical court rules I could never remember anyway. And the best thing is that I've never had to take the stupid bar exam. The only bar I've ever passed is Birdy's Tavern, and that's just when it's closed!" You later ask Barker what he knows about Porlock. Barker tells you that Porlock is quite successful at what he does: "Arbitrators love him, especially the ones who aren't lawyers. Plus, his rates are way below what you lawyers charge." Is there something going on here that the state bar needs to know about? What do you think?

The national and transnational nature of law practices is putting increasing strains on state bar admission rules. The following case examines those strains in the context of arbitration proceedings.

BIRBROWER, MONTALBANO, CONDON & FRANK, P.C. v. SUPERIOR COURT
Supreme Court of California
949 P.2d 1 (1998)

CHIN, JUSTICE.

Business and Professions Code section 6125 states: "No person shall practice law in California unless the person is an active member of the State Bar." We must decide whether an out-of-state law firm, not licensed to practice law in this state, violated section 6125 when it performed legal services in California for a California-based client under a fee agreement stipulating that California law would govern all matters in the representation.

Although we are aware of the interstate nature of modern law practice and mindful of the reality that large firms often conduct activities and serve clients in several states, we do not believe these facts excuse law firms from complying with section 6125. . . . We therefore conclude that, to the extent defendant law firm Birbrower, Montalbano, Condon & Frank, P.C. (Birbrower), practiced law in California without a license, it engaged in the unauthorized practice of law in this state. We also conclude that Birbrower's fee agreement with real party in interest ESQ Business Services, Inc. (ESQ), is invalid to the extent it authorizes payment for the substantial legal services Birbrower performed in California. . . .

I. BACKGROUND

The facts with respect to the unauthorized practice of law question are essentially undisputed. Birbrower is a professional law corporation incorporated in New York, with its principal place of business in New York. During 1992 and 1993,

Birbrower attorneys, defendants Kevin F. Hobbs and Thomas A. Condon (Hobbs and Condon), performed substantial work in California relating to the law firm's representation of ESQ [in connection with a breach of contract dispute with Tandem Computers, Inc.] Neither Hobbs nor Condon has ever been licensed to practice law in California. None of Birbrower's attorneys were licensed to practice law in California during Birbrower's ESQ representation.

. . .

While representing ESQ, Hobbs and Condon traveled to California on several occasions. In August 1992, they met in California with ESQ and its accountants. During these meetings, Hobbs and Condon discussed various matters related to ESQ's dispute with Tandem and strategy for resolving the dispute. They made recommendations and gave advice. During this California trip, Hobbs and Condon also met with Tandem representatives on four or five occasions during a two-day period. At the meetings, Hobbs and Condon spoke on ESQ's behalf. Hobbs demanded that Tandem pay ESQ $15 million. Condon told Tandem he believed that damages would exceed $15 million if the parties litigated the dispute.

Around March or April 1993, Hobbs, Condon, and another Birbrower attorney visited California to interview potential arbitrators and to meet again with ESQ and its accountants. Birbrower had previously filed a demand for arbitration against Tandem with the San Francisco offices of the American Arbitration Association (AAA). In August 1993, Hobbs returned to California to assist ESQ in settling the Tandem matter. While in California, Hobbs met with ESQ and its accountants to discuss a proposed settlement agreement Tandem authored. Hobbs also met with Tandem representatives to discuss possible changes in the proposed agreement. Hobbs gave ESQ legal advice during this trip, including his opinion that ESQ should not settle with Tandem on the terms proposed.

ESQ eventually settled the Tandem dispute, and the matter never went to arbitration. . . .

In January 1994, ESQ sued Birbrower for legal malpractice and related claims in Santa Clara County Superior Court. . . . ESQ moved for summary judgment and/or adjudication on the first through fourth causes of action of Birbrower's counterclaim, which asserted ESQ and its representatives breached the fee agreement. ESQ argued that by practicing law without a license in California and by failing to associate legal counsel while doing so, Birbrower violated section 6125, rendering the fee agreement unenforceable. Based on these undisputed facts, the Santa Clara Superior Court granted ESQ's motion for summary adjudication . . .

. . .

Birbrower petitioned the Court of Appeal for a writ of mandate directing the trial court to vacate the summary adjudication order. The Court of Appeal denied Birbrower's petition and affirmed the trial court's order, holding that Birbrower violated section 6125. . . .

We granted review to determine whether Birbrower's actions and services performed while representing ESQ in California constituted the unauthorized practice of law under section 6125 and, if so, whether a section 6125 violation rendered the fee agreement wholly unenforceable.

II. DISCUSSION

A. The Unauthorized Practice of Law

The California Legislature enacted section 6125 in 1927 as part of the State Bar Act (the Act), a comprehensive scheme regulating the practice of law in the state. Since the Act's passage, the general rule has been that, although persons may represent themselves and their own interests regardless of State Bar membership, no one but an active member of the State Bar may practice law for another person in California. The prohibition against unauthorized law practice is within the state's police power and is designed to ensure that those performing legal services do so competently.

A violation of section 6125 is a misdemeanor. Moreover, "No one may recover compensation for services as an attorney at law in this state unless [the person] was at the time the services were performed a member of The State Bar."

Although the Act did not define the term "practice law," case law explained it as "the doing and performing services in a court of justice in any matter depending therein throughout its various stages and in conformity with the adopted rules of procedure." . . . [I]ncluded in its definition [was] legal advice and legal instrument and contract preparation, whether or not these subjects were rendered in the course of litigation. . . .

In addition to not defining the term "practice law," the Act also did not define the meaning of "in California." In today's legal practice, questions often arise concerning whether the phrase refers to the nature of the legal services, or restricts the Act's application to those out-of-state attorneys who are physically present in the state.

Section 6125 has generated numerous opinions on the meaning of "practice law" but none on the meaning of "in California." In our view, the practice of law "in California" entails sufficient contact with the California client to render the nature of the legal service a clear legal representation. In addition to a quantitative analysis, we must consider the nature of the unlicensed lawyer's activities in the state. Mere fortuitous or attenuated contacts will not sustain a finding that the unlicensed lawyer practiced law "in California." The primary inquiry is whether the unlicensed lawyer engaged in sufficient activities in the state, or created a continuing relationship with the California client that included legal duties and obligations.

Our definition does not necessarily depend on or require the unlicensed lawyer's physical presence in the state. Physical presence here is one factor we may consider in deciding whether the unlicensed lawyer has violated section 6125, but it is by no means exclusive. For example, one may practice law in the state in violation of section 6125 although not physically present here by advising a California client on California law in connection with a California legal dispute by telephone, fax, computer, or other modern technological means. Conversely, although we decline to provide a comprehensive list of what activities constitute sufficient contact with the state, we do reject the notion that a person automatically practices law "in California" whenever that person practices California law anywhere, or "virtually" enters the state by telephone, fax, e-mail, or satellite. . . . We must decide each case on its individual facts.

This interpretation acknowledges the tension that exists between interjurisdictional practice and the need to have a state-regulated bar. . . .

If we were to carry the dissent's narrow interpretation of the term "practice law" to its logical conclusion, we would effectively limit section 6125's application to those cases in which nonlicensed out-of-state lawyers appeared in a California courtroom without permission. . . . Indeed, the dissent's definition of "practice law" ignores [this court's prior decisions] altogether, and, in so doing, substantially undermines the Legislature's intent to protect the public from those giving unauthorized legal advice and counsel.

Exceptions to section 6125 do exist, but are generally limited to allowing out-of-state attorneys to make brief appearances before a state court or tribunal. . . .

In addition, with the permission of the California court in which a particular cause is pending, out-of-state counsel may appear before a court as counsel pro hac vice. A court will approve a pro hac vice application only if the out-of-state attorney is a member in good standing of another state bar and is eligible to practice in any United States court or the highest court in another jurisdiction. The out-of-state attorney must also associate an active member of the California Bar as attorney of record and is subject to the Rules of Professional Conduct of the State Bar.

. . .

The Legislature has recognized an exception to section 6125 in international disputes resolved in California under the state's rules for arbitration and conciliation of international commercial disputes. (Code Civ. Proc., § 1297.11 et seq.) This exception states that in a commercial conciliation in California involving international commercial disputes, "The parties may appear in person or be represented or assisted by any person of their choice. A person assisting or representing a party need not be a member of the legal profession or licensed to practice law in California." . . .

B. The Present Case

The undisputed facts here show that . . . Birbrower engaged in unauthorized law practice in California on more than a limited basis, and no firm attorney engaged in that practice was an active member of the California State Bar. . . .

Birbrower contends, however, that section 6125 is not meant to apply to any out-of-state attorneys. Instead, it argues that the statute is intended solely to prevent nonattorneys from practicing law. This contention is without merit because it contravenes the plain language of the statute. Section 6125 clearly states that no person shall practice law *in California* unless that person is a member of the State Bar. The statute does not differentiate between attorneys or nonattorneys, nor does it excuse a person who is a member of another state bar. . . .

Birbrower next argues that we do not further the statute's intent and purpose — to protect California citizens from incompetent attorneys — by enforcing it against out-of-state attorneys. Birbrower argues that because out-of-state attorneys have been licensed to practice in other jurisdictions, they have already demonstrated sufficient competence to protect California clients. But Birbrower's argument overlooks the obvious fact that other states' laws may differ substantially from California law. Competence in one jurisdiction does not necessarily guarantee competence in another. By applying section 6125 to out-of-state attorneys who engage in the extensive practice of law in California without becoming licensed in our state, we serve the statute's goal of assuring the competence of all attorneys practicing law in this state.

. . .

Assuming that section 6125 does apply to out-of-state attorneys not licensed here, Birbrower alternatively asks us to create an exception to section 6125 for work incidental to private arbitration or other alternative dispute resolution proceedings. Birbrower points to fundamental differences between private arbitration and legal proceedings, including procedural differences relating to discovery, rules of evidence, compulsory process, cross-examination of witnesses, and other areas. As Birbrower observes, in light of these differences, at least one court has decided that an out-of-state attorney could recover fees for services rendered in an arbitration proceeding.

. . .

We decline Birbrower's invitation to craft an arbitration exception to section 6125's prohibition of the unlicensed practice of law in this state. Any exception for arbitration is best left to the Legislature, which has the authority to determine qualifications for admission to the State Bar and to decide what constitutes the practice of law. Even though the Legislature has spoken with respect to *international* arbitration and conciliation, it has not enacted a similar rule for private arbitration proceedings. Of course, private arbitration and other alternative dispute resolution practices are important aspects of our justice system. Section 6125, however, articulates a strong public policy favoring the practice of law in California by licensed State Bar members. In the face of the Legislature's silence, we will not create an arbitration exception under the facts presented.

. . .

In its reply brief to the State Bar's amicus curiae brief, Birbrower raises for the first time the additional argument that the Federal Arbitration Act (FAA) preempted the rules governing the AAA proposed arbitration and section 6125. . . . Although we need not address the question under California Rules of Court, rule 29(b)(1), and note the parties' settlement agreement rendered the arbitration unnecessary, we reject the argument for its lack of merit. First, the parties incorporated a California choice-of-law provision in the Tandem Agreement, indicating they intended to apply California law in any necessary arbitration, and they have not shown that California law in any way conflicts with the FAA. Moreover, in interpreting the California Arbitration Act stay provisions, the high court observed that the FAA does not contain an express preemptive provision, nor does it "reflect a congressional intent to occupy the entire field of arbitration."

. . .

C. Compensation for Legal Services

. . .

. . . [W]e conclude the Court of Appeal erred in determining that the fee agreement between the parties was entirely unenforceable because Birbrower violated section 6125's prohibition against the unauthorized practice of law in California. Birbrower's statutory violation may require exclusion of the portion of the fee attributable to the substantial illegal services, but that violation does not necessarily entirely preclude its recovery under the fee agreement for the limited services it performed outside California.

. . .

III. DISPOSITION

We conclude that Birbrower violated section 6125 by practicing law in California. To the extent the fee agreement allows payment for those illegal local services, it is void, and Birbrower is not entitled to recover fees under the agreement for those services. The fee agreement is enforceable, however, to the extent it is possible to sever the portions of the consideration attributable to Birbrower's services illegally rendered in California from those attributable to Birbrower's New York services. Accordingly, we affirm the Court of Appeal judgment to the extent it concluded that Birbrower's representation of ESQ in California violated section 6125, and that Birbrower is not entitled to recover fees under the fee agreement for its local services. We reverse the judgment to the extent the court did not allow Birbrower to argue in favor of a severance of the illegal portion of the consideration (for the California fees) from the rest of the fee agreement, and remand for further proceedings consistent with this decision.

GEORGE, C.J., and MOSK, BAXTER, WERDEGAR and BROWN, JJ., concur. KENNARD, JUSTICE, dissenting.

. . .

[T]he practice of law is the representation of another in a judicial proceeding or an activity requiring the application of that degree of legal knowledge and technique possessed only by a trained legal mind.

. . .

[U]nder this court's decisions, arbitration proceedings are not governed or constrained by the rule of law; therefore, representation of another in an arbitration proceeding, including the activities necessary to prepare for the arbitration hearing, does not necessarily require a trained legal mind. Commonly used arbitration rules further demonstrate that legal training is not essential to represent another in an arbitration proceeding. . . .

The American Arbitration Association and other major arbitration associations . . . recognize that nonattorneys are often better suited than attorneys to represent parties in arbitration. The history of arbitration also reflects this reality, for in its beginnings arbitration was a dispute-resolution mechanism principally used in a few specific trades (such as construction, textiles, ship chartering, and international sales of goods) to resolve disputes among businesses that turned on factual issues uniquely within the expertise of members of the trade. In fact, "rules of a few trade associations forbid representation by counsel in arbitration proceedings, because of their belief that it would complicate what might otherwise be simple proceedings." The majority gives no adequate justification for its decision to deprive parties of their freedom of contract and to make it a crime for anyone but California lawyers to represent others in arbitrations in California.

. . .

NOTES

1. The California legislature responded to the *Birbrower* case by amending the state arbitration statute to permit "an attorney admitted to the bar of any other state" to represent a party "in the course of, or in connection with, an arbitration proceeding this state," but only if the non-California attorney retains local counsel and the arbitrators approve. CAL. CIV. PROC. CODE § 1282.4(b), (c). Is that an appropriate solution? Even if it is, it is only a temporary one in California, because the provision expires January 1, 2013. *See also* Fought & Co. v. Steel Eng. & Erection, Inc., 951 P.2d 487, 498 (Hawaii 1998) (following *Birbrower* in connection with representation in mediation, but holding fees recoverable because Oregon attorney retained local counsel who was "at all times 'in charge' of . . . representation within the jurisdiction").

A contrary view was stated by Judge Jed S. Rakoff of the United States District Court for the Southern District of New York:

> Although . . . arbitration proceedings have become more protracted and complex, not to mention costly, they still retain in most settings their essential character of private contractual arrangements for the relatively informal resolution of disputes. Indeed, the Court notes that the rules of the New York Stock Exchange, where the . . . arbitration [at issue here] was held, do not require members of the arbitration panel to be lawyers at all. *See* N.Y. Stock Exch. Rule 607. It would be incongruous to apply a state's unauthorized practice rules in such an informal setting. Whatever beneficent purposes New York's prohibition against the unauthorized practice of law may serve in protecting clients and regulating lawyers' conduct, it is not designed as a trap for the unwary or as a basis on which New York lawyers can extend a monopoly over every private contractual dispute-resolving mechanism.

Prudential Equity Group, LLC v. Ajamie, 538 F. Supp. 2d 605, 608 (S.D.N.Y 2008); *see also* Superadio Ltd. P'ship v. Winstar Radio Prods., L.L.C., 844 N.E.2d 246, 252

(Mass. 2006); Donald J. Williamson, P.A. v. John D. Quinn Constr. Corp., 537 F. Supp. 613, 615-16 (S.D.N.Y 1982).

2. As the court notes in *Birbrower*, the California international arbitration statute provides that the parties may "be represented or assisted by any person of their choice" and that person "need not be a member of the legal profession or licensed to practice law in California." CAL. CIV. PROC. CODE § 1297.351. But that provision appears in the section of the statute dealing only with conciliation, not arbitration. Thus, the majority describes the statute as applicable to a "a commercial conciliation in California involving international commercial disputes." Should conciliation (*i.e.*, mediation) be treated differently than arbitration? Should it matter whether the dispute is an international one rather than a domestic one?

3. In 2002, the American Bar Association amended its Model Rules of Professional Conduct to provide as follows:

> Rule 5.5: Unauthorized Practice of Law; Multijurisdictional Practice of Law
>
> (c) A lawyer admitted in another United States jurisdiction, and not disbarred or suspended from practice in any jurisdiction, may provide legal services on a temporary basis in this jurisdiction that:
>
> . . .
>
> > (3) are in or reasonably related to a pending or potential arbitration, mediation, or other alternative dispute resolution proceeding in this or another jurisdiction, if the services arise out of or are reasonably related to the lawyer's practice in a jurisdiction in which the lawyer is admitted to practice and are not services for which the forum requires pro hac vice admission.

According to Comment 14 to the Model Rule, the "necessary relationship" between the legal services and the lawyer's practice in another jurisdiction "might arise when the client's activities or the legal issues involve multiple relationships, such as when the officers of a multinational corporation survey potential business sites and seek the services of their lawyer in assessing the relative merits of each." Another possibility listed in the Comment is when "the legal services may draw on the lawyer's recognized expertise developed through the regular practice of law on behalf of clients in matters involving a particular body of federal, nationally-uniform, foreign, or international law." Would *Birbrower* come out differently under the Model Rule? *See* Colmar, Ltd. v. Fremantlemedia North America, Inc., 801 N.E.2d 1017, 1026 (Ill. App. 2003) (relying on Model Rule 5.5(c) as persuasive authority that "an out-of-state attorney's representation of a client during arbitration does not violate the rules prohibiting the unauthorized practice of law").

4. Most other countries do not require that a party be represented by an attorney in an international commercial arbitration. *See* David Rivkin, *Keeping Lawyers out of International Arbitrations*, INT'L FIN. L. REV., Feb. 1990, at 11, 11. One commentator has criticized the *Birbrower* decision as "run[ning] against the trend of judicial precedents and legislative enactments that have been liberalizing the right of representation in a number of countries — often, ironically, under

American pressure. The decision is thus an embarrassment to those in the United States who have been preaching liberal policies in such matters to the rest of the world." Richard A. Eastman, 94 AM. J. INT'L L. 400, 403 (2000).

PROBLEM 6.3

You get a phone call from Ettie Shaffer, the general counsel of West Gilmerton General Mining Co., a Wyoming coal mining company. After reminiscing about law school ("What ever happened to Fred Porlock, anyway?" she asks), she gets down to business: "My company has just received demands for arbitration from three different customers who are unhappy with the coal we've been selling them. The arbitrations are going to be held in the customers' home states: one in Colorado, one in Wyoming, and one in California. I think it makes sense to have the same lawyer handle all three cases, since the contracts are so similar and the factual issues will be almost identical. I want you to represent us in all of them." As a member only of the Colorado bar, can you represent West Gilmerton in the arbitrations? If you foresee any possible problems with doing so, do you have any advice for Shaffer as to what she might do to make sure the same law firm can handle all of her arbitration matters in the future?

§ 6.04 SELECTING ARBITRATORS

A central difference between arbitration and litigation is that in arbitration parties get to choose who decides their case. Who the parties choose obviously can be of critical importance in how the case comes out. In addition, the fact that arbitrators are chosen rather than assigned (and that an arbitrator gets paid only if he or she is chosen) gives arbitrators different incentives in deciding cases than judges have, as we have already discussed. This section takes a closer look at selecting arbitrators. First, it examines the mechanics of selecting arbitrators, including the most common default mechanisms provided by arbitration rules and statutes. Second, it looks at problems of arbitrator bias and partiality.

[A] The Mechanics of Selecting Arbitrators

Parties are free to specify whatever mechanism they wish to choose the arbitrator or arbitrators, subject to the fundamental requirement of a neutral decision maker. The first question is how many arbitrators there will be. In domestic arbitrations, the default ordinarily is one arbitrator, although for more complex cases there may be three. AAA Commercial Arbitration Rules, Rule R-15; *id.* Rule L-2(a) (governing complex disputes). International arbitration rules and statutes provide either one or three arbitrators as the default. UNCITRAL Arbitration Rules, art. 7(1) (three arbitrators); UNCITRAL Model Law, art. 10(2) (same); AAA/ICDR Int'l Rules, art. 5 (default of one arbitrator, unless case administrator decides that three should be selected "because of the large size, complexity or other circumstances of the case"); ICC Rules of Arbitration, art. 12(2) ("the Court shall appoint a sole arbitrator, save where it appears to the Court that the dispute is such as to warrant the appointment of three arbitrators").

Why would parties prefer a particular number of arbitrators? A clear advantage of having only one arbitrator is cost: the parties only have to pay the fees of one arbitrator instead of three. Scheduling also is easier with a single arbitrator, and the arbitrator does not need to consult with others is making the award, so there is less possibility of delay. A panel of three arbitrators has the advantage of collegial decision making, and probably has less likelihood of an aberrational award. In addition, the three arbitrators may have a broader range of expertise relevant to the case than a single arbitrator. There is no universal consensus on which is preferable. In a sample of franchise contracts, almost half of the arbitration clauses provided for a single arbitrator, while less than 15 percent specified a panel of three. (The remaining clauses did not address the issue.)

The parties also can specify that the arbitrators have certain qualifications. For example, a handful of franchise contracts require that arbitrators have experience in franchise law. The obvious reason for such requirements is to ensure that the arbitrator has expertise in the subject matter of any dispute. In international arbitrations, the nationality of the arbitrators can be important. Thus, when the ICC Court of Arbitration selects an arbitrator, it must "consider the prospective arbitrator's nationality, residence and other relationships with the countries of which the parties or the other arbitrators are nationals and the prospective arbitrator's availability and ability to conduct the arbitration in accordance with the Rules." Art. 13(1). Indeed, the ICC Rules provide that a sole arbitrator or chairman shall be of different nationality than that of the parties. Art. 13(5). The concern with nationality has less to do with expertise (although language abilities are important) than with perceptions of neutrality.

A simple mechanism to select a sole arbitrator is to name in the arbitration agreement the person who will serve as the arbitrator. While that approach is not unusual when parties submit an existing dispute to arbitration, it is much less common (and often ill-advised) when parties enter into a pre-dispute arbitration agreement. (What if the arbitrator is unable or unwilling to serve when a dispute arises?) Alternatively, the parties can specify in their arbitration agreement that they will agree on an arbitrator once the dispute arises. Because any arbitrator chosen must be satisfactory to both parties, this mechanism provides at least some assurance of neutrality.

Arbitration rules provide other default means of arbitrator selection. The Commercial Arbitration Rules of the American Arbitration Association use a "listing" procedure, under which the AAA sends to each party a list of prospective arbitrators chosen from the AAA's panel. Rule R-11(a). If the parties do not agree to a single name, then the parties are to "strike names objected to," rank the remaining names, and return the list to the AAA. Rule R-11(b). The AAA then chooses the arbitrator from the names that neither party objected to, "in accordance with the designated order of mutual preference." Usually that means the name with the cumulative lowest ranks; in the case of ties, the AAA may respect the claimant's preference. If for whatever reason the AAA cannot select an arbitrator using this procedure, it can select the arbitrator itself. Under the AAA Expedited Rules, only five names are submitted to the parties, and they get only two strikes each. Rule E–4(a) & (b). The JAMS Employment Rules are similar to the AAA Expedited Rules. *See* Rule 15(b) & (c).

By comparison, the default mechanism for selecting arbitrators contained in most international arbitration rules — at least when there are to be three arbitrators — is for each party to select one arbitrator, with the two party-appointed arbitrators to select the third, presiding arbitrator. UNCITRAL Arbitration Rules, art. 9(1); UNCITRAL Model Law, art. 11(3)(a). This mechanism also is used in domestic arbitrations involving a panel of three arbitrators; there traditionally has been a key difference between domestic and international arbitrations with respect to party-appointed arbitrators (although this has been changing), which we will discuss later.

What if one party fails or refuses to participate in choosing the arbitrator? Or what if there is some problem with the method of selecting arbitrators provided in the arbitration agreement? The following case offers one solution.

KHAN v. DELL INC.
United States Court of Appeals for the Third Circuit
669 F.3d 350 (2012)

RoTH, Circuit Judge:

This appeal involves a matter of first impression for this Circuit — whether Section 5 of the Federal Arbitration Act (FAA) requires the appointment of a substitute arbitrator when the arbitrator designated by the parties is unavailable. Dell, Inc., appeals from the District of New Jersey's denial of Dell's Motion to Compel Arbitration and Stay Plaintiff's Claims. Dell contends that the District Court erred in denying its motion to compel arbitration based on the District Court's belief that the arbitration provision was rendered unenforceable because it provided for the parties to arbitrate exclusively before a forum that was unavailable when Khan commenced suit. The District Court also refused to appoint a substitute arbitrator, finding that it could not compel the parties to submit to an arbitral forum to which they had not agreed.

I. FACTUAL BACKGROUND

Dell designed, manufactured, and distributed the 600m computer from 2003 to 2006. Khan purchased a Dell 600m computer in September 2004 for approximately $1,200. Khan purchased the computer online through Dell's website, www.Dell.com. To complete the purchase, Khan was required to click a box stating "I AGREE to Dell's Terms and Conditions of Sale." . . . [Dell's] Terms and Conditions of Sale contained an arbitration provision that reads as follows:

> **13. Binding Arbitration.** ANY CLAIM, DISPUTE, OR CONTROVERSY (WHETHER IN CONTRACT, TORT, OR OTHERWISE, WHETHER PREEXISTING, PRESENT OR FUTURE, AND INCLUDING STATUTORY, COMMON LAW, INTENTIONAL TORT AND EQUITABLE CLAIMS) BETWEEN CUSTOMER AND DELL, its agents, employees, principals, successors, assigns, affiliates (collectively for purposes of this paragraph, "Dell") arising from or relating to this Agreement, its interpretation, or the breach, termination or validity

thereof, the relationships which result from this Agreement (including, to the full extent permitted by applicable law, relationships with third parties who are not signatories to this Agreement), Dell's advertising, or any related purchase SHALL BE RESOLVED EXCLUSIVELY AND FINALLY BY BINDING ARBITRATION ADMINISTERED BY THE NATIONAL ARBITRATION FORUM (NAF) under its Code of Procedure then in effect (available via the Internet at http://www.arb-forum.com, or via telephone at 1-800-474-2371). The arbitration will be limited solely to the dispute or controversy between customer and Dell. NEITHER CUSTOMER NOR DELL SHALL BE ENTITLED TO JOIN OR CONSOLIDATE CLAIMS BY OR AGAINST OTHER CUSTOMERS, OR ARBITRATE ANY CLAIM AS A REPRESENTATIVE OR CLASS ACTION OR IN A PRIVATE ATTORNEY GENERAL CAPACITY. This transaction involves interstate commerce, and this provision shall be governed by the Federal Arbitration Act 9 U.S.C. sec. 1-16 (FAA). Any award of the arbitrators shall be final and binding on each of the parties . . . . Information may be obtained and claims may be filed with the NAF at P.O. Box 50191, Minneapolis, MN 55405.

Rule 1 of the NAF's "Code and Procedure" . . . provided that "[t]his Code shall be administered only by the National Arbitration Forum or by any entity or individual providing administrative services by agreement with the National Arbitration Forum." Also, . . . the arbitration provision did not designate a replacement forum in the event that NAF was unavailable for any reason. But . . . the Terms and Conditions did incorporate the Federal Arbitration Act.

. . .

Khan alleged that his 600m suffered from design defects, causing his computer to overheat and thereby destroy the computer's motherboard. Khan replaced the motherboard multiple times. After the third replacement, Dell refused to issue another replacement, claiming the warranty had expired. The 600m allegedly suffered from other design defects, which prevented it from being used in a manner consistent with Dell's marketing.

On July 24, 2009, Khan filed a putative consumer class action on behalf of himself and other similarly situated purchasers and lessees of defectively designed 600m computers sold from approximately 2003 through 2006. . . . At the time the lawsuit was filed, the NAF had been barred from conducting consumer arbitrations by Consent Judgment, which resolved litigation brought by the Attorney General of Minnesota. The Consent Judgment "barred [the NAF] from the business of arbitrating credit card and other consumer disputes and [ordered the NAF to] stop accepting any new consumer arbitrations or in any manner participate in the processing or administering of new consumer arbitrations." This was the result of government investigations revealing that the NAF engaged in various deceptive practices that disadvantaged consumers.

According to Khan, such practices included:

(1) representing to consumers and the public that it was neutral;

430 THE ARBITRATION PROCEEDING CH. 6

(2) convincing credit card companies and other creditors to include exclusive arbitration forum provisions in their contracts and making representations to such entities that it would favor the entities in the arbitrations; and

(3) identifying and appointing anti-consumer arbitrators and withholding referrals to arbitrators who decided cases against companies.

Khan also alleged that the Minnesota investigations found that these practices encouraged some corporations to select the NAF as their arbitration forum because of this prospect of favorable results. However, although Khan suggested that Dell must have chosen the NAF based on its corporate-friendly disposition, the record does not show that Dell was aware of these practices at the time that it selected the NAF as the arbitral forum governing Khan's purchase or that Dell selected the NAF for any improper reason.

On October 2, 2009, Dell moved to compel arbitration, arguing that the arbitration provision was binding and covered all of Khan's claims. Khan did not dispute that the Terms and Conditions governed the contract. Khan did, however, assert that the arbitration provision was unenforceable because the NAF, which the arbitration provision designated as the arbitral forum, was no longer permitted to conduct consumer arbitrations. Khan further contended that the NAF's designation was integral to the arbitration provision. He argued, for that reason, that, because the NAF could not perform its function, the arbitration provision in the Terms and Conditions should not be enforced and the parties should proceed to litigation.

On August 18, 2010, the District Court denied Dell's motion to compel arbitration and stay claims. . . . The court concluded that granting Dell's motion to compel and appointing a substitute arbitrator would improperly force the parties to "submit to an arbitration proceeding to which they have not agreed."

. . .

III. ANALYSIS

In this appeal, we must determine whether the provision in the Terms and Conditions that the NAF be the arbitrator is exclusive to the NAF and is an integral part of the agreement between Dell and Khan, thus preventing the appointment of a substitute arbitrator. . . .

The particular problem presented in this case — the unavailability of the NAF — is addressed in section 5 of the FAA, which provides a mechanism for substituting an arbitrator when the designated arbitrator is unavailable. In determining the applicability of Section 5 of the FAA when an arbitrator is unavailable, courts have focused on whether the designation of the arbitrator was "integral" to the arbitration provision or was merely an ancillary consideration. . . . In other words, a court will decline to appoint a substitute arbitrator, as provided in the FAA, only if the parties' choice of forum is "so central to the arbitration agreement that the unavailability of that arbitrator [brings] the agreement to an end." In this light, the parties must have unambiguously expressed their intent not to arbitrate their disputes in the event that the designated arbitral forum is unavailable.

According to Khan, this standard has been met because the Terms and Conditions designate the NAF as the exclusive arbitral forum, implying that disputes should not be arbitrated if the NAF is unavailable. Khan relies on the contract language that states that all disputes "SHALL BE RESOLVED EXCLUSIVELY AND FINALLY BY BINDING ARBITRATION ADMINISTERED BY THE NATIONAL ARBITRATION FORUM."

In our view, this language is ambiguous: "EXCLUSIVELY" could be read to modify "BINDING ARBITRATION," "THE NATIONAL ARBITRATION FORUM," or both.

Khan, however, points out that the NAF's rules are incorporated into the contract, and that these rules provide that all arbitrations must be conducted by the NAF or an entity having an agreement with it. We conclude, however, that this requirement is also ambiguous as to what should happen in the event that the NAF is unavailable. The NAF's rules provide that they shall be interpreted in a manner consistent with the FAA and that, if any portion of the NAF rules are found to be unenforceable, that portion shall be severed and the remainder of the rules shall continue to apply.

Our finding of ambiguity is confirmed by the conflicting interpretations of this language adopted by the courts that have considered it.

Although courts are divided on the issue, we conclude that the "liberal federal policy in favor of arbitration" counsels us to favor . . . [construing the agreement as not making the NAF the exclusive arbitration forum]. The language relied on by Khan is at best ambiguous as to whether the parties intended to have their disputes arbitrated in the event that NAF was unavailable for any reason. Because of the ambiguity, it is not clear whether the designation of NAF is ancillary or is as important a consideration as the agreement to arbitrate itself. Therefore, we must resolve this ambiguity *in favor* of arbitration.

We note moreover that the arbitration provision in the Terms and Conditions specifically incorporated the FAA, suggesting that, in the event of the NAF's unavailability, the FAA's procedures for addressing such a problem should apply.

Khan, however, argues that, even if the NAF's designation as the arbitral forum was not integral to the Terms and Conditions, Section 5 of the FAA nevertheless did not apply here because NAF's unavailability was not a "lapse" within the meaning of statute. . . . Khan argues that the word "lapse" in Section 5 of the FAA means "a lapse in the naming of the arbitrator or in the filling of a vacancy on a panel of arbitrators or some other mechanical breakdown in the arbitrator selection process," not . . . the NAF's unavailability to do so.

We find [Khan's argument] unpersuasive. . . . [W]e do not see why the NAF's unavailability is not a "mechanical breakdown in the arbitrator selection process." Apparently, the NAF's Consent Judgment with the State of Minnesota prevents it from acting as an arbitrator. This unavailability appears to us to be a breakdown in the mechanics of the appointment process. To take a narrower construction of Section 5 would be inconsistent with the "liberal federal policy in favor of arbitration" articulated in the FAA.

We conclude therefore that the unavailability of NAF to hear the disputes between Khan and Dell constitutes a "lapse" within the meaning of Section 5.

IV. CONCLUSION

The contract's language does not indicate the parties' unambiguous intent not to arbitrate their disputes if NAF is unavailable. Section 5 of the FAA requires a court to address such unavailability by appointing a substitute arbitrator. The District Court's contrary conclusion is at odds with the fundamental presumption in favor of arbitration. We will therefore vacate the judgment of the District Court and remand this case for further proceedings consistent with this opinion.

SLOVITER, *Circuit Judge*, dissenting.

The majority opinion acknowledges that the Supreme Court has stated the "fundamental principle that arbitration is a matter of contract." . . . I dissent because the majority has given mere lip service to this "fundamental principle," and its holding as applied in this particular case violates that principle. There is no ambiguity in the arbitration agreement.

The plain text of the arbitration agreement clearly states that the selection by Dell of the NAF as arbitrator was integral to the agreement, and leads me to conclude that Section 5 of the FAA is inapplicable and the unavailability of the NAF precludes arbitration.

. . .

The majority reasons that this language is "ambiguous" because " 'EXCLUSIVELY' could be read to modify 'BINDING ARBITRATION,' 'THE NATIONAL ARBITRATION FORUM,' or both," and that the "liberal federal policy in favor of arbitration" thus compels the court to resolve this "ambiguity" in favor of arbitration. However, "the FAA's proarbitration policy does not operate without regard to the wishes of the contracting parties." The majority's conclusion focuses solely on the language used rather than giving appropriate weight to the additional clues that demonstrate the parties' clear intent.

The phrase "EXCLUSIVELY AND FINALLY BY BINDING ARBITRATION ADMINISTRATED BY THE NATIONAL ARBITRATION FORUM" is written in all capital letters yet surrounded by clauses written in lower case letters. This aesthetic prominence indicates the parties' intent for the entire phrase to be read together and emphasized as an essential part of the agreement. Moreover, as noted by the District Court, "[t]he NAF is expressly named, the NAF's rules are to apply, . . . no provision is made for an alternate arbitrator [, and the] language used is mandatory, not permissive." The agreement also states that "[i]nformation may be obtained and claims may be filed with the NAF at P.O. Box 50191, Minneapolis, MN 55404," again illustrating the central role that NAF was intended to play in arbitrations pursuant to this agreement.

Given "the consensual nature of private dispute resolution," courts must respect the principle that "parties are generally free to structure their arbitration agreements as they see fit." Here, the parties agreed only to binding arbitration administered by the NAF. Full analysis of the plain text of the agreement as a whole shows that the selection of the NAF as arbitrator was an integral part of the agreement to arbitrate. Therefore, Section 5 of the FAA is inapplicable and the unavailability of the NAF precludes arbitration. I respectfully dissent.

There is yet another reason why Dell's request to proceed via arbitration rather than trial should not be granted, and that reason applies to this defendant in this case. The majority avoids any discussion of the underlying reason why arbitration by NAF is unavailable. In an action pending in Minnesota, the Minnesota Attorney General made public the results of its year-long investigation that showed that NAF, far from being the neutral arbitration forum contemplated by Congress when it enacted the Federal Arbitration Act, represented to corporations that it would appoint anti-consumer arbitrators and discontinue referrals to arbitrators who decided cases in favor of consumers.

Rather than disputing the allegations, NAF accepted a consent judgment that barred it from administering and participating in all consumer arbitrations. It cannot be insignificant that Dell named NAF as the exclusive forum in its arbitration clauses. It followed that the District Court refused Dell's request to designate a substitute arbitrator. It was certainly not error for the District Court in this case to deny substitution at the behest of Dell. Even assuming that in the usual case, substitution of a neutral arbitrator would be an acceptable alternative, it is evident that this is not an ordinary case and we should affirm the District Court's denial of Dell's motion.

NOTES

1. *Kahn* illustrates the gap-filling function of arbitration statutes. Because the arbitration institution agreed to by the parties in their contract no longer conducted arbitrations, the arbitration agreement had a gap as to arbitrator selection. Section 5 of the FAA filled that gap by providing for a court to appoint the arbitrator. 9 U.S.C. § 5. The Uniform Arbitration Act and the Revised Uniform Arbitration Act are similar. UAA § 5; RUAA § 11; *see also* UNCITRAL Model Law, art. 11(3) (arbitrator to be appointed by "court or other authority specified in article 6").

2. Having a third party able to step in and appoint an arbitrator also is important when one of the parties to the arbitration agreement fails or refuses to participate in selecting an arbitrator. Without such an "appointing authority," a party to an arbitration agreement could frustrate the arbitration process by refusing to appoint an arbitrator. When the parties have agreed to institutional arbitration, the institution itself ordinarily acts as the appointing authority. *E.g.*, AAA Commercial Arbitration Rules, Rules R-11(b), R-13(b); ICC Arbitration Rules, art. 12(2), (3), (4), (5) (ICC Court of Arbitration). When there is no administering institution, some other entity must be chosen as the appointing authority. Thus, under the UNCITRAL Arbitration Rules, if the parties have not agreed to an appointing authority, the Permanent Court of Arbitration in The Hague selects the appointing authority. Art. 6(2). As already noted, arbitration statutes generally

provide for a court to act as the appointing authority unless the parties have agreed otherwise.

3.   At several points, the majority refers to the NAF as the "arbitrator" rather than the "arbitration provider" or "arbitration institution." That is incorrect. The NAF was not to serve as the arbitrator under the parties' contract; it was to administer the arbitration and select the arbitrator. Does that clarification affect the majority's legal analysis?

4.   Does it matter why the arbitrator selection mechanism failed? In some cases, the parties simply do not address the issue in their arbitration agreement. In other cases, it is a drafting error — the parties specify a non-existent arbitration provider in their contract. Here, the arbitration provider was unavailable because it settled allegations of wrongdoing by agreeing to stop administering new consumer arbitrations. The dissent argues that under those circumstances the court should refuse to compel arbitration, even if ordinarily it would appoint an arbitrator. Do you agree?

5.   Like the Third Circuit panel in *Khan*, the courts are divided on whether the choice of the NAF as provider was integral to the parties' arbitration agreement. *Compare* Jones v. GGNSC Pierre LLC, 684 F. Supp. 2d 1161, 1168 (D.S.D. 2010) ("Under all of the circumstances, the Court finds no reason to believe the specification of the NAF rules was integral to the Arbitration Agreement. Thus, the Court finds that Section 5 of the Federal Arbitration Act authorizes and requires the Court to appoint an arbitrator."); Meskill v. GGNSC Stillwater Greeley LLC, 2012 U.S. Dist. LEXIS 72798, at *24-*25 (D. Minn. May 25, 2012) (same); Levy v. Cain, Watters & Assocs., 2010 U.S. Dist. LEXIS 9537, at *12 (S.D. Ohio Jan. 15, 2010) (same); *and* Adler v. Dell Inc., 2009 U.S. Dist. LEXIS 112204, at *11 (E.D. Mich. Dec. 3, 2009) (same) *with* Ranzy v. Tijerina, 2010 U.S. App. LEXIS 17872, at **4 (5th Cir. Aug. 25, 2010) (unpublished) (holding that because "designation of NAF as the sole arbitration forum is an integral part of the arbitration agreement," "a federal court need not compel arbitration in a substitute forum if the designated forum becomes unavailable"); Klima v. Evangelical Lutheran Good Samaritan Soc'y, 2011 U.S. Dist. LEXIS 129486, at *19 (D. Kan. Nov. 8, 2011) (same); Carideo v. Dell, Inc., 2009 U.S. Dist. LEXIS 104600, at *18 (W.D. Wash. Oct. 26, 2009) (same); Carr v. Gateway, Inc., 944 N.E.2d 327, 336-37 (Ill. 2011) (same); Rivera v. Am. Gen. Fin'l Servs., Inc., 259 P.3d 803, 815 (N.M. 2011); *and* Apex 1 Processing, Inc. v. Edwards, 962 N.E.2d 663, 667 (Ind. Ct. App. 2012).

PROBLEM 6.4

Barker Business Supplies, Inc. (BBS) and Douglas Distribution Co. (from Problems 6.1 and 6.2) resolve their previous dispute amicably and are able to continue dealing with each other as before. But this newly harmonious state of affairs cannot last. And it doesn't. BBS, complaining that Douglas is failing to carry out its end of the deal, files a demand for arbitration with the AAA and serves a copy on Douglas. Douglas in turn files an answering statement with a counterclaim alleging that it was BBS that was in breach of contract.

The AAA determines that one arbitrator will be appointed and sends the following list of prospective arbitrators to the parties: Mike Scanlan, Ted Marvin,

Jill Carnaway, Simon Bird, and Joan Pinto.

(a) Douglas fails to return the list of arbitrators in time, and the AAA chooses Marvin to serve as arbitrator. Can Douglas then object that Marvin is unacceptable?

(b) Douglas strikes Scanlan and ranks the remaining arbitrators: 1-Pinto; 2-Bird; 3-Marvin; and 4-Carnaway. BBS strikes Pinto and ranks the remaining arbitrators: 1-Scanlan; 2-Marvin; 3-Bird; and 4-Carnaway. Who is likely to be chosen to serve as arbitrator?

(c) Douglas strikes Scanlan, Carnaway, and Marvin as unacceptable. BBS strikes Bird and Pinto. Who is likely to be chosen to serve as arbitrator?

PROBLEM 6.5

Mary Morstan is President of 4-M Co., a New York manufacturer of consumer products. She comes to see you concerning a dispute her company has with Kahn & Co., located in Turkey. Kahn manufacturers components for several of 4-M's biggest selling items. The contract between 4-M and Kahn provides that all disputes arising out of or relating to the contract shall be resolved by arbitration under the UNCITRAL Arbitration Rules. Morstan has several questions about what this means. First, she wants to know how many arbitrators there will be. "If I'm going to be paying their outrageous fees, I hope there will only be one and not three," she says. Second, she wants to know how the arbitrator or arbitrators will be selected. Third, Morstan tells you that although she has repeatedly contacted Kahn, it refuses to participate in the arbitration process. "How are we going to pick an arbitrator if Kahn won't cooperate?" How do you answer her questions?

[B]   Challenging Arbitrators for Partiality

What do parties look for when choosing an arbitrator? Interestingly, one study of labor arbitration suggests that sometimes parties look for pretty much the same thing. In a study of disputes involving police officers under the New Jersey Fire and Police Arbitration Law, Professors Bloom and Cavanagh found that "employer and union preferences tend to be at least moderately similar," with both parties preferring more experienced to less experienced arbitrators, for example. David E. Bloom & Christopher L. Cavanagh, *An Analysis of the Selection of Arbitrators*, 76 AM. ECON. REV. 408, 415, 418 (1986). Indeed, the union and the employer ranked the same prospective arbitrator first in 21 of the 75 arbitrations they studied. On the other hand, some lawyers involved in arbitration suggest that they are trying to get the greatest tactical advantage they can for their client: "[W]hen I am representing a client in an arbitration, what I am really looking for in a party nominated arbitrator is someone with the maximum predisposition towards my client, but with the minimum appearance of bias." Martin Hunter, *Ethics of the International Arbitrator*, 53 ARBITRATION 219, 223 (1987).

Possible sources or indications of bias are numerous, including business, personal, or family ties (present or former) to a party, attorney, witness, or other arbitrator; a significant involvement (financial or otherwise) in the project or dispute; public statements taking a position on the subject matter of the dispute;

participating in the parties' settlement discussions (perhaps as a mediator); and so on. For a thorough listing and analysis, see Doak Bishop & Lucy Reed, *Practical Guidelines for Interviewing, Selecting and Challenging Party-Appointed Arbitrators in International Commercial Arbitration*, 14 ARB. INT'L 395 (1998).

Arbitration rules require prospective arbitrators to disclose "any circumstance likely to give rise to justifiable doubt as to the arbitrator's impartiality or independence, including any bias or any financial or personal interest in the result of the arbitration or any past or present relationship with the parties or their representatives." AAA Commercial Arbitration Rules, Rule R-16(a); see also UNCITRAL Arbitration Rules, art. 11 ("any circumstances likely to give rise to justifiable doubts as to his or her impartiality or independence"); RUAA § 12(a). The disclosure permits the parties to decide whether to challenge the arbitrator or to waive the possible conflict.

An arbitrator's failure to disclose a possible basis for partiality may provide a ground for vacating the award. *See* FAA § 10(a)(2) ("[w]here there was evident partiality or corruption in the arbitrators, or either of them"); UAA § 12(a)(2) ("evident partiality by an arbitrator appointed as a neutral"). Indeed, under the Revised Uniform Arbitration Act, if the arbitrator fails to disclose a "known, direct, and material interest in the outcome of the arbitration proceeding or a known, existing, and substantial relationship with a party," the arbitrator "is presumed to act with evident partiality." RUAA § 12(e). The standard courts use when reviewing awards for evident partiality is not necessarily the same as the standard for disclosure under institutional rules. Indeed, the standard is not altogether clear, as the following cases suggest.

COMMONWEALTH COATINGS CORP. v. CONTINENTAL CASUALTY CO.
United States Supreme Court
393 U.S. 145 (1968)

MR. JUSTICE BLACK delivered the opinion of the Court.

At issue in this case is the question whether elementary requirements of impartiality taken for granted in every judicial proceeding are suspended when the parties agree to resolve a dispute through arbitration.

The petitioner, Commonwealth Coatings Corporation, a subcontractor, sued the sureties on the prime contractor's bond to recover money alleged to be due for a painting job. The contract for painting contained an agreement to arbitrate such controversies. Pursuant to this agreement petitioner appointed one arbitrator, the prime contractor appointed a second, and these two together selected the third arbitrator. This third arbitrator, the supposedly neutral member of the panel, conducted a large business in Puerto Rico, in which he served as an engineering consultant for various people in connection with building construction projects. One of his regular customers in this business was the prime contractor that petitioner sued in this case. This relationship with the prime contractor was in a sense sporadic in that the arbitrator's services were used only from time to time at irregular intervals, and there had been no dealings between them for about a year immediately preceding the arbitration. Nevertheless, the prime contractor's patronage was repeated and significant, involving fees of about $12,000 over a period of four of five years, and the relationship even went so far as to include the rendering of services on the very projects involved in this lawsuit. An arbitration was held, but the facts concerning the close business connections between the third arbitrator and the prime contractor were unknown to petitioner and were never revealed to it by this arbitrator, by the prime contractor, or by anyone else until after an award had been made. Petitioner challenged the award on this ground, among others, but the District Court refused to set aside the award. The Court of Appeals affirmed, we granted certiorari.

In 1925 Congress enacted the United States Arbitration Act, which sets out a comprehensive plan for arbitration of controversies coming under its terms, and both sides here assume that this Federal Act governs this case. Section 10 . . . sets out the conditions upon which awards can be vacated. The two courts below held, however, that § 10 could not be construed in such a way as to justify vacating the award in this case. We disagree and reverse. Section 10 does authorize vacation of an award where it was "procured by corruption, fraud, or undue means" or "where there was evident partiality . . . in the arbitrators." These provisions show a desire of Congress to provide not merely for *any* arbitration but for an impartial one. It is true that petitioner does not charge before us that the third arbitrator was actually guilty of fraud or bias in deciding this case, and we have no reason, apart from the undisclosed business relationship, to suspect him of any improper motives. But neither this arbitrator nor the prime contractor gave to petitioner even an intimation of the close financial relations that had existed between them for a period of years. We have no doubt that if a litigant could show that a foreman of a jury or a judge in a court of justice had, unknown to the litigant, any such relationship, the judgment would be subject to challenge. This is shown beyond doubt by Tumey v. Ohio, 273 U.S. 510 (1927), where this Court held that a conviction could not stand because a small part of the judge's income consisted of court fees collected from convicted defendants. Although in *Tumey* it appeared the amount of the judge's compensation actually depended on whether he decided for one side or the other, that is too small a distinction to allow this manifest violation of the strict morality and fairness Congress would have expected on the part of the arbitrator and the other party in this case. Nor should it be at all relevant, as the Court of Appeals apparently thought it was here, that "the payments received were a very small part of [the arbitrator's] income. . . ." For in *Tumey* the Court held that a decision should be set aside where there is "the slightest pecuniary interest" on the part of the judge, and specifically rejected the State's contention that the compensation involved there was "so small that it is not to be regarded as likely to influence improperly a judicial officer in the discharge of his duty. . . ." Since in the case of courts this is a *constitutional* principle, we can see no basis for refusing to find the same concept in the broad statutory language that governs arbitration proceedings and provides that an award can be set aside on the basis of "evident partiality" or the use of "undue means." It is true that arbitrators cannot sever all their ties with the business world, since they are not expected to get all their income from their work deciding cases, but we should, if anything, be even more scrupulous to safeguard the impartiality of arbitrators than judges, since the former have completely free rein to decide the law as well as the facts and are not subject to appellate review. We can perceive no way in which the effectiveness of the arbitration process will be hampered by the simple requirement that arbitrators disclose to the parties any dealings that might create an impression of possible bias.

While not controlling in this case, § 18 of the Rules of the American Arbitration Association, in effect at the time of this arbitration, is highly significant. It provided as follows:

> "Section 18. Disclosure by Arbitrator of Disqualification — At the time of receiving his notice of appointment, the prospective Arbitrator is requested to disclose any circumstances likely to create a presumption of bias or which he believes might disqualify him as an impartial Arbitrator. Upon receipt of such information, the Tribunal Clerk shall immediately disclose it to the parties, who if willing to proceed under the circumstances disclosed, shall, in writing, so advise the Tribunal Clerk. If either party declines to waive the presumptive disqualification, the vacancy thus created shall be filled in accordance with the applicable provisions of this Rule."

And based on the same principle as this Arbitration Association rule is that part of the 33d Canon of Judicial Ethics which provides:

> "33. Social Relations.

> ". . . [A judge] should, however, in pending or prospective litigation before him be particularly careful to avoid such action as may reasonably tend to awaken the suspicion that his social or business relations or friendships, constitute an element in influencing his judicial conduct."

This rule of arbitration and this canon of judicial ethics rest on the premise that any tribunal permitted by law to try cases and controversies not only must be unbiased but also must avoid even the appearance of bias. We cannot believe that it was the purpose of Congress to authorize litigants to submit their cases and controversies to arbitration boards that might reasonably be thought biased against one litigant and favorable to another.

Reversed.

Mr. Justice White, with whom Mr. Justice Marshall joins, concurring.

While I am glad to join my Brother Black's opinion in this case, I desire to make these additional remarks. The Court does not decide today that arbitrators are to be held to the standards of judicial decorum of Article III judges, or indeed of any judges. It is often because they are men of affairs, not apart from but of the marketplace, that they are effective in their adjudicatory function. This does not mean the judiciary must overlook outright chicanery in giving effect to their awards; that would be an abdication of our responsibility. But it does mean that arbitrators are not automatically disqualified by a business relationship with the parties before them if both parties are informed of the relationship in advance, or if they are unaware of the facts but the relationship is trivial. I see no reason automatically to disqualify the best informed and most capable potential arbitrators.

The arbitration process functions best when an amicable and trusting atmosphere is preserved and there is voluntary compliance with the decree, without need for judicial enforcement. This end is best served by establishing an atmosphere of frankness at the outset, through disclosure by the arbitrator of any financial transactions which he has had or is negotiating with either of the parties. In many cases the arbitrator might believe the business relationship to be so insubstantial that to make a point of revealing it would suggest he is indeed easily swayed, and perhaps a partisan of that party. But if the law requires the disclosure, no such imputation can arise. And it is far better that the relationship be disclosed at the outset, when the parties are free to reject the arbitrator or accept him with knowledge of the relationship and continuing faith in his objectivity, than to have the relationship come to light after the arbitration, when a suspicious or disgruntled party can seize on it as a pretext for invalidating the award. The judiciary should minimize its role in arbitration as judge of the arbitrator's impartiality. That role is best consigned to the parties, who are the architects of their own arbitration process, and are far better informed of the prevailing ethical standards and reputations within their business.

Of course, an arbitrator's business relationships may be diverse indeed, involving more or less remote commercial connections with great numbers of people. He cannot be expected to provide the parties with his complete and unexpurgated business biography. But it is enough for present purposes to hold, as the Court does, that where the arbitrator has a substantial interest in a firm which has done more than trivial business with a party, that fact must be disclosed. If arbitrators err on the side of disclosure, as they should, it will not be difficult for courts to identify those undisclosed relationships which are too insubstantial to warrant vacating an award.

Mr. Justice Fortas, with whom Mr. Justice Harlan and Mr. Justice Stewart join, dissenting.

I dissent and would affirm the judgment.

. . .

The third arbitrator is a leading and respected consulting engineer who has performed services for "most of the contractors in Puerto Rico." He was well known to petitioner's counsel and they were personal friends. Petitioner's counsel candidly admitted that if he had been told about the arbitrator's prior relationship "I don't think I would have objected because I know Mr. Capacete [the arbitrator]."

Clearly, the District Judge's conclusion, affirmed by the Court of Appeals for the First Circuit, was correct, that "the arbitrators conducted fair, impartial hearings; that they reached a proper determination of the issues before them, and that plaintiff's objections represent a 'situation where the losing party to an arbitration is now clutching at straws in an attempt to avoid the results of the arbitration to which it became a party.' "

The Court nevertheless orders that the arbitration award be set aside. It uses this singularly inappropriate case to announce a *per se* rule that in my judgment has no basis in the applicable statute or jurisprudential principles: that, regardless of the agreement between the parties, if an arbitrator has any prior business relationship with one of the parties of which he fails to inform the other party, however innocently, the arbitration award is always subject to being set aside. This is so even where the award is unanimous; where there is no suggestion that the nondisclosure indicates partiality or bias; and where it is conceded that there was in fact no irregularity, unfairness, bias, or partiality. Until the decision today, it has not been the law that an arbitrator's failure to disclose a prior business relationship with one of the parties will compel the setting aside of an arbitration award regardless of the circumstances.

I agree that failure of an arbitrator to volunteer information about business dealings with one party will, prima facie, support a claim of partiality or bias.

But where there is no suggestion that the nondisclosure was calculated, and where the complaining party disclaims any imputation of partiality, bias, or misconduct, the presumption clearly is overcome.

I do not believe that it is either necessary, appropriate, or permissible to rule, as the Court does, that, regardless of the facts, innocent failure to volunteer information constitutes the "evident partiality" necessary under § 10(b) of the Arbitration Act to set aside an award. "Evident partiality" means what it says: conduct — or at least an attitude or disposition — by the arbitrator favoring one party rather than the other. This case demonstrates that to rule otherwise may be a palpable injustice, since all agree that the arbitrator was innocent of either "evident partiality" or anything approaching it.

Arbitration is essentially consensual and practical. The United States Arbitration Act is obviously designed to protect the integrity of the process with a minimum of insistence upon set formulae and rules. The Court applies to this process rules applicable to judges and not to a system characterized by dealing on faith and reputation for reliability. Such formalism is not contemplated by the Act nor is it warranted in a case where no claim is made of partiality, of unfairness, or of misconduct in any degree.

POSITIVE SOFTWARE SOLUTIONS, INC. v. NEW CENTURY MORTGAGE CORP.

United States Court of Appeals for the Fifth Circuit (en banc)
476 F.3d 278 (2007)

EDITH H. JONES, Chief Judge . . . :

The court reconsidered this case en banc in order to determine whether an arbitration award must be vacated for "evident partiality," 9 U.S.C. § 10(a)(2), where an arbitrator failed to disclose a prior professional association with a member of one of the law firms that engaged him. We conclude that the Federal Arbitration Act ("FAA") does not mandate the extreme remedy of vacatur for nondisclosure of a trivial past association, and we reverse the district court's contrary judgment . . . .

BACKGROUND

The facts are undisputed. In January 2001, New Century Mortgage Corporation ("New Century") licensed an automated software support program from Positive Software Solutions, Inc. ("Positive Software"). In December 2002, during negotiations for a renewal of that license, Positive Software alleged that New Century copied the program in violation of the parties' agreement and applicable copyright law. Positive Software then filed this lawsuit against New Century in the Northern District of Texas alleging breach of contract, misappropriation of trade secrets, misappropriation of intellectual property, copyright infringement, fraud, and other causes of action. Positive Software sought specific performance, money damages, and injunctive relief.

In April 2003, the district court granted Positive Software's motion to preliminarily enjoin New Century from using the program and, pursuant to the parties' contract, submitted the matter to arbitration. Following American Arbitration Association ("AAA") procedures, the AAA provided the parties with a list of potential arbitrators and asked the parties to rank the candidates. After reviewing biographical information, the parties selected Peter Shurn to arbitrate the case, as he had the highest combined ranking. The AAA contacted Shurn about serving as an arbitrator, and he agreed, after stating that he had nothing to disclose regarding past relationships with either party or their counsel.

After a seven-day hearing, Shurn issued an eighty-six page written ruling, concluding that New Century did not infringe Positive Software's copyrights, did not misappropriate trade secrets, did not breach the contract, and did not defraud or conspire against Positive Software. He ordered that Positive Software take nothing on its claims and granted New Century $11,500 on its counterclaims and $1.5 million in attorney's fees.

Upon losing the arbitration, Positive Software conducted a detailed investigation of Shurn's background. It discovered that several years earlier, Shurn and his former law firm, Arnold, White, & Durkee ("Arnold White"), had represented the same party as New Century's counsel, Susman Godfrey, L.L.P., in a patent litigation between Intel Corporation and Cyrix Corporation ("the Intel litigation"). One of Susman Godfrey's attorneys in the New Century arbitration, Ophelia Camina, had been involved in the Intel litigation.

The Intel litigation involved six different lawsuits in the early 1990s. Intel was represented by seven law firms and at least thirty-four lawyers, including Shurn and Camina. The dispute involved none of the parties to the arbitration. Camina participated in representing Intel in three of the lawsuits from August 1991 until July 1992, although her name remained on the pleadings in one of the cases until June 1993. In September 1992, Shurn, along with twelve other Arnold White attorneys, entered an appearance in two of the three cases on which Camina worked. Although their names appeared together on pleadings, Shurn and Camina never attended or participated in any meetings, telephone calls, hearings, depositions, or trials together.

Positive Software filed a motion to vacate the arbitration award . . . . In September 2004, the district court granted Positive Software's motion and vacated the award, finding that Shurn failed to disclose "a significant prior relationship with New Century's counsel," thus creating an appearance of partiality requiring vacatur. New Century appealed, and a panel of this court affirmed the district court's vacatur on the ground that the prior relationship "might have conveyed an impression of possible partiality to a reasonable person." Neither the district court nor the appellate panel found that Shurn was actually biased toward New Century. This court granted New Century's petition for rehearing en banc.

DISCUSSION

To assure that arbitration serves as an efficient and cost-effective alternative to litigation, and to hold parties to their agreements to arbitrate, the FAA narrowly restricts judicial review of arbitrators' awards. The ground of vacatur alleged here is that "there was evident partiality" in the arbitrator. The meaning of evident partiality is discernible definitionally and as construed by the Supreme Court and a number of our sister circuits.

On its face, "evident partiality" conveys a stern standard. Partiality means bias, while "evident" is defined as "clear to the vision or understanding" and is synonymous with manifest, obvious, and apparent. Webster's Ninth New Collegiate Dictionary 430 (1985). The statutory language, with which we always begin, seems to require upholding arbitral awards unless bias was clearly evident in the decisionmakers.

The panel decision here disagreed with the straight forward interpretation, however, and concluded that, in "a nondisclosure case in which the parties chose the arbitrator," the "arbitrator selected by the parties displays evident partiality by the very failure to disclose facts that might create a reasonable impression of the arbitrator's partiality." The panel acknowledged a lack of any actual bias in this award even as it substituted a reasonable impression of partiality standard for "evident" partiality in cases of an arbitrator's nondisclosure to the parties. The panel believed this different standard to be required by the Supreme Court's decision in Commonwealth Coatings Corp. v. Continental Cas. Co. . . .

How *Commonwealth Coatings* guides this court is a critical issue. Reasonable minds can agree that *Commonwealth Coatings*, like many plurality-plus Supreme Court decisions, is not pellucid. . . . Justice Black delivered the opinion of the Court and imposed "the simple requirement that arbitrators disclose to the parties any dealings that might create an impression of possible bias." He noted that, while arbitrators are not expected to sever all ties with the business world, courts must be scrupulous in safeguarding the impartiality of arbitrators, who are given the ability to decide both the facts and the law and whose decisions are not subject to appellate review. Thus, arbitrators "not only must be unbiased but also must avoid even the appearance of bias," in order to maintain confidence in the arbitration system.

Justice White, the fifth vote in the case, together with Justice Marshall, purported to be "glad to join" Justice Black's opinion, but he wrote to make "additional remarks." Justice White emphasized that "[t]he Court does not decide today that arbitrators are to be held to the standards of judicial decorum of Article

III judges, or indeed of any judges." Indeed, Justice White wrote that arbitrators are not "automatically disqualified by a business relationship with the parties before them if . . . [the parties] are unaware of the facts but the relationship is trivial." While supporting a policy of disclosure by arbitrators to enhance the selection process, Justice White also concluded, in a practical vein, that an arbitrator "cannot be expected to provide the parties with his complete and unexpurgated business biography." His opinion fully envisions upholding awards when arbitrators fail to disclose insubstantial relationships.

If one lays primary emphasis on Justice White's statement that he was "glad to join" the plurality, his opinion can be deemed reconcilable with that of Justice Black. Only in that event is the plurality opinion binding on lower courts.

Another compelling reading of the opinions is also possible, however. Justice Black's opinion uses an egregious set of facts as the vehicle to require broad disclosure of "any dealings that might create an impression of possible bias." Justice White, for his part, hews closely to the facts and finds it "enough for present purposes to hold, as the Court does, that where the arbitrator has a *substantial interest* in a firm which has done *more than trivial business* with a party, that fact must be disclosed." (emphasis added). Justice White, thus read, supports ample but not unrealistic disclosure, and he supports a cautious approach to vacatur for nondisclosure. His "joinder" is magnanimous but significantly qualified.

The latter reading is more persuasive, because it accords scope to the full White opinion, unlike the view that focuses on the introductory "glad to join" sentence. Thus, Justice White's concurrence, pivotal to the judgment, is based on a narrower ground than Justice Black's opinion, and it becomes the Court's effective ratio decidendi.

A majority of circuit courts have concluded that Justice White's opinion did not lend majority status to the plurality opinion. While these courts' interpretations of *Commonwealth Coatings* may differ in particulars, they all agree that nondisclosure alone does not require vacatur of an arbitral award for evident partiality. An arbitrator's failure to disclose must involve a significant compromising connection to the parties.

. . .

Only the Ninth Circuit has interpreted *Commonwealth Coatings*, as the panel majority did, to de-emphasize Justice White's narrowing language. See Schmitz v. Zilveti, 20 F.3d 1043 (9th Cir. 1994). In *Schmitz*, the court criticized case law suggesting "that an impression of bias is sufficient while an appearance [of bias] is not." *Commonwealth Coatings*, it held, does not merit such a "hairline distinction." *Schmitz* not only interpreted *Commonwealth Coatings* to mandate a "reasonable impression of bias" standard in nondisclosure cases but went on to vacate an arbitral award where the arbitrator had not himself been aware of the potential conflict and had failed to undertake due diligence to ascertain and then disclose it to the parties.[4] Even if one ignores the extension of *Commonwealth Coatings* by

---

[4] In *Schmitz*, the arbitrator's law firm previously had represented Prudential Insurance Co., the parent of Pru-Bache Securities, the prevailing party in the arbitration. The representation involved at

Schmitz, the undisclosed relationship between the arbitrator's firm and Pru-Bache's parent company was more current, concrete and financially meaningful than the co-counsel relationship in the present case. *Schmitz* is an outlier that lends little support to Positive Software.

As we have concluded, the better interpretation of *Commonwealth Coatings* is that which reads Justice White's opinion holistically. The resulting standard is that in nondisclosure cases, an award may not be vacated because of a trivial or insubstantial prior relationship between the arbitrator and the parties to the proceeding. The "reasonable impression of bias" standard is thus interpreted practically rather than with utmost rigor.

According to this interpretation of *Commonwealth Coatings*, the outcome of this case is clear: Shurn's failure to disclose a trivial former business relationship does not require vacatur of the award. The essential charge of bias is that the arbitrator, Peter Shurn, worked on the same litigation as did Ophelia Camina, counsel for one of the parties. They represented Intel in protracted patent litigation that lasted from 1990 to 1996. Camina and Shurn each signed the same ten pleadings, but they never met or spoke to each other before the arbitration. They were two of thirty-four lawyers, and from two of seven firms, that represented Intel during the lawsuit, which ended at least seven years before the instant arbitration.

No case we have discovered in research or briefs has come close to vacating an arbitration award for nondisclosure of such a slender connection between the arbitrator and a party's counsel. In fact, courts have refused vacatur where the undisclosed connections are much stronger. See, e.g., Montez v. Prudential Sec., Inc., 260 F.3d 980, 982, 984 (8th Cir. 2001) (no vacatur; as general counsel for a company, arbitrator had employed sixty-eight attorneys, paying them $2.8 million in fees, from the law firm representing one of the parties in the arbitration); ANR Coal [Co., Inc. v. Cogentrix of N.C., Inc., 173 F.3d 493, 495-96] (4th Cir. 1999) (no vacatur; arbitrator's law firm represented company that indirectly caused the dispute in the arbitration by buying less from the defendant, who in turn sought to buy less from the plaintiff); Al-Harbi v. Citibank, N.A., 85 F.3d 680, 682, 318 U.S. App. D.C. 114 (D.C. Cir. 1996) (no vacatur where arbitrator's former law firm represented party to the arbitration on unrelated matters); Lifecare Int'l, Inc. v. CD Med., Inc., 68 F.3d 429, 432-34 & n.3 (11th Cir. 1995) (no vacatur where arbitrator had memorialized prior scheduling dispute with an attorney from the law firm representing one of the parties and mentioned it eighteen months later at the arbitration; arbitrator also failed to disclose that he became "of counsel" to a law firm the prevailing party had interviewed for the purpose of obtaining representation in the instant dispute and that had reviewed the contract involved in the case two years prior; court found this, at best, showed a "remote, uncertain, and speculative partiality"); Health Servs. Mgmt. Corp. v. Hughes, 975 F.2d 1253, 1255, 1264 (7th Cir. 1992) (arbitrator knew one of the parties, had worked in the same office with him twenty years ago, and saw him about once a year since; the court found this relationship "minimal" and

---

least nineteen cases over a thirty-five year period, including a case that ended less than two years before the arbitration. The arbitrator had reviewed documents naming the parent company, but did not run a conflict check for the parent or disclose any of his firm's earlier representations of the parent company prior to the arbitration.

insufficient to vacate); Merit Ins. [Co. v. Leatherby Ins. Co., 714 F.2d 673, 677, 680 (7th Cir. 1983)] (no vacatur; arbitrator had worked directly under the president and principal stockholder of one of the parties for three years, ending fourteen years prior to the arbitration; the Seventh Circuit noted that "[t]ime cools emotions, whether of gratitude or resentment"); Ormsbee Dev. Co. [v. Grace, 668 F.2d 1140, 1149-50 (10th Cir. 1982)] (no vacatur where arbitrator and law firm representing a party had clients in common; requiring vacatur under such facts would "request that potential neutral arbitrators sever all their ties with the business world" (internal quotation omitted)).

The relationship in this case pales in comparison to those in which courts have granted vacatur. See, e.g., *Commonwealth Coatings* (business relationship between arbitrator and party was "repeated and significant"; the party to the arbitration was one of the arbitrator's "regular customers"; "the relationship even went so far as to include the rendering of services on the very projects involved in this lawsuit"); Olson v. Merrill Lynch, Pierce, Fenner & Smith, Inc., 51 F.3d 157, 159 (8th Cir. 1995) (arbitrator was a high-ranking officer in a company that had a substantial ongoing business relationship with one of the parties); Schmitz, 20 F.3d at 1044 (arbitrator's law firm represented parent company of a party for decades, including within two years of the arbitration); Morelite [Constr. Corp. v. N.Y. Dist. Council Carpenters Benefit Funds, 748 F.2d 79, 81 (2d Cir. 1984)] (arbitrator's father was General President of the union involved in the arbitrated dispute).

Finally, even if Justice White's "joinder" is not read as a limitation on Justice Black's opinion in *Commonwealth Coatings*, and the controlling opinion emphatically requires arbitrators to "disclose to the parties any dealings that might create an impression of possible bias," we cannot find the standard breached in this case. The facts of *Commonwealth Coatings* are easily distinguishable. In *Commonwealth Coatings*, the arbitrator and a party had a "repeated and significant" business relationship. The relationship involved fees of about $12,000 paid to the arbitrator by the party, extended over a period of four or five years, ended only one year before the arbitration, and even included the rendering of services on the very projects involved in the arbitration before him. Such a relationship bears little resemblance to the tangential, limited, and stale contacts between Shurn and Camina. Nothing in *Commonwealth Coatings* requires vacatur for the undisclosed relationship in this case.

CONCLUSION

Awarding vacatur in situations such as this would seriously jeopardize the finality of arbitration. Just as happened here, losing parties would have an incentive to conduct intensive, after-the-fact investigations to discover the most trivial of relationships, most of which they likely would not have objected to if disclosure had been made. Expensive satellite litigation over nondisclosure of an arbitrator's "complete and unexpurgated business biography" will proliferate. Ironically, the "mere appearance" standard would make it easier for a losing party to challenge an arbitration award for nondisclosure than for actual bias.

Moreover, requiring vacatur based on a mere appearance of bias for nondisclosure would hold arbitrators to a higher ethical standard than federal Article III judges. In his concurrence, Justice White noted that the Court did not decide whether "arbitrators are to be held to the standards of judicial decorum of Article III judges, or indeed of any judges." This cannot mean that arbitrators are held to a higher standard than Article III judges. Had this same relationship occurred between an Article III judge and the same lawyer, neither disclosure nor disqualification would have been forced or even suggested. While it is true that disclosure of prior significant contacts and business dealings between a prospective arbitrator and the parties furthers informed selection,[5] it is not true, as Justice White's opinion perceptively explains, that "the best informed and most capable potential arbitrators" should be automatically disqualified (and their awards nullified) by failure to inform the parties of trivial relationships.

Finally, requiring vacatur on these attenuated facts would rob arbitration of one of its most attractive features apart from speed and finality — expertise. Arbitration would lose the benefit of specialized knowledge, because the best lawyers and professionals, who normally have the longest lists of potential connections to disclose, have no need to risk blemishes on their reputations from post-arbitration lawsuits attacking them as biased.

Neither the FAA nor the Supreme Court, nor predominant case law, nor sound policy countenances vacatur of FAA arbitral awards for nondisclosure by an arbitrator unless it creates a concrete, not speculative impression of bias. Arbitration may have flaws, but this is not one of them. The draconian remedy of vacatur is only warranted upon nondisclosure that involves a significant compromising relationship. This case does not come close to meeting this standard.

The judgment of the district court is REVERSED, and the case is REMANDED FOR FURTHER PROCEEDINGS.

WIENER, Circuit Judge, Specially Concurring in Judge Reavley's dissent . . . . :

As I wholeheartedly concur in Judge Reavley's dissent, I write separately only to add a perspective that I find helpful in analyzing this case and demonstrating that Judge Reavley has gotten it right. I refer in general to the key differences between arbitration under the FAA and litigation in federal court; I refer in particular to one difference that is of prime significance in this case, viz., the disparate ways that the decision maker — an Article III judge on the one hand and an arbitrator on the other — is selected, and the unique role of the potential arbitrator's unredacted disclosure of his relationships with the parties and their counsel to ensure selection of an impartial arbitrator. These general and particular differences underscore why such full and fair disclosure by a potential arbitrator of every conceivable relationship with a party or counsel, however slight, is a prerequisite. No relationship with a party or a lawyer is too minimal to warrant its disclosure, even if, in the end, it might be deemed to be too minimal to warrant disqualification. Such an

---

[5] The American Arbitration Association ("AAA"), whose rules governed this proceeding, requires broad prophylactic disclosure of "any circumstance likely to affect impartiality or create an appearance of partiality," so that parties may rely on the integrity of the selection process for arbitrators. Whether Shurn's nondisclosure ran afoul of the AAA rules, however, is not before us and plays no role in applying the federal standard embodied in the FAA.

evaluation by the potential arbitrator, and any withholding of information based on it, are simply not calls that he is authorized to make, yet ones that Lawyer Shurn obviously made.

.   .   .

In exchange for the actual or perceived economies of time, money, expertise and confidentiality, the parties to arbitration alone are responsible for who it is that will decide their fates. Subject to only relatively insignificant limitations, the parties (or in the case of panels, each party's selected arbitrator) have virtually absolute control over accepting or rejecting a nominee for the role of decision maker. It cannot therefore be left to the fox, who is the potential arbitrator, to guard the arbitration henhouse, secretly identifying to himself alone all "prior or present relationships," then just as secretly deciding which are worthy of disclosure and which are not. On the contrary, avoidance of partiality in the selection of the arbitrator can be achieved only if, in discharging his duty of disclosure, the potential arbitrator objectively disgorges absolutely every conceivable fact of prior or present relationships with parties or counsel, regardless of how tenuous or remote they might seem to him. He must leave to the parties the value judgment as to which (if any) among those fully disclosed facts constitutes a basis for rejecting the potential arbitrator for bias or the appearance of bias. Only of and after that is done can disclosure translate into disqualification or rejection.

.   .   .

REAVLEY, Circuit Judge, dissenting . . . :

In 1968 the Supreme Court held that an arbitral award could not stand where the arbitrator had failed to disclose a past relationship that might give the impression of possible partiality. The Court has never changed that holding; it is the law that rules us today. But the majority of this court disapprove of that law because they prefer to protect arbitrators and their awards when they fail to disclose prior relationships with parties or counsel. They therefore change the law for this case and, to make it appear as if their transgression does not matter, trivialize their report of the past relationship. I dissent because this court may not overrule a decision of the Supreme Court.

.   .   .

The majority opinion manages to substitute actual bias, or the reasonable impression of bias, or concrete impression of bias for the Supreme Court's ruling that dealings that might create only an impression of possible bias must be disclosed. And it purports to join other circuits to hold that non-disclosure alone does not require vacatur of an arbitral award. If the circuit courts could overrule the Supreme Court, the majority might be on a bit firmer ground, because the *Commonwealth Coatings* ruling has not been well received by some of the circuit courts. . . .

.   .   .

While I can understand the desire to protect the finality of arbitration awards and avoid a return to extended court expense and delay, this does not justify evading the law of the Supreme Court by misstating it or by avoiding it by bleaching the evidence of possible partiality. Nor should we miss the need to promote the impartiality of arbitrators in this time when that is the favored method of dispute resolution. Influence can so easily corrupt the decision-making process even when it is not recognized by the magistrate or arbitrator himself. And to prove bias or improper influence is rarely possible. It is imperative that we not allow even the good faith or memory of the potential arbitrator to control the disclosure decision for, as the Justices made clear in *Commonwealth Coatings*, it is the protection and reassurance of the party that matters most.

. . .

NOTES

1. What is the legal standard for "evident partiality" after *Commonwealth Coatings*?

2. Justice Black takes the position that arbitrators should be held to higher standards of impartiality than judges. His view is that the limited court review of arbitration awards makes more stringent standards appropriate. Judge Richard Posner takes the opposite position:

> The ethical obligations of arbitrators can be understood only by reference to the fundamental differences between adjudication by arbitrators and adjudication by judges and jurors. No one is forced to arbitrate a commercial dispute unless he has consented by contract to arbitrate. The voluntary nature of commercial arbitration is an important safeguard for the parties that is missing in the case of the courts. Courts are coercive, not voluntary, agencies, and the American people's traditional fear of government oppression has resulted in a judicial system in which impartiality is prized above expertise. Thus, people who arbitrate do so because they prefer a tribunal knowledgeable about the subject matter of their dispute to a generalist court with its austere impartiality but limited knowledge of subject matter. . . .
>
> There is a tradeoff between impartiality and expertise. The expert adjudicator is more likely than a judge or juror not only to be precommitted to a particular substantive position but to know or have heard of the parties (or if the parties are organizations, their key people). . . . The different weighting of impartiality and expertise in arbitration compared to adjudication is dramatically illustrated by the practice whereby each party appoints one of the arbitrators to be his representative rather than a genuine umpire. No one would dream of having a judicial panel composed of one part-time judge and two representatives of the parties, but that is the standard arbitration panel . . . .

Merit Ins. Co. v. Leatherby Ins. Co., 714 F.2d 673, 679 (7th Cir. 1983). Justice Black certainly is correct that standards of impartiality are to some extent a substitute for appellate review. Conversely, Judge Posner no doubt is right that at least some parties choose arbitration because of the greater expertise of arbitrators, and that "[t]here is a tradeoff between impartiality and expertise." Who, in your view, gets the better of the argument?

3. As these cases suggest, determination of when failure to disclose potential conflicts requires vacating an arbitration award depends to a large degree on the facts of each case. What are the key variables? One court has identified the following four factors to be considered:

> (1) the extent and character of the personal interest, pecuniary or otherwise, of the arbitrator in the proceeding; (2) the directness of the relationship between the arbitrator and the person he is alleged to favor; (3) the connection of that relationship to the arbitration; and (4) the proximity in time between the relationship and the arbitration proceeding.

ANR Coal Co. v. Cogentrix of North Carolina, Inc., 173 F.3d 493, 500 (4th Cir.), *cert. denied*, 528 U.S. 877 (1999). Can you reconcile *Commonwealth Coatings* and *Positive Software Solutions* on the basis of these factors?

4. The California Judicial Council has promulgated ethics standards applicable to all neutral arbitrators in California. The standards (reprinted in the Documentary Supplement) require extensive and controversial disclosures by arbitrators of possible conflicts of interest. *See also* Cal. Civ. Proc. Code §§ 1281.85, 1281.9, & 1286.2(a). The NASD and the New York Stock Exchange challenged the application of the ethics standards to securities arbitration proceedings, arguing that the rules were preempted by the FAA and the federal securities laws. Both the Ninth Circuit and the California Supreme Court have held that the ethics standards as applied in securities arbitrations are preempted by the federal securities laws. Credit Suisse First Boston Corp. v. Grunwald, 400 F.3d 1119 (9th Cir. 2005); Jevne v. Superior Court, 111 P.3d 954 (Cal. 2005).

Subsequently, in Ovitz v. Schulman, 35 Cal. Rptr. 3d 117 (Cal. App. 2005), the California Court of Appeal rejected an FAA preemption challenge to the state ethics standards (as applied to vacate an arbitration award for nondisclosure under Cal. Civ. Proc. Code § 1286.2(a)(6)(A)), reasoning that (1) sections 10 and 12 of the FAA by their terms apply only in federal court, not state court; (2) "section 1286.2(a)(6)(A) does not undermine the enforceability of arbitration agreements" — instead, "[i]f an award is vacated, the result is not a preclusion of further arbitration, but rather a new arbitration held in accordance with the disclosure requirements"; and (3) the statute "does not reflect hostility to arbitration" but rather "seeks to enhance both the appearance and reality of fairness in arbitration proceedings, thereby instilling public confidence." *Id.* at 132-36. You may wish to consider the holding in *Ovitz* when thinking about preemption and vacatur of arbitration awards in Chapter 7.

5. The American Arbitration Association, the American Bar Association, and the International Bar Association have promulgated ethical codes for arbitrators. *See* AAA & ABA, Code of Ethics for Arbitrators in Commercial Disputes; IBA, Ethics for International Arbitrators; *see also* IBA, Guidelines on Conflicts of Interest in International Arbitration, all in the Documentary Supplement. As the IBA states, "[t]he rules cannot be directly binding either on arbitrators, or on the parties themselves, unless they are adopted by agreement." *See* IBA, Introductory

Note to Ethics for International Arbitrators. Nonetheless, they provide important sources on what constitutes ethical (and unethical) conduct by arbitrators.

6.   Are there any exceptions to the requirement that arbitrators be impartial and independent? One possible exception, at least in domestic arbitrations in the United States, is for party-appointed arbitrators — those arbitrators, on a three-member panel, who are selected by only one of the parties. In reversing a district court judgment vacating an arbitration award for evident partiality, the Seventh Circuit (Easterbrook, J.), had this to say about the traditional approach to neutrality of party-appointed arbitrators in the United States:

> As far as we can see, this is the first time since the Federal Arbitration Act was enacted in 1925 that a federal court has set aside an award because a party-appointed arbitrator on a tripartite panel, as opposed to a neutral, displayed "evident partiality." The lack of precedent is unsurprising, because in the main party-appointed arbitrators are *supposed* to be advocates. In labor arbitration a union may name as its arbitrator the business manager of the local union, and the employer its vice-president for labor relations. Yet no one believes that the predictable loyalty of these designees spoils the award. This is so because the parties are entitled to waive the protection of § 10(a)(2), as they can waive almost any other statutory entitlement. The Federal Arbitration Act makes arbitration agreements enforceable to the same extent as other contracts, so courts must "enforce privately negotiated agreements to arbitrate, like other contracts, in accordance with their terms." *Volt Information Sciences, Inc. v. Stanford University.*

> Parties are free to choose for themselves to what lengths they will go in quest of impartiality. Section 10(a)(2) just states the presumptive rule, subject to variation by mutual consent. Industry arbitration, the modern law merchant, often uses panels composed of industry insiders, the better to understand the trade's norms of doing business and the consequences of proposed lines of decision. The more experience the panel has, and the smaller the number of repeat players, the more likely it is that the panel will contain some actual or potential friends, counselors, or business rivals of the parties. Yet all participants may think the expertise-impartiality tradeoff worthwhile; the Arbitration Act does not fasten on every industry the model of the disinterested generalist judge. To the extent that an agreement entitles parties to select interested (even beholden) arbitrators, § 10(a)(2) has no role to play.

Sphere Drake Insurance, Ltd. v. All American Life Insurance Co, 307 F.3d 617, 620 (7th Cir. 2002).

The AAA/ABA Code of Ethics for Arbitrators rejects the traditional American approach to party-appointed arbitrators, instead "establish[ing] a presumption of neutrality for all arbitrators, including party-appointed arbitrators, which applies unless the parties' agreement, the arbitration rules agreed to by the parties or applicable laws provide otherwise." *See* Code of Ethics for Arbitrators in Commercial Disputes, Note on Neutrality. The American Arbitration Association thereafter revised its Commercial Arbitration Rules to reflect such a presumption. *See* AAA,

Commercial Arbitration Rules, Rule R-17(a)(iii).

7. In international arbitration, by contrast, party-appointed arbitrators are always expected to be neutral. *E.g.*, IBA, Ethics for International Arbitrators, §§ 5.1, 5.3. Nonetheless, a party can ethically have some ex parte contacts with a neutral party-appointed arbitrator. First, the IBA Ethics rules permit a limited pre-appointment interview with a prospective arbitrator, "provided that such enquiries are designed to determine his suitability and availability for the appointment and provided that the merits of the case are not discussed." § 5.1. In addition, party-appointed arbitrators can obtain the views of the appointing party on possible candidates for the third, presiding arbitrator. § 5.2; *see also* AAA/ICDR Int'l Rules, art. 7(2) (no ex parte communications except to "advise the candidate of the general nature of the controversy and of the anticipated proceedings and to discuss the candidate's qualifications, availability or independence in relation to the parties, or to discuss the suitability of candidates for selection as a third arbitrator"). Otherwise, ex parte communications between arbitrators and parties are to be avoided.

How effective is the requirement of neutrality for party-appointed arbitrators, do you think? For a critical view, see Jan Paulsson, *Moral Hazard in International Dispute Resolution*, 25 ICSID Rev.: Foreign Inv. L.J. 339 (2010) (arguing that "unilateral appointments are inconsistent with the fundamental premise of arbitration: *mutual* confidence in arbitrators" and pointing out that "dissenting opinions [in international commercial arbitrations] are almost invariably (in more than 95% of the cases) written by the arbitrator nominated by the losing party").

PROBLEM 6.6

Which of the following facts or relationships would provide a basis for challenging an arbitrator under institutional arbitration rules? Which should be disclosed by the arbitrator? Which, if not disclosed, constitutes "evident partiality" within the meaning of the Federal Arbitration Act? In addition to the preceding cases, you should consider the Code of Ethics for Arbitrators in Commercial Disputes, Ethics for International Arbitrators, and the Guidelines on Conflicts of Interest in International Arbitration, reprinted in the Documentary Supplement.

(a) The arbitrator is an employee of one of the parties to the arbitration.

(b) The arbitrator is a partner in a law firm that regularly represents a subsidiary of one of the parties, but did not know of this representation.

(c) Same as (b), except that the law firm represented the subsidiary only on three minor matters unrelated to the arbitration, and the most recent was five years ago.

(d) The arbitrator is the president of a bank that has loaned a sizable sum of money to one of the parties.

(e) The arbitrator owns 100 shares of stock in one of the parties, which is a large publicly-held corporation.

(f) The arbitrator was an employee of the president of one of the parties ten years ago, but the two have had little contact since then.

(g) The arbitrator is a law school classmate of the attorney for one of the parties and socializes with the attorney once or twice a year.

(h) The arbitrator is a partner in a law firm that regularly represents one of the parties to the arbitration, and the arbitrator is appointed by that party to serve in a domestic arbitration as a member of a three-arbitrator panel.

(i) Same as (h) except that the arbitration is an international arbitration.

(j) The arbitrator served as a mediator for the parties in this dispute. (This one differs from the others because it is a relationship of which both parties obviously would be aware.)

————

Who decides a party's challenge to an arbitrator? Arbitration rules generally provide for the administering institution or other appointing authority to decide the challenge. AAA Commercial Arbitration Rules, Rule R-17(b); UNCITRAL Arbitration Rules, Art. 12(1). Under the UNCITRAL Model Law, the default rule is for the arbitral tribunal to decide the challenge. Art. 13(2). If the tribunal rejects the challenge, the party may request the appointing authority (usually a court) to decide the challenge, with no right to appeal. Art. 13(3). Such a pre-award court challenge is not available under the FAA, as the following case holds.

AVIALL, INC. v. RYDER SYSTEM, INC.
United States Court of Appeals for the Second Circuit
110 F.3d 892 (1997)

Lumbard, Circuit Judge:

Plaintiff-appellant Aviall is a former wholly-owned subsidiary of defendant-appellee Ryder. Following a spin-off of Aviall to Ryder's shareholders, Aviall disputed Ryder's allocation of certain pension-related assets and liabilities in the spin-off. Pursuant to the contract governing the spin-off, Aviall sought arbitration of the dispute before KPMG Peat Marwick ("KPMG"), Ryder's outside auditor. Subsequently, however, Aviall brought this suit in the Southern District of New York . . . to disqualify KPMG as arbitrator, claiming that KPMG was partial to Ryder on account of its business relationship with Ryder, and that KPMG had assisted Ryder in preparing for the arbitration. [The district judge] granted summary judgment to Ryder, and Aviall appeals. We affirm.

. . .

On appeal, Aviall argues that KPMG's relationship with Ryder as its regular outside auditor, as well as KPMG's conduct in connection with this dispute since it arose, demonstrate partiality which disqualifies KPMG from arbitrating the dispute. We agree with the district court that neither KPMG's relationship with Ryder, nor its conduct in connection therewith, is a valid ground for removing KPMG before an award has been rendered.

This dispute is governed by the FAA. . . . Although the FAA provides that a court can vacate an award "[w]here there was evident partiality or corruption in the arbitrators," § 10(a)(2), it does not provide for pre-award removal of an arbitrator. Thus, an agreement to arbitrate before a particular arbitrator may not be disturbed, unless the agreement is subject to attack under general contract principles "as exist at law or in equity." § 2. Indeed, we have stated in dicta that "it is well established that a district court cannot entertain an attack upon the qualifications or partiality of arbitrators until after the conclusion of the arbitration and the rendition of an award." District courts within this circuit have so held on at least two occasions.

Although Aviall points to cases in which an arbitrator was removed prior to arbitration on account of a relationship with one party to the dispute, those cases simply manifest the FAA's directive that an agreement to arbitrate shall not be enforced when it would be invalid under general contract principles. In [Erving v. Virginia Squires Basketball Club, 349 F. Supp. 716 (E.D.N.Y.), aff'd, 468 F.2d 1064 (2d Cir. 1972)], for example, the basketball star Julius Erving had entered into a contract which provided for arbitration by the Commissioner of the American Basketball Association. When the dispute arose, a new Commissioner — who was a partner of the law firm representing the defendant — had been appointed, resulting in frustration of the parties' contractual intent to submit their dispute to a neutral expert. Accordingly, the district court reformed the contract by substituting a neutral arbitrator in the Commissioner's stead.

. . .

Here, in contrast, Aviall was fully aware of KPMG's relationship with Ryder when the Distribution Agreement was executed. The Distribution Agreement also clearly contemplated that KPMG would arbitrate the dispute even were it no longer to be outside auditor to both companies. . . . Admittedly, as a wholly-owned subsidiary, Aviall played no role in the drafting of the Distribution Agreement and had no power to bargain over its terms. But that in no way points to any infirmity in the contracting process, for Ryder was obligated to draft those terms in the manner most advantageous to its shareholders, who would also be the shareholders of Aviall immediately following the spinoff. Thus, Aviall can hardly object to the Distribution Agreement being enforced according to its terms.

The FAA's lack of provision for pre-award removal of an arbitrator likewise prevents us from removing KPMG on account of whatever assistance it may have lent to Ryder so far in connection with the arbitration. Aviall points us to no authority to the contrary. Thus, Aviall's evidence of any such conduct by KPMG is not material, and cannot defeat Ryder's summary judgment motion. Aviall, of course, remains free to challenge on the ground of evident partiality any award ultimately rendered by KPMG.

. . .

We therefore affirm the judgment of the district court.

PROBLEM 6.7

You get an urgent phone call from James Barker, President of Barker Business Supplies, Inc. (BBS) (most recently from Problem 6.4). He has just learned that Ted Marvin, the arbitrator agreed to by the parties in BBS' arbitration with

Douglas Distribution Co., has done some legal work for Douglas that he did not disclose to BBS in the arbitration. He wants to know what the company should do. He says: "I'd like to get a new arbitrator now, before we get too far into the proceeding. Otherwise, we'll just have to do everything all over again and it'll be twice as expensive getting this resolved."

(a) Can BBS challenge Marvin in the arbitration proceeding? In court?

(b) Would your answer change if you were in a jurisdiction governed by the UNCITRAL Model Law?

§ 6.05 PROVISIONAL REMEDIES

Provisional remedies (also known as interim or conservatory measures) are remedies such as temporary restraining orders, preliminary injunctions, garnishment, and attachment. These remedies are designed either to maintain the status quo pending resolution of a dispute or to preserve the effectiveness of any ultimate award. Most arbitration rules grant arbitrators the authority to award provisional measures. AAA Commercial Arbitration Rules, Rule R-34(a); UNCITRAL Arbitration Rules, art. 26. The FAA and the UAA are both silent on the authority of arbitrators to award provisional relief. The RUAA and the UNCITRAL Model Law, by comparison, both provide arbitrators such authority. RUAA § 8(b); UNCITRAL Model Law, arts. 17 & 17A-17G. Indeed, the RUAA makes the arbitrator's authority nonwaivable until after a dispute arises. RUAA § 4(b)(1).

Parties sometimes want to seek provisional relief from courts rather than arbitrators. (Why do you think that is?) Section 8 of the FAA, dealing with admiralty cases, provides that "the party claiming to be aggrieved may begin his proceeding hereunder by libel and seizure of the vessel or other property of the other party according to the usual course of admiralty proceedings." 9 U.S.C. § 8. Otherwise, the FAA does not address the authority of courts to award provisional relief in support of arbitration. Does statutory silence mean that courts have the authority to award provisional remedies? Or does it mean they do not have such authority?

JANVEY v. ALGUIRE
United States Court of Appeals for the Fifth Circuit
647 F.3d 585 (2011)

EDWARD C. PRADO, Circuit Judge:

. . .

The Securities Exchange Commission ("SEC") brought suit against Stanford Group Company ("SGC"), along with various other Stanford corporate entities, including Stanford International Bank ("SIB"), for allegedly perpetrating a massive Ponzi scheme. The district court appointed Robert Janvey (the "Receiver") to marshal the Stanford estate . . . . [T]he Receiver subsequently obtained a preliminary injunction against numerous former financial advisors and employees of SGC, freezing the accounts of those individuals pending the outcome of trial.[4]

[The Employee Defendants opposed the preliminary injunction and moved to compel arbitration. They based their motion to compel on the existence of Promissory Notes between the Employee Defendants and SGC, which contained a broad arbitration clause. The district court did not decide the merits of the motion to compel arbitration, finding that it had the power to issue a preliminary injunction pending resolution of that matter.]

In this interlocutory appeal, the Employee Defendants contend that . . . the district court had no power to grant the preliminary injunction when the motion to compel arbitration was pending. Additionally, the Employee Defendants claim that the district court abused its discretion when it granted the preliminary injunction

. . . .

. . .

II. DISCUSSION

. . .

B. Power to Grant Preliminary Injunction

1. The Parties' Arguments

The Employee Defendants argue that the district court lacked power to issue a preliminary injunction because the Receiver's claims against them are subject to arbitration. The Receiver argues that case law, the FINRA rules, and common sense allows the district court to issue a preliminary injunction pending its resolution of a motion to compel arbitration. The district court found that it had power to grant preliminary injunctive relief before deciding whether to compel arbitration. We agree with the district court.

While the Employee Defendants acknowledge that the grant of a preliminary injunction lies within a district court's discretion, they posit that a motion to compel arbitration strips the district court of its power to grant an injunction. The Employee Defendants contend that (1) SGC is and was subject to arbitration for this dispute at all relevant times because it is a member of FINRA and it is bound under the broad arbitration clause of each Promissory Note, which requires that any controversy arising out of or related to the Note be submitted to arbitration pursuant to FINRA rules; (2) the dispute in this action is arbitrable because the Receiver became subject to the FINRA rules and the arbitration clauses when he stepped into the shoes of the received entity he represents; and (3) the FINRA rules do not contemplate pre-arbitration injunctive relief nor allow court-ordered injunctions lasting longer than 15 days. The Employee Defendants argue that because the dispute is arbitrable and subject to the FINRA rules, the district court

---

[4] There are numerous appellants, represented by various counsel. The district court describes the approximately 330 former Stanford employees collectively as "Employee Defendants." We will continue this practice for the appellants in this proceeding. . . .

did not have the discretion to issue injunctive relief; it only had the power to decide the motion to compel arbitration.

The Employee Defendants also argue that cases from both sides of a circuit split support their contention that the district court does not have power to enter an injunction. The circuit split concerns the power of a district court to issue an injunction while arbitration is pending. The Fifth Circuit acknowledged the circuit split in *RGI, Inc. v. Tucker & Associates, Inc.*, 858 F.2d 227, 229 (5th Cir. 1988), but did not enter the fray. The Employee Defendants contend that once again we may avoid the fray and still decide the issue in their favor because both the Eighth Circuit, on one side of the split, and the Seventh Circuit, on the other side of the split, would not permit an injunction here. The Eighth Circuit held that "where the [Federal Arbitration Act ("FAA")] is applicable to the dispute between the parties and no qualifying language has been alleged, the district court errs in granting injunctive relief" because the judicial inquiry required to determine "the propriety of injunctive relief necessarily would inject the court into the merits of issues more appropriately left to the arbitrator." *Merrill Lynch, Pierce, Fenner & Smith, Inc. v. Hovey*, 726 F.2d 1286, 1292 (8th Cir. 1984). The Seventh Circuit held that the district court may only issue injunctive relief that is effective only until the arbitration panel is able to address whether the equitable relief should remain in effect. *See Merrill Lynch, Pierce, Fenner & Smith, Inc. v. Salvano*, 999 F.2d 211, 215-16 (7th Cir. 1993).

The Receiver responds that the district court's broad power to preserve the status quo is well-established and supported by case law, FINRA rules, and common sense. The Receiver notes that "even after a district court decides that a case is subject to arbitration, most federal authority permits the district court to issue a preliminary injunction to maintain the status quo pending arbitration." Further, the Receiver points out that under FINRA Rule 13804, (1) parties can seek court-ordered temporary injunctive relief even where the case is subject to mandatory arbitration, and (2) if a court issues a temporary injunction in a dispute subject to arbitration, an arbitration panel will hold a hearing within 15 days to determine whether to continue the injunctive relief. The Receiver argues that if FINRA rules allow court-ordered injunctive relief when a party loses on the motion to compel arbitration, then he is entitled to such relief while the motion is still pending. Finally, the Receiver notes that a rule that would prohibit the district court from preserving the status quo when a motion to compel arbitration is filed would enable any party "to strip the trial court of its authority to enjoin the party's conduct simply by filing a motion to compel arbitration."

2. Analysis

In its order, the district court relied on its equitable powers to preserve the status quo, and expressly reserved the question of whether the Receiver's claims were subject to arbitration. In so doing, the district court noted that the cases in the circuit split did not specifically address the issue in this case: whether a court may preserve the status quo *pending its resolution of a motion to compel arbitration*, not pending the actual arbitration itself. We agree with the district court that it court can grant preliminary relief before deciding whether to compel arbitration.

The language of the FAA does not touch on the ancillary power of the federal court to act before it decides whether the dispute is arbitrable. The federal law of arbitration is governed by the FAA. . . . However, these sections do not provide guidance on the issue of whether a court may issue a preliminary injunction before deciding whether the dispute is arbitrable. . . . Section 3 only speaks to what the court should do once it is satisfied that the issue is referable to arbitration. Similarly, § 4 mandates that the court must direct the parties to proceed to arbitration *only after it is satisfied* that there is no issue as to whether a party failed to comply with the arbitration agreement. Both of these sections speak only to situations after the court has decided arbitration must ensue.

Here, the district court has yet to make up its mind as to arbitrability. The district court relied on its equitable powers to preserve the status quo, but expressly reserved the issue of whether the Receiver's claims were subject to arbitration for resolution at a later date. Nothing in the FAA controls a district court's approach to its docket. While the Supreme Court has stated that "Congress'[s] clear intent, in the [FAA], [was] to move the parties to an *arbitrable* dispute out of court and into arbitration as quickly and easily as possible[,]" there is nothing to control the district court's expeditious determination of arbitrability.

The cases cited by the Employee Defendants also do not bar the exercise of the district court's equitable powers here. The *RGI* Court found that "[t]he crux of the problem [in the circuit split] is whether the commands of the [FAA] require that a federal court immediately divest itself of any power to act to maintain the status quo *once it decides that the case before it is arbitrable.*" *RGI* (emphasis added). Here, however, the district court has not yet decided whether the case is arbitrable and thus the circuit-split cases are not applicable. The Receiver's request for a preliminary injunction was entered before the motion to compel arbitration. We agree with the district court that if we were to reverse and hold that the district court must stop everything and consider the motion to compel arbitration, such a holding

> would create a harsh procedural rule: in order to avoid irreparable injury, motions to compel arbitration where a request for injunctive relief is involved must be resolved before any temporary restraining order expires. Such a rule would be both burdensome for district courts and impracticable, given the time it takes motions to compel arbitration to become ripe for ruling, even if no discovery is required.

Though the circuit-split cases do not apply here, the reasoning of those circuits holding that a court may issue an injunction pending arbitration applies here.[7] As explained by the First Circuit, "the congressional desire to enforce arbitration agreements would frequently be frustrated if the courts were precluded from issuing preliminary injunctive relief to preserve the status quo pending arbitration and, *ipso facto*, the meaningfulness of the arbitration process." *Teradyne v. Mostek Corp.*, 797 F.2d 43, 51 (1st Cir. 1986). Here, the district court merely sought to preserve the status quo *before* deciding the motion to compel arbitration, and by

---

[7] Given that the facts at issue here do not require us to enter the circuit split, we reserve for another day the issues of whether a district court divests itself of the discretion to maintain the status quo once it decides the case before it is arbitrable and, if not, what the limits of that discretion may be.

doing so [it] sought to preserve the meaningfulness of any arbitration that might take place.

Even if applicable to the facts here, the Seventh Circuit case cited by the Employee Defendants would not bar the preliminary injunction issued by the district court. In *Salvano*, the Seventh Circuit held that the district court may issue injunctive relief only until the arbitration panel is able to address whether the equitable relief should remain in effect. In the instant case, the district court expressly stated that if it decides to compel arbitration, the defendants may ask the district court to reconsider the preliminary injunction in light of Fifth Circuit precedent and the terms of the contracts.

The matter of arbitrability has not yet been decided, and the district court did not overreach when it decided the preliminary injunction motion.

C. Decision to Grant Preliminary Injunction

The four elements a plaintiff must establish to secure a preliminary injunction are:

> (1) a substantial likelihood of success on the merits, (2) a substantial threat of irreparable injury if the injunction is not issued, (3) that the threatened injury if the injunction is denied outweighs any harm that will result if the injunction is granted, and (4) that the grant of an injunction will not disserve the public interest.

The Receiver bore the burden of establishing each element. The district court analyzed each of the elements in its grant of the preliminary injunction to the Receiver. The Employee Defendants challenge all aspects of the district court's analysis. We disagree with the Employee Defendants that the district court abused its discretion in issuing the preliminary injunction. . . .

. . .

CONCLUSION

The Receiver is in an unenviable position: although the Stanford estate has many thousands of claimants, there are startlingly few assets to disperse to the Stanford victims. In this appeal concerning the Receiver's attempt to marshal estate assets, we hold: (1) The district court acted within its power when it considered and decided the motion for preliminary injunction before deciding the outstanding motion to compel arbitration; [and] (2) The district court did not abuse its discretion in issuing the preliminary injunction . . . .

AFFIRMED and REMANDED.

NOTES

1. *Janvey* illustrates a fundamental difficulty with relying on arbitrators to award provisional remedies: that the parties have to appoint the arbitrators before they can rule on a request for provisional relief. What do you suppose would have

happened to the frozen assets if the receiver had to wait for the arbitrators to be appointed before obtaining the freeze order?

The American Arbitration Association, like other arbitration providers, has responded to this difficulty by maintaining an emergency panel that can rapidly rule on requests for provisional remedies before the arbitrators have been appointed. *See, e.g.*, American Arbitration Association, Optional Rules for Emergency Measures of Protections, Rules O-1 to O-8. In franchise contracts, at least, this option is selected only rarely.

2.   What do you think of the court of appeals' holding that the district court can issue a preliminary injunction before it rules on whether the dispute must be arbitrated? Given that court proceedings on petitions to compel arbitration are supposed to be summary in nature, wouldn't it be easier for the court to decide whether the dispute needs to be arbitrated first? Of course, that would then raise the issue the court of appeals was able to avoid given its holding — whether a court can grant provisional remedies after it has compelled arbitration. Does the court of appeals' holding here give district courts the incentive to postpone sending cases to arbitration so that they can preserve their orders granting provisional relief?

3.   Once the arbitration panel is appointed and functioning, there is much less reason for courts to order provisional relief. The *Janvey* court discusses the Seventh Circuit's decision in *Salvano*, which held that the trial court erred by continuing the preliminary injunction beyond the time when the arbitrators were appointed. The Revised Uniform Arbitration Act reflects a similar dichotomy. RUAA § 8. Before the arbitration panel is appointed, a court "may enter an order for provisional remedies to protect the effectiveness of the arbitration proceeding to the same extent and under the same conditions as if the controversy were the subject of a civil action." § 8(a). After the arbitrators are named, a court can intervene "only if the matter is urgent and the arbitrator is not able to act timely or the arbitrator cannot provide an adequate remedy." § 8(b). In addition, RUAA permits a party to go to court to enforce the award of provisional relief. *See* § 18.

4.   The *Janvey* case avoids the circuit split over the authority of federal courts to order provisional relief in support of arbitration. That said, it is not much of a split, since the substantial majority of the federal courts of appeals have held that the FAA does not preclude a court from granting provisional relief in aid of arbitration. The one exception is Merrill Lynch, Pierce, Fenner & Smith, Inc. v. Hovey, 726 F.2d 1286 (8th Cir. 1984), in which the Eighth Circuit held that "where the Arbitration Act is applicable and no qualifying contractual language has been alleged, the district court errs in granting injunctive relief." *Id.* at 1292; *see also* Manion v. Nagin, 255 F.3d 535, 539 (8th Cir. 2001). However, the Eighth Circuit limited *Hovey* in Peabody Coalsales Co. v. Tampa Electric Co., 36 F.3d 46 (8th Cir. 1994). *Peabody* held that injunctive relief pending arbitration is permissible when the contract contains "qualifying language" to the effect that the parties' performance of their obligations under the contract "shall be continued in full by the parties during the dispute resolution process." *Id.* at 47–48. Note that half of arbitration clauses in a sample of franchise agreements exclude claims for provisional remedies from arbitration altogether, presumably seeking to assure

that parties (or at least the franchisor) can go to court to get emergency relief if they so desire.

5.   Does a party waive its right to arbitrate when it seeks provisional relief in support of arbitration? As we discussed in § 2.03, arbitration rules commonly state that seeking court-ordered provisional remedies is not inconsistent with the right to arbitrate and so is not a waiver. AAA Commercial Arbitration Rules, Rule R-48(a); UNCITRAL Arbitration Rules, art. 26(9).

We have considered whether the FAA precludes courts from ordering provisional remedies in a matter otherwise subject to arbitration. How about the New York Convention?

McCREARY TIRE & RUBBER CO. v. CEAT S.P.A.
United States Court of Appeals for the Third Circuit
501 F.2d 1032 (1974)

GIBBONS, CIRCUIT JUDGE.

. . . The case commenced with the filing of a Praecipe and Complaint in Foreign Attachment in the Court of Common Pleas of Allegheny County. The plaintiff, McCreary Tire & Rubber Company (McCreary), a Pennsylvania corporation, sued CEAT, S.p.A. (CEAT), an Italian corporation, for alleged breaches of a distributorship contract and Mellon Bank, N.A. (Mellon), garnishee. CEAT filed a petition for removal to the United States District Court for the Western District of Pennsylvania. CEAT then . . . moved to dissolve the foreign attachment on the ground that at the time of service of the writ Mellon had none of its property in Mellon's custody; . . . and it moved for an order transferring the case to the United States District Court for the District of Massachusetts, where a prior action by McCreary against CEAT is pending, and in which CEAT has made a general appearance. It also moved for a stay of the within action so as to permit arbitration of the dispute in accordance with the terms of the contract upon which McCreary sued. The court denied each motion, denied a motion for a certification pursuant to 28 U.S.C. § 1292(b) and denied a motion for reconsideration. This appeal followed.

It is undisputed that a suit by McCreary against CEAT on essentially the same claims is pending in the United States District Court for the District of Massachusetts, that in the Massachusetts case CEAT has made a general appearance, that the Massachusetts district court ordered arbitration in accordance with the contract and stayed the suit pending arbitration and that the order compelling arbitration has been affirmed by the Court of Appeals for the First Circuit. At oral argument we were advised by counsel for McCreary and CEAT that the arbitration proceeding had actually commenced.

. . .

III. THE CONTINUANCE OF THE ATTACHMENT

. . . [R]esort to a Praecipe and Complaint in Foreign Attachment in the Court of Common Pleas of Pennsylvania is a violation of McCreary's agreement to submit the underlying disputes to arbitration, and . . . the [New York] Convention obliges the district court to recognize and enforce the agreement to arbitrate. Quite possibly foreign attachment may be available for the enforcement of an arbitration award. This complaint does not seek to enforce an arbitration award by foreign attachment. It seeks to bypass the agreed upon method of settling disputes. Such a bypass is prohibited by the Convention if one party to the agreement objects. Unlike § 3 of the federal Act, article II(3) of the Convention provides that the court of a contracting state shall "refer the parties to arbitration" rather than "stay the trial of the action." The Convention forbids the courts of a contracting state from entertaining a suit which violates an agreement to arbitrate. Thus the contention that arbitration is merely another method of trial, to which state provisional remedies should equally apply, is unavailable. . . . Here, although the suit is in the federal court after removal from a state court, the governing law with respect to arbitration is the Convention. . . .

. . . The obvious purpose of the enactment of Pub. L. 91-368, permitting removal of all cases falling within the terms of the treaty, was to prevent the vagaries of state law from impeding its full implementation. Permitting a continued resort to foreign attachment in breach of the agreement is inconsistent with that purpose. The relief requested, a release of all property from the attachment, should have been granted.

. . .

The order of the district court will be reversed and the case remanded for the entry of an order (1) discharging the foreign attachment and (2) referring the disputed claims to arbitration. . . .

CAROLINA POWER & LIGHT CO. v. URANEX
United States District Court for the Northern District of California
451 F. Supp. 1044 (1977)

PECKHAM, CHIEF JUDGE.

In 1973 Carolina Power & Light Company ("CP&L"), a North Carolina public utility company, contracted with defendant Uranex for the delivery of uranium concentrates to CP&L during the period 1977 to 1986. Uranex is a French *groupement d'intérêt économique* that markets uranium internationally. Following the recent and dramatic rise in the price of uranium fuel in the world market, Uranex either would not or could not deliver at the contract price, and requested renegotiation. CP&L has refused to enter any discussions aimed at contract modifications.

Earlier this year CP&L filed the present action against Uranex, and proceeded *ex parte* to attach an 85 million dollar debt owed to Uranex by Homestake Mining Company ("Homestake"), a San Francisco based corporation that markets uranium throughout the United States. The 85 million dollars is due to Uranex pursuant to a uranium supply contract between Homestake and Uranex, and has no relationship to the present litigation except as a potential source for CP&L to satisfy any judgment that might issue. But for the attachment the funds would have been transferred out of the country in the ordinary course of business.

The contract between CP&L and Uranex provides that disputes are to be submitted to arbitration in New York. At the time this lawsuit was filed CP&L sought to compel Uranex to enter arbitration. Since that time, however, Uranex voluntarily has entered arbitration and those proceedings are now going on in New York. Both parties agree that because of the arbitration agreement this court cannot adjudicate the merits of the dispute, but CP&L contends that the court should stay this action and maintain the attachment in order to protect any award that CP&L might receive in the New York arbitration. CP&L claims that Uranex has no other assets in this country with which to satisfy a judgment, and Uranex apparently does not dispute this proposition. Uranex has moved the court . . . to dismiss the complaint and quash the writ of attachment.

. . .

. . . There is little question that the [New York] Convention would apply to the contract at issue in this litigation. As described above, both Uranex and CP&L agree that they must pursue arbitration in New York as provided in the arbitration clause of their contract. Uranex, however, argues that it would be inconsistent with the Convention for this court to maintain the attachment pending the arbitration.

The Convention and its implementing statutes contain no reference to prejudgment attachment, and provide little guidance in this controversy. Article II of the Convention states only that a "court of a Contracting State . . . shall, at the request of one of the parties, refer the parties to arbitration." To implement this aspect of the Convention, section 206 of Title 9 provides that "[a] court having jurisdiction under this chapter may direct that arbitration be held in accordance with the agreement at any place therein provided for, whether that place is within or without the United States." The language of these provisions provides little apparent support for defendant's argument. Uranex, however, relies upon the decision[] of the Third Circuit in *McCreary Tire & Rubber Co. v. CEAT, S.p.A.* . . .

This court, however, does not find the reasoning of *McCreary* convincing. As mentioned above, nothing in the text of the Convention itself suggests that it precludes prejudgment attachment. The United States Arbitration Act, which operates much like the Convention for domestic agreements involving maritime or interstate commerce, does not prohibit maintenance of a prejudgment attachment during a stay pending arbitration:

> After declaring (§ 2 [of the U.S. Arbitration Act]) such agreements [to arbitrate] to be enforceable, Congress, in succeeding sections, implemented the declared policy. By § 3 it provided that "if any suit or proceeding be brought in any of the courts of the United States upon any issue referable to arbitration under an agreement in writing for such arbitration, the court . . . shall on application of one of the parties stay the trial . . . until such arbitration has been had" if the applicant is not in default in proceeding with such arbitration. The section obviously envisages action in a court on a cause of action and does not oust the court's jurisdiction of the action, though the parties have agreed to arbitrate. And, it would seem there is nothing to prevent the plaintiff from commencing the action by attachment if such procedure is available under the applicable law. This section deals with suits at law or in equity. The concept seems to be that a power to grant

a stay is enough without the power to order that the arbitration proceed, for, if a stay be granted, the plaintiff can never get relief unless he proceeds to arbitration.

Barge "Anaconda" v. American Sugar Refining Co., 322 U.S. 42, 44–45 (1944). The *McCreary* court makes two rather elliptical comments to distinguish the United States Arbitration Act from the Convention. First, the court notes that the Arbitration Act only directs courts to "stay the trial of the action," while the Convention requires a court to "refer the parties to arbitration." From this difference the *McCreary* court apparently concludes that while the Arbitration Act might permit continued jurisdiction and even maintenance of a prejudgment attachment pending arbitration, application of the Convention completely ousts the court of jurisdiction. The use of the general term "refer," however, might reflect little more than the fact that the Convention must be applied in many very different legal systems, and possibly in circumstances where the use of the technical term "stay" would not be a meaningful directive. Furthermore, section 4 of the United States Arbitration Act grants district courts the power to actually order the parties to arbitration, but this provision has not been interpreted to deprive the courts of continuing jurisdiction over the action.

Second, the *McCreary* court found support for its position in the fact that the implementing statutes of the Convention provide for removal jurisdiction in the federal courts. . . . It must be noted, however, that any case falling within section 4 of the United States Arbitration Act also would be subject to removal pursuant to 28 U.S.C. § 1441. Furthermore, removal to federal court could have little impact on the "vagaries" of state provisional remedies, for pursuant to Rule 64 of the Federal Rules of Civil Procedure the district courts employ the procedures and remedies of the states where they sit. Finally, it should be noted that in other contexts the Supreme Court has concluded that the availability of provisional remedies encourages rather than obstructs the use of agreements to arbitrate.

In sum this court will not follow the reasoning of *McCreary Tire & Rubber Company v. CEAT, S.p.A.* There is no indication in either the text or the apparent policies of the Convention that resort to prejudgment attachment was to be precluded. . . .

NOTES

1. A few American courts have followed the Third Circuit's opinion in *McCreary. See, e.g.*, I.T.A.D. Assocs. Inc. v. Podar Bros., 636 F.2d 75 (4th Cir. 1981); Cooper v. Ateliers de la Motobecane, S.A., 456 N.Y.S.2d 728 (N.Y. 1982). Many, however, have not. *See, e.g.*, Filanto S.p.A. v. Chilewich Int'l Corp., 789 F. Supp. 1229, 1241 (S.D.N.Y. 1992) (describing *McCreary* as "facially absurd"), *appeal dismissed*, 984 F.2d 58 (2d Cir. 1983); Chloe Z Fishing Co. v. Odyssey Re (London) Ltd., 109 F. Supp. 2d 1236, 1261 (S.D. Cal. 2000) (following *Filanto*). Indeed, the Fourth Circuit has indicated that its decision in *Podar Bros.* (and, by implication, the Third Circuit's decision in *McCreary*) has been effectively overruled by subsequent Supreme Court case law. Aggarao v. MOL Ship Mgmt. Co., Ltd., 675 F.3d 355, 377 n.19 (4th Cir. 2012) ("The decision in *McCreary*, however, predates [*Vimar Seguros y Reaseguros, S.A. v. M/V Sky Reefer*, 515 U.S. 528 (1995),] where

the Supreme Court endorsed a district court's retention of jurisdiction over a dispute subject to arbitration under the Convention Act. Because the Supreme Court has rejected the *McCreary* premise, *Podar Bros.* has been effectively overruled by the Court on the jurisdictional point and is not controlling precedent with respect to Aggarao's injunction request.").

Commentators have roundly criticized the decision as well. *See, e.g.,* Charles N. Brower & W. Michael Tupman, *Court Ordered Provisional Measures and the New York Convention,* 80 AM. J. INT'L L. 24 (1986); Douglas D. Reichert, *Provisional Remedies in the Context of International Commercial Arbitration,* 3 INT'L TAX & BUS. L. 368 (1986). Courts in other countries likewise have rejected the *McCreary* holding. *See* Peter J.W. Sherwin and Douglas C. Rennie, *Interim Relief Under International Arbitration Rules and Guidelines: A Comparative Analysis,* 20 AM. REV. INT'L ARB. 317, 333 (2009) ("[I]t appears that no court outside of the United States has found court-ordered interim relief in aid of arbitration to be inconsistent with the New York Convention.").

2. Despite the criticisms of its reasoning, on its facts the *McCreary* court may well have gotten the right result because the party seeking the attachment was trying to avoid arbitration and proceed in court instead. GARY B. BORN, INTERNATIONAL COMMERCIAL ARBITRATION 2032-2033 (2009). At least some of the cases following *McCreary* cannot be so reconciled, however.

Assuming that neither the FAA nor the New York Convention precludes a federal court from granting provisional relief in support of an arbitration proceeding, how should the court go about deciding whether to grant such relief?

CONTICHEM LPG v. PARSONS SHIPPING CO.
United States Court of Appeals for the Second Circuit
229 F.3d 426 (2000)

POOLER, CIRCUIT JUDGE:

ContiChem LPG ("ContiChem") appeals from the October 27, 1999, Memorandum and Order of the United States District Court for the Southern District of New York . . . denying its motion for a preliminary injunction and for an order of attachment and granting respondent Parsons Shipping, Ltd.'s ("Parsons") motion to vacate the temporary restraining order and order of maritime attachment granted October 13, 1999. ContiChem primarily argues that the district court's refusal to grant provisional remedies in aid of arbitration under New York Civil Practice Law and Rules ("C.P.L.R.") 7502(c) on the ground that no arbitration was pending in New York was erroneous. . . . ContiChem [also] maintains that it was entitled to a maritime attachment under Admiralty Supplemental Rule B(1). For the reasons set forth below, we reject ContiChem's contentions and affirm the order of the district court.

BACKGROUND

At the root of this dispute is ContiChem's attempt to obtain security in New York for damages resulting from a breach of a charter party. . . .

On August 14, 1999, ContiChem and Parsons entered into a charter party for the ship M/V World Rainbow. Under the charter party, Parsons agreed to deliver its ship to ContiChem at ContiChem's nominated port of Ras Tanura, Saudi Arabia for a voyage in which it would carry 40,500 metric tons of cargo for ContiChem. Parsons, the owner of the ship, warranted the vessel's "being seaworthy and having all pipes, pumps and compressors, boiler coils in good working order, and being in every respect fitted for the voyage." The charter party specified "[t]he place of General Average and arbitration proceedings to be London." The underlying breach of charter party claim stems from ContiChem's contentions that Parsons' vessel was unseaworthy and its tanks were unable to cool down sufficiently to enable loading of ContiChem's cargo. This problem delayed loading, which allegedly resulted in damages to ContiChem of $2,955,143.

ContiChem attempted to obtain security for its claims in a number of ways. First, ContiChem had the M/V World Rainbow arrested while at anchorage in Yosu, South Korea. Although the assessed value of the ship was $1.95 million, it was encumbered by a first preferred mortgage of $5 million and a second preferred mortgage of $1.3 million, both in favor of Den Norske Bank ASA ("Den Norske").

Next, on October 13, 1999, ContiChem petitioned the United States District Court for the Southern District of New York for an order pursuant to 9 U.S.C. § 1 *et seq.* compelling Parsons to proceed with arbitration in London. ContiChem also sought an order of attachment pursuant to Supplemental Admiralty Rule B(1) of Parsons' bank accounts as security for its arbitration claim against Parsons. ContiChem stated that it was due to make a $722,145.09 telephonic transfer to Unibank, S.A., one of the banks from which attachment was sought, for the benefit of Parsons' agent. ContiChem also sought a temporary restraining order and/or preliminary injunction prohibiting garnishee Unibank from transferring Parsons' assets out of the district pending arbitration. In the alternative, ContiChem sought a temporary restraining order and preliminary injunction pursuant to the equitable and discretionary powers of the court under the common law and Rules 64 and 65 of the Federal Rules of Civil Procedure.

On October 13, 1999, the district court issued an order directing Parsons to show cause before the court on October 25, 1999, why an order should not be issued . . . temporarily restraining garnishee Unibank from transferring Parsons' money out of the district. The court issued a temporary restraining order that prohibited Unibank from transferring or removing Parsons' property from the district pending the October 25 hearing. The court further ordered service of maritime attachment and garnishment on Unibank, so as to prevent removal of Parsons' property from the district. The following day ContiChem served the temporary restraining order on Unibank. ContiChem advised Unibank that it was due to make a freight payment to Parsons' agent's account there, but that Unibank could not transfer those funds to Den Norske due to the temporary restraining order it had served. Thereafter, ContiChem wired the freight payment to Unibank and later served the process of maritime attachment on Unibank.

Finally, one day after serving the order to show cause, ContiChem also sought to freeze assets of Parsons in London.

Upon Parsons' request, the return date of the motion in New York was accelerated and the district court conducted a hearing on October 22, 1999. On that date, Den Norske moved by order to show cause to intervene, claiming that it was entitled to the restrained funds. Parsons and Den Norske asked the district court to vacate the temporary restraining order as well as the order of maritime attachment. . . . [T]he district court denied petitioner's motion for a preliminary injunction and order of attachment and granted Parsons' motion to vacate both the temporary restraining order and maritime attachment order issued on October 13, 1999. ContiChem now appeals.

DISCUSSION

I. Standards

. . .

As a preliminary matter, we agree with the district court's determination that because ContiChem did not have a judgment against Parsons, the court had no equitable power to issue a preliminary injunction preventing any entity from disposing of Parsons' assets pending arbitration of the dispute. *See* Grupo Mexicano de Desarrollo, S.A. v. Alliance Bond Fund, Inc., 527 U.S. 308, 333 (1999) (district court is without power pursuant to Federal Rule of Civil Procedure 65 to order injunctive relief preventing party from disposing of assets pending adjudication of contract claims for money damages). Absent a prior judgment, the district court properly denied ContiChem's request. However, ContiChem also sought relief pursuant to Supplemental Rule B(1) of the Rules for Certain Admiralty and Maritime Claims, which supplement the Rules of Civil Procedure. Rule B(1) provides for prejudgment maritime attachment and garnishment in maritime in personam actions. In addition, Rule B(1) authorizes a plaintiff pursuant to Federal Rule of Civil Procedure 4(e) to "invoke the remedies provided by state law for attachment and garnishment or similar seizure of the defendant's property." We first consider whether the district court properly refused to grant pre-arbitration remedies under state law and then turn to federal law.

II. Relief

A. State Remedies

ContiChem rests its claim to provisional remedies partly on C.P.L.R. 7502, under which a court may consider an application for an attachment order or preliminary injunction in connection with an arbitrable controversy. Specifically, Rule 7502(c) provides:

> The supreme court in the county in which an arbitration is pending, or, if not yet commenced, in a county specified in subdivision (a), may entertain an application for an order of attachment or for a preliminary injunction in

connection with an arbitrable controversy, but only upon the ground that the award to which the applicant may be entitled may be rendered ineffectual without such provisional relief. The provisions of articles 62 and 63 of this chapter shall apply to the application, . . . except that the sole ground for the granting of the remedy shall be as stated above.

N.Y. C.P.L.R. 7502(c). Although the district court initially granted ContiChem's request for a temporary restraining order and order of attachment on October 13, 1999, it subsequently vacated the temporary restraining order, concluding that C.P.L.R. 7502(c) applies only to arbitration proceedings in New York.

. . .

ContiChem assumes that C.P.L.R. Article 75 is available to it, even though it agreed to arbitrate its disputes with Parsons in London pursuant to an arbitration agreement that is subject to the United Nations Convention on the Recognition and Enforcement of Foreign Arbitral Awards ("Convention"). However, these facts raise several issues that must be considered in turn. In analyzing ContiChem's claim for relief under Rule 7502(c), it is helpful to step back and consider the landscape of rules before us. In New York, the leading case on attachments in aid of arbitration is Cooper v. Ateliers de la Motobecane, S.A., 57 N.Y.2d 408, 442 N.E.2d 1239 (1982). In *Cooper*, the New York Court of Appeals refused to grant a pre-arbitration attachment in an international matter involving litigants governed by the Convention, finding that pre-award remedies violated the Convention. However, the New York Court of Appeals noted federal arbitration law "specifically permits attachment to be used in admiralty cases." ContiChem seizes on the apparent exception for maritime cases to argue that *Cooper* is not a barrier to application of C.P.L.R. Article 75.

. . .

. . . [W]e conclude that although this case involves a maritime attachment, and *Cooper* is therefore not necessarily a bar to relief, ContiChem nevertheless is not entitled to provisional remedies in aid of arbitration under C.P.L.R. 7502(c) because this is not a domestic arbitration. The charter party in this case specifically provided for arbitration of disputes in London, and Rule 7502 by its terms applies only to domestic arbitrations. Therefore, we reject ContiChem's attempt to expand the purview of this statute beyond the limits of its language and affirm the district court's conclusion that C.P.L.R. 7502(c) does not permit provisional remedies in aid of a maritime arbitration in London.

. . .

B. Federal Remedies

ContiChem also appeals the district court's order vacating the order of maritime attachment it granted pursuant to Supplemental Rule B on October 13, 1999. . . .

. . . Rule B(1) provides that "[w]ith respect to any admiralty or maritime claim in personam a verified complaint may contain a prayer for process to attach the defendant's goods and chattels, or credits and effects in the hands of garnishees . . . if the defendant shall not be found within the district." . . . However, Rule B(1) relief is not valid where the attachment and garnishment is served before the garnishee comes into possession of the property.

. . .

The district court properly vacated the attachment order. We hold that ContiChem improperly attempted to circumvent the rule against attachment of property not yet in Unibank's possession, by using a temporary restraining order that the court subsequently found had been issued in error to prohibit the transfer of Parsons' funds out of the district; making a payment to Unibank; and, once the funds ceased to be a moving target, serving the maritime attachment and garnishment. . . . If ContiChem made the freight payment to Unibank first, before obtaining the attachment order, Unibank would automatically transfer the funds to Den Norske in London, pursuant to already existing transfer instructions, and the funds would be gone. . . . [H]owever, ContiChem could not serve the attachment and garnishment order on Unibank when the bank was not yet in possession of the funds. To circumvent this problem, ContiChem sought, and the district court granted, a temporary restraining order prohibiting Unibank from transferring Parsons' money out of the district. . . .

We conclude that it was well within the district court's discretion to vacate the maritime attachment and garnishment order, having determined that it had erroneously issued the temporary restraining order that anchored the funds in New York. Absent the temporary restraining order, which the district court vacated . . . , there could be no attachment of funds in this case. . . . Therefore, the district court properly vacated the order of attachment. Although ContiChem's attempt to obtain security in New York failed, ContiChem is not without recourse to seek relief by appropriate means in an appropriate jurisdiction.

CONCLUSION

For the foregoing reasons, we affirm the order of the district court denying petitioner's request for a preliminary injunction and order of attachment and vacating the attachment order issued on October 13, 1999.

NOTES

1. The availability of provisional remedies in federal district courts is governed by Federal Rules of Civil Procedure 64 and 65. Rule 64(a) provides that "[a]t the commencement of and throughout an action, every remedy is available that, under the law of the state where the court is located, provides for seizing a person or property to secure satisfaction of the potential judgment." Rule 65 sets out rules governing the issuance of temporary restraining orders and preliminary injunctions. Injunctive relief is available under Rule 65 to the extent "traditionally accorded by courts of equity." Grupo Mexicano de Desarrollo v. Alliance Bond Fund, Inc., 527 U.S. 308, 319 (1999).

2. Relying on the admiralty equivalent of Rule 64, the *Contichem* court examined the permissibility of attachment pending arbitration under section 7502(c) of the New York Civil Practice Law & Rules. As the opinion suggests,

section 7502(c) was enacted in response to the decision of the New York Court of Appeals in *Cooper* and expanded the availability of provisional remedies in support of arbitration as a matter of state law. On the facts of *Contichem*, however, section 7502(c) did not authorize an attachment because the arbitration was not pending in New York.

In 2005, New York amended section 7502(c) to read as follows:

> The supreme court in the county in which an arbitration is pending or in a county specified in subdivision (a) of this section, may entertain an application for an order of attachment or for a preliminary injunction in connection with an arbitration that is pending or that is to be commenced inside or outside this state, whether or not it is subject to the United Nations convention on the recognition and enforcement of foreign arbitral awards, but only upon the ground that the award to which the applicant may be entitled may be rendered ineffectual without such provisional relief.
>
> . . .

The sponsor of the bill was quoted as saying that "[t]his amendment will make New York law consistent with the laws of other states of the United States, with the laws of other countries, and with the rules of national and international arbitration organizations." How would the amendment affect the result in *Contichem*? What effect does it have on *Cooper*?

3. The injunctive relief sought by the claimant in *Contichem* was a freeze of certain of the respondent's assets pending the outcome of the arbitration proceeding, which essentially would accomplish the same end as an attachment. The court of appeals affirmed the district court's refusal to grant that relief. It relied on the Supreme Court's opinion in *Grupo Mexicano*, which held that "[b]ecause such a remedy was historically unavailable from a court of equity, . . . [a] District Court ha[s] no authority to issue a preliminary injunction preventing petitioners from disposing of their assets pending adjudication of respondents' contract claim for money damages." 527 U.S. at 333. The Court in *Grupo Mexicano* refused to permit what are known as *Mareva* injunctions, after the leading case from the English Court of Chancery, Mareva Compania Naviera S.A. v. International Bulkcarriers S.A., 2 Lloyd's Rep. 509 (1975).

PROBLEM 6.8

Your client, Mary Morstan of 4-M Co. (from Problem 6.5), comes to you with another matter. It seems that 4-M is having a dispute with one of its suppliers, Singh Products Co. (a Massachusetts company), that is likely to end up with 4-M pursuing a claim for breach of contract in arbitration. (The contract between 4-M and Singh provides for arbitration in New York under the Commercial Arbitration Rules of the American Arbitration Association, although no proceeding has yet been begun.) Morstan is very worried about the prospects of collecting a possible award against Singh. She has learned that another one of Singh's customers is about to make a substantial payment to Singh's New York bank account. Singh's usual practice is to transfer the money out of the country almost immediately after it receives the payment.

(a) Morstan wants to know if there is anything 4-M might do, either in arbitration or in court, to keep the money available to satisfy a possible arbitration award. What do you tell her?

(b) Same as (a) except that Singh is located in Agra, India. What do you tell Morstan?

§ 6.06 CONSOLIDATION AND CLASS ARBITRATION

Multi-party disputes can be difficult to resolve in arbitration. All the parties might not have agreed to arbitrate. Or they might have agreed to arbitrate but under different procedures. This section examines the extent to which consolidation and (especially) class relief — procedures courts use to resolve multi-party disputes — are available in arbitration.

STOLT-NIELSEN S.A. v. ANIMALFEEDS INT'L CORP.
United States Supreme Court
130 S. Ct. 1758 (2010)

JUSTICE ALITO delivered the opinion of the Court.

We granted certiorari in this case to decide whether imposing class arbitration on parties whose arbitration clauses are "silent" on that issue is consistent with the Federal Arbitration Act (FAA).

I

A

Petitioners are shipping companies that serve a large share of the world market for parcel tankers — seagoing vessels with compartments that are separately chartered to customers wishing to ship liquids in small quantities. One of those customers is AnimalFeeds International Corp. (hereinafter AnimalFeeds), which supplies raw ingredients, such as fish oil, to animal-feed producers around the world. AnimalFeeds ships its goods pursuant to a standard contract known in the maritime trade as a charter party. Numerous charter parties are in regular use, and the charter party that AnimalFeeds uses is known as the "Vegoilvoy" charter party. . . .

Adopted in 1950, the Vegoilvoy charter party contains the following arbitration clause:

> Arbitration. Any dispute arising from the making, performance or termination of this Charter Party shall be settled in New York, Owner and Charterer each appointing an arbitrator, who shall be a merchant, broker or individual experienced in the shipping business; the two thus chosen, if they cannot agree, shall nominate a third arbitrator who shall be an Admiralty lawyer. Such arbitration shall be conducted in conformity with the provisions and procedure of the United States Arbitration Act [i.e., the

FAA], and a judgment of the Court shall be entered upon any award made by said arbitrator.

In 2003, a Department of Justice criminal investigation revealed that petitioners were engaging in an illegal price-fixing conspiracy. When AnimalFeeds learned of this, it brought a putative class action against petitioners in the District Court for the Eastern District of Pennsylvania, asserting antitrust claims for supracompetitive prices that petitioners allegedly charged their customers over a period of several years.

The parties agree that . . . AnimalFeeds and petitioners must arbitrate their antitrust dispute.

B

In 2005, AnimalFeeds served petitioners with a demand for class arbitration, designating New York City as the place of arbitration and seeking to represent a class of "[a]ll direct purchasers of parcel tanker transportation services globally for bulk liquid chemicals, edible oils, acids, and other specialty liquids from [petitioners] at any time during the period from August 1, 1998, to November 30, 2002." The parties entered into a supplemental agreement providing for the question of class arbitration to be submitted to a panel of three arbitrators who were to "follow and be bound by Rules 3 through 7 of the American Arbitration Association's Supplementary Rules for Class Arbitrations (as effective Oct. 8, 2003)." These rules (hereinafter Class Rules) were developed by the American Arbitration Association (AAA) after our decision in *Green Tree Financial Corp. v. Bazzle*), and Class Rule 3, in accordance with the plurality opinion in that case, requires an arbitrator, as a threshold matter, to determine "whether the applicable arbitration clause permits the arbitration to proceed on behalf of or against a class."

The parties selected a panel of arbitrators and stipulated that the arbitration clause was "silent" with respect to class arbitration. Counsel for AnimalFeeds explained to the arbitration panel that the term "silent" did not simply mean that the clause made no express reference to class arbitration. Rather, he said, "[a]ll the parties agree that when a contract is silent on an issue there's been no agreement that has been reached on that issue."

After hearing argument and evidence, including testimony from petitioners' experts regarding arbitration customs and usage in the maritime trade, the arbitrators concluded that the arbitration clause allowed for class arbitration. They found persuasive the fact that other arbitrators ruling after *Bazzle* had construed "a wide variety of clauses in a wide variety of settings as allowing for class arbitration," but the panel acknowledged that none of these decisions was "exactly comparable" to the present dispute. Petitioners' expert evidence did not show an "inten[t] to preclude class arbitration," the arbitrators reasoned, and petitioners' argument would leave "no basis for a class action absent express agreement among all parties and the putative class members."

The arbitrators stayed the proceeding to allow the parties to seek judicial review, and petitioners filed an application to vacate the arbitrators' award in the District Court for the Southern District of New York. The District Court vacated the award, concluding that the arbitrators' decision was made in "manifest disregard" of the law insofar as the arbitrators failed to conduct a choice-of-law analysis. Had such an analysis been conducted, the District Court held, the arbitrators would have applied the rule of federal maritime law requiring that contracts be interpreted in light of custom and usage.

AnimalFeeds appealed to the Court of Appeals, which reversed. As an initial matter, the Court of Appeals held that the "manifest disregard" standard survived our decision in *Hall Street Associates, L.L.C.* v. *Mattel, Inc.*, as a "judicial gloss" on the enumerated grounds for vacatur of arbitration awards under 9 U.S.C. § 10. Nonetheless, the Court of Appeals concluded that, because petitioners had cited no authority applying a federal maritime rule of custom and usage *against* class arbitration, the arbitrators' decision was not in manifest disregard of federal maritime law. Nor had the arbitrators manifestly disregarded New York law, the Court of Appeals continued, since nothing in New York case law established a rule against class arbitration.

We granted certiorari.

II

A

Petitioners contend that the decision of the arbitration panel must be vacated, but in order to obtain that relief, they must clear a high hurdle. It is not enough for petitioners to show that the panel committed an error — or even a serious error. "It is only when [an] arbitrator strays from interpretation and application of the agreement and effectively 'dispense[s] his own brand of industrial justice' that his decision may be unenforceable." *Major League Baseball Players Assn. v. Garvey*, 532 U.S. 504, 509 (2001) *(per curiam)* (quoting *Steelworkers v. Enterprise Wheel & Car Corp.*, 363 U.S. 593, 597 (1960)). In that situation, an arbitration decision may be vacated under § 10(a)(4) of the FAA on the ground that the arbitrator "exceeded [his] powers," for the task of an arbitrator is to interpret and enforce a contract, not to make public policy. In this case, we must conclude that what the arbitration panel did was simply to impose its own view of sound policy regarding class arbitration.[3]

B

. . .

Rather than inquiring whether the FAA, maritime law, or New York law contains a "default rule" under which an arbitration clause is construed as allowing class

---

[3] We do not decide whether " 'manifest disregard' " survives our decision in *Hall Street Associates, L.L.C.* v. *Mattel, Inc.*, as an independent ground for review or as a judicial gloss on the enumerated grounds for vacatur set forth at 9 U.S.C. § 10. AnimalFeeds characterizes that standard as requiring a showing that the arbitrators "knew of the relevant [legal] principle, appreciated that this principle controlled the outcome of the disputed issue, and nonetheless willfully flouted the governing law by refusing to apply it." Assuming, *arguendo*, that such a standard applies, we find it satisfied for the reasons that follow.

arbitration in the absence of express consent, the panel proceeded as if it had the authority of a common-law court to develop what it viewed as the best rule to be applied in such a situation. Perceiving a post-*Bazzle* consensus among arbitrators that class arbitration is beneficial in "a wide variety of settings," the panel considered only whether there was any good reason not to follow that consensus in this case. The panel was not persuaded by "court cases denying consolidation of arbitrations," by undisputed evidence that the Vegoilvoy charter party had "never been the basis of a class action," or by expert opinion that "sophisticated, multinational commercial parties of the type that are sought to be included in the class would never intend that the arbitration clauses would permit a class arbitration." Accordingly, finding no convincing ground for departing from the post-*Bazzle* arbitral consensus, the panel held that class arbitration was permitted in this case. The conclusion is inescapable that the panel simply imposed its own conception of sound policy.

. . .

. . . As a result, under § 10(b) of the FAA, we must either "direct a rehearing by the arbitrators" or decide the question that was originally referred to the panel. Because we conclude that there can be only one possible outcome on the facts before us, we see no need to direct a rehearing by the arbitrators.

III

A

The arbitration panel thought that *Bazzle* "controlled" the "resolution" of the question whether the Vegoilvoy charter party "permit[s] this arbitration to proceed on behalf of a class," but that understanding was incorrect.

. . .

When *Bazzle* reached this Court, no single rationale commanded a majority. The opinions of the Justices who joined the judgment — that is, the plurality opinion and JUSTICE STEVENS' opinion — collectively addressed three separate questions. The first was which decision maker (court or arbitrator) should decide whether the contracts in question were "silent" on the issue of class arbitration. The second was what standard the appropriate decision maker should apply in determining whether a contract allows class arbitration. (For example, does the FAA entirely preclude class arbitration? Does the FAA permit class arbitration only under limited circumstances, such as when the contract expressly so provides? Or is this question left entirely to state law?) The final question was whether, under whatever standard is appropriate, class arbitration had been properly ordered in the case at hand.

The plurality opinion decided only the first question, concluding that the arbitrator and not a court should decide whether the contracts were indeed "silent" on the issue of class arbitration. . . . The plurality therefore concluded that the decision of the State Supreme Court should be vacated and that the case should be remanded for a decision by the arbitrator on the question whether the contracts were indeed "silent." The plurality did not decide either the second or the third question noted above.

JUSTICE STEVENS concurred in the judgment vacating and remanding because otherwise there would have been "no controlling judgment of the Court," but he did not endorse the plurality's rationale. He did not take a definitive position on the first question, stating only that *"[a]rguably* the interpretation of the parties' agreement should have been made in the first instance by the arbitrator." (emphasis added)." But because he did not believe that Green Tree had raised the question of the appropriate decision maker, he preferred not to reach that question and, instead, would have affirmed the decision of the State Supreme Court on the ground that "the decision to conduct a class-action arbitration was correct as a matter of law." Accordingly, his analysis bypassed the first question noted above and rested instead on his resolution of the second and third questions. Thus, *Bazzle* did not yield a majority decision on any of the three questions.

B

Unfortunately, the opinions in *Bazzle* appear to have baffled the parties in this case at the time of the arbitration proceeding. For one thing, the parties appear to have believed that the judgment in *Bazzle* requires an arbitrator, not a court, to decide whether a contract permits class arbitration. In fact, however, only the plurality decided that question. But we need not revisit that question here because the parties' supplemental agreement expressly assigned this issue to the arbitration panel, and no party argues that this assignment was impermissible.

Unfortunately, however, both the parties and the arbitration panel seem to have misunderstood *Bazzle* in another respect, namely, that it established the standard to be applied by a decision maker in determining whether a contract may permissibly be interpreted to allow class arbitration. The arbitration panel began its discussion by stating that the parties "differ regarding *the rule of interpretation* to be gleaned from [the *Bazzle*] decision." The panel continued:

> Claimants argue that *Bazzle* requires clear language that forbids class arbitration in order to bar a class action. The Panel, however, agrees with Respondents that the test is a more general one — arbitrators must look to the language of the parties' agreement to ascertain the parties' intention whether they intended to permit or to preclude class action.

As we have explained, however, *Bazzle* did not establish the rule to be applied in deciding whether class arbitration is permitted. The decision in *Bazzle* left that question open, and we turn to it now.

IV

While the interpretation of an arbitration agreement is generally a matter of state law, the FAA imposes certain rules of fundamental importance, including the basic precept that arbitration "is a matter of consent, not coercion." *Volt.*

A

. . . Whether enforcing an agreement to arbitrate or construing an arbitration clause, courts and arbitrators must "give effect to the contractual rights and expectations of the parties." In this endeavor, "as with any other contract, the parties' intentions control." This is because an arbitrator derives his or her powers from the parties' agreement to forgo the legal process and submit their disputes to private dispute resolution.

Underscoring the consensual nature of private dispute resolution, we have held that parties are " 'generally free to structure their arbitration agreements as they see fit.' " For example, we have held that parties may agree to limit the issues they choose to arbitrate, and may agree on rules under which any arbitration will proceed. They may choose who will resolve specific disputes.

We think it is also clear from our precedents and the contractual nature of arbitration that parties may specify *with whom* they choose to arbitrate their disputes. It falls to courts and arbitrators to give effect to these contractual limitations, and when doing so, courts and arbitrators must not lose sight of the purpose of the exercise: to give effect to the intent of the parties.

B

From these principles, it follows that a party may not be compelled under the FAA to submit to class arbitration unless there is a contractual basis for concluding that the party *agreed* to do so. In this case, however, the arbitration panel imposed class arbitration even though the parties concurred that they had reached "no agreement" on that issue. The critical point, in the view of the arbitration panel, was that petitioners did not "establish that the parties to the charter agreements intended to *preclude* class arbitration." Even though the parties are sophisticated business entities, even though there is no tradition of class arbitration under maritime law, and even though AnimalFeeds does not dispute that it is customary for the shipper to choose the charter party that is used for a particular shipment, the panel regarded the agreement's silence on the question of class arbitration as dispositive. The panel's conclusion is fundamentally at war with the foundational FAA principle that arbitration is a matter of consent.

In certain contexts, it is appropriate to presume that parties that enter into an arbitration agreement implicitly authorize the arbitrator to adopt such procedures as are necessary to give effect to the parties' agreement. Thus, we have said that " ' "procedural" questions which grow out of the dispute and bear on its final disposition' are presumptively not for the judge, but for an arbitrator, to decide." *Howsam* (quoting *John Wiley & Sons, Inc. v. Livingston*, 376 U.S. 543, 557 (1964)). This recognition is grounded in the background principle that "[w]hen the parties to a bargain sufficiently defined to be a contract have not agreed with respect to a term which is essential to a determination of their rights and duties, a term which is reasonable in the circumstances is supplied by the court." Restatement (Second) of Contracts § 204 (1979).

An implicit agreement to authorize class-action arbitration, however, is not a term that the arbitrator may infer solely from the fact of the parties' agreement to arbitrate. This is so because class-action arbitration changes the nature of arbitration to such a degree that it cannot be presumed the parties consented to it by simply agreeing to submit their disputes to an arbitrator. In bilateral arbitration, parties forgo the procedural rigor and appellate review of the courts in order to realize the benefits of private dispute resolution: lower costs, greater efficiency and speed, and the ability to choose expert adjudicators to resolve specialized disputes. But the relative benefits of class-action arbitration are much less assured, giving reason to doubt the parties' mutual consent to resolve disputes through class-wide arbitration.

Consider just some of the fundamental changes brought about by the shift from bilateral arbitration to class-action arbitration. An arbitrator chosen according to an agreed-upon procedure no longer resolves a single dispute between the parties to a single agreement, but instead resolves many disputes between hundreds or perhaps even thousands of parties. Under the Class Rules, "the presumption of privacy and confidentiality" that applies in many bilateral arbitrations "shall not apply in class arbitrations," thus potentially frustrating the parties' assumptions when they agreed to arbitrate. The arbitrator's award no longer purports to bind just the parties to a single arbitration agreement, but adjudicates the rights of absent parties as well. And the commercial stakes of class-action arbitration are comparable to those of class-action litigation, even though the scope of judicial review is much more limited. We think that the differences between bilateral and class-action arbitration are too great for arbitrators to presume, consistent with their limited powers under the FAA, that the parties' mere silence on the issue of class-action arbitration constitutes consent to resolve their disputes in class proceedings.[10]

The dissent minimizes these crucial differences by characterizing the question before the arbitrators as being merely what "procedural mode" was available to present AnimalFeeds' claims. If the question were that simple, there would be no need to consider the parties' intent with respect to class arbitration. See *Howsam* (committing "procedural questions" presumptively to the arbitrator's discretion). But the FAA requires more. Contrary to the dissent, but consistent with our precedents emphasizing the consensual basis of arbitration, we see the question as being whether the parties *agreed to authorize* class arbitration. Here, where the parties stipulated that there was "no agreement" on this question, it follows that the parties cannot be compelled to submit their dispute to class arbitration.

V

For these reasons, the judgment of the Court of Appeals is reversed, and the case is remanded for further proceedings consistent with this opinion.

It is so ordered.

[Dissenting opinion omitted.]

---

[10] We have no occasion to decide what contractual basis may support a finding that the parties agreed to authorize class-action arbitration. Here, as noted, the parties stipulated that there was "no agreement" on the issue of class-action arbitration.

NOTES

1.　Consolidation and class actions both are ways to combine multiple proceedings into a single case. Consolidation permits the decision maker to combine several pending actions into one. Class actions permit class representatives to sue on behalf of claimants who are not, individually, parties to the lawsuit. If these procedural devices work properly, they can reduce litigation costs significantly and avoid inconsistent results in multi-party disputes. For general discussions of consolidation and class actions in the arbitration context, see Thomas J. Stipanowich, *Arbitration and the Multi-Party Dispute: The Search for Workable Solutions*, 72 Iowa L. Rev. 473 (1987); Jean R. Sternlight, *As Mandatory Arbitration Meets the Class Action, Will the Class Action Survive?*, 42 Wm. & Mary L. Rev. 1 (2000).

2.　Institutional arbitration rules generally do not address the authority of arbitrators to order consolidated arbitration proceedings involving multiple parties. An exception is Article 10 of the 2012 ICC Rules, which provides as follows:

> The Court may, at the request of a party, consolidate two or more arbitrations pending under the Rules into a single arbitration, where:
>
> a) the parties have agreed to consolidation; or
>
> b) all of the claims in the arbitrations are made under the same arbitration agreement; or
>
> c) where the claims in the arbitrations are made under more than one arbitration agreement, the arbitrations are between the same parties, the disputes in the arbitrations arise in connection with the same legal relationship, and the Court finds the arbitration agreements to be compatible.
>
> In deciding whether to consolidate, the Court may take into account any circumstances it considers to be relevant, including whether one or more arbitrators have been confirmed or appointed in more than one of the arbitrations and, if so, whether the same or different persons have been confirmed or appointed. When arbitrations are consolidated, they shall be consolidated into the arbitration that commenced first, unless otherwise agreed by all parties.

In addition, occasionally an arbitration clause will authorize some degree of consolidation of related proceedings.

3.　Can a court order separate arbitration proceedings to be consolidated? The answer appears to be no: "courts have uniformly held that, absent a clear agreement to the contrary, the question of whether arbitration proceedings should (or should not) be consolidated is a procedural matter to be decided by the arbitrators, not by a court." Rice Co. v. Precious Flowers LTD, 2012 U.S. Dist. LEXIS 78269 at *12 (S.D.N.Y. June 5, 2012). Whatever the rule might be for class arbitration, the Seventh Circuit has made clear that it does not apply to consolidated arbitration:

> Class actions always have been treated as special. One self-selected plaintiff represents others, who are entitled to protection from the repre-

sentative's misconduct or incompetence. Often this requires individual notice to class members, a procedure that may be more complex and costly than the adjudication itself. As a practical matter the representative's small stake means that lawyers are in charge, which creates a further need for the adjudicator to protect the class. Finally, class actions can turn a small claim into a whopping one. Unsurprisingly, Fed. R. Civ. P. 23 imposes stringent requirements on class certification. Consolidation of suits that are going to proceed anyway poses none of these potential problems. That's why Fed. R. Civ. P. 42(a) leaves to a district judge's discretion — and without any of Rule 23's procedures and safeguards — the decision whether to consolidate multiple suits. Just as consolidation under Rule 42(a) does not change the fundamental nature of litigation, so consolidation of the plans' claims would not change the fundamental nature of arbitration.

Blue Cross Blue Shield of Mass. v. BCS Ins. Co., 671 F.3d 635, 640 (7th Cir. 2011).

4. Some state arbitration laws permit courts to order separate arbitration proceedings to be consolidated. *See* CAL. CIV. PROC. CODE § 1281.3 (Deering 2012); GA. CODE ANN. § 9-9-6 (2012); MASS. GEN. LAWS ch. 251, § 2A (2012); N.J. STAT. ANN. § 2A:23A-3 (2012). In addition, § 10 of the Revised Uniform Arbitration Act permits court-ordered consolidation under appropriate circumstances unless the arbitration agreement "prohibits consolidation." RUAA § 10(a), (c). Does the FAA preempt such statutes?

5. Most litigation in recent years has involved class arbitration rather than consolidation. Class arbitration differs from a consolidated arbitration proceeding in several respects, as discussed in the *Blue Cross* case in note 3. The most fundamental difference is that in class arbitration (like class actions in court) a representative acts on behalf of absent class members. Thus, class arbitration is subject to all the criticisms of representative litigation generally, *see, e.g.,* Bruce Hay & David Rosenberg, *"Sweetheart" and "Blackmail" Settlements in Class Actions: Reality and Remedy*, 75 NOTRE DAME L. REV. 1377 (2000) (arguing risks overstated), perhaps more so because of the need for arbitrators in such proceedings to protect the interests of third parties who are not participating in the arbitration. On the other hand, unlike consolidated arbitration, class arbitration may be less likely to result in conflicts among arbitration agreements and may be necessary for some claims economically to be brought. *See* Sternlight, *supra*, at 86-88. The availability of class arbitration may be particularly important because courts have held that the parties who have agreed to arbitrate a dispute may not participate in a class action in court. *See, e.g.,* Ex Parte Green Tree Fin'l Corp., 723 So. 2d 6, 10 & n.3 (Ala. 1998); Zawikowski v. Beneficial Nat'l Bank, 1999 U.S. Dist. LEXIS 514 (N.D. Ill. Jan. 7, 1999); Collins v. International Dairy Queen, Inc., 169 F.R.D. 690, 694 (M.D. Ga. 1997); Hunt v. Up North Plastics, 980 F. Supp. 1046, 1048 (D. Minn. 1997).

6. In *Bazzle*, discussed in *Stolt-Nielsen*, the Supreme Court granted certiorari to resolve the following question: "Whether the Federal Arbitration Act, 9 U.S.C. § 1 *et seq.*, prohibits class-action procedures from being superimposed onto an arbitration agreement that does not provide for class-action arbitration." Petition for Writ of Certiorari at i, Green Tree Fin'l Corp. v. Bazzle, 539 U.S. 444 (2003) (No.

02-634). Because the case arose in state court and the class arbitration rule was based on state law, the question presented by the petitioner was one of federal preemption: did the FAA preempt the state rule providing for class arbitration? The Court did not resolve that preemption question (only the dissenting Justices even reached it), issuing four separate opinions none of which commanded a majority.

The plurality in *Bazzle* (Justices Breyer, Scalia, Souter, and Ginsburg) concluded that the FAA required the arbitrator to determine "whether the arbitration contracts forbid class arbitration," vacating the South Carolina Supreme Court's judgment and remanding for further proceedings. Justice Stevens concluded that "nothing in the Federal Arbitration Act" precludes the South Carolina court's decision that the parties' agreement was silent on class arbitration and so as a matter of state law class arbitration was permissible, but concurred in the judgment so that there would be a controlling judgment of the court. Chief Justice Rehnquist dissented, joined by Justices O'Connor and Kennedy. The dissenting justices construed the parties' agreement as precluding class arbitration: petitioner's "contractual right to choose an arbitrator for each dispute with the other 3,734 individual class members . . . was denied when the same arbitrator was foisted upon petitioner to resolve those claims as well." Because "the Supreme Court of South Carolina imposed a regime that was contrary to the express agreement of the parties as to how the arbitrator would be chosen," its decision was contrary to the FAA. Finally, Justice Thomas dissented on the ground that the FAA does not apply in state court and so "the FAA cannot be a ground for pre-empting a state court's interpretation of a private arbitration agreement."

What, if anything does *Bazzle* stand for? Is anything left of the decision after *Stolt-Nielsen*?

7. After *Bazzle*, the American Arbitration Association issued Supplementary Rules for Class Arbitrations (effective Oct. 8, 2003), reprinted in the Documentary Supplement. According to the AAA, it "will administer demands for class arbitration pursuant to its Supplementary Rules for Class Arbitrations if (1) the underlying agreement specifies that disputes arising out of the parties' agreement shall be resolved by arbitration in accordance with any of the Association's rules, and (2) the agreement is silent with respect to class claims, consolidation or joinder of claims." It will not administer an arbitration on a class basis if the "underlying agreement prohibits class claims, consolidation or joinder, unless an order of a court directs the parties to the underlying dispute to submit any aspect of their dispute involving class claims, consolidation, joinder or the enforceability of such provisions, to an arbitrator or to the Association."

Gregory A. Litt and Tina Praprotnik describe the trends in class arbitration filings with the AAA as follows:

> As set out in the table below, class arbitration filings with the American Arbitration Association (AAA) — widely believed to be the leading provider of class arbitration — exploded immediately after the AAA promulgated its class arbitration rules in 2003. The filings continued in large numbers up to the decision in *Stolt-Nielsen*, which many in the field read as a death knell for class arbitration in the United States. Indeed, class arbitration filings at the AAA dipped to 27 in 2010, the lowest full-year total since the AAA

procedure was initiated. . . . But the number of class arbitration filings surprisingly increased in 2011, rising to 36 new filings, and though 2012 appears to be slow, there were 9 additional class cases filed in the first half of the year.

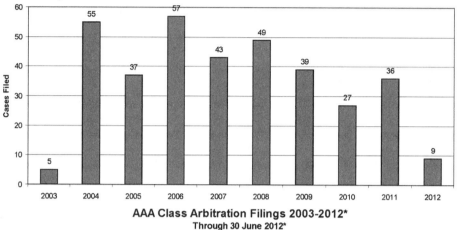

AAA Class Arbitration Filings 2003-2012*
Through 30 June 2012*

Gregory A. Litt & Tina Praprotnik, *After* Stolt-Nielsen, *Circuits Split, but AAA Filings Continue*, MEALEY'S INT'L ARB. REP., July 2012, at 1. What is the future of class arbitration after *Stolt-Nielsen* (and *Concepcion*), do you think?

8. So what about the decision in *Stolt-Nielsen* itself? *Stolt-Nielsen* is a complex case that raises perhaps more questions than it answers. The case can be read very narrowly — the sole issue before the arbitrators was whether the parties had agreed to class arbitration, and the arbitrators exceeded that authority by looking to public policy when the parties had stipulated that there was no agreement. But the Supreme Court went on to decide for itself whether the parties had agreed to class arbitration. Contrary to the Court's assertion, while section 10(b) of the FAA authorizes a court to remand a case to the arbitrators, it does not authorize the court to decide the issue itself instead. To the contrary, the Court has made clear (even summarily reversing a court of appeals' decision to the contrary) that the matter remains one to be decided by the arbitrators even after a court vacates the award, unless the ground for vacating the award is that the agreement to arbitrate is unenforceable. *See, e.g.*, Major League Baseball Players' Ass'n v. Garvey, 532 U.S. 511-12 (2001) (per curiam); *see also* JULIAN D.M. LEW ET AL., COMPARATIVE INTERNATIONAL COMMERCIAL ARBITRATION ¶ 25-61, at 682 (2003) ("If an award is set aside for reasons other than invalidity of the arbitration agreement, the agreement would survive the award and the parties would still be bound to have their disputes settled by arbitration.").

Moreover, the opinion raises serious questions about the authority of arbitrators to fill procedural gaps in contracts. The Court suggests that arbitrators do not have the same power to fill gaps in contracts as common law courts, and relies on labor arbitration cases (rather than cases decided under the FAA) in describing when courts can vacate arbitration awards. Are these characterizations of arbitrator authority consistent with cases such as *Mitsubishi* and *Gilmer* in Chapter 3, in which the Court stated that resolving cases in arbitration rather than in court does not affect the substantive rights of the parties? Do arbitrators have more power to fill gaps in statutes than they do in contracts? Are arbitrators' substantive powers greater than their procedural ones?

9.　One important question that the Court does not address in *Stolt-Nielsen* is what sort of evidence would be sufficient to show that the parties had agreed to class arbitration (see footnote 10 of the opinion). One would think that if the contract included a class arbitration waiver, it would be pretty good evidence the parties had not agreed to arbitrate on a class basis — perhaps even if the waiver is held unenforceable. Conversely, only very rarely do parties expressly agree to class arbitration. In addition, *Stolt-Nielsen* itself dealt with a maritime arbitration case. Will courts be more likely to find agreement on class arbitration in consumer and employment contracts? What sort of evidence of agreement would suffice in those types of cases? Interestingly, in five of the eight AAA clause construction awards (62.5%) issued since *Stolt-Nielsen* and available on the AAA web site, the arbitrator construed the arbitration agreement as permitting class arbitration — despite the decision in *Stolt-Nielsen*. Christopher R. Drahozal & Peter B. Rutledge, *Contract and Procedure*, 94 MARQUETTE L. REV. 1103, 1157-58 (2011). While that percentage is significantly lower than the percentage before *Stolt-Nielsen*, more life appears to remain in the class arbitration mechanism than some predicted.

In reviewing awards construing silent agreements as permitting class arbitration, the circuits have split since *Stolt-Nielsen*. *Compare* Jock v. Sterling Jewelers Inc., 646 F.3d 113, 126-27 (2d Cir. 2011), *cert. denied*, 132 S. Ct. 1742 (2012) (upholding award when "[i]n divining the parties' intent on the issue of class arbitration, the arbitrator relied solely on the terms of the agreement and Ohio law") *and* Sutter v. Oxford Health Plans LLC, 675 F.3d 215, 224 (3d Cir. 2012) (upholding award when "the arbitrator construed the text of the arbitration agreement to authorize and require class arbitration") *with* Reed v. Florida Int'l Univ., Inc., 681 F.3d 630, 646 (5th Cir. 2012) (vacating award when "the arbitrator . . . order[ed] the parties to submit to class arbitration without a contractual or legal basis"). Which approach is more true to *Stolt-Nielsen*?

10.　Who decides whether an arbitration agreement authorizes class arbitration after *Stolt-Nielsen*? As noted above, courts have consistently held that determining whether an arbitration agreement permits consolidation is an issue for the arbitrators, and have distinguished class arbitration from consolidation in so deciding. Interestingly, the Fifth Circuit in *Reed v. Florida International University, Inc.*, although ultimately vacating the arbitrators' award, concluded on the facts of the case that the issue was one for the arbitrators to decide:

> The Supreme Court has not definitively decided this issue. In *Green Tree Financial Corp. v. Bazzle*, four Justices concluded that the class arbitration issue did not constitute a "gateway" or arbitrability matter that is generally decided by a court, but was instead a procedural matter for the arbitrator. In *Stolt-Nielsen*, the Court confirmed that *Green Tree* "did not yield a majority decision" on this issue. The *Stolt-Nielsen* Court declined to revisit the question because the parties in that case had agreed to submit the question to the arbitrator rather than the court. At least at the Supreme

Court level, therefore, the question remains open.

[In this case,] [t]he parties' consent to the [AAA] Supplementary Rules, therefore, constitutes a clear agreement to allow the arbitrator to decide whether the party's agreement provides for class arbitration. As such, we need not determine whether, in the absence of such an agreement, the threshold matter of bilateral or class arbitration should be decided by a court or an arbitrator.

681 F.3d at 633-35; *see also* Brookdale Senior Living, Inc. v. Dempsey, 2012 U.S. Dist. LEXIS 57731, at *9 (M.D. Tenn. Apr. 25, 2012) ("numerous courts have continued to apply the plurality's ruling in *Bazzle* even after *Stolt-Nielsen* was decided").

11. *AT&T Mobility, LLC v. Concepcion* in § 4.04 also addresses the relationship between individual arbitrations and class arbitrations. Is it consistent with *Stolt-Nielsen*? What does it add?

PROBLEM 6.9

Ettie Shaffer, the general counsel of West Gilmerton Mining Co. (see Problem 6.3), calls you up and tells you about an arbitration proceeding brought against her company by one of its customers, Lawler & Co. It seems that West Gilmerton sold some coal to Lawler, which Lawler in turn resold to Andrews & Co. Both contracts contained arbitration clauses. Andrews has now filed a demand for arbitration against Lawler alleging that the coal did not meet contractual standards. Lawler in turn has filed a demand for arbitration against West Gilmerton, asserting that West Gilmerton breached its contract with Lawler.

Shaffer tells you that just today Lawler's general counsel phoned her and asked if she would agree to combine the two arbitration proceedings. Shaffer tells you that she believes West Gilmerton fully complied with its contract with Lawler. But she has no interest in agreeing to Lawler's request. "There's no reason to make things any easier for Lawler than we have to," she says. "If Lawler has to deal with multiple arbitration proceedings that's its problem, not mine." She wants your opinion, however, on whether consolidation could be ordered over her objection.

(a) If Lawler requests the arbitrators to consolidate the proceedings, are they likely to grant its request?

(b) If Lawler requests a federal court to order the arbitration proceedings consolidated, how is the court likely to rule?

(c) If Lawler requests a state court (located in a state that has enacted the Revised Uniform Arbitration Act) to order the arbitration proceedings consolidated, how is the court likely to rule?

(d) Same as (c) except that Lawler and Andrews agreed to arbitrate under the JAMS arbitration rules (instead of the AAA as in the West Gilmerton-Lawler contract) and have agreed to use three arbitrators (instead of one as in the West Gilmerton-Lawler contract). How is the court likely to rule?

(e) Same as (c) except that the contract between West Gilmerton and Lawler does not contain an arbitration clause. How is the court likely to rule?

(f) Same as (c) except that the arbitration clause in the contract between West Gilmerton and Lawler provides that no arbitration proceeding under the clause shall be consolidated with any other arbitration proceeding. How is the court likely to rule?

PROBLEM 6.10

Recall once again the facts of the *Gateway 2000* case from § 2.05[A]. Assume that you are representing the plaintiff in that case, who has a claim worth roughly $2,000. You know there are thousands of other consumers who have bought similar Gateway computers, at least some of whose computers likely have the same problem as your client's computer has. You also anticipate that the court likely will hold (as the court of appeals did in the actual case) that your client and the other consumers have agreed to arbitrate by using their computers for more than 30 days after receiving them.

(a) Can you bring the lawsuit in federal court as a class action on behalf of all similarly situated buyers of Gateway 2000 computers?

(b) Can you get either the arbitrator or the federal court to order that the case proceed on a class basis in arbitration? What other information would you need to evaluate your chances?

(c) How, if at all, would your answer change if the arbitration clause expressly precludes class arbitration?

(d) Is it economical to proceed with your client's claim in arbitration as an individual (rather than a class) action? What if the value of the claim were $20 instead of $2,000? Is there anything else that you might want to know?

§ 6.07 DISCOVERY

"Limitations on discovery . . . remain one of the hallmarks of American commercial arbitration. . . ." 3 IAN R. MACNEIL ET AL., FEDERAL ARBITRATION LAW § 34.1, at 34.2 (1994). Sophisticated commercial parties who agree to arbitration are willing to trade a reduced ability to discover facts in the other side's possession for a reduction in litigation costs. Unsophisticated parties who agree to arbitration may be doing the same thing — or they may be giving up their ability to get evidence essential for proving their claim, to the benefit of the more sophisticated parties with whom they are dealing.

The limited discovery available in domestic arbitration is reflected in institutional arbitration rules. Rule R-21 of the AAA Commercial Arbitration Rules, which addresses the "exchange of information," gives the arbitrator authority, "consistent with the expedited nature of arbitration," to "direct (i) the production of documents and other information, and (ii) the identification of any witnesses to be called." The AAA Procedures for Large, Complex Commercial Disputes contemplate more extensive discovery: the parties shall "cooperate in the exchange of documents, exhibits and information within such party's control if the arbitrator(s) consider such production to be consistent with the goal of achieving a just, speedy and cost-effective resolution," Rule L-4(b); the arbitrator is authorized to order document discovery "consistent with the expedited nature of arbitration," Rule L-4(c); and "upon good cause shown and consistent with the expedited nature of arbitration, the arbitrator(s) may order depositions of, or the propounding of interrogatories to, such persons who may possess information determined by the arbitrator(s) to be necessary to determination of the matter," Rule L-4(d). The JAMS Employment Arbitration Rules and Procedures provide for the exchange of "all non-privileged documents and other information (including Electronically Stored Information ('ESI') relevant to the dispute or claim" and the names of all individuals "whom they may call as witnesses," Rule 17(a), and permit at least one deposition to be taken of the opposing party, Rule 17(b). The arbitrator is authorized to order additional discovery. Rule 17(a) & (b).

The FAA and the UAA, with one possible exception discussed below, do not address the availability of discovery in arbitration. *See* FAA § 7; UAA § 7. By comparison, the Revised Uniform Arbitration Act provides that the arbitrator "may permit such discovery as the arbitrator decides is appropriate in the circumstances, taking into account the needs of the parties to the arbitration proceeding and other affected persons and the desirability of making the proceeding fair, expeditious and cost effective." RUAA § 17(c). Comment 3 to § 17 of the RUAA explains that the "discovery contemplated by section 17(c) . . . is not coextensive with that which occurs in the course of civil litigation under federal or state rules of civil procedure." *See also* RUAA § 4(b)(1) (permitting pre-dispute waiver of section 17(c)).

Ultimately, of course, the amount of discovery that takes place is within the parties' control. They can agree once a dispute arises to permit more or less discovery than authorized in the governing institutional rules. In addition, the parties can include provisions addressing the extent of discovery in their arbitration clauses. In a sample of franchise contracts, for example, a handful of clauses specified precisely how much discovery would be available and when. Interestingly, and perhaps surprisingly, several arbitration clauses in the sample actually *expanded* the scope of discovery to the full scope provided in the Federal Rules of Civil Procedure.

Even less extensive discovery is likely to be available in international arbitration than in domestic arbitration. This should not be surprising given that American discovery practices in court litigation tend to be much more liberal than in other parts of the world. The UNCITRAL Arbitration Rules, for example, provide only that the tribunal may require a party to "produce documents, exhibits or other evidence within such period of time as the arbitral tribunal shall determine." Art. 27(3); *see also* AAA/ICDR Int'l Rules, art. 19(2) & (3). *Compare* ICC Rules of Arbitration, art. 25(1) ("The arbitral tribunal shall proceed within as short a time as possible to establish the facts of the case by all appropriate means"). The IBA Rules on the Taking of Evidence in International Commercial Arbitration provide for document requests that contain "(*i*) a description of a requested Document sufficient to identify it, or (*ii*) a description in sufficient detail (including subject matter) of a narrow and specific requested category of Documents that are reasonably believed to exist." Art. 3(3)(a). The IBA Rules do not authorize the taking of depositions. Instead, parties submit written witness statements containing the substance of a witness' testimony. Art. 4.

Because an arbitrator's authority comes from the parties' contract, obtaining discovery from non-parties to the arbitration agreement is difficult: the contract can give the arbitrator no authority over them. Thus, any authority to order discovery from non-parties to the arbitration would have to come from an arbitration statute, such as the FAA. The following case addresses whether § 7 of the FAA permits discovery from non-parties to the arbitration.

HAY GROUP, INC. v. E.B.S. ACQUISITION CORP.
United States Court of Appeals for the Third Circuit
360 F.3d 404 (2004)

ALITO, CIRCUIT JUDGE:

PriceWaterhouseCoopers ("PwC") and E.B.S., non-parties to an arbitration, seek to avoid compliance with an arbitration panel's subpoena requiring them to turn over documents prior to the panel's hearing. The District Court enforced the subpoena. We reverse.

I.

Hay Group ("Hay") is a management consulting firm. David A. Hoffrichter left Hay's employment and joined PwC in September 1999. In early 2002, PwC sold the division employing Hoffrichter to E.B.S.

Hoffrichter's separation agreement from Hay contained a clause that forbade him from soliciting any of Hay's employees or clients for one year. The agreement further provided for arbitration to resolve any dispute arising under the agreement. In February 2000, Hay commenced such an arbitration proceeding in Philadelphia, Pennsylvania, against Hoffrichter, claiming that he had violated the non-solicitation clause.

In an attempt to obtain information for the arbitration, Hay served subpoenas for documents on E.B.S. at its Pittsburgh office and on PwC at its Philadelphia office. Hay sought to have the documents produced prior to the panel's arbitration hearing. PwC and E.B.S. objected to these subpoenas, but the arbitration panel disagreed. When PwC and E.B.S. still refused to comply with the subpoenas, Hay asked the United States District Court for the Eastern District of Pennsylvania to enforce the subpoenas. PwC and E.B.S. again objected, claiming, among other things, that the Federal Arbitration Act ("FAA") did not authorize the panel to issue subpoenas to non-parties for prehearing document production. . . .

In November 2002, the District Court issued a decision enforcing the subpoenas and ordering the parties to resolve any remaining differences. In doing so, the District Court accepted the view of the Eighth Circuit and several district courts that the FAA authorizes arbitration panels to issue subpoenas on non-parties for pre-hearing document production. The District Court also held that even under the view of the Fourth Circuit, which permits such production only when there is a "special need," the panel's subpoenas would be valid. . . .

PwC and E.B.S. then filed the present appeal. The District Court denied their motion to stay its order pending appeal, but our Court granted their emergency motion for a stay.

II.

A.

On appeal, PwC and E.B.S. . . . argue that, under Section 7 of the FAA, a non-party witness may be compelled to bring documents to an arbitration proceeding but may not simply be subpoenaed to produce documents. We agree.

An arbitrator's authority over parties that are not contractually bound by the arbitration agreement is strictly limited to that granted by the Federal Arbitration Act. Accordingly, we must look to the FAA to determine whether an arbitrator may issue a subpoena requiring pre-hearing document production by a person or entity that is not bound by the arbitration agreement (hereinafter a "non-party").

. . .

[The language of § 7] speaks unambiguously to the issue before us. The only power conferred on arbitrators with respect to the production of documents by a non-party is the power to summon a non-party "to attend before them or any of them as a witness *and* in a proper case *to bring with him or them* any book, record, document or paper which may be deemed material as evidence in the case." 9 U.S.C. § 7 (emphasis added). The power to require a non-party "to bring" items "with him" clearly applies only to situations in which the non-party accompanies the items to the arbitration proceeding, not to situations in which the items are simply sent or brought by a courier. In addition, the use of the word "and" makes it clear that a non-party may be compelled "to bring" items "with him" only when the non-party is summoned "to attend before [the arbitrator] as a witness." Thus, Section 7's language unambiguously restricts an arbitrator's subpoena power to situations in which the non-party has been called to appear in the physical presence of the arbitrator and to hand over the documents at that time.

This interpretation is supported by the interpretation of similar language in a previous version of Federal Rule of Civil Procedure 45. From its adoption in 1937 until its amendment in 1991, Rule 45 did not allow federal courts to issue pre-hearing document subpoenas on non-parties. . . .

Under this version of Rule 45(a), a subpoena was required to command the person to whom it was directed "to attend and give testimony." The court could then add a requirement that the subpoenaed witness bring documents with him. *See* Fed. R. Civ. Proc. 45(b). The accepted view was that nothing in Rule 45 gave the court the power to issue documents-only subpoenas to non-parties.

Some courts have argued that the language of Section 7 implies the power to issue such pre-hearing subpoenas. *See* In re Security Life Insurance Co. of America, 228 F.3d 865, 870-71 (8th Cir. 2000) ("We thus hold that implicit in an arbitration panel's power to subpoena relevant documents for production at a hearing is the power to order the production of relevant documents for review by a party prior to the hearing.").

We disagree with this power-by-implication analysis. By conferring the power to compel a non-party witness to bring items to an arbitration proceeding while saying nothing about the power simply to compel the production of items without summoning the custodian to testify, the FAA implicitly withholds the latter power. If the FAA had been meant to confer the latter, broader power, we believe that the drafters would have said so, and they would have then had no need to spell out the more limited power to compel a nonparty witness to bring items with him to an arbitration proceeding. . . .

Since the text of Section 7 of the FAA is straightforward, we must see if the result is absurd. We conclude that it is not. Indeed, we believe that a reasonable argument can be made that a literal reading of Section 7 actually furthers arbitration's goal of "resolving disputes in a timely and cost efficient manner." . . . [I]t is not absurd to read the FAA as circumscribing an arbitration panel's power to affect those who did not agree to its jurisdiction. The requirement that document production be made at an actual hearing may, in the long run, discourage the issuance of large-scale subpoenas upon nonparties. This is so because parties that consider obtaining such a subpoena will be forced to consider whether the documents are important enough to justify the time, money, and effort that the subpoenaing parties will be required to expend if an actual appearance before an arbitrator is needed. Under a system of pre-hearing document production, by contrast, there is less incentive to limit the scope of discovery and more incentive to engage in fishing expeditions that undermine some of the advantages of the supposedly shorter and cheaper system of arbitration. Thus, contrary to Hay's claim, heeding the clear language of Section 7 does not lead to absurd or even unreasonable results.

Of course, one may well think that it would be preferable on policy grounds for arbitrators to be able to require non-parties to produce documents without also subpoenaing them to appear in person before the panel. But if it is desirable for arbitrators to possess that power, the way to give it to them is by amending Section 7 of the FAA, just as Rule 45 of the Federal Rules of Civil Procedure was amended in 1991 to confer such a power on district courts. The Fourth Circuit has interpreted Section 7 in a way that is largely consistent with our reading. In COMSAT Corp. v. Natl. Science Foundation, [190 F.3d 269 (4th Cir. 1999)], the court held that the plain meaning of Section 7 did not empower an arbitrator to issue prehearing discovery subpoenas to nonparties. . . . In dicta, however, the *COMSAT* court suggested that an arbitration panel might be able to subpoena a non-party for pre-hearing discovery "under unusual circumstances" and "upon a showing of special need or hardship." While we agree with *COMSAT*'s holding, we cannot agree with this dicta because there is simply no textual basis for allowing any "special need" exception. Again, while such a power might be desirable, we have no authority to confer it.

We have carefully considered but must respectfully disagree with the Eighth Circuit's holding in *Security Life* that Section 7 authorizes arbitrators to issue pre-hearing document-production subpoenas on non-parties. In *Security Life*, the

Eighth Circuit reasoned that the "the interest in efficiency is furthered by permitting a party to review and digest relevant documentary evidence prior to the arbitration hearing." In our view, however, this policy argument cannot supersede the statutory text.

Even if we were to look outside the statutory text to make our decision, any argument in favor of ignoring the literal meaning of the FAA in the name of efficiency seems to cut against Supreme Court precedent regarding the role of efficiency considerations in interpreting the Act. Although efficiency is certainly an objective of parties who favor arbitration over litigation, efficiency is not the principal goal of the FAA. Rather, the central purpose of the FAA is to give effect to private agreements.

. . .

In sum, we hold that the FAA did not authorize the panel to issue a prehearing discovery subpoena to PwC and E.B.S. We further reject any "special needs exception" to this rule. If Hay wants to access the documents, the panel must subpoena PwC and E.B.S. to appear before it and bring the documents with them.

. . .

III.

For the reasons set out above, the order of the District Court is reversed.

CHERTOFF, CIRCUIT JUDGE, concurring:

I join Judge Alito's opinion in full. . . . I write separately to observe that our opinion does not leave arbitrators powerless to require advance production of documents when necessary to allow fair and efficient proceedings.

Under section 7 of the Federal Arbitration Act, arbitrators have the power to compel a third-party witness to appear with documents before a single arbitrator, who can then adjourn the proceedings. This gives the arbitration panel the effective ability to require delivery of documents from a third-party in advance, notwithstanding the limitations of section 7 of the FAA. In many instances, of course, the inconvenience of making such a personal appearance may well prompt the witness to deliver the documents and waive presence.

To be sure, this procedure requires the arbitrators to decide that they are prepared to suffer some inconvenience of their own in order to mandate what is, in reality, an advance production of documents. But that is not necessarily a bad thing, since it will induce the arbitrators and parties to weigh whether advance production is really needed. And the availability of this procedure within the existing statutory language should satisfy the desire that there be some mechanism "to compel pre-arbitration discovery upon a showing of special need or hardship."

NOTES

1. The circuits are divided over the proper interpretation of section 7:

The Sixth and Eighth Circuits have held that the power to compel pre-hearing discovery from a third party is implicit in the power of an arbitrator to compel production of documents from a third party for a hearing. *See In re Sec. Life Ins. Co. of Am.*, 228 F.3d 865, 870-71 (8th Cir. 2000); *Am. Fed'n. of Television and Radio Artists, AFL-CIO v. WJBK-TV (New World Communications of Detroit, Inc.)*, 164 F.3d 1004, 1009 (6th Cir. 1999). The Second and Third Circuits have ruled to the contrary. *Life Receivables Trust v. Syndicate 102 at Lloyd's of London*, 549 F.3d 210, 212 (2d Cir. 2008); *Hay Group., Inc. v. E.B.S. Acquisition Corp.*, 360 F.3d 404, 408-09 (3d Cir. 2004). The Fourth Circuit has read section 7 of the FAA in more or less the same way as the Third, though it has suggested that an arbitration panel may subpoena a non-party for prehearing discovery upon a showing of a "special need." *See COMSAT Corp. v. Nat'l. Sci. Found.*, 190 F.3d 269, 275-76 (4th Cir. 1999).

Alliance Healthcare Servs., Inc. v. Argonaut Private Equity, LLC, 804 F. Supp. 2d 808, 810-11 (N.D. Ill. 2011).

2. Does the suggestion in Judge Chertoff's concurring opinion provide a simple way around the apparent constraints of § 7? *See* Stolt-Nielsen SA v. Celanese AG, 430 F.3d 567, 580 (2d Cir. 2005) (avoiding question whether § 7 permits pre-hearing discovery and denying motion to quash subpoena when subpoenaed parties were ordered to testify before arbitrators).

3. Section 7 of the Uniform Arbitration Act contains language similar (although not identical) to that of § 7 of the FAA. UAA § 7 ("The arbitrators may issue (cause to be issued) subpoenas for the attendance of witnesses and for the production of books, records, documents and other evidence"). By comparison, the Revised Uniform Arbitration Act makes clear that "the arbitrator may . . . issue subpoenas for the attendance of a witness and for the production of records and other evidence at a discovery proceeding." RUAA § 17(d).

4. An arbitrator (or the other party) has several ways to enforce a discovery order once made. First, and perhaps most commonly, the arbitrator can simply presume that the evidence not produced would have been unfavorable to the non-producing party. *See, e.g.*, IBA Rules, art. 9(5) ("If a Party fails without satisfactory explanation to produce any Document requested in a Request to Produce to which it has not objected in due time or fails to produce any Document ordered to be produced by the Arbitral Tribunal, the Arbitral Tribunal may infer that such Document would be adverse to the interests of that Party"). Second, some arbitration rules and statutes expressly authorize the arbitrator to impose some other form of sanctions against the recalcitrant party, such as assessing costs, excluding evidence, or the like. *See* JAMS Employment Arbitration Rules and Procedures, Rule 29; RUAA § 17(d) ("the arbitrator may . . . take action against a noncomplying party to the extent a court could if the controversy were the subject of a civil action in this State"). Third, the party seeking the discovery can go to court to try to enforce a subpoena issued by the arbitrator. *See* FAA § 7; RUAA § 17(d), (g).

PROBLEM 6.11

The arbitration between Barker Business Supplies (BBS) and Douglas Distribution Co. has finally gotten moving again (the parties having worked out their dispute in Problem 6.7 by agreeing to have Joan Pinto serve as the arbitrator). Fred Porlock, who continues to act as Douglas' representative, serves you with a number of discovery requests.

(a) Douglas requests all documents relating to the contract between BBS and Douglas, as well as all similar contracts BBS has with other distributors. Douglas also notices the deposition of James Barker, President of BBS, as well as two Vice Presidents and the entire Board of Directors. When you object to the requests as overbroad, Douglas asks the arbitrator, Joan Pinto, to order you to produce the requested documents and make available the requested witnesses. Does Pinto have the authority to make such an order? Is she likely to grant the request? Would your answer be any different if the arbitration were an international one instead of a domestic one?

(b) After you respond to Douglas' requests, you submit your own document request to Douglas for any notes taken during negotiation of the contract at issue. Douglas refuses to produce the requested documents. You then obtain an order from Pinto directing Douglas to produce the documents. Douglas still refuses. What do you do now?

Can courts ever order discovery in support of arbitration? The next two cases consider when courts may have the power to do so.

DEIULEMAR COMPAGNIA DI NAVIGAZIONE S.P.A. v. M/V ALLEGRA
United States Court of Appeals for the Fourth Circuit
198 F.3d 473 (1999)

WILLIAMS, CIRCUIT JUDGE:

Deiulemar Compagnia Di Navigazione (Deiulemar) filed a petition to perpetuate testimony in the United States District Court for the District of Maryland pursuant to Federal Rule of Civil Procedure 27. Deiulemar sought to preserve evidence of the condition of a ship it chartered from Pacific Eternity and Golden Union Shipping Co. (collectively, Pacific Eternity) that was undergoing repairs and was soon scheduled to leave United States waters. Deiulemar, which expected to file an arbitration action against Pacific Eternity in London pursuant to its Charter Party agreement, asserted that "extraordinary circumstances" justified the district court's intervention in preserving evidence that was crucial to its arbitration case and unable to be recreated. . . . The district court granted Deiulemar's Rule 27 petition and permitted Deiulemar to inspect and perpetuate the evidence of the ship's condition. It then sealed the evidence pending appeal. For the reasons stated below, we affirm the district court's exercise of jurisdiction to preserve evidence in aid of arbitration in the extraordinary circumstances presented and remand with instructions to transfer the sealed evidence to the arbitrator in the now-pending London arbitration proceeding.

I.

On June 4, 1997, Deiulemar time-chartered the *M/V Allegra* from Pacific Eternity. The written Charter Party agreement required, among other things, that Pacific Eternity maintain the "hull, machinery and equipment in a thoroughly efficient state." The agreement also specified that the vessel would maintain a guaranteed speed of twelve to thirteen knots. . . .

Deiulemar began its voyage from Australia to the United States, with its final port in Baltimore, Maryland. During this voyage, Deiulemar discovered that the ship was traveling below the guaranteed speed, at just seven plus knots. . . . On February 12, 1999, the ship entered the Chesapeake Bay and reached the Port of Hampton Roads. The U.S. Coast Guard inspected the vessel and discovered several mechanical problems. Citing safety concerns, the Coast Guard detained the vessel until the Owners could repair a lengthy list of problems. As a result, the *Allegra* spent several weeks in anchorage at Hampton Roads undergoing inspection and repairs. Finally, after Pacific Eternity addressed many of the more critical deficiencies, the Coast Guard released the *Allegra.* On March 6, 1999, the ship proceeded to Baltimore to unload its cargo and complete further repairs. According to Deiulemar, Pacific Eternity intended to install new cylinder heads to the main engine in Baltimore.

On March 8, 1999, while the ship was in port in Baltimore, Deiulemar dispatched Captain Heiner Popp, a marine expert, to inspect the vessel. . . . Deiulemar anticipated that Captain Popp would determine that engine problems were the cause of the ship's slow pace of travel. Pacific Eternity denied Captain Popp access to the ship and ordered him off the vessel. Pacific Eternity asserts that marine growth on the hull, and not engine problems, was the cause of the ship's subpar speed.

On March 9, 1999, Deiulemar filed a Rule 27 petition to perpetuate testimony with the United States District Court for the District of Maryland. . . . Deiulemar stated that it sought to perpetuate the evidence "to determine the nature and extent of Petitioner's claim for a breach of the attached [Charter Party agreement]."

On March 10, 1999, Pacific Eternity filed a motion to dismiss the Rule 27 petition. Along with its motion to dismiss, Pacific Eternity filed a sworn declaration from English legal counsel. The declaration, which describes the English rules of arbitration, suggests that "[a]ll of the information sought in Deiulemar's Rule 27 petition could be requested through the arbitration process." On the same day, Deiulemar initiated arbitration proceedings in London, as required by the Charter Party agreement. Neither party filed a motion to stay this action pending arbitration.

On March 16, 1999, the district court . . . issued an order granting Deiulemar's Rule 27 petition. The order . . . simply states that "upon good cause shown," Captain Popp and his staff could inspect the vessel, observe repairs, and copy documents from the ship. . . .

Pursuant to the district court's order, Captain Popp and his staff inspected the *Allegra*. . . . After the crew completed inspection and repairs, the *Allegra* left United States waters. The district court is presently holding the collected information in camera pending appeal. None of the parties have seen this material, nor do they know the precise nature of the information collected.

. . .

III.

We first address whether a district court may, under limited "extraordinary circumstances," grant discovery in aid of arbitration. Federal discovery rules typically do not apply to disputes governed by arbitration provisions. *See COMSAT Corp. v. National Science Found.* Some lower courts, however, allow discovery in aid of arbitration "where a movant can demonstrate 'extraordinary circumstances,' " such as "where a vessel with crew members possessing particular knowledge of the dispute is about to leave port," or where there is a "special need for information which will be lost if action is not taken immediately." Courts typically find "extraordinary circumstances" where evidence is likely to disappear before a claimant can file suit in federal court.

In *COMSAT*, we recently recognized the concept of "extraordinary circumstances" when we stated that a district court could, upon a showing of "special need or hardship," compel pre-hearing discovery. . . . In the present case, Pacific Eternity was repairing the ship's main engine and hull and the condition of these items was crucial to Deiulemar's arbitration claim. Deiulemar's effort to preserve the evidence on the *Allegra* was disrupted by Pacific Eternity, which denied Deiulemar access to the ship. In addition, the *Allegra* was going to leave United States waters once Pacific Eternity completed repairs. As a result, Deiulemar was in danger of losing access to any evidence of the ship's condition. Although Deiulemar arguably could have sought emergency discovery from the London arbitrator, Deiulemar represented that it could not do so in time to preserve the rapidly changing condition of the ship. Given the time-sensitive nature of Deiulemar's request and the evanescent nature of the evidence sought, we do not believe that the district court abused its discretion in accepting Deiulemar's representation. Accordingly, we believe that Deiulemar adequately demonstrated that "the information it [sought was] otherwise unavailable."

Moreover, these facts fit squarely within the "extraordinary circumstances" exception as applied by the trial courts in [other cases.] . . . Deiulemar sought evidence from a ship that was soon leaving United States waters. It requested perpetuation of evidence that, if not preserved, was going to disappear or be materially altered. The evidence that Deiulemar sought was necessary to its arbitration claim and Deiulemar was reasonably uncertain whether it could timely preserve the evidence outside the district court. In this narrow set of facts, we agree with the district court's conclusion that Deiulemar faced a "special need" that justified preserving the evidence on the *Allegra*.

IV.

We next address whether Federal Rule of Civil Procedure 81 prohibited the district court from granting Deiulemar's Rule 27 petition. Rule 81(a)(3) provides that "[i]n proceedings under Title 9, relating to arbitration, . . . these rules apply only to the extent that matters of procedure are not provided for in [Title 9]." . . .

. . .

. . . Rule 81(a)(3) does not affirmatively authorize application of the federal rules to matters that are incident to an arbitrable dispute because Rule 81 does not apply to an underlying arbitration proceeding. Rather, it applies only to allow or prohibit use of the federal rules in Title 9 proceedings. Consequently, a district court could invoke Rule 81(a)(3) to use federal discovery rules to determine whether a dispute is arbitrable. The district court could not, however, invoke Rule 81 to authorize discovery in aid of arbitration because Rule 81 simply does not apply with respect to the arbitration proceeding itself. The flip side is also true; Rule 81 does not preclude discovery incident to arbitration because it does not apply in this context at all. The present case does not involve a Title 9 proceeding; it involves discovery related to the merits of the underlying arbitration. For that reason, we conclude that Rule 81, by its language, did not prohibit the district court from considering Deiulemar's request for discovery in aid of arbitration.[13]

V.

Pacific Eternity also argues that the district court lacked subject matter jurisdiction over Deiulemar's Rule 27 petition because Deiulemar failed to satisfy Rule 27's requirements. . . . We agree with the district court that Deiulemar established a cognizable action and that Deiulemar did not seek to use Rule 27 as an impermissible discovery device. . . .

A.

Deiulemar maintains that it established subject matter jurisdiction by demonstrating three cognizable actions — "either to compel arbitration, seek security or to enforce an award" — that it was unable to bring in federal court when it filed its Rule 27 petition. Pacific Eternity argues that these asserted actions are not "cognizable" because they are too speculative. Pacific Eternity contends that it never affirmatively disputed arbitration, and, therefore, Deiulemar had no basis to anticipate any future action to enforce or compel arbitration. We conclude that the district court did not abuse its discretion in implicitly finding that Deiulemar had

---

[13] Pacific Eternity also appears to argue that it is improper for Deiulemar to perpetuate evidence in aid of arbitration, as opposed to preserving evidence solely for the anticipated federal action that serves as its jurisdictional predicate. Pacific Eternity correctly notes that Deiulemar's anticipated actions to enforce or compel arbitration are Title 9 actions that, by themselves, would probably not entitle Deiulemar to discovery on the merits of the underlying arbitrable dispute. We recognize that permitting Rule 27 perpetuation in aid of arbitration may create a slight anomaly to the extent that Deiulemar could use Rule 27 to preserve evidence that it could not otherwise discover through its anticipated federal court actions. But the very idea of "extraordinary circumstances" is to preserve evidence in aid of arbitration rather than in aid of anticipated federal court actions. . . .

established potentially cognizable actions to support its Rule 27 petition.

Rule 27 is a means of perpetuating testimony before trial. A Rule 27 petitioner must show, among other things, that it expects to be a party to an action "that may be cognizable in any court of the United States but is presently unable to bring it or cause it to be brought." Fed. R. Civ. P. 27(a)(1). . . .

. . .

In the present case, Deiulemar filed its Rule 27 petition the day after Pacific Eternity denied Captain Popp access to the *Allegra*. At the time of filing, Deiulemar had not yet initiated arbitration. Thus, it was not certain that Deiulemar would have to compel or enforce arbitration. Under the circumstances, however, Deiulemar reasonably believed that it could not wait and see whether Pacific Eternity would comply with arbitration because Pacific Eternity was repairing the ship and crucial evidence was rapidly disappearing or changing. Moreover, Deiulemar asserted that Pacific Eternity demonstrated bad faith and dilatory intent by stonewalling Deiulemar and denying Captain Popp access to the ship. Given the district court's reasonable reliance on Deiulemar's allegations at the time of filing, as well as the clear exigency of the moment, we cannot say that the district court abused its discretion. . . .

B.

Pacific Eternity next argues that Deiulemar abused Rule 27 by using it to discover new evidence, as opposed to perpetuating known evidence. . . . We disagree.

. . .

. . . At the time Deiulemar filed its petition, . . . the Coast Guard had already revealed several engine-related defects on the *Allegra*. . . . [T]he district court could reasonably conclude that Deiulemar knew of and sought to preserve the present condition of the defective engine parts, as described by the Coast Guard's safety reports. The district court, therefore, did not abuse its discretion in implicitly finding that Deiulemar sought to perpetuate, rather than discover, the evidence on the *Allegra*.

. . .

VI.

Having determined that the district court did not err in considering Deiulemar's Rule 27 petition, we now must decide whether to unseal the preserved evidence. . . .

. . .

In the present case, the perpetuation of the evidence has already occurred and Deiulemar has already initiated arbitration in London. Neither party has seen the evidence gathered from the *Allegra*, and, as a result, the arbitrator will have an opportunity to rule on Deiulemar's discovery request as if Deiulemar had brought it for the first time in the arbitral forum. Neither party will be prejudiced by this action. To the contrary, the parties are in the exact positions they would have held had Deiulemar sought discovery from the arbitrator in the first place. The arbitrator does not have to admit the evidence, nor does he have to suppress it; that choice is left entirely to the arbitrator.

We find no unfairness in returning this issue, preserved in a pristine state, to the forum that will ultimately hear the merits of the underlying dispute. To the contrary, we can think of nothing fairer than leaving each party where it began. In doing so, we decline Pacific Eternity's invitation to destroy evidence that is already gathered and impossible to regain, and we decline Deiulemar's invitation to reveal the evidence in advance of any ruling by the arbitrator. . . .

CONSORCIO ECUATORIANO DE TELECOMUNICACIONES S.A. v. JAS FORWARDING (USA), INC.
United States Court of Appeals for the Eleventh Circuit
685 F.3d 1987 (2012)

Marcus, Circuit Judge:

This appeal arises out of a foreign shipping contract billing dispute between Consorcio Ecuatoriano de Telecomunicaciones S.A. ("CONECEL") and Jet Air Service Equador S.A. ("JASE"). CONECEL filed an application in the Southern District of Florida under 28 U.S.C. § 1782 to obtain discovery for use in foreign proceedings in Ecuador. . . . CONECEL's application seeks discovery from JASE's United States counterpart, JAS Forwarding (USA), Inc. ("JAS USA"), which does business in Miami and was involved in the invoicing operations at issue in the dispute. The district court granted the application and authorized CONECEL to issue a subpoena. Thereafter, JASE intervened and moved to quash the subpoena and vacate the order granting the application. The district court denied the motion, as well as a subsequent motion for reconsideration. JASE now appeals the denial of both.

After thorough review and having had the benefit of oral argument, we affirm the orders of the district court. We hold that the arbitral tribunal before which JASE and CONECEL's dispute is now pending is a foreign tribunal for purposes of the statute. The arbitral panel acts as a first-instance decisionmaker; it permits the gathering and submission of evidence; it resolves the dispute; it issues a binding order; and its order is subject to judicial review. The discovery statute requires nothing more. We also hold that the district court did not abuse its considerable discretion in granting the section 1782 discovery application over JASE's objections that it would be forced to produce proprietary and confidential information. The application was narrowly tailored and primarily requested information concerning JASE's billing of CONECEL, which is undeniably at issue in the current dispute between the parties. . . .

I.

CONECEL and JASE have had a lengthy contractual relationship that reaches back at least a decade. JASE agreed to provide transportation logistics services in connection with the international transportation of cell phones and accessories for CONECEL. The contracts between the parties contain descriptions of the potential services to be provided by JASE and detailed terms pertaining to the rate to be charged per applicable unit of weight transported. According to CONECEL, between 2002 and 2007 JASE invoiced, and CONECEL paid, more than $88 million for services rendered under the contracts. The relationship between the parties soured in 2008, and CONECEL contends that an internal investigation and audit "using the limited documentation in its possession" revealed that CONECEL had been improperly overbilled by millions of dollars.

CONECEL says that the agreements between the parties provided that CONECEL would pay the rate specified by the agreements (in terms of dollars per unit of weight) multiplied by the weight of the shipment. CONECEL contends that JASE introduced an "extra-contractual multiplication factor" into the equation, which "varied from shipment to shipment based on factors that are not known to CONECEL." CONECEL also claims that the calculation of the "chargeable weight" of the shipments was erroneous.

. . .

Not surprisingly, JASE tells a wholly different story. It claims that in 2008 CONECEL failed to pay several invoices. Pursuant to the contractual agreements between the parties, JASE has pursued arbitration in Ecuador before the Center for Arbitration and Conciliation of the Guayaquil Chamber of Commerce. CONECEL's primary defense in the pending arbitration proceeding is that the invoices do not correspond to the parties' agreed-upon price.

II.

On July 14, 2010, CONECEL filed an ex parte application for judicial assistance in the Southern District of Florida in order to obtain evidence pursuant to 28 U.S.C. § 1782. . . .

CONECEL's detailed application, accompanied by two declarations and a memorandum of law, sought evidence from JAS USA relating primarily to the invoicing and calculation of rates charged to CONECEL. The application was also accompanied by a sample air waybill purporting to show that JAS USA's Miami office was involved in the provision and invoicing of transport services to CONECEL.

On July 20, 2010, the district court granted the ex parte application and authorized CONECEL to issue and serve a subpoena on JAS USA seeking the discovery outlined in CONECEL's application. JASE moved to intervene to vacate the order granting the application. After full briefing, the district court permitted the intervention but denied the motion to vacate.

. . .

III.

. . .

A.

A district court has the authority to grant an application for judicial assistance under section 1782 if four statutory requirements are met:

> (1) the request must be made "by a foreign or international tribunal," or by "any interested person"; (2) the request must seek evidence, whether it be the "testimony or statement" of a person or the production of "a document or other thing"; (3) the evidence must be "for use in a proceeding in a foreign or international tribunal"; and (4) the person from whom discovery is sought must reside or be found in the district of the district court ruling on the application for assistance.

In re Clerici, [481 F.3d 1324, 1331-32, (11th Cir. 2007)] (quoting 28 U.S.C. § 1782(a)). JASE does not dispute that requirements (1), (2), and (4) have been met here. As a party to the dispute, CONECEL plainly is an "interested person"; CONECEL's application seeks evidence in the form of document production and deposition testimony; and the application seeks discovery from JAS USA, which has an office and does business in Miami and is therefore "found in the district of the district court ruling on the application for assistance" — namely, the Southern District of Florida.

At issue is the third requirement — that the evidence sought must be *for use in a proceeding in a foreign or international tribunal.* . . . [W]e now hold that the pending arbitration proceeding is a "proceeding in a foreign or international tribunal."

Although an issue of first impression in this Circuit, the determination of whether a foreign arbitration falls within the scope of section 1782 is guided in substantial measure by the Supreme Court's seminal decision in *Intel Corp. v. Advanced Micro Devices, Inc.*, 542 U.S. 241 (2004). Most significantly for our purposes, the Court in *Intel* emphasized the breadth of the statutory term "tribunal." In discussing the legislative history of section 1782, Justice Ginsburg, writing for the Court, observed that Congress in 1964 introduced the word "tribunal" into the statute to replace the previous version's term "judicial proceeding," quoting with approval from a Senate Report "explain[ing] that Congress introduced the word 'tribunal' to ensure that 'assistance is not confined to proceedings before conventional courts,' but extends also to 'administrative and quasi-judicial proceedings.' " *Id.* at 248-49 (quoting S. Rep. No. 88-1580, at 7 (1964)). And then, in determining whether the Directorate-General for Competition of the European Commission was a "tribunal" under the statute, the Supreme Court reiterated that the legislative change from the phrase "any judicial proceeding" to the current phrase — "a proceeding in a foreign or international tribunal" — was intended to "provide the possibility of U.S. judicial assistance in connection with administrative and quasi-judicial proceedings abroad." (alterations and internal quotation marks omitted). . . .

Moreover, the Court quoted with approval the following broad definition of "tribunal" set forth by a leading scholar on international procedure: "[t]he term 'tribunal' . . . includes investigating magistrates, administrative and *arbitral tribunals*, and quasi-judicial agencies, as well as conventional civil, commercial, criminal, and administrative courts." *Id.* at 258 (emphasis added) (quoting Hans Smit, *International Litigation Under the United States Code*, 65 Colum. L. Rev. 1015, 1026 n.71 (1965)).[4] Applying this broad definition to the case, the Supreme Court concluded that because the European Commission acted as a "proof-taking" body and a "first-instance decisionmaker," the Court had "no warrant to exclude the European Commission . . . from § 1782(a)'s ambit."

Thus, while the Supreme Court in *Intel* was not tasked with specifically deciding whether a private arbitral tribunal falls under the statute, its broad functional construction of the term "tribunal" provides us with substantial guidance. Consistent with this functional approach, we examine the characteristics of the arbitral body at issue, in particular whether the arbitral panel acts as a first-instance adjudicative decisionmaker, whether it permits the gathering and submission of evidence, whether it has the authority to determine liability and impose penalties, and whether its decision is subject to judicial review.

The pending arbitration between JASE and CONECEL meets the functional criteria articulated in *Intel*. In connection with its section 1782 application, CONECEL submitted declarations from its Ecuadorian counsel explaining that the arbitral panel has the "authority to receive evidence, resolve the dispute, and award a binding decision." The declaration further states that after the conclusion of the arbitration proceedings,

> the parties will be able to appeal the decision before an ordinary court of the Ecuadorian state for causes related to procedural defects during the proceedings, for example, for the lack of service of the complaint to the defendant or lack of notification relating to some relevant decision that prevented one of the parties to exercise its defense rights, or a violation of the rules regarding designation of arbitrators or the selection of the tribunal, etc. The nullification action is resolved by the Provincial Court in the jurisdiction in which the arbitral award is rendered. Against the decision of the Provincial Court, an appeal can be made before the National Court of Justice.

The declaration also opined that "another possible option is to attack an arbitral award through an extraordinary action of protection provided for in the new Constitution of 2008." This kind of constitutional attack on the arbitral award is "made before the Constitutional Court," and the action would be viable if "a guaranteed right under the Constitution has been violated, whether by act or omission."

Notably, JASE does not contest that the arbitral tribunal at issue is a first-instance decisionmaking body that can receive evidence and bind the parties with its ruling; it only contests whether the arbitral tribunal's decision is subject to judicial review. JASE submitted in the district court its own declaration from

---

[4] Professor Smit, whose articles are repeatedly cited by the Supreme Court in *Intel*, is more than a leading scholar in the field. Indeed, one of the reasons offered for citing his views as persuasive authority on the interpretation of section 1782 is that, as then-Judge Ginsburg explained in an earlier D.C. Circuit opinion, Professor Smit is "the dominant drafter of, and commentator on, the 1964 revision of 28 U.S.C. § 1782."

Ecuadorian counsel stating *only* that "[t]he sum and substance of [arbitrators'] rulings, including determinations of fact and law are not reviewable by appeal."

The parties' declarations are in no way inconsistent. JASE's declaration does not dispute that the award of the arbitral panel is subject to nullification based on procedural defects in the arbitration proceeding and to constitutional attack if the constitutional rights of one of the parties has been violated. The opposing declarations read together demonstrate that judicial review of arbitration awards in Ecuador, much like a federal court's review of an arbitration award, is focused primarily on addressing defects in the arbitration proceeding, not on providing a second bite at the substantive apple that would defeat the purpose of electing to pursue arbitration in the first instance.

One could not seriously argue that, because domestic arbitration awards are only reviewable in court for limited reasons (notably excluding a second look at the substance of the arbitral determination), this amounts to no judicial review at all. . . . Yet JASE urges us, for section 1782 purposes, to conclude that the functional requirement of being subject to judicial review is only satisfied when the sum and substance of the arbitral body's decision is subject to full judicial reconsideration on the merits. This definition is far too stringent, and we can discern no sound reason to depart from the common sense understanding that an arbitral award is subject to judicial review when a court can enforce the award or can upset it on the basis of defects in the arbitration proceeding or in other limited circumstances. Based on the undisputed record before this Court, the arbitral panel in Ecuador, after receiving evidence from the parties, will render a first-instance binding decision on the merits that is subject to judicial review. This arbitral panel is, in the words of the Supreme Court, "a first-instance decisionmaker" whose judgment is subject to judicial review, and we therefore "have no warrant to exclude [it] . . . from § 1782(a)'s ambit."[7] In short, CONECEL's application satisfied the prima facie requirements of 28 U.S.C. § 1782(a).

---

[7] We are aware that two of our sister circuits, prior to the Supreme Court's decision in *Intel*, had reached a different conclusion, holding that private arbitral tribunals fall outside of section 1782's scope because the statute was only "intended to cover governmental or intergovernmental arbitral tribunals and conventional courts and other state-sponsored adjudicatory bodies." *Nat'l Broad. Co. v. Bear Stearns & Co.*, 165 F.3d 184, 190 (2d Cir. 1999); *accord Republic of Kazakhstan v. Biedermann Int'l*, 168 F.3d 880, 881 (5th Cir. 1999). Most notably for our purposes, these decisions, and the categorical distinction they drew between governmental and private tribunals, were rendered without the benefit of the Supreme Court's subsequent *Intel* decision, in which the Court set forth a far broader and wholly functional definition of the term "tribunal," and declined to impose "categorical limitations" on the scope of section 1782(a). . . . As the Supreme Court explained, Congress in 1964 replaced the term "judicial proceeding" with the term "tribunal" precisely in order to broaden the reach of section 1782 and extend the authority of district courts to provide assistance in connection with quasi-judicial proceedings abroad. And the view that the statutory term "tribunal" includes "arbitral tribunals," strongly endorsed by the Supreme Court, albeit in dicta, was not qualified in any way or limited only to governmental arbitral tribunals. Indeed, we note that Professor Smit has also written that "[c]learly, private arbitral tribunals come within the term the drafters used" and that "the term 'tribunal' in Section 1782 includes an arbitral tribunal created by private agreement." Hans Smit, *American Assistance to Litigation in Foreign and International Tribunals: Section 1782 of Title 28 of the U.S.C. Revisited*, 25 Syracuse J. Int'l L. & Com. 1, 5-6 (1998).

. . .

B.

Our inquiry does not end with the statutory requirements. The law is clear that "a district court is not required to grant a § 1782(a) discovery application simply because it has the authority to do so." Thus, JASE argues that, even if the statutory requirements have been met, the district court abused its discretion in granting CONECEL's application anyway.

. . . [A]s we have said, "[w]hether, and to what extent, to honor a request for assistance pursuant to § 1782 has been committed by Congress to the sound discretion of the district court" and "this court may overturn the district court's decision only for abuse of discretion." . . .

Interpreting the Supreme Court's decision in *Intel*, a panel of this Court already has spelled out four factors that should be considered by the district court in exercising its discretion:

> Once the prima facie requirements are satisfied, the Supreme Court in *Intel* noted these factors to be considered in exercising the discretion granted under § 1782(a): (1) whether "the person from whom discovery is sought is a participant in the foreign proceeding," because "the need for § 1782(a) aid generally is not as apparent as it ordinarily is when evidence is sought from a nonparticipant"; (2) "the nature of the foreign tribunal, the character of the proceedings underway abroad, and the receptivity of the foreign government or the court or agency abroad to U.S. federal-court judicial assistance"; (3) "whether the § 1782(a) request conceals an attempt to circumvent foreign proof-gathering restrictions or other policies of a foreign country or the United States"; and (4) whether the request is otherwise "unduly intrusive or burdensome." The Supreme Court in *Intel* added that "unduly intrusive or burdensome requests may be rejected or trimmed."

In re Clerici, 481 F.3d at 1334 (quoting *Intel*, 542 U.S. at 264-65). JASE's argument that the district court abused its discretion only focuses on the fourth factor. JASE claims that CONECEL's request for discovery from JAS USA is overbroad and improperly seeks confidential and proprietary information related to how both JAS USA and JASE price their services.

The main problem with JASE's claim is that it fails to provide us with any sound basis for overturning the district court's exercise of discretion or for upending the district court's determination that the discovery request was narrowly tailored. . . .

CONECEL's discovery requests in the instant section 1782 application were undeniably relevant to CONECEL's defense in the pending arbitration. CONECEL's defense in the arbitration is based on establishing that JASE overbilled in violation of the contractual arrangement between the parties. Evidence in JAS USA's possession relating to, for example, "the rates charged or to be charged to CONECEL" or "the procedure or methodology for applying the rates to be charged to CONECEL" is plainly relevant to this defense. Moreover, we find unpersuasive JASE's unsubstantiated claim that JAS USA's compliance with the subpoena would require the disclosure of confidential pricing information that would harm its competitiveness in the marketplace. On its face, CONECEL's application does not seek general price information from JASE or JAS USA or information about how JASE or JAS USA bills any other clients besides CONECEL. Rather, every request in the application that bears on pricing information uses language limiting the request to information relating directly to CONECEL, such as "the rates charged or to be charged to CONECEL," or "services provided by JAS Ecuador or its affiliates to CONECEL," or "billing or invoicing to CONECEL," or "services rendered . . . in connection with shipments to CONECEL." The district court did not abuse its discretion in concluding that the subpoena requests information that "relates directly to the contract at issue" and was "narrowly tailored."

Moreover, JASE does not appear to have taken any steps to meet CONECEL somewhere in the middle or to narrow the discovery request in any particular way; rather, it has taken an all-or-nothing approach seeking to remove JAS USA from the burden of having to produce any documents or deposition testimony, even those that seem unambiguously relevant. We have previously recognized that such an approach is problematic:

> Finally, as to the fourth *Intel* factor — whether the § 1782 request is unduly intrusive — the district court's order granting the § 1782 application specifically indicated that if Clerici wished to pursue his "unduly intrusive" argument, Clerici should file a motion to limit discovery. Clerici never did so and instead chose to appeal the grant of any discovery whatsoever. On appeal, as in the district court, Clerici does not identify the terms of the written request that are overly broad or assert how the scope of the request should be narrowed. Thus, we, like the district court, have no occasion to address the scope of the Panamanian Court's discovery request.

In re Clerici, 481 F.3d at 1335.

. . . These concerns are persuasive. In this case, JASE has failed to identify which particular discovery requests in CONECEL's application are unduly burdensome or to provide any specific evidence to support its blanket claim that JAS USA should be exempted from having to comply with any and all discovery obligations due to overarching concerns about confidentiality that are stated only at the highest order of abstraction.

. . .

The district court's denial of JASE's motion to vacate the order granting CONECEL's 28 U.S.C. § 1782 application and the denial of JASE's motion for reconsideration are **AFFIRMED**.

NOTES

1. One court has expressed the concern that permitting court-ordered discovery even for exceptional circumstances "risks a plunge into judicial control over arbitration." Suarez-Valdez v. Shearson Lehman/American Express, Inc., 858 F.2d 648, 649 n.1 (11th Cir. 1988). Consistent with that fear, those federal courts permitting discovery have recognized only very limited "exceptional circumstances" as permitting court-ordered discovery. The most common example is that presented in *M/V Allegra*: a ship about to leave port. *See, e.g.*, In re Compania de Navegacion

Interoceana S.A., 2004 U.S. Dist. LEXIS 6408 (E.D.N.Y. Jan. 29, 2004); In re Deiulemar di Navigazione S.p.A., 153 F.R.D. 592 (E.D. La. 1994); Koch Fuel Int'l Inc. v. M/V South Star, 118 F.R.D. 318 (E.D.N.Y. 1987); *see also* Oriental Commercial & Shipping Co. v. Rosseel, N.V., 125 F.R.D. 398 (S.D.N.Y. 1989) (refusing discovery concerning location of defendant's assets as not involving exceptional circumstances). Other federal courts, like the Third Circuit in *Hay Group*, seem skeptical of permitting discovery even on such limited grounds. *See also* Life Receivables Trust v. Syndicate 102 at Lloyd's of London, 549 F.3d 210, 216 (2d Cir. 2008) (citing "growing consensus" that " 'the arbitrator's subpoena authority under FAA § 7 does not include the authority to subpoena nonparties or third parties for prehearing discovery *even if a special need or hardship is shown*' " (emphasis added) (quoting Thomas H. Oehmke, 3 Commercial Arbitration § 91:5 (2008)).

2.   What is the authority for federal courts to permit discovery in support of an arbitration proceeding, even under exceptional circumstances? The court in *M/V Allegra* relied on Federal Rule of Civil Procedure 27, which permits a deposition "to perpetuate testimony" to be taken before a court action has been filed. Rule 27(a)(1) requires a petitioner to show that it "expects to be a party to an action cognizable in a court of the United States but cannot presently bring it or cause it to be brought." The petitioner here claimed that it expected to bring a petition to compel arbitration or an action to enforce an award. But isn't the respondent right that the condition of the vessel is not relevant to whether the arbitration should be compelled or an award enforced but instead goes to the merits of the arbitration? Is there some other authority on which a federal court could rely?

3.   Doesn't section 1782 raise the same sorts of concerns about court involvement in the arbitration process? Does the Eleventh Circuit's interpretation of section 1782 permit greater court-assisted discovery in international arbitration than in domestic arbitration?

4.   In the end, any comparison between discovery in arbitration and discovery in court litigation needs to use the proper baseline. In many cases, there will be little difference between the two. Indeed, one study of discovery practices in "ordinary litigation" found "no evidence of discovery in over half our cases" based on data from court records. David M. Trubek et al., *The Costs of Ordinary Litigation*, 31 UCLA L. REV. 72, 89–90 (1983). In those cases, the limited availability of discovery in arbitration would have made little or no difference. What about the rest? In what sorts of cases would you expect the limited discovery available in discovery to be most likely to affect the outcome of the proceeding?

PROBLEM 6.12

As you continue your investigation into the dispute underlying the BBS-Douglas Distribution Co. arbitration (see Problem 6.11), you realize that a key witness is likely to be Jonathan Wild, a former employee of Douglas. You know you could probably have him subpoenaed to attend at the hearing, but you'd like to find out what Wild knows before the hearing itself.

(a) How would you arrange his deposition if you were litigating the case in federal court? Can you follow the same procedure here? How else might you find out what Wild has to say?

(b) You learn that Wild is getting ready to leave the country for a six-month trip following his favorite soccer team around the world. He is unlikely to be back in the United States until after the hearing is completed. You want to take his deposition so you can introduce his testimony (which you believe will be favorable to your client) in the arbitration hearing when it is held. How should you proceed?

(c) What if the BBS-Douglas Distribution Co. arbitration were seated in France, and you wanted to obtain evidence from Wild in the United States — how might you proceed?

§ 6.08   CONFIDENTIALITY

One of the touted benefits of arbitration, at least from the perspective of the parties, is privacy. Unlike court filings, which are a matter of public record, and court proceedings, which generally are open to the public, arbitration proceedings traditionally have been perceived as private. Thus, arbitration rules generally provide that arbitration proceedings are private and that awards can be made public only if both parties consent. AAA Commercial Arbitration Rules, Rule R-23; UNCITRAL Arbitration Rules, arts. 28(3), 34(5). Arbitration rules (and arbitration statutes) ordinarily do not impose a broader duty of confidentiality on the parties. (Ethics rules, however, impose such a duty on the arbitrator. *See* AAA & ABA, Code of Ethics for Arbitrators in Commercial Disputes, Canon VI(B) (imposing duty of confidentiality on arbitrators); IBA, Ethics for International Arbitrators § 9 (same).)

As a result, commentators often recommend that parties take steps to protect the confidentiality of arbitration proceedings in their arbitration agreements. One simple clause is suggested by the American Arbitration Association: "Except as may be required by law, neither a party nor an arbitrator may disclose the existence, content, or results of any arbitration hereunder without prior written consent of both parties." AAA, Drafting Dispute Resolution Clauses — A Practical Guide (2007) (reprinted in Documentary Supplement). But sometimes confidentiality provisions (in arbitration clauses and rules) can result in legal challenges, as the following cases demonstrate.

ZUVER v. AIRTOUCH COMMUNICATIONS, INC.
Supreme Court of Washington
103 P.3d 753 (2004)

Bridge, J.

— This case requires us to consider the enforceability of a predispute arbitration agreement between an employer, Airtouch Communications, Inc. (Airtouch), and its employee, Therese R. Zuver. Zuver appeals a superior court order granting Airtouch's motion to compel arbitration and stay proceedings. She principally argues that the arbitration agreement is both procedurally and substantively unconscionable, and thus, this court should strike down the entire arbitration agreement. Conversely, Airtouch claims that the arbitration agreement is neither procedurally nor substantively unconscionable; however, in the event that we find any of the agreement's provisions substantively unconscionable, Airtouch asserts that the agreement's severability clause requires this court to sever the offending provisions and enforce the remainder. We hold that the provisions of the agreement pertaining to confidentiality [among others] . . . are substantively unconscionable but agree with Airtouch that the agreement's severability clause requires us to sever these provisions and enforce the remainder of the agreement.

. . .

Confidentiality Provision

Relying on the Ninth Circuit's decision in Ting v. A.T.&T., 319 F.3d 1126, 1151-52 (9th Cir.), *cert. denied*, 540 U.S. 811 (2003), and a federal district court decision applying Washington law, Luna [v. Household Fin. Corp., 236 F. Supp. 2d 1166 (W.D. Wash. 2002)], Zuver asserts that the confidentiality provision unduly favors Airtouch and thus, is substantively unconscionable.[9] In *Ting*, the Ninth Circuit held that an arbitration agreement's confidentiality provision was unconscionable because "A.T.&T. ha[d] placed itself in a far superior legal posture by ensuring that none of its potential opponents have access to precedent while, at the same time, A.T.&T. accumulates a wealth of knowledge on how to negotiate the terms of its own unilaterally crafted contract." Similarly, in *Luna*, the court there held that a confidentiality provision in an arbitration agreement was substantively unconscionable since "repeat arbitration participants enjoy advantages over one-time participants [and] . . . the . . . confidentiality provision magnifies the effect of those advantages."

In response, Airtouch urges us to adopt the analysis articulated by the California Court of Appeal in Woodside Homes of California, Inc. v. Superior Court, 132 Cal. Rptr. 2d 35 (2003). There the court considered whether a confidentiality provision in a contract between two sophisticated parties was substantively unconscionable. The party seeking to void the contract argued that the confidentiality provision would impair the public's interest in open proceedings. The court rejected its argument reasoning that "[t]hese concerns have nothing to say about the fairness or desirability of a secrecy provision with respect to the parties themselves, and we see nothing unreasonable or prejudicial about it."

However, unlike the party in *Woodside Homes*, Zuver does not argue that the public interest in open arbitration proceedings *alone* renders this provision substantively unconscionable. Rather, she contends that the effect of this confidentiality provision is harsh and blatantly benefits only Airtouch because it "serves no purpose other than to tilt the scales of justice in favor of the employer by denying access to any information about other claims against the employer to other potential victims of discrimination." Consequently, we do not find the court's analysis in *Woodside Homes* compelling in these circumstances.

---

[9] The arbitration agreement requires that "[a]ll arbitration proceedings, including settlements and awards, under the Agreement will be confidential."

Airtouch alternatively argues that since confidentiality provisions are routinely included in arbitration agreements, such provisions cannot be substantively unconscionable. Indeed, this court has acknowledged that arbitrations are often confidential. Parties in labor arbitrations also routinely include confidentiality provisions in their collective bargaining agreements. *See* Cole v. Burns Int'l Sec. Servs., 105 F.3d 1465, 1477 (D.C. Cir. 1997). Nonetheless, although courts have accepted confidentiality provisions in many agreements, it does not necessarily follow that *this* confidentiality provision is conscionable. As the court aptly noted in *Cole*,

> [W]hile a lack of public disclosure of arbitration awards is acceptable in the collective bargaining context, because both employers and unions monitor such decisions and the awards rarely involve issues of concern to persons other than the parties, in the context of individual statutory claims, a lack of public disclosure may systematically favor companies over individuals.

Id. at 1477. The effect of the provision here benefits only Airtouch. As written, the provision hampers an employee's ability to prove a pattern of discrimination or to take advantage of findings in past arbitrations. Moreover, keeping past findings secret undermines an employee's confidence in the fairness and honesty of the arbitration process and thus, potentially discourages that employee from pursuing a valid discrimination claim. Therefore, we hold that this confidentiality provision is substantively unconscionable.[11]

CONCLUSION

. . . [W]e agree with Zuver that the confidentiality . . . provisions of the agreement are substantively unconscionable. While we conclude that these . . . provisions are substantively unconscionable, pursuant to the severance clause in the parties' agreement, we now sever those provisions and affirm the trial court's order compelling arbitration.

PARILLA v. IAP WORLDWIDE SERVICES VI, INC.
United States Court of Appeals for the Third Circuit
368 F.3d 269 (2004)

STAPLETON, CIRCUIT JUDGE:

IAP Worldwide Services VI, Inc. ("IAPVI"), IAP Worldwide Services, Inc. ("IAP"), Gene Ludlow, and Roy Varner (collectively, "Appellants") appeal from an order of the District Court of the Virgin Islands denying their motion to compel arbitration pursuant to the Federal Arbitration Act ("FAA"). Appellee Virgen Parilla, a former employee of IAPVI, brought suit against Appellants alleging, *inter alia*, discriminatory conduct in violation of Title VII of the Civil Rights Act of 1964, 42 U.S.C. § 2000e *et seq.* Invoking the provisions of an arbitration agreement in

---

[11] Zuver also argues that article I, section 10 of the Washington Constitution requires open civil and criminal proceedings and thus requires us to hold that this confidentiality provision is substantively unconscionable. However, since we conclude that the confidentiality provision is substantively unconscionable on other grounds, we need not consider this argument.

Parilla's employment contract, Appellants filed a motion to compel arbitration of Parilla's claims. The District Court denied Appellants' motion, holding that the agreement to arbitrate was unenforceable. For the reasons that follow, we will reverse the District Court's order and will remand to the District Court for further proceedings consistent with this opinion.

. . .

III. Enforceability of the Arbitration Provisions

. . . We next address whether the challenged contract terms are substantively unconscionable.

3. The Confidentiality Provisions

Paragraph 19 of the Agreement provides that "[a]rbitration shall take place pursuant to the Federal Arbitration Act, and in accordance with the . . . National Rules for the Resolution of Employment Disputes of the American Arbitration Association [("AAA Rules")]." The District Court . . . held that [the] AAA Rule[s,] . . . as incorporated by reference into the Agreement, were unconscionable to the extent they provide for confidentiality. Those rules provide, in accordance with the traditional arbitration practice, that the arbitrator will "maintain the confidentiality of the arbitration," may control who is present during any portion of the proceedings, and "shall provide written reasons for the award unless the parties agree otherwise." The rules also provide that while all awards will be "publicly available," the names of the parties will not be publicly available "unless a party expressly agrees to have its name made public in the award." In support of its conclusion that these rules, while facially neutral, favor the employer and unduly burden the employee, the District Court gave the following explanation:

> [T]he ability of a party to unilaterally prevent the inclusion of its name in the award favors the repeat participant and makes it difficult for a potential plaintiff to build a case of intentional misconduct or to establish a pattern or practice of discrimination by a particular company.

Without further explanation, the District Court went on to hold that "[s]imilarly, AAA Rule 18 making the arbitration itself confidential and AAA Rule 17 allowing the arbitrator to hold closed hearings also favor [the employer] and unduly burden [the employee]." We conclude that the District Court erred in so holding.

The unconscionability doctrine seeks to prevent substantial unfairness between contracting parties having grossly unequal bargaining power. The District Court did not and could not, we believe, identify any such unfairness as between Parilla and the Appellants resulting from the confidentiality provisions which the District Court refused to enforce. Each side has the same rights and restraints under those provisions and there is nothing inherent in confidentiality itself that favors or burdens one party *vis-à-vis* the other in the dispute resolution process. Importantly, the confidentiality of the proceedings will not impede or burden in any way Parilla's ability to obtain any relief to which she may be entitled.

The District Court's concern was not about any potential unfairness between two contracting parties *vis-á-vis* each other. Rather, that concern related to whether allowing an employer the right to prevent its name from appearing in an award in one proceeding would make it more difficult for claimants in subsequent proceedings to prove their cases. This concern has to do, not with unfairness between contracting parties, but with public policy and, more specifically, with whether confidentiality in arbitration proceedings of this kind is consistent with the public policy reflected in Title VII, the Virgin Islands' civil rights laws, and the Virgin Islands Wrongful Discharge Act ("WDA").

Concerns similar to those noted by the District Court were presented to the Supreme Court in *Gilmer v. Interstate Johnson Lane Corp.* in support of an argument that the arbitration of an age discrimination claim under the arbitration rules of the New York Stock Exchange ("NYSE rules") was inconsistent with the policy underlying the ADEA. . . . [The Supreme Court's] response persuades us that it would not find confidentiality in Title VII arbitrations unenforceable as against public policy.

In the course of upholding the agreement to arbitrate ADEA claims under the NYSE rules, the Court pointed to the ADEA's flexible approach to the resolutions of claims, noting that the United States Equal Employment Opportunity Commission ("EEOC") is directed to pursue "informal methods of conciliation, conference, and persuasion," all of which produce no publicly available records. In specific response to the concerns about some arbitrations remaining outside the public domain, the Court pointed out that such "concerns apply equally to settlements of ADEA claims, which . . . are clearly allowed."

This suggests to us that the Supreme Court would not view as a fatal defect the fact that, under Appellants' employment contract, some resolutions of Title VII claims will remain outside the public domain. This rationale, we conclude, applies equally to claims brought under the Virgin Islands' civil rights laws and the WDA. . . . Moreover, we do not perceive the potential for confidentiality in arbitrations as posing a substantial threat to employees' future ability to prove a case under these statutes. As in *Gilmer*, the governing arbitration rules provide for discovery and "there has been no showing in this case that [those] discovery provisions . . . will prove insufficient to allow [plaintiffs] . . . a fair opportunity to present their claims."

We conclude that the confidentiality provisions incorporated in ¶ 19 of the Agreement are not unconscionable or violative of the public policy embodied in Title VII, the Virgin Islands' civil rights laws, or the WDA. They are, accordingly, enforceable.

NOTES

1. Is there any way to reconcile the courts' opinions in *Zuver* and *Parilla*?

2. What effect, if any, does *Concepcion* have on the unconscionability holding in *Zuver*?

3. Both courts consider whether confidentiality in arbitration benefits the businesses drafting the arbitration clause. Does confidentiality ever benefit consumers or employees? What about sophisticated commercial parties (who can, of

course, enter into confidentiality agreements as part of the arbitration process as well)?

4.   What if the parties do not enter into a confidentiality agreement, either as part of their arbitration clause or after a dispute arises? What is the default rule governing confidentiality in arbitration? As UNCITRAL has explained, countries take varying approaches to the issue:

> 64. A survey of arbitration rules and the very few national laws which address confidentiality indicates a variety of approaches. One approach to formulating a confidentiality provision that could apply to all classes of cases has been to include a general provision that material produced for, or generated by, an arbitration cannot be disclosed to third parties without the consent of the other party or leave of the court. Another approach has adopted a more detailed provision which addresses the parameters of the duty of confidentiality including, for example, (i) the material or information that is to be kept confidential; (ii) the persons to whom the duty of confidentiality is to extend and how it is to be applied; and (iii) permissible exceptions to prohibitions on disclosure and communication.

> 65. In terms of the material or information that is to be kept confidential, some provisions include a general description of "facts or other information relating to the dispute or arbitral proceedings." Other provisions adopt a more particular description of the information to be covered and include various categories of information which are accorded different treatment. These categories include, for example, reference to the evidence given by a party or a witness; written and oral statements; the fact that the arbitration is taking place; the identity of the arbitrators; the contents of the award; communications between parties themselves or their advisors prior to, or in the course of, the arbitration; and information that is inherently confidential, such as trade secrets and commercial-in-confidence information.

> 66. As to the persons to whom the duty of confidentiality is to extend, a range of persons are covered such as the arbitrators; the staff of the arbitration institution, where the arbitration is institutional; parties and their agents; witnesses, including experts; counsel and advisors. Since the duty may not be able to be applied to all of these persons in the same way, one approach requires arbitrators and parties' representatives, and perhaps witnesses, to sign a confidentiality agreement. Another approach regarding witnesses is to require the party calling the witness to guarantee that the witness observes the same degree of confidentiality as that required of the party. Some provisions also deal with the period for which the duty of confidentiality continues to apply.

> 67. Some of the circumstances in which disclosure of information is permitted have included those where the parties consent to disclosure; where the information is in the public domain; where disclosure is required by law or a regulatory body; where there is a reasonable necessity for the protection of a party's legitimate interests; and, where it is in the interests of justice or in the public interest. While the scope of some of these exceptions may be susceptible of clear definition and application, others,

such as disclosure of information "in the public interest," are generally regarded as requiring some careful consideration. It has been suggested, for example, that a balance may need to be struck between a genuine public interest in the information in question and threatened disclosure of commercially sensitive information as a means of putting one party under pressure to settle.

United Nations Commission on International Trade Law, Note by the Secretariat on Possible Future Work in the Area of International Commercial Arbitration A/CN.9/460, at ¶¶ 64–67 (Apr. 6, 1999).

5. The handful of American cases dealing with the confidentiality of arbitration proceedings have, with little discussion, permitted discovery of arbitration materials in a subsequent case. *See, e.g.*, Galleon Syndicate Corp. v. Pan Atlantic Group, Inc., 637 N.Y.S.2d 104, 105 (N.Y. App. Div. 1996) ("There is no confidentiality privilege precluding disclosure of the material requested as the parties to the arbitration proceeding governed by the Rules of the American Arbitration Association are, in the absence of a confidentiality provision, not prohibited from disclosing documents generated or exchanged during the arbitration and since evidentiary material at an arbitration proceeding is not immune from disclosure"); Contship Container Lines, Ltd. v. PPG Industries, Inc., 2003 U.S. Dist. LEXIS 6857 (S.D.N.Y. Apr. 17, 2003); Industrotech Constructors, Inc. v. Duke Univ., 314 S.E.2d 272, 274 (N.C. App. 1984); United States v. Panhandle Eastern Corp., 118 F.R.D. 346 (D. Del. 1988).

6. Although traditionally arbitration proceedings have been private, some commentators have pointed to signs that "arbitral secrecy is eroding." Michael D. Goldhaber, *Big Arbitrations*, Am. Lawyer: Focus Europe (Summer 2003). For example, every other year since 2003, the American Lawyer magazine has published a list of "big arbitrations," including the names of the parties, lawyers, arbitrators, and a description of the dispute. In 2011, the magazine reported "on 113 billion-dollar cases: 65 based on old-fashioned contracts and 48 based at least in part on investment treaties or legislation." Michael D. Goldhaber, *High Stakes; Arbitration Scorecard 2011*, The American Lawyer (Online) July 1, 2011. According to Goldhaber, "[m]any big cases may enter the public domain through collateral litigation, press coverage, or securities disclosures;" the details of American Lawyer's lists were based "primarily on information supplied by lawyers involved in the cases, supplemented in some cases by arbitration or court papers, securities disclosures, and media reports." Michael D. Goldhaber, *Arbitration Scorecard: Methodology*, The American Lawyer (Online) July 1, 2011.

Investment treaty arbitrations have been at the forefront of the move toward transparency, with UNCITRAL preparing draft rules on the subject, *see* United Nations Commission on International Trade Law, Note by the Secretariat on Preparation of a Legal Standard on Transparency in Treaty-Based Investor-State Arbitration A/CN.9/WG.II/WP.171, at ¶¶ 5-16 (July 13, 2012), and some investment arbitration tribunals allowing third parties to participate as amici curiae and permitting the public to attend hearings. *See* Statement by the OECD Investment Committee, *Transparency and Third Party Participation in Investor-State Dispute Settlement Procedures* ¶¶ 22-35 (June 2005). On the domestic front, arbitration remains largely a private process, although a clear exception is the AAA's class arbitration docket. Rule 9(a) of the AAA's Supplementary Rules for Class Arbitrations provides that "[t]he presumption of privacy and confidentiality in arbitration proceedings shall not apply in class arbitrations" and that "all class arbitration hearings and filings may be made public, subject to the authority of the arbitrator to provide otherwise in special circumstances." As noted in § 6.06, the AAA's class arbitration docket, including case filings, is available on the AAA web site (although the web page is not always current).

What effect will this increasing transparency have on the arbitration process? Is it good for the parties? For the public?

PROBLEM 6.13

The arbitration between 4-M Co. and Singh Products (see Problem 6.8) is continuing, and Mary Morstan of 4-M calls you up. She is rather upset, to say the least. She tells you that just this morning there was an article in a prominent trade publication by a reporter named Dost Akbar. The article described in detail 4-M's dispute with Singh and the ongoing arbitration proceeding between the two. "The article is biased in favor of Singh, and it's obvious that Singh is Akbar's source," she complains. "I thought arbitration was supposed to be private, yet everything that's happened so far is right there in print for everyone to see." She says that the hearing is scheduled to take place in a couple of days. "I'm afraid that Akbar is going to show up and try to attend the hearing," she says. "What's worse, our other suppliers have now read all about the arbitration in the paper. If we later have a dispute with them, I just know the first discovery request we get will be for the award the arbitrators issue here."

Assuming that Morstan is correct that Singh was the source for the article, has Singh done anything wrong? Are Morstan's other fears justified? Is there anything 4-M might have done differently?

§ 6.09 PRE-HEARING PROCEDURE AND MOTIONS PRACTICE

Arbitration statutes and rules give arbitrators broad powers to control the course of the arbitration proceeding. For example, section 15(a) of the Revised Uniform Arbitration Act provides that "[a]n arbitrator may conduct an arbitration in such manner as the arbitrator considers appropriate for a fair and expeditious disposition of the proceeding." *See also* UNCITRAL Model Law, art. 19(2); AAA Commercial Arbitration Rules, Rule R-30(b); UNCITRAL Arbitration Rules, art. 17(1). In particular, many arbitration rules authorize or require arbitrators to conduct pre-hearing conferences to consider "the future conduct of the case, including clarification of the issues and claims, a schedule for the hearings and any other preliminary matters." AAA Commercial Arbitration Rules, Rule R-20 (b), (a) ("[a]t the request of any party or at the discretion of the arbitrator or the AAA"), Rule L-3 (for complex commercial disputes, "a preliminary hearing shall be held" to address lengthy list of possible matters); AAA/ICDR Int'l Rules, art. 16(2).

The 2012 ICC Arbitration Rules combine the requirement of a case management conference with a traditional — and unique — feature of the ICC rules: the requirement that the parties and the arbitral tribunal early in the proceeding prepare and agree on "a document defining [the tribunal's] Terms of Reference." Arts. 23 & 24. The terms of reference include "a summary of the parties' respective claims and of the relief sought by each party" and, "unless the Arbitral Tribunal considers it inappropriate, a list of issues to be determined." Art. 23(1).

Criticisms of the ICC's terms-of-reference procedure have included the difficulty of defining the issues in dispute so early in the case and the costs of preparing detailed terms of reference. One commentator put it bluntly as follows: "the fact that no other arbitral institution, no other arbitration rules, and, to the writer's knowledge, no ad hoc tribunals require terms of reference is sufficient proof that the notion is ill-conceived and that the requirement should be abolished in the interest of both economy and justice." J. Gillis Wetter, *The Present Status of the International Court of Arbitration of the ICC: An Appraisal*, 1 AM. REV. INT'L ARB. 91, 102 (1990). In reply, the ICC has asserted a number of benefits of the terms of reference procedure: it enables the arbitrators "to establish a rational structure and organization for the future path of the entire arbitration"; precludes the introduction of new claims as a delaying tactic; ensures that the arbitrators decide all issues submitted by the parties, and only those issues; promotes early settlement; educates the parties on the issues; and promotes the enforceability of the award in certain countries, by serving as an agreement to submit an existing dispute to arbitration. Stephen R. Bond, *The Present Status of the International Court of Arbitration of the ICC: A Comment on an Appraisal*, 1 AM. REV. INT'L ARB. 108, 116 n.13 (1990).

The current version of the ICC rules reflects significant modifications that have been made over the years in response to some of the criticisms. For example, the rules permit the arbitrators to dispense with the list of issues in the terms of reference if they consider it "inappropriate." Art. 23(1)(d). In addition, the rules authorize the arbitrators to permit a party to raise new claims or counterclaims even after the terms of reference have been signed. Art. 23(4). For another perspective on the ICC terms of reference, see GARY B. BORN, INTERNATIONAL COMMERCIAL ARBITRATION 1819 (2009) ("An experienced tribunal will usually attend to all of the issues required by the ICC Rules, even without an institutional requirement to do so. Nonetheless, no harm, and potentially much benefit, comes from requiring less experienced tribunals to complete these same tasks in a systematic manner.").

Another way courts can control the course of the proceedings is by ruling on dispositive motions. Motions practice is not as common in arbitration as it is in court litigation. Institutional arbitration rules ordinarily do not provide for dispositive motions, although they may permit the arbitrators to control the "order of proof" and "direct the parties to focus their presentations on issues the decision of which could dispose of all or part of the case." AAA Commercial Arbitration Rules, Rule R-30(b). Neither the FAA, the UAA, nor the UNCITRAL Model Law address dispositive motions. The Revised Uniform Arbitration Act, by contrast, provides that "[a]n arbitrator may decide a request for summary disposition of a claim or particular issue" if all parties agree, or on the request of one party on notice and an opportunity to respond. RUAA § 15(b). In the absence of an express provision of an arbitration statute or rule, do arbitrators have the authority to consider and decide dispositive motions?

SCHLESSINGER v. ROSENFELD, MEYER & SUSMAN
California Court of Appeal
47 Cal. Rptr. 2d 650 (1995)

MASTERSON, ASSOCIATE JUDGE

Gary Schlessinger, an attorney, and Rosenfeld, Meyer & Susman (RM&S), his former law firm, could not agree on the payment due Schlessinger upon his resignation from the partnership. Pursuant to the partnership agreement, the dispute proceeded to arbitration before the American Arbitration Association. The arbitrator disposed of the principal issues by way of two motions for summary adjudication and ultimately rendered an award in favor of RM&S.*

Schlessinger petitioned the superior court to vacate the arbitration award on the ground that the arbitrator had refused to hear evidence material to the controversy. In the petition, he asserted that the California Arbitration Act precluded the use of summary adjudication motions in an arbitration proceeding. The trial court dismissed the petition. We conclude that the arbitrator could entertain such motions and affirm.

. . .

DISCUSSION

The contention that the arbitrator lacked authority to entertain summary adjudication motions requires that we interpret provisions of the Act, the AAA rules, and the agreement. . . .

Neither the agreement, the Act, nor the AAA rules incorporate the state's summary adjudication statute. Nor do any of those sources expressly provide for such a motion. However, the lack of explicit authorization does not mean summary adjudication motions are precluded. While an authorizing statute may be necessary to permit summary adjudication motions in an action at law, the "rules of judicial procedure need not be observed [in an arbitration]." We conclude that the arbitrator had implicit authority to rule on such motions. We begin by examining the statutes on which Schlessinger relied in seeking to vacate the award.

A. The Statutory Basis of Schlessinger's Petition

An arbitration award must be vacated if the rights of a party were substantially prejudiced by the arbitrator's "refusal . . . to *hear* evidence material to the

---

* We use the term "summary adjudication" motion to describe a motion in which a party seeks a ruling on an issue of law based on evidence submitted in written form (e.g., exhibits, declarations). . . . Unlike a summary judgment motion, a motion for summary adjudication does not dispose of all legal issues in the case.

controversy." ([I]talics added.) Schlessinger contends that the arbitrator did not "hear" any evidence because he disposed of the principal issues by way of summary adjudication motions. According to Schlessinger, an arbitrator "hears" evidence only if he learns of it through his auditory sense; thus, the evidence had to be presented orally through witnesses.

An award must also be set aside if the arbitrator engaged in prejudicial conduct contrary to any of the Act's provisions. Schlessinger asserts that one provision of the Act required a hearing at which he could cross-examine witnesses. He claims that the arbitrator violated this provision because the summary adjudication motions deprived him of the right of cross-examination. We disagree with these contentions.

B. The Arbitrator's Duty to "Hear" the Evidence

Under section 1286.2, subdivision (e), the arbitrator's obligation "to hear evidence" does not mean that the evidence must be orally presented or that live testimony is required. "Legally speaking the admission of evidence is to hear it." An arbitrator "hears" evidence by providing a "legal hearing," that is, by affording an "opportunity to . . . present one's side of a case." An arbitrator also "hears" a matter by "consider[ing] a motion upon presentation thereof by counsel." Thus, a "hearing" does not necessarily include "an opportunity to present live testimony or be subject to cross examination." "Unless required by the express language, or the context of the particular rule, the use of the word 'hearing' does not necessarily contemplate either a personal appearance or an oral presentation to the court."

We decline to read section 1286.2, subdivision (e), as requiring that an arbitrator always resolve disputes through the oral presentation of evidence or the taking of live testimony. To do otherwise would lead to anomalous results. The purpose of arbitration, as reflected in the Act, is to provide a "speedy and relatively inexpensive means of dispute resolution." Having chosen arbitration over civil litigation, a party should "reap the advantages that flow from the use of that nontechnical, summary procedure."

Yet, Schlessinger's position would require full-blown trials even where, as here, one of the parties believes that no material facts are in dispute. In a case where a legal issue or defense could possibly be resolved on undisputed facts, the purpose of the arbitration process would be defeated by precluding a summary judgment or summary adjudication motion and instead requiring a lengthy trial. Moreover, taking Schlessinger's argument to its logical extreme, an arbitrator could not consider any documentary evidence, with or without a trial, unless one of the parties first read it to him. The Act certainly does not countenance such a wasteful use of the parties' resources and the arbitrator's time.

C. Schlessinger's Alleged Right to Cross-Examine Witnesses

We reject Schlessinger's argument that section 1282.2, subdivision (d), mandated a hearing at which witnesses presented live testimony and were subject to cross-examination. While that portion of the Act entitles a party to cross-examine witnesses if they appear at a hearing, it does not give a party an absolute right to present oral testimony in every case. Indeed, section 1282.2, subdivision (c), states that the arbitrator "shall rule on . . . questions of hearing procedure and shall exercise all powers relating to the conduct of the hearing." This language is sufficiently broad to permit an arbitrator to conduct a hearing on a summary adjudication motion in lieu of a hearing with oral testimony.

Equally important, all of the provisions of section 1282.2 are prefaced with the words "[u]nless the arbitration agreement otherwise provides." Thus, even if section 1282.2, subdivision (d), mandates a hearing with live testimony, the introductory language of the statute permits the parties to adopt a different procedure. They did so here. The partnership agreement required application of AAA rules to the parties' arbitration. Consistent with Rule 10, the arbitrator held a "preliminary hearing" at which he was authorized to "specify the issues to be resolved, to [have the parties] stipulate to uncontested facts, and *to consider any other matters that will expedite the arbitration proceedings.*" (Rule 10, italics added.) Further, while Rule 29 describes the method for conducting a "hearing," including the questioning of witnesses, it also provides that "[t]he arbitrator has the discretion to vary this procedure." Significantly, Rule 32 permits the arbitrator to "receive and consider the evidence of witnesses by affidavit." We believe that these rules implicitly sanctioned the use of summary adjudication motions.

Finally, Schlessinger's position, if correct, would exalt form over substance. . . . Had the summary adjudication motions not been made, RM&S could have presented its case at trial by calling two of its partners as witnesses (the ones who executed the declarations) and by reading from Schlessinger's deposition transcript. Schlessinger could have cross-examined the RM&S witnesses (whom he had already deposed) and could have taken the stand himself. At the close of the testimony, the arbitrator would have decided that RM&S's evidence alone was sufficient, that Schlessinger's evidence was irrelevant or cumulative, that no material facts were in dispute, and that RM&S was entitled to prevail. In other words, the inefficient use of a trial would have accomplished the same result as a summary adjudication motion. Neither the Act nor the AAA rules require a trial in such circumstances.

D. Non-California Authorities

While no California case has addressed the issue before us, other authorities shed some light on the question. For instance, a number of decisions by arbitrators indicate that they occasionally consider motions for summary judgment.

Commentators, on the other hand, generally assume or conclude that such motions are not available in an arbitration proceeding. But none of these secondary authorities has considered whether the Act, in conjunction with AAA rules, permits the use of summary judgment or summary adjudication motions.

. . .

In sum, we conclude that the arbitrator had authority under the Act and AAA rules to entertain the parties' cross-motions for summary adjudication.

. . .

In closing, we caution that our holding should not be taken as an endorsement of motions for summary judgment or summary adjudication in the arbitration context. By concluding that, under the Act and AAA rules, the arbitrator was permitted to entertain summary adjudication motions, we do not suggest that he was required to do so. Further, in any given arbitration, the propriety of summary adjudication motions will depend upon a variety of factors, including the nature of the claims and defenses, the provisions of the arbitration agreement, the rules governing the arbitration, the availability of discovery, and the opportunity to conduct adequate discovery before making or opposing a motion. Finally, especially where the arbitration lacks an explicit procedure for dispositive motions, courts must ensure . . . that the party opposing such a motion is afforded a fair opportunity to present its position.

DISPOSITION

The order dismissing the petition to vacate the arbitration award is affirmed.

NOTES

1.   Does the introduction of motions practice in arbitration constitute an excessive judicialization of arbitration? Or does it simply reflect the parties' ability to define by agreement the procedures in arbitration?

2.   What standards must arbitrators use in ruling on dispositive motions? *See* Prudential Securities, Inc. v. Dalton, 929 F. Supp. 1411 (N.D. Okla. 1996) (vacating award when arbitrators granted motion to dismiss "without hearing evidence": "Before an arbitration panel should be able to dismiss a claim for failure to state a claim upon which relief can be granted, the claim should be facially deficient. Such is not the case here for if the allegations of the claimant's complaint are taken to be true, he would be entitled to some form of relief"); Neary v. Prudential Insurance Co., 63 F. Supp. 2d 208 (D. Conn. 1999) (vacating award on grounds that "the arbitration panel manifestly disregarded the standard for summary judgment": "The record in this case provides overwhelming evidence to support an inference that Neary was wrongfully terminated. . . . These facts undeniably raise a genuine issue of material fact in regard to Prudential's motivation for terminating Neary. On a motion for summary judgment, that is all the law requires."). Do these cases require arbitrators to abide by court rules of procedure?

PROBLEM 6.14

James Barker of Barker Business Suppliers (BBS) (most recently from Problem 6.12) is getting very tired of its arbitration with Douglas Distribution Co., represented by Fred Porlock. "You said we had a slam dunk case," Barker complains, "but it's already cost me a small fortune and there hasn't even been a hearing yet. Can't we somehow cut this thing short?" You agree completely when Barker says that "we've got the best witnesses and the arbitrator's never going to believe anything that Douglas has to say." Then Barker (as clients often do) cuts to the bottom line. He says: "Can't we just file some sort of motion or something and get this thing over with once and for all?" What do you tell him? Barker also wants to know if there's anything he should consider doing differently in future arbitrations. He tells you that "I'm a firm believer that if the parties are forced to sit down right at the beginning of a case and see what it's all about, more often than not they can work it out then and there." Is there anything you might suggest?

§ 6.10   THE HEARING

Implicit, if not explicit, in all arbitration statutes and rules is that a party has the right to a hearing before the arbitrators issue their award. FAA §§ 7, 10; UAA § 5(b); RUAA § 15(c), (d); UNCITRAL Model Law, art. 24(1); AAA Commercial Arbitration Rules, Rule R-22, R-30(a), (c); UNCITRAL Arbitration Rules, art. 17(3). Of course, what the hearing looks like can vary dramatically, as the *Schlessinger* case in the previous section illustrates.

As already noted, the arbitrators have substantial control over the conduct of the proceeding, including the hearing. The overriding principle, as stated in the UNCITRAL Model Law, is that "[t]he parties shall be treated with equality and each party shall be given a full opportunity of presenting his case." Art. 18; *see also, e.g.*, AAA Commercial Arbitration Rules, Rule R-30(a); ICC Rules of Arbitration, art. 22(4).

One way in which arbitration hearings differ from court proceedings is that they ordinarily are not subject to the rules of evidence. For example, the Commercial Arbitration Rules of the AAA provide that "[t]he parties may offer such evidence as is relevant and material to the dispute. . . . Conformity to legal rules of evidence shall not be necessary." Rule R-31(a). It is up to the arbitrator to "determine the admissibility, relevance, and materiality of the evidence offered," and the arbitrator "may exclude evidence deemed . . . to be cumulative or irrelevant." Rule R-31(b); *see also* UNCITRAL Model Law, art. 19(2); UNCITRAL Arbitration Rules, art. 27(4). Although arbitrators have the authority to exclude evidence from the hearing, "the penchant of commercial arbitrators to 'let it all in' is well documented." 3 IAN R. MACNEIL ET AL., FEDERAL ARBITRATION LAW § 35.1.2, at 35:9 (1994). The following cases suggest one reason why that might be.

BOWLES FINANCIAL GROUP, INC. v. STIFEL, NICOLAUS & CO.
United States Court of Appeals for the Tenth Circuit
22 F.3d 1010 (1994)

BRORBY, CIRCUIT JUDGE.

The sole issue presented is whether an arbitration award should be vacated when the attorney for the prevailing party deliberately, intentionally, affirmatively and repeatedly communicated to the arbitrators an offer of settlement from the non-prevailing party in an effort to influence the arbitrators' decision. . . . We hold, in the absence of any evidence indicating the arbitrators were influenced by the settlement offer, the arbitration award should be confirmed.

BACKGROUND

The essential facts are not disputed. A quarrel arose between the parties as to the amount of compensation, if any, owed by Stifel, Nicolaus & Co. (Stifel) to Bowles Financial Group (Bowles). The matter was submitted to arbitration whose governing procedural rules gave arbitrators sole authority to determine materiality and relevance of proffered evidence. Counsel for Bowles, an attorney, repeatedly submitted to the arbitrators an offer of settlement made earlier by Stifel. Counsel argued, *inter alia*, the settlement offer evidenced Stifel's admission of liability; the offer proved nonpayment; and the settlement offer evidenced a scheme to trick Bowles. The district court properly characterized the stated reasons as "preposterous." When questioned by this court during oral argument as to the reason for counsel's action, counsel candidly replied that the arbitration rules provide that the arbitrators shall determine the materiality and relevance of any evidence offered and are not bound by rules governing the admissibility of evidence. Counsel also indicated he routinely submitted settlement offers to the arbitrators in the cases where he represented clients in arbitration. In short, counsel felt he owed to his client the duty to communicate the settlement offer to the arbitrators. The arbitrators, after receiving the settlement offer commented they would not consider it and their decision would not be based upon having seen the settlement offer. The arbitrators subsequently awarded Bowles $300,000, which was more than the offer of settlement.

When presented with the issue, the district court expressed shock at counsel's affirmative actions in communicating the settlement offer to the arbitrators, but concluded, in light of the arbitrators' comments, that the arbitration hearing was not fundamentally unfair. The district court thus allowed the arbitration award to stand.

The losing party, Stifel, appeals and asserts, with the benefit of little authority, that if this action is allowed to stand no person will ever again make a settlement offer knowing the controversy will terminate in arbitration. This court agrees. Counsel in a similar context would be derelict in advising a client to make a settlement offer knowing the offer would be communicated to the arbitrators. The next panel of arbitrators may well believe the settlement offer is an admission of liability. However, this is not the issue before this court.

DISCUSSION

The question before this court is whether deliberate, egregious, and repeated breaches of the judicial rules of evidence before an arbitration panel warrant the vacation of the arbitration award.

We commence by discussing what arbitration is and what it is not. Arbitration is a creature born of a contract between parties who are desirous of avoiding litigation in a court of law. Arbitration requires the parties agree to rules of arbitration. Frequently, rules of arbitration specifically exclude the application of judicial rules of evidence and, instead, the arbitrators determine the materiality and relevance of all evidence offered. Arbitrators are not judges of a court nor are they subject to the general superintending power of a court. Arbitration provides neither the procedural protections nor the assurance of the proper application of substantive law offered by the judicial system. Those who choose to resolve a dispute by arbitration can expect no more than they have agreed. One choosing arbitration should not expect the full panoply of procedural and substantive protection offered by a court of law. In short, "by agreeing to arbitrate, a party 'trades the procedures and opportunity for review of the courtroom for the [perceived] simplicity, informality, and expedition of arbitration.' " *Gilmer v. Interstate/Johnson Lane Corp. (quoting Mitsubishi Motors Corp. v. Soler Chrysler-Plymouth, Inc.).*

. . .

"[F]ederal courts have never limited their scope of review [of an arbitration award] to a strict reading of [9 U.S.C.A. § 10]." Courts have created a basic requirement that an arbitrator must grant the parties a fundamentally fair hearing.

. . .

. . .

Stifel has not proven it was subjected to a fundamentally unfair hearing. Conduct by Bowles' attorney was within the broad procedural rules of arbitration agreed to by Stifel. Courts have no power to draft a contract between the parties. The rules of arbitration agreed to by the parties do not explicitly condemn the communication of settlement offers to the arbitrators. What the reasons for this omission might be, this court does not know. It could be that the professionalism of counsel has previously prevented this problem from arising. In view of counsel's statement to this court during oral argument that he routinely conveys settlement offers to arbitrators, it could mean the arbitration rules mean what they say; i.e., the arbitrators will decide what evidence is material and relevant. This court has no power to judicially impose our rules of evidence on an arbitration proceeding.

Also, this court cannot ignore the comments of the arbitrators. The arbitrators stated the settlement offer would not be considered by them and their decision would not be based upon having seen the settlement offer. Undoubtedly the arbitrators were selected because of their reputations for truth and fairness and for their expertise. There exists no evidence in this record to show, or even indicate, that the decision of the arbitrators was not well grounded in either fact or law or that the settlement offer somehow influenced their decision. It would be improper for this court to speculate that knowledge of the settlement offer somehow trumps the arbitrators' statements to the contrary when there exists no evidence to support this conclusion.

We therefore conclude no factual evidence supports Appellant's contention that Stifel failed to receive a fundamentally fair hearing. The communication of a settlement offer to arbitrators who declare they would ignore it, standing alone, does not produce a fundamentally unfair hearing.

CONCLUSION

The result of this opinion may well be to encourage counsel to communicate settlement offers to arbitrators. This opinion might also encourage counsel to communicate other evidence to arbitrators which a court would regard as highly improper. This is for the parties to arbitration to decide and control as arbitration is possible only if the parties agree to arbitrate and how to arbitrate. A court can set aside an arbitration award only if one of the statutory or judicial grounds for vacation have been proven. The record shows proof of neither. We decline to adopt a rule that would ignore the statements of the arbitrators.

The judgment of the district court is AFFIRMED.

TEMPO SHAIN CORP. v. BERTEK, INC.
United States Court of Appeals for the Second Circuit
120 F.3d 16 (1997)

PARKER, CIRCUIT JUDGE:

Neptune Plus Corporation ("Neptune"), an affiliate of Tempo Shain Corporation ("Tempo Shain"), entered into an agreement with Bertek, Inc. ("Bertek") to purchase a license agreement from Gelman Sciences, Inc. ("Gelman") for a patented process to treat materials to enhance their repellency characteristics. Under the agreement, Bertek was to manufacture the treated material, which Neptune intended to sell to the apparel and footwear industries. Disagreements arose and the parties entered arbitration to resolve claims brought by Neptune against Bertek for fraudulent inducement to contract and breach of contract. Bertek counterclaimed with its own fraudulent inducement and breach of contract charges.

Bertek intended to call Wayne Pollock, former President of Bertek's Laminated Products Division, as a witness to provide what Bertek considered to be crucial testimony concerning the negotiations and dealings between the parties about which it claims only Pollock could testify. Pollock became temporarily unavailable to testify, however, after his wife was diagnosed with a recurrence of cancer. The arbitration panel was advised that Pollock remained willing to testify, but that the expected duration of his unavailability was indeterminate. Bertek urged the panel to keep the record open until Pollock could testify either in person or by deposition.

After deliberation, the panel concluded the hearings without waiting for Pollock's testimony. . . .

The panel subsequently rendered an award in favor of Tempo Shain and Neptune, and denied Bertek's counterclaims. Appellees petitioned the United States District Court for the Southern District of New York pursuant to sections 9 and 10 of the Federal Arbitration Act ("FAA" or "Act") to confirm the arbitration award. Bertek cross-moved to vacate the award, arguing that the arbitrators were guilty of misconduct pursuant to FAA section 10(a)(3), 9 U.S.C. § 10(a)(3). . . . The district court . . . granted the petition to confirm the arbitration award and denied the motion to vacate. . . . Bertek appealed.

The question on appeal is whether the panel's refusal to continue the hearings to allow Pollock to testify amounts to fundamental unfairness and misconduct sufficient to vacate the arbitration award pursuant to section 10(a)(3) of the Act. We believe that it did, and therefore vacate the court's endorsement of the award.

. . .

Federal courts may vacate an arbitration award only in limited circumstances as proscribed by section 10(a) of the Act. . . . In this case, we are primarily concerned with whether the arbitration panel committed misconduct in refusing to hear evidence pertinent or material to the controversy.

. . .

We find that there was no reasonable basis for the arbitration panel to determine that Pollock's omitted testimony would be cumulative with regard to the fraudulent inducement claims. Said differently, the panel excluded evidence plainly "pertinent and material to the controversy," 9 U.S.C. § 10(a)(3). The panel did not indicate in what respects Pollock's testimony would be cumulative, but stated that there were "a number of letters in the file" and that Pollock was "speaking through the letters [he wrote], and the reports he[ ] received." These letters and reports were not specifically identified by the arbitration panel. However, after a review of the record, it appears that the letters are correspondence between Pollock and Neptune's President, Robin Delaney, which the panel dubbed the "fight letters," and the reports are certain progress and accounting reports which were the basis for many of these fight letters. These so-called fight letters and reports are not at all representative of what Pollock's testimony would likely have been in connection with the fraudulent inducement allegations. The fight letters arose from individual problems that were ongoing at the time, and did not devolve into recriminations about earlier representations. Their focus was not on the inducement to enter the contracts — rather, they were attempts to solve problems which were giving rise to disputes. As Delaney explained, the parties were trying "[t]o keep the relationship going." The reports, like the letters, addressed discrete problems and possible courses of action. While the letters and reports might have been sufficient to represent what Pollock would have testified to in rebuttal of Neptune's breach of contract claims, which we do not decide, there is nothing to suggest that Pollock's intended testimony concerning appellees' fraudulent inducement claim and Bertek's counterclaim for fraudulent inducement was addressed by the documents admitted into evidence.

Because Bertek's alleged misrepresentations were not documented, appellees' unsupported oral testimony concerning such representations was unrebutted because Pollock, who allegedly made the representations on Bertek's behalf, was not allowed to testify, and he is the only person who could have done so.

As for Bertek's counterclaim for fraudulent inducement, Bertek contends, and there was no evidence to the contrary before the arbitration panel, that Pollock was the only individual involved in the negotiation of the contract with Neptune on Bertek's behalf. Pollock was identified several times throughout the testimony as Bertek's exclusive point-man in the negotiations. Neptune's Robin Delaney admitted this in her testimony. When asked to describe who was involved in the negotiations on each side, she responded: "Mainly it was just Wayne Pollock and myself and our attorneys."

. . . Because Pollock as sole negotiator for Bertek was the only person who could have testified in rebuttal of appellees' fraudulent inducement claim, and in support of Bertek's fraudulent inducement claim, and the documentary evidence did not adequately address such testimony, there was no reasonable basis for the arbitrators to conclude that Pollock's testimony would have been cumulative with respect to those issues.

. . .

III. CONCLUSION

On the facts of this case, the panel's refusal to continue the hearings to allow Pollock to testify amounts to fundamental unfairness and misconduct sufficient to vacate the award pursuant to section 10(a)(3) of the FAA. For the reasons stated above, we vacate the district court's endorsement of the arbitration award and remand for further proceeding consistent with this opinion.

NOTES

1. Section 10(a)(3) of the FAA provides for courts to vacate an arbitration award "[w]here the arbitrators were guilty of misconduct in refusing to postpone the hearing, upon sufficient cause shown, or in refusing to hear evidence pertinent and material to the controversy; or of any other misbehavior by which the rights of any party have been prejudiced." 9 U.S.C. § 10(a)(3); *see also* UAA § 12(a)(4); RUAA § 23(a)(3). As *Bowles* and *Tempo Shain* indicate, courts review awards under those grounds using an overall standard of fundamental fairness. *See* Restatement (Third) of the U.S. Law of International Commercial Arbitration § 4-21(b) ("such misconduct affected the fundamental fairness of the arbitral proceedings or resulted in significant prejudice to the basic procedural rights of a party").

2. Rule 22(f) of the JAMS Employment Arbitration Rules and Procedures provides that "[t]he Parties will not offer as evidence, and the Arbitrator shall neither admit into the record nor consider, prior settlement offers by the Parties." Other arbitration rules do not address the issue. Would the result in *Bowles* have been different if the JAMS rule applied in that case?

3. Interestingly, on occasion arbitration agreements in fact depart from the usual approach in arbitration and actually require the parties to follow the Federal Rules of Evidence. Why might that be?

4. Although the issue in *Tempo Shain* was whether the arbitrator should have granted a continuance, the arbitrator's decision to deny the continuance effectively excluded Mr. Pollock's testimony from the hearing. What were the key facts on which the court based its decision to vacate the award?

5. With the availability of video conferencing, arbitrators may hear live witness testimony without everyone involved being in the same room or even in the same country. Will improved technology reduce scheduling difficulties that may slow down arbitration proceedings or jeopardize the ultimate award? What about holding hearings over the Internet? Are such hearings likely to replace more traditional arbitration hearings? What are their risks and benefits? For a discussion of online arbitration generally, see § 6.12.

PROBLEM 6.15

James Barker informs you that a hearing has been scheduled on Barker Business Supplies' claim against Douglas Distributors, Inc. (Your efforts from Problem 6.14 to help cut the matter short have not been successful.) Barker asks you to sit in at the hearing (which is being handled by an in-house attorney for BBS). Three events occur during the hearing on which Barker wants your opinion.

(a) First, Fred Porlock, who represents Douglas, asks Jack Douglas about conversations Douglas had with several other suppliers concerning their dealings with BBS. When BBS' attorney objects to the testimony as hearsay and irrelevant, the arbitrator (Joan Pinto) says she will "admit it for what it's worth."

(b) Second, Porlock, during his cross-examination of Barker, insists on reading to Barker virtually the entire transcript of his deposition, asking Barker after each sentence whether that sentence was really true. After each objection by BBS' attorney, Pinto warns Porlock to "get to the point" but makes no effort to cut off the questioning. (Not surprisingly, Barker is particularly incensed when he talks to you about this one.)

(c) Third, just before Pinto is ready to close the hearing, Porlock requests a continuance of the hearing for one week. Porlock explains that one of his witnesses, J.W. Windle, could not be at the hearing today because she was out of town on business. According to Porlock, Windle will corroborate testimony by Douglas as to representations Barker made while negotiating the contract. Porlock admits that had he checked with Windle before agreeing to the hearing date, he would have discovered the conflict. BBS' attorney opposes the continuance on various grounds, including that BBS doesn't dispute that Douglas made any of the statements at issue. Pinto grants the continuance.

As to each event, Barker wants to know whether Pinto ruled properly and whether Pinto's ruling gives BBS any ground on which to challenge the award? In addition, Barker asks bluntly, "Why is Pinto so biased that she always rules against BBS?" How do you respond?

Arbitration procedures generally and hearings in particular tend to resemble the legal system with which the arbitrators and lawyers involved are most familiar. Domestic arbitration hearings in the United States tend to resemble a trial, with testimony by witnesses and cross-examination, albeit often much less formal. In international arbitrations, hearings may reflect a hybrid of procedures because the arbitrators, lawyers, and parties may be from very different legal traditions. The following excerpts are illustrative.

Paul D. Friedland, COMBINING CIVIL LAW AND COMMON LAW ELEMENTS IN THE PRESENTATION OF EVIDENCE IN INTERNATIONAL COMMERCIAL ARBITRATION, MEALEY'S INT'L ARB. REP., Sept. 1997*

The suggestion that international commercial arbitration combines civil law and common law approaches to the presentation of evidence may invite immediate skepticism on two counts. First, practitioners of international arbitration know that every arbitration differs, and one must therefore be cautious in positing a standard procedure. Second, there is enormous diversity within the civil law and common law worlds, and it is therefore difficult to describe any system as representing a harmonization of two supposedly definable approaches.

There is nevertheless an equal risk of excessive caution in describing the practice of international commercial arbitration. Despite variation and diversity, experience shows that it is possible to identify the basic components of a standard practice for presenting evidence in international commercial arbitration. Moreover, such practice combines what can legitimately be called civil law and common law approaches to the presentation of evidence.

. . .

The remainder of this article addresses the components that comprise the standard practice for presenting evidence in international commercial arbitration.

Memorials with Exhibits

The submission of memorials accompanied by exhibits is a practice so familiar to those experienced in international arbitration that it seems not to require comment. For American litigators, the practice may seem additionally familiar because it can be considered analogous to the submission of pretrial briefs. The analogy is flawed, however, in one critical respect: pre-trial briefs are not accompanied by exhibits that are automatically accepted into evidence by the trier of fact. Memorials are. It is by the mechanism of submitting documents as exhibits accompanying memorials that parties to international arbitration bypass the entire common law concept of the introduction of documents into evidence at the hearing. In this respect, therefore, the first basic component of the standard practice for presenting evidence in international commercial arbitration contains a significant compromise from the common law approach to presenting evidence.

The main variable with respect to the submission of memorials is the number of sequential exchanges that arbitrators will order or tolerate. This number evidently depends upon the complexity of the case. In contrast to litigation in common law nations, when one compares international arbitrations for complexity or difficulty, the differences are expressed primarily in the number and volume of memorials, and in the intervals required to draft materials, and only secondarily in the number of hearing days. This is another tilt away from the common law approach, where there is usually a more one-to-one correspondence between the complexity of the

---

case and the length of the hearing or trial.

. . .

Witness Statements

Witness statements may be on the cusp of what constitutes a standard feature of arbitration practice. This author has participated in and heard of many arbitrations done without witness statements, but many more done with witness statements. The rules of the leading arbitral institutions make witness statements optional. . . .

The variable here is to what extent witness statements will preclude direct testimony. It is difficult to identify a consensus in this regard. The author's personal view is that, in most cases, it is possible and appropriate to present direct testimony that does not repeat what was presented in a witness statement. New issues invariably arise in the last written pleading or memorial, which is usually after one side, if not both, has submitted its witness statements. In the interval between the end of the written phase and the hearing, moreover, the time for further reflection often gives rise to new points that can be made legitimately through witnesses.

The Hearing

There is an endless variation in the details of how a hearing may proceed in an international commercial arbitration. The most interesting variable is the arbitrators' attitude toward and control over cross-examination. That some cross-examination will be permitted is a standard feature of international commercial arbitration. This author has had only one experience where a tribunal actually forbade cross-examination, but that was the exception, and may also have been motivated as much by the arbitrators' attitude toward the merits as by their attitude toward cross-examination.

More typically, what changes from case to case is the extent to which arbitrators will preempt cross-examination by interrogating witnesses before counsel does, or take other steps to restrict the length and scope and aggressiveness of cross-examination. This is one area where differing backgrounds matter. Civil law arbitrators, more so than common law arbitrators, tend to be sympathetic to witnesses subjected to lengthy cross-examination, even if the cross-examination by common law standards is polite. Civil law arbitrators, more so than common law arbitrators, also tend to show a lack of appreciation for the uneven odds dividing cross-examiner and witness, where the cross-examiner has all the documents at his disposal and has the power to ask and avoid any question that he or she wishes.

BUCKAMIER v. ISLAMIC REPUBLIC OF IRAN
Iran-United States Claims Tribunal
Award No. 528-941-3 (1992)

[Among other claims, W. Jack Buckamier sought to recover $4500 he allegedly deposited in his account at Bank Mellat for transfer to the United States. The Bank admitted that it had not transferred the money to the United States, but argued that "Claimant has not produced evidence of the deposit." Buckamier responded that "the deposit records were among the documents that he alleges were seized from him at the airport when he fled Iran."]

67. The virtual absence of documentary support for Mr. Buckamier's claim raises the issue what the probative value is of the Claimant's affidavit. The importance of this question makes it appropriate to elaborate on the considerations the Tribunal must take into account in weighing this kind of evidence. In a memorandum dated 17 February 1988 the Tribunal's distinguished former member and Chairman of this Chamber, the late Professor Virally, expressed these considerations as follows.

> The Tribunal has often been presented with notarized affidavits or oral testimony of claimants or their employees. [Rare] are the cases where such an issue does not arise. The probative value of such written or oral declarations is usually hotly debated between the parties, each of them relying on the pecul[i]arities of its own judicial system. The U.S. parties insist that such evidence must be recognized with full probative value, as would be the case before U.S. courts. The Iranian parties contend that such declarations are not admissible as evidence under Iranian law, as in many other systems of law, because they emanate from persons whose interests are at stake in the proceedings, or who are, or were, dependent upon the claimants.
>
> . . .
>
> As an international Tribunal established by agreement between two sovereign States, the Tribunal cannot, in the field of evidence as in any other field, make the domestic rules or judicial practices of one party prevail over the rules and practices of the other, in so far as such rules or practices do not coincide with those generally accepted by international Tribunals. In this context, it can be observed that declarations by the parties, or employees of the parties, in the form of notarized affidavits or oral testimony, are often submitted as evidence before such Tribunals. They are usually accepted, but, apparently, their probative value is evaluated cautiously. . . .
>
> It is clear that the value attributed to this kind of evidence is directly related not only to the legal and moral traditions of each country, but also to a system of sanctions in case of perjury, which can easily and promptly be put into action and is rigorous enough to deter witnesses from making false statements. Such a system does not exist within international Tribunals and recourse to the domestic courts of the witness or affiant by the other party would be difficult, lengthy, costly and uncertain. In the absence of any practical sanction (other than the rejection by the international Tribunal of the discredited evidence), oral or written evidence of this kind cannot be accorded the value given to them in some domestic systems. Also it cannot be discounted that the ethical barriers which prevent the making of statements not in conformity with the truth before national courts will not have the same strength in international proceedings, notably when the other party is a foreign government, the conduct of which was severely condemned by public opinion in the country of the other party.

On the other hand, it must be recognized that in many claims filed with the Tribunal, claimants face specific difficulties in the matter of evidence, for which they are not responsible. Such is particularly the case when U.S. claimants were forced by revolutionary events and the chaotic situation prevailing in Iran at the time, to rush out of Iran without having the opportunity or the time to take with them their files, including documents which normally should be submitted as evidence in support of their claims. . . . Obviously, these facts made it very difficult for the claimants who did not keep copies of their files outside Iran to sustain their burden of proof in the ways which would be expected in normal circumstances. In view of these facts, the Tribunal could not apply a rigorous standard of evidence to the claimants without injustice. In adopting a flexible approach to this issue, however, it must not lose sight of its duty to protect the respondents against claims not properly evidenced. At any rate, it must be satisfied that the facts on which its awards rely are well established and fully comply with the provisions of . . . its Rules of procedure.

In order to keep an equitable and reasonable balance between those contradictory requisites, the Tribunal must take into consideration the specific circumstances of each case, as well as all the elements which can confirm or contradict the declarations submitted by the Claimants. The list of such elements is practically unlimited and varies from case to case. The absence or existence of internal contradictions within these declarations, or between them and events or facts which are known by other means, is obviously one of them. Explicit or implied admission by the other party is another, as well as the lack of contest or the failure to adduce contrary evidence, when such evidence is apparently available or easily accessible. In relation to this last element, however, the Tribunal must not disregard the fact that destruction due to revolutionary events or to the war, the departure from Iran of persons responsible for the conduct of the business at the time of the facts referred to in the claim, changes in the direction or the management of the undertakings concerned, can also impair the Respondents' ability to produce evidence. It is often a delicate task to determine if and to what extent respondents would be responsible for such a difficulty.

68. Bearing in mind these considerations, the Tribunal notes that the Claimant's pleadings appear to contain inconsistent statements with respect to the deposit records. While in his initial reply to the Bank's Statement of Defense Mr. Buckamier stated that "[e]vidence of these document's [sic] existence [sic] will be presented to the Tribunal during the 'oral arbitration,' " later in his affidavit he suggested that these records had been seized from him when he left Iran. Considering this apparent contradiction, the Tribunal is not convinced that the Bank actually received the deposit. . . . The Tribunal therefore dismisses Mr. Buckamier's claim against Bank Mellat.

NOTES

1. These two excerpts highlight some of the differences in practice between domestic arbitration in the United States and international commercial arbitration. Further, as they suggest, the practice in any particular international arbitration can vary significantly depending on the legal background and experience of the parties, lawyers, and arbitrators. In short, lawyers who practice in the area of international commercial arbitration need to be aware of other legal cultures and have to be flexible enough to adapt to differing legal perspectives.

2. One attempt to set out a framework for presenting evidence in international arbitration is the International Bar Association's Rules on the Taking of Evidence in International Commercial Arbitration, issued in revised form on May 29, 2010. The IBA Rules are "intended to govern in an efficient and economical manner the taking of evidence in international commercial arbitrations, particularly those between Parties from different legal traditions." Preamble to the IBA Rules. For a listing of procedural issues that may arise in international commercial arbitrations, see UNCITRAL Notes on Organizing Arbitral Proceedings (1996) (stating that "[t]he purpose of the Notes is to assist arbitration practitioners by listing and briefly describing questions on which appropriately timed decisions on organizing arbitral proceedings may be useful").

3. One other difference between American domestic and international arbitration practice worth noting is the greater frequency with which international tribunals appoint their own experts to assist in resolving disputes. International arbitration rules and statutes expressly authorize such a practice. *See, e.g.*, UNCITRAL Arbitration Rules, art. 29; ICC Rules of Arbitration, art. 25(4); UNCITRAL Model Law, art. 26; IBA Rules, art. 6. Although the practice is more common in international arbitration than in domestic arbitration, it is still, in the words of Paul Friedland (in a section omitted from the excerpt above), "an option that is rarely used."

The next case provides more background on the Iran-United States Claims Tribunal. It also is one of the rare American cases that refuses to enforce an award subject to the New York Convention.

IRAN AIRCRAFT INDUSTRIES v. AVCO CORP.

United States Court of Appeals for the Second Circuit
980 F.2d 141 (1992)

LUMBARD, CIRCUIT JUDGE:

Iran Aircraft Industries and Iran Helicopter Support and Renewal Company (collectively the "Iranian parties"), both agencies and instrumentalities of the Islamic Republic of Iran, appeal from the December 10, 1991 order of the District Court for the District of Connecticut . . . granting defendant Avco Corporation's motion for summary judgment.

In granting Avco's motion, which was not timely opposed by the Iranian parties, the district court declined to enforce an award of the Iran-United States Claims Tribunal which resulted in a net balance of $3,513,086 due from Avco to the Iranian parties (the "Award"). . . . Because we find that the district court properly denied enforcement of the Award, we affirm.

Beginning in 1976, Avco entered into a series of contracts whereby it agreed to repair and replace helicopter engines and related parts for the Iranian parties. After the Iranian Revolution of 1978–79, disputes arose as to Avco's performance of, and the Iranian parties' payments under, those contracts. On January 14, 1982, the parties' disputes were submitted to the Tribunal for binding arbitration.

The Tribunal was created by the Algiers Accords (the "Accords"), an agreement between the United States and Iran, through the mediation of Algeria, which provided for the release of the 52 hostages seized at the American Embassy in Tehran on November 4, 1979. In addition to providing conditions for the release of the hostages, the Accords established the Tribunal to serve as a forum for the binding arbitration of all existing disputes between the governments of each country and the nationals of the other. Accordingly, the Tribunal was vested with exclusive jurisdiction over claims by nationals of the United States against Iran, claims by nationals of Iran against the United States, and counterclaims arising from the same transactions.

On May 17, 1985, the Tribunal held a pre-hearing conference to consider, *inter alia*, "whether voluminous and complicated data should be presented through summaries, tabulations, charts, graphs or extracts in order to save time and costs." At the conference, Avco's counsel, Dean Cordiano, requested guidance from the Tribunal as to the appropriate method for proving certain of its claims which were based on voluminous invoices. . . . After noting that the Iranian parties "obviously have had those invoices all along," Cordiano stated that he would:

> like the Tribunal's guidance as to whether, uh, you would like this outside certifying agency to go through the underlying invoices and certify as to the summary amounts or that the Tribunal feels at this point that the, uh — that you would rather have the, uh, raw data, so to speak — the underlying invoices. Uh, we're prepared to do it either way.

The Chairman of Chamber Three, Judge Nils Mangard of Sweden, then engaged in the following colloquy with Cordiano:

Mangard:	I don't think we will be very, very much enthusiastic getting kilos and kilos of invoices.
Cordiano:	That, that's what I thought so . . .
Mangard:	So I think it will help us . . .
Cordiano:	We'll use . . .
Mangard:	To use the alternative rather.
Cordiano:	Alright . . .
Mangard:	On the other hand, I don't know if, if any, if there are any objections to any specific invoices so far made by the Respondents. But anyhow as a precaution maybe you could . . .

Cordiano: Yes sir.

Mangard: Get an account made.

Neither counsel for the Iranian parties nor the Iranian Judge attended the pre-hearing conference.

On July 22, 1985, Avco submitted to the Tribunal a Supplemental Memorial, which stated in part:

> In response to the Tribunal's suggestion at the Prehearing Conference, Avco's counsel has retained Arthur Young & Co., an internationally recognized public accounting firm, to verify that the accounts receivable ledgers submitted to the Tribunal accurately reflect the actual invoices in Avco's records.

Attached to the Supplemental Memorial was an affidavit of a partner at Arthur Young & Co. which verified that the accounts receivable ledgers submitted by Avco tallied with Avco's original invoices, with the exception of one invoice for $240.14.

The Tribunal held its hearing on the merits on September 16–17, 1986. By that time, Judge Mangard had resigned as Chairman of Chamber Three and had been replaced by Judge Michel Virally of France. At the hearing, Judge Parviz Ansari of Iran engaged in the following colloquy with Cordiano:

Ansari: May I ask a question? It is about the evidence. It was one of the first or one of the few cases that I have seen that the invoices have not been submitted. So what is your position on this point about the substantiation of the claim?

Cordiano: Your Honor, this point was raised at the pre-hearing conference in May of last year.

Ansari: I was not there.

Cordiano: I remember that you weren't there. I think we were kind of lonely that day. We were on one side of the table, the other side was not there . . . We could have produced at some point the thousands of pages of invoices, but we chose to substantiate our invoices through . . . the Arthur Young audit performed specifically for this tribunal proceeding.

The Tribunal issued the Award on July 18, 1988. Of particular relevance here, the Tribunal disallowed Avco's claims which were documented by its audited accounts receivable ledgers, stating, "[T]he Tribunal cannot grant Avco's claim solely on the basis of an affidavit and a list of invoices, even if the existence of the invoices was certified by an independent audit."

Judge Brower, the American judge and the only judge of the panel who was present at the pre-hearing conference, filed a separate Concurring and Dissenting Opinion in which he stated:

> I believe the Tribunal has misled the Claimant, however, unwittingly, regarding the evidence it was required to submit, thereby depriving Claimant, to that extent, of the ability to present its case . . .

. . .

Since Claimant did exactly what it previously was told to do by the Tribunal the denial in the present Award of any of those invoice claims on the ground that more evidence should have been submitted constitutes a denial to Claimant of the ability to present its case to the Tribunal.

. . .

Avco argues that the district court properly denied enforcement of the Award pursuant to Article V(1)(b) of the New York Convention because it was unable to present its case to the Tribunal. . . .

We have recognized that the defense provided for in Article V(1)(b) "essentially sanctions the application of the forum state's standards of due process," and that due process rights are "entitled to full force under the Convention as defenses to enforcement." *Parsons & Whittemore Overseas Co., Inc. v. Societe Generale de L'Industrie du Papier (RAKTA).* Under our law, "[t]he fundamental requirement of due process is the opportunity to be heard 'at a meaningful time and in a meaningful manner.' " Accordingly, if Avco was denied the opportunity to be heard in a meaningful time or in a meaningful manner, enforcement of the Award should be refused pursuant to Article V(1)(b).

At the pre-hearing conference, Judge Mangard specifically advised Avco not to burden the Tribunal by submitting "kilos and kilos of invoices." Instead, Judge Mangard approved the method of proof proposed by Avco, namely the submission of Avco's audited accounts receivable ledgers. Later, when Judge Ansari questioned Avco's method of proof, he never responded to Avco's explanation that it was proceeding according to an earlier understanding. Thus, Avco was not made aware that the Tribunal now required the actual invoices to substantiate Avco's claim. Having thus led Avco to believe it had used a proper method to substantiate its claim, the Tribunal then rejected Avco's claim for lack of proof.

We believe that by so misleading Avco, however unwittingly, the Tribunal denied Avco the opportunity to present its claim in a meaningful manner. Accordingly, Avco was "unable to present [its] case" within the meaning of Article V(1)(b), and enforcement of the Award was properly denied.

Affirmed.

CARDAMONE, CIRCUIT JUDGE, dissenting:

The issue before us is whether Avco was denied an opportunity to present its case before the Iran-United States Claims Tribunal at the Hague. . . . I respectfully dissent because it seems to me that a fair reading of this record reveals that Avco was not denied such an opportunity. Thus, in my view the arbitral award is enforceable under the New York Convention.

. . .

One of the reasons for this dissent is because until today no federal or foreign case appears to have used article V(1)(b)'s narrow exception as a reason to refuse to enforce an arbitral award due to the arbitration panel's failure to consider certain evidence. . . .

. . .

Further support for finding that Avco was not denied due process arises from a like exception to enforceability that appears in the Federal Arbitration Act, 9 U.S.C. § 10. . . . The more extensive case law available under § 10 supports the conclusion that Avco was not denied due process before the Iran-U.S. Claims Tribunal. . . . A reading of those cases reveals that they either involve arbitration hearings actually cut short and not completed before an award was rendered, or a panel's outright refusal to hear certain relevant evidence at all.

The present picture is vastly different. Avco had a full opportunity to present its claims, and was on notice that there might be a problem with its proof, especially given Judge Ansari's concerns voiced at trial. The earlier panel surely had never said that the invoices themselves would not be accepted or considered as evidence at trial. Nor did the pre-trial colloquy clearly indicate that the earlier panel had issued a definitive ruling that account summaries would be sufficient substitute proof for the invoices. Avco did not declare, after hearing Judge Ansari's comments, that it had been precluded by the pre-trial colloquy from producing the invoices, nor did it then attempt to introduce them before the panel. Rather than address Judge Ansari's concerns through producing the invoices themselves, Avco reiterated its "choice" to produce only a summary of the invoices. In so doing it took a calculated risk. Under these circumstances, Avco can scarcely credibly maintain that it was prevented from presenting its case before the Tribunal.

. . .

NOTES

1. Did the Tribunal's actions leave Avco "unable to present [its] case"? Or did Avco, in the words of the dissent, take "a calculated risk" in producing only a summary of the invoices? Does it matter that, at most, the Tribunal "unwittingly" rather than intentionally misled Avco about what sort of evidence was required?

2. American claimants before the Tribunal are entitled to collect awards in their favor from a security account maintained by Iran. There is no similar security account to pay awards in Iran's favor. As a result, Iran must go to court to enforce awards against recalcitrant American parties.

3. In a final twist, Iran thereafter filed a claim with the Claims Tribunal against the United States, alleging that the Second Circuit's decision in *Iran Aircraft* violated obligations the United States owed to Iran under the Algiers Accords. The Tribunal found in favor of Iran and awarded it as damages the amount awarded against Avco in the original proceeding. Islamic Republic of Iran v. United States of America, Award No. 586-A27-FT (Iran-United States Claims Tribunal 1998). The Tribunal reasoned that: (1) the Second Circuit's decision "was erroneous" because the award in Avco "was based not on the absence of the invoices underlying Avco's claims, but on a lack of proof that those invoices were payable"; (2) the United States should have filed a statement of interest with the Second Circuit "point[ing]

out why the Avco award deserved enforcement"; and (3) by relying on the dissenting opinion of the American arbitrator, "[t]he Second Circuit thus reconsidered a specific question raised and conclusively decided by the Tribunal; in effect, the Second Circuit repudiated the merits of the Tribunal's award in Avco." As a result, the Tribunal held that "the United States has violated its obligation under the Algiers Declarations to ensure that a valid award of the Tribunal be treated as final and binding, valid, and enforceable in the jurisdiction of the United States." So Iran ended up with its money, but from the United States Government instead of Avco.

4.   For a history of the Tribunal as well as a summary of its awards and decisions up to the time of publication, see GEORGE H. ALDRICH, THE JURISPRUDENCE OF THE IRAN-UNITED STATES CLAIMS TRIBUNAL (1996).

PROBLEM 6.16

Mary Morstan has a number of questions for you about the ongoing arbitration her company (4-M Co.) is involved in with Singh Products. The arbitration agreement provides that it is to be governed by the UNCITRAL Arbitration Rules. In addition, both parties have agreed to follow the International Bar Association's Rules on the Taking of Evidence in International Commercial Arbitration. How do you respond to the following questions from Morstan? (In addition to the rules cited below, you should of course also think about how the readings might help in answering the questions.)

(a) We have a number of witnesses we're going to want to call. Do we have to tell Singh who they are? If so, when do we have to do that by? *See* UNCITRAL Rules art. 28; IBA Rules arts. 4 & 8.

(b) Our best witness is one of the senior officers of the company. Is there any problem with that? *See* UNCITRAL Rules art. 27(2); IBA Rules art. 4(2).

(c) One of our lawyers said it might be a little tricky to interview the witnesses before they testify. Certainly that can't be true, can it? We need to know what the witnesses are going to say to decide whether to call them. IBA Rules art. 4(3).

(d) I've been told that the arbitration tribunal is requiring us to provide written witness statements. What are they? *See* UNCITRAL Rules art. 27(2); IBA Rules art. 4.

(e) If we provide written witness statements, does that mean the witnesses don't have to testify at the hearing? For some of the witnesses, at least, I'd like us to be able to ask follow-up questions without having to have the witness repeat everything that's in the witness statement. Can we do that? IBA Rules arts. 4 & 8.

(f) A book on international arbitration that I've been reading said something about the arbitrators appointing their own expert witness. Can they really do that? The idea makes me really nervous — I don't like the idea of the arbitrators having only one expert to listen to. You know they'll just do what that expert says. Can we hire our own expert? What do we have to do? *See* UNCITRAL Rules, arts. 28 & 29; IBA Rules arts. 5 & 6.

(g) Where will the hearing be held? *See* UNCITRAL Rules arts. 18(2), 28(1).

(h) What's going to happen at the hearing? Does the claimant get to go first? What language will the witnesses testify in? Will the witnesses be under oath? Will there be a transcript? UNCITRAL Rules arts. 19, 28; IBA Rules art. 8.

(i) Will our lawyers be able to cross-examine Singh's witnesses? Will the arbitrators ask any questions? IBA Rules art. 8.

(j) How will we introduce documents into evidence? Do we need to lay a foundation like we would in court? How will I be able to read the documents that aren't in English? UNCITRAL Rules, art. 19; IBA Rules art. 3.

(k) Are there any limits on the evidence that can come in? Can I be called to testify to conversations with my clients? UNCITRAL Rules art. 27(4); IBA Rules art. 9.

§ 6.11 THE AWARD

The end result of the arbitration proceeding is for the arbitrators to issue an award — "the judgment of the arbitrators on the merits of the case." 3 IAN R. MACNEIL ET AL., FEDERAL ARBITRATION LAW § 37.1 (1994). When there is more than one arbitrator, the default rule is that a majority must agree to the award. UNCITRAL Model Law, art. 29 (except for questions of procedure); UNCITRAL Arbitration Rules, art. 33(1), (2) (same); AAA Commercial Arbitration Rules, Rule R-40. Under the ICC Rules of Arbitration, however, if there is no majority, "the Award shall be made by the president of the arbitral tribunal alone." ICC Rules of Arbitration, art. 31(1). How are these different decision-making rules likely to affect the dynamics of deliberations among the arbitrators?

The arbitrators' award must be in writing and signed by those arbitrators who join the award. AAA Commercial Arbitration Rules, Rule R-42(a); UNCITRAL Model Law, art. 31(1); UNCITRAL Arbitration Rules, art. 34(2), (4); UAA § 8. In American domestic arbitrations, "[t]he arbitrator need not render a reasoned award unless the parties request such an award in writing prior to the appointment of the arbitrator or unless the arbitrator determines that a reasoned award is appropriate." *See, e.g.*, AAA Commercial Arbitration Rules, Rule R-42(b). By contrast, the usual practice in international arbitrations is for arbitrators to give reasons for their awards. *See, e.g.*, UNCITRAL Arbitration Rules, art. 34(2); UNCITRAL Model Law, art. 31(2).

Arbitration rules and arbitration agreements sometimes specify time limits in which arbitrators must make their award. *See, e.g.*, AAA Commercial Arbitration Rules, Rule R-41 ("no later than 30 days from the date of closing the hearing"); AAA Expedited Procedures, Rule E-9 (14 days from closing of hearing); ICC Rules of Arbitration, art. 30(1) (six months from the date of the last signature on the terms of reference). What happens if the arbitrators fail to meet that deadline?

GOVERNMENT OF INDIA v. CARGILL INC.
United States Court of Appeals for the Second Circuit
867 F.2d 130 (1989)

PIERCE, CIRCUIT JUDGE:

The Government of India appeals from an order of the United States District Court for the Southern District of New York . . . denying India's motion to vacate an arbitration award for certain carrying charges owed Cargill, Inc. India seeks to vacate the arbitrators' award on [the grounds] . . . that the arbitrators failed to make the award in a timely manner; and . . . that the award was too indefinite, because made in a lump sum without differentiating between the individual claims contested by the parties. . . . Since we find that the arbitrators acted well within their discretion, we affirm.

BACKGROUND

Underlying this controversy are four contracts for the sale of wheat, entered into between Cargill, Inc. and the Government of India ("India") in August 1982 and September 1983. The contracts were all essentially identical. Clause 17 of each contract required India to pay Cargill carrying charges for storage, insurance, and interest, if India's designated ships failed to begin loading within the periods prescribed by contract. . . . Under Clause 24 of the contracts, "any controversy or claim arising out of, in connection with or relating to [the] contract[s]" was to be settled by arbitration before the American Arbitration Association, pursuant to the Association's Grain Arbitration Rules.

The grain was delivered, per the contracts, to five different ships from March 1983 to January 1984. In each instance, India's designated vessel was late in beginning the loading process, and thus India incurred carrying charges. Cargill issued invoices to India for the carrying charges, and India concedes that the invoices were issued in a timely manner. Cargill's five invoices claimed, in total, carrying charges of $186,333.02.

. . . Cargill, having failed to settle its invoiced claims against India, demanded arbitration of the dispute over the carrying charges [and the parties proceeded to arbitration]. . . .

. . . In a letter dated February 3, 1987, the American Arbitration Association notified the parties that their briefs on the merits had been received. The panel informed the parties in a letter dated March 27, 1987 that the hearings were officially closed as of March 23, and that the award would issue within thirty days thereafter. On April 13, 1987, the arbitrators awarded Cargill the lump sum of $156,846.69, plus interest, on Cargill's original claim of $186,333.02. The arbitrators' decision did not set forth any rationale for the size of the award, and did not specify the carrying charges due on each of the five disputed deliveries.

On July 14, 1987, India commenced an action in the United States District Court for the Southern District of New York, pursuant to 9 U.S.C. §§ 10, 12, seeking to vacate the award. . . .

DISCUSSION

. . .

II. *Timeliness of the Award*

India . . . challenges the award on the ground that it was not made within the time limit set by the Grain Arbitration Rules. Rule 33 states that the award "shall be made . . . no later than 30 days from the date of closing the hearings." India argues that, because briefs were filed in this case, the hearings before the arbitration panel, per Rule 27 of the Grain Arbitration Rules, technically closed on February 3, 1987, when the arbitrators acknowledged receipt of the parties' briefs on the merits. On March 27, however, the arbitration panel notified the parties that the hearings had closed as of four days earlier, March 23. The arbitrators thus in effect extended their deadline to April 22, which they met by filing their award on April 13. No objection was made by India.

India argues now that the arbitrators did not have the power to extend their deadline. India therefore claims that the award was late and thus was invalid. That argument fails because the arbitrators' decision to delay was within the scope of their power under the contract and the Grain Arbitration Rules, and because India has failed to show any prejudice attributable to the arbitrators' delay.

A. *The Delay Was Within the Arbitrators' Discretion*

As this court has consistently held, "any limitation upon the time in which an arbitrator can render his award [should] be a directory limitation, not a mandatory one." It cannot be gainsaid that an arbitrator's decision must be made within a reasonable time, and a belated award will be invalid if the parties' "agreement itself makes the deadline [for filing the award] jurisdictional."

Of importance herein, Rule 46 of the Grain Arbitration Rules gives arbitrators the power to "interpret and apply" the Rules. Moreover, even if the arbitrators' decision to delay issuance of the award had been beyond their discretion under Rule 46, Rule 30 states that a party that proceeds in an arbitration knowing that a provision of the Rules has been violated, without protesting, waives any right to object. India failed to object to any delay during the proceedings. Since the arbitrators' delay did not constitute a cognizable breach of the Grain Arbitration Rules, and was not unreasonably protracted, we conclude that the delay did not invalidate the award.

B. *No Showing of Prejudice*

Furthermore, India has also failed to show that it suffered prejudice as a result of delay. As we have noted, "[b]ecause of the strong federal policy in favor of arbitration, a party must demonstrate prejudice before it can defeat efforts to resolve a dispute through arbitration." As this court [has] held . . . , it is within a court's discretion to uphold a late award if no objection to the delay has been made prior to the rendition of the award or there is no showing that actual harm to the losing party was caused by the delay.

Since India has failed to show that it suffered any such prejudice attributable to the delay, and since India did not object to the delay during the arbitration itself, we hold that the delay in this instance did not invalidate the award.

III. The Propriety of the Lump-Sum Award

Finally, India argues that the arbitrators' award, because it was simply for a lump sum amount, should be vacated as too indefinite. We start from the well-settled proposition that

> arbitrators may render a lump sum award without disclosing their rationale for it, and that when they do, courts will not inquire into the basis of the award unless they believe that the arbitrators rendered it in "manifest disregard" of the law or unless the facts of the case fail to support it.

The arbitrators' award herein reflected no disregard — manifest or otherwise — of the law. India, in fact, does not seem to challenge the substance of the award itself. Instead, India argues that the *form* of the award was improper, because the arbitrators failed to indicate *which* of the five invoices for carrying charges were being addressed. India now claims that it will be nearly impossible for it to recover against the five ships whose delay caused India to incur those carrying charges, since India's claims against the individual ships will be indefinite because of the arbitrators' lump-sum award to Cargill.

This contention is without merit, since, as was acknowledged at oral argument, India never asked the arbitrators to differentiate in the first instance among Cargill's five claims. The burden rests with the party seeking an itemized award to request one from the arbitrator; if that party fails to do so, this court will not invalidate a lump-sum award absent a showing that the form of the award was in manifest disregard of settled law, or that there was no support in the facts of the case for a lump-sum award. India has failed to make such a showing.

CONCLUSION

For these reasons, and substantially the reasons stated by the district court, the judgment is affirmed. . . .

NOTES

1.   Once the arbitration hearing is completed and any post-hearing filings have been submitted, the arbitrators close the hearing. *E.g.*, AAA Commercial Arbitration Rules, Rule R-35; UNCITRAL Arbitration Rules, art. 31(1). Under the AAA Commercial Arbitration Rules, like the Grain Arbitration Rules involved in the *Government of India* case, "[t]he time limit within which the arbitrator is required to make the award shall commence, in the absence of other agreements by the parties, upon the closing of the hearing." Rule R-35.

2. If the time limit for the arbitrators to decide had been "jurisdictional," in the terminology of the court, then presumably the arbitrators would have lost the power to act when the time for issuing an award ran out. Any award they then issued would have been in excess of their authority. In the *Government of India* case, the Second Circuit held that the time limit in the AAA Grain Arbitration Rules was merely "directory" and, thus, the running of the time limit did not divest the arbitrators of the authority to act. In addition, the court concluded, India had waived any objection by not acting sooner and was not prejudiced by the arbitrators' action. What good is a time limit if the arbitrators don't have to abide by it? What should India have done to preserve its objection?

3. Notice what the award in this case looked like: essentially a statement of the amount Cargill was to recover from India. The arbitrators did not state any reasons for their award or even identify which contracts the award was based on. Is that enough? Why don't arbitrators have to do more? What remedies can arbitrators grant in their award? Arbitration rules and statutes may expressly grant arbitrators broad remedial powers. *See, e.g.*, AAA Commercial Arbitration Rules, Rule R-43(a) ("The arbitrator may grant any remedy or relief that the arbitrator deems just and equitable and within the scope of the agreement of the parties, including, but not limited to, specific performance of a contract"); RUAA § 21(c) ("arbitrator may order such remedies as the arbitrator considers just and appropriate under the circumstances of the arbitration proceeding"). But how broad are those powers? As broad as the equitable powers of a judge? Broader? The next case considers that question.

ADVANCED MICRO DEVICES, INC. v. INTEL CORP.
Supreme Court of California
885 P.2d 994 (1994)

WERDEGAR, JUSTICE.

California law allows a court to correct or vacate a contractual arbitration award if the arbitrators "exceeded their powers." . . . This case requires us to decide the standard by which courts are to determine whether a contractual arbitrator has exceeded his or her powers in awarding relief for a breach of contract.

        . . .

FACTS AND PROCEEDINGS

[Advanced Micro Devices, Inc. (AMD)] and Intel [Corporation (Intel)] are both engaged in the creation, design, production and marketing of complex integrated circuits, also known as computer chips. In the period 1978–1981 both AMD and Intel were pursuing strategies for producing and marketing 16-bit microprocessors and the 32-bit microprocessors that were expected to follow. . . . Intel had developed its own 16-bit microprocessor, the 8086. Intel, needing another producer to "second source" the 8086, approached AMD.

Intel hoped to establish the 8086's basic architecture, known as iAPX, as the market standard, guaranteeing future sales of the 8086's expected progeny as well. AMD, having had what it saw as a bad experience in a previous second-source agreement with Intel, wanted to be sure it would not be cut off from second sourcing future generations of the 8086 family. . . .

The parties entered into the contract at issue in February 1982. . . . During the ten-year term of the contract (cancelable after five years on one year's notice by either party), either company could elect to be a second source for products offered it by the other. The nondeveloping company would receive technical information and licenses needed for it to make and sell the part. The developing company would receive a royalty. In addition, the developing company would earn the right to be a second source for products developed by the other party. The terms of exchange — the respective value of the products — were to be calculated by a specified equation from the complexity and size of the parts.

. . .

The contract provided for arbitration of "disagreements aris[ing] under this Agreement. . . ." Arbitration was to be by a single arbitrator, whose decision would be considered "a final and binding resolution of the disagreement." Disagreements over product exchanges led AMD to petition the superior court to compel arbitration in April 1987. The parties agreed on an arbitrator and to the rules he would follow, including section 42, entitled "Scope of the Award," which provided: "The Arbitrator may grant any remedy or relief which the Arbitrator deems just and equitable and within the scope of the agreement of the parties, including, but not limited to, specific performance of a contract." . . .

The arbitration lasted four and one-half years and included three hundred and fifty-five days of hearings. As the current dispute focuses narrowly on two items of relief awarded, only a small portion of the arbitrator's extensive findings need be summarized here.

. . .

The arbitrator found Intel extensively breached its obligations to act in good faith and deal fairly. Beginning in mid-1984 Intel, anxious to be the sole source for the 80386 (its 32-bit chip, which was to prove vastly successful) and convinced the contract was to its disadvantage, decided to frustrate the operation of the contract by taking no more products from AMD. Intel also resolved to keep this decision from AMD and the public, leaving AMD and others in the industry with the belief AMD would be a second source for the 80386. This "ke[pt] AMD in the Intel competitive camp" and avoided public knowledge of Intel's sole-source strategy for the 80386, a strategy Intel feared could limit its market if known. The plan succeeded: AMD continued for about two years to believe, incorrectly, its agreement with Intel "had a future."

. . .

. . . Apart from Intel's breach, . . . the arbitrator found AMD had unnecessarily delayed in seeking alternative ways to enter the 32-bit chip market. Having inferred by mid-1985 that Intel was not going to accept the AMD parts that could earn AMD the 80386, AMD should have sought arbitration at that time or immediately begun reverse engineering the 80386 when it became available in July 1986. Instead, AMD did not begin reverse engineering the 80386 until a later time and did not produce its own 80386 chip — known as the Am386 — until March 1991. "In short, Intel's plan succeeded . . . because of AMD's inertia." For this reason, the arbitrator declined to award AMD the hundreds of millions of dollars it sought in lost 80386 profits.

Despite AMD's delay, the arbitrator found AMD had actually been damaged by Intel's breach: "One *knows* that AMD lost *some* goodwill as the result of the Intel conduct; one *knows* that AMD lost *some* profits from not having the 80386 as the result of the Intel conduct. . . . The actual damages are immeasurable; and nominal damages only are inequitable." (Underlining in original.) The proper remedy, the arbitrator decided, was to relieve AMD from "legal harassment by Intel over AMD's alleged use of Intel intellectual property in the reverse engineered AMD 386."

The arbitrator therefore awarded AMD a permanent, nonexclusive and royalty-free license to any Intel intellectual property embodied in the Am386 (paragraph 5 of the award). He also awarded AMD a further two-year extension of certain patent and copyright licenses, insofar as they related to the Am386, that originated in a 1976 agreement between the parties, which had been extended under the 1982 contract to 1995 (paragraph 6 of the award). The arbitrator designated these items as remedies for breach of the covenant of good faith and fair dealing, as well as . . . for other breaches.

AMD petitioned the superior court to confirm the award; Intel petitioned for the award to be corrected by vacating paragraphs 5 and 6, on the ground they exceeded the arbitrator's powers. The superior court confirmed the award, but the Court of Appeal reversed. . . . The Court of Appeal found itself unable to locate a "rational nexus" between paragraphs 5 and 6 of the award and the contract itself. Therefore, the court concluded, the arbitrator had improperly "rewr[itten] the parties' agreement" in paragraphs 5 and 6 of the award. . . . We granted review.

DISCUSSION

I. Standard of Review of the Remedies Fashioned by a Private Arbitrator

. . .

Deference to the arbitrator is . . . required by the character of the remedy decision itself. Fashioning remedies for a breach of contract or other injury is not always a simple matter of applying contractually specified relief to an easily measured injury. It may involve, as in the present case, providing relief for breach of implied covenants, as to which the parties have not specified contractual damages. It may require, also as in this case, finding a way of approximating the impact of a breach that cannot with any certainty be reduced to monetary terms. Passage of time and changed circumstances may have rendered any remedies suggested by the contract insufficient or excessive. As the United States Supreme Court explained in the leading case on review of arbitral remedies in the collective bargaining context, the arbitrator is required "to bring his informed judgment to bear to reach a fair solution of a problem. . . . There the need is for flexibility in meeting a wide variety of situations. The draftsmen may never have thought of what specific remedy should be awarded to meet a particular contingency."

The choice of remedy, then, may at times call on any decision maker's flexibility, creativity and sense of fairness. In private arbitrations, the parties have bargained for the relatively free exercise of those faculties. Arbitrators, unless specifically restricted by the agreement to following legal rules, " 'may base their decision upon broad principles of justice and equity. . . .' As early as 1852, this court recognized that, 'The arbitrators are not bound to award on principles of dry law, but may decide on principles of equity and good conscience, and make their award *ex aequo et bono* [according to what is just and good].' " Were courts to reevaluate independently the merits of a particular remedy, the parties' contractual expectation of a decision according to the arbitrators' best judgment would be defeated.

. . .

We distill from the[] cases what we believe is a meaningful, workable and properly deferential framework for reviewing an arbitrator's choice of remedies. Arbitrators are not obliged to read contracts literally, and an award may not be vacated merely because the court is unable to find the relief granted was authorized by a specific term of the contract. The remedy awarded, however, must bear some rational relationship to the contract and the breach. The required link may be to the contractual terms as actually interpreted by the arbitrator (if the arbitrator has made that interpretation known), to an interpretation implied in the award itself, or to a plausible theory of the contract's general subject matter, framework or intent. The award must be related in a rational manner to the breach (as expressly or impliedly found by the arbitrator). Where the damage is difficult to determine or measure, the arbitrator enjoys correspondingly broader discretion to fashion a remedy.

The award will be upheld so long as it was even arguably based on the contract; it may be vacated only if the reviewing court is *compelled* to infer the award was based on an extrinsic source. In close cases the arbitrator's decision must stand.

. . .

II. Application to this Case

. . .

Paragraphs 5 and 6 of the award did not exceed the arbitrator's power under the standard previously stated. The contested items of relief were rationally drawn from the arbitrator's conception of the contract's subject matter and the effects on AMD of Intel's breach. The available facts do not compel the conclusion the arbitrator fashioned a remedy by reaching outside the contract to some extrinsic source; we are not constrained, in other words, to find he attempted "to dispense his own brand of industrial justice."

. . .

Paragraph 6 of the award, which extends for two years (insofar as they related to the Am386) certain licenses to Intel patents and copyrights originally granted

AMD in 1976 and extended to 1995 under the 1982 agreement, bears a clear and rational relationship to the contract and the effects of Intel's breach. Having found Intel succeeded in keeping AMD in the Intel camp for about two years through its bad-faith conduct, the arbitrator extended for that same period rights that AMD had enjoyed under the contract and that could be useful to it in recovering from the breach's effects.

Paragraph 5 awards AMD a nonexclusive, royalty-free license to any Intel copyrights, patents, trade secrets or maskwork rights contained in the Am386. . . .

. . . [T]he record demonstrates paragraph 5 derived rationally from his interpretation of the contract and the breach he found Intel to have committed. As already discussed, the arbitrator found AMD had been damaged by Intel's breach: the breach "to some extent contributed to AMD's delay in reverse engineering the 80386." Finding the amount of actual damages indeterminable and nominal damages alone inequitable, the arbitrator determined the "proper remedy" was to block Intel's interference with AMD's own attempts to mitigate its damage by marketing its reverse-engineered 32-bit chip. The award was thus rationally related to the arbitrator's plausible findings as to the subject matter of the contract and the effects of the breach. We repeat that in doubtful cases the arbitrator's choice of remedies must stand.

. . .

The dissent, while accepting the principle an award must be rationally linked to the contract or breach, would hold in addition that "the potential remedies available to an arbitrator are limited to those that a court could award on the same claim." In the present dispute over a breach of the implied covenant of good faith and fair dealing, the dissent would limit the possible equitable remedies to specific performance as it could have been ordered by a court, and would vacate the award because it does not order performance in the exact terms of the contract, i.e. because the licenses awarded in paragraphs 5 and 6 do not correspond precisely to licenses that could have been earned under the contract's technology exchange provisions.

We believe this approach is inconsistent with the principles of contractual arbitration and with the agreement of the parties in this case. As already discussed, arbitrators are not generally limited to making their award " 'on principles of dry law.' " For that reason, parties who submit their disputes to arbitration " 'may expect not only to reap the advantages that flow from the use of that nontechnical, summary procedure, but also to find themselves bound by an award reached by paths neither marked nor traceable and not subject to judicial review.' "

. . .

The parties in the present case did not by agreement restrict the arbitrator to remedies available in a court of law. To the contrary, they adopted an AAA rule authorizing the arbitrator to grant "any remedy or relief which the Arbitrator deems just and equitable and within the scope of the agreement." . . .

The test proposed by the dissent would impermissibly embroil the courts in reviewing the legal correctness of an arbitrator's decision on submitted issues. To determine whether a remedy is within the range a court could award on the same claim, a reviewing court would inevitably have to interpret the contract and resolve factual and legal disputes on questions such as the nature of the breach and the extent of the cognizable injury to the nonbreaching party. Reference to "normal contract remedies" is not sufficient, because what remedies are legally and equitably available for breach of contract may depend on the nature of the contract, the breach and the injury. Consequently, the dissent's approach would require judicial reexamination of the award's legal and factual sufficiency. . . . In addition, to measure the award of an arbitrator, who may have been chosen for practical experience or technical expertise rather than legal training, strictly against the legal limits of contract damages is, we believe, unrealistic and contrary to the parties' expectations.

. . .

CONCLUSION

We conclude the challenged portions of the arbitrator's award were within his authority to fashion remedies for a breach of contract. The superior court correctly confirmed the award under section 1286. The judgment of the Court of Appeal, reversing that of the superior court, is reversed.

Lucas, C.J., and Arabian and George, JJ., concur.

Kennard, Justice, dissenting.

. . .

Under the majority's decision an arbitrator in a commercial contract dispute may award an essentially unlimited range of remedies, whether or not a court could award them if it decided the same dispute, so long as it can be said that the relief draws its "essence" from the contract and not some other source. This standard, taken from the far different realm of federal labor law, imposes only the most minimal scrutiny on an arbitration award. In particular, it permits an arbitrator to award a remedy that a court would be prohibited from awarding.

The majority's decision will make businesses think twice about whether they should agree to resolve disputes by arbitration. Businesses choose arbitration for the same reasons they make any business decision — because they believe that, on balance, arbitration maximizes benefits and minimizes risks and costs. By permitting arbitrators deciding commercial contract disputes to award relief beyond that which a court could award and by imposing no limitation on the relief an arbitrator may award other than the minimal requirement that the award draw its essence from the contract, the majority has greatly increased the risks and uncertainty of arbitration.

In my view, an arbitrator's award must both fall within the range of remedies that a court could award for the same claim and, in the case of a contract dispute, bear a rational relationship to the contract. Because the arbitrator's award in this case does not meet either test, I dissent. . . .

. . .

NOTES

1. Counsel for the parties had estimated that the Intel-AMD arbitration would take six to eight weeks. As it turned out, the arbitration lasted four-and-a-half years, with 355 hearing days and 42,000 pages of transcript. *See* Tom Arnold, *Booby Traps in Arbitration Practice and How to Avoid Them, in* ALTERNATIVE DISPUTE RESOLUTION: HOW TO USE IT TO YOUR ADVANTAGE (ALI-ABA Course of Study Materials Mar. 19, 1998). Not all arbitrations are fast and inexpensive!

2. The California Supreme Court in *AMD* refused to vacate the arbitration award merely because the remedy awarded was not one that a court could have ordered, at least when the parties had agreed to give the arbitrators broad powers in their arbitration agreement. The UAA similarly provides that "the fact that the relief was such that it could not or would not be granted by a court of law or equity is not ground for vacating or refusing to confirm the award." UAA § 12(a); *see also* RUAA § 21(c).

3. Is the fact that arbitrators can exercise such broad powers (at least if the parties so agree) consistent with the use of arbitration to enforce statutory rights? Some commentators have argued that it is not:

> Commercial arbitration, at least as it is practiced in America, is a method of dispute resolution, but not necessarily a method of enforcing legal rights. . . . [T]he arbitrator has been under no duty to resolve a dispute in compliance with the parties' legal rights. A Latin phrase sometimes employed to describe the spirit of much American commercial arbitration is *ex aequo et bono* — a resolution is sought that is equitable, minimizes harm to either party, and enables potential adversaries to maintain a valuable commercial relationship; the role of such an arbitrator is said in Europe to be that of an *amiable compositeur.* . . .

Paul D. Carrington & Paul H. Haagen, *Contract and Jurisdiction*, 1996 SUP. CT. REV. 331, 344–45. Professors Carrington and Haagen point out that international arbitration rules generally forbid arbitrators from acting *ex aequo et bono* or as *amiable compositeur* unless the parties agree. *Id.* at 345–46; *see, e.g.*, UNCITRAL Arbitration Rules, art. 35(2). Interestingly, the AAA Consumer-Related Disputes Supplementary Procedures provide: "In the award, the arbitrator should apply any identified pertinent contract terms, statutes, and legal precedents. The arbitrator may grant any remedy, relief or outcome that the parties could have received in court." Rule C-7(c). Is the concern in the AAA Consumer Rules with arbitrators who have too much remedial power, or too little?

4. We have already considered, at least indirectly, the authority of arbitrators to award punitive or exemplary damages. In the *Mastrobuono* case in § 4.05, the United States Supreme Court stated that "if the contracting parties agree to *include* claims for punitive damages within the issues to be arbitrated" — which the Court found to be the case — "the FAA ensures that their agreement will be enforced according to its terms even if a rule of state law would otherwise exclude such claims from arbitration." Under the AAA/ICDR International Arbitration

Rules, by comparison, the default rule is that "the parties expressly waive and forego any right to punitive, exemplary or similar damages unless a statute requires that compensatory damages be increased in a specified manner." Art. 28(5). The RUAA takes an intermediate approach: it makes clear that "[a]n arbitrator may award punitive damages or other exemplary relief if such an award is authorized by law in a civil action involving the same claim," § 21(a), but it requires the arbitrator to "specify in the award the basis in fact justifying and the basis in law authorizing the award and state separately the amount of the punitive damages or other exemplary relief," § 21(e), presumably to enhance the possibility of judicial review.

The RUAA permits the parties in their arbitration agreement to modify section 21 by contract, such as by excluding the arbitrators' authority to award punitive damages or otherwise restricting the arbitrators' remedial powers. *See* RUAA § 4(a). Some courts have found restrictions on the remedial power of arbitrators to be unconscionable, however, and, the Ninth Circuit in *Graham Oil* (see § 3.03[C]) invalidated the entire arbitration clause after finding that a remedy restriction (and several other provisions) conflicted with a federal statute. In short, the scope of arbitrators' power to order remedies remains a highly controversial topic.

5.   Arbitration rules generally provide for the arbitrator to apportion the costs of the arbitration among the parties in the award. See AAA Commercial Arbitration Rules, Rule R-43(c). Some rules include attorneys' fees within the definition of costs. UNCITRAL Arbitration Rules, art. 40(2)(e) ("The legal and other costs incurred by the parties"). Article 42 of the UNCITRAL Arbitration Rules sets out the following standards for apportionment:

> The costs of the arbitration shall in principle be borne by the unsuccessful party or parties. However, the arbitral tribunal may apportion each of such costs between the parties if it determines that apportionment is reasonable, taking into account the circumstances of the case.

The FAA and the UNCITRAL Model Law are silent on the apportionment of costs. The UAA excludes attorneys' fees from the costs subject to allocation, § 10; the RUAA by contrast, provides that "[a]n arbitrator may award reasonable attorney's fees . . . if such an award is authorized by law in a civil action involving the same claim or by the agreement of the parties to the arbitration proceeding." RUAA § 21(b).

6.   As we already have discussed, who bears the costs of the arbitration proceeding can affect a court's decision whether to enforce an arbitration agreement, particularly one in a consumer contract or an employment contract. *See* § 3.03[C]. Does the arbitrator's ability to reallocate the costs of arbitration change your view on this issue? Some arbitration clauses preclude the reallocation of costs and/or the award of attorneys' fees as costs. In *Graham Oil* (see § 3.03[C]), the Ninth Circuit held that such a provision (along with several others, including a remedy limitation), which conflicted with the remedies available under a federal statute, required the invalidation of the entire agreement to arbitrate. Courts also have held such provisions to be unconscionable. *See Samaniego v. Empire Today* in § 2.05[C].

PROBLEM 6.17

Ettie Shaffer, general counsel of West Gilmerton Mines, just today has received the arbitrators' award in its arbitration with Lawler & Co. She is not happy. "The award," she says, "concludes that we breached our contract with Lawler by selling it substandard coal. That's bad enough. But then the arbitrators found that we acted in bad faith and awarded punitive damages!" After you confirm that her understanding of contract law is correct and that punitive damages are not ordinarily available for breach of contract, she continues: "Our contract even says that no punitive damages can be awarded. And then to top it all off, the arbitrators are making us pay all of the arbitration costs, including the arbitrators' own fees and Lawler's attorney's fees. You'd think in the three months they had to work on it since they closed the hearing they could have gotten it right." Assuming that the arbitration was conducted under the AAA Commercial Arbitration Rules, has the arbitration panel acted within its authority in making the award?

§ 6.12   ONLINE ARBITRATION PROCEEDINGS

We have touched at various points in this chapter (and elsewhere in the book) on how arbitration practice and procedure have been affected by technological advances, more particularly, electronic means of communication. The following excerpt considers in detail the workability of a system of online arbitration.

United Nations Commission on International Trade Law, Note by the Secretariat, ONLINE DISPUTE RESOLUTION FOR CROSS-BORDER ELECTRONIC COMMERCE TRANSACTIONS A/CN.9/WG.III/WP.105 (Oct. 13, 2010)

I. Introduction

. . .

3. ODR is a means of dispute settlement which may or may not involve a binding decision being made by a third party, implying the use of online technologies to facilitate the resolution of disputes between parties. Online dispute resolution has similarities with offline conciliation and arbitration, although the information management and communication tools which may be used during all or part of the proceedings can have an impact on the methods by which disputes are resolved. ODR may be applied to a range of disputes affecting B2B and B2C transactions. It could be logical to apply ODR for the resolution of disputes relating to transactions involving the use of Internet. Online arbitration raises specific legal issues stemming from the formal requirements contained in national and international arbitration laws and conventions.

4. The concept of ODR is particularly relevant in addressing disputes arising out of low value, high volume transactions that require an efficient and affordable dispute resolution process. This suggests the need for specific legal standards for ODR, being more than a simple adaptation of existing arbitration and electronic communication rules. The purpose of this note is to provide background information

on ODR, and to suggest matters that may need to be addressed in the formulation of legal standards on ODR.

II. Examples of online dispute resolution models and systems

. . .

C. Online arbitration

9. An example of online arbitration is the joint project of the International Centre for Dispute Resolution (ICDR) and General Electric for the online resolution of disputes between manufacturers and suppliers. Online arbitration is conducted under the American Arbitration Association (AAA) Commercial Arbitration Rules and no rules specific to online arbitration apply. Another model is that of the China Council for the Promotion of International Trade and the China Chamber of International Commerce, which adopted the China International Economic and Trade Arbitration Commission Online Arbitration Rules ("the CIETAC Rules") in 2009. The CIETAC Rules apply mostly to larger volume business to business electronic commerce disputes.

10. In an online arbitration, electronic file management can be used. Electronic file management is a closed system whose access is limited to the parties and arbitrators (i.e. website) or is only used by the arbitration institution (i.e. Intranet). Examples of electronic file management include AAA WebFile organized by AAA, and NetCase housed at the ICC International Court of Arbitration. Both systems provide an ODR online platform for filing complaints; uploading, downloading and transferring documents; and communicating with other participants in the dispute.

. . .

IV. Issues for possible consideration

. . .

C. Identification and authentication

28. Proper mechanisms of identification and authentication will be required at different stages of the ODR proceedings. A party's identity in an electronic setting can be verified through the use of a variety of technologies associated with electronic signature or identity management. The terms "electronic authentication" and "electronic signature" refer to various techniques for the purpose of replicating, in an electronic environment, some or all of the functions identified as characteristic of handwritten signatures or other traditional authentication methods. Identity management refers to the currently prevailing business model that requires service providers and other businesses to identify and authenticate users seeking access to services or databases. Given that in ODR trust is an important factor, the Working Group may wish to consider whether the legal standards dealing with it should incorporate any existing standard on electronic signatures.

. . .

D. Commencement of proceedings

. . .

32. A prerequisite for resorting to online . . . arbitration is that participants must have access to the relevant technology required by the respective ODR provider. An issue the Working Group may wish to consider is the extent to which such requirements must be specified in the terms and conditions of the ODR provider, to which the parties must consent. . . .

. . .

35. In online arbitration, the arbitration agreement serves as the basis of the arbitration. An option that online merchants may choose, in practice, is to include an arbitration agreement in the contract concluded between the parties or in a separate document, such as the general terms and conditions applicable to the transaction, that is, clicking on the corresponding button or ticking a box certifying that it consents to the terms and conditions. Regarding the conclusion of arbitration agreements in an online environment, the Working Group may consider the relevance of consumer law in this regard.

36. Where an arbitration agreement is concluded entirely online, for instance, by the online acceptance of general terms and conditions, a question may arise as to whether its form satisfies the written form requirement under Article II(2) of the New York Convention on the Recognition and Enforcement of Foreign Arbitral Awards (New York Convention). In that context it may be noted that UNCITRAL has adopted a Recommendation to promote flexible interpretation of Article II(2) of the New York Convention . . . .

. . .

E. Submission of complaint, statements and evidence

1. Complaint and statements of claim and of defence

37. In ODR, the complaint and statements of claim and defence can be expected to be submitted electronically through the ODR online platform of the ODR provider. In addition, documents are accessible to the parties, as well as the conciliator or arbitral tribunal, on the ODR online platform throughout the process. Access to certain documents may be restricted to certain participants.

38. In some systems the statement of claim may be submitted in an electronic form on the ODR online platform . . . , and a party might wish to attach documents thereto. Electronic document submission systems, such as NetCase at the ICC or the AAA's WebFile, already exist (see paras. 9-10 above). The question of confidentiality and security of the notice of arbitration and other documents submitted electronically, as well as the amendment of electronically submitted documents, need to be considered also through the application of appropriate technology.

. . .

H. Confidentiality and issues related to security of communications

. . .

49. In ODR, the confidentiality requirement is closely connected with the requirement of security within the online environment where resolution of the dispute takes place. In addition to technical measures providing security of electronic data and communications, the issue arises of making certain that participants are subject to conditions ensuring that electronic data and communications are not disclosed to unauthorized parties. Such mandatory provisions on confidentiality may already be contained in the policies of the ODR provider, to which the parties would become subject when entering the process.

50. Security issues arise with respect to both transmission and retention of electronic communications. The purpose of confidentiality, i.e. the requirement not to make accessible certain information to persons not entitled to it and not to allow intermediaries to share information with others, is intended to protect sensitive data and information involved in the dispute.

. . .

J. Hearings

59. Hearings of witnesses or independent experts could be needed in online arbitration. Such hearings could take place by video or telephone conference, services which could be integrated into the ODR online platform. Keeping a record of such hearings, whether electronically or in paper form, may be required for various reasons and would need to be taken into account in the establishment of an ODR system.

60. Hearings could take place on the ODR online platform in writing (where the parties and the conciliator or arbitrator communicate with each other in dialogue boxes), or orally. Oral hearings could occur through video or telephone conference or similar methods, which could be integrated services on the ODR online platform. Again, keeping a record of such hearings is an important matter.

. . .

L. Place of arbitration

64. The place of arbitration has a legal impact on a number of matters, such as the applicable domestic procedural law, procedures for setting aside, determining the court having jurisdiction to grant interim measures or assist and supervise the arbitral tribunal in certain matters, and the recognition and enforcement of the arbitral award.

65. In online arbitration, determining the place of arbitration may be problematic. For instance, parties and arbitrators may be in different geographical locations, or the actual location of a party may differ from the address that it has submitted. In order to avoid controversies during the arbitration process and, subsequently, with recognition and enforcement of arbitral awards, it may be useful to ascertain the place of arbitration, rather than leaving it to the agreement of the

parties. The place of arbitration may also affect the application of mandatory laws and public policy considerations on online arbitration.

. . .

N. Enforcement issues

68. The attractiveness of . . . online arbitration would presumably be increased if any settlements reached were to enjoy a regime of expedited enforcement, and this is a matter the Working Group may wish to consider.

. . .

71. In international commercial arbitration, foreign arbitral awards are recognized and enforced under the New York Convention. The New York Convention does not refer to the admissibility of electronic communications with regard to aspects of arbitration that are important regarding recognition and enforcement (e.g. the requirement that an arbitration agreement be in writing, and the formal requirements for the award to be submitted for recognition and enforcement). . . .

. . .

73. . . . [I]t should be noted that the Commission . . . adopted, at its thirty-ninth session in 2006, a "Recommendation regarding the interpretation of article II, paragraph 2, and article VII, paragraph 1, of the Convention on the Recognition and Enforcement of Foreign Arbitral Awards, done in New York, 10 June 1958." The Recommendation was drafted in recognition of the widening use of electronic commerce and enactments of domestic legislation as well as case law, which are more favourable than the New York Convention in respect of the form requirement governing arbitration agreements, arbitration proceedings, and the enforcement of arbitral awards. The Recommendation encourages States to apply article II(2) of the New York Convention "recognizing that the circumstances described therein are not exhaustive." . . .

74. Article V(1)(a) of the New York Convention provides that recognition and enforcement of a foreign arbitral award may be refused if the arbitration agreement is not valid under the law of the country where the award was made (provided that the parties did not subject the arbitration agreement to any other law). Under Article V(1)(d) of the New York Convention, recognition and enforcement may be refused if the composition of the arbitral authority or the arbitral procedure was not in accordance with the law of the country where the arbitration took place. The meaning of "the country where the award was made" and "the country where the arbitration took place" may be ambiguous in the case of online arbitration for the reasons discussed above in relation to the determination of the place of arbitration (see paras. 64-65 above).

. . .

Q. Costs and speed of proceedings

88. The services of ODR providers may be offered either free of charge or for a fee. The issue of the cost of the process to parties may have an impact on their

willingness to make use of it.

. . .

90. Research and experimentation with ODR indicate that the availability of dispute resolution which is faster than regular litigation or ADR may motivate parties to use ODR. If offered the opportunity to resolve their disputes without the need to travel and with the help of rapid electronic communications, parties may become more willing to embrace ODR. Since the speed of proceedings is a key motivating factor, it seems reasonable to consider tailoring the legal framework for ODR to promote this aspect.

. . .

NOTES

1.   Online dispute resolution is not limited to arbitration, of course, and many of the efforts at ODR have involved facilitated settlement rather than arbitration. The focus here is on online arbitration.

2.   Are any sorts of disputes particularly well suited for online arbitration? One possibility is low-value claims (brought by either consumers or businesses) — claims that could not economically be brought in court (e.g., claims for which class relief is unavailable, for whatever reason). Consistent with that possibility, an UNCITRAL Working Group currently is preparing draft procedural rules for ODR, with the aim of "provid[ing] a practical avenue — which in practice did not exist at present — for the quick, simple and inexpensive resolution of low-value cross-border disputes, matters for which it is not generally practicable to bring an action in the courts." United Nations Commission on International Trade Law, Report of Working Group III (Online Dispute Resolution) on the Work of Its Twenty-Fifth Session (New York, 21-25 May 2012) A/CN.9/744, at ¶ 15 (June 7, 2012). What do you think of such efforts? Are they likely to be useful? Are the barriers legal ones (of the sort raised in the excerpt above), practical ones, or perhaps political ones? Would you be willing to participate in ODR to resolve any disputes you might have with providers of consumer goods or services? Why or why not?

3.   A highly publicized use of an online dispute resolution process — sometimes called arbitration   is to resolve disputes over Internet domain names. The Internet Corporation for Assigned Names and Numbers ("ICANN") has promulgated a Uniform Domain Name Dispute Resolution Policy ("UDRP") and approved four providers of dispute resolution services (the Asian Domain Name Dispute Resolution Centre, the National Arbitration Forum, the World Intellectual Property Organization, and the Czech Arbitration Court Center for Internet Disputes; two others, eResolution and the CPR Institute for Dispute Resolution, were approved but have stopped handling UDRP cases) to administer what ICANN calls "mandatory administrative proceedings" under the Policy. The UDRP Rules provide that "any written communication to Complainant or Respondent provided for under these Rules shall be made electronically via the Internet (a record of its transmission being available), or by any reasonably requested preferred means stated by the Complainant or Respondent, respectively." Rules for Uniform Domain

Name Dispute Resolution Policy, Rule 2(b). The Rules discourage in-person hearings, although they seem to permit the panel to use electronic means for such hearings if held. Rule 13 ("There shall be no in-person hearings (including hearings by teleconference, videoconference, and web conference), unless the Panel determines, in its sole discretion and as an exceptional matter, that such a hearing is necessary for deciding the complaint."). The first proceeding was filed by the World Wrestling Federation Entertainment, Inc. against Michael Bosman, challenging Bosman's registration of the domain name worldwrestlingfederation.com. The sole arbitrator found in favor of the complainant, *see* Wrestling Federation Entertainment, Inc. v. Bosman, Case No. D99-0001 (WIPO Administrative Panel Decision Jan. 14, 2000) <http://www.wipo.int/amc/en/domains/decisions/html/1999/d1999-0001.html>, as has happened in the majority of proceedings under the rules (the decisions in which are all available on the Internet). Interestingly, under the Policy, panel decisions do not preclude prior or subsequent actions in court to resolve the dispute. Policy 4(k). Under such circumstances, are the ICANN administrative proceedings properly called arbitration? *See* Dluhos v. Strasberg, 321 F.3d 365 (3d Cir. 2003) (holding that "judicial review of . . . decisions [under the UDRP] is not restricted to a motion to vacate arbitration award under § 10 of the FAA, which applies only to binding proceedings likely to 'realistically settle the dispute' "); Parisi v. Netlearning, Inc., 139 F. Supp. 2d 745 (E.D. Va. 2001) (FAA provisions on judicial review do not apply to UDRP proceedings). For a critical view of ICANN dispute resolution (and "privatized" Internet dispute resolution generally), see Elizabeth G. Thornburg, *Going Private: Technology, Due Process, and Internet Dispute Resolution*, 34 U.C. Davis L. Rev. 151 (2000).

4. What if the online arbitration proceeding is fully automated? In other words, what if the "arbitrator" is a computer that is programmed to resolve the dispute? Can the current legal framework be applied to such a proceeding? What changes (if any) would be needed? Do you think parties would accept such a system?

PROBLEM 6.18

The Senate Committee on which Senator Grace Dunbar (see Problem 1.5) is a very junior member has decided to hold hearings on online dispute resolution as a means of facilitating electronic commerce. Senator Dunbar asks you, as the member of her staff with the greatest expertise on arbitration, to brief her before the hearing on the promise and pitfalls of online arbitration. What do you tell her?

PROBLEM 6.19

You are a law clerk for D.C. Circuit Judge Grant Munro, who has just been named to a committee considering possible revisions to the Federal Rules of Civil Procedure. He asks you to compare the procedures in arbitration with procedures in federal court. His reason for asking, he tells you, is that he wonders whether the Federal Rules would work better if they were more like typical arbitration rules. What differences can you identify between "typical" arbitration procedures and the Federal Rules of Civil Procedure? Should arbitration procedures serve as a model for amendments to the Federal Rules? Or vice versa? Why or why not?

Chapter 7

ENFORCING ARBITRAL AWARDS

§ 7.01 OVERVIEW

Most arbitration awards, like most arbitration agreements, are complied with voluntarily. Richard W. Naimark & Stephanie E. Keer, *Post-Award Experience in International Commercial Arbitration, in* Towards a Science of International Arbitration: Collected Empirical Research 269, 270-271 (Christopher R. Drahozal & Richard W. Naimark eds., 2005). In those cases, no court action is necessary to obtain payment of amounts awarded or otherwise to ensure compliance with the award. But that is not always true. Arbitration statutes generally establish procedures by which an arbitration award can be confirmed — turned into a judgment of a court — and thus enforced in the manner of any court judgment. In addition, even if the award is not confirmed, a court or subsequent arbitrator may nonetheless recognize the award by giving it preclusive effect in a future case.

This chapter examines the enforceability of arbitration awards. First, it looks at the procedures by which parties challenge arbitration awards before the rendering tribunal. Second, it considers the enforcement of domestic arbitration awards, including the grounds on which courts can refuse to enforce awards (some of which we have already seen) and procedural issues relating to enforcement actions. Third, this chapter examines similar issues with respect to the enforcement of international arbitration awards. Fourth, it addresses the extent to which parties can alter by contract the standard for judicial review of arbitration awards. Finally, fifth, it looks at the preclusive effect of awards in future cases.

§ 7.02 CHALLENGING AWARDS BEFORE THE ARBITRAL TRIBUNAL

Commercial arbitration rules ordinarily provide only a limited ability to challenge an award before the arbitral tribunal itself. Rule R-46 of the American Arbitration Association's Commercial Arbitration Rules, for example, permits any party, on notice and within 20 days of the award, to request correction of "any clerical, typographical, or computational errors in the award." The Rule makes clear, however, that "[t]he arbitrator is not empowered to redetermine the merits of any claim already decided." *See also* UNCITRAL Arbitration Rules, art. 38(1). In addition, the UNCITRAL Arbitration Rules permit the parties to request the arbitral tribunal to "give an interpretation of the award," art. 37(1), or "to make an additional award as to claims presented in the arbitral proceedings but not decided by the arbitral tribunal," art. 39. The Federal Arbitration Act is silent as to the grounds on which arbitrators can revisit an award, but both the Uniform Arbitration Act and the Revised Uniform Arbitration Act permit arbitrators to modify awards under similar circumstances. UAA § 9 ("evident miscalculation of figures or an evident mistake in the description of any person, thing or property referred to in the award"; "award is imperfect in a matter of form, not affecting the merits of the controversy"; "to clarify the award"); RUAA § 20 (same). The following award from the Iran-United States Claims Tribunal, which uses the UNCITRAL Arbitration Rules, shows how parties sometimes attempt to obtain review of the merits of an award despite the limits in the rules.

DEVELOPMENT & RESOURCES CORP. v. GOVERNMENT OF THE ISLAMIC REPUBLIC OF IRAN
Iran-United States Claims Tribunal
26 Iran-U.S.C.T.R. 256 (1991)

I. INTRODUCTION

1. The Claimant DEVELOPMENT AND RESOURCES CORPORATION filed its Statement of Claim on 17 November 1981, naming as Respondents THE GOVERNMENT OF THE ISLAMIC REPUBLIC OF IRAN, THE KHUZESTAN WATER AND POWER AUTHORITY, THE STATE ORGANIZATION FOR ADMINISTRATION AND EMPLOYMENT, THE MINISTRY OF ENERGY, THE MINISTRY OF AGRICULTURE, THE NATIONAL IRANIAN OIL COMPANY, as successor in interest to THE OIL SERVICES COMPANY OF IRAN, THE MINISTRY OF ECONOMY, and BANK MARKAZI.

2. The Parties submitted pleadings on all issues in this Case. A Pre-Hearing Conference was held on 26 April 1984 and a Hearing was held on 27 and 28 February 1986. The Parties made various submissions and requests that raised procedural issues.

3. The Tribunal signed and filed the Award in this Case in English on 25 June 1990. The Award was filed in Persian on 15 October 1990.

4. Subsequent to the filing of the Award, three of the Respondents, The Ministry of Agriculture ("MOA"), The Ministry of Energy ("MOE") and the State Organization for Administration and Employment ("SOAE"), filed documents with the Tribunal's Registry commenting on the Award.

. . .

III. THE TRIBUNAL'S FINDINGS

8. As a matter of principle, the Claims Settlement Declaration and the Tribunal Rules do not allow for the reopening or reconsideration of awards once rendered. Article IV, Paragraph 1, of the Claims Settlement Declaration states that "[a]ll decisions and awards of the Tribunal shall be final and binding." Likewise, Article 32(2) of the Tribunal Rules provides that the "award shall be made in writing and

shall be final and binding on the parties."[1] However, once a final award has been rendered, the Tribunal Rules explicitly allow for (i) a request by one or more of the parties to the relevant case that the Tribunal give an interpretation of the award (Article 35), (ii) a request that the Tribunal make an additional award as to claims presented in the arbitral proceedings but omitted from the award (Article 37), and (iii) a request that the Tribunal correct errors in computation, clerical or typographical errors, or any errors of a similar nature (Article 36). Each of these requests has to be made within thirty days of the receipt of the Award.

9. In view of the above, before deciding on the merits of any request the Tribunal must first decide whether the submissions of MOE, MOA and SOAE fall within the parameters set by the Tribunal Rules and — if so — whether all procedural requirements are met.

A. The Ministry of Energy

10. MOE refers in its submission to Articles 32(2) and 37 of the UNCITRAL Rules. Article 32(2) merely confirms the binding nature of awards. MOE makes reference to Article 32(2) in connection with its request that the Tribunal provide additional explanation and clarification concerning the basis for one of its holdings; the Tribunal assumes therefore that MOE intended to refer to Article 32(3) of the Tribunal Rules, which requires the Tribunal to state "the reasons upon which the award is based."

11. The holding that seems to have given rise to MOE's first request dealt with the Claimant's claim of $517,239.66 in arbitration costs. The Award granted $45,000 towards these costs. In this connection, MOE requests that the Tribunal "clarify the basis of issuance the said Award" as well as to "specify the portion of [MOE] in the judgment debt." The Award's decision to grant arbitration costs makes reference to the Parties' contentions, specific Tribunal rules authorizing the payment of costs, as well as Tribunal precedents interpreting those rules. The Tribunal finds that sufficient explanation has been given in the Award as to the exercise of its authority under Tribunal Rules 38 and 40 to award reasonable costs of arbitration and that there is no need for it to apportion the amount of costs awarded. The Tribunal notes further that the Rules do not provide for the right of an arbitrating party to exchange views with the Tribunal as to the question whether the Tribunal has — to the satisfaction of such arbitrating party — complied with Article 32(3), nor do the Rules provide for appeal or reconsideration of an award.

12. MOE's second request refers to the Tribunal's holding that MOE is to pay an amount of $260,903.50 (plus interest) to the Claimant. MOE refers to certain arguments that were made in its written submissions as well as at the Hearing, but that were not considered persuasive by the Tribunal. The specific arguments

---

[1] Article III, Paragraph 2, of the Claims Settlement Declaration provides inter alia that the "Tribunal shall conduct its business in accordance with the arbitration rules of the United Nations Commission on International Trade Law (UNCITRAL) except to the extent modified by the Parties or by the Tribunal to ensure that this Agreement can be carried out." Article 32(2) of the Tribunal Rules adopted on 3 May 1983 is unchanged from Article 32(2) of the UNCITRAL Rules. However, the note added to Article 32(2) of the UNCITRAL Rules points out that "the term 'parties' means the arbitrating parties."

referred to by MOE were not explicitly rejected in the Award. However, the Tribunal's ruling on the claim at issue clearly indicates that the Tribunal was not convinced by these arguments. MOE now repeats these arguments and concludes that it "duly established the basis for the dismissal of the claim at issue." . . .

13. As noted above, Article 37 of the Tribunal Rules gives the arbitrating parties the right to request the Tribunal to make an additional award as to claims presented to the arbitral proceedings but omitted from the award. In this case, however, the Award rules unequivocally on the claims brought by the Claimant against MOE, as well as MOE's counterclaims against the Claimant. No claim was omitted. Therefore, MOE's request cannot be based on Article 37 of the Tribunal Rules. Although presented as a request for an additional award, MOE's request essentially is an appeal or a request to reconsider the Award. As noted above, however, the Tribunal Rules do not provide for any appeal or reconsideration of an Award. The Tribunal denies MOE's second request.

B. The State Organization for Administration and Employment

14. Although SOAE makes reference in its request to Articles 32(3) and 35 of the UNCITRAL Rules, SOAE's submission simply reargues its position and requests "restitution of [its] lawful rights and provision of evidence on behalf of [SOAE]." SOAE's request, in fact, is for the Tribunal to reopen a case already concluded by award. As the Tribunal Rules do not provide for such reopening of a case, the Tribunal is unable to grant SOAE's request.

C. The Ministry of Agriculture

15. MOA states that its request is based on Articles 36 and 37 of the Tribunal Rules. MOA does not, however, make a request for correction of the award, as provided for in Article 36, nor does it make a request for an additional award, as provided for in Article 37 of the Tribunal Rules. Instead, MOA seeks to reargue certain aspects of the case and to submit additional evidence, in the form of an alleged Settlement Agreement, dated 18 December 1981. The Tribunal finds that MOA has had ample opportunity to present all arguments and submit all evidence it considered relevant. The Tribunal Rules do not provide for additional arguments and evidence after a case has been concluded by Award. The arguments and evidence contained in this filing are therefore rejected.

IV. DECISION

16. For the foregoing reasons,

THE TRIBUNAL DECIDES AS FOLLOWS:

The requests by the Respondents THE MINISTRY OF ENERGY, THE STATE ORGANIZATION FOR ADMINISTRATION AND EMPLOYMENT and THE MINISTRY OF AGRICULTURE contained in their submissions of 12 and 15 November 1990 concerning Award No. 485-60-3 are denied.

Even if the arbitration panel is willing to revisit the substance of the award after it has been made, such attempts face serious obstacles in the courts, as the next case demonstrates.

COLONIAL PENN INSURANCE CO. v. OMAHA INDEMNITY CO.
United States Court of Appeals for the Third Circuit
943 F.2d 327 (1991)

SLOVITER, CHIEF JUDGE.

After an arbitration panel issued a final award in favor of one of the parties, a majority of the panel issued a new award "clarifying" the original award and increasing the amount awarded. The district court granted the successful party's motion to confirm the second award, and denied the other party's motion to confirm the first award. This appeal presents the question whether the arbitrators exceeded their powers when they issued a second award, and, if so, the circumstances under which an arbitral award may be corrected because of an erroneous assumption of fact.

I.

Background Facts and Procedural History

In October 1984, Colonial Penn Insurance Company entered into a reinsurance agreement, signed by Royal American Managers, Inc. (RAM) on behalf of Omaha Indemnity Company, pursuant to which Omaha (the reinsurer) was to indemnify Colonial Penn (the reinsured) against ninety percent of the losses Colonial Penn might experience on a book of short-term auto rental policies. Omaha apparently honored the agreement by accepting Colonial Penn's premiums and paying the agreed upon share of claims and expenses until September 1986 when it ceased funding the claims and asserted that RAM lacked authority to bind Omaha to the contract.

Colonial Penn filed this diversity action for breach of contract in the United States District Court for the Eastern District of Pennsylvania against Omaha, its parent Mutual of Omaha Insurance Company, and RAM. . . . In December 1987, the district court . . . granted Omaha's motion to compel binding arbitration of its dispute with Colonial Penn as provided in the reinsurance agreement. . . .

A panel of three arbitrators was formed, whereby each party appointed an arbitrator and the two arbitrators together selected an umpire. Colonial Penn claimed that it had incurred losses and expenses of approximately $29 million as a result of Omaha's repudiation. . . . After the parties engaged in extensive discovery and briefing of legal and factual issues, they participated in an eight-day arbitration hearing.

The panel issued a unanimous "Final Award" on January 18, 1990, which provided in pertinent part:

. . .

1. Omaha Indemnity shall pay the sum of $10 million to Colonial Penn without further delay in satisfaction of Omaha Indemnity's obligations to Colonial Penn under the Reinsurance Agreement between the parties dated October 1, 1984.

2. Omaha Indemnity Company *shall further release any and all claims to the reserves* (including IBNR)[2] *currently held by Colonial Penn to pay losses and loss adjustment expenses* arising out of the business which was the subject of the Reinsurance Agreement between the parties.

3. Upon payment of the sum of $10 million to Colonial Penn and release of all claims to such reserves, Omaha Ind[em]nity shall be relieved of any further liability for the payment of losses and loss adjustment expenses under the Reinsurance Agreement between the parties and also released from any other claims arising out of or related to the performance or nonperformance of its duties under that Agreement.

([E]mphasis added).

After reading the final award, Colonial Penn's counsel initiated a conference call to the umpire and Omaha's counsel. Colonial Penn's counsel stated that he was puzzled by the award because Colonial Penn was not holding any reserves on this program and that Omaha was not claiming any Colonial Penn reserves. . . . [C]ounsel for Omaha responded that he thought the Final Award was clear and unambiguous. . . .

On January 29, 1990, Colonial Penn's arbitrator and the umpire, constituting a majority of the panel, issued a second (and substitute) order "[i]n response to a request from the parties for clarification . . . and after review of the submissions of the parties in support of their joint request for clarification." The second order deleted the reference to any release by Omaha of a claim to Colonial Penn's reserves. Instead, it provided that in addition to the $10 million previously awarded to Colonial Penn, Omaha would also be required to pay to Colonial Penn "the sum of $8,988,783 which represents Omaha Indemnity's share of the reserves (including IBNR) which will be necessary to pay losses and loss adjustment expenses arising out of the business which was the subject of the Reinsurance Agreement between the parties."

In a letter accompanying this second award, the umpire explained that "at least a majority of the Panel was under the mistaken assumption that Colonial Penn was holding Omaha's 90% share of the reserves on the book of business in question and, therefore, that portion of the Award directing Omaha . . . to release any and all claims to those reserves was designed to make that sum ($8,988,783) available to Colonial Penn for the purpose of paying claims in the run-off of the business." The

---

[2] When an insurer sets up a reserve, it designates part of its capital to fund policyholders' claims and makes these funds unavailable for other purposes. In addition to reserves set up for reported claims, actuaries estimate the amounts that will be necessary to pay claims for losses that have been incurred but not yet reported. The reserves based on these actuarial estimates are characterized as Incurred But Not Reported (IBNR) reserves.

third arbitrator dissented from this order. On February 1, 1990, as directed in the first award, Omaha forwarded $10 million to Colonial Penn and stated in the covering letter that Omaha "hereby releases any and all claims to the reserves (including IBNR) currently held by Colonial Penn to pay losses and loss adjustment expenses arising out of the business which was the subject of the reinsurance agreement." On February 2, 1990, Colonial Penn filed a motion in the district court for an order confirming the second arbitration award and directing entry of judgment against Omaha. On February 16, 1990, Omaha moved to confirm the first arbitration award. The district court denied Omaha's motion, granted Colonial Penn's motion confirming the second arbitration award in the amount of $18,988,783, and ordered Omaha to pay the unpaid balance and post-judgment interest.

Omaha appealed. . . .

II.

Discussion

. . .

B.

The Functus Officio *Doctrine*

As a general rule, once an arbitration panel renders a decision regarding the issues submitted, it becomes *functus officio*[3] and lacks any power to reexamine that decision. . . . [T]he *functus officio* doctrine has been routinely applied in federal cases brought pursuant to the Federal Arbitration Act.

The policy underlying this general rule is an "unwillingness to permit one who is not a judicial officer and who acts informally and sporadically, to reexamine a final decision which he has already rendered, because of the potential evil of outside communication and unilateral influence which might affect a new conclusion." Further, notwithstanding the fact that an increased utilization of arbitration in recent years has to some extent created the office of the specialized professional arbitrator, "[t]he continuity of judicial office and the tradition which surrounds judicial conduct is lacking in the isolated activity of an arbitrator."

. . . [A]s recognized by the district court, the common law *functus officio* doctrine contains its own limitations[:] . . . (1) an arbitrator "can correct a mistake which is apparent on the face of his award," (2) "where the award does not adjudicate an issue which has been submitted, then as to such issue the arbitrator has not exhausted his function and it remains open to him for subsequent determination," and (3) "[w]here the award, although seemingly complete, leaves

---

[3] *Functus officio* derives from the Latin meaning "[a] task performed" and is defined by Black's as, "[h]aving fulfilled the function, discharged the office, or accomplished the purpose, and therefore of no further force or authority." BLACK'S LAW DICTIONARY 606 (5th ed. 1979).

doubt whether the submission has been fully executed, an ambiguity arises which the arbitrator is entitled to clarify."

Colonial Penn does not argue that either the second or third exception is applicable here. The award did not fail to adjudicate an issue submitted. The "ambiguity," if any, does not arise from doubt as to the full execution of the submission. However, Colonial Penn argued and the district court agreed that there was a mistake evident on the face of the first arbitration award because the panel ordered Omaha to release its claim to Colonial Penn's reserves when Colonial Penn was holding no reserves to which Omaha had any claim. In a related vein, the district court also concluded that it was impossible to comply with the award because Omaha could not release any claims to reserves it was not holding.

We agree with Omaha that the district court's interpretation and application of the "mistake on the face of the award" standard cannot be sustained. The exception for mistakes apparent on the face of the award is applied to clerical mistakes or obvious errors in arithmetic computation. Possibly, it could also be applied in a situation where the award on its face is contrary to a fact so well known as to be subject to judicial notice, but we take no position on that here.

In this case, it was not possible to tell from the face of the award either that Colonial Penn held no reserves to which Omaha might have a claim or that Omaha had not submitted a claim for any reserves allegedly held by Colonial Penn. The fact that there was a provision for release from claims does not on its face and without more suggest any mistake. In extending the limited exception for mistakes apparent on the face of the award to a situation where extraneous facts must be considered, the district court opened a Pandora's box which could subvert the policies on which the application of *functus officio* to arbitral decisions are predicated. Parties could, under the guise of a mistake in fact, seek recourse directly from the arbitrators in an attempt to overturn an adverse award. The need to regard arbitral awards as final and protect the arbitrators from outside influence is too strong to permit diminution of the *functus officio* doctrine.

. . .

C.

Remand for Mistake

It should be apparent that the policy reasons for the *functus officio* doctrine precluding an arbitration panel from reconsidering its award are not applicable with the same force to action by the district court. In the first place, the court is not subject to the concerns about the arbitrator's lack of continuity and "isolated activity." Second, the court is not likely to be subject to the "evil of outside communication and unilateral influence." Third, and most important, the court must necessarily exercise some review of the arbitral award when a motion to confirm is before it.

. . .

Because our reversal of the district court's order confirming the second arbitration award necessarily requires that it reconsider the motion to confirm the first arbitration award, the district court will need to know the parameters of its authority. It is generally recognized that there are circumstances, albeit limited, under which a district court can remand a case to the arbitrators for clarification. Although there is no explicit provision in the Act for such a remand, courts have uniformly stated that a remand to the arbitration panel is appropriate in cases where the award is ambiguous.

. . .

Because an arbitration award must be upheld even when there have been "errors . . . in the determination of factual issues," a remand that allows the arbitrators to reexamine their decision on the merits is not permissible. On the other hand, when the remedy awarded by the arbitrators is ambiguous, a remand for clarification of the intended meaning of an arbitration award is appropriate. . . . "[A] district court itself should not clarify an ambiguous arbitration award but should remand it to the arbitration panel for clarification." Such a remand avoids the court's misinterpretation of the award and is therefore more likely to give the parties the award for which they bargained.

Unlike the exception to the *functus officio* doctrine which confines the arbitrators to correcting mistakes apparent on the face of the award, an ambiguity in the award for which the court may remand to the arbitrators may be shown not only from the face of the award but from an extraneous but objectively ascertainable fact. Thus, for example, if an arbitration award directed the transfer of real property, and the district court could ascertain that such property was no longer in the possession of the party directed to transfer it, the remedy would be unenforceable and hence ambiguous. This case may fall within the same category.

. . .

The first arbitration award entered January 18, 1990 not only provides in paragraph 2 that Omaha "shall release any and all claims to the reserves (including IBNR) currently held by Colonial Penn arising out of the business between the parties," but provides in paragraph 3 that Omaha should provide "$10 million to Colonial Penn *and* release of all claims to such reserves" (emphasis added). This suggests that the award may have contemplated that Colonial Penn's compensation for the breach of contract by Omaha would be paid in two components, cash and release of a valuable monetary claim against it. If the district court can ascertain by clear and convincing evidence that Colonial Penn had no reserves to which Omaha made a claim, then the intent of the arbitrators as to the remedy would be ambiguous.

Under such circumstances, the district court would be authorized to remand so that the arbitrators themselves could clarify their intent as to the remedy awarded. Put differently, the arbitral award would be deemed unenforceable if part of the consideration awarded did not, in fact, exist. . . . We do not discount the possibility that the arbitrators merely intended that Omaha pay $10 million and provide a form release, even if Omaha had no claim to the reserve. That is, however, the essence of the ambiguity.

We caution that we are not suggesting that the district court should order a remand in this case but merely instruct that such a remand is within its power upon a finding of ambiguity. . . .

III.

Conclusion

For the reasons set forth above, we will reverse the district court's order granting Colonial Penn's motion to confirm the second arbitration award. We will vacate the district court's order denying Omaha's motion to confirm the first arbitration award and will remand to the district court for further proceedings consistent with this opinion. . . .

NOTES

1.   Arbitration proceedings, unlike actions in court, generally have no procedure for rehearing on the merits by the arbitrators. The award, once made, is final and binding. The arbitrators have completed their job. Hence the phrase, functus officio, meaning "office performed." As the Supreme Court stated long before the FAA: "Arbitrators exhaust their power when they make a final determination on the matters submitted to them. They have no power after having made an award to alter it; the authority conferred on them is then at an end." Bayne v. Morris, 68 U.S. 97, 99 (1863). Several exceptions to the doctrine are discussed in *Colonial Penn.* In addition, "the doctrine of functus officio does not apply where the parties agree to go back to the arbitrator after an award." 3 Ian R. Macneil et al., Federal Arbitration Law § 37.6.1 (1994).

2.   If the arbitrators bifurcate the proceeding into multiple stages — such as, say, a jurisdictional phase, a liability phase, and a damages phase — the award at the end of each stage (known as a partial award) can finally resolve the issues presented in that phase of the dispute. If it does, then the partial award is a final award as to those issues and the arbitrators cannot revisit it, even if other issues remain unresolved. *See* Julian D.M. Lew et al., Comparative International Commercial Arbitration 632-633 (2003) ("a final award may put an end to a part of the dispute or the entire proceedings"). Likewise "[a]s with all awards, partial awards may be the subject of confirmation, set-aside, and enforcement actions before competent authorities." Restatement (Third) of the U.S. Law of International Commercial Arbitration § 1-1, cmt. w.

3.   Not only is there no rehearing procedure in arbitration, there also generally is no appeals process. The parties certainly are free to establish an arbitral appeals process by contract. Trade association arbitrations often include an appeals process, *see* Derek Kirby Johnson, International Commodity Arbitration (1991), and the JAMS Employment Arbitration Rules and Procedures include an optional appeals procedure. *See* Rule 34. In the international arena, although not an appeals process, the Rules of Arbitration of the ICC provide for some oversight of arbitration awards by the International Court of Arbitration of the ICC. *See* ICC Rules of Arbitration, art. 27 ("The Court may lay down modifications as to the form of the Award and,

without affecting the arbitral tribunal's liberty of decision, may also draw its attention to points of substance.").

4. Courts have the authority to modify or correct arbitration awards under narrow circumstances, similar to those under which arbitrators can do so. FAA § 11; UAA § 13; RUAA § 24. In addition, as the *Colonial Penn* court held, courts have authority to remand to the arbitrators to clarify ambiguities in the award. *See also* UAA § 9; RUAA § 20(d). *See generally* Restatement (Third) of the U.S. Law of International Commercial Arbitration §§ 4-35 & 4-36.

PROBLEM 7.1

H. Boone & Co. institutes an arbitration proceeding against Aberdeen Shipping Co. asserting a claim for breach of contract. The arbitration agreement between the parties provides that the arbitration is to be administered by the American Arbitration Association under its Commercial Arbitration Rules, and that the proceedings are to be held in New York. The arbitration panel issues a unanimous award in favor of Boone, awarding Boone substantial damages.

(a) Aberdeen files a motion with the arbitrators seeking an "interpretation or correction" of the award. It argues that (1) the panel misunderstood its defense of commercial impracticability and disregarded the undisputed testimony of Aberdeen's witnesses; and (2) the panel made a mathematical error in calculating damages, as shown by a comparison of the award to an exhibit in Boone's posthearing memorandum. Boone does not dispute any of the facts underlying Aberdeen's assertions, but instead argues simply that the arguments are impermissible under the AAA Rules. How should the arbitrators rule on Aberdeen's motion?

(b) Same as sub-part (a) except that Aberdeen does not file its motion with the arbitrators. Instead, Aberdeen files the motion in federal court, and requests the court to modify or correct the award, or, in the alternative, to remand the award to the arbitrators. How should the court rule on the motion?

(c) Same as sub-part (a) except that the arbitral tribunal grants the motion and issues a revised award. The revised award provides that Aberdeen's nonperformance of the contract was excused on grounds of commercial impracticability. Boone then seeks to have the federal court vacate the award, which Aberdeen opposes. How should the court rule?

§ 7.03 ENFORCING AND CHALLENGING DOMESTIC ARBITRATION AWARDS

Once the arbitrators have made a final award, the prevailing party can seek to have the award confirmed in court. When a court enters a judgment confirming an award, "[t]he judgment so entered shall have the same force and effect, in all respects, as . . . a judgment in an action; and it may be enforced as if it had been rendered in an action in the court in which it is entered." 9 U.S.C. § 13; *see also* UAA § 14; RUAA § 25(a). The losing party in the arbitration can request the court to vacate the award, i.e., issue an order setting aside the award. The effect of such an order varies depending on the circumstances, but, at a minimum, "[t]he most obvious consequence of vacation is that the award is not confirmed." 4 IAN R. MACNEIL ET AL., FEDERAL ARBITRATION LAW § 42.1.1 (1994). Of course, court review of an arbitration award for purposes of vacating or confirming the award is not the same as an appeals court's review of a trial court decision on appeal. To the contrary, the grounds on which courts review arbitration awards are much narrower than the grounds on which appeals courts review decisions of trial courts, as the material in the next section makes clear.

[A] Grounds for Vacating Domestic Arbitration Awards

Section 10 of the Federal Arbitration Act sets out the following grounds on which an arbitration award can be vacated:

> (1) where the award was procured by corruption, fraud, or undue means;

> (2) where there was evident partiality or corruption in the arbitrators, or either of them;

> (3) where the arbitrators were guilty of misconduct in refusing to postpone the hearing, upon sufficient cause shown, or in refusing to hear evidence pertinent and material to the controversy; or of any other misbehavior by which the rights of any party have been prejudiced; or

> (4) where the arbitrators exceeded their powers, or so imperfectly executed them that a mutual, final, and definite award upon the subject matter submitted was not made.

9 U.S.C. § 10(a). The grounds for vacating an award under the Uniform Arbitration Act and the Revised Uniform Arbitration Act are similar. UAA § 12; RUAA § 23.

We already have seen cases addressing several of these grounds in Chapter 6. The following cases revisit some of these grounds, and take a first look at others. We start with section 10(a)(1), when an award has been "procured by corruption, fraud, or undue means."

A.G. EDWARDS & SONS, INC. v. McCOLLOUGH
United States Court of Appeals for the Ninth Circuit
967 F.2d 1401 (1992)

PER CURIAM:

A.G. Edwards & Sons appeals the district court's order vacating an arbitration award against the McColloughs. We reverse and remand.

I

The McColloughs, investors, agreed to arbitration in lieu of a federal court suit to resolve a dispute with their brokers, Edwards & Sons, as to the cause of a considerable loss in their account. The McColloughs then filed with the New York Stock Exchange Director of Arbitration, their complaint alleging in conclusory fashion violation of federal and Arizona RICO, securities, and Consumer Protection statutes. Edwards & Sons answered, raising fourteen affirmative defenses, two of which the district court below found facially meritless. The McColloughs responded by filing a brief which sought to rebut these defenses, and specifically argued that the two defenses in question were without merit. At the close of arbitration, the panel found in favor of Edwards & Sons and awarded the firm $310,850.12. The panel did not state the reasons for its award.

The brokers filed an Application to Confirm Arbitrator's Award in federal court in Arizona. In response, the McColloughs moved to vacate the award or to remand for a statement of reasons.

The district court rejected the McColloughs' argument that the arbitrators were guilty of misconduct in refusing to hear material evidence. It also rejected their argument that the award was procured through fraud because Edwards & Sons made knowing misstatements of the law by raising the meritless defenses. . . . The court also rejected the McColloughs' motion to remand for a statement of reasons, finding it well settled that arbitrators are not required to state their reasons.

The court did, however, accept the McColloughs' third argument for vacatur — that the award was procured through "undue means" within the meaning of 9 U.S.C. § 10(a)(1). The McColloughs argued that two of the defenses put forth by Edwards & Sons were so facially meritless that to offer them was to engage in "undue means." The court agreed, finding that such behavior constituted grounds for vacatur. The court then remanded the case to a different arbitration panel.

II

As the district court noted, federal court review of arbitration awards is extremely limited. . . . The courts should not reverse even in the face of erroneous interpretations of the law.

The district court did not state whether (1) in the face of a lack of findings, it would presume the arbitrators had been persuaded by the meritless defenses; or (2) the mere act of putting forth the arguments, whether they were relied upon or not, constituted "undue means." In either case, the court's decision is in conflict with the law of this circuit.

If the district court employed a presumption that the meritless defenses had an impact on the arbitrator's decision, its holding is in obvious tension with the applicable case law. As the district court recognized, arbitrators are not required to state the reasons for their decisions. The rule that arbitrators need not state their reasons presumes the arbitrators took a permissible route to the award where one exists. Under the district court's rationale in this case, courts would be free to vacate an award in any case in which the winning side had raised even one meritless defense and the arbitrators had not specifically identified the reasons for their award. Panels of arbitrators wishing to avoid relitigation would be forced to state the reasons for their decisions in direct contradiction of the universally accepted rule that a statement of reasons is not required and arbitrators are presumed to have relied on permissible grounds.

If the district court meant to hold that no reliance by the arbitrators on the meritless arguments need be demonstrated because the mere offering of the defenses itself constitutes "undue means," its holding conflicts with the language of § 10 and cases interpreting it. The statute allows for vacation of an award "procured by corruption, fraud, or undue means." 9 U.S.C. § 10(a)(1). Thus the statute requires a showing that the undue means caused the award to be given.

Nor do we agree with the district court that mere sloppy or overzealous lawyering constitutes "undue means." Although the term has not been defined in any federal case of which we are aware, it clearly connotes behavior that is immoral if not illegal. *See* BLACK'S LAW DICTIONARY 1697 (Rev. 4th ed. 1968) ("Undue" means "more than necessary; not proper; illegal," and "denotes something wrong, according to the standard of morals which the law enforces." . . .). Offering a meritless defense, however unfortunate, is part and parcel of the business of litigation; it carries no connotation of wrongfulness or immorality. In addition, it occurs with such frequency that, were the district court's rule to be adopted, the federal courts would be required to overturn arbitration awards regularly as procured by "undue means." This would be inconsistent with the extremely limited scope of judicial review of such awards.

Moreover, the McColloughs have not satisfied the first part of this court's three part test for vacating an arbitration award under 9 U.S.C. § 10(a). We have held that, in order to justify vacating an award because of fraud, the party seeking vacation

> must show that the fraud was (1) not discoverable upon the exercise of due diligence prior to the arbitration, (2) materially related to an issue in the arbitration, and (3) established by clear and convincing evidence.

We see no reason not to apply this test to cases raising claims of "undue means."

An obvious corollary to the first prong of the test stated above is that, where the fraud or undue means is not only discoverable, but discovered and brought to the attention of the arbitrators, a disappointed party will not be given a second bite at the apple. This rule is consistent with "the extremely narrow scope of our review of the arbitration panel's decision."

In this case, the alleged "undue means" — the assertion of facially meritless defenses — were known to the McColloughs and the arbitrators from the outset of the arbitration. In fact, as mentioned above, in discussing and rejecting the McColloughs' fraud argument, the district court concluded that "all the alleged 'misstatements' [of the law] were known to, and pointed out to the arbitrators by, [the McColloughs'] counsel," and thus that the requirement that the fraud must not have been discoverable upon the exercise of due diligence was not satisfied.

The decision vacating the arbitration award is REVERSED. The district court shall enter an order confirming the arbitration award. . . .

NOTES

1. As the court points out, and as noted in § 6.11, in domestic arbitration proceedings arbitrators often do not give reasons for their awards. In addition, "[a]s a general rule arbitrators may be neither required nor allowed to testify regarding their award or the process by which it was reached." 4 IAN R. MACNEIL ET AL., FEDERAL ARBITRATION LAW § 38.5.1 (1994); RUAA § 14(d). Not surprisingly, the absence of evidence of the arbitrator's reasoning can make judicial review of an award very difficult. As a result, as the court explained in the *A.G. Edwards* case, the usual approach is to "presume[ ] the arbitrators took a permissible route to the award where one exists."

2. Is offering a meritless defense really "part and parcel of litigation process"? Isn't instead what the court is saying is simply that vacating the entire arbitral award is too great a sanction for A.G. Edwards' behavior here, even if wrongful?

3. Courts rarely vacate an award on grounds of fraud, corruption, or undue means. One of the rare exceptions is Bonar v. Dean Witter Reynolds, Inc., 835 F.2d 1378 (11th Cir. 1988), in which the Eleventh Circuit held that perjury by an expert witness as to his qualifications required vacating the damages portion of an award. The party challenging the award demonstrated (1) by clear and convincing evidence that the expert committed perjury about his qualifications (he "never graduated from the University of Alabama, and had never attended Columbia University," nor had he ever worked for one of the employers he claimed to have worked for); (2) that it could not have discovered the perjury before or during the arbitration hearing (because there was no pre-hearing exchange of witness lists); and (3) the perjury was "materially related to an issue in the arbitration" (because the perjured testimony "establish[ed] the foundation that allowed the panel to hear the influential expert testimony on the central issue of negligent supervision)." *Id.* at 1384–85.

———

Section 10(a)(2) provides for an award to be vacated for "evident partiality or corruption in the arbitrators," which was the subject of *Commonwealth Coatings v. Continental Casualty Co.* in § 6.04[B]. The following case reflects a different sort of challenge for evident partiality than that involved in *Commonwealth Coatings*.

HARTER v. IOWA GRAIN CO.
United States Court of Appeals for the Seventh Circuit
220 F.3d 544 (2000)

CUDAHY, CIRCUIT JUDGE.

The recent proliferation of so-called "hedge-to-arrive" contracts for the sale of grain has pitted many American farmers against their counterparts in the grain storage and marketing industry. The case before us involves these contracts, and these players, but it also wends its way into questions of arbitration. . . .

I. INTRODUCTION

Farmers often contract to sell grain to grain elevators at some specific time in the future. Such contracts guarantee farmers a buyer for their grain and guarantee grain elevators a supply of a commodity. The contracts generally specify the quantity and quality of grain to be sold, as well as a delivery date and a price for the grain. Both parties, by agreeing in advance to the grain price, take a risk that the market will move against them. The farmer's risk is that grain prices will be higher at the time of delivery, thus causing him to forego profit by selling at too low a price; the elevator's risk is that prices will drop, causing it to purchase unduly expensive grain. "Hedge-to-arrive" contracts (HTA contracts) attempt to alleviate these risks by introducing price flexibility. HTA contracts use two price indices — a "futures reference price," set by the Chicago Board of Trade for some time in the future, and a "local cash basis level," which is a local adjustment to the national price. In an HTA contract, the parties generally agree at the time of contracting on the national portion of the price, and defer agreement on the local part of the price. Many HTA contracts are "flexible," meaning the parties may "roll" the established delivery date to some point in the future. When an elevator enters an HTA contract, it usually "hedges," or tries to offset the risk of paying unduly high prices, by buying an equal and opposite position in the futures market. If either party to an HTA contract rolls the delivery date forward, the elevator buys back its original hedge and rehedges by purchasing a new futures contract. The spread between the original hedge position and the "rolled" hedge position is attached to the price per bushel of the original HTA contract, and the farmer runs the risk of assuming a debit.

. . .

II. BACKGROUND

Lowell Harter was, until his retirement, a corn farmer in Grant County, Indiana. "The Andersons" is a corporation that operates grain elevators around the Midwest. . . . In 1993, The Andersons began marketing HTA contracts. The Andersons solicited Harter, who entered into five such contracts in November 1994. Harter contends that an employee of The Andersons told him the contracts were "no risk" plays on the futures market. The Andersons counters that the contracts clearly stated that "the commodities represented under this contract will be tangibly exchanged." The Andersons implies that Harter understood that the contracts called for him to turn over corn or its cash equivalent at some point in the future, suggesting that the risk of loss was apparent.

Harter claims that a few months later, presumably at the delivery obligation date, The Andersons notified him that he owed them $16,941.69 (we assume — neither party specifies — that The Andersons requested and Harter refused delivery of the corn, thus giving rise to an obligation to furnish its cash equivalent). Harter was surprised, he says, because he thought the HTAs were "no risk." Harter says that the parties agreed he would tender a check for the amount, and they would simultaneously enter into new HTA contracts designed to capitalize on the market and generate enough profit to cover the initial loss. The Andersons does not directly respond to this, but states that the parties agreed to extend the delivery periods for the contracts, or roll the contracts forward.

In May of 1995, apparently when the new delivery obligation date arrived, The Andersons sought delivery of the corn, which Harter again refused. The Andersons then told Harter he owed it approximately $50,000. The Andersons explains that this figure represents "the difference between the market price of corn and the price for the corn established by the contracts." Harter says that the figure represents the entire loss throughout the HTA contract period, less a $16,000 payment Harter made to cover the initial loss.

Harter filed a class action lawsuit in the Northern District of Illinois against The Andersons, its subsidiary AISC and introducing broker Iowa Grain. Harter later dropped Iowa Grain, which Harter had erroneously believed to be The Andersons' principal, from the suit. Harter alleged that The Andersons had violated the Commodity Exchange Act, the federal Racketeer Influenced and Corrupt Organizations Act (RICO), the Indiana RICO statute, and had committed common law fraud, breach of fiduciary duty and intentional infliction of emotional distress. The contracts Harter had signed expressly provided that in the event of a dispute, the National Grain & Feed Association (NGFA) would arbitrate. After Harter filed suit, The Andersons petitioned the district court, pursuant to the Federal Arbitration Act, to stay proceedings and to compel arbitration. The district judge granted the motion. The NGFA arbitrators entered an award in favor of The Andersons, and ordered Harter to pay contract damages of $55,350 plus interest, as well as $85,000 in attorney's fees plus interest. Harter moved to vacate or modify the award; The Andersons moved to confirm it. On July 24, 1998, the district court entered an order confirming the arbitration award in its entirety. . . . Harter now appeals . . .

. . .

IV. Structural Bias Of The NGFA Arbitration Panel

The Andersons asked the district court to confirm the NGFA panel's award, which it did. Harter now argues to us, as he did below, that this decision was erroneous because the NGFA panel was biased against him. When reviewing the district court's confirmation of the arbitration award, we decide questions of law *de novo* and review findings of fact for clear error.

Parties to an arbitration contract agree to trade procedural niceties for expeditious dispute resolution. The Federal Arbitration Act permits us to upset the parties' bargain by vacating an arbitration award only in very specific situations. Harter argues that this arbitration is such a situation because there was "evident partiality . . . in the arbitrators . . ." in violation of section 10(a)(2) of the Act. We have stated that "evident partiality" exists when an arbitrator's bias is "direct, definite and capable of demonstration rather than remote, uncertain, or speculative." Harter now asks us to recognize a subset of arbitral partiality, "structural bias." He contends that the NGFA is "structurally biased" against farmers because its members include grain elevators like The Andersons. Thus, he was "placed in the unenviable position of having to attempt to persuade NGFA members that a widespread practice of the association's membership is illegal." Harter no doubt feels that the farmers' traditional adversaries were sitting in judgment over him.

Some notable jurists have harbored similar suspicions about the fate of customers appearing before arbitration panels populated by industry "insiders." For instance, when the Second Circuit required a securities buyer to arbitrate a fraud claim under the 1933 Securities Act against his broker, Judge Clark dissented. *See* Wilko v. Swan, 201 F.2d 439, 445–46 (2d Cir.), *rev'd* 346 U.S. 427 (1953). Judge Clark stated that "the persons to [adjudicate the dispute] would naturally come from the regulated business itself. Adjudication by such arbitrators . . . is surely not a way of assuring the customer that objective and sympathetic consideration of his claim which is envisaged by the Securities Act." *Id.* at 445 (Clark, J., dissenting). The Supreme Court adopted Judge Clark's point of view, stating that Congress's intent in passing section 14 of the Securities Act was to "assure that sellers could not maneuver buyers into a position that might weaken their ability to recover under the Securities Act." *Wilko v. Swan.* Section 14 created a non-waivable right to bring suit in federal court for such maneuvers, the Court determined.

However perceptive . . . Judge Clark may have been, the opposing view favoring arbitration has firmly won out. In 1989, the Supreme Court explicitly overruled *Wilko*, stating that it had "fallen far out of step with our current strong endorsement of the federal statutes favoring [arbitration as a] method of resolving disputes." *Rodriguez de Quijas v. Shearson/American Express, Inc. Rodriguez de Quijas* was the culmination of a series of pro-arbitration cases decided in the 1980s.[10]

To avoid the arbitration pitfalls identified by Judge[ ] . . . Clark, we have required arbitrators to provide a "fundamentally fair hearing." We guarantee fairness by steering clear of "evident partiality." And, in settings where arbitrators and litigants were structural adversaries, as Harter suggests they are here, we have never found evident partiality. For instance, we refused to set aside an award rendered in favor of a financial services company by a panel whose members were "drawn from persons in the commodities business." We reasoned that disqualifying arbiters with experience in the business would eviscerate the goals of arbitration. . . . We have elsewhere stated that by virtue of their expertise in a field, arbitrators may have interests that overlap with the matter they are considering as arbitrators. Such overlap has not amounted to prima facie partiality. Thus, even a prior business association between an arbitrator and a party is not sufficient evidence of bias to vacate an award. Reviewing these cases, we find it difficult to imagine how courts might apply the "structural bias" standard Harter advocates. In an economy increasingly populated by large conglomerates with diverse interests, many individual arbitrators could be affiliated with companies only arguably adverse to one of the parties. Harter's standard would require disqualification, despite the practical reality that the arbitrators themselves would quite likely be impartial.

Although as a matter of first impression we might sympathize with Harter's

---

[10] Notably, the legislative and judicial enthusiasm for arbitration does not extend to arbitration clauses contained in contracts of adhesion. The Federal Arbitration Act explicitly allows the courts to give relief where the party opposing arbitration presents "well-supported claims that the agreement to arbitrate resulted from the sort of fraud or overwhelming economic power that would provide grounds 'for the revocation of any contract.' " *Mitsubishi.* . . . . Harter does not argue on appeal that these HTA contracts were contracts of adhesion. Therefore, we cannot weigh any commercial oppression that The Andersons may have brought to bear on this individual farmer, and we cannot vacate the award on this ground. . . .

frustration, we are in the mainstream in rejecting his "structural bias" argument. The First Circuit recently rejected an argument that an arbitration panel comprising financial employers was so inclined to side with employers that it could not adjudicate the claim of a female worker alleging gender discrimination. *See* Rosenberg v. Merrill Lynch, Pierce, Fenner & Smith, Inc., 170 F.3d 1, 14–15 (1st Cir.1999). The Eleventh Circuit has affirmed the impartiality of a panel whose members were in the business of collecting futures debit balances from customers in a situation where the panel held a customer liable for such obligations. *See* Scott v. Prudential Sec., Inc., 141 F.3d 1007, 1015–16 (11th Cir. 1998). And, of particular relevance to us, the Sixth Circuit recently found in favor of The Andersons in a challenge to an NGFA arbitral award involving an HTA contract almost identical to Harter's. [The Andersons, Inc. v. Horton Farms, Inc., 166 F.3d 308, 328–30 (6th Cir. 1998).]

So precedent in this circuit and others, as well as the broad policy goals served by arbitration, require us to reject Harter's argument of "structural bias" in the NGFA. This issue is no longer open.

Thus, we will vacate the arbitration award only if Harter can show that the NGFA panel had *direct* bias against him. This standard is difficult to meet. . . .

Harter observes that the NGFA is an organization of grain merchandisers and their affiliates. Apparently, however, a number of farmer-owned cooperatives are also NGFA members. On the other hand, one of The Andersons' top employees sits on the NGFA board. The Andersons pays more than $26,000 in dues annually to the NGFA. And the NGFA has taken the public position that HTA contracts are not futures instruments. Harter charges that a significant portion of NGFA members have written HTA contracts, and that NGFA arbitration rules do not disqualify arbitrators who have written HTA contracts. Harter also charges that, prior to the influx of HTA cases, the NGFA arbitrated fewer than twenty cases involving farmers, and only vindicated farmers twice. Harter alleges that almost half of the NGFA's members have written HTA contracts, while the NGFA points out that just half of those members responding to an HTA survey have done so. Even if all of these facts are true, they do not establish the direct, definite, demonstrable bias required. . . .

Under NGFA arbitration rules, an aggrieved party must first file a complaint with the NGFA national secretary. The parties then fully brief the dispute, and either party may request oral argument, though the requesting party bears the cost. The NGFA national secretary then appoints a three-member arbitration committee selected from the membership. The individual arbitrators must have expertise in the industry sector at issue, but must be commercially disinterested in the particular dispute. Arbitrators must disclose any bias or financial interest that could influence their analysis; either party may object to any of the arbitrators. The panel issues written opinions, and the parties may appeal. These facts suggest significant procedural safeguards for the parties.

. . .

. . . We therefore affirm the district court's confirmation of the arbitral award.

. . .

PROBLEM 7.2

Recall the facts of Problem 2.12, in which Mawson & Williams adopts a dispute resolution program for its current and future employees. One aspect of the program is that it requires all arbitrators to have 25 years of experience in the financial services industry. Due to the demographics of the industry, it turns out that virtually every person who meets that standard is a white male. A female employee asserts a sex discrimination claim against M&W in arbitration. The arbitration panel, which consists of three white men (all of whom have worked in the financial services industry for more than 25 years), makes an award in favor of M&W. In a subsequent action to vacate the award on grounds of evident partiality, how should a court rule? Is the result you expect the same or different from the result if the challenge had been raised before the award was made?

Section 10(a)(3) provides for vacatur of awards when an arbitrator engages in misconduct. The arbitrators' refusal to postpone the hearing or to admit material evidence was addressed in § 6.10 in connection with the *Tempo Shain* case. Another form of arbitral misconduct is ex parte contacts with one of the parties, which is the subject of the next case.

GOLDFINGER v. LISKER
Court of Appeals of New York
500 N.E.2d 857 (1986)

ALEXANDER, JUDGE.

In the circumstances of this case, the private communication between the arbitrator and one party-litigant, which related to the credibility of the party-litigant and the validity of the amount in dispute, and occurred without the knowledge or consent of the other party-litigant, constitutes misconduct sufficient to warrant vacating the arbitration award.

I.

In 1981, Abraham Goldfinger and Leo Lisker, both members of a trade organization called the Diamond Dealers Club (DDC), became embroiled in a controversy involving diamond transactions. Pursuant to the DDC bylaws, both agreed to submit their dispute to a three-member panel of DDC arbitrators, and the matter proceeded to arbitration in accordance with the DDC bylaws and CPLR article 75. Goldfinger claimed that Lisker owed him $500,000 as the result of a joint venture, while Lisker denied the existence of any such partnership or obligation. After a hearing spanning five months, the arbitrators awarded Goldfinger $162,976. Thereafter, Goldfinger commenced this proceeding in Supreme Court to confirm the award (CPLR 7510); Lisker cross-moved to vacate, alleging various instances of arbitrator misconduct. . . . Special Term referred the matter to a Referee, who, after a hearing on the allegations of misconduct, recommended that the motion to confirm be granted and the cross motion to vacate be denied, concluding that Lisker had failed to sustain his burden of proving misconduct by clear and convincing evidence. Special Term adopted the Referee's findings and conclusions and confirmed the arbitration award. The Appellate Division affirmed, and the matter is before us by leave of this court. For the reasons that follow, we now reverse.

The Referee found that the arbitrators had engaged in several private communications, two of which — one involving Weinman, the chairman of the arbitration panel, and Horowitz, a third party, and another involving Weinman and Goldfinger, a party to the proceeding — we deem critical. Horowitz was a member of the DDC and one of Lisker's business associates, but also was known to Goldfinger. The Referee found that during the pendency of the arbitration, Horowitz and Goldfinger engaged in a conversation in which Goldfinger, referring to Lisker, stated "he could have settled it for $70,000 . . . now it will cost him three times the amount," and that Horowitz subsequently repeated these statements to Weinman, who called one of his fellow arbitrators to relay the story. Both arbitrators, without consulting the third on the panel, decided that Horowitz would not have to testify at the arbitration to his conversation with Goldfinger because the panel had already heard testimony concerning the settlement disputes and Horowitz's testimony would be cumulative.

Thereafter, Weinman, on his own initiative, and without the knowledge or consent of Lisker or the other arbitrators, engaged Goldfinger in conversation in an attempt "to force Mr. Goldfinger to break down and change his story," and "to break Goldfinger down from his original claim" of $500,000, on the assumption that if Goldfinger in fact had refused a $70,000 settlement offer from Lisker, then Goldfinger would not "break down." According to Weinman, Goldfinger remained steadfast, handling himself in Weinman's words "to my satisfaction." The Referee concluded that the communications between Weinman, Horowitz and Goldfinger, although they concerned the pendency of the hearing, did not concern the subject matter of the underlying dispute and therefore did not rise to the level of misconduct.

Lisker argues that Weinman pursued a private conversation with Goldfinger in part to test Goldfinger's credibility and in part to evaluate the amount of Goldfinger's claim in view of the conflicting evidence about who offered to settle the case with whom. Lisker maintains that the Referee erred in concluding that credibility of a party is not central to the substance of the dispute, arguing that when an arbitrator privately discusses a case with a litigant, the prejudice stems as much from the private access itself as from the substance of what was said between them. He therefore urges the adoption of a per se rule that private communications between an arbitrator and a party-litigant constitute misconduct. Goldfinger argues that in order to constitute misconduct sufficient to warrant vacating an arbitration award, such communications must result in prejudice to the complaining party and because the Referee found that Weinman's conversations with Horowitz, and with Goldfinger did not result in any prejudice to Lisker, the award should be confirmed. Additionally, Goldfinger argues that any conversations between the arbitrators and third parties were authorized by the DDC bylaws [which provide in pertinent part that the "Arbitration Committee, acting in each case, shall have the authority and power to investigate the facts charged in the complaint"].

II.

Our State has long sanctioned arbitration as an effective alternative method of settling disputes. Those engaged in commercial affairs have routinely resorted to arbitration for an expeditious resolution of their disputes by persons with a practical knowledge of the subject area, and as long as arbitrators act within their jurisdiction, their awards will not be set aside because they have erred in judgment either upon the facts or the law. Courts are reluctant to disturb the decisions of arbitrators lest the value of this method of resolving controversies be undermined. Precisely because arbitration awards are subject to such judicial deference, it is imperative that the integrity of the process, as opposed to the correctness of the individual decision, be zealously safeguarded.

Arbitration by its nature contemplates a less formal environment than the judicial forum, and accordingly, arbitrators are not held to the standards prescribed for members of the judiciary. Nevertheless, arbitrators must take a formal oath, are expected to "faithfully and fairly" hear the controversy over which they have been chosen to preside and ought to conduct themselves in such a manner as to safeguard the integrity of the arbitration process. Arbitrators must afford the parties the opportunity to present evidence and to cross-examine witnesses and may act only upon proof adduced at a hearing of which due notice has been given to each party. They may not predicate their award on the strength of independent investigation unless so authorized by the parties.

Although courts generally will not interfere with the judgment of arbitrators, arbitration awards are not to be confirmed without question where there is evidence of misconduct prejudicing the rights of the parties. . . . While arbitrators often are chosen because of their expertise in a particular area and are generally permitted independent recourse to third-party sources when necessary to confirm technical information or to further focus their expertise on a particular point, for an arbitrator to privately consult a party-litigant without the knowledge or consent of the other party to the proceeding raises serious concerns as to whether the award was procured by improper means.

. . .

While the bylaws of the DDC authorize arbitrators to "investigate the facts charged in the complaint," it does not follow that the bylaws sanction the kind of private communications that occurred between Weinman and Goldfinger and Horowitz. Weinman's communication with Goldfinger following the conversation with Horowitz was deliberate in nature and designed clearly to enable Weinman to resolve in his own mind any doubt he may have had as to Goldfinger's credibility or the validity of the claim itself. In so contacting Goldfinger, Weinman denied Lisker the opportunity to respond and created the appearance of impropriety if not actual partiality. Such actions amounted to misconduct which prejudiced Lisker's rights under CPLR 7506(a), (b) and (c). Furthermore, the fact that Weinman initiated the contact with the goal of testing whether he could break Goldfinger down from his original claim hardly permits characterizing the inquiry as one directed toward "facts of trifling importance" or "facts of such a nature as to preclude reasonable contest." Indeed, the record demonstrates the importance attached by the arbitrator to the substance and specifics of the alleged settlement offers. Our general reluctance to disturb arbitration awards must yield in this case to the clear necessity of safeguarding the integrity of the arbitration process.

For the foregoing reasons, the order of the Appellate Division should be reversed, the motion to confirm the award denied, and the cross motion to vacate the award granted.

NOTES

1.   Does it matter that the arbitration here was among members of a trade association and that the arbitrators were members of the same trade association?

2.   As the court notes, the bylaws of the Diamond Dealers Club authorize the arbitrators to "to investigate the facts charged in the complaint." Why doesn't that provision authorize the ex parte contacts here?

3.   The New York Diamond Dealers Club, including its dispute resolution system, has been studied by Professor Lisa Bernstein. *See* Lisa Bernstein, *Opting Out of the Legal System: Extralegal Contractual Relations in the Diamond Industry*, 21 J. LEGAL STUD. 115 (1992). Professor Bernstein concluded that because of reputational sanctions within the trade association, "[i]n practice . . . it is rarely necessary for a party to a DDC arbitration to seek confirmation of a judgment." *Goldfinger* obviously is an exception.

PROBLEM 7.3

A new client, John Hardy, comes to see you having just had a disastrous experience in an arbitration proceeding. Hardy tells you that he had brought a claim against his former employer, Maynooth Manufacturing, alleging that he had been wrongfully fired. "It wasn't just that I lost (which I did)," he says, "it's the way I lost." "I told the arbitrators that Mr. Maynooth, my ex-boss, lied through his teeth about my performance reviews but they didn't believe me. My best witness, Edith Woodley, missed the hearing because she had just gotten married. My attorney was totally incompetent — he slept through half the hearing! I even saw Maynooth's lawyer having lunch with one of the arbitrators the day after the hearing. And then all I got after spending all that money was a single piece of paper saying that I lost! I don't even know why!" Hardy asks if there is anything you can do for him. What do you advise him? (You may find reviewing some material in Chapter 6 helpful in formulating your advice.)

The other principal statutory ground for vacating an arbitration award is that the arbitrators exceeded their powers. *See* 9 U.S.C. § 10(a)(4). We have just seen one circumstance in which arbitrators exceeded their powers in *Colonial Penn* in § 7.02. Another case in which the arbitrators were alleged to have exceeded their powers is *First Options of Chicago, Inc. v. Kaplan* in § 2.02: when one party has not agreed to arbitrate at all. Because the arbitrators' authority comes from the parties' agreement, if there is no agreement, the arbitrators lack authority to issue an award and it should be set aside. As *First Options* illustrates, the result effectively is de novo court review of the question whether the parties have agreed to arbitrate.

The following case raises the issue of what a party must do to preserve that question for subsequent court review.

COMPREHENSIVE ACCOUNTING CORP. v. RUDELL
United States Court of Appeals for the Seventh Circuit
760 F.2d 138 (1985)

Posner, Circuit Judge.

This appeal from an order enforcing an award by a commercial arbitrator raises the question whether a person against whom such an award is made can be barred from challenging the validity of the original agreement to arbitrate if he delays his challenge until the person in whose favor the award was made sues to enforce it. The Rudells signed a contract with Comprehensive Accounting Corporation to acquire an accounting franchise. The contract, which both Rudells signed (Mrs. Rudell attesting the validity of her husband's signature), contained a standard arbitration clause, which Comprehensive later invoked after terminating the Rudells' franchise. Although notified of the arbitration, the Rudells refused to participate. Mr. Rudell wrote the arbitrator, "I can't afford to go to Chicago [for the arbitration] and can't see that there is anything left to arbitrate." But the arbitration went forward anyway, and resulted in an award to Comprehensive of both damages and equitable relief. Pursuant to the arbitration clause, Comprehensive moved for confirmation by a federal district court in this circuit under section 9 of the United States Arbitration Act — that is, moved for a judicial order that the Rudells comply with the arbitrator's award. The Rudells opposed confirmation on a variety of grounds, all of which the district court rejected. On appeal the Rudells argue only that the court should not have rejected, as too late, their offer to prove that they did not actually know about the arbitration clause. The basis of the offer is a letter to them from Comprehensive's counsel, acknowledging that he had not sent them a copy of the executed contract and that they might therefore not be "fully aware of all the nuances" of certain restrictions (restrictions not related to the arbitration clause) in the contract.

If a party refuses to arbitrate a dispute, and an order that he arbitrate it is sought in federal district court under section 4 of the Arbitration Act, the issue whether there was an agreement to arbitrate is for the court to decide. *Prima Paint Corp. v. Flood & Conklin Mfg. Co.* But once a matter has gone through arbitration and an award has been issued, the grounds on which a court asked to confirm (enforce) the award can refuse to do so are limited, so far as pertinent here, to cases "where the arbitrators exceeded their powers." 9 U.S.C. § 10(d). If there had been no arbitration clause, or if the Rudells had claimed that the clause was invalid and nevertheless the arbitrator had gone ahead and made an award against them, he might well (in the first case, clearly would) have exceeded his powers. But that is not this case. There is an arbitration clause, and the Rudells concede that it covers this dispute. They were notified of the arbitration, and while refusing to participate in it did not challenge the arbitrator's authority to proceed in their absence, as the clause (by incorporation of the American Arbitration Association's rules) allowed if the Rudells had notice of the arbitration — as they did — and refused to participate —

as they also did.

They now say they did not agree to the arbitration clause, which seems hard to believe, given the evidence of their signatures. In the absence of fraud or duress, a person who signs a contract cannot avoid his obligations under it by showing that he did not read what he signed. Maybe a claim of fraud can be teased out of the letter to the Rudells from Comprehensive's counsel, implying knowledge by Comprehensive that its franchisees didn't know what was in the franchise agreement — though this seems very doubtful, and is in any event irrelevant. If the Rudells did not agree, this would not show that the arbitrator had exceeded his power, given that he had every right to think they had agreed — for they never suggested otherwise to him. Agreement would be as we have said an issue under section 4 of the Arbitration Act, for the premise of that section is the existence of an agreement to arbitrate, and the section sets out a procedure for determining whether there was such an agreement in the particular case. But after an award has been entered, section 4 is no longer in play; sections 9 and 10 are, and section 10 does not permit the person resisting enforcement of the award to go back and litigate the question whether there was an agreement to arbitrate. He must show (so far as relevant here) that the arbitrator exceeded his powers, and the Rudells have failed to show this.

The difference between section 4 and section 10 makes perfectly good sense. No one should be forced into arbitration without an opportunity to show that he never agreed to arbitrate the dispute that is the subject of the arbitration. The Rudells had that opportunity when they were notified of the arbitration, and they let it pass by. It was then too late for them to sit back and allow the arbitration to go forward, and only after it was all done, and enforcement was sought, say: oh by the way, we never agreed to the arbitration clause. That is a tactic that the law of arbitration, with its commitment to speed, will not tolerate.

This would be clear enough if the Rudells had actually participated in the arbitration without challenging the arbitrator's authority till the arbitration was completed and they had lost. But, it may be asked, what concretely could the Rudells have done when they were notified of the arbitration, given that the arbitration clause allowed the arbitration to proceed in their absence? They might have brought suit to enjoin the arbitration. At the very least, they could have told the arbitrator that they did not recognize his authority to proceed, because they had not agreed to arbitration. That would have put the arbitrator and Comprehensive on notice that the arbitrator's jurisdiction was questioned. Comprehensive might then have moved under section 4 of the Act for an order to arbitrate, and the Rudells would have gotten their day in court to challenge the existence of an agreement to arbitrate, before Comprehensive was put to the expense of the arbitration. If Comprehensive had not moved under section 4, but had gone ahead with the arbitration in the Rudell's absence, then the Rudells, having put Comprehensive on notice of their reservation, might be allowed in the confirmation proceeding to litigate the question whether there was a valid agreement to arbitrate, though we need not decide in this case whether they should instead have sought to enjoin the arbitration. They did neither. They waited too long.

. . .

Affirmed.

NOTES

1. The court in *Comprehensive Accounting*, although perhaps influenced by a perceived lack of merit to the Rudells' defense that they did not agree to arbitrate, held that the defense was not raised in a timely manner. Under the court of appeals' holding in *Comprehensive Accounting*, a party cannot simply ignore a notice of arbitration. Instead, the party must at least raise an objection that it did not agree to arbitrate at some point before an action is brought to enforce the award. Compare this approach to how courts deal with a defense of lack of personal jurisdiction. When served with a complaint, "the defendant need not appear at all, and, if judgment is entered on the basis of invalid service or improper jurisdiction, jurisdiction may be attacked collaterally in any action brought to enforce the defective judgment." JACK H. FRIEDENTHAL ET AL., CIVIL PROCEDURE § 3.26, at 196 (4th ed. 2005). Is that an apt analogy?

2. The Uniform Arbitration Act and the Revised Uniform Arbitration Act take a somewhat different approach. Section 12 of the UAA provides that "the court shall vacate an award where . . . [t]here was no arbitration agreement and the issue was not adversely determined in proceedings under Section 2 and the party did not participate in the arbitration hearing without raising the objection." *See also* RUAA § 23(a)(5).

3. The *Comprehensive Accounting* court indicates that it "need not decide" whether the Rudells had to go to court to seek to enjoin the arbitration, or whether simply putting the arbitral tribunal on notice of their objection would have been sufficient to preserve it for later judicial review. *But see* Mays v. Lanier Worldwide, Inc., 115 F. Supp. 2d 1330, 1342–43 (M.D. Ala. 2000) (dicta) (merely putting arbitrator on notice of objection insufficient to preserve objection, when party fails to seek stay of arbitration). As discussed in § 5.03[A], French arbitration law in fact requires parties to wait until the arbitration proceeding is completed before raising challenges to the arbitrators' jurisdiction in court. Which approach is more consistent with what the court calls arbitration law's "commitment to speed"?

4. Recall *Stolt-Nielsen* from § 6.06. The Supreme Court there held that the arbitrators exceeded their powers by "imposing [their] own view of sound policy regarding class arbitration":

> Rather than inquiring whether the FAA, maritime law, or New York law contains a "default rule" under which an arbitration clause is construed as allowing class arbitration in the absence of express consent, the panel proceeded as if it had the authority of a common-law court to develop what it viewed as the best rule to be applied in such a situation.

Stolt-Nielsen S.A. v. AnimalFeeds Int'l Corp., 130 S. Ct. 1758, 1768-69 (2010). What are the implications of *Stolt-Nielsen* for how arbitrators can decide cases? Does it require them to follow prior court decisions (rather than "develop[ing] what [they] view[] as the best rule to be applied")? What if there is no existing legal rule? Common law courts can develop a rule in such case. Can arbitrators? Or is *Stolt-Nielsen* limited to the narrow context of class arbitration?

5.　The following excerpt discusses other applications of the "excess of authority" ground for vacating arbitral awards:

> . . . [E]fforts to secure vacatur of commercial arbitration awards on the ground that the arbitrator exceeded his powers seldom succeed. As the analysis that follows shows, the courts have consistently given this dimension of section 10(a)(4) a narrow reading. A clear majority view can be inferred from the case law: the "powers" of the arbitrator referred to in the first clause of section 10(a)(4) are contractual in nature. Consistent with this view of the reach of the "exceeded powers" standard, "a court can (vacate) an arbitrator's decision under section 10(a)(4) only if the arbitrator exceeds the powers *delegated to him by the parties*. . . . Section 10(a)(4) does not provide the courts authority to "examine the merits of an [arbitration] award." (Emphasis added).

As long as a commercial arbitration award "is grounded on the agreement of the parties and the issues they present for resolution," further judicial scrutiny is not sanctioned by the "exceeded powers" ground of section 10(a)(4). If the arbitrator actually interprets the contract in dispute and decides only the issues placed before the arbitration tribunal for resolution, the award is immune from vacatur under section 10(a)(4) and a reviewing court must defer to the arbitrator's interpretation of law and contract and findings of fact. It is the submission of issues to the arbitrator, and the definition of the arbitrator's authority as set forth in the arbitration agreement, that establishes the parameters for the section 10(a)(4) "exceeded powers" inquiry.

The relevant case law provides several examples of circumstances where application of the above principles has resulted in vacatur of commercial arbitration awards. If an arbitrator rules on an issue not submitted to arbitration by the parties, he exceeds his authority and the award will be vacated. Similarly, if an arbitrator decides an issue involving a nonparty to the arbitration argument, vacatur is appropriate under section 10(a)(4). If an arbitrator fails to comply with an express requirement set forth in the arbitration agreement as to the form, nature, or content of the arbitration award, the award will be vacated. An arbitrator who determines an issue beyond the scope of the arbitration clause similarly exceeds his powers under the contract and subjects the award to vacatur.

Vacatur is also warranted if the arbitrator directs one remedy, when another remedy is clearly specified in the parties' underlying contract. However, the case law also indicates that, at least with regard to questions of remedy, an arbitrator does not exceed her powers in contravention of section 10(a)(4) when she directs a remedy not expressly contemplated or sanctioned by the arbitration agreement, provided that remedy is either sanctioned by relevant law or not expressly barred thereby.

Because "arbitration is . . . a matter of contract, and the contours of the arbitrator's authority in a given case are determined by reference to the arbitral agreement," it is apparent that a commercial arbitrator does not exceed his powers under section 10(a)(4) merely because the arbitration award is the product, in whole or in part, of faulty arbitral reasoning or error. Thus, attempts to seek vacatur based on a claim that the arbitrator made an error of law cannot properly be brought under the "exceeded powers" clause of section 10(a)(4).

A court can properly vacate a commercial arbitration award under the section 10(a)(4) "exceeded powers" standard "only if the arbitrator exceeds the powers delegated to him by the parties (in the agreement to arbitrate and the submission to arbitration). . . . (W)hether or not the claim is permitted under the applicable law is irrelevant." In the same manner, an error in contract interpretation does not constitute an action in excess of the arbitrator's power warranting vacatur of the award under section 10(a)(4). Finally, an award is not subject to vacatur under the "exceeded powers" ground because the arbitrator made an error in determining the facts of the case.

Stephen L. Hayford, *Law in Disarray: Judicial Standards for Vacatur of Commercial Arbitration Awards*, 30 GA. L. REV. 731, 751–56 (1996).[*]

PROBLEM 7.4

Consider again the facts of *First Options* (see § 2.02), here summarized in slightly simplified form. The Kaplans are the sole shareholders of a corporation, MK Investments, Inc. (MKI). MKI enters into a contract with First Options. The contract contains an arbitration clause. First Options files a demand for arbitration against both MKI and the Kaplans. The arbitrators find in favor of First Options and against both MKI and the Kaplans. The Kaplans then seek to vacate the award in federal court, arguing that the arbitrators had no authority over them personally because they never agreed to arbitration. Under which of the following sets of facts will the court reach the merits of the Kaplans' argument?

(a) The Kaplans participated in the arbitration proceeding raising a variety of defenses, but did not argue before the arbitrators that they had never agreed to arbitrate.

(b) The Kaplans participated in the arbitration proceeding and argued that they had never agreed to arbitrate, but the arbitrators rejected the defense on the merits.

(c) The Kaplans did not participate in the arbitration proceeding, having never received notice that it was to take place.

(d) The Kaplans did not participate in the arbitration proceeding, instead simply ignoring the demand for arbitration directed to them personally.

(e) The Kaplans did not participate in the arbitration, although they did write a letter to the arbitrators stating that they had never agreed to arbitrate. The Kaplans did not, however, file an action in court to enjoin the arbitration.

PROBLEM 7.5

In which of the following cases should the award be vacated under the FAA on the ground that the arbitrators exceeded their powers?

(a) The contract provides that "[a]ny claim for breach of this contract shall be settled by arbitration." The arbitrators award damages for libel.

(b) The contract provides that the arbitrators have no authority to award punitive damages. In a reasoned award, the arbitration panel finds that this provision is void as contrary to public policy and proceeds to award punitive damages.

(c) Same as sub-part (b) except that the panel does not explain the basis for its decision to award punitive damages.

In addition to the statutory grounds for vacating awards set out in section 10, some courts have relied on non-statutory vacatur grounds as well. The most commonly cited such ground is that the arbitration award was in "manifest disregard of the law." As the following case discusses, whether manifest disregard of the law is available as a vacatur ground is very much an open question.

WACHOVIA SECURITIES, LLC v. BRAND
United States Court of Appeals for the Fourth Circuit
671 F.3d 472 (2012)

Duncan, Circuit Judge:

Wachovia Securities, LLC ("Wachovia") appeals from the district court's refusal to vacate an arbitration award entered against it after it sued several former employees on what the arbitrators determined were frivolous claims. Wachovia argues that the arbitrators (the "Panel") violated § 10(a)(3) of the Federal Arbitration Act (the "FAA") and "manifestly disregarded" the law when they awarded $1.1 million in attorneys' fees and costs under the South Carolina Frivolous Civil Proceedings Act (the "FCPA"), codified at S.C. Code Ann. 15-36-10. For the reasons that follow, we affirm.

I.

A.

Wachovia initiated an arbitration proceeding by filing a Statement of Claim with the Financial Industry Regulatory Authority ("FINRA") against four former employees — Frank J. Brand, Stephen N. Jones, Marvin E. Slaughter, and George W. Stukes (collectively, the "Former Employees") — on June 27, 2008. The Former Employees, all individual financial advisors, were previously employees of A.G. Edwards & Sons, Inc. ("A.G. Edwards"), which merged with Wachovia on October 1, 2007. After the merger, the Former Employees became employees of Wachovia's

Florence, South Carolina branch office. Wachovia terminated their employment on June 26, 2008. Following their termination by Wachovia, the Former Employees went to work for a competitor brokerage firm, Stifel Nicolaus & Co., Inc. ("Stifel").

In the arbitration proceeding, Wachovia alleged that the Former Employees had violated their contractual and common law obligations when they joined Stifel. Specifically, Wachovia claimed that the Former Employees conspired with Stifel to open a competitor office in Florence, South Carolina, and that they had misappropriated confidential and proprietary information in the process. Wachovia further complained that the Former Employees were soliciting current Wachovia clients and employees to join their new firm. In addition, Wachovia sought a permanent injunction, the return of records, and an award of costs and attorneys' fees associated with the arbitration. . . .

The Former Employees' Answer described this dispute as "meritless" . . . . The Former Employees requested that the Panel award them attorneys' fees and costs incurred in defending themselves "from Wachovia's baseless and unwarranted claims." . . . They did not assert any claims under the FCPA.

The arbitration proceeded before a panel of three arbitrators in accordance with FINRA's rules for "industry disputes." The first month of arbitration proceedings, during which both sides presented evidence, was unremarkable. Then, on October 22, 2009, the panel asked the parties to submit accountings or proposals regarding requested attorneys' fees, forum fees, expert fees and any costs or expenses during the final two days of hearings, scheduled for November 23 and 24, 2009. Wachovia requested that the parties brief the fees issues and the Panel agreed, asking that the parties submit their briefs by November 23. There was no discussion of response briefs.

Despite the deadline, Wachovia was unprepared to submit its brief on fees on November 23, 2009 and requested a one-day extension. The Panel permitted the extension, and the parties therefore submitted their briefs on November 24, 2009, the last planned day of hearings. Both parties' briefs contained new arguments regarding attorneys' fees. Wachovia argued, despite its own request for attorneys' fees in its Statement of Claim, that under the South Carolina Arbitration Act, neither party was entitled to attorneys' fees. The Former Employees argued for the first time that they were entitled to attorneys' fees under the FCPA.

As its name suggests, the Frivolous Civil Proceeding Act provides a mechanism for litigants to seek sanctions against attorneys who file frivolous claims. It contains a number of procedural safeguards for litigants facing sanctions. Significantly for our purposes, the statute provides for a notice period affording the accused 30 days to respond to a request for sanctions and a separate hearing on sanctions after the verdict. No such procedures were followed here.

Upon learning that the Former Employees were seeking sanctions under the FCPA, Wachovia expressed concern that the arbitrators were not affording them 30 days' response time or a post-verdict hearing on the issue of fees. Toward the end of the hearing on November 24, the chairman of the Panel asked Wachovia if "you have been given a fair opportunity to present your case in its entirety in these proceedings." Wachovia responded that it had not been given a fair opportunity with respect to "the issues raised and argued as to attorneys' fees." The Panel then asked whether additional briefing would cure the concerns. Wachovia replied:

> I don't know. Because the standard and the [FCPA] from what I saw, there's notice and opportunity to be heard. So that means in other words, we need some evidence. That's why I don't think it's appropriate at the end, after our record is closed, that new issues have been injected. The statute is not referred to in the pleadings. So it's not just the element of surprise. It's a complete surprise.

After listening to Wachovia's objections to the Panel reaching any decision on the issue of attorneys' fees, the Panel stated: "The issue on attorneys' fees, I'm sure there will be something that will occur to the panel where we need to seek clarification from parties. And if that becomes necessary, be assured we will be in touch with you." The Panel subsequently asked the parties for an accounting of their November fees but did not hold any additional hearings or request additional briefing. Nor, however, did Wachovia request additional briefing.

On December 18, 2009, the Panel issued an award in which it denied all of Wachovia's claims. It awarded the Former Employees $15,080.67 in treble damages on their Wage Act claims, as well as $1,111,553.85 for attorneys' fees under the FCPA. . . .

. . .

II.

. . .

B.

In this appeal, Wachovia argues that the Panel was "guilty of misconduct in refusing to postpone the hearing . . . or in refusing to hear evidence" in violation of § 10(a)(3) when it failed to hold a separate hearing on the issue of attorneys' fees.

. . .

. . . Wachovia argues that the Panel must comply with the FCPA's procedural provisions if it relies on the FCPA's substantive provisions when awarding attorneys' fees. In *Concepcion*, . . . the Supreme Court explained that "the informality of arbitral proceedings is itself desirable, reducing the cost and increasing the speed of dispute resolution." Parties may, of course, consent to particular procedures in arbitration, but it is inconsistent with the FAA for one party to demand ex post particular procedural requirements from state law. We similarly conclude that the Panel was not compelled to follow the FCPA's procedural mandates insofar as Wachovia attempts to import them into this arbitration.

. . .

Wachovia argues that the Panel's refusal to schedule another day of hearings at which it could present evidence on the question of attorneys' fees deprived it of a fundamentally fair hearing. We disagree.

To the contrary, we find that Wachovia is the architect of its own misfortune. Wachovia, not the arbitrators, cut short the hearing on the issue of attorneys' fees. The arbitrators set the deadline for submitting briefs on the issue of attorneys' fees for the penultimate day of hearings. Wachovia inexplicably missed this deadline and submitted its brief on the final day of arbitration, thereby leaving no time for the parties to debate the issue. Moreover, after Wachovia complained that it had not received a fair hearing on the issue of fees, the arbitrators asked Wachovia if it wanted to submit additional briefs. Wachovia turned down this opportunity. Even if Wachovia is correct in its contention that the FCPA requires a hearing in the context of arbitration, it could have used the additional briefing to explain why a hearing was necessary.

. . . [A]rbitrators have broad discretion to set applicable procedure. Accordingly, we will not overturn an award for violating § 10(a)(3)'s protection against "any other misbehavior by which the rights of any party have been prejudiced" where the arbitrators attempted to address one party's unhappiness with the fairness of the hearing and that party refused to take advantage of the opportunity provided.

C.

. . . Wachovia argues that the Panel "manifestly disregarded" the law when it refused to import the FCPA's procedural requirements into the arbitration. "Manifest disregard" is, as we will explain, an old yet enigmatic ground for overturning arbitral awards. Wachovia contends the Supreme Court's 2008 decision in *Hall Street* rendered "manifest disregard" a judicial gloss on §§ 10(a)(3) and (4) — rather than a separate common law ground for relief — perhaps hoping that this "gloss" would help it where the text of the statute offers little relief. We do not find Wachovia's argument persuasive.

To lay a foundation for our analysis, we look first at "manifest disregard" as a basis for vacatur and our interpretation of the doctrine pre-*Hall Street*. We then consider how the Supreme Court's decisions in *Hall Street* and, more recently, *Stolt-Nielsen v. AnimalFeeds*, have affected this analysis. Although we find that manifest disregard did survive *Hall Street* as an independent ground for vacatur, we conclude that Wachovia has not demonstrated that the arbitrators manifestly disregarded the law here.

1.

The origins of modern manifest disregard as an independent basis for reviewing American arbitration decisions likely lie in dicta from the Supreme Court's decision in *Wilko v. Swan*, 346 U.S. 427 (1953). In *Wilko*, the Court explained that when interpreting the agreements at issue, "the interpretations of the law by the arbitrators in contrast to manifest disregard are not subject, in the federal courts, to judicial review for error in interpretation." We have read *Wilko* as endorsing manifest disregard as a common law ground for vacatur, separate and distinct from § 10's statutory grounds.[6]). Before *Hall Street*, we stated that for a court to vacate

---

[6] Pre-*Hall Street*, most other circuits agreed. . . . The Seventh Circuit alone took a more limited

an award under the manifest disregard theory, the arbitration record must show that " '(1) the applicable legal principle is clearly defined and not subject to reasonable debate; and (2) the arbitrator[ ] refused to heed that legal principle.' " We note that under this standard, proving manifest disregard required something beyond showing that the arbitrators misconstrued the law, especially given that arbitrators are not required to explain their reasoning.

2.

The Supreme Court's decision in *Hall Street* has been widely viewed as injecting uncertainty into the status of manifest disregard as a basis for vacatur. There, a commercial landlord and tenant had contracted for greater judicial review of any arbitral award during a dispute about the tenant's alleged failure to comply with applicable environmental laws. The Supreme Court concluded that, by permitting review for legal errors, this contract impermissibly circumvented the FAA's limited review for procedural errors. The Court rejected this approach and held that the FAA prohibited parties from contractually expanding judicial review on the theory that the grounds for vacatur in the FAA are "exclusive." This circuit has not yet interpreted manifest disregard in light of *Hall Street*, although it has acknowledged the uncertainty surrounding the "continuing viability of extra-statutory grounds for vacating arbitration awards."[7]

We find that the Supreme Court's more recent decision in *Stolt-Nielsen* sheds further light on the operation of "manifest disregard" post-*Hall Street* . . . .

The Supreme Court's reasoning in *Stolt-Nielsen* closely tracked the majority of circuits' approach to manifest disregard before *Hall Street*: it noted that there was law clearly on point, that the panel did not apply the applicable law, and that the panel acknowledged that it was departing from the applicable law. Nonetheless, the Court said,

---

approach to manifest disregard. In *Wise v. Wachovia Securities, LLC*, 450 F.3d 265 (7th Cir. 2006), the Seventh Circuit explained that "although courts will also set aside arbitration awards that are in manifest disregard of the law, and this is often described as a nonstatutory ground, we have defined 'manifest disregard of the law' so narrowly that it fits comfortably under the first clause of the fourth statutory ground —— 'where the arbitrators exceeded their powers.' " This approach rejected the notion that "manifest disregard" was a common law ground for vacatur.

[7] Our sister circuits have split into three camps about the meaning of the word "exclusive" in *Hall Street*. The Fifth and Eleventh Circuits have read *Hall Street* as holding that the common law standards are no longer valid grounds for vacatur because the FAA's grounds are exclusive. *Citigroup Global Mkts., Inc. v. Bacon*, 562 F.3d 349, 358 (5th Cir. 2009); *Frazier v. CitiFinancial Corp.*, 604 F.3d 1313, 1323-24 (11th Cir. 2010). Similarly, the First Circuit has noted in dicta that *Hall Street* held that manifest disregard was not a valid ground for vacating or modifying an arbitral award in cases brought under the FAA. *Ramos-Santiago v. UPS*, 524 F.3d 120, 124 n.3 (1st Cir. 2008). The Second and Ninth Circuits have held that since *Hall Street*, manifest disregard exists as a shorthand or judicial gloss for §§ 10(a)(3) and (4). *See Stolt-Nielsen SA v. AnimalFeeds Int'l Corp.*, 548 F.3d 85, 93-94 (2d Cir. 2008), *rev'd on other grounds by Stolt-Nielsen S. A. v. AnimalFeeds Int'l Corp.*, 130 S. Ct. 1758 (2010); *Comedy Club, Inc. v. Improv W. Assocs.*, 553 F.3d 1277, 1290 (9th Cir. 2009). The Sixth Circuit, in an unpublished opinion, has read *Hall Street* narrowly and found that it only prohibited private parties from contracting for greater judicial review. *Coffee Beanery, Ltd. v. WW, L.L.C.*, 300 F. App'x 415, 419 (6th Cir. 2008). It reasoned that "[i]n light of the Supreme Court's hesitation to reject the "manifest disregard" doctrine in all circumstances, we believe it would be imprudent to cease employing such a universally recognized principle," then applied the manifest disregard standard. *Id.* at 419.

We do not decide whether "manifest disregard" survives our decision in *Hall Street Associates*, as an independent ground for review or as a judicial gloss on the enumerated grounds for vacatur set forth at 9 U.S.C. § 10. AnimalFeeds characterizes that standard as requiring a showing that the arbitrators knew of the relevant [legal] principle, appreciated that this principle controlled the outcome of the disputed issue, and nonetheless willfully flouted the governing law by refusing to apply it. Assuming, *arguendo*, that such a standard applies, we find it satisfied.

(quotation marks omitted). We read this footnote to mean that manifest disregard continues to exist either "as an independent ground for review or as a judicial gloss on the enumerated grounds for vacatur set forth at 9 U.S.C. § 10." Therefore, we decline to adopt the position of the Fifth and Eleventh Circuits that manifest disregard no longer exists.

3.

Although we find that manifest disregard continues to exist as either an independent ground for review or as a judicial gloss, we need not decide which of the two it is because Wachovia's claim fails under both. Wachovia argues that the Panel acknowledged that it was applying the substantive provisions of the FCPA but did not follow the statute's procedural provisions when it declined to give Wachovia 30 days to respond to the request for fees or hold a separate hearing on the issue of fees. However . . . [w]hether manifest disregard is a "judicial gloss" or an independent ground for vacatur, it is not an invitation to review the merits of the underlying arbitration. Therefore, we see no reason to depart from our two-part test which has for decades guaranteed that review for manifest disregard not grow into the kind of probing merits review that would undermine the efficiency of arbitration. In this case, we find that whether the Panel erred by not applying the FCPA's procedural requirements is a question that was itself not clearly defined and was certainly subject to debate. Accordingly, we cannot hold that the arbitrators manifestly disregarded the law when they awarded Appellees $1.1 million in attorneys' fees and costs under the FCPA.

III.

For the foregoing reasons, the decision of the district court is

AFFIRMED.

NOTES

1. Be clear on the source of the "manifest disregard of law" ground for vacating arbitration awards. That ground is not listed in section 10 of the FAA. Instead, as the court of appeals notes, it is traced to *Wilko v. Swan* (see § 3.03[A]), now overruled, in which the Supreme Court held that claims under the Securities Act of 1933 could not be arbitrated. There, the Court stated that "the interpretations of the law by the arbitrators *in contrast to manifest disregard* are not subject, in the federal courts, to judicial review for error in interpretation" (emphasis added).

Subsequent courts have relied on that language (as well as a subsequent citation to that language in *First Options* (see § 2.02)) as the underpinnings for this ground for vacatur. Interestingly, Professor Michael Scodro points out that historically (i.e., prior to enactment of the FAA), courts would vacate arbitration awards when the arbitrator sought to apply the law but did so incorrectly, but enforce awards when the arbitrator knowingly disregarded the law. In other words, the historical conception of "manifest disregard" was exactly the opposite of the view today. Michael A. Scodro, *Deterrence and Implied Limits on the Powers of Commercial Arbitrators*, 55 DUKE L.J. 549 (2005); *see, e.g.*, 2 JOSEPH STORY, COMMENTARIES ON EQUITY JURISPRUDENCE 792 (1886) ("If arbitrators refer any point of law to judicial inquiry by spreading it on the face of their award and they mistake the law in a palpable and material point, their award will be set aside. . . . If they admit the law but decide contrary thereto upon principles of equity and good conscience, although such intent appear upon the face of the award, it will constitute no objection to it."). Is this historical understanding of arbitration law relevant to interpreting and applying manifest disregard today? If so, how?

2.   Prior to the Supreme Court's decision in *Hall Street*, every United States Court of Appeals had recognized the availability of "manifest disregard" (in some form) as a nonstatutory ground for court review of arbitration awards. *See* Birmingham News Co. v. Horn, 901 So. 2d 27, 48-49 (Ala. 2004) ("every federal circuit has expressly recognized 'manifest disregard of the law' as a basis for vacating an arbitration award") (citing representative cases). The Fourth Circuit's statement of the test for manifest disregard in *Wachovia* is consistent with the approach taken by most of the circuits. By comparison, the Seventh Circuit has defined manifest disregard to mean that "an arbitrator may not direct the parties to violate the law." George Watt & Son, Inc. v. Tiffany & Co., 248 F.3d 577, 580 (7th Cir. 2001); *see also* Wise v. Wachovia Securities, LLC, 450 F.3d 265 (7th Cir. 2006). When would a court vacate an award under the Seventh Circuit's test? Under the Fourth Circuit's test?

The answer, evidently, was very rarely. *See* Duferco Int'l Steel Trading v. T. Klaveness Shipping A/S, 333 F.3d 383, 389 (2d Cir. 2003) ("since 1960 we have vacated some part or all of an arbitral award for manifest disregard in the following four out of at least 48 cases where we applied the standard"); Dawahare v. Spencer, 210 F.3d 666, 670 (6th Cir.), *cert. denied*, 531 U.S. 878 (2000) (identifying only two U.S. court of appeals cases vacating awards for manifest disregard of the law). What is the significance of the fact that few cases vacate awards for manifest disregard of the law? That it is too limited a ground for review? Or that arbitrators generally do a pretty good job?

3.   The Supreme Court's decision in *Hall Street* [see § 7.05], however, has created substantial uncertainty over the continuing availability of manifest disregard as a ground for vacating arbitration awards. *Hall Street* held that parties cannot expand the grounds for vacating an award by contract, reasoning that the grounds for vacatur stated in section 10 are exclusive. In so holding, the Court cast serious doubt on the viability of manifest disregard of the law as a nonstatutory ground for vacating awards. Indeed, the Court referred to the "vagueness" of the *Wilko* dictum, explaining:

Maybe the term "manifest disregard" was meant to name a new ground for review, but maybe it merely referred to the § 10 grounds collectively, rather than adding to them. See, *e.g., Mitsubishi Motors Corp. v. Soler Chrysler-Plymouth, Inc.* (STEVENS, J., dissenting) ("Arbitration awards are only reviewable for manifest disregard of the law, 9 U.S.C. §§ 10, 207"). Or, as some courts have thought, "manifest disregard" may have been shorthand for § 10(a)(3) or § 10(a)(4), the subsections authorizing vacatur when the arbitrators were "guilty of misconduct" or "exceeded their powers."

552 U.S. at 585.

As indicated in footnote 7 in *Wachovia*, the circuits are divided since *Hall Street* over the current status of manifest disregard review. To date, the Supreme Court has denied review in cases raising the question whether arbitration awards can be vacated for manifest disregard of the law.

4. In *Stolt-Nielsen* [see § 6.06], the Court only worsened the confusion. In a footnote, the Court noted the uncertainty about the continued existence of manifest disregard review and stated it was not going to resolve the issue. But it then assumed that manifest disregard was still available and held that the award should be vacated for manifest disregard of the law. How can the Court vacate an award on a ground that it acknowledges may not exist? At most, the holding was an alternative one, since the Court also held that the award should be vacated because the arbitrators exceeded their authority in finding that the arbitration agreement permitted class arbitration.

Is the court of appeals in *Wachovia* correct to read *Stolt-Nielsen* as "mean[ing] that manifest disregard continues to exist either 'as an independent ground for review or as a judicial gloss on the enumerated grounds for vacatur set forth at 9 U.S.C. § 10.' "? Is that a fair reading of the Court's statement that it was "not decid[ing] whether 'manifest disregard' survives our decision in *Hall Street Associates*"?

5. The Restatement concludes that manifest disregard is not available under FAA section 10:

> According to the most common definition, an arbitral tribunal manifestly disregards the law if it knowingly refuses to follow a controlling legal rule. That definition is inconsistent with the historical evidence on the availability of manifest disregard review as well as the limited nature of court review of arbitral awards. Under the alternative definition of manifest disregard used by the United States Court of Appeals for the Seventh Circuit, a tribunal manifestly disregards the law only if it directs the parties to violate the law. So defined, manifest disregard is essentially an application of the public policy ground . . . and has no independent substantive force.

Restatement (Third) of the U.S. Law of International Commercial Arbitration § 4-22, cmt. g.

6. The availability of some review of an arbitrator's legal decisions may have a bearing on whether statutory claims should be arbitrable, the issue discussed in

Chapter 3. As the D.C. Circuit explained in Cole v. Burns Int'l Security Services, 105 F.3d 1465 (D.C. Cir. 1997):

> Two assumptions have been central to the Court's decisions in this area. First, the Court has insisted that, " '[b]y agreeing to arbitrate a statutory claim, a party does not forego the substantive rights afforded by the statute; it only submits to their resolution in an arbitral, rather than a judicial, forum.' " *Gilmer* (quoting *Mitsubishi*). Second, the Court has stated repeatedly that, " 'although judicial scrutiny of arbitration awards necessarily is limited, such review is sufficient to ensure that arbitrators comply with the requirements of the statute' at issue." *Gilmer* (quoting *McMahon*). These twin assumptions regarding the arbitration of statutory claims are valid only if judicial review under the "manifest disregard of the law" standard is sufficiently rigorous to ensure that arbitrators have properly interpreted and applied statutory law.

> The value and finality of an employer's arbitration system will not be undermined by focused review of arbitral legal determinations. Most employment discrimination claims are entirely factual in nature and involve well-settled legal principles. In fact, one study done in the 1980s found that discrimination cases involve factual claims approximately 84% of the time. As a result, in the vast majority of cases, judicial review of legal determinations to ensure compliance with public law should have no adverse impact on the arbitration process. Nonetheless, there will be some cases in which novel or difficult legal issues are presented demanding judicial judgment. In such cases, the courts are empowered to review an arbitrator's award to ensure that its resolution of public law issues is correct. . . . Because meaningful judicial review of public law issues is available, Cole's agreement to arbitrate is not unconscionable or otherwise unenforceable.

Id. at 1487. Do you agree with the *Cole* court's view? What if "manifest disregard" is not available as a ground for setting aside an arbitration award? Does it undermine the Supreme Court's decisions holding statutory claims to be arbitrable?

7.   Drawing on labor arbitration cases, *see, e.g.*, Paperworkers Int'l Union v. Misco, Inc., 484 U.S. 29, 42–43 (1987), some courts have held that an award can be vacated when enforcement of the award would be "contrary to a 'well defined and dominant' [public] policy embodied in laws and judicial precedent." PaineWebber, Inc. v. Agron, 49 F.3d 347, 350 (8th Cir. 1995). The Tenth Circuit has explained the justification for this "public policy" exception as follows:

> The public policy exception is rooted in the common law doctrine of a court's power to refuse to enforce a contract that violates public policy or law. It derives legitimacy from the public's interest in having its views represented in matters to which it is not a party but which could harm the public interest.

Seymour v. Blue Cross/Blue Shield, 988 F.2d 1020, 1023 (10th Cir. 1993). But FAA section 10 does not mention public policy as a ground for vacating an award. Does that mean it is not available?

The Restatement, while rejecting the availability of manifest disregard of the law, concludes that public policy is available, as an application of the excess of powers ground in section 10(a)(4). Restatement (Third) of the U.S. Law of International Commercial Arbitration § 4-22(b)(5); *see also id.* § 4-22 rptrs. note to cmt. f (explaining that "such a ground is a necessary part of a national arbitration law" and reasoning that "public policy limits the powers of a tribunal, and if enforcing the award would violate public policy the tribunal exceeds its powers"). Is the Restatement right to treat public policy and manifest disregard of the law differently, even though neither is mentioned in section 10?

PROBLEM 7.6

Jane Stewart files an arbitration claim against her former employer, James Barclay, alleging that she was a victim of sexual harassment in violation of federal law. Henry Wood is selected as the sole arbitrator.

(a) At the hearing, Wood tells the parties that he doesn't believe that sexual harassment should be unlawful. He then issues an unreasoned award dismissing Stewart's claim. When Stewart seeks to vacate the award under the FAA, how should the federal court rule?

(b) Same as (a) except that Wood makes no comments about his views on sexual harassment law. However, the evidence presented at the hearing is overwhelming that Barclay sexually harassed Stewart and that she is entitled to recover damages. Nonetheless, Wood issues an unreasoned award dismissing Stewart's claim. When Stewart seeks to vacate the award under the FAA, how should the federal court rule?

PROBLEM 7.7

You are a law clerk for D.C Circuit judge Grant Munro (see Problem 6.19). Judge Munro gives you a copy of a very recent opinion from another circuit holding that after *Hall Street*, courts may not review arbitration awards for manifest disregard of the law, and tells you that the Supreme Court has just granted certiorari to review the case. The judge asks your views on how the Supreme Court likely will come out in that case and what impact its decision may have on the arbitrability of Title VII cases under the Circuit's decision in *Cole*. What do you tell the judge?

We saw in Chapter 4 that the Federal Arbitration Act preempts inconsistent state statutes. That chapter dealt with preemption of state statutes concerning the enforceability of agreements to arbitrate. How does the preemptive effect of the FAA impact state statutes dealing with the enforceability of arbitration *awards*?

SIEGEL v. PRUDENTIAL INSURANCE CO.
California Court of Appeal
79 Cal. Rptr. 2d 726 (1998)

TURNER, P.J.

I. INTRODUCTION

Defendants, the Prudential Insurance Company of America (Prudential) and James Dinges, appeal from a judgment denying their petition to vacate an arbitration award. Additionally, they appeal from a judgment confirming the award in favor of plaintiff, Howard Siegel. Defendants argue that the manifest disregard for the law standard of review of the merits of an arbitration award must be applied to this case because California's rule, which prohibits such, is preempted by the provisions of 9 United States Code sections 10 and 12 of the United States Arbitration Act (USAA). . . . [W]e reject defendants' contention that section 10 of the USAA preempts California's rule precluding judicial review of the merits of an arbitrator's award. We conclude the present effort to vacate the award is subject to judicial review pursuant to California's arbitration statute, Code of Civil Procedure section 1286.2.

II. BACKGROUND

On December 10, 1993, plaintiff filed a wrongful termination action against defendants in the superior court. The complaint alleged causes of action for: wrongful termination; breach of the implied contract of continued employment; breach of the implied covenant of good faith and fair dealing; defamation; breach of written contract; and negligent infliction of emotional distress. On March 4, 1994, the trial court granted defendants' petition to compel arbitration and stayed further judicial proceedings. The order was based on a written agreement between the parties that disputes arising from the plaintiff's employment with defendants would be subject to arbitration before the National Association of Securities Dealers, Inc. (NASD).

. . .

On May 13, 1997, the arbitrators issued their decision. They unanimously determined that defendants were jointly and severally liable to plaintiff for $113,016 in actual damages and for $225,000 in general damages. The arbitrators also determined Prudential was liable to plaintiff for $1,000,000 in punitive damages for acting with oppression, fraud, and malice in discharging plaintiff for reporting wrongdoing by its employees.

On June 13, 1997, plaintiff filed a petition to confirm the arbitration award. Defendants opposed the petition to confirm the award. Defendants filed a petition to vacate the award. Defendants sought to vacate the award on the ground . . . [that] the arbitrators acted in "manifest disregard of [the] law" by awarding $1,000,000 in punitive damages without any evidence to support such an award.

The trial court held a hearing on July 18, 1997. . . . [T]he trial court granted the petition to confirm the arbitration award. Also, the trial court denied the petition to vacate the award. Defendants filed a timely notice of appeal from the judgment.

III. DISCUSSION

. . .

Defendants argue that sections 10 and 12 of the USAA, which they argue includes the manifest disregard of the law test, applies to post-award litigation that raises issues concerning the merits in state court. More specifically, defendants argue that both California appellate courts and trial judges have the authority to determine whether the arbitrator manifestly disregarded the law in reaching the merits of a dispute in arbitration. Defendants reason that the California rule under this state's arbitration law, which precludes on the merits review of an award, is preempted by the USAA. In resolving the scope of preemption and potential application of the manifest disregard of the law test under the USAA, we examine: the preemption analysis set forth in *Rosenthal v. Great Western Fin. Securities Corp.*; United States Supreme Court analysis of the limited preemptive effect of the USAA; the legislative history of the USAA; and the non-statutory basis of the manifest disregard of the law rule. . . .

. . .

. . . [W]e conclude neither sections 10 and 12 nor the manifest disregard of the law rule preempt the California rule which prevents reweighing the merits of an arbitrator's decision. The language of section 10 with its reference to courts of the United States and the "district" where the award was made is inconsistent with it being applicable to litigation before state judges. Further, the reference in section 12 of the USAA to the district where service can be made is consistent with application to federal court post-arbitration litigation involving the merits of the award. Moreover, the reference to service by a "marshal" on a nonresident party of an application to set aside an award is consistent with the application to federal courts. Further, *Rosenthal* and relevant United States Supreme Court decisions make it clear not all elements of the USAA apply to state court litigation involving arbitrations. The United States Supreme Court has noted that the principal purpose of the USAA is to ensure the enforcement of arbitration agreements. Nothing in the legislative history of the USAA indicates in any fashion that Congress intended that state courts be compelled to vacate an award under sections 10 and 12 or in the face of a manifest disregard of the law in connection with the merits of the controversy. Moreover, the principal preemptive effect of the USAA occurs when a state law conflicts with the purpose of "ensuring that private agreements to arbitrate are enforced according to their terms." (*Volt Info. Sciences v. Leland Stanford Jr. U.*) Finally, contrary to defendants' arguments the manifest disregard of the law test is not premised on the USAA; it is a common law rule applied by the federal courts. Therefore, we reject defendants' contention that the USAA permits us to evaluate whether merits of the award were the result of a manifest disregard of the law. Instead, we apply the provisions of Code of Civil Procedure section 1286.2.

IV. DISPOSITION

The judgments are affirmed. . . .

NOTE

Siegel involved a state arbitration statute that did not include one of the grounds for vacating awards that (arguably) is available under the FAA. Would the analysis be any different if the state arbitration law contained a ground for vacatur that was not available under federal law? For example, Georgia arbitration law expressly lists manifest disregard of the law as a ground for vacating an award. *See* GA. CODE ANN. § 9-9-13(b)(5) ("The award shall be vacated . . . if the court finds that the rights of that party were prejudiced by . . . [t]he arbitrator's manifest disregard of the law."). If the United States Supreme Court were to hold that manifest disregard of the law is not a ground for vacating an award under the FAA, would the Georgia statute be preempted?

PROBLEM 7.8

Hayling, Inc. seeks to vacate an arbitration award against it in Texas state court under the newly enacted Revised Texas Arbitration Act. Which of the following provisions of the Act would be preempted by federal law?

(a) A provision stating that a court may not vacate an award for manifest disregard of the law.

(b) A provision permitting a court to vacate an award for manifest disregard of the law.

(c) A provision stating that no review of the merits of an arbitration award is permitted.

(d) A provision permitting de novo review of all arbitration awards.

(e) A provision permitting de novo review of arbitration awards presenting "important and unsettled issues of law."

[B]   Procedural Issues in Enforcing Domestic Arbitration Awards

Actions to enforce or challenge domestic arbitration awards raise many of the same procedural issues as actions to enforce arbitration agreements. Section 9 of the Federal Arbitration Act governs actions to confirm awards, while section 12 of the FAA deals with procedural aspects of actions to vacate awards.

Section 9 first provides that the parties must "in their agreement have agreed that a judgment of the court shall be entered upon the award made pursuant to the arbitration." (No similar language appears in sections 10-12, however.) In most cases this seeming requirement is not a problem, either because the arbitration clause itself tracks the statutory language or because the clause incorporates institutional arbitration rules that contain a provision tracking that language. *See, e.g.*, AAA Commercial Arbitration Rules, Rule R-48(c) ("Parties to an arbitration under these rules shall be deemed to have consented that judgment upon the arbitration award may be entered in any federal or state court having jurisdiction thereof."). Courts have consistently held that such incorporation by reference is sufficient to satisfy section 9. *See, e.g.*, P & P Industries, Inc. v. Sutter Corp., 179 F.3d 861 (10th Cir. 1999). If the arbitration clause does not contain such an entry-of-judgment clause, language that the award is "final and binding" also may be sufficient. 4 IAN R. MACNEIL ET AL., FEDERAL ARBITRATION LAW § 38.2.2 (1994 & Supp. 1999). Without some basis on which a court can imply a consent to judgment, however, at least one court has held that a federal court cannot confirm the award. Oklahoma City Assocs. v. Wal-Mart Stores, Inc., 923 F.2d 791 (10th Cir. 1991) (holding no subject matter jurisdiction).

Section 9 and section 12 also set out time limits. Under section 9, a party "may at any time within one year after the award is made" seek an order confirming the award. Under section 12, "[n]otice of a motion to vacate, modify, or correct an award must be served upon the adverse party or his attorney within three months after the award is filed or delivered." Courts have been clear that actions to vacate that fall outside the three-month time limit are untimely, subject to very limited exceptions. 4 IAN R. MACNEIL ET AL., FEDERAL ARBITRATION LAW § 38.4.2 (1994 & Supp. 1999). At least one court has held, however, that an action to confirm an award can be brought more than a year after the award is made, because the one-year time limit is not mandatory. *See, e.g.*, Sverdrup Corp. v. WHC Constructors, Inc., 989 F.2d 148 (4th Cir. 1993). *But see* Photopaint Techs., LLC v. Smartlens Corp., 335 F.3d 152 (2d Cir. 2003) (rejecting *Sverdrup* and holding that "section 9 of the FAA imposes a one-year statute of limitations on the filing of a motion to confirm an arbitration award under the FAA"). *See generally* Hare v. Hosto & Buchan PLLC, 774 F. Supp. 2d 849, at 853 (S.D. Tex. 2011) (explaining that "there is a division of authority on the issue of whether the one-year limit is absolute. It is commonly held that the Second Circuit has ruled that the statute of limitations is mandatory, while the Fourth, Sixth and Eighth Circuits have held it to be permissive.").

What if an action to confirm is brought after the three-month time limit for an action to vacate the award has run? On what grounds can a party rely to avoid enforcement of the award?

FLORASYNTH, INC. v. PICKHOLZ
United States Court of Appeals for the Second Circuit
750 F.2d 171 (1984)

CARDAMONE, CIRCUIT JUDGE:

On this appeal we consider whether a party aggrieved by an award at the conclusion of an arbitration proceeding must raise his defenses to it within the period prescribed, or whether he may sit that time out and make his motion to vacate as a defense to his opponent's motion to confirm. The United States District Court for the Southern District of New York . . . held that the Federal Arbitration Act's three month statute of limitations for motions to vacate barred appellant Alfred Pickholz' attempt to interpose such a motion as a defense to a motion made by appellee, Florasynth, Inc., to confirm its favorable arbitration award. Fully recognizing that New York permits such a defensive motion after the time for making it has elapsed and that a contrary view will create "one rule for Athens and another rule for Rome," we nonetheless affirm. When a losing party has important defenses to an arbitration award he should raise them promptly instead of later attempting to oppose what should be a routine confirmation motion.

I

Pickholz was a Vice-President of Florasynth pursuant to an employment contract dated November 2, 1979. On December 1, 1981 Florasynth gave him six months notice of termination under the "no cause" termination provision of the contract. A dispute arose about whether, according to the contract, Florasynth owed Pickholz certain commissions. The employment contract provided for arbitration of disputes before a tripartite arbitration panel. Pickholz demanded arbitration and chose his arbitrator. Florasynth agreed to arbitrate and chose its arbitrator. These two selected a third person as the neutral arbitrator.

Following Pickholz' presentation of his claim to the panel, but prior to any determination on its merits, Florasynth challenged the qualifications of the arbitrator chosen by Pickholz. The other two arbitrators investigated the challenges to that arbitrator's qualifications and decided that any determination on such issue would be time-consuming, extraneous to the merits of the claim before them, and probably beyond their powers. Accordingly, they wrote a letter dated September 8, 1982 stating that they had "a duty to resign and dissolve the panel" so that the parties would be free to conduct another proceeding *de novo*, with a new panel that would not be concerned with this question. Pickholz' attorney then initiated a *de novo* proceeding by naming a different arbitrator. Florasynth did the same and the two chose a third arbitrator. The second panel found in Florasynth's favor two to one — with Pickholz' choice dissenting — and rendered its award on April 14, 1983. Four months later on August 9, 1983 Florasynth successfully moved to confirm the award.

Appellant now claims that he is not bound by this final arbitration award. . . . In effect, appellant argues that the first panel of arbitrators had no right to resign, and it was their duty to decide the dispute before them. Appellant further contends that because two members of the original panel of arbitrators improperly resigned and dissolved the panel, the second panel never had jurisdiction to resolve the contract dispute, and for that reason its award must be vacated.

Pickholz remained silent for four months after the panel of arbitrators found against him. He made no attempt to correct what he apparently believed was an injustice by moving to vacate the final arbitration award within the three month time period allotted for such a motion under the Federal Arbitration Act. Not until Florasynth moved to confirm the award did appellant object. We agree with the district court judge that this was too late.

. . .

III

. . . [W]e hold that . . . defendant's failure to move to vacate the award within the three month time provided precludes him from later seeking that relief when a motion is made to confirm the award.

A

To support this conclusion we first examine the Federal Arbitration Act. . . . [The court here quoted section 12 of the Act.] No exception to this three month limitations period is mentioned in the statute. Thus, under its terms, a party may not raise a motion to vacate, modify, or correct an arbitration award after the three month period has run, even when raised as a defense to a motion to confirm.

Further, there is no common law exception to the three month limitations period on the motion to vacate. The action to enforce an arbitration award is a creature of statute and was unknown in the common law. . . .

B

The fact that the federal act is modeled substantially on similar New York State legislation has caused doubt about when a party must move to vacate. New York law permits a party to oppose a motion to confirm with a motion to vacate even after three months have passed. . . . Although the language of New York's present statute, CPLR §§ 7510 and 7511, is very similar to 9 U.S.C. §§ 9 and 12, there is a legislative basis for the different construction New York courts have given their statute.

Congress passed the present Federal Arbitration Act in 1947. It aimed to continue the original act passed in 1925, which it had modeled after New York arbitration legislation. . . . Section 1459 (later § 1463) of the old New York C.P.A. dealt with the time limit for motions to vacate, modify, or correct. That section, like the present 9 U.S.C. § 12, required notice of a motion to vacate, modify or correct to be made within three months after the award was filed. In 1937 the New York legislature added an exception to the section on the timing of these motions. It stated that the three month period of limitations should apply except that in opposition to a motion to confirm an award, any of the grounds specified in section fourteen hundred sixty-two [the grounds for vacation of an award] may be set up. . . .

Congress did not adopt this exception when it passed the present arbitration act in 1947.

In 1962 the New York legislature enacted its current arbitration law in the Civil Practice Law and Rules, which it patterned closely on the earlier Civil Practice Act. When New York adopted CPLR § 7511, which contains the time limit on motions to vacate, it did not retain the language quoted above, but the legislature expressly indicated its intent to continue the practice of allowing motions to vacate in opposition to motions to confirm even after the three month time limit has expired. This historical background explains why New York courts faced with statutory language almost identical to that contained in the Federal Arbitration Act §§ 9 and

12 allow persons in appellant's position to bring a motion to vacate as a defense to a motion to confirm, even after the three month limitation period has passed.

C

The grounds for vacation of an award are narrow. Courts may not question provisions of the award itself; rather, they may vacate only for conduct that has prejudiced the rights of the parties. The purpose of the motion to vacate is to prevent an award from being enforced when some injustice in the proceedings taints its validity. Although it is important to the fair administration of arbitration that a party have the means to vacate an unjustly procured award, there is also good reason for the Act's three month limitation on this right.

An examination of the underlying purposes of the arbitration mechanism amply demonstrates the sound policies that support our conclusion. First, the confirmation of an arbitration award is a summary proceeding that merely makes what is already a final arbitration award a judgment of the court. The award need not actually be confirmed by a court to be valid. An unconfirmed award is a contract right that may be used as the basis for a cause of action. In fact, in the majority of cases the parties to an arbitration do not obtain court confirmation. A party, successful in arbitration, seeks confirmation by a court generally because he fears the losing party will not abide by the award. Armed with a court order the winning party has a variety of remedies available to enforce the judgment.

Second, parties choose to arbitrate because they want quick and final resolution of their disputes. The role of arbitration as a mechanism for speedy dispute resolution disfavors delayed challenges to the validity of an award. Thus, when a party to an arbitration believes that he has been prejudiced in the proceedings by behavior that the Act condemns he must bring a motion to vacate within the allotted time. When the three month limitations period has run without vacation of the arbitration award, the successful party has a right to assume the award is valid and untainted, and to obtain its confirmation in a summary proceeding.

It is for these reasons that we hold . . . that a party may not move to vacate after three months from the time the arbitration panel issued its award.

The judgment is accordingly affirmed.

NOTES

1.   The other courts of appeals facing this issue likewise have held that failure to file a motion to vacate within the three-month time limit precludes raising grounds for vacating the award in response to a motion to confirm. *See* Val-U Constr. Co. v. Rosebud Sioux Tribe, 146 F.3d 573, 578–79 (8th Cir. 1998); Cullen v. Paine, Webber, Jackson & Curtis, Inc., 863 F.2d 851, 853–54 (11th Cir.), *cert. denied*, 490 U.S. 1107 (1989); Professional Administrators, Ltd. v. Kopper-Glo Fuel, Inc., 819 F.2d 639, 642 (6th Cir. 1987); Taylor v. Nelson, 788 F.2d 220, 225 (4th Cir. 1986).

2.   The Restatement, however, takes the opposite position. *See* Restatement (Third) of the U.S. Law of International Commercial Arbitration § 4-32(e) ("A party opposing confirmation of an award may raise defenses to confirmation, even if the

limitations period for seeking vacatur of the award on those grounds has passed."). The Reporters' Notes explain that "the position adopted in *Florasynth* sets a trap for the unwary," and that "it seems highly unlikely that Congress intended to make a party's entitlement to defeat confirmation conditional upon that party's bringing an independent action for vacatur." *Id.* § 4-32, rptrs. note to cmt. e.

In addition, as with enforcing arbitration agreements, actions to enforce domestic arbitration awards must satisfy basic procedural prerequisites, such as personal jurisdiction, subject matter jurisdiction, and venue. The following two cases address subject matter jurisdiction and venue in federal court over actions to confirm and vacate arbitral awards.

GREENBERG v. BEAR, STEARNS & CO.
United States Court of Appeals for the Second Circuit
220 F.3d 22 (2000)

JOHN M. WALKER, JR., CIRCUIT JUDGE:

Petitioner-appellant Howard Greenberg appeals from the August 25, 1999 judgment of the United States District Court for the Southern District of New York . . . denying his petition to vacate an arbitration award that dismissed his securities fraud claims against respondents-appellees Bear, Stearns & Co., Inc., and Bear, Stearns Securities Corp. (collectively, "Bear Stearns"). On appeal, Greenberg argues that the district court's judgment should be reversed and the arbitration award against him vacated because the arbitrators manifestly disregarded federal law in rendering the award. Bear Stearns responds that there was no basis for federal subject matter jurisdiction in this case and that, in any event, the arbitral award easily withstands review.

This appeal squarely presents the question of whether and under what circumstances federal courts have jurisdiction to hear motions to vacate arbitration awards. We conclude that the district court had jurisdiction in this case because Greenberg challenged the award primarily on the grounds of manifest disregard of federal law. Nevertheless, Greenberg has not met the very stringent burden of demonstrating the sort of manifest disregard required to vacate the award. Therefore, we affirm the judgment of the district court.

BACKGROUND

At the time of the events underlying Greenberg's claim, Bear Stearns (a "clearing broker") provided securities clearing services to Greenberg's primary broker, Sterling Foster (an "introducing broker"). According to Greenberg, Bear Stearns violated federal and state securities laws because it knew of and participated in a fraudulent scheme perpetrated by Sterling Foster; sent false and misleading confirmations in connection with this scheme; and failed to send out a required prospectus. . . .

. . .

In May 1997, the petitioner filed a claim with the National Association of Security Dealers ("NASD") against Bear Stearns alleging, among other things, fraud and market manipulation in connection with Bear Stearns's provision of securities clearing services to Sterling Foster. A panel of three arbitrators heard arguments and testimony through extensive briefing and seven days of hearings. The arbitrators first dismissed Greenberg's claim based on Bear Stearns's purported failure to send him a prospectus and thereafter dismissed his remaining claims. On March 9, 1999, the arbitrators issued a written award confirming their decision to dismiss.

On January 18, 1999, Greenberg moved in federal district court to vacate the award on the basis that it "violated public policy and manifestly disregarded the law." In an opinion and award dated August 23, 1999, the district court denied the motion on the grounds that the petitioner had failed to demonstrate manifest disregard of the law in the arbitrators' treatment of his claims. This appeal followed.

DISCUSSION

I. *Federal Jurisdiction*

The principal question presented in this appeal is whether the district court had federal question jurisdiction over Greenberg's motion to vacate the arbitration award. Jurisdiction would plainly lie if, among other things, the parties were diverse, *see* 28 U.S.C. § 1332, the claim arose in admiralty, *see* 28 U.S.C. § 1333, or the dispute concerned the interpretation of a collective bargaining agreement, *see* 29 U.S.C. § 185(a). However, we must decide whether and under what circumstances a federal court may entertain a motion to vacate an award where, as in this case, alternative bases for jurisdiction are absent. We conclude that: (1) the fact that the arbitration itself concerns issues of federal law does not, on its own, confer subject matter jurisdiction on a federal district court to review the award; but (2) federal jurisdiction may lie where the petitioner seeks to vacate the award primarily on the ground of manifest disregard of federal law.

Federal courts have jurisdiction over "all civil actions arising under the . . . laws . . . of the United States." 28 U.S.C. § 1331. Federal question jurisdiction exists where a well-pleaded complaint "establishes either that federal law creates the cause of action or that the plaintiff's right to relief necessarily depends on resolution of a substantial question of federal law." Franchise Tax Bd. v. Construction Laborers Vacation Trust, 463 U.S. 1, 27–28 (1983).

Federal law plainly does not create the cause of action in this case. . . . [I]t is well-settled that the FAA does not confer subject matter jurisdiction on the federal courts even though it creates federal substantive law. *See Southland Corp. v. Keating.* Therefore, federal question jurisdiction does not arise simply because a petitioner brings a claim under § 10 of the FAA; there must be "an independent basis of jurisdiction" before district courts may entertain petitions to vacate.

Simply raising federal-law claims in the underlying arbitration is insufficient to supply this "independent basis." In the context of a motion to compel arbitration under § 4 of the FAA, we have specifically held that there is no federal subject matter jurisdiction "merely because the underlying claim raises a federal question."

Westmoreland Capital Corp. v. Findlay, 100 F.3d 263, 268 (2d Cir.1996). Petitions to compel arbitration "must be brought in state court unless some other basis for federal jurisdiction exists, such as diversity of citizenship or assertion of a claim in admiralty." Language in § 4 seemingly authorizing the federal courts to hear such petitions "is not intended to confer jurisdiction, but should instead be read as a response to the antiquated common law principle that an agreement to arbitrate would oust the federal courts of jurisdiction."

The holding in *Westmoreland* logically extends to motions to vacate an arbitration award under § 10 of FAA. Indeed, we implied as much in *Westmoreland* itself, and other courts have explicitly so held. As with a motion under § 4, the only federal rights that a motion under § 10 necessarily implicates are those created by the FAA itself, which rights do not give rise to federal question jurisdiction. In both contexts, there is no necessary link between the requested relief and the character of the underlying dispute. For example, a petition to compel arbitration because the dispute falls within the scope of an arbitration clause, or to vacate an award because the arbitrators exceeded their powers under that clause, will turn on the interpretation of the clause, regardless of whether the actual dispute implicates any federal laws. Accordingly, the fact that the arbitration concerns issues of federal law does not, standing alone, confer subject matter jurisdiction on a federal district court to review the arbitral award.

Nevertheless, federal jurisdiction may still lie if the ultimate disposition of the matter by the federal court "necessarily depends on resolution of a substantial question of federal law." Thus we must decide whether the petition in this case to vacate an arbitral award presents a substantial question of federal law.

"[I]n determining federal question jurisdiction, courts must make principled, pragmatic distinctions, engaging in a selective process which picks the substantial causes out of the web and lays the other ones aside." "[E]xamining only those allegations which are properly raised in a well-pleaded complaint, we look to the nature of the federal question raised in the claim to see if it is sufficiently substantial to warrant federal jurisdiction." The greater the federal interest at stake, the more likely it is that federal jurisdiction will be found.

In our view, under these standards, whether or not a petition to vacate under § 10 raises a substantial federal question turns on the ground for the petitioner's challenge to the award. The FAA and federal case law supply various bases for review of an arbitral award. Section 10 itself lists several grounds, including fraud in procuring the award; corruption, partiality, or prejudicial misconduct on the part of the arbitrators; abuse of power; and failure to render "a mutual, final, and definite award." 9 U.S.C. § 10(a). Judicial interpretation has added additional grounds, such that awards may be vacated under limited circumstances where the arbitrators manifestly disregarded the law, or where enforcement would violate a "well defined and dominant public policy."

We hold that where, as here, the petitioner complains principally and in good faith that the award was rendered in manifest disregard of federal law, a substantial federal question is presented and the federal courts have jurisdiction to entertain the petition. In contrast to grounds of review that concern the arbitration process itself — such as corruption or abuse of power — review for manifest disregard of federal law necessarily requires the reviewing court to do two things: first, determine what the federal law is, and second, determine whether the arbitrator's decision manifestly disregarded that law. This process so immerses the federal court in questions of federal law and their proper application that federal question subject matter jurisdiction is present.

Where the arbitrators' alleged manifest disregard of federal law forms a key part of the petitioner's complaint about the award, the federal questions thereby presented are substantial enough to support federal jurisdiction. First, although review for manifest disregard is "severely limited," if engaging in such review is essentially all that is required of the reviewing court, it is plain that federal questions will predominate. Second, there is a clear federal interest in resolving these questions. While federal claims may appropriately be resolved through arbitration, the federal courts have a strong interest in ensuring that arbitrators interpret and apply federal law properly, even if within a wide range of tolerance. Indeed, . . . this interest "would seem to be far greater" than the federal interest implicated by a petition to compel arbitration under § 4 — that is, the "interest in seeing that the claims be arbitrated" in the first place.

We note that, by and large, the rulings of other courts are not inconsistent. Many courts have found the simple presence of federal claims in the arbitration itself insufficient as an independent basis for federal jurisdiction. These cases, however, generally did not involve a petition to vacate on the grounds of manifest disregard of federal law in the arbitrators' resolution of the underlying federal claims. Instead, the petitioners challenged arbitration awards on grounds that plainly did not require resolution of a uniquely federal issue, including perjury, "alleged misdeeds of the arbitrators," "fraud, corruption, undue means, evident partiality, and failure to consider pertinent and material evidence," and manifest disregard of state law. . . . Where the petitioner seeks vacatur chiefly on the ground of manifest disregard of federal law, a federal question is plainly presented.

. . .

Accordingly, the district court had jurisdiction to consider Greenberg's petition, and this appeal is properly before us. We turn now to the merits.

II. *Review of the Award for Manifest Disregard of the Law*

. . . [T]he arbitrators did not ignore or refuse to apply well-defined and clearly applicable law in rejecting any of the appellant's claims in such a way that would amount to manifest disregard.

. . . Accordingly, we affirm the judgment of the district court.

NOTES

1.   What effect does the Supreme Court's decision in *Vaden v. Discover Bank* (in Chapter 4) have on cases like *Greenberg*? The question is very much an open one. *Vaden* relied almost exclusively on the language of section 4 of the FAA as the basis for its "look-through" approach to federal jurisdiction under that section. Sections 9 and 10 of the FAA do not contain similar language. *See, e.g.*, Francis v. Landstar

Sys. Holdings, 2009 U.S. Dist. LEXIS 118897, at *13, n.9 (M.D. Fla. Nov. 25, 2009). To the contrary, the plain language of those sections might be read as permitting actions to confirm or vacate any arbitration award subject to the FAA to be brought in federal court, even if no federal issue was involved in the underlying arbitration. On the other hand, the Second Circuit in *Greenberg* clearly was relying in part on its now discredited decision in *Westmoreland*, which had rejected the "look-through" approach. Moreover, the FAA certainly contemplates that a party that brings a petition to compel arbitration in a federal court can go back to that court to seek confirmation of the award — effectively extending the look-through approach to such actions. Why should the result be different if no petition to compel arbitration was filed in the first place?

2. If the Supreme Court were to reject manifest disregard of the law as a ground for vacating awards under the FAA, what bases for subject matter jurisdiction are available under *Greenberg*?

3. In many cases, actions to vacate arbitration awards will be brought in federal court on the basis of diversity rather than federal question jurisdiction. In those cases, how should a court determine whether the amount in controversy exceeds the $75,000 jurisdictional minimum? Courts have taken various approaches to the question:

> [S]ome courts have held that the amount in controversy is equal to the amount of the award regardless of how much was sought at the beginning of the arbitration proceeding. *See Baltin v. Alaron Trading Corp.*, 128 F.3d 1466, 1472 (11th Cir. 1997) (holding that because the amount sought to be vacated was only $36,284.69, there was a "legal certainty" the amount in controversy could not be met). Other courts appear to measure the amount in controversy by examining the amount sought in arbitration, as opposed to the actual amount awarded. *See Am. Guar. Co. v. Caldwell*, 72 F.2d 209, 211 (9th Cir. 1934) ("It is the amount in controversy which determines jurisdiction, not the amount of the award."). Finally, most courts appear to adopt a mixed approach when confronted with an application to vacate an award and reopen the arbitration. Under such an approach, "the amount in controversy in a suit challenging an arbitration award includes the matter at stake in the arbitration, provided the plaintiff is seeking to reopen the arbitration." *Sirotzky v. N.Y. Stock Exchange*, 347 F.3d 985, 989 (7th Cir. 2003). Thus, the amount in controversy in such situations is the amount awarded in arbitration in addition to the amount that would be at play if arbitration was reopened.

Choice Hotels Int'l, Inc. v. Shiv Hospitality, LLC, 491 F.3d 171, 175 (4th Cir. 2007). Which approach is the best?

CORTEZ BYRD CHIPS, INC. v. BILL HARBERT
CONSTRUCTION CO.
United States Supreme Court
529 U.S. 193 (2000)

JUSTICE SOUTER delivered the opinion of the Court.

This case raises the issue whether the venue provisions of the Federal Arbitration Act, 9 U.S.C. §§ 9-11, are restrictive, allowing a motion to confirm, vacate, or modify an arbitration award to be brought only in the district in which the award was made, or are permissive, permitting such a motion either where the award was made or in any district proper under the general venue statute. We hold the FAA provisions permissive.

I

Petitioner Cortez Byrd Chips, Inc., and respondent Bill Harbert Construction Company agreed that Harbert would build a wood chip mill for Cortez Byrd in Brookhaven, Mississippi. One of the terms was that "[a]ll claims or disputes between the Contractor and the Owner arising out or relating to the Contract, or the breach thereof, shall be decided by arbitration in accordance with the Construction Industry Arbitration Rules of the American Arbitration Association currently in effect unless the parties mutually agree otherwise."

. . .

After a dispute arose, Harbert invoked the agreement by a filing with the Atlanta office of the American Arbitration Association, which conducted arbitration in November 1997 in Birmingham, Alabama. The next month, the arbitration panel issued an award in favor of Harbert.

In January 1998, Cortez Byrd filed a complaint in the United States District Court for the Southern District of Mississippi seeking to vacate or modify the arbitration award, which Harbert then sought to confirm by filing this action seven days later in the Northern District of Alabama. When Cortez Byrd moved to dismiss, transfer, or stay the Alabama action, the Alabama District Court denied the motion, concluding that venue was proper only in the Northern District of Alabama, and entering judgment for Harbert for $274,256.90 plus interest and costs.

The Court of Appeals for the Eleventh Circuit affirmed. It held itself bound by pre-1981 Fifth Circuit precedent to the effect that under the Act's venue provisions, venue for motions to confirm, vacate, or modify awards was exclusively in the district in which the arbitration award was made. The arbitration here having been held in Birmingham, the rule as so construed limited venue to the Northern District of Alabama.

We granted certiorari to resolve a split among the Courts of Appeals over the permissive or mandatory character of the FAA's venue provisions. We reverse.

II

. . .

The precise issue raised in the District Court was whether venue for Cortez Byrd's motion under §§ 10 and 11 was properly laid in the southern district of Mississippi, within which the contract was performed. It was clearly proper under the general venue statute, which provides, among other things, for venue in a diversity action in "a judicial district in which a substantial part of the events or omissions giving rise to the claim occurred, or a substantial part of property that is the subject of the action is situated." 28 U.S.C. § 1391(a)(2). If §§ 10 and 11 are permissive and thus supplement, but do not supplant, the general provision, Cortez Byrd's motion to confirm or modify was properly filed in Mississippi, and under principles of deference to the court of first filing, the Alabama court should have considered staying its hand. But if §§ 10 and 11 are restrictive, there was no Mississippi venue for Cortez Byrd's action, and the Northern District of Alabama correctly proceeded with the litigation to confirm. Although § 9 is not directly implicated in this action, since venue for Harbert's motion to confirm was proper in the northern district of Alabama under either a restrictive or a permissive reading of § 9, the three venue sections of the FAA are best analyzed together, owing to their contemporaneous enactment and the similarity of their pertinent language.

Enlightenment will not come merely from parsing the language, which is less clear than either party contends. Although "may" could be read as permissive in each section, as Cortez Byrd argues, the mere use of "may" is not necessarily conclusive of congressional intent to provide for a permissive or discretionary authority. Certainly the warning flag is up in this instance. While Cortez Byrd points to clearly mandatory language in other parts of the Act as some indication that "may" was used in a permissive sense, cf. 9 U.S.C. §§ 2, 12, Harbert calls attention to a contrary clue in even more obviously permissive language elsewhere in the Act. See § 4. Each party has a point, but neither point is conclusive. The answer is not to be had from comparing phrases.

Statutory history provides a better lesson, though, which is confirmed by following out the practical consequences of Harbert's position. When the FAA was enacted in 1925, it appeared against the backdrop of a considerably more restrictive general venue statute than the one current today. At the time, the practical effect of 28 U.S.C. § 112(a) was that a civil suit could usually be brought only in the district in which the defendant resided. The statute's restrictive application was all the more pronounced due to the courts' general inhospitality to forum selection clauses. Hence, even if an arbitration agreement expressly permitted action to be brought in the district in which arbitration had been conducted, the agreement would probably prove to be vain. The enactment of the special venue provisions in the FAA thus had an obviously liberalizing effect, undiminished by any suggestion, textual or otherwise, that Congress meant simultaneously to foreclose a suit where the defendant resided. Such a consequence would have been as inexplicable in 1925 as it would be passing strange 75 years later. The most convenient forum for a defendant is normally the forum of residence, and it would take a very powerful reason ever to suggest that Congress would have meant to eliminate that venue for postarbitration disputes.

The virtue of the liberalizing nonrestrictive view of the provisions for venue in the district of arbitration is confirmed by another obviously liberalizing venue provision of the Act, which in § 9 authorizes a binding agreement selecting a forum for confirming an arbitration award. Since any forum selection agreement must coexist with §§ 10 and 11, one needs to ask how they would work together if §§ 10 and 11 meant that an order vacating or modifying an arbitration award could be obtained only in the district where the award was made. The consequence would be that a proceeding to confirm the award begun in a forum previously selected by agreement of the parties (but outside the district of the arbitration) would need to be held in abeyance if the responding party objected. The objecting party would then have to return to the district of the arbitration to begin a separate proceeding to modify or vacate the arbitration award, and if the award withstood attack, the parties would move back to the previously selected forum for the confirming order originally sought. Harbert, naturally, is far from endorsing anything of the sort and contends that a court with venue to confirm under a § 9 forum selection clause would also have venue under a later-filed motion under § 10. But the contention boils down to denying the logic of Harbert's own position. The regime we have described would follow from adopting that position, and the Congress simply cannot be tagged with such a taste for the bizarre.

Nothing, indeed, would be more clearly at odds with both the FAA's "statutory policy of rapid and unobstructed enforcement of arbitration agreements," or with the desired flexibility of parties in choosing a site for arbitration. Although the location of the arbitration may well be the residence of one of the parties, or have some other connection to a contract at issue, in many cases the site will have no relation whatsoever to the parties or the dispute. The parties may be willing to arbitrate in an inconvenient forum, say, for the convenience of the arbitrators, or to get a panel with special knowledge or experience, or as part of some compromise, but they might well be less willing to pick such a location if any future court proceedings had to be held there. Flexibility to make such practical choices, then, could well be inhibited by a venue rule mandating the same inconvenient venue if someone later sought to vacate or modify the award.

A restrictive interpretation would also place § 3 and §§ 9-11 of the FAA in needless tension, which could be resolved only by disrupting existing precedent of this Court. Section 3 provides that any court in which an action "referable to arbitration under an agreement in writing" is pending "shall on application of one of the parties stay the trial of the action until such arbitration has been had in accordance with the terms of the agreement." If an arbitration were then held outside the district of that litigation, under a restrictive reading of §§ 9-11 a subsequent proceeding to confirm, modify, or set aside the arbitration award could not be brought in the district of the original litigation (unless that also happened to be the chosen venue in a forum selection agreement). We have, however, previously held that the court with the power to stay the action under § 3 has the further power to confirm any ensuing arbitration award. Marine Transit Corp. v. Dreyfus, 284 U.S. 263 (1932). Harbert in effect concedes this point, acknowledging that "the court entering a stay order under § 3 retains jurisdiction over the proceeding and does not 'lose venue.' " But that concession saving our precedent still fails to explain why Congress would have wanted to allow venue liberally where motions to confirm, vacate, or modify were brought as subsequent stages of actions antedating the arbitration, but would have wanted a different rule when arbitration was not preceded by a suit between the parties.

Finally, Harbert's interpretation would create anomalous results in the aftermath of arbitrations held abroad. Sections 204, 207, and 302 of the FAA together provide for liberal choice of venue for actions to confirm awards subject to the 1958 Convention on the Recognition and Enforcement of Foreign Arbitral Awards and the 1975 Inter-American Convention on International Commercial Arbitration. But reading §§ 9-11 to restrict venue to the site of the arbitration would preclude any action under the FAA in courts of the United States to confirm, modify, or vacate awards rendered in foreign arbitrations not covered by either convention. Although such actions would not necessarily be barred for lack of jurisdiction, they would be defeated by restrictions on venue, and anomalies like that are to be avoided when they can be. True, "[t]here have been, and perhaps there still are, occasional gaps in the venue laws, [but] Congress does not in general intend to create venue gaps, which take away with one hand what Congress has given by way of jurisdictional grant with the other. Thus, in construing venue statutes it is reasonable to prefer the construction that avoids leaving such a gap." Attention to practical consequences thus points away from the restrictive reading of §§ 9-11 and confirms the view that the liberalizing effect of the provisions in the day of their enactment was meant to endure through treating them as permitting, not limiting, venue choice today. As against this reasoning, specific to the history and function of a statute addressing venue where arbitration is concerned, Harbert's citations of cases construing other special venue provisions are beside the point. . . . [T]he authority of these cases is not that special venue statutes are deemed to be restrictive; they simply show that analysis of special venue provisions must be specific to the statute. With that we agree in holding the permissive view of FAA venue provisions entitled to prevail.

The judgment of the Court of Appeals is reversed, and the case is remanded for further proceedings consistent with this opinion.

It is so ordered.

PROBLEM 7.9

Biddle, Haywood & Moffat, Inc. (BHM), a Delaware corporation with its principal place of business in New York, is a securities brokerage firm. It entered into an account agreement with Dr. Percy Trevelyan, who lives in Delaware, under which Trevelyan agreed to have BHM manage his extensive investments. The account agreement provided that "[a]ny controversy or claim arising out of or relating to this contract, or the breach thereof, shall be settled by arbitration to be held in New Jersey and administered by the American Arbitration Association under its Commercial Arbitration Rules." After suffering significant losses on his account, Trevelyan filed a demand for arbitration with the AAA alleging various violations of the federal securities laws. After lengthy hearings (in fact held in New Jersey), the arbitrators issued their award on March 1, 2000, awarding Trevelyan $100,000 in compensatory damages and $250,000 in punitive damages.

(a) On April 1, 2001, Trevelyan files a motion to confirm the award in United States District Court for the Southern District of New York. How should the court rule on the motion?

(b) Assume instead that on April 1, 2001, BHM files a motion to vacate the award in United States District Court for the Southern District of New York. BHM contends that the award should be vacated because the arbitrators exceeded their authority in awarding punitive damages and "manifestly disregarded" the federal securities laws in making the award. How should the court rule on the motion?

(c) Assume instead that on August 1, 2000, Trevelyan (who lives in New Jersey) files a motion to confirm the award in United States District Court for the Southern District of New York. BHM then files a cross-motion seeking to vacate the award. How should the court rule on the motion and the cross-motion?

§ 7.04   ENFORCING AND CHALLENGING INTERNATIONAL ARBITRATION AWARDS

Article III of the New York Convention provides that "[e]ach Contracting State shall recognize arbitral awards as binding and enforce them in accordance with the rules of procedure of the territory where the award is relied upon, under the conditions laid down in the following articles." Those conditions include, Article III continues, that "[t]here shall not be imposed substantially more onerous conditions or higher fees or charges on the recognition or enforcement of arbitral awards to which this Convention applies than are imposed on the recognition or enforcement of domestic arbitral awards." Article IV of the Convention then sets out procedures that Contracting States are to follow in adjudicating requests for enforcement of awards. Finally, Article V of the Convention lists the grounds on which recognition and enforcement of an arbitration award may be refused. This section examines the enforcement of international arbitration awards under the New York Convention, with particular (but not exclusive) emphasis on the United States.

[A]   Actions to Enforce International Arbitration Awards

The United States has implemented its obligations under the New York Convention with respect to arbitral awards in Chapter 2 of Federal Arbitration Act. The central provision is section 207 of the FAA, which provides:

> Within three years after an arbitral award falling under the Convention is made, any party to the arbitration may apply to any court having jurisdiction under this chapter for an order confirming the award as against any other party to the arbitration. The court shall confirm the award unless it finds one of the grounds for refusal or deferral of recognition or enforcement of the award specified in the said Convention.

The following case examines the procedural options available to a party seeking to enforce an international arbitration award.

ORIENTAL COMMERCIAL & SHIPPING CO. v. ROSSEEL, N.V.

United States District Court for the Southern District of New York
769 F. Supp. 514 (1991)

SWEET, DISTRICT JUDGE.

Defendant Rosseel, N.V. ("Rosseel") has moved pursuant to Rule 12(b)(6), Fed. R. Civ. P., to dismiss the complaint of plaintiffs Oriental Commercial & Shipping Co. (U.K.), Ltd. ("OC & S-UK"), Oriental Commercial & Shipping Co., Ltd., ("OC & S") and Abdul Hamid Bokhari ("Bokhari") (collectively, "Oriental"), or in the alternative, for summary judgment under Rule 56. For the following reasons, the motion for summary judgment is granted and the complaint is dismissed.

The Parties

OC & S is a Saudi Arabian corporation engaged in the petroleum business. OC & S-UK is an English corporation affiliated with OC & S. Bokhari is a citizen and resident of Saudi Arabia and is the principal owner of both OC & S and OC & S-UK. Rosseel is a Belgian corporation also engaged in the petroleum business.

The Facts

In 1984, OC & S-UK and Rosseel entered into a contract for the sale of oil. When the transaction was not completed as planned, Rosseel sought arbitration in New York pursuant to an arbitration clause in the contract. In support of this goal, Rosseel applied to the Honorable Peter K. Leisure of this district for an order compelling OC & S-UK to submit to arbitration. OC & S-UK resisted this application on the grounds that the arbitration clause was unenforceable. After Judge Leisure granted Rosseel's request, . . . Oriental filed a timely notice of appeal. . . . However, during a pre-argument conference in connection with the appeal the Staff Counsel for the Second Circuit suggested that the Circuit Court lacked jurisdiction over the appeal and Oriental agreed to withdraw it. . . . [I]n order to preserve its rights for future resolution, Oriental insisted on the addition of a stipulation to the standard Second Circuit form for withdrawing an appeal. The language agreed upon read as follows:

> The parties agree that any proceedings to confirm or vacate the arbitration award will be brought in the U.S.D.C., S.D.N.Y. In any appeal therefrom, the issues sought to be raised here can be raised at that time.

. . .

The arbitration between Rosseel and OC & S-UK, OC & S and Bokhari took place in January and May, 1990, and in June the arbitrators awarded Rosseel over $4 million. An amended award was issued on August 16, 1990 ("the Award").

Thereafter, Rosseel initiated proceedings before the High Court of Justice in London ("the London Action") seeking to enforce the Award under the provisions of the New York Convention on the Recognition and Enforcement of Foreign Arbitral

Awards ("the Convention"). Oriental argued that this action was barred by the Stipulation, which required Rosseel to seek confirmation of the award in the Southern District of New York before attempting to enforce it abroad. After reviewing the language of the Stipulation and the other evidence presented and arguments raised by Oriental, the High Court ruled that Stipulation did not bar Rosseel's action and proceeded to grant the application to enforce the award ("the London Judgment").

During the pendency of the London action, Oriental filed the present complaint, seeking declaratory judgment that the London Action was barred by the Stipulation, that Rosseel was required to seek confirmation of the Award in this jurisdiction and that the Award was not binding on the parties until such confirmation was granted. Oriental's stated goal in this proceeding is to preclude Rosseel from recovering on the Award until Oriental obtains appellate review of Judge Leisure's rulings enforcing the arbitration clause and extending its reach to OC & S and Bokhari. Oriental did not move to vacate the Award and its time to do so has expired.

Rosseel filed the present motion on January 29, 1991, and it was argued and fully submitted on March 8, 1991.

Discussion

Rosseel's motion seeks dismissal of the complaint or summary judgment. Because both sides have submitted affidavits and have relied on materials outside of the pleadings, the motion will be treated as one for summary judgment.

. . .

1. Arbitration Terminology and Procedure.

Of primary importance in this case is the distinction between confirming an arbitral award and enforcing one. . . . [B]efore the Convention was adopted a party seeking to enforce an arbitration award rendered in one jurisdiction against a defendant in a second jurisdiction was generally required to seek leave to enforce the award in both the rendering jurisdiction and the enforcing jurisdiction. Under the Convention, it is no longer necessary to seek leave to enforce in the rendering jurisdiction: the party seeking to enforce an award may proceed directly to the jurisdiction in which it wishes to enforce the award and may apply directly to that jurisdiction's court for an order of enforcement.[3]

Thus, with the advent of the Convention, a party to an American arbitration which seeks to enforce the award abroad need not seek any order from an American court. Therefore, confirmation proceedings in federal court are now usually filed only where the prevailing party seeks to enforce the award in this country, when the Convention procedures would be of no assistance.

---

[3] In addition, a party may often avoid relying on the Convention by applying in the rendering jurisdiction for an order confirming the award, which converts the award into a judgment which may be enforced abroad under the appropriate procedures for enforcement of foreign judgments.

The Second Circuit has explained the difference between an action to enforce a foreign arbitral award under the Convention and one to enforce a foreign judgment confirming an arbitral award, which must proceed according to the normal rules for the enforcement of foreign judgments. . . . [T]he court specifically commented that even after an award had been confirmed in the foreign jurisdiction — making it enforceable as a foreign judgment — it was still enforceable as a foreign award under the Convention; the foreign confirmation had simply increased the options available to the enforcing party. It is not clear whether such a broad approach to enforcement would be adopted by the United Kingdom. During oral argument, Rosseel suggested that it would not be, that confirmation here would have irrevocably converted the Award to a judgment and made it impossible to enforce it as an award under the Convention, although it has cited no authority in support of this contention.

Thus in the absence of the Stipulation there would be no question as to the propriety of Rosseel's action in refraining from further proceedings in this jurisdiction and instituting the London Action to enforce its award. The only remaining question is whether the Stipulation altered this conclusion.

2. The Stipulation is Not Ambiguous.

Oriental's primary argument is that . . . the parties specifically agreed that there would be post-award proceedings in this district. . . .

. . .

Oriental argues that the first sentence of the Stipulation — "any proceedings to confirm or vacate the arbitration award will be brought in the U.S.D.C., S.D.N.Y." — can and should be interpreted to compel Rosseel to seek confirmation in this jurisdiction. In the absence of some specific language indicating that the parties intended by their agreement to create a condition that further proceedings would necessarily take place, the first sentence is most naturally understood as identifying the proper forum for any actions for confirmation or vacation of the Award which either party elected to bring, with no requirement that any such action be brought at all.

. . .

Oriental's error in this case was in not filing a timely motion to vacate the Award. Particularly when it became clear that Rosseel did not intend to seek confirmation in this jurisdiction, a motion to vacate would have been the proper vehicle for reopening the prior proceedings and for obtaining appellate review of the prior orders of Judge Leisure compelling OC & S and Bokhari to participate in the arbitration. Although a motion to vacate is not generally to be encouraged where the losing party disclaims any basis for the motion, given the context of this case and the course of prior proceedings it would not have been improper for Oriental to have made such a motion, which would have obviated the problem here.

For all of the foregoing reasons, Oriental has failed to present evidence sufficient to establish that the Stipulation required Rosseel to bring a confirmation action in this district or that the Award was not intended to be binding until such a proceeding had been brought. Therefore, Rosseel's motion for summary judgment dismissing the complaint is granted.

It is so ordered.

NOTES

1. As the *Oriental Commercial* court indicated, the New York Convention did away with the requirement that an award be confirmed in the arbitral seat before it can be enforced elsewhere. As the Second Circuit explained in Yusuf Ahmed Alghanim & Sons, W.L.L. v. Toys "R" Us, Inc., 126 F.3d 15 (2d Cir. 1997), *cert. denied*, 522 U.S. 1111 (1998):

> The [New York] Convention succeeded and replaced the Convention on the Execution of Foreign Arbitral Awards ("Geneva Convention"), Sept. 26, 1927, 92 L.N.T.S. 301. The primary defect of the Geneva Convention was that it required an award first to be recognized in the rendering state before it could be enforced abroad, the so-called requirement of "double *exequatur.*" This requirement "was an unnecessary time-consuming hurdle," and "greatly limited [the Geneva Convention's] utility."

> The Convention eliminated this problem by eradicating the requirement that a court in the rendering state recognize an award before it could be taken and enforced abroad. In so doing, the Convention intentionally "liberalized procedures for enforcing foreign arbitral awards."

Id. at 22.

2. In addition, as the *Oriental Commercial* court suggested, even once an award has been confirmed in the arbitral seat, a party can still bring an action in another country to enforce the award under the New York Convention. *See* Albert Jan van den Berg, *Refusals of Enforcement under the New York Convention of 1958: The Unfortunate Few*, ICC INT'L CT. ARB. BULL. 75, 93 (Supp. 1999) ("[m]ost courts hold that the merger of the award into the judgment in the country of origin does not have extra-territorial effect and that therefore the award remains a cause of action for enforcement in other countries on the basis of the Convention").

3. But does it follow, as the court concludes, that the parties' stipulation did not require Rosseel to bring an action to confirm the award in the United States? The court distinguishes between actions to confirm the award (to be brought in the arbitral seat) and actions to enforce the award (to be brought in another jurisdiction). But section 207 of the FAA makes no such distinction, referring only to an action to "confirm" the award. What did the parties intend by entering into the stipulation here?

PROBLEM 7.10

You represent Melas & Associates, an American import firm, in an arbitration in Greece against Kratides & Kratides (K&K), a Greek supplier of metalworks. Mr. Melas is none too happy when you tell him that the arbitrators just issued an award requiring Melas & Associates to pay K&K $950,000. As you start to explain to him where the arbitrators went wrong, he says to you: "I certainly have no intention of paying K&K one dime of this award, and we will, of course, fight it every step of the way." He continues: "What I really want to know now, though, is what K&K can do to me. Can they force me to pay this travesty? And if they can, how do they go about doing it?" What possible avenues can K&K take to recover on this arbitration award?

For section 207 to apply, the award must be one "falling under" the New York Convention. The discussion of the scope of the New York Convention in § 5.02 thus applies here as well: the award must be foreign or non-domestic, commercial, and the reciprocity requirement must be satisfied (*i.e.*, the award must be made in a country that is a party to the New York Convention). In addition, the award likely must arise out of a written arbitration agreement. *See* Restatement (Third) of the U.S. Law of International Commercial Arbitration § 4-4(b). The next case looks at several of these requirements in the context of an action to enforce an arbitral award.

LANDER CO. v. MMP INVESTMENTS, INC.
United States Court of Appeals for the Seventh Circuit
107 F.3d 476 (1997)

POSNER, CHIEF JUDGE.

This is a suit by the Lander Company against MMP Investments to enforce an arbitration award. The district court dismissed the suit for want of federal jurisdiction, and Lander appeals. The parties are American firms that made a contract (actually two contracts, but we can ignore that detail) for the distribution by MMP in Poland of shampoos and other products manufactured by Lander in the United States. The contract provides that disputes under it shall be settled by binding arbitration in New York City pursuant to the arbitration rules of the International Chamber of Commerce. The parties had a falling out, Lander notified MMP that it was terminating the contract, and the latter filed a request for arbitration with the International Court of Arbitration, an organ of the International Chamber of Commerce. Lander did not contest the jurisdiction of the Court of Arbitration. The dispute proceeded to arbitration in New York City before a New York lawyer designated by the Court, who after five days of evidentiary hearings decided in favor of Lander, awarding it more than $500,000 plus interest.

. . . MMP refused to pay the award, so Lander brought this suit to enforce it in the federal district court in Chicago, which is MMP's home. . . .

MMP moved to dismiss the suit on the ground that the New York Convention was inapplicable to the parties' arbitration; but in addition it moved to vacate the award. The Federal Arbitration Act allows only three months for mounting a judicial challenge to an arbitration award that is subject to the Act, 9 U.S.C. § 12, and MMP was concerned, as it explained to the district court, that "although Lander takes the position now that the Arbitral Award is covered by the New York Convention, other allegations in its Petition to Confirm suggest that if it is unsuccessful under the Convention, it will seek to enforce the Arbitral Award under the Federal Arbitration

Act." Under the Act, if you fail to move to vacate an arbitration award you forfeit the right to oppose confirmation (enforcement) of the award if sought later by the other party. In contrast, the New York Convention contains no provision for seeking to vacate an award, although it contemplates the possibility of the award's being set aside in a proceeding under local law, Art. V(1)(e), and recognizes defenses to the enforcement of an award.

. . . [The district judge] held that the New York Convention did not apply, and went on to dismiss the suit without mention of the Federal Arbitration Act. The Act's one-year statute of limitations (9 U.S.C. § 9) would bar Lander from filing a new suit under the Act. So far as appears, Lander has no other judicial remedy to enforce its award, though conceivably it could sue to enforce it in Poland, hoping MMP has assets there.

The judge should not have dismissed Lander's suit, at least on jurisdictional grounds. The complaint sufficiently alleged jurisdiction under the Federal Arbitration Act as well as under the New York Convention. No other purpose than to allege jurisdiction under the Act can be assigned to the allegation of diversity jurisdiction and the citation of 28 U.S.C. § 1332, the diversity statute. . . . The allegation of diversity was necessary because the substantive law applicable to the resolution of the parties' dispute is not federal, and the Federal Arbitration Act is limited to arbitration agreements or awards that arise out of disputes that could be litigated in federal court. Chapter 2 of Title 9, the chapter that creates jurisdiction to enforce awards made under the New York Convention, is not so limited, 9 U.S.C. § 203, and citation of the diversity statute would thus have been unnecessary had Lander thought that the district court had jurisdiction only by virtue of the Convention.

. . .

We cannot stop here. We have assumed rather than established that the district court had jurisdiction under the Federal Arbitration Act. And even if it does, if there are differences between that Act and the New York Convention that are material to the resolution of Lander's suit, we may have to decide whether the Convention applies. The Convention (including its implementing legislation) is more than a statute that confers jurisdiction; it contains procedural provisions besides; if it is inapplicable, but the court has jurisdiction on some other basis, its inapplicability may still affect the course of the suit. It has, for example, a longer statute of limitations — three years rather than one. 9 U.S.C. § 207. That is not a factor here. But if a court asked to enforce an arbitration award has less authority to turn down the request (in whole or part) under the Convention than under the Federal Arbitration Act, this could make a difference in this case — and may be why Lander, the enforcing party, was so eager to bottom jurisdiction on the Convention. One court, noting that manifest disregard of the law is an implied ground for vacating an award under the Act, but neither an express nor, the court thought, an implied defense to enforcement under the Convention, has held that it is indeed harder to knock out an award under the Convention. We need not decide whether this is right; the issue (expressly left open by the Second Circuit in *Parsons & Whittemore Overseas Co. v. Societe Generale De L'Industrie Du Papier (RAKTA)*) has not been argued to us. It is enough that it *may* be right, meaning that whether the

Convention is applicable may make a difference even though jurisdiction is secure under the Federal Arbitration Act.

. . .

. . . The only substantive defense to the enforcement of the award that MMP claims to have, however, is a defense that part of the award was based on a matter that had not been submitted to the arbitrator; in other words, that the arbitrator had exceeded his terms of reference. And that is a defense under both the Federal Arbitration Act and the New York Convention. *Compare* 9 U.S.C. §§ 10(a)(4), 11(b), *with* Article V(1)(c) of the Convention. The wording is slightly different but there is no reason to think the meaning different. So we do not have to decide whether the Convention also applies to this case. But we think we should decide. The possible difference in the scope of judicial review that we mentioned earlier could still make a difference in the outcome of this case, because the litigation is in an early stage and MMP may want and be permitted by the district court to interpose a defense of manifest disregard of law by the arbitrator. Moreover, the issue of the Convention's applicability has been fully and ably briefed and vigorously argued, and is bound to recur (under conditions no more favorable for decision) with the expansion of foreign activities by U.S. firms.

Article I(1) provides that the Convention shall apply not only to arbitral awards made in a different country from the one in which enforcement is sought (not the case here) but also to "arbitral awards not considered as domestic awards" in the country in which enforcement is sought. Article I(3), however, authorizes a country "on the basis of reciprocity [to] declare that it will apply the Convention to the recognition and enforcement of awards made only in the territory of another Contracting State." And in its declaration of accession the United States along with many other signatories announced that it "will apply the Convention, on the basis of reciprocity, to the recognition and enforcement of only those awards made in the territory of another Contracting State." Read no further, says MMP; the arbitration award in this case was made in the United States, not in another contracting state. But as natural a way to read the declaration is that the United States will enforce pursuant to the Convention only arbitral awards made in nations that also adhere to the Convention. This is the significance of the reference to reciprocity. The United States will not enforce an arbitration award made in a country that, by failing to adopt the Convention, has not committed itself to enforce arbitration awards made in the United States. Granted, "a Contracting State" would be clearer, but "another Contracting State" is clear enough in context; it means "another signatory of the Convention, like the United States, as opposed to nonsignatories."

This reading of Article I, in contrast to a reading that would preclude enforcement in U.S. courts of awards rendered in this country, is supported by the U.S. implementing legislation: Chapter 2 of Title 9 authorizes the enforcement of arbitration awards in disputes wholly between U.S. citizens if, as here, the dispute arose out of a contract involving performance in a foreign country. 9 U.S.C. § 202. It could be argued that in so providing section 202 goes further than the Convention. An arbitration award made in *and* sought to be enforced in the United States is a domestic award according to traditional principles of Anglo-American conflicts of law, under which the law of the place of the award determines whether the award is valid. And the Convention excludes domestic awards. The alternative is to view section 202 as defining nondomestic award in Article I(3) (more precisely as redefining it, altering the traditional Anglo-American approach) — or indeed as going beyond the Convention. We need not decide. MMP does not argue that section 202 is invalid, whether or not it tracks the Convention; nor could it argue that, for the statute is comfortably within Congress's commerce power. And if it thus is valid, it doesn't matter whether it goes beyond the Convention.

This makes the language of section 202 critical. The section adopts the provisions of the Convention for any "arbitration agreement or arbitral award arising out of a legal relationship, whether contractual or not, which is considered as commercial, including a transaction, contract, or agreement described in section 2 of this title" — that is, either a "maritime transaction or a contract evidencing a transaction involving commerce," 9 U.S.C. § 2 — provided only that if the relationship is entirely between U.S. citizens, it must involve performance abroad or have some other reasonable relation with a foreign country. There is no ambiguity; the relationship between Lander and MMP falls squarely within the inclusion and outside the exclusion. Congress may have believed that confining enforcement under the Convention to awards rendered abroad would drive away international arbitration business from New York. Or it may have been seeking to secure the Convention's benefits, on the basis of reciprocity, to American businesses seeking judicial enforcement of foreign arbitration awards in the countries in which the award was made. Or it may simply have wanted to simplify the procedures governing the foreign activities of American firms, since American firms doing business abroad are bound to have contracts with foreign firms as well as other American firms. Whatever Congress's precise thinking on the matter, it spoke clearly.

. . .

The judgment of the district court is reversed with instructions to reinstate Lander's suit.

NOTES

1. Why didn't the Seventh Circuit simply end its opinion after finding that Lander sufficiently alleged diversity jurisdiction? Did the court need to decide whether the New York Convention applied?

2. Is the court of appeals correct that "the [FAA]'s one-year statute of limitations (9 U.S.C. § 9) would bar Lander from filing a new suit under the Act" and so "Lander has no other judicial remedy to enforce its award"? What about the three-year time limit in section 207? Does it preclude actions to enforce an award brought more than three years after the award is made?

3. Other courts likewise have held that an award made in the United States is a "non-domestic" award and within the scope of the New York Convention so long as it falls "within the inclusion and outside the exclusion" of section 202. *See, e.g.,* Industrial Risk Insurers v. M.A.N. Gutehoffnungshütte GmbH, 141 F.3d 1434 (11th Cir. 1998) (one party not citizen of the United States), *cert. denied,* 525 U.S. 1068 (1999); Bergesen v. Joseph Muller Corp., 710 F.2d 928 (2d Cir. 1983) (neither party citizen of the United States); Freudensprung v. Offshore Tech. Servs., 379 F.3d 327,

340-41 (5th Cir. 2004) (both parties citizens of the United States).

4. Article I(1) of the New York Convention makes clear the Convention "shall apply to the recognition and enforcement of arbitral awards made in the territory of a State other than the State where the recognition and enforcement of such awards are sought." Would an award made in the United Kingdom, in an arbitration between two American parties concerning conduct that took place in the United States, fall under the Convention? Would it satisfy section 202 of the FAA? If so, does that give you any second thoughts about *Jones v. Sea Tow Services* (in § 5.02[B]), dealing with the enforceability of arbitration agreements under the New York Convention?

Section 203 of the FAA provides subject matter jurisdiction in federal court over "[a]n action or proceeding falling under the Convention." 9 U.S.C. § 203 ("shall be deemed to arise under the laws and treaties of the United States"). This basis for subject matter jurisdiction may not be very important in cases like *Lander*, in which there also is diversity of citizenship. But because of the requirement of complete diversity, section 203 can be essential in cases in which an alien is suing another alien. *See, e.g.*, U. S. Motors v. General Motors Europe, 551 F.3d 420, 424 (6th Cir. 2008), *cert. denied*, 130 S. Ct. 1524 (2010) (holding no complete diversity); Eze v. Yellow Cab Co., 782 F.2d 1064 (D.C. Cir. 1986) (same). Note that section 205 permits removal from state court of cases falling under the Convention. Finally, in addition to subject matter jurisdiction over an action to enforce an arbitration award, a court also must have personal jurisdiction, as the following case holds.

BASE METAL TRADING, LTD. v. OJSC "NOVOKUZNETSKY ALUMINUM FACTORY"
United States Court of Appeals for the Fourth Circuit
283 F.3d 208 (2002)

WILKINSON, CHIEF JUDGE:

Plaintiff Base Metal Trading, Inc. ("Base Metal"), a Guernsey, Channel Island corporation brought the present action to confirm a foreign arbitration award against Defendant OJSC "Novokuznetsky Aluminum Factory" ("NKAZ"), a Russian corporation. The district court dismissed the case for lack of personal jurisdiction over NKAZ. Because the mere presence of seized property in Maryland provides no basis for asserting jurisdiction when there is no relationship between the property and the action, we affirm.

I.

From 1995 to 1999, plaintiff Base Metal, a Guernsey, Channel Islands corporation engaged in trading in raw materials associated with the aluminum industry, had various business dealings with defendant NKAZ, a Russian corporation engaged in the manufacture and sale of aluminum. A dispute arose between the two parties and in 1999, they agreed to arbitrate the dispute in the private Commercial Arbitration

Court of the Moscow Chamber of Commerce and Industry. On December 10, 1999, the Commercial Arbitration Court issued an arbitration award in favor of Base Metal in the amount of approximately $12,000,000. However, Base Metal was unable to collect the award at that time.

On June 29, 2000, Base Metal filed a Verified Complaint to Confirm a Foreign Arbitration Award in Maryland district court, pursuant to the Convention on the Recognition and Enforcement of Foreign Arbitral Awards (the "Convention"), implemented by 9 U.S.C. §§ 201 *et seq.* On that same day, Base Metal filed a motion seeking seizure or attachment of an aluminum shipment alleged to belong to NKAZ that had arrived in Baltimore Harbor on June 28. *See* Fed. R. Civ. P. 64. The attachment motion was granted by the district court and the property was taken into custody by the U.S. Marshal. . . .

. . . NKAZ moved . . . to have the case dismissed for, *inter alia*, lack of personal jurisdiction.

On April 3, 2001, the district court dismissed the case for lack of jurisdiction. The court noted that NKAZ's contacts with Maryland related exclusively to the fact that aluminum manufactured by NKAZ in Russia was unloaded in Baltimore Harbor. And the court held that, "By no stretch could the single shipment, or even several such shipments, constitute continuous and systematic contacts with Maryland so as to justify general jurisdiction over NKAZ."

. . . Base Metal appeals.

II.

Base Metal argues that the presence of NKAZ's property in Maryland confers jurisdiction over NKAZ for the purpose of confirming and enforcing the foreign arbitration award.

A.

As a preliminary matter, the Convention and its implementing legislation give federal district courts original jurisdiction over actions to compel or confirm foreign arbitration awards. *See* 9 U.S.C. §§ 203, 207. However, while the Convention confers subject matter jurisdiction over actions brought pursuant to the Convention, it does not confer personal jurisdiction when it would not otherwise exist. In other words, a plaintiff still must demonstrate that personal jurisdiction is proper under the Constitution.

The personal jurisdiction inquiry is a well-established one. . . . Since Maryland's long-arm statute expands the exercise of personal jurisdiction to the limits allowed by the Due Process Clause, . . . the question is simply whether the exercise of personal jurisdiction would be consistent with due process. Due process requires only that a defendant "have certain minimum contacts with [the forum] such that the maintenance of the suit does not offend 'traditional notions of fair play and substantial justice.'" Int'l Shoe Co. v. Washington, 326 U.S. 310, 316 (1945) (quoting Milliken v. Meyer, 311 U.S. 457 (1940)). For these minimum contacts to exist, there must "be some act by which the defendant purposefully avails itself of the privilege of conducting activities within the forum State, thus invoking the benefits and protections of its laws." Hanson v. Denckla, 357 U.S. 235, 253 (1958); *see also* Burger King Corp. v. Rudzewicz, 471 U.S. 462, 474-76 (1985).

In examining whether the exercise of jurisdiction is reasonable, a distinction is made between specific and general jurisdiction. When the cause of action arises out of the defendant's contacts with the forum, a court may seek to exercise specific jurisdiction. *See* Helicopteros Nacionales de Colombia, S.A. v. Hall, 466 U.S. 408, 414 (1984). However, when the cause of action does not arise out of the defendant's contacts with the forum, general jurisdiction may be exercised upon a showing that the defendant's contacts are of a "continuous and systematic" nature.

This basic analysis is not altered when the defendant's property is found in the forum state. The Supreme Court's decision in Shaffer v. Heitner, 433 U.S. 186 (1977), eliminated all doubt that the minimum contacts standard in *International Shoe* governs *in rem* and *quasi in rem* actions as well as *in personam* actions. The Court held that "in order to justify an exercise of jurisdiction *in rem*, the basis for jurisdiction must be sufficient to justify exercising jurisdiction over the interests of persons in a thing." And "the standard for determining whether an exercise of jurisdiction over the interests of persons is consistent with the Due Process Clause is the minimum-contacts standard elucidated in *International Shoe.*"

Of course, the presence of property in a state may have an impact on the personal jurisdiction inquiry. Indeed, "when claims to the property itself are the source of the underlying controversy between the plaintiff and the defendant, it would be unusual for the State where the property is located not to have jurisdiction." Yet, when the property which serves as the basis for jurisdiction is completely unrelated to the plaintiff's cause of action, the presence of property alone will not support jurisdiction. While, "the presence of the defendant's property in a State might suggest the existence of other ties among the defendant, the State, and the litigation," when those "other ties" do not exist, jurisdiction is not reasonable.

Overall, courts "must consider the burden on the defendant, the interests of the forum State, and the plaintiff's interest in obtaining relief" when determining whether the exercise of jurisdiction is reasonable in any given case. Asahi Metal Indus. Co. v. Superior Court, 480 U.S. 102, 113 (1987). And "the unique burdens placed upon one who must defend oneself in a foreign legal system should have significant weight in assessing the reasonableness of stretching the long arm of personal jurisdiction over national borders." But, "when minimum contacts have been established, often the interests of the plaintiff and the forum in the exercise of jurisdiction will justify even the serious burdens placed on the alien defendant." We must, therefore, examine whether Base Metal has alleged significant minimum contacts between NKAZ and Maryland to justify the exercise of jurisdiction on the Russian corporation in this case.

B.

Base Metal contends that Maryland has jurisdiction to confirm the foreign arbitration award in large part because 2,563 tons of aluminum, alleged to be the property of NKAZ, arrived in Baltimore Harbor. Because Base Metal does not contend that this action arises out of NKAZ's alleged contacts with Maryland, there is no assertion of specific jurisdiction. Base Metal only alleges that the district court has general jurisdiction over NKAZ. Therefore, due process requires Base Metal to establish that NKAZ's contacts with Maryland are "continuous and systematic." Yet, sufficient minimum contacts are simply not present in this case.

Base Metal focuses on one shipment of aluminum to Maryland as a basis for jurisdiction, but it is not clear that the aluminum in question belonged to NKAZ. Even assuming, however, that the aluminum did belong to NKAZ, this single shipment does not amount to "continuous and systematic" contacts. There is no dispute that the aluminum bears no relationship to the arbitration award Base Metal seeks to confirm. And Base Metal has failed to show that NKAZ has "purposefully availed itself of the privilege of conducting activities within the forum State, thus invoking the benefits and protections of its laws."

Indeed, the evidence fails to demonstrate NKAZ even attempted to do business in Maryland at all. NKAZ is a Russian corporation with its principal place of business in Novokuznetsk, Kemerevo Oblast, Russia. The evidence shows that NKAZ's business consists entirely of manufacturing aluminum in its Russian plant and it does not maintain an office of any kind outside of Russia. NKAZ does not contract directly with American companies or purchasers. It has no sales force or other agents in the United States. NKAZ has no subsidiaries, affiliates or shareholders in Maryland. Nor has it ever been authorized to do business in Maryland, transacted or solicited business in Maryland, or designated an agent to accept service of process in Maryland. NKAZ also neither owns nor rents any property in Maryland, has never conducted a financial transaction in Maryland, and has no assets of any kind in Maryland.

The mere fact that metal NKAZ manufactured in Russia was shipped to the United States does not amount to significant contacts with Maryland. Nor do vague references to possible contacts with New Jersey, "negotiations" with Kaiser Aluminum Company, "negotiations" in 1997 and 1998 in Pittsburgh concerning a possible joint venture with Alcoa, purchases of secondary aluminum from the United States in 1994 and 1995, other vague allegations of "negotiations" in the United States in 1998, and the attendance of NKAZ representatives at trade conferences in the United States amount to systematic contacts with the United States, much less Maryland. Base Metal simply cannot support jurisdiction in Maryland by making vague, unsubstantiated claims based on the affidavit of a former NKAZ employee. Without establishing the minimum contacts required by *International Shoe* and *Shaffer*, the burdens the exercise of jurisdiction would place on NKAZ simply cannot be justified.

Furthermore, Base Metal has failed to demonstrate what, if any, interest Maryland has in the resolution of this dispute. NKAZ is not a Maryland corporation and does no business in Maryland. The dispute that led to the arbitration award has nothing to do with the United States or Maryland. And even more telling, Base Metal itself is not a Maryland corporation, nor is its principal place of business in Maryland or even in the United States. The fact that the plaintiff in this case is not a Maryland corporation or resident "considerably diminishes" Maryland's interest in the dispute. While it is true that there is a general public policy interest in encouraging and enforcing arbitration agreements, that interest is not paramount to the interests protected by the Due Process Clause.

III.

As a final attempt to assert jurisdiction, Base Metal argues that jurisdiction is proper under Rule 4(k)(2) of the Federal Rules of Civil Procedure. . . .

[F]or jurisdiction over NKAZ to be proper under Rule 4(k)(2), Base Metal must demonstrate that NKAZ is not subject to personal jurisdiction in any state and that NKAZ's contacts with the United States as a whole support the exercise of jurisdiction consistent with the Constitution and laws of the United States. This Base Metal has failed to do. Base Metal has never attempted to argue that NKAZ is not subject to personal jurisdiction in any state. . . .

Even assuming that Base Metal could successfully argue that NKAZ is not subject to personal jurisdiction in any state, Base Metal has failed to proffer any evidence to demonstrate that NKAZ has sufficient contacts with the United States as a whole to justify general personal jurisdiction. Even when the allegations and declarations before the district court are credited, the contacts relied upon by Base Metal are insufficient. . . . As we have explained, NKAZ's alleged contacts with the United States appear sparse and limited to a few shipments of aluminum arriving in American ports. It is not clear why the limited resources of the federal courts should be spent resolving disputes between two foreign corporations with little or no connection to our country. And the burdens of subjecting a foreign company to suit in this country in this case are not justified. Therefore, a finding of jurisdiction in this case would turn the notion of "fair play and substantial justice" on its head.

IV.

For the foregoing reasons, the judgment of the district court is

AFFIRMED.

NOTES

1. For a different view of the exercise of personal jurisdiction in actions to enforce arbitration awards, albeit in dicta, see Glencore Grain Rotterdam B.V. v. Shivnath Rai Harnarain Co., 284 F.3d 1114 (9th Cir. 2002):

> Considerable authority supports Glencore Grain's position that it can enforce the award against Shivnath Rai's property in the forum even if that property has no relationship to the underlying controversy between the parties.[8] In Shaffer v. Heitner, 433 U.S. 186 (1977), the Supreme Court endorsed the position urged by Glencore Grain:

---

[8] Tormented souls of first-year civil procedure will recognize this strain of jurisdiction as quasi in rem type II, where "the plaintiff seeks to apply what he concedes to be the property of the defendant to the satisfaction of a claim against him."

> Once it has been determined by a court of competent jurisdiction that the defendant is a debtor of the plaintiff, there would seem to be no unfairness in allowing an action to realize on that debt in a State where the defendant has property, whether or not that State would have jurisdiction to determine the existence of the debt as an original matter.

Shaffer, 433 U.S. at 210 n.36.

> Nevertheless, as even Shivnath Rai seems to concede by the very terms of its argument, the sine qua non of basing jurisdiction on a defendant's assets in the forum is the identification of some asset. Glencore Grain fails to identify any property owned by Shivnath Rai in the forum against which Glencore Grain could attempt to enforce its award. Indeed, the best Glencore Grain can say is that it believes in good faith that Shivnath Rai has or will have assets located in the forum. This is simply not enough. Given the record before us, we must reject Glencore Grain's argument for jurisdiction based on property in the forum.

Id. at 1127-28; *see also* Dardana Ltd. v. A.O. Yuganskneftegaz, 317 F.3d 202, 206 (2d Cir. 2003) (citing *Base Metal Trading* and *Glencore* and describing personal jurisdiction question as "a difficult one").

2. The Restatement rejects the Fourth Circuit's holding in *Base Metal Trading. See* Restatement (Third) of the U.S. Law of International Commercial Arbitration § 4-27(a) ("Unless forum law provides otherwise, jurisdiction over the defendant in a post-award action may be based on the presence of the defendant's property within the jurisdiction, whether or not the property bears any relationship to the underlying dispute."). Commentators likewise have been critical. *See, e.g.,* Joseph E. Neuhaus, *Current Issues in the Enforcement of International Arbitration Awards*, 36 U. MIAMI INTER-AM. L. REV. 23, 30 (2004) ("Nothing in the constitutional limits on personal jurisdiction provides a reason not to enforce a foreign arbitral award in any jurisdiction in which property of the respondent can be found, up to the limits of the property found"); Linda Silberman, *International Arbitration: Comments from a Critic*, 13 AM. REV. INT'L ARB. 9, 15 (2002) (describing Fourth Circuit's decision as "egregious" and as "overlook[ing] the critical distinction made by the Supreme Court in its decision in *Shaffer v. Heitner*").

3. In Monegasque de Reassurances S.A.M. (Monde Re) v. NAK Naftogaz of Ukraine, 311 F.3d 488 (2d Cir. 2002), the Second Circuit affirmed the dismissal of an action to enforce an arbitration award on grounds of forum non conveniens. The arbitration, which took place in Russia, involved a dispute between an insurer in Monaco and a Ukranian pipeline company. The insurer prevailed and sought to enforce the award in New York. The district court dismissed the action on grounds of forum non conveniens, and the court of appeals affirmed. The court of appeals reasoned that "[t]he doctrine of forum non convenience, a procedural rule, may be applied in domestic arbitration cases brought under the provisions of the Federal Arbitration Act, and it therefore may be applied under the provisions of the Convention." *Id.* at 496. Important issues of Ukranian (and Russian) law were involved in the case and "court congestion is no more a problem in Ukraine than it is here"; accordingly, the court concluded that Ukranian courts were "better suited

than United States courts for the resolution of these legal questions." *Id.* at 500; *see also* Figueiredo Ferraz e Engenharia de Projeto Ltda v. Republic of Peru, 665 F.3d 384, 389-94 (2d Cir. 2011).

Is the decision in *Monde Re* consistent with the New York Convention? The Restatement rejects *Monde Re* and concludes that actions to confirm or enforce awards subject to the New York Convention are "not subject to a stay or dismissal in favor of a foreign court on forum non conveniens grounds." Restatement (Third) of the U.S. Law of International Commercial Arbitration § 4-29(a). Which is the better approach?

PROBLEM 7.11

Yemen Enterprises, a Yemeni import company, enters into a contract with Thai Supply, located in Thailand, for the purchase of rice to be imported into Yemen. The contract provides for arbitration under the rules of the International Chamber of Commerce. The parties have a dispute, and Yemen Enterprises files a request for arbitration with the ICC.

(a) The arbitration agreement provides that the arbitration will be held in Yemen. After lengthy hearings, held in Yemen, the arbitrators award Yemen Enterprises sizable damages. Yemen Enterprises learns that Thai Supply has significant assets in the United States and files an action to enforce the award in federal district court in California. Thai Supply moves to dismiss the action. How should the court rule on the motion?

(b) Same as sub-part(a) except that the arbitration agreement provides for the arbitration to be held in California, and the proceeding is, in fact, held in California. How should the court rule on the motion?

[B] Grounds for Non-Enforcement of International Arbitration Awards

The New York Convention reflects a strong bias in favor of enforcing arbitration awards. If the party seeking enforcement provides certified copies of the award and the arbitration agreement, as required by Article IV, it has made out a prima facie case in favor of enforcing the award. The other party then must establish one of the grounds for non-enforcement in Article V or the court "shall confirm the award." 9 U.S.C. § 207. American courts construe the grounds for non-enforcement narrowly and generally reject challenges to awards on those grounds, as the following cases illustrate. As you read them, consider how the grounds for non-enforcement of awards under the New York Convention compare to the grounds for vacating awards under the Federal Arbitration Act.

PARSONS & WHITTEMORE OVERSEAS CO. v. SOCIETE GENERALE DE L'INDUSTRIE DU PAPIER (RAKTA)

United States Court of Appeals for the Second Circuit

508 F.2d 969 (1974)

J. JOSEPH SMITH, CIRCUIT JUDGE:

Parsons & Whittemore Overseas Co., Inc., (Overseas), an American corporation, appeals from the entry of summary judgment on February 25, 1974, by . . . the Southern District of New York on the counter-claim by Societe Generale de L'Industrie du Papier (RAKTA), an Egyptian corporation, to confirm a foreign arbitral award holding Overseas liable to RAKTA for breach of contract. . . . We affirm the district court's confirmation of the foreign award. . . .

In November 1962, Overseas consented by written agreement with RAKTA to construct, start up and, for one year, manage and supervise a paperboard mill in Alexandria, Egypt. The Agency for International Development (AID), a branch of the United States State Department, would finance the project by supplying RAKTA with funds with which to purchase letters of credit in Overseas' favor. Among the contract's terms was an arbitration clause, which provided a means to settle differences arising in the course of performance, and a "force majeure" clause, which excused delay in performance due to causes beyond Overseas' reasonable capacity to control.

Work proceeded as planned until May, 1967. Then, with the Arab-Israeli Six Day War on the horizon, recurrent expressions of Egyptian hostility to Americans — nationals of the principal ally of the Israeli enemy — caused the majority of the Overseas work crew to leave Egypt. On June 6, the Egyptian government broke diplomatic ties with the United States and ordered all Americans expelled from Egypt except those who would apply and qualify for a special visa.

Having abandoned the project for the present with the construction phase near completion, Overseas notified RAKTA that it regarded this postponement as excused by the force majeure clause. RAKTA disagreed and sought damages for breach of contract. Overseas refused to settle and RAKTA, already at work on completing the performance promised by Overseas, invoked the arbitration clause. Overseas responded by calling into play the clause's option to bring a dispute directly to a three-man arbitral board governed by the rules of the International Chamber of Commerce. After several sessions in 1970, the tribunal issued a preliminary award, which recognized Overseas' force majeure defense as good only during the period from May 28 to June 30, 1967.

In so limiting Overseas' defense, the arbitration court emphasized that Overseas had made no more than a perfunctory effort to secure special visas and that AID's notification that it was withdrawing financial backing did not justify Overseas' unilateral decision to abandon the project. After further hearings in 1972, the tribunal made its final award in March, 1973: Overseas was held liable to RAKTA for $312,507.45 in damages for breach of contract and $30,000 for RAKTA's costs; additionally, the arbitrators' compensation was set at $49,000, with Overseas responsible for three-fourths of the sum.

Subsequent to the final award, Overseas in the action here under review sought a declaratory judgment to prevent RAKTA from collecting the award out of a letter of credit issued in RAKTA's favor by Bank of America at Overseas' request. The letter was drawn to satisfy any "penalties" which an arbitral tribunal might assess against Overseas in the future for breach of contract. RAKTA contended that the arbitral award for damages met the letter's requirement of "penalties" and counter-claimed to confirm and enter judgment upon the foreign arbitral award. Overseas' defenses to this counterclaim, all rejected by the district court, form the principal issues for review on this appeal. Four of these defenses are derived from the express language of the applicable United Nations Convention on the Recognition and Enforcement of Foreign Arbitral Awards (Convention), and a fifth is arguably implicit in the Convention. . . .

I. OVERSEAS' DEFENSES AGAINST ENFORCEMENT

In 1958 the Convention was adopted by 26 of the 45 states participating in the United Nations Conference on Commercial Arbitration held in New York. For the signatory state, the New York Convention superseded the Geneva Convention of 1927. The 1958 Convention's basic thrust was to liberalize procedures for enforcing foreign arbitral awards: While the Geneva Convention placed the burden of proof on the party seeking enforcement of a foreign arbitral award and did not circumscribe the range of available defenses to those enumerated in the convention, the 1958 Convention clearly shifted the burden of proof to the party defending against enforcement and limited his defenses to seven set forth in Article V. Not a signatory to any prior multilateral agreement on enforcement of arbitral awards, the United States declined to sign the 1958 Convention at the outset. The United States ultimately acceded to the Convention, however, in 1970, and implemented its accession with 9 U.S.C. 201-208. . . .

A. *Public Policy*

Article V(2)(b) of the Convention allows the court in which enforcement of a foreign arbitral award is sought to refuse enforcement, on the defendant's motion or *sua sponte*, if "enforcement of the award would be contrary to the public policy of [the forum] country." The legislative history of the provision offers no certain guidelines to its construction. . . .

Perhaps more probative, however, are the inferences to be drawn from the history of the Convention as a whole. The general pro-enforcement bias informing the Convention and explaining its supersession of the Geneva Convention points toward a narrow reading of the public policy defense. An expansive construction of this defense would vitiate the Convention's basic effort to remove preexisting obstacles to enforcement. Additionally, considerations of reciprocity — considerations given express recognition in the Convention itself — counsel courts to invoke the public policy defense with caution lest foreign courts frequently accept it as a defense to enforcement of arbitral awards rendered in the United States.

We conclude, therefore, that the Convention's public policy defense should be construed narrowly. Enforcement of foreign arbitral awards may be denied on this basis only where enforcement would violate the forum state's most basic notions of morality and justice.

Under this view of the public policy provision in the Convention, Overseas' public policy defense may easily be dismissed. Overseas argues that various actions by United States officials subsequent to the severance of American-Egyptian relations — most particularly, AID's withdrawal of financial support for the Overseas-RAKTA contract — required Overseas, as a loyal American citizen, to abandon the project. Enforcement of an award predicated on the feasibility of Overseas' returning to work in defiance of these expressions of national policy would therefore allegedly contravene United States public policy. In equating "national" policy with United States "public" policy, the appellant quite plainly misses the mark. To read the public policy defense as a parochial device protective of national political interests would seriously undermine the Convention's utility. This provision was not meant to enshrine the vagaries of international politics under the rubric of "public policy." Rather, a circumscribed public policy doctrine was contemplated by the Convention's framers and every indication is that the United States, in acceding to the Convention, meant to subscribe to this supranational emphasis.

To deny enforcement of this award largely because of the United States' falling out with Egypt in recent years would mean converting a defense intended to be of narrow scope into a major loophole in the Convention's mechanism for enforcement. We have little hesitation, therefore, in disallowing Overseas' proposed public policy defense.

B. *Non-Arbitrability*

Article V(2)(a) authorizes a court to deny enforcement, on a defendant's or its own motion, of a foreign arbitral award when "the subject matter of the difference is not capable of settlement by arbitration under the law of that (the forum) country." Under this provision, a court sitting in the United States might, for example, be expected to decline enforcement of an award involving arbitration of an antitrust claim in view of domestic arbitration cases which have held that antitrust matters are entrusted to the exclusive competence of the judiciary. *See, e.g.,* American Safety Equipment Corp. v. J.P. Maguire & Co., 391 F.2d 821 (2d Cir. 1968). On the other hand, it may well be that the special considerations and policies underlying a "truly international agreement," Scherk v. Alberto-Culver Co., call for a narrower view of nonarbitrability in the international than the domestic context. *Compare id. with Wilko v. Swan.*

Resolution of Overseas' non-arbitrability argument, however, does not require us to reach such difficult distinctions between domestic and foreign awards. For Overseas' argument, that "United States foreign policy issues can hardly be placed at the mercy of foreign arbitrators 'who are charged with the execution of no public trust' and whose loyalties are to foreign interests," plainly fails to raise so substantial an issue of arbitrability. The mere fact that an issue of national interest may incidentally figure into the resolution of a breach of contract claim does not make the dispute not arbitrable. Rather, certain *categories* of claims may be non-arbitrable because of the special national interest vested in their resolution. *Cf. American Safety Equipment Corp.* Furthermore, even were the test for nonarbitrability of an ad hoc nature, Overseas' situation would almost certainly not meet the standard, for Overseas grossly exaggerates the magnitude of the national interest involved in the resolution of its particular claim. Simply because acts of the United States are somehow implicated in a case one cannot conclude that the United States is vitally interested in its outcome. Finally, the Supreme Court's decision in favor of arbitrability in a case far more prominently displaying public features than the instant one, *Scherk v. Alberto-Culver Co.*, compels by analogy the conclusion that the foreign award against Overseas dealt with a subject arbitrable under United States law.

. . .

C. *Inadequate Opportunity to Present Defense*

Under Article V(1)(b) of the Convention, enforcement of a foreign arbitral award may be denied if the defendant can prove that he was "not given proper notice . . . or was otherwise unable to present his case." This provision essentially sanctions the application of the forum state's standards of due process.

Overseas seeks relief under this provision for the arbitration court's refusal to delay proceedings in order to accommodate the speaking schedule of one of Overseas' witnesses, David Nes, the United States Charge d'Affairs in Egypt at the time of the Six Day War. This attempt to state a due process claim fails for several reasons. First, inability to produce one's witnesses before an arbitral tribunal is a risk inherent in an agreement to submit to arbitration. By agreeing to submit disputes to arbitration, a party relinquishes his courtroom rights — including that to subpoena witnesses — in favor of arbitration "with all of its well known advantages and drawbacks." Secondly, the logistical problems of scheduling hearing dates convenient to parties, counsel and arbitrators scattered about the globe argues against deviating from an initially mutually agreeable time plan unless a scheduling change is truly unavoidable. In this instance, Overseas' allegedly key witness was kept from attending the hearing due to a prior commitment to lecture at an American university — hardly the type of obstacle to his presence which would require the arbitral tribunal to postpone the hearing as a matter of fundamental fairness to Overseas. Finally, Overseas cannot complain that the tribunal decided the case without considering evidence critical to its defense and within only Mr. Nes' ability to produce. In fact, the tribunal did have before it an affidavit by Mr. Nes in which he furnished, by his own account, "a good deal of the information to which I would have testified." Moreover, had Mr. Nes wished to furnish *all* the information to which he would have testified, there is every reason to believe that the arbitration tribunal would have considered that as well.

The arbitration tribunal acted within its discretion in declining to reschedule a hearing for the convenience of an Overseas witness. Overseas' due process rights under American law, rights entitled to full force under the Convention as a defense to enforcement, were in no way infringed by the tribunal's decision.

D. *Arbitration in Excess of Jurisdiction*

Under Article V(1)(c), one defending against enforcement of an arbitral award may prevail by proving that:

> The award deals with a difference not contemplated by or not falling within the terms of the submission to arbitration, or it contains decisions on matters beyond the scope of the submission to arbitration.

. . .

This provision tracks in more detailed form § 10(d) of the Federal Arbitration Act. . . . Both provisions basically allow a party to attack an award predicated upon arbitration of a subject matter not within the agreement to submit to arbitration. This defense to enforcement of a foreign award, like the others already discussed, should be construed narrowly. Once again a narrow construction would comport with the enforcement-facilitating thrust of the Convention. In addition, the case law under the similar provision of the Federal Arbitration Act strongly supports a strict reading.

In making this defense as to three components of the award, Overseas must therefore overcome a powerful presumption that the arbitral body acted within its powers. Overseas principally directs its challenge at the $185,000 awarded for loss of production. Its jurisdictional claim focuses on the provision of the contract reciting that "neither party shall have any liability for loss of production." The tribunal cannot properly be charged, however, with simply ignoring this alleged limitation on the subject matter over which its decisionmaking powers extended. Rather, the arbitration court interpreted the provision not to preclude jurisdiction on this matter. . . . [T]he court may be satisfied that the arbitrator premised the award on a construction of the contract and that it is "not apparent" that the scope of the submission to arbitration has been exceeded.

. . .

Although the Convention recognizes that an award may not be enforced where predicated on a subject matter outside the arbitrator's jurisdiction, it does not sanction second-guessing the arbitrator's construction of the parties' agreement. The appellant's attempt to invoke this defense, however, calls upon the court to ignore this limitation on its decision-making powers and usurp the arbitrator's role. The district court took a proper view of its own jurisdiction in refusing to grant relief on this ground.

E. *Award in "Manifest Disregard" of Law*

Both the legislative history of Article V and the statute enacted to implement the United States' accession to the Convention are strong authority for treating as exclusive the bases set forth in the Convention for vacating an award. On the other hand, the Federal Arbitration Act . . . has been read to include an implied defense to enforcement where the award is in "manifest disregard" of the law. *Wilko v. Swan.*

This case does not require us to decide, however, whether this defense stemming from dictum in *Wilko* obtains in the international arbitration context. For even assuming that the "manifest disregard" defense applies under the Convention, we would have no difficulty rejecting the appellant's contention that such "manifest disregard" is in evidence here. Overseas in effect asks this court to read this defense as a license to review the record of arbitral proceedings for errors of fact or law — a role which we have emphatically declined to assume in the past and reject once again. "Extensive judicial review frustrates the basic purpose of arbitration, which is to dispose of disputes quickly and avoid the expense and delay of extended court proceedings."

Insofar as this defense to enforcement of awards in "manifest disregard" of law may be cognizable under the Convention, it, like the other defenses raised by the appellant, fails to provide a sound basis for vacating the foreign arbitral award. We therefore affirm the district court's confirmation of award.

. . .

Affirmed.

FERTILIZER CORP. OF INDIA v. IDI MANAGEMENT, INC.
United States District Court for the Southern District of Ohio
517 F. Supp. 948 (1981)

SPIEGEL, District Judge.

Fertilizer Corporation of India (FCI) brings this petition for enforcement, under the Convention on the Recognition and Enforcement of Foreign Arbitral Awards (the Convention) of an arbitral award rendered in India in FCI's favor against respondent IDI Management, Inc. (IDI). FCI asks that judgment be entered in its favor for 9,679,000 rupees ($1.3 million) with interest. . . . IDI has interposed a number of affirmative defenses to enforcement of the award, and has also counterclaimed for enforcement of a prior arbitration award. . . .

. . .

FACTUAL SUMMARY

Petitioner FCI, a wholly-owned entity of the Government of India, is engaged in the manufacture, marketing and sale of fertilizers. Rashtriya Chemicals & Fertilizers is FCI's legal successor in interest with respect to the manufacturing facility located at Trombay, Bombay, India. IDI, the successor in interest to Chemical & Industrial Corp. (C & I) is an Ohio corporation whose business includes the design, engineering and construction of complex fertilizer plants.

In 1962 FCI and IDI's predecessors in interest entered into a contract for construction of a nitrophosphate plant near Bombay, India. The contract provided that all disputes between the parties "shall be finally settled by arbitration in conformity with the rules of conciliation and arbitration of the International Chamber of Commerce by one or more arbitrators appointed in accordance with the rules." After the facility was built, a dispute arose concerning the quantity of daily production from the plant. FCI requested arbitration through the International Chamber of Commerce (ICC) in 1968.

Pursuant to the rules of the ICC, each party designated an arbitrator, Mr. Sen by FCI and Mr. Wilson by IDI. Lord Devlin was appointed as the third member and chairman. The arbitrators met on numerous occasions between 1971 and 1976, including twenty-five evidentiary sessions in 1974 and 1975. On November 1, 1976, the arbitrators unanimously awarded to FCI 9,679,000 rupees plus $10,118.31. IDI failed to pay to the ICC its share of the arbitration's costs and expenses; therefore, the award was not released to the parties until FCI deposited the full amount of those fees in 1979. This award, known as the "Nitrophosphate Award," is a so-called "speaking award" in which the panel, in a lengthy document, gave reasons for its findings.

Prior to 1968, the same arbitrators were appointed to resolve a dispute between the same parties over the construction of a methanol plant, also near Bombay, India. A contract for that project had been entered into in 1964. This contract also contained an arbitration clause; it provided for arbitration under the provisions of the Indian Arbitration Act, rather than under the rules of the ICC. In 1974, an award of more than $300,000 was issued in favor of IDI. This Methanol Award, the subject of the counterclaim in this case, was a so-called "non-speaking" award in which no reasons for the findings were given. Mr. Sen did not concur; he wrote a dissent after the majority published its award. FCI appealed this award to an Indian court which, however, found for IDI and entered judgment on the award. FCI appealed, and that appeal is pending. FCI has deposited a portion of the judgment; IDI has furnished guarantees required by the Indian court before withdrawing the deposit. Because of foreign exchange regulations, the Government of India has not allowed withdrawal up to this time.

With respect to the Nitrophosphate Award, the subject of the petition and motion in this case, IDI has filed in an Indian court to set aside the award, and FCI has petitioned another Indian court for confirmation of the award. Both actions are pending. FCI then petitioned this Court for enforcement of the Nitrophosphate Award under the Convention.

Since FCI has submitted to the Court the documents required by the Convention, we must confirm the award unless we find in favor of IDI on one of its asserted defenses or choose to adjourn our decision under Article VI. We will analyze each defense in turn before reaching a decision.

I. FIRST AFFIRMATIVE DEFENSE, RETROACTIVITY

FCI and IDI entered into the nitrophosphate contract on May 8, 1962. The United States did not accede to the Convention until 1970. IDI contends that the Convention may not be applied to an arbitration under a contract which predates the Convention's adoption by the United States and that, consequently, FCI has not properly invoked the jurisdiction of this Court. . . .

. . .

We hold . . . that the jurisdiction of this Court under the Convention has been properly invoked and that the Convention should be applied, even though the parties contracted before the United States adopted the Convention.

II. SECOND AFFIRMATIVE DEFENSE, RECIPROCITY

IDI argues that India would not enforce the Nitrophosphate Award had it been rendered in the United States in IDI's favor and that therefore the reciprocity between India and the United States required by the Convention is absent. India has adopted various evasive devices, IDI submits, to avoid enforcement of awards adverse to Indian parties. Moreover, Article I, paragraph 3 of the Convention states that contracting states may choose to apply the Convention only to legal relationships considered "commercial" under the law of the acceding state, and may also choose to apply the Convention only to awards made in another contracting state's territory. Both India and the United States chose to adopt these restrictions. Citing Indian Organic Chemicals, Ltd. v. Chemtex Fibers, Inc., A.I.R. 1978 Bombay 106, IDI alleges that India has narrowly defined the term "commercial" so as to exclude many or most legal relationships which would be considered "commercial" in the normal sense of the word. IDI argues further that Article XIV of the Convention sweeps broadly and, in effect, requires this Court to determine the extent to which India is applying the Convention and to react in like manner.

. . .

The Court is persuaded that the reciprocity required by the Convention is satisfied in this case. With regard to the wording of Article I, paragraph 3, it is an elementary rule of statutory construction that where express language is used in one part of a statute, its omission from another part is presumed to be deliberate. It is undisputed that India is a signatory to the Convention; therefore, the reciprocity of the first sentence in question is satisfied. It is equally undisputed that the contract between the parties is considered commercial under the laws of the United States; thus, the requirement of the second sentence is met.

As to Article XIV, Leonard Quigley has said, "The adoption of this Article (XIV) gives states a defensive right to take advantage of another state's reservations with regard to territorial, federal or other provisions." L. Quigley, "Accession by the United States to the United Nations Convention on the Recognition and Enforcement of Foreign Arbitral Awards," 70 Yale L.J. 1049, 1074 (1961). Quigley also mentions that this clause "presumably will also cover the case where the courts of a State have placed a restrictive interpretation upon its obligations under the Convention," but we do not find this comment determinative.

In any case, we are satisfied that the Indian courts are not engaged in a devious policy to subvert the Convention by denying non-Indians their just awards. The Methanol Award, which is in IDI's favor, helps persuade us that the Indian judiciary is functioning in a responsible manner. Moreover, FCI has cited other cases and arbitrations showing that Indian courts will enforce awards against Indian parties and that Indian parties do arbitrate outside of India. As IDI itself has counseled, United States courts should "construe exceptions narrowly lest foreign courts use holdings against application of the Convention as a reason for refusing enforcement of awards made in the United States."

III. THIRD AFFIRMATIVE DEFENSE, PUBLIC POLICY ARBITRATOR SEN'S RELATIONSHIP WITH FCI

IDI asserts that enforcement of the Nitrophosphate Award would violate the public policy of the United States, in violation of Article V(2)(b) of the Convention. They allege that Mr. B. Sen, the arbitrator nominated by FCI for the Nitrophosphate case (as well as for the Methanol case) had served as counsel for FCI in at least two other legal or arbitral proceedings and that these facts were not disclosed to IDI. Respondent cites *Commonwealth Coatings Corp. v. Continental Casualty Co.* to support the claim that American public policy demands that arbitrators be not only unbiased but free from even the appearance of bias. . . .

FCI responds that Mr. Sen was chosen properly under the ICC rules as well as under the Convention. . . . FCI contends that even today it is not clear whether an "independent" arbitrator need be neutral. Moreover, they argue, Mr. Sen is a Senior Advocate and, as such, his relationship with FCI was not that of attorney and client. Rather, Senior Advocates in India are hired by the client's advocate (similar to the retention of a barrister by a solicitor under the British system), are paid by the advocate (who is normally reimbursed by the client), and the Senior Advocate is thus insulated from the client. He is an officer of the Court, like a British Queen's Counsel, and may argue for and against the same client at different times.

. . .

The Court does not take lightly IDI's charge. In view of the unanimity of the Nitrophosphate Award, there is nothing to suggest actual bias or prejudice on Mr. Sen's part, yet we strongly believe that full disclosure of any possible interest or bias is the better rule whenever one is in a position to determine the rights of others. However, we do not find that nondisclosure of Mr. Sen's relationship with FCI has so tainted the proceedings as to nullify the award.

FCI relies upon *Commonwealth Coatings* as the statement of American public policy with respect to neutrality of arbitrators. . . .

. . . *Commonwealth Coatings* is distinguishable on the facts. That case dealt with a so-called tri-partite arbitration where one party chose one arbitrator, the other party chose a second, and those two arbitrators selected the third. The controversy centered on the third arbitrator, "the supposedly neutral member of the panel." In the present case, we are dealing, not with the third member of the panel, but with the member appointed by the party, FCI, with whom the alleged undisclosed relationship existed. The third member of the panel was Lord Devlin. . . . [T]here is nothing at all to suggest that Lord Devlin was other than totally impartial. In fact, it is undisputed that the identical panel of arbitrators found for IDI in the Methanol arbitration, with Mr. Sen dissenting, but with Lord Devlin and Mr. Wilson favoring IDI.

The Court of Appeals for the Second Circuit has concluded that the Convention's public policy defense should be narrowly construed. "Enforcement of foreign arbitral awards may be denied on this basis only where enforcement would violate the forum state's most basic notions of morality and justice." *Parsons and Whittemore Overseas Co., Inc. v. Societe Generale de l'Industrie du Papier (RAKTA)*. Even in domestic arbitrations, that Court has "viewed the teachings of *Commonwealth Coatings* pragmatically, employing a case-by-case approach in preference to dogmatic rigidity." . . . We believe, also, that the Court has given wise advice in counseling courts "to invoke the public policy defense with caution lest foreign courts frequently accept it as a defense to enforcement of arbitral awards rendered in the United States."

We therefore find that recognition or enforcement of the Nitrophosphate Award would not be contrary to the public policy of the United States, and enforcement may not be denied on this basis. . . .

IV. FOURTH AFFIRMATIVE DEFENSE, BINDING EFFECT OF THE AWARD

IDI's fourth defense is that the Nitrophosphate Award is not enforceable because it is not binding within the Convention's meaning. . . . IDI argues that the award is not binding until it has been reviewed by an Indian court for errors of law. The award is presently before the Indian courts for a ruling, among other things, on whether the arbitrators could award consequential damages despite an express contract clause to the contrary. While American courts, they contend, review arbitration awards only for errors which are totally irrational or in manifest disregard of the law, Indian courts review "speaking awards" for any error of law. IDI contends that this kind of review is one on the merits and that it prevents any meaningful binding effect or finality.

FCI counters that under Indian law, both statutory and decisional, as well as under the ICC Rules and under the parties' contract, an arbitral award is final and binding. They argue that merely because an award has been challenged in an Indian court, its binding effect is not destroyed, just as a district court decision is binding on the parties, even though it is appealable, and a judgment may be executed upon unless the loser posts an appeal or supersedeas bond. . . .

     . . .

We find that the Nitrophosphate Award is final and binding, for purposes of the Convention. Therefore, Article V, paragraph (1)(e) does not apply to prevent enforcement. We note the comment of Professor Gerald Aksen, General Counsel of the American Arbitration Association:

> The award will be considered "binding" for the purposes of the Convention if no further recourse may be had to another arbitral tribunal (that is, an appeals tribunal). The fact that recourse may be had to a court of law does not prevent the award from being "binding." This provision should make it more difficult for an obstructive loser to postpone or prevent enforcement by bringing, or threatening to bring, proceedings to have an award set aside or suspended.

G. Aksen, "American Arbitration Accession Arrives in the Age of Aquarius: United

States Implements United Nations Convention on the Recognition and Enforcement of Foreign Arbitral Awards," 3 Sw. U.L. Rev. 1, 11 (1971).

V. FIFTH AFFIRMATIVE DEFENSE, CONSEQUENTIAL DAMAGES

It is IDI's position that the arbitrators exceeded their authority in awarding consequential damages and that the award is therefore unenforceable under Article V, section 1(c) of the Convention. This argument is based on the parties' contract which expressly excludes from damages any amount for lost profits.

FCI contends that Article V(1)(c) of the Convention covers only the case where a particular issue was not *submitted* to the arbitrators. Here, the question of consequential damages was included in the terms of reference, signed by both parties, which constituted the framework of the arbitration. Therefore, they argue, IDI has no defense under the Convention based on the award of consequential damages.

. . .

It is beyond dispute that the contract between these parties clearly excluded consequential damages. It is also undisputed that the arbitrators rendered a large award, based almost exclusively on consequential damages, in FCI's favor. The award is a long one and, after reviewing it carefully, the Court finds it to be a thorough and scholarly opinion, written for a unanimous panel by Lord Devlin, a well-respected jurist and former Law Lord of the English House of Lords.

. . .

. . . [T]he arbitrators found that, as of a certain date, IDI's predecessors "repudiated" the contract by failing to hold, within a reasonable time, tests which were to demonstrate that the plant could meet its guarantee, and that FCI "rescinded" the contract based on respondent's repudiation. Using the concept of "fundamental breach," the arbitrators found that, in such a situation, the limitation of damages clause no longer applied. They awarded to FCI damages based on profits lost between the date the contract was "repudiated" and the date when the plant became profitable. Otherwise, there would have been virtually nothing on which to base damages, even though the panel found that, as of the date representing the outside limit of reasonable time, the plant's production was significantly below that promised. . . .

Without engaging in an in-depth analysis of the law of contract in the United States, we cannot say with certainty whether a breach of contract found to be material or "fundamental" would abrogate an express clause limiting damages to those other than consequential. The answer, however, is irrelevant. The standard of review of an arbitration award by an American court is extremely narrow. The Convention "does not sanction second-guessing the arbitrator's construction of the parties' agreement," nor would it be proper for this Court "to usurp the arbitrator's role." *Parsons & Whittemore.*

We find under the Convention that the arbitrators did not exceed their authority in granting consequential damages in the Nitrophosphate Award. . . . In the present case the award is within the submission to the arbitrators, there were numerous hearings, and we are impressed with the thoroughness and scholarship of the arbitrators' decision.

The Court of Appeals for the Second Circuit has stated:

> When arbitrators explain their conclusions . . . in terms that offer even a barely colorable justification for the outcome reached, confirmation of the award cannot be prevented by litigants who merely argue, however persuasively, for a different result.

We find at least colorable justification for the result reached in the Nitrophosphate Award.

. . .

We therefore agree with FCI that this Court, acting under the narrow judicial review of arbitral awards granted to American courts, may not substitute its judgment for that of the arbitrators. However, this arbitration was held in India, and, while the contract does not state specifically whose law shall govern, no party has claimed that American law should control. Since the contract was executed and was to be performed in India, and the venue of arbitration was expressly stated to be New Delhi, India, the Court concludes that the law of India governs the contract rights of the parties.

Indian courts are given broader review of arbitral awards than are American courts, when reasons for the award are given by the arbitrators. When a proposition of law is stated in the award and forms a basis of the award, that award can be set aside or remitted on the ground of error of law apparent on the face of the record, if the stated proposition of law is found by a court to be erroneous. We interpret this to mean that an Indian court could set aside the Nitrophosphate Award if it were to find that the law of fundamental breach, upon which a substantial portion of the award is based, is erroneous under Indian law. Therefore, while we do not find under the Convention that the arbitrators exceeded their authority in awarding consequential damages, as the issue was properly submitted to them, we believe that we must consider seriously IDI's contention that we should adjourn our decision, under Article VI, pending resolution of this issue by the Indian court.

VI. ARTICLE VI OF THE CONVENTION

Article VI . . . appears to be an unfettered grant of discretion [to adjourn pending a proceeding to vacate the award]; the Court has been unable to discover any standard on which a decision to adjourn should be based, other than to ascertain that an application to set aside or suspend the award has been made. Here, it is undisputed that IDI has made such an application in India.

. . .

We believe it is important in making this decision to consider the purpose of the Convention. The primary thrust of the Convention is to make enforcement of arbitral awards more simple by liberalizing enforcement procedures, limiting defenses, and placing the burden of proof on the party opposing enforcement.

The Supreme Court discussed at some length the goal of the Convention in

Scherk v. Alberto-Culver:

> The goal of the Convention, and the principal purpose underlying American adoption and implementation of it, was to encourage the recognition and enforcement of commercial arbitration agreements in international contracts and to verify the standards by which agreements to arbitrate are observed and arbitral awards are enforced in the signatory countries.

The Court also observed:

> A parochial refusal by the courts of one country to enforce an international arbitration agreement would not only frustrate these purposes, but would invite unseemly and mutually destructive jockeying by the parties to secure tactical litigation advantages.

The same would be true of a parochial refusal to enforce an arbitral award under the Convention.

We are not unmindful of the fact that IDI has been unable to collect in India its judgment on the Methanol Award. However, to allow that fact to influence our decision on enforcement of the Nitrophosphate Award would be "parochial" indeed. It is clear, as even IDI has conceded, that the Indian courts have enforced the Methanol Award and have required FCI to post security, but, as FCI apparently concedes, the Indian Government has not so far allowed the funds to be removed from the country. Whatever this Court may think of the propriety of the refusal, it is simply not a matter over which we have any jurisdiction, nor are we sufficiently informed of all the circumstances to have formed an educated opinion.

Nevertheless, in order to avoid the possibility of an inconsistent result, this Court has determined to adjourn its decision on enforcement of the Nitrophosphate Award until the Indian courts decide with finality whether the award is correct under Indian law. FCI, of course, may apply to this Court for suitable security, as provided by Article VI.

When we are informed that the Indian courts have reviewed the Nitrophosphate Award and rendered a decision, we will proceed to either grant or deny enforcement, based on that decision.

VII. . . . COUNTERCLAIM

. . . [R]emaining to be determined . . . [is] whether the Methanol Award may be enforced in this Court, as requested in IDI's counterclaim.

. . .

We find that IDI's counterclaim must be dismissed for two reasons. First, under 9 U.S.C. § 207, a party must apply to this Court for enforcement within three years after an award is made. The Methanol Award was made in 1974, while IDI's counterclaim seeking enforcement was filed in this Court on January 2, 1980. Thus, the counterclaim is time-barred since this Court finds that the Convention does apply to this case.

Second, we find that a counterclaim is inappropriate in a confirmation proceeding. In Chapter One of the Arbitration Act, 9 U.S.C. § 6, it is provided that a confirmation proceeding is to follow the rules for motion practice. Chapter One applies to proceedings brought under the Convention, which is codified as Chapter Two, insofar as no conflicts exist between the two. We find no conflict here. This matter is in fact before us on FCI's motion for confirmation, and a counterclaim may not be interposed in response to a motion. Furthermore, a confirmation proceeding is not an original action; it is, rather, in the nature of a post-judgment enforcement proceeding. In such a proceeding a counterclaim is clearly inappropriate.

Accordingly, IDI's counterclaim is dismissed.

SUMMARY

Having determined that IDI's defenses to enforcement of the Nitrophosphate Award fail, we adjourn our final decision on enforcement, pursuant to Article VI of the Convention, until the Indian courts resolve with finality pending actions relating to this award. If it is determined in India that the award is in accord with Indian law, we will enter judgment for FCI for 9,679,000 Indian rupees plus $10,118.31 plus $46,765, all with interest at 6% from the date of filing of this Opinion.

SO ORDERED.

NOTES

1. How do the grounds for non-enforcement of arbitral awards under the New York Convention compare to the grounds for vacating awards under the FAA? One possible difference, as noted in *Parsons & Whittemore* and *Lander*, involves review for manifest disregard of the law. Are there any others? For those grounds that are the same, did the courts in *Parsons & Whittemore* and *Fertilizer Corp.* construe them consistently with the same grounds under the domestic FAA?

As noted earlier, the Restatement takes the position that manifest disregard of the law is not available under FAA § 10, *see* Restatement (Third) of the U.S. Law of International Commercial Arbitration § 4-16, cmt. g, and construes the remaining FAA § 10 grounds as comparable to the New York Convention Article V grounds, at least as applied in international transactions, *see, e.g., id.* § 4-22(a). For a detailed analysis of the Article V grounds, see *id.* §§ 4-12 through 4-18.

2. "In approximately 10% of the reported cases involving the New York Convention, a court has refused enforcement of a foreign arbitral award." Albert Jan van den Berg, *Refusals of Enforcement under the New York Convention of 1958: The Unfortunate Few*, ICC INT'L CT. ARB. BULL. 75, 75 (Supp. 1999). Of course, that does not mean that ten percent of *all awards* are not enforced, since opinions enforcing awards are less likely to be published and the substantial majority of awards are never challenged in court. One of the rare American cases refusing enforcement of an award under the New York Convention, which is included in the ten percent figure, is *Iran Aircraft*, discussed in § 6.10.

PROBLEM 7.12

Kratides and Kratides (K&K) (from Problem 7.10) now has filed an action against your client, Melas & Associates, to enforce the $950,000 Greek arbitration award in federal court in the United States. Mr. Melas relates the following facts to help you prepare your response:

(1)   One of the arbitrators, Harold Latimer, was a British barrister. Mr. Melas learned after the arbitration hearing that Latimer had appeared on behalf of K&K in several previous arbitrations.

(2)   One of the claims on which the arbitrators based their award was that Melas & Associates had violated Greek competition law. However, Greek law makes competition law claims nonarbitrable. In addition, the theory on which the claim was based (that of vertical maximum resale price maintenance) has been rejected by the United States Supreme Court for purposes of American antitrust law on the ground that such contracts benefit, rather than harm, consumers.

(3)   At the hearing, the arbitrator permitted much less cross-examination of witnesses than would be available in a United States court.

(4)   Mr. Melas' Greek law firm has already filed an action to vacate the award in Greece.

On what possible grounds might you try to resist enforcement of the award in the United States? Are you likely to succeed?

PROBLEM 7.13

In *Fertilizer Corp.*, IDI argued that "India has adopted various evasive devices . . . to avoid enforcement of awards adverse to Indian parties," including "narrowly defin[ing] the term 'commercial' so as to exclude [from the New York Convention] many or most legal relationships which would be considered 'commercial' in the normal sense of the word." The court rejected that argument as a factual matter, concluding that "we are satisfied that the Indian courts are not engaged in a devious policy to subvert the Convention by denying non-Indians their just awards." *See also RM Investment & Trading*, discussed in § 5.02[C] (re the definition of "commercial"). But what if a country did adopt such a policy, such as by construing the term "commercial" so narrowly that most ordinary business transactions were noncommercial and thus not subject to the New York Convention. What could a company such as IDI do under those circumstances?

[C]   Actions to Vacate International Arbitration Awards

The New York Convention does not specify the circumstances under which courts may vacate arbitration awards (as opposed to declining to enforce them). The cases in this section address the proper court for such an action, the grounds on which an international arbitration award can be vacated, as well as the consequences of a successful action to vacate.

KARAHA BODAS CO. v. PERUSAHAAN PERTAMBANGAN MINYAK DAN GAS BUMI NEGARA
United States Court of Appeals for the Fifth Circuit
364 F.3d 274 (2004)

ROSENTHAL, DISTRICT JUDGE:

. . . This appeal arises from an arbitral award (the "Award") made in Geneva, Switzerland, involving contracts negotiated and allegedly breached in Indonesia. The Award imposed liability and damages against Perusahaan Pertambangan Minyak Dan Gas Bumi Negara ("Pertamina"), which is owned by the government of Indonesia, in favor of Karaha Bodas Company, L.L.C.("KBC"), a Cayman Islands company. KBC filed this suit in the federal district court in Texas to enforce the Award under the United National Convention on the Recognition and Enforcement of Foreign Arbitral Awards (the "New York Convention"), and filed enforcement actions in Hong Kong and Canada as well. While those enforcement proceedings were pending, Pertamina appealed the Award in the Swiss courts, seeking annulment. When that effort failed, and after the Texas district court granted summary judgment enforcing the Award, Pertamina obtained an order from an Indonesian court annulling the Award.

Pertamina appealed to this court. During the appeal, Pertamina filed in the district court a motion to set aside the judgment under Federal Rule of Civil Procedure . . . 60(b)(5), based on the Indonesian court's decision annulling the arbitration Award. This court remanded to the district court for consideration of Pertamina's Rule 60(b) motion. On remand, the district court denied Pertamina's Rule 60(b) motion. This appeal consolidates Pertamina's challenges to the grant of summary judgment and to the denial of the Rule 60(b) motion.

We reject Pertamina's argument that the Indonesian court's order annulling the Award bars its enforcement under the New York Convention; this argument is inconsistent with the arbitration agreements Pertamina signed and with its earlier position that Switzerland, the neutral forum the parties selected, had exclusive jurisdiction over an annulment proceeding. . . .

. . .

A. The New York Convention

The New York Convention provides a carefully structured framework for the review and enforcement of international arbitral awards. Only a court in a country with primary jurisdiction over an arbitral award may annul that award. Courts in other countries have secondary jurisdiction; a court in a country with secondary jurisdiction is limited to deciding whether the award may be enforced in that country. The Convention "mandates very different regimes for the review of arbitral awards (1) in the [countries] in which, or under the law of which, the award was made, and (2) in other [countries] where recognition and enforcement are sought." Under the Convention, "the country in which, or under the [arbitration] law of which, [an] award was made" is said to have primary jurisdiction over the arbitration award. All other signatory states are secondary jurisdictions, in which parties can only contest whether that state should enforce the arbitral award. It is clear that the district court had secondary jurisdiction and considered only whether to enforce the Award in the United States.

Article V enumerates specific grounds on which a court with secondary jurisdiction may refuse enforcement. In contrast to the limited authority of secondary-jurisdiction courts to review an arbitral award, courts of primary jurisdiction, usually the courts of the country of the arbitral situs, have much broader discretion to set aside an award. While courts of a primary jurisdiction country may apply their own domestic law in evaluating a request to annul or set aside an arbitral award, courts in countries of secondary jurisdiction may refuse enforcement only on the grounds specified in Article V.

. . .

B. The Choice-of-Law Issues

In [their contracts], the parties stipulated that "the site of the arbitration shall be Geneva." The Tribunal concluded that under the arbitration agreements, Swiss procedural law applied as the law of the arbitral forum. From 1998 to April 2002, Pertamina consistently and repeatedly took the position before the Tribunal, the Swiss courts, and the United States district court, that Swiss procedural law applied to the arbitration. In April 2002, after the Swiss court had rejected Pertamina's annulment proceeding and the district court had held the Award enforceable in the United States, Pertamina moved in the district court for a stay of the Award pending the outcome of the annulment proceeding Pertamina had filed in Indonesia. For the first time, Pertamina raised in the district court the argument that Indonesian, not Swiss, procedural law had applied to the arbitration. Pertamina took this position in the district court as part of its argument that Indonesia had primary jurisdiction over the Award and therefore had the authority to set it aside rather than merely decline to enforce it.

Article V(1)(e) of the Convention provides that a court of secondary jurisdiction may refuse to enforce an arbitral award if it "has been set aside or suspended by a competent authority of the country in which, or under the law of which, that award was made." Courts have held that the language, " 'the competent authority of the country . . . under the law of which, that award was made' refers exclusively to procedural and not substantive law, and more precisely, to the regimen or scheme of arbitral procedural law under which the arbitration was conducted, and not the substantive law . . . applied in the case." In this appeal, Pertamina and the Republic of Indonesia (the "Republic"), as amicus, argue that the Tribunal and the district court erred in finding that Swiss procedural law, rather than Indonesian procedural law, applied. Pertamina and the Republic argue that in the arbitration agreements, the parties chose Indonesian procedural, as well as substantive, law to govern the arbitration. Pertamina and the Republic assert that, as a result: (1) the arbitration must be examined for compliance with Indonesian procedural law; and (2) the Indonesian court had primary jurisdiction to annul the Award, providing a defense to enforcement in the United States. KBC responds that the Tribunal properly interpreted the parties' contracts in deciding that Swiss procedural law applied and the district court properly applied the New York Convention in affirming that decision. This court agrees with KBC.

Under the New York Convention, the rulings of the Tribunal interpreting the parties' contract are entitled to deference. Unless the Tribunal manifestly disregarded the parties' agreement or the law, there is no basis to set aside the determination that Swiss procedural law applied. The parties' arbitration agreements specified that the site of the arbitration was Geneva, Switzerland and that the arbitration would proceed under the UNCITRAL rules. Those rules specify that the "arbitral tribunal shall apply the law designated by the parties as applicable to the substance of the dispute." It is undisputed that the parties specified that Indonesian substantive law would apply. It is also undisputed that the contracts specified the site of the arbitration as Switzerland. The contracts did not otherwise expressly identify the procedural law that would apply to the arbitration. The parties did refer to certain Indonesian Civil Procedure Rules in the contracts. Pertamina and the Republic argue that these references evidence an intent that while Switzerland would be the place of the arbitration, Indonesian procedural law would apply as the lex arbitri.

Under the New York Convention, an agreement specifying the place of the arbitration creates a presumption that the procedural law of that place applies to the arbitration. Authorities on international arbitration describe an agreement providing that one country will be the site of the arbitration but the proceedings will be held under the arbitration law of another country by terms such as "exceptional"; "almost unknown"; a "purely academic invention"; "almost never used in practice"; a possibility "more theoretical than real"; and a "once-in-a-blue-moon set of circumstances." Commentators note that such an agreement would be complex, inconvenient, and inconsistent with the selection of a neutral forum as the arbitral forum.

In [their contracts], the parties expressly agreed that Switzerland would be the site for the arbitration. This agreement presumptively selected Swiss procedural law to apply to the arbitration. There is no express agreement in the [contracts] that Indonesia would be the country "under the law of which" the arbitration was to be conducted and the Award was to be made. The Tribunal recognized the parties' selection of Switzerland by issuing the Award as "made in Geneva." In selecting Switzerland as the site of the arbitration, the parties were not choosing a physical place for the arbitration to occur, but rather the place where the award would be "made." Under Article 16(1) of the UNCITRAL rules, the "place" designated for an arbitration is the legal rather than physical location of the forum. The arbitration proceeding in this case physically occurred in Paris, but the Award was "made in" Geneva, the place of the arbitration in the legal sense and the presumptive source of the applicable procedural law.

The references in the contracts to certain Indonesian civil procedure rules do not rebut the strong presumption that Swiss procedural law applied to the arbitration.[41]

---

[41] Robert N. Hornick, one of the authorities on international arbitration and Indonesian law who submitted an affidavit and report in the district court, provided an explanation for the references to the Indonesian laws in the arbitration clauses unrelated to any intent to designate Indonesia as the country

These references fall far short of an express designation of Indonesian procedural law necessary to rebut the strong presumption that designating the place of the arbitration also designates the law under which the award is made.

As the district court, another panel of this court, and the Hong Kong Court of First Instance have all recognized, Pertamina's previous arguments that Swiss arbitral law applied strongly evidence the parties' contractual intent. Pertamina represented to the Tribunal that Swiss procedural law applied. . . . Pertamina at no point argued to the Tribunal that Indonesian procedural law applied. Pertamina initially sought to set aside the Award in a Swiss court. Pertamina asked the Texas district court to stay its enforcement proceeding until Pertamina's appeal in Switzerland was resolved. In making this argument, Pertamina stated that "the arbitration . . . was conducted according to the laws of Switzerland, and the Swiss court is empowered to vacate an award rendered in Switzerland. . . . KBC is asking this Court to act prematurely to confirm an award that might be overturned in the country whose law governed the arbitration."

The Tribunal's decision that Swiss arbitral law applied does not make the Award unenforceable. The combination of the parties' selection of Switzerland as the site of the arbitration; the failure clearly or expressly to choose Indonesian arbitral law in their agreements, as required to select arbitral law other than that of the place of the arbitration; and the clear evidence provided by the parties' own conduct that they intended Swiss law to apply to the arbitration, amply supports the district court's determination that the Tribunal properly applied Swiss procedural law.

. . .

F. The Effect of the Indonesian Court's Annulment of the Arbitral Award

Pertamina filed an annulment action in the Central District Court of Jakarta, Indonesia in March 2002. That court annulled the Award on August 27, 2002. Pertamina now contends that the Indonesian court's annulment is a defense to enforcement under the New York Convention. KBC responds that Indonesia cannot be a proper forum for annulment because Switzerland is the country of primary jurisdiction.

Pertamina argues that the New York Convention permits more than one country to have primary jurisdiction over an arbitration award. Pertamina contends that the Convention's language permitting annulment by a court in "the country in which, or under the law of which, that award was made" allows for two potential primary jurisdiction countries — the country who hosted the arbitration proceeding, and the country whose arbitral procedural law governed that proceeding. Using this reasoning, Pertamina suggests that both Switzerland (the host country) and Indonesia (the country of governing law) have primary jurisdiction over the arbitration in this case.

---

under the law of which the Award would be made. Hornick explained that each article of Indonesian law cited in the contracts imposes a requirement inconsistent with the contemplated arbitration. These articles could have been invoked to oppose later enforcement of the Award in Indonesia unless waived. By waiving in advance provisions that could later be invoked to block enforcement of the Award in an Indonesian court, the parties facilitated future enforcement efforts in Indonesia.

Pertamina correctly observes that the Convention provides two tests for determining which country has primary jurisdiction over an arbitration award: a country in which an award is made, and a country under the law of which an award is made. The New York Convention suggests the potential for more than one country of primary jurisdiction. Courts and scholars have noted as much. . . .

Although an arbitration agreement may make more than one country eligible for primary jurisdiction under the New York Convention, the predominant view is that the Convention permits only one in any given case. "Many commentators and foreign courts have concluded that an action to set aside an award can be brought only under the domestic law of the arbitral forum." Pertamina's expert on international arbitration filed a report in the district court, stating that "there can be only one country in which the courts have jurisdiction over an annulment." In its motion to the district court to set aside judgment under Rule 60(b), Pertamina conceded that "[a] primary jurisdiction has exclusive authority to nullify an award on the basis of its own arbitration law." Such "exclusive" primary jurisdiction in the courts of a single country is consistent with the New York Convention's purpose; facilitates the "orderliness and predictability" necessary to international commercial agreements; and implements the parties' choice of a neutral forum.

In this case, both of the New York Convention criteria for the country with primary jurisdiction point to Switzerland — and only to Switzerland. The Award was made in Switzerland and was made under Swiss procedural law. The parties' arbitration agreement designated Switzerland as the site for the arbitration. This designation presumptively designated Swiss procedural law as the *lex arbitri*, in the absence of any express statement making another country's procedural law applicable.

Pertamina's own conduct during and after the arbitration evidences its intent to have Swiss procedural law apply and to have Switzerland be the country of primary jurisdiction over the Award. During the arbitration, Pertamina asserted that Swiss procedural law applied. When it lost the arbitration, Pertamina asked the Swiss court to set aside the Award, acknowledging that the Swiss courts had primary jurisdiction. While that appeal was pending, Pertamina urged the district court in the enforcement proceeding that the Swiss court had exclusive primary jurisdiction — until the Swiss courts rejected Pertamina's appeal.

Under the New York Convention, the parties' arbitration agreement, and this record, Switzerland had primary jurisdiction over the Award. Because Indonesia did not have primary jurisdiction to set aside the Award, this court affirms the district court's conclusion that the Indonesian court's annulment ruling is not a defense to enforcement under the New York Convention.

. . .

Pertamina's challenges to the district court's decision affirming the Award are without merit. The summary judgment enforcing the Award is AFFIRMED.

NOTES

1.   The court in *Karaha Bodas* holds that an action to vacate an international arbitration award can be brought only in the arbitral seat, or in another country if the parties agreed that the other country's arbitration law governed the proceeding. *See also* Restatement (Third) of the U.S. Law of International Commercial Arbitration § 4-2. By comparison, an action to enforce the award can be brought in any court with jurisdiction. Indeed, actions to enforce an award may be brought in multiple jurisdictions, depending on where assets are located. Why do you think the losing party in an arbitration might prefer to bring an action to vacate the award rather than simply resisting enforcement of the award?

2.   Why should the arbitral seat (or the country whose arbitration law applies) have the authority to vacate the arbitration award? In *Karaha Bodas*, for example, one party was from the Cayman Islands, while the other was from Indonesia. The parties chose Switzerland as the seat, at least in part, because it was a neutral site. Given that, why should Swiss courts have the authority to vacate the arbitral award? Some commentators have advocated the "delocalization" of arbitration awards, freeing them from oversight by the arbitral seat: "the award, once rendered, would be cast adrift, its effects to be controlled by no other authority than its (unvarying) contractual foundation and the (varying) requirements of the particular jurisdictions in which it may be sought to be relied on." Jan Paulsson, *Arbitration Unbound: Award Detached from the Law of Its Country of Origin*, 30 INT'L & COMP. L.Q. 358, 358 (1981); *see also* Jan Paulsson, *Delocalisation of International Commercial Arbitration: When and Why It Matters*, 32 INT'L & COMP. L.Q. 53 (1983). We will revisit this issue shortly in connection with the *Chromalloy* case.

3.   As the court notes, it is rare for parties to choose the arbitration law of a country other than the arbitral seat to govern the proceeding. More commonly, for the convenience of the parties, some of the arbitral hearings might be held in locations other than the seat. Article 13(2) of the International Arbitration Rules of the AAA, for example, provides that "[t]he tribunal may hold conferences or hear witnesses or inspect property or documents at any place it deems appropriate."

4.   The Fifth Circuit's opinion in *Karaha Bodas* was another step in a heated battle between KBC and Pertamina over enforcement of the award in the United States. Michael D. Goldhaber of the *American Lawyer* magazine describes some earlier phases of that battle as follows:

> In November 2001 Judge Nancy Atlas of the U.S. district court in Houston confirmed the arbitral award, citing the narrow scope allowed courts in reviewing arbitrators.

> Tensions between the U.S. and Indonesian courts rose quickly. In mid-March 2002 Pertamina filed an action in Central District Court in Jakarta to enjoin enforcement of the award on public policy grounds. Seeing this as an end-run on the arbitral system, Judge Atlas ordered Pertamina to suspend its Jakarta suit. Three days later, the Jakarta court defiantly enjoined KBC against enforcing the arbitral award, and assessed a $500,000 penalty for each day that KBC pressed forward with its effort to collect. The Texas court held Pertamina in contempt the following day.

See Michael D. Goldhaber, *Arbitral Terrorism*, AM. LAWYER: FOCUS EUROPE (Summer 2003). On appeal, the Fifth Circuit vacated the district court's injunction against Pertamina as well as its contempt holding. The court of appeals explained:

> Although Indonesia has already purported to annul the Award, such annulment in no way affects the authority of the district court (or this court) to enforce the Award in the United States — which is, after all, the principal task of a U.S. court under the [New York] Convention. And, the Award can be enforced here with or without the district court's injunction against Pertamina. Similarly, other enforcement jurisdictions will be forced independently to weigh the Indonesian annulment with or without awareness of a U.S. court's injunction. Inasmuch as the Convention provides for multiple proceedings and a more limited role for enforcement jurisdictions, Pertamina's actions in Indonesia, even if spurious, are less vexatious and oppressive than they would be outside of this treaty structure. Finally, given the absence of a practical, positive effect that any injunction could have, more weighty considerations of comity dictate that the better course for U.S. courts to follow is to avoid the appearance of reaching out to interfere with the judicial proceedings in another country and to avoid stepping too far outside its limited role under the Convention.

Karaha Bodas Co. v. Perusahaan Pertambangan Minyak Dan Gas Bumi Negara, 335 F.3d 357, 374 (5th Cir. 2003). Do actions like those of the Indonesian court jeopardize the international arbitration system? Or are they necessary to preserve the national sovereignty of developing nations? Are they "arbitral terrorism" or "fair play"? *See* Goldhaber, *supra*.

In the United States, what are the grounds on which an international arbitration award can be vacated?

YUSUF AHMED ALGHANIM & SONS, W.L.L. v. TOYS "R" US, INC.
United States Court of Appeals for the Second Circuit
126 F.3d 15 (1997)

MINER, CIRCUIT JUDGE.

Appeal from a judgment entered in the United States District Court for the Southern District of New York . . . denying respondents' cross-motion to vacate or modify an arbitration award and granting the petition to confirm the award. . . .

For the reasons that follow, we affirm.

BACKGROUND

In November of 1982, respondent-appellant Toys "R" Us, Inc. . . . and petitioner-appellee Yusuf Ahmed Alghanim & Sons, W.L.L. ("Alghanim"), a privately owned Kuwaiti business, entered into a License and Technical Assistance

Agreement (the "agreement") and a Supply Agreement. Through the agreement, Toys "R" Us granted Alghanim a limited right to open Toys "R" Us stores and use its trademarks in Kuwait and 13 other countries located in and around the Middle East (the "territory"). Toys "R" Us further agreed to supply Alghanim with its technology, expertise and assistance in the toy business.

From 1982 to the December 1993 commencement of the arbitration giving rise to this appeal, Alghanim opened four toy stores, all in Kuwait. . . . It is uncontested that Alghanim's stores lost some $6.65 million over the 11-year period from 1982 to 1993, and turned a profit only in one year of this period.

. . .

On July 20, 1992, Toys "R" Us purported to exercise its right to terminate the agreement, sending Alghanim a notice of non-renewal stating that the agreement would terminate on January 31, 1993. Alghanim responded on July 30, 1992, stating that because its most recently opened toy store had opened on January 16, 1988, the initial term of the agreement ended on January 16, 1993. Alghanim asserted that Toys "R" Us's notice of non-renewal was four days late in providing notice six months before the end of the initial period. According to Alghanim, under the termination provision of the agreement, Toys "R" Us's failure to provide notice more than six months before the fifth year after the opening of the most recent store automatically extended the term of the agreement for an additional two years, until January 16, 1995.

. . .

Through the balance of 1992 and 1993, the parties unsuccessfully attempted to renegotiate the agreement or devise a new arrangement. . . .

. . .

On December 20, 1993, Toys "R" Us invoked the dispute-resolution mechanism in the agreement, initiating an arbitration before the American Arbitration Association. Toys "R" Us sought a declaration that the agreement was terminated on December 31, 1993. Alghanim responded by counterclaiming for breach of contract.

On May 4, 1994, the arbitrator denied Toys "R" Us's request for declaratory judgment. The arbitrator found that, under the termination provisions of the agreement, Alghanim had the absolute right to open toy stores, even after being given notice of termination, as long as the last toy store was opened within five years. The parties then engaged in substantial document and expert discovery, motion practice, and a 29-day evidentiary hearing on Alghanim's counterclaims.

On July 11, 1996, the arbitrator awarded Alghanim $46.44 million for lost profits under the agreement, plus 9 percent interest to accrue from December 31, 1994. The arbitrator's findings and legal conclusions were set forth in a 47-page opinion.

Alghanim petitioned the district court to confirm the award under the Convention on the Recognition and Enforcement of Foreign Arbitral Awards of June 10, 1958 ("Convention"). Toys "R" Us cross-moved to vacate or modify the award under the Federal Arbitration Act ("FAA"), arguing that the award was clearly irrational, in manifest disregard of the law, and in manifest disregard of the terms of the agreement. The district court concluded that "[t]he Convention and the FAA afford overlapping coverage, and the fact that a petition to confirm is brought under the Convention does not foreclose a cross-motion to vacate under the FAA, and the Court will consider [Toys "R" Us's] cross-motion under the standards of the FAA." By judgment entered December 20, 1996, the district court confirmed the award, finding Toys "R" Us's objections to the award to be without merit. This appeal followed.

DISCUSSION

I. Availability of the FAA's Grounds for Relief in Confirmation Under the Convention

Toys "R" Us argues that the district court correctly determined that the provisions of the FAA apply to its cross-motion to vacate or modify the arbitral award. . . . We agree that the FAA governs Toys "R" Us's cross-motion.

A. Applicability of the Convention

. . .

The Convention's applicability in this case is clear. The dispute giving rise to this appeal involved two nondomestic parties and one United States corporation, and principally involved conduct and contract performance in the Middle East. Thus, we consider the arbitral award leading to this action a non-domestic award and thus within the scope of the Convention.

B. Authority Under the Convention to Set Aside an Award Under Domestic Arbitral Law

Toys "R" Us argues that the district court properly found that it had the authority under the Convention to apply the FAA's implied grounds for setting aside the award. We agree.

Under the Convention, the district court's role in reviewing a foreign arbitral award is strictly limited: "The court shall confirm the award unless it finds one of the grounds for refusal or deferral of recognition or enforcement of the award specified in the said Convention." 9 U.S.C. § 207. Under Article V of the Convention, the grounds for refusing to recognize or enforce an arbitral award are:

[The court here quoted the text of Article V.]

. . . These seven grounds are the only grounds explicitly provided under the Convention.

In determining the availability of the FAA's implied grounds for setting aside, the text of the Convention leaves us with two questions: (1) whether, in addition to the Convention's express grounds for refusal, other grounds can be read into the Convention by implication, much as American courts have read implied grounds for relief into the FAA, and (2) whether, under Article V(1)(e), the courts of the United

States are authorized to apply United States procedural arbitral law, i.e., the FAA, to nondomestic awards rendered in the United States. We answer the first question in the negative and the second in the affirmative.

1. Availability Under the Convention of Implied Grounds for Refusal

We have held that the FAA and the Convention have "overlapping coverage" to the extent that they do not conflict. However, by that same token, to the extent that the Convention prescribes the exclusive grounds for relief from an award under the Convention, that application of the FAA's implied grounds would be in conflict, and is thus precluded.

In *Parsons & Whittemore Overseas Co. v. Societe Generale de L'Industrie du Papier (Rakta)*, we declined to decide whether the implied defense of "manifest disregard" applies under the Convention, having decided that even if it did, appellant's claim would fail. . . .

There is now considerable caselaw holding that, in an action to confirm an award rendered in, or under the law of, a foreign jurisdiction, the grounds for relief enumerated in Article V of the Convention are the only grounds available for setting aside an arbitral award. This conclusion is consistent with the Convention's pro-enforcement bias. We join these courts in declining to read into the Convention the FAA's implied defenses to confirmation of an arbitral award.

2. Nondomestic Award Rendered in the United States

Although Article V provides the exclusive grounds for refusing confirmation under the Convention, one of those exclusive grounds is where "[t]he award . . . has been set aside or suspended by a competent authority of the country in which, or under the law of which, that award was made." Convention art. V(1)(e). Those courts holding that implied defenses were inapplicable under the Convention did so in the context of petitions to confirm awards rendered abroad. These courts were not presented with the question whether Article V(1)(e) authorizes an action to set aside an arbitral award under the domestic law of the state in which, or under which, the award was rendered. We, however, are faced head-on with that question in the case before us, because the arbitral award in this case was rendered in the United States, and both confirmation and vacatur were then sought in the United States.

We read Article V(1)(e) of the Convention to allow a court in the country under whose law the arbitration was conducted to apply domestic arbitral law, in this case the FAA, to a motion to set aside or vacate that arbitral award. . . .

. . .

Our conclusion also is consistent with the reasoning of courts that have refused to apply non-Convention grounds for relief where awards were rendered outside the United States. . . . [I]n [International Standard Electric Corp. v. Bridas Sociedad Anonima Petrolera, 745 F. Supp. 172 (S.D.N.Y 1990)], the district court decided that only the state under whose procedural law the arbitration was conducted has jurisdiction under Article V(1)(e) to vacate the award, whereas on a petition for confirmation made in any other state, only the defenses to confirmation listed in

Article V of the Convention are available.

This interpretation of Article V(1)(e) also finds support in the scholarly work of commentators on the Convention and in the judicial decisions of our sister signatories to the Convention. There appears to be no dispute among these authorities that an action to set aside an international arbitral award, as contemplated by Article V(1)(e), is controlled by the domestic law of the rendering state. . . .

. . .

There is no indication in the Convention of any intention to deprive the rendering state of its supervisory authority over an arbitral award, including its authority to set aside that award under domestic law. . . .

. . .

. . . [U]nder the Convention, the power and authority of the local courts of the rendering state remain of paramount importance. "What the Convention did not do . . . was provide any international mechanism to insure the validity of the award where rendered. This was left to the provisions of local law. The Convention provides no restraint whatsoever on the control functions of local courts at the seat of arbitration." . . . From the plain language and history of the Convention, it is thus apparent that a party may seek to vacate or set aside an award in the state in which, or under the law of which, the award is rendered. Moreover, the language and history of the Convention make it clear that such a motion is to be governed by domestic law of the rendering state, despite the fact that the award is nondomestic within the meaning of the Convention as we have interpreted it. . . .

In sum, we conclude that the Convention mandates very different regimes for the review of arbitral awards (1) in the state in which, or under the law of which, the award was made, and (2) in other states where recognition and enforcement are sought. The Convention specifically contemplates that the state in which, or under the law of which, the award is made, will be free to set aside or modify an award in accordance with its domestic arbitral law and its full panoply of express and implied grounds for relief. However, the Convention is equally clear that when an action for enforcement is brought in a foreign state, the state may refuse to enforce the award only on the grounds explicitly set forth in Article V of the Convention.

II. Application of FAA Grounds for Relief

Having determined that the FAA does govern Toys "R" Us's cross-motion to vacate, our application of the FAA's implied grounds for vacatur is swift. . . .

. . .

. . . [A]wards may be vacated, see 9 U.S.C. § 10, or modified, see id. § 11, in the limited circumstances where the arbitrator's award is in manifest disregard of the terms of the agreement, or where the award is in "manifest disregard of the law." We find that neither of these implied grounds is met in the present case.

. . .

CONCLUSION

For the foregoing reasons, the judgment of the district court is affirmed.

NOTE

The circuits are divided on whether the FAA § 10 grounds or the grounds in Article V of the New York Convention apply in actions to vacate Convention awards made in the United States. The majority approach is that taken by the Second Circuit in *Toys "R" Us.* By comparison, the Restatement adopts the minority approach, concluding, based on its reading of FAA § 207, that the Article V grounds apply. § 4-11(a). For a detailed analysis of the issue, see Restatement (Third) of the U.S. of International Commercial § 4-11, rptrs. note to cmt. a. Under the Restatement, the practical effect of the issue is minimal (if not nonexistent), because as noted above it construes the two sets of grounds as essentially the same. *See, e.g., id.* § 4-22(b).

PROBLEM 7.14

You are general counsel to Adair Inc., an American company that is involved in two ongoing international arbitrations. In one proceeding your client is the claimant, seeking $1.5 million in damages for breach of contract against Bombay Mining, an Indian company. The arbitration is being held in India. In the other, your client is the respondent, defending against a claim by Balmoral Chemicals (a British company) seeking almost as much ($1.2 million) for breach of a different contract. That arbitration is taking place in New York. The contract between Adair and Balmoral provides that the law of England is the governing law. By some strange twist of fate, both awards are issued and served on your client on the same day.

In *Adair Ltd. v. Bombay Mining*, your client prevailed, receiving an award of $1 million. Adair's president, Ronald Adair, already has been in contact with Bombay, which made clear to him that it will not come up with the money voluntarily. Adair tells you, however, that Bombay has significant assets in Wyoming from which he thinks the company should be able to collect the award.

The result in *Balmoral Chemicals v. Adair Ltd.* was not so favorable, however. The award was in favor of Balmoral in the amount of $900,000. Adair is convinced that the *Balmoral* award is a travesty of justice, and wants you immediately to go about getting the award thrown out.

(a) How do you proceed in each case?

(b) Adair wants to know the possible grounds on which you might (depending of course on the underlying facts) have the award in *Balmoral* thrown out. What do you tell him? How do those grounds compare to the grounds on which Bombay might rely to defend against any action you bring against it?

If a court in the arbitral seat vacates the award, the award is no longer enforceable in the seat itself. But under the arbitration law of France, French courts may nonetheless enforce such an award if it meets French standards for enforceability. *See, e.g., Polish Ocean Line v. Jolasry* (Cour de cassation 1993), *in* XIX Y.B. Comm. Arb. 662, 663 (1994) ("a French court may not deny an application for leave to enforce an arbitral award which was set aside or suspended by a competent authority in the country in which the award was rendered, if the grounds for opposing enforcement, although mentioned in Art. V(1)(e) of the 1958 New York Convention, are not among the grounds specified in Art. 1502 NCCP"). As one of the leading commentators on the New York Convention has stated, "[i]f an award is set aside in the country of origin, a party still can try its luck in France." Albert Jan van den Berg, *Consolidated Commentary, in* XIX Y.B. Comm. Arb. 475, 592 (1994). At least one American case has reached a similar result.

IN RE CHROMALLOY AEROSERVICES
United States District Court for the District of Columbia
939 F. Supp. 907 (1996)

June L. Green, District Judge.

I. Introduction

This matter is before the Court on the Petition of Chromalloy Aeroservices, Inc., ("CAS") to Confirm an Arbitral Award, and a Motion to Dismiss that Petition filed by the Arab Republic of Egypt ("Egypt"), the defendant in the arbitration. This is a case of first impression. The Court GRANTS Chromalloy Aeroservices' Petition to Recognize and Enforce the Arbitral Award, and **DENIES** Egypt's Motion to Dismiss, because the arbitral award in question is valid, and because Egypt's arguments against enforcement are insufficient to allow this Court to disturb the award.

II. Background

This case involves a military procurement contract between a U.S. corporation, Chromalloy Aeroservices, Inc., and the Air Force of the Arab Republic of Egypt.

On June 16, 1988, Egypt and CAS entered into a contract under which CAS agreed to provide parts, maintenance, and repair for helicopters belonging to the Egyptian Air Force. On December 2, 1991, Egypt terminated the contract by notifying CAS representatives in Egypt. On December 4, 1991, Egypt notified CAS headquarters in Texas of the termination. On December 15, 1991, CAS notified Egypt that it rejected the cancellation of the contract "and commenced arbitration proceedings on the basis of the arbitration clause contained in Article XII and Appendix E of the Contract." Egypt then drew down CAS' letters of guarantee in an amount totaling some $11,475,968.

On February 23, 1992, the parties began appointing arbitrators, and shortly thereafter, commenced a lengthy arbitration. On August 24, 1994, the arbitral panel ordered Egypt to pay to CAS the sums of $272,900 plus 5 percent interest from July 15, 1991 (interest accruing until the date of payment), and $16,940,958 plus 5 percent interest from December 15, 1991 (interest accruing until the date of payment). The panel also ordered CAS to pay to Egypt the sum of 606,920 pounds sterling, plus 5 percent interest from December 15, 1991 (interest accruing until the date of payment).

On October 28, 1994, CAS applied to this Court for enforcement of the award. On November 13, 1994, Egypt filed an appeal with the Egyptian Court of Appeal, seeking nullification of the award. On March 1, 1995, Egypt filed a motion with this Court to adjourn CAS's Petition to enforce the award. On April 4, 1995, the Egyptian Court of Appeal suspended the award, and on May 5, 1995, Egypt filed a Motion in this Court to Dismiss CAS's petition to enforce the award. On December 5, 1995, Egypt's Court of Appeal at Cairo issued an order nullifying the award. This Court held a hearing in the matter on December 12, 1995.

Egypt argues that this Court should deny CAS' Petition to Recognize and Enforce the Arbitral Award out of deference to its court. CAS argues that this Court should confirm the award because Egypt "does not present any serious argument that its court's nullification decision is consistent with the New York Convention or United States arbitration law."

III. Discussion

. . .

B. Chromalloy's Petition for Enforcement

A party seeking enforcement of a foreign arbitral award must apply for an order confirming the award within three years after the award is made. 9 U.S.C. § 207. The award in question was made on August 14, 1994. CAS filed a Petition to confirm the award with this Court on October 28, 1994, less than three months after the arbitral panel made the award. CAS's Petition includes a "duly certified copy" of the original award as required by Article IV(1)(a) of the Convention, translated by a duly sworn translator, as required by Article IV(2) of the Convention, as well as a duly certified copy of the original contract and arbitration clause, as required by Article IV(1)(b) of the Convention. CAS's Petition is properly before this Court.

1. The Standard under the Convention

This Court *must* grant CAS's Petition to Recognize and Enforce the arbitral "award unless it finds one of the grounds for refusal . . . of recognition or enforcement of the award specified in the . . . Convention." 9 U.S.C. § 207. Under the Convention, "Recognition and enforcement of the award *may* be refused" if Egypt furnishes to this Court "proof that . . . [t]he award has . . . been set aside . . . by a competent authority of the country in which, or under the law of which, that award was made." Convention, Article V(1) & V(1)(e) (emphasis added). In the present case, the award was made in Egypt, under the laws of Egypt, and has been nullified by the court designated by Egypt to review arbitral awards. Thus, the Court *may*, at its discretion, decline to enforce the award.

While Article V provides a discretionary standard, Article VII of the Convention *requires* that, "The provisions of the present Convention *shall not* . . . deprive any interested party of any right he may have to avail himself of an arbitral award in the manner and to the extent allowed by the law . . . of the count[r]y where such award is sought to be relied upon." ([E]mphasis added). In other words, under the Convention, CAS maintains all rights to the enforcement of this Arbitral Award that it would have in the absence of the Convention. Accordingly, the Court finds that, if the Convention did not exist, the Federal Arbitration Act ("FAA") would provide CAS with a legitimate claim to enforcement of this arbitral award. . . .

2. Examination of the Award under 9 U.S.C. § 10

Under the laws of the United States, arbitration awards are presumed to be binding, and may only be vacated by a court under very limited circumstances. . . .

. . .

[T]he arbitrators in the present case made a procedural decision that allegedly led to a misapplication of substantive law. After considering Egypt's arguments that Egyptian administrative law should govern the contract, the majority of the arbitral panel held that it did not matter which substantive law they applied — civil or administrative. At worst, this decision constitutes a mistake of law, and thus is not subject to review by this Court.

In the United States, "[W]e are well past the time when judicial suspicion of the desirability of arbitration and of the competence of arbitral tribunals inhibited the development of arbitration as an alternative means of dispute resolution." *Mitsubishi Motors Corp. v. Soler Chrysler-Plymouth, Inc.* In Egypt, however, "[I]t is established that arbitration is an exceptional means for resolving disputes, requiring departure from the normal means of litigation before the courts, and the guarantees they afford." Egypt's complaint that, "[T]he Arbitral Award is null under Arbitration Law, . . . because it is not properly 'grounded' under Egyptian law," reflects this suspicious view of arbitration, and is precisely the type of technical argument that U.S. courts are not to entertain when reviewing an arbitral award.

The Court's analysis thus far has addressed the arbitral award, and, as a matter of U.S. law, the award is proper. The Court now considers the question of whether the decision of the Egyptian court should be recognized as a valid foreign judgment.

As the Court stated earlier, this is a case of first impression. There are no reported cases in which a court of the United States has faced a situation, under the Convention, in which the court of a foreign nation has nullified an otherwise valid arbitral award. This does not mean, however, that the Court is without guidance in this case. To the contrary, more than twenty years ago, in a case involving the enforcement of an arbitration clause under the FAA, the Supreme Court held that:

> An agreement to arbitrate before a specified tribunal is, in effect, a specialized kind of forum-selection clause. . . . The invalidation of such an agreement . . . would not only allow the respondent to repudiate its solemn promise but would, as well, reflect a parochial concept that all disputes must be resolved under our laws and in our courts.

Scherk v. Alberto-Culver Co.

. . .

. . . The Court finds this argument equally persuasive in the present case, where Egypt seeks to repudiate its solemn promise to abide by the results of the arbitration.

C. The Decision of Egypt's Court of Appeal

1. The Contract

"The arbitration agreement is a contract and the court will not rewrite it for the parties." The Court "begin[s] with the 'cardinal principle of contract construction: that a document should be read to give effect to all its provisions and to render them consistent with each other.' " . . . Appendix E to the contract defines the "Applicable Law Court of Arbitration." The clause reads, in relevant part:

> It is . . . understood that both parties have irrevocably agreed to apply Egypt (sic) Laws and to choose Cairo as seat of the court of arbitration.
>
> . . .
>
> The decision of the said court shall be final and binding and cannot be made subject to any appeal or other recourse.

This Court may not assume that the parties intended these two sentences to contradict one another, and must preserve the meaning of both if possible. Egypt argues that the first quoted sentence supersedes the second, and allows an appeal to an Egyptian court. Such an interpretation, however, would vitiate the second sentence, and would ignore the plain language on the face of the contract. The Court concludes that the first sentence defines choice of law and choice of forum for the hearings of the arbitral panel. The Court further concludes that the second quoted sentence indicates the clear intent of the parties that any arbitration of a dispute arising under the contract is not to be appealed to any court. This interpretation, unlike that offered by Egypt, preserves the meaning of both sentences in a manner that is consistent with the plain language of the contract. The position of the latter sentence as the seventh and final paragraph, just before the signatures, lends credence to the view that this sentence is the final word on the arbitration question. In other words, the parties agreed to apply Egyptian Law to the arbitration, but, more important, they agreed that the arbitration ends with the decision of the arbitral panel.

2. The Decision of the Egyptian Court of Appeal

The Court has already found that the arbitral award is proper as a matter of U.S. law, and that the arbitration agreement between Egypt and CAS precluded an appeal in Egyptian courts. The Egyptian court has acted, however, and Egypt asks this Court to grant *res judicata* effect to that action.

The "requirements for enforcement of a foreign judgment . . . are that there be 'due citation' [*i.e.*, proper service of process] and that the original claim not violate U.S. public policy." The Court uses the term 'public policy' advisedly, with a full understanding that, "[J]udges have no license to impose their own brand of justice in determining applicable public policy." Correctly understood, "[P]ublic policy emanates [only] from clear statutory or case law, 'not from general considerations of supposed public interest.' "

The U.S. public policy in favor of final and binding arbitration of commercial disputes is unmistakable, and supported by treaty, by statute, and by case law. The Federal Arbitration Act "and the implementation of the Convention in the same year by amendment of the Federal Arbitration Act," demonstrate that there is an "emphatic federal policy in favor of arbitral dispute resolution," particularly "in the field of international commerce." *Mitsubishi v. Soler Chrysler-Plymouth.* A decision by this Court to recognize the decision of the Egyptian court would violate this clear U.S. public policy.

3. International Comity

"No nation is under an unremitting obligation to enforce foreign interests which are fundamentally prejudicial to those of the domestic forum." Laker Airways Ltd. v. Sabena, Belgian World Airlines, 731 F.2d 909, 937 (D.C. Cir. 1984). "[C]omity *never* obligates a national forum to ignore 'the rights of its own citizens or of other persons who are under the protection of its laws.' " *Id.* at 942 (emphasis added) (quoting Hilton v. Guyot, 159 U.S. 113, 164 (1895)). Egypt alleges that, "Comity is the chief doctrine of international law *requiring* U.S. courts to respect the decisions of competent foreign tribunals." However, comity does not and may not have the preclusive effect upon U.S. law that Egypt wishes this Court to create for it.

The Supreme Court's unanimous opinion in W.S. Kirkpatrick & Co., Inc. v. Environmental Tectonics Corp., Int'l, 493 U.S. 400, 408 (1990), defines the proper limitations of the "act of state doctrine" and, by implication, judicial comity as well. *Kirkpatrick* arose out of a dispute between two U.S. companies over a government construction project in Nigeria. Kirkpatrick, the losing bidder, sued Environmental Techtonics, ("ETC"), the winning bidder, alleging that ETC acquired the contract by bribing Nigerian officials in violation of U.S. law. ETC argued that the act of state doctrine precluded U.S. courts from hearing the case because to do so "would impugn or question the nobility of a foreign nation's motivations," and would "result in embarrassment to the sovereign or constitute interference in the conduct of [the] foreign policy of the United States." The Supreme Court rejected this argument:

> The short of the matter is this: Courts in the United States have the power, and ordinarily the obligation, to decide cases and controversies properly presented to them. The act of state doctrine does not establish an exception for cases and controversies that may embarrass foreign governments, but merely requires that, in the process of deciding, the acts of foreign sovereigns taken within their own jurisdictions shall be deemed valid. *That doctrine has no application to the present case because the validity of no foreign sovereign act is at issue.*

([E]mphasis added). Similarly, in the present case, the question is whether this Court should give res judicata effect to the decision of the Egyptian Court of Appeal, not whether that court properly decided the matter under Egyptian law.

Since the "act of state doctrine," as a whole, does not require U.S. courts to defer to a foreign sovereign on these facts, comity, which is but one of several "policies" that underlie the act of state "doctrine," does not require such deference either.

4. Choice of Law

Egypt argues that by choosing Egyptian law, and by choosing Cairo as the sight [sic] of the arbitration, CAS has for all time signed away its rights under the Convention and U.S. law. This argument is specious. When CAS agreed to the choice of law and choice of forum provisions, it waived its right to sue Egypt for breach of contract in the courts of the United States in favor of final and binding arbitration of such a dispute under the Convention. Having prevailed in the chosen forum, under the chosen law, CAS comes to this Court seeking recognition and enforcement of the award. The Convention was created for just this purpose. It is untenable to argue that by choosing arbitration under the Convention, CAS has waived rights specifically guaranteed by that same Convention.

5. Conflict between the Convention & the FAA

As a final matter, Egypt argues that, "Chromalloy's use of [A]rticle VII [to invoke the Federal Arbitration Act] contradicts the clear language of the Convention and would create an impermissible conflict under 9 U.S.C. § 208," by eliminating all consideration of Article V of the Convention. As the Court has explained, however, Article V provides a permissive standard, under which this Court *may* refuse to enforce an award. Article VII, on the other hand, mandates that this Court must consider CAS' claims under applicable U.S. law.

. . . Article VII does not eliminate all consideration of Article V; it merely requires that this Court protect any rights that CAS has under the domestic laws of the United States. There is no conflict between CAS' use of Article VII to invoke the FAA and the language of the Convention.

IV. Conclusion

The Court concludes that the award of the arbitral panel is valid as a matter of U.S. law. The Court further concludes that it need not grant *res judicata* effect to the decision of the Egyptian Court of Appeal at Cairo. Accordingly, the Court **GRANTS** Chromalloy Aeroservices' Petition to Recognize and Enforce the Arbitral Award, and **DENIES** Egypt's Motion to Dismiss that Petition.

NOTES

1. American courts have addressed the enforceability of vacated arbitration awards in several cases since *Chromalloy*. In Baker Marine (Nig.) Ltd. v. Chevron (Nig.) Ltd., 191 F.3d 194 (2d Cir. 1999), the Second Circuit affirmed a district court decision declining to enforce an arbitration award vacated in Nigeria, the arbitral seat. The court emphasized that the parties had agreed to arbitrate in Nigeria under Nigerian law and that "Baker Marine has made no contention that the

Nigerian courts acted contrary to Nigerian law." *Id.* at 197. It distinguished *Chromalloy* in a footnote:

> Unlike the petitioner in *Chromalloy*, Baker Marine is not a United States citizen, and it did not initially seek confirmation of the award in the United States. [Baker Marine initially sought to confirm the award in Nigeria.] Furthermore, Chevron . . . did not violate any promise in appealing the arbitration award within Nigeria. Recognition of the Nigerian judgment in this case does not conflict with United States policy.

Id. at 197 n.3. Subsequently, the United States District Court for the Southern District of New York followed *Baker Marine* in an attempt by an American citizen to enforce an award vacated in Italy. Spier v. Calzaturificio Tecnica, S.p.A., 71 F. Supp. 2d 279, *on reargument,* 77 F. Supp. 2d 405 (S.D.N.Y. 1999). The district court acknowledged that "[i]n some respects *Chromalloy* bears a superficial resemblance to the case at bar, since Spier is a United States citizen and seeks confirmation of the award in the United States." 71 F. Supp. 2d at 287. But, according to the court, *Baker Marine* found the "decisive circumstance" in *Chromalloy* to be "Egypt's repudiation of its contractual promise not to appeal an arbitral award." *Id.* Because no such repudiation occurred here, the *Spier* court refused to enforce the award.

Most recently, in 2007, the D.C. Circuit followed *Baker Marine* in refusing to enforce an arbitration award vacated in Colombia. Termorio S.A. E.S.P. v. Electranta S.P., 487 F.3d 928 (D.C. Cir. 2007). The court of appeals distinguished *Chromalloy* on the ground that in that case " 'an express contract provision was violated by pursuing an appeal to vacate the award,' " whereas in *Termorio* " 'Electranta preserved its objection that the panel was not proper or authorized by law, promptly raised it in the Colombian courts, and received a definitive ruling by the highest court on this question of law.' " *Id.* at 937 (quoting appellee's brief). The D.C. Circuit in *Termorio* expressly did "not decide whether the holding in *Chromalloy* is correct." *Id.* But — particularly given that *Chromalloy* was decided by the U.S. District Court for the District of Columbia — little may remain of its holding.

    2.   What is the significance of the Egyptian court judgment vacating the award in *Chromalloy*? Did the district court correctly decline to recognize that judgment? If the relevant United States public policy is one "in favor of final and binding arbitration of commercial disputes," when will a foreign court judgment vacating an award ever be consistent with that policy?

The Restatement provides that a U.S. court can enforce a Convention award vacated in the seat "if the judgment setting it aside is not entitled to recognition under the principles governing the recognition of judgments in the court where such relief is sought, or in other extraordinary circumstances." Restatement (Third) of the U.S. Law of International Commercial Arbitration § 4-16(a). Examples of such extraordinary circumstances include "if the set-aside court knowingly and egregiously departed from the rules governing set-aside in that jurisdiction" or "when other facts give rise to substantial and justifiable doubts about the integrity or independence of the foreign court with respect to the judgment in question." *Id.* § 4-16, cmt. d. Is the Restatement consistent with *Chromalloy*?

3. As for the contractual waiver of the right to appeal the award, one way to construe the Egyptian court's holding was that it concluded that the waiver was unenforceable. Why should American courts disregard such a holding, given that, as we will see in the next section, waivers of the right to appeal likely do not preclude court review of arbitration awards in the United States either? One commentator relies on *Chromalloy* and *Baker Marine* to argue that "no-appeal clauses in arbitration agreements, especially international ones, now have some prospect of enforceability in U.S. courts." David R. Foley, *Agreements Precluding Review of Awards: Are They Now Enforceable in U.S. Courts?*, MEALEY'S INT'L ARB. REP., May 2000. Do you agree?

4. *Chromalloy* has prompted extensive commentary, both supportive and critical. One prominent debate took place between Jan Paulsson and Albert Jan van den Berg. Paulsson took the position that "annulment of an award by the courts in the country where it was rendered should not be a bar to enforcement elsewhere unless the grounds are ones that are internationally recognized." Jan Paulsson, *Enforcing Arbitral Awards Notwithstanding a Local Standard Annulment (LSA)*, ICC INT'L CT. ARB. BULL., May 1998, at 14, 14. According to Paulsson, annulments based solely on local standards (which he calls "Local Standard Annulments" or "LSAs") would have effect only in the arbitral seat, a rule he then proceeds to defend against a variety of objections. *Id.* at 17–28. In response, van den Berg supported the "generally accepted rule . . . that if an award has been annulled . . . in the country of origin (usually the place of arbitration), it cannot be enforced in other countries." Albert Jan van den Berg, *Enforcement of Annulled Awards?*, ICC INT'L CT. ARB BULL., Nov. 1998, at 15, 15. Such a rule "concentrat[es] judicial control over the arbitral process at the place of arbitration," and gives greater consistency and more predictable results. *Id.* at 15, 19–20. For more of the extensive commentary about the issue presented in *Chromalloy*, see, *e.g.*, William W. Park, *Duty and Discretion in International Arbitration*, 93 AM. J. INT'L L. 805 (2000); Eric A. Schwartz, *A Comment on* Chromalloy: *Hilmarton, á l'américaine*, 14 J. INT'L ARB., June 1997, at 125; Gary H. Sampliner, *Enforcement of Nullified Foreign Arbitral Awards:* Chromalloy *Revisited*, J. INT'L ARB., Sept. 1997, at 141.

PROBLEM 7.15

Ronald Adair (President of Adair Inc. from Problem 7.14) stops by your office for a progress report. You have mixed news for him. You just found out minutes before that the court has vacated the *Balmoral* award for manifest disregard of the law (that's the good news). The bad news is that a court in India has just vacated the *Bombay Mining* award under Indian arbitration law, which permits de novo review of legal rulings by an arbitrator. The federal district court in Wyoming had suspended proceedings pending the outcome of the Indian case, and is soon to decide what to do.

Adair is pleased with the *Balmoral* news, although he asks if there is anything more to worry about on that front ("We've been doing a lot of work in France lately; is that a problem?"). He is quite troubled by the *Bombay* ruling, however, saying that he "thought we took care of that possibility by getting Bombay to waive its rights to appeal in the contract." The Indian court ruling, you tell him, holds that such an agreement cannot override the mandatory provisions of Indian arbitration law. Adair then asks you what to expect from the Wyoming federal court. Is there any chance, he asks, of getting that court simply to disregard the Indian court's ruling? What do you tell him?

§ 7.05 MODIFYING THE STANDARD OF REVIEW BY CONTRACT

This section examines the extent to which parties can modify by contract the grounds for court review of arbitration awards. Or to put the question another way, are the grounds on which courts can set aside arbitration awards mandatory rules, default rules, or some combination of the two?

United States courts have generally held (subject to the questions raised by the *Chromalloy* and *Termorio* cases above) that parties cannot by contract preclude courts from vacating an award when one of the statutory grounds for vacating the award is met. Thus, the parties cannot avoid judicial review of an award by providing (as arbitration rules commonly do) that "[a]ll awards shall be final and binding on the parties" or that the "parties also waive irrevocably their right to any form of appeal, review or recourse to any state court or other judicial authority, insofar as such waiver may be validly made." LCIA Arbitration Rules, art. 26.9. As the court stated in the *Iran Aircraft* case from § 6.10: "The terms 'final' and 'binding' [in arbitration agreements] merely reflect a contractual intent that the issues joined and resolved in the arbitration may not be tried de novo in any court"; the statutory grounds remain available to challenge the award. *See also* M&C Corp. v. Erwin Behr GmbH & Co., 87 F.3d 844 (6th Cir. 1996) (same); Restatement (Third) of the U.S. Law of International Commercial Arbitration § 4-24.

The international arbitration laws of some countries, by contrast, permit parties (under limited circumstances) to reduce the scope of judicial review by the country's courts. The Swiss international arbitration law, for example, provides that:

> If none of the parties have their domicile, their habitual residence, or a business establishment in Switzerland, they may, by an express statement in the arbitration agreement or by a subsequent written agreement, waive fully the action for annulment or they may limit it to one or several of the grounds listed in Art. 190(2).

Swiss Private International Law Act, art. 192 (Dec. 18, 1987), *in* 5 INT'L HANDBOOK ON COMMERCIAL ARBITRATION, *Switzerland*: at Annex II-5 (Mar. 2008). Article 1717.4 of the Belgian arbitration law is similar, and constitutes a retrenchment from the previous Belgian law, which precluded actions to vacate some international awards in Belgium even without an agreement to that effect by the parties. *See* Luc Demeyere, *1998 Amendments to Belgian Arbitration Law: An Overview*, 15 ARB. INT'L 295, 307–08 (1999) (explaining that previous law "was highly criticized and for some, including arbitration institutions, Belgium became a forum to be avoided"); *see also* Code of Civil Procedure, Book IV, Arbitration, art. 1522 (Jan. 13, 2011), *in* 2 INT'L HANDBOOK ON COMMERCIAL ARBITRATION, *France*, at Annex I-14 (May 2011) ("By way of a specific agreement the parties may, at any time, expressly waive their right to bring an action to set aside."). In each case, of course, the award could still be subject to scrutiny in an action to enforce the award wherever brought.

Although limited judicial review is touted as one of the advantages of arbitration, the finality of the award may increase the risk of an incorrect award. In litigation, if the trial court makes a mistake, the appellate court can correct it. In arbitration, an error of law or fact is not a ground on which a court can set aside an award. Are parties that are concerned about such a risk permitted to contract for a higher degree of court scrutiny than provided in the FAA?

HALL STREET ASSOCIATES, L.L.C. v. MATTEL, INC.
United States Supreme Court
552 U.S. 576 (2008)

JUSTICE SOUTER delivered the opinion of the Court.*

The Federal Arbitration Act (FAA or Act) provides for expedited judicial review to confirm, vacate, or modify arbitration awards. §§ 9-11. The question here is whether statutory grounds for prompt vacatur and modification may be supplemented by contract. We hold that the statutory grounds are exclusive.

I

This case began as a lease dispute between landlord, petitioner Hall Street Associates, L.L.C., and tenant, respondent Mattel, Inc. The property was used for many years as a manufacturing site, and the leases provided that the tenant would indemnify the landlord for any costs resulting from the failure of the tenant or its predecessor lessees to follow environmental laws while using the premises.

Tests of the property's well water in 1998 showed high levels of trichloroethylene (TCE), the apparent residue of manufacturing discharges by Mattel's predecessors between 1951 and 1980. . . .

After Mattel gave notice of intent to terminate the lease in 2001, Hall Street filed this suit, contesting Mattel's right to vacate on the date it gave, and claiming that the lease obliged Mattel to indemnify Hall Street for costs of cleaning up the TCE, among other things. Following a bench trial before the United States District Court for the District of Oregon, Mattel won on the termination issue, and after an unsuccessful try at mediating the indemnification claim, the parties proposed to submit to arbitration. The District Court was amenable, and the parties drew up an arbitration agreement, which the court approved and entered as an order. One paragraph of the agreement provided that

> "[t]he United States District Court for the District of Oregon may enter judgment upon any award, either by confirming the award or by vacating, modifying or correcting the award. The Court shall vacate, modify or correct any award: (i) where the arbitrator's findings of facts are not supported by substantial evidence, or (ii) where the arbitrator's conclusions of law are erroneous."

Arbitration took place, and the arbitrator decided for Mattel. In particular, he held

---

*   JUSTICE SCALIA joins all but footnote 7 of this opinion.

that no indemnification was due, because the lease obligation to follow all applicable federal, state, and local environmental laws did not require compliance with the testing requirements of the Oregon Drinking Water Quality Act (Oregon Act) . . . .

Hall Street then filed a District Court Motion for Order Vacating, Modifying And/Or Correcting the arbitration decision on the ground that failing to treat the Oregon Act as an applicable environmental law under the terms of the lease was legal error. The District Court agreed, vacated the award, and remanded for further consideration by the arbitrator. The court expressly invoked the standard of review chosen by the parties in the arbitration agreement, which included review for legal error, and cited *LaPine Technology Corp.* v. *Kyocera Corp.*, 130 F.3d 884, 889 (CA9 1997), for the proposition that the FAA leaves the parties "free . . . to draft a contract that sets rules for arbitration and dictates an alternative standard of review."

On remand, the arbitrator followed the District Court's ruling that the Oregon Act was an applicable environmental law and amended the decision to favor Hall Street. This time, each party sought modification, and again the District Court applied the parties' stipulated standard of review for legal error, correcting the arbitrator's calculation of interest but otherwise upholding the award. Each party then appealed to the Court of Appeals for the Ninth Circuit, where Mattel switched horses and contended that the Ninth Circuit's recent en banc action overruling *LaPine* in *Kyocera Corp.* v. *Prudential-Bache Trade Servs., Inc.*, 341 F.3d 987, 1000 (2003), left the arbitration agreement's provision for judicial review of legal error unenforceable. Hall Street countered that *Kyocera* (the later one) was distinguishable, and that the agreement's judicial review provision was not severable.

The Ninth Circuit reversed in favor of Mattel in holding that, "[u]nder *Kyocera* the terms of the arbitration agreement controlling the mode of judicial review are unenforceable and severable." . . . After the District Court again held for Hall Street and the Ninth Circuit again reversed, we granted certiorari to decide whether the grounds for vacatur and modification provided by §§ 10 and 11 of the FAA are exclusive. We agree with the Ninth Circuit that they are, but vacate and remand for consideration of independent issues.

II

Congress enacted the FAA to replace judicial indisposition to arbitration with a "national policy favoring [it] and plac[ing] arbitration agreements on equal footing with all other contracts." *Buckeye Check Cashing, Inc.* v. *Cardegna.* As for jurisdiction over controversies touching arbitration, the Act does nothing, being "something of an anomaly in the field of federal-court jurisdiction" in bestowing no federal jurisdiction but rather requiring an independent jurisdictional basis.[2] But in cases falling within a court's jurisdiction, the Act makes contracts to arbitrate "valid, irrevocable, and enforceable," so long as their subject involves "commerce." § 2. And this is so whether an agreement has a broad reach or goes just to one

---

[2] Because the FAA is not jurisdictional, there is no merit in the argument that enforcing the arbitration agreement's judicial review provision would create federal jurisdiction by private contract. The issue is entirely about the scope of judicial review permissible under the FAA.

dispute, and whether enforcement be sought in state court or federal. See *Southland Corp.* v. *Keating.*

The Act also supplies mechanisms for enforcing arbitration awards: a judicial decree confirming an award, an order vacating it, or an order modifying or correcting it. §§ 9-11. An application for any of these orders will get streamlined treatment as a motion, obviating the separate contract action that would usually be necessary to enforce or tinker with an arbitral award in court. § 6. Under the terms of § 9, a court "must" confirm an arbitration award "unless" it is vacated, modified, or corrected "as prescribed" in §§ 10 and 11. Section 10 lists grounds for vacating an award, while § 11 names those for modifying or correcting one.

The Courts of Appeals have split over the exclusiveness of these statutory grounds when parties take the FAA shortcut to confirm, vacate, or modify an award, with some saying the recitations are exclusive, and others regarding them as mere threshold provisions open to expansion by agreement. . . . We now hold that §§ 10 and 11 respectively provide the FAA's exclusive grounds for expedited vacatur and modification.

III

Hall Street makes two main efforts to show that the grounds set out for vacating or modifying an award are not exclusive, taking the position, first, that expandable judicial review authority has been accepted as the law since *Wilko* v. *Swan.* This, however, was not what *Wilko* decided, which was that § 14 of the Securities Act of 1933 voided any agreement to arbitrate claims of violations of that Act, a holding since overruled by *Rodriguez de Quijas* v. *Shearson/American Express, Inc.* Although it is true that the Court's discussion includes some language arguably favoring Hall Street's position, arguable is as far as it goes.

The *Wilko* Court was explaining that arbitration would undercut the Securities Act's buyer protections when it remarked (citing FAA § 10) that "[p]ower to vacate an [arbitration] award is limited," and went on to say that "the interpretations of the law by the arbitrators in contrast to manifest disregard [of the law] are not subject, in the federal courts, to judicial review for error in interpretation." Hall Street reads this statement as recognizing "manifest disregard of the law" as a further ground for vacatur on top of those listed in § 10, and some Circuits have read it the same way. Hall Street sees this supposed addition to § 10 as the camel's nose: if judges can add grounds to vacate (or modify), so can contracting parties.

But this is too much for *Wilko* to bear. Quite apart from its leap from a supposed judicial expansion by interpretation to a private expansion by contract, Hall Street overlooks the fact that the statement it relies on expressly rejects just what Hall Street asks for here, general review for an arbitrator's legal errors. Then there is the vagueness of *Wilko*'s phrasing. Maybe the term "manifest disregard" was meant to name a new ground for review, but maybe it merely referred to the § 10 grounds collectively, rather than adding to them. See, *e.g., Mitsubishi Motors Corp.* v. *Soler Chrysler-Plymouth, Inc.* (STEVENS, J., dissenting) ("Arbitration awards are only reviewable for manifest disregard of the law, 9 U.S.C. §§ 10, 207."). Or, as some courts have thought, "manifest disregard" may have been shorthand for § 10(a)(3) or § 10(a)(4), the subsections authorizing vacatur when the arbitrators were "guilty of misconduct" or "exceeded their powers." We, when speaking as a Court, have merely taken the *Wilko* language as we found it, without embellishment, see *First Options of Chicago, Inc.* v. *Kaplan*, and now that its meaning is implicated, we see no reason to accord it the significance that Hall Street urges.

Second, Hall Street says that the agreement to review for legal error ought to prevail simply because arbitration is a creature of contract, and the FAA is "motivated, first and foremost, by a congressional desire to enforce agreements into which parties ha[ve] entered." . . . But to rest this case on the general policy of treating arbitration agreements as enforceable as such would be to beg the question, which is whether the FAA has textual features at odds with enforcing a contract to expand judicial review following the arbitration.

To that particular question we think the answer is yes, that the text compels a reading of the §§ 10 and 11 categories as exclusive. To begin with, even if we assumed §§ 10 and 11 could be supplemented to some extent, it would stretch basic interpretive principles to expand the stated grounds to the point of evidentiary and legal review generally. Sections 10 and 11, after all, address egregious departures from the parties' agreed-upon arbitration: "corruption," "fraud," "evident partiality," "misconduct," "misbehavior," "exceed[ing] . . . powers," "evident material miscalculation," "evident material mistake," "award[s] upon a matter not submitted;" the only ground with any softer focus is "imperfect[ions]," and a court may correct those only if they go to "[a] matter of form not affecting the merits." Given this emphasis on extreme arbitral conduct, the old rule of *ejusdem generis* has an implicit lesson to teach here. Under that rule, when a statute sets out a series of specific items ending with a general term, that general term is confined to covering subjects comparable to the specifics it follows. Since a general term included in the text is normally so limited, then surely a statute with no textual hook for expansion cannot authorize contracting parties to supplement review for specific instances of outrageous conduct with review for just any legal error. "Fraud" and a mistake of law are not cut from the same cloth.

That aside, expanding the detailed categories would rub too much against the grain of the § 9 language, where provision for judicial confirmation carries no hint of flexibility. On application for an order confirming the arbitration award, the court "must grant" the order "unless the award is vacated, modified, or corrected as prescribed in sections 10 and 11 of this title." There is nothing malleable about "must grant," which unequivocally tells courts to grant confirmation in all cases, except when one of the "prescribed" exceptions applies. This does not sound remotely like a provision meant to tell a court what to do just in case the parties say nothing else.

In fact, anyone who thinks Congress might have understood § 9 as a default provision should turn back to § 5 for an example of what Congress thought a default provision would look like . . . . "[I]f no method be provided" is a far cry from "must grant . . . unless" in § 9.

Instead of fighting the text, it makes more sense to see the three provisions, §§ 9-11, as substantiating a national policy favoring arbitration with just the limited review needed to maintain arbitration's essential virtue of resolving disputes straightaway. Any other reading opens the door to the full-bore legal and evidentiary appeals that can "rende[r] informal arbitration merely a prelude to a more cumbersome and time-consuming judicial review process," and bring arbitration theory to grief in post-arbitration process.

. . .

When all these arguments based on prior legal authority are done with, Hall Street and Mattel remain at odds over what happens next. Hall Street and its *amici* say parties will flee from arbitration if expanded review is not open to them. One of Mattel's *amici* foresees flight from the courts if it is. We do not know who, if anyone, is right, and so cannot say whether the exclusivity reading of the statute is more of a threat to the popularity of arbitrators or to that of courts. But whatever the consequences of our holding, the statutory text gives us no business to expand the statutory grounds.[7]

IV

In holding that §§ 10 and 11 provide exclusive regimes for the review provided by the statute, we do not purport to say that they exclude more searching review based on authority outside the statute as well. The FAA is not the only way into court for parties wanting review of arbitration awards: they may contemplate enforcement under state statutory or common law, for example, where judicial review of different scope is arguable. But here we speak only to the scope of the expeditious judicial review under §§ 9, 10, and 11, deciding nothing about other possible avenues for judicial enforcement of arbitration awards.

. . .

One unusual feature, however, prompted some of us to question whether the case should be approached another way. The arbitration agreement was entered into in the course of district-court litigation, was submitted to the District Court as a request to deviate from the standard sequence of trial procedure, and was adopted by the District Court as an order. Hence a question raised by this Court at oral

---

[7] The history of the FAA is consistent with our conclusion. The text of the FAA was based upon that of New York's arbitration statute. Section 2373 of the code said that, upon application by a party for a confirmation order, "the court must grant such an order, unless the award is vacated, modified, or corrected, as prescribed by the next two sections." 2 N.Y. Ann. Code Civ. Proc. (Stover 6th ed. 1902) (hereinafter Stover). The subsequent sections gave grounds for vacatur and modification or correction virtually identical to the 9 U.S.C. §§ 10 and 11 grounds.

In a brief submitted to the House and Senate Subcommittees of the Committees on the Judiciary, Julius Henry Cohen, one of the primary drafters of both the 1920 New York Act and the proposed FAA, said, "The grounds for vacating, modifying, or correcting an award are limited. If the award [meets a condition of § 10], then and then only the award may be vacated. . . . If there was [an error under § 11], then and then only it may be modified or corrected . . . ." Arbitration of Interstate Commercial Disputes, Joint Hearings before the Subcommittees of the Committees on the Judiciary on S. 1005 and H. R. 646, 68th Cong., 1st Sess., 34 (1924). . . .

In a contemporaneous campaign for the promulgation of a uniform state arbitration law, Cohen contrasted the New York Act with the Illinois Arbitration and Awards Act of 1917, which required an arbitrator, at the request of either party, to submit any question of law arising during arbitration to judicial determination.

argument: should the agreement be treated as an exercise of the District Court's authority to manage its cases under Federal Rules of Civil Procedure 16? . . .

We are, however, in no position to address the question now, beyond noting the claim of relevant case management authority independent of the FAA. . . . We express no opinion on these matters beyond leaving them open for Hall Street to press on remand. If the Court of Appeals finds they are open, the court may consider whether the District Court's authority to manage litigation independently warranted that court's order on the mode of resolving the indemnification issues remaining in this case.

* * *

Although we agree with the Ninth Circuit that the FAA confines its expedited judicial review to the grounds listed in 9 U.S.C. §§ 10 and 11, we vacate the judgment and remand the case for proceedings consistent with this opinion.

It is so ordered.

JUSTICE STEVENS, with whom JUSTICE KENNEDY joins, dissenting.

May parties to an ongoing lawsuit agree to submit their dispute to arbitration subject to the caveat that the trial judge should refuse to enforce an award that rests on an erroneous conclusion of law? Prior to Congress' enactment of the Federal Arbitration Act (FAA or Act) in 1925, the answer to that question would surely have been "Yes."[1] Today, however, the Court holds that the FAA does not merely authorize the vacation or enforcement of awards on specified grounds, but also forbids enforcement of perfectly reasonable judicial review provisions in arbitration agreements fairly negotiated by the parties and approved by the district court. Because this result conflicts with the primary purpose of the FAA and ignores the historical context in which the Act was passed, I respectfully dissent.

. . .

. . . As I read the Court's opinion, it identifies two possible reasons for reaching this result: (1) a supposed *quid pro quo* bargain between Congress and litigants that conditions expedited federal enforcement of arbitration awards on acceptance of a statutory limit on the scope of judicial review of such awards; and (2) an assumption that Congress intended to include the words "and no other" in the grounds specified in §§ 10 and 11 for the vacatur and modification of awards. Neither reason is persuasive.

While § 9 of the FAA imposes a 1-year limit on the time in which any party to an arbitration may apply for confirmation of an award, the statute does not require that the application be given expedited treatment. Of course, the premise of the entire statute is an assumption that the arbitration process may be more expeditious and less costly than ordinary litigation, but that is a reason for interpreting the statute liberally to favor the parties' use of arbitration. An unnecessary refusal to

---

[1] See *Kleine* v. *Catara*, 14 F. Cas. 732, 735, F. Cas. No. 7869 (C.C.D. Mass. 1814) ("If the parties wish to reserve the law for the decision of the court, they may stipulate to that effect in the submission; they may restrain or enlarge its operation as they please") (Story, J.).

enforce a perfectly reasonable category of arbitration agreements defeats the primary purpose of the statute.

That purpose also provides a sufficient response to the Court's reliance on statutory text. It is true that a wooden application of "the old rule of *ejusdem generis*" might support an inference that the categories listed in §§ 10 and 11 are exclusive, but the literal text does not compel that reading — a reading that is flatly inconsistent with the overriding interest in effectuating the clearly expressed intent of the contracting parties. A listing of grounds that must always be available to contracting parties simply does not speak to the question whether they may agree to additional grounds for judicial review.

Moreover, in light of the historical context and the broader purpose of the FAA, §§ 10 and 11 are best understood as a shield meant to protect parties from hostile courts, not a sword with which to cut down parties' "valid, irrevocable and enforceable" agreements to arbitrate their disputes subject to judicial review for errors of law.

Accordingly, while I agree that the judgment of the Court of Appeals must be set aside, and that there may be additional avenues available for judicial enforcement of parties' fairly negotiated review provisions, I respectfully dissent from the Court's interpretation of the FAA, and would direct the Court of Appeals to affirm the judgment of the District Court enforcing the arbitrator's final award.

NOTES

1.   The Court in *Hall Street* resolved a longstanding split among the circuits over the enforceability of expanded review provisions — i.e., provisions that seek to expand the grounds for court review of arbitration awards. Most commonly, the provisions provide for de novo court review of the arbitrators' legal conclusions. Somewhat less commonly, they provide for some degree of court review of the arbitrators' fact findings. The clause at issue in *Hall Street* provided for both.

2.   Who is in a better position to determine how extensive court review of an arbitration award should be — the parties? the courts? or Congress? Don't courts determine questions of law all the time, and frequently review factual determinations (such as by juries) for evidentiary support? How would reviewing arbitration awards on those grounds differ? What if parties chose a different standard of review — such as directing the district judge to "review the award by flipping a coin or studying the entrails of a dead fowl?" *See* Lapine Tech. Corp. v. Kyocera Corp., 130 F.3d 884, 891 (9th Cir 1997) (Kozinski, J., concurring). Should that be permissible?

3.   The Court leaves open the possibility of expanded review on some basis other than the FAA. One possibility is under the district court's inherent powers, since the settlement agreement in *Hall Street* containing the expanded review provision was approved by the court. Another possibility is to use state law, at least in state court. *See* Cable Connection v. DIRECTV, Inc., 190 P.3d 586, 599 (Cal. 2008) (holding that California law permits parties to contract for expanded vacatur grounds and is not preempted by the FAA); Nafta Traders, Inc. v. Quinn, 339 S.W.3d 84, 101 (Tex. 2011) (holding that "the FAA does not preempt enforcement of an agreement for expanded judicial review of an arbitration award enforceable under the TAA").

A third possibility is by defining the scope of the arbitrators' authority so as to make errors of law reviewable under the section 10(a)(4) excess of authority ground. This approach to expanded review was standard at the time the FAA was enacted. *See* Christopher R. Drahozal, *Contracting Around RUAA: Default Rules, Mandatory Rules, and Judicial Review of Arbitral Awards*, 3 PEPP. DISP. RESOL. J. 419, 432 (2003) ("[A]t common law (i.e., prior to the enactment· of modern arbitration statutes), parties could contract for court review of arbitral awards for legal error by requiring the arbitrators to follow the law. In such a 'restricted submission,' arbitrators exceeded their authority by making a legal error, permitting a court to vacate the award."). Courts are divided on whether this latter device is available after *Hall Street*. *Compare* Cable Connection v. DIRECTV, Inc., 190 P.3d 586, 599 (Cal. 2008) (under California law); Nafta Traders, Inc. v. Quinn, 339 S.W.3d 84, 97 (Tex. 2011) (under Texas law) *with* Wood v. PennTex Resources LP, 2008 U.S. Dist. LEXIS 50071, at *21 (S.D. Tex. 2008) ("This reading would impermissibly circumvent *Hall Street*."), *aff'd on other grounds*, 2009 U.S. App. LEXIS 8813 (5th Cir. Apr. 23, 2009) (per curiam); *and* Feeney v. Dell Computer Corp., 2008 Mass. Super. LEXIS 104, at *6-*7 (Mass. Super. Ct. Apr. 4, 2008) (rejecting argument that National Arbitration Forum rules, which require arbitrators to follow the law, make legal rulings in awards reviewable de novo), *rev'd on other grounds*, 908 N.E.2d 53 (Mass. 2009). *See also* Restatement (Third) of the U.S. Law of International Commercial Arbitration, § 4-23, rptrs. note to cmt. c ("While there are conflicting judicial authorities, the Restatement rejects the notion that parties may effectively expand judicial review through language that defines the arbitrators' mandate as limited to application (or to the correct application) of legal principles. Allowing the parties to do so would invite judicial review of the merits of an award and circumvention of the limitations imposed by *Hall Street*.").

4.   The California Supreme Court in *Cable Connection* and the Texas Supreme Court in *Nafta Traders*, not only construed their state arbitration laws as permitting parties to agree to expanded review, but also held that the FAA did not preempt application of expanded review in state court. Do you agree?

PROBLEM 7.16

Your client, Ronald Adair of Adair, Inc. (see Problems 7.14 and 7.15), tells you he is frustrated with the grounds available for judicial review of arbitration awards. He says that "it's either too much or too little. Courts should be able to take a good look at these things, I mean, the awards, or just leave them alone altogether." He's come up with some variations on standard arbitration clauses that he asks you to take a look at. He wants to know what courts will do with each of the following clauses. What do you tell him?

(a) The arbitration clause provides that the arbitration award is final and binding and is not subject to any appeal.

(b) The arbitration clause provides that a court may vacate the arbitration award on any ground in the FAA as well as for errors of law.

(c) The arbitration clause provides that a court may vacate the arbitration award on any ground in the FAA as well as for errors of fact or law, and that the court's review of all issues shall be de novo.

(d) The arbitration clause provides that the arbitrator lacks the authority to make errors of law.

PROBLEM 7.17

Your boss, Senator Grace Dunbar (see problem 1.6), continues to be interested in proposals to revise and update the Federal Arbitration Act. One of the issues she asks you about is whether the FAA should be amended so as to permit parties to contract into a higher standard of judicial review than otherwise provided in the Act.

(a) What do you recommend?

(b) Should Chapters 2 and 3 of the FAA be included in the amendment?

(c) How would your answer be different if you were considering whether to amend a state arbitration statute to permit contracting for a higher standard of judicial review?

§ 7.06   PRECLUSIVE EFFECT OF ARBITRATION AWARDS

So far we have focused on actions to enforce and vacate arbitration awards — turn them into court judgments so that the prevailing party can collect on them — or set them aside. But courts (and arbitrators) also can give effect to arbitration awards by recognizing them in subsequent litigation, either to preclude relitigation of claims (res judicata) or to preclude relitigation of issues (collateral estoppel). Some courts, however, have been reluctant to treat arbitration awards, even when confirmed by a court, as fully equivalent to court judgments in this respect.

VANDENBERG v. SUPERIOR COURT
Supreme Court of California
982 P.2d 229 (1999)

BAXTER, J.

[W]o must consider when, if ever, a judicially confirmed award in an arbitration governed by California's private arbitration law (Code Civ. Proc., § 1280 et seq.) is entitled to collateral estoppel, or "issue preclusion," effect in favor of a *nonparty* to the arbitration. . . .

We [conclude that] . . . a private arbitration award, even if judicially confirmed, may not have nonmutual collateral estoppel effect under California law unless there was an agreement to that effect in the particular case.[2]

---

[2] Our holding is narrowly circumscribed. Nothing in our decision imposes or implies any limitations on the strict res judicata, or "claim preclusive," effect of a California law private arbitration award. (*See, e.g.*, Thibodeau v. Crum (1992) 4 Cal.App.4th 749, 756–761, 6 Cal.Rptr.2d 27 [unconfirmed award in private arbitration between homeowner and general contractor is res judicata barring homeowner's identical claim against subcontractor]; Sartor v. Superior Court (1982) 136 Cal.App.3d 322, 327–328, 187 Cal.Rptr. 247 [confirmed private arbitration award in favor of architectural firm is res judicata barring homeowner's identical causes of action against firm's employees].) We also do not address the

FACTUAL AND PROCEDURAL BACKGROUND

The underlying litigation involves damage to a parcel of land that Vandenberg used as an automobile sales and service facility. Before 1958, owners Eugene and Kathryn Boyd operated an automobile dealership on the property. From 1958 to 1988, Vandenberg leased the property from Boyd under a series of leases. In 1988 Vandenberg discontinued the business and possession of the land reverted to Boyd.

To prepare the property for sale, Boyd removed three underground waste oil storage tanks. Testing revealed contamination of soils and groundwater underlying the property. Boyd filed an action against Vandenberg, alleging . . . Vandenberg had installed and operated the waste oil storage tanks and the tanks were the source of the petroleum contamination.

Vandenberg had obtained CGL insurance from several companies over the years, including . . . Centennial Insurance Company (Centennial) . . . and United States Fidelity and Guaranty Company (USF&G) (collectively insurers). The policies provided coverage to Vandenberg for sums he was "legally obligated to pay as damages" because of property damage. However, certain of the policies, including policies issued by USF&G and Centennial, also contained a so-called pollution exclusion, under which property damage caused by a pollutant or contaminant was not covered except for a "sudden and accidental" discharge.

Vandenberg tendered defense of the Boyd action to his insurers, but only USF&G agreed to provide a defense. During judicially supervised settlement proceedings, Vandenberg, Boyd, and USF&G reached an agreement among themselves to resolve the Boyd litigation. The agreement provided that its parties would contribute jointly to the investigation and remediation of the contamination, with USF&G bearing the largest share of the cost. . . . Boyd released all claims against Vandenberg except those based on the theory that the contamination constituted a breach of the lease agreements. *Boyd and Vandenberg* agreed to resolve the reserved *breach of lease* issues through arbitration . . . USF&G agreed to defend Vandenberg, but the ultimate issues of USF&G's coverage and indemnity obligations, as well as any claim by Vandenberg for . . . counsel fees were "*reserved for [future] resolution.*" (Italics added.)

The arbitration between Vandenberg and Boyd took place before a retired federal judge, Raul Ramirez. Formal discovery was conducted, and the transcribed proceedings included representation by counsel, and extensive evidence, briefing, and argument. In a lengthy and detailed decision, the arbitrator ruled for Boyd. Among other things, the arbitrator found that the contamination stemmed primarily from the underground waste oil tanks and was caused in part by Vandenberg's improper installation, maintenance and use of the tanks. The arbitrator indicated the discharge of contaminants was not sudden and accidental. The arbitrator's award of over $4 million to Boyd was confirmed by a superior court judgment.

The insurers rejected Vandenberg's request for indemnification. He then filed the

---

circumstances, if any, in which a private arbitration award may have "issue preclusive" effect in subsequent litigation between the same parties on different causes of action. No party has suggested the arbitration here at issue is governed by the Federal Arbitration Act (FAA), and we have no occasion to consider whether application of the FAA would alter our ruling. . . .

underlying action against his insurers, alleging various causes of action arising out of the failure to defend, settle, or indemnify in the Boyd action.

The insurers filed [a motion for summary adjudication, arguing that] . . . they had no duty to defend or indemnify because the pollution exclusion in their policies was triggered by the arbitrator's determination in the Boyd action that the contamination was not sudden and accidental. These two insurers contended that Vandenberg's relitigation of the "sudden and accidental" issue was precluded by principles of collateral estoppel. . . .

The trial court granted [the motion.] . . . [It] ruled that relitigation of issues regarding the source and causation of the contamination was precluded by collateral estoppel. The court reviewed the arbitration transcript and concluded the "only reasonable inference is that the leaks or spills were occurring over a considerable period of time." . . .

. . . [T]he Court of Appeal [reversed, holding] . . . that absent a contrary agreement by the arbitral parties, a party to private arbitration is not barred from relitigating issues decided by the arbitrator when those issues arise in a different case involving a different adversary and different causes of action. . . .

We granted the insurers' petitions for review to consider the circumstances, if any, in which private contractual arbitration decisions may have collateral estoppel effect in favor of nonparties. . . .

DISCUSSION

. . .

Collateral estoppel is one of two aspects of the doctrine of res judicata. In its narrowest form, res judicata " 'precludes parties or their privies from relitigating a *cause of action* [finally resolved in a prior proceeding].' " But res judicata also includes a broader principle, commonly termed collateral estoppel, under which an *issue* " 'necessarily decided in [prior] litigation [may be] conclusively determined *as [against] the parties [thereto] or their privies* . . . in a subsequent lawsuit on a *different cause of action.*' " ([I]talics added.)

Thus, res judicata does not merely bar relitigation of identical claims or causes of action. Instead, in its collateral estoppel aspect, the doctrine may also preclude a party to prior litigation from redisputing *issues* therein decided against him, even when those issues bear on different claims raised in a later case. Moreover, because the estoppel need not be mutual, it is not necessary that the earlier and later proceedings involve the identical parties or their privies. Only the party *against whom* the doctrine is invoked must be bound by the prior proceeding.

Accordingly, the collateral estoppel doctrine may allow one who was not a party to prior litigation to take advantage, in a later unrelated matter, of findings made against his current adversary in the earlier proceeding. This means that the loss of a particular dispute against a particular opponent in a particular forum may impose adverse and unforeseeable litigation consequences far beyond the parameters of the original case.

Collateral estoppel (like the narrower "claim preclusion" aspect of res judicata) is intended to preserve the integrity of the judicial system, promote judicial economy, and protect litigants from harassment by vexatious litigation. However, even where the minimal prerequisites for invocation of the doctrine are present, collateral estoppel " 'is not an inflexible, universally applicable principle; policy considerations may limit its use where the . . . underpinnings of the doctrine are outweighed by other factors.' "

Whether collateral estoppel is fair and consistent with public policy in a particular case depends in part upon the character of the forum that first decided the issue later sought to be foreclosed. In this regard, courts consider the judicial nature of the prior forum, i.e., its legal formality, the scope of its jurisdiction, and its procedural safeguards, particularly including the opportunity for judicial review of adverse rulings.

Moreover, a particular danger of injustice arises when collateral estoppel is invoked by a nonparty to the prior litigation. (*See, e.g.*, Parklane Hosiery Co. v. Shore (1979) 439 U.S. 322.) Such cases require close examination to determine whether nonmutual use of the doctrine is fair and appropriate.

. . .

An agreement to arbitrate particular claims reflects each party's conclusion that the immediate stakes make it preferable to avoid the delay and expense of court proceedings, and instead to resolve the matter between themselves without resort to the judicial process. Under such circumstances, each party is willing to risk that the arbitration will result in a "final" and "binding" *defeat* with respect to the *submitted claims*, even though the party would have won in court, and even though the arbitrator's errors must be accepted without opportunity for review. But this does not mean each arbitral party also consents that issues decided against him by this informal, imprecise method may bind him, in the same manner as a court trial, in *all future* disputes, *regardless* of the stakes, against *all* adversaries, known and unknown.

On the contrary, common sense weighs against the assumption that parties contemplate such remote and collateral ramifications when they agree to arbitrate controversies between themselves. Logic equally suggests that conscious agreements to give arbitrators' decisions nonmutual collateral estoppel effect would not be routine. *The very fact* that arbitration is by nature an informal process, not strictly bound by evidence, law, or judicial oversight, suggests reasonable parties would hesitate to agree that the arbitrator's findings in their own dispute should thereafter bind them in cases involving different adversaries and claims. Even where, as here, the arbitral parties have imposed some formality on their proceedings, have aired their dispute thoroughly, and have received a detailed decision, there is no reason to assume they agreed to "issue preclusive" effect in favor of nonparties. In the usual case, tactical considerations would weigh against such an agreement. Most often, the effect would be to burden whichever party *lost* the arbitration, while affording no corresponding benefit to either arbitral party.

Accordingly, there is little basis to surmise that mere silence implies the arbitral parties' acceptance of nonmutual collateral estoppel. A general rule that confirmed private arbitration awards may have such effect would thus violate the fundamental premise that private arbitration is a contractual proceeding *whose scope and effect are defined and limited by the parties' consent.* For similar reasons, such a rule would chill, rather than promote, the voluntary use of the arbitral forum as an efficient and informal alternative means of resolving particular controversies.

Under these circumstances, the public policy reasons against applying the collateral estoppel doctrine well outweigh those in favor of doing so. In fact, the traditional justifications for collateral estoppel — factors which "strongly influence whether its application in a particular circumstance would be fair to the parties and constitute[ ] sound [public] policy" — have diminished force when the nonmutual prong of the doctrine is applied to private arbitration without the arbitral parties' specific consent.

As noted above, the primary purposes of collateral estoppel are to "preserv[e] the integrity of the judicial system, promot[e] judicial economy, and protect litigants from harassment by vexatious litigation." But because a private arbitrator's award is *outside* the judicial system, denying the award collateral estoppel effect has no adverse impact on judicial integrity. Moreover, because private arbitration does not involve the use of a judge and a courtroom, later relitigation does not undermine judicial economy by requiring duplication of judicial resources to decide the same issue. Finally, when collateral estoppel is invoked by a *nonparty* to the private arbitration, the doctrine does not serve the policy against harassment by vexatious litigation. In such cases, the doctrine is asserted not to protect one who has already once prevailed against the same opponent on the same cause of action, but simply to gain vicarious advantage from a litigation victory *won by another.*

We therefore face a situation in which the policies underlying the doctrine of collateral estoppel must yield to the contractual basis of private arbitration, i.e., the principle that the scope and effect of the arbitration are for the parties themselves to decide. Accordingly, we are compelled to conclude that a private arbitration award, even if judicially confirmed, can have no collateral estoppel effect in favor of third persons unless the arbitral parties agreed, in the particular case, that such a consequence should apply.

We realize that some commentators, and most other courts addressing the issue, have taken a contrary approach. The predominant view is that unless the arbitral parties agreed otherwise, a judicially confirmed private arbitration award will have collateral estoppel effect, even in favor of nonparties to the arbitration, if the arbitrator actually and necessarily decided the issue sought to be foreclosed and the party against whom estoppel is invoked had full incentive and opportunity to litigate the matter. To determine whether particular arbitration proceedings provided a full and fair opportunity to litigate, courts typically proceed case-by-case, assessing multiple factors including the extent to which the arbitration resembled a court trial.

When justification for these rules is offered, it centers on one or more of three premises. The first is the general policy against relitigation of issues already decided. The second is that collateral estoppel causes no injustice when the party to be bound had a full and fair opportunity to litigate the issues to be foreclosed. The third, and most sophisticated, is that "final" and "binding" arbitration necessarily implies the possibility of collateral estoppel, particularly when (as in California) the law gives judicially confirmed arbitration awards the force and effect of civil judgments.

Respectfully, we find these rationales unpersuasive. As our earlier discussion suggests, we believe they give insufficient consideration and weight to the voluntary, contractual, and informal nature of private arbitration, and to the consequent reasonable expectations of the arbitral parties.

In particular, we reject the notion, strongly urged by the concurring and dissenting opinion, that California's statutory provision giving confirmed private arbitration awards the force and effect of civil judgments (*see* Code Civ. Proc., § 1287.4) automatically implies that such awards "may have nonmutual collateral estoppel effect *with or without* the [specific] consent of the arbitral parties." Under California law, collateral estoppel will apply in any setting *only* where such application comports with fairness and sound public policy. . . .

. . . [T]he informal nature of arbitration, the usual reasons for its use, the potentially disproportionate consequences of nonmutual collateral estoppel, and the fact that such consequences may not be immediately apparent to the arbitral parties, all suggest that their silence on the subject does not imply consent. Fairness and public policy thus counsel against application of nonmutual collateral estoppel in this setting, unless the parties specifically agree thereto. That California law treats confirmed arbitration awards as judgments does not compel us to conclude otherwise.

Moreover, we believe the case-by-case approach prevalent in other jurisdictions has particular adverse effects on the choice, use, and effectiveness of private arbitration as a faster, cheaper alternative to litigation in court. . . .

This "ad hoc, post hoc" standard eliminates a prime benefit of choosing the arbitral over the judicial forum — the right to shape, control, know, and predict *at the outset* the scope and effect of the arbitrator's decision. Moreover, the case-by-case approach encourages both the arbitral parties, and the arbitrator himself, to "hedge" against the future possibility that the decision will be deemed binding in different litigation with other parties. "By creating the possibility that some arbitral findings will [have] collateral estoppel [effect], the case-by-case approach puts subtle but strong pressure on the arbitration process to conform its perspective and methods to those of litigation, in order to justify the confidence in its findings that collateral estoppel represents. [A] compelling reason to abandon the case-by-case approach to arbitral collateral estoppel is to ease or eliminate this pressure, in order to maintain arbitration as a useful, distinct alternative to litigation."

Accordingly, we adopt, for California purposes, the rule that a private arbitration award cannot have nonmutual collateral estoppel effect unless the arbitral parties so agree. It remains to apply this rule to the facts before us. . . . USF&G and Centennial seek to give the arbitrator's decision nonmutual collateral estoppel effect against Vandenberg. They may not do so unless Vandenberg and Boyd so agreed.

We find no such agreement. On the contrary, the terms of the three-way settlement among Boyd, Vandenberg, and USF&G strongly suggest the parties' intent that, while the arbitration would be "binding" between Vandenberg and

Boyd, it should *not* have collateral estoppel effect in favor of Vandenberg's insurers.
. . .

. . .

The Court of Appeal therefore correctly reversed the trial court order granting the motion of USF&G and Centennial for summary adjudication.

. . . Dissenting Opinion by Brown, J.

. . . I strongly disagree with [the majority's] conclusion . . . that judicially confirmed arbitration awards do not have "nonmutual" collateral estoppel effect absent a specific agreement between the arbitral parties.

The majority conveniently disregards the fact that the Legislature has already resolved this question. Section 1287.4 of the Code of Civil Procedure (section 1287.4) establishes that a confirmed arbitration award has *"the same force and effect as, and is subject to all the provisions of law relating to,* a judgment in a civil action of the same jurisdictional classification. . . ."* (Italics added.) This language is clear and unambiguous: confirmed arbitration awards are equivalent in all respects to other court judgments. Thus, a confirmed arbitration award, like any other judgment, may have nonmutual collateral estoppel effect *with or without* the express or implied consent of the arbitral parties.

. . .

The majority's use of public policy considerations to circumvent section 1287.4 is just as specious. This case does not present a question of common law policy; it presents a question of statutory interpretation. The court is not at liberty to reject the plain meaning of a statute merely because it believes the statute implements an unwise policy.

In any event, most of the cited public policy considerations actually repudiate the majority's position. . . . First, denying judicially confirmed arbitration awards collateral estoppel effect creates the risk of inconsistent rulings. Because the Legislature has given these arbitration awards "equal status" to court judgments, any inconsistencies between the rulings of the arbitrator and court would have a profoundly negative impact on the integrity of our judicial system.

. . .

Denying judicially confirmed arbitrations collateral estoppel effect also undermines judicial economy. . . . If arbitration awards have collateral estoppel effect, relitigation — including additional discovery, motions and trials — would not be necessary. Thus, courts could avoid this needless dissipation of judicial resources by deciding just *one* motion addressing the collateral estoppel effect of the award.

Finally, in perhaps the greatest irony of all, the majority's foray into legislative enactment will likely have the very "adverse effects" on arbitrations that it seeks to prevent. . . .

. . . Commercial disputes often involve nonparties to the arbitration agreement. If the majority is correct and tactical considerations weigh against agreements according nonmutual collateral estoppel effect to a judicially confirmed arbitration award, then the guaranteed "possibility of conflicting rulings on a common issue of law or fact" in disputes involving nonparties will lead to two probable outcomes. (Code Civ. Proc., § 1281.2, subd. (c).) Courts will either deny or stay arbitration or order arbitration and stay the action against nonparties to the arbitration agreement. The first outcome makes otherwise arbitrable disputes inarbitrable in direct contravention of the strong public policy in favor of arbitration. The second outcome gives a party asserting claims against nonarbitrating parties an undeserved second bite at the apple if they are not satisfied with the arbitration award. . . .

. . .

Accordingly, I believe the only reasoned view is to determine the applicability of collateral estoppel on a case-by-case basis. If the parties have a full and fair opportunity to litigate the issues in arbitration, then a judicially confirmed arbitration award has nonmutual collateral estoppel effect. If the parties do not, then the award does not have nonmutual collateral estoppel effect. By rejecting this approach, the majority ignores the plain language of section 1287.4, the overall statutory scheme governing arbitrations in California and the clear weight of authority — including the decisions of our sister states with similar statutes, the Restatement of Judgments, and most commentators and treatises. In doing so, the majority sends a clear message to the Legislature — "judicial hostility" to arbitration still trumps.

CHIN, J., concurs.

NOTES

1. The court in *Vandenberg* held that a judicially-confirmed arbitration award does not have non-mutual collateral estoppel (i.e., issue preclusive) effect unless the parties to the arbitration so agreed. The court indicates in footnote 2 that it does not question the res judicata (i.e., claim preclusive) effect of arbitration awards (confirmed or unconfirmed), nor does it address mutual (as opposed to non-mutual) collateral estoppel. Indeed, at least some degree of preclusive effect seems inherent in the nature of binding (as opposed to non-binding) arbitration.

2. Why would parties agree that an arbitration award will have non-mutual collateral estoppel effect? Presumably the agreement must be between the parties to the arbitration, not the third party that later seeks to claim the benefit of the award. But that third party will not be bound by the award since it was not a party to the arbitration proceeding. In other words, the parties to the agreement have everything to lose and seemingly nothing to gain from permitting nonmutual collateral estoppel. Indeed, arbitration clauses in a sample of franchise contracts never provide that arbitration awards are to have nonmutual collateral estoppel effect, but sometimes disclaim any such effect. Does that mean that the California Supreme Court correctly determined what the default rule here should be? Or should the applicability of preclusion doctrines be a mandatory rule? Is that what the California statute (section 1287.4 of the Code of Civil Procedure) provides? Are you persuaded by the majority's interpretation of that statute?

3. Who does the rule in *Vandenberg* benefit? Here, the court's holding benefits the insureds, who are now free to relitigate policy coverage issues with their insurers. More commonly, however, it seems likely that the party trying to avoid the non-mutual collateral estoppel effect of a prior arbitration award will be a corporation, attempting to relitigate an issue decided adversely in an arbitration with a similarly situated individual. Did the court here let what it saw as the equities of the case give rise to an undesirable result? Or did the court adopt a rule in an unusual setting knowing full well what the consequences would be in other cases?

4. The *Vandenberg* court notes that the majority of courts, including some federal courts, hold that confirmed arbitration awards do have non-mutual collateral estoppel effect. In cases covered by the FAA, does that rule preempt the rule adopted in *Vandenberg*? Does the FAA apply on the facts of *Vandenberg*? Does the McCarran-Ferguson Act? Why didn't the insurance companies rely on the FAA here?

5. One of the requirements for issue preclusion is that "the court first must find that the issues on which collateral estoppel is being asserted are identical in both actions." JACK H. FRIEDENTHAL ET AL., CIVIL PROCEDURE §§ 14.10, 14.11 (4th ed. 2005). How can a party make that showing if there is no reasoned arbitration award? The answer is that "it can be difficult": "[t]he lack of a written opinion with findings frequently forces courts to search the pleadings and briefs filed in the arbitration to determine identity of issues." 4 IAN R. MACNEIL ET AL., FEDERAL ARBITRATION LAW § 39.3.2.2 (1994) (chapter authored by G. Richard Shell).

6. *Vandenberg* involved an arbitration award that had been confirmed by a court. What about an unconfirmed award? In Dean Witter Reynolds, Inc. v. Byrd, 470 U.S. 213 (1985), which involved just such an award, the Supreme Court stated that "[w]e believe that the preclusive effect of arbitration proceedings is significantly less well settled than the lower court opinions might suggest." *Id.* at 222. Why should that be? Certainly it is true that statutes providing for confirmed awards to be treated the same as court judgments (*see, e.g.*, 9 U.S.C. § 13) do not apply. Nonetheless, "[a]s a matter of practice, and without a great deal of discussion, the courts have held repeatedly and authoritatively that confirmation is not required to apply preclusion so long as the award is final under the applicable arbitration rules." 4 IAN R. MACNEIL ET AL., *supra*, § 39.6, at 39:65.

7. Additional complications come into play when the arbitration award is international rather than domestic. For a detailed consideration of those complications, see Restatement (Third) of the U.S. Law of International Commercial Arbitration §§ 4-9 & 4-10.

———

Who should decide the preclusive effect of an arbitration award? In *Vandenberg*, Vandenberg and the insurance companies had not agreed to arbitrate their dispute, so there was no question but that the issue was one for the court to decide. But what if the preclusion issue arises between the parties to a previous arbitration?

CHIRON CORP. v. ORTHO DIAGNOSTIC SYSTEMS, INC.
United States Court of Appeals for the Ninth Circuit
207 F.3d 1126 (2000)

McKeown, Circuit Judge:

This case requires us to decide whether the res judicata effect of a prior arbitration award on a subsequent arbitration is an issue to be determined by an arbitrator or by the court. . . . Because res judicata is a legal defense that is necessarily intertwined with the merits, we [hold] . . . that this is a matter for the arbitrator. Our holding is consistent with the strong federal policy favoring arbitration, and with the Federal Arbitration Act. We have jurisdiction under 28 U.S.C. § 1291 and 9 U.S.C. § 16(a)(3), and we affirm.

BACKGROUND

In the late 1980s, Chiron Corporation, a biotechnology company, successfully developed and patented a blood test used to detect a previously unidentified form of hepatitis, the hepatitis C virus ("HCV"). Chiron also made significant strides in the development of AIDS-related blood tests, obtaining certain patents in that field. In 1989, Chiron and Ortho Diagnostic Systems, a wholly owned subsidiary of Johnson & Johnson, combined forces to undertake a joint business arrangement — a 50 year collaboration — aimed at developing, marketing, and selling Chiron's HCV and AIDS tests.

The parties memorialized the terms of this joint undertaking in a written agreement (the "Agreement"). Under the Agreement, Chiron assumed primary responsibility for research and manufacturing while Ortho assumed an exclusive license to the technology and primary responsibility for product development, distribution, marketing, and sales. The parties agreed to share equally all proceeds from the sale of the tests. All budgetary and strategic decisions were vested in a Supervisory Board comprised of three representatives from each company. In the event of a Board deadlock, the Agreement authorized Ortho to set the budget and strategic plan in its discretion for the succeeding year. Chiron and Ortho agreed to arbitrate "any dispute, controversy or claim arising out of or relating to" the Agreement.

In 1994 a dispute arose, ultimately leading Ortho to invoke the arbitration provision. The dispute stemmed from the parties' decision to expand the venture's marketing and sales efforts to diagnostic testing. . . . Entry into the diagnostic testing market . . . required the business to customize its AIDS and HCV tests for use on the diagnostic machines, otherwise known as "random access instruments." Through a series of unrelated transactions, Chiron and Ortho each secured ownership rights to competing random access instruments and, consequently, each company developed a strong interest in customizing the AIDS and HCV tests for use on its respective machine.

In setting the business's plan and budget for 1995, the Supervisory Board deadlocked as to which random access machine or machines the joint arrangement would focus its sales efforts. Per the terms of the Agreement, Ortho adopted a strategic plan and budget that authorized the venture to customize the blood tests for use only on Ortho's Vitros machine, effectively precluding use of the tests on Chiron's Centaur machine. When Chiron announced its intention to market the tests for use on its Centaur machine, Ortho objected, claiming that Chiron was prohibited from independently selling, marketing, or licensing the AIDS and HCV tests outside the joint arrangement.

To arbitrate their dispute, the parties chose former federal district judge Joseph W. Morris, who issued his arbitration decision in April 1997. He determined that in light of the deadlock, the express terms of the Agreement gave Ortho the right to establish the budget and strategic plan for the successive year. He further concluded that Ortho's decision to limit the sale of the tests to the Vitros machine was permitted so long as Ortho continued to share all profits with Chiron. The arbitration award "constitute[d] a full and complete resolution of all claims and counterclaims submitted or urged by either party in this Arbitration," and was "final and binding upon the parties."

Following Judge Morris's decision, Chiron submitted a new proposal to Ortho that involved amending both the then-current 1997 and the 1998 strategic plans and budgets to allow the joint business access to the Centaur. Although Chiron maintained that such an amendment would serve the parties' stated intent by maximizing the business's profits, Ortho rejected Chiron's proposal without submitting it to all members of the Supervisory Board. . . . Chiron sought a second arbitration proceeding to resolve the disagreement. Ortho, however, refused on the ground that the new claims raised by Chiron were the same as the claims presented to Judge Morris and were thus precluded from further arbitration under the doctrine of res judicata.

Chiron filed a declaratory judgment action seeking an order compelling arbitration and later moved for such an order under § 4 of the Federal Arbitration Act ("FAA" or "Act"). Ortho filed a cross-motion for summary judgment on the ground that the earlier arbitration award operated as res judicata to all claims Chiron sought to raise in a second arbitration proceeding. . . . Applying federal law, the district court concluded that Ortho's res judicata defense was itself an arbitrable issue within the scope of the parties' agreement to arbitrate. The Court without reaching the merits of Ortho's objection therefore granted Chiron's motion to compel arbitration and denied Ortho's motion for summary judgment. . . . This appeal stems from Ortho's timely appeal of the district court's grant of Chiron's motion to compel arbitration.

ANALYSIS

We review de novo the district court's decision to compel arbitration. We begin our analysis by recognizing that an agreement to arbitrate is a matter of contract: "it is a way to resolve those disputes — but only those disputes — that the parties have agreed to submit to arbitration." *First Options of Chicago, Inc. v. Kaplan.* As with any other contract dispute, we first look to the express terms which in this case require Chiron and Ortho to arbitrate "[a]ny dispute, controversy or claim arising out of or relating to the validity, construction, enforceability or performance" of the

Agreement. . . . These express terms unambiguously reflect the parties intent both to arbitrate disputes arising from the joint business and to be bound by the arbitration decisions that resolve such disputes. . . .

. . .

Recognizing that the dispute itself is subject to arbitration, Ortho attempts to shift the debate by arguing that, unlike a determination on the merits of a claim, the defense of res judicata is not arbitrable. Whether Ortho's res judicata objection to Chiron's claims is itself arbitrable also raises the separate issue of *who* determines the preclusive effect of an earlier arbitration award, the court or the arbitrator. Chiron counters that a res judicata defense goes to the merits of the dispute and is thus arbitrable under the broad terms of the parties' arbitration agreement. Ortho, on the other hand, points out that the district court entered judgment upon the arbitration award as provided for by § 9 of the Act. . . . Ortho argues that because courts generally determine the preclusive effect of a court judgment on a subsequent court proceeding, the court rather than an arbitrator should reach the merits of its res judicata objection. We address each argument in turn.

The simplest answer to Ortho's argument is to look once again at the parties' agreement, which requires arbitration of "any" dispute. Nowhere is the defense of res judicata treated differently or singled out for exclusion. Rather, Ortho's argument to treat res judicata as a special case appears premised on the notion that the court will make a better decision than the arbitrator or that it is somehow unfair to leave this issue to an arbitrator. We need not go down that path. Ortho already opted to arbitrate all disputes arising under the Agreement and this election was not a casual one, evidenced by not only an unambiguous arbitration clause, but also by the negotiated, detailed, and extensive procedures for alternate dispute resolution that were included in the joint business agreement.

The question of whether Ortho's res judicata defense to arbitration is itself an arbitrable issue is bound up with the question of who should make such a determination. Although we have not had previous occasion to consider this issue, we find the Second Circuit's analysis persuasive: a res judicata objection based on a prior arbitration proceeding is a legal defense that, in turn, is a component of the dispute on the merits and must be considered by the arbitrator, not the court. *See* National Union Fire Ins. Co. v. Belco Petroleum Corp., 88 F.3d 129 (2d Cir. 1996); *see also* John Hancock Mutual Life Ins. Co. v. Olick, 151 F.3d 132 (3d Cir. 1998) (holding res judicata objection based on prior arbitration is issue to be arbitrated under National Association of Securities Dealers arbitration procedures).

. . .

Ortho urges us to . . . look to other provisions of the FAA to support its position that the court should reach the merits of its res judicata defense. . . .

. . . Relying on the language of [§ 13 of the FAA], Ortho argues that we must treat the district court's confirmation of the arbitration award as if it were a judgment rendered in a judicial proceeding. This approach, however, begs the question because the statute says nothing about which forum or *who* determines the effect of the judgment. Moreover, it obscures the fact that while a judgment entered upon a confirmed arbitration award has the same force and effect under the FAA as a court judgment for enforcement purposes, it is not wholly parallel to a court judgment for all purposes.

Indeed, there are fundamental differences between confirmed arbitration awards and judgments arising from a judicial proceeding. Absent an objection on one of the narrow grounds set forth in sections 10 or 11, the Act requires the court to enter judgment upon a confirmed arbitration award, without reviewing either the merits of the award or the legal basis upon which it was reached. A judgment upon a decision or order rendered by the court at the conclusion of a judicial proceeding, by contrast, confirms the merits of that decision. Along the same lines, a judgment under § 13 of the FAA is not subject to Federal Rules of Civil Procedure 59 or 60 whereas a judgment arising from a judicial proceeding is subject to reopening and challenge under those rules. And, unless the provisions of the parties' agreement provides to the contrary, there is no right under the FAA to appeal the merits of a confirmed arbitration award. In sum, a judgment upon a confirmed arbitration award is qualitatively different from a judgment in a court proceeding, even though the judgment is recognized under the FAA for enforcement purposes.

Even were we to accept Ortho's position that § 13 requires us to treat a confirmed arbitration award as a court judgment for all purposes, the primary cases on which Ortho relies are distinguishable in that both involved the court determining the res judicata effect of its *own* prior judgment on a subsequent arbitration proceeding. . . . [Those decisions rest] on the presumption that the court issuing the original decision is best equipped to determine what was considered and decided in that decision and thus what is or is not precluded by that decision. The policy underlying these decisions is not served in this case, however, when the district court merely confirmed the decision issued by another entity, the arbitrator, and was not uniquely qualified to ascertain its scope and preclusive effect. Nor do these cases take into consideration the FAA's policy limiting the role of the court once arbitrability is determined.

. . . Chiron and Ortho's arbitration agreement is undeniably broad. Ortho's res judicata defense to a subsequent arbitration proceeding necessarily involves an inquiry into Chiron's underlying claims. As with other affirmative defenses such as laches and statute of limitations, we agree . . . that a res judicata defense is a "component" of the merits of the dispute and is thus an arbitrable issue.

CONCLUSION

The court's role under the Federal Arbitration Act is limited to enforcing the agreement to arbitrate between Chiron and Ortho. Their broad arbitration clause binds them to arbitrate "any dispute, controversy or claim arising out of or relating to" the Agreement. Because Ortho's res judicata objection to Chiron's petition to compel arbitration is intertwined with the merits of the dispute, it too falls within the scope of the agreement to arbitrate. Accordingly, we AFFIRM the district court's order to compel arbitration.

PROBLEM 7.18

James Wilder has a credit card issued by Capital and Counties Bank, and has been assessed substantial late payment fees several times over the past year. Capital & Counties has reported Wilder's allegedly late payments to credit rating bureaus, with the result that Wilder has been unable to get a home mortgage loan. Wilder believes that the late payment fees violated his account agreement (his payments actually were on time under the terms of the agreement, in his view). Wilder initiates an arbitration proceeding against Capital & Counties to resolve the dispute. Among other terms, the arbitration clause in the account agreement provides that "any arbitration award may not be used to collaterally estop either party from raising any similar issues, claims or defenses in any subsequent arbitration or litigation involving third parties." After a hearing, the arbitrator awards Wilder $5,000 in damages.

(a) The only claim Wilder included in his demand for arbitration was a breach of contract claim. He now files suit against Capital & Counties in California state court alleging a claim for fraud based on the same conduct. Capital & Counties moves for summary judgment. How should the court rule?

(b) Same as sub-part (a) except that Wilder included both breach of contract and fraud claims in his demand for arbitration. The arbitration award did not include any statement of reasons, nor did it even indicate whether the award was based on the breach of contract claim or the tort claim (or both). In addition, the arbitration clause in the account agreement between Wilder and Capital & Counties provided that the arbitrator had no authority to award punitive damages, and Wilder never sought punitive damages from the arbitrator. Wilder now files suit in California state court seeking (1) to have the arbitration award confirmed; and (2) to recover punitive damages from Capital & Counties for its conduct. He relies on the prior arbitration award as establishing the factual basis for his claim for punitive damages. At the same time, Capital & Counties relies on the prior award as precluding Wilder from bringing the punitive damages claim in a separate action. Who will prevail? Does it matter whether the court confirms the arbitration award?

(c) Reuben Hayes, a Capital & Counties Bank credit card holder who has had difficulties with late payment fees similar to Wilder's, learns of Wilder's success in arbitration "through the grapevine." He files his own demand for arbitration asserting claims for breach of contract and fraud, and seeking compensatory and punitive damages. He wants to rely on Wilder's arbitration award to preclude Capital & Counties from relitigating any liability issues. Capital & Counties opposes the request, on a variety of grounds, including that the confidential nature of arbitration makes it particularly inappropriate for Hayes to be able to rely on Wilder's award. Assuming that California law applies, how should the arbitrator rule?

(d) Same as sub-part (c) except that federal law applies. How should the arbitrator rule?

(e) Same as sub-part (c) except that Capital & Counties prevailed in its arbitration proceeding with Wilder. Capital & Counties then asserts the prior arbitration award as a defense in its arbitration with Hayes. How should the arbitrator rule?

Chapter 8

DRAFTING ARBITRATION CLAUSES

§ 8.01 OVERVIEW

This final chapter deals with what ordinarily is the first step in the entire process: drafting the arbitration clause. That topic is saved for last, however, because drafting an effective arbitration clause requires an understanding of all aspects of the arbitration process. As such, this topic provides a useful opportunity to review much of what has been covered in previous chapters. This chapter begins by looking at a pair of empirical studies of dispute resolution clauses and concludes with a discussion of how to draft an arbitration clause.

§ 8.02 EMPIRICAL STUDIES OF ARBITRATION AGREEMENTS

A helpful starting point in the drafting process can be to see what other drafters have done. The following empirical studies offer a look at what sorts of provisions commonly are included in arbitration agreements. The first study looks at arbitration clauses in credit card agreements. The second examines arbitration clauses in international contracts. What types of provisions appear in the credit card contracts (which typically are standard form contracts drafted by the business) that are not in the international contracts (which are more likely to be negotiated by the parties)? What additional provisions are included in the international contracts that are not in the domestic ones?

Peter B. Rutledge & Christopher R. Drahozal, CONTRACT AND CHOICE, 2013 BYU L. Rev. ___ (forthcoming)[*]

II. What Do Arbitration Clauses in Credit Card Agreements Look Like?

This Part undertakes a comprehensive examination of the use of arbitration clauses in credit card agreements. It first examines trends in the use of arbitration clauses: to what extent do issuers provide for arbitration of disputes and to what extent can cardholders opt out of the obligation to arbitrate? It then takes a detailed look at the provisions included in arbitration clauses in credit card agreements. . . .

---

[*] Copyright © 2013 by Peter B. Rutledge & Christopher R. Drahozal. Reprinted with permission.

A. Sample

The Credit Card Accountability, Responsibility, and Disclosure Act (Credit CARD Act) of 2009 required all issuers to provide electronic copies of their consumer credit card agreements to the Federal Reserve, which, in turn, was to "establish and maintain on its publicly available Internet site a central repository of the consumer credit card agreements received from creditors."[41] Our sample consists of 293 credit card agreements submitted by issuers to the Federal Reserve as of December 31, 2009 and 2010, and made available via the Internet. We collected the arbitration clauses, if any, from the credit card agreements and classified the provisions of the clauses as described throughout this part.

We report our findings by number of issuers and by market share of the issuer, as measured by its share of the dollar value of credit card loans outstanding for all issuers in the relevant sample. Data on the amount of credit card loans outstanding come from the December 31, 2009, and December 31, 2010, call reports filed by issuers with the appropriate federal regulators. Our sample is limited to those issuers for which such data is available.

. . .

B. Trends in the Use of Arbitration Clauses

Until recently, credit card agreements have been a standard example of a consumer contract that always, or almost always, included an arbitration clause. Most often, commentators (accurately) stated that most credit card *agreements* included arbitration clauses. Less often (and less accurately), commentators sometimes stated that most credit card *issuers* included arbitration clauses in their credit card agreements. The limited empirical evidence in support of those statements focused on the very largest credit card issuers, which, given the degree of concentration in the credit card market, provided a reasonable view of what most credit card agreements included. But because the studies focused on the very largest issuers, they provided little evidence of what most issuers did.

. . .

1. Use of arbitration clauses

As of December 31, 2009, most credit card agreements included arbitration clauses but most credit card issuers did not use arbitration clauses[:] 95.1% of the dollar value of outstanding credit card loans by issuers in the sample was subject to credit card agreements with arbitration clauses. But only 17.4% of credit card issuers in the sample included arbitration clauses in their credit card agreements. A minority of very large issuers used arbitration clauses; the majority of much smaller issuers did not.

---

[41] At the time we collected the data, the credit card agreements were available on a web page maintained by the Federal Reserve. Subsequently, responsibility for making credit card agreements publicly available has shifted to the Consumer Financial Protection Bureau, which now posts the agreements on its web page.

. . .

In mid-to-late 2009, two events occurred that had a significant effect on the use of arbitration clauses in credit card agreements. First, in July 2009, the National Arbitration Forum (NAF) settled a consumer fraud lawsuit with the Minnesota Attorney General by agreeing to stop administering new consumer arbitration cases. Prior to the settlement, the NAF had the largest caseload of consumer arbitrations (almost all debt collection arbitrations) in the United States. Second, in December 2009, four of the largest credit card issuers settled a pending antitrust suit (*Ross v. Bank of America*) by agreeing to remove arbitration clauses from their consumer and small business credit card agreements for three-and-one-half years. Bank of America, Capital One, Chase, and HSBC were the settling defendants; other large issuers — Citibank and Discover Bank (with American Express and Wells Fargo alleged to be co-conspirators but not named as defendants) — remained in the case and continue to use arbitration clauses.

. . . [As a result, the] percentage of issuers using arbitration clauses declined from 17.4% on December 31, 2009, to 15.0% on December 31, 2010. More dramatically, the percentage of credit card loans subject to arbitration clauses declined from 95.1% to only 48.0%. In the aggregate, eight fewer issuers used arbitration clauses at the end of 2010 than at the end of 2009. Ten issuers switched away from arbitration (including the four settling issuers), while two switched to arbitration.

2. Carve-outs

Parties do not always agree to arbitrate all disputes that arise under their contract. Even if the contract includes a broad arbitration clause, the parties may agree to exclude, or "carve out," certain claims from arbitration. . . .

. . .

Far and away the most common carve-out in credit card arbitration clause is for small claims (defined either by the dollar amount sought or by the claims being brought in small claims court). Of the issuers studied, thirty-two (of fourty-seven, or 68.1%) excluded small claims from arbitration. Most of the agreements that did not exclude small claims were from small issuers (the fifteen issuers not including a small claims carve-out comprised only 1.6% of credit card loans outstanding, while the thirty-two including a small claims carve-out comprised 98.4% of credit card loans outstanding).

. . .

Relatedly, five issuers (of forty-seven, or 10.6%; but 51.4% of credit card loans outstanding) excluded debt collection claims from arbitration. (Four of the five also excluded issuer and cardholder small claims cases from arbitration.) One clause (of forty-seven, or 2.1%; 0.0% of credit card loans outstanding) by a very small issuer sought to obtain a similar result by expressly providing that the issuer's filing of a debt collection action does not waive its right to demand arbitration in the event the cardholder files a counterclaim. Whether a court would honor such a no-waiver provision is uncertain.

Other types of carve-outs are less common in credit card arbitration clauses. Nine issuers (of forty-seven, or 19.1%; 3.8% of credit card loans outstanding) excluded from arbitration claims for interim relief, such as preliminary injunctions and attachments. Twelve issuers (of forty-seven, or 25.5%; 11.2% of credit card loans outstanding) excluded repossession and other self-help remedies, while six issuers (of forty-seven, or 12.8%; 3.6% of credit card loans outstanding) excluded claims in bankruptcy.

3. Opt-out provisions

Some courts consider whether cardholders have the ability to opt out of an arbitration clause in deciding whether the clause is procedurally unconscionable. . . . [M]ost arbitration agreements in our sample (thirty-five of forty-seven, or 74.5% of issuers; 76.3% of credit card loans outstanding) do not include an opt-out provision. For those that do, the amount of time in which the cardholder can exercise the right to opt out varies from thirty days (the most common — seven of forty-seven, or 14.9% of issuers; 17.4% of credit card loans outstanding) to sixty days (four of forty-seven, or 8.5% of issuers; 6.2% of credit card loans outstanding).

. . .

C. Provisions of Arbitration Clauses

By agreeing to arbitration, parties agree to a form of dispute resolution that differs from litigation in court. Parties retain the ability to customize the arbitration process to a large degree . . . . But even if the parties do not customize the process, arbitration still differs in important ways from court: juries are not available; discovery tends to be more limited; and courts do not review awards on the merits but rather only on the limited grounds set out in the governing arbitration statute.

. . .

Parties to an arbitration agreement may modify these typical characteristics of arbitration or otherwise define the arbitration process in their arbitration clause. The rest of this section examines the extent to which credit card agreements in our sample contain provisions that (1) set out the governing arbitration law, (2) select a provider to administer the arbitration, (3) delegate certain decisions to the arbitrators, (4) provide a minimum recovery to a prevailing cardholder, (5) contain possibly "unfair" provisions, (6) regulate the costs of arbitration, and (7) establish an arbitral appeals panel or address the scope of court review of awards.

1. Governing arbitration law

In *Volt Information Sciences, Inc. v. Board of Trustees of Leland Stanford Junior University*, the Supreme Court held that parties can incorporate state arbitration law by reference into their contract, even if the provision of state arbitration law otherwise would be preempted by the FAA. If the parties so agree, the provisions of the state arbitration law are treated as part of the arbitration agreement, and are to be enforced as such by courts under the FAA.

. . .

The more difficult issue is deciding when the parties have agreed to incorporate state arbitration law by reference into their agreement. In *Volt*, the Supreme Court did not decide that issue; instead the Court deferred to the California court's interpretation of a general choice-of-law clause in the contract as constituting the parties' agreement to state arbitration law. Following *Volt*, numerous lower courts construed general choice-of-law clauses as incorporating state arbitration law. Given how frequently parties include choice-of-law clauses in their contracts, the result was to restrict the scope of FAA preemption substantially. In subsequent cases, however, the Supreme Court rejected that interpretation of a general choice-of-law clause. In *Mastrobuono v. Shearson Lehman Hutton, Inc.*, the Court refused to construe a general choice-of-law clause (which specified New York law as the governing law) as "mean[ing] 'New York decisional law, including that State's allocation of power between courts and arbitrators, notwithstanding otherwise-applicable federal law.' " Instead, as reiterated in *Preston v. Ferrer*, "the 'best way to harmonize' the parties' adoption of the AAA rules and their selection of [state] law is to read the latter to encompass prescriptions governing the substantive rights and obligations of the parties, but not the State's 'special rules limiting the authority of arbitrators.' "

Data from the credit card agreements we studied . . . are consistent with the view reflected in *Mastrobuono* and *Preston v. Ferrer* that parties do not ordinarily intend to incorporate state arbitration law, to the exclusion of federal arbitration law, into their arbitration agreements. Only one very small issuer (of forty-seven, or 2.1%; 0.0% of credit card loans outstanding) in our sample contracted solely for application of a state's arbitration law to the arbitration proceeding. By contrast, forty-three issuers (of forty-seven, or 91.5%; 99.9% of credit card loans outstanding) specified that the FAA applies, ordinarily with either no mention of state law or expressly excluding the application of state arbitration law.

Presumably the provisions specifying the governing arbitration law were included in response to *Volt* to make clear that parties were not trying to incorporate state arbitration law by reference. Such a wholesale rejection strongly suggests that, at least for credit card issuers, the contract interpretation in *Mastrobuono* and *Preston v. Ferrer* is more in accord with the parties' agreement.

. . .

2. *Provider rules*

All of the arbitration clauses in the sample provide for administered arbitration — that is, arbitration in which an arbitration provider handles the administrative aspects of the case, makes available detailed rules governing the proceeding, and serves as an appointing authority if the parties cannot otherwise agree on an arbitrator. The arbitration rules promulgated by providers, which the parties incorporate into their arbitration agreement, also modify the default characteristics of arbitration.

. . . The AAA is named as the exclusive provider in sixteen (of thirty-nine, or 41.0%; 16.3% of credit card loans outstanding) of the arbitration clauses as of

December 31, 2010, and is listed as one of two or three permissible providers in an additional sixteen (of thirty-nine, or 41.0%; 82.3% of credit card loans outstanding). Two clauses (of thirty-nine, or 5.1%; 0.1% of credit card loans outstanding) name JAMS as the exclusive provider, and another seventeen (of thirty-nine, or 43.6%; 82.3% of credit card loans outstanding) list it as one of two or three permissible providers. Two (of thirty-nine, or 5.1%; 0.1% of credit card loans outstanding) continue to name the National Arbitration Forum as the exclusive provider, despite the fact that it no longer administers consumer arbitrations. One clause (of thirty-nine, or 2.6%; 0.0% of credit card loans outstanding) gives the parties a choice between JAMS and National Arbitration and Mediation, a less well known provider, and another clause (one of thirty-nine, or 2.6%; 1.2% of credit card loans outstanding) specifies only that the provider shall be "a national arbitration organization with significant experience in financial and consumer disputes."

The data illustrate how credit card issuers responded to the National Arbitration Forum's ceasing all administration of new consumer arbitrations in July 2009. A number of large issuers (reflecting 47.6% of credit card loans outstanding and subject to arbitration in the sample) still specified the NAF as a possible provider in the credit card agreements they filed with the Federal Reserve as of December 31, 2009. By December 31, 2010, all of those issuers (with the exception of one very small issuer) had replaced the NAF with JAMS as an approved provider. Even a year and a half after the NAF ceased administering new consumer arbitrations, a surprising number of issuers continued to include the NAF in their arbitration clauses. When the NAF is listed as one of multiple providers, the risks of not updating the arbitration clause are limited because another provider continues to be available. The persistence of the NAF in some credit card arbitration agreements for at least a year and a half after it was no longer available suggests that the costs of updating the issuer's arbitration clauses exceed the benefits, or that the provision for some other reason is "sticky."

. . .

3. Delegation clauses

In *Rent-A-Center, West, Inc. v. Jackson*, the Supreme Court held that parties can agree by contract to delegate to the arbitrators the exclusive authority to rule on unconscionability challenges to the arbitration clause. . . .

Commentators predicted that after *Rent-A-Center* businesses would likely revise their consumer and employment arbitration clauses to include delegation clauses. If so, courts would lose their ability to police arbitration clauses on unconscionability grounds, unless the court first held the delegation clause unenforceable. And to do so, challenges to that clause must be directed specifically to that clause, not the contract as a whole or the arbitration clause as a whole. Our data provide an early look at whether credit card issuers have revised their arbitration clauses to include delegation clauses.

None of the arbitration clauses in our sample included the sort of definitive language ("The Arbitrator, and not any federal, state, or local court or agency, shall have the exclusive authority to resolve . . .") that is in the *Rent-A-Center* arbitration clause. That said, the majority of the clauses in the sample, both before and after *Rent-A-Center*, do state that the arbitrators have the authority to rule on the validity of the arbitration agreement, which courts treat as comparable to the language in *Rent-A-Center.* So defined, as of December 31, 2010, twenty (of thirty-nine, or 51.3%) clauses included a delegation clause; and 52.6% of credit card loans outstanding in the sample were subject to a delegation clause.

. . .

Although not as common as delegation clauses, twelve (of 39, or 30.8%; 12.8% of credit card loans outstanding) arbitration clauses included a delegation clause that excludes issues of class arbitration from the scope of the clause. In other words, the clauses provided that arbitrators are to decide issues of the validity of the arbitration clause, except for issues related to class arbitration, which are to be decided by courts. Such clauses likely reflect an attempt to avoid the empirical reality that (at least prior to the Supreme Court's decision in *Stolt-Nielsen SA v. AnimalFeeds Int'l*) AAA arbitrators almost unanimously construed arbitration clauses as permitting class arbitration, even though almost no clauses expressly permit arbitration on a class basis.

Four issuers (of thirty-nine, or 10.3%; but 29.2% of credit card loans outstanding) used an "anti-delegation clause" — expressly providing that the validity of the arbitration agreement shall be resolved only in court and not in arbitration. Finally, three of the clauses included no provision on point. But all three issuers did incorporate provider rules, which give arbitrators authority to rule on the validity of the arbitration clause, into their arbitration clauses. Given that most courts construe such provider rules as falling under *Rent-A-Center*, these clauses effectively include delegation clauses, although not by express language.

Interestingly, though, the use of delegation clauses declined slightly and the use of anti-delegation clauses actually increased after *Rent-A-Center.* Between 2009 and 2010, two issuers added a class exception to their arbitration clauses, and one (relatively large) issuer replaced its class exception with an anti-delegation clause. No issuers in our sample added delegation clauses to their arbitration clauses after *Rent-A-Center.*

Again, these are early results. The Supreme Court issued the *Rent-A-Center* decision on June 21, 2010, just six months prior to the December 31, 2010 filings we consider in this study. Given the slow speed of issuer response to the NAF's demise as a provider of consumer arbitration services, it may be too early to conclude that credit card issuers will not respond to *Rent-A-Center* by including delegation clauses in their arbitration clauses. So far, however, we find no such trend.

4. Minimum recovery provisions

The arbitration clause in *AT&T Mobility v. Concepcion* provided that a consumer who recovered more in arbitration than AT&T's last settlement offer would recover a minimum of $7500 and double attorney's fees. The district court in that case found that "[b]ecause the arbitration provision provides sufficient incentive for individual consumers with disputes involving small damages to pursue (a) the informal claims process to redress their grievances, and (b) arbitration in the event of an unresolved claim, the subject provision is an adequate substitute for class arbitration." The Supreme Court likewise referred to the provision in its opinion, characterizing the district court's decision as finding that "the Concepcions were *better off* under their arbitration agreement with AT&T than they would have been as participants in a class action."

Only one clause in our sample (which predated the Supreme Court's decision in *Concepcion*) included a similar provision. The arbitration clause in the World Financial Network National Bank (WFNNB) credit card agreement provided for a "special payment" to a prevailing cardholder as follows:

> **14. Special Payment:** If (1) you submit a Claim Notice in accordance with Paragraph 30.B. on your own behalf (and not on behalf of any other party); (2) we refuse to provide you with the relief you request; and (3) an arbitrator subsequently determines that you were entitled to such relief (or greater relief), the arbitrator shall award you at least $5,100 (plus any fees and costs to which you are entitled).

Although the amount of the "special payment" is less than that in the AT&T Mobility clause, the structure of the clause is the same: if the cardholder asserts a claim that the issuer does not pay, and the cardholder then recovers in arbitration at least as much as the amount claimed, the issuer will make a minimum payment that might exceed the cardholder's actual damages. It remains to be seen whether additional issuers will incorporate such a clause into their arbitration agreement after *Concepcion*; our data are not able to answer that question.

5. *"Unfair" provisions*

Courts and commentators have identified an array of provisions in arbitration clauses as "unfair" to consumers and employees. This section examines the use of some of those provisions in credit card agreements. The short answer is that, with the exception of class arbitration waivers, most of these types of provisions are rare or nonexistent in credit card agreements.

. . . [S]everal . . . types of provisions [have been] identified by courts and commentators as unfair or at least potentially unfair: clauses resulting in biased decision makers; class arbitration waivers; remedy limitations (such as waivers of punitive damages); shortened time limits for filing claims; distant hearing locations; limits on discovery; provisions precluding the cardholder from disclosing the existence of a dispute; and provisions denying a right to counsel or an in-person hearing. The list includes many if not most of the provisions most frequently challenged as unconscionable; those not included (e.g., provisions setting up a nonmutual arbitral appeals process and provisions dealing with arbitral costs) are excluded from this [list] only because of the greater variety of approaches reflected in such clauses (but "unfair" variations of those provisions are nonetheless rare).

. . .

The only type of provision in this list of "unfair" provisions that is common in credit card agreements is a class arbitration waiver, the provision at issue in *Concepcion*. Of the arbitration clauses in the sample, forty-four of forty-seven clauses (or 93.6%) (covering 99.9% of the credit card loans outstanding) waived any right to class arbitration. Because arbitration clauses themselves preclude a party from being a member of a class action in court, the vast majority of arbitration clauses in the sample would preclude cardholders from obtaining class relief.

By comparison, as already stated, the other types of "unfair" provisions in the list almost never appear in the arbitration clauses in the sample. None of the clauses in the sample contained a biased arbitrator selection mechanism, specified biasing arbitrator qualifications, or denied the right to counsel. Only three clauses (of forty-seven, or 6.4% of clauses; 1.2% of credit card loans outstanding) included a limitation on the award of punitive damages. Only one clause included a nondisclosure provision, although it covered 5.7% of credit card loans outstanding. The other provisions . . . — time limits for filing claims, potentially distant hearing locations, limits on available discovery, and restrictions on the availability of an in-person hearing — are included in at most two clauses and apply to no more than 0.2% of credit card loans outstanding in the sample.

A few other points worth noting about provisions dealing with issues related to those listed [above]:

- Twenty-five of the clauses (of forty-seven, or 53.2%; 44.4% of credit card loans outstanding) contained no provision requiring particular qualifications for arbitrators. Of the twenty-two clauses that did set out some sort of required qualifications: one (of forty-seven, or 2.1%; 0.0% of credit card loans outstanding) required expertise in the subject matter of the dispute; one (of forty-seven, or 2.1%; 1.2% of credit card loans outstanding) required that the arbitrator be a retired federal judge if a party so requests; while the remaining twenty (of forty-seven, or 42.6%; 54.4% of credit card loans outstanding) required that the arbitrator be either a lawyer (with varying degrees of experience) or a retired judge (one clause provided that "registered arbitrator" was an option as well).

- Although the substantial majority of arbitration clauses included class arbitration waivers, two (of forty-seven, or 4.3%; 0.1% of credit card loans outstanding) contained no provision on the issue and one (of forty-seven, or 2.1%; 0.0% of credit card loans outstanding) was silent on class arbitration while expressly authorizing consolidation of related claims.

- Slightly under half of the clauses (twenty-one of forty-seven, or 44.7%) from issuers with slightly more than half the market share (53.6%) contained an "anti-severability provision." Such clauses provide that if a court invalidates the class arbitration waiver, the invalid waiver should not be severed from the rest of the arbitration clause, with the result that the entire arbitration clause is unenforceable and the case proceeds as a class action in court.

- Two clauses (of forty-seven, or 4.3%; 6.6% of credit card loans outstanding) provided by contract that constitutional restrictions on the award of punitive damages, which courts have held are not otherwise applicable to arbitration awards, would apply.

- Ten clauses (of forty-seven, or 21.3%; 40.0% of credit card loans outstanding) provided that the arbitrator had the authority to award all remedies available under applicable law, and another five (of forty-seven, or 10.6%; 6.4% of credit card loans outstanding) specified that all remedies that were available in court would also be available in arbitration. In one respect, those provisions might be seen as limitations on remedies that otherwise could be available in arbitration, because courts have held that arbitrators are not limited in fashioning remedies to the remedies courts can award. On the other hand, given that arbitration clauses have been criticized as denying consumers remedies that would be available to them in court, these provisions also might be seen as protecting the rights of cardholders by ensuring that the same remedies are available in arbitration as in court.

- Of the clauses in the sample, seven (of forty-seven, or 14.9%; 40.1% of credit card loans outstanding) expressly provided that parties can be represented by counsel in arbitration; the rest of the clauses did not address the issue.

- Six clauses (of forty-seven, or 12.8%; 52.2%% of credit card loans outstanding) expressly authorized the arbitrator to protect the confidentiality of customer information upon request.

6. Arbitration costs

Because arbitration is private rather than public dispute resolution, parties to the arbitration proceeding must pay the full cost of the process. Typically, when a party files a claim in arbitration, it must pay at least some of the administrative fees upfront and put down a deposit to cover expected arbitrator's fees. For larger claims, these upfront costs can exceed the costs of filing a comparable case in court. For smaller claims, both the AAA and JAMS cap the costs to consumers. For all claims, providers may waive their fees in the event of hardship. Nonetheless, a number of court decisions have invalidated arbitration agreements on the ground that they imposed excessive costs on consumers.

Almost all of the arbitration clauses in our sample selected either the AAA or JAMS as the arbitration provider. Arbitrations under those clauses are subject to the provider's cost schedule and rules governing costs, which thus provide the backdrop against which the more detailed provisions in the clauses are operating. Beyond those basics, most of the arbitration clauses in our sample address arbitration costs to some degree, but the details of the provisions vary . . . .

Only one clause in the sample (of forty-seven, or 2.1%; 0.1% of credit card loans outstanding) went as far as the clause in *Concepcion* and provided that the issuer pays all arbitration fees. Another (one of forty-seven, or 2.1%; 5.9% of credit card loans outstanding) provided that the issuer would pay all fees when the cardholder makes a good faith request for assistance. At the other end of the spectrum, none of the clauses in the sample required the cardholder and issuer to share costs equally. In its internal review of arbitration clauses for compliance with the Consumer Due Process Protocol, the AAA requires businesses to waive such cost-sharing provisions before it will administer consumer arbitrations seeking $75,000 or less because such provisions would impose higher costs on consumers than provided under the AAA's consumer arbitration fee structure.

A handful of clauses capped the fees for which the cardholder is responsible —

at a fixed dollar amount (three of forty-seven, or 6.4% of clauses; 1.4% of credit card loans outstanding); at the amount of court filing fees (one of forty-seven, or 2.1% of clauses; 13.4% of credit card loans outstanding); or for small claims (two of forty-seven, or 4.3% of clauses; 0.2% of credit card loans outstanding). A number of clauses addressed the circumstances under which the issuer would advance the upfront filing and arbitrators fees on behalf of a cardholder. (Fourteen (of forty-seven, or 29.8%; 7.2% of credit card loans outstanding) contained no provision on point.) Again, the details varied widely, with the most common clauses providing that the issuer would advance arbitration fees for good cause (eight of forty-seven, or 17.0%; 60.2% of credit card loans outstanding); would consider advancing the fees in good faith (four of forty-seven, or 8.5%; 13.5% of credit card loans outstanding); or simply would consider advancing the fees (ten of forty-seven, or 21.3%; 4.1% of credit card loans outstanding). Finally, just under half the clauses (twenty of forty-seven, or 42.6%; 45.7% of credit card loans outstanding) dealt with how costs would be allocated at the end of the case, with the most common such provision stating that the issuer will reimburse the cardholder for his or her arbitration fees if the cardholder prevails or for good cause (three of forty-seven, or 6.4% of clauses; 38.8% of credit card loans outstanding).

. . .

Provisions specifying the number of arbitrators also can affect the cost of the arbitration proceeding: three arbitrators will almost certainly cost more than one. Accordingly, in applying the Consumer Due Process Protocol, the AAA requires businesses to waive any contract provision requiring three arbitrators before it will administer consumer arbitrations seeking $75,000 or less.

In our sample, none of the arbitration agreements imposed an across-the-board requirement that the parties use a three-arbitrator panel to decide the case. Sixteen agreements (of forty-seven, or 34.0%; 57.9% of credit card loans outstanding) provided expressly for a single arbitrator, and twenty more (of forty-seven, or 42.6%; 21.0% of credit card loans outstanding) seemed to do so implicitly by always referring to "the arbitrator" in the singular. By comparison, one clause provided that any dispute will be resolved by "one or more" arbitrators, and three clauses refer to the "arbitrator(s)," leaving open the possibility that more than one arbitrator would be chosen but not requiring it. One clause (of forty-seven, or 2.1%; 0.2% of credit card loans outstanding) provided for a single arbitrator unless the claim is larger than $250,000, while three (of forty-seven, or 6.4%; 13.4% of credit card loans outstanding) provided for three arbitrators only if the arbitration provider specified in the contract is unavailable, otherwise leaving the decision to the provider and its rules.

. . .

7. Appeals and court review

As noted above, a common characteristic of arbitration is that court review of awards is limited. However, parties can set up an arbitral appeals process if they wish, appointing a panel of arbitrators to review the decision of the initial decision maker. In consumer and employment cases, some courts have found provisions establishing arbitral appeals panels to be unconscionable when they are one-sided — i.e., structured so that only the business is likely to be able to appeal (such as by limiting appeals to cases in which an award exceeds a threshold dollar amount).

Just under half of the arbitration clauses in the sample established an arbitral appeals process. Of the forty-seven clauses in the sample, twenty-four (51.1%; 23.9% of credit card loans outstanding) did not set up an arbitral appeals process (although, of course, the award remains subject to review under Section 10 of the FAA). Two of the clauses (4.3%; 0.1% of credit card loans outstanding) provided for an appeal if a right to appeal is available under the FAA, again, apparently adding nothing to the usual FAA grounds. But the remaining twenty-one clauses — 44.7% of the clauses but covering 76.0% of credit card loans outstanding — authorized an appeal to an arbitral appeals panel.

The triggering event for the availability of an appeal varied . . . . Nine clauses (of forty-seven, or 19.1%; 57.4% of credit card loans outstanding) permitted an appeal upon request, making the right to appeal available to both issuers and consumers. Seven clauses (of forty-seven, or 14.9%; 18.5% of credit card loans outstanding) permitted an appeal when the amount claimed exceeded a specified threshold (either $50,000 or $100,000). Given the added expense of an appeal, limiting its availability to higher stakes claims seems to make sense. And setting the threshold as based on the amount claimed permits either consumers (who might make claims exceeding the threshold) or issuers (who might be subject to claims exceeding the threshold) to appeal. By contrast, five clauses (of forty-seven, or 10.6%) from small issuers (with 0.2% of credit card loans outstanding) specified the threshold (either $100,000 or $200,000) based on the amount awarded rather than the amount claimed. These provisions, while relatively rare, are potentially problematic under the cases cited above because consumers are relatively less likely than businesses to be subject to such awards.

Interestingly, the arbitration clauses studied included a varying degree of provisions that might affect the scope of court review. . . .

          . . .

One clause in the sample might run afoul of *Hall Street*. The USAA Bank Credit Card Arbitration Addendum (one of forty-seven, or 2.1%; 4.9% of credit card loans outstanding) provided that:

> The arbitrator's decision . . . may be judicially reviewed on all grounds set forth in 9 U.S.C. § 10, as well as on the grounds that the decision is manifestly inconsistent with the terms of the Agreement or any applicable laws or regulations.

The standard of review echoes the "manifest disregard of the law" vacatur ground, which is of uncertain validity under the FAA. If manifest disregard review is no longer available, this provision would have the same flaw as the one in *Hall Street*: it would specify a vacatur ground not listed in Section 10 of the FAA. If manifest disregard continues to be available, the provision would be superfluous.

Other clauses might affect the scope of court review indirectly, by requiring the arbitrator to follow the law or to make decisions supported by substantial evidence.

Both the California Supreme Court and the Texas Supreme Court have construed such provisions as limitations on the arbitrators' authority, and held that courts can vacate an award for excess of authority when arbitrators fail to comply with those provisions (i.e., make an error of law or decide without substantial evidence support). By contrast, some federal courts have rejected this mechanism for obtaining court review of arbitral awards as an attempt to evade *Hall Street*, even though its use long pre-dates that case. Alternatively, rather than attempts to expand the scope of court review, these sorts of clauses might be attempts to ensure that arbitrators do not ignore the law or facts in their decisions (or to reassure cardholders and courts that substantive legal rights remain available in arbitration).

In our sample, the substantial majority of clauses (thirty-five of forty-seven, or 74.5%; 94.0% of credit card loans outstanding) contained some requirement that the arbitrators follow the substantive law in making their awards. The verbal formulations varied slightly (*e.g.*, "must apply"; "must follow"; "shall follow"; "shall resolve"; "will apply"; "will render"), but the substance of the provisions appears to be identical. By comparison, arbitration clauses providing that the arbitrators were bound by the facts or were required to have substantial evidence for their decisions were much rarer. Only three clauses (of forty-seven, or 6.4% of clauses in the sample, and 0.1% of credit card loans outstanding) provided that the arbitrators were bound by the facts, and two more (of 47, or 4.3%; 0.0% of credit card loans outstanding) required the award to be supported by substantial evidence. At bottom, clauses requiring the arbitrators to follow the law are common in the sample, while clauses addressing the facts are uncommon.

Stephen R. Bond, HOW TO DRAFT AN ARBITRATION CLAUSE (REVISITED),
ICC INTERNATIONAL COURT OF ARBITRATION BULLETIN (vol. 1/no. 2), Dec. 1990, at 14, 16–21[*]

a. *Ad Hoc* or Institutional Arbitration

While this question can itself be the subject of entire seminars, it is a fundamental choice which must be made before going any further as the decision on this point affects everything else in the arbitration clause. My own view, which I hope is objective, is that in international arbitration the arbitration clause should provide for institutional arbitration. You pay an administrative charge, but with a good institution you get value for the money. For example, with the ICC you have an arbitration system tested by over 7,000 cases, with an experienced International Secretariat and special features, such as scrutiny of draft arbitral awards by the ICC Court, that result in an overwhelming number of ICC awards being honored voluntarily by the parties and the balance overwhelmingly upheld by national tribunals. For these reasons, the majority of international contracts that provide for arbitration provide for it to be carried out under the auspices of the ICC Rules.

It appears that to shift from an *ad hoc* arbitration clause to one specifying an institution is extremely difficult once a dispute has broken out. Accordingly, wisdom and prudence — two watchwords of good attorneys — mandate an effort to incorporate institutional arbitration into the clause. Then, after a dispute arises, if for any reason it subsequently appears desirable for the parties actually to resort to *ad hoc* arbitration experience indicates that the parties can often reach agreement to do this.

. . .

b. The Standard Arbitration Clause

The choice of an institution naturally presents you with the standard or model arbitration clause advocated by the chosen institution. The ICC, for example, has the following model clause:

> "All disputes arising in connection with the present contract shall be finally settled under the Rules of Conciliation and Arbitration of the International Chamber of Commerce by one or more arbitrators appointed in accordance with the said Rules."

It is short, simple, but contains what has been called the three "key expressions" to any effective arbitral clause. "All disputes" . . . "in connection with" . . . "finally settled." How often is this standard clause actually used? Of 1987's 237 arbitration clauses, the standard clause, word-for-word, was used exactly once. Of 1989's 215 clauses, it was used thrice.

Does this mean that the standard clause is valueless? Not at all. It is a basic clause, intended to create an enforceable agreement to arbitrate. However, many parties wish to add elements to it. In fact, the publication containing the amended ICC Arbitration Rules in force from 1 January 1988 itself notes, following the standard clause, that:

> "Parties are reminded that it may be desirable for them to stipulate in the arbitration clause itself the law governing the contract, the number of arbitrators and the place and language of the arbitration."

Thus, the standard ICC clause, with perhaps minor variations of wording, was used in 47 arbitration clauses (20%) in 1987 and in 21 arbitration clauses (10%) in 1989, generally with the addition of the place of arbitration.

Let us return to the standard ICC clause, which has certainly withstood the test of time, to examine some of its basic elements.

Scope of the Clause: "In connection with"

The standard ICC clause refers to all disputes "in connection with" the contract. Many of the arbitration clauses submitted to the ICC refer to disputes "arising out of or related" to the contract, disputes "arising under" the contract, disputes "related directly and/or indirectly to the performance" of the contract, etc.

These various phrases may all appear to mean about the same thing. However, a line of legal analysis has developed that draws a sharp distinction between a so-called "narrow" arbitration clause and a "broad" arbitration clause. . . .

. . .

This language and the surrounding reasoning clearly demonstrate the advantages of utilizing the key phrases of the ICC clause as well as referring arbitration to a widely-used arbitration institution which is well-known by judges in national courts.

Thus, parties should be extremely careful not to narrow inadvertently the scope of the arbitration clause by restricting the clause simply to disputes "arising under" the contract or "related to execution or performance" of the contract.

"Finally settled"

This point is considered below.

"The International Chamber of Commerce"

Difficulties arising from incorrect references to the ICC are discussed below.

Which Version of the ICC Rules is Applicable?

This question was especially pertinent two years ago because as of 1 January 1988, amended ICC Rules came into force. In a cover-letter to the amended Rules I stated that:

> "The amended ICC Rules of Arbitration will govern arbitrations which commence on or after 1 January 1988. Parties may also agree to have the amended Rules govern arbitrations initiated prior thereto. Where the parties had provided in an arbitration clause agreed to by them prior to 1 January 1988, to apply the ICC Arbitration Rules then in force, such agreement will be respected regardless of when the arbitration is commenced."

During 1987 some ten arbitration clauses specifically dealt with this question. Two of the clauses referred to the ICC Rules "then in force," presumably meaning at the time of the submission of the dispute to the ICC. The other six clauses provided for the ICC Rules "as modified from time to time" or "as amended," thus also accepting any future version of the Rules. Only three clauses dealt with this question in 1989, two of which referred to the ICC Rules "then in force."

I would note that when the ICC Rules were last modified in 1975, the question of what version of the Rules applied very rarely went to the arbitrators and, so far as I am aware, went before national courts a mere handful of times. This has also been our experience with the 1988 Rules. Indeed, a great many Terms of Reference have specifically stated that the 1988 Rules govern the case even though the arbitration commenced prior to 1 January 1988.

c. The Place of Arbitration

The importance of the place of arbitration cannot be overestimated. Its legislation determines the likelihood and extent of involvement of national courts in the conduct of the arbitration (either for judicial "assistance" or "interference"), the likelihood of enforceability of the arbitral award (depending on what international conventions the situs State is a party to), and the extent and nature of any mandatory procedural rules that you will have to adhere to in the conduct of the arbitration. (For example, in Saudi Arabia, the arbitrators must be Muslim and male.) Such factors are of far greater importance than the touristic attractions of any particular place that sometimes appear to be the decisive factor in making this decision.

Parties generally appear to be aware of the importance of the situs, at least if one can judge by the fact that in 1987 some 136 arbitration clauses (57%) specified the city or country in which any arbitration held pursuant to the clause would take place. In 1989, the figures were even higher: 146 clauses (68%). This mention of situs is, along with the choice of applicable law, the element most often added to the basic ICC arbitration clause.

. . .

I would like to add here a special comment related to the choice of a place of arbitration. In 57 (24%) of the arbitration clauses submitted to the ICC in 1987 (and in 56 (26%) of the arbitration clauses in 1989), reference was made not simply to the ICC, but to the ICC "in" Paris or "of" Paris or "de" Paris. As discussed above, this is, in fact, unnecessary as there is only one "International Chamber of Commerce" in the world. Understandably, however, many parties feel more comfortable with this additional clarification. (Indeed, in one relatively recent ICC case, the arbitrator's award on jurisdiction had to deal with a defendant's allegation that the arbitration clause was not intended to refer to ICC arbitration precisely because it did not specify "in Paris" and because there were, defendant alleged, "a large number of international chambers of commerce in the world." The arbitral tribunal quite correctly dismissed this line of reasoning.)

Parties should be aware, however, that reference to the ICC "of" Paris or "in" Paris will be interpreted by the ICC Court of Arbitration as an indication of the intended place of arbitration, unless another *situs* is clearly indicated in the clause (as does often happen). A breakdown of the figures for 1989 shows that out of those 56 cases where reference was made to the ICC and "Paris," 33 of the clauses contained in addition a specific mention as to the place of arbitration.

The "rule of interpretation" noted above was thus applied in 11% of cases in 1989. It is equally used when an arbitration clause mistakenly refers to the ICC "of" Geneva, or "in" Zurich or any other place. After all, as there is only one ICC, the reference to another city can, logically, have no other meaning. This position of the ICC Court has been given solid support in several ICC awards and Court decisions.

d. Applicable Law

While the choice of the law to be applied by the arbitrators to determine the substantive issues before them is not an element necessary for the validity of an arbitration clause, it is certainly desirable for the parties to agree upon the applicable law in the arbitration clause if at all possible. Failure to do so is a significant factor in increasing the time and cost of an arbitration. Moreover, the decision of the arbitral tribunal on the matter (for it is an issue to be decided by the arbitrators, even if institutional arbitration is used) may bring an unpleasant surprise to one of the parties. Finally, where an institution is to select the chairman or sole arbitrator it is, as a practical matter, far easier to appoint the best possible person when it is known in what country's law the arbitrator should be most expert.

For these reasons, the element most often added to the contract, often directly in the arbitration clause itself, is that of the law applicable to the contract. Some 178 contracts (75%) in 1987 and 146 contracts (66%) in 1989 contained reference to a specific applicable law, either by naming the law of a particular country or of the country of one of the parties (e.g., "law of seller's country"). The applicable law was included in the arbitration clause itself some 81 times in 1987 (111 times in 1989). Also of interest is the rarity of clauses which authorize the arbitral tribunal to resolve the dispute on the basis of equity, amiable composition, *ex aequo et bono*, or with the arbitrators acting as mediators. In 1987, only some 9 clauses (3%) incorporated any such basis for resolving the dispute. (Some other clauses specifically forbade amiable composition, although in ICC arbitration the arbitral tribunal may not act as *amiable compositeur* unless specifically authorized to do so by the parties). Out of the 8 1989 clauses (4%) providing for amiable composition, some specified that a national law could be applied at the same time.

One contract between Yougoslavian and Kenyan parties in a case submitted before the ICC Court in 1987, provided that any dispute should be settled "on the basis of international law." Another provided that disputes would be settled according to "traditional Rules Covering International Contracts." Yet another contract stated that "General Principles of Law applicable in Western Europe" would apply. No clause in 1987 or in 1989 mentioned *lex mercatoria*.

While the object of this article is certainly not to examine the "philosophy" of arbitration, I cannot help but note that the statistics just cited support the view that arbitration is generally not sought by the parties because they wish an "extra-legal" resolution to their disputes. Rather, the parties appear to desire a resolution based on a specified, predictable legal system. What they clearly do not want is such a legal system being applied by the national court of the other party.

A few points should be borne in mind in deciding upon an applicable law and I will very briefly mention them.

First, it is preferable that the legal system agreed upon is adequately developed in regard to the specific issues likely to arise in any eventual dispute.

Second, you may wish to exclude the conflict of laws principles of the chosen law, either explicitly or by specifying the "substantive law" of the particular country concerned.

Third, be sure that the national law chosen permits the subject matter of the contract to be resolved by arbitration. Copyright or patent law questions, antitrust matters, etc. often may not be resolved by arbitration, but only by the national courts.

e. Composition of the Arbitral Tribunal

The next element which should be given the most serious attention is that of the composition of the arbitral tribunal. How many arbitrators do you want?

How should they be selected? Should they have any particular qualifications? No broad generalities can cover all the situations likely to arise.

Regarding the number of arbitrators, in 1987's arbitration clauses some 58, — 24% — (in 1989, 62 clauses — 29%) specified either one or three arbitrators. Of these, 11 (7 in 1989) specified one arbitrator and 47 clauses (55 in 1989) specified three. It is interesting to note that in some 83 of the 1987 cases where the arbitration clause did not determine the number of the arbitrators, the parties were able to reach agreement between themselves on the point prior to the ICC Court having to make a decision. This would indicate that, as a practical matter, it will often be possible to reach agreement on this element even after a dispute has developed. Consequently, it is less urgent to reach agreement on this point in negotiating the arbitration clause than on certain others.

In 1987, four of the arbitration clauses (2 in 1989) specified one arbitrator if the parties could agree upon him, otherwise there would be three arbitrators. Although the statistics are too meager on this point to draw general conclusions, I do believe that these few clauses provide a key to a major concern of the parties, namely the need to have an arbitral tribunal in which the parties can have confidence. Confidence is engendered either by knowing and agreeing upon an individual or, if this cannot be done, by having a three-person tribunal, one of whom can be proposed by each party. Probably for these reasons the ICC's experience has been that parties from developing countries and Eastern European countries have a strong preference for three-person arbitral tribunals. They seem to believe that even though co-arbitrators must be independent of the party proposing them, pursuant to the ICC Rules, a co-arbitrator of the same nationality can explain to his fellow arbitrators the legal, economic and business context within which that party operates.

Of course, three-person arbitral tribunals are more expensive and the arbitration tends to take longer, considerations that cannot be ignored when drafting the arbitration clause.

Arbitration clauses tend to include no mention of other elements relating to the arbitral panel. Only three clauses in 1987 specified the nationality of the chairman and each time he had to be Swiss. Only a single clause set out professional qualifications, namely that the chairman should be "fully educated and trained as a lawyer."

In 1989, out of 13 clauses containing special requirements, 10 concerned the nationality either of the Chairman or of all arbitrators. Some gave positive indications such as "the chairman shall be a Swiss professional judge." Others excluded certain nationalities, such as the following mentioned in three different cases, which, confirming the analysis above, did not involve parties from developing countries or Eastern Europe: "none of the arbitrators shall be nationals of either of the parties hereto."

It may well be that ICC clauses are not typical in this regard because parties know that the quality of ICC arbitrators is excellent and the ICC Rules require that the Chairman or sole arbitrator be from a country other than those of the parties. Thus, with regard to the selection of arbitrators, confidence in the arbitral institution may well have reduced the amount of detail parties would otherwise have put in an *ad hoc* arbitration clause, for example.

f. Language of the Arbitration

Many parties may mistakenly believe that the language in which the contract is written will automatically be the language of any arbitration arising out of that contract. It is true that the ICC Rules, for example, state in Article 15(3) that the arbitrator shall give "due regard . . . in particular to the language of the contract" in determining the language of the arbitration. It will, however, be for the arbitral tribunal to decide the question should the parties not have agreed on it.

As can well be imagined, simultaneous interpretation at hearings and translation of all documents into two or more languages are enormously expensive and time-consuming. If it is not possible to agree on a language in the arbitration clause then it would be desirable to try to agree either that costs for interpretation and translation are shared or else borne by the party requiring the interpretation or translation. However, not a single clause in 1987 or in 1989 contained such a provision, although some 32 clauses — 13.5% — in 1987 (and 40 clauses — 19% — in 1989) did select a language. English was specified in 25 clauses (31 in 1989), French in 6 (4 in 1989) French and/or English in 1 clause. (In 1989, one clause provided for French and Spanish, another for English and German).

g. Waiver of Appeal/"Exclusion Agreement"

A primary advantage of arbitration is that it is, in principle, essentially free from judicial involvement during the arbitration itself and an arbitral award is "final" in the sense that it is intended to be free from judicial examination of its substance. Article 24 of the ICC Rules provides that "the arbitral award shall be final" and the parties are deemed to waive their right to any appeal insofar as such waiver can validly be made. Despite this language, in 1987 some 49 arbitration clauses (21%), and in 1989 56 clauses (26%) specifically provided, in essence, that the award issued is to be "Final and binding upon the Parties who agree to waive all right of appeal thereon."

Depending on the nationalities of the parties, the place of arbitration and the location of assets that may need to be used to satisfy the award, a specific waiver of appeal in the arbitration clause could well be useful. . . .

h. Entry of Judgement Stipulation

In the U.S., arbitration clauses often provide that judgement may be entered upon the award in any court of competent jurisdiction. The model clause of the AAA contains language to this effect and it has been said that it is better to include such a phrase in clauses with U.S. parties or where execution may be sought in the U.S. Some 31 clauses (13%) in 1987 and 21 clauses (10%) in 1989 had such a stipulation, and not always where U.S. parties were involved. In one instance, the parties relied on a contractual penalty clause to ensure that the arbitral proceedings and the enforcement procedure would run smoothly. The clause provided that any party who refuses to go to arbitration or to enforce an award and by doing so forces the other party to bring the case in front of local courts, shall be bound to pay to the other party a sum of 1,000,000 French Francs.

i. Other Matters

Much could be said about the advantages of including various other elements in the arbitration clause where, according to circumstances, they could prove useful in facilitating a less expensive and time consuming arbitration. However, in 1987 and 1989 these other elements were virtually never mentioned. This does not, of course, detract from their utility, but is probably a reflection of the practical difficulties of negotiating a too-detailed arbitration clause and of the fact that it takes the incentive and stimulation of an actual arbitration before most minds can adequately focus on such matters.

Nevertheless, for the sake of completeness I will list these other elements so that they may be borne in mind should the occasion arise where one or more of them might one day prove to be important in a particular arbitration. (The number of times each element was included in an arbitration clause in 1987 and 1989 is also noted.)

(a) The applicable procedural law (1987-1:1989-1).

(b) Power of the arbitrator to adapt the contract (1987-1, refusing any such power: none in 1989).

(c) Extent of discovery and cross-examination (1987-1:1989-0).

(d) Waiver of sovereign immunity (1987 and 1989-0).

(e) Accommodation for multiparty disputes (1987-4:1989-2).

(f) Division of costs of arbitration between parties (1987-6:1989-2).

(g) Partial awards either forbidden or required (1987 and 1989: 0).

(h) Technical expertise (1987-0:1989-2).

Finally, three 1989 clauses in construction contracts specified in essence that "the works shall continue pending the arbitral proceedings."

CONCLUSIONS

I will not end this presentation by revealing the all-purpose, miraculous arbitration clause because there is no single clause that is appropriate in every case. You cannot escape the need, each time you negotiate an arbitration clause, to engage in a rigorous analysis of the circumstances related to the particular transaction in order to produce an arbitration clause tailored to the situation at hand. In the long run, this work will result in immeasurable savings of time and money.

PROBLEM 8.1

As an aide to Senator Grace Dunbar (see, *e.g.*, Problem 7.17), you have learned a lot about arbitration these past several months. After you prepare a report for the Senator summarizing the available empirical evidence on the terms and provisions contained in arbitration agreements, she asks you whether that evidence provides any insight into the fairness of consumer arbitration. How would you respond to the Senator?

PROBLEM 8.2

Your first job out of law school is with a large law firm that represents a number of banks with extensive credit card operations. You are given the task of redrafting the standard form agreement that one of the banks uses for all of its credit card customers. The client tells you to be sure and include an arbitration clause in the revised form. "Do what you can to discourage busybodies from filing claims against us," the client says. "A really short time limit for filing claims, no attorneys' fees or punitive damages, all those sorts of things would be good." "And," the client adds, "make sure the arbitrator has to be a manager from another bank — then we won't have to worry about the award coming out the wrong way."

Although you say nothing to the client at the time, you are uneasy about drafting such a one-sided arbitration clause. Is it ethical to draft a clause that you believe to be unfair? Is it ethical to refuse to do so? What sort of practical considerations come into play? What do you do?

§ 8.03   DRAFTING AN ARBITRATION CLAUSE

John M. Townsend, DRAFTING ARBITRATION CLAUSES: AVOIDING THE 7 DEADLY SINS,
DISP. RESOL. J. Feb./Apr. 2003[*]

From time to time, someone tries to define what a perfect arbitration clause would look like. Efforts to do so usually founder on one of the strengths of arbitration, which is its adaptability to the particular circumstances of the parties and the dispute. Therefore, while it is difficult to generalize about what would make a "perfect" clause, it is not nearly as difficult to identify some of the features that

---

[*] Copyright © 2003 by the American Arbitration Association. Reprinted with permission.

make for a bad one. This article identifies seven of the most damning "sins" that plague arbitration clauses and offers suggestions for addressing the most important issues drafters face.

Equivocation

Credit for identifying the sin of equivocation as the cardinal sin of arbitration-clause drafting goes to Laurence Craig, Rusty Park and Jan Paulsson, who so named it in their book *International Chamber of Commerce Arbitration*. The essence of this sin is the failure to state clearly that the parties have agreed to binding arbitration. Because arbitration is a creature of contract, if there is no contract, there is no agreement to arbitrate.

Craig, Park and Paulsson's example of an equivocating clause has a certain Gallic simplicity:

> *In case of dispute, the parties undertake to submit to arbitration, but in case of litigation the Tribunal de la Seine shall have exclusive jurisdiction.*

What this clause commits the parties to is nothing other than years of litigation about how to resolve any dispute that may arise. That is the sulfur and brimstone that threatens the drafter who puts such a clause in the client's contract: The client will spend what will seem like an eternity, and a great deal of money, trying to resolve the dispute.

The overriding goal of the drafter of an arbitration clause should be to draft a provision that, if a dispute arises, will help the parties obtain an arbitration award without a detour through the court system. First and foremost, that means that the drafter must produce an enforceable agreement to arbitrate. . . . [A]n unequivocal clause that does not firmly commit the parties to arbitrate their disputes will not be enforced . . . .

Inattention

Anyone who regularly deals with arbitration has no doubt heard someone say, "No one really paid any attention to the arbitration clause," explaining that the drafters decided at around 2:00 a.m. on the morning on the day of the closing that they should provide for arbitration and pasted in a copy of the nearest clause available.

What this describes is the sin of inattention: drafting an arbitration clause with insufficient attention to the transaction to which it relates. This is far from the ideal approach. An arbitration clause should be designed to fit the circumstances of the transaction and the parties' needs. The drafter may well select a standard "off-the-shelf" clause prepared by one of the well-known arbitration institutions — one can do far worse — but the off-the-shelf clause should only be selected because it is right for the deal.

. . .

When advising a client about dispute resolution options and deciding on the type of clause to use, the drafter, at a minimum, should ask the following questions:

- What type of dispute resolution process is best suited to the client and the transaction?

Arbitration is not the only option. There are many alternative dispute resolution processes and there is always litigation. In particular circumstances it may be preferable to litigate in court, provided that the parties can agree on which court to designate and whether that court will have jurisdiction. Litigation, however, may not be an option in an international agreement.

- If arbitration is selected, does the client understand that the arbitration clause will commit the client to a binding process that involves certain trade-offs?

Arbitration has advantages, prominent among them privacy, as well as the possibility of crafting a process that will be speedier and more economical than litigation. It also provides the opportunity for the parties to choose a fair and neutral forum — and to participate in the selection of the decision maker and the rules that will be applied. On the trade-off side, the client should understand that it is giving up some rights provided by law to litigants. These may include the right to a jury trial, the right to an appeal and, under certain institutional arbitration rules (such as the arbitration rules of the International Centre for Dispute Resolution (an arm of the American Arbitration Association) and those of the CPR Institute for Dispute Resolution), the right to claim punitive damages, unless the contract provides otherwise.

The drafter should be especially cautious about giving in to the temptation to advise the client to agree to arbitrate some types of disputes and go to court for others. This may be inevitable in some countries that do not allow certain types of disputes to be arbitrated (e.g., patent disputes) — but dividing jurisdiction should be the subject of an advanced course in drafting. Do not try it at home.

- Have the parties considered providing for steps preceding arbitration, especially if the relationship between the parties is an ongoing one?

It may be that, in light of their prior relationship, the parties should agree to mediate or negotiate before heading into arbitration. They can always arbitrate if less adversarial techniques are unsuccessful. A "step clause" can be drafted with as many steps preceding arbitration as the parties desire.

- Have the parties considered where they may want to enforce an award or a judgment based on an award?

This is particularly critical in an international contract. The New York Convention and the Panama Convention make arbitration awards enforceable in most countries involved in international commerce, as long as the country where the arbitration takes place and the country where the award is to be enforced are parties to the same convention. No similar treaty to which the United States is a party makes judgments enforceable across national lines. Foreign judgments are enforced in the United States and U.S. judgments are enforced abroad only as a matter of comity.

The key is to pay sufficient attention to the underlying transaction so that the arbitration clause can be tailored to the client's particular requirements and to possible disputes that may reasonably be anticipated. The drafter should consider in what country the client is most likely to need to enforce an eventual award (such as where assets of the adversary are located) and determine whether that country is a participant to a treaty on the enforcement of arbitral awards. The arbitration should be sited in a country that is a party to the same treaty.

Omission

A drafter who omits a crucial (or even a useful) element from an arbitration clause commits the sin of omission. This can result in a clause that expresses an agreement to arbitrate, but fails to provide guidance as to how or where to do so. Here is an extreme example:

> *Any disputes arising out of this Agreement will be finally resolved by binding arbitration.*

This clause is probably enforceable because it clearly requires the parties to arbitrate disputes. However, it does not achieve the goal of an arbitration clause, which is to stay out of court. Unless the parties can agree on the details concerning their arbitration, they will have to go to court to have an arbitrator or arbitral institution selected for them.

Section 5 of the FAA provides a partial remedy for the incomplete arbitration clause. . . .

FAA Section 5 only gets the parties an arbitrator, however. In the arbitration, the parties will still have to resolve disputes about when, where and how to conduct the arbitration. It is far better to provide in the arbitration clause for the minimum fundamentals needed to get an arbitration under way without the intervention of a court. Ten essential provisions are:

- the agreement to arbitrate,

- what disputes will be arbitrated (broad or narrow clause),

- the rules that will govern the arbitration,

- the institution, if any, that will administer the arbitration,

- the place of arbitration,

- in an international agreement, the language of the arbitration,

- the applicable law, if not provided elsewhere in the agreement,

- the procedural law that will apply to the arbitration,

- the number of arbitrators and how they will be chosen, and

- an agreement that judgment may be entered on the award.

There are many other subjects that can and should be dealt with in the arbitration clause, some of which will be touched on later, but these are the ones that must be addressed if the drafter wants to avoid the sin of omission.

Over-Specificity

The opposite of the sin of omission is the sin of over-specificity. Rather than providing insufficient detail, the drafter provides too much. Drafters occasionally take the job of crafting an arbitration clause as a challenge to show how many terms they can invent. This can produce a clause that is extremely difficult to put into practice. For example:

> *The Arbitration shall be conducted by three arbitrators, each of whom shall be fluent in Hungarian and shall have twenty or more years of experience in the design of buggy whips, and one of whom, who shall act as chairman, shall be an expert on the law of the Hapsburg Empire.*

This may seem like a comic exaggeration, but if you substitute computer chips for buggy whips, with appropriate adjustment of the language and law in question, you will find this example chillingly similar to many that make their way to arbitration.

Basically, it is a big mistake to over-draft an arbitration clause. When the arbitration clause is excessively detailed, those layers of detail can make it difficult or impossible to arbitrate a dispute when one arises. The standard clauses recommended by the major arbitral institutions are used by many knowledgeable people because they have been tested by the courts and they do the job.

Unrealistic Expectations

A companion sin to over-specificity is the sin of unrealistic expectations. We have all encountered arbitration clauses along the following lines:

> *The claimant will name its arbitrator when it commences the proceeding. The respondent will then name its arbitrator within seven (7) days, and the two so named will name the third arbitrator, who will act as chair, within seven (7) days of the selection of the second arbitrator. Hearings will commence within fifteen (15) days of the selection of the third arbitrator, and will conclude no more than three (3) days later. The arbitrators will issue their award within seven (7) days of the conclusion of the hearings.*

There are circumstances that may justify, indeed even require, tight time limits. It may be reasonable to provide for accelerated resolution of an urgent matter, such as the need for provisional relief of a dispute involving the use of a trademark or one that would delay a major construction project. But most commercial arbitration proceeds at a more stately pace. While clients and their attorneys understandably become impatient with that pace, they should be aware that too tight a timeframe for an arbitration can cripple the process before it gets started. The risk is, as usual, collateral litigation. American courts have been less rigid than their European counterparts in finding that a failure to meet a deadline in an arbitration agreement deprives an arbitrator of jurisdiction to proceed with the arbitration. However, drafters should not invite a challenge on that basis by imposing unrealistic deadlines on the parties, the case administrator, or the arbitrator.

Litigation Envy

Sometimes the drafter of an arbitration clause cannot be reconciled to the thought of letting go of the familiar security blanket of litigation. What sometimes results is a clause that calls for the arbitration to follow court rules. This is the sin of litigation envy. Take the following clause, which the author once had to deal with as the chair of an ad hoc arbitration panel:

> *The arbitration will be conducted in accordance with the Federal Rules of Civil Procedure applicable in the United States District Court for the Southern District of New York, and the arbitrators shall follow the Federal Rules of Evidence.*

Trying to conduct the arbitration under rules designed for an entirely different kind of proceeding produced predictable and needlessly expensive wheel-spinning. The arbitrators had to decide whether and how to apply the local rules of the Southern District, whether a pre-trial order was required, whether the parties were obligated to make the mandatory disclosures required by the Federal Rules, and other controversies about discovery of the sort that people resort to arbitration to escape.

Whether administered or non-administered arbitration is desired, there are many good sets of procedural rules available that can be incorporated in an arbitration clause. Any one of them is preferable to requiring an arbitration to be conducted according to the rules governing litigation.

. . .

Overreaching

Sometimes the drafter of an arbitration clause cannot resist the temptation to tilt the arbitration process in favor of his or her client. This is the sin of overreaching. Where this sometimes comes up in a painfully obvious way is in contracts of adhesion. A notorious example is the clause the Hooters chain of restaurants used in employment agreements. . . .

. . .

The temptation to overreach in drafting the arbitration clause should be strongly resisted. It is not only wrong, but it is also counterproductive.

Doing it Right

If one knows what to avoid in drafting the arbitration clause, how does the drafter go about drafting it correctly? Here is a do-it-yourself kit for drafting a simple arbitration clause.

The beginning drafter is well advised to begin with a standard clause by one of the many respected arbitral institutions. The Web sites of the principal arbitral institutions provide recommended provisions for both administered and non-administered arbitration that have been tested by the courts and that work. The arbitration clause used here for illustration starts with the clause from the

Commercial Arbitration Rules of the American Arbitration Association (AAA) (numbered items 1-4). The steps below correspond to these numbers in the "basic clause" pictured below.

Step 1: Define what is arbitrable.

Step 2: Commit the parties to arbitration.

Step 3: Pick a set of rules (and, in this case, an arbitration institution to administer the case).

Step 4: Provide for entry of judgment. This is essential to enforcement in the United States.

The Basic Clause

[1] Any dispute arising out of or relating to this contract, or the breach thereof,

[2] shall be finally resolved by arbitration

[3] administered by the American Arbitration Association under its Commercial Arbitration Rules,

[4] and judgment upon the award rendered by the arbitrators may be entered in any court having jurisdiction.

[5] The arbitration will be conducted in the English language

[6] in the city of New York, New York,

[7] in accordance with the United States Arbitration Act.

[8] There shall be three arbitrators, named in accordance with such rules.

Recommended Clauses

After Step 4 you basically have the AAA standard clause, which is enforceable and can stand on its own. There are, however, some additional details that it is wise to add. These details are added by going through the following steps (see the corresponding numbers in the basic clause . . .).

Step 5: Specify the language in which the arbitration will be conducted. Obviously, this is most important in an international arbitration.

Step 6: Specify the location of the arbitration.

Step 7: Specify the procedural law that will govern the arbitration. This is important in domestic clauses when one wants the FAA to trump state arbitration law.

Step 8: Specify the number of arbitrators. The parties usually will require only one arbitrator in small domestic disputes, but in large cases and international disputes, they often will want a panel of three. The parties can choose the method of arbitrator selection stated in step 8 in the [basic clause], or provide for each party to select one arbitrator and the third arbitrator (the chair) to be appointed by the two party-appointed arbitrators. Other variations are also possible.

Optional Additions

After all eight steps are taken, the clause will normally contain all that is needed. However, there are some optional provisions that could be considered.

Step 9: Provide for mediation first. Because mediation offers the possibility of reaching a mutually agreed-upon settlement, it may be useful to include a "mediation first" clause. This dispute resolution clause is adapted from the AAA standard clause:

> *(a) If a dispute arises out of or relates to this contract, or the breach thereof, and if said dispute cannot be settled through negotiation, the parties agree first to try in good faith to settle the dispute by mediation under the Commercial Mediation Rules of the American Arbitration Association, before resorting to arbitration.*

> *(b) Any dispute arising out of or relating to this contract, or the breach thereof, that cannot be resolved by mediation within 30 days shall be finally resolved by arbitration administered by the American Arbitration Association under its Commercial Arbitration Rules, and judgment upon the award rendered by the arbitrators may be entered in any court having jurisdiction. The arbitration will be conducted in the English language in the City of New York, New York, in accordance with the United States Arbitration Act. There shall be three arbitrators, named in accordance with such rules.*

Step 10: Provide for a reasoned award. The drafter may want to specify whether the arbitrators should provide reasons for their award in the written decision, which is not required unless the parties request it. This can be accomplished by adding a sentence at the end of clause (b) above.

> *The award of the arbitrators shall be accompanied by a statement of the reasons upon which the award is based.*

Step 11: Address the substantive law. If the substantive law that will govern is not dealt with elsewhere in the document (or in a document incorporated by reference), the drafter could include a governing law provision in paragraph (b) above by adding the following:

> *The arbitrators shall decide the dispute in accordance with the substantive law of the state of New York.*

This wording has the effect of requiring the arbitrators to apply the law. Care should be taken not to add a substantive law clause if one already exists, since to do so could produce an ambiguous clause.

Step 12. Address the need for interim relief. In any dispute there is a possibility that one party will need to obtain emergency relief before the arbitrators are appointed. To authorize the appointment of an emergency arbitrator, the parties may specifically provide in their arbitration agreement that the AAA's Optional Rules for Emergency Relief will apply. (These rules are part of the AAA Commercial Dispute Resolution Procedures but they do not apply unless the parties' agreement so states.)

The parties also agree that the AAA Optional Rules for Emergency Measures of Protection shall apply to the proceedings.

The parties could provide, instead, for interim relief by a court, as is explicitly permitted under the AAA Commercial Rules (Rule R-36(c)).

Other Issues

The parties can also address other issues in the arbitration clause, including:

- whether claims by or against parents or affiliates are covered or not covered by the arbitration agreement;

- issues arising from the presence of multiple parties, such as whether or not related arbitration proceedings may be consolidated, or whether provisions (other than those stated in the selected arbitration rules) should apply to selecting the arbitrator.

The usual solution in commercial disputes is for the administering institution to select all the arbitrators when there are more than two parties.

- whether there should be limits on the authority of the arbitrators to award punitive or similar damages, although some courts have refused to enforce such limits.

The drafter should not try to limit the arbitrators' authority to award statutory remedies because the result may be either to invalidate the arbitration clause or leave an adversary free to pursue a parallel court proceeding for such remedies.

- whether to address the scope of discovery.

Institutional arbitration rules usually address the need for information exchange, so the drafter should know what the selected rules provide. Many international lawyers choose to provide for discovery under the International Bar Association (IBA) Rules on the Taking of Evidence in International Commercial Arbitration. These rules articulate a middle ground between the type of "discovery" practiced in common law and in civil law jurisdictions, and it has gained widespread acceptance.

- whether there is a need for a waiver of sovereign immunity.

- whether special confidentiality protection is needed.

Most institutional arbitration rules require the institution and the arbitrators to maintain confidentiality, but not the parties. The principal countervailing concern is to preserve the ability of the parties to comply with legal obligations, such as securities law disclosures.

- whether to authorize arbitrators to award attorney's fees.

Some institutional arbitration rules, such as the ICDR International Rules, allow the arbitrators to award attorney's fees to a prevailing party. Others, such as the AAA Commercial Arbitration Rules, do not. Almost all arbitration rules permit the parties to provide otherwise in their arbitration agreement.

The list of optional provisions could be extended almost indefinitely. To avoid drafting an over-specific arbitration clause, which can get the drafter's client into trouble, the safest course is to start with a standard, proven clause that the courts have regularly enforced. Then, add to it only necessary, consistent provisions that are tailored to the particular transaction. Do not overload the clause with excessive detail, unrealistic deadlines, bias toward either party, or matter already dealt with satisfactorily in the arbitration rules that will apply. The result should be a serviceable, if not necessarily perfect, arbitration clause, free, at least, from the seven deadly sins that drafters are often tempted to commit.

NOTES

1. What are the "seven deadly sins" of arbitration clause drafting? Is one sin "deadlier" than the others?

2. For other guides to drafting arbitration clauses, see, *e.g.*, American Arbitration Association, Drafting Dispute Resolution Clauses — A Practical Guide (2007) and International Bar Association, Guidelines for Drafting International Arbitration Clauses (2010).

PROBLEM 8.3

The General Counsel of Anerly Oil, Inc. (Anerly) (see Problem 1.4) asks you to review an arbitration clause contained in a draft contract she just received. The clause provides simply that "disputes arising under the agreement shall be settled by arbitration." She tells you she knows that the clause is inadequate. But she asks you to come up with ways in which the clause might be improved. More specifically, she wants you to identify provisions that should be included in the clause, as well as others that might be included in the clause depending on the circumstances. How would your answer to her change if the clause was contained in a contract between (1) Anerly and another oil company for purchase of oil on the spot market in the United States; (2) Anerly and a consumer who wishes to use an Anerly gas station credit card; or (3) Anerly and an oil pipeline company located in Turkey?

PROBLEM 8.4

Peter Steiler, a lawyer at your law firm who did not take a course on commercial arbitration while in law school, asks you to look over several contracts he drafted recently that included arbitration clauses. Steiler tells you that he has had a recent run of bad luck: courts regularly have refused to enforce the arbitration agreements he has drafted. You gently explain to him that perhaps the fact that so many disputes have arisen from contracts he drafted is a warning sign. Then you look over the dispute resolution clauses in the contracts Steiler gives you. What would you tell him about each of the clauses below?

(A) In case of a dispute, the parties agree to submit to arbitration. If the arbitrator's decision is not acceptable to either party, a court of law shall resolve the dispute.

(B) [Mr. X, of X organization], shall act as arbitrator to settle all disputes.

(C)   Disputes shall be referred to arbitration, to be carried out by arbitrators named by the American Arbitration Association in New York, in accordance with the arbitration procedures set out in the Federal Arbitration Act and the Revised Uniform Arbitration Act, with due regard for the law of the place of arbitration.

(D)   All disputes under the present agreement shall be submitted to arbitration. The arbitration shall be administered by a well-known arbitration institution on which the parties agree.

(E)   All disputes arising in connection with this agreement shall be subject to arbitration before the Chamber of Commerce in Paris.

TABLE OF CASES

[References are to pages]

[References are to pages]

C

[References are to pages]

[References are to pages]

[References are to pages]

[References are to pages]

[References are to pages]

[References are to pages]

Z

INDEX

[References are to sections.]

A

AD HOC ARBITRATION
Institutional arbitration, versus . . . 6.01; 8.02

ALTERNATIVE DISPUTE RESOLUTION (See ARBITRATION, MEDIATION, NEGOTIATION)

AMERICAN ARBITRATION ASSOCIATION (AAA)
Arbitration Rules . . . 6.01–2; 6.04[A]–[B]; 6.07–9; 6.11; 7.03[B]; 8.02
International Centre for Dispute Resolution (ICDR) . . . 5.03[A]; 6.04[A]; 6.07; 6.09

ANTI-INJUNCTION ACT
Enjoining state court proceedings . . . 4.06

ANTITRUST LAWS (See ARBITRABILITY)

APPEALS PROCESS (See ARBITRATION PROCEDURE, ENFORCING ARBITRATION AGREEMENTS)

APPLICABLE CONTRACT DEFENSES
Federal arbitration act preemption . . . 4.04

APPLICABLE LAW (See CHOICE OF LAW)

APPOINTING AUTHORITY (See ARBITRATORS)

ARBITRABILITY (See also NONARBITRABILITY DOCTRINE)
Generally . . . 2.02
Contract law defenses . . . 2.05; 5.03[B]–[C]
Separability doctrine . . . 2.02
Substantive arbitrability . . . 2.05[E]
Who decides . . . 2.02; 2.05[A]; 5.03[A]; 7.06

ARBITRAL AWARDS, ENFORCING
Generally . . . 7.01
Arbitral tribunal, challenging awards before . . . 7.02
Domestic arbitration awards, enforcing and challenging
    Generally . . . 7.03
    Grounds for vacating award . . . 7.03[A]
    Procedural issues . . . 7.03[B]
International arbitration awards, enforcing and challenging
    Generally . . . 7.04
    Enforce, actions to . . . 7.04[A]
    Non-enforcement, grounds for . . . 7.04[B]
    Vacate award, actions to . . . 7.04[C]
Preclusive effect of . . . 7.06
Standard of review by contract, modification of . . . 7.05

ARBITRATION (See also ARBITRATION CLAUSE, ARBITRATION PROCEDURE, ARBITRATORS, INTERNATIONAL COMMERCIAL ARBITRATION)
Consumer . . . 1.05
Employment . . . 1.05; 4.03; 5.02[C]
Franchise . . . 1.05; 3.03[C]; 4.02; 6.01; 6.04[A]; 6.07
Historical overview . . . 1.05
Merchant guilds . . . 1.05
Nonbinding . . . 1.03
Online . . . 6.12
Outcomes . . . 1.05
Securities . . . 3.01; 3.03[A]
Trade Associations . . . 1.02; 1.05; 7.03
Unions . . . 6.08
Why parties agree to arbitrate . . . 1.04

ARBITRATION CLAUSE (See also ENFORCING ARBITRATION AGREEMENTS, INTERNATIONAL COMMERCIAL ARBITRATION)
Generally . . . 8.01
Arbitration agreements, empirical studies of . . . 8.02
Damage limitations . . . 3.03[C]
Drafting of . . . 8.03
Empirical studies . . . 6.01; 6.04[A]; 6.07; 8.01–2
Entry-of-judgment clause . . . 1.04; 7.03[B]
Exclusion agreement . . . 8.02
Expanded review clause . . . 1.01; 7.05; 8.03
Forum selection clause . . . 2.05[A]; 4.04; 5.04
Location clause . . . 5.04; 8.02
Model clause . . . 8.02
Pre-dispute . . . 2.01
Scope . . . 1.01; 2.02; 2.04; 3.02; 3.03; 4.05; 6.06; 6.09; 7.03[A]; 8.02
Voluntary compliance with . . . 2.01
Waiver of review . . . 8.02

ARBITRATION PROCEDURE (See also ARBITRATORS, CONFIDENTIALITY, ETHICS, INTERNATIONAL COMMERCIAL ARBITRATION, REPRESENTATION)
Appeals process . . . 1.04
Class relief . . . 6.06
Consolidation . . . 6.06
Continuance . . . 6.02; 6.10; 7.04[B]
Depositions . . . 6.02; 6.07
Discovery . . . 1.04; 1.05; 6.01; 6.07
Dispositive motions . . . 6.09
Document requests . . . 6.07
Evidence rules . . . 1.03; 6.10
Hearing . . . 6.01; 6.10; 7.04[B]
Initiating the proceeding . . . 6.02
Interim measures . . . 6.05
Interpreters . . . 8.02
Interrogatories . . . 6.07
"Judicialization" . . . 6.02
Language . . . 6.04[A]; 8.02
Location of hearing . . . 5.04; 8.02

[References are to sections.]

CONVENTION ON CONTRACTS FOR THE INTERNATIONAL SALE OF GOODS
Contract formation issues . . . 5.03[B]

CONVENTION ON THE RECOGNITION AND ENFORCEMENT OF FOREIGN ARBITRAL AWARDS (See NEW YORK CONVENTION)

COSTS
Generally . . . 1.04; 3.03[C]
Attorneys' fees . . . 1.04; 3.03[C]
Vindicating statutory rights . . . 3.03[C]

D

DAMAGE LIMITATIONS (See ARBITRATION CLAUSE)

DEFAULT RULES
Arbitration statutes . . . 6.02
Mandatory rules, versus . . . 6.02

DISCOVERY (See ARBITRATION PROCEDURE)

DISPOSITIVE MOTIONS (See ARBITRATION PROCEDURE)

DUE PROCESS
Lack of fundamental fairness . . . 1.03; 6.10; 7.04[B]
U.S. Constitution . . . 7.04[A]

E

ELECTRONIC COMMUNICATIONS
Contract formation . . . 2.05[A]
Online arbitration . . . 6.12

EMPIRICAL STUDIES
Arbitration Clauses . . . 6.01; 6.04[A]; 6.07; 8.01–2
Outcomes . . . 1.05

EMPLOYMENT DISCRIMINATION CLAIMS (See NONARBITRABILITY DOCTRINE)

ENFORCING ARBITRATION AGREEMENTS (See also ARBITRABILITY, ARBITRATION CLAUSE, FEDERAL ARBITRATION ACT, INTERNATIONAL COMMERCIAL ARBITRATION, NEW YORK CONVENTION, NONARBITRABILITY DOCTRINE)
Appealability . . . 2.07
Express statutory restrictions on . . . 3.02
Federal law restrictions on . . . 3.01
Implied statutory restrictions on
    Generally . . . 3.03
    Federal statutory claims, issues of . . . 3.03[B]
    Nonarbitrability doctrine, rise and decline of . . . 3.03[A]
    Statutory rights and remedies . . . 3.03[C]
Jury trial right . . . 2.07; 4.04
Motion for stay pending arbitration . . . 2.02
Personal jurisdiction . . . 5.04
Petition for stay of arbitration . . . 2.01; 4.05

ENFORCING ARBITRATION AGREEMENTS (See also ARBITRABILITY, ARBITRATION CLAUSE, FEDERAL ARBITRATION ACT, INTERNATIONAL COMMERCIAL ARBITRATION, NEW YORK CONVENTION, NONARBITRABILITY DOCTRINE)—Cont.
Petition to compel arbitration . . . 2.01; 2.07; 4.04; 4.06
Power to compel arbitration . . . 4.06; 5.04
Revocability doctrine . . . 1.05
Specific peformance . . . 1.05
Subject matter jurisdiction . . . 4.06; 5.–02[A]; 5.04
Venue . . . 4.06; 5.04

ENFORCING ARBITRATION AWARDS (See also AWARD, FEDERAL ARBITRATION ACT, INTERNATIONAL COMMERCIAL ARBITRATION, PRECLUSION)
Generally . . . 7.04[A]
Challenging the award before the arbitral tribunal . . . 7.02
Confirming award . . . 7.03; 7.04[A]
Error of law . . . 7.04[B]; 7.05
Evident partiality . . . 6.04[B]; 7.03[A]; 7.04[B]
Excess of authority . . . 2.02; 6.11; 7.02; 7.03[A]; 7.04[B]
Expanding review by contract . . . 1.01; 7.05; 8.03
Functus Officio . . . 7.02
Fundamental fairness . . . 1.03; 6.10; 7.04[B]
Grounds for nonenforcement of award . . . 7.04[B]
Manifest disregard of the law . . . 2.02; 7.03[A]–[B]; 7.04[A]–[C]
Personal jurisdiction . . . 7.03[B]; 7.04[A]
Recognition . . . 7.01–2
Subject matter jurisdiction . . . 7.03[B]; 7.04[A]
Time limits . . . 7.03[B]; 7.04[A]
Undue means . . . 2.02; 6.04[B]; 7.03[A]
Vacating award . . . 6.04[B]; 7.04[C]
Venue . . . 7.03[B]

ENFORCING DOMESTIC ARBITRATION AGREEMENTS
Generally . . . 2.01
Adhesion, unconscionability and contracts of . . . 2.05[C]
Arbitral awards, enforcing (See ARBITRAL AWARDS, ENFORCING, subhead:Domestic arbitration awards, enforcing and challenging)
Assent and formalities . . . 2.05[A]
Binding non-signatories to . . . 2.06
Default proceeding . . . 2.03
Fiduciary duty, fraud and breach of . . . 2.05[D]
General contract law defenses
    Generally . . . 2.05
    Adhesion, unconscionability and contracts of . . . 2.05[C]
    Assent and formalities . . . 2.05[A]
    Fiduciary duty, fraud and breach of . . . 2.05[D]
    Formalities, assent and . . . 2.05[A]
    Lack of consideration . . . 2.05[B]
    Material breach . . . 2.05[E]
Material breach . . . 2.05[E]

[References are to sections.]

[References are to sections.]

[References are to sections.]